Foreign Relations
of the
United States
1947

Volume III

The British Commonwealth;
Europe

United States
Government Printing Office
Washington : 1972

DEPARTMENT OF STATE PUBLICATION 8625

HISTORICAL OFFICE

BUREAU OF PUBLIC AFFAIRS

———

For sale by the

Superintendent of Documents, U.S. Government Printing Office

Washington, D.C. 20402 - Price $5.75 (Buckram)
Stock Number 4400–1411

PREFACE

This volume was prepared under the direct supervision of S. Everett Gleason, Chief of the Foreign Relations Division, assisted by Fredrick Aandahl.

Ralph R. Goodwin, and former staff member Marvin W. Kranz were responsible for the documentation on European economic recovery (the Marshall Plan), and on other aspects of United States foreign economic policy.

David H. Stauffer compiled the documentation on United States policies with respect to Iceland, Canada (including Newfoundland), India, Pakistan, and the Kashmir dispute.

Former staff member, Howard M. Smyth, prepared the materials on Italy, and on the disposition of the former Italian colonies. He also compiled the documentation on the peace treaties with Italy, Romania, Bulgaria and Hungary.

Documentation on United States policies with respect to Portugal, Spain and France was the work of former staff member Owen Sappington, in the last mentioned instance in collaboration with Mr. Aandahl. Mr. Aandahl was also responsible for the compilation on the publication by the Department of State of *Nazi-Soviet Relations, 1939–1941*.

Rogers P. Churchill compiled the materials on American concern over Soviet demands on Norway with respect to Spitsbergen and Bear Island.

William Slany prepared the documentation on arrangements with Denmark for the defense of Greenland.

The Publishing and Reproduction Services Division (Jerome H. Perlmutter, Chief) was responsible for the technical editing of this volume.

WILLIAM M. FRANKLIN
Director, Historical Office
Bureau of Public Affairs

III

Principles for the Compilation and Editing of "Foreign Relations"

The principles which guide the compilation and editing of *Foreign Relations* are stated in Department of State Regulation 2 FAM 1350 of June 15, 1961, a revision of the order approved on March 26, 1925, by Mr. Frank B. Kellogg, then Secretary of State. The text of the regulation, as further amended, is printed below:

1350 Documentary Record of American Diplomacy

1351 *Scope of Documentation*

The publication *Foreign Relations of the United States* constitutes the official record of the foreign policy of the United States. These volumes include, subject to necessary security considerations, all documents needed to give a comprehensive record of the major foreign policy decisions within the range of the Department of State's responsibilities, together with appropriate materials concerning the facts which contributed to the formulation of policies. When further material is needed to supplement the documentation in the Department's files for a proper understanding of the relevant policies of the United States, such papers should be obtained from other Government agencies.

1352 *Editorial Preparation*

The basic documentary diplomatic record to be printed in *Foreign Relations of the United States* is edited by the Historical Office, Bureau of Public Affairs of the Department of State. The editing of the record is guided by the principles of historical objectivity. There may be no alteration of the text, no deletions without indicating where in the text the deletion is made, and no omission of facts which were of major importance in reaching a decision. Nothing may be omitted for the purpose of concealing or glossing over what might be regarded by some as a defect of policy. However, certain omissions of documents are permissible for the following reasons:

a. To avoid publication of matters which would tend to impede current diplomatic negotiations or other business.

b. To condense the record and avoid repetition of needless details.

c. To preserve the confidence reposed in the Department by individuals and by foreign governments.

d. To avoid giving needless offense to other nationalities or individuals.

e. To eliminate personal opinions presented in despatches and not acted upon by the Department. To this consideration there is one qualification—in connection with major decisions it is desirable, where possible, to show the alternatives presented to the Department before the decision was made.

1353 *Clearance*

To obtain appropriate clearances of material to be published in *Foreign Relations of the United States*, the Historical Office:

a. Refers to the appropriate policy offices of the Department and of other agencies of the Government such papers as appear to require policy clearance.

b. Refers to the appropriate foreign governments requests for permission to print as part of the diplomatic correspondence of the United States those previously unpublished documents which were originated by the foreign governments.

CONTENTS

LIST OF ABBREVIATIONS, SYMBOLS, AND CODE NAMES

Editor's Note.—This list does not include standard abbreviations in common usage; unusual abbreviations of rare occurrence which are clarified at appropriate points; and those abbreviations and contractions which, although uncommon, are understandable from the context.

A– (plus number), airgram

A–1, –2, –3, –4, sections of an air staff

A–A, Assistant Secretary of State for Political Affairs, Mr. Armour

AAF, Army Air Forces (U.S.)

AC, Allied Commission

AC of S, Assistant Chief of Staff

AF, Division of African Affairs, Department of State

ACA, Allied Control Authority

AFA, Allied Financial Agency

Afem (Mefa), indicators for messages relating to the Foreign Aid Act of 1947 (Public Law 389)

AFHQ, Allied Force Headquarters (Mediterranean Theater)

AFL, American Federation of Labor

AFRA, Allied Forces Record Administration

AGWar, Adjutant General, War Department

AICC, All-India Congress Committee

AMG, Allied Military Government

AMGVG, Allied Military Government, Venezia Giulia

AmVat, American mission at Vatican City

ANFD, *Alianza Nacional de Fuerzas Democraticas* (Spanish political group)

AOA, American Overseas Airlines

APC, Allocation Policy Committee of the European Coal Organization

ARAR, *Azienda Rilievo Alienazione Residuati*, the Agency of the Italian Government to receive surplus materiél, and to dispose of it on a commercial basis

ASAA, Allied Supply Accounting Agency

ASC, Advisory Steering Committee on European Recovery Program

ASGI, Army Survey Group, Italy

AT, Assistant Secretary of State for Economic Affairs

ATC, Air Transport Command

AUS, Army of the United States

AUSA, *Assistenza degli Stati Uniti d'America*, Assistance of the United States of America, the Italian designation of the U.S. Foreign Aid Program

BC, Division of British Commonwealth Affairs, Department of State

Benelux, Belgium, Netherlands, Luxembourg

BETFor, British Element, Trieste Forces

BMA, British Military Administration

BOAC, British Overseas Airways Corporation

BOT, Board of Trade (United Kingdom)

BTA, British Troops, Austria

CA, Constituent Assembly, India

CAA, Civil Aeronautics Administration

CBI, China-Burma-India

CCC, Commodity Credit Corporation

CCF, Cooperative Commonwealth Federation (Canada)

CCS, Combined Chiefs of Staff

CEEC, Committee (or Conference) of European Economic Cooperation

CFM, Council of Foreign Ministers

CGIL, *Confederazione Generale Italiana del Lavoro* (General Confederation of Labor in Italy)

CGMTO, Commanding General, Mediterranean Theater of Operations

CGT, *Confédération Générale du Travail* (French labor group)

c.i.f., cost, insurance, freight

CIG, Central Intelligence Group

C–in–C, Commander-in-Chief

CIO, Congress of Industrial Organizations

cirtel, circular telegram

CLNAI, *Comitato di Liberazione Nazionale dell' Alta Italia,* Committee of National Liberation of Upper Italy

CMF, Central Mediterranean Force (British)

CNT, *Confederación Nacional del Trabajo* (Spanish labor group)

Colit (Itcol), indicators for messages from (to) London dealing with the question of convening the Deputies (of the CFM) for the Former Italian Colonies

ComGenMed, Commanding General, Mediterranean

CP, Division of Commercial Policy, Department of State

CPF, Communist Party of France (PCF)

CRO, Commonwealth Relations Office (United Kingdom)

CSGID, Ground Intelligence Division, War Department General Staff, Office of the Chief of Staff, U.S. Army

Delsec (Secdel), indicators for messages to (from) the Secretary of State while heading a U.S. delegation away from Washington

DepItCol, Deputies (of the CFM) for the Italian Colonies

Deptel, telegram from Department of State

DP's, displaced persons

DRE, Division of Research for Europe, Department of State

EAD, External Affairs Department

ECE, Economic Commission for Europe

ECO, European Coal Organization

ECOSOC, Economic and Social Council, United Nations

ED, Division of Investment and Economic Development, Department of State

EM, enlisted man, enlisted men

Embdes, Embtel, despatch, telegram from an American Embassy

ETA, ETD, estimated time of arrival, departure

ETO, European Theater of Operations

EUCOM, European Command

EUR, Office of European Affairs, Department of State

EXIM, Export-Import Bank of Washington

F, code letter used in 1946 and 1947 by the War Department to indicate a message from Caserta to a single addressee

FAA, Foreign aid and assistance

Fan (Naf), indicators for messages from (to) Combined Chiefs of Staff to (from) Supreme Allied Commander Mediterranean, AFHQ

FLC, Foreign Liquidation Commission

FN, Division of Financial Affairs, Department of State

FNA, French North Africa

FonMin, FonOff, foreign minister, ministry, office

FX, code letters used in 1946 and 1947 by the War Department to indicate a message from Caserta directed to several addressees

G–1, –2, –3, –4, –5, sections of a military staff, in a division or larger unit

GA, General Assembly

GATT, General Agreement on Tariffs and Trade

GHQ, General Headquarters

GOC, General Officer Commanding

GOI, Government of India

GOP, Government of Pakistan

GPU, Soviet secret police

GSC, General Staff Corps

GREEN, Greenland

HMG, His Majesty's Government in the United Kingdom

IAC, Iceland Airport Corporation

IARA, Inter-Allied Repatriations Agency

IBRD, International Bank for Reconstruction and Development

ICAO, International Civil Aviation Organization

ICS, Indian Civil Service

IEFC, International Emergency Food Council

IMF, International Monetary Fund

IMI, *Istituto Mobiliare Italiano* (Italian financial institution)

INA, Indian National Army

INS, International News Service

InterCross, International Red Cross

IR, International Resources Division, Department of State

IRI, Institute for Industrial Reconstruction (in Italy)

Itcol, see Colit

ITO, International Trade Organization

ITP, Office of International Trade Policy, Department of State

JCS, Joint Chiefs of Staff

Kosmos (Moskco), indicators for messages from (to) the United States delegation at the Fourth Session of the Council of Foreign Ministers at Moscow on subjects other than C.F.M. business

Lasco (Salco), indicators for messages from (to) Department of State to (from) U.S. representative to the European Coal Organization

LE, Office of the Legal Adviser, Department of State

LP, Division of Lend-Lease and Surplus War Property Affairs, Department of State

MA, military attaché

MAR, military attaché report

Martel (Telmar), indicators for telegrams from (to) the Secretary of State at the Fifth Session of the Council of Foreign Ministers at London, November–December 1947

MEA, Mission for Economic Affairs, U.S. Embassy, London

Mefa, see Afem

MILA, Military Liquidating Agency

MOFP, Ministry of Fuel and Power (United Kingdom)

Moskco, Kosmos

MRP, *Mouvement Républicain Populaire* (French political party)

MTO, Mediterranean Theater of Operations

MTOUSA, Mediterranean Theater of Operations, United States Army

mydes, mytel, my despatch, telegram

NAC, National Advisory Council on International Monetary and Financial Problems

Naf, see Fan

Niact, night action (urgent message)

NKVD, Soviet secret police

NWFP, North West Frontier Province (India)

ODT, Office of Defense Transportation

OFD, Office of Financial and Development Policy, Department of State

OFLC, Office of Foreign Liquidation Commissioner

OIE, Office of Information and Educational Exchange, Department of State

OIR, Office of Intelligence Research, Department of State

OMGUS, Office of Military Government (for U.S. Zone of Germany)

Par (Rap), indicators for messages relating to the U.S. Foreign Relief Program

PCF, *Parti Communiste Français*, the French Communist Party

PL, Public Law

PM, Prime Minister

PCI, *Partito Comunista Italiano*, the Italian Communist Party

POL, petroleum, oil, lubricants

PolAd, Political Adviser

POW's, PW, prisoners of war

PriMin, Prime Minister

PRL, *Parti Républicain de la Liberté* (French political party)

PSLI, *Partito Socialista dei Lavoratori Italiani*, Socialist Party of Italian Workers, or Saragat Socialists

PTT, posts, telephone, telegraph

R–Day, Ratification Day (as applied to the Treaty of Peace with Italy)

RAF, Royal Air Force (British)

Rap, see Par

reemb, with reference to embassy's (message)

refdes, reftel, despatch, telegram under reference

remy, with reference to my (message)

reourad, reurade, with reference to our, your, radiogram

reourtel, reurtel, with reference to our, your telegram

RFC, Reconstruction Finance Corporation

RGR, *Rassemblement des Gauches Républicaines* (French political party)

RJ, Ratification by Yugoslavia of the Treaty of Peace with Italy

RPF, *Rassemblement du Peuple Français* (French political party)

S-Day, Signature Day (as applied to the Treaty of Peace with Italy)

SAC, Supreme Allied Commander

SACMED, Supreme Allied Commander, Mediterranean

SAFEHAVEN, a program directed against efforts by the Axis governments to secrete funds or other assets in neutral countries

Salco, see Lasco

SAS, Scandinavian Airlines System

SC, Security Council

SCAP, Supreme Commander for the Allied Powers (in Japan)

SD, social democrats

SE, Division of Southern European Affairs, Department of State

Secdel, see Delsec

SecState, Secretary of State

SHAEF, Supreme Headquarters, Allied Expeditionary Force

SOA, Division of South Asian Affairs, Department of State

SPITS, Spitsbergen, Svalbard

SWN, designation for a series of papers presented to the State-War-Navy Coordinating Committee

SWNCC, State, War, Navy Coordinating Committee, and also a designation of a series of papers presented to that Committee

SYG, Secretary General

TA, Trade Agreement

TAC, Interdepartmental Committee on Trade Agreements

Telmar, see Martel

TIAS, Treaties and Other International Acts Series, official publication by the Department of State superseding the Treaty Series and the Executive Agreement Series

TRUST, Trieste United States Troops

UDSR, *Union Démocratique et Socialiste de la Résistance* (French political party)

UE, Office of the Under Secretary of State for Economic affairs

UGT, *Unión General del Trabajadores* (Spanish labor group)

UNESCO, United Nations Educational, Scientific and Cultural Organization

UNGA, United Nations General Assembly

UQ, *Uomo Qualunque* (Mr. Everyman), a movement, and then a political party, founded in Italy in 1946 by Guglielmo Giannini, a movement of protest against the anti-Fascists

urdes, urtel, your despatch, telegram

USAFE, United States Air Forces in Europe

USAF, United States Air Force

USFET, United States Forces, European Theater

USDel, U.S. Delegation

USFA, United States Forces in Austria

USFAP, United States Foreign Aid Program

USFRP, United States Foreign Relief Program

USG, United States Government

USIS, United States Information Service

USPolAd, United States Political Adviser

VG, Venezia Giulia

WAA, War Assets Administration

WARX, War Department call sign, for messages emanating from the War Department or from Army Headquarters, Washington

WD, War Department

WDSCA, War Department Special Staff, Civil Affairs Division

WE, Division of Western European Affairs, Department of State

WFTU, World Federation of Trade Unions

WPA, Works Progress Administration

YMS, Auxiliary Motor Mine Sweeper (Navy symbol)

yrdes, yrtel, your despatch, telegram

Z.I., Zone of the Interior

THE BRITISH COMMONWEALTH OF NATIONS

UNITED KINGDOM

CONCERN OF THE UNITED STATES OVER THE FOREIGN EXCHANGE POSITION OF THE UNITED KINGDOM [1]

841.50/1–1847

The Secretary of State to the Embassy in the United Kingdom

SECRET   WASHINGTON, January 18, 1947.

No. 714

The Secretary of State refers to the Embassy's report No. 1449, the *Commercial and Economic Weekly* for December 2, 1946.[2]

The Department has taken special note of the section in the foregoing report entitled "Export Drive and Dollar Parsimony," in which the Embassy refers to recent pronouncements on the part of British Government officials dealing with the allegedly unsatisfactory dollar exchange position of the United Kingdom. In general, the Department is inclined to agree with the Embassy's belief that this series of statements has been undertaken with an eye to the future rather than the present. The possible motives for such action advanced by the Embassy appear to be plausible. Another motive that had been suggested in the Department before receipt of the Embassy's report was a possible desire on the part of the British to utilize the sterling balances as a means of strengthening the United Kingdom's export position after the present seller's market will have run its course. According to this view, the British may not object to the passage of some time before they reach settlements on the sterling balances. In the meantime, they will use those balances to maintain or extend the United Kingdom's trade position in the creditor countries. It was also suggested that the recent emphasis on balance-of-payments difficulties might be a first step in an attempt by the British to obtain a concession with regard to Section 10 of the Financial Agreement,[3] such concession to consist of the privilege of paying the funded part of the sterling settlements in inconvertible sterling, that is with British exports.

---

[1] For previous documentation, see *Foreign Relations*, 1945, vol. VI, pp. 1 ff.
[2] Not found in Department of State files.
[3] For text, see Department of State Treaties and Other International Acts Series (TIAS) No. 1545, or 60 Stat. (pt. 2) 1841.

For the confidential information of the Embassy two British officials, in conversation with officers of the Department, have already intimated that the United Kingdom may wish to postpone implementation of some of the provisions of the Financial Agreement.

Sir David Waley [4] and Mr. Gordon Munro (the latter attached to the United Kingdom Treasury Delegation in Washington) met with Mr. Ness, Director of OFD, on November 21.[5] Sir David reported the following area-by-area estimates of the gold and dollar deficits (–) and surpluses (+) anticipated in calendar 1947:

		Billions of $
1.	United States and Canada	$–1.9
2.	Argentina and other "hard currency" areas	–0.4
3.	Sterling-area dollar requirements	–0.2
4.	Gold from sterling area	+0.4
5.	Total (net)	$–2.1

He stated that because of political uncertainty in India, it was not deemed possible to approach that country for settlement before April, and that Egypt and other countries must be approached later. When Mr. Ness observed that this schedule left but little time before July 15, 1947, when the most important convertibility provisions of the Agreement go into effect, Sir David agreed and said that the United States might have to be prepared to consider postponement of these provisions under the "mutual agreement" clause. He alluded several times to the possibility that this Government might be asked to explain to the American people the difficulty under which the British are laboring. Mr. Ness observed that postponement would have grave political consequences here.

About a week before the foregoing conversation took place, Mr. Thompson-McCausland of the Bank of England spoke to Mr. W. G. Brown, Chief of CP, on the same general subject. Mr. Thompson-McCausland referred briefly to the sterling settlement negotiations and asked whether it would cause great concern in the United States if these negotiations were not concluded within one year from the date of the loan. He also asked what this Government's reaction would be if the British Government should say that it would be of help to them in getting satisfactory results in their negotiations if they could use the convertibility of exchange arising from current transactions as an additional bargaining weapon. In other words, would the United States be willing to waive this provision of the Agreement for a while in order to assist the British in working out a more satisfactory over-

---

[4] Third Secretary, British Treasury.

[5] A memorandum of conversation, not printed, is in file 611.4131/11–2146.

all solution of their financial problems. Mr. Brown stated that his immediate personal reaction was that this Government would find it almost impossible to agree to a modification of the Financial Agreement requirement that exchange from current transactions be made convertible within a year. Mr. Thompson-McCausland further said that he regretted that Lord Keynes, during the loan negotiations, had always talked in terms of sterling balances as a debt and in terms of funding a portion of them. Actually, they were not a debt; London was really holding the balances as banker. The balances were not blocked, but the British would want to control the rate at which they were expended in order to stop too great a drain on their production.

The Embassy's further comments from time to time on this subject will be welcomed.

Editorial Note

The Departments of State and Treasury viewed with concern certain provisions of the Anglo-Argentine Agreement of September 17, 1946, which appeared to have been inconsistent with the U.S.–U.K. Financial Agreement. Excerpts of correspondence exchanged between Secretary of the Treasury John W. Snyder and the British Chancellor of the Exchequer, Hugh Dalton, October 31, 1946–February 4, 1947, are in Department of State Wireless Bulletin 30, February 5, 1947.

841.51/2–647 : Telegram

The Secretary of State to the Embassy in the United Kingdom

SECRET   WASHINGTON, February 6, 1947—6 p.m.

620. For Embassy and Gunter from State and Treasury. 1. Munro, UK Treasury Delegation, has informed Treas that British Govt (presumably President of the Board of Trade) intends to invite Emb representation to British interdepartmental meetings at which implementation of Section 9 of Financial Agreement is being discussed. Dept and Treas recommend that Peterson attend for Emb and Gunter for Treas [1] since they are fully acquainted with Dept's and Treasury's views concerning matter.

2. No statements should be made committing US Govt beyond restating general assumption that British will fully and completely implement Section 9. However, Peterson and Gunter should feel free to discuss problems fully, in order to obtain fullest possible delineation of British attitudes and plans. Dept and Treas particularly interested in British attitude toward use of provisions under Section 9 which

---

[1] Avery F. Peterson, First Secretary at the U.S. Embassy in the United Kingdom; John W. Gunter, U.S. Treasury Representative in the United Kingdom.

release Britain from full implementation of non-discrimination in exceptional cases. This includes prospective census of inconvertible currencies accumulated before Dec 31, 1946 (which, confidentially, Munro indicates will be made available to us) and British attitude on relation of these accumulations to implementation. Peterson and Gunter should also attempt to obtain explicit commitment with respect to application of Section 9 to colonial possessions, together with statement of British plans for insuring implementation in those possessions where control may not be exerted by British Govt through legislative channels. In this connection refer Dept instructions to London 596, Nov 29 and 618, Dec 9;[2] Dept instruction to Nairobi Dec 26;[3] secret despatch 301, Dec 9 from Nairobi to Dept (copy to London);[4] and Dept telegram 372, Jan 22.[5]

MARSHALL

---

[2] Instruction 596 not printed. Instruction 618 dealt with British alleged discrimination against the United States in Palestine, and requested that this situation be discussed with British authorities. (667N.1112/11–1346)

[3] Not printed.

[4] Despatch 301 was a response to telegram 92 of December 4, 1946, which said: "Since London discussions likely please prepare documented report types and instances violations U.S. treaty rights in Tanganyika, Kenya, Uganda and Zanzibar for possible use." The despatch was a memorandum commenting on the East African system of economic controls and the apparent importance of the violation of the treaty rights of American nationals. (648T.0031/11–2646, 12–946)

[5] Not printed.

841.51/2–1747 : Circular Instruction

The Secretary of State to Consular Officers in British Colonial Dependencies

RESTRICTED   WASHINGTON, February 17, 1947.

The Secretary of State refers to the Anglo-American Financial Agreement of December 6, 1945, and invites attention to the bearing of this Agreement on the import and exchange control policies of the British colonial dependencies.

The Agreement as such obligates only the signatories thereto, namely the United States and the United Kingdom. However, a supplementary note from the British Government, a copy of which is enclosed,[1] made most of the British colonial dependencies subject to the provisions of Sections 8 and 9 of the Agreement. The British Government undertook to enforce the principles of these sections in those colonial dependencies in which it has the required authority through normal legislative or administrative channels to do so. In the case of the more

---

[1] The supplementary note of December 15, 1945, is not printed here, but see the U.S. reply of January 11, 1946, which is printed in Foreign Relations, 1945, vol. VI, p. 199.

autonomous dependencies, it undertook to use every endeavor to persuade the local authorities to comply with the principles in question.

Section 8 of the Financial Agreement provides that after July 15, 1946 the United Kingdom "will not apply exchange controls in such a manner as to restrict . . . payments or transfers in respect of . . ."[2] current transactions" with the United States. It also provides (with certain exceptions) that after July 15, 1947 the United Kingdom will not impose any restrictions on payments or transfers for current transactions with any country.

Section 9 provides that, beginning January 1, 1947, any quantitative import restrictions imposed or maintained by either country will not discriminate against imports from the other country in respect of any product. This section specifies three types of exceptions to the general rule of non-discriminatory quantitative import restrictions.

Clause (a) permits discrimination where necessary in order to use up inconvertible currencies accumulated up to December 31, 1946. By "inconvertible currencies" in this context is meant currencies which are not readily convertible into dollars or other "hard" currencies. It should be noted that, so far as the colonial dependencies are concerned, this clause is not regarded as permitting discrimination in favor of the United Kingdom. However, if a colonial dependency were to be in possession of French francs or Polish zloty, for example, and could not use up such currencies otherwise, it would be permitted to discriminate in favor of France or Poland under this clause.

Clause (b) of Section 9 permits discrimination where necessary to assist countries "whose economy has been disrupted by war." The Department, however, invites particular attention to the restrictive phraseology of this clause. Discrimination is allowed only when there is "special necessity" for the type of assistance mentioned. Moreover, the discriminatory measures should be circumscribed and should not involve "a substantial departure from the general rule of non-discrimination." Thus while a colonial dependency might have the privilege of imposing on some product a quota which would discriminate in favor of, say, Holland or Belgium, it should not use this clause as a means of substantially avoiding its obligation under Section 9 to give the United States most-favored-nation treatment with respect to quantitative import controls. In other words, clause (b) should be given a strict and narrow construction.

Clause (c) of Section 9 refers to the "scarce currency" provisions of the Monetary Fund Agreement. This clause merely permits colonial dependencies to impose discriminatory quantitative restrictions which would have equivalent effect to any exchange restrictions which they

---

[2] Omissions indicated in the source text.

would be authorized to impose on some currency declared to be scarce under Article VII of the Fund Agreement.

The officer in charge is requested to keep the Department informed regarding developments in local import and exchange controls with particular reference to their conformity with Sections 8 and 9 of the Anglo-American Financial Agreement. He is authorized to discuss with the local authorities any case involving an apparent departure from the provisions of these sections; and is requested to report such discussions in full to the Department, which will issue further instructions when warranted.

A list of the British colonial dependencies is attached hereto.[3] It is to be noted that the present instruction does not apply to any territory not named on this list.

------

[3] Not printed.

Lot 60 D 137, Box 1

Minutes of the Sixtieth Meeting of the National Advisory Council on International Monetary and Financial Problems, Washington, D.C., April 17, 1947

TOP SECRET

[Here follows a list of the 25 persons present, and a discussion of other subjects.]

4. *Settlement of Sterling Balances.* Mr. Schmidt[1] recalled that it had been reported to the Council several meetings earlier that the Staff Committee had set up a working group to follow the implementation of the U.S.–U.K. Financial Agreement in view of the fact that the Secretary of the Treasury in consultation with the Council was responsible for the implementation of the Agreement. The Staff Committee had considered the following three aspects of the Agreement:

(1) The requirement that as of July 15, 1947 newly acquired sterling and sterling released from accumulated balances be made generally convertible.

While there had been an informal suggestion that the United States might have to consider the possibility of postponing the convertibility requirement, the Staff Committee did not feel there was indication at present that such postponement would be requested.

(2) The possibility that accumulated balances will not be funded by the British Government.

At the time of the negotiation of the Anglo-American Agreement it was expected by the United States that the sterling held by third countries would fall into three categories and that balances in the first two would be free, while balances in the third category (sterling accumulated in the past and not yet available for current expenditure,

------

[1] Orvis A. Schmidt, Acting Secretary to the National Advisory Council.

in the U.K. or elsewhere) would either be deposited in a separate, fully blocked account, or funded. It appears that it is the present intention of the British Government not to set up separate accounts for sterling not available for current expenditure, but rather to work out with each creditor country the over-all rate of use of the global balance held by such country. If the balances are not funded or segregated it will be of great importance that this Government be regularly informed as to the rate and manner of release.

(3) The possibility that temporary rather than permanent settlements will be reached.

Section 10(i) obligates the United Kingdom to "make every endeavor to secure the early completion" of settlements of the sterling balances. Section 10(ii) obligates the British Government in effect to grant full convertibility to all sums made available for current transactions out of the accumulated balances. It has been learned that British officials are considering 4 or 5-year settlements with the understanding that the agreements will be renegotiated at the end of that period. While the plan for temporary settlements raises the question as to whether the United Kingdom has carried out its obligations, it would seem that we could not object if we are assured the British have made every endeavor to secure complete settlements and were unable to do so. This Government, however, would be concerned that the temporary settlements do not result in the use of sterling in a discriminatory manner. In any event the British are required by the Agreement to make every endeavor to secure the early completion of final settlements.

The recommendations of the Staff Committee with respect to these several points were contained in NAC Document No. 399.[2]

Mr. Acheson [3] stated that he agreed with the recommendations. Mr. Eccles [4] also agreed but commented upon the impressions he had gained during the course of the negotiations. The United States had expected so far as possible that the British would obtain permanent settlements and that temporary settlements would be a very secondary choice. We could not obligate the British to make permanent settlements but it was the impression that they intended to try to do so. There would be great advantage to the British if they could make permanent settlements and in turn there would be an advantage to us so far as the British loan was concerned. In view of their present straitened circumstances, the British as a great debtor nation are in a position to dictate terms. Within five years the British could be expected to be in a stronger financial position and hence less likely to obtain favorable terms. The United States would be very desirous of having settlements favorable to the British because many of the obligations were created on the basis of inflated prices and in a sense the obligations were comparable to those under lend-lease. However,

the further the war recedes into the background the less likelihood
there is that these obligations will be related to the sacrifices the
British made during the war. There will be more of a feeling that
these are obligations that should be paid. The experience of the
United States after the first World War could be cited as a parallel.
Mr. Eccles felt strongly that everything possible should be done to
get permanent settlements, including every encouragement this country could give.

The Chairman [5] agreed that this was a sound argument but pointed
out that some countries were taking an adamant position. Mr. Blaisdell [6] commented upon the political difficulties that stood in the way
of permanent settlements with certain areas at this time but suggested that it might be desirable to brief the new Ambassador to
India on this matter.

Action. The following action was taken:

The Secretary of the Treasury should at the earliest possible date
explore fully with the appropriate officials of the British Government the nature and progress of British plans for implementation
of Sections 8 and 10 of the Financial Agreement. In particular, he
should:

(*a*) express his appreciation of the efforts on the part of the British
negotiators to keep this Government informed of the sterling settlement negotiations;
(*b*) obtain additional detailed information as to the nature and
progress of the negotiations, and plans for further negotiations;
(*c*) inform the British of the importance to the United States of
being regularly informed as to the rate and manner of releases from
accumulated sterling balances after July 15; especially in the event the
British propose not to segregate sterling which is not available for
current expenditure;
(*d*) in the event the British propose to make temporary settlements
of the sterling balances

(*i*) express, if it appears appropriate, his confidence that the
decision to reach temporary settlements will be made only after
every possible effort has been exerted to reach satisfactory permanent settlements;
(*ii*) express his confidence that, should temporary settlements
prove necessary, the U.K. will at the earliest favorable opportunity endeavor to obtain the completion of final settlements
consistent with the principle of non-discriminatory use of accumulated sterling balances.

[Here follows discussion of other subjects.]

---

[5] Secretary of the Treasury John W. Snyder.
[6] Thomas C. Blaisdell, Jr., Department of Commerce.

841.51/5–947

Memorandum by the United States Treasury Representative in the United Kingdom (Blaser)[1]

SECRET

LONDON, May 5, 1947.

THE PROBLEM OF THE STERLING BALANCES

ORIGIN AND GROWTH OF THE BALANCES

Prior to the war sterling balances held in London by various foreign countries ranged between one-half and one billion pounds. These were kept largely as working balances due to the importance of London as a commercial and financial center and also as a monetary reserve for certain countries which operated a sterling exchange standard.

During and after the war these balances increased each year, though at various rates, to a peak of £3,480 million at the end of 1946. This large increase represents an important method by which the United Kingdom financed its participation in the war and its postwar deficit in its international balance of payments. The following types of transactions were important in building up the balances: United Kingdom military expenditures abroad; United Kingdom purchases abroad; and the proceeds of United States dollar expenditures abroad which were acquired by the dollar pool and paid for by the United Kingdom in sterling. The rapid increase in prices due to inflationary pressure generated by these activities in the countries concerned contributed substantially to the amount of the balances. No important exchange rate adjustments were made between sterling and the other currencies which would have offset these price increases.

RELATION OF THESE BALANCES TO UNITED STATES–UNITED KINGDOM FINANCIAL AGREEMENT

Section 10 of the Financial Agreement provides that after July 15, 1947, any sterling balances released or otherwise available for current payments will be freely available for current transactions in any currency area without restriction. This means that if any country is permitted to use any portion of its accumulated sterling holdings for payments (even in the sterling area) the entire portion so released may be spent in any currency area. The correspondence between Secretary Snyder and Chancellor Dalton with reference to this point in the United Kingdom–Argentine Agreement is well known.[2]

What Britain must do, therefore, is to come to some agreement with each of the holders of the balances as to what portion is to be con-

---

[1] This memorandum was submitted to the Department as enclosure No. 1 to despatch 945, from London, May 9, 1947. (841.51/5–947)

[2] See editorial note, p. 3.

sidered available for current payments and what portion not so available. The British must then be prepared to furnish gold, dollars, or other foreign exchange for that portion which has been released for current payments.

BRITISH POSITION ON THE STERLING BALANCES QUESTION

It has been suggested in many British quarters that the problem of the sterling balances might not exist at all, and certainly not in its present magnitude if lend-lease principles had been uniformly applied, and supplies furnished by each of the allies were regarded as a contribution to the common cause. Now that the war is over the British find around their neck this financial "mill stone" which was acquired as a result of their magnificent effort in resisting the forces of aggression throughout the world.

Since these obligations do now exist, in the British view the best solution would be the cancellation of a substantial portion of the balances and the funding of the remainder over a long period of time so that the yearly burden of repayment would be as small as possible.

The conditions and methods under which these balances were built up vary considerably from country to country. These differences among the countries include their financial contributions to the war in relation to their resources, the degree of inflation experienced, and certain technical differences in the way in which the balances are held, i.e., privately or on government account. Thus, the negotiated settlements will presumably vary somewhat from country to country.

The British feel strongly that in their present difficult economic position they cannot go very far in the direction of "unrequited exports." This was forcefully pointed out by Chancellor Dalton in his budget speech. Current British exports must be devoted to the procurement of essential imports and not applied to any appreciable extent to the settlement of past debts.

Various schemes and rates of repayment have been suggested by way of a formula to work out this problem. It is not yet clear what will be the yearly total of the obligations which will be undertaken by the British in their efforts to settle these debts. This will depend upon the individual settlements which are reached country by country. Some general indication as to the possible magnitude of the problem and its impact on the British financial position is given by the following figures. A rate of release of 2 percent per annum on the total of reported balances of £3,480 million would represent a potential annual burden of £70 million in "unrequited exports" or a corresponding loss in foreign exchange. This is a little less than 5 percent of a total import program of £1,450. The prospective balance of payments deficit for

1947 has been variously estimated at £350 to £400 million. It should be less in succeeding years. Gold and dollar reserves amounted to £642 at the end of 1946. In addition, considerable foreign exchange will be still available after July 15, 1947, from the unused portions of the United States and Canadian lines of credit.

BRITISH PROGRESS IN NEGOTIATING SETTLEMENTS OF ACCUMULATED STERLING BALANCES

Settlements have already been reached with Portugal, Argentina, Iran, the Netherlands, Belgium, and Italy about the treatment of all sterling balances held by each of these countries. In addition, suitable arrangements have been made with the United States and Canada, although neither of these countries emerged from the war with a sterling balance problem of the type with which this review is concerned.

Preliminary negotiations have been completed or are under way with a number of other countries which hold important amounts of accumulated sterling balances. Such countries are India, Egypt, Iraq, Brazil, Uruguay, Sweden, Switzerland, and possibly others. Negotiations are contemplated prior to July 15, 1947, with all countries holding accumulated sterling balances with which suitable arrangements have not already been made. The prospect of successfully reaching agreement with all countries concerned in the time remaining is not bright.

POSITION TAKEN BY HOLDERS OF BALANCES

Preliminary negotiations with India (balances about £1,250 million) and Egypt (balances about £450 million), the largest creditors, have not given promise of final agreement. The political situation in both these countries is such that any settlement with Britain will be most difficult. On the economic side these countries have maintained that these balances were built up by the sale of goods and services taken from people who have a very slender margin above the base subsistence level. Military expenditures disrupted the economy of each country. The balances represent honest debts, which upon repayment will be used to buy much needed capital equipment.

Negotiations with Brazil have been protracted and their outcome is still uncertain. The Brazilians are understood to be insisting on the right to spend a larger portion of the balances which they hold than the British feel they can afford to release.

Satisfactory arrangements have been reached with Argentina and Portugal both of which hold substantial amounts of sterling.

No difficulty is anticipated in reaching agreement with Australia and New Zealand. These countries have demonstrated their good-will by agreeing to cancel £20 million and £10 million, respectively, of the balances which they hold.

The settlement with Italy is interesting in that it is the first agreement by a country to hold a certain minimum balance below which it will not draw down its sterling. The Argentine accepted an agreement which provided for the release of £5 million per annum for four years, but this arrangement will probably be superseded by the repatriation of the railroad securities which will wipe out all the balances.

From this brief review it is evident that the position taken by holders of the balances varies widely. Some have accepted the British proposals and others have found them completely unacceptable.

THE SITUATION ON JULY 15, 1947

As noted above suitable arrangements have been completed or are in prospect with many of the countries holding the balances. It is probable that agreement will not be reached with other countries before Section 10 of the Financial Agreement becomes operative on July 15. The British will then be required either to take unilateral action in these latter cases or to request a postponement of the effective date of Section 10. Both of these alternatives are extremely distasteful to the British and the choice is an unpleasant one. On the one hand, unilateral action, whatever it is called, will have to be tantamount to blocking some portion of the balances. The whole concept of "blocked sterling" is something which the British are very anxious to avoid so far as possible because of the harmful effect it will have upon sterling as an international means of payment. A currency which has tendency to get itself "blocked" is not a very useful medium of exchange or a safe repository for foreign exchange reserves. These are important considerations for many reasons, not the least of which is that any increase in sterling balances represents essentially a credit to Britain which contributes to its ability to finance its deficit in current payments. British officials in discussing this problem usually object to the use of the word "blocked" in reference to the balances. They point out that they may now be used freely anywhere in the sterling area. After July 15 this will no longer be possible except for whatever portion of the balances is freed for payments anywhere.

Presumably unilateral action by the British would take the form of a statement to each country not voluntarily consenting, that from July 15 a specified portion of its balance is at its free disposition, possibly over a four year period, and that the remainder cannot be used for any purpose (blocked). Considerable administrative and mechanical difficulties will arise for the British if this unilateral action is taken, particularly since they probably cannot expect to have the friendly cooperation of the exchange control authorities of the other country which is so vital to effective control. Otherwise there seems to be a very fine line to be drawn between the effect of such unilateral action and a similar state of affairs set up by mutual agreement.

Perhaps one further explanation of the British reluctance to admit the use of the expression "blocked" and to "block" by unilateral action is that this definitely suggests frozen and long term. On this basis a suitable investment for the funds would be long dated, high yield, United Kingdom Government or other securities rather than the one-half percent short dated Government issues which are deemed suitable for "liquid" reserves. It is a little difficult to see how funds which may not be used until after four years, and even then probably not in their entirety, can still be considered liquid and their investment restricted to one-half percent issues. The one-half percent interest provision was, of course, agreed to by Argentina in the original settlement of balances with that country.

The other alternative facing the British, namely postponement of the effective date of Section 10, would engender strong opposition in the United States where it would be widely construed as the first in a series of moves by the British to recoil from fulfilling commitments which they made in the Financial Agreement and which were accepted by the United States in good faith.

There is no clear indication at this time as to how this dilemma will be resolved. Unilateral action in difficult cases seems more probable than an appeal to the United States for postponement of the obligation accepted under Article 10.

ARTHUR F. BLASER, JR.

841.51/5–1647 : Telegram

The Ambassador in the United Kingdom (Douglas) to the Secretary of State

SECRET   LONDON, May 16, 1947—4 p. m.

2772. On May 12, I lunched with Dalton, Chancellor of the Exchequer. He discussed in general terms and at considerable length the British dollar position and the problem of sterling balances.

In regard to the dollar position he said that he was drawing down dollars against the line of credit more rapidly than was anticipated. This was due to a rise in our price level and the unanticipated slowness of European recovery and the winter crises. I told him that our calculations of British dollar position, based upon the assumptions on which the calculations were made, did not indicate a serious situation but that I would appreciate it if he would submit for my confidential information the Treasury estimate. This he agreed to do.

As to the settlement of the sterling balances, particularly Egypt and India, he asked for my informal opinion as to the application of the following principle; namely, that the difference between the sterling balances as they stood on V–J Day and as they stand now should represent the amount that should be recognized as a liability. Informally, I replied that in principle this might appear to be a valid approach but that before expressing a view it would be necessary to see the figures.

Yesterday I received a personal note from him in which he stated that at the present rate of drawing the dollar line of credit would be exhausted in the early part of next year but that he did not intend to refrain from taking every possible step to make the line of credit last for a much longer period. I suggested that Gunter discuss with the appropriate UK Treasury officials their estimates, together with ours to determine wherein the discrepancies lay, solely for the purpose of determining the facts and without discussing policy. This he thought a good idea. Clayton,[1] with whom I talked on the telephone, approves the suggestion. Accordingly, Gunter will review the facts with Sir Wilfrid Eady.[2] This is of interest to our Treasury Department and the Department of Commerce and possibly others.

DOUGLAS

---

[1] William L. Clayton, Under Secretary of State for Economic Affairs.
[2] Second Secretary of the British Treasury.

841.51/5–2047 : Telegram

The Ambassador in the United Kingdom (Douglas) to the Secretary of State

SECRET   LONDON, May 20, 1947—6 p. m.

2834. For State and Treasury. In general discussion of British financial position with Sir Wilfrid Eady and R.W.B. Clarke at British Treasury the following statements were made:

1. British position has deteriorated beyond the estimates given by Dalton in his budget speech. UK deficit on current account for 1947 may reach pounds 600 million.

2. Britain not stock-piling dollars as result of recent heavy drawings on credits. In fact, Treasury dollar balance was recently insufficient to take care of purchase of ships negotiated by another Ministry without due notice to Treasury. No figure volunteered for present gold and dollar holdings.

3. Canadian credit now half used. Eady stated that one purpose of recent visit to Canada was to explain to Canadians reasons for recent large drawings on Canadian credit representing more rapid use than previously contemplated.

4. Greatly increased prices of imported goods an important factor. Due to forward contracts marked rise in US prices has just begun to be felt in recent weeks. During 1946 stocks of consumers goods at local distributing points reduced to dangerous point. While no extensive stock-piling is contemplated, UK Government feels that some additional stocks must be built up in order to protect the public against shortages due to possible local strikes in distribution and transport.

5. February fuel crisis will affect export drive for nine months. It is now anticipated that 1947 target of 140 per cent of pre-war exports by volume will not be reached until second quarter of 1948. Estimate of level at close of 1947 is 125 percent. Apparently British do not count on total export value in 1947 to appreciably exceed 1946. Fuel and other dislocations so serious that at conclusion of crisis, production could not rapidly return to level reached before breakdown. Eady stated crisis had broken pattern of economic revival and it proved difficult to get things back into gear.

6. In addition to above, timetable envisioned during Washington negotiations for British transitional period has been upset by disappointingly slow economic and political recovery of Europe and Asia. Dutch East Indies cited as outstanding example.

7. British recognize that test of their competitive position in exports is impending but test cannot be made in present sellers market.

8. British equilibrium contemplated during 1945 negotiations was equilibrium at a satisfactory level including exports at 175 per cent of pre-war by volume, and British imports at corresponding high levels based on full employment. It may be necessary to postpone the attainment of this sort of equilibrium but British hope that it will not have to be entirely abandoned. Eady pointed out that it will be necessary to feed the people better since they cannot be expected to reach the high level of productivity required for Britain's needs on the basis of 1946 level of consumption, 70 per cent of pre-war.

DOUGLAS

FW 841.51/7–2547

The Chancellor of the Exchequer (Dalton) to the Secretary of the Treasury (Snyder)

[LONDON] 23rd May, 1947.

MY DEAR JOHN: Thank you for your letter of the 7th May [1] on the Sterling Balances negotiations. We are pressing forward, and Gordon

---

[1] Not printed.

Munro will be keeping you informed of what we are doing and what we have in mind.

The broad picture is as follows. The two largest of our problems—India and Egypt—will come to a head in June. The Egyptians should be arriving at the beginning of the month, and the Indians in the second half. We shall be able to handle Iraq, either over here or at Baghdad, towards the end of the month.

In the meantime, we are continuing with other negotiations. We have completed arrangements with some European countries—Portugal, Belgium, Holland and Italy—and are proceeding with others, including Czecho-Slovakia, Norway, Denmark, Spain, Sweden and Switzerland. The Argentine problem is settled, and we have carried discussions with Brazil some distance, possibly within sight of a conclusion. The Uruguayan Delegation arrives in a few days. Australia and New Zealand have been very helpful with their willing cancellations, and we expect to complete arrangements—less formal than would be appropriate to other holders of balances—in due course. All our various arrangements will be within the framework of the Loan Agreement.

As regards the "segregation" of that part of the Sterling Balances of each creditor which is not to be released for current transactions, I think the technique must vary according to the capacity of the other party to control its financial affairs. With some countries, an informal agreement that they will maintain their balances at such and such a level should suffice; with others—and these, I fear, include the largest holders of sterling—something more stringent may prove to be inevitable. But, whatever the exact arrangements, they will have the same effect: that what we agree to release for current purposes will be for use in any currency area, while what is not released cannot be drawn upon for current transactions at all. It is against our own interests to allow drawings on the accumulated balances, for, in the end, this means using up current productive effort in unrequited exports. If we fail to reach agreement with any creditor, we shall probably have no alternative but to take the steps necessary to segregate past accumulations while leaving future accumulations free.

Like you, I should have liked to make permanent settlements between us and each of our creditors, but it is not easy to see how we could commit ourselves at this time to details of the rate of release after 1951. The rise in prices in the United States, coupled with slow recovery in other parts of the world, has left the future obscure. Given the tremendous demand for dollars in the world at large, we can offer much less than we would have hoped in the way of releases in the short run. On the other hand, the countries with whom we are negotiating will insist, in these circumstances, on waiting for several years in the hope of securing better terms in any final arrangements. I am sure that, in these conditions, it is wiser to make provisional settlements for five years. Before the end of the period we shall, of course, discuss further arrangements, which will be either for another period of five years, or, if things go well, for longer.

The inescapable fact is that all releases are, in the end, an added charge either on our current production or on our dollar credit. The first is as yet inadequate to our current needs, and the second is exhausting itself fast. We shall have to be modest in what we attempt accordingly.

With my warm personal regards,

Yours very sincerely,

HUGH DALTON

Editorial Note

For an analysis of June 11 by Douglas of the interrelation of economic and strategic factors affecting British policy, see the compilation in volume I on United States national security policies.

841.51/6–1847

The British Embassy to the Department of State [1]

MEMORANDUM

UNITED KINGDOM FINANCIAL POSITION AND THE WORLD DOLLAR SHORTAGE

1. This is an account of how the United Kingdom Foreign exchange position has developed since the Anglo-American Financial Agreement was signed in December, 1945; of the situation which now faces us, and of the relation of this to the world dollar shortage.

[I.] THE EXHAUSTION OF THE CREDIT

2. In the loan negotiations we estimated our 1946 balance of payments deficit at pounds 750 millions, to be followed by a further deficit of pounds 500 millions in 1947 & 1948 and some deficit in 1949 & 1950 before stable equilibrium could be reached. Thus we expected a cumulative deficit of some dollars five billion (pounds 1250 millions) by the

---

[1] This memorandum was delivered under cover of a note from the British Ambassador, Lord Inverchapel, to the Secretary of State, dated June 18th, 1947. In this note Lord Inverchapel said: "His Majesty's Government hope that there will be time for this memorandum to be studied by the United States Administration before Mr. Clayton leaves for London." An accompanying chit bears the following handwritten notation by Mr. Edward Thompson Wailes, Chief of the Division of British Commonwealth Affairs: "After discussion it was decided that no reply was necessary in light of the Clayton talks etc."

end of 1948 and a further deficit in the following period. Against this, we had gold and dollar reserves at end of 1945 of nearly dollars two and a quarter billion (after allowing for payment of subscription to International Monetary Fund), plus the United States credit of dollars three and three quarter billions plus the subsequent Canadian credit of dollars one and one quarter billion—dollars seven and a quarter billion in all. The margins were already narrow, and it was likely that we should be dependent upon our reserves by the end of 1948. But the underlying assumption was that the world would then be well on the way to recovery and that our own resources (together with International Monetary Fund etc.) would cover us until we reached a stable equilibrium.

3. The results of the year 1946 were, in fact, much better than expected. The deficit was only pounds 400 millions, instead of pounds 750 millions. This was because :—

(1) Exports recovered very fast, and in 1946 averaged nearly 100 percent of 1938 volume.

(2) Imports were restricted by world supply shortages to 65–70 percent of 1938 volume; this gain was illusory, for we had to draw heavily on our stocks of food and raw materials, which we must later replace at higher prices.

4. The position in 1946 seemed to develop even more favourably than the total deficit implies, for the net drain upon our ultimate resources—our gold and dollar reserves and the United States and Canadian credits—was only pounds 227 millions. The remainder of the pounds 400 millions deficit was financed by growth in sterling area and other countries sterling balances, etc.

5. The drain upon our ultimate resources, however, was tending sharply upwards towards the end of 1946 and this year has accelerated rapidly :—

Net drain upon reserves and credits ($Millions a month)

1946	1st quarter	31
	2nd quarter	82
	3rd quarter	70
	4th quarter	123
1947	January	137
	February	224
	March	323
	April	307
	May	334

Net monthly outgoings of gold, United States dollars and Canadian dollars.

The result is that we have now used over one-half of the United States and Canadian credits. At the end of June, we shall have gold and dollar resources of about $2.4 billion, undrawn United States credit of $1.7 billion, and undrawn Canadian credit of $0.57 billion—total resources of some $4.7 billion.

6. If the present drain of over $300 millions a month continues, not only will the United States and Canadian credits be gone in a few months time, but also our reserves will be down to $1 billion by the middle of 1948. If we were unable to draw upon the Canadian credit and the Canadians' difficulties are such that they cannot afford to allow us to draw on the credit as we please—our effective reserves would be exhausted even earlier.

7. Our reserves are those of the whole Commonwealth (except Canada), the financial strength of which is essential to world stability. We regard pounds 250,000,000 ($1 billion) as a final reserve to be used as a war chest against international political crises and the like. Our effective reserves are the excess above this figure, and in order to have sufficient financial strength to meet the uncertainties of the next few years, we regard a further $1 billion as essential.

8. We are, of course, taking measures to deal with this critical situation—cutting imports, devoting more of our production to exports, etc. but our reserves at the middle of 1948 will certainly not exceed $2.5 billion (compared with the present $4.7 billions) and they may be substantially below this figure. Even the higher figure, however, leaves us little margin for 1948–49—a year in which the world will still be very far from recovery.

9. These are the facts. There has been a real change for the worse in the last six months.

II. THE CAUSES OF THE DRAIN

10. This worsening of our position results partly from our fuel and raw materials crises and partly from the unfavourable development of the world economy. We attach the greater weight to the latter, for in a favourable world background we should have much more time in which to solve our internal problems; in an unfavourable world background, on the other hand, even the best possible development of our own industry would leave us very badly placed.

The fuel crisis

11. Six months ago, we were well satisfied with our reconversion. We had reached a level of business activity which compared favourably with that of a good pre-war year. The ordinary indicators—steel consumption, railroad traffics, power output and the like—all pointed the same way. There were bad spots—in particular the industries which had been disrupted by the war, such as coal and cotton textiles. It was becoming apparent that the real losses caused by war-time deferment

of maintenance were greater than had previously been believed. But nevertheless progress was good and compared favourably with that of any other country which had been in the front line. In particular, the record of industrial peace which had been achieved was second to none, and the system of rationing and other internal controls, while preventing the superficial appearance of prosperity which was apparent in many other countries, was ensuring a much fairer distribution of the available goods and was, in fact, providing a higher standard of living than ever before for the poorest sections of the community.

12. As shown above, the recovery was particularly marked in exports. We were working to a target of 150 percent of 1938 volume by the second half of 1947, and this looked wholly practicable, for a level of 110–115 percent was established in the latter part of 1946, and the labour force engaged on work for export was rising at the appropriate rate.

13. The February coal and power crisis—the result of unprecedented weather conditions impinging upon a critically low stock position—has set this process of recovery back. It has left in its wake a continuing shortage of coal and steel, which will continue to hamper output for the rest of this year, despite the encouraging coal output figures for the first weeks working of the 5-day week, and the continuous efforts which are being made to save coal.

14. These are grave difficulties. But there is no reason to suppose that they are permanent. The crisis has set back the export drive by nine months in a period in which time is of the utmost importance. But, as far as exports are concerned, its effects can be and are being offset to some extent by a further diversion of supplies from the home market to export, which primarily means a postponement of increases in civil consumption. The loss of exports resulting from the fuel crisis—and particularly from its delayed effects over a period of several months—is an important factor in the dollar drain, but it is not a decisive one. Indeed, our exports have already recovered to the level reached before the fuel crisis.

The rise in prices

15. The rise in world prices is of more far-reaching importance. We are now feeling the full impact of the price increases in world markets which begin to develop seriously in the second half of 1946. These increases are now costing us $60–70 millions a month—a large item in the figures in paragraph 5 above. Indeed, the 40 percent increase in the United States wholesale price index since the loan negotiations really means that the buying power of the credit is about $1 billion less than it was at the time of the negotiation.

16. This element in the situation can completely distort all forecasts. The loan negotiation forecasts of our balance of payments assumed sterling prices double pre-war. The prices which we are now paying, over our whole import programme, are over 250 percent of 1938. The prices of exports have not improved to nearly the same extent—they are about 220 percent of 1938. This deterioration in the terms of trade is crucial to us. It reduces our purchasing power by the last 10–15 percent of our import programme which makes all the difference between getting along quite comfortably and drastic restriction.

Slow world recovery

17. Our expectations at the time of the loan negotiations have been even more seriously falsified by the disappointing speed of world recovery. Two years have elapsed since VE–Day, and Europe's recovery has hardly begun. Nearly two years have passed since VJ–Day, and no significant supplies have yet come forward (except of rubber) from the whole South East Asia Command Area. The world food situation has hardly eased at all; the raw material situation has become worse rather than better.

18. Our interests in world recovery are probably greater than those of any other country. We have made available huge resources to foster it. We have contributed to relief and rehabilitation, in loans and gifts, some pounds 750 millions—equivalent, in proportion of national income, to a contribution of some dollars 15 billions by United States. But this has done little more than shore up the disrupted economies of Europe and Asia.

19. The importance to us of world recovery is threefold :—

(1) The failure of recovery of primary production is a basic cause of world price inflation. Moreover it is keeping us short of food and raw materials; the cereals crisis of the last two years has prevented us from restoring our own livestock, and forces us to choose between doing without bacon, eggs and meat or importing them at high prices.

(2) We are unable to get enough supplies from our traditional suppliers and are therefore compelled to depend to a far greater extent upon Western Hemisphere supplies than we can afford.

(3) We have difficulty in getting acceptable payment for our exports to European and Asiatic countries. Our economy is the bridge between the Western and Eastern Hemisphere. Traditionally we have deficits with the West which are financed by surpluses with the East. The effect of the world supply crisis is that our deficit with the West is inflated to quite unmanageable proportions, while we are unable to get full benefit, in goods or in gold, from our surplus with the East.

20. We are seeking to right this, as far as we can, by developing sources of supply in the Eastern Hemisphere, and by increasing our exports to the Western Hemisphere. But the scope of the former is very limited in a short period of time and we cannot, in fact give more

than indirect stimulus to our exports to the Western Hemisphere. A system of comprehensive export licensing control is clearly out of the question on administrative grounds and we can, therefore, seek to influence exporters' choice of markets only by exhortation and by such indirect means as are open to the Government.

21. There is no manipulation, indeed, which can solve this problem for us. The only solution to our problem is in the recovery of these disrupted territories to bring the world supply structure back into balance again. We cannot afford to contribute more to the financing of this recovery ourselves.

22. In financial terms, the situation described in the previous paragraphs is that we have rapidly growing deficits with the Western Hemisphere—which require to be settled in dollars or the equivalent—while we are unable to secure dollars in settlement of our surpluses with the Eastern Hemisphere (because these countries have no dollars to provide). This is the central explanation of the growing drain upon our gold and dollar resources, and it is intimately related to the world supply of dollars.

III. THE WORLD DOLLAR SHORTAGE

23. This is the crux of our problem. The increase in our dollar drain from less than dollars 100 million a month in the second half of 1946 to over dollars 300 million a month in April and May 1947, corresponds with the rapid growth in the United States surplus of exports over imports from less than dollars 400 million a month in the second half of 1946 to over 700 million dollars a month in the first quarter of 1947 and nearly dollars 800 million in April.

24. The facts of the developing shortage of United States dollars are, of course well known to the United States administration; we are only concerned here to explain the impact upon us. The dominating consideration for us is the appearance of a world dollar shortage. This is critical for United Kingdom for the following reasons:—

(1) It hampers the growth of production in Europe and the East and thus prevents us from reducing our huge import bill with the American continent.

(2) It prevents us from securing enough dollars from the rest of the world to finance our deficit with the American continent.

(3) It threatens to make convertibility a serious drain upon our resources. If countries are short of dollars they will conduct their affairs so that they can earn sterling from us and convert it into dollars and so pass their dollar difficulties on to us.

(4) Our interests lie in the expansion of multilateral world trade which is impossible if the world is short of dollars.

25. In fact the shortage of dollars affects us wherever it occurs.

Europe

26. We explained earlier the difficulties created for us by the slowness of European recovery, which prevents us from getting urgently needed supplies from Europe and also prevents us from securing effective payment for our exports to Europe. In addition to this is the increasing drain which Germany makes upon our dollars.

27. We would emphasise that if the European countries are so short of dollars that they must use them exclusively for buying the basic essentials of life, they are unable to buy the supplies they need for reconstruction, thus prolonging the crisis and preventing any effective solution.

28. Furthermore, their shortage of dollars involves us in grave risks that convertibility will be a heavy drain upon us, for this is one source of dollars for them. This difficulty arises in the stronger countries of Europe such as Sweden as well as in the weaker, for Sweden's lack of dollars compels her to seek to earn more convertible sterling by cutting down her imports from us, and in this way we are caught up in a declining spiral of trade.

Asia

29. A similar problem arises for us in the belt of countries stretching from the Middle East to Indonesia. Supplies from this area are of paramount importance fats, sugar, fibres, etc. To set these supplies moving again involves large work on rehabilitation which is proceeding only very slowly. These countries are all faced to a greater or lesser extent with acute economic difficulties.

At present their economies are under-pinned by their ability to draw upon their sterling balances. It is only by this means for example that India can buy cereals and materials which she must have to avert calamity. We cannot afford to continue to provide this substantial assistance. It not only represents a direct drain upon our dollars (e.g. for United States wheat for India and Japanese textiles for our Far Eastern colonies), but it also means that we are supplying exports without securing effective payment. The supply of financial resources to the countries in this belt is as important to us as the reconstruction of Europe.

Western Hemisphere

30. The shortages of United States dollars in Canada and Latin America also affect us severely. Our deficit with them is as large as our deficit with the United States. The effect of Canada's shortage of United States dollars is that we are unable to draw as much as we need from our Canadian credit and in effect have to pay Canada United States dollars for our supplies from her. Latin America is also running short of dollars very fast and this means that these countries will have

to take full advantage of our convertibility obligations to convert their earnings from us into dollars. Their balance of payments difficulties indeed are forcing them to cut down their imports from us in order to secure as large a surplus of sterling as they can for conversion into dollars to meet their deficits with the United States.

31. The Western European countries will be confronted with similar difficulties in financing their payments to Canada and Latin America.

Multilateral Trade

32. These are illustrations of the difficulties which the world dollar shortage creates for us. Our whole economy depends upon multilateral trade—that is on being able to earn dollars from the rest of the world in order to finance our trade with the American continent. If there are not enough dollars in the world to enable us to do this, our position becomes critical. Either we are forced into import restrictions on a scale which would make it impossible for us to provide for our people even their present threadbare standards, or we are compelled to abandon the whole concept of multilateral trading and seek to eke out a painful existence on the best terms of bilateral trade which we can secure. Neither of these prospects is tolerable to us. But unless sufficient steps can be taken to fill the gap in the world's dollar supply we shall be confronted with the choice as a hard fact which has to be faced.

841.51/6–1847 : Telegram

The Ambassador in the United Kingdom (Douglas) to the Secretary of State

SECRET   LONDON, June 18, 1947—4 p. m.

3347. Embtel 2772, May 16; Embtel 3116, June 6.[1] On Bevin's[2] instructions, Roger Makins[3] today handed me document entitled "UK Position and the World Dollar Shortage"[4] which I am informed, was delivered to the Secretary of State by the British Ambassador in Washington either late yesterday or early this morning.

In response to the question as to whether any further information was desired by us I repeated the request which I had made to Mr. Bevin some ten days ago and to the Chancellor of the Exchequer almost exactly a month ago, that we be given the following information:

1. The way in which dollars drawn down against the line of credit over the past four months have been expended; and
2. The purposes for which the estimated draw down of dollars in the future will be expended.

[1] Not printed.
[2] Ernest Bevin, British Secretary of State for Foreign Affairs.
[3] Roger Makins, British Assistant Under Secretary of State for Foreign Affairs.
[4] *Supra.*

This information, I believe, is essential if we are to have a clear understanding of the present British dollar position and her estimated dollar position in the future.

I hope this information will be made available to us prior to Mr. Clayton's arrival. Without it, it is difficult to make an intelligent comment and to have a considered appraisal.

DOUGLAS

841.51/6–2047 : Telegram

The Ambassador in the United Kingdom (Douglas) to the Secretary of State

SECRET   LONDON, June 20, 1947—4 p. m.

3393. For State and Treasury. Reembtel 3347, June 18. Peterson and Gunter discussed with Clarke and Grant [1] of British [Treasury] factors leading to drain British dollar resources. Following summary:

1. We presented analysis indicating at least one-third 1947 dollar drain attributable to factors other than current deficit. British agreed this roughly correct. Our figures put current deficit at pounds 215 million for 5 months, leaving pounds 116 million to be accounted for.

2. We discussed possible causes of this drain, including use of accumulated sterling balances, British exports against inconvertible sterling and against proceeds of sales of sterling securities, and accumulation of monetary reserves in gold and dollars by other countries in British Commonwealth. British stated that inconvertible currency factor negligible, that sales of sterling securities important only in French case, and that any increase in gold and dollar holding of Commonwealth outside UK was very small.

3. British agreed only possible explanation seemed to be drawing down of sterling balances. They claimed not to know just what is happening, since sterling balance figures for end first quarter 1947 do not indicate drain from this source. Balances held by sterling area declined by only about pounds 12 million, while non-sterling-area balances increased by about pounds 47 million. (Transfer relative to sale of Argentine railroads has not taken place.[2]) Bank of England is working on study apparently designed to clarify what is happening which is expected to be ready soon. We will be informed. Later figures on sterling balances will be included.

4. We asked if capital transactions could obscure drawing down balances for current transaction. British stated capital outpayments

---

[1] A. T. K. Grant, British Treasury official.
[2] The British were in the process of disposing of their Argentine railroad security holdings in return for a reduction in British sterling obligations to Argentina.

by UK residents to rest of sterling area could occur without knowledge of British Treasury, since no control of these transactions.

5. Estimates of size of 1947 deficit in current payments also discussed briefly. British stated their estimate of pounds 650–700 million did not contemplate price increases in imports above 250% of 1938 and in exports above 220%. They now place cost of import program contemplated in economic survey [3] at pounds 1600–1650 million. We pointed out this seemed high on their price assumptions and questioned possibility of importing volume of goods planned, since even at high level of imports in April and May they probably hadn't reached annual rate contemplated in economic survey. We pointed out also that they apparently hadn't allowed for any effect of price increases on income from exports. They did not dispute any of these statements.

6. Additional information will be cabled as it becomes available. This will be of interest to Harriman personally.

DOUGLAS

---

[3] British Cmd. 7046, *Economic Survey of 1947*, February, 1947.

841.5151/6–2347 : Telegram

The Ambassador in the United Kingdom (Douglas) to the Secretary of State

SECRET   LONDON, June 23, 1947—8 p. m.
US URGENT

3443. From Clayton [1] and Ambassador for State and Treasury.
1. For our information only, it would be helpful to know:

(a) Whether as a matter of policy, it would be feasible to grant extension of time for any British obligations relating to sterling convertibility in exceptional cases under Sections 7, 8, and 10 of financial agreement;
(b) Whether it is feasible to take up at this session of Congress under Section 12, relaxation of British obligations under Section 9 relating to nondiscrimination in imports or a general relaxation of UK convertibility obligations.

2. What action has been taken on British proposal for discrimination in imports between UK and colonies having common quota in IMF?

3. None of these questions have been raised with us by British.

[Clayton and Douglas]
DOUGLAS

---

[1] Under Secretary Clayton was in London to meet with leading British officials. These discussions, held June 24–26, covered a wide range of subjects related to economic and financial affairs; the major focus was on matters related to European recovery and the role that the United Kingdom might play therein. Aspects of the British financial crisis and the sterling convertibility obligation were discussed. Substantially complete records of these conversations are printed in the compilation dealing with the creation of a European recovery program (the Marshall Plan), pp. 197 ff.

841.51/6–2547 : Telegram

The Ambassador in the United Kingdom (Douglas) to the Secretary of State

TOP SECRET   LONDON, June 25, 1947—2 p. m.

3475. For Eyes Only of the Secretary, Acheson, Lovett [1] and Snyder from Clayton and Ambassador. Beginning last Friday, British Treasury began to supply promised data relative British international financial position. Please guard this information with extreme secrecy and take every possible precaution to insure against leaks. Four tables covering period ending June 30, 1947 have been presented and further tables relating future prospects will be forthcoming soon. They are not final but they reflect critical dollar exchange position. Copies of tables are being sent airmail.[2] Following is summary of information received.

Table 1 analyzes British operations in US dollars in considerable detail. Not only have UK direct dollar expenditures gone up considerably in first half 1947 as compared with second half 1946 but also allocations of dollars to sterling area for transactions in US and western hemisphere have considerably increased. In second half 1946 net dollar outgoings were 510 million dollars compared to drawings on US credit of 600. In first half of 1947 net outgoings were 1510 million dollars compared to drawings on credit of 1450. While there are certain non-recurring items in first half of 1947 British expect they will be offset by other adverse factors and that therefore the rate of draw down of dollar credits will not change in next six months.

Table 2 analyzes drawings upon resources of US and Canadian dollars and gold. It is estimated that gold and dollar reserves on June 30 will amount to 2400 million dollars while undrawn portion of credits will be 2250 million dollars giving total ultimate reserves of 4650 million dollars. The decrease in ultimate reserves from 7040 million dollars on June 30, 1946 is analyzed in terms of transactions with US, with Canada and Latin America, with sterling area, and with other countries. Important feature is fact that sterling area has changed from net contributor of 135 million dollars in the last half of 1946 to net drawer of 100 million dollars so far in 1947.

Table 3 presents UK balance of payments by six months periods for 1946 and first half 1947. Deficit on current account in first half 1947 estimated at 375 million pounds compared to total deficit in 1946 of 400 million pounds. In first half of 1947 imports (fob) estimated at 792 million pounds while net government expenditure placed at 141

---

[1] Robert A. Lovett, Special Assistant to the Secretary of State, who was to become the Under Secretary of State on July 1.
[2] Ambassador Douglas' letter of June 25 and the tables prepared by the British, not printed here, are in Department of State file 841.5151.

million pounds giving total payments of 933 million pounds. Exports and re-exports expected to yield 515 million pounds while net income from other sources placed at 43 million pounds giving total of 558 million pounds. British admit that actual deficit may well be less than 375 million pounds since import target may not be reached by as much as 40 million pounds. They, however, point to uncertainties in estimates of net income from invisibles.

Table 4 attempts to reconcile dollar drain and UK balance of payments. It is pointed out that dollar drain exceeds balance of payments deficit by 20 million pounds. Sterling balance picture shows that in first quarter 1947, sterling balances of sterling area countries decreased by 12 million pounds while balances of non-sterling countries increased by 58 million pounds. At the same time, RFC loan and Canadian interest free loan were reduced by 11 million pounds. Thus net change in current liabilities of UK in first quarter was increase of 35 million pounds. British state that further fall in sterling area balances likely in second quarter, that there will be further decline in obligations under RFC loan and Canadian loan but that no net decline in non-sterling area balances is expected. Figures for second quarter will not be available for some weeks after end of second quarter. British estimate that over half year period net current liabilities as a whole are likely to have increased by about 15 million pounds. This increase, plus 20 million excess of dollar outpayments over current deficit, is accounted for primarily in terms of British overseas investment. British state that net investment outside sterling area is not likely to have been significant. However, there is no control over capital transactions between UK and sterling area and overseas investment in sterling area likely to have been of magnitude of 35 million pounds. One big element is purchase of South African securities which is estimated at about 10 million pounds in 1946 and has probably been at substantially higher rate so far this year.

[Clayton and Douglas]
DOUGLAS

841.51/6–2647 : Telegram

The Ambassador in the United Kingdom (Douglas) to the Secretary of State

TOP SECRET   LONDON, June 26, 1947—noon.

3499. For Eyes Only of Secretary, Acheson, Lovett and Snyder from Clayton and Ambassador. Reference Embtel 3475, June 25. 1. British have now presented us with two additional preliminary tables relating to their international financial position. Copies of tables are being sent air mail. One table sets forth estimates of dollar drain for last half 1947 and first half 1948 while other table gives various data relative to course of British trade in recent periods as compared with 1938.

2. Estimates for 1947–48 based on imports at 80% of 1938 volume. This import program designed to maintain present level of food consumption and provide essential raw materials, machinery, etc., for industry and agriculture. Estimates also rely upon expansion of exports to 140% of 1938 volume by second quarter of 1948. On production and commercial grounds this level of exports considered by British possible of achievement but would not be achieved if world shortage of foreign exchange intensifies causing other countries to restrict imports from UK.

3. On this basis balance of payments deficit of pounds 325 million expected in second half of 1947 and deficit of pounds 125 million in first half 1948 giving total deficit of pounds 450 million in coming year.

4. In second half 1947 total payments deficit with western hemisphere which can be met in US dollars or equivalent expected to reach $1,350,000,000. Moreover, dollar drain of transactions with eastern hemisphere estimated to involve additional dollar drain of $150,000,000 giving total dollar drain of $1,500,000,000. British indicate this is optimistic estimate involving average dollar drain of $60,000,000 per week compared to present rate of $80,000,000. When asked about this discrepancy, British indicated primary reliance on estimate rather than present rate of drain. British estimate that $1,500,000,000 drain may be met as follows: $150,000,000 from Canadian credit, $150,000,-000 from sale of public utilities to Argentina and $1,200,000,000 from US credit. This would leave $500,000,000 of US credit for 1948. At present rate of drain, however, US credit would be exhausted by end of 1947.

5. In first half 1948 payments deficit with western hemisphere placed at $1,050,000,000. No attempt is made to estimate effect of transactions with eastern hemisphere on dollar position but is pointed out that if there is no net dollar income from this area, remaining part of US credit and significant part of reserves will be exhausted by middle of 1948. In this period British expect to be able from production standpoint to export enough to achieve near balance of current payments. Thus, British consider that their position depends primarily on their ability to earn gold and dollars from trade with eastern hemisphere.

[Clayton and Douglas]
DOUGLAS

841.5151/6–2347 : Telegram

The Secretary of State to the Embassy in the United Kingdom

SECRET   WASHINGTON, June 26, 1947—6 p. m.

2759. For Clayton and Ambassador from State and Treasury. Urtel 3443 June 23. When subject matter was discussed today's meeting NAC Staff question was raised in which of two following ways phrase "in exceptional cases" appearing in para one (*a*) of reftel should be interpreted: (1) in the case of sterling owned by particular countries only (2) in exceptional circumstances applying to Britain's financial position as whole.

Please inform Dept which interpretation is correct. If interpretation (1) is correct please inform Dept which countries you have in mind.

In meantime State and Treas are assuming that second interpretation is correct one. Your inquiry is being submitted to NAC for its opinion. However definitive answer will await clarification of question raised herein. [State and Treasury.]

MARSHALL

841.5151/6–2747 : Telegram

The Ambassador in the United Kingdom (Douglas) to the Secretary of State

SECRET   LONDON, June 27, 1947—6 p. m.

3552. From Clayton and Ambassador for State and Treasury. Reference urtel 2759, June 26. 1. In paragraph 1(*a*) of Embtel 3443 we had in mind only cases of sterling owned by particular countries. This based on our interpretation of language of financial agreement. "In exceptional cases" would appear to refer to particular countries in context used. In fact, we have expressed this view to British, stating that broad relief from obligations would involve congressional action. Paragraph 1(*b*) in our cable 3443 intended to refer to problem of general relief from obligations.

2. British appear quite definite in their intention to meet obligations under financial agreement. As indicated in Embtel 3512, June 26, they will probably request postponement of convertibility obligations in cases of small number of countries to give them additional time to reach agreements.[1] No indication of request for general relaxation of any obligations has been given us by British.

3. We consider it desirable, however, for NAC to determine if financial agreement can be interpreted to provide for general relaxation

---

[1] In telegram 3512, Ambassador Douglas also noted that "Countries involved will be those with whom negotiations will not have been completed by July 15. Presumably request will be for short extension." (102.1/6–2647)

without congressional action in exceptional circumstances applying to Britain's financial position as whole. In this connection Clayton's testimony before Congress should be examined. British may find themselves later in such a difficult financial position that only alternative is to request postponement of obligations, and we should be prepared for this possibility. It is not our intention to suggest to British possibility of proceeding along these lines.

4. Please inform us fully of action by NAC. [Clayton and Douglas.]

DOUGLAS

841.5151/6–2747

The Ambassador in the United Kingdom (Douglas) to the Secretary of State

TOP SECRET   LONDON, June 27, 1947.

DEAR MR. SECRETARY: We have now received from the British Treasury two additional tables primarily concerned with estimating the future British international financial position, to which I referred in my letter of June 25.[1] The contents of these tables are summarized in cable No. 3499 of June 26, and copies are attached.[2]

These tables are preliminary, as were the tables which I sent you the other day. One of the tables presents estimates of the British balance of payments and the dollar drain over the coming year, while the other table gives certain relevant statistics concerning the volume and distribution of U.K. trade. It is important to note with regard to the estimates that they are probably cast in a pessimistic light, and the table presenting the estimates should be read with this reservation in mind.

The tables do, however, indicate quite clearly the very significant point that the British economy is greatly dependent on the recovery of the rest of the world. The British have always experienced a deficit in their balance of payments with the Western Hemisphere which they have traditionally covered by achieving a surplus in their transactions with the Eastern Hemisphere. The failure of the Eastern Hemisphere to recover as had been hoped has resulted in a situation in which the British payments deficit with the Western Hemisphere has been intensified and in which the British have been unable to earn sufficient foreign exchange in their trade with the Eastern Hemisphere to meet this deficit. The economic recovery of the Eastern Hemisphere would enable the British to reduce their dependence on the Western Hemis-

---

[1] Not printed.
[2] Not printed. The Embassy sent an additional table "Estimated Overseas Expenditure" in despatch 1549, June 30, 1947, not printed. (841.51/6–3047)

phere and to earn foreign exchange from the Eastern Hemisphere with which to settle their debts with the Western Hemisphere.

In the light of this basic dependence of the United Kingdom on trade with the Eastern Hemisphere, I believe that we can count on British leadership in an overall approach to solving Europe's economic problems.

Sincerely yours,

L. W. DOUGLAS

841.5151/6–2347 : Telegram

The Secretary of State to the Embassy in the United Kingdom

SECRET   WASHINGTON, July 7, 1947—8 p. m.

2906. From Marshall and Snyder to Clayton and Douglas. Re urtel 3443, June 23. Following are replies to your questions:

1 (*a*). We are informed that British Treasury Representative in Washington will shortly present a memorandum outlining arrangements which have been made or are contemplated by the UK Govt in this connection and specifically requesting extension of time in certain cases.[1]

1 (*b*). It is not feasible to take up with Congress modification of Financial Agreement.

2. No decision has been reached on British proposal for discrimination in imports. NAC consideration of problem is being expedited.

[Marshall and Snyder]
MARSHALL

---

[1] Allan Cristelow, the United Kingdom Treasury Representative, in a letter of July 3 (received by Secretary of the Treasury Snyder on July 7) discussed in detail the negotiations which the British had had or were having with respect to making sterling convertible. The text comprises NAC Document 470, July 7, 1947, not printed.

841.51/7–947 : Telegram

The Ambassador in the United Kingdom (Douglas) to the Secretary of State

CONFIDENTIAL   LONDON, July 9, 1947—5 p.m.

3758. For Marshall from Douglas. Reference urtel 2901, July 7, 1947.[1] 1. Statement in British Treasury representative's letter to Secretary Snyder that I was kept informed through course of negotiations with Egypt is not correct. Following completion of Egyptian negotia-

---

[1] Not printed.

tions, Sir Wilfrid Eady informed Gunter of various aspects of Egyptian negotiations and substance of this conversation was reported by cable No. 3655, July 3.[2]

2. We assume that reference cable was sent prior to receipt by Secretary Snyder from British in Washington of long British memorandum concerning their negotiations with various countries relative to sterling convertibility. Copy of this memorandum received by Embassy on July 7.[3]

3. We have always followed policy of reporting promptly to State and Treasury either by cable or airpouch any information received by Embassy relative to British financial negotiations with third countries and her general financial position. We will continue this practice. It would be helpful to us to receive information supplied to State and Treasury by British in Washington. In this way Department, Treasury and Embassy will be fully informed at all times of information supplied by British. It would be helpful also to know what information you have requested from British. It may be embarrassing to us here to find that communications of which we have no knowledge have passed in either direction between Washington and London.

4. British Treasury usually supplies information requested by Embassy relative to their financial negotiations, although this information not always supplied promptly. Recently because of large number of negotiations underway, it has been impossible to follow in detail the course of each negotiation. However, memorandum referred to in Paragraph 2 presumably brings us up to date. With reference to Secretary Snyder's letter of May 7 to Dalton,[4] Gunter has learned from British Treasury that they consider Dalton's letter of May 23 to Secretary Snyder [5] at least partial reply.[6] We do not know contents this letter.

5. Have previously reported that request made soon after arrival and repeated on several occasions for detailed information on British exchange position was not finally given us until late June.

DOUGLAS

---

[2] Not printed.

[3] Not printed, but see footnote 1 to telegram 2906, p. 32. The Department informed Ambassador Douglas in telegram 3466 on August 13 that "your assumption correct that Deptel 2901 July 7 was prepared prior to receipt by Secretary Snyder of UK Treasury Delegation's letter." (841.51/7–947)

[4] Not printed.

[5] Ante, p. 15.

[6] The Department, in telegram 3466, August 13, agreed that "Dalton's letter to Secretary Snyder of May 23 is regarded as having been only partial and rather general response to Secretary Snyder's letter May 7." (841.51/7–947)

Lot 60 D 137, Box 1

Minutes of the Sixty-Eighth Meeting of the National Advisory Council on International Monetary and Financial Problems, Washington, D.C., July 10, 1947

TOP SECRET

[Here follows consideration of unrelated material.]

2. *British Plan for Colonial Implementation of Section 9 of the Financial Agreement*

(a) *Statement of the Problem*

Mr. Schmidt said that the basic question was whether or not either Section 9 of the Financial Agreement or a letter of Lord Halifax, dated December 15, 1945,[1] prevents the U.K., its colonial dependencies or its mandated areas from discriminating in favor of each other's products in the administration of their quantitative import controls. In no case is there any question of discrimination against the U.S. in favor of any other area. Section 9 of the Agreement provides that, with certain exceptions, the United Kingdom will after December 31, 1946 administer its quantitative import restrictions in such a manner as not to discriminate against imports from the United States. On April 28, 1947, copies were informally made available by a British official of a draft telegram [2] outlining the procedures by which the dependencies should implement Section 9. An essential feature of the plan is that any member within the group composed of the U.K. and the colonial dependencies may discriminate in favor of any other member of the group in administering its quantitative import controls.

The text of the Financial Agreement does not specifically mention the application of Section 9 to the British colonial dependencies, but Lord Halifax subsequently wrote a letter to Secretary Byrnes which stated that the United Kingdom Government would, so far as possible, seek "to use every endeavor to see that the practice of the Colonial dependencies accords in these matters with that of the United Kingdom." [3] American exports to the colonies have more than doubled

---

[1] Not printed, but see Under Secretary Acheson's reply to Halifax, January 11, 1946, *Foreign Relations*, 1945, vol. VI, p. 199.

[2] Not printed. Texts of the British memorandum of April 28, 1947, and the proposed circular telegram were included as attachments to NAC Document 467, July 7, 1947, which was circulated to Council members. (Lot 60 D 137, Box 7)

[3] An NAC staff study had pointed out that: "Although the Halifax letter was not made public, it provided the basis for certain statements which have tended to lead American exporters to think that when Section 9 came into force the United States would receive equal treatment with the United Kingdom in colonial markets, and with the colonies in the United Kingdom market." (NAC Document 467, July 7, 1947)

since 1938, and exporters have indicated an expectation of further increase as a consequence of the termination of restrictions favoring the United Kingdom. However, it is probable that certain quota restrictions will be imposed which will cause exports to fall.

There is some justification for discrimination since the colonies are, for the most part, included in the United Kingdom quota in the International Monetary Fund. Britain must be prepared to supply the dollars necessary to maintain the par value of the currency of any part of such area which incurs a dollar deficit. It was the opinion of some Staff Committee representatives of member agencies that discriminations of this type were understood to be permitted under the terms of Section 9 of the Financial Agreement.

The situation is complicated with respect to mandated territories by the existence of agreements giving the United States equal access to the markets of the territories.

Section 9 does not contain any provision for relaxing the British commitment after consultation between the two governments. If the British proposal were deemed to include discrimination within the meaning of Section 9, the proposal could only be accepted after reference to the Congress and the Parliament under the provisions of Section 12 of the Financial Agreement.

It was the opinion of the Staff Committee that the British proposal did not involve discrimination but that without admitting such the United States should attempt to obtain as favorable conditions as possible in the administration of quotas or restrictions. The formal action recommended that representatives of the United States need not take the position that Section 9 of the Financial Agreement or the Halifax letter prohibit the United Kingdom, its colonial dependencies or its mandated areas from discriminating in favor of one another's products in the administration of their quantitative import controls (NAC Document No. 467 [4]).

The recommendation was accepted without objection.

(*b*) *Action.* The following action was taken:

The National Advisory Council is of the opinion that in their discussions with respect to the British plan of April 28, 1947, representatives of the United States need not take the position that Section 9 of the US–UK Financial Agreement or the Halifax letter of December 15, 1945, prohibit the United Kingdom, its colonial dependencies or its mandated areas from discriminating in favor of one another's products in the administration of their quantitative import controls.

---

[4] Not printed.

3. *British Request for Postponement of Date on Which Sections 8 and 10 of the U.S.–U.K. Financial Agreement Must be Implemented in Certain Cases*

(a) *Statement of the Problem*

Mr. Schmidt pointed out that under the Financial Agreement the United Kingdom is required to arrange by July 15, 1947 that sterling accruing to third countries after that date or released from sterling balances accruing before that date shall be freely convertible for current transactions. The date can be postponed in exceptional cases after consultation with the two countries. On July 7, 1947 the Secretary of the Treasury received a letter requesting postponement in certain cases and had requested the advice of the Council with respect to this communication.

British Requests.—The British letter concludes with the request for an indefinite extension of the date with respect to China and short extension in the case of nine other countries. In addition, it states that before July 15 a request may be made for an indefinite extension with respect to Switzerland and shorter extensions with respect to six other countries.

The British indicate that they would not request extension under Section 7 which requires that after July 15, 1947 "the sterling receipts from current transactions of all sterling area countries will be freely available for current transactions in any currency area without discrimination."

Section 8 (*ii*) requires that the British "impose no restrictions on payments and transfers for current transactions" after July 15 for sterling acquired after that date. The British propose accomplishing this through the Transferable Accounts System which is an arrangement permitting countries having transferable accounts to approve all transfers for current transactions and placing the responsibility on the particular country to insure that the conditions are lived up to. The British say it would be impossible to make the technical arrangements with all countries before July 15 and ask for a brief extension with respect to Austria, Bulgaria, Greece, Hungary, Poland, Roumania, Siam, Turkey and Yugoslavia. They may be forced to ask for similar extensions with respect to Ethiopia, France, Paraguay, Sweden, Uruguay and the USSR.

Secondly, the British indicate certain areas, particularly Switzerland, may not be willing to accept sterling freely from all countries and they may, therefore, ask the United States to agree to an indefinite extension for Switzerland until that country agrees to set up a Transferable Accounts System.

Thirdly, the British do not feel that the authorities in China can guarantee that payments from Chinese sterling accounts will be for current transactions only or that the matter can be handled through London and they may ask for an indefinite postponement. For smaller areas they are willing to assume the administrative burden of control.

Analysis and Recommendations.—Mr. Schmidt said that the Staff Committee felt that some weight should be given to the British argument and that extension of time could be permitted without sacrificing the principles of the Financial Agreement by providing that all sterling after July 15 become freely available for current payment from the date when the agreement is signed. With respect to China the Staff Committee felt that the situation was not likely to improve in the near future and that it would be impossible to grant an indefinite extension. The British should be held to the Agreement and should be informed that the United States trusts that the British will make every effort to insure that applications to transfer sterling will be freely granted for current transactions. The Staff Committee also felt that the British should give assurances that applications will be granted for current transactions involving such non-sterling area countries as Afghanistan, Albania, Korea, Liberia, Nepal, Saudi Arabia and Tangier.

The Staff Committee was concerned with the Swiss case. The British state that "we cannot, of course, ask that a country should accept sterling freely from countries which will not accept sterling from it." It was felt that this argument could not be accepted. So long, for example, as Belgium could use sterling for payments to the United States it would not matter whether the sterling came from Switzerland or from some other country. Secondly, the British say that the Swiss "may not be willing to accept sterling from all sources, in which case they cannot expect . . . [5] to be entitled to transfer sterling in all directions." The British, therefore, propose postponement until the Swiss change their minds. The Financial Agreement imposes a unilateral obligation on the United Kingdom to make current sterling available and it does not contain any provision that fulfillment of the obligations may be made contingent upon reciprocal undertakings.

With respect to certain countries that are heavily indebted to Britain (Czechoslovakia, Denmark and France) the British say that limitations might be placed on the transfer of sterling to assure that receipts are used for payment to the sterling area on current transactions or on accumulated debts. The Staff Committee felt that the British could accomplish this objective without imposing restrictions on the transferability of sterling for current transactions.

---

[5] Omission indicated in original minutes.

With respect to the Bizonal Agency and SCAP the British do not think the Transferable Accounts System need be extended since the obligations under the Financial Agreement will be lived up to in agreements they are negotiating with those agencies. It was not clear whether any further action should be taken until clarification is obtained of the provisions of the proposed agreements and assurances are received that there will be no deviation from the Financial Agreement.

The Staff Committee felt that the British letter left unanswered several questions concerning future sterling area arrangements and the settlement of accumulated sterling balances.

The Staff Committee recommended for consideration the action indicated in NAC Document No. 473,[6] the substance of which had already been indicated.

(b) Discussion

Mr. Thorp [7] thought that recognition should be taken of the extraordinary job the Staff Committee had done in preparing analyses and recommendations on such short notice. The Chairman commented that the British letter had not been received until July 7 but that fortunately the Staff Committee had been working on the problem so it was prepared to act promptly. He agreed that the Staff Committee had done an excellent job in presenting recommendations on a most difficult and involved problem. He felt that the United States should take a firm position vis-à-vis the British on future requests for action. The Council could not be expected to provide an answer with the rapidity which had been required in the present instance.

Mr. Thorp said that he did not disagree with the position taken by the Staff Committee with respect to China but thought that it left the matter rather completely in the hands of the British without indicating our concern as to how they proceeded. He thought we should indicate to the British that at some later time, a few months hence, we should like to review with them the operations and procedures in the Chinese case. He thought it was too lenient merely to urge them to take a particular action without requiring them to report back and consult with us. The Chairman [8] agreed that the matter should be followed through. Mr. Overby [9] commented that reviewing the steps taken was inherent in the whole Agreement. Any letter would indicate that the United States would want to be informed on what the British worked out in China. The Chairman added that the United States had indi-

---

[6] Not printed.
[7] Willard Thorp, Assistant Secretary of State for Economic Affairs.
[8] John W. Snyder, Secretary of the Treasury.
[9] Andrew N. Overby, Special Assistant to the Secretary of the Treasury.

cated that it was not at all satisfied with the information so far furnished.

Mr. Martin [10] said that he assumed that the Staff Committee's recommendation constituted a general approach and was not intended to bind any postponement to two months. The Chairman observed that the two months' period applied only to certain items. Mr. Martin thought the British should have some latitude in their discussions with respect to Switzerland. Mr. Eccles commented that the Agreement does not give the United States latitude to extend an indefinite extension.

Mr. Overby pointed out that the British in their letter had asked for an extension of "a month or two" and suggested that the matter might be worked out administratively. An extension of two months could be granted and a further extension proffered if necessary. Mr. Knapp pointed out that the two months' period would lapse on September 15 and that there would be an opportunity to review the matter in London. The Chairman suggested, and it was agreed, to strike out the reference in paragraph (d) of the recommendation to "paragraph (a) above" so that the recommendation with respect to Switzerland would be that favorable consideration should be given to a request for a postponement of short duration without defining the latter term.[11]

Mr. Eccles stated that the Staff Committee had done an excellent job but as a member of the Council he was left rather unprepared. He had not had time to consider the problem adequately and he liked to have confidence in his own judgment. However, he was willing to vote his confidence in the Staff Committee by accepting the recommendation.

The Chairman said that his Staff had consulted frequently with him and he assumed that the Staff members had kept their principals informed. However, he did not wish to exert pressure on the Council and he inquired whether any member of the Council would like to postpone action. It was pointed out that very little postponement was possible and Mr. Thorp commented that the worst that could happen was to postpone some of the issues two months.

The recommendations were adopted unanimously with the one modification that with respect to Switzerland postponement of "short duration" should not be defined in terms of a maximum of two months.

The Chairman requested that a firm letter on the matter be prepared immediately for transmittal to the British. Mr. O'Connell [12] in

---

[10] William M. Martin, Jr., Chairman and President, Export-Import Bank of Washington.

[11] The recommendation of the NAC Staff in NAC Document 473, paragraph (d) read: "but favorable consideration should be given to a request for a postponement of short duration as in paragraph (a) above, which would allow the British time to complete whatever arrangements may be necessary."

[12] Joseph J. O'Connell, Jr., General Counsel, Treasury Department.

quired whether there would be any publicity with respect to the July 15 date, and possible postponements thereunder. Mr. Overby commented that questions had already been raised with him on this matter by the press. The Chairman suggested that a press release be prepared jointly with the British on this matter.

(*c*) *Action.* The following action was taken:

The National Advisory Council advises the Secretary of the Treasury in reference to the British communication of July 3, 1947, as follows:

(*a*) Favorable consideration should be given to granting the British request of a maximum of two months' postponement of the July 15, 1947, deadline in those cases where it is impossible for the British to complete technical arrangments with the particular countries before July 15. In these cases, the Secretary of the Treasury should attempt to secure an agreement that all sterling accruing to these countries after July 15, 1947, shall become freely available for current payments retroactively upon the date of completion of the necessary arrangements.

(*b*) The British request for an indefinite postponement with respect to China should be denied. The British should be informed that, while the U.S. Government is conscious of the difficulties which will be faced in administering Chinese accounts, it trusts that the British Government will make every effort to ensure that applications to transfer sterling will be freely granted whenever the current nature of the transaction is established.

(*c*) The British should be advised that, in the case of other nonsterling area countries with which no formal transferability agreements are contemplated, the British will be expected to administer their foreign exchange control in such a way as to permit transfers freely for all current transactions.

(*d*) The British request for an indefinite extension for Switzerland until that country agrees to accept sterling and set up a Transferable Accounts System should be denied, but favorable consideration should be given to a request for a postponement of short duration which would allow the British time to complete whatever arrangements may be necessary.

(*e*) The British should be informed that arrangements relating to the debts of those countries which are indebted to the United Kingdom should be effected by means which do not limit the transferability of sterling for current transactions.

(*f*) In the event that additional requests are made by the British in the immediate future, the Secretary of the Treasury should, in considering his reply, take account of the general approach set forth above.[13]

[Here follows discussion of other subjects.]

[13] Under Secretary Clayton was informed of the actions taken by the NAC on July 10 in telegram 784 to Geneva, July 11, 1947, and the same information was repeated to London in telegram 2985. (841.51/7–1147)

Editorial Note

Secretary of the Treasury Snyder conveyed the substance of the National Advisory Council's July 10 actions in a letter of the same date to British Chancellor of the Exchequer Hugh Dalton. The British were asked to clarify certain points raised in their July 3 letter, and for their assurances along the lines suggested by the NAC actions. Mr. Gordon Munro of the British Treasury Delegation in a letter of July 12 thanked Secretary Snyder for agreeing to the postponement of the convertibility obligation in the case of the named countries, and asked that these provisions be extended to cover France, the U.S.S.R., Denmark, and Paraguay. Confirming the understanding that sterling accruing to those countries would be made convertible retroactively after agreements had been reached, Mr. Munro asked that a postponement until December 31, 1947, be granted in the case of China. He added that: "In the case of Switzerland I am now happy to confirm that full convertibility will be in effect as of July 15, 1947."

Secretary Snyder, on July 14, agreed to Mr. Munro's request, except that in the case of China, a two months' delay was granted "in the hope that you may be able to complete the necessary arrangements within that period of time."

841.51/7–2447

The Department of State to the British Embassy

AIDE-MÉMOIRE

1. The Government of the United States has given very careful consideration to the British Embassy's memorandum of April 28, 1947 and to the attached directive which the Government of the United Kingdom proposes to send to the colonial dependencies and trust territories, outlining the procedure by which the latter are to implement Section 9 of the Anglo-American Financial Agreement.[1] The Government of the United States regrets that the Government of the United Kingdom considers it necessary for the colonial dependencies and trust territories to institute quantitative import controls which, while not

[1] Not printed, but see footnote 2, p. 34.

discriminatory against the United States in favor of imports from the Dominions, India and many other countries, would result in discrimination against American products with respect to similar products from the other dependencies and trust territories and from the United Kingdom. Nevertheless, the Government of the United States recognizes that so long as it is necessary for the United Kingdom rigidly to control imports for balance of payments reasons it is not unreasonable to expect the colonial dependencies to spend scarce currencies with equal care.

2. The Government of the United States is concerned, however, with the possible effects of the proposed import control regime on commercial relations between the United States, the United Kingdom and the colonial dependencies. The Government of the United States therefore suggests that a small number of technicians selected by each government meet together as soon as convenient to discuss the various problems which may arise in the implementation of the plan suggested, with a view to possible modifications which would be in the joint interest of the two countries. These discussions would be limited to a review of the effects of the system proposed and to an exchange of views with respect to various alternatives, and would be conducted wholly at the technical level.

3. If the Government of the United Kingdom considers it essential to establish a discriminatory import control regime, the Government of the United States also hopes that in any directive issued to the colonial dependencies and in the initial colonial announcements of the new import control regime, it will be emphasized that the discrimination is a temporary measure to be continued only so long as necessary on balance-of-payment grounds.

4. In addition to the consultations suggested above, the Government of the United States assumes that the Government of the United Kingdom will be prepared to consider at any time such representations as the Government of the United States may find it necessary to make regarding the application of the discriminatory import regimes.

5. In the territories in which the United States is entitled to equality of treatment under mandate and trusteeship agreements at present in force, the Government of the United States assumes that there will be no discrimination against the United States in favor of any other country including the United Kingdom. Such territories include Palestine (under the Mandate Convention of December 3, 1924); and Cameroons, Togoland, and Tanganyika (under the Trusteeship Agreements approved by the General Assembly of the United Nations on December 13, 1946). The Government of the United States also assumes that there will be no discrimination in the territories of the Congo Basin (covered by the Convention of St. Germain-en-Laye of 1919).

6. In the case of the former Italian Colonies, to which the Government of the United Kingdom also proposes to extend the discriminatory import control regime (according to information received by the American Embassy at London from the Board of Trade), the Government of the United States requests that in view of the temporary and special nature of the British administration of these territories as envisaged by Article 23 of the treaty of peace with Italy, there be no discrimination against the United States in these territories.

WASHINGTON, July 24, 1947.

841.51/7–2547 : Telegram

The Ambassador in the United Kingdom (Douglas) to the Secretary of State

SECRET   LONDON, July 25, 1947—4 p. m.
US URGENT

4071. For the Secretary and Lovett. Bevin informed me this morning that he was sending you today an urgent cable describing the critical British financial position.[1] A copy of this will be delivered to me as soon as it has been prepared.

Convertibility of sterling on the 15th of July has caused a heavy drain on dollars. (The extent to which the British situation has been aggravated by convertibility, I do not at the moment know, but I have feared that it would be more than they or we anticipated.

He says that we are pressing too hard and too fast in the discussions at Geneva [2] on the matter of non-discrimination, which, although he agrees to it as a long run policy, is not adapted or suitable to the present emergency conditions. By the year 1951 he thinks that they would be applicable but for the year 1948 he believes they are not applicable.

Before Parliament rises on the 8th of August, there will be a two days debate on the state of the nation. Prior to this debate, the government will have to decide whether:

a. To cut imports "violently";
b. To cut multi-lateral trade;
c. To "withdraw from Germany"; and
d. Possibly to declare a state of emergency.

Bevin says he is trying to provide the leadership, so far with considerable success, in the organization of an integrated economic pro-

---

[1] This message presumably was incorporated in the *aide-mémoire* which Sir John Balfour, the British Chargé, left with Secretary Marshall on July 28, p. 45.
[2] Reference here is to the Second Session of the Preparatory Committee of the United Nations Conference on Trade and Employment. Documentation concerning this subject is found in volume I.

gram for Western Europe; and there are other things approaching—such as the General Assembly of the United Nations—in which it is important that Britain play a significant part.

He doubts, in the face of the present British crisis, that their prestige will be such as to provide the leadership and to play a significant role.

If some temporary relief for Britain can be found, the moral position of Britain will be greatly strengthened among other countries. She will be able to provide the direction and leadership, and she will be able to play the role which only Britain can play in integrating the economic program for Europe. Without relief, he doubts that Britain will be able to play this part, and thinks that the consequences on France and Italy and elsewhere may be disastrous.

He suggests personally and informally the possibility that the International Bank might be able to provide this relief to the tune of a billion dollars which, he believes, will be sufficient to carry them over the hump by the middle of next year, and which, he believes, will place Britain in a position where she can provide assistance to France and play her role in Germany.

From my knowledge, I can say that the British position is critical. This has been reported to you by me before.

As to whether Bevin's personal suggestion is a feasible one or not, I have no judgment, but it is my view that we run the serious risk of losing most of Western Europe if the crisis here develops as it now seems almost certain to develop.

That the British have not come to grips with their coal problem and other issues, I am certain.

I would not suggest temporary relief, if it is feasible, to UK on straight economic grounds, but I think that if we are to be successful in Western Europe, we cannot afford to permit the British position so to deteriorate that her moral stature will be reduced to a low level.

If some relief is feasible, it should not, I think, be of a nature or an amount which will permit Britain to avoid grappling in earnest with some of her problems.

DOUGLAS

841.10/7–2847

Memorandum of Conversation, by the Secretary of State

TOP SECRET   [WASHINGTON,] July 28, 1947.

Participants: The Secretary
                Sir John Balfour, British Chargé d'Affaires
                Sir John Magowan, Minister, British Embassy
                Mr. Matthews [1]

---

[1] H. Freeman Matthews, Director, Office of European Affairs, until July 21, 1947.

Sir John Balfour called this morning at his request and left with me the attached *aide-mémoire* [2] and annexes concerning the British financial position. He emphasized the importance which his Government attaches to the subject and proceeded to read aloud most of the *aide-mémoire*.

He then said that he had been instructed to tell me orally that his Government considered this as an informal approach and not the formal notification envisaged in Article 12 of the Anglo-American Financial Agreement. Under that article either the British or American Government reserves the right to initiate formal consultation if it finds itself unable to comply with the provisions of the Agreement. He had also been instructed to say that should this Government consider such an approach desirable the British Government would consider taking the formal step called for by Article 12. Sir John Magowan then read the text of Article 12.

Mr. Balfour asked if there was any word which I would like him to communicate to Mr Bevin. I said that I would wish to study his *aide-mémoire* first and that there was nothing which I wished to say at this time.

[Enclosure]

The British Embassy to the Department of State

AIDE-MÉMOIRE [3]

British Ministers have recently had a valuable exchange of views with Mr. Clayton on the United Kingdom financial position, on some of the implications of Mr. Marshall's Harvard speech,[4] and other matters.[5] After preliminary discussion with the United States Ambassador and Mr. Clayton, a memorandum was drawn up on the subject of action to implement Mr. Marshall's speech. A copy of this memorandum, which was accepted by Mr. Clayton is attached at Annexe A.[6]

The United Kingdom Government has also drawn up a note on the results of the second Paris Conference which shows the extent to which they have been able to carry out Mr. Clayton's informal advice. A copy of this note is attached at Annexe B.[6]

His Majesty's Chargé d'Affaires has been instructed to assure the United States Government that the United Kingdom Government will

---

[2] On the previous evening, Sir John Balfour gave to Charles E. Bohlen, Special Assistant to the Secretary of State, an advance copy of the message which Foreign Secretary Bevin wished delivered to Secretary Marshall. The message is substantially the same as the *aide-mémoire*. (841.51/7–2847)

[3] This *aide-mémoire* and its enclosures are in Lot 56 D 510, Box 17.

[4] For text of speech, see p. 237.

[5] Memoranda of conversations covering these meetings held June 24–26 in London are printed on pages 268 to 294.

[6] Not printed.

do their utmost to see that a European scheme is produced by the beginning of September which, they hope, will afford the basis of further governmental action by the United States. It is, however, a matter of doubt to the United Kingdom Government whether any assistance to Europe which may flow from Mr. Marshall's proposals will come early enough or be large enough to meet the special difficulties and position of the United Kingdom as a world-wide trading nation.

The United Kingdom Government have gone ahead unhesitatingly in an attempt to fulfil by July 15th their obligations under the Anglo-American Financial Agreement. They assumed this heavy burden in the hope that by doing so they were taking the first steps in the construction of a healthy world economy and in the faith that by measures taken on a large scale to assist Europe on the one hand and to relieve the world dollar shortage on the other, the United States would ensure that these first steps were not taken in vain. It has been common knowledge between the United States and United Kingdom Governments that, without further measures either through the International Monetary Fund and the International Bank for Reconstruction and Development or by direct United States Government action, these first steps were doomed to failure.

Mr. Marshall has had the figure of drawings on the United States credit and a full statement of the position by the United Kingdom Government.[6] At the present rate of drawings, and there is no reason to expect any significant change in them in the immediate future, they will by the fall have exhausted the credit and shall be left only with their final reserves. These comprise not only their own working reserves but those of other sterling countries. With all the uncertainties before them they could not contemplate serious depletion of these already inadequate reserves.

In the face of this situation the United Kingdom Government will be compelled in any case early in the fall to take corrective measures affecting not only their own internal economy, but their trading relations with other countries. They are urgently studying these measures already. They will have to cut their imports from the Western Hemisphere to a point where their productive capacity is damaged because of deficiency of food and also of raw materials. This means at once that any contribution from the United Kingdom to restore European economy will be drastically lessened. They will have to explore all possible alternative sources of supply. They will have to curtail the supply of dollars for India, for the Middle East and for other coun-

---

[6] Reference here is to the tables mentioned in Ambassador Douglas' letter to Secretary Marshall of June 25 (see footnote 2, p. 27) and to other financial information supplied to the American Embassy.

tries, and will not be able to find the dollars necessary to finance the Canadian deficit with the United States. They will be able to provide no further dollars for Germany. Their difficulties will spread to other countries and they will no longer be able to act as the differential gear between the United States economy and much of the rest of the world. Mr. Marshall will realize also that their dollar shortage is bound to react on their military commitments abroad.

Moreover, unless assistance is forthcoming, the United Kingdom Government will be forced by circumstances beyond their control to retreat from one position to another, and further and further from the concept of a multilateral world economy. They will not be able to progress towards multilateral trade and non-discrimination over a large part of the world. Instead they will have to manage their affairs on the basis of a series of bargains by which they can get what they can, where they can and on the best terms they can arrange.

The United Kingdom Government wish to make it clear to Mr. Marshall that these are not groundless fears. They are the stark facts of the situation. It is because they are aware of these facts that they are bending every effort to secure an early and satisfactory response to Mr. Marshall's Harvard speech. But at the same time they feel they must leave Mr. Marshall in no doubt of what kind of policy, both at home and abroad, will be forced upon them when they have no dollar resources available. They recognise that the first result of this policy will be a general restriction of international trade. They will suffer from that and they are aware of this fact. But they see no alternative line of policy open to them.

As regards Germany, the United Kingdom Government, on the facts given above, could not possibly go to Parliament for a supplementary estimate above their existing appropriation knowing that much of any appropriation for Germany means dollars. Indeed, they are very doubtful whether they can afford to provide the dollars due under their existing appropriation. This will certainly be the case if there is a crisis in the autumn. Further, they cannot ask Parliament for an appropriation largely in dollars for next year unless there is a radical transformation of the whole situation. While they believe, as the United States Government do, that it is vitally necessary to raise and maintain at a higher level the present low standard of German economy, they themselves shall be unable to play any part in providing the dollar funds which will be required for this purpose.

The United Kingdom Government are most anxious that Mr. Marshall should be left in no doubt of the urgency and gravity of the situation as they see it and as they have explained it to Mr. Clayton. They think it necessary to place on record the full implications of the situation with which the United Kingdom Government are now faced.

It is their intention to keep in very close touch with the United States Government on the development of the situation.

WASHINGTON, 28th July, 1947.

841.51/7–3047

Memorandum by the Secretary of State to President Truman

SECRET   [WASHINGTON,] August 1, 1947.

Subject: Reported Impending British Dollar Crisis

The British Chargé d'Affaires has left with me an *Aide-Mémoire* expressing his government's concern at the rapid depletion of its dollar resources. The *Aide-Mémoire* stated that at the present rate of depletion the balance remaining from the $3–¾ billion U.S. loan will be exhausted by fall. There will then be left only basic monetary reserves, which at the current rate of loss would not last beyond April or May of 1948.

The British question whether in these straitened circumstances they could contribute leadership for a European recovery program. Moreover, they feel compelled to consider: (*a*) reducing their financial commitments in Germany and elsewhere, (*b*) further curtailing imports and (*c*) withdrawing from multilateralism in international trade.

Background. The British have now drawn $2–¾ billion, leaving a balance of only $1 billion. This situation has arisen in part because British purchases abroad have been made at prices higher than when the loan was made. The rate of world recovery has been slower than anticipated, with the result that Britain has been forced to buy largely in the western hemisphere. A contributing factor has been the recent undertaking by the United Kingdom to make sterling convertible as required by the Anglo-American Financial Agreement. Britain's own failure to muster the full force of its productive resources has retarded the expansion of exports.

Comment: Ambassador Douglas comments that the British position is critical. He believes that "we run the serious risk of losing most of Western Europe if the crisis here develops as it now seems almost certain to develop." [1] I agree that the possible developments are most disturbing.

---

[1] Evidence of mounting economic anxiety was reported by the Embassy in London in telegram 4142, July 30: "Daily headlines, articles, editorials, speeches, announcements, and meetings on Britain's economic crisis during past two weeks are driving home the realities which face British when loan is exhausted and is producing a state of mounting anxiety and tension here, which will likely reach crescendo middle next week when economic situation is to be debated in Commons." (841.50/7–3047)

We have talked to Treasury on this matter. They will confer with the British to determine more precisely what the situation is and what the British themselves can do. We will keep you advised of developments.

G. C. MARSHALL

841.50/8–247

The British Chargé (Balfour) to the Secretary of State

WASHINGTON, 2nd August, 1947.

(Ref.G. 190/ /47)

DEAR MR. SECRETARY: I have just received instructions from Mr. Bevin to inform you that in the last few days British Ministers have had under consideration the steps that they should take forthwith to increase the nation's productivity and to relieve the strain on the balance of payments of the United Kingdom. Measures to this end will be announced in a two-day debate in Parliament on Wednesday the 6th and Thursday the 7th August.

2. In this connexion His Majesty's Government in the United Kingdom wish to suggest that, as a first step, a discussion with the United States Government should take place forthwith on a high official level about our position and its immediate implications. His Majesty's Government propose to announce in Parliament that they have made this approach to the United States Government. They hope that it will prove acceptable and it would be a great help to Ministers if they could inform Parliament that it had been accepted.

3. I am instructed to emphasize that this approach is not intended to settle matters which are proper for discussion at the Paris Conference,[1] or subsequent developments in response to your initiative. But His Majesty's Government feel strongly that it might be embarrassing to both our Governments if we were to attempt too close a definition at this stage as to the matters to be discussed.

4. I am asked to add that the United States Government may prefer that His Majesty's Government should now invoke consultation under Clause 12 of the Anglo-American Financial Agreement, to which I referred in the course of my conversation with you on the 28th July. In that event, His Majesty's Government would be ready to do so.

5. His Majesty's Government would greatly appreciate your early comments on the foregoing proposals.

Yours sincerely,

JOHN BALFOUR

---

[1] Reference here is to the Committee of European Economic Cooperation, which began its deliberations on July 12, 1947, in Paris. For documentation see pp. 249 ff.

841.51/8–447

The Secretary of State to the British Chargé (Balfour)

TOP SECRET   [WASHINGTON,] August 4, 1947.

MY DEAR MR. CHARGÉ D'AFFAIRES: In reply to your communication to me of August 2 I wish to inform you that the United States Government is prepared to accept the suggestion of His Majesty's Government that a discussion should take place forthwith between us, on a high official level, concerning your position and its immediate implications. I assume from your communication that you contemplate sending an official of high rank to Washington for any such discussions.

My Government is in entire agreement with the view expressed in your communication that such discussions should not be regarded as affecting the matters under consideration at the Paris Conference. In order to avoid any misunderstanding on this point my Government feels that any reference to or announcement of such discussions make it clear that they are to deal with problems arising out of the Anglo-American Financial Agreement.

We feel the decision whether or not to invoke Clause 12 of the Anglo-American Financial Agreement is one which, at this juncture, would appear to rest with the British Government. You will understand, however, that this Government could agree to no action under this clause without prior authorization by the Congress.

I agree that it is not necessary at this stage to attempt to define too closely the matters which are to be discussed.[1]

Faithfully yours,   G. C. MARSHALL

---

[1] The texts of this reply and of the British letter of August 2 were sent to London in telegram 3374 on August 6 (841.51/8–647).

841.51/8–647 : Telegram

The Secretary of State to the Embassy in the United Kingdom

TOP SECRET   WASHINGTON, August 6, 1947—3 a. m.
NIACT

3364. From Wood. Following Top Secret letter received Sect [Secretary] from Balfour 7 : 25 p. m., EDT, August 5 :

"I have been instructed to notify you that in the debate in the House of Commons on the 6th August, His Majesty's Government in the United Kingdom will announce that they have decided that they must make an immediate and substantial reduction in their purchases of foodstuffs from hard currency areas. They are, therefore, making a reduction in the rate of these purchases of the order of £12,000,000.

(twelve million pounds sterling) a month. Such a reduced rate of buying from hard currency sources will mean that they will completely stop the buying from those sources of luxury foods. Bulk long term contracts for staple foodstuffs from these areas will not be interfered with.

The effect of this decision on the level of distribution of foodstuffs in the immediate future will depend upon a number of factors. The first is the degree to which His Majesty's Government are able to buy their foodstuffs from soft currency sources. So far as these soft currency sources are, all things considered, more favorable from the commercial point of view, the question of discrimination under Article 9 of the Loan Agreement will not, of course, arise. Where, however, such purchases cannot be justified under the Loan Agreement, His Majesty's Government will be exploring the situation with the United States Government to see what steps can be taken to enable them to obtain supplies from soft currency areas. A second factor will be the length of time for which this policy must be continued.

In asking me to inform you of the above-mentioned statement, which will give an account of the effect of this policy on rationing in the immediate future, His Majesty's Government are confident that the United States Government are fully aware of the reasons that have led them to take these steps. They emphasize that the application of this policy will involve no unilateral breach by His Majesty's Government of Article 9 of the Loan Agreement. Such questions as involve Article 9 will, of course, come within the scope of the forthcoming official talks."

Following draft of reply which intended give them formally August 6 handed informally to Magowan and Hutton [1] midnight EDT August 5 with request they transmit urgently British Government:

"I refer to your letter to me of August 5th in which you inform me of your government's decision to announce in Parliament on August 6th the reduction by £12,000,000 monthly of purchases of foodstuffs in hard currency areas.

I am happy to note your statement that the application of the policy which the British Government proposes to announce will involve no breach of Article 9 of the Anglo-American Financial Agreement.

I shall, of course, be questioned by the press and public as to the effect of this announcement on the Loan Agreement. Until we have a fuller understanding as to the specific measures your government proposes to adopt, it seems appropriate to limit my replies to a general statement to the effect that your government has advised me that no breach of the agreement will be involved.

It is my understanding, of course, that all matters of interpretation relative to the Loan Agreement will continue to be the subject of discussion and mutual agreement between our two governments."

---

[1] Maurice I. Hutton, head of the British Mission in the United States.

When we handed draft reply [2] to Magowan and Hutton, we advised them in following sense:

1. That it was a draft of letter we proposed sending on August 6 and that it represented the only official statement we felt we could make at this time.

2. That there were certain points raised by British letter which gave us some concern and that we believed it desirable to indicate them in most unofficial manner. We stressed that our unofficial comments should not be considered as US position nor as a suggestion to British as to manner in which they should handle this matter under difficult circumstances confronting them at home.

3. British letter seemed to contradict itself. Although it stated that policy to be announced would not involve a breach of loan agreement, this was hard to reconcile with statement that reduction in buying from hard currency sources of luxury foods would completely stop. We suggested that if purchases from hard currency sources of these items was completely stopped, it would result in breach of Article 9 of agreement. British pointed out that ways and means might be found to avoid this, particularly if intended cut imports and consumption in these items was drastic enough. We repeated here that we were accepting their statement that there would be no breach, despite our qualms.

4. We expressed view that if Attlee [3] states or implies publicly that there will be a 12 million pound monthly reduction in purchases of "luxury foods", the public reaction in this country might be bad. The implications involved in this might leave British open to charge that they have been frittering away large parts of loan on luxury items. British agreed on this point and are apparently suggesting to London that terminology "less essential" be substituted for "luxury".

5. In response to direct inquiry British assured us that existence of soft currency was not among commercial considerations although it was mutually agreed that no meeting of minds had been reached on elements involved commercial considerations and hence matter for further consultation.

6. British on most confidential basis listed hard currency countries as Canada, U.S., Argentina, Brazil, Paraguay, Uruguay, possibly Cuba with Switzerland special case.

---

[2] The telegraphed text of Secretary Marshall's proposed reply to the British Chargé, Sir John Balfour, is substantially that which was made on August 6. The final paragraph of the latter follows: "It must be understood that I can make no commitment at this time other than to explore the situation with your government at the forthcoming official talks which you have requested and that all matters of interpretation relative to the Anglo-American Financial Agreement will continue to be subject to mutual agreement between our two governments." (841.51/8–647)

[3] Clement Richard Attlee, British Prime Minister.

British emphasized throughout that they were speaking unofficially and without complete information.

Repeated to Paris for Clayton and Douglas 2912; repeated to Geneva for Wilcox 957.

MARSHALL

841.51/8–747 : Circular Instruction

The Secretary of State to Certain Diplomatic and Consular Officers [1]

SECRET WASHINGTON, August 7, 1947.

The Secretary of State refers to that portion dealing with Section 9 in a circular instruction dated February 17, 1947 sent to certain American Consular Officers under the title "Relation of Sections 8 and 9 of Anglo-American Financial Agreement to British Colonial Dependencies."

For the information of the Officers in Charge, a copy of each of the following documents is attached:

1) Memorandum handed to Assistant Secretary of State for Economic Affairs by Sir John Magowan of the British Embassy, Washington, on April 28, 1947.[2]

2) Proposed directive to be sent to British dependencies by the British Colonial Office.[2]

3) Statement read by the Secretary of State at his press conference on July 23, 1947.[3]

4) *Aide-Mémoire* sent to Sir John Magowan of the British Embassy, Washington, by Assistant Secretary of State for Economic Affairs on July 24, 1947.

The Officers in Charge will note that the Government of the United Kingdom proposes to implement Section 9 of the Financial Agreement in those colonial dependencies in which it has the authority to do so. However, as will be noted from the proposed British directive, the dependencies in question as well as Burma and Southern Rhodesia which share with the United Kingdom a common membership and quota in the International Monetary Fund would be free mutually to discriminate in favor of one another in the administration of their quantitative import restrictions.

The National Advisory Council on International Monetary and Financial Problems carefully considered this proposal of a variation from nondiscrimination. The Council decided that the proposal was not inconsistent with the Financial Agreement.

---

[1] Sent to 36 posts, primarily consular offices in British colonial dependencies.
[2] Not printed, but see footnote 2, p. 34.
[3] Printed in Department of State *Bulletin*, August 3, 1947, pp. 228–229.

In considering this question, the Council gave considerable weight to the fact that the original *Proposals for Expansion of World Trade and Employment* [5] and the Financial Agreement were negotiated at the same time and as parts of the same series of negotiations. The text of the Financial Agreement and of a Joint Statement on Commercial Policy by the United States and the United Kingdom, announcing agreement in principle of the two countries on the Proposals, was issued by this Government in a single document in December 1945.[6] Section C(5) of the Proposals states that Members (of the proposed International Trade Organization) should not be prohibited from applying quantitative restrictions in a manner designed to maintain the par value of the currencies of the territories having a common quota in the Monetary Fund. A similar provision was included in the proposed Charter for an International Trade Organization published by the United States in September 1946,[7] and in the London and New York redrafts of the proposed Charter. It is also included in the Draft General Agreement on Tariffs and Trade which it is proposed to conclude at the meeting now in progress at Geneva [8] with the object of bringing into force certain parts of the Charter prior to the time it will be possible for the entire Charter to be approved and implemented. Moreover it was the understanding of the American negotiators at the time of negotiation of Section 9 that if balance-of-payments requirements made it necessary the United Kingdom and those dependencies sharing with it a common quota and membership in the International Monetary Fund could discriminate in favor of imports from one another. The current balance-of-payments position of the United Kingdom and the fact that unrestricted colonial expenditures would be a serious drain on the dollar availabilities of the United Kingdom appear to make the common quota exception fully applicable at the present time.

It will be noted that in its *Aide-Mémoire* to the British Embassy of July 24, 1947 the Department has proposed discussions at the technical level with respect to the form of quantitative import controls to be adopted in the dependencies. The Officers in Charge will be informed of further developments.

In view of recent constitutional changes in Burma and the omission of Burma from the list of colonial dependencies in the Halifax letter,[9] the Department is studying the question whether common quota discrimination applies to Burma.

---

[5] Department of State publication 2411.
[6] Department of State publication 2439, Commercial Policy Series 80.
[7] For documentation regarding this subject, see the index entry in *Foreign Relations*, 1946, volume I.
[8] For documentation on the negotiations at Geneva, see volume I.
[9] See footnotes 1 and 3, p. 34.

FW 841.51/8–647

Memorandum by the Assistant Secretary of State for Economic Affairs (Thorp) to the Under Secretary of State (Lovett)

[WASHINGTON,] August 8, 1947.

The British Chargé d'Affaires has asked the Secretary whether the first stages of the conversations to which we have agreed might be held in London. I have recommended to the Secretary that he indicate his firm belief that all conversations be held here in Washington. One reason for this is our conviction that the interests of the British themselves would be prejudiced with American opinion were we put in the position (to use Secretary Snyder's words) of "a banker running to the convenience of his debtor." The British, anticipating that we might be of this opinion, have indicated that they will, if we so desire, make arrangements for meetings here.

We may assume, I think, that the conversations will commence within the next ten days or two weeks. It is planned that the American side be the National Advisory Council. As you know, it was the Council which conducted the original negotiations with the British; moreover, "the Secretary, in consultation with the National Advisory Council" is authorized by the British Loan Act, "to carry out the (Financial) Agreement." In this way, too, the Secretary of Commerce, the Chairman of the Board of Governors of the Federal Reserve System, and the Chairman of the Export-Import Bank will be drawn officially into the negotiations along with State and Treasury.

Conversations with Treasury indicate that negotiations are likely to be divided into two parts, one concerning convertibility, the other involving discrimination. The former will probably be directed by Treasury, whereas the latter involves us primarily. Mr. Ness has advanced to Treasury the suggestion that Agriculture should be represented on the latter group, and has met with favorable response from his opposite numbers.

We are undertaking to keep Mr. Clayton advised by cable.

FW 841.51/8–1247

The Acting Secretary of State to the British Chargé (Balfour)

[WASHINGTON,] August 14, 1947.

MY DEAR MR. CHARGÉ D'AFFAIRES: I have received your letter of August 12 [1] advising me that your government's delegation for the forthcoming talks on financial matters will arrive in Washington this weekend in anticipation of discussions beginning Monday.

---

[1] Not printed.

On our side these discussions will be conducted by the National Advisory Council on International Monetary and Financial Problems, of which, as you know, the Secretary of Treasury is Chairman. I have informed Mr. Snyder of the contents of your letter.

Sincerely yours,

ROBERT A. LOVETT

841.51/8–1947

Memorandum by the Sub-Committee on Commercial Policy of the NAC Staff Committee [1]

SECRET

[WASHINGTON,] August 16, 1947.

Subject: Relaxation of the Provisions of Section 9

Before any decision is taken to relax the provisions of Section 9, it must be conclusively proved that such action will materially alleviate the British dollar position. If this is proved, it will be necessary to determine the procedure by which this relaxation can best be effected. This paper attempts to indicate in general terms the possible significance of a relaxation of Section 9 and to outline the possible procedures for effecting it.

POSSIBLE BRITISH REQUEST

There has been no indication of the specific proposals the British intend to make, and it will be necessary to ascertain these in the forthcoming discussions before any conclusive evaluation of the significance of the proposals can be made. The general nature of the probable British proposals is apparent from official statements, however. They want to be free to discriminate in favor of the Dominions* and other countries (Argentina, for example), and possibly to use such discrimination as one means of requiring other countries to discriminate in their favor. There are also indications that recent events and pressure from other countries may be causing the British to move away from acceptance of the general principle of nondiscrimination.

BENEFITS TO THE BRITISH FROM DISCRIMINATORY MEASURES

It is difficult to see how any significant benefits will be obtained by the British solely from a relaxation of Section 9. It should be noted first of all that unless there is some relaxation of the sterling convertibility requirement, the benefits in the form of dollar savings which the British will obtain will be negligible. As long as such convertibility obligations remain in force, countries short of dollars would convert

---

[1] This memorandum was addressed to the NAC Staff Committee and is Anglo-American Financial Discussion Staff document No. 6.

*The NAC has already decided that Section 9 does not apply to the British colonial dependencies. [Footnote in the source text.]

the sterling proceeds of their sales to the United Kingdom into dollars. It may also be noted that in the present situation of a seller's market, many countries would refuse to sell to the United Kingdom unless they could be assured of payment in free or convertible sterling. It therefore follows that a relaxation of Section 9 would help the United Kingdom to save dollars only to the extent that countries like Australia, New Zealand and South Africa would voluntarily refrain from converting their net sterling proceeds.

It is not possible to make, in the short time available, an adequate statistical analysis of the situation to indicate how trade might be diverted by discriminatory measures, but the following considerations indicate some of the limitations which apply:

1. During the period July 1946–March 1947, 36 per cent of U.K. imports from the U.S. consisted of food. Most of this was bought on bulk-purchase arrangements and was presumably obtained from the U.S. because it could not be obtained elsewhere, or could not be obtained as cheaply elsewhere. There are certain types of fruits, however, which might be obtained from other sources at a dollar saving.

2. Another 20 per cent of U.K. imports from the U.S. consisted of tobacco. An increased amount of tobacco might be obtained from Southern Rhodesia if production can be expanded, but this source could not begin to supply the U.K. demand. Moreover, discrimination in favor of Southern Rhodesia is already permitted under the "common quota" principle. Increased amounts of Greek and Turkish tobacco might also substitute for a small part of the U.K. consumption, but this possibility is limited by British "taste" which prefers Virginia leaf. Incidentally, the present supply of American tobacco does not depend on the size of the requirements (which have been reduced somewhat by recent duty increases), but on the fact that British tobacco purchases are limited by a procedure under which the British Government makes dollars available only for the purchase of less than the present British requirements of the U.S. tobacco.

3. Another 6 per cent consisted of raw cotton, all bought through a central government buying agency, and presumably purchased from the U.S. because it could not be obtained elsewhere.

4. Petroleum products accounted for about 10 per cent of U.K. imports from the U.S. Possibly some of these purchases might be diverted by discriminatory arrangements, but in view of the petroleum supply situation such diversion is unlikely to amount to much.

5. The remaining 28 per cent consisted of a wide range of products including wood and timber, metals, machinery and chemicals, which were probably obtainable for the most part only in the U.S. or Canada.

As long as the United Kingdom abides by the convertibility provisions of the Financial Agreement, and as long as the nondiscrimination provisions of the ITO Charter remain the basis of international trade policy, it is not possible to foresee how there will be any really significant benefits to the British from a setting aside of the provisions of Section 9. The privilege of discriminating in favor of non-dollar countries would be important to the United Kingdom only to the extent that (*a*) the United Kingdom could pay such countries in convertible sterling or enter into firm commitments for future deliveries of goods; and (*b*) it aided the United Kingdom in compelling other countries to discriminate in its favor, through bilateral trade arrangements or otherwise.

Nevertheless, we should be prepared to consider sympathetically whatever specific proposals the British may make. We should insist, however, on conclusive proof that the specific measures which the British would take would in fact result in a substantial saving of dollars. We should therefore request full details of all arrangements or transactions which the British contemplate taking, including the following information.

(*a*) Goods involved
(*b*) Countries involved
(*c*) Types and general terms of arrangements contemplated
(*d*) Estimated dollar savings or other benefits

It is understood, of course, that in determining this Government's position, consideration would also be given to the effects of the British proposals on American export interests.

Possible Method of Meeting the British Request

Proceeding on the assumption that in the course of the discussions we are convinced by the facts presented by the British that some relaxation of the nondiscrimination commitment is necessary, there are a number of methods which might accomplish this result in varying degrees.

1. *Liberal Interpretation of Section 9(b)*. One possible method is the liberal interpretation of the exception for discrimination in favor of countries having war-disrupted economies (Section 9(*b*)). Indications are, however, that this method would not go as far as the British desire. It would be difficult to extend the definition of countries having war-disrupted economies much beyond that suggested by the NAC Working Committee, that is, countries of Europe, North Africa and the Far East which were under enemy occupation. Furthermore, there is a proviso which limits its application to cases where there is special necessity for the U.K. to assist the other country.

2. *"Liberal Attitude" Toward Bulk-Purchase Arrangements*. Although the Section 9 commitment does not refer specifically to state trading, the British Government has indicated that it recognizes that bulk-purchasing arrangements are subject to the nondiscrimination rule, and that such arrangements would not conform to the rule unless they involve purchases which are "all things considered, more favor-

able from the commercial point of view"† than purchases from the U.S.

There is considerable scope for interpretation in such cases, however, and it might be possible to give the British some leeway without contravening Section 9. At any rate any specific proposals for contracts of a short-term nature which the British may make could be considered with this possibility in mind.

3. *Modification of Section 9.* The most direct method for making discrimination permissible would be by the formal modification of Section 9. The most logical modification would be to replace the existing commitment with one conforming in general to the new article on discrimination agreed for inclusion in the ITO Charter. Such modification would, however, require the consent of Congress and hence would involve considerable delay. However, it has been suggested by the U.S. Delegation at the Geneva Conference that this Government could agree to offer not to invoke the rule against discrimination in Section 9 pending action by the Congress on the Charter, with the understanding that, upon coming into effect, the more flexible provisions of the Charter supersede the provisions of Section 9. (These provisions, incidentally, already represent a substantial concession to the British point of view. One argument in justification for such action would be that the Financial Agreement itself (Section 8 (*iii*)) contemplates that the provisions of Section 9 are "in anticipation of more comprehensive arrangements by multilateral agreement". Before such an offer could be made, it would however be necessary to consult and obtain the agreement of Congressional leaders.

There are precedents for this procedure and it is believed that the much-publicized British crisis and its international political implications would justify, in the public mind, this emergency action. It should also be emphasized that this procedure (assuming, of course, we are convinced of its necessity) is probably the only one by which we can give the British the relief they desire in time to afford them any significant assistance in the present crisis.

Conditions of Such a Concession

In view of the political difficulties and dangers which may be involved in making such a concession, however, it will be necessary that this Government be able to demonstrate to Congress and the public that it has agreed to this course of action only as a temporary, emergency measure, and that in return for the concession we have obtained from the British long-run commitments which hold forth a firm promise to return to nondiscrimination and multilateral trading as soon as

---

†Statement by the British Prime Minister in the House of Commons, August 6, 1947. [Footnote in the source text.]

conditions permit. These commitments can best be obtained by the successful conclusion of the Geneva negotiations. The U.S. Delegation at Geneva considers that satisfactory British action on the following points must be the *quid pro quo* for any such concession on our part and as evidence of their good faith and good intentions.

(1) Fulfillment of the previous British commitment to eliminate preferences of material importance to the U.S. in the U.K., the Dominions and the Colonies;

(2) Support for the U.S. position with respect to outstanding points in the Charter;

(3) Signature of the General Agreement on Trade and Tariffs at the close of the Geneva negotiations and its provisional entry into force during November 1947.

Any action along these lines will of course be subject to reconsideration in the light of Mr. Clayton's current discussions with top British officials in London.

841.51/8–1847 : Telegram

The Ambassador in the United Kingdom (Douglas) to the Secretary of State

SECRET   LONDON, August 18, 1947—3 p.m.
NIACT

4459. For Lovett and Snyder. Bevin asked me to call on him at his office this morning. He explained to me the crisis that had developed during the last week and the decision in principle which the Cabinet had made at its extraordinary meeting yesterday.

1. During the five days, August 10–15, there had occurred a drain on British dollar resources in the amount of $175,900,000. This figure compares with an average weekly drain during the proceeding six weeks of $115,000,000 and with an average weekly drain during the second quarter of this year of $77,000,000.

2. The Bank of England and the Treasury estimate the very minimum future drain at $175,000,000 each week and a probable maximum drain of about $300,000,000 each week.

3. The British calculate that on this basis, the remaining $700,000,-000 of the American loan may last about two weeks.

4. The run on sterling that commenced prior to July 15 has therefore now assumed huge proportions. Much of the drain is on current account, a substantial part is on capital account, but, whatever the cause, the drain is very heavy.

5. If, Bevin said, the issue were purely a monetary and financial one, he would oppose taking any steps. He felt, however, that it was not purely a financial and monetary one, that a break in sterling would necessarily lead to bilateral arrangements, shrinking of trade at the very time they were attempting to expand trade. That it would have

profound effect, adversely, on the attitude of both France and Italy, with the possibility of political crisis there. A break in sterling probably would, he felt, impair if not destroy all the efforts that had been made over the course of the last two years in the political field and would create so much confusion that even the present position might never be recovered. Certainly he felt that it would aggravate aggressive action throughout Europe and particularly in the danger spots by the Soviet.

6. Because of this broad political question which Bevin felt is of such significance to US and to Britain, the Cabinet had decided to take unilateral action (Embtel 4382, August 13 [1]) to protect sterling. He was particularly anxious that this be not construed in the US as a repudiation of any commitment made or of the terms of the loan agreement and he pressed the view that this sort of action was taken purely as a stop-gap to hold the status quo while we with the UK could survey all the facts and review the whole situation. I am confident that he was expressing an honest and sincere view of the British Government when he made this statement.

7. Bevin was not able to give me officially the precise measures which the British Government would take. They were still in the formulation period. He hoped, however, to be able to get a communication to Sir Wilfred Eady for the meeting with John Snyder this afternoon in Washington at 3 o'clock.[2] This statement would include precise measures which Britain proposed to take.

8. At the risk of reiteration, Bevin expresses the deep hope that you will not construe this action as a violation or repudiation of the commitments but rather as a purely stop-gap measure which he believed absolutely essential be taken within the next 48 hours to prevent the sort of catastrophe which he outlined.

DOUGLAS

[1] Not printed.
[2] Reference here is to the Anglo-American financial discussions which began on August 18.

841.51/8–1947 : Telegram

The Acting Secretary of State to the Secretary of State at Petropolis [1]

TOP SECRET
US URGENT

WASHINGTON, August 19, 1947—11 a. m.

30. Humelsine to Carter.[2] Eyes Only Secretary Marshall from Lovett. We were notified by British yesterday afternoon through

[1] Secretary Marshall was head of the U.S. Delegation to the Inter-American Conference for the Maintenance of Continental Peace and Security at Quintandinha, near Petropolis, Brazil, between August 15 and September 2, 1947.
[2] Carlisle H. Humelsine was Director of the Executive Secretariat, Office of the Secretary of State; Marshall S. Carter was Special Assistant to the Secretary of State.

Deputy Governor, Bank of England, flown in for purpose, that special British Cabinet meeting Sunday night reached decision to impose through Bank of England dollar exchange rationing in desperate effort halt what amounts to full scale flight from pound sterling. This reached rate of 237 million dollars in six days. All but 550 million dollars of loan has been notified for withdrawal. British proposed to make announcement their action at four o'clock Washington time today.

Obviously this announcement and action will be tremendous shock and will have widest repercussions, notably on economies non-sterling areas, including particularly certain South American countries. We pointed out that notice given us was completely inadequate permit any attempt to soften impact of this unilateral action and in late night session at Treasury which I attended at Snyder's request we urged British postpone announcement and effective date for at least another twenty-four hour period. Answer on this due this morning.

While British claim their action is within broad intent of loan agreement and possibly covered by Section 8 Subdivision 2, we feel this may constitute breach of loan agreement and therefore suggested last night arrangement under which we in effect freeze the loan, preventing withdrawals beyond those presently notified for a period of one week's grace during which lawyers can consider fundamental problems involved. In absence of such temporary arrangement which only postpones day of reckoning, contemplated British action represents desperate attempt Britain to go it alone regardless of consequences to herself and Europe.

Britain gives positive assurances that under exchange rationing there will be no defaults by her on existing dollar contracts with U.S. exporters. She admits however that it may require action approaching breach of bilateral trade agreements with sixteen other countries.

It begins to appear that Churchill's [3] charge that loan was largely "frittered away" is not far off mark. In interest of over-all recovery, we are and will continue to do utmost to keep Britain afloat but it is clear she must stop biting our hand.

Answers from London on controlling questions due this morning. Will report later on day's developments. All above information is top secret.

Postscript: flash message received before dispatch British Treasury agrees further postponement twenty-four hours.

LOVETT

---

[3] Winston S. Churchill, former Prime Minister.

841.5151/8–1947 : Telegram

The Acting Secretary of State to the Consulate at Geneva

TOP SECRET · · · · · · · · · · WASHINGTON, August 19, 1947—5 p. m.

1028. For Clayton's Eyes Only from Lovett. Eady informed Snyder yesterday morning of his government's intention to suspend as of close of business today transfer of sterling to dollar accounts, in effect terminating convertibility. Cited rapid increase rate of weekly drawing from 77 million in second quarter, 115 million in July to 237 million last six days. Eady gave assurance however that this action would not effect transactions between UK and US. Specifically proposed that following this action UK would ration dollars against sterling.

Eady asserted restriction would extend beyond elimination capital transfers to limitation current items. In these circumstances we are confronted with question whether breach agreement involved. At present seems clear only escapes must be found in Section eight-two, especially para B. Also seems equally clear that phrase "exceptional cases" refers individual countries. Br insist cannot at this time apply restrictions basis individual countries.

In this situation informed Br last night that unless they could limit action within agreement if confronted by unilateral action we would have to assert breach agreement and freeze unnotified balance credit (550 million). Suggested as alternative (*a*) that Br advise us by letter of (1) proposed act (2) continued Br stake in securing convertibility of sterling, (3) consistency of action with purpose and intent agreement, (4) desire to consult reference section 8 and (*b*) that we reply (1) expressing sympathy gravity British problem, (2) indicating uncertainty re consistency terms agreement (3) agreeing week consultation during which unnotified portion credit frozen. Br demurred especially re implications last two items. Br suggested asking London twenty-four hour postponement action during which explore alternatives. Br have now informed us London agrees this postponement.

LOVETT

841.51/8–1947

Minutes of the Combined United States–United Kingdom Technical Committee, Anglo-American Financial Discussions, August 19, 1947, Washington, D.C.

SECRET

Participants:

U.K. MEMBERS:

Sir John Magowan, U.K. Embassy, Washington

Mr. Edgar Jones, Treasury Delegation, Washington
Mr. H. J. Lintott, Board of Trade
Mr. P. S. Beale, Bank of England
Mr. L. P. Thompson-McCausland, Bank of England
Mr. Marcus Fleming, Cabinet Offices
Miss G. M. Jennings, U.K. Treasury
Mr. G. Parker, Board of Trade

U.S. MEMBERS:

Mr. Harold Glasser, Treasury Department [Chairman]
Mr. Paul H. Nitze, State Department
Mr. Emilio G. Collado, State Department
Mr. J. J. Stenger, State Department
Mr. Clarence I. Blau, Commerce Department
Mr. John M. Cassels, Commerce Department
Mr. J. Burke Knapp, Board of Governors, Federal Reserve System
Mr. Frank M. Tamagna, Board of Governors, Federal Reserve System
Mr. Charles R. Harley, Board of Governors, Federal Reserve System
Mr. Hal Lary, Export-Import Bank
Mr. Orvis A. Schmidt, Treasury Department
Mr. John S. Richards, Treasury Department
Mr. John Gunter, Treasury Department
Mr. George H. Willis, Treasury Department
Mr. Joseph B. Friedman, Treasury Department
Mr. Charles R. McNeill, Treasury Department
Mr. Fred B. Smith, Treasury Department
Mr. Philip P. Schaffner, Treasury Department

RÉSUMÉ OF COMBINED TOP COMMITTEE MEETING [1]

Prior to the arrival of the British delegation at the meeting, Mr. Knapp gave a résumé of the combined U.S.–U.K. Top Committee meeting of August 18. Sir Wilfrid Eady had pointed out that the relatively favorable appearance of the 1946 U.K. balance of payments on current account was superficial. Exports were made in a sellers market and imports were supplemented by the drawing down of stocks. He had also stated that the required minimum level of imports for the U.K. was 85 percent of the prewar volume. The domestic situation during 1946 demonstrated a straining of the U.K. economy resulting from (a) inadequate stocks of materials, (b) accumulated under-maintenance of equipment and (c) excessive demands on production facilities for reconstruction, increase of living standards and exports. Due to the inadequacy of stocks, the fuel and transportation crisis cost the British an estimated $800 million of exports.

---

[1] No other record of this meeting found in Department of State files.

Sir Wilfrid had also stated that convertibility and non-discrimination formed the underlying basis of the Financial Agreement and had emphasized that sterling had to be an international currency or nothing. The basic assumptions of the Financial Agreement, however, had been nullified by subsequent events—mainly the world scarcity of dollars. This situation had increased the burden of convertibility since many countries were unwilling to accumulate sterling balances. He had not mentioned the subject of additional U.S. financial aid but implied that certain terms of the Financial Agreement should be waived. He had described the difficult task of recruiting labor for coal production and said the situation in textiles was weak.

Mr. Knapp concluded his résumé by suggesting that the British be asked to furnish a statement of sterling balances by countries, at semi-annual intervals beginning with June 30, 1945.

Working Group and Agendas

The setting up of working groups and agendas was discussed. It was agreed that a Commercial Policy Group and a Financial Group should be established and that a small combined group should work on the statistics required by the Financial Group. Mr. Jones pointed out the difficulties of preparing estimates for 1948 and 1949 in the absence of agreed-upon assumptions concerning such factors as convertibility and the Marshall Plan. He added that the British delegation planned to return to London on Monday, August 25.

It was agreed that the possibilities for relaxation of Section 9 of the Financial Agreement should constitute the agenda of the Commercial Policy Group. In this connection, a British representative mentioned the difficulties of forecasting the benefits that might result to the U.K. from a relaxation of Section 9.

It was agreed that the Financial Group should concern itself with the convertibility problem. The Chairman asked if the U.S. side could be furnished estimates of the U.K. dollar drain in 1948 and 1949 on the assumption that there would be no modification of convertibility. The British representatives indicated that no precise estimates of the drain could be given. They promised, however, to elaborate the statistical data for the period since June 30, 1947, particularly with reference to changes in the U.K. monetary reserves and the uses to which dollars had been put.

The Chairman inquired about the form in which the Committee's conclusions should be presented. The head of the British delegation expressed the hope that a substantial degree of agreement could be reached by the Committee before presenting conclusions for consideration by the National Advisory Council. He thought, however, that a few matters, such as the German problem, would have to be presented to the Council directly.

The Committee then divided into the Commercial Policy and Financial Groups for further discussion.[2]

---

[2] Minutes of these meetings are in Department of State file 841.51/8–1947.

841.5151/8–1947 : Telegram

The Acting Secretary of State to the Embassy in the United Kingdom

SECRET   WASHINGTON, August 19, 1947—9 p. m.

NIACT

3572. For Clayton. This message covers only technical discussions with U.K. subdelegation on commercial policy which began today with presentation of types of discrimination permitted by Art. 28 [1] but not by Section 9 which British desire to undertake. The examples given did not indicate that any large savings in dollar exchange or increase in imports could be expected. However Lintott emphasized the public relations importance in U.K. of even limited benefits. Lintott further repeated Cripps statement that complete freedom to use full economic pressures to secure favorable bilateral compensation agreements might be needed if U.K. had back to wall and that they might not even be able to agree to an amendment to Section 9 which would bind them to provisions of Art. 28. Meeting terminated with no position being taken our side other than to point out the implications of the U.K. position and the difficulty of significant relaxation Section 9 without Congressional approval.

LOVETT

---

[1] Reference is to Article 28, "Exceptions to the Rule of Non-Discrimination", of the draft charter of the International Trade Organization.

841.51/8–2047 : Telegram

The Acting Secretary of State to the Secretary of State at Petropolis

TOP SECRET   WASHINGTON, August 20, 1947—2 p. m.

NIACT

46. Humelsine to Carter Eyes Only Secretary Marshall from Lovett. Meetings with Treas yesterday on Brit financial agreement and proposed Brit action to impose through Bank of Eng dollar exchange rationing as of 4 p.m. Wash time today, highlighted by fol:

(1) Treas disposition to strain interpretation financial agreement in order permit Brit to stop convertibility pounds to dollars for countries other than those in sterling area and United States. While specific

proposal advanced by Treas and acceptable to Sec of Treas was ingenious, it nevertheless opened us to serious Congressional charge that our action would be in effect a modification of agreement which under terms agreement can only be done after consultation between govts and submission modifications to respective legislatures.

(2) Our basic position was that we cannot risk approving any Brit action as falling within terms of agreement which would, however, in effect really constitute breach of agreement. While agreement does not provide for any penalties for breach, nevertheless it is clear that a substantial breach by Brit would require us to stop performance on our part contract by prohibiting the Brit from making any further withdrawals from balance of fund remaining under loan. While agreement does provide for Brit suspending convertibility in exceptional cases, it is clear from legislative history and particularly from Clayton's testimony that such proviso was intended to be applied only on a case-by-case basis and on proof by Brit to our satisfaction that financial relations between Britain and particular country for which exception requested require suspension convertibility. However, to permit an across-the-board suspension of convertibility on basis of exceptional cases, would require us to misinterpret agreement and to ignore legislative history.

(3) Proposal finally worked out which met our objections and which was approved by Sec of Treas and me last evening for submission to Brit was as fol:

(a) Brit to address letter to us advising that they find it necessary to take stringent measures to counter recent excessive drains on dollar resources which drains, if permitted to continue, would defeat objectives of financial agreement. Accordingly Brit advise that control of transferability to be imposed at close business today. Action is taken as an emergency and temporary measure which Brit consider to be within intention and purposes of agreement and which they hope will enable them to take appropriate action to assure limited dollar resources of UK available for purposes contemplated by agreement. Brit confirm that payments between UK and US will not be affected by this action and that restrictions now contemplated should not be interpreted as indicating modification of Brit view of desirability maintaining full and free convertibility of sterling which, as long-run objective, is indispensable to Brit financial policy. Brit state that under circumstances, financial agreement provides for consultation prior to agreement if exceptions are to be made to the principle of convertibility. Brit would not propose to notify any further withdrawals from remaining balance of loan until consultation has been carried out.

(b) US reply takes sympathetic note of grave drains on Brit dollar resources in excess of normal flow of current transactions with consequent peril to re-creation multilateral payment system which is major objective financial agreement. Letter advises that we understand action Brit taking today is of emergency and temporary nature deemed essential to afford Brit opportunity to take measures to protect system of convertibility from abuses endangering its survival. US notes with satisfaction assurances of UK that it will be possible to work out proposed action within terms and purposes of agreement. Also notes statement in last sentence in (*a*) above.

(4) At meeting last night Brit agreed to transmit to UK for its approval exchange of letters outlined (3) above. We have just been advised that Brit Government has approved and announcement is being made at 4 p. m. this afternoon.[1]

LOVETT

[1] The texts of the letters exchanged by Secretary of the Treasury Snyder and Chancellor Dalton are printed in "Report of Activities of the National Advisory Council on International Monetary and Financial Problems, April 1, 1947 to September 30, 1947", Appendix "C", House Document No. 501, 80th Cong., 2nd sess., pp. 22–23. The letters were released simultaneously in Washington and London and were printed in the *New York Times*, August 21, 1947.

841.5151/8–2047 : Telegram

The Ambassador in the United Kingdom (Douglas) to the Secretary of State

US URGENT   LONDON, August 20, 1947.

4529. British Treasury announced at 9 :20 British Standard Time that a Treasury order (SRO 1947 No. 1785) has been issued effective August 21 with regard to suspension of sterling convertibility. The order repeats the substance of the existing payments orders with the following amendments:

(1) Sterling can no longer be freely transferred from transferable account (of nonresidents of the sterling area) to American accounts or Canadian accounts but remains otherwise transferable as hitherto.
(2) Sterling on Canadian account may only be used in Canada or the sterling area. Canadian transferable accounts disappear. Instruc-tions to banks are being issued by the Bank of England.
Text of Dalton's broadcast follows.[1]

DOUGLAS

[1] Telegram 4530, not printed. In a BBC broadcast Mr. Dalton had announced the suspension of convertibility.

841.50/8–2247 : Telegram

The Acting Secretary of State to the Embassy in the United Kingdom

CONFIDENTIAL   WASHINGTON, August 22, 1947—8 p. m.

3648. For Douglas. NAC meeting this afternoon confined to presen-tation by Eady of problem presented to UK by Section 9 in view of increased dollar shortage and potential increased availability of goods in areas in which other payment possibilities might be available to UK. He went on to say that discussions at the technical level had indicated UK may have been interpreting Section 9 too strictly but that a solution of the UK problem would probably require some form of agreed modification of Section 9. No decision taken by NAC other than work at the technical level should continue. Eady returning London tomorrow.

LOVETT

841.51/8–2347 : Telegram

The Acting Secretary of State to the Secretary of State at Petropolis

TOP SECRET   WASHINGTON, August 23, 1947.

78. Humelsine for Carter. For Secretary Marshall from Lovett. British financial talks at top level terminating today with leaders British Delegation returning to London to report progress of conference to their Government and discuss policy requirements. Other members Delegation are remaining to continue technical discussions next week. Conferences have been divided into two broad categories, one dealing with the convertibility and foreign exchange problem, and the other with the non-discriminatory clauses relating to US–UK trade.

As indicated in previous cables, temporary procedures for dealing with financial aspects have been worked out under Section 8, Subsection 2, and trade aspects to be covered in general by adjustments coming within terms of section[s] 8 and 9.[1]

In my opinion British must show far more managerial competence and more flexibility in their control measures than heretofore exhibited if they are to operate within the broad terms and purposes of the loan agreement. Even with improved operations and elastic policy I feel that the measures taken here in these conferences are temporary and that a renewal of the crisis is likely in about two months. This time is important since it gives opportunity to obtain proposals from the Paris conference and try to work out integrated program.

LOVETT

---

[1] In a Cabinet meeting on August 29, "the Secretary of the Treasury reported on the concluding stages of the British loan agreement talks and indicated that it was expected that the British would continue to operate within the terms and conditions of the Act, using such latitude as was permitted in Sections 8 and 9." (811.5043/8–2947)

841.51/9–447 : Telegram

The Ambassador in the United Kingdom (Douglas) to the Secretary of State

SECRET   LONDON, September 4, 1947—7 p. m.

4809. For Lovett from the Ambassador. Public statements by British officials interpret Article 9 of financial agreement as preventing purchases by Britain of needed imports because this would also require purchases in dollar area and expenditure of dollar resources urgently needed for other purposes.

I have been considering desirability of suggesting to Bevin that steps be taken to avoid erroneous and provocative interpretations of this character but clearly the only way of allaying completely criticism and misunderstanding on this point would be relaxing Article 9 by exchange of letters possibly along line of State Department draft brought back by Hawkins from Washington.[1]

Understand that Treasury had doubts about this draft but that effort was to be made to reach agreement with Treasury by beginning of this week. Not advised whether any decision reached. I feel that if we are going to relax the obligations of Article 9 it is desirable from the standpoint of British public opinion that this action should not be too long delayed.

DOUGLAS

---

[1] Draft not found in Department of State files.

641.006/9–547

Memorandum of Conversation, by the Acting Assistant Chief of the Division of Commercial Policy (Lewis)

CONFIDENTIAL   [WASHINGTON,] September 5, 1947.

Participants: Mr. Anthony E. Percival, Commercial Counselor, British Embassy
Mr. Corse, Acting Chief, Division of Commercial Policy
Mr. Lewis, Acting Assistant Chief, Division of Commercial Policy

Mr. Percival said he had instructions to give the Department copies of the attached directive [1] which was being sent out on September 5 from London to the Colonial dependencies explaining how colonial import licensing policy should be implemented, particularly with regard to the nondiscrimination provisions of the Anglo-American

---

[1] Not printed.

Financial Agreement. He said a copy was also being handed to our Embassy in London.

Mr. Percival explained that the directive differed in a number of respects from the draft directive which had been submitted to the Department on April 28, 1947 [2] and which was the subject of the Department's *aide-mémoire* of July 24. In the first place, the present crisis in the United Kingdom had made it necessary to stiffen the part of the directive which called on the colonies to curtail purchases from the United Kingdom.[3] In the second place the new directive did not include the "token import" control regimes which had been previously contemplated (whereby imports up to 150 percent of prewar were to be permitted in the West Indian colonies and 50 percent in the other colonies). Instead the colonies were merely being instructed to keep imports from outside the United Kingdom plus Colonies group lower than imports from countries within the group, so far as practicable having regard to supply availabilities. The reason for this was that it was not certain that the token-import plan in the United Kingdom could be continued, and it would not be desirable to have such a system operating in the colonies and not in the United Kingdom.

With regard to the mandates, trust territories and Congo Basin area, Mr. Percival said his Government had not been able to accept the United States position as set forth in the *aide-mémoire* of April 28 [*July 24*] (in which we requested that there be no discrimination against us in these areas in favor of any other country including the United Kingdom). He said he had thought it unfortunate that in the Department's press release of July 23, 1947 reference had been made to this problem, although he realized the release had merely stated that the Department was studying the pertinent international commitments. Mr. Lewis asked whether the new directive was being sent out to the mandates and trust territories. Mr. Percival said it was. Mr. Lewis expressed surprise that this action had been taken without at least discussing the problem with us further, and asked whether Mr. Percival could say upon what reasoning the British Government had rejected our request for non-discrimination in these areas. Mr. Percival said he had not been given any detailed explanation to present to us. He said he presumed the argument was that these territories were a part of the common quota area and hence did not differ from the other colonies. He said the Colonial Office must have considered it important to include them in the scope of the directive. Mr. Lewis said he thought the importance to the United Kingdom of discrimination in these

---

[2] Not printed, but see footnote 2, p. 34.

[3] The directive pointed out that by decreasing intra-Empire trade it would be possible to maximize exports to hard currency areas and to narrow the foreign exchange gap.

areas was not very great. He pointed out that the United States had been willing to concede discrimination in the United Kingdom in favor of the mandates, (so that the United Kingdom could buy Palestine oranges, for example), but he had felt that the principle of equality of treatment ought to be maintained in the mandates themselves. Mr. Corse emphasized the special nature of these territories, referring to the fact that they had been given to the United Kingdom to administer in trust, and to the probability that there would be criticism in this country that the United Kingdom was now attempting to build up its long-term position at the expense of other countries. Mr. Percival suggested it was unlikely that occasion for any public reaction would arise. Mr. Lewis expressed the opinion that on the contrary there would probably be considerable criticism, particularly in the case of Palestine. He referred to the special importance of Palestine because of its large net dollar receipts and possibility that such receipts might not all be used by Palestine directly.

Mr. Lewis also referred to the former Italian colonies and said it seemed to the Department it would be very difficult to explain why there should be discrimination in favor of the United Kingdom in these areas. Here again the adverse reaction might be out of all proportion to any slight benefit which the United Kingdom might obtain.

Mr. Percival mentioned the temporary nature of the arrangement and repeated that he had not been instructed to present any detailed explanation. He said, however, that he had already asked London to provide him with a fuller explanation, and suggested that the Department make a formal request for such an explanation if it desired one. Mr. Corse said it would be helpful if Mr. Percival could let us have informally anything further he received from London on the subject.

Mr. Percival then referred to the proposal in the Department's *aide-mémoire* for discussions at the technical level. He said his Government preferred that these take place in Washington. Mr. Lewis said this was acceptable to us. Mr. Percival said he presumed we would want to wait until specific problems arose in particular colonies and then to discuss them. Mr. Lewis replied that on the contrary we desired some discussion in advance, since the Department of Commerce in particular wanted to point out certain aspects of the import control system which might cause trouble and to make certain suggestions which might be advantageous to both countries. Mr. Percival suggested that Mr. Heatherington of Commerce might talk with him immediately and let him know some of the problems Commerce had in mind so that he could inform London. Mr. Lewis said he would suggest this to Mr. Heatherington.

Mr. Percival was informed that the Department would study the new directive and would consult the other interested agencies, before deciding what further action we might wish to take.

841.51/9–1047 : Telegram

The Secretary of State to the Embassy in the United Kingdom

SECRET WASHINGTON, September 10, 1947—7 p. m.

3944. To Gunter from State and Treas. Postponement of obligation of UK under Financial Agreement granted Jul 14 and 15 with respect to fourteen countries expires Sept 15. The August 20 action relates to modification of transferable account system and apparently not applicable to countries for which postponement granted. In any event it appears desirable to clarify situation by specific extension of postponement for those countries with which the UK has not yet been able to complete arrangements and for which a postponement was previously granted. The following exchange of letters between Dalton and Snyder which has been approved by NAC Staff Committee is suggested as a basis for discussions with the Treas Delegation, other members of the NAC, and the British:

"DEAR MR. SECRETARY : I refer to your letter of Jul 14, 1947 [1] relating to the postponement of certain obligations of the United Kingdom under the Anglo-American Financial Agreement. In accordance with the request of H.M. Government, the United States Government thereby agreed to the postponement until Sept 15, 1947, if necessary, of the obligations under Sections 8 (ii) and 10 of the Financial Agreement in the case of Austria, Bulgaria, China, Denmark, France, Greece, Hungary, Paraguay, Poland, Rumania, Siam, Turkey, the U.S.S.R., and Yugoslavia.

Because of the modification of the system of transferable accounts on Aug. 20, 1947 and the necessity of revising agreements with countries formerly operating under the transferable accounts system, H.M. Government have been unable to complete the necessary arrangements with the countries referred to above. Accordingly, I should be most grateful if the postponement of the obligations of Sections 8 (ii) and 10 of the Financial Agreement with respect to those countries were extended until Nov 15, 1947.

MY DEAR CHANCELLOR : I have received your letter of Sept 15, 1947, requesting a further postponement of the obligations of the United Kingdom under Sections 8 (ii) and 10 of the Anglo-American Financial Agreement.

In accordance with your request the United States Government agrees to the postponement until Nov 15, 1947, if necessary, of the obligations of your Government under the Anglo-American Financial

---

[1] See the editorial note, p. 41.

Agreement in the case of Austria, Bulgaria, China, Denmark, France, Greece, Hungary, Paraguay, Poland, Rumania, Siam, Turkey, the U.S.S.R. and Yugoslavia."

Under the July postponement arrangement the UK agreed to make all sterling accruing after July 15 convertible when the necessary arrangements were completed with the countries for which a postponement was granted. The British may suggest that this retroactive feature be eliminated in connection with further postponement. We see no objection to a waiver to retroactivity if requested as it appears to be of relatively little practical importance. It should be noted however that the Treas press release of Jul 15 stated that Sec Snyder emphasized that the two months postponement does not involve any modification of the obligation of the British Government to permit these countries to dispose freely of sterling accruing between Jul 15 and the date the arrangements are agreed to but involves only the postponement of such disposition.

If it is agreed to dispense with retroactivity, the following paragraph might be added to Mr. Dalton's letter:

In view of recent developments and the reduced amount of dollars available to the United Kingdom, H.M. Government believe it is no longer appropriate that all sterling accruing to those countries between Jul 15, 1947 and the date of completion of the necessary arrangements be made available for payments on current account. I should appreciate being advised whether you agree with this proposal.

In answer the following paragraph might be added to Mr. Snyder's letter:

For the reasons advanced in your letter, the United States agrees that all sterling accruing to those countries before completion of arrangements with them need not be made available for current transactions retroactively to Jul 15, 1947.

MARSHALL

Lot 60 D 137 Box 6

Minutes of the Eighty-Seventh Meeting of the National Advisory Council Staff Committee, Washington, D.C., September 10, 1947

SECRET

Participants:

Mr. Harold Glasser (Chairman), Treasury Department
Mr. Walter M. Day, War Assets Administration, Visitor
Mr. Norman T. Ness, State Department
Mr. Paul H. Nitze, State Department
Mr. Walter S. Surrey, State Department
Mr. James Lewis, State Department
Mr. Clarence I. Blau, Commerce Department

Mr. John M. Cassels, Commerce Department
Mr. Lewis Dembitz, Board of Governors, Federal Reserve System
Mr. Frank M. Tamagna, Board of Governors, Federal Reserve System
Mr. Charles R. Harley, Board of Governors, Federal Reserve System
Mr. Hal Lary, Export-Import Bank
Mr. Walter C. Louchheim, Jr., Securities and Exchange Commission
Mr. John S. Hooker, International Bank
Mr. Frank A. Southard, Jr., Treasury Department
Mr. John S. Richards, Treasury Department
Mr. Andrew M. Kamarck, Treasury Department
Mr. Elting Arnold, Treasury Department
Mr. M. E. Locker, Treasury Department
Mr. George Bronz, Treasury Department
Mr. William L. Hebbard, Treasury Department
Mr. Allan J. Fisher, (Secretary), NAC Secretariat

[Here follows discussion of an unrelated topic.]

2. *Prospective Problems Concerning the U.S.–U.K. Financial Agreement*

The Chairman pointed out that both State Department and Treasury representatives in London had requested guidance from Washington on this matter and said that it was proposed that the Staff Committee send a paper along the lines of Staff Draft No. 152 to London.[1]

The discussion brought out the following points among others:

(1) The British are apparently not considering consultations under Section 12, but an interpretation under Section 9 which would permit them to increase their purchases from third countries.

(2) Unilateral action by a creditor country to limit drawings on sterling accounts would be unobjectionable, whereas a formal agreement to such effect would probably constitute a violation of the Financial Agreement.

(3) If an arrangement is worked out whereby credit is extended to the British, there would be no objection under the terms of the Financial Agreement, but if an agreement is entered into to accumulate sterling, the question of violation of the Financial Agreement might be raised. In this connection, it was agreed that the Staff Committee should give further consideration to the Spanish and Portuguese cases which had previously been reviewed.

(4) The British may consider agreements for acquiring commodities now against the delivery of British goods several years hence. Such a proposal was made to Brazil but was finally rejected by the latter country. The credit aspect of such an arrangement would presumably be unobjectionable but question might be raised as to the attempts to provide an assured market for foreign goods in the United Kingdom and for British goods in the foreign country.

---

[1] Not printed.

(5) The several discriminations which might be permissible within the framework of the Financial Agreement might result in permitting Britain to import a maximum of some $200 million worth of additional goods. While the magnitude of this addition appears relatively small, the political repercussions of failure to secure these imports would be serious.

(6) The evidence is inconclusive as to whether the British are more concerned about the future prospects of their trade than they are about the present emergency. A recent cable indicates that the British have presented schedules on preferences and, apparently, have gone far in meeting the United States position. Since the discussions between Mr. Clayton and Sir Stafford Cripps, the British Government has reviewed its position and is making concessions.[2]

(7) The legislative history of the language "exceptional cases" in Section 8 (*ii*) of the Financial Agreement indicates that a country-to-country basis was contemplated rather than exceptional circumstances in terms of time. However, it was felt that no position should be taken on this point at the present time.

(8) It would appear that under Article VIII of the Articles of Agreement, the British could request the International Monetary Fund's permission to impose exchange controls. The British have not suggested such action and they may be reluctant to be the first to make such a request of the Fund. There are doubts as to whether Article VIII was intended to permit action of this character in view of Articles VII and XIV, and the Fund would probably be reluctant to grant permission. It was agreed that further consideration should be given to this point although it would not be included in the paper.

The SEC representative commented that the paper did not mention British assets in this country, which include excess collateral pledged with the Reconstruction Finance Corporation, unpledged securities, and substantial direct investments. The total of that type of potential relief would far exceed what might be made available under the conditions outlined in the paper. The Chairman pointed out that the paper had to do only with the United States policy with respect to the Financial Agreement and that there were various possibilities of relief outside of convertibility and trade which were not covered. It was agreed that the paper should indicate that no attempt was being made to reassess the financial position of the British at this time.

With respect to the conclusions to be presented in the paper, the Treasury Department representatives pointed out that so far as the

---

[2] On July 31, in Paris, Under Secretary Clayton and Sir Stafford Cripps, British Minister of Economic Affairs, discussed the British critical dollar situation with regard to the ITO negotiations then in progress in Geneva. For documentation concerning U.S.–U.K. discussions and matters related to the proposed establishment of an International Trade Organization, see volume I.

convertibility section of the Agreement was concerned, no breach of the Financial Agreement was involved, since the British had agreed to try to work out a solution within the terms of the Agreement. Only if they were unsuccessful in such attempts would there be need for consultation under Section 12, say by November. The Treasury Department felt, however, that the proposed exchange of letters, with respect to Section 9, saying that because of changed circumstances it was necessary to interpret Section 9 in terms of the Financial Agreement as a whole, would be admitting a breach of the Agreement. The Treasury Department felt the Financial Agreement was unique and tightly drawn, and that it was dangerous to accede to an interpretation which might appear to have the effect of bringing about a modification of the Agreement in a way contrary to the procedure specifically provided for in Section 12. The Treasury Department therefore felt that the British should also try to live within the Agreement with respect to Section 9 and only if that proved to be impossible, should there be consultation under Section 12.

The State Department representatives felt that it was necessary to interpret the Agreement as a whole and that it was logical to interpret it in the light of the present situation, which would mean that the British could import commodities into Britain where they have means of payment in soft currencies, whereas if they were to apply Section 9 strictly, they would not be able to import because they have no dollars. They felt that a unilateral breach of the Agreement by the British would undermine the U.K.'s contractual stature internationally. State Department lawyers had pointed out that the Executive Branch has greater latitude in the interpretation of international treaties than it has with respect to domestic matters, but had gone on to say that in the present instance the question was political rather than legal. The State Department representatives further said that in view of the fact that Congress, or important Congressional committees, might be in session earlier than was previously anticipated, the State Department might wish to re-examine its position and might be inclined to go along with the Treasury position in the meantime, if Section 12 were in any case to be involved.

It was agreed that the State Department would either redraft the conclusions of the paper, or would state their position as an alternative for inclusion in the paper.[3]

---

[3] In reporting on this meeting the Department informed the Embassy in London in telegram 3995, September 15, that "no agreement reached and alternative State and Treasury recommendations along above lines have been circulated today for indication of other agencies' views. Alternatives with such indication will then be forwarded NAC London for decision." (841.51/9–447)

3. *Further Postponement of United Kingdom July 15 Obligations with Respect to Certain Countries*

The Chairman referred to Staff Document No. 179 [4] which contained a proposed exchange of letters extending the postponement of the obligations of the United Kingdom under Sections 8 (*ii*) and 10 of the Anglo-American Financial Agreement from September 15 to November 15, 1947, for the fourteen countries which had been covered by the exchange of letters of July 14 and July 15, 1947. It was pointed out that the action taken on August 20, 1947, which related specifically to modification of the transferable account system, was not applicable to these fourteen countries.

The Staff Committee agreed to the proposal that the draft letters be communicated to Secretary Snyder for his consideration.

[4] Not printed, but see telegram 3944, *supra*.

The Ambassador in the United Kingdom (Douglas) to the Secretary of State

SECRET   LONDON, September 12, 1947—7 p. m.
URGENT

4943. For State and Treasury from Gunter. Reurtel 3944, September 10. 1. Exchange of letters between Secretary Snyder and Chancellor Dalton without additional paragraphs concerning retroactive feature has been approved by Secretary Snyder, Clayton, Martin and Knapp.[1]

2. Question has been discussed also with Playfair of British Treasury who has agreed tentatively to exchange of letters with minor changes in text of letter from Chancellor to Secretary. He agreed that mention of retroactive feature introduced unnecessary complications at this time. He will clear matter with Dalton and inform us Monday, September 15. It is now proposed that letters both be dated September 15 and released to public Wednesday, September 17 simultaneously in Washington and London.

3. Following is revised text of letter from Chancellor to Secretary:

"Dear Mr. Secretary: I refer to your letter of July 14, 1947 relating to the postponement of certain obligations of the United Kingdom under the Anglo-American financial agreement. In accordance with the request of H. M. Government, the United States Government thereby agreed to the postponement until September 15, 1947 if

[1] Secretary of the Treasury Snyder, Under Secretary of State Clayton, William McC. Martin (Chairman and President, Export-Import Bank), and J. Burke Knapp (a representative of the Federal Reserve Board) were in London for the annual meetings of the Boards of Governors of the International Bank for Reconstruction and Development and of the International Monetary Fund.

necessary, of the obligations under Sections 8 (*ii*) and 10 of the financial agreement in the case of Austria, Bulgaria, China, Denmark, France, Greece, Hungary, Paraguay, Poland, Rumania, Siam, Turkey, the USSR and Yugoslavia.

Because of the modification of the system of transferable accounts on August 20, 1947 and the need to revise arrangements with the countries operating under that system, H. M. Government have been unable to complete the necessary arrangements with the countries referred to above. Accordingly, I should be grateful if the postponement of the obligations of Sections 8 (*ii*) and 10 of the financial agreement with respect to those countries could be extended until November 15, 1947."

DOUGLAS

841.51/9–1847

The Ambassador in the United Kingdom (Douglas) to the Secretary of State

SECRET   LONDON, September 18, 1947.

No. 2110

SIR: I have the honor to refer to the Department's cable No. 3944, dated September 10, 1947, concerning further postponement of certain obligations of the U.K. under the Anglo-American Financial Agreement.

Upon receipt of this cable the recommendation of the NAC staff committee outlined in the cable was taken up with the NAC who were present in London, including Secretary Snyder and Messrs. Clayton, Martin and Knapp. The letters recommended by NAC staff committee were approved without inclusion of the paragraphs dealing with retroactive convertibility.

On the basis of this NAC action, Messrs. Friedman, Pumphrey and Gunter of the U.S. Treasury discussed the proposed exchange of letters with Messrs. Playfair and Grant of the British Treasury. In the course of these discussions the British Treasury representatives (after first tentatively accepting the U.S. drafts as reported in Embassy's cable No. 4943, dated September 12, 1947) suggested a revision of the letters, which instead of granting a further postponement of the convertibility obligations in relation to the 14 countries concerned, would have the effect of extending the August 20 action of suspending convertibility to these countries. The British also suggested that the letters should not be published, and that the exchange should take place between Mr. Grant and the Treasury Representative in London, rather than between Secretary Snyder and Chancellor Dalton.

These proposed alterations were taken up with the members of the NAC and were approved. Accordingly, the attached letters [1] were exchanged between Mr. Grant and the Treasury Representative.

---

[1] Not printed.

Copies of this despatch with attachments should be sent to the Treasury Department for appropriate action by the NAC Secretariat.

Respectfully yours,

For the Ambassador

JOHN W. GUNTER

U. S. Treasury Representative

841.51/9–447 : Telegram

The Acting Secretary of State to the Embassy in the United Kingdom

SECRET   WASHINGTON, September 18, 1947—6 p. m.

4057. Deptel 3995, Sep 15, rptd Geneva for Wilcox as 1193, Paris for Clayton as 3483. After further discussions between Dept and Treasury on Section nine financial agreement it was decided not to submit alternative recommendations to NAC but merely to agree on position paper [1] outlining problems involved and listing possible courses of action open to British consistent with strict interpretation Financial Agreement. Paper then refers to data to be supplied by British and states that same may reveal there is reasonable prospect they can work out import program within such possible courses of action. If so no difficult question would arise under Section 9 and appropriate public announcements could be released in both countries. If British program and prospects reveal there is clear necessity for import programs which could not be carried out under possibilities outlined in position paper "further analysis of alternative possible courses of action will be necessary".

Dept presumes Embassy will telegraph at least summary of British data and that Embassy will keep Dept informed of any developments in connection with statements made at Secretary Snyder's press conference on Sept. 15.[2]

LOVETT

---

[1] National Advisory Council document 511, September 18, 1947, not printed.

[2] Excerpts from Secretary of the Treasury Snyder's comments to the press are printed in the *New York Times*, September 16, 1947. Snyder agreed that a press release would be made through the U.S. Embassy concerning section 9. The text transmitted to the Department in telegram 5049, September 18, and released the same day follows: "In his statement to the press on September 15 last Mr. John W. Snyder, the US Secretary of the Treasury, pointed out that when any two governments work out an agreement, it must be kept flexible. This was the spirit of the original loan negotiations, and it is the purpose and intention of the officials of the two governments who are presently dealing with this problem. The framers of the Anglo-American financial agreement specifically recognized the existence of unusual aspects of the UK position requiring certain deviations from the inflexible rule of non-discrimination. It is basic to an understanding of section nine of the agreement to appreciate that it was never intended to constitute a strait jacket on British trade." (FW841.51/10–1047)

841.51/10–1047

Memorandum by the Deputy Director of the Office of International Trade Policy (Nitze)[1] *to the Under Secretary of State (Lovett)*

SECRET [WASHINGTON,] October 10, 1947.

Subject: Treasury Department proposal with respect to the release of the remaining $400 million of British credit and institution of negotiations for modification of loan agreement

DISCUSSION

The Treasury Department has proposed that the Chancellor of the Exchequer advise Secretary Snyder that, since the number of countries with which it has been impossible for the United Kingdom to complete satisfactory arrangements consistent with the terms of the Anglo-American Financial Agreement is too large to consider as exception cases under a reasonable interpretation of Section 8(*ii*)(*b*), consultations between the two governments should be held under Section 12 for modification of Sections 7 and 8. The Chancellor's communication would also advise that while Section 9 (trade discrimination section) has not heretofore constituted a hindrance to the British import program, it is foreseen that discriminations will arise in a small area, and the British would therefore also propose a modification of this Section under Section 12. The British would also re-state their adherence to the general principles of the loan agreement, and would propose a resumption of drawing of the $400 million remaining under the line of credit. The United States reply would accept the proposal for discussions for modification of the Agreement under Section 12 and acquiesce in the British request for resumption of withdrawals.

As a matter of law, the Executive of the Government can adopt the policy of full compliance by the United States with its obligations under the Agreement, even though the British do not comply. However, it is clear that such a course of conduct by the Executive would raise serious problems with respect to its relationship to the Congress which may prejudice Congressional action on (*a*) the eventual modification of the British agreement and (*b*) the Marshall Plan. Congress may take the position that it was its intention that continued withdrawals after British failure to comply completely with the agreement should be subject to prior Congressional approval of the modifications. It is, however, most urgent from an economic and political point of

---

[1] This memorandum was also prepared by Walter S. Surrey, Deputy Assistant Legal Adviser for Economic Affairs.

view that the British be in a position to know that they can definitely count on the $400 million during the coming months. In the event that the British cannot definitely rely upon the availability of the $400 million, they may have to institute controls which would not only retard their recovery program, but which would probably lead them into larger violations of the loan agreement and may force them into complete bilateralism.

RECOMMENDATIONS

It is recommended that the State Department member of the NAC propose to the NAC that Secretary Snyder immediately approach the available Congressional leaders along the following lines:

1. A presentation of the serious situation in which Britain now stands and the undesirable effects which would result were the $400 million credit not to be made available without delay.

2. To the extent that the British are permitted to withdraw the $400 million credit now and their situation is correspondingly ameliorated, the necessity on the part of the British to resort to restrictive trade practices will be less urgent than otherwise. Conversely, failure to authorize withdrawals may prejudice continued British adherence to basic principles of the agreement.

3. In the event that the Congressional leaders personally approve the release of the remainder of the credit, and state that they will support before Congress an executive decision to release the $400 million, but also advise that they cannot commit the Committees or the Congress as a whole, it is recommended that withdrawals be permitted.

4. In the event that the Congressional leaders advise that they oppose withdrawals from the credit prior to consideration by Congress of the proposed modifications, it is recommended that no withdrawals will be permitted prior to Congressional action.

5. In the event that the Congressional leaders state that they are not in a position either to approve or disapprove current withdrawals during the period of the modification negotiations, it is recommended that the matter be brought back to the NAC in order to determine whether there is anything in the attitude of the Congressional leaders which would permit the Executive on its own responsibility to authorize withdrawals.[2]

---

[2] At the seventy-first meeting of the National Advisory Council on October 13, the following action was taken: "The National Advisory Council is of the opinion that the Chairman of the Council should discuss with appropriate Congressional leaders the question of whether the United Kingdom shall be permitted to draw the $400 million balance remaining to its credit under the terms of the Anglo-American Financial Agreement. If Congressional approval is obtained the Council agrees that the Chairman should proceed with the program of reopening drawings under this credit. If Congressional reaction is unfavorable the Council requests that the matter be referred to it for reconsideration." (60 D 137 Box 1)

CONCURRENCES

This memorandum was concurred in by OFD, ITP, and Ambassador Douglas.

841.51/10–1447 : Circular Instruction

The Secretary of State to Certain Diplomatic and Consular Officers [1]

SECRET WASHINGTON, October 14, 1947.

DISCRIMINATION IN FAVOR OF IMPORTS FROM ONE ANOTHER AND FROM THE UNITED KINGDOM BY DEPENDENCIES SHARING COMMON MEMBERSHIP AND QUOTA IN INTERNATIONAL MONETARY FUND

The Secretary of State refers to the circular instruction dated August 7, 1947 sent to certain American Consular Officers under the above title.

For the information of the Officers in Charge a copy of each of the following documents is attached:

1) Directive sent to British Dependencies by the British Colonial Office, handed to Officers of the Department by Mr. Anthony Percival, Commercial Counselor, British Embassy, Washington, on September 5, 1947; [2]

2) Memorandum of Conversation between Mr. Percival and Officers of the Division of Commercial Policy on September 5, 1947.

The Officers in Charge will note that the directive which has been sent to the British Colonial Dependencies differs in a number of respects from the draft directive submitted to the Department April 28, 1947, a copy of which was enclosed with the instruction under reference.

Of particular interest is the fact that the directive does not include the "token import" control schemes which had previously been contemplated. It has been transmitted moreover, to the trust territories, former Italian colonies, Palestine, and those dependencies located in the Congo Basin area, notwithstanding the fact that the Department in its *aide-mémoire* of July 24 assumed that there would be no discrimination against the United States in those areas in favor of any third country including the United Kingdom. As stated in the instruction under reference this Government recognizes the right of mutual discrimination in the administration of import controls among the metropole and its dependent areas which share a common quota and membership in the International Monetary Fund. The Department is however studying the British action in including among this group those territories covered by international acts guaranteeing

---

[1] Sent to 36 posts, primarily consular offices in British colonial dependencies.
[2] Not printed.

equality of treatment, and the Officers in Charge will be informed of any further developments concerning this matter.

With the exception of this latter point this Government feels that the British directive is both reasonable and necessary as a temporary measure in view of the current dollar shortage on the part of the British Empire as a whole. Problems, however, will doubtlessly arise in the various areas through the interpretation and implementation of the Colonial Office directive. Any discriminatory action on the part of the colonial governments will have to be examined not only on the basis of the facts of any specific case but also in light of the general British situation.

The Consular Officers are therefore requested to study carefully the methods used by the local colonial authorities in implementing the new directive. Cases of undue discrimination should be examined for the facts, which then should be reported to the Department. No action, other than that arising from investigation of a complaint or the settling of minor problems, should be taken by the Consular Officers concerning the general policy until the Department's approval has been obtained, so that a uniform policy may be followed throughout all of the British dependent areas.

The majority of American exporters, understanding the seriousness of the present shortage in the British dollar availabilities, appreciates the inevitability of import restrictions during this emergency period. It must be remembered, however, that for some time American exporters have been expecting a nondiscriminatory import control regime to be effected in the colonial areas. Consequently, they may be inclined to be critical of this new and more severe import control program, especially if it is felt that the United Kingdom is using the present financial crisis to secure long-term advantages for goods from the United Kingdom as opposed to those from the United States.

The British are being informed unofficially of certain practical steps that could be taken in the administration of the directive to assure American exporters that they are not being placed in a permanently disadvantageous position in the colonial markets. The Consular Officers, bearing in mind that the British have not committed themselves with respect to these steps, are requested to observe and report, without disclosure to either importers or exporters, whether the following suggestions made by the United States are being carried out by the local authorities:

(1) Import samples of goods and advertising literature having no commercial value should generally be admitted;

(2) Imports needed for the maintenance and repair of goods already in the colonies, such as auto and radio parts, should in any event be considered as in the category of essential goods and imports of these permitted from the original sources.

(3) A reasonable interpretation of the section of the directive relating to the honoring of orders already placed and for which licenses have been granted so long as a confirmed letter of credit in the seller's country has been opened should be given. In certain instances where payment has been arranged other than by letter of credit, inequities may result from cancellation of orders. Each case will have to be considered on its individual merits.

(4) Orders for goods connected with long-term development projects should not unduly discriminate against United States goods, recognizing, of course, the limitations of the dollar supply.

(5) So far as it is possible, American exporters should be given an advance estimate of the dollar allocations anticipated by individual colonial importers, in order to facilitate reasonable future planning by producers and exporters.

It is realized that considerable leeway is granted to local colonial authorities in so far as implementation of the new import control regime is concerned. Reliance will be placed on the Consular Officers in the various dependent areas to evaluate the implementation of the directive in light of local conditions. As already noted it is expected that lesser cases may be settled by discussions between the Consular Officers and the local colonial authorities. Cases involving general policy and repeated infringements of the directive should be reported to the Department so that appropriate action may be taken through the British Embassy in Washington or the Colonial Office in London. Special treatment accorded imports from the war disrupted countries under Section 9(b) of the Financial Agreement should also be reported to the Department for consideration.

The Consular Officers should take positive action to encourage colonial exports to the United States in order to increase the supply of dollars by:

1) Watching for and reporting export opportunities to the Department of Commerce, which will notify interested individuals and groups in this country;

2) Continued reporting on export controls which are restricting colonial exports to the United States. This Government is endeavoring to secure the elimination of such restrictions in cases where it would appear to be to the mutual advantage of the United States and those areas sharing the common quota to do so.

641.006/9–547

The Secretary of State to the British Ambassador (Inverchapel)

CONFIDENTIAL

The Secretary of State presents his compliments to His Excellency the British Ambassador and has the honor to refer to the directive on import licensing policy in the British colonial dependencies, which the Commercial Counselor of the British Embassy handed to officers of the Department of State on September 5, 1947.[1]

In the Department's *aide-mémoire* of July 24, 1947 on this subject, it was stated that in the territories in which the United States is entitled to equality of treatment under mandate and trusteeship agreements at present in force, the Government of the United States assumed there would be no discrimination against the United States in favor of any other country including the United Kingdom. It was also assumed that there would be no discrimination in the territories of the Congo Basin and in the former Italian colonies. The Secretary of State notes that, nevertheless, the British Government has sent the present directive, calling for the establishment of import control regimes which discriminate against the United States in favor of the United Kingdom, to the mandates, trust territories, the Congo Basin area and the former Italian colonies.

The principle of equality of treatment is one to which this Government attaches importance both in general and in its application to these territories. In so far as the trust territories are concerned, the British action may involve questions of general policy which must be considered in the light of their relation to trust territories administered by other states and of their interest to the Trusteeship Council of the United Nations. Furthermore, this Government is not aware how discrimination in any of these territories will be of significant benefit to the United Kingdom in its present difficulties.

The Secretary of State would therefore appreciate receiving a statement setting forth the reasons why the British Government considers it necessary to pursue this policy with respect to the territories in question, and indicating its views as to how this action is reconciled with the pertinent international agreements which were cited in the Department of State's *aide-mémoire* of July 24, 1947.[2]

WASHINGTON, October 16, 1947.

---

[1] Not printed.
[2] On December 17 Mr. Anthony Percival, Commercial Counselor, British Embassy, informed Mr. Wilson Beale, Assistant Chief of the Division of Commercial Policy, that he had had no further response from London regarding the Department's note of October 16. (641.006/12–1747)

841.51/10–1047 : Telegram

The Acting Secretary of State to the Embassy in the United Kingdom

SECRET   WASHINGTON, October 17, 1947—7 p. m.

4491. From State and Treasury. Urtel 5482, Oct 10.[1] We believe interpretation of Section 9 in Emb press release of Sep 18 as reported

---

[1] Not printed.

in Embtel 5049, Sep 18 [2] provides sufficiently broad basis for answer to possible parliamentary inquiries on relation of that Section to Brit imports. It is not believed necessary to have formally agreed statement but Emb should indicate to appropriate Brit officials this Govt's hope that if foregoing interpretation of Sec 9 is used in Parliament it will be accompanied by strong reaffirmation of adherence to principles of Sec 9.

For urinfo NAC has decided that before reaching final decision to release remaining $400 million circumstances should be discussed with foreign relations committees House and Senate scheduled to meet about Nov 10. Accordingly you should do all you can to impress Brit that it would be most helpful if parliamentary discussion respecting any aspect of financial agreement could be kept to minimum during this period. NAC has further decided there should be no exchange of letters between the two governments at this time concerning any phase of financial agreement. We are proposing to Brit here that official but unannounced exploratory discussions be initiated immediately in Washington. Discussions can begin with Brit officials already at Emb and UK Treas Del, leaving to later determination need additional officials from London.

LOVETT

---

[2] For text, see footnote 2, p. 80.

841.51/10–1847 : Telegram

The Chargé in the United Kingdom (Gallman) to the Secretary of State

SECRET LONDON, October 18, 1947—4 p. m.

5589. For State and Treasury. Prior receipt your 4491, October 17, BOT had indicated desire discuss with us today draft statement to be made in Parliament reference Section Nine financial agreement. Substance your telegram communicated to them. Following draft not yet considered by Ministers but being sent British Embassy Washington for comment and with instructions to communicate to you.

"During the visit of the Eady mission to Washington in August, discussions took place between the mission and officials of the US administration about the present position as regards the non-discrimination provisions of the American loan agreement. During these talks the officials of the two governments were able to discuss and explore together in detail the practical interpretation of the provisions of Section Nine of the loan agreement against the background of the overseas financial position of the United Kingdom. These discussions revealed that there existed very substantial agreement between the two governments about the meaning of these provisions relating to non-discrimination. When Mr. Snyder came to this country in September for the I. M. F. meetings, these discussions continued on the official plane. At the conclusion of Mr. Snyder's visit to this country, the following statement was issued by the US Embassy in London. (Here follows Snyder statement quoted Embtel 5049.) In the light of the discussions which have taken place between the two governments and of the above statement, His Majesty's Government are satisfied that, for the present, and in the light of the existing supply and availabilities position throughout the [apparent garble] the provisions of Section Nine of the loan agreement are not operating to prevent the United Kingdom from importing any goods, including foodstuffs, which we are anxious to take and which we can afford to buy. As regards the future position, discussions with the US Government are continuing." [1]

Regarding reaffirmation adherence to principles of Section Nine, BOT pointed out difficulty and inadvisability doing this in text of above statement but promised to recommend to Ministers that reaffirmation of principle be worked in at some point in discussion in Parliament.

GALLMAN

---

[1] Marginal notation: "Statement cleared in Treasury, OFD and ITP, and British Emb. notified 10/20/47 11:30 a. m. AMR[osenson]". London telegram 5764, October 29, reported that the statement was issued on October 28 "with only minor changes in wording from text quoted in reference telegram." (841.51/10-2947)

841.5151/11-547 : Telegram

The Ambassador in the United Kingdom (Douglas) to the Secretary of State

TOP SECRET   LONDON, November 5, 1947—6 p. m.
US URGENT

5894. For the Secretary and Lovett from the Ambassador. 1. Purely personal and informal discussions have been had with Bevin, and on one occasion with Attlee, Bevin, Cripps and Dalton, on the British financial position and the ways of supplementing British dollar resources during the interim period before Congress shall have approved, if it does approve, a program for European recovery. Following these discussions, a personal memorandum summarizing the present British position and suggested methods of reinforcing the British dollar resources during the period in question, was submitted to me. I should emphasize that the British Cabinet, as a whole, has no knowledge neither of these discussions, nor of the memorandum [sic]. The British officials referred to are extremely anxious that the suggestions be guarded with the greatest discretion.

2. This memorandum suggests loan by Export-Import Bank of $700 million against collaterals now held for RFC loan, which would provide new money. I informed the British that even though the suggestion, in principle, were acceptable to us, I had grave doubts that the

collateral would justify a loan of this size, and that the principal amount of the loan would necessarily have to be less. It is my further thought that if such a loan were made by the Export-Import Bank, the terms of the RFC loan should be altered so that the present principal amount secured by the collateral would remain in the RFC, and so that the Export-Import Bank would advance only the new funds, taking a secondary position to the loan remaining in the RFC. This would conserve bank funds, which I realize are short. The income from the collateral could be used first to pay interest on the two loans and secondly to repay principal on RFC loan until it is repaid.

3. British memorandum assumes interest at 2 per cent. Interest rate in excess of 2 per cent not desirable since this is rate on unsecured $3,750 million credit. British indicate that loan of $700 million would be extinguished in 22 years.

4. Memorandum also suggests loan should be untied, but, if not, should be available for purchases by rest of sterling area as well as UK.

5. I plan no further discussions as to the practicability of the suggestion put forward until I hear from you. I feel, however, that it has merit and should be explored with Secretary Snyder and Martin of Export-Import Bank. The suggestion seems to provide a method by which the British reserves can be substantially protected, thus avoiding imposition of greater restriction on imports, and the danger of change or modification of foreign policy which a shrinkage of reserves to a dangerous level would, I believe, probably entail. At the same time it avoids the necessity of going to Congress for an outright interim appropriation as is necessary in the case of both France and Italy.

6. Memorandum states British gold and dollar reserves for sterling area amounted to pounds 574 million on October 25, and that continued decline is expected because of dollar needs of UK and sterling area. Argument made that if reserves fall below pounds 500 million stability of UK and sterling area economies will be endangered.

7. On basis present British calculation reserves will fall to pounds 310 million by June 30, 1948. This estimate allows for:

(*a*) Drastic cuts in food imports recently announced which will reduce food consumption to or below lowest level reached in the war.

(*b*) Maximum development of exports to dollar destinations involving further cuts in home consumption and severe cuts in investment process including housing.

(*c*) Big reduction in dollar deficit of rest of sterling area.

(*d*) No dollar expenditure for Germany.

(*e*) Net dollar expenditure by UK and sterling area in first half 1948 at only half present rate.

Estimate does not include pounds 80 million South Africa loan, which for purpose of estimate is set aside as cushion for excess expenditure over estimates. Further drawings on IMF in first half 1948 also excluded.

8. On basis these estimates British calculate reserves can be prevented from falling below pounds 500 million, if (*a*) remaining $400 million of financial agreement credit is released, (*b*) Export-Import Bank loan proposed this cable is made.

9. British have agreed to supply US with monthly statistics on their financial position. First figures in this series will be cabled soonest.

10. The British Embassy in Washington is being informed of the personal discussions that have been had here, but is being advised toward the matter with great secrecy and to take no action.

11. Will appreciate your comments on the proposal in principle.[1]

12. Dalton is writing a personal letter to Snyder.

DOUGLAS

---

[1] Marginal notation: "No action required. Problem discussed with Douglas 11–15 N[orman] T. N[ess]".

841.51/11–1947

Memorandum from the Acting Director of the Office of European Affairs (Reber) to the Under Secretary of State (Lovett)

[WASHINGTON,] November 19, 1947.

You are scheduled to appear soon before Congressional Committees with Secretary Snyder and Secretary Forrestal to discuss the release of the $400,000,000 balance of the line of credit to the United Kingdom established under the Financial Agreement. The basic approach to the Congressional Committees was outlined in a memorandum to you, dated November 7, 1947, from Mr. Gross[1] and Mr. Ness (copy attached). In your exposition of the foreign policy aspects of the availability of the undrawn balance to the British, you may wish to make the following points:

1. Our basic objectives in the Financial Agreement have been twofold. First, we desire British recovery, in our own economic interest, in order to make possible a high level of world trade, and to enable Britain to participate ultimately in multilateral and non-discriminatory trade. Secondly, a strong and healthy Britain is essential to our basic foreign political objectives. She is our most important friend in supporting the United Nations, in dealing with the Soviet Union, and in preserving peace.

2. Britain is now drawing on her basic gold and dollar reserves (which serve the entire Sterling area) to meet her balance of payments deficit. The $400,000,000 balance of the loan, given British dollar losses during the financial crisis, is an important bridge to carry

---

[1] Ernest A. Gross, Legal Adviser of the Department of State.

Britain through the difficult interim period before the Congress takes action on the European Recovery Program. (Secretary Snyder will take the lead in developing this line.)

3. If the balance of the loan were not available to alleviate Britain's present dollar shortage, it would be more difficult for the United Kingdom to implement the undertakings it has accepted in the ITO Charter and would delay the United Kingdom's return to a multilateral and freer trading system.

4. The political results within Britain of withholding the balance of the loan cannot be gauged with precision. However, some political consequences which we wish to avoid would undoubtedly follow, even though these would not include changes in fundamental British foreign policies.

The British regard our present attitude with respect to the convertibility and non-discrimination clauses of the Financial Agreement as demonstrations of sympathy for their economic situation. A freezing of the balance would offset this favorable British reaction. It would give ammunition to the Left Wing critics of Bevin who have charged him with "subservience" to, and "dependence" upon, the United States. The anti-Americanism of these critics within the Labor Party has been their principal common denominator and Bevin has at times had to be responsive to their views.

Withholding the balance of the loan might also have some political consequences in our general relations with Britain and Russia, although they would not be of major significance. The Russians and the Communists would say that our action is additional proof that the United States is in fact not interested in British recovery, and that the freezing of the balance is simply another example of Anglo-American economic rivalry which will eventually destroy the friendship between the two countries. On the other hand, making the $400,000,000 available would be a demonstration of the continuing solidarity of the United States and the United Kingdom, and of our vital interest in British recovery and welfare.

S. REBER

[Enclosure]

Memorandum from the Legal Adviser (Gross) and the Director of the Office of Financial Development Policy (Ness) to the Under Secretary of State (Lovett) [2]

The basic approach to the Congressional committees with respect to the release of the balancé of the line of credit established under the Loan Agreement should be substantially as follows:

1. As an introductory statement, the Secretary of the Treasury would comment briefly on the action taken on August 20. This would

---

[2] The file copy is undated.

involve a brief statement to the effect that the situation in Great Britain became so serious that it was necessary for the British Government to suspend convertibility.

In this connection the British voluntarily proposed that no further withdrawals be made against the line of credit. Accordingly, withdrawals were discontinued by mutual consent of both Governments.

2. A brief statement should be made dealing with the results of the efforts made by the British Government to reach bilateral agreements with respect to convertibility. It should be indicated further that continuing balance of payments pressure upon the British has compelled them to resort to rigid measures to restrict imports from dollar areas.

3. An explanation should be made concerning the situation existing at the present time. The elements which should be stressed include the continued rate of decline of the gold and dollar resources left to the U.K., the importance of the unnotified 400,000,000 dollars for the British to enable them to continue with the policies of multilateralism and convertibility which constituted the basic purposes of the Anglo-American Financial Agreement from the viewpoint of the United States. In this exposition Under Secretary Lovett would emphasize the important foreign policy aspects of making available the undrawn balance to the British. Secretary Forrestal would outline the security aspects of the problem.

4. The next step in the presentation of the problem to Congressional committees should be with reference to Section 12. This discussion should center on the fact that in the opinion of the Executive Branch of the Government it is impossible at this time for the U.S. and U.K Governments jointly to reconsider the Agreement with a view to presenting to their respective legislatures specific recommendations for modification. In outlining the reasons why such consultations are not feasible at the present time, particular attention should be given to the facts that world conditions are at the moment so uncertain as to make it impossible for the U.K. accurately to determine in what degree she can safely undertake to abide by the commitments to which she dedicated herself in the Loan Agreement and to which she continues to wish to abide as fully as possible. Particularly is this true because of the uncertainty both of the British and U.S. Governments of the extent to which the implementation of the Marshall Plan will enable the British to continue multilateralism and convertibility. If an attempt were made now to specify modifications, it is almost certain that the extent of modification would be greater than would subsequently prove necessary.

5. Having demonstrated that action under Section 12 is neither practical nor in the best interests of U.S. long-range policy favoring multilateralism and convertibility, it should next be pointed out to the

Congressional committees that the unblocking of the balance of the loan is an act which in itself would be in furtherance of our basic objectives. The distinction should be drawn between substantive modifications of the Agreement pursuant to Section 12 based upon reconsideration designed to take account of prevailing conditions of international exchange, and the effects of refusing to permit further withdrawals. It should be made clear that in the view of the Executive Branch of the Government, the continued freezing of the balance would intensify the difficulties which have compelled the U.K. Government to take the steps which have been described. The Executive Branch considers it appropriate to discuss informally with Congressional representatives the effects which continued freezing of the balance of the loan would have upon our national interest in order that Congressional representatives will have been informed concerning the basis of future action by the Executive Branch.

6. The definitive action by the Executive Branch should be taken in the light of Congressional reaction to the foregoing exposition.

841.51/12–347 : Telegram

The Acting Secretary of State to the Embassy in the United Kingdom

SECRET WASHINGTON, December 3, 1947—5 p. m.

5072. Secretary Snyder, accompanied by Ness and Gross of Department, appeared this morning before Senate Banking and Currency Committee and discussed U.S. interest in release of $400 million balance U.K. loan. Statement generally followed lines discussed with Douglas when he was in Washington.

Committee members asked numerous questions but attitude was friendly throughout and it was indicated by Chairman Tobey at end of meeting that there was no objection to the proposed action.

Snyder and State representatives also called on Congressman Wolcott, Chairman House Committee on Banking and Currency. Wolcott personally favorable but wishes explore matter further. Snyder expressed hope he might obtain definite clearance from Wolcott within next few days.

Will report further developments.

LOVETT

Editorial Note

At the seventy-sixth meeting of the NAC, December 3, Secretary of the Treasury Snyder reported that he had consulted with both the Senate and the House Banking and Currency Committees, and that

they had agreed that the British should be permitted to resume drawings against the $400 million credit still undrawn. The Committees
"felt, however, that approval should likewise be obtained from Senator
Taft as Chairman of the Joint Economic Committee." On December 4,
the Department in telegram 5093 to London reported that Snyder had
obtained the approval of Wolcott and Taft for release of the funds.

A press statement reviewing the events leading to the resumption
of British drawings and an exchange of letters between Secretary
Snyder and Chancellor of the Exchequer Cripps are printed in Department of State *Bulletin*, December 21, 1947, pages 1222–1223.

EFFORTS TO NEGOTIATE AN AGREEMENT WITH NEWFOUNDLAND RESPECTING USE OF LEASED BASES BY CIVIL AIRCRAFT; CONCERN OF THE UNITED STATES OVER RESULTANT DELAY OF SIMILAR NEGOTIATIONS WITH THE UNITED KINGDOM [1]

843.7962/3–2047

*Memorandum by the Assistant Secretary of State for Transportation
and Communications (Norton) to the Under Secretary of State
(Acheson)*

[WASHINGTON,] March 20, 1947.

Under the Bases Agreement of March 27, 1941,[2] the United States
has established naval and air bases for military purposes on leased
areas in Newfoundland, Bermuda, Jamaica, St. Lucia, Antigua, Trinidad and British Guiana.

At the Bermuda Conference in February 1946, the United States
and the United Kingdom drafted an agreement for opening the bases
airfields to use by civil aircraft. The bases airfields in Newfoundland
were not included because Newfoundland was not represented at the
Conference. The United States reserved the right not to sign the agreement until a satisfactory agreement had also been reached with Newfoundland regarding the civil use of the fields in Newfoundland.

A US–Newfoundland agreement was drafted in July 1946. At your
direction I have been insisting on the inclusion therein of a provision
that American flag carriers may transfer their operations from Newfoundland's international airport (Gander) to Harmon Field (a bases
airfield) if and when they consider the fees at Gander to be unreasonable. Newfoundland has steadfastly refused to include the provision as
irrelevant to the agreement and as incompatible with its concept of
sovereignty.

---

[1] For previous documentation on this subject, see *Foreign Relations*, 1946, vol.
I, pp. 1450–1481.
[2] For text of the agreement and exchange of notes, see Department of State
Executive Agreement Series No. 235, or 55 Stat. (pt. 2) 1560.

The stalemate is preventing the conclusion of the US–UK agreement drafted at Bermuda as well as the Newfoundland agreement. Kindley Field in Bermuda therefore remains closed to the civil aircraft of third nations. Venezuela is refusing to conclude a bilateral air transport agreement with the United Kingdom until Kindley Field is open to her flag carrier. British bilaterals with a number of other Latin American countries are also in suspense owing to the inability of the British to guarantee the availability of the bases airfields. The United States will also be faced with the necessity of making these fields available before bilaterals can be concluded with Venezuela, Cuba and possibly other Latin American countries.

Because of the foregoing developments, I recommend that we insist no longer on the inclusion of the controversial provision in the Newfoundland agreement and that a compromise be developed in collaboration with the interested American flag carriers. In the past the carriers have opposed any compromise in this regard, but their position was taken without reference to more recent developments. They have considered the controversial provision as a necessary restraining influence over Newfoundland in the setting of fees at Gander Airport. It should be pointed out, however, that the United States has demanded no such control over the setting of fees at international airports in other foreign countries. The poor financial status of Newfoundland and the probable high cost of airport maintenance there does not justify the assumption that Newfoundland will charge unreasonable fees if not restrained. A right in the American carriers to remove their operations from Gander would place an undue burden on Newfoundland which has already incurred considerable expense at Gander on the theory that it would be the international airport.

GARRISON NORTON

843.7962/9–647

The Consul at St. John's, Newfoundland (Millet) to the Assistant Chief of the Division of British Commonwealth Affairs (Foster)

CONFIDENTIAL   ST. JOHN'S, September 6, 1947.

DEAR MR. FOSTER: Here is a copy for you of my despatch No. 459 of yesterday's date.[1] You will note that we get no further as to mandatory rather than permissive coverage on Newfoundland's designating a substitute base for Gander. I found it impossible to get anything helpful out of Mr. Neill,[2] although he seemed well disposed and received me very pleasantly.

---

[1] Not printed.
[2] James Neill, Newfoundland Commissioner for Public Utilities.

It seems to me that the Commissioners' insistence on "may" arises out of their wish to avoid yielding to us in something that they fear might be used by political opponents in the accusation that the Commissioners had again failed in their duty of guarding the interests of the country in having further extended what many people consider the lamentably foolish generosity of concessions granted to the United States without any *quid pro quo*. This is probably the important reason for the stubbornness of the Government on this point, while the fear of running into the costly maintenance of an uneconomic airport is surely not the whole reason for their stubbornness.

Note also that Neill couldn't or wouldn't give me any idea of the effect of London's pressure on the Government here.

I should like to know what you think of all this, and what suggestions you may have for me in the premises.

Do you think we could undertake to back strongly any request that Newfoundland might make for ICAO aid to maintain Gander? If so, could we promise to enlist similar support of the other several nations whose civil aircraft operate through Gander?

Possibly Neill will attempt to work out some other wording which might be accepted as a compromise. You can be sure that I shall report promptly on anything of the sort.

One more possibility, but rather a dim one: are there no earlier commitments obliging this Government to maintain Gander or some other airfield? If so, it might be possible to fall back on such an undertaking by Newfoundland, perhaps even insert reference to it in Article I(d). By this I mean such things as treaties covering American and other civil aircraft flying through the Island, commitments in the American civil airlines' franchises (if any) with Newfoundland, or even the undertakings embodied in the ICAO and Chicago Conference. You will appreciate that I have not sufficient time to go deeply into this. Could the Department's Aviation Division and Treaty Division people be asked to use their own files to work out a swift answer to this question?

Please send what comments you can on the whole thing. I seem to have run into an impasse at present, but hope that something will work out as time goes on.[3]

Yours sincerely,

CHARLES S. MILLET

[3] In answer to the questions raised in this letter, Foster wrote to Millett on October 16 saying: "We consider very reasonable your suggestion that strong backing be given Newfoundland in any request she might make for ICAO aid for the maintenance of Gander and feel reasonably sure that the other nations whose civil aircraft operate through Gander would support such a move. Since your negotiations with Newfoundland are now at a standstill, it seems unnecessary and unwise at this time to promise to enlist the support of other nations. According to the Aviation Division, there seems to be no earlier commitment on which the maintenance of Gander or other airfields might be based. The only such agreement along those lines is that embodied in general ICAO principles." (843.7962/9–647)

843.7962/9–2547

The Ambassador in Canada (Atherton) to the Secretary of State

RESTRICTED   OTTAWA, September 25, 1947.
No. 5519

SIR: I have the honor to refer to the Department's Restricted telegram No. 161 of September 22, 1947, 5 p.m., and to the Embassy's reply No. 141 of September 24, 2 p.m.,[1] both on the subject of the Newfoundland Air Bases Agreement.

In accordance with the promise made by the Department of External Affairs, as mentioned in the Embassy's telegram, there is enclosed herewith copy of an *Aide-Mémoire* dated September 25, 1947, which is entitled "Newfoundland-United States Base Fields Agreement", which the Department of External Affairs has transmitted to the Canadian High Commissioner in St. John's, Newfoundland, for delivery to the Newfoundland Commission of Government. The Embassy believes that this *Aide-Mémoire* goes as far as it is possible for the Canadian Government to go, particularly in view of the present very delicate relationships which exist between the Dominion and Newfoundland over confederation.

Respectfully yours,

For the Ambassador
JULIAN F. HARRINGTON
American Minister

[Enclosure]

The Canadian Department of External Affairs to the Newfoundland Commission of Government

AIDE-MÉMOIRE

NEWFOUNDLAND—UNITED STATES BASE FIELDS AGREEMENT

The use of Kindley Field, Bermuda which is essential to the operation of any Canadian commercial air service to the West Indies is at present contingent on the exchange of notes between the United States and the United Kingdom in relation to the United States–United Kingdom Agreement on Leased Air Bases. A wording acceptable to both the Canadian and the United States Governments has been reached in respect to this exchange of notes, but the United States as they had previously made clear at Bermuda in 1946, would only approve this Agreement conditional to a satisfactory agreement being

---

[1] Neither printed.

reached with Newfoundland regarding the use by the United States Civil Aircraft of Newfoundland air fields.

In June of this year negotiations appeared to be progressing favourably on the United States–Newfoundland Agreement when the Commission of Government of the latter announced that they had reconsidered the wording of Article 1 (d) to the draft agreement, which provided that, "in the event of Gander Air Field being closed temporarily or permanently, or otherwise unavailable as a regular civil international airport, the Government of Newfoundland will designate (subject in the case of Argentia and Stephenville to the concurrence of the United States Military Authorities) another suitable airport in Newfoundland, either temporarily or permanently, as the case may be, as a regular civil international airport;" The Commission of Government said they preferred to amend the Article to read "the Government of Newfoundland may designate etc. etc.," insofar as they feel, in view of the nature of the present Government, that they should not bind their successors to the automatic designation of an alternative air field in the event of Gander being closed. It is understood that this week the United States agreed to accept the latter wording, provided that in the event of Gander being closed, the United States should be allowed to automatically use Argentia and Stephenville as temporary fields (subject to the concurrence of the military officials) during the interim period whilst Newfoundland considered the designation of a new airport.

The delay in the signing of this agreement affects the future civil aviation programme of both Canada and the United Kingdom. It is understood that the latter Government have already forwarded a memorandum to the Newfoundland Commission of Government explaining their own position and their urgent desire to discover a way out of the present impasse.

In this respect the position of Canada is similar to that of the United Kingdom. Failure of the United States and Newfoundland to reach an agreement has resulted in the denial to Canadian aircraft of the only air field in Bermuda suitable for commercial operations. Such a result would be out of keeping with the discussions at Bermuda in December 1945 in which Newfoundland participated.

The Canadian Government appreciates the spirit of co-operation which has at all times been evidenced by Newfoundland in respect to the development of civil aviation and it is hoped that a satisfactory agreement can be reached in the near future between the Government of Newfoundland and the United States which will allow the implementation of the decisions reached at Bermuda in 1945.

September 25, 1947.

843.7962/10–947 : Telegram

The Acting Secretary of State to the Consulate General in
Newfoundland

CONFIDENTIAL   WASHINGTON, October 15, 1947.

60. Pls suspend further Newf negotiations in view Newf rejection
US proposal re Art I (*d*) Reurtels 68 Oct 7 and 73 Oct 9.[1] Dept has
decided proceed with US–UK Agreement[2] re Kindley and Caribbean
Bases and conclusion thereof will no longer be contingent on reaching
satisfactory agreement with Newf.[3]

Sent St. John's; rptd London as 4445; Ottawa as 175.

LOVETT

---

[1] Neither printed.

[2] For text of agreement and exchange of notes, signed at Washington, February
24, 1948, see Department of State Treaties and Other International Acts Series
(TIAS) No. 1717, or 62 Stat. (pt. 2) 1860.

[3] As a result of the Union of Newfoundland with Canada in April 1949, this
agreement was effected by an exchange of notes between the United States and
Canada signed at Ottawa June 4, 1949. For text of this agreement respecting the
use by civil aircraft of Stephenville and Argentia military air bases in Newfoundland, see Department of State Treaties and Other International Acts
Series (TIAS) No. 1933, or 63 Stat. (pt. 3) 2486.

AGREEMENT BETWEEN THE UNITED STATES AND THE UNITED KINGDOM RESPECTING AIR TRANSPORT SERVICES CONCERNING GANDER AIRPORT, NEWFOUNDLAND

[For text of this Agreement, effected by exchange of notes signed
at London, May 21 and 23, 1947, see Department of State Treaties
and Other International Acts Series (TIAS) No. 1641, or 61 Stat. (pt.
3) 3092.]

AGREEMENT BETWEEN THE UNITED STATES AND THE UNITED KINGDOM RESPECTING THE UNITED STATES LEASED BASE AT ARGENTIA, NEWFOUNDLAND

[For text of Agreement, delimiting the area within Newfoundland
territorial waters, effected by exchange of notes signed at London,
August 13 and October 23, 1947, see Department of State Treaties and
Other International Acts Series (TIAS) No. 1809.]

AGREEMENTS AND ARRANGEMENTS BETWEEN THE UNITED STATES AND THE UNITED KINGDOM CONCERNING MEASURES TO IMPROVE ECONOMIC COOPERATION AND COORDINATION IN THE UNITED STATES-UNITED KINGDOM BIZONAL AREA OF GERMANY

[For documentation and text of agreements and arrangements, see
volume II, pages 909 ff.]

AGREEMENT BETWEEN THE UNITED STATES AND THE UNITED KINGDOM RESPECTING CLAIMS FOR DAMAGES RESULTING FROM ACTS OF MEMBERS OR CIVILIAN EMPLOYEES OF ARMED FORCES

[For text of Agreement, effected by exchange of notes signed at Washington, October 23, 1946 and January 23, 1947, see Department of State Treaties and Other International Acts Series (TIAS) No. 1622, or 61 Stat. (pt. 3) 2876.]

AGREEMENT BETWEEN THE UNITED STATES AND THE UNITED KINGDOM RESPECTING INTERGOVERNMENTAL CLAIMS

[For text of Agreement, effected by exchange of notes signed at Washington, February 19 and 28, 1947, see Department of State Treaties and Other International Acts Series (TIAS) No. 1635, or 61 Stat. (pt. 3) 3012.]

AGREEMENT BETWEEN THE UNITED STATES AND THE UNITED KINGDOM RESPECTING MARINE TRANSPORTATION AND LITIGATION

[For text of Agreement, effected by exchange of notes signed at Washington, June 17 and 27, 1947, see Department of State Treaties and Other International Acts Series (TIAS) No. 1636, or 61 Stat. (pt. 3) 3014.]

AGREEMENT BETWEEN THE UNITED STATES AND THE UNITED KINGDOM RESPECTING AIR TRANSPORT SERVICES ROUTES TO AND FROM FIJI ISLAND

[For text of Agreement, effected by exchange of notes signed at Washington, December 20, 1946 and January 27, 1947, see Department of State Treaties and Other International Acts Series (TIAS) No. 1640, or 61 Stat. (pt. 3) 3089.]

AGREEMENT BETWEEN THE UNITED STATES AND THE UNITED KINGDOM RESPECTING STANDARDIZATION OF DISTANCE MEASURING EQUIPMENT FOR TELECOMMUNICATIONS

[For text of Agreement, signed at Washington, October 13, 1947, see Department of State Treaties and Other International Acts Series (TIAS) No. 1652, or 61 Stat. (pt. 3) 3131.]

AGREEMENT BETWEEN THE UNITED STATES AND THE UNITED KINGDOM SUPPLEMENTING THE GENERAL AGREEMENT ON TARIFFS AND TRADE OF OCTOBER 30, 1947

[For text of Agreement, signed at Geneva, October 30, 1947, see Department of State Treaties and Other International Acts Series

(TIAS) No. 1706, or 61 Stat. (pt. 4) 3725. For documentation concerning United States participation in the formulation of the GATT agreements, see volume I.]

ARRANGEMENT BETWEEN THE UNITED STATES AND THE UNITED KINGDOM RESPECTING MILITARY AID TO GREECE

[For text of Arrangement, effected by exchange of notes signed at Washington, July 25 and October 9, 1947, see Department of State Treaties and Other International Acts Series (TIAS) No. 1718, or 61 Stat. (pt. 4) 3763.]

TERMINATION OF THE ANGLO-AMERICAN AGREEMENT FOR THE TRANSFER OF AMERICAN CARGO VESSELS TO THE BRITISH FLAG FOR TEMPORARY WARTIME DUTY (THE LAND-LEATHERS AGREEMENT OF 1944)

Editorial Note

Documentation on this Agreement, which was entered into on December 9, 1944, is printed in *Foreign Relations*, 1944, volume II, pages 740 ff. For a statement on legal aspects of the Agreement by Under Secretary of State Clayton on February 6, 1947, before the Subcommittee on Ships Sales, Charters, and Lay-ups of the Committee on Merchant Marine and Fisheries, House of Representatives, see Department of State *Bulletin*, February 23, 1947, pages 347–348.

On November 1, 1946, Sir Cyril Hurcomb submitted to the United States Maritime Commission on behalf of the United Kingdom certain detailed proposals "for winding up the arrangements for bareboat chartering of ships covered by the agreements recorded in the exchange of letters between Lord Leathers and Admiral Land dated November 24, 1944, and in exchange of letters between the Acting Administrator, War Shipping Administration, and the Secretary of the British Merchant Shipping Mission of the 15th February, 1946." These proposals were later amended by the British Embassy's note of February 3, 1947. In a reply dated March 13 the United States Government submitted certain "proposals for the disposal or redelivery of the vessels presently under the Land-Leathers Agreement," and these proposals were accepted by the United Kingdom on March 25. On May 13 the Department of State, taking note of these exchanges and various specific points mentioned in the British note of March 25, informed the British Embassy that the United States Maritime Commission had instructed its staff to do everything necessary to carry out the arrangements. Documentation on the termination of the Agreement, not printed, is in Department of State file No. 800.85.

AUSTRALIA

DISCUSSIONS OF THE AMERICAN COMMANDER-IN-CHIEF IN THE PACIFIC WITH AUSTRALIAN OFFICIALS

Editorial Note

The following joint press statement by Herbert V. Evatt, Australian Minister for External Affairs, and Robert Butler, the American Ambassador, was released at Canberra on June 11, 1947:

"Admiral Denfeld, Commander-in-Chief of United States Navy, Army and Air Forces in Pacific area is leaving today for his headquarters at Pearl Harbour after discussions with Australian Government and service authorities on matters of mutual interest in Pacific.

"Purpose of the Admiral's visit was to ensure continuance of close cooperation between United States and Australian services which existed all through war period and which contributed so much to victory in Pacific.

"There is practical identity of Pacific interest and most excellent relationships existing between United States and Australia. Discussions Admiral Denfeld has had with Prime Minister, Minister External Affairs, Minister Navy and service authorities have covered mutual interests of our two countries in Pacific and it is natural that such discussions should be repeated from time to time. They are natural outcome of close association between two governments which characterized war period and being purely defensive in character are completely in accord with principles and purposes of UN.

"Discussions Admiral has had during last few days in Australia have been entirely successful from all points of view." (Text transmitted in telegram 185 from Canberra, June 12, 1947; 811.2347/6–1247)

In despatch 241 of June 20, Ambassador Butler reported that in the conversations Dr. Evatt had expressed great disappointment that the United States would not take part in maintenance of the naval base on Manus Island and had stated that Australia and the United States should have a broad regional agreement such as was provided for in the United Nations Charter and such as the United States already had with Canada and the American Republics. (811.2347/6–2047)

AGREEMENT BETWEEN THE UNITED STATES AND AUSTRALIA RESPECTING AIR SERVICE FACILITIES AT EAGLE FARM AND AMBERLEY IN AUSTRALIA

[For text of Agreement, signed at Canberra, March 10, 1947, see Department of State Treaties and Other International Acts Series (TIAS) No. 1732, or 61 Stat. (pt. 4) 3843.]

**EFFORTS OF THE UNITED STATES TO RESOLVE CERTAIN DIFFER-
ENCES WITH AUSTRALIA CONCERNING DISPOSAL OF WAR SUR-
PLUS MATERIALS AND FIXED MILITARY INSTALLATIONS IN THE
SOUTHWEST PACIFIC**

[For documentation on this subject, involving unfulfilled pipeline
shipments to Australia, unauthorized sales of U.S. war surplus at
Milne Bay, Finschhafen, etc., disposal of U.S. fixed installations at
New Guinea, maintenance of custodial services for Lend-Lease materials at Brisbane and Sydney, and continued operation of the military base at Manus Island, see Department of State files 847.24FLC
and 841.24FLC.]

CANADA

MILITARY COOPERATION AND POLITICAL RELATIONS OF THE UNITED STATES AND CANADA [1]

Press Release Issued by the Department of State, February 12, 1947

Announcement was made in Ottawa and Washington today of the results of discussions which have taken place in the Permanent Joint Board on Defense on the extent to which the wartime cooperation between the armed forces of the two countries should be maintained in this postwar period. In the interest of efficiency and economy, each Government has decided that its national defense establishment shall, to the extent authorized by law, continue to collaborate for peacetime joint security purposes. The collaboration will necessarily be limited and will be based on the following principles:

1. Interchange of selected individuals so as to increase the familiarity of each country's defense establishment with that of the other country.
2. General cooperation and exchange of observers in connection with exercises and with the development and tests of material of common interest.
3. Encouragement of common designs and standards in arms, equipment, organization, methods of training and new developments. As certain United Kingdom standards have long been in use in Canada, no radical change is contemplated or practicable and the application of this principle will be gradual.
4. Mutual and reciprocal availability of military, naval and air facilities in each country; this principle to be applied as may be agreed in specific instances. Reciprocally each country will continue to provide with a minimum of formality for the transit through its territory and its territorial waters of military aircraft and public vessels of the other country.
5. As an underlying principle all cooperative arrangements will be without impairment of the control of either country over all activities in its territory.

While in this, as in many other matters of mutual concern, there is an identity of view and interest between the two countries, the decision of each has been taken independently in continuation of the practice developed since the establishment of the Joint Defense Board in 1940. No treaty, executive agreement or contractual obligation has been entered into. Each country will determine the extent of its practical

---

[1] For previous documentation, see *Foreign Relations*, 1946, vol. v, pp. 53 ff.

collaboration in respect of each and all of the foregoing principles. Either country may at any time discontinue collaboration on any or all of them. Neither country will take any action inconsistent with the Charter of the United Nations. The Charter remains the cornerstone of the foreign policy of each.

An important element in the decision of each government to authorize continued collaboration was the conviction on the part of each that in this way their obligations under the Charter of the United Nations for the maintenance of international peace and security could be fulfilled more effectively. Both Governments believe that this decision is a contribution to the stability of the world and to the establishment through the United Nations of an effective system of world wide security. With this in mind, each Government has sent a copy of this statement to the Secretary-General of the United Nations for circulation to all its members.

In August 1940, when the creation of the Board was jointly announced by the late President Roosevelt and Prime Minister King, it was stated that the Board "shall commence immediate studies relating to sea, land and air problems, including personnel and material. It will consider in the broad sense the defense of the north half of the Western Hemisphere".[2] In discharging this continuing responsibility the Board's work led to the building up of a pattern of close defense cooperation. The principles announced today are in continuance of this cooperation. It has been the task of the governments to assure that the close security relationship between Canada and the United States in North America will in no way impair but on the contrary will strengthen the cooperation of each country within the broader framework of the United Nations.[3]

[2] For text of this statement of August 18, 1940, and related documentation concerning the establishment of the Permanent Joint Board on Defense, see *Foreign Relations*, 1940, vol. III, pp. 144-145.

[3] For related information, see Stanley W. Dziuban, *Military Relations between the United States and Canada 1939–1945*, in the official Army history *United States Army in World War II: Special Studies* (Washington, Government Printing Office, 1959), pp. 334-339.

842.20 Defense/2–1447

The Canadian Minister in the United States (Stone) to the Chief of the Division of British Commonwealth Affairs (Hickerson)

WASHINGTON, February 14, 1947.

MY DEAR MR. HICKERSON: With reference to the public statement on joint defence which was released on February 12th by the United States and Canadian Governments,[1] I have been instructed by my government

[1] *Supra.*

to write to you in the matter of Principle No. 4 therein, which includes the following sentence:

"Reciprocally each country will continue to provide, with a minimum of formality, for the transit through its territory and its territorial waters of military aircraft and public vessels of the other country."

In the view of the Canadian Government, this Principle in no way infringes on the complete jurisdiction which each country maintains over its territorial and boundary waters. The Canadian Government would be glad to learn whether the United States Government agrees with this interpretation.[2]

Yours sincerely,   THOMAS A. STONE

---

[2] Hickerson replied, in a letter to Stone dated February 19, that the United States Government was in accord with the Canadian Government's interpretation of principle No. 4 of the February 12 statement (842.20 Defense/2–1447).

842.20 Defense/2–1747

The Canadian Minister in the United States (Stone) to the Deputy Director of the Office of European Affairs (Hickerson)[1]

TOP SECRET   WASHINGTON, February 17, 1947.

MY DEAR MR. HICKERSON: As you know, the matter of standardization of military equipment as between the United Kingdom, the United States and Canada has been a cause of some concern because of the unauthorized reports and stories which have appeared in the press in recent months. Statements on this subject have had to be made by your Under-Secretary of State as well as in the United Kingdom House of Commons.

Except for the short paragraph included in our joint release[2] the other day, no specific statement on standardization has been made in Canada. The matter has, however, been considered by the Cabinet Defence Committee and in case it should prove necessary or advisable for the Canadian authorities to make some statement on the subject, a draft has been prepared which is, as you will see, in very general terms only. It is not intended that this draft would be used unless, as is not unlikely, the Government is questioned closely on the subject during discussions of defence questions in the House of Commons. It was thought wise, however, to have an agreed statement ready, and the Cabinet Defence Committee wished to have the text communicated to

---

[1] A marginal notation on this document indicates that copies of this letter and its enclosure were forwarded for comment on February 19 to General Lincoln (presumably Brigadier General George A. Lincoln, General Staff, War Department) and to Vice Admiral Forrest P. Sherman, Deputy Chief of Naval Operations.
[2] Department of State press release, February 12, p. 104.

the United States and United Kingdom authorities in advance. I am, therefore, instructed to pass on to you the enclosed text [3] and to let the authorities in Ottawa know as soon as possible whether you have any observations to offer.

Yours sincerely,

THOMAS A. STONE

[3] Not printed. For revised draft, altered after Hickerson transmitted to Stone the first comment from the War and Navy Departments, see *infra*.

842.20 Defense/4–1447

Draft Statement on Standardization of Military Equipment Between the Armed Forces of the United Kingdom, United States and Canada [1]

TOP SECRET   [undated].

(For use only if it is found necessary to make a statement on this subject)

There have been many references in the Press to standardization of arms and equipment between the Armed Forces of the United Kingdom, Canada and the United States. It seems desirable to state the position of Canada in this matter.

The Canadian Armed Services have always been, and still are, organized and equipped along generally similar lines to the forces of the United Kingdom and other Commonwealth countries. During World War II they used equipment of United Kingdom, Canadian and United States origin.

Canadian industry produced a wide variety of military equipment, using both United Kingdom and United States designs, modified in some cases to suit Canadian production methods. Such articles were not used solely by Canadian Forces but formed a part of the common pool for distribution in accordance with operational requirements. This is shown by the fact that of all Canadian production, seventy per cent was made available by Canada for use by other allied forces. On the other hand, Canadian Forces used almost no equipment peculiar to themselves and much of the equipment was of other than Canadian manufacture.

This reciprocal exchange of weapons between the allies inevitably resulted in some standardization of equipment; aided in marked degree the efficient prosecution of the war, and resulted in substantial economies. In these circumstances it is natural that there should now be informal exchanges of views on the continuation and extension of these wartime practices.

[1] Transmitted to Hickerson by Stone in his letter dated April 14, not printed; point of origin is unspecified. Copies of this draft were transmitted by Hickerson on April 15 to Major General Lauris Norstad, Director, Plans and Operations Division, War Department, and to Admiral Sherman (842.20 Defense/4–1447).

It will be appreciated that manufacturing standards and processes differ as between the United Kingdom and the United States. Canadian industry is patterned generally along United States lines, yet a considerable part of Canadian equipment was of original British design. It therefore follows that the problem of equipping Canadian Forces, should the need arise, would be greatly simplified if, in fact, common standards were in use in the United Kingdom and the United States.

A typical example of the problem is the present variation in screw thread designs. The National Physical Laboratory of the United Kingdom, the American Bureau of Standards and the National Research Council of Canada have collaborated for several years in an effort to set suitable common standards for screw threads and have reached the stage where agreed designs are now being tested by the three countries. It is hoped that this will lead to the adoption of uniform designs in due course.

If collaboration in design is extended to include military equipment, production will be simplified and Canada will benefit accordingly. We welcome such collaboration and are prepared to support measures designed to achieve a greater degree of standardization with the United Kingdom and the United States.[2]

---

[2] General Norstad commented in a letter to Hickerson dated April 18 that he could discover nothing objectionable in this proposed statement and that he concurred with its use, if necessary, by the Canadian government (842.20 Defense/4–1847). Admiral Sherman, in a letter to Hickerson dated April 23, suggested substitution in paragraph 5 of the words "could be adopted" for the phrase "were in use in the United Kingdom and the United States". He further suggested deletion in paragraph 7 of the words "with the United Kingdom and the United States", and commented that the statement appeared quite innocuous and therefore unobjectionable for use if necessary by the Canadian authorities. (842.20 Defense/4–2347) There is no indication that this statement was ever issued.

842.00/4–2347

Memorandum of Conversation, by the Chief of Protocol (Woodward)

CONFIDENTIAL   [WASHINGTON,] April 23, 1947.

Participants: Mr. President
The Prime Minister of Canada
The Chief of Protocol

The Prime Minister of Canada, Mr. Mackenzie King, called on the President today at 12 : 00 Noon.

After an exchange of courtesies, the Prime Minister said that he looked forward with great pleasure to the President's visit to Canada in June, and that he was especially happy June 10th was to be the date of the President's arrival in Ottawa as that was his own twentieth anniversary as Prime Minister. The President said that he would make every effort to be there on schedule, and that only the Congress could interfere with his plans. Against this eventuality he preferred to make no announcement concerning the date of his Canadian visit for another week or two.

The Prime Minister then congratulated the President on the result of the Greek-Turkish aid vote in the Senate and said that in stating his approval he expressed the sentiment of all Canadians. The President thanked the Prime Minister for his endorsement of the American position.[1]

The Prime Minister then referred to the International Trade Conference now meeting at Geneva [2] and said that he hoped for important results. The President agreed and said that we had a strong and well qualified delegation at Geneva and that he too hoped for the best. Mr. King said that Canada was very much interested in its trade relations with the world in general and with the United States in particular, and that there was a growing shortage of American dollars in Canada, which he hoped might be corrected. What he feared was restrictive action on the part of Canada with respect to imports from the United States.[3] A subject not immediately urgent but one which was beginning to give him concern. He thought that the United States might like to increase its reserve supply of aluminum for example. The President said he knew we needed lead, zinc and copper and that he was sure the "financiers" of our two countries could sit down and work out a solution to this problem. The President added that we had in this country quite a stock of aluminum producing plants which had been greatly expanded during the war.

The Prime Minister then referred to Senator Vandenberg's recent speech advocating that Canada join the Pan American Union. Mr. King declared this to be a fine gesture on the part of the Senator but hoped that the subject would not be pressed at this time. He said that to do so would certainly give rise to misunderstanding in the rest of the British Commonwealth if nowhere else, and that the inference would be drawn that Canada was giving up its ties with the Commonwealth for the sake of its neighbors in the Western Hemisphere. The President agreed that Canada had an important role to play in both the British Commonwealth and the Americas and said that he understood the Prime Minister's position.

Before leaving the Prime Minister referred to the position taken by the United States with respect to the peace treaties and thanked the President for our insistence upon the participation of all cobelligerents in drafting the terms of the peace. He admired General Mar-

[1] For documentation on United States Economic and Military Aid to Greece and Turkey, see vol. v, pp. 1 ff.
[2] For documentation on this subject, see volume I.
[3] See pp. 116 ff.

shall's firm stand at Moscow which he declared to be splendid.[4] To this President Truman responded that we had tried everything else with the Russians and that we were left no choice but to be firm.

[4] For documentation on the meeting of the Council of Foreign Ministers at Moscow, see vol. II, pp. 139 ff.

842.00/6–547

Memorandum by the Secretary of State to President Truman

[Extract]

SECRET   [WASHINGTON,] June 5, 1947.

The following background information concerning problems and personalities may be of possible usefulness during your visit to Ottawa on June 10–12 : [1]

UNITED STATES-CANADIAN RELATIONS

United States-Canadian relations continue to be excellent. Economically, Canada is our best customer and our foremost supplier.

Joint military cooperation is proceeding very satisfactorily. In accordance with the recommendations of the Permanent Joint Board on Defense, United States–Canada, the two Governments are exchanging information, interchanging personnel, cooperating in the establishment of weather and Loran stations in the Far North, conducting joint experiments under Arctic conditions at Fort Churchill, and developing plans for the defense of the continent. United States troops are stationed at present at Fort Churchill (about 130), at the Army Airfield at Edmonton, and in comparatively small numbers at the weather and Loran stations. While joint military cooperation has the strong support of a majority of Canadians, there is an element in the country which declares that the arrangements threaten a violation of Canadian sovereignty and prejudice the chance of Canada maintaining peaceful relations with the Soviet Union.

The Hyde Park Agreement concluded by President Roosevelt and Prime Minister King in 1941 to mobilize the economic resources of the continent for defense and extended in May 1945 during the period of reconversion, continues in force although its effectiveness necessarily declines with the relaxation or abandonment of economic controls on both sides of the border.

The St. Lawrence Seaway project is the subject of special interest in Canada at the moment because of the hearings now being held by Senator Wiley's Sub-Committee of the Senate Foreign Relations

[1] No records of the President's discussions with Prime Minister Mackenzie King in Ottawa have been found in Department of State files.

Committee. The two aspects of the enterprise under particular consideration at present are the new principle of self-liquidation through tolls on shipping, championed by Senator Vandenberg, and the importance of the project to the defense of the continent. In response to our request in March 1947 the Canadian Government informed us that it "is prepared to agree to the principle of making the St. Lawrence Seaway self-liquidating by means of toll charges subject however to the conclusion of arrangements satisfactory to both governments for the implementation of this principle". In the event you may be interested in details concerning the tolls and national defense aspects of the project, I attach a copy of my statement before the Sub-Committee on May 28.[2] There are the same kinds of support for, and of opposition against, the project in Canada as in the United States. Generally speaking the Canadian railroads, power interests, and eastern seaports are opposed.

[Here follows information on Canada's government, politics and internal problems.]

---

[2] See Department of State Press Release No. 437, May 28, 1947. Documentation on the Seaway Project may be found in Department of State file 711.42157 SA 29. See also Canadian Department of External Affairs, *External Affairs*, vol. I, No. 2 (February 1949), pp. 3–11, and *St. Lawrence Seaway Manual: A Compilation of Documents on the Great Lakes Seaway Project and Correlated Power Development*, Senate Document No. 165, 83d Cong., 2d sess.

811.203/6–747 : Airgram

The Ambassador in Canada (Atherton) to the Secretary of State

RESTRICTED   OTTAWA, June 7, 1947.

A–124. Reference Embassy's despatch 5271, May 23 [1] and previous. House of Commons last night defeated by 104 votes to 26 CCF amendment to government bill providing for jurisdiction of US service courts over members of US armed forces in Canada. Amendment would have effectively killed measure by referring it to committee for "study".

Vote climaxed three days of unexpectedly sharp debate during which many CCF members objected to presence of any US armed forces in Canada and Progressive-Conservative members voiced miscellaneous objections to bill. Progressive-Conservatives however joined with Government in defeating CCF motion. Embassy now regards passage as certain.

In course of debate External Affairs Secretary St. Laurent stated that any American troops who operate in Canada do so under Canadian

---

[1] Not printed.

command and that there was no intention of establishing American bases on Canadian soil but that "no man can undertake to say that there may not unfortunately be some time when all Canadians will be glad to see posts established here".

Despite favorable outcome of vote, protracted debate on this bill has been unfortunate in that it may tend to create less favorable atmosphere for consideration of future joint defense requests and has supplied Canadian Government with excuse for cautious handling of such requests.

ATHERTON

842.20 Defense/6–947

Memorandum by the Secretary of State to President Truman

SECRET   [WASHINGTON,] June 9, 1947.

You may wish to consider mentioning to Prime Minister King at some time during your visit to Ottawa on June 10–12 your interest in the proposed "Inter-American Military Cooperation Act".[1] I attach a copy of House Document No. 271 containing your message of May 23, 1947, and the draft of the proposed Act.[2]

The proposed Act would considerably strengthen the basis of our joint defense arrangements with Canada. It is true that we are already interchanging personnel between the armed forces of each country and that we have already made transfers of arms, ammunition and implements of war to Canada by sale through the Foreign Liquidation Commissioner. The new Act would, however, facilitate the interchange of personnel and would make it possible to transfer arms and matériel directly and affirmatively rather than through the surplus property procedure. The provisions for the transfer of services and technical information would also be helpful.

If you decide to discuss the matter with the Prime Minister, it is my thought that you would wish to do so informally and privately. I have in mind that, as we mentioned in the general memorandum submitted to you on June 5, joint military cooperation has the strong support of a majority of Canadians but there is an element in the country which declares that the arrangements constitute a violation of Canadian sovereignty and prejudice the chance of Canada maintaining peaceful relations with the Soviet Union. As of possible interest I attach clippings from the *New York Times* of June 6 and 8 relating to the debate which took place late last week in the House of Commons on the subject of our joint military cooperation. These two articles are symptomatic

---

[1] For documentation concerning this proposed act, which failed to pass Congress in 1947, see vol. VIII, pp. 101 ff.

[2] Draft not found in Department of State files.

of the situation and constitute further evidence, if any were needed, that our joint defense relationship requires careful and tactful handling on both sides.

With further reference to my thought that the matter should be mentioned only informally and privately to the Prime Minister, I also have in mind the fact that the proposed bill has not yet been reported out of Committee in either the House or the Senate and we cannot be sure what its fate will be. In other words, it would be a mistake to leave with the Prime Minister an impression that we expected to be able to take action under the bill in the immediate future.

Finally, I suggest that if you do discuss the matter with the Prime Minister [3] you might want to tell him that you would ask Ambassador Atherton to talk with him later in detail about the bill and our plans to implement it.

G. C. MARSHALL

---

[3] No record has been found of such discussion in Ottawa between the President and Prime Minister Mackenzie King.

Editorial Note

For texts of an address by President Truman before the Canadian Parliament in Ottawa, June 11, and of a special news conference with Prime Minister Mackenzie King near Ottawa, June 12, see *Public Papers of the Presidents of the United States: Harry S. Truman, 1947* (Washington, Government Printing Office, 1963), pages 272–277.

842.20 Defense/11–1247

Memorandum by the Chairman of the United States Section of the Permanent Joint Board on Defense, United States–Canada (Acheson) to President Truman [1]

SECRET WASHINGTON, November 12, 1947.

At its meeting at New York on September 11–12, 1947, the Permanent Joint Board on Defense, U.S.–Canada, adopted the following Recommendation:

"*Recommendation of September 11, 1947*

"That as a measure contributing directly to the efficiency of joint United States–Canadian defense arrangements, the service personnel (civil and military) of each country should be carried reciprocally in the military airplanes of the other country without charge for reimbursement."

[1] Marginal notation dated November 14: "Approved, Harry S. Truman."

The Departments of State, the Army, the Navy, and the Air Force have signified their agreement with the Board's Recommendation.

I recommend that you approve the Board's Recommendation of September 11, 1947.

DEAN ACHESON

Department of State Departmental Announcement No. 920

RESTRICTED　　　　　　　　　　　　　　[WASHINGTON,] December 29, 1947.

DIRECTIVE CONCERNING PUBLICITY RELATING TO JOINT CANADIAN–UNITED STATES DEFENSE PLANS AND OPERATIONS

In order to inform personnel of the Department regarding the policy and procedure governing publicity relating to joint Canadian–United States defense plans and operations, and to provide the information necessary to insure conformity thereto, the covering directive is quoted herein.

The Secretaries of State and Defense have agreed that a uniform and clearly defined policy and procedure shall apply in connection with publicity relating to plans and operations jointly conducted by Canada and the United States or conducted by either country in the territory of the other. This directive will be followed by all personnel of the Department of State.

1. It is considered a fundamental principle that Canadian–United States defense arrangements should, within the limitations necessarily imposed by the requirements of military security and in the light of the international situation, be made known to the peoples of the two countries. Apart from the fact that secrecy is counter to the traditions of the United States and of Canada, the strength of the defense arrangements depends in the last analysis upon their general acceptance and support by the two peoples. Again undue secrecy has led occasionally to sensational stories in the press—stories embarrassing to the two Governments and harmful to the joint defense program.

2. It is therefore the policy of the United States and Canadian Governments that simple factual announcements should be issued at an early stage in the case of those projects which can be classified as "Unrestricted" from the point of view of military security and of the international political situation.

3. Such public announcements must always have the approval of both the United States and Canadian Governments.

4. The primary responsibility for such public announcements rests with the country whose territory is utilized in connection with the project in question.

5. Each project must be examined on its own merits in so far as possible publicity is concerned and must be reviewed in terms of military

security (which is for determination by the United States National Military Establishment and the Canadian Department of National Defense) and of the prevailing international political situation (which is the province of the Canadian Department of External Affairs and the United States Department of State).

6. To implement the foregoing policy and procedure the State Department and Military Service members of the U.S. section of the Permanent Joint Board on Defense, U.S.–Canada, are designated to consider each case that may arise concerning possible publicity relating to U.S.–Canadian plans and operations. The members will:

(*a*) review, along the lines indicated in paragraph No. 5 above, each U.S.–Canadian defense project;

(*b*) ascertain the views of the Canadian Government concerning possible publicity relating to the project;

(*c*) decide, in so far as the United States is concerned, whether such publicity would be in accord with the policy described in paragraphs Nos. 1 and 2 above; and

(*d*) if so, determine (in cooperation with the appropriate Canadian authorities) to what extent, at what time, and by whom the publicity should be issued.

7. The members of the U.S. section of the Board will normally deal with the representatives of the press through their respective public relations officers.

8. Officers of the several departments, including those in the press or public relations units, will submit to the senior Board member of their Department (the Canadian desk officer in BC is the State Department member of the Board) for review, as specified in paragraph No. 6 above, any draft publicity releases or announcements which it is desired to issue and any other matters relating to publicity on U.S.–Canadian defense arrangements (e.g. visits of newspapermen to the far north, furnishing of "background" information to the press, et cetera).

9. Officers of the several departments, including those in the press or public relations units, will not communicate with the Canadian Embassy at Washington or with officials of the Canadian Government at Ottawa concerning publicity matters but will address themselves only to the senior Board member of their Department.

10. It is the purpose of this directive to further the national security in general and to coordinate the joint responsibilities of the National Military Establishment, the Department of State, and the Canadian Government. Officers are therefore particularly cautioned against giving the press the impression that they would be willing to release information about a given project but that another Department or the Canadian Government has refused to agree.

11. This directive is effective immediately.

EFFORTS BY THE UNITED STATES TO RELIEVE THE CANADIAN SHORTAGE OF DOLLARS; COOPERATIVE STUDY OF CLOSER ECONOMIC TIES

842.5151/8–2247 : Airgram

The Ambassador in Canada (Atherton) to the Secretary of State

CONFIDENTIAL   OTTAWA, August 22, 1947.

A–189. The Embassy has learned from a responsible source that as one measure to prevent further deterioration of her United States dollars position Canada is considering the imposition of restrictions on imports from the United States and that studies of various commodities likely to be affected are now being made. Specifically suggested as likely items for restriction are fresh and canned fruits, fruit juices, and automobiles, as well as such key imports as steel, gasoline and other fuels. There will probably be many others.

Rather than restrict imports it is probable that Canada would prefer to receive a dollar loan as the lesser of the two evils. The Embassy understands, however, that feelers put out recently in Washington by Mr. Graham Towers, Governor of the Bank of Canada, did not give rise to much optimism for a loan of the size needed by Canada to tide her over the next six or eight months. Mr. Towers reportedly was talking in terms of a loan of $750,000,000 but received encouragement only to the extent of $250,000,000. The Canadians apparently regard $500,000,000 as their minimum needs in the form of a United States Government loan, and this amount they would probably attempt to supplement by means of private loans in New York. It is more than likely that the initial list of imports proposed for restriction would be impressive in the hope that Washington would view a loan application in a more favorable light. Even if Canada should be successful in obtaining a loan this step would undoubtedly be coupled with a number of domestic "austerity" measures.

There seems to be little doubt that the Canadian dollar position vis-à-vis the United States is rapidly approaching a critical point, and evidence of this situation is the fact that high Canadian officials are considering the restriction of American imports and/or seeking an American loan, or loans, both of which steps are considered drastic. The present record high level of Canadian production and income is, of course, due in a large measure to exceptionally heavy imports from the United States, and the restriction of American imports, doubtless involving decreased Canadian production and lower incomes, as well as the virtual certainty of rationing many commodities, would be extremely unpopular. A loan is equally unpalatable in view of the excellent financial condition in which Canada emerged from the war and the creditor position which she has assumed with many countries. Nevertheless, the Embassy believes that the Canadian Government will take some affirmative action in the near future to protect its dollar exchange position. Devaluation of the Canadian dollar is unlikely unless the United Kingdom should devalue the pound.

The press in recent weeks has given unusual prominence to the growing American dollar shortage. Official figures just released disclose an adverse balance of $488,000,000 for the first six months of 1947, and since July 1 the rate of deficit has been reportedly higher. Although the Minister of Finance [1] announced yesterday that no change has yet been made in the United Kingdom–Canada Agreement under which the British since early this year have been paying half the purchase price of Canadian goods with United States dollars, giving the Dominion in the first six months of this year U.S. $220,000,000, Canadian officials apparently feel that some modification will now have to be made in this agreement thus drying up an important source of American dollars.

Such measures as restrictions on imports and loans are temporary expedients at best. Canada's real hope is to increase her exports to the United States and thus offset her large volume of exports on credit to the United Kingdom and other areas. Food shipments which could be integrated in our relief problem [*program?*] might be one solution. There may be other commodities that present similar opportunities. In any event it seems to us that the broad considerations affecting our relations with Canada justify the most energetic efforts to assist her constructively at this time.

ATHERTON

---

[1] Douglas Abbott.

842.5151/9–847

*The Assistant Chief of the Division of British Commonwealth Affairs
(Foster) to the Ambassador in Canada (Atherton)*

SECRET [WASHINGTON,] September 8, 1947.

DEAR MR. AMBASSADOR: This is an effort to give you the story of what has happened at this end concerning the Canadian dollar problem and of what the feeling is here about the future. I must remind you that I am not an economist, nor have I been present at all the meetings relating to the problem. I would like to recall, also, that I am writing about matters which it has been impossible to talk about on the telephone—in which connection you will have in hand by now my recent letter concerning the tip we had that the line may be tapped.

As you know, the discussions began in June when Graham Towers came to Washington and talked one evening with Messrs. Acheson,

Clayton, and Hickerson.[1] Mr. Wrong and Mr. Rasminsky [2] were also present. It was evidently the purpose at this first meeting to warn our people of the increasing gravity of the situation, which of course centered in the fact that the Canadians were selling on credit to "soft" currency countries and buying refrigerators, automobiles, et cetera, for dollars in the United States at a rate which was depleting their dollar balance by nearly $100,000,000 per month.

There followed a meeting at the Department in late June between Mr. R. B. Bryce, Director of the Economic Division, Department of Finance; Mr. V. W. Scully, Deputy Minister of Reconstruction and Supply; Mr. J. R. Beatie, Chief of the Research Department of the Bank of Canada; and Mr. J. R. Murray of the Canadian Embassy; and Mr. Wayne Jackson of EUR; Mr. Harold Spiegel of FN; Mr. Morse of the Federal Reserve Board; myself and other officers of the Economic Offices and Divisions. I enclose a memorandum [3] concerning this meeting from which you will see that it was devoted entirely to the question whether it would be possible for the U.S. to assist Canada by throwing some government procurement her way. We had in mind procurement for the relief programs in Europe and the Near East and also possibly procurement for the needs of the U.S. armed forces. It was generally agreed that the most we could possibly hope to provide for Canada by these means would be somewhere between $25,000,000 and $50,000,000. The Canadians were talking about $500,000,000 or $700,000,000. The meeting was adjourned on the understanding that the Canadians would explore further in Ottawa concerning items that might be offered under the relief and armed services procurement programs, while the Americans would explore in Washington concerning the requirements of the programs.

Early in July Mr. Bryce returned to Washington and we had the second meeting. I enclose a copy of a secret memorandum dated July 8 [3] concerning this meeting, which you will see was devoted to the same general subject, namely assistance through procurement for the relief programs and the needs of the armed forces.

Throughout these meetings in June and July the Canadians were emphatic in declaring that they would not under any circumstances devalue their dollar or impose import restrictions. They also said that they did not want to try to solve the problem by borrowing money. They felt that any of these three alternatives would be merely a stopgap palliative and not a fundamental cure.

---

[1] Dean Acheson, then Under Secretary of State; William L. Clayton, Under Secretary of State for Economic Affairs; and John D. Hickerson, then Deputy Director of the Office of European Affairs.

[2] Hume Wrong, Canadian Ambassador in Washington, and Louis Rasminsky, Canadian representative on the International Monetary Fund.

[3] Not printed.

There have been no further talks along the lines of procurement and evidently the Canadians have dropped this possible solution as inadequate.

The next chapter consists in a call made on August 13 by Graham Towers on the Acting Secretary, Mr. Lovett. Mr. Towers was accompanied by the Canadian Chargé, Tommy Stone. I enclose a copy of Mr. Lovett's own memorandum of conversation,[4] which related to both the Canadian dollar problem and freight car embargo.

It now looks here, as it seems to look to you at Ottawa, as if the Canadians were now more intent upon getting a loan than upon seeking any other solution of their problem. Within the past several days I have begun to hear talk for the first time about the possibility of the Canadians imposing import restrictions—a possibility which they had previously denied. As far as I can gather at this end they are still as firm as ever against a devaluation of their dollar.

I have been unable to ascertain whether further visits from Graham Towers are expected in the near future. In fact, I can't seem to find out what the next move by the Canadians is likely to be. You are probably far better informed on this angle than I am. In fact, you mentioned on the phone today that Mr. Clifford Clark [5] might come to town a week hence.

The Canadians themselves have of course repeatedly told us, and they have said the same thing publicly, that the permanent solution of their problem lies in the reconstruction of Western Europe. That brings me to the very important point that top side in Washington is so preoccupied with the crisis in the U.K. and Western Europe that I fear it is going to be difficult to get much of a hearing for Canada's problem at present. I have an impression that there is an increasing feeling in Washington that the capacity of the United States to assist the world is limited and that our resources ought to go first for the salvation of the U.K. and Western Europe. It is all very well to say that the United States cannot let Canada suffer an economic crisis. There is nobody in Washington who would disagree with that. The point is that most people in Washington will find it difficult to believe that Canada really is facing something grave. In every respect except the miserable problem of the dollar balance the Canadians seem to be just fine and dandy. The dollar problem seems to arise largely because of the spree of buying U.S. refrigerators, automobiles, et cetera. There seems on the surface to be nothing in the Canadian scene comparable to the truly desperate conditions of the U.K., France, and the rest.

If the Canadians are going to stake the solution on a loan or perhaps on a loan plus import restrictions, they will be up against the

---

[4] Memorandum by Robert A. Lovett, Under Secretary of State, not printed.
[5] William Clifford Clark, Canadian Deputy Minister of Finance.

difficulty that $750,000,000 is not to be had for the asking in Washington these days. The loan would have to be authorized by Congress, and you know the job of persuasion which lay behind a loan to the U.K.[6] The worst of it is the Congress is probably going to be very skeptical about a big loan for Canada. I don't say this difficulty can't be got over but I do say that it must be faced as a very great difficulty.

Under these circumstances I feel sure you will agree that you and I and the others concerned will have to be careful not to do anything that might arouse false or premature hopes among the Canadians. It is going to be difficult, though it should not be impossible, to follow the problem closely and to present a sympathetic attitude toward the Canadians while at the same time avoiding any action that might cause them to think that we were able and willing to make them a large loan without more ado.

September 9.

I had my talk last night with Jack Hickerson. I told him that you and I were deeply concerned by the increasingly grave situation and that we both wondered whether we shouldn't be taking some sort of affirmative action rather than merely waiting about for Canadian proposals or requests. Jack said he fully appreciated that the Canadian situation is serious. He referred to the point which I made earlier in this letter: namely, that the situation in the U.K. and Western Europe is so much more serious that we have to put first things first. He added that of course we would never let Canada go down the drain. He felt, however, that for the present you and I should wait for approaches from the Canadians. "Under present circumstances", he said, "I don't see how you can do anything else". He said he was not aware of any approach from this end more recent that Mr. Towers' call on Mr. Lovett on August 13.

I shall of course be very much interested to read the despatch which you told me you were sending in towards the end of this week. I have no doubt it will throw a lot of light on the situation, particularly from the point of view of the present thinking and intentions of the Canadians.

I apologize for the hodgepodge nature of this letter, the dictation of which was interrupted at least thirty times between the beginning and the end. I shall not fail to let you know of any significant developments at this end.

With all best wishes,

Ever sincerely,

ANDREW B. FOSTER

---

[6] For documentation on the negotiation of this loan, see *Foreign Relations,* 1945, vol. VI, pp. 1 ff.

842.5151/9–1147

The Ambassador in Canada (Atherton) to the Secretary of State

RESTRICTED   OTTAWA, September 11, 1947.
No. 5487

SIR: Contributing further to the Embassy's previous reports on the Canadian financial and economic situation, I have the honor to emphasize the seriousness of the rapidly developing United States dollar crisis.

Although Canada currently enjoys a slightly favorable balance on her global trade—at the end of the first six months of 1947 $88,500,000—she had an adverse balance with the United States of $488,000,000 at the end of the same period. At the end of the calendar year Canada's adverse trade balance with the United States will exceed $1,000,000,000 U.S.

Canada entered the present year with gold and United States dollar reserves of $1,244,900,000. It is known that these reserves have been very heavily depleted. Making allowances for United States dollar funds which Canada may obtain from the United Kingdom and other sources, it is increasingly evident that when the balance is struck at the end of the present calendar year Canada's gold and United States dollar reserves will be approaching the vanishing point.

Canada does not have sufficient United States dollars to finance purchases from the United States at their present volume. There is no single avenue at present open through which she can obtain these dollars. Relief, which must come unless a major crisis is to be suffered, may well be furnished in part from various sources which in the aggregate may be sufficient to ease the burden. Canada can restrict purchases from the United States and buy more from sterling areas. This she can do, however, only to a limited extent without causing harm to the domestic economy and forcing a lower standard of living. Canada can increase her exports to the United States, although she cannot go too far in this direction over and above her present volume at a time when she is enjoying the peak of industrial and agricultural production. The main immediate hope lies in diverting to the United States and dollar areas agricultural, mineral and manufactured products which in the past and even now are going to sterling areas.

Although the average Canadian official and man on the street is critical of alleged high United States tariffs, it is only too evident that the United States tariff wall is not responsible for the failure of Canada to export even vaster quantities of materials to the United States. Since the war United States tariffs have remained constant, whereas commodity prices have soared. The element of duty in an imported product is consequently less than formerly. It is not unlikely that in relation to price, United States tariffs have actually decreased by at least 50 percent. As a matter of fact, approximately 75 percent of all Canadian exports to the United States enter free of duty. The average rate, figured on an ad valorem basis, on those dutiable, taking into account present expanded prices, runs substantially less than 25 percent. Certainly on most agricultural products the disparity in price between Canada and the United States is such that they would find ready acceptance in the United States and other dollar areas were it not for the fact that exports have been subject to special restrictive license in order that Canada might be able to fulfill her commitments to the United Kingdom. It is not a valid argument that a further reduction of United States tariffs would be of material benefit to Canada or, conversely, that present tariffs are a serious detriment to her export position vis-à-vis the United States. The Embassy is completing a despatch going into detail on the subject of tariffs which will be forwarded within the next few days.[1] Although Canada cannot be regarded normally as a supplier of wheat to the United States, she could dispose of wheat in other areas in exchange for United States dollars if it were not for United Kingdom commitments. With the removal of export restrictions against poultry, large volumes are now moving into the United States in exchange for United States dollars. Canada's foreign fiscal policies rather than United States tariffs must bear the responsibility for the deepening dollar crisis.

As of the end of the fiscal year 1946–1947 (ended March 31, 1947) Canada had loan commitments to the United Kingdom of $1,250,000,-000 and to other countries, including Belgium, China, Czechoslovakia, France, the Netherlands and the U.S.S.R. of $594,500,000, a total of $1,844,500,000. Appreciation of the significance of these credits may be had by comparing the volume with Canada's total national income, which for 1946 was $9,212,000,000. The simple fact is that Canada, through external credits, has diverted to debtor countries a large volume of available exports for which she will presumably one day be repaid but from which she is presently failing to receive the United States dollars of which she is in such dire need. The countries to whom Canada has extended this credit, prior to the war supplied her with sufficient dollars to balance her United States account. These areas are themselves today critically short of dollars and their ability to have supplied any substantial number of dollars over the past two years is open to question.

A United States dollar loan, if available, would protect the Canadian gold and dollar reserves by exactly that amount. It would

---

[1] Despatch No. 5490, September 12, 1947, not printed.

not go to the root of the question. At this point it is difficult to see how a loan could be extended to Canada at a time when it has been made clear to Latin American neighbors that they cannot expect help until the European situation is better.

Although the Embassy is fully conversant with the Department's desire to encourage multilateral trade as well as to discourage government-to-government trading, it is submitting to the Department under cover of a separate despatch [2] a list of agricultural, industrial and military items which can be had through the Canadian Goverment's Canadian Commercial Corporation, the purchase of which might be consummated under the Marshall Plan with resultant immediate benefit to the Canadian Government.

The Embassy wishes to point out that in the situation shaping up here there are elements of discord which might not only impair Canadian-American relations at a time when solidarity is essential but which might conceivably present us with an unpleasant economic situation immediately across the border rather than on the other side of the Atlantic. Unfortunately government circles appear unable or unwilling to face the situation and evolve some plan of action to correct it before it is out of control. The Honorable John Bracken, Leader of the Government's Opposition, referred in a radio address last night to this attitude of the Government as a "Micawber attitude" hoping that something would turn up.

The radio address of Mr. Bracken last evening is the first serious public examination into the mounting dollar crisis which has been made by any of the Canadian leaders. He attributes much of it to inept fiscal policy. Unfortunately he suggested no remedy other than the unpalatable one of a customs union with the United Kingdom, as suggested by Foreign Secretary Bevin, or the devaluation of the Canadian dollar.

It is the Embassy's earnest desire that on our part consideration be given the dollar situation on a high level in order that we may move promptly and effectively when called upon. It is most probable that Canada herself will take no action until the termination of present economic discussions [3] at London and the results of the Geneva talks,[4] both as to tariffs and the ITO charter, are made public.

Respectfully yours,   RAY ATHERTON

---

[2] Despatch No. 5498, September 18, 1947, not printed.
[3] Reference here is to British–Canadian discussions attended by Canada's Minister of Finance, Douglas Abbott.
[4] For documentation on the Geneva talks, see volume I.

842.5151/9–2747

Memorandum by the Assistant Chief of the Division of British Commonwealth Affairs (Foster) to the Director of the Office of European Affairs (Hickerson)

SECRET   [WASHINGTON,] September 27, 1947.

CANADIAN DOLLAR PROBLEM

The following is a summary of the developments of the past two weeks:

On September 18 Mr. Clifford Clark (Acting Minister of Finance in the absence of Abbott, who is still in London) visited Washington with the intention of talking with you, Thorp, and Southard of the Treasury.[1] He spent an hour or so with Southard in the morning, and in the afternoon he met with Messrs. Ty Wood, Nitze, Jackson, Rosenson,[2] and myself. We compared notes afterwards and found that the talks in State and Treasury were very similar.

I attach a copy of the memo relating to the State meeting,[3] which you may wish to read. In brief, Clark (who was accompanied by Hume Wrong) emphasized the gravity of the Canadian problem and said that his Government was going to be compelled in the near future to apply import restrictions against the radios, refrigerators, etc., from the U. S. He scarcely mentioned the loan angle. He wanted to know whether we could give him any indication whether Canada was being included in our framing of the Marshall plan (not in terms of direct aid but as a partner in the reconstruction of the U. K. and western Europe). If Canada was included in our thinking, and he appreciated that we couldn't say what Congress may do, his Government would apply the least drastic remedies to the present emergency and would declare them to be temporary. But if Canada was not included and if we felt that a "multilateral" trading world of comparative free trade and comparatively interchangeable currencies was a thing of the past, Canada would be obliged to apply very drastic and long-term remedies.

---

[1] Willard L. Thorp, Assistant Secretary of State for Economic Affairs, and Frank A. Southard, Director of the Office of International Finance, Treasury Department.

[2] C. Tyler Wood, Deputy to the Assistant Secretary of State for Economic Affairs; Paul H. Nitze, Deputy Director of the Office of International Trade Policy; Wayne G. Jackson, Special Assistant to the Director of the Office of European Affairs; and Alexander M. Rosenson, Assistant Chief of the Division of Financial Affairs.

[3] Memorandum dated September 18, 1947, not printed.

Mr. Ty Wood underlined to Mr. Clark and Ambassador Wrong that we were deeply concerned by the Canadian problem and anxious to do what we could to assist; he added, however, that there was no magic cure available to us in Washington. He said that the ITO and the Marshall plan would simply have to be made to succeed but he said he thought it would be a mistake for Canada to rely on either for any immediate solution of her problem. Even under optimum conditions the effect of the ITO and the Marshall plan might not be felt for a long time, perhaps years.

We feel that the meeting served two useful purposes. It brought us up to date on details concerning the problem and Canadian thinking about its solution. Secondly, it acquainted the Canadians with the fact that there is no easy remedy available at present at this end. As to the loan, it would have to be appropriated by Congress (which I suspect will be somewhat astonished to be asked to lend $500,000,000 to Canada) ; and as to the Marshall plan, it is in a very early stage. There isn't much sign that Congress will give us in the Marshall plan, even if it is adopted, any great degree of flexibility in placing procurement in Canada or making US dollars available to the U. K. and western Europe for purchases in Canada.

On September 25 I talked with Hume Wrong for an hour about the problem. I attach a copy of my memo of conversation,[4] which I recommend you read if you have time. This meeting served chiefly to set the record straight concerning the word which Hume had sent us, after the Clark meeting on the 18th, that he and Clark understood that "the next move was up to the U. S.".

Ray Atherton arrives in Washington on Monday morning, September 29, for a week's consultation. On Tuesday morning at 11.00 the following are meeting in Mr. Ty Wood's office to talk further about the problem: Wood, Atherton, Southard (of the Treasury), Wayne Jackson, Nitze, Rosenson, and myself. I think you should be there: you'd get the latest developments at first hand and I think the group needs your wisdom. (Incidentally, Hume Wrong said, after the Clark meeting, "I think we need to have Jack's imagination brought to bear on the problem".)

ANDREW B. FOSTER

P.S. As you will note in my memo of conversation with Hume, he told me that within a matter of weeks there will be a very high level approach, possibly by the P. M. to the President, about the Canadian

---

[4] Memorandum dated September 25, 1947, not printed.

problem. No doubt the approach will relate to a loan and to inclusion in the Marshall plan.

842.5151/10–1447 : Telegram

The Acting Secretary of State to the Consulate at Geneva

SECRET   WASHINGTON, October 14, 1947—2 p. m.

1321. Personal for Brown.[1] Deptel 1102, August 28.[2] Further recent discussions Canadian dollar position with Clark, Acting Minister Finance and Canadian Ambassador indicate likelihood imposition soon restrictions imports from US including some items specified Schedule I, 1938 agreement.[3] Probable items already decided but Can feel they cannot discuss with us.

Canadians emphatically deny possibility devaluating Can dollar, which may or may not be true since this is line any Can official bound to take until and unless the moment for devaluation comes.

Believe impossible solve problem through 1) increased US procurement Can, 2) increased Can exports US, 3) loan or borrowing New York though all three would help. We are obviously unable at present give Can any assurance re Marshall Plan and effects on Can position. All foregoing under study by interdepartmental committee.

Believe here Can should not take unilateral action in announcing restrictions. Hope to persuade them advisability releasing simultaneously with list of restricted goods an exchange of memoranda similar to exchange between US and Sweden regarding restrictions imposed by latter.

Can memo, if they agree, would refer to present dollar difficulties, their causes and the need of measures now to prevent more drastic controls later, as well as to permit continued Can participation in European reconstruction, would emphasize intention administer controls in manner consistent Gen Agreement Trade and Tariffs,[4] remove controls as soon as possible, allow imports in transit and, with appropriate cut-off dates, goods for which *bona fide* contracts made. Would agree discuss any individual cases with us. Would express hope US not invoke pertinent provisions 1938 trade agreement and would sug-

---

[1] Winthrop G. Brown, Chief of the Division of Commercial Policy and U.S. delegate to the Second Meeting of the United Nations Preparatory Committee, International Conference on Trade and Employment, at Geneva, 1947.

[2] Not printed.

[3] For text of Reciprocal Trade Agreement between the United States and Canada, signed at Washington, November 17, 1938, see Department of State Executive Agreement Series No. 149, or 53 Stat. 2348. For documentation on the negotiation of the Agreement, see *Foreign Relations*, 1938, vol. II, pp. 164–177.

[4] For documentation on the negotiation of this Agreement, see volume I.

gest early consultation re future under 1938 agreement if Gen Agreement did not come into effect early 1948.

US memo would note appreciation of Can difficulties and extent of Can contribution to European reconstruction. Would acknowledge Can intention to follow Gen Agreement, and their statement re temporary nature and transitional measures. Would comment particularly on desirability opportunity discuss individual cases as no opportunity given before announcement restrictions. Would agree not to invoke provisions 1938 agreement for duration of arrangement and to consult early in 1948 if 1938 agreement not superseded.

US press release issued same time would note foregoing stressing traditional cooperation, friendship US and Can. Action contemplated is predicated on need and desirability assisting Can whose action would be consistent Gen Agreement though not with 1938 TA. Since 1938 TA would presumably be in effect until Jan, TAC decision to waive rights under that agreement necessary. Does TAC agree course of action outlined above?

Proposed exchange of memoranda not yet submitted to Canadians but expect to submit possibly within one week.

Reply soonest.[5]

LOVETT

---

[5] In telegram No. 1147, October 16, 4 p. m., Brown answered as follows: "TAC members feel they have no basis decision as to necessity proposed Canadian action reported Deptel 1321, October 14. If Department convinced Canadian action necessary, TAC members agree we must concur. Procedure outlined telegram 1321 satisfactory." (842.5151/10–1647)

611.4231/10–2947

The Ambassador in Canada (Atherton) to the Secretary of State

RESTRICTED   OTTAWA, October 29, 1947.
No. 5596

[Extracts]

SIR: I have the honor to report that Canadian public opinion, particularly as reflected in the press, has reached probably an all time high in favoring a closer integration of the economies of Canada and the United States. Economic union between the two countries is taken as a natural parallel development with intimate military ties existing since early in the late war and close political collaboration as now manifest at the UN. Sentiment favoring economic integration is a logical outgrowth of the growing realization that Canada's pre-war international trade position founded on the triangular exchange of commodities with the United States and the United Kingdom is no longer valid, and there has been widespread acceptance of Finance Minister Abbott's doctrine that the solution of Canada's present external economic difficulties calls for "radical and wholesale changes" in the Dominion's position as a world economic power. The changes adumbrated clearly imply Canada's secession from the Empire trading unit in so far as Empire ties interfere with Canada's development as an independent North American nation.

It is well known that for some time Canadian Government departments have been studying as a long term solution to Canada's trade difficulties the expansion of the Dominion's economy along lines complementary to that of the United States. Such expansion is said to involve, first, the intensified development of natural resources, both for export to the United States and for supplanting raw material imports from the United States (such as Alberta coal and Labrador iron ore) and, second, a greater interchange of finished products between North American companies with emphasis on increased exports to the United States. While trade restrictions may prove to be necessary in the short term to conserve a dwindling United States dollar supply, the long term solution is founded on trade expansion, probably to be promoted in the first stages by Canadian participation in an American aid program for Europe under a kind of "peacetime Hyde Park Plan".[1]

The new "national policy" for a "directed economy" is widely supported in the press and, with minor exceptions, apparently has the popular backing of the Canadian people.

[Here follows a summary of press comment on Canadian–American trade relationships.]

In brief, it may be said that Canada today more than ever before appears ready to accept virtual economic union with the United States as a necessary substitute for the multilateralism of the Atlantic triangle now believed to have disappeared for an indefinite time to come, if not permanently, and as a desirable corollary to American–Canadian cooperation in other fields. Such metamorphosis of thinking is a far cry from the pre-war Tory principle of "No truck or trade with the Yankees" and the French Canadian opposition to ties with the United States because of the latter's "godless imperialism".

Respectfully yours,   RAY ATHERTON

---

[1] Reference is to a statement made at Hyde Park, New York, by President Roosevelt and Prime Minister Mackenzie King on April 20, 1941, which announced agreement on plans for economic coordination during the war emergency. For text, see Department of State *Bulletin*, April 26, 1941, pp. 494–495.

611.4231/10–2947

Memorandum of Conversation, by the Associate Chief of the Division of Commercial Policy (Willoughby)

SECRET   [WASHINGTON,] October 29, 1947.

Participants: Mr. Hector B. McKinnon, Chairman of the Canadian
 Tariff Board
 Mr. John D. Deutsch, Director of Economic Relations,
 Canadian Department of Finance
 Mr. Wilcox,[1] Mr. Nitze—ITP
 Mr. Foster—BC
 Mr. Willoughby—CP

UNITED STATES—CANADA TRADE RELATIONS

Mr. McKinnon and Mr. Deutsch prefaced their remarks with a brief review of the statement they had made the day before in Mr. Wood's office concerning the balance-of-payments situation of Canada. Mr. McKinnon then said that Program B (less drastic restriction of imports) [2] could be adopted if there were some likelihood of assistance under the Marshall Plan and of substantial further relaxation of trade barriers between the two countries. The Canadian Cabinet authorized him to explore with United States officials the possibility of concluding a comprehensive agreement involving, wherever possible, the complete elimination of duties. It would be necessary to obtain Congressional approval. Mr. McKinnon indicated that the Canadian Government would be willing to enter into an agreement even if it necessitated a major readjustment and reorientation of Canada's international economic relations. They feel that Canada must either integrate her economy more closely with that of the United States or be forced into discriminatory restrictive policies involving greater self sufficiency, bilateral trade bargaining and an orientation toward Europe with corresponding danger of friction with the United States, if not economic warfare.

Mr. Wilcox explained some of the difficulties of obtaining at the coming regular session of Congress approval for tariff cuts beyond those authorized by the Trade Agreements Act but said that he did not want to close the door to the possibility of negotiating a new comprehensive agreement. He said that he would take the matter up with the higher officers of the Department.

---

[1] Clair Wilcox, Acting Deputy to the Assistant Secretary of State for Economic Affairs, and Director of the Office of International Trade Policy.

[2] The alternative programs, A and B, are outlined in a memorandum of conversation dated October 29, 1947 by Constant Southworth of the Division of Commercial Policy (642.116/10–2947).

(Mr. McKinnon and Mr. Deutsch later discussed this proposal further with officers of the Department and representatives of the Departments of Commerce and Agriculture. CP will make a quick survey of the possibilities for further tariff negotiations.)

The Canadian representatives urged the utmost caution to avoid leaks, which would lead to heavy imports and probably necessitate quicker imposition of restrictions.

842.5151/11–1447

Memorandum by Mr. C. Tyler Wood, Deputy to the Assistant Secretary of State for Economic Affairs, to the Under Secretary of State (Lovett)

WASHINGTON, November 14, 1947.

Subject: Canadian Dollar Problem

The present status of the Canadian dollar problem may be summarized as follows:

Import restrictions will be imposed by the Canadian Government next Tuesday, November 18. The restrictions will be aimed chiefly against consumer goods and luxury items, many of which will be prohibited entirely. Capital goods will in general be subject to quotas of 200% to 300% of pre-war levels. There will be no legal or outright discrimination against the United States although by selection the restrictions will hit chiefly goods from the United States. The restrictions are intended to save a net of $175 million per annum. Details are being closely guarded by the Canadians although they have told us about the general range and scope of the restrictions.

Loan from the Export-Import Bank to the Canadian Government in the amount of $300 million has been agreed to,[1] subject to certain conditions including the provision that Canada will borrow (perhaps $200 million) in the private market. (Copies of letters exchanged between the Canadians and the Bank are attached as tab A.[2])

Exchange of notes will be completed tomorrow, November 15, we hope by you and Ambassador Wrong. (Attached as tab B is a suggested informal statement which you might wish to make to Ambassador Wrong at the time.[2]) The exchange is required chiefly because the U.S. has to agree not to invoke the 1938 Trade Agreement against the Canadian import restrictions, which would be a violation of the Agreement. (Copies of the proposed notes, the text of which has been widely cleared in the Department and by the Departments of the

---

[1] Mr. A. B. Foster, Assistant Chief of the Division of British Commonwealth Affairs, added the following marginal notation: "Mr. Ness of OFD states that the loan of $300 million was specifically approved by the NAC on November 8, 1947."

[2] Not found in Department of State files.

Treasury, Commerce, and Agriculture, and by the Canadians at Ottawa, are attached as tab C.[3])

Announcements relating to the Canadian import restrictions will be made at Ottawa and Washington on the evening of Monday, November 17, simultaneously with the announcement concerning the Geneva Agreement. Prime Minister King, who is in London for the Royal wedding, will broadcast concerning the achievements at Geneva and will be followed immediately on the air by Finance Minister Abbott at Ottawa, who will tell about the import restrictions. Needless to say, both sides have had the gravest misgivings about the timing but the Canadian decision has been taken and there is no help for it. (A copy of the announcement to be made by the Department is attached hereto as tab D.[4]) This announcement has been widely cleared in the Department, in the Departments of the Treasury, Agriculture, Commerce, and by the Canadians. It takes the line that we understand the difficulties of the Canadian situation and appreciate the necessity for the imposition of Canadian import controls; it expresses the hope that the controls will be lifted as soon as possible and touches upon our agreement not to invoke the 1938 Trade Agreement.

C. TYLER WOOD

---

[3] Not found in Department of State files; presumably reference is to the *aide-mémoire* included in the Department's press release of November 17 and printed *infra*.

[4] Not found in Department of State files. Presumably this announcement is the statement published in the Department's press release of November 17, the first paragraph of which is printed *infra*.

Press Release Issued by the Department of State, November 17, 1947

[Extract]

The Department of State has not yet had time to study in detail the restrictions which the Canadian Government has just imposed on Canadian imports from abroad. The Department has been aware for some months past, however, that Canada might be compelled to adopt temporary measures of this sort because of the increasing difficulty she has had in obtaining United States dollars to finance her imports from the United States. During recent weeks representatives of the two Governments have discussed the Canadian position in general terms. The discussions culminated in the exchange of memoranda released today.

. . . .

The text of the exchange of memoranda follows:

"AIDE-MÉMOIRE

"The Government of Canada refer to the discussions which have taken place recently between its representatives and those of the Government of the United States of America regarding the problems confronting Canada because of the rapid and marked decline during 1947 of its gold and United States dollar reserves.

"It was noted in the course of the discussions that this condition was due 1) to an unprecedented increase in Canadian imports from the United States unmatched by an equivalent increase in Canadian exports to the United States, 2) to the disruption in consequence of the war of normal trade and currency relationships, which ordinarily would have allowed Canada to discharge its deficit with the United States with the receipts from Canadian exports to other countries and 3) to the necessity which Canada, in common concern with the United States, has felt for extending very substantial financial assistance to various European Nations in their urgent problems of postwar reconstruction.

"The deterioration of Canada's gold and United States dollar reserves has proceeded at such a rate and to such an extent that the Government of Canada are compelled to take immediate remedial measures. Failure to take effective action now could only mean, in the circumstances, that in the near future measures more drastic than contemplated at present would be necessary.

"The Government of Canada find it necessary as one part of a general programme to curtail imports immediately in order to conserve their limited supplies of gold and United States dollars. It is a matter of special concern that such an action is necessary at this time when Canada is working with the United States and other Nations of the world to provide a sound basis for the expansion of world trade on a multilateral basis.

"The Government of Canada wish to emphasize that it is their intention to administer their controls in a manner consistent with the General Agreement on Tariffs and Trade recently concluded at Geneva which will govern trade relations between the signatory countries in the near future.

"The Government of Canada propose to remove the controls which they now find necessary to impose at the earliest possible moment that circumstances permit. They will moreover allow imports of any items which are now in transit to Canada. At any time during the period when control of imports is necessary the Government of Canada will give sympathetic consideration to representations in regard to any matter connected therewith which because of unusual circumstances involving particular hardships to the principals concerned would seem to merit special attention.

"In order to effect the necessary savings of gold and United States dollars, it is necessary to limit, among other imports from the United States, some items specified in Schedule I of the 1938 Trade Agreement between the United States and Canada. The Government of Canada express the hope that the Government of the United States will not in the circumstances, consider it necessary to invoke the pertinent provisions of the Trade Agreement of 1938 during the brief interval before the provisional coming into force on January 1st next, of the General Agreement on Tariffs and Trade which will replace the provisions of the earlier agreement.

"WASHINGTON, November 14, 1947."

"Aide-Mémoire

"The Government of the United States of America refers to the *aide-mémoire* of the Government of Canada, dated November 14, 1947, concerning the problems confronting Canada because of the serious decline in its gold and United States dollar reserves, and concerning the limitation on imports from the United States which the Government of Canada therefore considers necessary.

"The Government of the United States takes note of the information presented by the representatives of the Government of Canada in support of its contention that temporary controls on imports are necessary in view of the current situation respecting Canada's gold and United States dollar reserves. It appreciates the repercussions on Canada's exchange position resulting from the economic and financial difficulties which various European Nations are now experiencing as a result of the war. It is aware of the extent to which Canada has been participating in European reconstruction and of the fact that this effort has contributed to Canada's present foreign exchange reserve position.

"Acknowledgment is made of the statement by the Government of Canada of its intention to administer its controls in a manner consistent with the General Agreement on Tariffs and Trade which was recently concluded at Geneva.

"The Government of the United States takes note also of the statement of the Government of Canada with respect to the duration and the administration of the controls. In view of the prolonged efforts our two countries have made to promote world trade and world recovery, the Government of the United States attaches the highest importance to this indication of the Canadian Government's intention. Having in mind, also, that the conditions of the controls contain elements which might become unduly prejudicial to the position of individual commodities, it is particularly concerned that an opportunity be given for discussion of the detailed effects where, in its opinion, the circumstances are sufficiently grave. In the circumstances the Government of the United States agrees for the duration of the present arrangement not to invoke the provisions of Articles II, III and X of the Trade Agreement of 1938 between the United States of America and Canada in respect of the measures to be taken by the Government of Canada as set forth in its *aide-mémoire*.

"It is recognized that the Trade Agreement between the United States of America and Canada remains in full force and effect during the present arrangement, save for those temporary modifications in its operation provided for in this exchange of *aides-mémoire*.

"WASHINGTON, November 15, 1947."

AGREEMENT BETWEEN THE UNITED STATES AND CANADA AMENDING THE AGREEMENT OF FEBRUARY 17, 1945, RESPECTING AIR TRANSPORT SERVICES

[For text of Agreement, effected by exchange of notes signed at Ottawa, April 10 and 12, 1947, see Department of State Treaties and

Other International Acts Series (TIAS) No. 1619, or 61 Stat. (pt. 3) 2869.]

_____

AGREEMENT BETWEEN THE UNITED STATES AND CANADA RESPECTING TERMINATION OF THE RECIPROCAL TRADE AGREEMENT SIGNED DECEMBER 13, 1940, RELATING TO FOX FURS AND SKINS

[For text of Agreement, effected by exchange of notes signed at Washington, March 18, 1947, and for proclamation by the President of the United States terminating proclamations of December 18, 1940 and August 21, 1941, relating to the reciprocal trade agreement signed December 13, 1940, see Department of State Treaties and Other International Acts Series (TIAS) No. 1638, or 61 Stat. (pt. 3) 3054.]

_____

INTERIM ARRANGEMENT BETWEEN THE UNITED STATES AND CANADA RESPECTING MOBILE RADIO TRANSMITTING STATIONS

[For text of Agreement, effected by exchange of notes signed at Washington, June 25 and August 20, 1947, see Department of State Treaties and Other International Acts Series (TIAS) No. 1670, or 61 Stat. (pt. 4) 3349.]

_____

AGREEMENT BETWEEN THE UNITED STATES AND CANADA AMENDING THE PROVISIONAL AGREEMENT OF DECEMBER 8 AND 19, 1942, RESPECTING FUR SEALS

[For text of Agreement, effected by exchange of notes signed at Washington, December 26, 1947, see Department of State Treaties and Other International Acts Series (TIAS) No. 1686, or 62 Stat. (pt. 2) 1821.]

_____

AGREEMENT BETWEEN THE UNITED STATES AND CANADA RESPECTING ALLOCATION OF FM CHANNELS IN RADIO BROADCASTING

[For text of Agreement, effected by exchange of notes signed at Washington, January 8 and October 15, 1947, see Department of State Treaties and Other International Acts Series (TIAS) No. 1726, or 61 Stat. (pt. 4) 3800.]

_____

AGREEMENT BETWEEN THE UNITED STATES AND CANADA RENDERING INOPERATIVE THE TRADE AGREEMENT OF NOVEMBER 17, 1938, AND SUPPLEMENTING THE GENERAL AGREEMENT ON TARIFFS AND TRADE OF OCTOBER 30, 1947

[For text of Agreement and accompanying letters, signed at Geneva, October 30, 1947, effective January 1, 1948, see Department of State

Treaties and Other International Acts Series (TIAS) No. 1702, 61 Stat. (pt. 4) 3695.]

AGREEMENT BETWEEN THE UNITED STATES AND CANADA RESPECTING SURPLUS PROPERTY DISPOSAL OPERATIONS

[For text of Agreement, effected by exchange of notes signed at Ottawa, January 9, 1947, see Department of State Treaties and Other International Acts Series (TIAS) No. 1603, or 61 Stat. (pt. 3) 2738.]

ARRANGEMENTS BETWEEN THE UNITED STATES AND CANADA RESPECTING JOINT DEVELOPMENT AND OPERATION OF WEATHER OBSERVATION STATIONS IN THE CANADIAN ARCTIC REGION

Editorial Note

These arrangements, initiated by the Department of State in early 1946, were postponed until 1947 by a decision of the Canadian Cabinet. The matter was reopened by Canadian note No. 16 of February 13, 1947, addressed to Ambassador Ray Atherton. Technical aspects of the operation were agreed upon at a conference held in Ottawa on February 25 and 26, and summarized in Canadian note No. 32 of March 18, 1947. United States confirmation of the agreement, which pertained to 1947 and 1948 operations only, was delayed by planning for 1949 developments in the weather station program. These plans were referred to in Canadian note No. 181 of December 22, 1947. A further attempt to formalize the 1947–1948 agreement was made in Canadian note No. 661 of October 4, 1948, to the Secretary of State from the Canadian Chargé d'Affaires at Washington. It was not followed up by the Department because of the lateness in the time period of the first agreement and the possibility of negotiating an altered arrangement for 1949.

Documentation on this subject, including the above-mentioned notes and a related memorandum dated June 11, 1946, from Acting Secretary of State Acheson to William L. Clayton, Chairman of the interdepartmental Air Coordinating Committee, concerning existing and potential territorial claims in the Arctic region, and United States policy regarding the so-called "sector" claims, is in Department of State file No. 842.9243.

INDIA AND PAKISTAN

INTEREST OF THE UNITED STATES IN THE EMERGENCE OF THE DOMINIONS OF INDIA AND PAKISTAN; ELEVATION OF THE STATUS OF DIPLOMATIC MISSIONS [1]

845.00/1–447 : Telegram

The Chargé in India (Merrell) to the Secretary of State

SECRET　　　　　　　　　　　NEW DELHI, January 4, 1947—11 a.m.

4. Deptel 953, December 31.[2] Since Jinnah[3] expected remain Karachi till January 12, following sent Karachi today.

Embassy on December 26 conveyed to Liaquat Ali Khan[4] Dept's view that it was doubtful Congress[5] attitude re provincial groupings could be modified unless Muslim League made declaration or gave other tangible evidence of willingness cooperate within framework Indian Federal Union established accordance Cabinet mission plan.[6] We stressed fact that we are fully aware as indicated in Acheson's statement December 3 [7] of need for providing in Federal Union ample scope for Muslim political and economic aspirations but that atmosphere for creating necessary safeguards can never be achieved unless concept of union itself is generally accepted by principal parties. Liaquat was also informed that Embassy had conveyed to Nehru,[8] Patel[9] and other Congress leaders Dept's view that it is in interest of all United Nations that early and amicable settlement Indian con-

---

[1] For previous documentation on the political situation in India and elevation of the status of the Missions in the United States and India, see *Foreign Relations*, 1946, vol. v, pp. 77 ff.

[2] Not printed. See *Foreign Relations*, 1946, vol. v, p. 112, footnote 68.

[3] Mohammed Ali Jinnah, President of the Muslim League.

[4] General Secretary of the Muslim League.

[5] Indian National Congress.

[6] For text of plan, see British Cmd. 6821, *Statements by the Cabinet Mission and H.E. the Viceroy, 16 May 1946;* or V.P. Menon, *The Transfer of Power in India* (Princeton University Press, 1957), pp. 466–475.

[7] Statement by Acting Secretary of State Dean Acheson on "United States Interest in India," Department of State *Bulletin*, December 15, 1946, p. 1113, or *Foreign Relations*, 1946, vol. v, p. 99, telegram 7996 to London.

[8] Pandit Jawaharlal Nehru, Vice-President of Governor-General's Executive Council and Leader of the National Interim Government.

[9] Sardar Vallabhbhai Patel, Home and Information Minister of the Interim Government.

stitutional problem be reached and that it would be wise for Congress accept interpretation set forth in HMG's December 6 statement.[10]

Liaquat said he did not see how League could be expected give assurance re cooperation under Cabinet mission plan when Congress had not accepted plan as interpreted by HMG but that if Congress accepted December 6 statement, Jinnah would call meeting of League Council. When asked if he would convey Dept's views to Jinnah, Liaquat said he thought Jinnah would be unreceptive at this time but that if Congress accepted December 6 statement expression our views to Jinnah then might have its effect.

Unless AICC decision January 5 takes form of outright rejection of December 6 statement, you are requested to express to Jinnah on January 6, US Government's deep concern serious deterioration Indian political situation; to state it is our impression that in view Congress effort to accommodate itself to HMG and League's interpretation of plan, US public will be puzzled if League now declines enter Constituent Assembly; and to say Dept believes any halt in constitutional progress may well cause widespread chaos similar China with worldwide repercussions.

FYI when Gallman[11] talked with Jinnah in London December 12 Jinnah said he appreciated sympathetic interest shown by US Government and Acheson statement but much remained to be done to develop an informed world opinion and that this would take time.

MERRELL

[10] Reference is to a statement by the British Government supporting the Muslim League's contention that decisions by simple majority vote should prevail in the inter-provincial groups of the regional areas. The Congress Party had contended that each province should be allowed to vote separately on whether or not to join groups.

[11] Waldemar J. Gallman, Counselor of Embassy at London.

845.00/1–647 : Telegram

The Vice Consul at Karachi (Sparks) to the Secretary of State

SECRET   KARACHI, January 6, 1947—11 p. m.
US URGENT

3. Jinnah stated during interview tonight League in complete agreement Acheson statement December 3rd and three points presented him taken from penultimate paragraph Delhi telegram.[1] After review Congress-League relations June 6[2] to present said "if Congress made genuine effort accommodate itself His Majesty's Government's and

[1] Telegram 4, *supra*.
[2] June 6, 1946, when the Council of the All-India Muslim League passed a resolution accepting the Cabinet Mission's plan, subject to certain reservations.

Muslim League's interpretation Cabinet plan, League would enter Constituent Assembly at once but resolution passed today [3] can not be defined as such effort" (reference Delhi telegram January 4 re political situation). Called resolution "same Congress tactics; propaganda to fool world into believing Congress had accepted Cabinet December 6 statement and that only League was at fault for not entering Assembly when resolution is statement of contradictions that in fact says nothing".

Jinnah refused commit League's next action said "must consider in light new developments which are in fact not new". He welcomed expression Department's viewpoint with which he was "in complete agreement" said "tell your government we work toward same ends but for God's sake not to be chloroformed by meaningless Congress gestures made for purely propaganda effect. Congress had only to say we accept nothing more; that would have shown true faithful intent and League would have responded in same coin". Stressed confidential nature his statements.

My belief is Jinnah feels next move up to League even though under its interpretation Congress resolution is meaningless.

Sent Department No. 3; repeated Delhi No. 1.

SPARKS

---

[3] For text of resolution, presented by Nehru at the All-India Congress Committee meeting January 5 and passed by a majority of 91 to 55 on January 6 after two days of debate, see Menon, *The Transfer of Power in India*, pp. 332–333.

845.00/1–2147 : Telegram

The Chargé in India (Merrell) to the Secretary of State

CONFIDENTIAL   NEW DELHI, January 21, 1947—11 a. m.

47. Following is official text of statement issued yesterday by Nehru with reference to Reuter report dated January 18 from New York stating John Foster Dulles addressing National Publishers Association dinner January 17 had declared : "India Soviet Communism exercises a strong influence through interim govt."

"I have read with surprise and regret a report of a speech made by Mr. John Foster Dulles in New York in which he criticizes policy of interim govt. I can hardly believe that report is a correct one. Mr. Dulles was one of representatives of US Govt in UN General Assembly and his words therefore carry weight. His reported description of interim govt and its policy shows lack of knowledge of facts and want of appreciation of policy we are pursuing. I do not wish to say more at this stage except to repeat that our policy is to cultivate friendly and cooperative relations with all countries, notably USA, and not to align ourselves with any particular power grouping. Our policy is going to be an independent one based on furtherance of peace and freedom everywhere on lines laid down by UN Charter.

Mrs. Pandit [2] in press interview yesterday said she found it difficult to believe Dulles had made such a statement; suggested he might have based conclusion on cooperation of India and USSR at UN in efforts "to liberalize trusteeship agreements." "India", said Mrs. Pandit, "far from blindly following alien influences . . . will evolve her policy in accordance with her own interests and her own conception of right and wrong."

Embassy has observed no indication of Soviet influence on interim govt. Most individuals in govt which is primarily representative of propertied and conservative classes seem rather to fear Communist infiltration. As Dept is aware Congress has been making strenuous efforts during past year to counteract Communist activities in organizing labor and peasants and recent wide spread raids on Communist offices indicate anything but friendly attitude on part of Congress and Muslim League provincial authorities.

Please repeat London.

MERRELL

---

[2] Mrs. Vijayalakshmi Pandit, sister of Pandit Jawaharlal Nehru, was appointed in June 1947 to be the first Indian Ambassador to the Soviet Union.

845.00/1–2147

The Secretary of State to the Embassy in India

SECRET   WASHINGTON, January 22, 1947—6 p. m.
U.S. URGENT

43. Urtel 47 January 21. Re Dulles' speech suggest you discuss matter with Nehru along following lines first appropriate occasion.

Dulles' speech (full text being transmitted open air mail) completely unofficial and not seen before delivery by SecState or any Dept officials concerned with Indian affairs. Dulles spoke as a private citizen giving lengthy analysis Soviet ideological and territorial challenge.

Re the one sentence in speech re India ("In India, Soviet Communism exercises a strong influence through interim Hindu govt"), you may inform Nehru that we have followed with deep interest his various expressions of Indian foreign policy since inception interim govt and have been favorably impressed by India's avowed intention to pursue independent but cooperative policy based on UN Charter.

We are aware both Congress and Muslim League leaders in GOI recognize danger infiltration Indian political scene of outside totalitarian influences which would make even more difficult of solution complex constitutional problems now facing India.

We are confident US–India relations will continue on friendly and mutually advantageous basis.

Dulles may have obtained an impression Communist influence on GOI from attitude some members GOI delegation recent UN General Assembly session. It is undoubtedly true that activities of Indian reps abroad are being more closely observed than ever before and that many observers are inclined to believe that these activities reflect GOI policies.

For your confidential info we hope informally to let Dulles have more complete picture Indian situation.

MARSHALL

845.00/2–147 : Telegram

The Vice Consul at Karachi (Sparks) to the Secretary of State

CONFIDENTIAL   KARACHI, February 1, 1947—2 p. m.
PRIORITY

5. Reference Dept's 5, January 30, 7 p. m.[1] Despite heavy pressure from all interested outside parties including Viceroy, Muslim League working committee today published 3,000 word resolution[2] accepting [attacking?] HMG statement December 6 as dishonest trick; described Consultative [Constituent] Assembly as truncated rump and called its proceedings *ultra vires* and illegal. Resolution demands Consultative [Constituent] Assembly dissolution forthwith and called upon HMG to declare constitutional plan has failed. It stated Congress' rejection HMG's final appeal December 6 to accept interpretation fundamental procedure has destroyed May 16 and every possibility of compromise, on basis Cabinet mission's constitutional plan. Resolution concluded that as Congress as a major contracting party had not accepted clarification of May 16 statement, no useful purpose would be served by summoning meeting Council of All India Muslim League to reconsider decision of July 29[3] whereby it had withdrawn acceptance Cabinet Mission's plan May 16.

Repeated New Delhi 8.

SPARKS

---

[1] In telegram 5 to Karachi, the Department expressed interest in the outcome of the current Muslim League working committee meeting and requested cabled reports on any significant developments (845.00/1–3047).

[2] For discussion and partial text of the League's resolution, see Menon, *The Transfer of Power in India*, pp. 333–334.

[3] Reference is to the League's resolution of July 29, 1946, which rejected the Cabinet Mission Plan.

845.00/2–1147 : Telegram

The Secretary of State to the Embassy in the United Kingdom

CONFIDENTIAL WASHINGTON, February 11, 1947—7 p. m.

698. We have been following with concern recent developments in India [1] and would appreciate info re Brit thinking as to next steps. If you have opportunity we hope you will endeavor to ascertain whether or not Brit are disposed to instruct Viceroy dismiss Muslim League members from Council, whether they are planning to bring pressure on Princes to reach definitive agreement with Congress and whether they have been giving consideration to possibility of meeting problem Muslim League absence from Constituent Assembly by modifying Cabinet Mission plan to include provision for provincial ratification (either by popular plebiscite or legislative action) of constitutions drafted by Assembly.

Sent London 698 rptd New Delhi 77.

MARSHALL

[1] On February 5, the Congress and minority members of the Interim Government, reacting to the League's resolution of January 31 (see telegram 5, *supra*), had presented the Viceroy with a demand for the resignation of the Muslim League representatives.

845.00/2–1447 : Telegram

The Chargé in India (Merrell) to the Secretary of State

SECRET NEW DELHI, February 14, 1947—4 p. m.

113.1. Factors which might suggest possibility of a split in League in event of forced withdrawal of League members from interim government and continuation opposition (reference Department's telegram 78 Feb 11 [1]) are (a) desire of Muslim business interests—particularly in Sind and Bengal—for settlement of political deadlock one way or another; (b) current feeling among some League supporters that Karachi resolution [2] went too far and amounted to League's burning bridges; (c) the super-desire of Sind and Bengal League politicians to avoid situation which might increase difficulties of League in Ministries.

On other hand (a) Jinnah's influence with Muslim masses is such that if he declared League participation in Cabinet Mission plan impossible, Embassy questions whether League politicians would dare court his wrath by attempting formation of new party; (b) Muslims who resigned from League to serve in Central Government would un-

[1] Not printed.
[2] January 31 resolution of the Muslim League Working Committee.

doubtedly be branded by most Muslims as "traitors to Islam" and "Congress stooges"; (c) There is reason to believe, particularly in light of recent successes in Sind elections and remarkable discipline in provincial Muslim League civil disobedience campaign in Punjab, that League organization has never been stronger. Embassy attaches no importance to nationalist Muslims' efforts to organize non-League Muslims in united front; and feels Jinnah's apparent success in stigmatizing non-League Muslims would prevent such an organization from gathering effective numbers of followers.

No evidence that recent Muslim student demonstration against Bengal Premier signifies any abnormal discord in Bengal League.

2. Embassy believes strength and trouble making potentialities of League are such that His Majesty's Government will endeavor avoid if possible instructing Viceroy to dismiss League members. Scott [3] told Embassy officer yesterday that while Viceroy had as yet received no clear indication of what His Majesty's Government's decision would be it seemed unlikely League members would be dismissed immediately. Scott thinks wisest approach would be to endeavor persuade Congress to alter January 6 AICC resolution sufficiently to enable Viceroy to tell League Congress had accepted December 6 statement unconditionally and League would have to join CA or withdraw from interim govt.

3. Embassy believes course favored by Scott would be worth trying but in view of Nehru's difficulty in obtaining support of AICC even for conditional acceptance December 6 statement questions whether suggested "concession" could be obtained. Further efforts to bring League into CA would then have to be based on argument that AICC resolution in effect constituted acceptance December 6 statement and that League in interest of welfare of India as whole should enter CA and thresh out differences of interpretation there. If Jinnah still refused in hope that he might obtain Pakistan by default Viceroy and His Majesty's Government would probably feel they had no choice but to allow Congress and Princes to proceed with constitution-making in which case League opposition whether "violent" or non-violent would almost certainly result in disorders.

4. Embassy believes that if British Congress and Princes agree on constitutional plan Congress dissidents might well find it more difficult to promote civil strife since such agreement might represent a concrete step toward Indian independence and rob of some of its weight dissidents' argument that there must be a "final struggle" against Britain.

Until such time as tangible constitutional progress is made, however, Narain's [4] anti-British propaganda will undoubtedly continue to be effective among substantial numbers of Indians.

---

[3] Ian Scott, Assistant Private Secretary to the Viceroy.
[4] Jayprakash Narain, also known as Narayan.

5. Scott informed Embassy officer yesterday that on or about February 18 a critical situation will probably develop as a result of Viceroy's intention to use his special powers to prevent release of 15 INA officers convicted last year of "gross brutality". Scott says Viceroy has already overruled decision of Council in which both League and Congress members favored release of prisoners. Central Assembly is expected to vote for their release on February 18 but Viceroy with agreement of C-in-C and His Majesty's Government intends to use his veto power. This will give both League and Congress politicians new stick with which to beat British.

Please repeat London.

845.00/2–2047

Memorandum of Conversation, by the Secretary of State

TOP SECRET [WASHINGTON,] February 20, 1947.

Participants: The Secretary
The British Ambassador [1]
Mr. John Hickerson [2]

The British Ambassador came in to see me at 9:45 this morning by an appointment made at his request. He summarized briefly and then handed me the following papers:

1. Text of a statement to be made by Prime Minister Attlee on India in the House of Commons at 10:30 Eastern Standard Time this morning, announcing the British intention to transfer complete power to the Indians not later than June 1948.[3]

2. A Top Secret memorandum [4] giving a background analysis of the present Indian situation and stating that the only alternative to the British Government's transferring complete authority to the Indians would be for the British Government to use the necessary force to govern India indefinitely, a course which the British Government must reject.

3. A copy of an announcement to be made by Prime Minister Attlee in the House of Commons, following his statement on India, to the effect that Lord Wavell is being recalled and is being replaced by Lord Mountbatten.[5]

I thanked the British Ambassador for bringing me these papers and told him that they would receive my study. I stated that the U.S. Government is thoroughly convinced of the sincerity of the British

---

[1] Lord Inverchapel.
[2] Deputy Director, Office of European Affairs.
[3] For text, see *Parliamentary Debates*, House of Commons, 5th series, vol. 433, cols. 1395–1399, or S. L. Poplai, *Select Documents on Asian Affairs: India 1947–50*, (Oxford University Press, Bombay, 1959), vol. 1, pp. 10–13.
[4] *Infra.*
[5] For text, see Menon, *The Transfer of Power in India*, pp. 508–509.

Government in its efforts to bring about a satisfactory solution of the Indian problem. I stated that, as the Ambassador knows, the Department of State has during the past several months issued several statements in this general sense and in support of the British constitutional plan for India. I added that after a study of the above mentioned documents I would consider whether I could make any additional statement which might be helpful.[6] I went on to say that I would be glad to have the Ambassador let me know later on whether he feels that a further statement from the U.S. Government would be helpful. The Ambassador expressed his appreciation.

The Ambassador commented that I probably knew Lord Mountbatten. I replied that I did know him well and had a very high regard for him. I discussed briefly some of my war-time associations with Lord Mountbatten.

---

[6] On February 25, the Department released to the press a statement entitled "United States Interest in Self-Government for India." For text, see Department of State *Bulletin*, March 9, 1947, p. 450.

845.00/2–2047

The British Embassy to the Department of State [1]

TOP SECRET

1. The objective of United Kingdom policy in India has for many years past been, through a process of gradually developing the transfer of authority, ultimately to hand over power to a Federal system of Government commanding at least the assent of all the important elements in the Indian population and in which the Indian States would be co-operating parties. The unity of India which is the greatest single achievement of our rule would thus be preserved.

2. The policy of the present British Government has been in line with this tradition. Its main principles were stated in the Prime Minister's speech in Parliament on the 15th March [2] and developed in detail in the proposals of the Cabinet Mission. If operated wholeheartedly in a spirit of co-operation these proposals should make it possible for Indians to frame a Constitution which would both preserve the unity of India and meet the real and legitimate fears of the Muslim community and of other minorities. The intention was that formal and final transfer of authority would not take place until a Constitution framed in accordance with the Mission's proposals, or otherwise

---

[1] This memorandum, attachment No. 2 to the memorandum of conversation, *supra*, was handed to the Secretary of State by the British Ambassador, Lord Inverchapel, on February 20.
[2] March 15, 1946. For substance of Mr. Attlee's words, as he intervened in a House of Commons debate on the Cabinet Mission's imminent visit to India, see Menon, *The Transfer of Power in India*, pp. 234–235.

by agreement between the major communities, could be brought into operation. In this way the broad objective referred to in paragraph (1) above would have been realized, and United Kingdom responsibility in India have been terminated by an orderly and peaceful transition. In the meantime it was hoped that an interim government representative of all parties would operate harmoniously under the existing Constitution. Although the broad responsibility of the United Kingdom Government and Parliament for Indian affairs would continue, this Government would in practice have a wide measure of autonomy. Obviously great difficulties were to be expected in this interim period, which it was hoped would be not more than two years, unless there were mutual forbearance between ourselves and Congress Party, and a real spirit of compromise and co-operation between the Congress Party and the Muslim League.

3. Unfortunately these conditions have not been realized. The following is a broad assessment of events since the mission. After the mission left India the Congress Party interpreted the provisions of the mission's proposals regarding the procedure in sections in a way contrary to the mission's intention, as clearly explained to them. An essential element of the mission's proposals was that sections of the Constituent Assembly should decide by majority vote the constitutions of the provinces and whether groups of provinces should be formed subject to the right of provinces to opt out of a group by decision of the legislature under the new Constitution. The Congress Party argued that decisions on these questions should require a majority of representatives of each province within the section. This would almost certainly result in no group constitution being framed by sections B and C. Thus the Congress Party interpretation removed the basis of the compromise which is the whole basis of the proposals. The League reacted by withdrawing their acceptance of the mission's proposals, by reverting to the advocacy of the full Pakistan claim in provocative form, and by threatening direct action. Six months have passed without any substantial progress in drawing up the constitution and the Constituent Assembly is meeting without Muslim League representatives. Although the recent Congress Party resolution modified their position, there are still certain ambiguities in the acceptance by the Congress Party of our statement of December 6th. Certain rules of procedure have been framed by the Constituent Assembly which can hardly be reconciled with the principle of our statement that provincial constitutions and the decision whether there shall be a group shall be taken by sections of the Constituent Assembly by a majority vote. This has led the Muslim League again to refuse co-operation in the Constituent Assembly by their resolution of January 31st. These events have rendered the relations of the two parties in the Cabinet increasingly difficult and the Congress Party have now demanded that the

Muslim League members should resign from the government. We are being pressed to wind up the Secretary of State's services and to withdraw British troops from India. Although, in individual cases the Congress Party are putting strong pressure on Indian States whom we are bound by our existing relationship to protect from external interference from British India, recent conversations between the States' representatives and representatives of the Constituent Assembly were amicable and there seems a reasonable prospect that the States will enter the Constituent Assembly.

4. The communal situation deteriorated seriously between August and November and over 10,000 persons have been killed and many more injured. Since the London Conference [3] the situation has improved but the tension is still high. Any open and irrevocable breach between the parties might lead to a widespread recrudescence amounting almost to unorganised and spontaneous civil war. In this event the Indian army might disintegrate and take sides.

5. We have made every effort to bring the Indian parties together by negotiations and there is not much more that we can do without some move from them. The alternatives therefore are to place the responsibility for finding a solution, or for the consequences of failure to do so, finally and solely upon Indian leaders; or to reassert British authority and govern India for a substantial period. The latter course could only be feasible if we resorted to widespread and extreme measures of repression and publicly declared an intention to retain our authority in India for a substantial period of years. We do not consider that this course would be likely to lead to any solution of the Indian problem. In the long run it would lead rather to a spread of revolutionary extremism, probably in a communist form.

6. We have therefore come to the conclusion set out in the statement announcing our intention to hand over authority in India not later than June 1948. We are hopeful that the prospects of a settlement between the Congress Party and the Muslim League will be increased if it is clearly stated that we shall withdraw at a definite date and definite steps are taken to implement this decision. At present both sides hope to produce a situation in which we shall be forced to assist them in securing their own political objective and this fact impedes a settlement between them.

7. We, therefore, think that the statement provides the best prospect of being able to hand over the functions of the existing central government to a single government having the support of both major parties. But if, when the date for withdrawal is reached, this is not possible we shall have to hand over to whatever constituted authorities seem most representative of the different parts of the country when the

---

[3] December 3–6, 1946; attended by Nehru, Jinnah, Sardar Baldev Singh and Liaquat Ali Khan. Singh and Khan held the portfolios of Defense and Finance, respectively, in the Indian Interim Government.

time comes. Paragraph 10 of the statement is designed to avoid, on the one hand, a commitment to create Pakistan (which would encourage the League to be obstructive), and on the other, any indication that we should, whatever happens, hand over to one authority only (which would encourage the Congress Party to be uncompromising).

8. We realize, of course, that we are running the risk that no settlement will be arrived at and that as the date for our withdrawal draws near, the communal situation will deteriorate seriously. But this is just as likely to happen if we make no statement because both sides will hope that we shall assist them against the other. We believe, therefore, that the right course is for us to be definite as to our intentions.

9. It may be felt that a definite partition of India before our departure would, if there is no agreement, be preferable, in the last resort, to withdrawal in the way we propose. Cogent reasons were given in the opening paragraphs of the Cabinet mission's statement of the 16th May against any form of Pakistan because the area claimed by the Muslim League would contain far too great a minority of non-Muslim population while a smaller area having a substantial Muslim majority could not be capable economically of survival as an independent State. Partition would be violently resented by a large part of the Indian population including substantial elements in the areas affected. The equitable demarcation of the areas to be separated would be a matter of extreme difficulty but it is not totally excluded by Paragraph 10 of the statement if it is found to be inevitable at the latest stage.

WASHINGTON, February 19, 1947.

701.4511/2–2647

Memorandum of Conversation, by the Secretary of State

RESTRICTED [WASHINGTON,] February 26, 1947.

Participants: The Secretary of State, General Marshall
The Appointed Ambassador of India, Mr. Asaf Ali [1]
The Minister of the Indian Embassy, Mr. Binay Ranjan Sen
The Chief of Protocol, Mr. Woodward

The Appointed Ambassador of India called upon me today to present a copy of his Letter of Credence, and a copy of his remarks to be made to the President.[2]

---

[1] M. Asaf Ali, former Congress member of the 1946 (September–October) Indian Interim Government.
[2] The text of the Ambassador's remarks and the President's reply was issued to the press by the Department of State as press release 155 of February 28, 1947.

After I had read his remarks, I told the Ambassador that I was pleased it had fallen among my early duties to receive him as the Representative of India; that my knowledge of India was not very great, although I had probably read as much as most people on the subject; that during the war I had known India as the supply center for the China–Burma–India theatre; and that my relations with India were now of course entirely different from what they had been during the war.

The Ambassador replied to the effect that this was a momentous time in India's history and that he was pleased with his opportunity to represent his country in the United States on this historic occasion in Indian development. He referred to India's role in the war as the arsenal of the CBI theatre, and deplored that his country had been so ill prepared to serve the allied cause. He stated that he wished to repeat what he had told Mr. Bevin,[3] that had India been adequately prepared, the war would have been shortened by at least two years. He continued that he hoped to see the political and economic development of his country flourish, and that if India became strong it would be a bastion for the world against the great northern neighbor which now cast its shadow over two continents, Asia and Europe. To the left and right flanks of India the countries were weak but India might serve as a strong center between weaker neighbors.

I told the Ambassador that I was greatly interested in what he had said and inquired concerning his knowledge of the United States. Upon his reply that this was his first visit, I said that I hoped he would not be confused by our politics, that sometimes in the discussion of domestic issues, like the budget, international relations seemed to become involved, but of one thing he could be sure, the integrity of American foreign policy. I mentioned my experience in China where the situation was very confused and told the Ambassador that despite the confusion, there was never any doubt concerning our aim which was for only two things, first, unity in China and second, a reasonably democratic system of government, and that despite propaganda to the contrary and the allegation of ulterior motives to the United States in its dealings with China, it became clearer and clearer to all concerned that it was only unity and an orderly, democratic form of government that we wanted in that country.

In his final remarks to me, the Ambassador made no reference to unity, on which his predecessor, Bajpai,[4] had laid so much store, or an orderly, democratic system, but referred to my mention of propaganda and his own unhappy experiences in that field as Indian Minister of Transportation. Asaf Ali concluded his remarks with the statement

---

[3] Ernest Bevin, British Secretary of State for Foreign Affairs.
[4] Sir Girja Shankar Bajpai.

that politically India had nothing to fear, that it was greatly indebted to the British and to the stand the British had taken on Indian Independence, that India politically would get along all right but that economically the potential of four hundred million people had yet to be developed. A number of "Tennessee Valley Authorities" were projected for India and it was especially with respect to these that the Ambassador would call upon me for assistance.

G. C. M[ARSHALL]

845.00/3–847

The Consul General in India (Macdonald) to the Secretary of State

RESTRICTED · BOMBAY, March 8, 1947.

No. 24

SIR: I have the honor to report that, accompanied by Vice Consul J. Jefferson Jones, III, I called on Mr. M. A. Jinnah, President of the Muslim League, on March 5, 1947. Mr. Jinnah, who received us at his residence, was most affable and showed considerable enthusiasm at times during our forty-five minute conversation. Although Mr. Jinnah said nothing which he has not said numerous times before, the more pertinent parts of his conversation are reported herewith as of possible interest.

Referring to the British Government's statement regarding the transfer of power to responsible Indian hands not later than June, 1948, Mr. Jinnah said he is anxious to hear what the American reaction is to the proposal. He said that he could understand the American public's surprise as well as impatience with India for not finding a solution to its political problems following Britain's offer of independence. Mr. Jinnah then made the statement that news regarding Indian problems in the American press is influenced by false propaganda. He did not accuse the British of influencing the American press, but was very out-spoken in placing all the blame for the so-called false propaganda on the Congress party which, according to him, has a highly efficient propaganda organization that is on the alert for all foreign correspondents and journalists. I remarked that prior to my departure from the United States it was not my impression that news relating to India was affected by propaganda and also mentioned the fact that a number of American correspondents are assigned to India at present and it is their job to report facts free from all propaganda or prejudice. Mr. Jinnah admitted that some journalists who spend sufficient time in India obtain a correct view of the situation and mentioned several whom he had met and considers to be top rate reporters. He reiterated, however, his concern regarding the danger of new correspondents falling into the hands of the Congress party propaganda machine.

On his return from London in January, Mr. Jinnah said that at a reception given him in Cairo he was told by a group of prominent Egyptians that they had a warm heart for him as a brother Muslim, but found his policy annoying as they felt he was in league with the British instead of working for Indian independence. To this accusation he replied that he would be only too happy to prove his innocence if given an opportunity. He told the accusing group that if Congress really wanted to test his sincerity regarding his desire for Indian independence, they should agree to Pakistan. In the event, he said, that the Congress did come to such an agreement, he would immediately accept the responsibility placed upon him for taking the necessary steps to establish a constitutional government and he added "I would be the first to go down to the Gateway of India to wave farewell to the British".

The Muslims, according to Mr. Jinnah, cannot accept the idea of a united India because in so doing they would merely be substituting a Hindu Raj for the British Raj. He said that it is foolish to talk about a compromise because one cannot have compromise unless there is a basis for it. He added that the difference in culture, religion, and way of life between the Muslims and Hindus precludes any possibility of a compromise. He asked why a hundred million Muslims should become a minority in a Hindu dominated Government. Vice Consul Jones made reference to safeguards such as those contained in the Cabinet Mission's proposals, to which Mr. Jinnah replied that safeguards for the minority in a united India were worthless because in the event of an appeal by the minority the accused would sit as the judges of the accusers. The only recourse left to the Muslims in such eventuality would be an appeal to the United Nations.

Mr. Jinnah talked at some length on what he regards as the utter folly of compromise. He said "we have made sacrifices, we are willing to make more sacrifices, and even die for Pakistan, so why should people talk of compromise when there is no basis for compromise".

Despite several leading questions which I asked him during the course of our conversation, Mr. Jinnah did not touch upon the present political situation or shed any light upon the probable reaction of the League to the United Kingdom Government's statement of February 20. His emphatic reiteration that there could be no compromise regarding the basic principles of Pakistan does not lead to optimism that the attitude of the League will be any more conciliatory in the future than that which it exhibited at the time of the last meeting of the Working Committee of the League on January 28, 1947.

Respectfully yours,   JOHN J. MACDONALD

845.00/3–2747 : Airgram

The Acting Secretary of State to the Embassy in the United Kingdom

CONFIDENTIAL [WASHINGTON,] April 4, 1947.

A–391. We are disturbed by the implications of New Delhi's telegram No. 208 [*203*] March 27,[1] repeated to London, regarding purported plans of Hyderabad State to establish "direct relations with the British Crown" and presumably to maintain a status completely separate from that of the rest of India.

As is well known to the Embassy, we have during the past year given full support to the efforts of the British Government to effect a peaceful transfer of power to Indian hands on the basis of a federally unified India. This support has taken the form of several statements to the press by high American officials and of many informal conversations between our diplomatic representatives and important Indian leaders.

In following this course we have been fully aware of the serious obstacles in the path of Indian unity but for the excellent reasons against the division of India set forth in the British Cabinet Mission plan have inclined to the view that our political and economic interest in that part of the world would best be served by the continued integrity of India.

We have accordingly assumed that the British Government would not lend encouragement to plans such as those reported in New Delhi's telegram No. 208 [*203*]. We feel that a separatist move by Hyderabad may be a prelude to a fragmentation process which might have far reaching effects on any plan for ultimate Indian unity.

In the light of the foregoing please make informal inquiries of appropriate British officials to ascertain whether the British policy on the establishment of an Indian federal union, including the princely states, remains substantially as outlined in the Cabinet Mission Plan of May 16, 1946.[2] If there has been a change in British policy, we may have to reconsider our own position with regard to India. It is possible that the British may allude in this connection to our recent moves to establish diplomatic relations with Nepal. As pointed out in the Department's telegram No. 104 of February 25 to New Delhi,[3]

---

[1] Not printed.

[2] Ambassador Douglas in London informed the Department in telegram 2335, April 21, that Sir Paul Patrick, Assistant Under-Secretary of State, India Office, had stated informally but categorically that his Office shared the Department's view that in present circumstances neither Hyderabad nor any other Indian state should be allowed to establish a direct relationship with the British Crown. (845.00/4–2147)

[3] In telegram 104, the Embassy was directed to seek an early opportunity to discuss with Nehru and other high officials reasons why a special diplomatic mission was being sent to Nepal (611.45e31/2–2547).

repeated to London by airgram, these steps do not have any special significance vis-à-vis the political situation in India. The status of Nepal has long been sharply differentiated from that of the Indian princely states, and we do not feel that Nepal's position is in any way analogous to that of Hyderabad.

ACHESON

845.00/4–2247

The Chargé in India (Merrell) to the Secretary of State

SECRET   NEW DELHI, April 22, 1947.
No. 1061

[Extract]

SIR:

.   .   .   .

SIGNIFICANCE

The foregoing paragraphs leave no doubt as to Mr. Jinnah's official League policy. The demand for Pakistan or nothing, and the allegation that there is not the slightest possibility of the League's entering the Constituent Assembly are bargaining points which are a logical outcome of events of the past year. While in the light of Mr. Jinnah's past performance it would be rash to predict that there is now no possibility of compromise on the question of the League's associating itself with a Union Center, the League's declared fears of Congress domination are, unfortunately, not without a rational basis.

It is difficult to condone provocative, if not frenzied, outbursts in which League leaders, including Mr. Jinnah, have indulged during the past twelve months, and it may be argued that Congress has made certain concessions to the League. Perhaps the most important of these concessions was acceptance of the principle of "equal representation" of Muslims and caste Hindus in the Interim Government, though Congress knew that in practice it would control the majority of votes through its Sikh, Christian, Parsi, and Scheduled Castes appointees. So far as acceptance of the Cabinet Mission plan is concerned, however, the League is on logical ground when it maintains that Congress has never agreed unconditionally to the plan as interpreted by the British Government.

It will be recalled that in June 1946 the Muslim League Working Committee went on record as accepting the May 16 statement without reservations, while the Congress Working Committee accepted only the long-term portion of the statement. It will also be recalled that in July Mr. Nehru and other Congressmen made statements indicating quite clearly that Congress had no intention of adhering strictly to the provisions of the Cabinet Mission plan affecting the Constituent Assembly. As a result the League withdrew its acceptance of the Cabinet Mission plan. There followed the acceptance by the Congress Working Committee with reservations of the short-term provisions of the Plan and the formation late in August of the Interim Government which the League decided to join in October.

As has been indicated in previous reports, I am willing to believe that if the All-India Congress Committee, meeting January 6, 1947 had accepted unconditionally the British Government's statement of December 6 regarding the Cabinet Mission plan, Mr. Jinnah would have agreed to enter the Constituent Assembly. In any case, if Mr. Jinnah had then refused to enter the Constituent Assembly, Congress could have said with a clear conscience that they had done everything in their power to make it possible for the League to participate. Congress, however, fearful of losing its hold on Assam and its position among the Sikhs and the Pathans, and frightened by Jai Prakash Narain's efforts to wreck the Cabinet Mission plan, released a resolution which made it clear they were unwilling to commit themselves to the interpretation of the provincial grouping clause which had been accepted by both the British Government and the League.

Even though the British Government took the stand that Congress had, in effect, accepted the Cabinet Mission plan, the League was in a position to justify its claim that the January 6 resolution did not constitute unconditional acceptance, and in its meeting at the end of January the League Working Committee called for the dissolution of the Constituent Assembly. Annoying as Mr. Jinnah and his followers have been in many of their statements and declarations, I feel the Congress leaders have not only failed to show the magnanimity which so many observers have felt would have led to a peaceful settlement, but have demonstrated remarkable ineptitude as politicians. I question seriously whether their fear of a Muslim majority of two (36 Muslims, 34 non-Muslims) in the proposed Bengal-Assam Constituent Assembly, can be justified in the light of the larger issues involved. Had they been willing to agree to the British Government's interpretation of the grouping clause the League's civil disobedience campaigns in the Punjab, the Northwest Frontier Province, and Assam might never have materialized. As it is, the provincial League organizations concerned have demonstrated sufficient strength to encourage Mr. Jinnah in his demand for Pakistan, and the likelihood of his obtaining it in one form or another seems to be growing daily.

Most Congressmen with whom officers of the Embassy have talked during the past three months appear to have resigned themselves to the prospect of the League's staying out of the Constituent Assembly, and recently more and more Congress supporters have indicated that they feel some sort of Pakistan is inevitable. In their effort to make Pakistan as unattractive as possible—by demanding partition of the Punjab and Bengal—Congress leaders have in effect abandoned the tenets which they have supported for so many years in their campaign for a united India. They have also agreed by implication with Mr. Jinnah's allegation that Hindus and Muslims cannot live together, a charge which in the past Congress has—quite rightly I believe—denied.

I cannot help feeling, therefore, that the present unhappy situation is as much a result of Congress leaders' political ineptitude and lack of vision as of Mr. Jinnah's intransigence. Had Congress leaders put aside their fears regarding the effect of the Cabinet Mission plan on their party's position in Assam, the Punjab and the Northwest Frontier Province, Mr. Jinnah would not have been provided with a logical basis for the Muslim League's current stand, and India might today be laying the ground-work for a united country instead of facing the prospect of Balkanization.

Respectfully yours,   GEORGE R. MERRELL

845.00/5–247 : Telegram

The Chargé in India (Merrell) to the Secretary of State

SECRET   NEW DELHI, May 2, 1947—10 a. m.

299. In hour and half conversation with Hare and Weil [1] yesterday, Jinnah said Congress demand for partition Bengal and Punjab would not "frighten" him into joining union center; that even if "driven into Sind desert" he would refuse to join union. He said establishment Pakistan essential to prevent "Hindu imperialism" spreading into Middle East; Muslim countries would stand together against possible Russian aggression and would look to US for assistance. Reminded of *Dawn's* [2] frequent jibes re US economic imperialism and dollar diplomacy, he said *Dawn* editors simply reflected attitude of Indian Muslims in general towards US and added jokingly "they had to make a living". He said while he realized US Govt probably open-minded re Pakistan, most Indian Muslims felt Americans were against them (*a*) because most Americans seemed opposed to Pakistan and (*b*) US Govt and people backed Jews against Arabs in Palestine.

---

[1] Raymond A. Hare of the Division of Middle Eastern and Indian Affairs, and Thomas E. Weil, Second Secretary of Embassy at New Delhi.
[2] Daily newspaper published in New Delhi; official organ of the Muslim League.

Jinnah said he thought if Calcutta area were included in Pakistan, Hindus would adjust selves to situation but if they didn't they would have to be brought under control and he thought this would "not take very long". Apropos Punjab, he said Sikhs would be fairly treated and would have as many representatives in Pakistan Parliament as Sind or NWFP. Said he thought announcement HMG's decision on Pakistan would clear atmosphere and reduce communal tension.

Jinnah's manner was calm and gracious and he showed none of nervousness or effects of illness noted by Jones of *New York Times* on April 19 (mitel 280, April 21 [3]).

Difficult to believe eventual announcement HMG's decision on Pakistan with or without partition of Bengal or Punjab will clear communal atmosphere. Force will undoubtedly have to be employed to control rebellious elements in Bengal and Punjab no matter who receives power from HMG in those areas.

Please repeat London.

MERRELL

[3] Not printed.

845.00/6–247 : Telegram

The Ambassador in the United Kingdom (Douglas) to the Secretary of State

TOP SECRET
US URGENT

LONDON, June 2, 1947—7 p. m.

3001.1. When I called on Prime Minister Attlee this afternoon at his request he said he desired to extend to US the courtesy of advance information regarding the announcement [1] which, with brief introduction by Prime Minister, the Viceroy will broadcast to the Indian people and to UK tomorrow, and which he himself will lay before Parliament tomorrow afternoon (Embassy's 2979, May 29, paragraph 3).[2]

2. In sober mood, at times tinged with sorrow, because in his own words he has been working on the Indian problem "for 21 years", Attlee explained that Viceroy is to make one last attempt to secure

[1] For text of the Prime Minister's statement, see *Parliamentary Debates*, House of Commons, 5th series, vol. 438, pp. 35–40, or Menon, *The Transfer of Power in India*, pp. 510–515. For text of the Viceroy's broadcast, see Lord Louis Mountbatten, *Time Only to Look Forward* (London, 1949), pp. 10–13, or Poplai, *Select Documents on Asian Affairs: India 1947–50*, vol. I, pp. 18–21.
[2] In telegram 2979 from Ambassador Douglas at London, May 29, it was explained that only the American representative, among the several whose countries had missions in India, would receive the courtesy of advance briefing on the proposed statement. This, he was told, was because only the United States had closely followed the situation and had expressed its interest by helpful statements. (845.00/5–2947)

acceptance of Cabinet mission's plan. Failing such acceptance, which Attlee believed most unlikely, Viceroy would lay before Indian leaders a procedure for the partition of India into a Hindustan dominion and a Pakistan dominion. Power might be transferred to Hindustan sometime in August. Pakistan being without administrative machinery, power transfer to it might be delayed until this is available. As regards Punjab and Bengal, plan envisages a decision by their own elected representatives as to which of the two major dominions these provinces will adhere and failing agreement, the partition of these provinces between the two. Attlee himself thought a division of Punjab likely, but said that there was a distinct possibility that Bengal might decide against partition and against joining either Hindustan or Pakistan. In this event Bengal might form a separate dominion (Embassy's 2979, May 29, paragraph 9) an alternative also open to Punjab which he thought it improbable that it would elect to do.

3. In event India is divided, Attlee indicated that such problems as the partition of gold holdings, army, etc. would be carried out by joint commissions of Indians representing the several Indian dominions.

4. Attlee was hopeful that there would be no bloodshed but feared that there would be. In its efforts to restore order Indian Army would be acting under orders of Defense Minister of interim Government of India.

5. Prime Minister thought opposition in Parliament would not object to appropriate legislation and that it would therefore go through promptly. (Embassy's 2979 May 29, paragraph 11).

6. I thanked the Prime Minister warmly for his courtesy in providing the US with this advance information, courtesy which so far as I know has not been extended to any other power.

Sent Department 3001, repeated New Delhi 46.

DOUGLAS

845.00/6–2047 : Telegram

The Secretary of State to the Embassy in India

CONFIDENTIAL   WASHINGTON, June 20, 1947—5 p. m.

337. June 19 Reuter despatch reports selection Karachi as capital Pakistan and quotes Minnigerode [1] as stating that "question of establishing an American Embassy here was engaging the attention of US authorities".

---

[1] Holdsworth G. Minnigerode, **Consul at Karachi.**

Dept appreciates fact Minnigerode may have been misquoted [2] but wishes stress need avoid premature indication any US intentions re establishment additional dip missions in India or that question is engaging question [*attention?*] US authorities this time.

Sent New Delhi, repeated Karachi and London. Delhi to inform other consulates.

MARSHALL

[2] Minnigerode informed the Department, in telegram 39, June 23, from Karachi, that the Reuters dispatch allegedly quoting him was "utterly false," and that he had limited his June 17 remarks before a delegation of eight newspapermen to the comment that he had no information on the subject of establishing an American Embassy at Karachi and was unable and unauthorized to make any statement (845.00/6–2347).

845.00/6–2747 : Telegram

The Ambassador in India (Grady) [1] *to the Secretary of State*

SECRET NEW DELHI, June 27, 1947—5 p. m.

459. I called on Nehru at EAD today. Chief points his remarks to me were:

1. The present government will continue in office except for those members who are Muslim Leaguers and will resign to join Pakistan. He emphasized continuity of government in "India" re Pakistan as having seceded with the approval of India because India does not wish to force it to remain.

2. His government has asked British to retain Mountbatten as Governor General for both India and Pakistan. Nehru said there was of course no assurance Pakistan would be agreeable though he seemed not without hope.

3. Nehru said he hoped India would receive expert assistance from USA but was not specific re projects. He stated government was [*has?*] a number of projects which he will later take up with me. He feels and I agree that little can be done for six weeks or two months.

4. Only comment re Mrs. Pandit was that her mission was a "difficult one". [2]

5. Nehru was very cordial throughout conversation.

GRADY

[1] Henry F. Grady assumed charge of the Embassy at the close of business June 25.
[2] Reference here is presumably to the appointment of Mrs. Vijayalakshmi Pandit as Indian Ambassador to the Soviet Union.

845.00/7-247 : Telegram

The Ambassador in India (Grady) to the Secretary of State

SECRET   NEW DELHI, July 2, 1947—2 p. m.

475. In private conversation after lunch yesterday, Viceroy told me that during morning he had been going over draft of new India Act with Congress and League leaders (meeting separately) and that "things had been going very well." He said draft would be based on conception of continuing GOI and establishment Pakistan as a secession govt and indicated clearly he would like remain after August 15 as Governor General—at least of India, preferably of both Dominions. He seemed to feel it was important that he continue head of [*sic*] even after separation of Pakistan area from rest of India. (mytel 459, June 27, re Nehru's request that Mountbatten remain as Governor General both Dominions.)

In this connection Viceroy expressed hope I could talk with Jinnah in near future since he felt it would help matters if Jinnah had some indication US intended establish diplomatic relations with Pakistan. He said it might be possible for US set up a diplomatic mission in Pakistan under a Chargé responsible to AMA [*Amb?*] in Delhi. On other hand he said he had told UK High Commissioner Shone that UK should send High Commissioner to Pakistan (mytel 454, June 27 [1]). I gathered Viceroy would like US to make an early commitment to Jinnah re some kind of diplomatic representation to Karachi as an aid to him in his negotiations with Jinnah. I hope the opportunity will come soon to talk informally with Jinnah. I shall get his views without, of course, making any commitment so far as our Govt is concerned.

Please repeat to London.

GRADY

_____

[1] Not printed.

_____

845.00/7-547 : Telegram

The Ambassador in India (Grady) to the Secretary of State

SECRET   NEW DELHI, July 5, 1947—1 p. m.

488. In conversation with Hare, Jai Prakash Narain stated that Communist Party of India had circulated written instructions to members to refrain from attacking interim government following acceptance June 3 partition plan. This ties in with reports from other Indian sources. It seems safe to assume these orders originated outside India. Possible reasons for adoption this policy: Russian leaders may wish avoid at this time any appearance of unfriendliness toward new

dominion government and may not wish discourage fissiparous tendencies in India which might facilitate future infiltration.

Please repeat to London.

GRADY

845.00/7–747 : Telegram

The Ambassador in India (Grady) to the Secretary of State

CONFIDENTIAL NEW DELHI, July 7, 1947—9 a. m.

491. I shall issue following statement at press conference today:

"I have no instructions from my Government but speaking for myself I can see no reason why, on the establishment of the two Dominions, there should not be prompt recognition of the fact by Washington. As to diplomatic representation, I would point out that all the Dominions are represented in Washington and, similarly, we have representation in all the Dominions."

Any attempt to evade or escape this issue would only arouse ill-feeling and give rise to distorted reports re diplomatic recognition Pakistan.

It would be helpful to our future relations with Pakistan if the Secretary would at a press conference confirm and possibly elaborate my statement. I have avoided use of word Pakistan.

Trevelyan [1] had told Donovan [2] Pakistan plan have Embassy Washington but no indication who will fill post.

Sysons, Deputy High Commissioner, says quarters for five Embassies reserved Karachi: Great Britain, USA, France and "Malaya" and "Arab States."

GRADY

---

[1] Humphrey Trevelyan, predecessor of Major M. O. Ali Baig as First Secretary to the Agent General for India.
[2] Howard Donovan, Counselor of Embassy at New Delhi.

845.00/7–747 : Telegram

The Secretary of State to the Embassy in India

CONFIDENTIAL WASHINGTON, July 7, 1947—7 p. m.

381. We fully approve press statement urtel 491 Jul 7. Our attitude toward emerging Pakistan state was clearly foreshadowed in Dept press release No. 466 Jun 10 which states in part "Future constitutional pattern is matter to be determined by Indian people themselves and whatever that pattern may be US Govt looks forward to con-

tinuance of friendliest relations with Indians of all communities and creeds." [1]

We hope to have friendliest relations with new Pakistan state when it is established and as token that prospect I plan send message of good wishes to Pakistan constituent assembly when it convenes along same lines as recent messages to constituent assemblies New Delhi and Rangoon.[2] Please cable soon as known chairman this Assembly and expected date first meeting.

You will appreciate that until actual establishment Pakistan Govt and official intimation from that Govt that it wishes exchange dip reps with US it would be inappropriate issue formal press statement here on subject recognition. If reference made to your statement in my next press conference I shall of course confirm it and mention Depts press release No. 466 as background. It is obvious from your recent reports that only satisfactory form for US representation Pakistan would be independent Emb at Karachi with separate Amb accredited to Pakistan. Without making any official commitments suggest you discuss details informally with Jinnah and at same time ask him for any suggestions he may care to make on subject dip representation US and Pakistan.

Sent to New Delhi, repeated London.

MARSHALL

---

[1] For complete text, see Department of State *Bulletin*, June 22, 1947, pp. 1249–1250.
[2] Messages not found in Department of State files.

845.00/7–947 : Airgram

The Ambassador in India (Grady) to the Secretary of State

SECRET   NEW DELHI, July 9, 1947.

A–146. *Section I* Reference mytel No. 500, July 7,[1] re Nehru's expression of opinion that Afghanistan's agitation re NWFP probably represented effort to divert attention from domestic difficulties; and his criticism of India Bill [2]—particularly with regard to provisions affecting position of States.

In course of same conversation Nehru made following additional points:

1. India's foreign policy based on desire avoid involvement with any particular bloc, to refrain from meddling, and to avoid war. India desired friendly relations with U.S.

---

[1] Not found in Department of State files.
[2] For text of Indian Independence Bill, introduced in the House of Commons by the Prime Minister on July 4 and passed without amendment by the House of Commons and the House of Lords on July 15 and 16 respectively, see *British and Foreign State Papers*, vol. 147, pt. I, p. 158, or Menon, *The Transfer of Power in India*, pp. 516–532.

While there was some fear in India of U.S. economic penetration, India would want U.S. exports—particularly capital goods. In fact U.S. was only country from which quantities needed could be obtained. Need to conserve dollars to import food necessitated cutting down imports of consumer goods. India would probably apply to International Bank for loan.

2. While USSR had in past held considerable attraction for Indians internal troubles of India now such that interest in USSR had declined. Present interest more in Asiatic Russia than in European since conditions in former furnished Indians better clue to progress. International ideological conflicts currently less important to Indians than domestic problems.

3. Indian economy would probably tend to follow trend of British economy under Socialist government. Certain large industries would probably be nationalized; large proportion of business and industrial activity would remain in private hands.

Section II While in recent weeks Nehru has shown strain imposed by official duties and remarkably large number of receptions, etc., he seemed on this occasion unusually calm and rational, and did not talk, as on some occasions, in somewhat superficial or detached manner.

Re Afghanistan, mentioned in connection with Hare's itinerary, Nehru did not elaborate, but remarks reflected his support of policy indicated mytels No. 465, July 1 and No. 505, July 9 [3]—namely to make it clear to Afghans GOI strongly opposed to separation of NWFP, whether from Hindustan or Pakistan.

References to USSR seemed indicate a wary attitude—no wholehearted admiration. Remarks re U.S. seemed genuinely friendly.

GRADY

---

[3] Neither printed.

845.00/7–1147 : Telegram

The Ambassador in India (Grady) to the Secretary of State

SECRET NEW DELHI, July 11, 1947—1 p. m.

514. Deptel 381, July 7. I saw Jinnah last evening who said Pakistan CA would meet Karachi August 10 to elect chairman and organize government to take over power August 15; CA would continue in session August 10–15.

2. Election CA chairman will be first order business, I agree as soon as Embassy cables name a message of good wishes should be despatched and feel it should be over President's signature.

3. Jinnah said Mountbatten would go to Karachi August 14, turn over power in simple and brief ceremony morning of 15th, and fly back to Delhi to transfer power late afternoon (this is confirmed by Bajpai).

Jinnah pointed out reason Mountbatten must transfer power to Pakistan first is that this must be done while he is still Viceroy, since when he transfers power to what Jinnah insists on calling Hindustan, he will automatically become Governor General that dominion. It is significant Mountbatten will be chairman Joint Defense Council which will undoubtedly continue well into next year.

4. Jinnah said he expected Pakistan Government take up promptly question exchange Ambassador with US. I told him we would act with expedition. He was most cordial, expressed great admiration for US and said he was hopeful US would aid Pakistan in its many problems. I gave him warm assurances.

5. When I asked Jinnah if he had any matters to take up with me he said "not at this time".

6. Highly placed GOI official says Pakistan will probably send Ambassador to the Middle East with headquarters at Cairo, high commissioners to London and Delhi, a minister to Kabul and a representative of some sort to Rangoon.

Sent Department, repeated Kabul, Calcutta.

Department please repeat to London.

GRADY

845.6359/5–1447 : Telegram

The Secretary of State to the Consulate at Madras

CONFIDENTIAL   WASHINGTON, July 16, 1947—4 p.m.

40. Consideration being given to Travancore proposals (urdesp 786 Apr 15 and 808 May 14)[1] from viewpoint US Govt program acquisition strategic minerals. While we appreciate desirability informal and personal contact between US consular officials India and officials Indian princely states, direct and formal correspondence should be avoided since it definitely encourages assumption US Govt giving support to moves by certain Indian states to assert their independence from rest of India. Such correspondence inconsistent with standing instructions re handling matters affecting Indian states through Delhi which remain in effect at least until Aug 15 when Brit paramountcy lapses.

We are favorably impressed with present Brit policy of endeavoring bring states into one or another of two new Dominions and do not wish to take any action that might interfere with the sound objective of avoiding further Balkanization of India.

If some states eventually fail join Dominions, question direct US relations with states may arise, but we wish to avoid any premature

---

[1] Neither printed.

developments this regard. When answering informal inquiries, line to be taken is that US believes future of Indian states is up to Indians themselves to decide by peaceful negotiations between states and new Dominions and that we hope they will reach mutually satisfactory arrangements.

Sent to Madras, repeated to London and New Delhi.

Delhi to inform Consulates India.

MARSHALL

701.45F11/8–947 : Telegram

The Consul General at Karachi (Lewis) to the Secretary of State

RESTRICTED

KARACHI, August 9, 1947—4 p.m.

57. Reference Department's telegram 478, August 6 to Delhi.[1] I presented Secretary's message [2] this morning to Mr. Jinnah as President Constituent Assembly of Pakistan, which convenes tenth. Jinnah received me cordially and upon reading the message he asked that his warm thanks be conveyed to the Secretary. He stated that he would read the message to the Assembly upon its opening and was sure that the members would be pleased.

Mr. Jinnah stated that he was desirous of establishing diplomatic relations with United States as soon as possible and that he had already selected an Ambassador but did not mention his name.[3] I referred to the informal conversations between him and Ambassador Grady and between other officers of Embassy and officials of Pakistan Government on this subject and stated United States Government was prepared establish diplomatic relations as soon as officially advised of Pakistan Government's wishes. I inquired of Mr. Jinnah whether he wished his present conversation be regarded as an official intimation in that sense. He suggested, after moment's reflection, that upon formation of Cabinet prior to 15th he would present the matter to the Cabinet for approval and would then, after 15th, advise me formally of his government's desire that there be an exchange of Am-

---

[1] Not printed.

[2] For text, see Department of State *Bulletin*, August 17, p. 336.

[3] Presumably Mirza Abol Hassan Ispahani, who presented his credentials to Acting Secretary of State Lovett on October 3. For texts of Department announcements on 1) the agreement of the United States and Pakistan to exchange ambassadors, 2) the raising of the American Consulate at Karachi to the rank of Embassy effective August 15, with the concurrent raising of the Consulate at Madras to the rank of Consulate General, and 3) the presentation of credentials on August 28 of Mr. M.O.A. Baig as Chargé of the newly-established Embassy of Pakistan at Washington pending the arrival of an Ambassador, see respectively Department of State *Bulletin*, August 24, 1947, p. 396, August 31, 1947, p. 438, and September 7, 1947, p. 480.

bassadors.[4] He added, however, that as he is the one who has already made the decision all else was mere formality.

I told Mr. Jinnah that of course we would need working and living accommodations as present Consulate wholly unsuitable for Embassy. I said that from conversations in New Delhi I was aware that Pakistan Government was setting aside quarters for Embassy and Embassy residence and that this gesture was deeply appreciated. Mr. Jinnah confirmed that such facilities are being made available and he added that if any further facilities were needed I should inform him. Reference Department's telegram No. 67 to me at Casablanca,[5] subject quarters, I am looking into this matter and will inform Department. Upon solution working and living quarters problem depends question added staff. Therefore urge Department wait my further report before sending additional personnel as housing problem here desperate. At that time will also discuss question naval and military attachés on which Embassy New Delhi has made provisional report.

Sent Department as 57; repeated Delhi as 65.

LEWIS

---

[4] The request for an exchange of Ambassadors was formalized by a letter dated August 6 from Mohammed Ikramullah, Secretary of External Affairs and Commonwealth Relations, Government of Pakistan, to Ambassador Grady. The request was relayed to the Department (701.45F11/8–847) and answered affirmatively on August 9 by telegram No. 62 to Karachi, repeated No. 494 to New Delhi (701.45F11/8–847), neither printed.

[5] Not printed.

Editorial Note

For texts of messages from President Truman to Governors-General Mohammed Ali Jinnah and Lord Louis Mountbatten on the occasion of the coming into being of the new Dominions of Pakistan and India on August 15, see Department of State *Bulletin*, August 24, 1947, page 396.

102.78/9–247 : Telegram

The Ambassador in India (Grady) to the Secretary of State

RESTRICTED   NEW DELHI, September 2, 1947—6 p. m.

782. For Anderson [1] Agriculture. At request of Secretary General Bajpai, I called on him today where I met Secretary Food Department GOI. Secretary General stated GOI already faced with serious danger due short crops and partition disturbances. Failure on food

---

[1] Clinton P. Anderson, Secretary of Agriculture.

front would endanger foundation new formed state struggling maintain law and order.

Food Secretary stated food grain stocks in deficit areas first November estimated sufficient few days only and no internal surplus sources available due late autumn harvest result late monsoon. He requested (1) that everything possible be done to expedite delivery 270,000 tons USA allocation last quarter '47 emphasizing that shipments direly needed arrive India between October 15 and December 15; (2) that allocation be increased by 100,000 tons which would be great help maintaining "controlled hunger" at present low rationing scale which will have to be cut further.

Food Secretary stated GOI unable obtain further food shipments Australia or Middle East—have just obtained agreement Argentina but procurement and shipments too uncertain depend upon help from there.

I informed Indian officials I would transmit facts of situation to my government with recommendation that as much as possible be done to relieve crisis. It is particularly important that shipments be expedited to reach India between October 15 and December 15. Food will contribute a great deal in maintaining law and order especially in refugee settlements which are becoming quite a problem Delhi vicinity. GOI would not be inclined to overstage [*overstate*] food import requirements at this time when dollars are needed for other essential imports.

I urge and would greatly appreciate personally your earnest effort in this matter.

GOI also making representations through Indian Embassy Washington.

GRADY

845.01/9–347 : Airgram

The Ambassador in India (Grady) to the Secretary of State

CONFIDENTIAL NEW DELHI, September 3, 1947.

A–207. I discussed with Bajpai [1] yesterday the difficulties we were experiencing in getting favorable consideration, in fact any consideration, on a number of matters which I have taken up with the various departments of Government since my arrival here. Apparently the Office of External Affairs has as yet little influence on other departments. When the Government is in a position to have regular meetings of the Ministers, it is expected that there will be improvement. Bajpai stressed the great weakness of administration and properly observed

---

[1] Girja Shankar Bajpai, Secretary-General, Ministry of External Affairs and Commonwealth Relations.

that good and adequate administration is basic to the success of government. He pointed out in this connection that the Government of India should have at this time, based on conservative estimates of requirements, 1,200 ICS personnel, whereas it has actually 410.

He queried me quite unofficially on the matter of loans to India. I stated that I felt that if the Dominion Governments solve their initial problems of organization and the economic and political situation reverses the present downward trends so that the outlook is promising, I saw no reason why application for private credits on the part of industries from American banks would not be in order, and that the Government of India might for its large public works approach the International Bank and/or The Export-Import Bank.

I told him quite frankly that I could not at this time favor any loans for India. I hoped that in six months or a year the situation would warrant my cooperation if the Government of India wished to approach either of the above mentioned agencies.

GRADY

102.78/10–347 : Telegram

The Acting Secretary of State to the Embassy in India

RESTRICTED   WASHINGTON, October 3, 1947—5 p. m.

649. From Agriculture. Your 782, Sept. 2 and 909 Oct. 1.[1] Indian food situation constantly reviewed here along with that of other countries. In view of current grain situation growing out of our decreased production total grains, developing plans for Marshall-plan countries, and rapidly rising prices, impossible for us to assure all countries that even IEFC July–Dec proposed program from U.S.A. will be met. Not possible to add to July–Nov programs to India totaling 408,500 tons, and currently it appears that Dec program cannot be more than fraction of Nov. Advisable India maximize efforts to procure much larger share of imports from other areas. Indian Mission and Embassy fully acquainted with our position over past several months.[2] [Agriculture.]

LOVETT

---

[1] Telegram 909 not printed; in it Ambassador Grady reasserted the gravity of the food situation and pressed for an answer to telegram 782 (102.78/10–147).
[2] Documentation on the Ambassador's further unsuccessful effort to effect an increase in United States grain exports to the new Dominion is in Department of State file No. 102.78.

845.00/10–547 : Telegram

The Ambassador in India (Grady) to the Secretary of State

SECRET   NEW DELHI, October 5, 1947—11 a. m.

922. For the Secretary. Bajpai told me last night that a non-Muslim caravan of 500 moving on October 3 under guard from NWFP toward

East Punjab was attacked by Muslims and that about 400 killed and remainder including women and children wounded. These 500 were part of the concentration of about 50,000 non-Muslims who have during recent weeks fled from West Punjab into NWFP for safety.

Prime Minister through Bajpai makes formal request that US make available ten army transport planes to fly these 50,000 refugees from a concentration point, say at Peshawar, to Armtisar [*Amritsar*]. These refugees are in bad shape, are starving, and in immediate peril. They cannot be sent by caravan because of the physical weakness of so many and certainty of attack. GOI will pay full cost of operation and believes removal can be effected one week. GOI has available sixteen BOAC Dakotas only a few of which in condition to fly.

Attack on caravan has not been reported Delhi. When news gets out a new outburst against Muslims in Delhi is almost certain and if the 50,000 perish from hunger and/or attack communal war will reach proportions beyond anything yet seen. GOI is now under attack for not evacuating non-Muslims from NWFP and present government may fall if it cannot evacuate them. Could not MacArthur quickly send ten transport planes? It means much not only from humane standpoint but from standpoint of the whole future of India.

I ask that this appeal be taken up directly with Secretary of War and if necessary with the President.

Sent Department 922, repeated Calcutta 101; Karachi informed.

GRADY

845.00/10–747

Memorandum of Conversation, by the Acting Secretary of State

CONFIDENTIAL [WASHINGTON,] October 7, 1947.

Participants: The Acting Secretary, Mr. Lovett
The Indian Ambassador, Mr. Asaf Ali

Present: Mr. Mathews,[1] SOA

The Indian Ambassador called informally at 5:15 to express his appreciation of my statement to the press on September 24[2] and to give me his impressions of the Indian situation gained during his recent period of consultation in New Delhi.

STATEMENT OF SEPTEMBER 24

The Ambassador said that he and his Government were very grateful for the sympathy and understanding of India's problems shown in

[1] Elbert G. Mathews, Assistant Chief, Division of South Asian Affairs.
[2] For text, see Department of State *Bulletin*, October 12, 1947, pp. 748–749. This statement was the outcome of a request by Secretary-General Bajpai, in telephone conversation with Ambassador Grady September 13, that the Secretary of State make some form of statement supporting the Government of India in this difficult period when press despatches in American papers were showing an unfriendly tone (845.00/9–1447).

the statement of September 24, and that he believed that it had a salutary effect on the tone of American press reports and comments concerning conditions in India. I thanked him for his kind remarks.

THE RECENT DISTURBANCES

The Ambassador sketched the history of communal disturbances during the past several years, and said that although localized and involving only some one and one-half percent of India's (and Pakistan's) peoples, the troubles in the Punjab since August 15 had been on a much larger scale than the leaders of the new Dominions had expected, and that the displacement of population which has resulted was not anticipated. These developments originated spontaneously among the people and have created very serious problems for the two newly-formed Governments.

In Delhi by the end of August, the Ambassador said, a potentially dangerous situation existed as some 250,000 refugees from the Punjab had assembled in the city. However, serious disturbances were avoided until the arrival in early September of a second influx of refugees. The Ambassador's own investigations and those of his Government had convinced him that these refugees came prepared to make trouble. The instigators were the Sikhs, the militant Hindu organization Rashtriya Swayam Sewak Sangh, and "counter-revolutionary" elements. The last were certain rulers of princely states in the Punjab, notably Patiala and Faridkot who had stores of arms and ammunition. These rulers presumably hoped to discredit the new Government in New Delhi.

The Government of India has appointed a Minister of Refugees to handle the short-term aspects of the displaced persons problem and a Minister of Resettlement to develop long-term solutions. The Ambassador was not aware of the steps being taken by the Government of Pakistan, but he felt sure that it had a similar program.

INTERNATIONAL REPERCUSSIONS OF RECENT DISTURBANCES

The Ambassador referred to India's strategic position in Asia and expressed the view that disturbed conditions in the subcontinent encouraged aggressive powers, citing the explosive Indian situation in 1941 and 1942 as having enticed the Japanese into ever-expanding adventures in the belief that India would fall to them without a struggle. He saw certain similarities in the present situation and suggested that the USSR had decided to open a diplomatic offensive against the US [sic] on the assumption that India was in chaos. He pointed out that India's northernmost boundary lay only fifteen miles from Soviet territory (actually, this is a boundary of the domains of the Maharaja of Kashmir who has not yet acceded to India or Pakistan) and that the USSR had shown great interest in Indian developments. It was therefore unfortunate, the Ambassador felt, that press reports should emphasize the troubles of India. He implied that he was telling me this under instructions from his Government, and said that he had made his views known to Lord Mountbatten and to British officials in London. He added that he hoped to discuss these matters with the President when the latter was less occupied than at present.

I said that I found his analysis of the current position very interesting. I commented that the preoccupation of the press with dramatic events was an ever-present problem, and added that as long as Sikhs attacked Muslims and Muslims retaliated, the press would feature this news.

INDIA'S FOOD REQUIREMENTS

The Ambassador stated that India's need for grain imports was still very great and had been increased by the disturbances in the Punjab (an important grain producing area). His country had spent one billion rupees ($300,000,000) for foreign food grains and must continue these large and burdensome disbursements. He hoped that the US would be able to increase its allocation to India, which would be a concrete evidence of the American desire to aid the Dominion. His Government had approached the USSR for grain, but had been refused.

I pointed out that the US grain position was very difficult owing to the failure of the corn crop, and that we were faced with the necessity of reducing rather than increasing export allocations.

I told the Ambassador that we were very glad to have him with us again, and I appreciated his frank and helpful review of conditions in his country. Some of us in the Department had found it difficult to understand certain of the aspects and ramifications of the partition of India, but clarifications such as he had just given were of great assistance to us.

The Ambassador departed at 5 :45.

845.00/10–547 : Telegram

The Acting Secretary of State to the Embassy in India

SECRET   WASHINGTON, October 9, 1947—6 p. m.
US URGENT   NIACT

667. Convey substance following to Nehru (urtel 922 Oct 5) : President and Acting Secy have considered GOI request and Air Dept studying technical problems involved. President and Acting Secy

sympathetic but of opinion US could act only if request made jointly by GOI and GOP. Joint request should be accompanied by indication size and location refugee groups both Dominions in imminent danger and movable only by air, it being assumed two Govts will make every effort resume adequately protected rail and road movement refugees whose resettlement absolutely essential. However, this Govt would hesitate venture into undertaking this kind unless assured by two Govts that they would immediately establish intensive overall joint inter-Dominion program provide adequate protection minorities, prevent inflammatory statements, demonstrations and other incitements communal violence, and reduce displacement population.

If Nehru accepts suggestion GOI–GOP approach, inform him US Emb Karachi will apprise GOP of US position. Cable GOI decision urgently Dept, Karachi and London.

For your info, preliminary informal discussions with Air Dept indicate provision US planes technically feasible. Planes obviously could not be placed disposal two Dominions but would have remain under operational control US commanding officer. We would make no charge for planes but would expect two Dominions supply gasoline, oil and maintenance facilities, and quarters, food and adequate protection for crews. Thinking here is that transport refugees from both Dominions would almost certainly be involved, and that situation affords opportunity not only render humanitarian service but also press two Govts to closer cooperation in solving mutual problems.

Following for Karachi Action

If Emb Delhi reports GOI agreeable joint request, you should inform Liaquat Ali Khan GOI has requested US military planes assist movement refugees, that US Govt could act on joint GOP–GOI request only, and that if GOP wishes associate itself with GOI, this Govt will give resulting joint request sympathetic consideration, provided it is part overall inter-Dominion effort as indicated first para this tel.

For your background but not for disclosure GOP, GOI request related specifically movement some 50,000 non-Muslim refugees NWFP to Amritsar.

Following for London Action

Delhi's 922 already repeated to you for info. Inform HMG of US position as outlined herein and state US Govt would welcome HMG views and comments and appreciate being informed whether HMG has been similarly approached. If so, ample scope parallel assistance probably exists.

Sent New Delhi; repeated Karachi 134 and London 4360.

LOVETT

845.00/11–1047 : Telegram

The Ambassador in India (Grady) to the Secretary of State

SECRET   NEW DELHI, November 10, 1947—5 p. m.

1036. ReDeptel 707 to Delhi October 29.[1] Bajpai yesterday again requested on behalf of Prime Minister use American planes to expedite transfer non-Muslims from vicinity of Peshawar to Arerroj Amritsar. There are still about 40,000 vicinity Peshawar. According to press about 20,000 non-Muslims have up to date been moved into India by air. Our aid most important to hasten completion migrations and reduce tension. GOI has done all in its power to comply US Government's conditions. It cannot control attitude or actions GOP. ReEmbtel 940 October 11 and my recommendations next to last paragraph which Denning concurred in.[2] Department's conception interdominion program excellent idea but unrealistic. The roots of the conflict which brought about the division of India too deep to be healed or particularly ameliorated by loan of ten planes. I am convinced it is fundamental for US Government to support Nehru in every way possible. If he should fall disintegration in India could easily follow. We do not want, I am sure, India to become another Greece. Russia would in my opinion rather control India than several Greeces.

This Embassy has received no information re communications this subject between Karachi and Washington since Karachi wire October 28 No. 105.[3] Since Liaquat Ali Khan said (Lahore's 26 October 12 [3]) he had no objection in principle to landing planes in Pakistan Department could state willingness to go ahead with India, notify Pakistan, request their clearance for planes to land and invite their participation on return trip. If they refuse clearance, responsibility for our inability to comply this request will be only on Pakistan and goodwill US Government will have been demonstrated.

Sent Department 1036, repeated Karachi as 91, Lahore informed.

GRADY

---

[1] Not printed.
[2] Grady recommended in telegram No. 940 that the United States Government proceed with the airlift if technically feasible and not objectionable to the Government of Pakistan, regardless of whether the latter specifically requested such facilities (845.00/10–1147).
[3] Not printed.

845.00/11–1047 : Telegram

The Secretary of State to the Embassy in India

SECRET   WASHINGTON, November 14, 1947—7 p. m.

751. Convey substance following Bajpai (urtel 1036 Nov 10) : When original GOI request planes referred President he expressed sympathy

but stipulated planes could only be provided in response joint GOI–GOP request. Considerations which led President make this stipulation still exist, and US Govt regrets it cannot act on request one Dominion for planes to be used interdominion flights. Moreover, while US Govt recognizes protection and movement refugees still present great problems both Dominions, GOI and GOP efforts protect refugees have largely eliminated imminent mortal danger refugees which prevailed early Oct and which was then primary factor in leading US Govt give sympathetic consideration provision its planes.

Following for your info only. In view President's stipulation, Dept would have to refer matter White House again to obtain authority act on request from GOI only. Dept does not feel justified do this or press Air Force provide planes now for following reasons. (1) Improvement refugee situation noted above. Dept fully aware continuing potential danger but doubts that US aid on practicable scale would remove danger. (2) Karachi tel 158 Oct 30 [1] reported GOP had moved 8000 non-Muslim refugees from NWFP by rail. Hence, refugee group of primary concern GOI apparently can be moved without planes. (3) GOP obviously not enthusiastic about US planes as Lewis never approached, and GOP made special effort move NWFP group by rail. (4) GOI has obtained more than ten planes originally requested US from other sources including BOAC and internal airlines, although planes from latter source appear have been used for movement troops and military supplies to Kashmir and not for refugees. (5) Provision US planes at present obviously would not contribute improvement GOI–GOP relations which as you point out have so deteriorated that relatively small US gesture would be ineffective. As you are aware, Dept from outset emphasized view that primary justification for and objective of provision US planes was closer GOI–GOP cooperation.

Dept appreciates and has carefully considered Emb point of view this matter but feels factors enumerated foregoing paragraph impel negative response GOI request.

Sent Delhi 751 Rptd London 4852 and Karachi 179 Karachi pass to Lahore.

MARSHALL

---

[1] Not printed.

845F.51/11–2847

*The Acting Secretary of State to the Pakistani Ambassador
(Ispahani)*

The Acting Secretary of State presents his compliments to His Excellency the Ambassador of Pakistan and has the honor to refer to the Embassy's note of November 28, 1947 [1] asking whether this Government would be prepared to receive a financial mission from the Government of Pakistan to continue negotiations on the subject of a dollar loan; and to a note of the same date [1] addressed by the Chargé d'Affaires *ad interim* of Pakistan to the Acting Secretary of State with specific regard to a loan for the relief and rehabilitation of refugees who have entered Pakistan in a destitute condition from India.

As Mr. Laik Ali [2] was verbally informed by officers of the Department some weeks ago, the memoranda submitted by him in connection with proposed economic reconstruction and development projects in Pakistan appear to reflect a program which will require implementation over a period of years as foreign capital and technical assistance can be obtained, technical and managerial personnel can be trained, and adequate credits can be secured. He was also informed that this Government is not authorized to extend foreign credits for a comprehensive program of this magnitude without prior Congressional approval and appropriation. Since the Department is not prepared, at this time, to recommend such Congressional action, it was suggested to Mr. Laik Ali that the Government of Pakistan break down the comprehensive program envisaged in his memoranda into selected projects which might qualify for financing by the Export-Import Bank or ultimately by the International Bank. To assist in reviewing the projects eligible for such financing and to make clear the procedures to be followed, there is attached hereto a statement of principles governing the operations of the Export-Import Bank.[1]

In view of the limited availability of public funds, the possibility of drawing upon private funds to meet a part of Pakistan's capital needs should not be overlooked. It is the understanding of the Department that representatives of the Government of Pakistan have already taken preliminary steps in this direction. The growing restoration of order in Pakistan, and the continued improvement of economic and political relations between Pakistan and neighboring countries will, no doubt, encourage such private investment.

The Department would, of course, welcome a visit to this country at any time by the Finance Minister of Pakistan, but it would appear that the most advantageous step that could be taken now would be the submission of a fully documented application by the Government of Pakistan for credits to finance one or more specific projects by the Export-Import Bank in terms of the statement of principles transmitted herewith. Such an application should be sent directly to the Bank

---

[1] Not printed.
[2] Representative of Pakistan in Washington doing preliminary investigation on procurement of a short term $45 million loan for his country.

through the Embassy of Pakistan at Washington. An opportune time for high officials of your Government to be present in Washington would be during the period when the Bank has such an application under consideration.

With respect to the problem of relief and rehabilitation of refugees in Pakistan, it is noted that the Embassy of Pakistan has already taken steps to obtain some assistance from the War Assets Administration. This Government is fully aware of the grievous hardships that have been imposed upon millions of persons as a result of recent disturbances in Pakistan and India and is deeply sympathetic with the efforts that are being made for the relief and rehabilitation of these destitute groups. The full support of the Department will be given to the efforts which the Embassy of Pakistan is making to obtain assistance from the War Assets Administration. There is, however, no other channel through which additional relief supplies may be obtained except through volunteer American relief agencies. In this connection the attention of the Embassy is called to the efforts now being made by the Committee for Emergency Aid to Pakistan and India, which has its headquarters in care of Church World Service, Inc., 37 E. 36th Street, New York, New York. The Department is in close touch with this organization and has given it all possible moral support and appropriate information concerning the refugee situation. It is understood that the Committee for Emergency Aid to Pakistan and India has already shipped considerable quantities of relief supplies to the two countries and that one hundred volunteer workers are now engaged under its auspices in relief work on both sides of the Pakistan–India frontier.

Some weeks ago it was suggested in a communication addressed to the Government of Pakistan through the Embassy of the United States at Karachi, that the Government of Pakistan establish a fund in the rupee equivalent of $2,000,000 to enable the American Relief Committee to utilize such personnel and relief supplies as may be available locally. Thus far no response has been received to this suggestion.[3]

WASHINGTON, December 17, 1947.

---

[3] In a follow-up memorandum of December 29 the Department corrected this last paragraph by the following statement: "Subsequent investigation reveals that the Government of Pakistan's consideration of the establishment of a fund for the utilization of the American Relief Committee was not invited in the form of a communication from the Embassy of the United States at Karachi, but that the Government of Pakistan was approached through its Consulate at New York City directly by the Committee for Emergency Aid to India and Pakistan, with a suggestion that the volunteer agencies effecting shipments to Pakistan be reimbursed in rupees by the Government of Pakistan in the amount of the overseas freight charges incurred. The funds thus received by the agencies would be employed in Pakistan for the distribution of supplies and the maintenance of relief personnel." (845F.51/12–2947)

845.00/12–2647

Memorandum of Conversation, by Mr. Joseph S. Sparks of the Division of South Asian Affairs

[Extracts]

SECRET [WASHINGTON,] December 26, 1947.

The following notes compose an abstract in abbreviated form of the discussion on Tuesday morning, December 16, between the three Ambassadors [1] currently on consultation in SOA, and the appropriate Department officers: [2]

MR. HARE: Should we be thinking still in terms of an eventual return to a united India, and are there certain realms of cooperation between India and Pakistan on which we should concentrate our attentions?

AMBASSADOR GRADY: There is a chance for overall cooperation without disturbing the institutional independence of either country. The possibility of a Joint Parliamentary Committee is an example. This would not represent an about face on the question of the division of the country, but would be an attempt to cooperate along economic and defense lines. Real progress in this direction was made in the recent Lahore meetings with only Kashmir left unsettled.[3] Nehru is pessimistic about this one problem, but I do not feel that solution is hopeless. Even if Kashmir is not satisfactorily solved, the countries may well go ahead on other cooperative lines. For example, a Customs Union is possible and would serve to solve the jute problem. On the whole, a loose federal system is the maximum we could hope for. Earl Mountbatten hopes for concrete advances in this direction before his departure in April.

AMBASSADOR ALLING: You agree that it is unlikely that the two nations could get together?

AMBASSADOR GRADY: They could not on the pre-August 15 status. However, feelings at top level are not as antagonistic as the public utterances of the leaders suggest. Communal feelings will last a long time with sporadic uprisings, but this will not interfere with high level cooperation. At the top level, the troubles which have been experienced have taught a lesson and some humility. Chances are better than fifty-fifty there will be no more serious uprisings.

---

[1] Henry F. Grady, Paul H. Alling, appointed Ambassador to Pakistan September 25, 1947, and Jerome Klahr Huddle, appointed Ambassador to Burma October 17, 1947.

[2] Henry L. Deimel, NEA, Raymond A. Hare, Ray L. Thurston, E. G. Mathews, Ernest F. Fox, Edward Dahl and Joseph S. Sparks, SOA, and Hooker A. Doolittle, Consul General at Lahore. Mr. Hare was Chief of the Division of South Asian Affairs.

[3] For documentation on the Kashmir dispute, see pp. 179 ff.

Mr. Hare: What should our tactics be in political, economic, and defense fields?

Ambassador Grady: The economic field is the easiest to answer—defense is now being worked on in the two countries.

Mr. Thurston: The Joint Defense Council is being retained.

Mr. Mathews: Are possibilities of cooperation stronger if the two Dominions remain in the Commonwealth?

Ambassador Grady: We should encourage a loose federation, but I question our interfering in the Commonwealth problem. We are already accused of pulling British chestnuts out of the fire. I don't think the possibility of cooperation would be affected, although the countries might work together better if they were independent. It would be difficult if one country left the Commonwealth and the other stayed in, but, in my opinion, cooperation between the two does not depend on their Commonwealth status.

Ambassador Huddle: Are there any indications as to whether India will remain in the British Commonwealth?

Ambassador Grady: Not yet, although the Draft Constitution provides for a republic.

Ambassador Alling: If India withdrew, would that affect the status of the Princely States?

Mr. Thurston: That is possible.

Mr. Hare: Are you convinced of the sincerity of Patel's [4] change of approach to the communal problem?

Ambassador Grady: I am inclined to think Patel is sincere. He is confident of the future of India, but not so confident of the future of Pakistan. Patel may be counting on Pakistan falling back automatically to India as a result of the working of economic forces. He told me he expects East Bengal to want to go back to India within a year. Communal troubles have occurred in Calcutta, but were brought under control.

Mr. Thurston: Has there been any further talk about a united Bengal?

Ambassador Grady: No. There is a strong anti-British feeling among top Indians. They want the British out and the sooner the better. I think India will carry through on the question of separation.

Mr. Doolittle: Does resentment extend to British businessmen?

Ambassador Grady: Yes, but officials and major industrialists are the leaders among the Indians who wish to eliminate the British.

Ambassador Alling: Pakistan has not even considered going back to India.

---

[4] Sardar Vallabhbhai Patel, Minister for Home, Information, Broadcasting and States, Indian Dominion Government.

Mr. Hare : What should our attitude be ?

Ambassador Grady : Encourage cooperation—stay out of Commonwealth questions. There is no anti-American feeling in India (the newspapers do not really carry enough influence to count in this), but there would be, if we identified ourselves with the Commonwealth cause.

Mr. Thurston : We have taken on certain commitments in supporting Pakistan internationally which we could not now go back on.

Ambassador Grady : I agree we must be very careful. Indians are very jealous of everything we do for Pakistan. I am constantly questioned on this point in India. If we made a loan to Pakistan, India would resent it unless we gave the same to India. This applies to all matters right down the line.

Mr. Hare : Would you agree that our key note now should be good neighborliness rather than unity ?

Ambassador Grady : I would.

Ambassador Alling : There are international problems bringing the countries together, i.e., South Africa, Palestine, et cetera.

Ambassador Grady : Yes—and the number will increase as time goes on.

Ambassador Alling : What are the possibilities of a Customs Union ?

Ambassador Grady : Very good. They are working toward it. Rajagopalachari [5] deplores reference by Indian leaders to unity as he feels it accomplishes nothing, and offends Pakistan leaders.

Mr. Thurston : Pakistan needs revenue. Can they afford a Customs Union ?

Ambassador Grady : If they could jointly raise tariffs against the world, they could increase revenues, and I believe they will do just that.

Mr. Hare : Shall we agree then, that we will never question independence of either country in our policy, but will encourage cooperation wherever possible ?

Ambassador Grady : Yes—particularly economic.

. . . .

United States–British Cooperation

Ambassador Grady : The British have been friendly, but have made no attempt to consult with us on common problems or to ask our advice. Neither Shone nor Mountbatten thinks of us in any way as partners. They have over three hundred people working on trade relations. I have expressed more sympathy for British trade than the British have for American trade. On more than one occasion, Mountbatten has warned Nehru against dollar imperialism.

---

[5] H. E. Rajagopalachari, Governor of West Bengal.

Mr. Hare: Can we do anything about that attitude?

Ambassador Grady: I have waited patiently for a hand of cooperation from the British, but it has never come. Any change in this attitude would have to come on orders from London.

Mr. Hare: There is no reason why British–United States interests should clash in India?

Ambassador Grady: None whatever. The British are not happy about the strong position which we have in India, or about the weak position which they have. They are trying to salvage everything they can from the separation. Shone thinks only in terms of immediate British interests.

Mr. Thurston: How do you feel about the Department's point of view as outlined in the Consultation Memoranda?

Ambassador Grady: I think it is all right—quite sound. I think top level conversations in London at this time a good idea.

Mr. Hare: Could such general cooperation be sold to the British?

Ambassador Grady: There are many fields in which we should be cooperating, but are not. There are only minor relations between Shone's office and ours. The Deputy High Commissioner is more helpful. Shone is not a heavyweight and is the key to the problem. Certain British generals, however, have been very cooperative. I think Shone's attitude is personal rather than official.

General Economic
SPECIFIC AIMS

Aviation

Ambassador Grady: I don't believe American civil air lines are doing us much good in India because of their service (or lack of it). The situation is moving along rather satisfactorily, however, competition will be stronger, particularly from Indian lines which may look to the Government of India for help vis-à-vis United States lines.

Princely States

Ambassador Grady: I was asked if the United States Government would help in obtaining office space in Washington for Hyderabad. They talk in terms of tremendous business development, but are concerned about demands of material to carry out the Marshall plan, and its effect of [on?] India's needs. I think it a great mistake for our Government to overlook India in concentrating on Europe. There should be a real fight on the part of all of us here to see to it India isn't overlooked.

Mr. Hare: If Hyderabad sets up an independent office in Washington, would they deal separately with us? Mustn't we always think in terms of India as a whole?

AMBASSADOR GRADY: The emphasis will have to be placed on working through the Indian Embassy.

MR. MATHEWS: Particularly on any diplomatic point.

AMBASSADOR GRADY: There is danger of Hyderabad trying to use its trade representation as an entering wedge. It will have to be watched constantly. Mountbatten has really appreciated our attitude of not encouraging the ambitions of Hyderabad. This attitude has strengthened GOI's hand. I think their mission should be regarded strictly as any other purchasing office.

Food

MR. DEIMEL: There has been some feeling among United States allocation authorities that India was too large and remote to help. We have fought that and have been reasonably successful in keeping India from being cut down too much.

AMBASSADOR GRADY: GOI is anxious to reduce food purchases as soon as possible from the dollar area to their absolute minimum needs.

MR. THURSTON: What effect will abandonment of rationing controls have on food consumption in India?

AMBASSADOR GRADY: It was a spirited fight and results are not yet clear.

I think prices will advance which will cut consumption at the wrong level of the economy.

[Omitted here are final paragraphs concerning Ambassador Grady's request for increased administrative funds and a second plane for Embassy use at New Delhi.]

UNITED STATES CONCERN OVER DEVELOPMENT OF THE KASHMIR DISPUTE

845.00/10–2847 : Telegram

The Chargé in Pakistan (Lewis) to the Secretary of State

RESTRICTED KARACHI, October 28, 1947—11 a. m.

153. Alleging that GOP has been trying coerce Kashmir join Pakistan by economic strangulation and be [*by*] sending soldiers in plain clothes and tribesmen from northwest frontier into Kashmir to destroy life and property the Maharaja has appealed to GOI for assistance [1]

---

[1] For text of a letter dated October 26 from the Maharaja of the State of Jammu and Kashmir, Sir Hari Singh, to the Governor-General of India, Lord Louis Mountbatten, requesting acceptance of an instrument of accession and immediate military assistance, see Government of India, *White Paper on Jammu and Kashmir*, place and date of publication not indicated, pp. 46–47.

and signed on October 27 instrument of accession [2] which was accepted same day by Mountbatten. However, latter stated in letter acceptance that "as soon as law and order have been restored in Kashmir and her soil cleared of the invader the question of the state's accession should be settled by reference to the people." [3] Meanwhile, Mountbatten added in response Maharaja's appeal for military aid, troops of Indian army are being sent Kashmir. Maharaja has set up interim govt under Sheikh Abdullah and this accepted by GOI.

These developments have created sensation here and will certainly be taken seriously by GOP.

Developments this point summarized Embassy's despatch 196 October 27 mailed yesterday. [4]

LEWIS

---

[2] For text of Instrument of Accession signed by Hari Singh on October 26 and for statement by Lord Mountbatten on its acceptance dated October 27, see P. L. Lakhanpal, *Essential Documents and Notes on Kashmir Dispute* (New Delhi, 1958), pp. 57–58.

[3] For text of Mountbatten's letter of acceptance dated October 27, see Government of India, *White Paper on Jammu and Kashmir*, pp. 47–48.

[4] Not printed.

845.00/11–347 : Telegram

The Ambassador in India (Grady) to the Secretary of State

CONFIDENTIAL   NEW DELHI, November 3, 1947—noon.

1009. Bajpai [1] yesterday advised me as follows regarding Kashmir: some things he said were later covered in Nehru's radio address reported mytel 1004, November 3. [2]

In attempting arrange conference between two Governors General and Prime Ministers [3] at Lahore Mountbatten found Jinnah very difficult. Jinnah said he had no confidence in Government of India. Perhaps Mountbatten should not have communicated this to GOI but he stated it to GOI Defense Commission. Despite this Nehru was prepared to go to Lahore until he read Jinnah's statement accusing GOI of "fraud" in connection with accession of Kashmir. [4] Mountbatten is

---

[1] Sir Girja Shankar Bajpai, Secretary-General, Ministry of External Affairs and Commonwealth Relations.

[2] Not printed. Reference is to a broadcast on the night of November 2. For text, see Government of India, *White Paper on Jammu and Kashmir*, pp. 52–55.

[3] Governors-General Lord Mountbatten and Mohammed Ali Jinnah, Prime Ministers Pandit Jawaharlal Nehru and Liaquat Ali Khan.

[4] Reference here is presumably to the meeting of the Governors-General and Prime Ministers originally scheduled for October 29, and to a Pakistan Government press release of October 30 stating that the accession of Kashmir to India was based on fraud and violence and as such could not be recognized. For text, see S. L. Poplai, *Select Documents on Asian Affairs: India 1947–50*, Bombay, (Oxford University Press, 1959), pp. 374–377.

continuing negotiations with Jinnah. Jinnah first proposed that if Indian troops withdrawn from Kashmir, invaders would withdraw. This in opinion of GOI indicated control by Pakistan over invaders who Bajpai said have looted and destroyed at least 100 villages on border. GOI countered this proposal by promising to withdraw troops if invaders first withdrew and proposed plebiscite or referendum under UN auspices.[5] They had in mind observation similar to that which British, French and Americans conducted last year in Greece.[6] They are awaiting Jinnah's reply to this proposal.

Bajpai stated military situation as far as GOI forces are concerned seemed "under control".

He mentioned deep concern GOI naturally has for Kashmir and referred to three neighbors on north—China, Afghanistan and USSR. GOI not concerned about first two but definitely concerned about last if Kashmir becomes center of real conflict and chaos gets deeper. He observed specifically that Prime Minister concerned with regard to USSR.

When invasion first began Nehru wired Attlee urging him request Pakistan exert its influence on tribesmen to withdraw. Attlee's reply in form of general admonition that two Dominions should preserve peace. GOI felt his message patronizing and failed to appreciate position of GOI and necessity it was under to respond to appeal of a friendly neighbor for assistance when it was under attack. Nehru replied to Attlee at great length outlining whole situation as GOI sees it. GOI does not like what it regards as lecturing from London and feels HMG is taking its friendliness and good will for granted while it woos Pakistan. Bajpai promised keep me fully informed particularly with respect Jinnah's response to GOI's latest proposal.

Sent Department 1009, repeated Karachi 84.

Please repeat London.

GRADY

---

[5] See telegram dated November 8, 1947, from Pandit Nehru to Liaquat Ali Khan, Government of India, *White Paper on Jammu and Kashmir*, pp. 61–62.
[6] For documentation on this subject, see *Foreign Relations*, 1946, vol. VII, pp. 88 ff.

501.BB/12–247 : Telegram

The Acting Secretary of State to the Embassy in India

CONFIDENTIAL [WASHINGTON,] December 2, 1947.

55. The Acting Secretary of State transmits herewith for the information of the Embassy a copy of the position paper on the India–

Pakistan dispute over Kashmir prepared for the United States Delegation to the General Assembly of the United Nations.[1]

[LOVETT]

[Enclosure]

INDIA–PAKISTAN DISPUTE OVER KASHMIR

THE PROBLEM

Indications recently received from official sources in India and Pakistan and from unofficial sources, including Prime Minister Jawaharlal Nehru's speech of November 1, 1947,[2] are that the current dispute between India and Pakistan over Kashmir may be referred to the United Nations for settlement. Pandit Nehru stated in his speech when discussing the provisional accession of Kashmir to India that "as soon as Kashmir is free from the invaders our troops will have no further necessity to remain there and the fate of Kashmir will be left in the hands of the people of Kashmir". Nehru then suggested a referendum in Kashmir "under international auspices like the United Nations".

RECOMMENDATIONS

We would much prefer that the Kashmir question be settled by direct negotiation between India and Pakistan. However, in the event that a resolution requesting the intervention of the United Nations, and in particular requesting the United Nations to supervise a referendum in Kashmir, is introduced by India or Pakistan and supported by the United Kingdom, the United States Delegation should also support the resolution. Such a resolution should define the electoral body in terms of universal adult suffrage.

In the event that a resolution requesting the intervention of the United Nations should be introduced by a third power (including any other member of the British Commonwealth) or introduced by India or Pakistan and opposed by the United Kingdom, the United States position must be further studied.

COMMENT

It is increasingly apparent that this major difficulty between India and Pakistan probably cannot be removed without external assistance, or without resort to further armed conflict which may eventually involve some or all of the Afghan border tribes. Despite their vested interests in this area, because of the peculiarities of their position and the recentness of their withdrawal, the British are apparently not

---

[1] Copy of position paper also sent to the Embassy in Pakistan in Department instruction No. 12 to Karachi, December 2, 1947 (501.BB/12–247).

[2] Presumably Nehru's radio address on the night of November 2.

in a position to render this outside assistance, and rather than have the role fall either to the United States or to any other single third party, assumption by the United Nations of the problem would be preferred.

If a resolution of the nature suggested above is introduced, it will probably be by one of the interested parties. The Dominion of India may attempt to establish the extant electoral rolls as the basis for the referendum. As these rolls are said to contain less than 7% of the population and were compiled on a basis which served to weight the numbers of the wealthier educated Hindu minority who would obviously vote for accession to India, it is important that the electoral body should in fact be composed on a basis of complete adult suffrage in order that the result of the referendum may be representative of the actual wishes of the people of Kashmir.

The practical difficulties of supervising a general referendum in Kashmir should not be overlooked by the United Nations. No comprehensive electoral machinery is known to exist for conducting a general referendum. The population of Kashmir is scattered, and many sections will soon be isolated by winter. Few persons other than British political agents and missionaries have first hand knowledge of the people of Kashmir and finally, the people of Kashmir are largely illiterate and without political consciousness.

745.45F/12–2447 : Telegram

The Chargé in India (Donovan) to the Secretary of State

SECRET NEW DELHI, December 24, 1947—1 p. m.

1151. I saw Bajpai today at his request. He showed me copy of note from GOI to GOP delivered December 22.[1] After listing various forms of assistance GOI alleges GOP is giving raiders, GOI requested GOP "to deny to invaders all access to and use of Pakistan territory for operation against Kashmir, all military and other supplies, and all other kinds of aid which might tend to prolong the present struggle".

GOI stresses its desire to live on terms of friendship with Pakistan and expresses hope that GOP will "accede promptly and without reserve" to foregoing request.

Note ends by saying that "failing such response, GOI will be compelled to take such action, with due regard to its rights and obligations as a member of UN, as it may consider necessary to protect its own interests, and those of the people of Jammu and Kashmir".

Bajpai said he saw very little hope of agreement between GOI and GOP on Kashmir question and that unless favorable reply to note was

---

[1] For text, see Government of India, *White Paper on Jammu and Kashmir*, pp. 74–75.

received within a week, GOI would present matter to Security Council. He feels question is practically certain to go to UN and said GOI will not permit adjudication by UK or member British Commonwealth.

He has given similar information to French Ambassador and UK High Commissioner but has not decided whether to inform Australian High Commissioner.

Bajpai admitted GOP might not be able to stop all assistance to raiders but stressed that GOP had done absolutely nothing to check activities of raiders.

Sent Department 1151; repeated Karachi as 99. Department please repeat London.

DONOVAN

745.45F/12–2447 : Telegram

The Acting Secretary of State to the Embassy in India

SECRET   WASHINGTON, December 26, 1947—8 p. m.

814. Dept seriously concerned turn Kashmir situation has taken as indicated urtel 1151 Dec 24.

Nov 12 Mrs. Pandit [1] approached Dept officials New York re Kashmir situation stating she was doing so at instance Nehru. She expressed India's desire for Kashmir plebiscite on basis adult suffrage to be held next spring under UN supervision. She mentioned plan under which India and Pakistan would agree beforehand take case SC with joint request that commission of small and disinterested countries be sent supervise and observe Kashmir elections and definitely indicated desire that Great Powers including USSR not participate in plebiscite commission.

Question UN plebiscite also discussed informally with GOP Amb Ispahani [2] New York who stated that although he was without instructions, he seemed [3] favorably disposed toward such solution Kashmir problem.

Subsequently Dept noted that although London reported (6270 Dec 1 [4]) UN approach unlikely, Mountbatten was endeavoring (Delhi's 1119 Dec 12 [4]) persuade GOI and GOP agree appointment UN intermediaries including US.

---

[1] Vijaya Lakshmi Pandit, sister of the Indian Prime Minister and delegate to the 1947 second session of the United Nations General Assembly.
[2] M.A.H. Ispahani, Pakistan Ambassador to the United States and delegate to the 1947 second session of the General Assembly.
[3] The word "was" which originally appeared here, was changed to "seemed" before telegram was sent.
[4] Not printed.

Obviously best solution Kashmir problem would be amicable agreement among Kashmir authorities GOI and GOP. Failing that, it would be hoped parties to dispute would follow letter and spirit Art 33 UN Charter which enjoins recourse negotiation, inquiry, mediation, conciliation, etc., before reference UN. Dept not informed reasons why recent Lahore talks on Kashmir failed, but it appears from your 1147 Dec 23 [5] and particularly your 1151 Dec 24 direct settlement among parties concerned highly doubtful.

If Bajpai envisages recourse UN along lines Mrs Pandit indicated Nov 12, one possible procedure would be that GOI and GOP should each choose one or two UN Govts, not necessarily member SC, the two or four Govts chosen to select an additional Govt to comprise plebiscite commission. Obviously, this type approach to SC would be more effective if made jointly by GOI and GOP as suggested by Mrs Pandit, but conceivable that GOI could unilaterally make such proposal to SC. Dept believes SC technically competent authorize establishment such plebiscite commission under its auspices.

View foregoing Delhi requested informally convey GOI US regret breakdown Lahore talks, ascertain reasons for breakdown and present GOI plans for future Kashmir status; and inquire whether, in event recourse UN, plan along above lines for plebiscite SC auspices would be followed. US concerned lest recourse by India to UN without some such prearranged plan might lead to unnecessary complications and crystallize pattern GOI–GOP hostility.

Karachi requested likewise discuss Kashmir situation with GOP informally without divulging contents Delhi's 1151 and primarily with view ascertaining GOP reaction to plebiscite plan outlined above.

London should report Brit views which will be taken into account in final determination US position.

Sent New Delhi repeated Karachi 218 and London 5368.

LOVETT

---

[5] Not printed.

745.45F/12–2947 : Telegram

The Chargé in the United Kingdom (Gallman) to the Secretary of State

SECRET   LONDON, December 29, 1947—8 p. m.

6647. 1. Patrick [1] CRO described December 22 GOI note to GOP (Delhi's 1151, December 24 to Department, repeated Karachi 99) as "ultimatum" seriousness which can hardly be exaggerated. There is

[1] Sir Paul J. Patrick, British Commonwealth Relations Office.

ample reason in his view to fear GOI attack on Pakistan simultaneously with filing GOI complaint with SC. Attlee and ministers are now formulating HMG policy re various eventualities.

2. Patrick said CRO is without full account two meetings re Kashmir but he understands first talk failed because GOP while denying GOI charges, claimed it could not stop transit raiders. December 22 talk failed because in GOI note GOP was faced with ultimatum. Patrick understands GOP was willing to make joint approach to UN re broader problem long-term settlements Kashmir and Junagadh. GOP could not accept approach to UN on narrow question Pakistan complicity raiders. When GOI announced its intention to approach UN, GOP announced that it would file rejoinder with UN. This may be done December 30 because ultimatum expires today.

3. Patrick sees problem GOI–GOP relations as falling into two phases: First is finding UN means to stop conflict which may begin within next few days by GOI attack towards Lahore; second is finding way to decide long-term fate Kashmir by plebiscite or some other means (Department's 5368, December 26 [2]). Latter may take time because plebiscite could not begin until May and if carried out on basis adult suffrage, would require about eight months to complete. Preparatory to plebiscite, peaceful conditions would have to be established in Kashmir under UN auspices. This might mean, since British troops would not be available, and since SC has no force at its disposal, decision whereby both GOI and GOP troops would be supplied for pacification Kashmir under commander appointed by SC. If and when conditions favorable for plebiscite are established, Patrick thought some arrangement comparable to that suggested Paragraph 6, Department's reference telegram might be worked out. As minor point, he doubted that GOI which considers itself in possession Kashmir would unilaterally propose plebiscite to SC.

4. Some concession by GOP to GOI might relieve tension but Liaquat has made it plain that tribesmen regard Kashmir operations as Jihad [3] and are largely beyond GOP control. GOI on other hand is driven to its rash course by Nehru's "Brahmin logic" which argues that now Kashmir has adhered to GOI it is part India and consequently GOP is interfering with steps by GOI to put down rebels in GOI territory. As further factor Sikhs might get out of control and force GOI–GOP struggle.

5. If fight starts, Nehru will demand immediately and obtain withdrawal British officers from Pakistan Army thus crippling it. Patrick said "we will withdraw British officers as quickly as possible from both sides."

[2] Telegram 814 to New Delhi, *supra*.
[3] Holy war.

6. Although Pakistan Army is much smaller than Indian Army, latter is so extended Kashmir that initially Pakistan would not be overwhelmed. In event conflict Patrick believes Afghanistan would make deal with GOP and become GOP ally. "Because more trouble would be created that way" Patrick thinks USSR would probably take Pakistan side.

7. Patrick said he could not advise Embassy re course HMG plans to take in present crisis because thinking Prime Minister and Cabinet is unknown. However, this is clearly situation in which it is highly desirable USG and HMG should keep in close touch everywhere, i.e. New York, Washington, New Delhi, Karachi, London. Re reaction world public opinion to GOI–GOP conflict Patrick considers it likely that GOI will be considered aggressor. Asked whether warning to this effect by members SC might deter Nehru, Patrick said he did not know but it was an idea. Embassy will see Patrick tomorrow.

Sent Department 6647; repeat New Delhi 149; repeat Karachi 53; Moscow by pouch.

GALLMAN

745.45F/12–2947 : Telegram

The Chargé in India (Donovan) to the Secretary of State

SECRET   NEW DELHI, December 29, 1947—4 p. m.

1162. Deptel 814 December 29. 1. I saw Bajpai noon today and communicated to him Department's regret breakdown Lahore talks. I outlined Department's suggestions regarding settlement Kashmir problem under terms UN charter. Bajpai said he felt GOI had taken all possible steps as provided by Article 33 UN charter. He pointed out GOI had endeavored negotiate Kashmir question with GOP and it felt other means settlement outlined Article 33 not feasible since tribesmen were in fact stateless persons as GOP refused accept responsibility their entry Kashmir.

2. He said joint approach by GOI and GOP was impracticable since GOP had consistently adopted attitude it had nothing to do with raiders' activities.

3. GOI feels question plebiscite must not be confused with problem cessation hostilities and withdrawal of raiders. Therefore GOI believes Department's suggestion of requesting Security Council arrange impartial commission hold plebiscite Kashmir would only lead to confusion issues involved.

4. Embassy certain GOI feels only course practicable under circumstances is appeal SC and request SC instruct Pakistan prevent entry

raiders Kashmir from Pakistan territory. Note to UN already prepared and Bajpai thinks will be sent today or tomorrow. He indicated note to UN would state unless Pakistan took measures restrain entry raiders Kashmir and prevent use Pakistan territory as base for raiders GOI troops might be compelled enter Pakistan. Entry Indian troops Pakistan in Embassy's opinion could only result open hostilities between GOI and GOP. Cabinet meets 3 p.m. today when final decision regarding appeal UN will be taken. Bajpai will let me know immediately result Cabinet meeting.

5. Reasons breakdown Lahore talks was question administration of Kashmir until holding of plebiscite. Pakistan felt if Sheikh Abdullah continued as head of emergency administration he would be able after imprisoning opposition raiders to obtain majority in favor of the administration and in favor of approval of accession of Kashmir to India. GOI demanded raiders withdraw and that state remain under Abdullah's administration and then plebiscite be held.

6. Embassy advised by UK High Commissioner's office that it has been informed HMG believes feeling so strong between GOI and GOP regarding Kashmir issue that recourse UN only feasible solution.

7. Embassy's appraisal situation is as follows:

(a) GOP is in very difficult military position Kashmir with little hope success under present conditions supply and communications between India and Kashmir. GOI is deeply committed to support of Sheikh Abdullah and withdrawal from present position impossible from view prestige. GOP realizes difficulties GOI and will be correspondingly unyielding.

(b) Embassy views situation with grave concern and can see no solution other than appeal to UN by GOI.

(c) Only hopeful indication is Bajpai's statement to me that after withdrawal raiders GOI will abide by its previous statement agreeing to plebiscite Kashmir under international auspices.

Sent Department 1162, repeated Karachi 104. Department please repeat London.

DONOVAN

745.45F/12–3047 : Telegram

The Chargé in the United Kingdom (Gallman) to the Secretary of State

SECRET   LONDON, December 30, 1947—8 p. m.
US URGENT

6668. 1. Sir Archibald Carter permanent Under-Secretary CRO and Patrick showed Embassy officer today three documents regarding GOI–GOP dispute. (Embassy's 6647 December 29).

2. First document is text December 28 message from Nehru to Attlee in which Nehru refers to fact talks with Liaquat December 22 and 23 "yielded no result". He writes that to bring home Liaquat gravity situation he personally handed Liaquat letter briefly specifying aid which Kashmir invaders were deriving from Pakistan and restating GOI request such aid should be stopped. So far despite telegraphic reminder GOP has not replied. Meanwhile pressure invaders all along frontier Jammu Province has greatly intensified. GOI troops are under heavy attack at Jhangar where 6000 invaders attacked and GOI troops were outnumbered 30 to 1. Naushera has been scene severe fighting during last few days. 19,000 invaders are massed Uri area and GOI intelligence indicates approximately 100,000 tribesmen and Pakistan nationals located different districts West Punjab. Many are receiving military training preparatory joining battle against GOI.

3. Nehru writes that these developments have created military situation full of peril not only to Jammu and Kashmir state but to GOI. Unless Pakistan takes immediate steps stop all forms aid to attackers, operating from bases in Pakistan, and therefore strategically enjoying great advantage over GOI troops whose only hope of dealing with them effectively lies in striking at them at their Pakistan bases. This would involve GOI entering Pakistan territory. Such a step would be justified in international law as GOI is entitled to take this action in self-defence. What is now happening is definitely an act of aggression against GOI by GOP.

4. However, since GOI is most anxious to act in conformity with letter and spirit of UN Charter GOI is asking SC to repeat to GOP the request in Nehru's December 23 [22] letter,[1] i.e., that GOP should take immediate and effective action to deny to raiders:

(a) Access to and use of Pakistan territory for operations against Jammu and Kashmir states;
(b) Military and other supplies;
(c) All other kinds of aid that might tend to prolong present struggle.

5. This request, Nehru writes, was without prejudice to freedom of GOI to take, at any time, such military action as it might consider necessary in exercise of GOI right of self-defence.

6. Nehru expresses hope GOP will respond favorably to this request since it is still earnest desire GOI to live on terms peace and friendship with GOP. However this relationship cannot be one-sided and Pakistan must reciprocate. Letter states text of GOI reference to SC will

---

[1] The reference here is presumably to Nehru's letter of December 22 to the Prime Minister of Pakistan, which is summarized in telegram 1151 from New Delhi, p. 183, and printed in Government of India, *White Paper on Jammu and Kashmir*, pp. 74–75.

be telegraphed SC December 30 and is being communicated UK High Commissioner Delhi.[2] *End summary Nehru message.*

7. Second document is text GOI draft reference to SC which at some length gives account political developments and military operations in Kashmir since September 1947. It sets forth steps taken by GOI to reach amicable solution with GOP and failure of these efforts and then under Article 35 of UN Charter brings situation before SC as danger to international peace and security. Communication concludes with specific request that SC ask GOP:

(*a*) To prevent GOP personnel military and civil participating in or assisting invasion of Jammu and Kashmir state;

(*b*) To call upon other Pakistan nationals to desist from taking any part in fighting;

(*c*) To deny invaders access to and use of its territories for operations; military and other supplies; and all other kinds of aid that might tend to prolong present struggle.

8. Urgency of matter is stressed in communication because military operations in invaded area have in past few days been developing so rapidly that GOI must in self-defence reserve to itself freedom to take at any time when it may become necessary such military action as GOI may consider situation requires.

9. In body communication GOI cites as evidence it has not sought to take advantage Kashmir situation fact GOI has made it plain that once Kashmir has been cleared of invaders and normal conditions restored Kashmiri people would be free to decide their future by recognized democratic method of plebiscite or referendum which, in order to ensure complete impartiality, might be held under international auspices. *End summary GOI communication SC.*

10. Third document is message from Attlee to Nehru sent late December 30 [*29*] in reply Nehru message (Paragraph 2 above). In it Prime Minister makes following points:

11. Much as situation is regretted Attlee agrees "that it now seems that it is only under authority of UN that settlement can be achieved".

12. It is important there should be no delay in handling matter by SC and HMG will do its best through Cadogan [3] to assure very early consideration. "In meantime", Attlee writes, "I beg you as a friend that whatever the provocation and whatever the immediate difficulties you should do nothing that might lead to war and its incalculable consequences on the two dominions".

13. Reverting to Nehru's point in Paragraph 3 above Prime Minister states that he is disturbed by GOI assumption GOI will be within its

---

[2] Sir Terence Allen Shone.
[3] Sir Alexander George Montagu Cadogan, United Kingdom Permanent Representative to the United Nations.

rights in international law if GOI were to move forces into Pakistan in self-defence. Prime Minister doubts whether it is in fact correct juridically and is "afraid that it would be fatal from every other point of view" because in his opinion it would place GOI "definitely in the wrong in eyes of world and I can assure you from our experience on international bodies that it would gravely prejudice India's case before UN if after appealing to SC she were to take unilateral action of this kind".

14. Prime Minister makes point that GOI is being "very optimistic" in concluding that military action would bring about speedy solution because all military history shows how difficult it is to deal with NWF tribes even when operating from secure bases.

15. If peaceful settlement is brought about through SC it will redound greatly to credit GOI which laid matter before SC and will enhance international reputation already achieved by GOI.

16. HMG will do its best on SC to support any measures likely achieve peaceful settlement and if Nehru considers there is anything helpful which UK as sister member of Commonwealth can do to assist in ameliorating situation, Nehru can count on HMG.

17. Message ends with statement that GOP is not being advised of contents of Attlee message summarized above.

18. Carter and Patrick inquired whether, in view serious character GOI–GOP relations USG would be willing to instruct Am Embassy Delhi to approach Nehru immediately and without reference to Nehru-Attlee correspondence tell Nehru that USG is concerned by state GOI–GOP relations as outlined by Bajpai December 24 and that USG hopes GOI will rely upon UN to produce solution and not by any rash action such as invading Pakistan territory not only make UN aid more difficult but also prejudice irretrievably world public opinion against GOI case. In other words would USG at this juncture be willing to counsel Nehru generally along lines of Paragraphs 12, 13 and 15 of Attlee's message? If so, earliest possible action is desirable. Emb officer undertook to put question to Department. Sources also expressed hope USG would, if and when question goes before SC, urge in concert with Cadogan expeditious SC action (see Paragraph 12).

19. Embassy was advised that similar approach with regard to comparable advice to Nehru may be made in near future to Dominions having representation Delhi and possibly to other friendly foreign governments. Which governments is still undecided but Canada was advised by Carter this afternoon.

20. Queried as to what sources thought SC might do about problem, sources said they visualized that first gain would be that GOI–GOP dispute would be placed *sub-judice* SC. This in itself might restrain GOI

to some extent and at early SC meeting SC might formally freeze existing situation thus adding another deterrent. More long range might be steps by SC to investigate GOI complaint simultaneously with making arrangement for eventual Kashmir plebiscite when conditions make this possible. In view sources it is essential that SC couple these two aspects problem because "one hope is that both GOI and GOP have not abandoned plebiscite idea" (see Paragraph 9).

21. Queried regarding attitude GOP since December 23, sources said they understood GOP has been working since that date on draft reply Nehru's letter (see Paragraph 2). Consequently if GOI files complaint with SC today GOP rejoinder should follow soon.

22. Asked whether there was any ground to hope for eleventh hour resolution difficulties without recourse SC sources said they were afraid not. On December 28 Bajpai told Stone [Shone?] terms and date of SC reference were "immutable". GOI feels it may be on verge military disaster in Kashmir which would cause collapse Nehru government. Consequently GOI is desperate. HMG plans no *démarche* other than Attlee message (begins Paragraph 10).

23. Full brief situation is being telegraphed today to Cadogan. CRO is sending Curson next few days to assist Cadogan and other and higher officials may follow.

24. CRO is instructing UK High Commissioners Delhi and Karachi to make available to US missions full information as this question develops. It is suggested missions should keep in touch with High Commissioners.

Sent Department 6668, repeated New Delhi 151, Karachi 54, Moscow by pouch.

GALLMAN

745.45F/12–2947 : Telegram

The Acting Secretary of State to the Embassy in India

SECRET   WASHINGTON, December 31, 1947—6 p. m.
US URGENT   NIACT

817. Reference Bajpai's statement urtel 1162 Dec 29 that "GOI troops might be compelled enter Pakistan" notwithstanding expected reference Kashmir problem by India to UN, please convey urgently in person to FonMin Nehru by formal note following views US Gov't (London's 6668 Dec 30):

"The US as a firm friend of both India and Pakistan regrets that they have been unable by direct negotiation to solve the Kashmir problem. It now appears that the UNSC will soon be seized of this issue. USG will respond fully to its obligations as a member of SC to assist in the attainment of an early and peaceful settlement. We are certain that such a settlement can be achieved only if, during the critical period when this question is under SC consideration, the GOI and GOP will not only refrain from taking any provocative action but will also restrain those irresponsible elements on both sides who are not alive to the grave consequences of their actions. We fear that precipitate action by either Gov't at this stage would seriously jeopardize the international good-will and prestige which it now enjoys.

For your information an identic message is being delivered to the (GOP) (GOI)."

Karachi to present identic Note to GOP FonMin and cable urgently all available info GOP this subject.

Karachi and Delhi requested inform Brit colleagues in confidence of action taken.[1]

LOVETT

---

[1] Telegram 817 was repeated to New York as 624, Karachi as 221, and London as 5405. On January 1, 1948, in telegram 1 from London, Gallman informed the Department that the note to the GOI and GOP was characterized by Dening, Superintending Under-Secretary of the South-East Asia Department of the British Foreign Office, as "admirable and likely to be great help". Gallman added that Carter and Patrick were equally pleased with the Department's prompt and "very helpful" action, Carter remarking that the "US note coming at this critical moment may very possibly save situation" (745.45F/1-148).

AGREEMENT BETWEEN THE UNITED STATES AND INDIA RE-SPECTING FLIGHTS ACROSS INDIA BY MILITARY AIRCRAFT OF THE UNITED STATES, AND FACILITIES ACCORDED SUCH AIRCRAFT

[For text of Agreement, effected by exchange of notes signed at New Delhi, July 1 and 5, 1947, see Department of State Treaties and Other International Acts Series (TIAS) No. 2416, United States Treaties and Other International Agreements (UST), volume 3, (pt. 1), page 568.]

IRELAND

AGREEMENT BETWEEN THE UNITED STATES AND IRELAND RESPECTING AIR TRANSPORT SERVICES

[For text of Agreement amending the agreement of February 3, 1945, effected by exchange of notes signed at Washington, June 2 and 3, 1947, see Department of State Treaties and Other International Acts Series (TIAS) No. 1620, or 61 Stat. (pt. 3) 2872.]

194

UNION OF SOUTH AFRICA

AGREEMENT BETWEEN THE UNITED STATES AND THE UNION OF SOUTH AFRICA RESPECTING A MUTUAL AID SETTLEMENT

[For text of Agreement, effected by exchange of notes signed at Washington, March 21, 1947, see Department of State Treaties and Other International Acts Series (TIAS) No. 1593, or 61 Stat. (pt. 3) 2640. Related documents are in Department of State file 848A.24.]

AGREEMENT BETWEEN THE UNITED STATES AND THE UNION OF SOUTH AFRICA RELATING TO AIR SERVICES BETWEEN THEIR RESPECTIVE TERRITORIES

[For text of Agreement, signed at Cape Town, May 23, 1947, and related Agreement effected by exchange of notes on the same date, see Department of State Treaties and Other International Acts Series (TIAS) No. 1639, or 61 Stat. (pt. 3) 3057.]

195

EUROPE

THE COUNCIL OF FOREIGN MINISTERS

[For documentation regarding the Council of Foreign Ministers in 1947, see volume II.]

196

THE POLITICAL AND ECONOMIC CRISIS IN EUROPE AND THE UNITED STATES RESPONSE (THE MARSHALL PLAN)

I. UNITED STATES CONCERN WITH FOREIGN NEEDS FOR SUBSTANTIAL ECONOMIC AID: THE EUROPEAN CRISIS AND SECRETARY OF STATE MARSHALL'S SPEECH AT HARVARD (MARCH–JUNE)

SWNCC[1] Files

The Acting Secretary of State to the Secretary of War (Patterson)[2]

SECRET [WASHINGTON,] 5 March 1947.

MY DEAR MR. SECRETARY: Subsequent to our meeting Wednesday morning, February 25 [*26*], 1947, President Truman approved in principle the measures which you endorsed for immediate aid to Greece and Turkey as set forth in the memorandum entitled 'Position and Recommendations of the Department of State Regarding Immediate Aid to Greece and Turkey'.[3] Congressional leaders have been informed of the nature of the problem and the urgency of the need for our assistance to these countries. They also approve in principle the general program for aid.

In the course of our discussions on the Greek and Turkish problem, frequent reference was made to the fact that this is only part of a much larger problem growing out of the change in Great Britain's strength and other circumstances not directly related to this development. I believe it important and urgent that study be given by our most competent officers to situations elsewhere in the world which may require analogous financial, technical and military aid on our part.

I have asked Assistant Secretary Hilldring as Chairman of the State–War–Navy Coordinating Committee to direct the attention of that committee to this important problem and, in consultation with the

---

[1] State–War–Navy Coordinating Committee.
[2] Attached as Enclosure "B" to SWNCC document SWN–5231, March 18, 1947.
[3] For documentation regarding this subject, see vol. v, pp. 1 ff.

Treasury Department, undertake a thorough study to be submitted to me or Secretary Marshall as soon as possible.[4]

Sincerely yours,   [DEAN ACHESON]

---

[4] The State–War–Navy Coordinating Committee, at its 55th Meeting on March 11, 1947, agreed to appoint an *ad hoc* Committee to study and report on the problems incident to possible requests which might be made to the United States by foreign governments for substantial economic, financial or technical assistance, or for military equipment. Mr. W. A. Eddy, Department of State, Brig. Gen. George A. Lincoln, War Department, and Rear Adm. E. T. Wooldridge, Navy Department, were designated by their respective departments to serve on this committee. Document SWN–5231 was circulated by the SWNCC Secretariat to the *ad hoc* Committee.

SWNCC Files

Memorandum by the State Department Member, State–War–Navy Coordinating Committee (Hilldring)[1]

SECRET   [WASHINGTON,] 17 March 1947.

1. The Secretaries of the State, War, and Navy Departments desire that the SWNCC give immediate attention to the problems incident to possible requests which may be made to the United States by foreign governments for substantial economic, financial, or technical assistance, or for military equipment. This study and report should take into account decisions already made and action already taken or under way with respect to Greece and Turkey. In preparing its report upon the problems enumerated below, it is desired that the Committee include recommendations, within the scope of the President's message to Congress, concerning further policies and procedures necessary to the accomplishment of the United States program in Greece and Turkey.[2]

2. The study and report should be undertaken by a Special SWNCC Subcommittee consisting of competent officers from each of the three Departments, and in consultation with the Treasury Department. The more specific questions which should be considered and concerning which a report is desired are the following:

a. What are the countries to which, within the next few months, we may find it necessary to give analogous financial, technical and military aid?

---

[1] Attached as Enclosure "A" to SWNCC document SWN–5231, March 18, 1947, and entitled "Report by the State–War–Navy Coordinating Committee Regarding the Policies, Procedures and Costs of Assistance by the United States to Foreign Countries."

[2] For text of President Truman's message, see *Public Papers of the Presidents of the United States: Harry S. Truman, January 1 to December 31, 1947* (Washington, Government Printing Office, 1963), p. 176, or Department of State *Bulletin*, March 23, 1947, p. 534.

b. What are the relevant considerations of United States national security and interest which should govern the decision in the case of each country?

c. In the light of such considerations, what, in the case of each country, should be the character of such assistance? What would such assistance involve in the reasonably foreseeable future in terms of financial, economic, supply and technical demands upon our resources?

d. What arrangements should be made with foreign Governments in connection with the grant of assistance to assure to the maximum practicable extent the accomplishment of our objectives in granting such assistance?

e. What would be the effect upon each country concerned and upon our general foreign policy and security interests in the event that we refuse assistance or in the event of failure of any program undertaken?

3. The Department of State has designated Mr. William Eddy as the State member of the Special SWNCC Subcommittee. The Report of the Subcommittee should be made to SWNCC as a matter of urgency.[3]

---

[3] Within the Department of State, a Committee on Extension of U.S. Aid to Foreign Governments, with Mr. Eddy as chairman, was set up at the direction of Acting Secretary Acheson as a mechanism for formulating the Department's position with respect to the work of the *ad hoc* committee which had been established on March 11, 1947. The minutes of the committee are in Lot 122.

800.51/4–1047

Memorandum by Mr. Sherman S. Sheppard of the Bureau of the Budget to the Director of the Bureau (Webb)[1]

SECRET   [WASHINGTON,] April 7, 1947.

Subject: U. S. Program for Foreign Assistance

CURRENT AND PROPOSED PROGRAMS

1. At the present time there are pending before the Congress programs totalling $1.85 billion for foreign relief, rehabilitation and reconstruction: post-UNRRA relief ($350,000,000), proposed aid to Greece and Turkey ($400,000,000), a 1947 supplemental and 1948 appropriation for government and relief in occupied areas ($1,025,-000,000), and the International Refugee Organization ($75,000,000).

2. In addition, we have received informally a copy of a proposed three-year grant-in-aid program for Korea of $540 million. We have been informed that State is preparing a justification for a $40 million

---

[1] Transmitted under cover of a letter from Mr. Webb to Under Secretary of State Acheson, April 10, not printed.

contribution to the International Children's Fund. The Bureau has received for clearance a Navy program for additional aid to China in the form of ships and maritime services. There have been suggestions that additional aid to Austria in 1948, financial aid in connection with Palestine, and perhaps an additional loan to France are also contemplated.

BUDGETARY AND ADMINISTRATIVE IMPLICATIONS

3. There are increasing indications of Congressional desires to "see the whole picture at once". Certainly from the standpoint of the President's overall budgetary and international programs each succeeding proposal cannot be considered adequately unless total proposed commitments can be estimated. The implications for the Federal budget are obvious; in addition, these proposals will require either modifications in the administrative structure of existing departments, or the creation of new organizational units both here and abroad.

NEEDED INFORMATION

4. We need to obtain some idea of the overall pattern of U. S. foreign assistance, as well as the State Department's best prediction of whether it does or does not anticipate that it will propose (a) U. S. participation in the Children's Fund, (b) the use for China of funds earmarked for Export-Import Bank loans to it, (c) further aid for Austria in 1948, (d) financial requirements in connection with Palestine, and (e) further loans to France or other countries. It would likewise be helpful to know whether the Department contemplates any further extensions of existing aid programs beyond those thus far announced.

PRIORITIES

5. The number and size of the foreign assistance proposals now before the Congress, plus those in contemplation, make it desirable to ascertain the Department's judgment as to the legislative priority to be assigned to each item in the overall pattern; otherwise, legislative and budgetary "credit" may be exhausted by the President before highest priority needs are met.

6. There is attached a tabulation of the Government's present and thus far proposed program of foreign assistance arranged according to the apparent foreign policy objectives to be attained.

[Attachment]

PRESENT AND PROPOSED U.S. PROGRAMS FOR FOREIGN ASSISTANCE

Objective	Program	Authorized by Existing Legislation or Pending Before Congress	Probable Future Programs
1. To provide relief to sustain life and prevent economic and physical retrogression (appears to apply world-wide)	Post-UNRRA	X	?
	Occupied Areas	X	X
	Other	—	?
2. To rehabilitate national economies to the level of self-sufficiency for minimum needs. (Appears to be limited to countries U.S. has direct and major political interest)	Occupied Areas	X	X
	Greek Civilian Aid	X	?
	Korean Grant-in-Aid	—	?
	Additional Austrian Aid, 1948	—	?
	Other	—	?
3. To assist in rehabilitation and further development of national economies above the level of self-sufficiency for minimum needs (appears to apply world-wide)	British Loan	X	?
	Export-Import Bank Loans	X	?
	International Bank Participation	X	—
	Surplus Property Transfers	X	—
	Maritime Ship Transfers	X	—
	Philippine Aid	X	?
	Other	—	?
4. To achieve stable economic conditions (applies world-wide)	International Monetary Fund Participation	X	?
	Other	—	?
5. To provide military assistance to enable governments to resist aggression	Greek-Turkish military aid	X	?
	Military surplus property transfers	X	?
	Other	—	—
6. To provide aid to special categories of people without regard to nationality	Children's Fund Participation	X	?
	International Refugee Organization Participation	—	?
	Financial requirements in connection with Palestine	X	?
	Other	—	?

800.51/4–1047

Memorandum by Mr. C. Tyler Wood, Special Assistant to the Assistant Secretary of State for Economic Affairs (Thorp), to the Under Secretary of State (Acheson)

TOP SECRET   WASHINGTON, April 17, 1947.

A. A reply to the questions raised in the third paragraph of the memorandum attached to Mr. Webb's letter of April 10, 1947 (attached hereto) may be made along the lines indicated below.[1]

1. *United States Participation in the International Children's Fund*

The Department's justification for a $40 million contribution to the International Children's Fund will be sent to the Bureau of the Budget by April 18.

2. *The Use for China of Funds Earmarked in Export-Import Bank*

It is anticipated that, if developments in China are regarded as satisfactory in accordance with the President's statements of December 15, 1945 and December 18, 1946, the Department will support consideration of Chinese credit applications for well defined projects which show possibilities of assisting in an early improvement of China's foreign exchange position. It is unlikely that credits for such projects during fiscal 1948 would represent more than a small fraction of the $500 million earmarked by the Export-Import Bank for possible credits to China.

3. *Further Aid for Austria in fiscal 1948*

The pending post-UNRRA relief appropriation together with the deficiency appropriation for occupied areas and a possible Export-Import Bank loan would probably be adequate to cover Austria's anticipated balance of payments deficit in calendar 1947. During the last half of fiscal 1948, it may be necessary to obtain a further appropriation; whether this will be required depends on (a) whether funds for this period can be made available from the post-UNRRA appropriation, and (b) whether a substantial Eximbank credit on suitable terms can be obtained for Austria.

For fiscal 1949 it is anticipated that a further appropriation will be needed.

4. *Financial Requirements in Connection with Palestine*

No program of financial assistance to Palestine is at present under consideration in the Department. It is anticipated that the Special Session of the General Assembly of the United Nations to be held be-

---

[1] Reference is to lettered items in numbered paragraph 4 in the memorandum of April 7, *supra*. Letter of April 10 not printed.

ginning April 28, 1947 to consider the Palestine problem will set up a committee to report to the next regular General Assemby of the United Nations in September 1947. Whether any United Nations decisions in this respect will result in any financial requirements for Palestine which the United States would be expected to meet can not be determined at present.

5. *Further Loans to France or Other Countries*

I do not assume that you will choose to disclose to Mr. Webb that a Special *Ad Hoc* Committee of SWNCC is now considering whether there are other countries for which aid programs analogous to the Greek–Turkish program may have to be initiated during the next few months. This Committee is now drafting an interim report.[2] While I do not want to anticipate its findings or the outcome of their consideration by SWNCC, I understand the possibility of a new aid program for Italy and possibly Hungary and Austria is being seriously considered at the working level. Iran, also in this category, will not require special assistance beyond present programs (surplus credit and World Bank loan).

As far as France specifically is concerned, it is at present anticipated that existing financial institutions, particularly the International Bank, will be able to take care of France's financial needs through fiscal 1948. This assumes that the Bank will grant France the full $500 million which she has requested before the end of calendar 1947 or early 1948. It also assumes that adequate coal supplies will be available to France and that control of inflation in France can be maintained. If adverse conditions turn out to belie this latter assumption France may need further financial assistance in fiscal 1948 which would not be likely to be forthcoming from the International Bank or the Export-Import Bank. (Further, there are military and political considerations which have led the SWNCC working group on France to classify it as a critical area which may need assistance in the next several months.)

The financial needs of other countries through fiscal 1948 can probably be met from existing commitments, programs or lending institutions, to the extent that it is now considered in the United States interest to meet such needs.

While it would probably not be desirable at this stage to mention the work now going on in SWNCC, I should think the general outlines of the above could be indicated to Mr. Webb.

I have not attempted to indicate what I think is implicit in Mr. Webb's query regarding priorities, namely how would we reallocate any cut in an "overall program" among the several programs now pending.

---

[2] *Infra.*

B. The fourth [*fifth*] paragraph of the memorandum attached to Mr. Webb's letter, requests the Department's judgment as to the legislative priority to be assigned to each item in the overall pattern. The Department has, of course, indicated that urgent action is required on the Greek–Turkish Aid Bill. Almost equally pressing for economic and political reasons is the post-UNRRA Bill. Other legislation now pending has less priority but action is needed before the beginning of fiscal 1948.

SWNCC Files: Series 360

Report of the Special "Ad Hoc" Committee of the State–War–Navy Coordinating Committee

TOP SECRET	[WASHINGTON,] April 21, 1947.

References:	a. SWN–5231, March 20, 1947
	b. SWN–5255, March 21, 1947
	c. SWNCC 358/d, March 31, 1947 [1]

1. Attached hereto is the report of the Special *Ad Hoc* Committee of SWNCC in response to the reference memoranda, on policies, procedures and costs of assistance by the U.S. to foreign countries.

2. The Special *Ad Hoc* Committee states that this interim report, which is highly tentative in nature, has been prepared from information presently at hand and a hasty analysis of such information. It is intended to provide, in a single document, a survey of the present world-wide situation, and to indicate countries to which the U.S., for its own security and national interests may find it desirable to extend aid in the next few months. The preparation of a fuller report, containing more thorough analysis and refinements lacking in this interim report, has been initiated, with completion date estimated as mid-July, 1947.

3. This paper contains, in the first ten pages, (1) the conclusions reached by the committee, (2) a brief of assistance measures which may prove desirable, and (3) a statement of principles and policies pertaining to aid to foreign countries. The State–War–Navy Coordinating Committee is asked to *approve in principle* the contents of these ten pages as a basis for planning. The remainder of the paper consists of briefs based on the reports which were prepared by working sub-

---

[1] Enclosures "A" and "B" to SWN 5231 are printed on pages 197 and 198; the other reference memoranda are not printed.

committees for use of the Special *Ad Hoc* Committee.[2] The SWNCC is asked to *note* these briefs which are included in this paper, since it is considered they will be of help in guiding planning agencies in the three departments.

4. The Special *Ad Hoc* Committee does not believe that it has been able to adequately fulfill the requirements of SWN–5231 of March 20, 1947 as it relates to China. It has been unable to reach an agreement on a program for this country.

The *Ad Hoc* Committee recommends that SWNCC direct the Far Eastern Subcommittee to submit a more conclusive report on China as a matter of priority when the JCS study now being formulated is made available to the State–War–Navy Coordinating Committee for its consideration.

5. Attention is invited to the necessity for extraordinary security measures in view of the nature of the material contained in this report.

Enclosure

POLICIES, PROCEDURES AND COSTS OF ASSISTANCE BY THE UNITED STATES TO FOREIGN COUNTRIES [3]

THE PROBLEM

1. To prepare a broad determination of the measures which might be undertaken, in implementation of U.S. foreign policy, for the extension of aid, including money, food, military equipment and other forms of assistance, to foreign nations by the U.S., and to make recommendations as to the allocation and employment of the means likely to be available.

FACTS BEARING ON THE PROBLEM

2. See Appendix "A".

DISCUSSION

3. See Appendix "B".

CONCLUSIONS

4. It is concluded that:

a. A planned program of assistance to foreign countries should enable the U.S. to take positive, forehanded, and preventative action in

[2] The minutes of the Committee on the Extension of U.S. Aid to Foreign Governments describe the liaison effected by the Department of State and by working groups of other Departments and of SWNCC in the preparation of the report. Department of State action was completed on April 15, when the committee reached final agreement as to a priority listing of countries to be considered for U.S. assistance. This list was substantially the same as that incorporated into the "Main Report", *infra*, except that in the latter Korea was included among the highest priority group.

[3] This enclosure has been described as the "Main Report".

the matter of promotion of U.S. national interests by extending assistance under a system of priorities where it will do the most good from the standpoint of promoting U.S. security and other national interests.

b. Needs for such assistance will considerably exceed currently estimated availabilities. In order that aid as extended may be of maximum usefulness, it is necessary that the provision of U.S. aid to foreign countries should be carried out in accordance with a well-considered comprehensive world-wide program, developed in the maximum reasonable amount of detail.

c. The nations of the world which the United States may find it necessary and desirable to aid in the next few months are, in presently estimated order of the urgency of their need in the light of U.S. interest:

(1) Greece
(2) Turkey
(3) Iran–Italy   .
(4) Korea
(5) France (for political and not economic reasons)
(6) Austria (assuming conclusion of the treaty)
(7) Hungary

d. In these countries, concentrated U.S. programs of aid may be required. As appropriate (see Appendix "A"), these should include financial aid, economic aid, military aid, political support, and vigorous programs of information.

e. In the near future, China will need an undetermined amount of post UNRRA aid, credits for purchase of ships from the Maritime Commission, and a carefully conceived information program. As to additional aid, there is a divergence of view between the State Department on the one hand and the War and Navy Departments on the other, which is indicated in Appendix "A", Annex "E", Attachment II. A supplementary report with appropriate corrigendums to this paper will be submitted as a matter of priority when the conclusions of the JCS on the problem are made available to SWNCC for integration with the other factors involved.

f. In the following countries no urgent requirement for extension of U.S. aid or support over and above that now contemplated exists, although substantial requirements may develop at a later date:

(1) Great Britain
(2) Belgium and Luxembourg
(3) Netherlands–NEI
(4) The Philippines
(5) Portugal
(6) Czechoslovakia
(7) Poland

g. The situation of other countries is not so urgent as to warrant examination in this report.

h. In addition to the provision of military equipment and supplies to countries where urgent need exists, a well considered program of military collaboration, including one or more of (*a*) the provision of U.S. military equipment supplies, (*b*) the maintenance of military missions, and (*c*) the training of key foreign military personnel, should be continued or initiated for selected countries indicated at the end of this paragraph. Authorizing legislation now lacking should be submitted and supported. Convincing deliveries under all approved programs should be made thereafter without delay. Plans for the effective sustaining of the program from new manufacture should be developed. General priorities on a long-term basis are:

(1) Western Hemisphere ((a) Canada, (b) Latin America and the Philippines)
(2) Near and Middle East-Europe
(3) Far East (less Philippines)

Priorities for piece-meal acts of assistance, perhaps with a psychological objective, will vary from the foregoing. Programs now exist in one form or another not necessarily in order of priority for

(1) Canada
(2) The Philippines
(3) Latin American Republics
(4) Iran
(5) Italy
(6) China
(7) Greece and Turkey

i. In 1947 the U.S. will probably export to the rest of the world $7.5 billion more goods and services than it imports. The outflow of dollars to finance this deficit will probably include $4.8 billion financed by the U.S. Government in loans, grants, and expenditures in the occupied areas. The current volume of U.S. financing, and particularly its distribution between countries, is not adequate to the full accomplishment of world economic stability, the type of world trading system the U.S. seeks, or U.S. political objectives in several countries.

j. World-wide shortages and maldistribution will exist in the year ending 30 June 1948 in basic commodities, including grains, coal, nitrogenous fertilizer, steel, capital equipment. Legislation relating to materials priorities, domestic transportation, export controls, and shipping will be required in order to achieve a successful program for those exports which are available. Concurrently, economic policy must aim at the reintegration of the economies of critical countries into regional and world trading and production systems.

RECOMMENDATIONS

5. It is recommended that:

a. The above conclusions and interim program, relating to U.S. assistance to foreign nations, contained in Sections I and II of Appendix "A" be approved in principle for planning purposes as tentative, interim guidance for actions by the State, War and Navy Departments, subject to comment on this report from the military point of view by the Joint Chiefs of Staff and with the understanding that determination to implement each of the programs proposed for planning purposes is a matter for separate decision.

b. Annexes "A" to "E", inclusive, of Appendix "A" and Appendix "B" be noted as being the detailed exposition supporting the conclusions and Sections I and II of the Appendix.

c. This report be forwarded to the JCS with a request for comment from the military point of view, as a matter of urgency.

Appendix "A"

[Here follows Section I of Appendix A, a tabular summary of assistance measures to be undertaken in an interim program.]

SECTION II

POLICIES AND PRINCIPLES FOR EXTENSION OF U.S. AID TO FOREIGN NATIONS

PREAMBLE

It is taken to be the policy of the United States:

a. To support economic stability and orderly political processes throughout the world and oppose the spread of chaos and extremism.

b. To reduce or to prevent the growth or advancement of national or international power which constitutes a substantial threat to U.S. security and well-being and to oppose programs of coercion and infiltration, especially when effected by the use of armed minorities.

c. To orient foreign nations toward the U.S., toward support of the U.N. and toward procedures in international relations which are consistent with the purpose of the U.N.

A. *Objectives of the Aid Program*

1. To take positive, forehanded and preventative action in the matter of promotion of U.S. interests through assistance to foreign nations. By timely provision of moderate amounts of assistance to avoid the development of crises which will demand urgent, much larger expenditures.

2. To apply assistance, under a system of priorities, where it will do the most good from the standpoint of promoting U.S. security and national interest. Specifically, to give highest priority to the nations or areas which are vital to our national security and national interest.

B. *Consideration of the National Security and Interests of the U.S.*

1. It is essential in the national interest that the U.S. use its best efforts to insure that other nations, as well as ourselves, be able to work out a national life free from all forms of coercion.

2. The security of the U.S., and the foundations of international peace, are undermined whenever a totalitarian regime is imposed upon a free people by direct or indirect aggression.

3. For reasons of our national security and of vital national interests, our country should support free peoples who are resisting attempted subjugation, whether by armed minorities or by outside pressures.

4. The security of the United States is concerned not only with the dangers which threaten a free country, but also with the effect which those dangers may have on other countries. If the U.S. supports a freedom-loving people whose independence is threatened, other nations may be stiffened in their determination to remain free; conversely, if the U.S. neglects to support such a free people, other nations may be profoundly dismayed and may lose faith in the leadership of the U.S.

5. In helping free and independent nations to retain their freedom the U.S. will be giving support to the principles of the charter of the United Nations.

6. It is important to maintain in friendly hands areas which contain or protect sources of metals, oil and other national resources, which contain strategic objectives, or areas strategically located, which contain a substantial industrial potential, which possess manpower and organized military forces in important quantities, or which for political or psychological reasons enable the U.S. to exert a greater influence for world stability, security and peace.

7. It is desirable that military collaboration between the U.S. and foreign nations important to U.S. security be continued and extended.

[Here follows discussion of conditions to be attached for extension of aid, particularly that there be "a reasonable chance" for success, and that arrangements be made to maintain "adequate measures of supervision and control of the expenditures of U.S. funds, and of the distribution of U.S. goods and equipment, to insure that they are devoted to the purpose for which they have been approved". There is also a brief consideration of "public information aspects".]

Annex "A" to Appendix "A"
GENERAL ECONOMIC PROGRAM

Reference: Memorandum of Request to Working Group on Economic Aid (Food and Finance) dated March 21, 1947.

1. The war and the political changes consequent thereto destroyed in substantial part the former capacity of the countries of Europe to meet their manufacturing and agricultural needs through the normal operations of closely integrated economies. As a result the United States became for practical purposes the only country in the world capable of tiding Europe and other deficit areas over the period of reconstruction.

U. S. RESOURCES AVAILABLE FOR FOREIGN FINANCING

2. In 1947, the United States will export to the rest of the world approximately $16.2 billion of goods and services, taking into considera-

tion existing and probable foreign financial commitments. The United States will import in 1947 only about $8.7 billion of goods and services. In 1947 the economy of the United States will thus be supplying to the world $7.5 billion of goods and services more than it receives.

3. Only about $450 million of this $7.5 billion will be financed by private long-term loans and by private and government short-term credits. Most of the balance will be financed by the United States Government ($4.8 billion of which approximately $500 million is the cost of U.S. Army financing of occupied areas) and out of cash and gold holdings of foreign buyers ($1.2 billion). Disbursements by the International Bank during 1947 will provide about $300 million, and private remittances about $750 million.

4. The volume of United States Government foreign financing will, under present programs and policies,[4] taper off rapidly during the latter part of 1948 and 1949. Similarly, the ability of foreign purchasers to finance U.S. exports out of gold and dollar holdings will diminish as these reserves are drawn down. The volume of private remittances may also be expected to decline.

5. These factors will be offset only in small part by an increase in International Bank financing and possibly by some net increase in private long and short term loans and credits, and by an increase in United States imports.

6. The conclusion is inescapable that, under present programs and policies, the world will not be able to continue to buy United States exports at the 1946–47 rate beyond another 12–18 months.

7. The great weight of evidence indicates that even the current volume of United States foreign financing, and particularly its distribution between countries, is not adequate to the accomplishment either of world economic stability and the type of world trading system which is the object of our trade policy, or of our political objectives in several critical countries. Our political interests abroad, particularly in Italy, Austria and Hungary have suffered and will continue to suffer because existing financial institutions and policies tend to restrict present U.S. financial aid very largely to countries which are regarded as good credit risks.

8. Other than the United States, there are now no major sources of credits or supplies to which the needy countries can turn to meet the bulk of their balance of trade deficits and reconstruction and development needs over the next few years.

9. The President's Council of Economic Advisers has indicated that a slight business recession may be anticipated sometime within the next twelve months. A substantial decline in the United States export

---

[4] For documentation regarding U.S. foreign loan policy in the immediate postwar period, see *Foreign Relations*, 1946, volume I.

surplus would have a depressing effect on business activity and employment in the United States. The net effect would depend on the direction and strength of other economic forces, but, if the export decline happened to coincide with weakness in the domestic economy, the effect on production, prices and employment might be most serious.

10. The implications of these preliminary conclusions are most serious both for world recovery and stability and possibly for employment and business activity in the United States.

U.S. EXPORT PROGRAMS FOR CRITICAL COMMODITIES

11. As important to the democracies of the world as the problem of financing essential exports from the U.S. is the problem of insuring that maximum supplies of critical commodities are made available for export and properly distributed. War-time disruption of the world economy was so vast that severe shortages of a number of vital commodities persist. Recovery of production is frequently slow and tight situations will continue. The burden of meeting these shortages falls primarily on the strongest economy in the world—the U.S.

12. If U.S. financing is to achieve its purpose of strengthening the economies of friendly countries, this Government must maintain such controls as are necessary to insure that a limited number of essential commodities can be procured and shipped abroad to appropriate destinations.

These vital commodities fall into three main groups:

Food

13. In the year ending June 30, 1948, the world will continue to face shortages of bread grains, fats and oils, proteins and sugar.[5] In the case of bread grains, the most important single item, import requirements are estimated at 37 million metric tons wheat equivalent and exportable supplies at 28 million tons, including 11.2 million tons from the U.S., leaving a deficit of 9,000,000 tons. This means that the importing countries face another year in which their requirements, which are based in most cases on substandard feeding levels, cannot be met by a substantial margin. The U.S. export figure is based on the assumption of normal and non-controlled grain exports.

14. The importance of the U.S. in the world food picture is apparent from the fact that it is expected to supply almost half of the total exportable supplies of bread grains during the next crop year.

15. U.S. food exports, particularly of bread grains, must be increased to the maximum if the program of economic assistance abroad is to be successfully fulfilled. The maximum tonnage of grain which

---

[5] For documentation on U.S. policy regarding the world food crisis in 1946, see *Foreign Relations*, 1946, vol. I, pp. 1439 ff.

can be moved in 1947–48 over our internal transportation system to ports is approximately 15 million tons. According to present forecasts, the 1947 grain crop should be large enough to permit this volume of exports without any curtailment of domestic consumption.

16. In order to insure that U.S. exports in 1947–48 reach the 15 million ton maximum it will be necessary (a) to commit ourselves firmly to this export goal at an early date; and (b) to direct this amount of grain into export channels by continuing throughout the crop year the domestic controls outlined below. For this purpose continuation of some government procurement and efficient use of transportation will, of course, be essential.

17. Maximum U.S. efforts would reduce the 1947–48 deficit of bread grains from 9 million tons to between 5 and 6 million tons. This additional 4–5 million tons of grain would greatly increase the chances for success of our program for aid to foreign countries. This is particularly true in the critical countries of Western Europe. Unless we can assure maximum U.S. exports, we may face a situation next spring similar to the one which confronts us now, in which the problem is to determine which critical country will have to bear the brunt of inadequate supplies and ration cuts.

18. At the present time we are programming our grain exports in close collaboration with the International Emergency Food Council. This collaboration should continue since the major influences in the IEFC, in addition to our own, are exerted by areas for which we have great concern. The IEFC consequently provides a convenient forum for consulting countries with whom we would collaborate in any case and obtaining multilateral agreement, rather than unilateral decision, on our allocations.

Coal

19. Europe is the critical coal deficiency area of the world. The gap between 1947 requirements and availabilities for Europe will be at least 36 million metric tons. The major European coal importing countries are France, Italy, Belgium, Denmark, the Netherlands, Sweden and Norway—all countries of special interest to the U.S. These countries will obtain in 1947 about 40% of their probable imports from other European countries and the remainder from the United States.

20. It is essential to the progress of European recovery that United States coal exports to Europe should continue at a maximum rate throughout 1947 and for a considerable period thereafter.

21. Under present conditions, exports of U.S. coal entail a heavy drain upon European dollar resources. Ocean freight represents over half the cost of each ton of United States coal delivered at European

ports. A coordinated program to increase European coal production should, therefore, receive the highest priority.

22. We should continue to support the principle of international allocation in accordance with need in the distribution of available coal supply. The European Coal Organization has performed a useful function in this respect which should be continued by the Economic Commission for Europe.

Other Critical Commodities

Nitrogenous Fertilizer

23. The world faces an acute shortage of this essential commodity in the coming crop year. U.S. demand has reached unprecedented levels as a result of high farm income and production. Europe and the Far East have heavy requirements due to war-time soil depletion and the shortage of livestock. In order to secure exports from the U.S. controls will be required.

Steel

24. No adequate data are available to give an accurate picture of the world steel position. It seems clear, however, that for several years to come a number of countries, including several in Europe formerly dependent on Germany, will require substantial imports. The European steel shortage which restricts the progress of reconstruction is in part caused by the coal shortage.

25. The American mills simply cannot supply both the huge domestic demand and any substantial share of the export demands. They prefer Latin American and other markets where the long-range prospects are better than in European markets. An effort to meet all foreign requirements would entail restrictions on the domestic use of steel. Unless such restrictions can be imposed, the rate of European reconstruction will be substantially retarded.

Capital Equipment

26. A number of items of capital equipment, such as tractors, construction equipment, freight wagons, and mining machinery are tight. The import requirements of the critical countries are large and the U.S. is the only current source of exports. If domestic demand continues strong, some form of priorities to meet the critical export programs will be essential.

LEGISLATIVE ACTION REQUIRED

27. Successful export programs for food, coal, steel and capital equipment cannot be achieved without the following legislative action:

a. The first step is to insure equitable distribution of supplies as between the domestic economy and foreign economies. This requires extension of allocation powers with respect to a limited list of commodities certified by the Secretaries of State and Commerce as critical to the foreign economic policy of the U.S. Powers to assign priorities directly to producing firms will be necessary for a still more restricted group of items. Both of these powers now expire on June 30, 1947. Recommended legislative action along these lines is now being prepared in the White House.

b. Continuation of export controls is required in order to channel exportable supplies to proper countries and to cut down undesired foreign demand in the domestic market. These controls now expire on June 30, 1947. The President has recommended this legislation to the Congress in his message of March 18, 1947.

c. Finally extension of powers to assign priorities on transportation, which also expire on June 30, 1947, are needed. These powers are essential to insure efficient use of transportation facilities, particularly freight cars. Without them it would be difficult to move bulky export commodities such as coal and grain in the required quantities. The necessary legislation is being prepared in the White House.

d. Legislative action on shipping is also required, as indicated in the following section.

Ocean Shipping

28. To assure the success of our export programs which include tremendous quantities of bulky items such as coal and grain, the following legislative action is required to enable the Maritime Commission to insure maximum availability and efficient use of shipping:

a. Extension of authority of Maritime Commission to operate government-owned vessels. This authority now expires on June 30, 1947.

b. Extension of Maritime Commission authority to apply revenues from operation of ships for government account to meet expenses of operation, including expenses of withdrawing ships from the reserve fleet. This authority also expires June 30, 1947.

c. Extension of Maritime Commission authority to sell or charter war-built vessels under the Merchant Ship Sales Act of 1946. This authority expires December 31, 1947.

29. Recommended legislation along the above lines is now being prepared by the Maritime Commission. Failure to obtain this legislative action would result in a disastrous curtailment of available supplies of U.S. shipping and inability to fulfill essential export goals. For example, it would be necessary to decrease the size of the U.S. tanker fleet by about 230 tankers which would dry up a major portion of the world's present flow of oil.

ECONOMIC INTERDEPENDENCE OF CRITICAL COUNTRIES

30. The cost and duration of United States economic assistance are directly dependent upon the successful integration and coordination of the economic programs in the critical countries both with each other

and with similar programs in countries not receiving special United States aid.

31. Furthermore, the reintegration of these countries into healthy regional and world trading and production systems will accelerate their recovery and attainment of the ability to eventually enable them to finance their import needs, thus permitting the strain on the United States to be lifted.

32. Special attention must be given to the coordination of economic policy in occupied areas, particularly Germany and Japan, with general economic objectives in Europe and the Far East.

33. The interdependence of the various national economies is so great, particularly in Europe, that economic recovery of western-oriented areas will require a substantial increase in trade with Soviet-dominated areas, provided such trade can be arranged on terms compatible with the economic and political independence of western-oriented areas.

NEEDS OF THE OCCUPIED AREAS

34. The occupied areas of bi-zonal Germany, Japan and Korea deserve special consideration for the fiscal year 1948. They will require an estimated $1.4 billion of imports for that period, including foodstuffs, petroleum products and raw materials, principally for textile manufacturing. Not all of this sum will be a drain on American financial resources; however, the requirements for materials will be competitive with those of the countries to be given economic aid. The requirements of the occupied areas, to the extent that they are necessary to prevent disease and unrest, represent an urgent demand on world supplies.

35. The following estimated requirements in metric tons and dollar value, and covering the fiscal year 1948 are noteworthy:

	Metric tons	Dollars
Minimum food imports, US and British Zones of Germany	4, 030, 000	$510, 000, 000
Minimum food imports, Japan	1, 685, 000	255, 000, 000
Minimum total imports, US and British Zones of Germany		666, 000, 000
Minimum total imports, Japan		576, 000, 000
US appropriated funds required, Germany		283, 000, 000
US appropriated funds required, Japan		226, 500, 000

36. It should be noted in the case of bi-zonal Germany that the data are for the combined US and UK occupation zones; financing of these requirements is a joint and equal US–UK responsibility.

[Here follow Annexes "B" through "E" of Appendix "A"; Annex "B—General Military Aid Program"—is scheduled for inclusion in volume I. Detailed examinations of aid needs on a country and area basis in Europe, the Near East, and the Middle East are included in Annexes "C", "D", and "E", respectively, none printed.]

Appendix "B"

DISCUSSION

1. The determination of tangible means of assistance to be provided by the U.S. in implementation of its foreign policy requires that U.S. interests, in terms of its present and future security and well-being, be carefully established and considered. These interests were recently crystallized in the statement of general U.S. foreign policy enunciated by the President in connection with the situation in Greece and Turkey. The purpose of this study is to report on problems incident to foreign needs or demands for substantial U.S. assistance, and to make certain that commitments undertaken are consistent with U.S. interests and capabilities.

2. In considering this problem it is first in order to define the aid involved. This report is concerned with goods and services, available to the countries in question, and with the actions of the U.S. government relating thereto. The role of the U.S. government regarding these goods and services extends to positive measures of support, or to restrictions, beyond those normal in free international trade and exchange. This aid falls into the following main categories:

    a. Material resources—divided broadly into (1) military equipment and (2) non-military items such as food, machinery, clothing, etc.

    b. Money, in the form of grants, loans, or expenditures.

    c. Services, including advice and technical and administrative assistance.

    d. Political support, in the form of backing, encouragement and good offices in international affairs and organizations. (This category of aid is not considered further in this interim report.)

    e. Dissemination of information of [by] appropriate means.

3. U.S. security is the fundamental interest to be served by U.S. aid to foreign nations. National security can be maintained most effectively through the rebuilding of a stable peaceful world, in which each nation respects the sovereignty, integrity and way of life of the others in a friendly manner. This situation can best be attained through effective implementation of the charter of the United Nations, coupled with early satisfactory settlement of certain major world problems, which may be settled partially or wholly outside of the structure of the UN,

such as peace treaties with Germany and Japan. However, the UN charter has yet to be implemented with full effectiveness. A realistic appraisal of the world situation shows that there exist many problems which adversely affect the security interests of the U.S. and which may, particularly at their inception, be outside the purview of the UN.

4. Such problems form the basis from which U.S. aid programs should be determined. In certain countries economic weaknesses exist which may give rise to instability and subsequently to political shifts which adversely affect the security of the U.S. They include subversive and "boring from within" tactics or the threat of overwhelming force, all of which are difficult and sometimes impossible to combat under the United Nations Charter, particularly at its present stage of implementation. The United States has need of friends in the world today and particularly needs to take care that other nations do not pass under the influence of any potentially hostile nation. There are some countries which are at present in very close balance and it is to our advantage to strengthen their resolution to remain independent. As to the countries hostile to the U.S. every opportunity for assisting any of them to regain an independent national life should be reviewed to determine whether the probabilities of success and cost of undertaking the effort warrant any expenditure of resources by the U.S.

5. It should be noted that the results to be achieved by our program of aid may extend well beyond the countries being aided. There is a "bandwagon" quality attaching to the Communist movement, and efforts at infiltration and minority domination, which is vulnerable to positive measures of aid and encouragement undertaken by U.S. If such measures are taken early, they may be carried out with relatively small actual expenditures.

6. The broad purpose of U.S. aid and assistance is to extend in terms of the U.S. national interest the objective recently enunciated by the President for Greece and Turkey, by supporting economic stability and orderly political processes, opposing the spread of chaos and extremism, preventing advancement of Communist influence and use of armed minorities, and orienting other foreign nations toward the U.S. and the UN. In addition, the U.S. will probably continue to undertake to alleviate starvation and suffering as such where this action is consistent with U.S. interests.

7. The provision by the U.S. of carefully regulated quantities and types of military aid and assistance in the form of military equipment, advice, and training, is a powerful influence in orienting the recipient nations toward U.S. policy. Foreign armed forces which are supplied with U.S. equipment will look to the U.S. for replacement and maintenance. In addition to contributing to the internal order and integrity of the countries concerned, moderate security forces maintained by

those nations offer several benefits to the U.S. against the contingency of war. Foreign powers with aggressive designs would be faced with the necessity of committing openly overt acts. The reduction by an enemy of even the small countries may consume significant, though small, amounts of time and resources, thus affording a cushion of time and distance to the U.S.

8. It is believed that the following considerations are basis to decisions as to aid to be provided:

a. Taking the action will probably have consequences favorable for us, possibly carrying far beyond the limits of the nation concerned. Alternatively, if we do not take action the resulting situation might operate very decidedly to our disadvantage.

b. The problem at hand in the nation concerned is one within our economic, technical, and financial capabilities.

9. In order to be certain that aid is applied to the specific purpose for which provided in implementation of the policy enunciated by the President, controls and safeguards must be maintained which will ensure:

a. That misuse, diversion and waste are minimized.

b. That the U.S. have full knowledge of the manner in which the means provided are distributed and used.

c. That the government of the country being aided proceed with the development and support of free and democratic institutions as opposed to minority domination.

10. The necessity for an organized and comprehensive program of aid is apparent from the magnitude of the existing problem. The present and prospective needs and demands of foreign nations for U.S. aid will, in all probability, exceed availabilities. Hence a system of priorities must be installed if the provision of aid is to be closely related to the contribution thereby made to U.S. national interests and to attainment of the objectives of U.S. foreign policy. Further, it is probable that positive, forehanded and preventative actions will result in commitments considerably below those which would be required if situations were allowed to develop to the point of crisis. The interim comprehensive program set forth in Appendix "A" and the Annexes thereto has been prepared to provide such a system of priorities and such a basis for positive, forehanded, preventative action.

11. In order to establish the requirements which it may be desirable to fulfill within the next few months, it is considered necessary to develop an interim report, tentative in nature, which indicates:

a. Present urgent requirements for assistance which it is within the U.S. interest to provide.

b. Additional measures of assistance, derived from consideration of long-term U.S. programs and international assistance objectives, which it is in the U.S. interest to initiate without further delay.

The interim report is of necessity based upon fragmentary data and will be revised as better data is assembled. It must be followed by a more comprehensive and thorough report which will set forth a program and policy for U.S. aid over the next few years.[6]

---

[6] The final report was completed and circulated to the State–War–Navy Coordinating Committee as SWNCC document 360/3, dated October 3, 1947. In an accompanying memorandum the *Ad Hoc* Committee stated "that the recent rapid progress of events has made obsolete much of the data on which the report is based. It cannot therefore be considered current. . . . Attention is invited to the fact that the Marshall Plan was inaugurated *after* this report was in process of formulation under the Committee's original terms of reference . . . consequently this report relates only indirectly to the Plan." Elsewhere in the memorandum, the *Ad Hoc* Committee stated that the report "is intended to provide in a single document a survey of the present world situation and to indicate countries to which the United States for its own security and national interests may find it desirable to extend aid *during the next three to five years*. . . . The attached report recommends that U.S. capabilities be reviewed once the Marshall Plan becomes firm insofar as the application of U.S. support to other areas of the world is concerned."

Editorial Note

Secretary of State Marshall discussed problems of postwar reconstruction in a radio address of April 28 on the occasion of his return from the meeting of the Council of Foreign Ministers at Moscow. Concentrating upon the problem of effecting a peace settlement in "the vital center of Europe—Germany and Austria—an area of large and skilled population, of great resources and industrial plants", Mr. Marshall urged that "the complex character of the problems should be understood, together with their immediate effect on the people of Europe in the coming months . . . we cannot ignore the factor of time involved here. The recovery of Europe has been far slower than had been expected. Disintegrating forces are becoming evident. The patient is sinking while the doctors deliberate. . . . Whatever action is possible to meet these pressing problems must be taken without delay." (Department of State *Bulletin*, May 11, 1947, page 919.)

Under Secretary of State Acheson, speaking on May 8 before the Delta Council at Cleveland, Mississippi, on "The Requirements of Reconstruction", described in broad context Europe's acute dollar deficit, its desperate need for food, clothing, coal, steel, and machinery for relief and reconstruction purposes, the probable inability of the American economy operating at near-capacity to sustain any further substantial increase in the total volume of exports of these commodities, and what "these facts of international life mean for the United States and for United States foreign policy." (*Ibid.*, May 18, 1947, page 991.)

The drafting history of Mr. Acheson's speech is shown in the papers of Joseph M. Jones, special assistant to the Assistant Secretary of State for Public Affairs (Benton), who assisted Mr. Acheson on this occasion. Notes prepared for a conference of Acheson and Jones on April 9 indicate that the latter submitted a proposal "to elaborate our Greco-Turkish program into a more comprehensive statement of foreign policy" to be based on the concept of "further extension of aid to foreign countries". This statement was to draw on the conclusions of the SWNCC report, *supra*. The Jones Papers are at the Harry S. Truman Library, Independence, Missouri.

Policy Planning Staff Files

Memorandum by the Director of the Policy Planning Staff (Kennan)[1]

SECRET   [WASHINGTON,] May 16, 1947.

The Planning Staff is undertaking its work along the following lines of thought:

1. The most important and urgent element in foreign policy planning is the question of restoration of hope and confidence in Western Europe and the early rehabilitation of the economies of that area. The character and outcome of the action we may take with relation to western Europe will have overwhelming implications for our policy elsewhere. Therefore, the problems of this area must be considered first.[2]

---

[1] The Policy Planning Staff was established on May 5, 1947, in the office of the Under Secretary of State to assure the development of long-range policy. Minutes of the Staff are in Lot 64 D 563, files of the Policy Planning Staff, Department of State, 1947–1953.

On May 19 Mr. Kennan used the present memorandum as the basis for a discussion with Under Secretary Acheson about the activities of the Staff to that time.

[2] On April 24, before the Staff actually began functioning, Mr. Kennan had set this priority for its work. In a memorandum of that date he had called for the assembling of documents on current economic trends in the United Kingdom, France, Italy, and the Western zones of Germany and Austria in order to make an overall assessment of what these areas would need "(*a*) by way of relief, in order to keep human life going in case no programs of rehabilitation are undertaken beyond those already in existence, and (*b*) to effect complete rehabilitation [of the] economy and to render it self-supporting." (64 D 563, Box 2042, 1947 Chron File).

In the Staff's meeting on May 15, it was *"agreed* generally that the main problem in United States security today is to bring into acceptable relationship the economic distress abroad with the capacity and willingness of the United States to meet it effectively and speedily; that with Greece and Turkey taken care of and the Korean problem now being posed, the greatest and most crucial problem is in Western Europe; that the areas most urgently concerned are France, Italy, the occupied zones of Germany and Austria, and Great Britain; that the problem is both political and economic, and not military (except insofar as maintenance of US military effectiveness is concerned) ; that the approach to the political problem for the moment must be economic; that it will not be possible to evolve in a short space of time any program to meet the long-term problem, but that some sort of immediate action is necessary for psychological reasons; and that since coal is so vitally important to Western Europe, we should examine the problem to see what the United States can do immediately to bolster production in Europe." (64 D 563, Box 20036, 1947 Minutes of meetings.)

2. A special *ad hoc* committee of SWNCC is already at work on the study of "policies, procedures, and costs of assistance by the United States to foreign countries." This committee is completing an interim report and is beginning work on a final report scheduled for completion in mid-July. Its work relates to possible American assistance in all areas, and thus embraces the problems of western Europe.

3. The Policy Planning Staff recognizes the high quality and value of the work being performed by this SWNCC committee, and feels that the working out of detailed plans for American aid to Western Europe must continue to be the responsibility of that committee. There will be, however, a number of points on which the Planning Staff will have suggestions to make which will affect the assumptions and points of departure on which the committee is proceeding. The Planning Staff hopes to submit those to you at an early date in the form of a set of principles which it feels should be observed in framing a master plan for US assistance to western Europe. It believes that these principles may be useful not only to the SWNCC committee but also to other units in the Department and elsewhere in the Government which are occupying themselves with this problem.

The following is a tentative list of such principles:

(*a*) The program for American aid should be, if possible, supplementary to a program of intramural economic collaboration among the western European countries which should, if possible, be initiated by one of those countries and cleared through the Economic Commission for Europe. A clear distinction must be observed between these two programs.

(*b*) The schedule of American aid should be embodied in a master-program, which, like the European collaboration scheme which it is designed to support, would look ahead for a period of four to five years to a point where western Europe would no longer need to be the object of charity from outside.

(*c*) The scheme of American aid for western Europe must be tied in with some workable plan for the solution of England's difficulties and must be agreed in advance with the British.

(*d*) The over-all plan of American aid must rest on guarantees from the European countries which will preclude communist sabotage or misuse. It must be made possible for us to terminate the flow of assistance at once if we are not satisfied on this point.

(*e*) We should be careful not to talk in terms of loans when there is no plausible prospect of repayment and should make it clear to everyone that assistance in these cases will have to be by means of outright grants.

(*f*) The program should be designed to encourage and contribute to some form of regional political association of western European states. Our occupational policies in Germany and Austria must be shaped toward enabling the western zones of those countries to make the maximum contribution to economic restoration in western Europe in general.

(*g*) We should use our influence to see that the program to be agreed on for western Europe leaves the road open for Czechoslovakia and other states within the Russian orbit to come, as soon as they can give guarantee that their participation will be constructed [*constructive*].

4. The above refers to an over-all program of American aid which we would hope could be put before the American public and Congress by mid-summer. The Planning Staff feels, however, that there is great need, for psychological reasons, of some energetic and incisive American action to be undertaken at once in order to create in Europe the impression that the United States has stopped talking and has begun to act and that the problem is being taken in hand swiftly and forcefully.

The Planning Staff is searching for a suitable field in which such action could be taken without prejudice to the execution of the eventual over-all program. It feels that the most likely field would be that of the rapid restoration of the coal-producing capacity of the Rhine valley; and it is examining the feasibility of a scheme that could be put in hand at once of the enlistment of American energy and resources to this end.

It envisages here the launching of an undertaking

> which might be called "Coal for Europe" or something of that sort;
> which would aim at a specified increase in the coal production of that area during a specific period (say from July 1 to December 31, 1947);
> which would include every possible way in which the United States could help to boost production;
> which would be accomplished by maximum publicity and public dramatization; and
> which would be given as far as possible the character of an action not so much by the US Government to the French Government and other Governments of that area but by the US *public* to the peoples of those areas.

We conceive that this action might include, for example:

> measures to increase production and procurement of coal-mining machinery of every sort and rush it to the coal-producing areas;
> campaigns to make available food by popular sacrifice here (breadless days, etc.) to be sent specifically to coal-producing areas of ex-Allied states (such shipments to be accompanied direct to those areas by representatives of American organizations, such as Veterans' organizations or labor unions);
> special American government-grants to help the British overcome production difficulties in the Ruhr;
> maximum cooperation of our occupational authorities in Germany in providing labor, materials, etc. for the coal-producing areas; and possibly,
> assistance to various European countries in developing other sources of energy in order to ease coal allocations.

The purpose of the above action would be primarily to achieve the following psychological effect: (*a*) to instill into the minds of people associated with coal production in Europe the feeling that the United States was behind them and was determined to see that conditions would be provided which would help them to achieve maximum output; (*b*) to convince European peoples in general that this country is in earnest and is determined to do all in its power to see economic problems of that area taken energetically into hand; and (*c*) to capture the interest and imagination of the American public and channel it into the problem of reviving European productive facilities.

5. The Planning Staff hopes to be able to make formal suggestions along these lines very soon.

840.50 Recovery/5–2347

The Director of the Policy Planning Staff (Kennan) to the Under Secretary of State (Acheson)

SECRET [WASHINGTON,] May 23, 1947.

MR. ACHESON: Attached is the first recommendation of the Planning Staff. It deals with the question of aid to western Europe.

If approved it should serve as a general orientation, both for operations and for planning in the immediate future.

It is only a few days since the Planning Staff, with an incomplete and provisional complement of personnel, was able to begin to give attention to the substance of its work. Normally, I would consider this far too short a time in which to consider and make recommendations on matters of such importance. But I recognize that the need for a program of action on this problem is urgent and the best answer we can give today is perhaps more useful than a more thoroughly considered study one or two months hence.

If the views set forth here meet with the approval of the Secretary and yourself, we will make this paper the basis of further planning.[1]

GEORGE F. KENNAN

[Enclosure]

[WASHINGTON,] May 23, 1947.

SUMMARY

1. The Policy Planning Staff has selected as the first object of study the question of American aid to western Europe.

---

[1] On May 26, at a staff meeting in the office of the Under Secretary, it was decided to circulate this proposal for discussion at the meeting of May 28.

2. It sees here a long-term problem, namely of European rehabilitation in general, and a short-term problem, namely the immediate shoring up of confidence at home and abroad in the possibility of a constructive solution.

3. As to the short-term problem the Policy Planning Staff proposes that the United States, with a view to seizing the offensive and inspiring confidence, select some suitable bottleneck or bottlenecks in western European economy and institute immediate action which would bring to bear the full weight of this Government on the breaking of these bottlenecks. The Planning Staff attaches great importance to this suggestion, believing that only by means of some such action can we gain time to deal with the long-term problem in an orderly manner.

4. With respect to the long-term problem, the Policy Planning Staff feels that the formal initiative in drawing up a program for its solution and the general responsibility for such a program must come jointly from European nations and that the formal role of this Government should be to support that program at joint European request. It proposes that we aim at inducing the European governments to undertake soon the task of evolving such a program, and give them every assistance therein, in order that their request to us may reach us by the end of the year.

5. The Policy Planning Staff proposes the despatch of instructions to certain European missions designed to obtain a uniform digest of the views of the respective chiefs. It is also proposed that secret discussions with the British be undertaken at once with respect to the general approach to this problem.

6. It recommends that immediate measures be taken to straighten out public opinion on some implications of the President's message on Greece and Turkey.

POLICY WITH RESPECT TO AMERICAN AID TO WESTERN EUROPE
VIEWS OF THE POLICY PLANNING STAFF

I. GENERAL

1. The Policy Planning Staff has selected the question of American aid to western Europe as the first subject of its attention. This does not mean that the Staff is unmindful of the importance or urgency of problems in other areas or of its mission to coordinate long-term policy on a global basis. It means simply that western Europe appears to be the area for which long-term planning might most advantageously begin.

2. The Policy Planning Staff does not see communist activities as the root of the difficulties of western Europe. It believes that the pres-

ent crisis results in large part from the disruptive effect of the war on the economic, political, and social structure of Europe and from a profound exhaustion of physical plant and of spiritual vigor. This situation has been aggravated and rendered far more difficult of remedy by the division of the continent into east and west. The Planning Staff recognizes that the communists are exploiting the European crisis and that further communist successes would create serious danger to American security. It considers, however, that American effort in aid to Europe should be directed not to the combatting of communism as such but to the restoration of the economic health and vigor of European society. It should aim, in other words, to combat not communism, but the economic maladjustment which makes European society vulnerable to exploitation by any and all totalitarian movements and which Russian communism is now exploiting. The Planning Staff believes that American plans should be drawn to this purpose and that this should be frankly stated to the American public.

3. The Policy Planning Staff sees in this general question of American aid to western Europe two problems: a long-term one and a short-term one. The long-term problem is that of how the economic health of the area is to be restored and of the degree and form of American aid for such restoration. The short-term problem is to determine what effective and dramatic action should be taken in the immediate future to halt the economic disintegration of western Europe and to create confidence that the overall problem can be solved and that the United States can and will play its proper part in the solution.

4. The Policy Planning Staff feels that there is some misconception in the mind of the American people as to the objectives of the Truman Doctrine and of our aid to foreign countries and recommends that immediate action be taken to correct this misunderstanding.

II. The Short-Term Problem

5. With respect to the short-term problem, the Planning Staff feels that we should select some particular bottleneck or bottlenecks in the economic pattern of western Europe and institute immediate action which would bring to bear the full weight of this Government on the breaking of those bottlenecks. The purpose of this action would be on the one hand psychological—to put us on the offensive instead of the defensive, to convince the European peoples that we mean business, to serve as a catalyst for their hope and confidence, and to dramatize for our people the nature of Europe's problems and the importance of American assistance. On the other hand, this action would be designed to make a real contribution to the solution of Europe's economic difficulties.

The Planning Staff attaches great importance to this project and considers it almost essential to the success of the general scheme. It fears that unless something of this sort is done at once the result may be a further deterioration of morale in Europe which will seriously jeopardize the long-term program. For this reason it recommends that most careful and intensive consideration be given at once to this project.

The production of coal in the Rhine Valley and its movement to the places of consumption in Europe has suggested itself as the most suitable object of such an action. The Planning Staff has this question under consideration and expects to come up with more detailed suggestions in the near future.

It may be necessary as a matter of short time urgency to take certain other measures with respect to Italy supplementary to such aid as may be given to that country out of the $350,000,000 appropriation.[2] Since this question is already under advisement in operational sections of the Department the Planning Staff is not including it in this survey.

III. The Long-Term Problem

6. The Policy Planning Staff recognizes that the long-term problem is one of enormous complexity and difficulty. It should be the subject of a careful study which must of necessity extend over a period of at least several weeks. The Staff proposes to occupy itself with that study at once. In the belief, however, that this Government cannot afford to delay the adoption of some overall approach to the solution of the problem, the following tentative views are set forth:

a. It is necessary to distinguish clearly between a program for the economic revitalization of Europe on the one hand, and a program of American support of such revitalization on the other. It would be neither fitting nor efficacious for this Government to undertake to draw up unilaterally and to promulgate formally on its own initiative a program designed to place western Europe on its feet economically. This is the business of the Europeans. The formal initiative must come from Europe; the program must be evolved in Europe; and the Europeans must bear the basic responsibility for it. The role of this country should consist of friendly aid in the drafting of a European program and of the later support of such a program, by financial and other means, at European request.

b. The program which this country is asked to support must be a joint one, agreed to by several European nations. While it may be linked to individual national programs, such as the Monnet plan in France, it must, for psychological and political as well as economic

---

[2] This refers to the Joint Resolution, providing relief assistance to the people of countries devastated by war, which was approved by President Truman on May 31, 1947; 61 Stat. 125.

reasons, be an internationally agreed program. The request for our support must come as a joint request from a group of friendly nations, not as a series of isolated and individual appeals.

c. This European program must envisage bringing western Europe to a point where it will be able to maintain a tolerable standard of living on a financially self-supporting basis. It must give promise of doing the whole job. The program must contain reasonable assurance that if we support it, this will be the last such program we shall be asked to support in the foreseeable future.

d. The overall European program must embrace, or be linked to, some sort of plan for dealing with the economic plight of Britain. The plan must be formally a British one, worked out on British initiative and British responsibility, and the role of the United States, again, must be to give friendly support.

e. This does not mean that the United States need stand aside or remain aloof from the elaboration of the overall European program. As a member of the United Nations and particularly of the Economic Commission for Europe, and as a power occupying certain European territories, it is entitled and obliged to participate in working out the program. Our position as an occupying power also makes it incumbent upon us to cooperate whole-heartedly in the execution of any program that may be evolved. For this reason, and because we must know as soon as possible to what extent such a program is technically feasible, we must undertake an independent and realistic study of the entire problem of European rehabilitation. But we must insist, for the sake of clarity, for the sake of soundness of concept, and for the sake of the self-respect of European peoples, that the initiative be taken in Europe and that the main burden be borne by the governments of that area. With the best of will, the American people cannot really help those who are not willing to help themselves. And if the requested initiative and readiness to bear public responsibility are not forthcoming from the European governments, then that will mean that *rigor mortis* has already set in on the body politic of Europe as we have known it and that it may be already too late for us to change decisively the course of events.

f. While this program must necessarily center in the European area, it will admittedly have widespread ramifications in other areas. It will also have important connotations for the UN, and we should bear constantly in mind the need for maximum utilization of UN machinery.

g. American support for such a program need not be confined to financial assistance. It may involve considerable practical American cooperation in the solution of specific problems.

h. With respect to any program which this Government may eventually be asked to support, it will be necessary for it to insist on safeguards to assure

first, that everything possible be done to whittle down the cost of such support in dollars;

secondly, that the European Governments use the full force of their authority to see that our aid is employed in a purposeful and effective way; and

thirdly, that maximum reimbursement be made to this country in any forms found to be economically feasible and in United States interest.

i. The problem of where and in what form the initiative for the formulation of a European program should be taken is admittedly a tremendously difficult and delicate one. It cannot be definitely predetermined by us. Presumably an effort would first be made to advance the project in the Economic Commission for Europe, and probably as a proposal for general European (not just western European) cooperation; but then it would be essential that this be done in such a form that the Russian satellite countries would either exclude themselves by unwillingness to accept the proposed conditions or agree to abandon the exclusive orientation of their economies. If the Russians prove able to block any such scheme in the Economic Commission for Europe, it may be necessary for the key countries of western Europe to find means of conferring together without the presence of the Russians and Russian satellites. In general, however, the question of where and how this initiative should be taken is primarily one for the European nations, and we should be careful not to seek unduly to influence their decision.

7. Based on the above considerations, the Policy Planning Staff suggests the following course of action with relation to the long-term problem:

a. That the SWNCC Special *Ad Hoc* Committee studying "policy, procedures and costs of assistance by the United States to foreign countries" continue its studies, but that the State representation on this Committee maintain close contact with the Policy Planning Staff for purposes of coordination.

b. That by way of supplement to the SWNCC study, telegraphic instructions be despatched at an early date to the Chiefs of Mission in a number of western and central European countries designed to elicit their frank views on

(1) The economic situation of their respective country and the measures required for its remedy;

(2) Whether there is any element in the situation which makes it likely that the United States may be faced with any urgent and desperate demand from that quarter for assistance within the next year;

(3) Whether and to what extent the respective economic difficulties could be relieved by better exchanges (commodities, financial, manpower, etc.) with other areas of western and central Europe;

(4) The nature of the main obstacles to be overcome if such improved exchanges are to be made possible;

(5) To what extent the respective country might contribute to general European rehabilitation if these obstacles were removed; and

(6) The general state of mind of responsible government leaders in the respective country with respect to a possible program of European rehabilitation, the degree to which they are inhibited by Russian or communist pressure in considering such a program and the prospects for their initiative or cooperation in working it out.

c. That certain of these Missions be requested, at the discretion of the operational divisions of the Department, to detail qualified officers to Washington for a period of several weeks to participate in discussion and planning on this general subject.

d. That the Planning Staff, assisted by the operational sections of the Department, proceed to work out a general formulation of this Government's views on the long-term problem of European rehabilitation for use in discussions with European governments and for the guidance of the American representative on the Economic Commission for Europe.

e. That it be accepted as our general objective to induce and assist the European governments to undertake before autumn the development of a program of European rehabilitation which would show clearly what was expected of this country in the way of support, and to submit the request for such support to this Government by the end of the year.

f. That this overall approach be informally and secretly discussed with British leaders at an early date and their assurances of support solicited.

IV. Clarifying Implications of "Truman Doctrine"

8. Steps should be taken to clarify what the press has unfortunately come to identify as the "Truman Doctrine", and to remove in particular two damaging impressions which are current in large sections of American public opinion. These are:

a. That the United States approach to world problems is a defensive reaction to communist pressure and that the effort to restore sound economic conditions in other countries is only a by-product of this reaction and not something we would be interested in doing if there were no communist menace;

b. That the Truman Doctrine is a blank check to give economic and military aid to any area in the world where the communists show signs of being successful. It must be made clear that the extension of American aid is essentially a question of political economy in the literal sense of that term and that such aid will be considered only in cases where the prospective results bear a satisfactory relationship to the expenditure of American resources and effort. It must be made clear that in the case of Greece and Turkey we are dealing with a critical area where the failure to take action would have had particularly serious consequences, where a successful action would promise particularly far-reaching results, and where the overall cost was relatively small; and that in other areas we should have to apply similar criteria.

840.50 Recovery/5–2747

Memorandum by the Under Secretary of State for Economic Affairs (Clayton)[1]

THE EUROPEAN CRISIS

1. It is now obvious that we grossly underestimated the destruction to the European economy by the war. We understood the physical destruction, but we failed to take fully into account the effects of economic dislocation on production—nationalization of industries, drastic land reform, severance of long-standing commercial ties, disappearance of private commercial firms through death or loss of capital, etc., etc.

2. Europe is steadily deteriorating. The political position reflects the economic. One political crisis after another merely denotes the existence of grave economic distress. Millions of people in the cities are slowly starving. More consumer's goods and restored confidence in the local currency are absolutely essential if the peasant is again to supply food in normal quantities to the cities. (French grain acreage running 20–25% under prewar, collection of production very unsatisfactory—much of the grain is fed to cattle. The modern system of division of labor has almost broken down in Europe.)

3. Europe's current annual balance of payments deficit:

UK	$2¼	billions
France	1¾	”
Italy	½	”
US–UK Zone Germany................	½	”
	$5	billions

not to mention the smaller countries.

The above represents an absolute minimum standard of living. If it should be lowered, there will be revolution.

Only until the end of this year can England and France meet the above deficits out of their fast dwindling reserves of gold and dollars. Italy can't go that long.

---

[1] This memorandum was sent to Under Secretary Acheson on May 27, with a chit reading, "If you approve the attached, I would like to discuss it with the Secretary."

Mr. Clayton had temporarily returned to Washington from Europe, where he was attending, as head of the U.S. Delegation, the Second Session of the United Nations Preparatory Committee for an International Conference on Trade and Employment at Geneva. In Europe since early April, the Under Secretary of State for Economic Affairs had been in frequent consultation with leaders of many governments of Western Europe regarding the deterioration of their economies.

4. Some of the principal items in these deficits:

From the U.S.:	Coal, 30 million tons........	$ 600 million
" " " :	Bread grains, 12 million tons..	1,400 "
" " " :	Shipping services at very high rates on imports and exports	xxxxx "

Before the war, Europe was self-sufficient in coal and imported very little bread grains from the United States.

Europe must again become self-sufficient in coal (the U.S. must take over management of Ruhr coal production) and her agricultural production must be restored to normal levels. (Note: No inefficient or forced production through exorbitant tariffs, subsidies, etc., is here contemplated).

Europe must again be equipped to perform her own shipping services. The United States should sell surplus ships to France, Italy and other maritime nations to restore their merchant marine to at least prewar levels. (To do it, we will have to lick the shipping lobby, fattening as it is off the U.S. Treasury).

5. Without further prompt and substantial aid from the United States, economic, social and political disintegration will overwhelm Europe.

Aside from the awful implications which this would have for the future peace and security of the world, the immediate effects on our domestic economy would be disastrous: markets for our surplus production gone, unemployment, depression, a heavily unbalanced budget on the background of a mountainous war debt.

These things must not happen.

How can they be avoided?

6. Mr. Baruch [2] asks for the appointment of a Commission to study and report on our national assets and liabilities in order to determine our ability to assist Europe.

This is wholly unnecessary.

The facts are well known.

Our resources and our productive capacity are ample to provide all the help necessary.

The problem is to organize our fiscal policy and our own consumption so that sufficient surpluses of the necessary goods are made available out of our enormous production, and so that these surpluses are paid for out of taxation and not by addition to debt.

This problem can be met only if the American people are taken into the complete confidence of the Administration and told all the facts and only if a sound and workable plan is presented.

[2] Bernard M. Baruch had served as Chairman of the War Industries Board in 1918, as an adviser to the Director of War Mobilization, 1943–1945, and as U.S. Representative on the U.N. Atomic Energy Commission in 1946.

7. It will be necessary for the President and the Secretary of State to make a strong spiritual appeal to the American people to sacrifice a little themselves, to draw in their own belts just a little in order to save Europe from starvation and chaos (*not* from the Russians) and, at the same time, to preserve for ourselves and our children the glorious heritage of a free America.

8. Europe must have from us, as a grant, 6 or 7 billion dollars worth of goods a year for three years. With this help, the operations of the International Bank and Fund should enable European reconstruction to get under way at a rapid pace. Our grant could take the form principally of coal, food, cotton, tobacco, shipping services and similar things—all now produced in the United States in surplus, except cotton. The probabilities are that cotton will be surplus in another one or two years. Food shipments should be stepped up despite the enormous total (15 million tons) of bread grains exported from the United States during the present crop year. We are wasting and over-consuming food in the United States to such an extent that a reasonable measure of conservation would make at least another million tons available for export with no harm whatsoever to the health and efficiency of the American people.

9. This three-year grant to Europe should be based on a European plan which the principal European nations, headed by the UK, France and Italy, should work out. Such a plan should be based on a European economic federation on the order of the Belgium–Netherlands–Luxembourg Customs Union. Europe cannot recover from this war and again become independent if her economy continues to be divided into many small watertight compartments as it is today.

10. Obviously, the above is only the broad outline of a problem which will require much study and preparation before any move can be made.

Canada, Argentina, Brazil, Australia, New Zealand, Union of South Africa could all help with their surplus food and raw materials, but we must avoid getting into another UNRRA. *The United States must run this show.*

[WASHINGTON,] May 27, 1947.   W. L. CLAYTON

840.50 Recovery/5–2847

Memorandum by the Under Secretary of State (Acheson) to the Secretary of State [1]

SECRET   [WASHINGTON,] May 28, 1947.

In further reference to your question this morning as to how we should present the economic problems of Europe which we discussed

---

[1] Marginal notation: "GCM".

with you, an incident at luncheon in Les Biffle's [2] office indicates that we must begin to do so at once.

I lunched there with a dozen Senators, including Senator McMahon.[3] During the course of the luncheon he said that he thought they should be all told about what the Administration had in mind or at least what the problem was from the Administration's point of view. It was suggested that I might be asked to talk to the Policy Committee of the Democratic Minority in the Senate. Senator McMahon stated that for his part, if confronted with a *fait accompli*, he would refuse to go along and would vote against any credits or grants.

I assured them all that we were, as they were, in the stage of wrestling with the problem and that in the very near future, or as soon as it became a little clearer to us, we would want to talk it over with them. This means that we ought to begin to talk with Vandenberg [4] almost at once, not about solutions but about the growing seriousness of the problem.

My suggestion, therefore, is that you begin your talks with him as soon as possible and that within the next two or three weeks you make a speech which would not undertake to lay down any solution but would state the problem and that the great immediate problem is not an ideological one, but a material one.[5] This could be followed up by speeches by Cohen,[6] Clayton, and me, still dealing with the problem rather than the solution. A little later on, a new phase might be reached after full discussion within the Government and on the Hill, when the President, you, and other cabinet officers might begin to outline solutions.

DEAN ACHESON

---

[2] Leslie L. Biffle, staff director of the Minority Policy Committee, United States Senate.

[3] Brien McMahon, Senator from Connecticut.

[4] Arthur H. Vandenberg, Senator from Michigan.

[5] By May 20 a speech had been drafted by Joseph M. Jones, for delivery by the Secretary of State at an appropriate time and place. The draft entitled "Design for Reconstruction" was forwarded to Mr. Acheson by Mr. Jones in a memorandum of May 20 in which he said in part: "The attached draft speech was begun at the direction of the Secretary. . . . I believe the message came through you that the Secretary would like to 'develop further' the line taken by you in your Mississippi speech on May 8. . . .

"In writing this draft, I have again worked closely with the economic officers and I believe this represents the line which they think should be projected now. It is certainly the one which I think it is highly important to take. . . .

"Except for the first four pages which sound warnings similar to those of your speech in Mississippi, this speech is written primarily with a view to its effect abroad. The indications of suspicion and skepticism with which foreign people are beginning to view American aid are alarming and it would seem to be of first importance to spell out our design for reconstruction and to give a positive concept about which peoples of Europe especially can rally and upon which they can pin their hopes. The political and economic policy of the Department has led up to an expression of this sort and now seems the psychological time to launch it. We have a great deal to gain by convincing the world that we have something positive and attractive to offer, and not just anti-Communism." (Jones Papers, Truman Library)

[6] Benjamin V. Cohen, Counselor of the Department of State.

Lot 54 D 394, Box 538

*Summary of Discussion on Problems of Relief, Rehabilitation and
Reconstruction of Europe* [1]

[WASHINGTON,] May 29, 1947.

The following is a summary of Mr. Clayton's observations which
opened the discussion. The nations of Europe are now running a $5
billion deficit this year in their dollar exchange in seeking to maintain
an absolute minimum standard of living. The prospects for 1948 are
little better and the ability of the nations to meet this situation is
fast running out. Three major items in the balance of payments problem are:

1. 30 million tons of U.S. coal at $20 a delivered ton;
2. 12 million tons of bread grains at over $100 a delivered ton;
3. Transportation costs which for all items average 22 to 23 percent
of the total cost.

A basic element in the problem, in addition to nature-made shortages, is a breakdown in the modern system of division of labor in
European economy between peasants and city workers. Furthermore,
existing trade barriers (*a*) clog the flow of Europe's trade and (*b*)
will set an uneconomic pattern for any reconstruction efforts. The
constantly recurring political crises in Europe are only reflections of
the economic distress.

The situation must be faced immediately. If it is not remedied,
Europe will in early 1948 suffer increasingly severe economic, political,
and social disintegration, the impact of which on the U.S. will be a
falling-off of exports and a piling up of surpluses, leading to depression. The following action is necessary:

1. To help relieve the immediate coal crisis, the U.S. should consider taking over the Ruhr coal production, at which the U.K. has
failed.

2. A $6–7 billion annual expenditure by the U.S. should be made
for the next three years for rehabilitation purposes to provide more
consumer's goods, to restore confidence in European currencies, and
thus to help remedy the breakdown of the division of labor.

3. A total of no more than $2 or $3 billion annually in loans from the
Bank, the Fund, and other sources will be necessary in addition for
reconstruction purposes.

4. Some system for closer European economic cooperation must be
devised to break down existing economic barriers.

---

[1] The discussion took place in a meeting with Heads of Offices in the Department of State on May 28; the summary was prepared by Mr. Ward P. Allen of
the Executive Secretariat.

The last point which parallels the recommendation in the Policy Planning Staff paper was elaborated in the ensuing discussion. Three major problems presented themselves:

1. The inclusion or exclusion of Soviet-dominated Eastern Europe.
2. U.S. vs. European responsibility and initiative.
3. The timing and machinery to be utilized in developing the plan.

As to point 1, Mr. Clayton expressed the strong view that, while Western Europe is essential to Eastern Europe, the reverse is not true. Coal and grains from Eastern Europe are important to Western Europe, but these products will be exported westward in any event because the necessity of obtaining vital foreign exchange for necessary products from the west creates a suction which the U.S.S.R. is incapable of counteracting, and there can only be absolute and final Soviet domination of Eastern Europe by force of arms. It was concluded, therefore, that a European economic federation is feasible even without the participation of Eastern European countries. There was general agreement, however, that the plan should be drawn with such conditions that Eastern Europe could participate, provided the countries would abandon near-exclusive Soviet orientation of their economies.

Regarding the problem of European vs. U.S. initiative in the plan, Mr. Kennan pointed out the necessity of European acknowledgment of responsibility and parentage in the plan to prevent the certain attempts of powerful elements to place the entire burden on the U.S. and to discredit it and us by blaming the U.S. for all failures.

Messrs. Cohen and Thorp emphasized the importance of substantial U.S. responsibility and initiative because (a) experience has demonstrated the lack of ability of European nations to agree on such matters, (b) if agreement is reached, the scheme may not be a sound one and (c) the problem is so complex that no one can plot a definite, final plan now. It should, therefore, be approached functionally rather than by country, concentrating on the essentials, and this is an approach which the U.S. is in a better position than Europe to take.

Balancing the dangers of appearing to force "the American way" on Europe and the danger of failure if the major responsibility is left to Europe, Mr. Bohlen suggested that the alternative is to place strong pressure on the European nations to plan by underscoring their situation and making clear that the only politically feasible basis on which the U.S. would be willing to make the aid available is substantial evidence of a developing overall plan for economic cooperation by the Europeans themselves, perhaps an economic federation to be worked out over 3 or 4 years.

The third major problem discussed was the timing and machinery for developing the program. Mr. Acheson pointed out the practical impossibility of developing a program and obtaining congressional action between now and July 1. He suggested that the ensuing 4 to 6 months be employed in (a) working out agreement within the U.S. Government, (b) carrying on discussions with other governments, and (c) educating the public so that Congressional action would be sought either at a special Fall session or on January 3, 1948. The problem of introducing new elements and a definite time limit in order to obtain Congressional and public support was recognized.

As to the international machinery, Mr. Clayton stated his conviction that the Economic Commission for Europe is completely unusable as a forum, even to make a beginning, since the paralyzing fear of the U.S.S.R. by the small countries would permit her to carry out her undoubted intention to block all constructive action. He suggested that preliminary talks be held with key leaders in the U.K., France, and Italy with the Netherlands, Belgium, and Luxembourg also included. Mr. Cohen put forward the possibility of a high-grade technical-study commission in Europe this Summer, headed by a person commanding strength and respect.

Mr. Rusk urged that we should not decide now not to use the ECE for, unless we can demonstrate conclusively that it cannot be used for this, the purpose of its creation, the ground swell of public opinion against again by-passing the U.N. might wreck and would certainly jeopardize any program. Mr. Acheson was quite responsive to this danger. Although it was suggested that we might begin in the ECE with the understanding that the matter would be withdrawn from it if progress were blocked, Mr. Bohlen pointed out difficulties of withdrawing once the organization has been given jurisdiction.

In response to Mr. Acheson's question, Messrs. Vincent and Henderson expressed the opinion that there would be no untoward repercussions in the Near or Far East if the plan were concentrated on Europe.

Policy Planning Staff Files

Memorandum from the Executive Secretary of the Policy Planning Staff (Savage) to the Director of the Policy Planning Staff (Kennan)

[WASHINGTON,] June 3, 1947.

General Carter [1] phoned me at noon today to say that Secretary Marshall approves the sending of the messages to US Missions as suggested in the Policy Planning Staff's memorandum of May 23.[2]

---

[1] Brig. Gen. Marshall S. Carter, Special Assistant to the Secretary of State.
[2] *Ante,* p. 223.

General Carter said that the Secretary is still considering the other parts of the memorandum of May 23.

C[ARLTON] S[AVAGE]

Lot 64 D 563, Box 1(20027), 1947–50

Press Release Issued by the Department of State, June 4, 1947

Remarks by the Honorable George C. Marshall, Secretary of State, at Harvard University on June 5, 1947.

I need not tell you gentlemen that the world situation is very serious. That must be apparent to all intelligent people. I think one difficulty is that the problem is one of such enormous complexity that the very mass of facts presented to the public by press and radio make it exceedingly difficult for the man in the street to reach a clear appraisement of the situation. Furthermore, the people of this country are distant from the troubled areas of the earth and it is hard for them to comprehend the plight and consequent reactions of the long-suffering peoples, and the effect of those reactions on their governments in connection with our efforts to promote peace in the world.

In considering the requirements for the rehabilitation of Europe the physical loss of life, the visible destruction of cities, factories, mines and railroads was correctly estimated, but it has become obvious during recent months that this visible destruction was probably less serious than the dislocation of the entire fabric of European economy. For the past ten years conditions have been highly abnormal. The feverish preparation for war and the more feverish maintenance of the war effort engulfed all aspects of national economies. Machinery has fallen into disrepair or is entirely obsolete. Under the arbitrary and destructive Nazi rule, virtually every possible enterprise was geared into the German war machine. Long-standing commercial ties, private institutions, banks, insurance companies and shipping companies disappeared, through loss of capital, absorption through nationalization or by simple destruction. In many countries, confidence in the local currency has been severely shaken. The breakdown of the business structure of Europe during the war was complete. Recovery has been seriously retarded by the fact that two years after the close of hostilities a peace settlement with Germany and Austria has not been agreed upon. But even given a more prompt solution of these difficult problems, the rehabilitation of the economic structure of Europe quite evidently will require a much longer time and greater effort than had been foreseen.

There is a phase of this matter which is both interesting and serious. The farmer has always produced the foodstuffs to exchange with the city dweller for the other necessities of life. This division of labor is the basis of modern civilization. At the present time it is threatened with breakdown. The town and city industries are not producing adequate goods to exchange with the food-producing farmer. Raw materials and fuel are in short supply. Machinery is lacking or worn out. The farmer or the peasant cannot find the goods for sale which he desires to purchase. So the sale of his farm produce for money which he cannot use seems to him an unprofitable transaction. He, therefore, has withdrawn many fields from crop cultivation and is using them for grazing. He feeds more grain to stock and finds for himself and his family an ample supply of food, however short he may be on clothing and the other ordinary gadgets of civilization. Meanwhile people in the cities are short of food and fuel. So the governments are forced to use their foreign money and credits to procure these necessities abroad. This process exhausts funds which are urgently needed for reconstruction. Thus a very serious situation is rapidly developing which bodes no good for the world. The modern system of the division of labor upon which the exchange of products is based is in danger of breaking down.

The truth of the matter is that Europe's requirements for the next three or four years of foreign food and other essential products— principally from America—are so much greater than her present ability to pay that she must have substantial additional help, or face economic, social and political deterioration of a very grave character.

The remedy lies in breaking the vicious circle and restoring the confidence of the European people in the economic future of their own countries and of Europe as a whole. The manufacturer and the farmer throughout wide areas must be able and willing to exchange their products for currencies the continuing value of which is not open to question.

Aside from the demoralizing effect on the world at large and the possibilities of disturbances arising as a result of the desperation of the people concerned, the consequences to the economy of the United States should be apparent to all. It is logical that the United States should do whatever it is able to do to assist in the return of normal economic health in the world, without which there can be no political stability and no assured peace. Our policy is directed not against any country or doctrine but against hunger, poverty, desperation and chaos. Its purpose should be the revival of a working economy in the world so as to permit the emergence of political and social conditions in which free institutions can exist. Such assistance, I am convinced, must not be on a piece-meal basis as various crises develop. Any assistance that this Government may render in the future should provide a cure rather than a mere palliative. Any government that is willing to assist in the task of recovery will find full cooperation, I am sure, on the part of the United States Government. Any government which maneuvers to block the recovery of other countries cannot expect help from us. Furthermore, governments, political parties or groups which seek to perpetuate human misery in order to profit therefrom politically or otherwise will encounter the opposition of the United States.

It is already evident that, before the United States Government can proceed much further in its efforts to alleviate the situation and help start the European world on its way to recovery, there must be some agreement among the countries of Europe as to the requirements of the situation and the part those countries themselves will take in order to give proper effect to whatever action might be undertaken by this Government. It would be neither fitting nor efficacious for this Government to undertake to draw up unilaterally a program designed to place Europe on its feet economically. This is the business of the Europeans. The initiative, I think, must come from Europe. The role of this country should consist of friendly aid in the drafting of a European program and of later support of such a program so far as it may be practical for us to do so. The program should be a joint one, agreed to by a number, if not all European nations.

An essential part of any successful action on the part of the United States is an understanding on the part of the people of America of the character of the problem and the remedies to be applied. Political passion and prejudice should have no part. With foresight, and a willingness on the part of our people to face up to the vast responsibility which history has clearly placed upon our country, the difficulties I have outlined can and will be overcome.

Lot 122, Box 13113

The Assistant Chief of the Division of Commercial Policy (Moore) to the Director of the Office of International Trade Policy (Wilcox) at Geneva [1]

CONFIDENTIAL   [WASHINGTON,] July 28, 1947.

DEAR CLAIR: The "Marshall Plan" has been compared to a flying saucer—nobody knows what it looks like, how big it is, in what direction it is moving, or whether it really exists. Nevertheless, all of us here who must cope with this mysterious phenomenon—Paul, Bob,

---

[1] Clair Wilcox was vice-chairman of the U.S. Delegation to the trade negotiations then in progress at Geneva.

Joe, Bill Phillips [2]—feel that you should have a detailed account of the situation insofar as we have been able to follow it.

It gradually became increasingly clear last spring that a new approach would be needed. The balance-of-payments situation was obviously deteriorating. Paul kept pushing for adequate information and analysis of this problem (he sent you a copy of his memorandum). The first comprehensive study in the Department was a report prepared for a special SWNCC subcommittee (copy enclosed) [3] which Van Cleveland [4] and I pulled together on the basis of such information as we could collect at that time. This report led directly to Acheson's Mississippi speech (written by Joe Jones) which put the problem clearly before the people and Congres. [5]

In the meantime, Congressional reaction to the Greek–Turkish program indicated strongly that such a piece-meal approach to the problem of foreign aid could not be continued much longer. The next request would undoubtedly have raised an insistent demand for the total bill. For this reason the Korean legislation, although badly needed, was withdrawn.

The third element was a growing recognition of the serious character of the crisis in Western Europe. When Kennan was first appointed to the Policy Planning job he decided to concentrate on this area. He felt that the failure to reach agreement on Germany at Moscow was due primarily to Soviet anticipation of continued deterioration in France, Italy and Western Germany plus hope for a U.S. depression. It was essential to improve the Western European situation in order to prevent further weakening in our bargaining power.

This was the Departmental frame of mind when Mr. Clayton came back from Geneva. He prepared a memorandum shortly after his return outlining the basic elements of a new approach to the European problem. These were incorporated in a paper which the Planning Staff sent to the Secretary proposing this approach as a basis for further study. Kennan heard nothing further from it until he read the newspapers shortly thereafter, and realized that the basic elements had been presented at Harvard. The Secretary has tremendous power of decision and his batting average is phenomenally high. He made up his mind on most of the major decisions of the war in just as short a time.

---

[2] Probably Paul Nitze, Deputy Director; J. Robert Schaetzel, Special Assistant to the Director; Joseph Coppock, Adviser; all of the Office of International Trade Policy, and William T. Phillips, Special Assistant to the Chief of the International Resources Division.

[3] For text of report, see p. 204.

[4] Harold Van Buren Cleveland, Assistant Chief, Division of Investment and Economic Development.

[5] For text, see Department of State *Bulletin*, May 18, 1947, pp. 991–994.

[Here follow several pages detailing the progress of events and the thinking in the Department of State regarding the Marshall Plan from June 5 to July 28.]

Sincerely,

Ben [T. Moore]

840.50 Recovery/7–2248

Memorandum by Mr. Charles P. Kindleberger [1]

[WASHINGTON,] July 22, 1948.

MEMORANDUM FOR THE FILES

ORIGINS OF THE MARSHALL PLAN

The collection of gossip and rumors presented below is not vouched for in any way. It is set forth only because time is fleeting, memories fade, and the stuff of history is fragile. Even at this date, thirteen months later, I am unable to sort out what I know of my direct knowledge and what I have been told.

It is well known that the topic of European reconstruction was widely discussed during the winter of 1946–47. The Council on Foreign Relations had its entire winter program devoted to this topic. I talked twice on it: once in January on coal; and a second time in May on Germany.

Walter Lippmann,[2] without claiming credit for the origin of the Marshall plan, has told me that he wrote a series of columns (not the one on the cold war) setting forth the necessity for a plan for European reconstruction. This I do not recall and didn't when he told me.

In early 1946, Walt Rostow[3] had a revelation that the unity of Germany could not be achieved without the unity of Europe, and that the unity of Europe could best be approached crabwise through technical cooperation in economic matters, rather than bluntly in diplomatic negotiation. This suggestion was given to Secretary Byrnes for free examination through the kindly offices of Mr. Acheson. Joe and Stewart Alsop [4] wrote a column on the subject in April 1946, referring to what was in the Secretary's briefcase. In any event, the Secretary didn't buy. That summer, however, the US representation on the Devastated Areas Subcommission of the Commission on Employment of the Economic and Social Council of the United Nations bought the idea from Rostow and Kindleberger (who was by that time a member of the firm) and

---

[1] Mr. Kindleberger, Chief of the Division of German and Austrian Economic Affairs, Department of State, participated in the work of various departmental and interdepartmental committees on the Marshall Plan.

[2] Walter Lippmann, newspaper columnist.

[3] Walt W. Rostow, Assistant Chief, Division of German and Austrian Economic Affairs.

[4] Joseph and Stewart Alsop, newspaper columnists.

peddled it first to Mr. Lubin on the Commission on Employment, to the Poles and to others. This was the origin of ECE, of which *causa proxima* was Mr. Molotov's [5] decision, made in the corridors of the Waldorf after a midnight debate between the Poles (winners) and the Jugs (losers).

The ECE thought was inextricably wound up in a European recovery plan. ECOSOC in February 1947 wrote terms of reference for ECE (it thought it did; actually Miriam Camp [6] wrote the terms of reference and ECOSOC initialled them). These contained reference to planned recovery programs.

I have had a hard time seeing how the Acheson speech at Delta, Mississippi, was the midwife to the Marshall plan. Acheson made five points—including primarily the usual ones about multilateralism which the Department has stated so frequently that it is inclined to believe them. One point, however, referred to using United States assistance in future where it would do the most good in recovery in some planned way. This was hardly revolutionary, since there was no specific suggestion of a recovery program, and since there was no suggestion as to who should draw one up. And the point was only one of five.

In my book, Scotty Reston [7] gets a great deal of the credit for initiating the Marshall plan. As I reconstruct the plot, Reston would have lunch with Acheson. Mr. Acheson, as many of his warmest admirers are prepared to concede, converses with a broad brush. Reston would get him started on European recovery, and Mr. Acheson would allude to plans under consideration. The following day invariably Reston would have a first-page story in the *New York Times* referring to big planning going on in the State Department. This would give Mr. Kennan, who had just been appointed to the newly created planning staff in February, the jim-jams. If there was public talk of all this planning in the Department, and the planning staff had received so much publicity, maybe this was where the effort should be applied. As I say, I have no way of knowing what was going on in Mr. Kennan's mind. I do recall, however, learning that Kennan had been having lunch with Reston (this may have been later though). Perhaps Reston was acting as liaison man within the Department.

The Secretary got back from Moscow in April—about the 25th I recall. The Truman doctrine was making heavy weather of it, both on Capitol Hill and in the country as a whole. Its negative, retaliatory, counter-punching features were disliked. Its implications for economic and ultimately military warfare were regretted. I had the strong

---

[5] Vyacheslav M. Molotov, Minister of Foreign Affairs of the Soviet Union.

[6] Miriam Camp, a Foreign Service Staff Officer in London in 1946, returned to the Department of State in January 1947 as a divisional assistant.

[7] James Reston, a Washington correspondent of the *New York Times*.

impression from a chance conversation with Willard Thorp before I left for Moscow on February 20th (about), that the Department was in a panic as to what to do in Greece. Slapping together an anti-Russian policy to take over the British policing role there, was too much for the country to swallow. It gagged. The Secretary, whose attention to the Truman message of March 11 [8] must have been cursory at best, was obviously going to try something else. The Truman doctrine was no great shakes. Negotiation in the CFM was no way to get peace fast. He was receptive to new ideas.

Then Mr. Clayton came home from Geneva. I do not remember when he did return, but it was either April or May. It was common knowledge in the Department that Mr. Clayton was deeply exercised by what he had seen in Europe. He had the impression that Europe was collapsing rapidly. His interest lay in production—and he was deeply impressed by the prospective failure of the French wheat crop—and in organized markets. He was depressed by what he had seen and heard of black markets, hoarding, etc. He was worked up about the state of the economy of Europe and felt strongly that something should be done.

About this time, partly I guess in response to the Reston articles, Van Cleveland and Ben Moore started to write a long memo on a European recovery program. I was asked to contribute a couple of chapters on Germany, which I did. Cleveland and I had some difficulty getting together on the German passages. He felt that what I had written did not fit into his broader scheme, and I would not accept what he rewrote of my material as bearing any resemblance to the economic problems of Germany or their solution. This memo was finished sometime before the end of May, as I recall. It took a long time to duplicate in mimeograph. This was finally done and it appeared after the Harvard speech with a date of June 12, 1947.[9]

During April or May, Ty Wood [10] organized the Thursday luncheons in the Assistant Secretary's office for office directors. The purpose of these was to discuss wider problems of a sort a little too vague to warrant holding meetings for. Ed Martin [11] tells me that the Thursday meeting began to discuss the European recovery problem during May. It had, of course, heard from Mr. Clayton. It was, moreover, aware that Cleveland and Moore were writing the piece on a recovery pro-

---

[8] Presumably the President's Special Message to the Congress on Greece and Turkey, delivered in person before a joint session, March 12; for text, see *Public Papers of the Presidents of the United States: Harry S. Truman, January 1 to December 31, 1947* (Washington, Government Printing Office, 1963), p. 176, or Department of State *Bulletin*, March 23, 1947, p. 534.

[9] Not printed.

[10] Clinton Tyler Wood, Deputy to the Assistant Secretary of State for Economic Affairs.

[11] Edwin M. Martin, Acting Director, Office of Economic Security Policy.

gram. Some of the May discussion turned on how to organize the shop to deal with the problem of European recovery.

Bill Malenbaum [12] tells me that on June 3 or 4th, but in any event just before the Harvard speech, Mr. Wm. A. Eddy, Special Assistant to the Secretary for Intelligence, told him that the Secretary had called a meeting at the assistant-secretary level to discuss the proposed speech and that there had been a fundamental difference of opinion between Clayton and Kennan as to how to go about the European recovery program. This difference, of course, turned narrowly on how to write the speech. But it may be useful to turn first to the drafting of the speech.

On no good authority, and I have forgotten what, I have understood for some time that the speech is a merger of paragraphs from separate memos on the problem of European recovery written by Mr. Clayton and Mr. Kennan. The part laying out the analysis of what is wrong in Europe seems to be very much the product of Mr. Clayton's mind. The emphasis on trade and exchange is striking. The rest, and particularly the final paragraphs, are supposed to be the product of Mr. Kennan's pen.

The question which apparently divided Messrs. Clayton and Kennan was that of whether the initiative should be left to Europe. Mr. Clayton, as I later learned from him, was strongly opposed to a program of the UNRRA type, where the United States put up most of the funds and had only one vote in 17 on its distribution. He was accordingly opposed to reducing the role of the United States to that of supplying the assistance. It seems to me probable that his opposition to a European plan for US assistance sprang from this background of view. Mr. Kennan, on the other hand, presumably had in mind the political desirability of leaving the initiative to Europe. The clash between these views, of course, was ultimately resolved through the device of the multilateral *and* bilateral agreements, with Europe operating the program under a series of mutual pledges, but each country being responsible for its performance under the program to the US if it received assistance.

Bill Malenbaum also reports that Walter Salant [*sic*],[13] who had the task for the Council of Economic Advisers of estimating the net foreign balance of the United States for a period ahead, asked him just before the speech what his views were on whether there would be a foreign aid program. Salant said that he had canvassed the Department of State and that there was no unanimity of view as to what was

---

[12] Wilfred Malenbaum, Chief, Division of International and Functional Intelligence.

[13] William A. Salant, Assistant Chief, Division of German and Austrian Economic Affairs.

about to transpire, but that on balance he thought the majority view was that there would be no program of assistance.

A newspaper man—I forget which one—gave me a long story on how the speech happened to be delivered at Harvard which may be worth setting down, despite the fact that I cannot vouch for one word of it. First, however, I cannot help recalling a bit of dialogue which took place in the central corridor, fifth floor, New State Department Building, in about the second week of July between Philander P. Claxton [14] and me.

CLAXTON: Where have you been? I haven't seen you around lately.

KINDLEBERGER: I am not working on German matters any more. I have moved over and now work on the European recovery program.

CLAXTON: Oh, that's the program which developed out of the Secretary's speech at Princeton.

KINDLEBERGER: Phil, where did you go to college?

CLAXTON: Princeton, why?

KINDLEBERGER: That's what I thought.

According to the newsman's unsubstantiated story, the Secretary agreed with Messrs. Kennan and Clayton that there should be a speech and that it should read about as it eventually did. He then wondered where it might be given. Pat Carter [15] looked up and found that the Secretary had no speaking engagements until June 17, 1947, which all agreed was too far distant in the future in the nature of the existing European crisis.

At that point, the Secretary is said to have remembered that Harvard University had awarded him a degree during the war. He had refused it. Normally, he wrote letters to universities which offered him degrees during the war, saying that he was unable to accept because he felt that the soldiers overseas might misunderstand his position if he were to accept an honorary degree, leaving his desk for the purpose, when they couldn't get away. This type of letter could not be written to Harvard, however, since Admiral King and General Arnold had both been awarded degrees and had accepted. Accordingly, the Secretary merely wrote and refused it.

It had rarely if ever occurred before that Harvard had been refused an offer of an honorary degree, and the University was both surprised and puzzled. Suspecting, however, that the Secretary had some hidden motive for refusing, it wrote back to him saying that it would award the degree, which the Secretary could claim at any time when it suited his convenience.

---

[14] Philander P. Claxton, assistant to the Assistant Secretary of State for Occupied Areas.

[15] Brig. Gen. Marshall S. Carter, special assistant to Secretary Marshall.

All this the Secretary recalled. Accordingly, he got in touch with Harvard and said he wanted his degree. This again is reported to have surprised Harvard, which already had a speaker and whose commencement, only a few days away, was practically complete as to arrangements. But Harvard gracefully acquiesced. And the historic speech was given at Harvard. Ed Mason [16] says that he doesn't believe this story because, as he puts it, Harvard does not alter its arrangements even for the Secretary of State.

Joe Harsch of CBS and the *Christian Science Monitor* has printed this story as to why the Marshall plan should be called the Miall plan. [17] Leonard Miall is the BBC correspondent in Washington and incidentally a neighbor, car-pool mate and friend of mine. I recall very well that the evening of June 4, as we were driving home, he complained that he had just finished writing out a script for the next day's noon broadcast on plans for United States economic aid to Europe, when on his way home he had stopped by the newsroom of the Department and picked up a copy of the Harvard speech. This required him to tear up his script and start again. (It seems to me noteworthy in retrospect that aid to Europe was such a widespread thought in Washington that Miall would have written several scripts on the subject, starting out with the Acheson Delta speech. He was fairly close to Acheson, with whom, along with a group of British journalists, he had lunched once or twice.)

Miall handed me the text of the Marshall speech in the back of the car. I hastily read it as the car moved along and suggested that this was big news and that he would most certainly have to do a new script. I recall that Miall was irritated as well by the fact that there was no firm release date on the Marshall speech, release being the indeterminate hour the speech would begin at Harvard. This was a usual annoyance for him, however, in booking circuits to London.

Harsch's story runs to the effect that Philip Jordan, the information officer of the British Embassy asked Mr. Balfour, then the Chargé, whether he should cable the Foreign Office the text of the Secretary's speech. Balfour is reported to have said no—just another commencement speech.

The rest of the British and foreign press were all off running down some other story which they featured in their cables—United States note to some country like Hungary—if I recall correctly. Only Malcolm Muggeridge of the *Daily Telegraph* and Leonard Miall of BBC

---

[16] Edward S. Mason, professor of economics at Harvard University, and a consultant to the Department of State.

[17] Mr. Miall, BBC correspondent in Washington, 1945–53, wrote his own account in *The Listener*, London, May 4, 1961, in an article entitled "How the Marshall Plan Started."

gave it a big play (Harsch omits mention of Muggeridge, but Miall insists he should share the credit). And so the Marshall plan was communicated to Mr. Bevin [18] by the BBC (and possibly the *Daily Telegraph*) since the Foreign Office-Embassy, London *Times* and other avenues of communication were uninterested in it.

I have many times been asked whether the Department did not advise US missions abroad and/or foreign missions here of the importance which it attached to the speech. As far as I have gathered, without putting any effort into it, the answer is no. Asked why not, I have had no answer.

These random jottings are perhaps not worth recording. I record them just the same to help light the lamp of memory for my old age, waiting for me around the corner.

C. P. KINDLEBERGER

---

[18] Ernest Bevin, British Secretary of State for Foreign Affairs.

Lot 64 D 563, Box 20027

Memorandum Prepared for the Use of the Under Secretary of State for Economic Affairs (Clayton) [1]

SECRET

[WASHINGTON, June 1947.]

We Americans are deeply concerned over the production and exchange difficulties which you people in Europe are experiencing.

We had hoped that the outside aid which your countries have already received would have sufficed, together with the facilities of the agencies which have now been established for international financial assistance, to bring you to a point where your import requirements could be

---

[1] An early draft of this memorandum was prepared in Mr. Acheson's morning meeting of June 5, 1947. A revision of the above dated June 9, 1947, bears the following notation: "Mr. Secretary: The attached memorandum contains suggestions as to the line it would be advisable for Mr. Clayton to take in discussing with representatives of European Governments the question of further American aid to Europe.

"This memorandum has been concurred in by Mr. Acheson and Mr. Lovett.— George F. Kennan." Secretary Marshall in a chit made the following comments: "Dear Lovett: It seems to me that this statement indicates too much of American cash and too little of European organization, however elementary, to facilitate the European states in helping themselves and in making it possible for American aid to be more effective.—GCM." Mr. Lovett, then a Special Assistant to the Secretary, redrafted the memo and said: "Mr. Secretary, I have taken a crack at rewriting this memo which is designed for use by Mr. Clayton as a reminder of the points to be covered in any conversations he has on this subject. Do the changes meet your views? The first draft is attached for comparison.— L." (Lot 64 D 563, Box 20042, 1947 Chron File)

The Lovett draft was revised by Secretary Marshall and this revision is printed here. It bears the notation "O.K. as amended G.C.M."

Under Secretary Clayton arrived in London for talks with British officials which began on June 24, 1947.

handled on a normal commercial basis. We recognize that many of the factors which have caused these hopes to be disappointed are ones which were beyond anyone's control, and that for some of the others we share a measure of responsibility.

We are most anxious to find out from you the causes why the various measures undertaken by the European Governments themselves and the assistance furnished from the United States and other non-European countries have not further advanced the restoration of economic health in Europe. Only if we and you have a clear understanding of the real causes of the present serious economic situation of Europe can remedies to correct the situation be intelligently sought.

We regard the question of the restoration of economic health in Europe as a matter requiring joint consideration. Before the U.S. Government can take any effective action to be of help it must know from the European Governments directly concerned what measures these Governments either jointly or separately have in mind in order to remove the causes of the present troubles. This is particularly important because it affects the whole problem of future American aid for Europe.

It is generally recognized in the United States that a stable and self-supporting Europe is a matter of immediate interest to the American people. Our people have already demonstrated their willingness to aid Europe. But they are naturally concerned that any future aid shall be productive of more effective results than the aid they have extended in the past. And unless the American Congress can receive some convincing reassurance on this point, we doubt that its members would feel justified in making further appropriations of American money for this purpose.

You Europeans know your own continent and your own problems better than we ever can. Furthermore, it is you who are administering the economies of Europe. For these reasons we would like to have your ideas and plans as to the future course of European recovery and for joint or cooperative efforts among you. It would be much easier for us to consider the whole question of further American assistance to Europe if you could provide us with facts and figures showing just how you envisage the restoration of your economy.

What we are interested in here is in learning the size and character of the specific problems. What are the bottlenecks impeding recovery? What form of outside help added to your internal efforts would prove most effective, and what are the prospects of prompt cooperative efforts?

Our people would wish to have the assurance that in facing these problems maximum advantage has been taken of the possibilities for better exchange among European nations. We know that this is more a question of creating export surpluses than of reducing barriers. We also recognize as one of the powers occupying Germany, the importance of making surpluses from that country available to the other peoples in Europe. We will continue to do our best to make the US-UK zones in Germany useful and productive units in any European pattern.

In this connection, it would be a great help to us if any or all of you could get together and give us your common views on these matters. We have no desire to force on you any measures which you would not feel would be timely and useful. But Americans would feel greater confidence about the effectiveness of their support if there were some degree of agreement on the course of and the measures required for your recovery.

Many things have been said in Europe about the aims which underlie American assistance to other countries and the conditions which might be attached to this assistance. Most of these statements were foolish or unjust, or both. But there is one condition which Americans will attach to any future aid and with good reason: namely, that it should really do its work of putting the economies of European countries on their feet.

II. THE GENESIS OF A EUROPEAN RECOVERY PROGRAM (JUNE–SEPTEMBER): CONVERSATIONS AT LONDON; THE CONFERENCE OF EUROPEAN ECONOMIC COOPERATION, AT PARIS, AND ITS REPORT

840.00/6–1247 : Telegram

The Secretary of State to the Embassy in France

SECRET   WASHINGTON, June 12, 1947—7 p. m.

2143. Personal for the Ambassador. 1. As stated in my Harvard speech, before US Gov can proceed much further in efforts to alleviate European economic situation there must be some agreement among European countries as to requirements of situation and part those countries themselves will take in order to give proper effect to whatever action might be undertaken by US Gov.

2. It has become increasingly clear that US financial and economic aid to individual European countries on a piecemeal basis cannot alone solve the situation. There is definite limit to amount of such aid. American people and Congress will not support continued loans or grants or other tangible economic aid if no end in sight and if various steps taken by us are unrelated. Moreover, it would seem that economic health and public morale of the needy countries would be greatly improved if they sought to evolve a definite European program in lieu of continued individual shots in arm.

3. Role of US Gov is to give friendly aid in drafting European program and later to support program so far as may be practical. However, extent of any US assistance likely to be dependent on sincerity and effectiveness of effort and courageousness of approach displayed by European countries in attempting to help themselves. If initiative and readiness to bear public responsibility are not forthcoming from European Govts (whether through ineptness, fear of Soviet obstruction, or otherwise) it may be impossible for us to aid in changing decisively the course of events.

4. Because of our vital interest in European rehabilitation and our position as occupying power, it is important that we know as soon as possible to what extent a European program is politically and technically feasible. We have therefore undertaken independent and realistic study of entire problem European rehabilitation. In order further this study, I am seeking frank views Chiefs of certain European Missions on following among other points:

a. The economic situation of their respective countries and the measures required for its remedy;

b. Whether there is any element in the situation which makes it likely that US may be faced with any urgent and desperate demand from that quarter for assistance within the next year;

c. Whether and to what extent the respective economic difficulties could be relieved by better exchanges (commodities, financial, manpower, etc.) with other areas of western and central Europe or other countries;

d. The nature of the main obstacles to be overcome if such improved exchanges are to be made possible;

e. To what extent their respective countries might contribute to general European rehabilitation if these obstacles were removed; and

f. The general state of mind of responsible Govt leaders in their respective countries with respect to a possible program of European rehabilitation, the degree to which they are inhibited by Russian or communist pressure in considering such a program and the prospects for their initiative or cooperation in working it out.

5. The geographic coverage of and forum for considering any program of European countries will depend on answers to the above questions as well as on other imponderables. For example, if it should develop that there was some real hope that all European countries would cooperate in formulating and carrying out a European-wide program, its coverage could be broad and it could be developed in the Economic Commission for Europe. On the other hand, if it should be agreed that Soviets would oppose or employ obstructionist tactics against a European-wide program, the Western European nations should be able to find means of evolving a regional program. In such event it might be desirable to advance proposals in the Economic

Commission for Europe in first instance. In any event it would seem desirable to avoid any implication of commitment to use any one exclusive channel either in developing information or implementing program. The primary responsibility for this must rest with European countries.

6. Scope and nature of program is not yet foreseeable. It might be possible for program to be somewhat along lines Monnet Plan [1] but on much larger scale involving several countries. On the other hand, it might develop that most feasible thing is to concentrate on few matters of vital importance to Europe such as food, coal and transport.

7. Your despatches and telegrams over the past months have been most helpful to Dept in its attempts to come to grips with this overall problem. Many of the questions raised have already been dealt with by you. However, it would be particularly helpful now if you could give us benefit of your personal views on this difficult subject, with particular reference to questions outlined in paragraph 4 above. If you consider some type of European program feasible, please also give your opinion as to possible individuals who might spearhead its preparation, whether they be French or other nationals.

MARSHALL

---

[1] A plan for reequipping and modernizing French industry.

840.50 Recovery/6–1347

Memorandum of Conversation, by the Secretary of State

[WASHINGTON,] June 13, 1947.

Participants: M. Henri Bonnet, French Ambassador
               The Secretary
               Mr. Matthews [1]

The French Ambassador called at 11:30 this morning at his request and said that he had been instructed by his Government to have a preliminary conversation with me concerning the suggestions contained in my remarks at Harvard University. He said that his Government attached great importance to the Harvard speech which was why he had asked to see me urgently rather than wait until Monday. Since his time was short (he knew I had a 12 o'clock engagement) he had put what he wished to say in an *aide-mémoire* although his Government had suggested merely an oral discussion. He then outlined for twenty minutes the points made in the attached *aide-mémoire*.[2]

---

[1] H. Freeman Matthews, Director, Office of European Affairs.
[2] Not printed.

In his oral outline he emphasized the following points:

1. His Government was in full accord with the approach I suggested at Harvard and desired him to discuss with the American Government the best means of procedure.

2. France agreed with the importance of a determined European effort to bring about within the limits of possibility its own reconstruction.

3. European countries should first draw up an inventory of their total resources in the fields of agriculture, raw materials, industrial production, power and transportation.

4. This inventory would show the extent of the deficiency in equipment and materials which would remain in spite of all the individual efforts of countries of Europe and in spite of such plans for mutual aid to each other as they may be able to devise.

5. The resulting deficiency which must be supplied by outside aid, particularly American, to be of two sorts; that required for the rebuilding of Europe's productive apparatus and that needed for daily consumption during the next three or four years pending full reconstruction. These requirements unfortunately greatly exceed available dollar exchange.

6. In the opinion of the French Government the inventory and estimated balance of payments deficit should not be reached by calling a large conference which would be both long drawn out and dilatory. It should be done by forming a number of *ad hoc* committees composed of representatives of European producer states and of the United States.

7. The deficit in balance of payments resulting from lack of food and raw materials should be communicated in turn to distributive organizations such as ECO and IEFC. "Thus the needs could be determined of essential foodstuffs and raw materials needed by Europe, the importation of which should not be a charge on the balance of payments." As an example, an *ad hoc* committee to study coal production composed of representatives of the United States and European producing countries should be set up, Germany being represented by "delegates of the occupying powers". This committee might study which European coal fields should be the object of the principal effort to obtain the quickest possible results for the greatest number of countries. "It would be apparent that mine equipment and certain steel tonnage would be necessary. Part of this could be furnished by European countries. The remainder should be sought by them from the United States. It was important that during the period of reconstruction European countries should have their balance of payments re-

lieved of the charge represented by imports of American coal. On this question the coal committee should deal with ECO."

M. Bonnet also said that he hoped that the plan suggested at Harvard would not interfere with France's efforts to obtain her further loan this autumn from the World Bank. He said that heavy payments (on previous credits) are already falling due and the dollar question is daily one of considerable worry to France.

I told M. Bonnet that what he had said interested me greatly. I could say no more at this time but I would study his memorandum with great attention. I was impressed with the need for European countries to work together on the problem and I was impressed with the urgency in point of time. M. Bonnet said that he hoped to have further talks with me after I had studied his memorandum.

840.00/6–1447

The British Ambassador (Inverchapel) to the Secretary of State

SECRET   WASHINGTON, June 14, 1947.
URGENT

MY DEAR SECRETARY OF STATE: I have this morning received a telegram from Mr. Bevin asking me to inform you that, in pursuit of the intention to cooperate with the French in studying the new American approach to Europe adumbrated in your recent speech at Harvard, he proposes to take the initiative by visiting Paris early next week to discuss the matter personally with the Prime Minister of France and M. Bidault. The French Government are being informed that, subject to their agreement, Mr. Bevin would hope to arrive in Paris on Tuesday afternoon and return to London on Wednesday evening. He hopes that it may be possible to arrange for M. Monnet,[1] who is at present in Basle, to be available during the discussions.

In a speech which he delivered yesterday afternoon, Mr. Bevin indicated that His Majesty's Government in the United Kingdom are specially mindful of the part that France can play in the economic reconstruction of Europe and he stated that it had been decided to consult her and other European nations to see how best advantage could be taken of the great American proposal.

Mr. Bevin hopes that you will understand that in view of the postponement of Mr. Clayton's visit to London [2] and the urgency of making progress with the questions raised in your Harvard speech, he has

---

[1] Jean Monnet, head of the French Cabinet Planning Commission.
[2] Under Secretary Clayton's visit had been planned to permit an exchange of views between the United States and British Governments regarding the dollar shortage in international transactions.

thought it desirable to open early discussions with the French. These discussions will be exploratory only and Mr. Bevin hopes that His Majesty's Government will be in a better position to talk effectively to Mr. Clayton after they have heard the French views. Mr. Bevin specially asks me to say that he very much hopes that Mr. Clayton will not find it necessary further to postpone his departure for London on account of Mr. Bevin's proposed visit to Paris.

Mr. Bevin states that if the United States Government have any views to express about his talks with the French, he would be glad to have them.

I am also informed that I shall shortly receive instructions to approach the United States Government on the substance of your recent proposal and on the general subject of the shortage of dollars.

Yours sincerely,   INVERCHAPEL

840.50 Recovery/6–1647

The Italian Ambassador (Tarchiani) to the Secretary of State

WASHINGTON, June 16, 1947.

MY DEAR SECRETARY OF STATE: The Italian Minister for Foreign Affairs Count Sforza, has directed me to convey to you Italy's wholehearted solidarity in the aims you have expressed in your Harvard address with such outstanding statesmanship.

Count Sforza has asked me to communicate to you that the Italians are grateful, both as Italians and as Europeans, for this speech of yours which, as we all hope, will develop as the utmost contribution to peace throughout the world.

And he also has instructed me to assure you of Italy's readiness to warmly cooperate with the ideas you expressed.

Please accept [etc.]   TARCHIANI

840.00/6–1647 : Telegram

The Chargé in the United Kingdom (Gallman) to the Secretary of State

SECRET   LONDON, June 16, 1947—5 p. m.

3279. I saw Bevin this morning. He told me that he would leave tomorrow morning for Paris for the discussions with Ramadier [1] and Bidault on the Secretary's offer to [of] aid to Europe. He would return

---

[1] Paul Ramadier, President of the French Council of Ministers.

to London Wednesday night. On Thursday, the nineteenth, he would have to speak in the Commons on the opposition motion to debate recent developments in eastern Europe. He said he regretted a debate on this subject had been called for this time. He would have preferred to have it come somewhat later.

Immediately following the Secretary's Harvard speech, Bevin said, he approached the French about an exchange of views on it. It was not, however, until Friday night after his speech before the Foreign Press Association here that he decided to visit Paris. He had not made up his mind on just what to say to the French. He was thinking along the lines of a British–French Monnet plan for Europe as a first step. As a result of soundings made in Brussels, he felt certain the Belgians would support such a plan. The Dutch, he believed, would also be interested.

In this matter, he continued, he did not want to work outside the United Nations. At some point the United Nations should be brought in. He hesitated though about the ECE being used. He would have to have more time to consider this.

On his return from Paris he said he would give Ambassador Douglas a full account of his talks.

The Secretary's Harvard speech, Bevin then said, was an announcement of the greatest historic significance. It rightly placed responsibility on Europe to make the next move and formulate a plan of reconstruction. The three immediate problems to be considered in any plan were food, coal and transport.

Bevin's concluding observations were that the US was in the position today where Britain was at the end of the Napoleonic wars. When those wars ended Britain held about 30 percent of the world's wealth. The US today holds about 50 percent. Britain for 18 years after Waterloo "practically gave away her exports" but this resulted in stability and a hundred years of peace.

Sent Dept 3279; repeated Paris as 327.

GALLMAN

840.00/6–1647 : Telegram

The Ambassador in France (Caffery) to the Secretary of State

SECRET   PARIS, June 16, 1947—6 p. m.

2378. Bidault tells me that he is not too happy about Bevin coming here at this juncture because his visit is being interpreted here as a desire on Bevin's part to steal the show. (The truth of the matter is that Bidault wanted to steal the show and Bevin beat him by a day or two.) Also he does not want to give the impression to small nations in Europe that a Franco–British condominium is out to dominate western Europe. Nevertheless, he will work enthusiastically and wholeheartedly with Bevin and ardently hopes that they can come to an agreement as to the approach to be made to Washington. However, he would prefer that France and Great Britain make their approaches separately even if they say the same words.

Bidault showed me a telegram he sent to his Ambassador at Moscow instructing him to inform the Soviet Government that conversations would soon be under way between Paris and London in regard to the Secretary's Harvard speech and that conversations are now under way between Paris and Washington (Bonnet's conversation Saturday with the Secretary). He instructed his Ambassador to tell the Soviet Government also that he would be "disposed" to enter into conversations at Moscow on the same subject if Moscow so desired.

Sent Department 2378, repeated Moscow 373, and London 451.

CAFFERY

840.50 Recovery/6–1747

The British Ambassador (*Inverchapel*) *to the Secretary of State* [1]

SECRET

WASHINGTON, June 17, 1947.

DEAR MR. SECRETARY: Mr. Bevin has asked me to let you know that the talks which he is having with the French Government today are exploratory in character but that he hopes they may be the first step in a speedy and concerted response to your inspiring lead.

As soon as the talks are over, Mr. Bevin will, of course, let you have a full account of them and of any tentative conclusions reached; and shortly thereafter Mr. Bevin hopes that the British Government will have an opportunity of going over the ground with Mr. Clayton, from whom they will be interested to hear how your own thoughts are developing.

You may further like to know for your own confidential information that, as soon as the exploratory talks with the French are over, Mr. Bevin intends to bring in the Belgium and Netherlands Governments.

Mr. Bevin has further asked me to give you the following paraphrase of a message which he has asked Sir M. Peterson [2] to deliver to M. Molotov:—

"As the Soviet Government is aware, His Majesty's Government are deeply concerned about the economic rehabilitation of Europe. The

---

[1] Marginal notation by the Director of the Office of Departmental Administration: "Secretary has seen and this has been passed along to Clayton–Thorp–Matthews etc. C[arlisle] H[umelsine]."

[2] Sir Maurice D. Peterson, Ambassador of the United Kingdom in the Soviet Union.

suggestion made by Mr. Marshall in recent statements that European countries should take the initiative by preparing a reconstruction plan seems to offer a new hope that the solution of Europe's economic difficulties may be facilitated. It is, therefore, in the view of His Majesty's Government a matter of the utmost urgency that some concrete plan should be proposed by the European countries so that it can be discussed with the United States Government as soon as possible. The issue is an economic not a political one. His Majesty's Government would be glad of any observations which the Soviet Government may care to offer as regards the United States Government proposal."

Mr. Bevin would like you to know confidentially that he is making this communication to the Soviet Government because he wishes to know as soon as possible whether or not they intend to take part in the preparation of a reconstruction plan for Europe.

Yours sincerely,

INVERCHAPEL

840.50 Recovery/6–1747

The Netherlands Ambassador (Loudon) to the Secretary of State

WASHINGTON, June 17, 1947.

SIR: I have the honor to inform Your Excellency that the Netherlands Government with great interest and deep appreciation has taken cognizance of the speech which you made at Cambridge, Massachusetts, on the 5th of this month concerning the economic rehabilitation of Europe, which cannot come about without the helping hand of the United States and constitutes an indispensable requisite for a sound world economy and the consolidation of peaceful relations between the nations.

In this connection, it may not be amiss to call attention to the fact that the Netherlands, in conjunction with Belgium and Luxembourg, since a considerable time have been striving to create such economic relations in Europe as will meet the requirements of present economic conditions and circumstances, an aim which in some measure has taken shape and expression in the Customs Union between these countries. The Netherlands Government is, naturally, fully disposed to give serious consideration to any other suggestion for the rebuilding of Europe's economic structure.

I may further advise Your Excellency that for some time past Her Majesty's Government has made the economic collaboration between the European countries a subject of study and research, as *i.a.* may appear from its memorandum concerning Germany of January 14, 1947, submitted to the Department of State with my note of January 25, 1947, No. 352,[1] and it is expected that the result of this enquiry will be communicated to the Government of the United States and those of the countries of Europe after the elapse of two months from the present date. In case the Department of State has already some material on the subject-matter available, tending to assist in forming an opinion on some point or another, it would be very helpful if Your Excellency would be so kind as to place it at the disposal of the Netherlands Government, which courtesy on your part would be deeply appreciated.

Please accept [etc.]

A. LOUDON

---

[1] Ambassador Loudon's note of January 25 is not printed. The Netherlands Government's memorandum of January 14, 1947, on Allied policy with regard to Germany was circulated as document CFM (D) (47) (G) 9 to the Deputies for Germany, who met in London from January 14 to February 25, 1947. The salient aspects of the Netherlands Government's proposals for a German peace settlement are included in the Report of the Deputies for Germany to the Council of Foreign Ministers, February 25, 1947, vol. II, pp. 40, 50.

840.00/6–1847 : Telegram

The Ambassador in France (Caffery) to the Secretary of State

SECRET

PARIS, June 18, 1947—4 p. m.

URGENT

2412. The British tell me that the conversations between Bevin and Bidault are progressing satisfactorily. They and the French have agreed on the following points:

(1) The necessity for inviting the Soviets to join in these talks and of getting a reply from them before July 5 on which date the European Economic Committee is to meet. British feel that Russian participation would tend greatly to complicate things and that it might be best if Russians refused invitation. They tell me that French also offer [appear?] to share this feeling. In any event they intend to issue invitation to the Russians in such form as to receive a reply before July 5.

(2) The formation of *ad hoc* committees on coal, food, steel, etc. These committees would be drawn together by a steering committee the chairman of which might be the chairman of the European Economic Committee.

(3) Desirability once conversations take further shape of inviting Belgium, Netherlands and later Czechoslovakia and Yugoslavia to participate.

Bevin leaves for London tomorrow morning. Conversations will continue on technical level.

Sent Department as 2412; repeated to London as 456.

CAFFERY

840.00/6–1847 : Telegram

The Ambassador in France (Caffery) to the Secretary of State

SECRET   PARIS, June 18, 1947—11 p. m.
URGENT

2427. Bevin and Bidault separately this evening gave me copies of an *aide-mémoire* in English and in French [1] which they were to give to the Soviet Chargé d'Affaires here later this evening reading as follows:

"The British and French Governments have examined with interest the statement made by Mr. Marshall at Harvard University on 5 June last. The two governments welcome with the greatest satisfaction the suggestions made by the United States Secretary of State. Mr. Marshall has not made any official approach to the two governments but in his speech he clearly suggests the drawing up of economic programmes by the European nations themselves, and indicates that the United States will be ready to lend their aid to the fullest possible extent for the execution of these programmes.

The Foreign Ministers of Great Britain and France consider that this aid is necessary, but that it will only bear fruit to the extent that the countries of Europe make the maximum effort to develop once more the resources which in the main they produced for themselves before the war, and which they have to import today, along with indispensable industrial equipment largely from the American continent.

The two governments consider that the economic condition of Europe necessitates the rapid drawing up of comprehensive programmes. Such programmes should be drawn up by all the countries of Europe which are willing to participate in such action, in liaison with the appropriate organs of the United Nations.

The initiatives to be taken are of extreme urgency because of the economic and financial situation of a great number of European countries. In the view of the British and French Governments, these initiatives should be taken by the three principal European powers. In view of the above, before any examination of the practical measures which must be taken to implement the American proposals, Mr. Bevin and M. Bidault propose to Mr. Molotov that a meeting of the British, French and Soviet Foreign Ministers should be held during the week beginning 23 June at a place to be agreed, in order to discuss these problems as a whole.

The most convenient place for the meeting for Mr. Bevin and M. Bidault, would of course be Paris or London. If however, Mr. Molotov should consider that another European city mid-way be-

---

[1] The French text of this *aide-mémoire* is printed in Ministère des Affaires Étrangères, *Documents de la Conférence des Ministres des Affaires Étrangères de la France, du Royaume-Uni, de l'U.R.S.S. tenue à Paris du 27 Juin au 3 Juillet 1947* etc. (Paris : Imprimerie Nationale, 1947), p. 15. A translation which differs somewhat from the text of the telegram above is found in the *French Yellow Book: Documents of the Conference of Foreign Ministers of France, the United Kingdom, and the U.S.S.R., held in Paris from the 27th June to the 3rd July, 1947* etc. (London : Hutchinson and Co., 1947?), pp. 18–19. Some of the documents of the French official publication are reprinted in Margaret Carlyle, Ed., *Documents on International Affairs, 1947–1948*, issued under the auspices of the Royal Institute of International Affairs (London, Oxford University Press, 1952), pp. 26–58.

tween Moscow and London should be chosen, we are disposed to consider any suggestions he might make."

Bevin and Bidault also both told me separately that they hope the Soviets will refuse to cooperate and that in any event they will be prepared "to go ahead with full steam even if the Soviets refuse to do so."

They both expressed again their vast interest in and appreciation of what the Secretary's Harvard speech implied.

What they agreed to in their conversations here is along the lines reported in my 2412, June 18.

Repeated to London as 457; to Moscow as 375.

CAFFERY

840.50 Recovery/6–1847

Memorandum of Conversation, by the Counselor of the Department of State (Cohen)

Participants: The Polish Ambassador, Mr. Winiewicz
                Mr. Cohen
                Mr. Thompson [1]

The Ambassador said he had read with great interest the Secretary's Harvard speech and public remarks made by myself and others with reference to the economic rehabilitation of Europe. He said that he was somewhat confused as to what we had in mind by the "Marshall Plan". From the Secretary's remarks it appeared that Eastern European countries would be included, but from press interpretations, particularly in Britain, it had been suggested that it envisaged only Western Europe. His first question, therefore, was: Did we have in mind that Eastern European countries might be included?

I replied by suggesting that he should be guided by the Secretary's remarks rather than by press interpretations. I said I could only say that my understanding was that we had in mind that the European countries should develop a program that would help Europe as a whole insofar as this was possible. I pointed out, however, that we had been disappointed over the trend of events which seemed to divide rather than unite Europe. I said that, speaking personally, I felt that it might be well to begin with steps or plans which would clearly be in the interest of Europe as a whole to the extent that this might be practicable.

---

[1] Llewellyn E. Thompson, Chief, Division of Eastern European Affairs.

The Ambassador then inquired what practical steps could be taken? Did we have in mind that this would be handled through the ECE or independent of that body?

I replied that I gathered that our position was that this was a question which the European countries should work out for themselves, and that we would neither insist upon nor reject the use of the ECE. I observed, however, that we had been disappointed by the lack of progress made up to date in that body.

The Ambassador said he did not know what his Government's official views were; he only knew of its great interest. He felt that all of the countries of Eastern Europe were at present considering the *Pravda* article,[2] which was the only expression of opinion so far from the Soviet Union. He personally did not interpret this article as excluding the possibility of Soviet cooperation or that the Soviet Government would oppose the program. He said he thought that the best thing for his country to do was to approach the Czechoslovak Government in the first instance since their positions were similar and their relations had greatly improved recently. He referred to the role that Poland could play in the economy of Europe and mentioned particularly the coal which they were now in a position to supply and their efforts to increase their production and their exports to Western Europe. He mentioned the fact that they had succeeded in obtaining the consent of the Soviet Government to reducing their coal exports to the Soviet Union from the figure earlier agreed upon. He also said that next year Poland would be in a position to help European countries with food. He pointed to the role that Poland had played in the creation of the ECE and the fact that Poland had decreased the proportion of her exports going to the Soviet Union as evidence of Poland's desire to integrate her economy with that of Western Europe.

In the course of the conversation I observed that assistance from the United States depended upon the attitude of the American people and said that, speaking quite frankly, some of the public declarations and things that were said about American assistance in the countries of Eastern Europe did not put the American people in the best mood to support measures of assistance. I reminded the Ambassador of his presence in Paris at a time when some unfortunate remarks on the part of certain Delegates at the Peace Conference had interfered with measures of assistance to Czechoslovakia. The Ambassador said he fully realized this.

The Ambassador expressed the hope that he would be able to discuss these matters more fully after he had received instructions from his Government. BENJAMIN V. COHEN

---

[2] For an excerpt from Pravda, June 16, see W. P. and Zelda K. Coates, *A History of Anglo-Soviet Relations*, vol. II, *1943–1950* (London, Lawrence & Wishart, 1958), p. 257. See also telegram 2270 from Moscow, *post*, p. 294.

840.50 Recovery/6–1947 : Telegram

The Ambassador in France (Caffery) to the Secretary of State

SECRET   PARIS, June 19, 1947.
URGENT

2440. The British tell me that they have "a firm verbal commitment" from the French that they will go along with them even if the Soviets refuse the invitation to participate in the conversations. They showed me a tentative agenda listing the "form and nature of American aid" in order of importance:

(a) Supply of raw materials, foodstuffs and animal feeds.
(b) Supply of equipment and means of production.
(c) Financial credits.

Duff Cooper [1] expects the Ministers to meet again next week. Repeated to London as 459, sent Department 2440.

CAFFERY

---

[1] Alfred Duff Cooper, British Ambassador in France.

840.50 Recovery/6–1947

The British Ambassador (Inverchapel) to the Secretary of State

SECRET   WASHINGTON, June 19, 1947.

DEAR MR. SECRETARY: On instructions from Mr. Bevin I enclose a copy of a message from him setting out the results of his conversations in Paris with M. Bidault on the subject of your proposals for European reconstruction.[1] Mr. Bevin has instructed His Majesty's Ambassador at Moscow to communicate this message urgently to M. Molotov. I understand that copies of the message have also been given to the American Ambassador and to the Soviet Chargé d'Affaires at Paris and that a communiqué in similar terms has been issued to the press.

2. In instructing His Majesty's Ambassador at Moscow to transmit the enclosed communication to M. Molotov, Mr. Bevin stated that he thought it possible that M. Molotov might ask whether it was proposed (a) to make use of the Economic Commission for Europe to frame the reply to yourself, or (b) to set up new and separate bodies. Mr. Gunnar Myrdal, the Executive Secretary of the Economic Commission for Europe, who is now in Moscow, would presumably have told the Russians that in his view and in that of Mr. Trygve Lie,[2] the

---

[1] Substantially the same as the aide-mémoire quoted in telegram 2427 from Paris, p. 259.
[2] Secretary General of the United Nations.

Commission is the proper body to convoke such experts as are needed to provide the basis for framing the reply.

3. Mr. Bevin told Sir Maurice Peterson that the answer to such an enquiry is, that Great Britain and France are anxious, assuming that Russian cooperation is secured, to bring in the Economic Commission for Europe at a later stage in whatever ways are judged most appropriate. But the Commission has not yet a fully developed Secretariat and though Mr. Bevin and M. Bidault have full confidence in Mr. Myrdal, they are convinced that his staff could not successfully organise the initial steps needed to provide the basis for a reply to your proposal, more especially as the Secretariat has to deal with the second meeting of the Commission on the 5th July and will be taking over the essential functions of the European Central Inland Transport Organisation, the Emergency Economic Commission for Europe, and the European Coal Organisation. Mr. Bevin and M. Bidault are convinced, therefore, that the initial steps must be taken outside the Economic Commission for Europe, but it is their hope that the Commission, at its forthcoming session, will take note of and approve the steps taken, and it is the view of Mr. Bevin and M. Bidault that, assuming Russian cooperation, full use should be made of the Commission and its staff at a later stage.

Yours sincerely,

INVERCHAPEL

840.00/6–2047 : Telegram

The Secretary of State to the Embassy in the United Kingdom

SECRET

WASHINGTON, June 20, 1947.

2670. For Ambassador. I am repeating to you separately [1] a cable sent 19 June [2] from Secys War, Navy and myself to Clay [3] and Murphy which summarizes cables I have sent to Embs Paris, Brussels, Rome, Hague,[4] which outline principles enunciated in my Harvard speech and ask comments on certain general and specific matters relating to formulating a program of European rehabilitation. The cable to Clay and Murphy inquires re contribution western Germany can make to such a program. Mr. Clayton will discuss the whole matter

[1] Telegram 2671, to London, June 20, not printed.
[2] Telegram 1292 to the U.S. Political Adviser on German Affairs (Murphy), at Berlin, not printed.
[3] Gen. Lucius D. Clay, U.S. Military Governor for Germany.
[4] Telegram 2143, June 12, to Paris, p. 249; similar messages were sent to the other three Embassies on June 13.
Replies from the four diplomatic missions, not printed, are in files 840.00 and 840.50 Recovery. These replies were received in the Department over a period of several weeks. Situations described therein were frequently overtaken by events.

with you in detail. The valuable analysis and info you have sent us on UK position and prospects have been most helpful.

If, after reading cable mentioned above, you have further comments or recommendations to make which you believe would assist us. we should be glad to have them.

Of immediate concern is the question of what role, if any, the ECE can usefully play in developing a European program. While the use of a UN body whose terms of reference directly cover this type of problem would be desirable and in accord with our long-range objectives towards UN, we share the fear that effective and prompt action might be very difficult there, whether because of the inefficiency of a new and untried body or because of a continuance of the obstructive tactics pursued by the eastern countries at the first session. Further consideration must be given to whether FAO should be used in connection with the food aspects of any program. We are inclined to let the European countries, particularly the UK and France, take the initiative in determining whether ECE has a role but will urge, if it is used, that guarantees of prompt and effective action be given by setting a definite timetable with interim progress reports and reserving the position of interested countries to proceed outside ECE if delay occurs there. The desirability of improving coal production before winter and fertilizer and agricultural equipment production by the autumn planting season gives us targets to aim at. We would also consider it important that non-members particularly Italy and Austria should take full part.

We are inclined to feel that the most fruitful immediate action would be along the lines of specific subjects such as coal, food, clothing production and transport rather than more elaborate plans for general increased industrial activity which would take longer to plan and which must be based on reasonably adequate fuel, food, housing and transport

Pls bring to attention Porter, MEA.[5] Dept will comment on Embtel 3201 June 11 separately.[6]

MARSHALL

---

[5] Paul R. Porter, Acting Chief, Mission for Economic Affairs at London.
[6] Not printed.

Lot 64 D 563, Box 1 (20027)

Statement Issued to the Press by the White House, June 22, 1947

STATEMENT BY THE PRESIDENT

The impact upon our domestic economy of the assistance we are now furnishing or may furnish to foreign countries is a matter of grave concern to every American. I believe we are generally agreed that the recovery of production abroad is essential both to a vigorous democracy and to a peace founded on democracy and freedom. It is essential also to a world trade in which our businessmen, farmers and workers may benefit from substantial exports and in which their customers may be able to pay for these goods. On the other hand, the extent to which we should continue aiding such recovery is less easy to ascertain, and merits most careful study.

Much attention has already been given to these questions by various agencies of the Government, as well as by a number of well-informed and public-spirited citizens. The results of current study and discussion have not, however, been brought together and objectively evaluated in a form suitable for guidance in the formulation of national policy.

Accordingly, I am creating immediately three committees to study and report to me within the shortest possible time on the relationship between any further aid which may be extended to foreign countries and the interests of our domestic economy. Two of these studies will be conducted within the Government; the third will be conducted by a non-partisan committee of distinguished citizens headed by the Secretary of Commerce.[1]

Of the two studies to be conducted within the Government, one will deal with the state of our national resources, and will be made by a committee of specialists under the direction of the Secretary of the Interior.[2] The other governmental study will deal with the impact on our national economy of aid to other countries, and will be conducted by the Council of Economic Advisers.[3]

The non-partisan committee will be requested to determine the facts with respect to the character and quantities of United States resources available for economic assistance to foreign countries, and to advise me, in the light of these facts, on the limits within which the United States may safely and wisely plan to extend such assistance and on the relation between this assistance and our domestic economy. This committee will be drawn from representatives of American business, finance, labor, agriculture and educational and research institutions. In carrying out its work this committee will have the benefit of the studies which are to be made within the Government, as well as the materials already prepared by various Government agencies.

---

[1] The proposal for such studies was originally made in a Policy Planning Staff Memorandum of June 19, 1947, entitled "Studies Relating to the Impact of Aid to Foreign Countries on U.S. Domestic Economy and Natural Resources", not printed. The committee headed by the Secretary of Commerce was referred to as the Harriman Committee.

[2] This committee was known as the Krug Committee.

[3] This was commonly known as the Nourse Committee.

The names of those being asked to serve on the committee are as follows:

Hiland Batcheller, Pres.,
Allegheny–Ludlum Steel Corp.,
Pittsburgh, Pennsylvania.

Robert Earle Buchanan, Dean,
Graduate College,
Iowa State College,
Ames, Iowa.

W. Randolph Burgess,
Vice-Chairman,
National City Bank of N.Y.,
New York, N.Y.

Paul G. Hoffman, Pres.,
The Studebaker Corp.,
South Bend, Indiana.

Calvin B. Hoover, Dean,
Graduate School,
Duke University,
Durham, North Carolina.

Robert Koenig, Pres.,
Ayrshire Collieries Co.,
Big Four Building,
Indianapolis, Indiana.

840.00/6–2347 : Telegram

The Ambassador in France (Caffery) to the Secretary of State

SECRET   PARIS, June 23, 1947—11 a. m

URGENT

2481. Chauvel [1] informs me that Molotov has accepted invitation of Bidault and Bevin to discuss the proposals set forth in Secretary's Harvard speech and that he will come to Paris next Friday, June 27 for discussions.

Sent to Department as 2481; repeated London 468, Moscow 379.

CAFFERY

---

[1] Jean Chauvel, Secretary General of the French Foreign Office.

840.50 Recovery/6–2347 : Telegram

The Ambassador in the Soviet Union (Smith) to the Secretary of State

TOP SECRET   Moscow, June 23, 1947—5 p. m

2246. Although apparent now that Molotov will participate in conversations in Paris regarding a European economic plan, I feel sure that this participation will be for destructive rather than constructive purposes. British and French Ambassadors here have privately expressed same view to me. Reason for my opinion is that intelligent and well implemented plan for economical recovery would militate against the present Soviet political objectives.[1]

SMITH

---

[1] In telegram 2487, from Paris, not printed, Ambassador Caffery reported that French officials feared that Molotov's coming was designed to sabotage the Marshall plan. (840.00/6–2347)

Lot 122, Box 13113

Memorandum by the Director of the Policy Planning Staff (*Kennan*) *to the Assistant Secretary of State for Economic Affairs* (*Thorp*)

SECRET   [WASHINGTON,] June 24, 1947.

The Policy Planning Staff will require, in connection with its examination of the problems of European reconstruction, a series of brief background studies relating to certain important items of European economy. These are the items which may constitute the basis of the functional approach to problems of European recovery, now under discussion in many quarters of Europe.

The fields of European economy which I have in mind in this connection are the following:

> Coal
> Electric power
> Steel
> Agriculture
> Food
> Inland transport
> Shipping and shipbuilding

You may think of others which should be included. The principal criterion in my mind is that they should be fields of activity which might be supposed to have key significance in Europe's recovery and ones which would lend themselves to treatment on an overall European basis rather than a national basis.[1]

Since it is impossible to draw up any common set of terms of reference for these studies, I enclose individual papers [2] on each of the items mentioned setting forth the points in which I am particularly interested. They will serve at least to reveal the nature of the inquiry. The persons preparing the study are welcome to add other items if they consider them pertinent to the general purpose of the inquiry.

These studies need not be exhaustive. We merely want the main outlines of the facts which bear on the situation. I am afraid that we will need the completed studies at a very early date if they are to be useful in the work which the Planning Staff now has in hand. They should, if possible, be completed by the Fourth of July weekend or, if that is simply not possible in certain instances, by July 15. But we would prefer to have brief skeleton surveys at an early date rather than long and detailed studies later. If questions of priority are involved, I am sure that Mr. Lovett will agree with me on the

---

[1] On the previous day, a Working Group on European Reconstruction, drawn from the offices responsible to the Assistant Secretary of State for Economic Affairs, met to consider "ways and means of implementing the European Reconstruction program". (Memorandum of June 23 Meeting, Lot 122, Box 13113.)
[2] Enclosures not printed.

overriding importance of getting into the Secretary's hands at a very early date a workable study of the main elements of the European reconstruction problem and will be prepared to support any requests we may have to make of other people for rapid action on these inquiries.

I am addressing this request to you with the feeling that you will know better than I do what can be done in the sections of the Department under your supervision and what should be farmed out elsewhere in the Department and the Government. (Presumably the food study, for example, can be farmed out at once to Agriculture.) In general, there is a virtue in spreading responsibility for this type of study as widely as possible.

Many of the questions may look so naively broad as to horrify the scholarly economist. If so, tell your people to disregard their consciences, take a deep breath, and let us have their best guess.

G[EORGE] F. K[ENNAN]

840.50 Recovery/7–147

Memorandum of Conversation, by the First Secretary of Embassy in the United Kingdom (Peterson)

TOP SECRET   [LONDON,] June 24, 1947.

SUMMARY OF FIRST MEETING OF UNDER SECRETARY CLAYTON AND AMBASSADOR WITH BRITISH CABINET MEMBERS [1]

MR. BEVIN

The chronic troubles of Europe are interwoven with politics and our dollar problem really comes from Europe. Europe can contribute materially to the solution but Britain with an Empire is on a different basis.

I am looking for some temporary interim solution to enable the U.K. to play its part. The U.K. dollar problem is seen in Balkan countries as well as in the U.K. and all we try to do or say in Europe is conditioned by our own resources.

I went ahead on the Marshall Plan without asking questions and I feel that it is the quickest way to break down the iron curtain. My recent experience in France shows that Russia cannot hold its satellites against the attraction of fundamental help toward economic revival in Europe. If the U.K. in playing its part in this program should en-

---

[1] Meeting held at the Prime Minister's residence, 10 Downing Street, London. On July 1 Ambassador Douglas sent to the Secretary of State and other officials copies of this memorandum and the memoranda that follow summarizing the other four meetings.

counter snags we would desire and hope that the U.S. can put the U.K. in position to go ahead. We really ask to be in the position which we held in 1923–24 in economic reconstruction after the last war. I would impress upon everyone the importance of quick action if anything is to be done.

I am worried about the loan [2] and for practically all of my plans Mr. Dalton [3] puts in a caveat as regards our resources. The rise in prices has thrown us a year out and the U.K. position compelled me at Moscow to draw in my horns. For that reason I could not support Secretary Marshall to the extent I desired and I think it would pay the U.S. and the world for the U.S. and the U.K. to establish a financial partnership.

The first European need is for food. We need a better pipeline and a security of rations. I need six or eight weeks stockpile of grain to guarantee a ration of 1800 calories to 1949 (presumably referring to Germany.)

MR. DALTON

Reviewed the financial position and found rapid worsening of their position in the last six months. The rate of drawings upon the loan has risen rapidly and this loan (which they had expected would carry Britain through the "difficult" period) would be exhausted at the end of the year.

In ascertaining why this had happened he mentioned wholesale prices up by 40 per cent. This had in effect reduced the value of the loan by $1 billion. Secondly, Canada and Argentina had demanded dollars to a rapidly increasing extent in payment for Britain's imports from those countries and third, this action revealed a dollar shortage throughout the world which was fundamental to difficulties faced by Britain. The real reason for the difficulties was the slow rate of world recovery including recovery in the Far East and Indonesia which were important to the United Kingdom. The world problem had an impact requiring very urgent action.

In their own field they might take defensive action by cutting U.K. imports but this would start a circle of restrictionism which should be avoided. Sir Stafford Cripps [4] interjected that the U.K. had encountered increasing difficulties in earning foreign exchange, mentioning import handicaps in Latin America and recent cancellations of U.S. contracts for example for linen and hosiery. These troubles arose from a dollar shortage all over the world.

Mr. Clayton said Mr. Bevin's speed in acting after the Secretary's speech created a highly favorable impression in the United States.

---

[2] For documentation on implementation of the loan agreement, see pp. 1 ff.
[3] Hugh Dalton, Chancellor of the Exchequer.
[4] President of the British Board of Trade.

In the U.S. viewpoint, no further piecemeal assistance was feasible for Europe. The problem must be dealt with as a whole. Italy might today be in the worst position of European countries but solution of Italian problems must await a program for the whole problem. Thus speed was essential.

Mr. Clayton referred to an opening remark by Mr. Bevin to the effect that the U.K. wanted to be a partner in the European Plan and if it could not be equipped financially to carry out such a partnership its relations with the U.S. would become somewhat similar to relationship between the U.S.S.R. and Yugoslavia. Mr. Clayton could not see how the U.K. could find itself in a "Yugoslav" position. He asked how the U.K. problem was different from other European countries.

Mr. Clayton referred to the paper delivered at Washington regarding the U.K. financial and trading position [5] and understood the difficulties. As for Russia's Satellites in Eastern Europe he doubted with Mr. Bevin whether the U.S.S.R. could hold or improve its position there, because those countries would be compelled for a long time to trade actively with the rest.

Mr. Clayton reiterated that he was unable to visualize the Administration going to Congress regarding new proposals for any one country and he felt that a European plan must be worked out. In this, Mr. Bevin's continued leadership would be welcomed.

Mr. Bevin

Brief discussion indicated that Bevin is most anxious for some interim financial arrangement from the U.S. to stop a back-biting of his foreign affairs moves by people at home who were pinched by the British financial position. He considered the U.K. production and recovery record since the war as a good one. Mr. Clayton mentioned that not all of the financial difficulties were due to the U.S. price rise. Mr. Bevin said the "circle" must be broken. "Can't some temporary arrangement running to 1947 and '48 be worked out? Give me 5 million tons of grain and I will break the production problem in Germany".

Mr. Dalton interjected with reference to Mr. Clayton's question that one difference between the U.K. and other European countries was that the U.K. is helping in Germany. Mr. Bevin, reverting to food, said the U.S.S.R. was flush with cereals and he was trying to get grain from them. Poland was in balance. On the general European plan he had in mind dealing with food, coal, steel etc. in parallel columns to show requirements of individual countries. But he needed some assurance

---

[5] *Ante*, p. 17.

of continuity of supply in 1947–48—perhaps 1949—which he called "two desperate years".

Sir Stafford Cripps interjected that internal measures open to the U.K. could not make more than six weeks difference in the exhaustion of British resources and also expressed the opinion that there was a difference between the U.K. and other European countries because of U.K. trade with non-European countries.

Mr. Bevin said that if U.K. was considered just another European country this would fit in with Russian strategy, namely, that the U.S. would encounter a slump and would withdraw from Europe, the U.K. would be helpless and out of dollars and as merely another European country the Russians, in command of the Continent, could deal with Britain in due course. Speaking of food, the Prime Minister mentioned that Britain had to let Australian supplies go to India to avoid starvation and catastrophe for which Britain held political responsibility and similar considerations applied in parts of Africa.

Mr. Douglas

The Ambassador referred to figures received from the Treasury and asked whether the draw-down of the loan in the next six months would be as rapid as in the first six months of 1947. He mentioned that part of the recent drain was for the purpose of replenishing stocks which had been run down in the first spurt of U.K. economic revival and also that British purchase of ships was a non-recurring item. After momentary thought Mr. Dalton said he was not hopeful of improvement. He agreed that replenishment of stocks and ship purchase might not recur but replenishment would carry over a twelve-month period. Contra items were the cost of convertibility (see below) about which the British had argued at Washington, the dollar cost of which he could not estimate. Nondiscrimination in imports was also mentioned. Mr. Bevin interjected that convertibility and nondiscrimination obligations upon the U.K. had in his opinion been dated three years too soon. Sir Stafford Cripps mentioned that their export estimates might prove high and recent closing of markets raises the question that even though the British could make the goods they might not be able to sell them. In response to Mr. Clayton's question he said he thought Argentine marketing difficulties represented hit-or-miss measures by Miranda [6] of the Argentine Government.

Mr. Clayton then asked pointedly why Mr. Dalton had not come earlier with these troubles noting that Congress would adjourn July 26 and exceptional cases for relief from governmental commitments might be difficult to handle at this session. He would not prophesy inability to handle cases in this Congress but wondered why the British

---

[6] Miguel Miranda, President of the Argentine Economic Council.

authorities had not taken up the problem when it first arose. The British response was that Canada and Argentina demands for dollars caused much of the trouble and this had arisen rapidly and somewhat surreptitiously.

Mr. Dalton, in referring to convertibility of sterling made it clear he was *not* asking for or suggesting any change in this commitment under the Financial Agreement. Moreover, he pointed out that regardless of the terms of the Financial Agreement a large part of the difficulties now facing the British would have arisen anyway.

MR. CLAYTON

Referring to Mr. Bevin's need of food, Mr. Clayton said that food up till now was a question of production and not money, noting that the 15 million ton export of U.S. cereals was a vast effort and reached about the maximum which transport and transit facilities would allow.[7] He agreed the U.S. was well fed and possibly wasteful of food but this did not indicate unwillingness to share with others since the transit problem was the bottleneck. We did not have the boxcars, terminals, port facilities, etc. and could not create them over-night. Perhaps one million more tons of cereals could be gotten out but there was a limit. Mr. Bevin observed that in contrast to UNRRA operations the authorities could concentrate needs of food better at present and could avoid waste in Europe.

Mr. Bevin spoke of German affairs, mentioning recent conversations with General Robertson[8] and difficulties in working out plans because of U.S. budgetary limitations. "In our plans, will we be held up by appropriations?" "Clay and Robertson seem forever tied by appropriation questions". Mr. Clayton said that of course appropriations were a limiting factor in our form of government but he would look into the difficulty.

Mr. Clayton reiterated that the U.K. as a partner in the Marshall program rather than a part of Europe, with special assistance to the U.K. partner would violate the principle that no piecemeal approach to the European problem would be undertaken. He said that in the U.S. even a non-piecemeal approach would be hard to sell to the U.S. public and Congress and he frankly saw no possibility of interim arrangements for the U.K. as part of the European approach. (At this point I thought Sir Stafford Cripps raised two points in the Financial Agreement, namely, convertibility and nondiscrimination in imports which might be looked into as some relief to the British dollar problem. Mr. Gunter[9] is not quite sure if this was specifically raised by Cripps.)

---

[7] For documentation regarding U.S. concern about the world food shortage, see *Foreign Relations, 1946*, vol. I, pp. 1439 ff.

[8] Deputy Military Governor, British Zone of Occupation in Germany.

[9] John W. Gunter, U.S. Treasury Representative in London.

At this point Mr. Clayton raised the first of his criticisms of the U.K., namely, their handling of the Ruhr coal problem. He also then raised the question of U.K. action regarding measures in Japan, both of which had been covered separately.

To summarize, Mr. Clayton described the idea presented by Secretary Marshall as involving a really big problem. The U.S. Administration wanted information from all of the interested European countries as to why recovery in Europe had been so slow, what Europe could do to help itself, and how long it might take, with a minimum of assistance from the United States for Europe to get back on its own feet.

Following views on reasons for slow recovery and remedial measures, we would need information regarding food requirements, fuel requirements and other emergency essentials.

Prime Minister, referring to Mr. Clayton's remark on socialization, said that new socialist structures were created as alternatives to structures created by the Nazis which syndicates could not be allowed to reemerge and if they did would cause fears in neighboring countries. Mr. Bevin thought the trouble in Germany stemmed from unsettled level-of-industry questions and mentioned controversy of whether German steel production was to be 11 million tons or some other figure. He also deprecated dismantling of German industry and asked that Clay settle this question so the Germans will know where they stand, expressing willingness to fight out with the French any US–UK agreements which were not palatable. Besides level-of-industry problems, he thought the Potsdam Agreement, forced on him in his first day of office, left much to be desired. Syndicates in Germany were a war potential and could not be put back. In general, Mr. Bevin thought U.S. and U.K. plans for Germany were not far apart. Mr. Clayton said he would look into the level-of-industry problem in Germany.

On the point of German management, the Ambassador expressed his personal view that part of the problem hinged on the question of clothing managers of the industrial operations with enough authority to get production going. He also believed that the lack of a currency in Germany which commanded public confidence was a root difficulty, decreasing incentives, diverting resources, creating black markets and chicanery. (There was general agreement that the lack of confidence in currency was a problem which applied over all Europe). Mr. Bevin agreed on the currency question and mentioned his thought that the currency for the non-Russian zones could be linked with the French franc, the Belgian franc and the Dutch guilder. He referred to confusion of authority in coal operations and said he was trying to get this straightened out. The proposal of Clay for a single trustee he thought would not work.

840.50 Recovery/7–147

Memorandum of Conversation, by the First Secretary of Embassy in the United Kingdom (Peterson)

TOP SECRET   [LONDON,] June 24, 1947

RECAPITULATION OF MAIN POINTS OF DISCUSSIONS OF UNDER SECRETARY CLAYTON AND AMBASSADOR DOUGLAS WITH BRITISH OFFICIALS RE- GARDING THE DOLLAR PROBLEM

This meeting, under the chairmanship of Sir Edward Bridges,[1] was held at 4:00 o'clock June 24 in the Treasury Chambers. There were present Sir John Henry Wood and James Helmore of the Board of Trade; Sir Percivale Liesching, Ministry of Food; Sir Edmund Hall-Patch, Foreign Office; A.T.K. Grant and R.W.B. Clarke of the Treasury; and a representative of the Ministry of Fuel and Power Mr. Peterson and Mr. Gunter attended from the Embassy.

Sir Edward Bridges opened the discussion seeking elucidation of Mr. Clayton's plans for short-term assistance to Europe. Mr. Clayton contemplated the essential components of assistance as food, fuel and fiber but said that the present rate of Europe's imports, some $3 billion annually, could not continue but must be reduced by rehabilitation and enlarged production.

Mr. Clayton said the long-term assistance in reconstruction and development should be via the International Bank. He felt that the Bank's view of Europe and its repayment prospects depended on an attack on the immediate problem of food, fuel and fiber. He felt that it was up to Europe to agree on a program and he hoped this would contemplate minimum and decreasing calls on the U.S.

Sir Edward Bridges summarized these points as an inventory of Europe's needs and a cooperative agreement in Europe regarding economic rehabilitation. He understood that the U.S. plan would require commitments on rehabilitation and asked questions regarding the speed of the program and the number of nations which would be involved. Mr. Clayton reiterated the program could not be piece-meal—no dabs of assistance here and there.

Sir John Henry Wood discussed various aspects of European trade particularly as it related to the U.K. From what he understood about the nature of the possible short time assistance to Europe by the U.S. he was doubtful as to the advantage which would accrue to the U.K., particularly if no special consideration was given the U.K. position and if the plan involved submerging British national interests. In particular, he was worried about pooling of

---

[1] Permanent Secretary to the British Treasury.

European resources. He thought that if the plan put dollars into Europe this would automatically ease the U.K. position to some extent, but that the relief would not be of sufficient magnitude. The pooling of assistance would reduce the U.K. position to that of the "lowest" in Europe. If this was the case, in view of Britain's relative advance in production as compared to the rest of Europe, he thought the U.K. might be better outside of the plan since the British position could be maintained by bilateral deals.

Sir Percivale Liesching visualized the U.K. as a partner with the U.S. in world recovery and said the U.K. was examining the Marshall Plan to consider how far it would help the British position. He saw the plan as a partial solution.

Mr. Clayton indicated that he failed to understand the British argument that they would not benefit in the plan for Europe. In particular, he felt that U.K. would not gain from a restrictionist policy.

In answer to Sir Edward Bridges' question on timing Mr. Clayton said it would be impossible for the present Congress to consider assistance to Europe and as yet there was only talk of another session.

Mr. Helmore attempted to explain how some people in the British Government felt that the U.K. would be better off to follow at this time a policy based on bilateral trade deals. This discussion was rapid and not lucid to Peterson but seemed based on the thought that, given the relatively strong U.K. economic position as compared with Europe other than Belgium, the U.K. was in strong position to bargain and deal bilaterally with suppliers and thus induce a change in terms of trade in favor of Britain. Sir Edmund Hall-Patch felt that the Marshall Plan does not meet U.K. needs because Britain's lack of dollars made it impotent to act as a partner in the plan.

Mr. Clayton attempted to explain in more detail how he is visualized that short term assistance would be provided. In particular, he stated that he was not thinking in terms of limiting supplies that could be purchased in the U.S. For example, the plan might include purchases of food stuffs for the U.K. from Canada and Latin America.[2] The British representative indicated that they had not been clear on this point and that obviously if the plan took this form the British dollar position would be considerably relieved.

There was a flavor of critical examination of the Marshall idea in the comments of the British officials and at one stage Mr. Douglas pointed out to Sir Edward Bridges that we had been seeking the facts of the British financial position for three months, "but only last Friday were we able to get the figures". Sir Edward agreed and regretted

---

[2] Dollar credits authorized by the Export-Import Bank in 1946 to aid European recovery generally were in the form of "tied" loans, requiring the borrower to buy United States goods and services.

the delay, but said there was a most complex web of transactions to be analyzed in getting the present estimates and the Treasury had been loaded with work.

The discussion included brief resume of coal production, efficiency at the coal face, absenteeism and stock position. Stocks are expected to reach nine million tons by October 1. Sir John Henry Wood was optimistic regarding the coal and steel position. There was also a discussion of U.K. food imports totalling $1,600,000,000, of which approximately $220 million came from the U.S.; $270 from Canada; $190 from Argentina; $200 from Australia and New Zealand and perhaps $250 from the Colonial Areas. Mr. Gunter and Treasury officials analyzed the British financial tables and it was agreed that Mr. Gunter's method of analysis showing part of British difficulties as attributable to decreased sterling balances could be defended.

At the conclusion of the meeting Mr. Douglas referred to the need for budgetary rationalization among countries of Europe and thought the Marshall Plan would involve commitments regarding fiscal affairs. In the absence of commitments further assistance to European economy would be fruitless since the whole scheme would be undermined by inflationary pressures which would break through the existing mechanisms of control.

840.50 Recovery/7–147

Memorandum of Conversation, by the First Secretary of Embassy in the United Kingdom (Peterson)

TOP SECRET   [LONDON,] June 25, 1947.

SUBSTANCE OF SECOND MEETING OF UNDER SECRETARY CLAYTON AND AMBASSADOR WITH BRITISH CABINET MEMBERS

[Here follows a discussion of international rubber questions.]

Mr. Bevin as the next point sought elucidation of Mr. Clayton's belief that the UK problem must be lumped into the problem of Europe, because if that were the case, in forthcoming meetings, Mr. Bevin's approach would have to be changed. Mr. Bevin had planned (1) a steering committee (2) groups to analyze needs in relation to European production (3) groups on finance (4) groups on railway problems, their needs and organization (5) groups on motor transport (difficult because of cutdown in Germany, the biggest producer) and (6) groups regarding credits, currency, etc.

When the plans of these working parties were completed and in operation Bevin thought the only effect on the UK would be that—in time, a year or two—Europe would be in somewhat better position to pay for British imports but since in the interim period Europe would consume all she could produce there would be little effect on the UK position except perhaps for an increase in dollar receipts from German exports.

As to Germany, Mr. Dalton mentioned the cost of the Byrnes Agreement.[1] Originally for an eighteen-month period from January, 1947, total cost was contemplated as $860 million of which the UK share was $460 million which in terms of dollar drain on the UK was estimated as $200 million. This last figure, revised because of price changes was now $275 million. A further overall increase in costs for Germany to provide additional calories had added $150 million to the total bill ($75 million to the U.K.) which made the present rate of drain on the UK for Germany some $350 million. "Pretty poor", according to Dalton.

Mr. Bevin noted that if Poland feeds Europe, Poland demands dollars in exchange because the Polish Prime Minister has a solid case as to his needs of U.S. equipment. Bevin was cultivating the Polish Prime Minister, having decided to center British policy around the new leader whom he had consulted on return from Moscow. He believed this plan would be fruitful. Similar approaches were being made in Yugoslavia where Bevin had talked. He was convinced that Yugoslavia would gradually come west. Yugoslav needs were agricultural implements, railway equipment, timber-cutting equipment, etc. which Russia could not supply. In connection with Yugoslavia mention was made of Trieste and the effect of the opening of that port on Yugoslavia's western connections. But when Bevin asked Cripps what he could give up for Yugoslavia, Cripps could offer little, primarily because of the steel shortage. This was the pattern wherein Britain got into a dollar tangle in order to "get going" on constructive political relationships. Mr. Bevin did not foresee early solution of these political difficulties. We must have patience but he was confident. Mr. Bevin said that if the U.S. took the line that the U.K. was the same as any other European country this would be unfortunate because the UK could contribute to economic revival. The UK held stocks of rubber and wool and "we, as the British Empire", could assist materially. The British did not want to go into the program and not do anything—this would sacrifice the "little bit of dignity we have left".

---

[1] Presumably the agreement of December 2, 1946, between the United States and the United Kingdom on the economic fusion of their respective zones of occupation in Germany. For text, see Department of State Treaties and Other International Acts Series (TIAS) No. 1575, or 61 Stat. (pt. 3), 2475, and for related documentation, see *Foreign Relations*, 1946, vol. v, pp. 635–648.

Mr. Clayton did not quite see how the UK position was different from that of other European countries. The whole trouble arose from a shortage of dollars but this in turn represented failure of Europe to produce. The production bottleneck should be eased in a few years—perhaps by 1951. The UK had a dollar shortage the same as other European countries and if the US could do something to ease this shortage he wondered where the difference in impact upon the UK arose. Sir Stafford Cripps responded that the UK was a natural market for European goods for which the US were not buyers. Mr. Clayton had some question on this point but Cripps mentioned timber, foodstuffs (especially perishables, dairy products and dried fruits) and said "if you want to rehabilitate Europe that market (the UK) must be rehabilitated. The dollar drain is coming through the UK".

Mr. Clayton still could not see the difference. He thought if the UK received dollars from its trade with Europe their position would be satisfactory. Mr. Clayton thought the Marshall idea would put dollars into Europe by taking care of their essential imports, leaving more of the proceeds of their exports available for payment for goods imported from Britain.

Mr. Clayton said that in the US examination of the dollar problem it seemed to fall into two parts—(1) a short-range problem, mainly requirements of food and fuel—perhaps fiber—which might cost three and one-half to four billion dollars (2) reconstruction and development where responsibility fell on the International Bank. The Bank was getting well organized, had a good staff and US and UK controlled it. If there was a solution of the short-term European problem there would be a firm foundation for the Bank to go ahead with longer-term reconstruction and development. Mr. Clayton thought he may have given an incorrect impression that US aid would be set forth specifically in food and basic raw materials. If the UK needed food we did not mean that the US would necessarily supply it. There should be no "tied loan" principle. The US would simply look at the emergency European problem in bulk, mainly the three "f's"—food, fuel and fiber. In these observations Mr. Clayton was merely thinking aloud but it was his idea that whatever the US would do would probably be untied, just as was the British loan.

Mr. Bevin asked if the US could not bring Canada and Argentina into such a Lend-Lease conception and thus save the UK on dollars. In mentioning Lend-Lease, Mr. Bevin did not contemplate strict repetition of such a device but thought something akin to Lend-Lease would be the end result.

Sir Edward Bridges recapitulated the last point that Mr. Clayton gave—(1) short-term assistance for Europe (2) assurances from

Europe as to what it would do to help itself and (3) a certain integration of "degree of closeness" of economic relations in Europe as an essential component. He said the UK did not contemplate going into a European Customs Union. Even the UK–French plans for integration were not complete and although Belgium, Netherlands, and Luxembourg were going ahead with the Customs Union they had encountered difficulties. A full blueprint for Europe would take too long for the present emergency.

Sir Edward asked how Britain would fit into the plan. If the US was thinking of help in kind from the US the effect would be only to prolong by a few months the date when the credit would be exhausted. He thought Mr. Clayton's remarks showed an understanding that as far as the UK was concerned their requirements could not be confined to goods from the US but would be needed from usual sources. He understood there was a further point, namely, that Europe should join together in giving assurances. The UK had a fear of the "European pool" idea in the Marshall Plan which he thought would bring the UK down to the level of the lowest in Europe. Sir Edward also understood the US contemplated a series of bilateral agreements with individual European countries which would take into account the differences in economic needs of the various countries and yet permit the program to be put to Congress as a unified scheme. Mr. Clayton said there was no "pooling" idea current in Washington; it was his idea that there would be bilateral agreements within the framework of a European program of rehabilitation.

Sir Wilfrid Eady sought reassurance that the US considered the International Bank an effective mechanism for the second stage. Mr. Clayton said the primary need was to create investors' confidence in prospects of repayments of loans. Mr. Dalton noted the Bank had been slow in organization, with many changes in management and this caused much discouragement among the British. He asked if Mr. McCloy [2] thought the Bank would go into Europe and Mr. Clayton replied affirmatively. Mr. Bevin asked how far political consideration[s] would come into lending by the Bank. He presumed bank loaning would be dependent upon the conclusion of treaties with former enemies and that as for Allies there would be assurances under their United Nations obligations. With Europe striving to produce there would be reasonable chance of repayment.

Mr. Clayton said that the Bank's constitution required that political considerations should not enter into decisions on loans and noted that in connection with the Polish loan a delegation was making an on-the-

---

[2] John J. McCloy, President of the International Bank for Reconstruction and Development.

spot investigation and undoubtedly the Bank would require an agreement regarding Polish coal (both present production and that attributable to the new machinery) before funds for re-equipment would be forthcoming. Other details of operations of the International Bank were discussed.

Mr. Dalton raised the nondiscrimination clause in the Financial Agreement. The British dollar position required them to look at their import programs where they were unwilling (and shouldn't) reduce food imports. But certain articles, for example, fruit, could be purchased from soft currency countries yet this could not be the exclusive source under the nondiscrimination clause. Fruit from the US added "very much" to the dollar problem. Tobacco was a similar case in point. He had taken tax action to cut imports and in other directions the UK "may take action". In the case of films he had taken power to act which he felt the Government must have if it were necessary later to take some action.

In connection with nondiscrimination, discussion arose regarding the present British interpretation of Clause 9 of the Financial Agreement as applied to trade between the UK and its Colonial Areas for which the UK provided a common quota in the Monetary Fund. As the Department is aware, the British consider themselves free to discriminate in favor of trade within this UK–Colonial Area. The British express belief that this interpretation would ease the impact of the nondiscrimination clause. Mr. Clayton and the Ambassador agreed and did not challenge this interpretation of Clause 9.

Mr. Clayton said with emphasis that the matter of nondiscrimination "comes so late". The loan was an Act of Congress and relief on nondiscrimination meant passage of a joint resolution where many questions would be asked and this might call for exposure or some revelation of the UK situation.

Sir Edward Bridges mentioned the clause regarding imports from countries with war-shattered economies and Mr. Douglas agreed that we and the British could take a look at various commodities and their sources to see what could be done. Mr. Dalton said the last thing he wanted was a debate in Congress on nondiscrimination and Mr. Clayton thought an approach to Congress on this subject would endanger larger plans now underfoot.

Sir Stafford Cripps mentioned steel and UK dependence on imports. Two years ago he placed contracts in the US and because of understandable difficulties there the steel was not obtained. This had handicapped UK aid to Europe, the manufacture of tractors and other productive equipment. Was there any possible way of getting steel? The British had given UK steel producers their full coal requirements and would get thirteen million tons of steel this year but their requirements were sixteen million tons. Mr. Clayton outlined the difficulties arising from shortages at home, factories on short-time because of lack of steel and internal pressure for steel but thought there "was always a possibility". The Department of State was fighting for exports every day. Mr. Clayton asked for a memorandum from Sir Stafford on their steel needs.

Mr. Bevin then asked for a somewhat more concise statement of the present US attitude toward Europe and the Marshall program. In response Mr. Clayton said that he foresaw the following phases: (1) Europe should explain why more progress has not thus far been made since the cessation of hostilities with the help already received (2) European countries should set forth in a concrete and substantial way a statement of what they proposed to do to help themselves, how long it will take and by what steps—what minimum assistance is required from the US, why it is necessary and when the load on the US would be reduced—presumably on a sliding scale. Mr. Clayton again stressed it would not be easy to sell the idea in the US. There was much in the press of what the US "has got to do" and much about American needs for export markets. Mr. Clayton knew the US need for export markets but many of his fellow citizens had other views and in order to put the program across the US must know when Europe will be able to get on its own feet. To supplement this, if possible, the US would like some proposals regarding a closer integration of European economy. He did not assume that anything in great detail could be provided in a short time and cited his conversation with Senator Millikin [3] as an example of why a firm plan for Europe including European integration was necessary to convince Congress on the necessity of additional assistance by the US.

Mr. Bevin said integration raised an interesting point because whenever he took steps in this direction, for example with France and Belgium, Sir Stafford Cripps said he was violating ITO principles. Apparently to point out the US need for exports, he said in 1927 he had examined economic factors in the US and given the narrowing of our imports and the wasteful character of our investments, he had predicted the American slump two years in advance. But on the point of integration he found in Europe a desire to do what Mr. Clayton sought but found Europe in effect committed by ITO not to integrate. If Mr. Clayton could make a public statement on European integration this would help. "In Europe we can't reach a customs union at once", but Mr. Bevin suggested Europe should act sensibly. He had in mind an international board to develop and utilize water-

---

[3] Eugene D. Millikin, chairman, Senate Finance Committee.

power from the Alps. He also mentioned the Teschan political problem and thought a coal mine was at the root of this and the solution would be found in joint operation of the mine and sharing of the output. But these attempts toward rebuilding came into conflict with trading rules.

Mr. Clayton mentioned the progress made in the Benelux Customs Union and said this certainly did not violate ITO rules.

Mr. Bevin then mentioned Anglo-French plans for integration—tractors to be produced in the UK, food in France and a free exchange of the two; musical instruments to be produced in France, no competitive plant set up in the UK and French instruments freely admissible into the UK even though they might be taxed from other sources. Sir Stafford Cripps said such plans needed assurance of some permanence. Mr. Clayton agreed that the principle of nondiscrimination as now understood would be violated in such proposals.

Mr. Bevin said the British might obtain agreement in principle for a Customs Union and wondered if this would be enough to comply with ITO rules. "We have in ITO an ideological plan which thwarts reconstruction" and felt a five-year plan for the first stages of integration would be necessary. The very words "Customs Union" would be objected to in France by the Communists.

Mr. Douglas thought the integration problem raised two questions. First, decisions regarding interchanges arising from new plants and enlargements of old plants (to which point Sir Stafford Cripps interjected that the British must have free entry for the *products* concerned). This interjection precluded Mr. Douglas from defining the second category of goods, namely, production from existing plants (Mr. Douglas intended to explore the possibility of special treatment for integration of new production and nondiscrimination in trade arising from existing plant).

Mr. Clayton said that once the bars were let down on the principle of nondiscrimination all kinds of undesirable arrangements would take place tending toward bilateralism which had been proved unsound. Sir Stafford Cripps thought the ITO Delegation might make provision for certain phases of integration and we might look into the matter jointly. Mr. Clayton, thinking aloud, said something in the nature of special interim exceptions to nondiscrimination working gradually up to a Customs Union might be presented to our people at Geneva.

After the Prime Minister indicated the meeting must break up because of the hour, Mr. Douglas added one further point to the general plan for Europe: there must be acceptance in principle at least of constructive measures in the field of fiscal affairs. Budgetary reform, like integration of European economy, would be most acceptable to the present Congress and would be an important factor in action by the

International Bank relative to Europe. Mr. Douglas also raised with Mr. Dalton the matter of enabling legislation relative to films, which subject has been covered by separate telegram to the Department.

At the conclusion it was agreed that tabulations regarding the British financial position could be sent on to Washington for highly restricted use on the basis that the actual figures had not been "put through or checked" and might be changed in twenty-four hours. The tables had been prepared under pressure and Treasury experts looked upon them chiefly as an approach in presenting the problem.

840.50 Recovery/7–147

Memorandum of Conversation, by the First Secretary of Embassy in the United Kingdom (Peterson)

TOP SECRET [LONDON,] June 25 [26?], 1947.

MAIN POINTS IN DISCUSSIONS OF UNDER SECRETARY CLAYTON AND AMBASSADOR WITH BRITISH OFFICIALS REGARDING AIDE-MÉMOIRE FOR FOREIGN SECRETARY RE MARSHALL PLAN

This discussion on the afternoon of June 25 was held at the Embassy. Sir Edward Bridges, Sir Wilfrid Eady (Treasury) Sir Percivale Liesching (Food), Sir John Henry Wood (Board of Trade), Sir Edmund Hall-Patch (Foreign Office), Mr. R. W. B. Clarke (Treasury) attended. Mr. Peterson and Mr. Gunter were present from the Embassy.

The British distributed a memorandum entitled "Summary of Discussions with Mr. Clayton" [1] which was being prepared for guidance of Mr. Bevin in his Paris talks. Most of the discussion concerned changes in this paper.

Mr. Clayton thought it inadvisable to even mention "Lend Lease" in Paragraph VIII. He said that influential people in the US insist that the Marshall Plan should contain some reciprocal economic considerations from Europe; for example, items for stockpiling in the United States. Stockpiling operations were likely to commence soon. These operations would encompass US acquisitions over and above normal requirements; purchases would be outright and dollars paid to Europe, thus feeding European dollar needs. In response to a question, Mr. Clayton said stocks thus acquired would be "locked up" and not released into current demand although the legislation provided for some turnover of stocks to prevent depreciation.

---

[1] Copy attached to original only. [Footnote as in source text; the memorandum referred to, which is in the Department's files, is not printed, but a subsequent draft is printed *infra*.]

Mr. Douglas suggested a phrase in the part of Paragraph VIII to the effect that "although in appropriate instances the US Government may seek some sort of commodity considerations related to strategic stockpile programs".

Sir Edward Bridges then outlined the purpose of the document being considered. It would be useful for further discussion with Ministers and also useful to Mr. Bevin. There would be no publicity and it was agreed that the publicity question was important. Mr. Clayton said most of his views came out of his own head as he had only one talk with the Secretary and this concerned chiefly the coal problem. Mr. Clayton did not want to give the impression he had laid out any well thought-out plan or scheme. The Planning Staff was hard at work in the Department under George Kennan and when they completed their studies there might well be some alteration in the viewpoint which Mr. Clayton had outlined in a most preliminary way.

Mr. Douglas asked Sir Edward Bridges to confirm his understanding that the *aide-mémoire* did not constitute an agreement. Sir Ernest [*sic*] concurred and described the document as simply a statement along informal lines of the subjects of British and American thinking. A new heading to the document would make this clear.

Numerous other drafting and substantive changes were made in the statement. These will be apparent from a comparison of the first draft and the final draft reviewed at 10 Downing Street, June 26. This included a new paragraph suggested by the Ambassador regarding financial stability and budgetary affairs.

In the section of Paragraph VIII which was redrafted as "The first reaction of UK officials", Mr. Peterson asked if the British might desire to redraft the penultimate paragraph regarding the difficulties of integrated European production to include the idea that this subject might be considered and discussed at Geneva by delegations of European countries now considering trade policy. Sir John Wood said the British did not contemplate this approach, but that officials of the Board of Trade were looking into the general question of aid to Europe separately from the consideration given to ITO.

840.50 Recovery/7-147

Aide-Mémoire by the British Foreign Office for the Secretary of State for Foreign Affairs (Bevin) [1]

TOP SECRET

[This note has been prepared for the personal guidance of the Foreign Secretary after informal and preliminary discussion with the United States Ambassador and Mr. Clayton.

---

[1] See footnote 1, p. 283.

It has been shown to the United States Ambassador and Mr. Clayton but must not be regarded as in any sense a commitment].[2]

[I.] INTRODUCTORY

It is an essential point in the U.S. approach to the present situation that whatever scheme is drawn up should deal comprehensively with the needs of Europe, and not piecemeal with particular countries. A prime condition on which substantial help is likely to be forthcoming from the people of the United States (and it looks as though nothing effective could be done without help on a really substantial scale) is that they feel confident that this help will be used, not alone as a temporary alleviation of the ills of particular countries, but essentially for a well-thought-out scheme which is demonstrably directed to remedying the underlying causes of the European situation as a whole. In particular, the scheme must be directed to restoring European production within a stated period to a level which will render unnecessary Europe's present abnormal dependence on imports. U.S. thought also attaches importance to avoiding the perpetuation of uneconomic rivalries between the countries of Europe.

II. STATEMENT AS TO THE PRESENT POSITION

As a first step, therefore, it would be helpful if the countries of Europe could co-operate in preparing a statement themselves as to why in 1947—two years after the end of the war—they still find themselves in such serious economic and financial difficulties.

(The U.S. Administration have, of course, a good deal of information themselves on this. But from the point of view of Congress and public opinion it would be of great help to have such a statement carrying the authority of the Governments of the countries of Europe).

III. STATEMENT OF NEEDS

Next, the European countries concerned should draw up a statement of their own needs and production capabilities. Taking coal as an example, the statement would show:—

(a) Consumption: the present rate, and the requirements for consumption at the present time and over the ensuing (say) four years, and from what sources it is proposed that the requirement should be met.

(b) European production: the present rate, and the extent to which production can be expanded over the ensuing four years to meet home needs, and for export.

---

[2] Brackets appear in the source text.

(c) What special steps are proposed to increase the rate of production, and any special help required to this end, e.g. in the way of importation of additional equipment.

Statements on similar lines should be drawn up in regard to:—

> The principal foodstuffs;
> Fertilisers;
> Steel;
> Fibres;
> Transport: road and rail;
> Machinery for immediate expansion of output.

IV. Statement of Long-Term Objectives

The above relates primarily to immediate needs. Statements on broadly similar lines will also be required covering plans for longer term reconstruction and development.

V. Purpose of These Statements

These statements will enable comprehensive schemes to be drawn up which will show—both as regards primary needs and long-term reconstruction—

(a) what Europe needs in order to get on her feet again;
(b) how much of what is needed for the purpose can be found from within Europe itself and how much must be found from outside;
(c) the economic objectives towards which Europe will agree to work, over the next four years;
(d) how long the job will take, and—assuming for example that it will take four years—the minimum amount of help which will be required in each of those four years. Presumably this will be on a descending scale.

VI. Countries To Be Covered

More will be known about the attitude of the countries of Eastern Europe towards the scheme after the forthcoming meeting in Paris.

It is understood that, while it is hoped that the scheme will cover Europe as a whole, the U.S. Administration would be satisfied if it could be started with the Western countries of Europe as a nucleus, on the understanding that the scheme would be open to other countries if they so desired.

VII. Integration of Production

Public opinion in the United States attaches great importance to some assurance being given by the countries of Europe that their goods and products of all kinds will be freely available to each other so that the needs of Europe will, so far as is economically practicable, be met from European resources, and that this should be reflected in the pattern of reconstruction and development. United States opinion is thus thinking of a "continental" rather than a country approach to the present trade and production problems of Europe.

The first reaction of U.K. officials to this is as follows:—

Any proposal that went so far as asking for assurances even in principle that the European countries would constitute themselves into a customs union would present great difficulties and would almost certainly involve delay which in present circumstances would be disastrous.

On the other hand, as there is a great shortage of the essential resources for capital re-equipment, there is scope for considerable co-operation between countries in order to avoid unnecessary duplication of effort in capital expenditure.

It must be recognised, however, that schemes for integrated production must carry some security to the producer that he will have an assured market and to the user that he will obtain supplies.

The working out of this conception thus presents considerable difficulties. But it probably presents the natural line of evolution towards the conception of the continent of Europe as a viable economic unit.

Moreover, the position of Great Britain, which is not merely a European country but an international trader, presents very special difficulties.

VIII. FINANCIAL STABILITY

Public opinion in the United States also attaches great importance to satisfactory assurances that participating countries will take all reasonable action to place their budgetary affairs in a manageable position as soon as possible, as an essential preliminary step toward the stability and convertibility of their currencies.

IX. METHODS OF OPERATION

While no decision has yet been reached, it is presumed at the moment that the United States Government contemplate that the immediate help required might be provided by some means which would be generally equivalent in its financial effects to grants in aid, although in appropriate instances the United States Government may seek some sort of commodity consideration in connection with its strategic stockpile programme.

The needs of long-term reconstruction should, however, be met by the International Bank. It is true that the Bank has as yet only made one substantial loan. It is thought that the Bank would be much more ready to make funds available if:—

(a) a comprehensive scheme for Europe had been drawn up; and
(b) through the assistance of the United States, a firm economic foundation had been laid for Europe's recovery from her immediate problems.

X.

It is understood that the United States Administration contemplate that, although the approach to the problem is essentially European, the arrangements for giving help for immediate needs would take the form of a series of agreements between the United States Government and each of the countries concerned.

In this connection it is understood that there might well be differences in the objects or purposes for which help was given to different countries according to the varying needs and situations of such countries. For example, help to Great Britain would not necessarily be limited to help in regard to supplies which Great Britain draws from the United States. In her case, the help would have to be in a form which would enable her to obtain essential supplies from, e.g. Canada and Latin America.

XI. Timing

The U.K. officials regard it as essential that the statements in II, III, IV and V should have been completed not later than 1st September, 1947.

[London,] 25th June, 1947.

840.50 Recovery/7–147

Memorandum of Conversation, by the First Secretary of Embassy in the United Kingdom (Peterson)

TOP SECRET   [London,] June 26, 1947.

Summary of Third Meeting of Under Secretary Clayton and Ambassador With British Cabinet Members

Sir Stafford Cripps was not present at this meeting but Sir John Henry Wood and James Helmore represented the Board of Trade; Sir Edward Bridges and Sir Wilfrid Eady and Mr. R. W. B. Clarke were present for the Treasury; Sir Orme Sargent and Sir Edmund Hall-Patch represented the Foreign Office. As in previous meetings, Mr. Peterson and Mr. Gunter attended for the Embassy.

Participants at the meeting had copies of the revised "aide-mémoire" for the Foreign Secretary.*

Mr. Bevin thought the memorandum set forth accurately the views expressed and received at previous meetings. He could not tell what line would be taken at Paris or what the outcome would be but for his guidance he thought he could use the memorandum with reasonable

---

*Copy attached to original only. [Footnote as in the source text. The *aide-mémoire* is printed *supra.*]

safety as an approach in the Paris discussions. While he knew the memorandum was without commitment he sought assurance that it represented the U.S. Administration's approach to the European economic problem.

Mr. Clayton thought this was so. The memorandum contained some things which had not been discussed in Washington, for example the outline of the difference between the emergency phase and the long-term phase of European rehabilitation. There had been little discussion of the whole subject at Washington and none at all in the NAC, which committee was described, and practically all of the consideration thus far given—meager indeed—had been in the Department of State.

Mr. Bevin understood that the Marshall idea encompassed a relatively short-term, say four years, and involved help to Europe in its purchases from the Western Hemisphere while Europe itself was getting underway. This would be of tremendous help.

Mr. Clayton said he could only indicate what he thought the Administration would recommend to Congress and believed that the British authorities would understand this distinction in our form of government which understanding he thought was highly important. Mr. Clayton thought some countries would be found in no present difficulties as regards their balance of payments but that these might have some long-term development problem. For the latter the UN Organization had established a bank.

Mr. Bevin mentioned another thought regarding the four-year term of assistance. This was related to a question in the House of Commons June 23 by Mr. Warbey who asked Bevin to bear in mind the importance for the U.K. of securing a balanced economic development of Europe and ensuring that there should be no one-sided stimulation of the industrial West without a corresponding stimulation of the agrarian East.

In meeting Europe's food needs Mr. Bevin wanted to avoid sowing too much wheat and while he agreed with Mr. Clayton's idea of a sliding scale adjustment of agriculture in Europe he believed that if cereals production was stimulated too much an agricultural surplus would be created and would "burst things". Mr. Bevin thought it best to work to a balance in European agriculture in three years whereby it would revert to the 1934–35 levels of imports of human foods.

Discussion then analyzed the prewar pattern of European food production, Nazi methods and exceptionally high protection on grain resulting in exorbitant prices. Mr. Bevin did not think it would be possible for Europe to get into balanced agricultural production in less than three years.

Mr. Clayton mentioned the necessity of getting away from current abnormal imports of food and fuel. He did not wish to see a return to the abnormal grain production of the days of Hitler and Mussolini or other artificial stimulations which affected the pattern of distribution in 1936–38. Mr. Douglas mentioned that even before 1933–34 there was some artificial stimulation of wheat production in Italy.

At the end of the discussion on food production it was generally agreed that a European balance should not be supported by subsidies.

Mr. Bevin then discussed the long-term phase of European recovery. He assumed that if "we as a club go to the U.S. and find a willingness to support the putting up of a plant", he assumed that the lending bank would give consideration to (a) repayment prospects and (b) the rationality of the project. Mr. Clayton thought this was correct and that rationality meant that the plant would have reasonable prospects of economic survival.

Mr. Douglas believed the bank, for example in considering a new steel rolling mill, would analyze existing capacity, the new mill's competitive position, questions of tariff protection and if the project was not economically sound in these respects it might not receive bank support. In this Mr. Clayton agreed. In absence of these measures on the part of the bank's borrowers, investments markets would not absorb the securities of the institution.

Mr. Bevin remarked that Europe was so extensively devastated that he was anxious not to force it to export products too soon and as repayment of loans would arise from exports he inquired regarding the repayment terms of the International Bank.

Mr. Dalton interjected to ask the extent to which the Bank's loans must be at a uniform rate and at a uniform time of repayment. Mr. Douglas thought the Bank held wide authority in these fields, Mr. Clayton adding that certain minima in interest rates were established, namely, 3 per cent on loans to the public, plus a 1 per cent commission charge. Mr. Clayton mentioned 4 per cent as a minimum rate.

Mr. Dalton asked that if the Bank in making a series of loans could balance out its aggregate position to meet the required minimum by having higher rates and shorter repayment on one loan and lower rates and longer repayment on another individual loan. Mr. Clayton thought that a rate much above 4 per cent would be too high. Mr. Dalton mentioned that the Bank had interest-free contributions from participating governments and with reference to Mr. Clayton's understanding that reserves were invested in Treasury bills Mr. Dalton thought it might be possible to place some funds in higher-yield securities thus to permit a lower loaning rate.

Mr. Bevin suggested that at the forthcoming Paris meeting the USSR would demand priority in its application for credits and would sweep other applicants aside. Mr. Bevin expected a Russian demand in this direction and asked regarding the U.S. attitude. Mr. Clayton said he could not give a categorical answer regarding the U.S. attitude toward credits to Russia but stated as his opinion that there would have to be a radical change in the Russian position regarding European recovery and other related matters before the American people would approve the extension of financial assistance to Russia. Mr. Clayton referred to the Secretary's definition that Europe included territory west of Asia. On this subject many things had to be considered in the U.S. But Mr. Clayton suggested that Russia did not need food, fuel and fiber and would thus have little basis for participating in the short-term phase. The need for short-term assistance varied inversely as one went east. As for food, Russia had offered wheat to France (delivered actually 180,000 tons according to Hall-Patch) and Mr. Clayton understood there were suggestions that Russia furnish wheat to the U.K. The USSR also sent cotton to Balkan countries and as for fuel, acquired 5 million tons of coal annually from Poland as reparations, costing $2.50 to $3.00 a ton. Finally Russia held gold. Mr. Clayton thought the USSR would have difficulty in making a case for the short-term phase although for the long-term there might clearly be a basis for Russian needs of credits for capital equipment, for reconstruction, development, etc.

Mr. Bevin thought if Russia did not get in on the short-term scheme they would not play in the Marshall program. If so, he asked Mr. Clayton if the British would be supported by the U.S. in going along with the others. Mr. Clayton replied in the affirmative.

Mr. Dalton then mentioned with regard to the long-term that Russia was not a participant in the International Bank, and therefore, could not borrow. However, it was open to Russia to join the Bank but as mentioned by a Treasury representative, this seemed unlikely because as a member the USSR would be required to reveal its gold holdings.

Mr. Bevin then brought up the question of balanced budgets in Europe. Does this apply in the short or the long term? He mentioned France, wherein a balanced budget might create a difficult situation. But if a balanced budget was a consideration for the long-term that might be reasonable for France. Similar conditions obtained in Italy. Mr. Bevin would look with greater favor on balanced budgets as a condition in the longer term.

Mr. Douglas referred to the text of the memorandum and the words "as soon as possible".

Mr. Bevin applied this phrase to France noting the "gripes" already arising from fiscal measures courageously introduced and said he would not like the U.S. and the U.K. to appear as a source of pressure— deflationary pressure upon the French people.

Mr. Clayton thought the language of Article VIII could be accepted by any reasonable interpretation. Mr. Dalton thought Article VIII contemplated a manageable budgetary position, the sort of thing he was doing in the U.K. There might be surplus one year—deficit another—but over a term of years a balanced position should be sought.

Mr. Douglas agreed that Europe was in a dilapidated position, much of which had been inherited both as regards fiscal affairs and productivity. He did not think the statement contemplated drastic budgetary measures and thought it meant reasonable steps. Mr. Bevin interjected that that would be satisfactory. Mr. Douglas continued that there should be an intention to maintain a manageable budgetary position although he realized that one government could not bind its successors. Mr. Bevin then made what he called a friendly suggestion to the U.S. to use cautious language in these matters. In the U.K. during the depression an attitude arose tending to blame the U.S. for its difficulties and this caused ten years of unpleasantness. Caution was therefore warranted and he agreed the end result but said care must be taken to avoid a political row.

Mr. Clayton suggested that in European relief as a whole the distinction between short and long term assistance might not be precise in the thinking of various countries of Europe and the Paris meeting would of course find it necessary to take in both problems. The only distinction the U.S. desired was to draw a line between U.S. assistance and International Bank assistance.

Mr. Bevin mentioned the attraction of the prospect of free assistance for those in dire need with which Mr. Clayton agreed. Mr. Bevin summarized that we deal with the Congress on dire needs and on the long-term must deal with the Bank.

Mr. Bevin, outlining Paris plans, recognized the need for great speed. He wanted a small representative body, perhaps from five countries (mentioning France, Czechoslovakia and Italy) to work up some proposals by early August for use in the U.S. in September. Mr. Clayton thought this would be satisfactory and discussion then turned on the inclusion of Italy on the committee or sub-committee, substance of which has been previously reported.

Mr. Bevin then referred to the Mediterranean Area and expressed hope that what he called the "Genoa cycle" could be restored. The Board of Trade representatives confirmed the importance of this. Bevin said he had once calculated the employment of between 750,000 and 1 million persons in the U.K. depended on Italy, with particular emphasis in South Wales.

Mr. Dalton then referred to the convertibility obligation. Considering the short period before the effective date some cases of "squeeze" seemed likely to arise. He understood that in individual *cases* relief from convertibility could be arranged without reference to Congress. Mr. Clayton said this was correct. Mr. Dalton added he was merely airing his views so that if later he wished to raise the question he would have the proper basis. Mr. Douglas mentioned that the agreement provided for this to be done in exceptional cases.

Sir Wilfrid Eady said they had no cases at present and did not contemplate any general escape from the convertibility obligation but he anticipated the need for temporary relief in the case of countries holding sterling balances with which no agreement could be reached by July 15. He also mentioned China. The British would give an impressive list of countries with which convertibility would be made operative (and sterling balance agreements concluded) but they might have to use the escape clause for India. Mr. Douglas suggested that Mr. Dalton work out the proper procedure and inform us as promptly as possible because advance information would avoid embarrassment. The information suggested would be treated with extreme confidence.

Mr. Dalton closed on the note that the timetable of the Financial Agreement was "so wrong". He did not blame the U.S.—"it is our fault" but he doubted whether the Bretton Woods agreements which contemplated a five-year transition period would prove workable. In the meantime it was difficult for the U.K. to take the burden of convertibility.

840.50 Recovery/6–2647 : Telegram

The Ambassador in the United Kingdom (Douglas) to the Secretary of State

TOP SECRET   LONDON, June 26, 1947—7 p. m.
US URGENT   NIACT

3516. For the Secretary from Clayton and Ambassador. In discussions at 10 Downing St. today Foreign Secretary sketched his plans for forthcoming Paris meeting re European aid. Bevin wanted a small representative body, perhaps representing five countries from Western Europe, to prepare a program by early August for our use and consideration in September. He hoped Italy could work on this committee or on sub-committee but the delay in ratification of the peace treaty kept Italy in the same category as certain Balkan countries, for example, Bulgaria, which the USSR might nominate for the committee work Bevin contemplated.[1] To take a debating point away from USSR and to have valid reason for selecting Italy and not one of

---

[1] For documentation on problems of ratification, see pp. 515 ff.

Balkan satellites, Bevin had urged immediate ratification of the treaty by the Italian Constituent Assembly. De Gasperi informed Bevin that there was some difficulty because of the threatened resignation of President de Nicola in Italy but Bevin recommended extraordinary measures to get the treaty ratified.

We agree[d] to ask you to support Bevin's efforts in this direction and if you concur suggest Ambassador Dunn be asked to supplement the approaches by the British by urging De Gasperi to arrange for immediate ratification. If time is not too short perhaps a parallel approach to Italian Embassy, Washington would be in order.

[CLAYTON AND DOUGLAS]
DOUGLAS

840.50 Recovery/6–2647 : Telegram

The Ambassador in the Soviet Union (Smith) to the Secretary of State

Moscow, June 26, 1947.

2270. *Pravda* Ukraine June 11 just received here carries belated but most extensive comment on Secretary's Harvard address noted in Soviet press in form article by K. Morozov "Marshall Doctrine" highlights:

"American press calculates US expended on assistance to European countries i.e. to European reaction nearly 14 billion dollars with prospect of additional 5 billion this year. More lavish its assistance to its European clientele cruder becomes behavior of USA towards European powers. State Dept like firm governess issues instructions on behavior to European powers administering praise and censure dependent on degree of attention to Washington's orders. Lately, for example, Secretary gave full approval to Italian reaction's exclusion from govt of representatives of workers parties. . . .[1]

For those powers which don't wish to barter their independence for American dollars State Dept is not stinting in repressions and threats. Fact that young Hungarian democracy succeeded in warding off attack which reactionary plotters had prepared against it, that it unmasked and neutralized agents of Horthy,[2] arouses righteous anger in Washington. State Dept by way of repression cancelled American loan to Hungary and is preparing cancel considerable credit granted Hungary by Exim Bank.[3]

Sinister results of Truman Doctrine, of American policy of support for anti-popular forces and regimes and of gross interference in affairs of other countries, are felt with greater force each day by peoples of Europe. This doctrine is spread in bloodstains on slopes of Thessalian mountains where Greek Govt troops, equipped by British and Ameri-

---

[1] Ellipses throughout this document appear in the source text.
[2] Admiral Miklos Horthy, Regent of Hungary, 1920–1944.
[3] For documentation regarding U.S. relations with Hungary in 1947, see volume IV.

cans obliterate from face of earth insurgent villages; this doctrine has contributed to bitter economic conflicts in France and threatens French finances and whole French economy with confusion. It has called into action black forces of reaction and oppression in Italy and other lands.

But even Truman Doctrine in its present form does not satisfy appetites of American imperialists. Recent speech of Marshall at Harvard University is evidence of even wider plans of American reaction of new stage in Washington's campaign against forces of world democracy and progress . . .

If European powers work out general plan for their own salvation and if that plan is approved by America, then America will consent to help Europe by providing supplies and, of course, war materials.

Help will be offered only to such countries as join plan approved, or rather more accurately, dictated by America. Those powers, to whom this plan doesn't appeal, are threatened by Marshall with displeasure and with every kind of 'counteractivity' from Washington.

It is easy to see that Marshall proposes or rather demands quick formation of notorious western bloc but under unconditional and absolute leadership of American imperialism. Spiral of Truman Doctrine begins unroll. From retail purchase of separate European countries Washington has conceived design of wholesale purchase of whole European Continent. American horsemen of capitalist anarchy and 'free economy' have disclosed selves as defenders of all European plan—plan for stifling democratic progressive forces and conversion of all Europe into colony of dollar empire . . .

It is fact dissatisfaction is growing in Congress with policy of squandering billions on financing other countries . . . . limitation by Congress of budgetary expenses by billion dollars was signal for Congressmen to start finding Truman policy too unprofitable 'business'. This is reason why those in charge American policy have busied selves with such enthusiasm in running up structure of western bloc. They hope Congress will more speedily grant new *billions* for 'business' on European scale than on receipt of promissory notes from separate governments.

Whatever doctrines invented by American imperialists for enslavement of European peoples, their plans will only result in same inglorious failure which marked end of certain attempts create new order in Europe."

Repeated London 262, Paris 252.

SMITH

840.50 Recovery/ 6–2647 : Telegram

The Secretary of State to the Embassy in the United Kingdom

TOP SECRET   WASHINGTON, June 27, 1947—7 p.m.

2776. For Clayton and the Ambassador. Ur 3516 June 26. Dept has from time to time endeavored persuade Itals for their own good expedite treaty ratification, and reports from Dunn and Ital Amb Wash indicate Ital Govt will act as rapidly as Ital political situation permits. We have however resisted numerous Brit proposals to join them in exerting pressure on Itals, feeling such pressure would strengthen stand of Ital opponents of ratification and place Ital Govt in difficult position.

Pls inform FonOff and if possible get word to Bevin in Paris that we are convinced Ital Govt is aware of advantages early treaty ratification and will in fact ratify shortly. We do not agree however that Ital ratification is necessary before Italy can participate in discussions European aid. In fact, it seems wholly unrealistic to erect legalistic barrier to participation country whose economy bulks so large in European economy and whose recovery is essential to economic health of Europe and world. You shd add that we therefore feel Italy shd be brought into discussions at earliest possible date and would be keenly disappointed if Brit were to fail to support Italy for membership suggested committee.

MARSHALL

501.BD–Europe/ 6–2747 : Telegram

The Ambassador in France (Caffery) to the Secretary of State

SECRET   PARIS, June 27, 1947—11 a.m.

2548. Bidault told me last night that immediately upon his arrival Molotov asked him what he and Bevin had done behind his back. Bidault denied that they had done anything behind his back; said they met and agreed to invite Molotov to join them. Bidault said that he is leary of ECE and sympathizes with our point of view. He added that he hopes that Molotov has come here to cooperate, but whether he cooperates or not, France is determined to go ahead.

Finally he said: "I was frightened this morning by the newspaper account of some remarks of your Secretary of the Treasury but since I have seen the way your Radio Bulletin carries it and I feel better.[1] However, I devoutly hope that in case we on our side do accomplish something your Congress will do its part. If they failed us it would be sheer disaster here."

Sent Department as 2548; repeated London as 486.

CAFFERY

---

[1] See Department of State Wireless Bulletin, June 25, 1947, for the substance of Secretary Snyder's press conference comment and subsequent statement concerning Secretary Marshall's proposal that the initiative for drafting a European recovery program come from Europe.

840.50 Recovery/6–2847 : Telegram

The Ambassador in France (Caffery) to the Secretary of State

TOP SECRET   PARIS, June 28, 1947.
URGENT   NIACT

2577. I have just seen Duff Cooper who has given me a confidential account of the first Bevin–Bidault–Molotov meeting which opened at four o'clock this afternoon.[1]

At the outset, the question of how the press should be handled was raised by Bidault who said they should be told everything or nothing. It was agreed that for the present and until there was some progress to report the meetings would be secret with no press handouts of any kind whatsoever.

Molotov then said he wished to inquire what additional information the French and British Governments had received from the United States Government other than had been contained in the Secretary's Harvard speech.

Bidault and Bevin both replied that there had been no additional information from the US Government. Bevin added that he had seen Under Secretary Clayton in London but that the latter had nothing further to add to the imative [*initiative?*] which the Secretary had suggested that the European countries should take.

Molotov then said he wished to ask what agreements the French and British had arrived at during the Bidault–Bevin talks last week. Bevin and Bidault replied that the only decision they had made was to invite Molotov to meet with them to discuss a European economic plan as set forth in the terms of the invitation.

Bidault then distributed several papers. The only important one being a tentative form of agenda relating to the *ad hoc* committees outlined in my 2412, June 18; 2423, June 18 and 2440, June 19.[2]

It was then after six o'clock and Bidault suggested that the meeting might adjourn until tomorrow to give the delegations time to study the papers.

At this juncture, Molotov said that he wished to make a proposal. Since none of the three governments knew anything more about the seriousness of the United States Government's proposal than had

---

[1] The meeting actually was held on June 27. In telegram 2580 from Paris, not printed, Ambassador Caffery conveyed the French account of the meeting, given to him by M. Couve de Murville of the French Foreign Ministry.
[2] Telegram 2423 not printed. The Ambassador also transmitted the texts of the papers tabled by the French at the meeting in telegram 2581; for texts of the papers, see *French Yellow Book*, pp. 25–27.
In London telegram 3564, June 28, 7 p.m., Ambassador Douglas cabled a personal message" from Mr. Bevin to Secretary Marshall which described the meeting in general terms (840.50 Recovery/6–2847).

been contained in the Secretary's speech, he proposed that they should
ask the United States Government:

1. The exact sum of money which the United States was prepared to
advance to aid European recovery.
2. Whether the United States Congress would vote such a credit

Bevin at once replied that he could not agree to such a proposal
In the first place, he said, in a democracy the Executive Branch o
the Government cannot engage the responsibility of the Legislative
Branch. Secondly, the Secretary's speech had not contained any
United States offer of any specified sum of money but had suggested
that European countries get together and formulate a constructiv
plan for European rehabilitation. Thirdly, debtors do not lay down
conditions when seeking credits from potential creditors. It wa
therefore imperative that they get down to business and work out a
coherent plan.

Bidault then said he agreed with Bevin. However, since a passag
in the Secretary's speech seemed to suggest that the United State
Government might be willing to assist in the drafting of Europea
plan, he proposed that the three governments might ask the Unite
States for more specific enlightenment in this regard.

Bevin replied that he interpreted the passage in question to mea
that after a European plan had actually been drafted by the Euro
pean states, the United States would be willing, if the plan wer
realistic, to assist in the final stages, but that until such a plan ha
been drafted he did not think that any useful purpose would be serve
by Bidault's proposal.

It then being eight o'clock the meeting was adjourned by unanimou
consent. The Soviets requested that it not be reconvened until fou
tomorrow afternoon in order "to have sufficient time to study th
French papers", but obviously, as Duff Cooper put it, to gain tim
for further instructions from Moscow.

In conclusion Duff Cooper remarked to me that the Soviets toda
were obviously feeling out the ground and sparring for time. "Moloto
after the meeting and indeed during it was comparatively affable"

Duff Cooper is not sure what line Molotov will next take but sai
that Bevin is determined not to let the Soviets get away with an
obstructionist or delaying tactics. The British, he said, realize tl
vital importance of meeting rapidly and courageously the Secretary
suggestion. He believes that Bidault recognizes this equally well an
will go along in this sense, although "Bidault's position is more diff
cult because of the strength of the French Communist Party.["]

In Duff Cooper's opinion, the outcome of the present conference depends on what develops in the next two days.

CAFFERY

840.50 Recovery/6–2847 : Telegram

The Ambassador in France (Caffery) to the Secretary of State

SECRET
PARIS, June 28—midnight.
URGENT

2586. Duff Cooper described today's meeting, which lasted only from five to eight, as "unsatisfactory and inconclusive". (My telegram 2577 of June 28). Main items of discussion were:

1. Molotov was persuaded to drop his proposal to ask the US how much aid they were prepared to give.
2. Russians presented an agenda similar to that which the French had presented (central steering committee and *ad hoc* committees).
3. Russians opposed any inquiry being made into the resources of European nations. (Duff Cooper believes that the conference will probably split on this and that the French will side with the British).
4. Agreement that Germans would only be represented by the occupying powers.

Duff Cooper added that the French had showed "surprising firmness" at today's meeting.

Bevin is "not keen" on the inclusion of Italy because it might involve the inclusion of one of the Soviet satellite countries although the French share our opinion on this.

CAFFERY

840.50 Recovery/6–2947 : Telegram

The Ambassador in France (Caffery) to the Secretary of State

SECRET
PARIS, June 29—1 p. m.
NIACT

2588. Couve de Murville has just given me an account of yesterday's meeting (my 2586, June 28). He said that at outset of the meeting Molotov stated that the Soviets did not agree with certain of the proposals contained in the paper which the French had tabled the preceding day. In particular, the Soviets felt that inquiry into the resources of European nations would violate the sovereignty of the individual countries. He went on to say that the Soviet view was that each individual country should make its own study as to its needs which would establish the amount of credit it needed from the US. The coal [*total?*] credits of all the participating countries would then be pooled and this figure would be transmitted to the US Government as the credit needed for European reconstruction. In other words, as Couve put it, "The Soviets want to put the United States in a position where it must either shell out dollars before there is a real plan or refuse outright to advance any credits."

Both Bevin and Bidault strongly opposed this suggestion on the grounds that it did not constitute a European plan such as envisaged by Secretary Marshall and that it would not provide for maximum utilization of the sources of the individual European countries for the benefit of Europe as a whole.

The question of what European countries should participate was then discussed. The French proposal envisaged the participation of all European countries except Spain, which would be "provisionally" excluded. (Couve believes the British are disposed to go along on this) Molotov said that Soviets felt that only Allied countries which had suffered from the ravages of war should participate directly in the plan. The satellite and ex-enemy states could participate indirectly in a "consultative capacity". Bidault then made a strong plea for Italian participation on which Molotov made no comment.

Molotov then stated that he wished to talk about the question of German participation. He said that since the German question was to be discussed in the CFM meeting in London next November, he did not see how Germany could be represented until important decisions on Germany's future had been reached by the Council of Foreign Ministers. Both Bevin and Bidault rebutted this view and said that in view of the importance of German coal for Europe, in view of Germany's food problem, et cetera, they believe it indispensable that Germany should be represented in the planning stage by representatives of the Allied occupation powers.

With reference to Molotov's previous proposal that information be immediately requested from the US Government (my 2577, June 28), Couve said that Molotov had not raised this question again and he shares the British belief that it has probably been abandoned although he admitted that with the Soviets it was always possible they might return to it.

In summing up, Couve stated that it was abundantly clear that the Russians are in no hurry to get on with the meeting. Molotov, he said, has been unusually mild and the French believe that the Soviets wish at all cost to avoid giving the French or the British a valid pretext to break with them.

Couve believes that the Soviets will continue to proceed cautiously. He said that they are highly suspicious and at all costs do not wish to be helpful in setting up any plan which will permit the United

States to exercise influence in Europe. On the other hand, Bidault and Bevin are determined, he said, not to let the Soviets sabotage their efforts to formulate a realistic and effective plan.[1]

The three Foreign Ministers will not reconvene until tomorrow (Monday) afternoon at 4 o'clock.

Repeated Geneva 62 for Clayton.

CAFFERY

---

[1] In London telegram 3568, June 29, not printed, Ambassador Douglas transmitted Foreign Secretary Bevin's record of the meeting as well as the text of a personal message from Bevin to him, as follows: "I am asking that you should be shown my summary report of yesterday's meeting (June 28).

"You will see that there is a wide difference between Russians and ourselves as to what should go into the programme. They want to confine it to an uncoordinated statement of requirements on a national basis, without any attempt to present a constructive plan or to indicate what Europe can do to help herself. I propose to continue to insist that the only procedure likely to produce the desired results is a programme, which provides for the maximum of self-help and makes a demand on the US with respect only to residual requirements.

"M. Bidault is taking similar line." (840.50 Recovery/6–2947)

840.50 Recovery/6–2947 : Telegram

The Ambassador in France (Caffery) to the Secretary of State

SECRET   PARIS, June 29, 1947—4 p. m.
URGENT

2590. Bidault told me this morning he is very "uncertain". "Molotov", he said, "clearly does not wish this business to succeed but on the other hand his hungry satellites are smacking their lips in expectation of getting some of your money. He is obviously embarrassed".

Bevin told me this morning he is not optimistic. "Molotov is dragging his feet. However Bidault and I gave him to understand yesterday that we are determined in one way or another to go ahead with this with or without him".

CAFFERY

840.50 Recovery/7–147 : Telegram

The Ambassador in France (Caffery) to the Secretary of State

TOP SECRET   PARIS, July 1, 1947.
URGENT   NIACT

2603. For the Secretary of State. Bevin asked me to come to see him at 10 this evening.[1] He said that to all intents and purposes the conference had broken down today, that it would probably terminate

---

[1] June 30. The telegram was received in Washington at 1:11 a. m. on July 1.

tomorrow and that he wished you to know exactly what had happened and where he stood.

He began by stating that after the French had tabled their proposal Friday [2] (my 2577, June 28) and the Soviets had taken an obstructionist position on both Friday and Saturday [3] (my 2588, June 29) he had decided that the issues should be clearly stated and "laid on the line." Accordingly he had taken the French proposal (my 2581, June 28 [4]) and reduced it to a "single page" which embodied the French suggestions "but stripped them of words" (text of Bevin's (1) stripped proposal as well as his (2) clarifying statement which he made when the conference reconvened at four this afternoon [5] is transmitted in my immediately following telegram.[6])

Bevin sent his "single page" paper to Bidault and Molotov at eleven this morning.

When the conference convened this afternoon at four, Molotov immediately got to his feet and reiterated all his arguments of last Friday and Saturday to the effect that "there could be no infringement on the sovereignty of European states; that they should individually establish their needs and submit the total dollar costs of their combined needs to the US Government and ask it if it were prepared to advance the necessary credits; etc. ."

Bidault then took the floor and in a "very strong statement" supported Bevin's stand.

At this juncture, Molotov was handed what Bevin described as "an obviously partially decoded telegram from Moscow." In brief, "it reviewed all his previous arguments and added nothing to what he had previously elucidated." (Bevin said the telegram from which Molotov read was without doubt Moscow's reply to the paper he had given Molotov at eleven this morning).

Bevin then replied to Molotov: "I said with a smile, in effect what you are asking the United States Government to do is to give us a blank check. If I were to go to Moscow with a blank check and ask you to sign it I wonder how far I would get with your end."

Bidault supported Bevin again and the meeting adjourned on this general note.

Bevin then went on to discuss with me the implications of today's conference. He said that Bidault had shown "great courage and had given the fullest, and even surprisingly, solid and wholehearted support having in mind the present critical state of French internal politics." He continued, "this conference will break up tomorrow. I am glad that the cards have been laid on the table and that the

---

[2] June 27.
[3] June 27 and 28.
[4] See footnote 2, p. 297.
[5] June 30.
[6] Telegram 2604, July 1, not printed. For texts of Mr. Bevin's proposal and statement, see *French Yellow Book*, pp. 47–48.

responsibility will be laid at Moscow's door. They have tried to sabotage it in the conference room from the very beginning as I knew they would. In addition, however, Molotov after pressing for secrecy gave a complete handout of the Soviet position to the Tass Agency (my 2600, June 30 [7]). Accordingly I have given to the press this evening my clarifying statement made at the conference this afternoon (paragraph two (2) above) and I hope that it will convey clearly to your people where we stand."

"In the face of the breakdown this conference, which I had anticipated and even wished for—given my certainty that Molotov had come to Paris to sabotage our efforts—I wish to raise another point: whereas we (the British) are determined to go forward and do everything in our power to take advantage rapidly of the initiative—indeed the life-line thrown us by Secretary Marshall—and I must point out that my position with the Labor Party is happily strong—the French are in a very dangerous position both politically and financially. I repeat that the French have supported me wholeheartedly and with great courage in view of the precarious French political situation.[8] If the French in the face of the position they have taken and facing the critical political considerations they must meet in the next three weeks—have no hopes for even interim credits which can hold out to the French public until we can work out a plan to save Western Europe, I fear greatly that they may waver at a time when the battle can be won. If they stand with us I hope you will not abandon them. Give them something to hope for."

In conclusion Bevin said that after the conference breaks up tomorrow he intends to send you a message on Wednesday giving his over-all views of the situation. There is no doubt in my mind that he is determined to do his utmost to produce a worthwhile plan and to bolster and encourage the French to go along wholeheartedly despite their critical internal political situation.

Repeated to Geneva for Clayton, repeated to London for Douglas.

CAFFERY

[7] Not printed.
[8] For documentation on the situation in France, see pp. 688 ff.

840.50 Recovery/7–147 : Telegram

The Ambassador in France (Caffery) to the Secretary of State

SECRET
PARIS, July 1, 1947—11 a. m.
URGENT   NIACT

2606. For the Secretary. I have just seen Couve de Murville who confirms in detail the information given me by Bevin last night (my 2603, July 1). Couve also gave me text of proposal which Molotov tabled yesterday, which is being transmitted in my immediately following telegram.[1] The Molotov proposal is simply a résumé of position he took on Friday and Saturday.

Couve expects conference to break up shortly after it reconvenes at 4 o'clock this afternoon. He said that French regret that Soviets will not cooperate because it means that they will prevent countries of central and eastern Europe from cooperating in an effective European plan. Despite this he said French are as determined as British to try and work out an effective plan for western Europe. He believes Dutch, Belgians, Italians and possibly Denmark will be willing to join with them but at this juncture he is still not sure which, if any, other countries will be willing to go along.

He concluded by stating that French believe their efforts to include Soviets were worthwhile particularly since it should establish clearly to everyone that it is Moscow which has refused to cooperate.

Sent Department; repeat London as 503, repeated to Geneva for Clayton as 69.

CAFFERY

---

[1] Telegram not printed. For text of this proposal, see *French Yellow Book*, pp. 49–50.

840.50 Recovery/7–247 : Telegram

The Ambassador in France (Caffery) to the Secretary of State

SECRET

PARIS, July 2, 1947—noon.

NIACT

2631. Bevin says that at yesterday's session the French produced a proposal [1] "to reconcile the difference of views". Bidault said that "Europe must put up a coordinated plan of her economy" and that the United States would then be in a position to supply "the supplement". Europe was to help itself and this could be done without any "interference with sovereignty".

Molotov's first remark was with regard to a statement made by Bidault that German production was of interest, but would, of course, have to be dealt with subject to the assent of the four occupying powers. He asked whether Germany would be expected to contribute to the recovery of Europe before taking care of reparations. He then added that he had just received the French proposal and suggested that the meeting be adjourned until tomorrow in order to consider it.

Bevin then said that he would agree to adjourn on the understanding that an agreement would be reached tomorrow.

---

[1] For text of this proposal, see *French Yellow Book*, pp. 55–57.

Bevin tells me that if Molotov comes out with a proposal tomorrow, will be examined. If there is no modification in Molotov's attitude, e said, the British were prepared to go along without the Soviets and e expected the French to stay with them (the British).

CAFFERY

40.50 Recovery/7–247 : Telegram

The Ambassador in France (Caffery) to the Secretary of State

CRET   PARIS, July 2, 1947—noon.
RGENT   NIACT

2633. My 2631, July 2. Referring to yesterday's meeting Couve e Murville tells me that the French decision to submit a final com- romise proposition was dictated not in the belief that it would be cceptable to the Russians but for reasons of French internal politics. e explained that although the wording of the original French pro- osal had been modified the basic Franco-British position had not en changed in the latest draft. Therefore, in the absence of a reversal f Soviet position Molotov would be obliged to refuse it. Couve said at Bidault feels that a Soviet refusal after this last French effort compromise will greatly strengthen the French Government with rench public opinion; will tend to disarm the French Communists ho may be expected to attack the plan; and will make it much sier to proceed with the British to draw up a European plan with- t the Russians.

Bidault opened yesterday's meeting by tabling the new French oposal. Molotov made little comment other than to say that he would ve to study it but that a superficial perusal did not indicate that e French paper differed greatly from the one which they had eviously submitted. Molotov then said that before adjourning he shed to ask Bidault two questions:

(1) Is it correct that the French proposal envisages the immediate ilization of German resources to meet the needs of the countries nich will participate in a European plan without reference to parations? In other words, has the French Government changed views on German reparations and does it favor turning over in- ased German production for use in European reconstruction before parations are made?

(2) Does the French proposal mean that the French Government w favors raising the level of German industrial production?

Bidault replied evasively that the question of Germany had been d would continue to be the subject of discussion by the four occupying powers, et cetera, and that at this juncture the questions did not appear to relate to the question at issue.

Molotov then asked that the meeting be adjourned until this afternoon at 4 o'clock, Bevin immediately proposed instead that the meeting recess and meet later in the evening. Couve said "Molotov insisted on adjournment until today, obviously in order to refer the French proposal back to Moscow for final instructions." Bevin said he would agree if it were clearly understood that final agreement or disagreement between the three would be reached today. The meeting adjourned on this note.

Couve said that while there is always a possibility that Moscow may make an about-face, he does not believe that the Soviets will go along and he expects the meeting to break up today. If this occurs he says the French feel that the extra day's delay entailed by their final proposal will have been more than worthwhile from the point of view of French public opinion.[1]

CAFFERY

---

[1] Foreign Secretary Bevin conveyed substantially the same information to Ambassador Douglas, who reported it to the Department in telegram 3637, July 2, 1947 from London, not printed (840.50 Recovery/7–247).

840.50 Recovery/7–347 : Telegram

The Ambassador in the United Kingdom (Douglas) to the Secretary of State

TOP SECRET   LONDON, July 3, 1947—3 p. m

3644. For the Secretary from the Ambassador. Mr. Bevin has asked me to send you the following report of yesterday's meeting in Paris

"The final meeting of the 3 Foreign Ministers took place today. Molotov adopted a completely uncompromising attitude towards the French proposal, churning out in even stronger terms than before the Soviet accusations that the preparation of an over-all programme meant that smaller European States were being subjected to Big Power domination and would involve interference with national sovereignty. He concluded with a warning to the British and French Governments that action, if persisted in, would have grave consequences It would result not in the unification or reconstruction of Europe but in a division of Europe into two groups.

2. Bidault made a moving and eloquent reply in which he vigorously repudiated Molotov's accusations and hurled back the gage by saying that it was Soviet Russia, by her action, which was dividing Europe into two groups.[1]

---

[1] For texts of the statements made by Messrs. Molotov and Bidault at the July meeting, see *French Yellow Book*, pp. 58–65.

3. I said that Molotov's statement was based on a complete travesty of the facts and entirely misrepresented the position of the British Government. Mr. Molotov presumably repeated misrepresentations like this in the hope that by constant repetition they would be believed. I referred to the high hopes with which we had come to Paris and to my own efforts in the past to ensure that Europe was not divided into two hostile camps. Our policy was to cooperate with all and dominate none. With regard to the division of Europe, nobody had striven more than I for the unity of Europe, including the political and economic unity of Germany. I noted and regretted that M. Molotov had ended with a threat. Great Britain on other occasions had been threatened with grave consequences. Such threats had not and would not cause us to hesitate to pursue what we considered to be our duty. Therefore, we intended to proceed with the line of action which we had advocated in as close association as possible with the United Nations and should keep other governments informed whether they could see their way open to cooperate with us or not. We hoped that by our work we should be able to refute the nasty suspicions expressed in the room today.

4. Molotov said that he hoped the world at large would acquaint itself with the proposals of all three delegations. After being assured by Bidault that the full texts of the various proposals would be published Molotov said that he would consider it his duty on his return to Moscow to report what had been said and done in Paris. Bidault remarked that the French Government felt bound to pursue the study called for by Marshall. I said that I would also report to His Majesty's Government, and that I hoped we might yet find a common ground by which to lift Europe out of the misery in which war had left her. I added that I must make it clear that we intended to cooperate with such European states as were willing in the restoration of war-shattered Europe. The Conference then ended.

5. I am seeing M. Bidault early tomorrow when we hope to agree on a joint invitation to all European Governments (except Spain) to collaborate in appropriate degrees in the preparation of a reply to Mr. Marshall's suggestion.

6. The most satisfactory feature of these talks has been that the French have been quite unwavering in their attitude on the basic issue and I am sure that we can count on the full collaboration of the present Government in the work which we are now setting in hand together."

Mr. Bevin has informed me that he will be telegraphing to Washington the text of the invitation to European Governments as soon as this is agreed with M. Bidault today.

Mr. Bevin returns from Paris today, and I am seeing him at 6:15 this afternoon.

Repeated to Geneva for Clayton as 72.

Douglas

840.50 Recovery/7–347 : Telegram

The Secretary of State to the Embassy in France

SECRET   WASHINGTON, July 3, 1947—4 p. m.

URGENT   NIACT

2450. For Caffery from the Secretary. Please deliver immediately the following personal and private message from me to Bidault and Bevin:

"I have followed with complete understanding the course of your patient efforts to find agreement with the Soviet Government on a broad and constructive approach to the problems of European recovery. We realize the gravity of the problem with which you have been confronted and the difficulty of the decisions which you have been forced to take. At least the Soviet attitude in these questions has been clarified at this stage and will not continue to represent an uncertainty in the working out of a recovery program for other countries.

"We here are prepared to do all in our power to support any genuine and constructive efforts toward the restoration of economic health and prosperity in the countries of Europe." [1]

MARSHALL

---

[1] Marginal notation by the Director of the Office of European Affairs (Matthews) : "Approved by the President, the Secretary and Mr. Lovett in draft. H.F.M."

840.50 Recovery/7–347 : Telegram

The Ambassador in France (Caffery) to the Secretary of State

SECRET   PARIS, July 3, 1947—6 p. m.

NIACT

2667. Couve de Murville and Alphand [1] have just given me confidentially the text of the invitation agreed to by Bevin and Bidault at their meeting this morning (my 2656, July 3) which they state will be sent to 22 European countries tomorrow (excluding Spain and Russia and including Turkey). They also gave me the text of the proposals which will accompany the invitation. I am transmitting translations of both these documents in my immediately following telegram for the Department's confidential information. [2]

Couve told me that I was to be given officially the texts tomorrow. [3]

---

[1] Hervé Alphand, Director of Economic Services, French Ministry of Foreign Affairs.

[2] Paris telegram 2668, July 3, not printed. In Washington, the British Embassy transmitted texts officially to the United States Government in a note of July 4, not printed (840.50 Recovery/7–447). For texts of the invitation and accompanying proposals, see *French Yellow Book*, pp. 69–74.

[3] For text of the French note to the U.S. Embassy, July 4, see *French Yellow Book*, p. 76.

Both Couve and Alphand expressed the opinion that the results of the Three Power conference have the gravest implications and that Europe now stands at the crossroads. The Russians, they said, believe that the European nations will not be able to draw up an effective plan and more particularly that the US will be unwilling to advance the credits necessary to make it work because the Soviets believe that the US will undergo a profound depression within the next 18 months. They believe that the Soviets are counting on this depression to put an end to the American aid for European reconstruction. This will mean that European economies will disintegrate and economic, social and political chaos will follow. When this catastrophe occurs the Soviets hope to take over the Western European countries with their well organized Communist Parties.

In conclusion Couve said that the French had for internal political and other reasons never wished to take the lead in establishing a European bloc.

"The Soviets, however, by their actions there have forced Europe to band together to save itself. They are the persons who have established the European bloc. It is now up to the European countries and to the US to see that such a bloc succeeds. We intend to publish all the papers on the Three Power conference in French and English [4] and we hope they will be widely read and understood by the American people and the American Congress and that Moscow's desire to sabotage European reconstruction will be as clearly revealed as is our determination to do everything within our power to save ourselves and to profit from the splendid initiative taken by Secretary Marshall."

Sent Department 2667; repeated London 513, Geneva for Clayton 73, Moscow 404, Rome 158.

CAFFERY

---

[4] For references to the publications see footnote 1, p. 259.

840.50 Recovery/7–347 : Telegram

The Secretary of State to the Consulate at Geneva

SECRET
URGENT
WASHINGTON, July 3, 1947—10 p. m.

730. For Clayton.[1] Inability of Bevin, Bidault and Molotov to reach agreement on basic approach to formulation of European recovery plan suggested by US makes it seem extremely unlikely that any constructive action along this line could now be achieved in ECE. Soviet opposition to program of mutual assistance and cooperative attempt to

---

[1] Under Secretary Clayton had returned to Geneva as chief of the U.S. Delegation to the second meeting of the Preparatory Committee of the United Nations Conference on Trade and Employment. For documentation concerning this conference, see volume I.

formulate solutions to common problems is contrary to spirit if not letter of para 1 (*a*) ECE terms of ref. It is of greatest importance that US continue to support concept of prompt and effective cooperation and mutual assistance, which is underlying principle of UN as well as Marshall proposals. Assumed British and French will not favor discussion Marshall proposals in ECE. However, if any discussion of Secretary's suggestion for formulation of recovery program comes up in ECE or in conversations with delegates, US reps should continue to hold position that means for working out cooperative recovery program including place of ECE, should primarily be decided by Eur countries, that US does not believe solution of rehabilitation problems can be achieved through relief operations but only through measures which lead directly to ability of Europe to support itself by normal economic transactions in Europe and with rest of world. Relief, grants and loans must be temporary expedients. Although ECE was created to facilitate concerted action for reconstruction, most important to use whatever means will result in prompt and effective action. If decided to act outside ECE, which is still in organizational stage, liaison with ECE could and should be established.

Sent Geneva 730, repeated London 2893, Paris 2475.

MARSHALL

840.50 Recovery/7–447 : Telegram

The Ambassador in the United Kingdom (Douglas) to the Secretary of State

TOP SECRET   LONDON, July 4, 1947—1 p. m.

URGENT   NIACT

3668. For the Secretary. Had a long conversation with Bevin last night covering the Paris Conference of the three Foreign Ministers. He said that because of the very shaky political position of France and the strength of the Communists, Bidault had acted with very great courage, particularly was the position he had taken brave because Molotov had come with more than 100 in his entourage who had been carefully selected, he thought, because of their contacts with the French Communist organizations. These agents had attempted through the French Communists to put as much pressure as possible on Bidault and Ramadier. Notwithstanding, however, the influence the Communists brought to bear, Bidault had stood by his side with great firmness and Ramadier had given complete support. He said that both the French and he though[t] they had done everything which they reasonably could to prevent a breakdown without frustrating the prompt development of the program, had taken great risks. (I have formerly reported to you Bidault['s] and Bevin['s] respective responses to Molotov's "curiously worded warning").

While Bevin was worried about the effects of the impasse, he was, he said, more worried about the United States. Would she provide in time the assistance which Europe desperately needed? He was worried about the Soviets because he interpreted Molotov's warning to mean that they would use a very [every?] subversive device to prevent other European nations from joining in the formulation of a program and would employ every method to create internal trouble.

He believed that France would stand firmly in the immediate future, but that sometime, probably after the first meeting of the Cooperative Committee, if we could find some method of giving France some immediate and temporary assistance, it would have the effect of assuring French stability until such time as Congress might act. He was hopeful that we would be able to include the UK in this but that he was more concerned during the interim period with France than with the UK. I reminded him of our reluctance to act in a piece-meal way.

He went on to observe that the program would be completed by the first of September, but that we would be kept completely informed from time to time in the intervening period of the progress and development of the program in all of its details. This, he said, would enable us to digest the programme before it was finally formulated and would enable us, if we so concluded, to call a special session of Congress sooner than would otherwise be the case. If, he said, no action is taken by the United States until late fall or winter, he thought that France, and with her most of Europe, would be lost.

I asked him what nations in his judgment would join and made particular reference to Holland and Belgium which, because of their overseas possessions and the pool of natural resources, when combined with the resources of the British commonwealth, the British Crown colonies and the French colonies could make available on their own account large volume of raw materials for the reconstruction of such European countries as joined in the program. He replied that he was confident that Holland and Belgium would join (I have already given you his views about France), that Molotov had made particular reference to Norway and Bevin doubted, therefore, whether she would come in; that Sweden might join although she was in a difficult position; that while it was clear that Czechoslovakia and Poland want to participate, he questioned whether they would be permitted to do so. As to Austria, he was doubtful (I emphasized your concern with Austria). In regard to Italy, he said that she had been so vacillating and was under such pressure from Communists that while he recognized the extreme importance of Italian participation, he could not now give positive assurance that she would enter the scheme with them and he expressed the hope that such pressure as we could legitimately bring on Italy to participate would be exerted. Switzerland would participate.

If Poland does not participate, he emphasized his opinion that we should not at this juncture by-pass the European program and the Committee on Cooperation by making credits available to Poland either through the International Bank or from some other American source.

Invitations to all European countries, excepting Spain and Russia, will be sent out today and the first meeting of the Committee on Cooperation will be held on the tenth. He had himself suggested that Paris be the center for the Committee's work because he wanted to give France a feeling that she was important, restore her confidence, and thus give strength and support to her and particularly the Ramadier government.

As to the western zones in Germany and coal production in the Ruhr he had reviewed the proposals put up by Clay and Robertson and felt that unless we made some commitment that the coal properties, even though temporarily held by trustees or custodians, would be ultimately publicly owned, we would lose Germany to the Communists. He also referred to difference between US and UK proposals and stated UK plan for custodian under land [sic] was consistent with US position on decentralization.

I replied by referring to contemplated meeting in Washington at which presumably these questions would be discussed.

Bevin said he was meeting trade union leaders today to stiffen their support of his actions.

I suspect that Bevin's views regarding socialization Ruhr coal at least partly influenced by his need for strong trade union support and his fear that it may not be sufficiently strong if he even temporarily abandons programme for public ownership of German coal properties.

DOUGLAS

840.50 Recovery/7–447 : Telegram

The Ambassador in France (Caffery) to the Secretary of State

SECRET   PARIS, July 4, 1947—2 p. m.
URGENT   NIACT

2679. For the Secretary. I handed your message [1] to Bidault who was delighted. He said that he was particularly appreciative of your understanding his difficulties. He went on to say that he and Bevin are prepared to go full speed ahead and that they will first of all examine

---

[1] This is presumably a reference to telegram 2450, to Paris, July 3, p. 308.

just what the interested countries can do for themselves, either directly or by interchange, in the way of coal, wheat, steel and transportation. He said that he apprehends that some of the satellite countries will accept the invitation primarily to make difficulties. He has heard rumors that the Swiss will not take part and are even talking on the subject with the Scandinavian countries. If true, he would regret it.

He has had conversations with Bevin about Germany and fears there will be trouble in arriving at an agreement. He does not like the British idea of socializing the Ruhr mines, and among his reasons is the fact that French interests own a few of the mines. He is not hostile in principle to raising production levels in Germany but can give no blank check. In regard to Germany he will be subject to attack here on the one hand by the French Communists and on the other by De Gaulle's friends. The Gaullist press is already showing signs of this.

He is not apprehensive of any immediate unusual trouble here from the French Communists. In fact, he believes that the Soviets will strike first elsewhere but he does not know where.

CAFFERY

840.50 Recovery/7–747 : Telegram

The Counselor of Embassy in Poland (Keith) to the Secretary of State

SECRET   WARSAW, July 7, 1947—5 p. m.

1064. When Ambassador Griffis [1] called on Foreign Minister today latter took occasion to say that although final decision had not been made he certain Polish Government would accept British-French invitation and be present at meeting in Paris. This decision is different from that which was anticipated by British for British Ambassador told Ambassador Griffis evening sixth that neither he nor Bevin expected Poles would participate.

Sent Department 1064.

KEITH

[1] Stanton Griffis was actually the appointed ambassador, since he did not present his credentials to President Bolesław Bierut until July 9. See telegram 1089, from Warsaw, p. 320.

840.50 Recovery/7–747 : Telegram

The Ambassador in Czechoslovakia (Steinhardt) to the Secretary of State

SECRET   PRAHA, July 7, 1947—6 p. m.
URGENT

847. For Clayton. When British and French Ambassadors called on Masaryk [1] July 4 to tender invitation to Paris Conference, Masaryk

[1] Jan Masaryk, Czechoslovak Minister of Foreign Affairs.

accepted invitation immediately, as reported in my 837.[2] As Czechs are extremely anxious to participate in Marshall plan and will do so unless forbidden by Soviets, there would seem no necessity for being rushed at this time into decision to reconsider Czech application for Eximbank 50 million dollar loan.[3] I feel that any reconsideration of an Eximbank loan for general purposes as distinguished from commodity credits should be predicated on our over-all relations with Czechoslovakia and particularly extent to which proceeds of any such loan might be subject to diversion for benefit of Soviet Union or Czechoslovak Communist Party than that we be rushed into a reconsideration thereof to accomplish a purpose which has already been accomplished.

As reported my 836,[2] Gottwald,[4] Masaryk and Ripka[5] proceeding Moscow tomorrow where they will presumably receive instructions as to extent to which they may participate in any agreements which may be reached in Paris. Sent Geneva for Clayton as 19; repeated Department 847.

STEINHARDT

---

[2] Not printed.
[3] For documentation regarding this subject, see vol. IV, pp. 196 ff.
[4] Klement Gottwald, Prime Minister of Czechoslovakia.
[5] Dr. Hubert Ripka, Czechoslovak Minister of Foreign Trade.

840.50 Recovery/7–847 : Telegram

The Ambassador in France (Caffery) to the Secretary of State

SECRET   PARIS, July 8, 1947—7 p. m.
URGENT

2714. I asked Bidault today what responses the French are receiving to the Franco-British invitation to attend the July 12 conference to formulate a European plan.

He replied that the following countries had accepted unconditionally: Ireland, Portugal, Netherlands, Belgium, Luxembourg, Italy, Greece and Turkey. From what he hears from the Austrians he also believes they will accept.

Concerning the satellites he said Poland and Czechoslovakia say they wish to send delegates but that their final acceptance depends "on the scope of the plan, etc."

He believes Rumania, Bulgaria and Hungary are certain to refuse in view of Moscow's radio announcement last night and this morning to that effect.

Bidault is particularly concerned about Switzerland and Sweden. For political and psychological, even perhaps, more than economic reasons he said it is most important that they join in the formulation of a plan. He said, "Unless they are persuaded to do so by governments other than French and British (he obviously meant US) they may refuse to go along." Bidault is still hoping that the Scandinavian countries as well as Switzerland will go along and that a total of about 15 countries will meet in Paris.

CAFFERY

840.50 Recovery/7–947 : Telegram

The Ambassador in France (Caffery) to the Secretary of State

SECRET   PARIS, July 9, 1947—6 p. m.

2725. For the Secretary and Lovett from Clayton. At a meeting this morning with Jean Monnet, head of the Cabinet Planning Commission, and Alphand of the Foreign Office, I reviewed with them, along the same lines as in my talks with Bevin, our views regarding the European economic situation and its relation to the Secretary's Harvard address.

Monnet gave me a copy of a draft questionnaire which the French Government plans to present to each participant in the Paris Conference as a basis for developing a joint report to the United States. Draft is being transmitted by separate telegram. Monnet said that United Kingdom should frankly admit to conference its responsibility for failure of coal program in UK and Ruhr and that France should likewise take responsibility for failure of its agricultural program.

During conversation French raised three questions of special interest to Department:

(1) Monnet said that a member of his government was of the opinion that, while in some countries such as Great Britain (a) US grants for basic commodity imports and (b) international bank loans for reconstruction and modernization might be sufficient to assure recovery, in some other European countries, such as France, public finances were in such disorder that inflation could be arrested and production and distribution normalized only through massive imports of consumers' goods. Inquiry was made as to whether, in addition to grants and loans, a "stabilization fund" could be established for this purpose.

I replied that the only measures we had in mind were, (a) and (b) above; that I believed that budget balancing was the principal additional instrument to be used to arrest inflationary trends; and that we recognized that in some cases such as that of Great Britain and France the supply of essential consumers' goods had fallen to or below the danger point.

(2) Alphand raised the question of a possible conflict between provisions in the draft World Trade Charter and measures which participating countries might adopt to improve interchanges among European nations. He pointed out that European trade at present is largely conducted under a series of bilateral agreements which stipulate both import and export undertakings for specific commodities.

I replied, (a) that we regard bilateral and barter arrangements as restrictive to trade developments; (b) that on the other hand we approved of measures leading to a customs union in the Belgo–Dutch–Luxembourg pattern; and that I was confident that the Trade Charter as completed would not conflict with any European plan for interchanges if such a plan was based on sound economic principles.

(3) The French referred to the opening of the conference on July 12 and to the Secretary's statement of extending "friendly aid in the drafting of the European program", and inquired as to the means we had in mind for extending this aid. In reply I emphasized the European character of the plan and said that our drafting assistance would depend on what was requested of us.

Monnet suggested the desirability of establishing an agreed channel of liaison between the conference and the US, expressing the fear that otherwise the conference might be receiving divergent interpretations of the Department's views.

CAFFERY

840.50 Recovery/7–1047 : Telegram

The Ambassador in France (Caffery) to the Secretary of State

SECRET PARIS, July 10, 1947—noon.
URGENT

2744. Couve de Murville has just given me latest information on replies to invitation to the July 12 conference.

The following countries have accepted unconditionally: Ireland, Iceland, Portugal, Belgium, Netherlands, Luxembourg, Italy, Greece, Turkey, Austria, Switzerland. (Switzerland in accepting stated that it accepted on understanding that conference would not deal with political matters).

Czechoslovakia will be represented at the conference by Czech Ambassador in Paris but Czechs have informed French they will reserve final decision on participation until they know more about scope of plan.

French have now been informed that Sweden, Norway and Denmark will officially accept some time today.

No reply has been received from Finland but French still believe there is possibility that Finland may give a limited acceptance similar to Czechs.

No reply has been received from Poland, Yugoslavia, Rumania, Bulgaria and Hungary. In view of radio broadcasts from capitals of these countries, French consider their refusal although not yet officially announced is definite. Couve says that conference will convene probably at 11 Saturday morning. Bidault will preside. Conference will then proceed to elect president. Since conference is in Paris French candidate for presidency is Bevin and French and British are in agreement on this.

Couve says decision on composition of various subcommittees would probably take several days and he thinks this may possibly not be completed until July 15. French are strongly opposed to idea that all 17 participating countries be represented on each subcommittee. They take stand that the larger the subcommittees the more unwieldy they become and agreement is also more difficult.

French are very pleased over acceptance of Scandinavian countries not so much for economic reasons but because this broadens political and psychological composition of conference.

Sent Department; repeated London as 525, Moscow as 413, and Rome as 164.

CAFFERY

840.50 Recovery/7–1047 : Telegram

The Ambassador in France (Caffery) to the Secretary of State

SECRET

PARIS, July 10, 1947—7 p. m.

2757. To the Secretary and Lovett from Clayton. The Ambassador and I today continued with Jean Monnet and Couve de Murville the talks reported in Embtel 2725, July 9, 6 p. m., regarding the questions the French had raised concerning the Paris Conference on a European economic plan beginning July 12.

We placed emphasis on the following three points:

1—Any European report should include an analysis understandable to the man-in-the-street in the United States of reasons why European recovery has not progressed farther in spite of large sums already made available.

2—A sound production program designed progressively to put Europe on its feet within three or four years.

3—A program sketching in broad lines a type of European economic federation which would make economic sense and be designed to eliminate the small watertight compartments into which Europe's pre-war and present economy is divided. I suggested that Europe's case could be greatly strengthened if in this presentation they could actually agree to take at least one definite step in the direction of these objectives.

I am returning to Geneva this afternoon and have requested the Ambassador to keep the Department and me informed of all significant developments during the preliminary work of the conference. [CLAYTON]   CAFFERY

840.50 Recovery/7–1047 : Telegram

The Ambassador in Czechoslovakia (Steinhardt) to the Secretary of State

SECRET   PRAHA, July 10, 1947—1 p. m.

URGENT   NIACT

872. I have learned from sources which have heretofore been entirely reliable that a telegram was received at midnight from Gottwald in Moscow directing that an immediate meeting of Czech cabinet be summoned to withdraw Czechoslovakia's acceptance of Anglo-French invitiation to take part in Paris conference. My informants stipulate that in telegram Gottwald gave as his reason for insisting upon a withdrawal of acceptance fact that Paris meeting is to be a political and not an economic conference and that withdrawal of Czech acceptance would serve as conclusive evidence of Czechoslovakia's loyalty to its alliance with Soviet Union.

Cabinet is at present in session. Having regard to fact that Fierlinger [1] is leader of Social Democratic Party and that Social Democrats hold the balance of power in Cabinet there is little doubt in my mind but that Cabinet will acquiesce in Gottwald's demand.

I am inclined to view that Beneš [2] who appears to have been determining factor in acceptance of invitation to Paris prior to departure of Gottwald for Moscow and who approved of Gottwald's trip to Moscow has out-maneuvered Soviets and Czech Communists. Having anticipated a Soviet veto of Czech participation he is now in a position to make it clear to Czech public that Czechoslovakia's foreign policy is being dictated from Moscow, that country does not enjoy complete independence and that repeated charge in western press that Czechoslovakia is a Soviet satellite has been proven. He will also be in a position to suggest to moderate parties that they bring home to Czech public the fact that Czechoslovakia has been obliged by Soviet Union to act contrary to its own interests. In connection with foregoing see

---

[1] Zdeněk Fierlinger, Czechoslovak Deputy Prime Minister.
[2] Eduard Beneš, President of Czechoslovakia.

my 829 of July 3 [3] outlining probable course of action of both Czech and Soviet Governments.

STEINHARDT

---

[3] Not printed.

840.50 Recovery/7–1047 : Telegram

The Ambassador in Czechoslovakia (Steinhardt) to the Secretary of State

TOP SECRET   PRAHA, July 10, 1947—6 p. m.
NIACT

876. The same reliable source from which the information contained in my 872, July 10 was received has furnished me with a copy of Gottwald's telegram to Czechoslovak Government of which following is a free translation.

"I have had two audiences with Generalissimo Stalin.[1] The first shortly after our arrival, the second at 11 p. m. At the second visit there were present from the Czechoslovak side Masaryk, Drtina, Horak, Heidrich [2] and from the Soviet side Molotov and Bodrov (Soviet Counselor in Praha). The principal item of discussion was our participation at the Paris Conference, Stalin brought up first of all the questions which the governments of Yugoslavia, Poland and Rumania asked of Moscow before arriving at their decision. Both Stalin and Molotov did not conceal fact that they were surprised at the decision of the Czechoslovak Government in accepting the invitation to Paris. They emphasized their conviction that the real aim of the Marshall Plan and the Paris Conference is to create a western bloc and isolate the Soviet Union with loans which the initiators of the conference would not be able to grant and even if the loans should be granted sometime in the future by America they would not be without decisive limitations on the political and economic independence of the recipients. In view of this situation the Soviet Union would regard our participation as a break in the front of the Slav States and as an act specifically aimed against the USSR. Stalin declared that the question now under consideration involves our friendship with the USSR. There is no one in the Soviet Government who has any doubts about our friendship for the Soviets. However, our participation at Paris would be proof to the people of the USSR of the fact that we have allowed ourselves to be used as an instrument against the USSR, something which neither the Soviet public nor the Soviet Government could tolerate. Therefore, according to Stalin, we should withdraw our acceptance to participate and he thinks we could justify this action by pointing to the fact that the non-participation of the other Slav nations and the other eastern European states has created a new situa-

---

[1] Chairman of the Council of Ministers of the Soviet Union.
[2] Dr. Prokop Drtina, Czechoslovak Minister of Justice; Dr. Bohuslav Horak, of the Czechoslovak Ministry of Information; and Arnost Heidrich, of the Czechoslovak Foreign Office.

tion under which our participation could easily be aimed against the friendship with the Soviet Union and our other Allies.

Therefore, immediately call together all the members of the government within reach and inform them of the substance of our conference with Stalin and Molotov. We regard it as imperative that you agree to the withdrawal of our acceptance to joint conference at Paris and communicate it in such a way that it will reach here officially Thursday afternoon. In addition, telephone immediately your decision. We will bring a detailed report of the conference with us. Signed Gottwald, Masaryk, Drtina."

I have learned that after a lengthy debate in the Cabinet a decision was reached to comply with Gottwald's instruction; no vote was taken. The Cabinet is at present debating the text of the communiqué to be issued.

For obvious reasons I urge the Department to take every precaution to prevent the fact from becoming known that the Embassy has furnished the Department with the text of Gottwald's message to the Czechoslovak Government.

STEINHARDT

840.50 Recovery/7–1047 : Telegram

The Ambassador in Poland (Griffis) to the Secretary of State

SECRET   WARSAW, July 10, 1947—2 p. m.
URGENT

1089.   Following an apparently most cordial reception by all Polish officials whom I have thus far met here and unprecedented [apparent omission] arrangement to present credentials, my first diplomatic effort yesterday resulted in perfect score—100 percent failure.

As already advised reached Embassy Monday morning and was received by Foreign Minister within three hours. During general discussion he volunteered information that Polish Government expected send delegation Paris Conference 12th.

Yesterday I presented credentials to President and in following conference at which Keith was present I had general discussion on Polish–American questions. I expressed delight at news that Polish delegation would attend Paris Conference. I felt that good impression of such attendance on US public opinion would vary directly with extent of cooperation by Poles in Paris with other conferees. I stated that importance of this could not be over-estimated; that full cooperation might mean definite turning point in Polish–American relations and failure to cooperate would bring disastrous and adverse repercussions in US. We discussed this matter for nearly an hour Presiden stressing that England and France would largely control Conference and that most of its decisions had already been made in advance. He repeatedly referred to devastation in Poland to direct need of US aid and relief in Poland but expressed great antagonism to theory that Germany should be rehabilitated and put in position start another war as she had twice in past. He stated that in his opinion present policy of US was to rehabilitate the aggressor nation whereas assistance should be given nations which had suffered most from aggression during war. Nevertheless he stated that matter of Paris Conference would be decided at a govt meeting at six o'clock. The President also stated that there were many people today who did not realize that it was impossible to bring back the life which existed in Europe before war and that in all countries there had been great changes and that this was a new world. At 9:30 Keith and I were called to Foreign Minister's office where Modzelewski,[1] after various preliminary statements as to how fully Paris Conference had been considered, stated that Polish Government was giving a negative answer. He stated that he had desired have copy of govt's reply as a courtesy to US but he was simultaneously advising "our friend and ally Russia". He then gave me copy of their note, translation of which is being transmitted in following telegram.[2] He then gave reasons for this decision referring to copy of note (addressed to British Ambassador) replying to French and British.

Polish Government chief contention was that Poland would have little or nothing to say at Paris Conference; that whole trend of his discussion with British and French Ministers was to effect that plan was already substantially in form; that French Ambassador had told him previous evening that no political discussion should be permitted or included in Paris agenda. I stated that I did not quite understand where any political questions were involved as Marshall Plan was entirely an invitation to peoples of Europe to present a balance sheet of economic and reconstruction needs and a program of mutual co-operation. He replied that entire question of the rehabilitation of Germany, the aggressor nation, was a political question. The Foreign Minister stated that there was already an economic commission for Europe and that this proposal of the British and French brought into being a new organization to accomplish something which should be carried out by the UNO.

I expressed great regret at decision of Polish Government and asked if my strong representations to the President and to him that afternoon as to effect of such action on American public opinion had been

---

[1] Zygmunt Modzelewski, Polish Minister of Foreign Affairs.
[2] Not printed.

taken into consideration at the Ministers' meeting. Foreign Minister stated that this had been done but nevertheless Polish Government decision was adverse for reasons given. I reiterated my views as to the wisdom of sending a Polish delegation to Paris and of making an honest attempt to work out a plan even if Poles were unable finally agree to it. He replied in effect that cards were already stacked against Poland by the Western Powers.

Foreign Minister stated that he had in his portfolio a Polish plan for the rehabilitation of Europe and asked if our Government would care to have Polish Government submit it. I stated that I could not answer that question (my theory was that possibly Dept might wish me informally discuss plan later with the faint hope that whatever plan eventuated in Paris the Polish plan might somehow be reconciled with it, perhaps by a third party nation). Minister stated that despite decision of Polish Government the US could expect to have the fullest cooperation from Poland; that Poland intended to use surpluses for rehabilitation of Europe and that under those circumstances he hoped that great aid in rehabilitation could be obtained from US. He asked if I thought that this would be forthcoming. I stated that he must fully realize that both American Government and the Ambassador were the slaves of American public opinion and that such public opinion would give the answer to his question.

Sent Dept 1089; repeated Paris 153; London 888.

GRIFFIS

840.50 Recovery/7–1047 : Telegram

The Ambassador in Poland (Griffis) to the Secretary of State

SECRET   WARSAW, July 10, 1947—4 p. m.

1092. Continuing my 1089 July 10.[1] In reference to sudden change in Polish plans to send delegation Paris conference it is my distinct and firm impression that Foreign Minister was honest in statement on Monday that delegation would attend and again my firm impression last night that he himself if not entire Polish Cabinet had in the interim been overruled by higher authority. His attitude extremely apologetic and at least apparently regretful.

If Department has any desire receive Polish plan for reconstruction referred to 1089 please advise.

Sent Dept; repeated Paris 155, London 112.

GRIFFIS

---

[1] *Supra.*

840.50 Recovery/7–447 : Telegram

The Secretary of State to the Embassy in the United Kingdom

TOP SECRET   WASHINGTON, July 10, 1947—10 p. m.

2963. For the Ambassador. Pls express to Bevin gratitude for views and info given ur 3668 July 4. We share his concern for French position, and agree as to importance of French stability.

In this connection, you shd say to Bevin we are somewhat disturbed by apparent lack FonOff appreciation of present Ital situation. Far from requiring pressure to participate in European plan, Italy was one of first countries to indicate acceptance of Brit–French invitation, and Ital public opinion is so thoroughly behind plan that Ital Communists have found it expedient give their conditional endorsement Ital participation. Principal question which arises re Italy is similar to that suggested by Bevin re France namely need of some further immediate support. Ital political situation is roughly analogous to that in France, with added elements of danger in that moderate leftists have thus far been hesitant support present Govt fully in face determined Communist opposition and Ital needs for interim assistance are perhaps most critical of all European countries.

As we see it, there is urgent need in Italy of economic and moral support not only of US but of all Western powers if stability there is to be maintained until anticipated benefits from overall European plan can be felt. We are convinced that unless present Govt meets with success in its efforts to stop further deterioration Ital situation, both political and economic, there will be no way to prevent Communist rise to power in spring elections, with all of the serious consequences which this would entail, if indeed they do not take advantage before that time of growing difficulties to return to Govt in dominant position.

We recognize that certain fiscal and social reforms are just as necessary as foreign economic assistance for betterment general conditions of mass Ital people. De Gasperi [1] appears aware of need for these measures, however, and with adoption effective governmental program this nature we are hopeful moderate leftists, particularly Republicans and Saragat Socialists, will support him and perhaps eventually agree enter Govt on broader coalition basis.

We want to emphasize, however, that support of Western powers must be made plainly evident to Ital people if any democratic Ital Govt is to have reasonable opportunity to prove itself.

MARSHALL

[1] Alcide de Gasperi, Prime Minister of Italy.

840.50 Recovery/7–1047 : Telegram

The Secretary of State to the Consulate at Geneva

TOP SECRET   WASHINGTON, July 10, 1947—11 a. m.
URGENT

768. Personal from Lovett for Clayton and Ambassador only. I have
read with great interest the discussions you and Douglas have had with
Bevin, Cripps, Dalton etc. and the Brit *aide-mémoire* summarizing
them.[1] These documents are very helpful in giving us an insight into
your thinking and into the problems which the Secretary's suggestion
raises. In general I can say that our thinking has been running along
parallel lines, though you have developed some points further than
we have taken them. There are a number of points on which I should
like to comment.

It seems to me that yours is the right answer on the relation of the
special Brit dollar problem to the question of European recovery. A
correct solution to the European production and distribution difficulties will go a long way to help the Brit out of their troubles. The
European program, however, should not attempt to solve the world
dollar shortage. For one thing, I doubt that this country can stand the
pressure on its exports at the rate of the first quarter of this year. As
you know, the pinch is being felt in oil; lately we have been made
aware of worries in coking coal, steel and agriculture. Canadian and
Latin American purchases here are exerting very heavy pressure on
domestic supplies. If in the name of European recovery we help Brit
to pay Canada, Argentina etc. all the dollars the latter require, we are
going to find ourselves solving a world long-run problem via a short-
run European problem and we will run into Congressional difficulties.
We can make provision in European recovery aid for the transfer of
some dollars from Europe to points outside the US. The Brit commitment to convert annually agreed amounts of blocked sterling into
dollars should be taken into account for example, as well as the minimum amounts of dollars Europe will require to finance purchases from
non-US areas. In addition, we should try to get away from tied purchases, if Congress will permit, and procure commodities needed by
Europe under minimum aid programs outside the US, if this does not
interfere with supply arrangements on which Europe is already counting. Finally, I know that Dept is considering whether we should take
over the burden of the minimum support of the US–UK combined
zones of Germany, insofar as dollars are concerned. Beyond this, however, I think we have to be careful not to go, or we will find ourselves

---

[1] For documentation on conversations held June 24–26 in London, see pp. 268–
294. For *Aide-Mémoire* of June 25, see p. 284.

trying to solve the dollar problems of the whole world. This we cannot do.

Your distinction between short-term needs for consumption and long-term needs for reconstruction is a correct one, but I am somewhat uneasy about drawing too hard and fast a line. For general reconstruction needs, you are of course completely right. For bottleneck items, such as fertilizer, mining machinery, facilities needed to aid Europe in repairing rolling stock, I am not sure that we should not hold the question open a little longer. As you point out, the distinction between consumption goods and capital goods leads to geographic differences. Eastern Europe doesn't need coal and food so much as fertilizer, transport equipment, mining machinery etc. If we insist too rigorously from the beginning that all capital goods have to be obtained on a loan basis, while consumption goods may be financed through grants, we lose a little flexibility which may later stand us in good stead. I suggest only that this question be held open a bit longer on capital goods needed to produce consumption goods in a bottleneck field. I have not yet talked to McCloy [2] on this subject but hope to do so shortly.

We are all here in agreement with you on the point that a customs union is a desirable long-run objective but that to attempt to work it out now would bog Europe down in details and distract from the main effort. I leave to you how the integration which Bevin seems to want in such matters as farm implements and musical instruments can be squared with our ITO endeavors. Undoubtedly if rapid recovery is to be achieved we shall have to interpret various escape clauses in ITO liberally.

I agree with Douglas on the importance of steps to straighten out financial chaos, but think that the Brit are probably right in thinking that we should not press too hard on this from this end. Nevertheless fiscal stability should be pressed by someone. In addition to the budgetary aspects of the problem, there are of course exchange-rate questions (France and Germany) questions of external and internal prices (which must be solved shortly if trade—in other than critical bottleneck items which will presumably be allocated—is to flow in normal channels) and the restoration of internal monetary stability, including confidence in currencies. The last of course largely a budgetary question except that in some countries like Germany and Austria, budgets are balanced but outstanding currency and deposits are far too large in relation to prices.

I have not thought through the problem you raise in suggesting that while we should get individual and overall commitments from Europe

---

[2] John J. McCloy, President of the International Bank for Reconstruction and Development.

regarding their recovery, our aid should be arranged through a series of bilateral agreements with separate countries. I appreciate your worries about an UNRRA type distribution of aid. On the other hand, I don't see how a European coal program, based upon certain goals for production in deficit and exporting countries and certain minimum requirements for aid from the United States, can have the latter fixed by a series of European country agreements with us in view of the necessity for flexibility in allocations. As you know better than I, allocations cannot be made effectively much more than 3 to 6 months ahead (and in food there is frequent necessity to divert individual ships). If US coal is allocated by a European organization, and if our aid is linked in whole or part to commodities, how would the bilateral agreements work. I am not yet sure that we want to discard the commodity approach, the administrative aspects of which may be possible of solution in ways that would avoid the UNRRA difficulties, without having examined the question further. If we allocate dollars, rather than commodities, for example, we are in danger of returning to the piece-meal approach we are so anxious to avoid.

Finally, I am inclined to think that the commodity approach should not be pursued by Europe to the exclusion of trade and administrative problems. Some device must be found to rid Europe of the stultifying effects of bilateral trade, and steps must be taken within the separate economies (partly monetary but some administrative) to correct black markets, compensation deals, hoarding, diversion of resources to repair or expansion in low priority industries, etc. You cover these points indirectly when you asked Bevin for an account of why recovery in Europe had not progressed farther in the two years since the war, given the substantial quantities of US aid. But this account of the past, I think, should not be focussed exclusively on commodities, and it should produce an effort to handle the European economic problems more effectively, both inter-Europewise and internally in separate countries. This raises issues larger than food, coal, fibers, etc.

A word on timing. If Europe gives us a plan by September 1, the best we can do under present prospects is to have hearings this fall and try to get approval shortly after January 1, 1948. This is optimistic. Before this day, I am told, there may be financial crises in Italy and France. You know more about this than I. Do we have to envisage taking some piecemeal steps for France and Italy before January 1?

I do not like these emergency treatments because they are piecemeal and our whole approach is based on an overall solution. Yet I see no alternative. What are your views?

I am sending a copy of this to Douglas in London as Dept's 2952.

[Lovett]
Marshall

840.50 Recovery/7–1147 : Telegram

The Ambassador in the Soviet Union (Smith) to the Secretary of State

SECRET   Moscow, July 11, 1947.

2413. For the Secretary and Matthews. The Czechoslovak reversal on the Paris Conference, on Soviet orders, is nothing less than a declaration of war by the Soviet Union on the immediate issue of the control of Europe.

The Kremlin's assessment of the situation must be assumed to have convinced it of its ability to win, either by resignation and retirement of the West in face of their firm stand, as they hope, or in an open struggle, if necessary. With firm control of the continental bread basket in Eastern Europe and of important sectors of its industrial economy in Germany, Poland and Czechoslovakia, the Soviet leaders must expect that Bevin and Bidault will be unable to secure enough US support to establish a viable regional reconstruction plan for the free countries of Europe. Even if a workable plan should emerge from the Paris meetings and sufficient American support be initially forthcoming, it would soon be cut off by the "inevitable" crisis in the United States—a basic postulate of Soviet politico-economic thinking.

In no previous instance has the Soviet Govt been so firm in handling its satellites. It seems clear that the Kremlin was surprised by the original Czechoslovak acceptance on July 8, presumably without prior consultation, but thereafter no other satellite ventured out of line. The seriousness of the Soviet purpose has now been strikingly demonstrated by making the Czechoslovaks eat crow publicly, even though the reserved nature of their original acceptance would have provided a face-saving exit at a later stage. The words of the Czechoslovak communiqué that Czechoslovak participation would be interpreted as an "act aimed against friendship with the USSR" indicate that there was plain speaking in the Kremlin when the Czechoslovak delegation was whisked into that sanctuary so shortly after its arrival here.

The lines are drawn. Our response is awaited. I do not need to point out to the Dept the repercussions of a failure to meet the Soviet challenge, in terms not only of the control of Europe, but of the impact which such a failure would have in the Middle and Far East and throughout the colonial world.

Dept please repeat Paris as Moscow's 274; Berlin as 449; Praha as 5 and London as 277.

SMITH

840.50/7–1147 : Telegram

The Ambassador in France (Caffery) to the Secretary of State

SECRET   PARIS, July 11, 1947—5 p. m.

2766. For Secretary and Lovett from Caffery. Under Secretary Clayton, who had returned to Geneva, requested me to send you summary of conversation which we had with President Ramadier.

Ramadier opened conversation by referring to Europe's difficult economic position and to need to re-establish international exchanges, commenting that it was easier to re-establish exchange of goods than an exchange of ideas. In this conversation, which occurred before Czechoslovakia reversed its position concerning participation in conference, Ramadier stressed need for economic unity in Europe, expressing his pleasure at what he believed to be Czechoslovakian acceptance of membership in conference and referring to important position which Poland occupied as source of coal for both France and other European countries. In this connection he said, "indeed, it is indispensable that this unity should include Poland for it can be said that Europe extends as far as Vistula. Beyond, things are different. To wish to have Europe stop this side of Vistula would be equivalent to having United States stop at Mississippi.["]

Ramadier then said that independently of economic difficulties a profound moral uneasiness reigned in Europe. It could even be said that France's economic reconstruction is more advanced than its moral reconstruction. European nations are now comparable to customers of bank about to suspend its payments. Marshall concept therefore, in addition to its economic aspects, is also remedy for this moral uneasiness, but rapidity of execution is above all necessary. European countries must move rapidly in this task but it is also necessary the United States place itself rapidly in position to define aid it considers it can bring us.

Mr. Clayton, in reply, assured Ramadier that he appreciated difficulty of French position: Europe at moment is under pressure as concerns foodstuffs, fuel and all current consumption goods, that this pressure is so strong that Europe does not have respite necessary for it to review its difficulties and make its reconstruction plans. If it should prove possible for American Government to extend assistance in form of coal, cereals and other items, this would permit Europe to concentrate effectively on its production and reconstruction problems. In this connection, Mr. Clayton referred to staggering costs of European imports of coal and wheat, and fact that European nations could not recover economically if they had to dedicate their available foreign exchange to that purpose. Disruption of Europe's economy was much greater than indicated solely by physical destruction and it is now certain that economic reconstruction of Europe will require longer period than had been anticipated. Necessary measures for reconstruction, rehabilitation and development must be adopted and implemented by Europeans themselves, and it is Europe itself which will perfect means and methods which must be applied and which will permit it, with assistance of United States, once again get "back on its feet" economically. When Europe is economically "back on its feet" it is certain that it will also be "on its feet" politically.

Ramadier then turned to German problem stating that success of conference and subsequent work pre-supposes that German problem will be solved before end of the year, at least in its principal aspects. It must be solved from economic point of view and also, at least in part, from political point of view. Partition of Germany is inconceivable and, therefore, there could be no other solution than federal solution, at least during coming years.

Furthermore, from an economic point of view, solution must be found to problem of Ruhr. This, moreover, does not prejudice right to reparations of powers who can claim them, to extent, of course, that this right can be satisfied. These problems, which will not be brought up at conference, are, nevertheless, conditions for success of Marshall Plan. On this point Ramadier concluded by saying that American aid proposals implied pledge to resolve German problem, at least provisionally.

Ramadier then referred to fact that there were European countries with overseas areas and inquired: "Does contemplated assistance to Europe include overseas countries under jurisdiction of European countries?"

Clayton, in reply, said this question had not been considered up to moment but that it was his personal feeling that Marshall suggestion had in mind primarily granting of assistance to continental Europe and not to overseas territories. He was cognizant of fact, however, that in many respects North Africa had been treated economically as part of France proper. Clayton added that it was clear that Secretary's suggestion could not be considered as applying to Indo-China which is not regarded as European country. He added that assistance given to European countries would permit their overseas areas to profit from certain advantages but it was not contemplated that there would be direct aid to these territories. Clayton stated that with regard to undesirability of dividing Germany, at least economically, he concurred and that he also knew that Ruhr question is fundamental problem because it is reservoir of coal, steel and other raw materials located in middle of Europe. In closing Mr. Clayton mentioned that he had previously discussed same questions with Mr. Bevin and had spoken to him in same terms.

Sent Dept as 2766, repeated Geneva for Clayton as 81.

CAFFERY

840.50 Recovery/7–1147 : Telegram

The Ambassador in the United Kingdom (Douglas) to the Secretary of State

TOP SECRET   LONDON, July 11, 1947—8 p. m.

3812. For the Secretary. ReDeptel 2963, July 10. I expressed to Bevin this afternoon your gratitude for his views and the information contained in Embtel 3668, July 4 and your serious concern about the position of Italy. He shares your concern.

He said that he was very hopeful that Italy would have a representative at the forthcoming Paris meeting and was himself cabling to Rome urging that a representative attend. He suggested that we do likewise.

He said that he would do everything possible to provide moral support for Italy among the Western powers. He would at Paris suggest that under the General Committee on Cooperation there be established an Executive Committee of five on which he hoped the participating countries would designate one member from the Scandinavian countries, one member for Benelux (Belgium, Netherlands, Luxembourg) one member from the UK, one member from France, and one member from the Mediterranean area, the latter being a representative of Italy.

He thought that if successful this program would provide the moral support, on behalf of the Western European countries, which he recognized the present Italian Government needs.

In addition, he had been attempting to find some method by which the Italian Ambassador Designate, Carandini, could be officially recognized by the British Government but that he had so far been able to find no precedent which would fit this particular situation.

As soon as Italy ratifies the treaty and even before it is signed, he hoped to make a statement to the House of Commons that the "state of war" with Italy was ended and that His Majesty's Government was now "at peace" with her.

If you have any other suggestions as to how the participating Western European countries may add further moral support to the present Italian Government, please let me have them.

DOUGLAS

840.50 Recovery/7–1647

The British Chargé (Balfour) to the Secretary of State

PERSONAL   WASHINGTON, July 16, 1947.

DEAR MR. SECRETARY: I have just received a telegram from Mr.
Bevin in Paris asking me to convey to you the following personal mes-
sage from him. Mr. Bevin's telegram was despatched last night,
July 15th.

"The initial stages of our work in Paris have passed off with great
smoothness and rapidity and there is every evidence of good-will and
of a desire to cooperate on the part of all participating countries.[1] It
has been particularly interesting that in general countries have been
anxious to be represented on committees for commodities in which they
can make some contribution to European reconstruction.

A further point of interest which has emerged from these preliminary discussions is that the Scandinavian countries are prepared to
work as a team and all are somewhat anxious to know how far the
special arrangements which may be necessary in order to implement
the effective pooling of resources within Europe can be reconciled with
the general principle of non-discrimination. They have not at present
fully developed their thinking in any of these directions, but they are
obviously reflecting seriously upon this whole complex of problems
and are prepared to put their best people to work to try to help to
solve them.

I think that we can regard the limited size and actual membership
of the Executive as extremely satisfactory. I am sure that you will be
glad to see that Italy has obtained a seat on this Committee, which, I
anticipate, will be an important cog in the machine. The Turks, in
particular, made an attempt to enlarge the membership of this Committee by the addition of themselves, but the other Delegations felt that
this would have been quite inappropriate and their suggestion was
therefore withdrawn.

On the whole, I am glad to be able to tell you not only that the composition of these committees is satisfactory in itself, but also that it
has been arrived at without any visible ill-will or dissatisfaction. Our
final meeting today was conducted in a very genial atmosphere".[2]

Yours sincerely,   JOHN BALFOUR

[1] The Conference on European Reconstruction opened on July 12, and British
Foreign Secretary Bevin was elected president. By that evening, the working
committee, composed of representatives of all participants, reached agreement
on a plan for organizing the conference; this was presented to the conference's
second plenary session at 4 p.m. on July 13. A Cooperation Committee, Executive
Committee, and committees on Food and Agriculture, Energy-Power, Iron and
Steel, and Transportation were established. It was provided that the Cooperation
Committee's function would be to prepare a report on European availabilities and
requirements for the next four years, to be submitted to the United States before
September 1. It was decided that "the Cooperation Committee, as suggested by
the Secretary of State of the U.S.A., shall seek the friendly assistance of the U.S.
for the preparation of the report." (Telegram 2789 from Paris, 840.50 Recovery/7–
1347). Substantial documentation on the progress of the conference is in the
840.50 Recovery file.
[2] On July 17 Secretary of State Marshall handed to President Truman a
memorandum summarizing this message, and on the same day Under Secretary
Lovett conveyed the information to Senator Vandenberg and Congressman Eaton.
(840.50 Recovery/7–1647)

Policy Planning Staff Files

Memorandum Prepared by the Director of the Policy Planning Staff (Kennan)[1]

[WASHINGTON, July 18?, 1947.]

1. There is a serious gap between what is required of Germany for European recovery and what is being produced there today. Unless this gap can be overcome no European recovery program will be realistic.

2. It is clear that any attempt on the part of the British and ourselves to arrive at measures for eliminating this gap without consultation with the French will undermine Bidault's position and prejudice the success of the Paris talks.

3. I see no reason why we should not ask for early tri-partite conversations with the French and British on the subject of general policy toward Germany. The aim of such conversations would be to arrive at a general consensus on what has to be done and what ought to be done to raise German production. There would be no question of arriving at any written agreement, and it would be left to each of the three powers to translate into action in Germany, within the limits of its direct responsibilities, any common set of views that might be arrived at.

4. In this way we could place squarely before the French the choice between a rise in German production or no European recovery financed by the U.S. I believe that we could actually come to a meeting of the minds. What puts Bidault in a hard position is not to be consulted at all when we take decisions on Germany.

5. I can see no objection to having the coal talks merged with these tri-partite discussions if this would be preferable from the British standpoint.[2]

6. As for level of industry, I am afraid we must insist that instructions be sent to General Clay to the effect that the agreement arrived at between him and General Robertson [3] should be held in abeyance pending final approval by the two governments in the light of the development of the general situation in Europe. It could be made clear to Clay that this implies absolutely no criticism of his procedure or of his work in negotiating the agreement but that a situation has simply

---

[1] Marginal notation: "GFK Notes for Mr. Lovett July 18, 1947".

[2] For documentation regarding German production levels, coal distribution, and tripartite discussions, see volume II.

[3] For documentation, see vol. II, pp. 977 ff. For text of revised Plan for the Level of Industry in the United States–United Kingdom Zones of Occupation in Germany, signed August 27, 1947, see *Germany 1947–1949*, pp. 358–362, Department of State *Bulletin*, September 7, 1947, pp. 468–472. *Documents on International Affairs, 1947–1948*, pp. 626–632, or Ruhm von Oppen, *Documents on Germany*, pp. 239–245.

arisen in Europe which makes it advisable, as a matter of government policy, that this matter should be held open for a little while.

840.50 Recovery/7–2047 : Telegram

The Ambassador in France (Caffery) to the Secretary of State

SECRET   PARIS, July 20, 1947—6 p. m.
URGENT

2886. For Secretary and Lovett. I submit following preliminary appraisal of first week's activities of conference on European economic cooperation, based on day-by-day informal contacts which we have maintained with number of delegates from participating countries:

1. Organizational plan. There is general agreement that organizational plan provides workable basis, consisting of: (*a*) conference proper which is now adjourned but will probably reconvene to receive and approve final plan. (*b*) The committee of European economic cooperation. This is in effect conference proper but committee device is used to permit closed sessions. (Only criticism raised to date has been that Alphand, in his position as spokesman for committee, has tended to give French slant to information released. It has now been agreed that press relations will be handled by Secretariat). (*c*) Executive Committee. (UK, France, Netherlands, Norway and Italy) This is in effect steering committee. (*d*) Technical committees. Four of these (food and agriculture, energy, iron and steel and transportation) have already been established and will begin work tomorrow. It now appears that other committees may be established to deal with questions (1) labor supply and (2) housing and timber supply.

2. Plan of work. The basic document for scheme of work, which outlines objectives and types of statistical and other data required, was adopted last night and I am forwarding text by airgram. Supplementary detailed questionnaires will be prepared by technical committees for their respective fields.[1]

3. The first week's activities were characterized by desire to work as rapidly as possible and by disinclination to permit questions of procedure or minor detail to slow down progress of conference.

---

[1] The text and annex of the "Memorandum Outlining Object and Scheme of Work With a View to a Reply to Mr. Marshall" was transmitted in Paris airgram A–1212, July 21, 1947, not printed (840.50 Recovery/7–2147). The annex to this memorandum described the kinds of information to be sought by questionnaires. On August 6, the Paris Embassy in airgram A–1306 reported that the "technical questionnaires have been completed by virtually all the countries and it is hoped that they can be tabulated by the beginning of next week." The information contained in *Committee of European Economic Co-operation*, vol. II, *Technical Reports, July–Sept. 1947* (Department of State publication 2952) is based on replies to these questionnaires.

At same time, it is apparent that there are several fundamental policy differences which must be resolved if workable plan is to result. At some stage of negotiations views of Department may well be requested concerning these major questions. Differences which have already come into focus include:

(a) *Multilateral trading.* Benelux has already proposed that present network of bilateral trading and payment agreements should be placed on multilateral basis as among participating countries and I am informed that France and UK are not opposed to consideration of this proposal. Doubt has been expressed whether Scandinavian countries, in view of their commercial ties with east, will be prepared to go along on this project.

(b) *The question of emphasis in planning.* As I have already reported there has been good deal of discussion concerning question of whether planning should be primarily on short-term or long-term basis and cleavage is somewhat deeper than indicated by surface discussion. Benelux countries have taken approach that large part of imbalance in Europe's payments position is due to failure to utilize productive resources already in existence and that immediate plan should concentrate on this problem. French, with some support from British, have contended that each country should submit long-term reconstruction and modernization program, arguing (a) that this is necessary in order to show American people that self-supporting European economy will finally result and (b) because assistance from US will be extended under series of bi-lateral agreements, taking into account plan of each country. I am informed that real cleavages in these differences of emphasis arise from following:

1. It is implicit in Benelux approach that resources of western zones of Germany would be utilized at rapid rate and,

2. The smaller countries fear that long-term investment program, if adopted by September 1, would merely be composite of reconstruction programs already formulated by individual countries. In such case it is feared that countries, such as France, which already have adopted "very ambitious programs" would get "lion's share" of assistance from US. Furthermore, such composite plan would bear no necessary relationship to principle of comparative advantage.

(c) *Role of western zones of Germany.* As indicated above, Benelux countries believe there can be no western European economic recovery in true sense unless there is rapid utilization of resources of western Germany. They are prepared to rely on occupational controls, plus elimination of actual war industries, to deal with security problem. (I am informed that Benelux countries also believe that French zone should be merged with other two zones as part of European plan, but feel that for political reasons initiative in this matter should come from UK or US).

French, of course, have not abandoned outwardly their position of "pastoral" approach to German problem and contend that security lies in "pulling heavy industrial teeth" of Germany.

(*d*) *Standard of living.* British informed me that in anticipation of desire by some countries to use program for "spending spree" they obtained insertion of following provision in working plan:

> "Standards of consumption during period under review, while they should be determined with regard to their effect on ability and incentive to produce, should not exceed those which each country expects subsequently to be able to maintain without special external assistance."

It is believed that when combined programming is undertaken, particularly for food supplies, many questions will be raised regarding differentials in living standards both in absolute terms and relative to pre-war.

Sent Dept 2886, repeated Geneva for Clayton as 105, London as 564, Berlin as 266, to Moscow and Berlin by airpouch.

CAFFERY

Policy Planning Staff Files

Memorandum Prepared by the Policy Planning Staff [1]

[WASHINGTON, July 21?, 1947.]

1. *Marshall "plan".*

We have no plan. Europeans must be made to take responsibility. We would consider European plan only if it were a good one and promised to do the whole job.

Our main object: to render principal European countries able to exist without outside charity.

Necessity of this:

(*a*) So that they can buy from us;
(*b*) So that they will have enough self-confidence to withstand outside pressures.

2. *Russia and Communism.*

Strain placed on communist movement by effort to draw up plan for European rehabilitation. Communist Parties in West forced to show their hand.

Russians smoked out in their relations with satellite countries. Maximum strain placed on those relations.

Events of past weeks the greatest blow to European Communism since termination of hostilities. If same line can be continued on our part we can weaken movement still further but for this we need strong internal support.

---

[1] Marginal notation: "GFK Notes for Secy Marshall 7–21–1947".

Principal Communist argument today: that U.S. public and Congress will not pack [back] up program of aid to Europe.

3. *Germany.*

U.S. determination to keep Germany disarmed and demilitarized (Four-Power Pact).[2]

Meanwhile, urgent necessity for increased production:

(a) From standpoint of cost to U.S. taxpayer;
(b) From standpoint of contribution to European recovery.

French apprehensions: Communists making big capital out of assertion that "Marshall plan" spells preference to German reconstruction over that of France. True facts as to situation: German production less than 50% of pre-war; France—pre-war level substantially achieved. What French Government really wants: to be consulted on these matters so as to have an answer to Communist attacks.

Coal talks. Coal—the center of German and European recovery. British desire to widen talks. French fears.

4. *Other areas.*

European situation no precedent for other areas.

Suggestions made in Harvard speech applicable to Europe alone. Problems elsewhere require different approach, main exceptions being Korea and Japan.

Backward nations require not so much government loans as other forms of support: technical aid, business initiative, etc., which can come more directly from private sources in this country, with government support.

This problem will have to be studied carefully. There may well be instances where further expenditure of government funds in other areas may be warranted by U.S. interests; but certainly nothing is visible today which could rank with European recovery program in importance to U.S., in character of measures called for, in total costs or in benefits to be obtained.

5. *Britain.*

Britain's position—serious, more serious than most people know.

Her position beginning to improve; but it will be one year before she can be expected even to approach balance of payments.

Possibly, a program of European recovery worked out by the Europeans themselves might include provisions which would benefit Britain along with the others. Britain would benefit in any case, a would this country, from an increase in prosperity in western Europe

[2] For text of the draft treaty submitted on April 29, 1946, by Secretary of Stat Byrnes to the Council of Foreign Ministers meeting in Paris, see Department o State *Bulletin*, May 12, 1946, p. 815.

But this may not be enough; and some special aid may have to be provided for Britain. This is a problem which we are now studying.

It must be remembered that first loan really shrunk in significance from British standpoint, partly on account of rises in prices and partly on account of severe winter.

If Britain should not receive some aid, she would have no choice but to dismantle extensively her defense and imperial commitments. This would mean that serious vacuums would be created in other areas which could be most embarrassing to us, and cause us many headaches.

Some of these vacuums are ones we might have to fill. This could cost far more than a completion of aid to Britain at this time.

840.50 Recovery/7–2247

The Italian Embassy to the Department of State [1]

The new American policy towards Germany as announced through the instructions issued by the United States Government to General Clay [2] is of deep interest to the Italian Government. Italy views with favor that Germany be included again in the European system, also in view of the fact that Italian–German prewar exchanges (horticultural produce, coal and metals) would contribute to reduce the deficit of her balance of payments, thus representing a considerable saving to the American taxpayer.

Italian representatives have sustained this opinion at the Paris Conference in the conviction that the application thereof would fully meet the Marshall plan. A similar program, however, clashes with the firm attitude of France. On the other hand it seems that Switzerland, the Low Countries and Sweden would adhere to such a program.

---

[1] Marginal notations: "Left with me by Tarchiani 7/27/47 H F[reeman] M[atthews]"; "Tel. from Rome to Ital. Amb."
[2] The text of this directive to General Clay regarding the Military Government of Germany is printed in Department of State *Bulletin*, July 27, 1947, p. 186.

Editorial Note

A study by the Policy Planning Staff, "Certain Aspects of the European Recovery Problem from the United States Standpoint", top secret, begun in May, was completed on July 23, when what was called a "preliminary report" was submitted to Secretary Marshall. This 62-page study, an extension of the paper of May 23, page 223, presented the matured views of the Planning Staff, which in turn were based upon the studies, recommendations and suggestions of a wide cross-section of the operating and research units of the Department."

The report was designed to clarify the elements of the problem, to suggest approaches by the United States, and to serve other agencies as a guide to the views of the Department of State. A copy bearing the marginal notation "Noted G.C.M." is in Lot 64 D 563, Box 1 (20027) envelope "Foreign Assistance, 1947-50".

George F. Kennan, Director of the Policy Planning Staff, prepared a top-secret supplement describing certain additional considerations that contributed to the Staff's conclusions but that were omitted from the body of the report. A copy of this supplement is in Lot 64 D 563, Box 5 (718), envelope "Foreign Assistance, 1947-50".

840.50 Recovery/7–2347 : Telegram

The Ambassador in France (Caffery) to the Secretary of State

SECRET   PARIS, July 23, 1947—7 p. m.

2930. Sir Oliver Franks, president (in absence of Bevin) of Conference of European Economic Cooperation informs me that group will really come to grips with major policy questions in week beginning August 4. This week technical committees and subcommittees are drafting questionnaires and consulting with such bodies as ECO and ECITO in regard to statistics and information required. Next week many delegates will return to their countries to supervise execution of questionnaires. Balance of payments committee has also been established, composed of Sir David Waley, Great Britain, Guindey, France, Ansiaux, Belgium, and Italian and Danish representatives.

From informal talks with number of delegates, I gather that leading policy questions continue to be those listed in my 2886, of July 20.

Sent Dept; repeated Rome for Clayton as 181.

CAFFERY

840.50 Recovery/7–2747 : Telegram

The Ambassador in France (Caffery) to the Secretary of State

SECRET   PARIS, July 27, 1947—2 p. m.

2987. For Lovett. Sir Oliver Franks yesterday afternoon conveyed to me informally following comment concerning progress of Conference of European Economic Cooperation:

He has been somewhat concerned about controversy going on between Benelux group and French. In effort to get at root of problem, British first had Benelux group to dinner and found that Belgians took dim view of Monnet plan because in half dozen instances French were projecting large production increase for items which Belgian were either producing or expecting to produce and for which they regarded France normal market. He mentioned artificial nitrates as example.

Dutch problem was of somewhat greater proportions, because economies of western Germany and Netherlands were complementary, and because Dutch placed such great dependence on entrepot trade as source of foreign exchange. Magnitude of this source of income in turn is dependent very largely on level of economic activity in Germany.

British subsequently had dinner with French to explore this problem and found that French were quite conciliatory and prepared to make effort to adapt Monnet plan to meet in large part Belgian objections. It did not appear that solution to Dutch problem would prove as easy to find.

Sent Dept; repeated to London 588; repeated to Clayton at Geneva 121.

CAFFERY

840.50 Recovery/7-2947 : Telegram

The Ambassador in France (Caffery) to the Secretary of State

SECRET   PARIS, July 29, 1947—8 p. m.

3022. For the Secretary and Lovett from Clayton. Sir Oliver Franks at his request called on me today in his capacity as chairman of the Committee of European Economic Cooperation and gave me a review of the work of his group to date which closely paralleled the reports we have already received from Ambassador Caffery.

Franks then said that it was only this week that the members of the executive and cooperation committees were beginning to discuss key policy matters and that he expected that they would really come to grips with these problems in a fortnight's time, or when questionnaire data had been received and collated.

As a prelude to policy formulation, Franks has recalled the attention of his group to pertinent sections of the Secretary's Harvard address, which he interpreted as posing three major problems with which the conference should concern itself:

1. The immediate increase in European production of essential commodities.

2. The financial problem, subdivided into (a) external balance of payments, and (b) internal financial stabilization in European countries.

3. The problem of freeing trade movements within the European community.

In reply I said that this interpretation was quite sound and in line with our own thinking to date. I emphasized (*a*) the tremendous difference in the European balance of payments which would result if Europe could regain its pre-war position in coal and food production; (*b*) the close attention we were giving to the currency stabilization problem; and (*c*) the absurdly uneconomic lengths to which exchange controls had been carried in Europe. Examples cited were the day-by-day administrative interventions which intervened to prevent both export and import movements and the artificial exchange rate policies of some countries which were reducing the flow of goods to the United States to a mere trickle.

Franks then mentioned the following special questions which had or soon would arise in the conference:

1. *The German Problem.*

Franks mentioned that it was becoming apparent that German recovery was inseparably linked to European recovery and that the smaller countries all recognized this to one degree or another. The French attitude towards German recovery was an emotional one, but Franks was encouraged that the French, after some discussion, had abandoned their position that any approach had to be based on 1946 level of industry plan [1] and had agreed to the dispatch to zone commanders of technical questionnaires in same form as sent to participant countries.

Mention was also made of fact that French had also agreed to treatment of three western zones of Germany as a group in balance of payments study.

2. *Preparation of Report.*

Franks mentioned that question had been raised in conference concerning desirability obtaining services some American so that report could be drafted in such a manner that it would be attractively presented to the United States. I replied that I did not think it would be advisable to employ any public relations counsel for this purpose; that Europeans were quite capable of preparing an adequate report and that if they desired Department's views on special aspects, they could be obtained on a "within the family" basis.

3. *Possible Conflict With Trade Charter.*

Franks said that several delegates were honestly perplexed as to how program of reducing intra-Europe trade barriers could be adopted without violating proposed trade charter. In reply I pointed out that charter was a pioneer effort; that we felt that a customs union such as Benelux was progressive; but that a preferential system was discriminatory. If the conference should come up with a plan which provided for a series of definite, overall percentage reductions, culminating in the elimination of barriers at a definite time, I was confident

---

[1] This plan is printed in the Department of State *Bulletin*, April 14, 1946, pp. 636–639.

that the charter could be adapted to meet such a program; in fact consideration now being given to modification charter accordingly.

At Frank's suggestion and to dispel any feeling among the smaller countries that they are being left out of things, I am meeting informally on Thursday with the executive committee, which includes representatives of Benelux and the Scandinavian countries, as well as United Kingdom, France and Italy. [Clayton.]

CAFFERY

840.50 Recovery/7–3147 : Telegram

The Ambassador in France (Caffery) to the Secretary of State

SECRET   PARIS, July 31, 1947—1 p. m.

3044. For Lovett from Clayton. The Ambassador and I conferred yesterday with Belgian Prime Minister Spaak and the Belgian Ambassador here regarding the work of the Paris conference.

Spaak inquired as to the conditions under which assistance might be made available by the United States. I replied that the conditions were those set forth in the Secretary's Harvard address, including the survey of requirements, measures of self-help and those designed to increase mutual interchange of goods. The additional requirements of any program were those implicit in the necessity of convincing the American people that the plan made economic sense and would actually result in a self-supporting European economy after a transitional period of three or four years.

This led to a discussion of possible means to eliminate exchange and other trade barriers within the European group. Spaak mentioned that any plan for the transferability of currencies among member countries would have to deal with the question of ultimate convertibility into dollars of excess amounts accumulated by one member country of currencies of other members. I replied that we had been thinking in terms of commodity assistance to Europe, but that I would study carefully the letter which he said he would send me on this and other points.

Spaak also raised a question of means of allocating among member countries the increase in production which would result from the program. I replied that we were anxious to avoid any move in the direction of cartelization or bilateralism; that in some cases, such as France with wheat, the increase in production would be consumed within the producing country, and that I felt that economic distribution of output could best be effected by elimination of trade barriers, and adherence to principles of multilateralism.

Finally, Spaak expressed his concern that some countries would agree "in principle" to sound measures, but would fail at a later date to implement their commitments. I replied that we were thinking in terms of "concrete measures." [Clayton.]

CAFFERY

840.50 Recovery/8–147 : Telegram

The Ambassador in France (Caffery) to the Secretary of State

SECRET   PARIS, August 1, 1947—1 p. m.

3065. For Lovett from Clayton and Caffery. We believe there is reason to draw some encouragement from our conversations the past few days with a number of delegates to the Paris Conference on European Economic Cooperation. It was noted that members of the Executive Committee did not hesitate to wade into such questions of substance as multilateral elimination of quota restrictions and progressive reduction of tariff barriers with a view to reaching a customs union.

On the monetary front, Governor Monick of the Bank of France showed us a draft formula, already considered at a ministerial level in the United Kingdom, France and the Benelux countries, under which the participating countries would undertake:

1. To make the necessary internal financial and monetary measures (budget balancing, realistic exchange rate),
2. To establish transferability of their respective currencies for all current transactions among themselves (thus eliminating intra-European exchange controls except for capital movements),
3. And, ultimately, to establish convertibility into gold or dollars of net accruals of member currencies.

(It is, of course, at this point that the United States comes into the picture and we have cautioned our friends that Washington has been thinking largely in terms of commodity assistance).

In considering the foregoing it should be kept in mind that the home governments which have not been exposed to the contagion of the Paris meeting may not be as advanced in their thinking as are their respective delegates, and that any joint monetary plan might in its earlier stages be limited to such countries as Britain, France, Benelux and Italy.

Finally, a thought-provoking consideration was advanced by the Netherlands delegate who said that, if it should prove possible to have an assistance agreement concluded between the US and the participating countries as a group such an arrangement would prove to be a powerful catalytic agent in welding the western European economies into a unit.

Sent Department as 3065, repeated Berlin as 283 and to Moscow and Rome by pouch. Copy held Paris for Douglas. [Clayton and Caffery.]

CAFFERY

840.50 Recovery/8–647 : Telegram

The Ambassador in France (Caffery) to the Secretary of State

TOP SECRET   PARIS, August 6, 1947—1 p. m.

3122. For the Secretary and Lovett, from Clayton, Caffery, Douglas, Murphy and Nitze. In our discussions the past two days we have reviewed carefully the draft policy paper of the Planning Board [*Staff*] on the economic recovery of western Europe. We have been encouraged to find that the people in the Department and those in the field are generally thinking along similar lines.

It is our observation that many of the delegates to the Paris conference personally favor a bold constructive program; but that their governments, while agreeing in principle, shy away from many of the necessary specific measures. Furthermore, various delegates have repeatedly called to our attention the reference in the Secretary's Harvard address to friendly aid in drafting the plan. They now feel the need of such aid, without it their planning might crystallize into an unacceptable program, which would be extremely unfortunate.

We, therefore, believe that our views covering a few basic undertakings by each country should be promptly communicated informally and in an appropriate way to the Paris conference.

We believe that the following basic undertakings are essential parts of any comprehensive economic program for Western Europe which will most nearly assure the effective employment of our assistance, promote the recovery of Western Europe within three or four years so that it may proceed thereafter without further US aid, and which the Secretary may recommend to the administration, the Congress and the American people:

1. Coal and food are key items in the recovery of Europe. Countries whose production of these commodities is subnormal should undertake to give the highest priority to maximizing the output of such commodities. Failure to achieve a satisfactory level of production will be ground for discontinuance of aid.

2. Each participating country should be obligated to take the necessary internal financial and monetary measures to stabilize its money, establish and maintain proper rates of exchange with other countries and generally to restore confidence in its currency.

3. To facilitate the production, distribution and exchange of the products of each participating country, agreement should be reached among them for effective action in the financial and commercial fields, including tangible steps for the progressive reduction and eventual

elimination among the participating countries of exchange controls, tariffs and other trade barriers.

4. Failure by any country to take and maintain effective measures in any of the above respects will be ground for reconsideration of the aid to be extended to such country.

We have discussed the question of the form which our agreement with the participating countries should take. We believe that it will be necessary for us to make bilateral agreements but that such agreements should be clearly tied into a multilateral agreement, thus assuring individual and collective responsibility.

We have discussed in connection with paragraph number two above the proper use to which the local currency counterpart of our aid should be put. We have reached no definite conclusion. This is a technical subject which should have the attention of the National Advisory Council.[1] We do feel, however, that the permanency of the financial reforms which we seek may be jeopardized if the local currency counterparts of our aid were to be used to defray public expenditures.

Sent to Department as 3122 repeated Rome for Dunn only as 198. [Clayton, Caffery, Douglas, Murphy, and Nitze.]

CAFFERY

---

[1] The National Advisory Council on International Monetary and Financial Problems was established by the Bretton Woods Agreements Act, approved July 31, 1945 ; 59 Stat. 512.

840.50 Recovery/8–647 : Telegram

The Ambassador in France (Caffery) to the Secretary of State

TOP SECRET   PARIS, August 6, 1947—1 p.m.

3123. For the Secretary and Lovett from Clayton, Caffery, Douglas, Murphy, and Nitze. Supplementing our 3122 of August 6, we have canvassed position of the UK, France and Italy. The case of each is, we believe, critical. Failing additional assistance by the United States this year, the situation in these countries may so deteriorate economically, socially, politically, and their foreign policy may be necessarily so modified, that our objectives in Western Europe and elsewhere may become unattainable. We, therefore, suggest that every conceivable avenue of providing interim assistance be carefully reviewed, including possibly the calling of a special session of Congress.

We have not mentioned the critical state of affairs in Germany, which is recognized. However, United States responsibility as an occupying power places the German problem from the standpoint of interim relief in a separate category.

Sent Dept as 3123, repeated Rome for Dunn as 199.
[Clayton, Caffery, Douglas, Murphy, and Nitze.]

CAFFERY

USPolAd Files : Ambassador Murphy's Correspondence [1]

*Memorandum by Mr. Wesley C. Haraldson of the Office of the
United States Political Adviser for Germany (Murphy)* [2]

SECRET August 8, 1947.

Subject: Paris Discussions on the Marshall Plan, August 4 to August 6,
1947.

Under Secretary of State Clayton, Ambassadors Caffery, Douglas
and Murphy met in Paris from August 4 to August 6 to discuss the
Marshall proposal for rendering aid for the economic reconstruction
of Europe. Paul Nitze had been sent by the Department in order to
bring the most recent Washington thinking to the group. During a
series of sessions covering most of the three days, various topics briefly
outlined below were explored and recommendations were sent by the
group to the Secretary of State.

CRITICAL SITUATION

Ambassadors Caffery and Douglas informed the group of the critical
situation existing in France and Britain, respectively, and Under
Secretary Clayton told of the conditions existing in Italy. At the
present time England is exhausting its dollar resources at the rate
of 100 million dollars a week. At this rate, England will find it impossible to go beyond November 15 without cutting into her gold reserves.
Unless additional American aid is forthcoming shortly, she will be
completely out of dollar resources. Douglas indicated that on the basis
of his discussions with Bevin and other British officials, this situation
might lead, in the very near future, to the depreciation of the pound,
a drastic cut in imports, and force England to withdraw from many of
her foreign commitments and radically change her foreign policy.

Ambassador Caffery indicated that the situation with France was
very similar, that France could not get by beyond the end of this year
without substantial aid, that her reduced harvest this year would
provide bread for only five months at the present low ration.

Under Secretary Clayton felt that Italy might possibly scrape
through on her present resources up until the first of January, but

---

[1] Files of the U.S. Political Adviser for Germany, Lot F 169, Box 581.
[2] The memorandum was an enclosure to a letter of August 18, 1947 from Ambassador Robert D. Murphy to John D. Hickerson, Deputy Director of the Office
of European Affairs.

that unless aid was forthcoming very shortly she would not be in a position to contract for food deliveries for the first quarter of 1948.

The possibilities of interim aid were briefly explored. Because of the specialized purpose of the American Export-Import Bank, it was believed highly unlikely that this institution could provide any assistance. The Monetary Fund could grant Great Britain a small amount of aid, perhaps in the amount of 320 million dollars if dollars were declared a scarce currency, vis-à-vis the English pound. The United States could also assist Great Britain by assuming the full burden of necessary imports into the bizonal area of Germany, and by relaxation of certain commitments, such as the convertibility and non-discrimination clauses of the US–UK loan agreement. However, it was believed that Congressional action would be necessary to provide even this interim assistance. Because Congress does not meet again until the first of the year, it did not seem possible that any aid would be forthcoming under the Marshall Plan until March at the earliest. In view of this, recommendations were sent to Washington that all possibilities of rendering interim financial aid should be explored, even to the calling of a special session of Congress. Unless immediate aid were forthcoming, it was felt that the situation in these three countries might so deteriorate economically, politically, socially and in the field of foreign relations, that many of their objectives in Western Europe and elsewhere might be unobtainable.

The situation in Germany was recognized as critical. However, the direct responsibility of the United States as an occupying power placed the German problem in a somewhat different category.

Policy Paper of the Planning Board

Paul Nitze briefly outlined a memorandum prepared by the Planning Board of the State Department which summarized its thinking on the Marshall Plan. Briefly this paper set forth the following considerations:

A. *U. S. selfish interests involved*

(1) If the present trend of economic and political deterioration continues, Europe and its way of life will be lost for a long time.

(2) From a standpoint of trade, the U.S. was interested in a healthy European economy.

(3) For reasons of strategic necessity, it is highly desirable to support the existence of free and independent states and a United Nations organization made up of such states.

B. *Nature of the problem*

(1) Previous aid by the United States to the European countries in an amount of approximately 10 billion dollars has failed to fulfil the anticipated aims.

(2) Increased production is the only answer. Otherwise the European countries will continue to remain relief clients.

(3) Europe's transport system must be rebuilt.

(4) Conditions must be created in which the products of the several European countries can be exchanged among themselves. This should envisage initially some type of multilateral clearing agreement and finally to erase exchange restrictions, tariffs and other trade barriers so as to unite Europe economically.

C. Congress will appropriate money only on a declining scale over the period of any proposed plan. Hence, it will be necessary for the countries receiving aid to use the money in the most effective manner. Also, because of domestic political considerations, as well as for technical and administrative requirements, aid forthcoming under any plan will undoubtedly be concentrated to a relatively few commodities, such as coal, wheat, cotton, tobacco, etc.

The entire emphasis of the plan should be to help Europeans to help themselves. Hence, not only food and consumers goods should be sent to Europe, but wherever possible, short term capital equipment which will increase the productivity of the European farms and factories, should be included. Long term capital requirements should be satisfied by the World Bank.

In all the discussions at the Paris Conference and in Washington, it was emphasized that any plan for European aid should have as its goal a self-sustaining Europe at the end of three or four years. Hence, elaborate plans for reconstruction or industralization, such as the Monnet plan for France, cannot be supported by American aid.

D. The Planning Board's policy paper called for the following changes with respect to Germany:

(1) Simplification at Allied Control with more responsibility resting with the German people.

(2) Production controls, priorities and allocations which would assure that the scarce commodities were directed to the proper ends.

(3) Financial reform and readjustment of internal prices.

(4) Early clarification of reparations.

(5) Early termination of denazification. This would, perhaps, involve further amnesties. It would permit the employment of persons in capacities commensurate with abilities. No administrative or political power should be given to persons of pronounced Nazi taint.

(6) Remove existing barriers to foreign travel and trade except where security demands their continuation. Germans should be permitted to set up agencies outside of Germany.

(7) Special arrangements for coal production.

(8) Inclusion of Western Germany into any new arrangements for multilateral clearing or other devices for eliminating exchange restrictions.

Problem Discussed

During and following the presentation of the program as outlined by the Planning Board, a number of the specific points presented or closely related thereto, were discussed by the group, many in a detailed, definitive way which resulted in concrete recommendations to Washington and others in a more cursory manner. Among these problems discussed were the following:

> To what extent should America make its views known to the cooperating countries and in demanding reforms or concessions.
> Type of organization.
> Aid in the form of commodities or cash, or both.
> International allocation of scarce commodities.
> Centralized purchasing to reduce competitive buying.
> Internal budgetary reforms of participating countries.
> Elimination of trade barriers and present unreasonable exchange rates.
> Use of domestic currency counter-part of aid received.
> Technical assistance to be given by the United States in drafting plan.
> Time required for Congressional action and the possibility of Congressional approval.

Consensus of Group and Recommendations

It was the general consensus of the group that it would be impossible to get Congressional approval to any plan which did not spell out in great detail the use to which the funds would be put, and unless the participating countries not only promised to take steps but actually did take steps to put their own economies in order. For example, it would be necessary for Great Britain to improve coal production and to eliminate much of her housing program which is such a drain on steel and labor resources. In the case of France it would be necessary to take steps which would both increase her agricultural production and eliminate the present situation where the farmers are unwilling to sell their present limited products. It would be undesirable as well as impossible to get the American taxpayer to provide funds for the importation of scarce commodities into Europe unless the European countries themselves did everything possible to maximize their production of these commodities. This being the case, the group was in general agreement that the United States should make its wishes known at an early date to the participating countries, so that they might draw up the proper type of proposal, and be cognizant of the commitments for internal improvement which they would be called upon to make as a *quid pro quo* to the receipt of any aid. It was felt that a number of countries or certain groups within these countries were of the opinion that they were favoring the United States by participating in the Marshall Plan, that it was a device on the part of the United States to ward off a depression.

The following recommendations were made to Secretary Marshall and Under Secretary Lovett:

(1) That the participating countries be informed of the views of the United States prior to the adoption of any program. Unless this were done it was believed that the planning of the European countries might very well crystallize in an unacceptable program which would be extremely unfortunate.

(2) Top priority should be given by the countries of Europe in the production of coal and food (this was aimed specifically at France and Great Britain). Failure to achieve satisfactory levels in the production of these items should warrant the discontinuance of aid.

(3) Participating countries should be called upon to carry out internal financial reform which would stabilize their money, restore confidence in it and make possible the establishment and maintenance of proper exchange rates.

(4) Agreement should be reached among the participating countries for the reduction and eventual elimination of all tariffs and trade barriers so as to facilitate production, distribution and exchange of their commodities.

(5) Organizationally the plan should envisage bilateral agreements between the United States and the individual countries tied into a multilateral agreement among all the participating countries. This would insure individual and collective responsibilities.

(6) The problem of the disposition of the domestic currency counter-part of any aid received by a country was discussed, but no recommendation was made other than that the problem should be explored by technical experts with the view of preventing such currency from being used in ways which might jeopardize necessary monetary and budgetary reforms.

LEVEL OF INDUSTRY

The problem of the level of industry was discussed only incidentally as a result of the note which Ambassador Caffery was sending to the French Foreign Office asking, on the part of the United States Government, for France's view on level of industry, control of the Ruhr and related matters. Caffery indicated that publicly France would go on record for a modified version of the Morgenthau Plan, but that informally he was sure that France was willing to compromise on a mutually acceptable solution. He stated that Bidault had frequently told him "We know that we have to join with you in the control of Germany and reorganization of Western Europe, but please don't force us to do so at the point of a gun". Under Secretary Clayton analyzed France's position on the basis of what he called legitimate interests and illegitimate interests. Their legitimate interests were (a) military security, and (b) a desire to decrease the economic dependency of France on Germany. The illegitimate interest should be ignored completely and the French so informed, but that attempts should be made to satisfy their legitimate concerns. This he felt could be done outside of any level of industry plan.

At one stage of the discussion Mr. Clayton thought that in making recommendations to the Department the Conference should suggest that unless immediate steps were taken to extend aid to the United Kingdom and France "irreparable" damage would be done. Mr. Murphy expressed doubt that such damage would be irreparable and stated that it seemed to him that this question might then involve a fundamental change in our foreign policy. Mr. Clayton pointed out that what he had in mind was that if the United Kingdom for example were forced to pull out of a number of areas for financial reasons that a vacuum would be created which would be filled then by another foreign power—maybe the Soviet Union. He doubted that American public opinion would move fast enough to enable the necessary shift in our foreign policy which would permit the United States and not the Soviet Union to fill that vacuum.

Mr. Murphy commented also that it had been most interesting to listen to the exposition of the possible political effects of the deteriorating economic situation in France and the United Kingdom in view of the fact that the economic condition of Germany was so much worse than that existing in either the United Kingdom or France. He mentioned that the effect of this adverse German economic situation remained to be seen but that the political direction in which 66,000,000 Germans went might have a decisive effect on the European future.

W. C. HARALDSON

840.50 Recovery/8–647 : Telegram

The Secretary of State to the Embassy in France

SECRET   WASHINGTON, August 11, 1947—2 p. m.

2967. Personal for Clayton from Lovett and Wood. Agree that situation you describe makes decision on nature of our friendly aid in drafting the plan imperative now. We are giving urgent consideration this question and will communicate decision and comments soonest. In meantime suggest you defer any action such as proposed in Embtel 3122 of August 6. Very important consideration is not to make suggestions to conferees or consult with or advise them in manner allowing us to be maneuvered into position where, if they accept or act on our suggestions, they would regard us as being committed to their plan. Feeling in Congress very strong that they must not again be presented on a crisis basis with a virtual commitment to any precise course of action as they now claim was done in case of Greece and Turkey. If are to get Congress approval must carefully avoid this. Must also avoid charge we dictating plan.

Realize we are committed to friendly aid and importance of effective plan from Paris conference so vital we must do whatever practicable to help insure this result. Problem being considered urgently in light of all above factors. Hope to wire you in detail tomorrow.

Repeat to London 3428. [Lovett and Wood.]

MARSHALL

Lot 122 Box 19 B, Folder D–1

Memorandum by the Deputy Director of the Office of European Affairs (Hickerson)[1]

CONFIDENTIAL   [WASHINGTON,] August 11, 1947.

DISCUSSION

1. In your Harvard speech you stated that "The role of this country should consist of friendly aid in the drafting of a European program and of later support of such a program so far as it may be practical for us to do so". Subsequently, the British and French sent out invitations to the Paris Conference and accompanied the invitations with a set of proposals. Point No. 4 of the proposals states in part: "Information relating to the resources and needs of Germany shall be requested from the Commanders-in-Chief, members of the Control Council."Point No. 5 states: "The Committee of Cooperation shall seek the friendly aid of the United States in drafting the report, as suggested by the Secretary of State of that country."

2. No official approach has been made by us to the Paris Conference, or by any of the participating powers, to follow up the point on "friendly aid" (except that questionnaires were sent to the zone commanders in Germany). The Conference adopted an organization plan which contains practically the same language as used under points 4 and 5 of the British and French proposals. In addition, during his discussions with French officials in Paris, Mr. Clayton was asked what means we had in mind for extending the "friendly aid", and this question has been touched upon unofficially in other places. At the recent meeting in Paris between Messrs. Clayton, Caffery, Douglas and Murphy, it was agreed that the time had arrived for taking some action to carry out the offer of friendly aid. It is probable that an

---

[1] This memorandum was addressed to Secretary Marshall through Under Secretary Lovett.

official approach will be made to us in the near future and our course of action should be prepared and agreed upon in advance.

3. Obviously, the concept of "friendly aid" does not include full participation in the Conference. Further, it would be undesirable to take any action now which could be construed, either by the European countries or the U.S. Congress, as approval of any part of the program being developed by the Conference because it might be regarded as a commitment on our part which could later prove embarrassing. It is, however, of extreme importance that the plan which emerges from the Paris Conference be generally acceptable to the U.S. The consequences of a wholly unacceptable plan would be disastrous. Steps which could be taken to assist the Conference while avoiding any U.S. commitment are set forth in the following paragraphs 4, 5, 6 and 7. The steps suggested in paragraphs 4, 5, and 6 could be taken at once and before a first draft of the program is completed. Paragraph 7 refers to action to be taken with respect to a first draft program.

4. The Conference should be informed along the following lines:

    a. The basic essential of the U.S. suggestion was that the European countries themselves should devise a program and carry forward effective measures for bringing about European economic recovery. The U.S. will not assist in formulating the program nor, while in the process of formulation, will the U.S. comment on the adequacy or desirability of specific schemes or measures under consideration.

    b. There are certain basic objectives that should be achieved in connection with any program if it is to have a reasonable chance of support from the American public and Congress, including, but not limited to, the following:

    (1) The program must be designed to bring about the greatest practicable increase, within the European countries concerned, in production of materials needed to fill their basic requirements and to limit requests for supplies from the U.S. to those necessary to fill deficits which those countries cannot, with reasonable effort, themselves satisfy.

    (2) Further, the production program of a participating country should not be based only on its own needs but rather on the contribution that can be made to filling the needs of all participating countries.

    (3) The participating countries should adopt financial and monetary programs designed to correct as soon as practicable existing financial and monetary weaknesses and to accomplish stabilization of currencies, establishment and maintenance of proper rates of exchange and generally to restore confidence in currencies.

    (4) The participating countries should adopt measures looking to the most effective distribution and use of their own resources and the resources obtained from outside sources, including

measures to enforce farm collections and to prevent diversions of products into black markets.

(5) The participating countries should take steps to facilitate the greatest practicable interchange of goods and services among themselves, reducing and seeking to eliminate dependence on exchange controls, quota restrictions, compensation and barter agreements and other obstacles to a free flow of goods.

(6) The program should provide for the greatest possible European self-help and should be such as to warrant the belief that its carrying out would give reasonable assurance of European ability to maintain its economy without continued support from the U.S.

c. The points made under Item B above are given in the spirit of friendly aid to the Conference and as an indication of the type of action which the U.S. believes necessary to achieve European economic recovery. It should be clearly understood that, even if the participating countries adopt all the suggestions outlined above, there is no commitment on the part of the U.S. to accept or implement any plan.

5. The U.S. should make it possible for the Conference to ask for technical factual information from U.S. representatives such as statistical information, advice as to the physical possibility of producing certain goods in the U.S. (e.g., an indication of the length of time it would take to fill orders for locomotives).

6. The Conference should be able to obtain some information about the needs and potentialities of the bizonal area in Germany. Since the agreement on the bizonal level of industry is of special importance to the relationship between the German economy and the balance of the European economy, U.S. representatives should be prepared to submit to the Conference the level of industry plan as soon as agreement has been reached after the impending London talks. The method of presentation should be closely coordinated with the French to assure the greatest possible French support for the plan in the Paris Conference. The plan should be presented as the U.S. and British view as to the type of German economy we believe desirable to enable Germany to make a real contribution to European recovery and at the same time to cease being a financial burden to the United States and Britain. It should be pointed out that our main objectives are to expedite the recovery of Europe as a whole, to minimize the financial outlays which the U.S. is being called upon to make, and to insure against a militant Germany in the future. We should be prepared to listen to the views of other powers and to discuss them in a cooperative spirit. In the latter connection, the rate at which the revised level of industry is to be put into effect and the decision as to which industries are to receive priority in reactivation will obviously be of major importance in connection with the contributions that western Germany and the other

European countries can make to each other and to the general restoration of Europe. It is particularly these aspects which it is believed should be discussed with the countries participating in the Paris Conference. Unless exceptional circumstances dictate otherwise, it will normally be best to speak frankly about our guiding policies in Germany and the measures we have adopted or would like to adopt in furtherance thereof. If we proceed in this way, there is a good chance that we shall obtain considerable support for the early carrying out of the revised level of industry plan from the countries at Paris.

7. When the Conference has produced a first draft of a program, U.S. representatives could go over it informally with representatives of the Conference, seeking explanations and clarifications of points that are not clear and generally assisting in putting the program into form which could be understandable to those in the U.S. who would study it for substance. It would have to be made clear that such drafting assistance was not to be construed as approval or endorsement of the program but was merely to facilitate its presentation to the U.S. Government, including the Congress.

8. The matter of procedure for communicating with the Conference requires consideration. The United States must present a united front when talking to other powers. It would be undesirable to have two independent groups of U.S. representatives, one representing our interests in the over-all European recovery and the other representing our interests in Germany alone. As our interests in Europe are broader than, though inclusive of, our interests in Germany, it would appear that the State Department should head the U.S. representation and should coordinate the necessary assistants supplied by the War Department and OMGUS and, if any, by the civilian agencies. The OMGUS representatives need not be top ranking officers, but they should be capable and thoroughly familiar with the level of industry plan and with the general economic situation in the bizonal area.

9. The State Department should immediately select its head coordinator and the necessary civilian assistants. They should be sent to Paris and assigned to the staff of the Embassy. They should not form any official or unofficial liaison with the Conference independent of the Embassy. This staff, aside from being of assistance to the Ambassador in connection with paragraphs 5 and 7 above, would be able to study the program as information regarding it is made available to the Embassy. This would mean that less time would be required for evaluating the program after it has been completed and presented and, therefore, it could be presented to Congress sooner. In addition, the staff could advise the Ambassador if the program being developed was clearly inadequate, in which case we would be able to consider whether further positive action by the U.S. was appropriate.

10. It would not appear necessary for OMGUS representatives to be sent to Paris for the moment, but OMGUS should be instructed to be prepared to do so on very short notice. The OMGUS representatives should be further instructed to be prepared to carry on discussions along the lines set forth in Paragraph 6 above, taking the necessary guidance from the head coordinator referred to in Paragraphs 8 and 9 above.

11. The British should be consulted before final instructions are given concerning the course of action suggested in Paragraph 6 above. However, the U.S. governmental position on that course of action should be agreed immediately.

RECOMMENDATIONS

I. That you approve the interpretation of the "friendly aid" referred to in your Harvard speech as including the steps outlined in Paragraphs 4, 5, 6, and 7 above.

II. That you approve sending instruction to Ambassador Caffery to present to the Committee of European Economic Co-operation an informal memorandum covering the points set forth in Paragraphs 4, 5, and 7 above.

III. That you approve the attaching of additional staff to the Paris Embassy for the purpose outlined in Paragraph 9 above.

IV. That you seek agreement with the War Department on the course of action outlined in Paragraphs 6, 8, and 10 above.

V. That, if you and the War Department approve the course of action outlined in Paragraph 6 above, you approve consultation with the British on this matter through Ambassador Douglas in London.

840.50 Recovery/8–1247 : Telegram

The Ambassador in France (Caffery) to the Secretary of State

SECRET   PARIS, August 12, 1947—1 p. m.
URGENT   NIACT

3222. For Lovett and Wood from Clayton. All right, your 2967, will await further instructions but would like to point out that a clear-cut decision on this question is necessary. As you say, it is so vital that the plan be an effective and acceptable one that I strongly recommend against a negative approach. For example, until I talked with Spaak he was prepared to push the adoption of a wholly unworkable and unacceptable provision for allocating among sixteen nations all increased production resulting from our aid. He was doing this in the belief that he was following our wishes.

There may be some risks involved in a positive and affirmative position but I think they are minor and certainly not nearly so serious as those attendant upon a timid and negative approach.

I would confine our aid to a few broad policy suggestions such as those contained in our 3122 refusing to be drawn into details. I would make it perfectly clear that we are not dictating and that the plan must positively be a European plan to which the Secretary and the President are in no sense committed until the completed plan is received, carefully examined, approved and presented by them to Congress. I would further make it clear that, even then, Congress must take the final action. As a matter of fact, I have been saying just these things over and over to all these people. I feel sure they all clearly understand we are not committed. [Clayton.]

CAFFERY

840.50 Recovery/ 8–1447 : Telegram

The Acting Secretary of State to the Embassy in France

SECRET　　　　　　　　　　WASHINGTON, August 14, 1947—4 p. m.

URGENT

3029. For Clayton and Caffery. I. From your cables and other reports that reach us of the course of the Paris talks, we gain the impression that too little attention is being paid by the participants to the elements of self-help and mutual aid which constituted an integral part of the suggestions made by the Secretary in his Harvard speech. We are much concerned over this. We consider that the problem of the leading western European countries is not only to make up deficiencies caused by the vicissitudes of the war, but to adjust themselves to certain basic changes which have occurred and are continuing to occur in their international position. This adjustment calls for courageous and incisive action on their own part, both individually and collectively. Unless they are prepared to make this adjustment, no aid from this country could be really effective. It could achieve no more than a postponement of inevitable decisions. We are entirely serious about this and we will not be able to accept, even as a basis for recommendation to Congress, any plan which does not recognize this basic requirement. An itemized bill summing up prospective deficits against a background of present policies and arrangements will definitely not be sufficient.

In approaching this problem, the Europeans might make more progress if they were to assume there was no one to help them, to imagine that they had no choice but to try to work out an acceptable economic future without any outside support, to elaborate the best program they could, and only then to undertake to define the gaps which absolutely could not be filled out of their own resources even by the most strenuous individual and collective effort.

The above remains our basic position on these matters and you are at liberty to make it clear to any of the participants at the Paris talks.[1]

II. With respect to the specific points in your 3122 Aug 6, the following are our comments:

1. It is assumed that point one, although intended to emphasize coal and food, was not meant to exclude production increases through bold constructive action in other bottleneck industries, and in industries on which these in turn depend (i.e., fertilizer, mining machinery, etc.). Increases in production, moreover, should be accompanied by constructive action in distribution, particularly in food collection from farmers, and measures to deal with diversions of mining and factory products into black and compensation markets, etc. There should also be considered necessity for expansion of capital equipment in some lines, so as to reach for each country pay-as-you-go basis within brief period of time at satisfactory standards of living, but primary emphasis should be on efficient utilization of existing capacity rather than on capital development.

2. Re your point two, we regard financial and monetary stability as a goal toward which European efforts should be steadfastly directed, and we consider it important that every effort be made by the conference powers toward attainment of that goal. However, in view of fact that some financial and monetary disorders are basically symptoms of production difficulties and that some others reflect deep-seated differences between political groups which cannot be bridged immediately, we question advisability of making the adoption and carrying out of policies of, say, wage reduction or tax reforms the *sine qua non* of US aid. The importance of formulating and adopting as soon as practicable (keeping in mind the above considerations and without jeopardizing the program) measures to achieve the ends mentioned in your para 2 should be stressed.

3 (a) Your point three is regarded here as two separate though related points. First is necessity to which US attaches greatest importance for full collaborative effort of European countries to solve their production problems in concert. This involves agreement on rates of reactivation among the participating countries, sharing of commodities in short supply on equitable basis, special efforts in one country to direct production into fields helpful to others, etc.

(b) Tangible steps for progressive reduction and eventual elimination among participating countries of exchange controls, tariffs and other trade barriers in our judgment constitute a separate point.

---

[1] When French Ambassador Bonnet called on Acting Secretary Lovett on August 21 prior to a return to Paris for consultation, Lovett "stated that time was running short and that he was disturbed lest the conference of the 16 nations in Paris should produce little more than 16 'shopping lists' for which the United States would be expected to pay the bill." He then read the above portion of this telegram to M. Bonnet and "urged the Ambassador to impress on his government the necessity for bringing home to the governments of the smaller countries at Paris this basic conception of ours." (840.50 Recovery/8–2147)

4. We question the advisability at this time of overemphasizing that failure to achieve set levels of production or to maintain effective measures in the above respects will be ground for the discontinuance or reconsideration of aid. Production goals may not be met for variety of reasons, including Acts of God (flood, freeze, drought), Communist-inspired strikes, inept administration, or perverse unwillingness to live up to commitments. Withdrawal of aid would have to be weighed against reasons underlying failure, and against political as well as economic consequences. Suggest it is more appropriate to withhold discussion of specific conditions under which US would withdraw aid from individual countries until bilateral and multilateral agreements are negotiated after Congressional action on aid to Europe. At this time, main emphasis should be laid on unwillingness of US public and US Congress to aid Europe as a whole unless European countries take effective and cooperative steps to help themselves. Most effective present sanction lies, in our judgment, in likelihood of US refusal to support European plan unless there is real unified effort on their part in the sense of points covered in this message.

III. For your guidance in answering queries from participants in the Conference, the following are some of the basic objectives which we feel should be envisaged by any European program if it is to have a reasonable chance of winning support from the American public and Congress:

1. The program must be designed to bring about the greatest practicable increase, within the European countries concerned, in production of food and materials needed to fill their basic requirements and to limit requests for supplies from the US to those necessary to fill deficits which those countries cannot, with vigorous effort, themselves satisfy.

2. Further, the production program of a participating country should not be based only on its own needs but also on the contribution that can be made to filling the needs of all participating countries.

3. The participating countries should adopt financial and monetary programs designed to correct as soon as practicable existing financial and monetary weaknesses and to accomplish stabilization of currencies, establishment and maintenance of proper rates of exchange and generally to restore confidence in currencies.

4. The participating countries should adopt measures looking to the most effective distribution and use of their own resources and the resources obtained from outside sources, including measures to ensure farm collections and to prevent diversions of products into black markets.

5. The participating countries should take steps to facilitate the greatest practicable interchange of goods and services among themselves, reducing and seeking to eliminate dependence on exchange controls, quota restrictions, compensation and barter agreements and other obstacles to a free flow of goods.

6. The program should provide for the greatest possible European self-help, should provide for action on the part of the participating countries which they will in fact be able to carry out, and should be

such as to assure the maintenance of the European economy without continued support from the US.

The above points may be mentioned in response to inquiries in the spirit of friendly aid to the conference and as an indication of thinking in this Dept as to the type of action necessary to achieve European economic recovery. It should be clearly understood that, even if the participating countries adopt all the measures outlined above our action in giving friendly aid in drafting must not be construed as a commitment on the part of the US to accept or implement any plan. Furthermore, to avoid any possibility of misunderstanding we should caution inquirers that, even if the conference adopts a program which seems workable on its face, any aid which the US might determine to give must be conditioned upon the effective carrying out of such program.

IV. In addition to stating the objectives outlined in para III Dept believes that we could offer to furnish on request technical factual information such as statistical information, advice as to the physical possibility of producing certain goods in the US, etc. Further, the US could offer that, when the conference has produced a first draft of a program, responsive to the self-help and mutual help approach outlined earlier herein, US representatives could go over it informally with representatives of the conference, seeking explanations and clarifications of points that are not clear and generally assisting in putting the program into form most understandable to those in the US who would study it for substance. It should be clearly understood that such drafting assistance was not to be construed as approval or endorsement of the program but was merely to facilitate its presentation to the US Govt, including the Congress.

V. It is recognized that the carrying out of the functions described in para IV will require additional US personnel in Paris to assist Embassy and Clayton when in Paris. Also, it would seem helpful to have qualified staff in Paris who could return to Washington when program is completed, having studied it in process of development. This would mean that less time would be required for evaluating the program after it has been presented and, therefore, enabling earlier presentation to Congress. In addition, the staff could advise you if the program being developed was inadequate, in which case we would be able to consider whether further positive action by the US was appropriate. If inadequate, Dept believes it might be possible to authorize you to make substantive comments on specific parts of the program and on its omissions. Dept believes such staff should be attached to Embassy and not have liaison with conference independent of Embassy.

VI. If Clayton and Ambassador agree with suggestions herein, suggest informal talks with appropriate committee chairmen or others be held promptly. It may be considered desirable within the next few days for Dept to release to the press here a statement along the lines of paras III and IV above. Your comments requested.

VII. Dept believes further aid can be given re role of western Germany. Proposals will be discussed with War and then Brit and will be sent later.

Sent Paris, repeated to London for Ambassador as 3495.

LOVETT

Policy Planning Staff Files

Memorandum Prepared by the Policy Planning Staff

SECRET   [WASHINGTON,] August 14, 1947
PPS-6

SUMMARY

The Policy Planning Staff has examined in greater detail the time factor involved in the question of United States aid to a European recovery program.

The Staff concludes that if a program of U.S. aid is not acted upon by the Congress before the end of this year, there is little likelihood that such a program, as now conceived, could be successful. Moreover there is danger that unless we are able to maintain among the Europeans a firm expectation of early U.S. assistance, not only must we expect unfavorable political and moral reactions in Europe, but measures taken by European governments may set off a train of restrictive actions in international affairs which would affect adversely our economic interests in areas outside Europe and would further complicate the question of European recovery.

The Staff recommends that these conclusions be borne in mind in any decisions affecting the timing of Executive and Congressional action with respect to United States aid.

It further recommends that in order to expedite to the utmost the handling within this Department of questions connected with a European aid program, a special center be established at once within the Department to act as a clearing house for Departmental action and to conduct detailed advance planning for such machinery as the Department may later require in connection with such a program.

---

1. The Policy Planning Staff has reviewed the economic situation of the individual countries which are participating in the Paris Economic Conference. The Staff wishes to point out that the position of certain

of these countries is such that it is imperative not to leave the question of U.S. aid until the next regular session of Congress. If Congressional action on aid for Europe is not taken prior to the end of this year, there is serious danger of events in Europe taking such a course that the task of European recovery will be made much more difficult, and that much greater U.S. aid will be required in the long run. There is some danger that the whole purpose of the invitation to the European countries to cooperate in drawing up a European recovery program will be frustrated.

2. The situation in the United Kingdom is clearly critical and would alone warrant action prior to the next regular session of Congress. In addition, Italy will require additional assistance before the end of this year. France and Austria face serious difficulties early in 1948 and it is not certain that if the question of aid is left to the next session of Congress, action could be expected soon enough to ward off these difficulties. None of the other European countries appears to face economic difficulties as immediate as those mentioned above, but if the general European situation should deteriorate to a marked degree during the coming months, there is no guarantee that we might not be confronted with urgent requests for assistance from some of these countries. The margin of safety in Europe, both from an economic and political viewpoint, is extremely thin. Any sharp change in the economic picture for the worse might cause difficulties in areas which have not hitherto given occasion for concern.

3. The basic facts with regard to the four countries mentioned above, as they now appear, are as follows:

a. *United Kingdom*. If the dollar drain on Britain continues at its present rate, the loan will be exhausted and the British reduced to what they have considered their minimum reserve of gold and dollars by mid-October. The full facts of the British situation are not yet clear, but it is doubtful whether further analysis will disclose a radical difference in the basic situation. The measures which the British apparently propose to take to deal with the situation will not have important immediate effects, so that it is probable that the situation foreseen by them will arise some time during the fall. There are possibilities of financial assistance which would not require Congressional action, but these would merely postpone the day of final reckoning by a matter of a few weeks. A reduction in British gold and dollar reserves below what the British (and we ourselves) have regarded as a minimum figure also offers a way of dealing with the situation temporarily. The British will no doubt be strongly opposed to any such reduction unless they have greater assurance than we are now in a position to give, that they will obtain further U.S. aid at an early date.

b. *France*. The Embassy at Paris has reported that the French also will be reduced to their minimum reserves at some time during the remainder of this year and forecasts a French dollar deficit through March 1948 of $300,000,000 to $420,000,000. This picture appears in general to be accurate. The French situation can be dealt with in major part if the World Bank gives France another $250,000,000 loan during the latter part of this year. This would see the French through the present year and defer the problem of further assistance until the early part of next year.

c. *Italy.* Studies which have been made in the Department of the balance of payment for 1947 indicate a deficit during the remainder of the present year in the neighborhood of $75,000,000 to $100,000,000. No recent detailed estimates of the 1948 picture are available. However, it appears that unless further financial aid to Italy is forthcoming during the present year, there will have to be a significant adjustment in the scale of Italian imports with the probability of a serious deterioration in the Italian economic situation.

d. *Austria.* The Austrians will squeeze by during the present year, thanks to a variety of handouts of different kinds by the United States and the British. It is not easy to estimate when the funds will be exhausted; the probability is that this point will be reached perhaps by February or March 1948.

4. The fact that, at present rates of expenditure, a country will be confronted with a critical situation some weeks or months from now does not postpone the crisis until that time. As the facts become clear, steps will be taken to meet the situation. In this sense, the crisis is already upon us. The French, Italians, and Austrians will probably defer making adjustments in their import programs as long as possible, in the hope of receiving aid, although they will undoubtedly be required to take certain steps in the direction of cutting down their dollar expenditures. The British are already doing so.

5. One of the most serious aspects of the present situation is the danger that the steps taken by European countries, and particularly by Britain, to deal with the dollar shortage may set in motion a train of events with exactly the opposite effect of that intended in the Harvard speech. Restrictions on imports adopted by one country are likely to give rise to the imposition of new restrictions in other countries and to cut down the international flow of goods at a time when it is most important that the trend should be in the opposite direction. The effects are not likely to be confined to Europe, but would spread quite rapidly to Latin American countries and Canada. If this process should go on with any speed, we might find ourselves confronted with something far more serious than the present European situation.

6. In addition to the financial problems outlined above, there is growing evidence that there will be a serious food situation in Europe and possibly elsewhere during the coming winter. The French wheat

crop has been described as the worst since 1815. The general crop picture is not as yet clear, but as further indications are received they will deserve careful study.

7. As is well known, a number of leading members of Congress on Committees which will have to do with foreign aid expect to go to Europe and other parts of the world during the late summer and fall. The presence of many of these leaders in the United States will be essential, either for a special session of Congress or if consideration of the European aid program is to be undertaken in the early fall by the appropriate committees of the House and Senate. If their presence in the United States will be required later, presumably they should be given some warning of this fact now. The entire subject of Congressional action on the European aid program seems to require early discussion with the leaders of Congress.

8. Carefully coordinated action on a broad scale will also be necessary as far as the Executive branch of the Government is concerned, if the question of aid to Europe is to be handled expeditiously and effectively.

a. The critical period in the formation of the European program is being reached now, as the answers to the questionnaires by the various subcommissions are being received and the subcommissions turn to the substance of the program. If time-consuming delays are to be avoided after the completion of the Paris Conference, and if the United States is to influence the general character of the program developed at Paris, our influence must be brought to bear now. Presumably this should be done by the "friendly aid" offered by the Secretary in the Harvard speech.

b. There will be a task of considerable magnitude in translating the European program into a U.S. legislative program for submission to the Congress. The European program must be reconciled with the reports of the committees appointed by the President to consider the domestic aspects of the problem.[1] Legislation must be prepared and the program will have to be fitted in with the Government's general fiscal program. Numerous interdepartmental clearances will presumably have to be obtained. No organization now exists in the Department for undertaking this work. Indeed, no responsibility for seeing that it is done has been placed anywhere.

c. An administrative agency of some kind will be necessary to carry out the U.S. part of the European program. Such an agency cannot be organized over night. Much advance planning and the selection of some key personnel is called for. It would be most desirable if some of the people who will be responsible for the administration of the program from the U.S. end participated in its formative stages. This also calls for some action by the Department.

---

[1] See President Truman's press statement of June 22, p. 264.

840.50 Recovery/8-2047 : Telegram

The Ambassador in France (Caffery) to the Secretary of State

SECRET　　　　　　　　　　　　　　　PARIS, August 20, 1947—11 a. m.

3327. From Clayton and Caffery. With reference to the suggestions made in your 3029 August 14, 6 p. m. we met yesterday with Sir Oliver Franks, chairman, Committee of European Economic Cooperation. Ambassador Douglas was present and participated in the conversation but left for London before this telegram was drafted.

Franks gave us a report on the progress of the conference, first mentioning that the technical commodity reports were now going to the Executive Committee, after which they would be presented to the General Committee, but that these individual reports would not be finally approved until the entire report was adopted. It was expected that all these reports would have been submitted to the Executive Committee this week and that by the end of the week the balance of payments report, incorporating data from all of the countries, would be ready for committee consideration.

In reply to our inquiry, Franks said that the criterion used by individual countries in determining their requirements is based on the standard of living which they expect to be able to maintain after 1951 without special external assistance thereafter. It had already been learned that in some cases it would be necessary on a global basis to scale down requirements simply because they exceeded any possible availability. He cited specifically the case of bread grains but pointed out that the committee action would be limited to reducing the global amounts and that the actual allocations to be made to individual countries would have to be determined elsewhere.

Next Franks referred to the active discussions during the past week concerning a possible customs union (reference Embassy's 3195, August 9, 3269, August 14, and 3290, August 16 [1]). Franks mentioned that France and Italy had taken an affirmative position in regard to the development of a Customs Union among the participating countries; that the United Kingdom was not in a position at this time to commit itself to such a program but had no objection to other countries going ahead with such an arrangement. The Benelux group had previously indicated that it was not interested in participating in a general union which did not include the United Kingdom but he did not know whether this group still held the same view. The Irish delegate was even less favorably inclined towards the customs union proposal and the Turkish delegate had made a speech on the subject which did not clearly set forth his position. The other delegates were still awaiting instructions from their governments.

---

[1] None printed.

Franks set forth the position of his government as reported my 3290, August 16 and then inquired as to our view concerning the importance of the adoption of the Customs Union program in relation to public opinion in the US toward a European plan.

In reply we made it clear that the US was not making at this time a demand for a commitment in regard to the intentions of the participating countries to eventually form a Customs Union. We did, however, point to the need for a positive constructive program quoting the Department that "an itemized bill summing up prospective deficits against a background of present policies and arrangements will definitely not be sufficient". It was our belief that definite measures directed towards the eventual elimination of trade and other barriers among the European group would meet with a very favorable reception in the US, but that a mere statement of intentions to explore the matter would hardly be impressive.

We next mentioned to Sir Oliver that the Department had commented that the Europeans might make more progress if they were to imagine that they had no choice but to try to work out their problems without any outside support. He replied that if such a planning approach were used it would result in a program based on self sufficiency (as contrasted with a viable economy) and that the pattern would be entirely different from one based on fitting Europe into a world economy and on the assumption of some kind of outside assistance during the transitional period. We are inclined to agree with this point of view.

We next outlined to Sir Oliver the six basic principles mentioned in Section III of the Department's telegram under reference. He remarked that there were some delegates to the conference who were thinking in terms of forming a comprehensive organization to control the allocation of production, rates of reactivation, etc., among the participating countries, but that he had resisted this type of restrictive approach. On this point we refrained from setting forth the Department's position in detail as stated in your telegram under reference. We had previously given attention to Section II 3a of your telegram which called for the full productive effort of European countries to solve their production problems in concert, stating that "this involves agreement on rates of reactivation among the participating countries, sharing of commodities in short supply on equitable basis, special efforts in one country to direct production into fields helpful to others, etc."

We found this comment to be disturbing, not only because it would provide an excuse for resuming the cartel practices which so retarded industrial progress in Europe before the war, but also because it would tend to stimulate bilateral trade and to intensify the various economic controls which under the best of circumstances have removed incentives for maximum output and which in other cases, such as France and Italy, have so distorted the productive and distributive processes as to almost result in economic chaos.

We hope on reconsideration, the Department will agree that the language quoted above would be subject to a wrong interpretation (and will approve our action in not passing it on to Sir Oliver).

Sir Oliver next raised the question whether it would be desirable to have some form of continuing organization to deal with this program after the final report had been approved and forwarded to the US, pointing out that the Scandinavian countries (keeping one eye to the east) were reluctant to continue this activity in its present form beyond that point. In reply we said that, while at present we saw no need for an organization of participating countries beyond the period of assistance envisaged in the Marshall approach, it seemed to us that there would be such need during that period. We pointed out that an effective plan would require specific measures by each participating country in such fields as production, financial and monetary stabilization, and removal of trade barriers and that we believed that the American public and Congress would be impressed by a multilateral undertaking in which the individual countries would obligate themselves to the group to do specific things, their failure to do so constituting grounds for review and appropriate action by the group.

Sir Oliver next said that, while the order of magnitude of financial requirements from the US for the program would not be known until the end of the week it was quite possible the total sum would prove so large that "pruning down would be necessary before the US would find the program acceptable." He regarded it as a basic question whether this reducing procedure would be done by the US or by the conference itself. As an illustration he mentioned the very large steel output estimates submitted both by bizonal authorities for Germany and by the French govt under the Monnet plan, pointing out that there would not be enough coke available to meet global requirements. The difficulty was that this was a problem outside the jurisdiction of the conference but until it could be resolved the global deficit for the European balance of payments would be larger than would be the case if the level of industry and Ruhr questions were settled.

We next mentioned to Sir Oliver the suggestion made in Sections IV and V of the Department's telegram under reference regarding the assignment of additional personnel to the Paris Embassy to become familiar with the methods and work of the conference with a view to advising the Department concerning suggestions which it might find desirable to make to the conference. It was pointed out that such personnel would work with the Ambassador and White [2] in an informal

---

[2] Ivan B. White, first secretary and consul at the Paris Embassy.

apacity and as members of the Embassy, not having individual liaison vith the conference. Sir Oliver agreed enthusiastically with this suggestion and we recommend therefore that the officers mentioned in Department's 3048, August 14 be sent to Paris as soon as possible. We lso recommend that telegraphic travel authorization be transmitted mmediately to Geneva detailing Robert Terrill [3] to assist in this work n Paris.

Before closing the conversation Sir Oliver raised the question of he procedures under which the report was to be transmitted to the JS and made available to the American and European publics. We eplied that we had no instructions on this point but would request the Department's advice. It seemed to us, however, that under the circumtances it would be proper for Mr. Bevin as chairman of the conference o transmit the report to Secretary Marshall whose Harvard address nspired the calling and organization of the conference. Furthermore t was very important that publication of the report take place in the JS simultaneously with its release in Europe.

We agreed that the people in Washington at some stage would want o discuss the matter with some of the conference members, probably he Executive Committee and that the need for this would probably rise at the time the report was being studied by an inter-Departmental roup. It was believed that work on the drafting of multilateral and ilateral agreements could, in accordance with previous practice, go n while Congress was debating the program.

We would greatly appreciate receipt by telegram of the Department's views in regard to the foregoing.

Throughout the conversation we emphasized the informal character f our views; the fact that they constituted no commitment and that nal decisions regarding their program would be taken by the Jongress.

Sent Department as 3327, repeated to London for Douglas as 649.

[Clayton and Caffery]
CAFFERY

---

[3] Associate Chief, International Resources Division.

40.50 Recovery/8–1847 : Telegram

he Acting Secretary of State to the Embassy in the United Kingdom

ECRET WASHINGTON, August 20, 1947—9 p. m.

3596. For Ambassador Douglas. Dept deeply concerned by indicaons that Paris Conference is not facing necessity of subjecting stated equirements of participating countries to critical analysis with a iew to producing a final program whose statements of needed aid ould be justifiable as realistic and based on maximum self-help and utual aid. Study of questionnaires shows end use justifications of

requirements requested in very few cases. Other reports indicate tha
requirements statements and existing national plans of participatin
countries are being accepted without discussion of real analysis. Merel
adding up separate estimates would obviously result in unacceptabl
program and reductions would be more difficult than if made durin
formulation stage.

It seems inappropriate to consider offering revised level of industr
plan to Paris Conference for comment on rate of and priorities i
reactivation unless comparable comment made by Conference re plar
and statements of all participating countries. An opportunity to see
help from bizonal area as well as from US might further encourag
avoidance of critical discussion of proposals for self-help.

In absence of assurances that Paris Conference intends to analyz
separate country proposals with aim of securing integrated realisti
program embracing all participating countries, Dept feels any decisio
re discussion in Paris of reactivation rate bizonal level of industry pr
mature. (Re para 1 Douglas message from Paris, 3310 Aug 18 [1]). Wi
Clayton, Douglas and Caffery please comment re Depts appreher
sions? In meantime discussion of rate of reactivation bizonal industr
in London talks with French should be avoided. Clay's views regardin
appropriate position also requested. Sent London for Ambassado
repeated to Paris 3120 for Ambassador, and to Geneva 1043 fc
Clayton.

LOVE1

---

[1] Not printed.

840.50 Recovery/8–2147 : Telegram

*The Ambassador in the United Kingdom (Douglas) to the Secretar
of State*

SECRET   LONDON, August 21, 1947—8 p. n

4552. For Lovett. 1. I share your apprehensions that Paris Coi
ference is not critically analyzing the estimated production and r
quirements of participating countries and that there is danger tha
final program may be both unrealistic as to production and inord
nately large as to our assistance. (Department's telegram 3596, Augu
20). Agree important all countries at Paris adjust their productio
programs to realities and critically screen each other's requirements i
order to keep demands on US at minimum. For example: French mu
be persuaded to abandon present position that original Monnet pla
must be accepted practically unchanged no matter what the cost to U
or to general recovery.

2. Did not intend to propose that production program for bizon
area be subject to any more rigorous screening than that of any oth

country. Question is not, it seems to me, one of submitting bizonal production program to Paris or permitting it to be discussed there, for both of these steps have already been taken.

3. Question seems rather to be one of participation of US Government representative aided of course by OMGUS staff in discussions on behalf US zone Germany in order that our program may be defended and that other countries may have an opportunity of pointing out to US as they will to each other changes in our program which would in their judgment contribute to reducing overall bill or to facilitating economic recovery of Europe as whole. Do not believe that in absence US delegate UK representatives are, or are considered by Paris conferees to be, adequate spokesmen for whole bizonal area.

4. To hold ourselves aloof from such give-and-take cannot help but encourage other participants to consider that their national plans and requirements should be accepted without examination or discussion. While we perhaps need not take the lead, neither should we hang back. We cannot in my view too promptly make it clear that we are prepared to participate in any overall program of critical analysis affecting all countries alike, though reserving, as each country must, the right of final decision in the light of all the evidence.

5. I recognize that US zone participation may carry implication that US is contributing directly and is accordingly committed to any program which may be formulated at Paris Conference but this danger can, I believe, be minimized, even completely removed.

6. Clay will arrive tomorrow morning. Will discuss this further with him and request him to transmit his views.

Repeated to Geneva 121 for Clayton and Paris 469 for Caffery.

DOUGLAS

840.50 Recovery/8–2247

Memorandum by Lt. Col. Charles H. Bonesteel, III, Special Assistant to the Under Secretary of State (Lovett)

[WASHINGTON, undated.]

MINUTES OF MEETING ON MARSHALL "PLAN" 3:00 P. M., AUGUST 22, 1947

Present:　　C–Mr. Bohlen
S/P–Mr. Kennan
Le–Mr. Gross
EUR–Mr. Hickerson
EUR–Mr. Jackson
GA–Mr. Kindleberger
PA–Mr. Swihart
U–Mr. Bonesteel

Informal discussion revolved around the questions listed in Tab A attached. There follows a summary of the conclusions reached with regard to each of these questions.

The paragraph numbers below refer to the question numbers in Tab A.

1. A comprehensive departmental position has not been officially approved. Considerable work has been done and is expressed in the report of the Policy Planning Staff on European reconstruction and in a series of documents produced by the committee working under Mr. Kindleberger.[1]

It was concluded that the time has come to firm up the overall departmental position. It was the consensus that the two sets of documents mentioned above should be circulated to selected representatives within the Department for hasty review and comment to the end that a departmental position be established early next week.

a. It was the consensus that Mr. Clayton, while generally aware of departmental thinking with regard to the "Plan", holds fundamental divergent views on some aspects, notably the importance of a Customs Union for Europe, the over-riding importance of financial and multilateral exchange arrangements, and his aversion to continuing European machinery to implement the European reconstruction plan. These divergencies held by Mr. Clayton may fundamentally affect the form and acceptability of the final plan presented by the Europeans. It seems essential that, as soon as the departmental position is clarified, that every effort be made to bring Mr. Clayton's thoughts in line with the clarified position.

b. It was felt that the following procedure would be best to bring Mr. Clayton fully in line with the departmental position: Send him a comprehensive cable covering, in its first part, a review of basic political factors in the present European scene; in the next part, a brief but fairly detailed review of the essentials of the Department's position; a third part, asking him to prepare his comments on part two and be prepared to discuss them with Mr. Lovett by teletype. If the teletype conversation indicated any remaining divergencies of view, Mr. Kennan should make a quick trip to London for the purpose of discussing the outstanding matters with Mr. Clayton.

2. The consensus was that sufficient friendly aid is not being given. It seems fundamentally necessary that the European nations go through a screening procedure of the committee reports being presented with a view to substantially decreasing the aid requirements therein and making a greater showing of cooperative effort. This, in

---

[1] Charles Kindleberger was the executive secretary of the Committee on European Recovery Program organized on June 25. This Departmental Committee studied the projected aid program from many points of view and prepared a substantial corpus of background and operating materials. Copies of these are in Lot 122.

effect, would extend the present target of 1 September by some appreciable amount.

3. The screening of committee reports, suggested in 2 above, will almost inevitably lead to an extension of the target date. This will achieve the purpose suggested in question 3, and is a better way to delay submission of the report than to suggest directly to the European nations that the report should be further considered.

4. It was agreed that the critical situation in Britain [2] may have some serious effects on the cooperation expected under the European recovery plan. Mr. Kennan undertook to review, in light of the present situation, his basic paper, particularly the chapter on Great Britain therein.

5. Discussion on this question brought out the necessity for a clearer idea of the mechanics of presentation of the European plan to Congress. It appears highly desirable to establish that the initial report from the European countries will be reviewed by the Administration and further questions asked the Europeans if, in our opinion, the plan is not wholly satisfactory. Such a course is, in effect, a form of negotiation but it seems impossible to avoid it. If the first report from the European countries is to be passed directly to Congress it seems very likely that the best action from the Hill will not ensue.

6. All agreed that an Administration position should be established as soon as possible. We understand that the Treasury Department, Commerce, et cetera, are becoming somewhat restive since they have heard nothing as to State Department thinking with regard to the Marshall program. As soon as the departmental position is clear, it was felt that copies of the position papers should be transmitted to the appropriate Cabinet officers by a letter which asks them to have the paper reviewed in their departments and their comments transmitted to the State Department through a designated representative, who could meet in an *ad hoc* committee with Mr. Kennan and other State Department representatives. As soon as the Administration position was clear it should then be given Mr. Harriman's committee and appropriate Congressional leaders and interested Congressional committees.

7. A separate memorandum has been prepared on the public relations aspects of the Marshall Plan and will be reviewed in the light of such action as is taken in regard to the matters discussed above.

The important questions of the special session of Congress and the question of Germany in relation to the European plan were not completely discussed. Further meeting will be held on these subjects in the near future.

---

[2] For documentation, see pp. 1 ff.

[Enclosure]

QUESTIONS

1. Is the Department's position regarding the skeleton of the Plan sufficiently clear?

    a. Is Mr. Clayton fully aware of the Department's position?
    b. Would it be desirable to send a representative to Paris to make Mr. Clayton fully *au fait* with the Department's position?

2. Are we satisfied that all desirable "friendly aid" is being given?

3. Should we indicate to C.E.E.C. the desirability of extension of the target date for their report so as to permit full consideration of factors expressed in Deptel 3029,[3] etc.?

4. Are there important foreign political factors entering the picture that require recognition in our approaches on "friendly aid"?

    a. British political and financial situation?
    b. French–Italian relations?

5. Should consideration be given to making less clear-cut the alternatives which would have to be followed if C.E.E.C. submits an unacceptable report?

6. What should be the timing in bringing the Treasury Department, Commerce, Congress, et cetera, into the picture?

7. Are there any factors with regard to the public relations aspects of the Marshall Plan which we should consider?

---

[3] August 14, p. 356.

840.50 Recovery/8–2447 : Telegram

The Acting Secretary of State to the Secretary of State at Petropolis, Brazil [1]

TOP SECRET   WASHINGTON, August 24, 1947—7 p. m.

US URGENT   NIACT

80. Humelsine for Carter.[2] Eyes Only for Secretary Marshall from Lovett. Subject: Paris talks on unified economic plan. 1. Seven days from now the Paris Conference is scheduled to produce a plan. Progress so far is disappointing in that all that has come out so far is sixteen shopping lists which may be dressed up by some large-scale

---

[1] Secretary Marshall was head of the United States delegation at the Inter-American Conference for the Maintenance of Continental Peace and Security at Quitandinha, near Petropolis, Brazil. For documentation on this conference, see vol. VIII, pp. 1 ff.

[2] Carlisle H. Humelsine became Director of the Executive Secretariat, Office of the Secretary of State on June 29, 1947; Marshall S. Carter was Special Assistant to the Secretary of State.

ut very long-term projects such as Alpine power, etc. The present
grand total of the shopping list approach is unreasonable, not solely
because of its size but because on its face it indicates that even these
huge sums will not accomplish the rehabilitation over a four-year
period, still leaving a deficit at end of that time amounting to about
four billion dollars annually (mostly a food deficit according to their
experts).

2. This approach continued even after a message sent on August 14
to Clayton and Caffery [3] pointing out that from reports received "we
gain the impression that too little attention is being paid by the par-
icipants to the elements of self-help and mutual aid which constituted
an integral part of the suggestions made by the Secretary in his Harvard speech. We are much concerned over this. We consider that the
problem of the leading western European countries is not only to make
up deficiencies caused by the vicissitudes of the war, but to adjust
hemselves to certain basic changes which have occurred and are con-
inuing to occur in their international position. This adjustment calls
for courageous and incisive action on their own part, both individually
and collectively. Unless they are prepared to make this adjustment, no
aid from this country could be really effective. It could achieve no more
han a postponement of inevitable decisions. We are entirely serious
about this and we will not be able to accept, even as a basis for recommendation to Congress, any plan which does not recognize this basic
requirement. An itemized bill summing up prospective deficits against
a background of present policies and arrangements will definitely not
be sufficient.

"In approaching this problem, the Europeans might make more
progress if they were to assume there was no one to help them, to
imagine that they had no choice but to try to work out an acceptable
economic future without any outside support, to elaborate the best
program they could, and only then to undertake to define the gaps
which absolutely could not be filled out of their own resources even
by the most strenuous individual and collective effort.

"The above remains our basic position on these matters and you are
at liberty to make it clear to any of the participants at the Paris talks."

3. The remainder of the cable was devoted to pointing out that our
objective was to break the bottlenecks so as to increase production, both
industrial and agricultural, through the clearing of choke points in
coal, fertilizer, transportation, food, etc., and in improving systems of
distribution. We pointed out necessity for primary emphasis on effi-
ient utilization of existing capacity rather than on capital development. We then enumerated financial and monetary stability, tangible

---

[3] Telegram 3029, p. 356.

and progressive reduction of exchange controls, tariffs, etc., and necessity for removal of all obstacles in exchange of goods between European nations, etc. Clayton and Caffery have obviously endeavored to make these points clear but, as indicated at outset this message, adequate results have not ensued.

5. This morning *New York Times* front page article by Callender from Paris apparently giving considerable detail on European economic conference report. Article stresses that there will remain after 1951 annual deficit of four billion dollars due principally to food import requirements. Unless Western Europe's food supply can be made up from resumption trade relations with food producing countries behind Iron Curtain alternative is continuing provision these food requirements from Western Hemisphere, et cetera, which will continue the large annual dollar deficit. Article also stresses importance of Germany requirements for increased supplies of coke and finished steel. Article ends on disturbing note implying that report is in effect near [*mere?*] summation of national requirements based on individual national planning. Article ends with paragraph stating members of conference count on US officials to aid them in writing final report which would "strike the imagination" of US public and Congress. I believe the article was planted.

In these circumstances and against the background of our promise to lend friendly aid in drafting, I am convinced that the time has now arrived for us to give some indications that the present plan is not acceptable and to do so promptly. This can be done without commitments. If not done we will be criticized. I therefore recommend the following steps:

(*a*) That a message be dispatched to Clayton and Caffery reiterating our object to obtain from the Europeans a plan which will enable them to improve production to the point where they can become self-supporting at whatever minimum scale is tolerable through the principle of self-help and mutual help rather than have them lean on us to rebuild, on a long-term capital basis, their entire production machine. The latter, while desirable, cannot come into being for some years and we cannot support the drain of rebuilding Europe on a grand scale. In connection with this basic approach, we would emphasize the breaking of specific bottlenecks well known to them and to us. This overall tentative statement of Department's views will be held pending your comments on proposals submitted herewith.

(*b*) Since Clayton and Caffery have been out of touch with headquarters for some months and may not be wholly familiar with the work that has been done here and the difficulties any program must face, I would like to send George Kennan for a few days and Charles Bonesteel for a week to Paris Tuesday night carrying realistic proposals to Clayton and Caffery so that they can be of such assistance as possible in giving aid to Caffery and Clayton for the Executive Committee in particular.

(*c*) As is common in all such conferences, I suspect that no real progress will be made in obtaining real concessions involving the abandonment of national prestige or transitory competitive advantages until the deadline for adjournment approaches. Therefore it seems wise to me to keep this pressure on the conferees but to notify Franks, the British Chairman of the Executive or Steering Committee, through Caffery, that we would be prepared to have the conference extended for two weeks in order to avoid having them bring out a shopping list report instead of a constructive program. I believe this can be done and that it would be welcome. It would not materially delay our over-all study of the program since Harriman's committee will not report on U.S. potentialities for aid until October first.

(*d*) We are preparing a summarized memorandum using portion of Kennan's report as background and adding some material developed in economic sections as a top secret report to keep the Secretaries of Treasury, War and Commerce posted on current developments in light of British crisis. They have been asking for detailed indications from Paris talks and we are anxious to inform them and insure their cooperation in our efforts to find solution. We would like to have this go only to the three Departments mentioned above plus the President, and think we can have it ready by Thursday.

6. While the present outlook seems gloomy, I am not one bit discouraged, as we are only now coming up to the point where we have something concrete to work on and where we can point out the unsatisfactory measures so far taken. If we can keep the conferees from getting crystallized into a bad plan, perhaps we can swing them into a good one, or at least a better one. This seems to us here to be well worth our best efforts. The British financial crisis, plus the virtual British walkout on the ITO at Geneva,[4] were not foreseen by the conferees when their original time schedule was selected, and two weeks grace after September 1 may be the difference between failure and success.

Will you please authorize or amend the action outlined above at your earliest convenience.

All goes well here.

Best regards,[5]

LOVETT

---

[4] For documentation regarding the U.S. role at the Geneva conference, the Second Session of the Preparatory Committee of the United Nations Conference on Trade and Employment, see volume I.

[5] In top secret telegram 68 from Petropolis, Secretary Marshall answered: "I concur completely in your views and action proposed in your 80. I consider it essential that our people show great firmness and be most emphatic in stating our requirements. I suggest that proposed message to Caffery and Clayton be repeated to Douglas and Dunn for their supporting advice to respective government seats. We should also furnish Forrestal a copy of the summarized memorandum of developments you are preparing." (840.50 Recovery/8-2547)

840.50 Recovery/8–2247 : Telegram

The Acting Secretary of State to the Embassy in France

TOP SECRET   WASHINGTON, August 24, 1947—8 p. m.
URGENT   NIACT

3158. For Caffery. Caffery's 3395 (147 to Geneva for Clayton's eyes only)[1] reinforces view here that there must be major changes in both content and conclusions of CEEC report prior to completion. Realistic and workable program more important than meeting predetermined deadline for completion of report.

Program presently indicated by above message and other reports from Clayton, Caffery, and Douglas, does not appear to meet following essential standards: (1) achievement of European economy capable of maintenance without indefinitely prolonged outside support; (2) maximum realization of opportunities for mutual aid within the area; (3) concentration of aid at points where it will have maximum immediate recovery effects.

Coming to you soon is overall summary of Department's view on essentials of a workable European recovery program. While we must not create impression that we are directing specific content of report or slowing down its preparation, publication of a report not meeting standards in para 2 above would do irreparable harm by evoking serious criticism in US and by further undermining confidence and hope of Europeans that they can help themselves.

Pending receipt of summary you should express to Franks and such others as you think necessary our grave concern as to character of presently envisaged report. If Conference procedure follows para 2 urtel 3327 of Aug 20 from Paris, you might suggest that Exec Comm, with help of technical committees, take the time necessary to direct report toward standards in para 2 above before discussing draft report with US representatives as envisaged in para IV Dept's 3209 [*3029*] of 14 Aug to Paris. Overall summary mentioned above will contain further suggestions re procedures for consultation with US representatives, etc. To provide fullest and most expeditious amplification of departmental views I am consulting Secretary about sending George Kennan to Paris for short stay, leaving Washington

---

[1] In telegram 3395, August 22, 1947, from Paris, not printed, Caffery noted that "Marris informs us that preliminary findings are that deficit of 16 participants plus western Germany for 1948–51 period will be in 26–28 billion dollar range order of magnitude decreasing from eight billion 1948 to four billion dollars 1951 . . . . the disturbing aspect arising not only from the magnitude of the sum but also from the fact that a viable economy would not result by the end of 1951." (840.50 Recovery/8–2247)

Tuesday night. Would appreciate your immediate thoughts as to utility this move.

Repeated to Clayton, Geneva, as 1068.

Repeated to Douglas, London, as 3664.

LOVETT

840.50 Recovery/8–2547 : Telegram

The Consul at Geneva (Troutman) to the Secretary of State

TOP SECRET GENEVA, August 25, 1947—8 : 10 p. m.

US URGENT NIACT

909. Lovett from Clayton. Reagan,[1] White and I spent over two hours with Sir Oliver Franks Saturday discussing very disturbing total requirements 16 nations and western Germany. Sir Oliver emphasized that this summation is not yet a conference document as there is still much work to do on it.

Total balance of payments deficit with USA for four year period '48 to '51 is 19.9 billion dollars and with rest of American continent 8.3 billion. Grand total American continent 28.2 billions ranging from 8.1 in '48 gradually downwards to 5.8 in '51. Latter figure most disturbing of all because indicates their expectation that they will be far from self sustaining in '51. Also indicated that the agreed basis for preparation of figures was not observed. That basis is a standard of living which they expect to be able to maintain without special outside assistance after '51.

Figures of requirements are divided between food, steel, transport and fuel in one total and other goods in another total. Latter is stated at 3 billion for each of the four years former 6.7 for '48, 6.6 for '49, 6.3 for '50, 6.1 for '51. This also disturbing as showing unsatisfactory progress in recovery production particularly food and coal. Exports to American continent are to be deducted.

Figures for rest of world are almost in balance showing a total deficit of 1 billion for the four years.

Of course I told Sir Oliver in my opinion the 28.2 figure was out of the question.

I again stated to Sir Oliver that I believed presentation of figures for '48 at higher level than these 16 countries and western Germany showed as deficit with American continent in '46 would create very bad impression at home and of course subsequent years should show scaling down to very low figures for '51. None of us knows exactly

---

[1] Daniel J. Reagan, Counselor of Embassy for Economic Affairs at Paris.

what this '46 deficit was but my impression is it was between 5 and 6 billion dollars. Sir Oliver stated that this would mean a standard of living below prewar and would raise grave political problems for most of the countries. I replied that the destruction to European economy by two world wars was so enormous that I seriously questioned if Europe could achieve in the next decade a standard of living equal to prewar even with all the help which had been provided by the US and with such additional help from the US as might be practicable. This especially true because for several prewar years Europe was living off its investments abroad to extent 2 billions annually, three-fourths being interest and one-fourth disinvestment and that practically all this capital now lost.

Sir Oliver said a quick examination of the supporting documents indicated that the total could be trimmed by probably 5 billion dollars because some of the requirements included capital equipment which should be financed by the International Bank; in other cases requirements clearly exceeded available supplies; furthermore indicated exports by and to the group substantially exceeded indicated imports from the same source hence there would probably be further exports available for American continent from this source.

Sir Oliver added if the total had to be reduced, say to 15 billion, he was sure this could only be done if we told them it had to be done.

I informed Sir Oliver of the concern expressed by you in 1043 [2] to Geneva and inquired particularly regarding end use examination of requirements and whether the reports submitted by individual countries had been subjected to critical analysis.

Sir Oliver said that the work represented primarily an assembly of individual country estimates although some "shaking down" had been accomplished in cases where combined estimates were obviously greatly in excess of available supplies. As to end use examination this was impossible within the available time. He said it would take months.

Sir Oliver left me with the definite impression that he was very reluctant to open up in the conference the question of relative living standards current or prospective and that under its present system of procedures the conference was not likely to arrive at a program which would bring their actual dollar requirements much below the preliminary summation or which would give any assurance of a self sustaining economy by '52.

I think the trouble is that most of these countries have really not come to grips with their toughest problems. For example, Britain has not come to grips with the coal problem. I think we ought to tell

[2] Probably 1044 to Geneva, which was a repetition of 3596 to London of August 20, p. 367.

this conference and Britain and France that their plan must contemplate that Britain will again export annually 25 to 30 million tons of coal (exclusive of bunkers) by '51 and that France will again be practically self sustaining in bread grains by that time. If we don't tell them this, they won't do it. The French need agricultural workers and still they are sticky on receiving them from Italy where there is a great excess of such workers anxious to emigrate. France and Britain will not face the political hurdles they must take if they are to solve their coal and grain problems unless we make it clear that we will not consider assistance on any other basis. I am sure both problems can be satisfactorily solved but not if they think we will continue to furnish coal and grain in current volume. These are just examples of the situation we face.

I am convinced there is no other way to deal with this situation than to impose certain necessary conditions. If we fail to do so, we are going to be presented with a bill which I do not believe our people should or will meet. It will be much more difficult to take corrective measures then than now. I am repeating this to London and Paris for Ambassadors only with request that they wire you direct their comments.

My next meeting with Sir Oliver and perhaps his Executive Committee set for Paris Thursday morning. I am asking Ambassador Douglas come over if convenient and of course Ambassador Caffery will be present. Will appreciate receiving your instructions by that time.

Sent Dept 909, repeated London Ambassador's eyes only 89, Paris Ambassador's eyes only 82. [Clayton.]

TROUTMAN

840.50 Recovery/8–2547 : Telegram

The Ambassador in France (Caffery) to the Secretary of State

SECRET

US URGENT   NIACT

PARIS, August 25, 1947—7 p. m.

3431. I have informed Sir Oliver Franks of the pertinent comments in your 3158, August 24, emphasizing that a realistic and workable program was far more important than meeting a pre-determined deadline for completion of the report. In reply Franks mentioned that he agreed all along the line but as any undue delay might have unfortunate psychological effects on the sixteen countries the reports should be available for publication not later than September 15. He also expressed doubt whether western Europe, under any set of reasonable assumptions, could in fact reach a completely self-supporting status by 1952. A telegram follows of my views on this subject, with special reference to the considerations raised in your 3120, August 20.[1]

I am to see delegates of several other countries tomorrow on this.[2]

Repeated London 670; Geneva for Clayton 157.

CAFFERY

---

[1] This was a repetition of telegram 3596 to London, p. 367.

[2] In this connection Ambassador Caffery reported in telegram 3452, August 26, from Paris that "I talked today with several other delegates about the necessity of a realistic and workable program, irrespective of inability to meet deadlines. They agreed. I also referred to the view prevaling in some quarters that the US would have to save Europe financially, irrespective of type of program. I emphasized that American people and Congress would only underwrite a program which made good economic sense." (840.50 Recovery/8–2647)

840.50 Recovery/8–2647 : Telegram

The Ambassador in France (Caffery) to the Secretary of State

SECRET   PARIS, August 26, 1947—7 :41 p. m.
US URGENT   NIACT

3451. Lovett from Caffery. I submit the following comments in regard to Department's 3120, August 20; 3158, August 24; Geneva's 909, August 25 and my 3431, August 25.

From day by day talks with members of various delegations and from an examination of CEEC documents I conclude that the following three basic questions confront us :

1. Why does the preliminary summation show such astronomical deficits and lack of adequate progress towards a viable western European economy ?

2. Why is it unlikely that a satisfactory program will result from present conference procedures and attitudes ?

3. What can be done about it ?

I. The summary of the balance of payments work points to five conclusions :

a. Western Europe before the war was consuming annually two billion dollars in goods and service more than it was producing at that time. The resources for financing this deficit have now disappeared.

b. The commercial isolation of eastern Europe under Soviet controls has greatly reduced an important source for foodstuffs, timber and other materials which western Europe previously financed by the sale of its manufactured products to the same area. This has contributed to the shift in requirements to the western hemisphere with no correlative expansion in anticipated export shipments to dollar areas. (The anticipated 1948 ratio of exports to imports with the American continent is 1 to 4 and in the case of transactions with the United States alone the ratio is 1 to 7.2.)

c. Conference planning to date has been largely an assembly job of country estimates which in the words of one delegate "were aimed at prewar standard of living, western Germany excluded."

d. These estimates pre-suppose a continuation of the basic economic pattern of the European economy with all the implications regarding low labor productivity and maldistribution of effort which derive from segregating 270,000,000 people into 17 uneconomic principalities.

e. There is no indication of a determined effort to utilize Europe's own resources where they could be substituted for dollar items. (As an example the planning calls for 43,000,000 tons coal imports from the United States in 1948 and as reported my August 23, major conversion to fuel oil, all of which must be imported, in substitution for coal.)

II. As Sir Oliver Franks indicated to Clayton, as much as $5,000,-000,000 might be taken off the preliminary estimates through elimination capital equipment items, downward adjustments to meet available supplies and redirection to American continent of certain export items. In the absence of a fundamental change in the conference's approach, it is unlikely that reductions will go further unless it is done through a "tinkering with figures" for purposes of improving presentation. The reasons for my pessimism are:

a. Some participants, such as the Scandinavian countries for political reasons, and Switzerland, because it does not need direct assistance, favor a program restricted to listings of net requirements. This attitude tends seriously to reduce the conference's policy-making function.

b. The conference's terms of reference and general procedures are such that the majority of the participants on any specific issue do not feel that they can require any single participant to adjust its national program to meet the needs of the group.

c. Home governments tend to act as a brake on the enthusiasms of some individual delegates who would be disposed to push through a bold constructive program. (The Italian Ambassador called on me today to say that one of the difficulties was that none of the delegates here had any real authority and that most of them lacked influence with their governments.)

d. The United Kingdom has been reluctant to permit the question of living standards to come to the floor on the conference, a procedure which would be essential if requirement were to be geared to possible production plus outside assistance.

III. I thoroughly agree with Under Secretary Clayton's observation that it has become necessary to impose certain necessary conditions. Although I recognize that the course of action contains an element of risk, I believe that the danger would be much greater if the conference were permitted to continue its present course. It seems to me that in the light of the foregoing it is desirable:

a. To make a presentation of our views to the home governments through our respective missions at the same time the presentation is made to the conference here and,

b. That the presentations should be based on the points outlined in Section Three of Department's 3029, August 14, modified to eliminate any possible loophole which might permit a participating country to avoid its share of responsibility.

I have reviewed with Spiegel, Longstreet, Terrill, Bray and Moore [1] the six basic objectives outlined in Section Three urtel 3029, August 14, and we believe that they constitute a basis for a series of conditions on which the conference report must be based, modified along the following lines to take care of recent developments in the conference.

Point One. We suggest that the term "production of food and materials needed to fill their basic requirements" be changed to specify production of [garbled], coal, coke and major items essential to their production. The reason we suggest this change is that individual European countries regard a multitude of articles as necessary to fill their basic requirements and tend to disperse their labor and other means of production. We believe that the vital need is to concentrate their emergency productive effort on a few items which will mean direct dollar savings. We suggest the inclusion under this point of the following condition:

"Failure to achieve a satisfactory level of production will be ground for discontinuance of aid". Reference Embassy's Telegram 3122, August 6.

Point Two. We agree.

Point Three. Our only suggestion is that the word "must" be substituted for the word "should".

We believe that the retention of the term "as soon as practicable" leaves the necessary flexibility for situations such as Communist-inspired strikes which might prevent effective stabilization at any given moment.

Point Four will be discussed with Clayton on Thursday and our views telegraphed thereafter.

Point Five. In order to eliminate any reason for noncompliance by participating countries we recommend that this provision be reworded to read as follows: "The participating countries shall take steps to facilitate the greatest practicable interchange of foods and services

---

[1] Victor Longstreet, Associate Chief, Division of Investment and Economic Development; William H. Bray, Jr., Foodstuffs Branch, International Resources Division; Ben T. Moore, Assistant Chief, Division of Commercial Policy.

among themselves, adopting definite measures directed towards the eventual elimination of trade and other barriers among the participating countries".

Point Six. We agree.

We believe that the presentation of the foregoing should emphasize:

(*a*) That our views were being presented at this time because the conference had requested our friendly assistance in drafting its program and

(*b*) That final determination of what assistance, if any, will be forthcoming resides with the Congress and with the American people.

Finally the Department may wish to consider adding a statement to the effect that if the participating countries are willing to proceed with their work on the foregoing bases, the Department of State is prepared to recommend, through appropriate channels, to the occupation authorities that they assume an additional and final part [*sic*] behalf of western Germany, an active part in the formulation of the European program and that they undertake the same responsibility as the participating countries towards the principles outlined above.

Copies held for Clayton and Kennan, repeated London as 675.

CAFFERY

840.50 Recovery/8–2647 : Telegram

The Acting Secretary of State to the Embassy in France

TOP SECRET   WASHINGTON, August 26, 1947—6 p. m.
URGENT

3195. For Clayton and Caffery. Following is basic portion of summary referred to in para 3 of mytel 3158 [1] for your consideration pending arrival Kennan and Bonesteel Thursday. Additional portion relating to general political situation will be given you orally by Kennan. This summary is to be discussed with you by Kennan and Bonesteel in order to incorporate your views before it is firmed up.

A. FUNDAMENTAL OBJECTIVES

Department regards following features fundamental to U.S. concept of program:

1. Basic objective of program is to move entire area progressively from present condition to working economy independent of abnormal outside support, taking full account of basic changes in European conditions such as political developments in Eastern Europe, altered position of former colonial territories, and loss of overseas assets, merchant shipping and other prewar invisible exports.

---

[1] Not printed.

2. Participants must take concerted efforts to foster European recovery as a whole, and show genuine readiness to make national contributions to this common goal.

3. Program must realize maximum opportunities for self-help and for mutual help within the area and thus minimize outside aid requirements; program must therefore concentrate initially on elimination of bottlenecks and other opportunities for greatest immediate recovery at lowest cost in scarce resources.

4. Program must be directed primarily toward short-run recovery rather than long-run development; full use of existing or readily repairable capacity and restoration of normal domestic and intra-European intercourse therefore have priority, although not excluding longer-run capital development necessary to meet goal in 1 above.

B. Essential Elements of Program

Program submitted for U.S. consideration must contain these elements:

1. Concrete proposals for area-wide recovery of agriculture and basic industries—coal, steel, transport, and power—which are fundamental to viable European economy. Proposals must correlate individual national programs and individual industry programs and give priority to projects promising quickest expansion of output. Bizonal German area must be taken fully into account. Stopgap aid in coal, food, etc. pending European recovery must be minimized. Proposals must be fully justified through following steps:

a. Development of country requirements for food and end-products of basic industries (coal, steel, etc.) on realistic and defensible basis, with clearly stated standards, and intensive mutual criticism and screening.

b. Statement of specific national production goals in food and basic industries, with concrete proposed measures to attain those goals and specific stated requirements (if any) for extra-national aid in such items as fuel, fertilizer, mining and agricultural machinery, power, steel, or manpower. These requirements statements must be supported by justifications and must also be subjected to constructive mutual criticism and screening.

c. Development in concert of concrete proposals for mutual aid to meet requirements under (a) and (b) from sources within the area or under political control of the participants, including priorities in reactivation creating maximum mutual aid potentialities.

d. Adjustment of national agricultural and basic industry programs on area-wide basis, taking full account of mutual aid possibilities, and giving priority to bottleneck elimination and other opportunities for greatest speed in recovery.

e. Development of concrete and minimum requirements for outside aid as a residual of processes in (a), (b), (c), and (d).

DISCUSSION OF ITEM 1

Production recovery in agriculture and basic industries is cornerstone of entire program. Greatest hope lies in intensive attack on such problems as British and Ruhr coal production, French grain, railroad equipment repair, etc. Measures of planning, international allocations, and internal priorities to obtain promptest expansion are essential to speedy recovery with minimum outside aid at least while basic resources remain sharply limited. Such controls should be confined to fields of agriculture and basic industries and be progressively liquidated as output increases and normal economic forces come into play. As to U.S. public views on this item, note that NAM industrialists meeting with Ness [2] have expressed view that European program's main feature should be to set production goals for the basic industries and concentrate on their achievement.

2. Undertakings on domestic measures necessary for internal economic stabilization, efficient use of national resources to minimize outside aid, and fulfillment of mutual aid commitments. Proposals should recognize wide variations in need for remedial measures, which include:

a. Currency reform, correction of grossly inflationary fiscal practices, and price stabilization for essential commodities.

b. Collections, internal allocations and priorities, and rationing of essentials, during period of acute stringency.

c. Direction of supplies to fulfill mutual aid commitments, on priority equal to if not higher than internal use.

DISCUSSION OF ITEM 2

These measures complementary to Item 1.

Full restoration of economic fabric internally will be possible only after production has increased, although much can be done immediately to reduce currency in circulation, reform taxes, etc. Must be recognized, however, that breakdown in normal monetary exchange is to considerable extent symptom rather than cause, and that over-drastic monetary and fiscal remedies without foundation in increased production may actually retard recovery. Moreover political implications, including danger of widening cleavages among producer and consumer groups must be carefully considered. As to use of internal Government controls, hope that expanded production will permit early liquidation. However, normal price mechanism cannot function in face of present acute scarcities. U.S. cannot accept situation under which its aid goes directly into or replaces domestic supplies going into barter, compensation and black markets. U.S. also concerned as to

---

[2] Norman T. Ness, Director, Office of Financial and Development Policy.

internal political consequences of inequitable distribution of scarce vital commodities.

3. Comprehensive measures to foster multi-lateral intra-European trade, over and above any specific mutual aid arrangements. These measures should be directed toward:

a. Progressive replacement of bilateral trading arrangements by more effective multilateral arrangements for expanding intra-European trade, looking, if possible, toward an eventual European customs union. Bilateral trade and payments agreements within the group of participants in conflict with the mutual aid program should be abrogated. Possibilities of major trade barrier reductions, encompassing important commodity groups or smaller groups of nations, but short of general customs union, should be carefully considered. Recognize that partial measures of apparently preferential character may run counter to ITO principles. But in view short-run political and administrative obstacles to immediate commitment or rapid progress toward customs union, appears vital to explore means for European trade barrier reduction falling short of customs union.

b. Facilitating multilateral trade through foreign exchange clearing arrangements among the participants or other means for achieving currency convertibility and transferability. Conference may propose U.S. support of clearing system, under suitable safeguards, either through dollar fund or through direction of portion U.S. commodity aid to countries with export surpluses, although Department has as yet no appraisal of probable Congressional reaction.

DISCUSSION OF ITEM 3

While in many respects the long-run gains of European economic integration in terms of specialization of production and economic location—achieved ideally through both a customs and a currency union—would be the most beneficial consequences of a recovery program, these goals must be put in perspective in relation to more urgent short-run needs. Measures *a* and *b* above will contribute little to immediate restoration of production, but will grow in significance as production expands and domestic economies are stabilized. In first phase, therefore, Item 3 is subordinate to 1 and 2, although the groundwork must be laid immediately. In this connection Congressman Herter[3] has stated to Department that program merely aggregating national deficits and commiting participants to customs union would be completely inadequate and unacceptable to Congress.

C. FORMS OF POSSIBLE U.S. ASSISTANCE

Department regards formulation of program of maximum self-help and minimum outside aid requirements as primary Conference goal

---

[3] Christian A. Herter, of Massachusetts, was vice chairman of the Select Committee on Foreign Aid, House of Representatives.

but recognizes importance to realistic program guidance on general form of possible outside assistance. In this connection:

1. Assumed that in any event major part U.S. aid would be specified commodities or commodity groups. Extent of possible untied dollar assistance, either to support clearing system or otherwise, should be left open for review on merits.

2. Program should minimize dollar aid for purchases outside U.S. It is not intended to satisfy entire world's appetite for dollars under guise European Recovery program. Efforts should be made to maintain existing commitments from other suppliers (such as Argentine and Canadian contracts for wheat to U.K.), with dollar aid being limited to increments beyond these commitments. This approach desirable both to limit total assistance requested Congress and to limit inflationary effects within U.S. of maintaining heavy export demands from other areas as well as Europe. Partial relief for dollar shortages outside Europe may of course be subject of negotiations apart from European program. Moreover, program should not exclude expenditures outside U.S. which would increase flow of essential goods to Europe and make real contribution to European recovery. A firm position on this point should not be taken until appraisal is possible of cost of financing extra-European trade and alternative means of securing and financing supplies for Europe from non-U.S. sources. Note press reports of possible large-scale Canadian loan to be floated privately in New York.

3. Distribution of aid by U.S. should take into account recommendations by continuing European organization or where appropriate by other international allocating bodies (e.g., coal and food). However, U.S. aid will not be provided in totals for subdivision by Europeans. UNRRA precedent will not be followed. U.S. would hope to be guided by European recommendations but must retain freedom to modify allocations to assure most efficient use of aid and to enforce any agreed conditions.

D. RELATIONS WITH EASTERN EUROPE

On trade and financial relations of participating countries with Eastern Europe, Dept recognizes necessity of existing trade between Eastern and Western Europe and desirability of its increase. Program cannot, however, include provision of U.S. direct dollar or commodity aid to Eastern Europe because of political inacceptability here. U.S. will consider international measures of help for Eastern European countries designed to aid Western European recovery, e.g. World Bank loan to expand production and transport Polish coal; and recognizes necessity expanding production in Western countries in lines furnishing exports to Eastern Europe, to be exchanged against

Eastern European exports of essential commodities to West. U.S. does not require abrogation bilateral agreements with Eastern European countries. Foregoing views obtain so long as Eastern Europe not clearly engaged in economic warfare against Western Europe.

E. Place of Germany in Program

On relation of Germany to program, Dept considers that three western zones, as unit or bizonal area plus French zone, be covered fully into program. Revised level of industry agreement should be basis for inclusion of bizonal area, with changes required in interest of European-wide recovery recommended by conference on same basis that conference makes similar recommendations for changes in Monnet or other national plans. Rates of and priorities in reactivation of German industry should likewise be discussed by conference as part of similar discussion of achievement of other national plans. U.S. desires earliest possible self-supporting German economy, but recognizes that German recovery does not have priority over similar recovery elsewhere in Europe, and that recovery in Germany should not receive special impetus at expense of wider European recovery. On other hand, Dept will not agree to system of allocations of German resources or U.S. aid which would postpone German recovery until full recovery other countries has been assured.

F. Role of U.N.

Dept supports fullest practicable use of United Nations bodies and specialized agencies in carrying out of program. This includes continued international allocation of coal through ECE Coal Committee and food through IEFC Committees, and technical planning work in ECE Committees on transport and power. Sympathetic to assignment to ECE of additional functions related to program. But Dept recognizes that coordination of European program and integration of UN activities with needs of this special program will probably have to be retained in organization composed only of participants (including bizonal Germany). In view possibilities systematic obstruction to ECE effectiveness, special European recovery organization must be able to handle entire program and must be prepared to assume promptly functions assigned to other organizations if they prove ineffective.

G. Continuing Organization

Dept recognizes that present Conference cannot possibly make complete blueprint for European recovery over next several years. Initial program must conform to all above elements, but many details of its application will remain for further study. Modifications are also to be expected during negotiations with the U.S. before acceptance and in continuing development of any accepted program. Emphasis should be given to major role of continuing organization of participating countries (plus bizonal German area), both in implementing and in progressively refining any agreed program.

H. PROCEDURES

1. When the Conference has first draft of program, U.S. representatives in Paris should review it informally, presumably with Executive Committee. Review should cover both general policy matters and technical questions, and U.S. group in Paris should include technician qualified on all phases of program. Purpose of review is to afford U.S. representatives opportunity to seek explanations and clarifications of points that are not clear. In such discussions, U.S. representatives would be guided by above statements on essentials of workable program. This should be opportunity to guide both content and conclusions of Conference report. It should be made clear that U.S. representatives are taking this action to facilitate presentation of program to U.S. Government and that it is not final U.S. critical analysis of program looking toward approval.

2. When the Conference has completed report, it should be transmitted to U.S. Transmittal by Bevin as Conference Chairman to Secretary Marshall would be satisfactory. Desirable to have document physically in Washington prior to release to press in Paris so that copies can be made here for distribution. First impact on U.S. public should not be through newspaper accounts cabled from Paris.

3. After report has been received in Washington and given at least cursory examination, it would be desirable for Conference representatives, presumably Executive Committee, to discuss it in Washington with U.S. Executive Departments.

4. Drafting of multilateral and bilateral agreements would start simultaneously with submission of proposed legislation to Congress.

LOVETT

840.50 Recovery/8–2947

The Acting Secretary of State to President Truman

TOP SECRET [WASHINGTON,] August 29, 1947.

MY DEAR MR. PRESIDENT: I am enclosing herewith three documents which represent certain preliminary work of the Department of State setting forth the problems of European Recovery.

The complexity of the subject is such that it has taken some time to formulate worthwhile specific views on this question. It has also been necessary in order to reach this stage to obtain some concept of the developments in the Paris Conference on European Economic Cooperation. I feel now that progress has been sufficient to lay a basis for effective interdepartmental consideration of the policy issues involved in any European recovery program. It is especially necessary to have applied to this problem the best thinking of the interested Departments in order that a sound governmental position may be developed.

I should like to emphasize particularly the urgency of action on this question since the conference at Paris is expected to present a plan to the United States Government around September 15.

The documents enclosed herewith consist of:

(1) Memorandum entitled "Certain Aspects of the European Recovery Problem from the United States Standpoint." This is a background study prepared in the Policy Planning Staff of the Department during July.[1] It is outdated in certain respects by the rapid march of recent events, particularly in connection with the British dollar position.

(2) A summary statement of the Department of State's present views on the content of a European Economic Recovery Program, which has been communicated to Under Secretary Clayton in Paris, to guide him in his informal discussions with representatives at the Conference.[2] It should be noted that no U.S. representative has taken any part in the meetings of the Paris Conference, and that Mr. Clayton has at all times explicitly stated to representatives of other governments that he can in no way commit the United States Government to any course of action.

(3) A report, entitled "Problems of European Reconstruction"[3] which the Department of State is considering releasing informally at the appropriate time as background material on the nature of the economic problems being faced by European countries.

I hope to send you shortly (4) a more detailed statement of the Department's present views and (5) a rough draft of possible required legislation.[4]

You will note that the documents enclosed do not touch upon the capacity of the United States to aid Europe since this is a subject for study by the Committees appointed by the President on June 22, 1947.

---

[1] See editorial note, p. 337.

[2] This information was communicated to Under Secretary Clayton in telegram 3029 to Paris, August 14, p. 356.

[3] This document, prepared by the Economic Offices in the Department of State, is document D–4/19 of the Committee on European Recovery Program, not printed. A copy is in the Committee's records in Lot 122.

[4] On September 5 the Department sent to the President two additional documents: (a) "Questions of Policy and Procedure Regarding U.S. Aid to a European Program of Economic Recovery", which was presumably document D–16a, prepared on August 25, and (b) an initial draft of possible required legislation, prepared by the Committee on the European Recovery Program as document D–18. These documents are in Lot 22, and letters of transmittal of copies sent to other departments are in the 840.50 Recovery file.

I trust you will agree with me as to the urgency of arriving at an interdepartmental position on the host of complicated issues raised by these problems. I should appreciate it if you would designate someone on your staff to work with representatives of the Department of State. I have appointed Mr. Charles H. Bonesteel to coordinate work within the Department of State on the problems of European Recovery.

It seems to me essential to have a first meeting toward the end of next week to discuss the problems presented in the three documents enclosed with this letter.

In addition to your views on the substantive issues, I should very much appreciate your guidance on questions of procedure, particularly on the time and manner of getting the views of the members of the Non-Partisan Committee on Foreign Aid (Harriman Committee) and those of the Congressional leaders.

At your request these matters are being handled for the time being on a Top Secret basis.

Faithfully yours,

[ROBERT A. LOVETT]

840.50 Recovery/ 8–3147 : Telegram

The Ambassador in France (Caffery) to the Secretary of State

TOP SECRET   PARIS, August 31, 1947—1 p. m.

3543. For the Secretary and Lovett from Clayton. With reference to your 3201 August 26 and Caffery's 3489 August 28,[1] Ambassadors Caffery and Douglas and I spent Friday and Saturday morning with Kennan and Bonesteel in a comprehensive review of the Paris Conference. This mutual exchange of ideas was most helpful and enabled us to agree on a common position which we stated orally to the Conference's Executive Committee yesterday afternoon.

Following is a brief digest of discussions in a three hour meeting with the Committee:

1. *Introductory remarks:*

We have now had an opportunity to acquaint ourselves with the general work of this Conference and to review the reports of its committees. We believe that these reports represent a valuable contribution and provide a basis upon which its work might be carried forward.

Nevertheless, the conclusions of the Conference as reported to us are, in our opinion, disappointing and might, if formally advanced, prejudice the success of the entire Marshall program.

---

[1] Neither printed.

2. *Objective:*

The objective of the European recovery program, as we see it, is to provide for the speediest possible reactivation of the European economic machine and for its restoration to a self-supporting basis, while at the same time meeting the essential consumption requirements of the people. It is our belief that once determined steps toward this end are taken and tangible results achieved, the latent resources of Europe will begin to make their contribution to recovery. Common European effort, initially assisted by special American aid, should give rise to a further liberation of trade and to the emergence of fresh supplies of capital and technology, both from within Europe and from outside sources.

3. *General comment:*

The Conference's preliminary estimate of dollars 29.2 billion of required outside aid would appear in the US as much too large. The size of the estimated deficit and the fact that it remains same at the end of the period reflect the unsatisfactory nature of the methods by which it was calculated and the assumptions on which it was based. The most important standards by which the program will be judged in the US are the purposes which it is intended to serve and the basis on which it has been prepared. Congress and the American public will have to be convinced that there is an urgent need for this program, that its fundamental objectives are sound and can be accomplished within a specified period of time; that it represents a considered and critically analyzed statement of requirements; that the program has been prepared with a view to reducing to a minimum the outside aid required; and that at the end of the period the European economy will be restored to a balanced condition in order that its long run expansion will be assured.

4. *Conditions:*

It is believed that the probability of widespread acceptance of this program by the American public will be enhanced if it meets the following main essentials:

a. It must provide for the achievement within the four year period of a workable European economy independent of special, outside aid.

b. It must provide for continuous and progressive reduction in the special outside aid required by the participating countries to the point where it will become eliminated by the end of the period.

c. The participating countries must from time to time during the period of the program show convincing evidence that they have made substantial progress toward the scheduled goals of production of items essential to European recovery especially food and coal.

d. Long run development projects should not be allowed to interfere with the reactivation of the most efficient existing productive facilities.

The latter must have first priority. The financing of long term projects must be obtained from sources outside this program.

e. The participating countries must mutually undertake the necessary internal financial and monetary measures to stabilize their currencies, establish and maintain proper rates of exchange, and generally restore confidence in their monetary systems.

f. The participating countries must take concerted steps to facilitate the greatest practicable interchange of goods and services among themselves, adopting definite measures directed toward the progressive reduction and eventual elimination of barriers to trade within the area, in accordance with the principles of the ITO Charter.

g. The participating countries must regard the conditions mentioned above as a common European responsibility and must therefore provide for a multilateral organization which from time to time will review and take stock of the progress achieved by participating governments under the program.

We made it clear that we are not attempting to dictate to the Conference, and that no commitment by US was involved, but that we were merely stating our view of essentials for winning approval of American people.

Two of the committee members, Sir Oliver Franks and Alphand, discussed at length essentials *a* and *b*. Franks said that he was doubtful whether the European economy would in fact have reached a point by the end of 1951 where it could sustain itself without special external assistance. It seems to him that by the end of the period the deficit should have been reduced to moderate proportions but that complete viability, as far as the United Kingdom was concerned, and probably for the entire area, could be expected only on three assumptions:

1. Complete convertibility of currencies so that export receipts from one part of the world could be transferred to other areas to meet dollar needs.

2. Ability to find markets for export surpluses.

3. A readjustment in the terms of trade which would correct in large part the present disparity, as compared with the war, between prices of imported foods and raw materials and prices of exports. In reply to my comment that historically the pendulum of price relationships following wars tends to swing in the other direction and then to reach a normal balance, Sir Oliver said that his investigations indicated a prolonged shortage of cereals, livestock, iron ore, lead, and possibly zinc and he was not convinced that the correction in relative prices would occur by 1952. In completing his comments on this general question, Sir Oliver said, "It is not yet clear as to how zero can be reached by 1952. We can get to a low figure. If zero, we will have gone from area of reasonable assumptions to paper construction."

Alphand said that his list of assumptions necessary to viability are as follows:

1. That targets of production would be reached.
2. That exports to dollar areas would reach their goal.

3. That some important trade with eastern Europe be established.
4. That there be effective internal financial stabilization which in the case of France could bring out hidden resources in commodities, gold, and foreign exchange.

Kennan said that this was a vital question and that if the possibilities of a balanced position by 1952 were actually remote it would call for a reconsideration of the problem and a frank discussion of the matter with our own people. Bonesteel inquired whether Frank's pessimism was fused [based?] on the inadequacy of the time period or on a fundamental disequilibrium. Sir Oliver replied that the big question marks were terms of trade and marketability.

The Scandinavian representative (Coel Bjoernsen of Norway) said that it must be assumed that after 1951 Europe would be a capital importing country in the broad sense. Bonesteel replied that this was recognized and that what we had in mind was an end to the need for direct assistance from the US Government.

In commenting on the foregoing observations we pointed out that an inflow of foreign capital from the International Bank and other sources was a reasonable assumption if western Europe could make itself a going concern and get out of its red-ink status. We emphasized that a prime condition of any plan is that it should accomplish its purpose of placing Europe in a balanced position by the end of the contemplated period, saying that any other approach would be disastrous in terms of public reaction in the US. It seems evident that Sir Oliver's expectation that deficits will persist is based on a higher standard of living than Europe's productivity will support. It will also be noted that, while Franks was talking in terms of developments outside the immediate control of the European group, most of Alphand's conditions relate to objectives the attainment of which primarily depends on the Europeans themselves.

In discussing Point c (production of items essential to European recovery), we emphasized that it seemed to us that reasonable goals would be prewar fuel output by France and Italy and British coal production at level which would again result in annual shipment to continent of 25–30 million tons. We also recognized joint US–UK responsibility towards the European group for high level Ruhr output.

Alphand emphasized that while most European countries were projecting programs equal to or in excess of prewar coal production, the figures submitted by bizonal authorities gave a target below prewar output. Ambassador Douglas said it was his understanding that destruction to the mines was greater in the case of the Ruhr. Hirschfeld [2] confirmed this and said, furthermore as a result it is now necessary to open five new mines a year whereas under the Hitler regime it was necessary to open only one.

---

[2] M.H.M. Hirschfeld, Netherlands representative on the Committee of Cooperation at the CEEC.

The balance of the discussion centered on Point *g*, regarding the need for a joint organization. We explained that it seemed implicit in the program itself and from the other conditions outlined that some continuing organization would be needed for the period of the program and that we felt there should be a joint responsibility by all members of the group as to standard of performance. Thus there should be periodic and critical reviews of the programs by the participating governments. It would be our intention to recognize this mutuality of interest and responsibility and to tie in with the multilateral undertakings any bilateral agreements which we might negotiate with the individual participants. The conditions specified in the bilateral agreements would thus include those undertaken by the members towards each other. Four of the members of the Executive Committee, speaking in personal capacities, agreed that the program would require this kind of continuing organization.

The Scandinavian representative stated that on behalf of Sweden and Norway he wished to make full reservations on this point. He then commented that those countries believed that there were already organizations such as the European Economic Commission and proposed international trade organization which had been formed to fulfill many of the economic functions envisaged in this new project. He inquired whether we had in mind a large organization with a large secretariat.

We said that the need for the organization arose from the essentials of the program: That its activities would be limited to that sphere; that we saw no need for a large bureaucratic setup; and that other international organizations were not in a position to perform this work, which was essentially a matter of implementing the joint responsibilities of the participating countries in this particular enterprise.

We told the committee that a survey of the preliminary work indicated that the individual national requirements and production goals set forth in the committee reports do not reflect a concerted effort to direct European production, trade, and manpower, in the most efficient and economic manner, taking account of existing productive installations. For example, in determining the requirements of coal for steel production, account should be taken of the relative efficiencies of available plants, and other related matters. The report on steel avoided this problem by assuming that all existing steel capacity in the 16 participating countries would be operated at its maximum, beginning in 1948, and that there would be sufficient coal and transportation for this purpose. Since realistic estimates of coal and coke supplies indicate that the committee's optimistic expectations will not be fulfilled, attention must be given to an initial selective utilization of productive capacity, without regard to national boundaries.

Alphand remarked that the French Government had definite views on the question of utilization of productive steel capacity. Franks said that it was substantially correct that the basic approach to the Conference report had not been based on the establishment of standards or on the critical analysis of individual country programs. This was because:

(a) The terms of reference for the Conference made it clear that there would be no diminution of sovereignty and

(b) Lack of time prevented investigation of end use of required materials.

Nevertheless there had been scrutiny of the country reports and in two cases, pit-props and agricultural machinery, adjustments had been made. There were also one or two examples where country reports had undergone scrutiny because their stated requirements were out of line with their prewar consumption.

In closing we referred to the conversations which Ambassador Caffery had had during the week with individual members of the Committee regarding the necessity of coming up with a workable program even though it meant a major extension of the time period originally projected for the conference work. Sir Oliver replied that they had taken due note of this suggestion and had given up any idea of completing the report by September 1.

It is our understanding that Kennan will take up with you two matters of major importance:

(a) Our possible discussion directly at a high level of the objectives and conditions outlined above with the governments of certain countries and

(b) The question of full participation in the program by western Germany.

I am leaving today for a few days stay at St. Moritz, Palace Hotel, returning to Paris on September 6 or 7 where I shall stay until departing for London the evening of September 10.

Sent Department, repeated Geneva 162, London 690, Rome 223.

[Clayton]
CAFFERY

840.50 Recovery/8–3147 : Telegram

The Acting Secretary of State to the Secretary of State at Petropolis, Brazil

SECRET   WASHINGTON, August 31, 1947—10 a. m.
URGENT

137. For Carter from Humelsine. Eyes Only for Secretary Marshall from Lovett. Message from Kennan and Bonesteel indicates after con-

ferences Friday and Saturday morning with Clayton and Embassy staff they attended with Clayton meeting with Steering Committee of Conference. They say[:] "We both feel that visit thus far has been highly illuminating and worthwhile. In light of impressions gained Paris we strongly endorse Caffery's suggestion that time has come to present our views to governments directly". Kennan expected arrive Washington Wednesday evening Bonesteel one day later. Decision involved in quoted portion above can safely await your return and report of Kennan and Bonesteel.

Presidential party left on schedule this morning. All moving along well here.

See 4730, Aug 31, noon from London.[1]

Best regards,

LOVETT

---

[1] Not printed.

Policy Planning Staff Files

Memorandum by the Director of the Policy Planning Staff (Kennan)[1]

SECRET   [WASHINGTON,] September 4, 1947.

REPORT

SITUATION WITH RESPECT TO EUROPEAN RECOVERY PROGRAM [2]

I. PARIS

The representatives of the 16 European nations assembled at Paris have had the character of their work prescribed for them with considerable rigidity by the background of their meeting and the atmosphere in which it is taking place. By way of reaction to Soviet charges, there has been strong emphasis on national sovereignty (perhaps the only triumph of Molotov's visit to Paris). None of the delegates is a strong political figure domestically. There is none who could take any extensive liberties with the anxious reservations of the home governments. Finally, in the absence of the Russians the gathering has reverted, with a certain sense of emotional release, to the pattern of old-world courtesy and cordiality in which many of the participants were reared and for which they have instinctively longed throughout the rigors of a post-war diplomacy dominated by the Russian presence. This has practically ruled out any critical examination of the other fellow's figures—particularly as most of the delegates must have lively doubts as to the entire validity of some of their own, and cannot be eager to enter a name-calling contest between pot and kettle.

---

[1] Marginal notation: "Kennan Report on Paris Trip".
[2] Initialed "G.C.M."

It would be wrong to laugh at this gingerly approach or to put it all down to short-sighted timidity in the persons concerned. It reflects serious European realities which must be taken into account. Many of these governments are operating under formidable strains, internal and external. Some of them have internal economic problems with which they are politically too weak to cope. They do not want these problems spot-lighted and made critical issues by the Paris conference. Others, particularly the Scandinavians, are pathologically timorous about the Russians. Finding themselves somewhat unexpectedly in a gathering denounced by Molotov as politically wicked, they have the jumpy uncertainty of one who walks in pleasing but unaccustomed paths of sin. All of them are inhibited, I think, by the consciousness of what seem to them Herculean differences among the great powers over Germany and by the consequent feeling that the necessary center of any real European planning is beyond the effective scope of their activity. This conference reflects, in short, all the weakness, the escapism, the paralysis of a region caught by war in the midst of serious problems of long-term adjustment, and sadly torn by hardship, confusion and outside pressure.

In these circumstances, we must not look to the people in Paris to accomplish the impossible. That they can scale down their preliminary figure they have themselves admitted. That a further scaling down of that figure can be achieved by energetic pressure on the governments from our side, I think likely. That some sort of effort is being made to adjust the report in some measure to the suggestions advanced by Mr. Clayton on August 30 may be expected. As a result of all this, there will be a hopeful—and I think in large measure an honest—attempt to total up the cost of restoring production and of almost achieving "viability" throughout the region, in the light of such improvements of policy as the governments are now prepared to make. Perhaps a gesture or two will be made toward a reduction of the barriers to intra-European trade. A well-meant—and perhaps not entirely ineffective—appeal to the participating governments to put their financial houses in order may well be included.

But glaring deficiencies will remain. No bold or original approach to Europe's problems will be forthcoming. No startling design will emerge here for the removal of the pitiful dependence of much of this great peninsular area on overseas supplies for which it cannot pay. Worst of all: the report will not fulfill all of the essential requirements listed by Mr. Clayton in his remarks to members of the Executive Committee on August 30. And the total figure of aid required from outside will be considerably higher than it would need to be if it assumed the type of action by the governments, individually and collectively, which we would like to see.

II. CAUSES OF THE LIMITATIONS OF THE PARIS CONFERENCE

Before we attempt to draw conclusions from this state of affairs let us examine more carefully the causes of it. The main causes may be summed up as follows: (1) England, (2) Germany, and (3) general political conditions on the continent.

(1) *England.*

As late as September 3 the Committee was not intending to include in its report a breakdown by countries of the over-all balance of payments. I understand that the British opposed the inclusion of this item. The reason for this seems obvious: a breakdown would show the great extent to which western European viability, as a whole, is a question of the viability of the combined zones of Germany and even more of Britain itself. I do not have the exact figures; but I am sure it is no exaggeration to say that if these two areas could be eliminated from the calculations, the problem of most of the remainder would not be formidably difficult of solution.

Britain's position today is tragic to a point that challenges description. Her problems need no treatment here, except the reiteration that they are deep-seated and grave, and require for their solution all the coolness, the realism, the energy and the unity the British people can muster. In the face of this fact, as a body politic Britain is seriously sick. She is incapable of viewing her own situation realistically and dealing with it effectively.

This view is not confined to outsiders. It is admitted and even volunteered by individual Englishmen who have retained some clarity of vision; and it is coupled with an appeal to us, pitiable in the cost to national pride which it implies, to take responsibility, to find and announce the answer—to treat the British, in short, as a sick people and to tide them over until "they can recover their balance."

In these circumstances, it can be no great wonder that the largest component of the European recovery problem could not be treated on a basis which would satisfy our "essentials". The tragedy of the Labor Government lies in the fact that after waiting several decades for a chance to put certain principles into effect, it has finally come into power at precisely the moment when those principles became essentially inapplicable. It is too much to expect the leaders of that movement to recognize that, as an intellectual proposition, and to take the consequences out of their own logical deduction. Only the most dire practical necessity can push them to that point. But when they finally arrive there, they will have lost their justification for undertaking to rule the country; by that time conditions in England will have become quite intolerable; and the present leaders will be forced either to yield or to share governmental power with others. Only then, perhaps, will

England be prepared to take all the measures which she ought to take if she were to make a full contribution to European recovery. But by then, unless we have extended some further aid in the meantime, the deterioration may well have been so great that the cost of the problem will be greatly increased.

This deterioration is already progressing by leaps and bounds. It is exerting a cruel pressure on the government. This is probably desirable and necessary; and sensible Englishmen recognize this regretfully. But the usefulness of pressure has definite limits. It is incumbent on us to calculate those limits with the greatest of precision.

Meanwhile, we may hope that the British Government will come a certain distance toward a more realistic program and thus come closer to meeting our "essentials". But it is too much to hope that it can come all the way within the time allowed. A gap will remain—a gap in which British governmental behavior will be unrealistic, erratic, slap-happy.

It is our problem how to handle that gap. If we choose to hold the British Government fully responsible, as a rational body, and to treat it accordingly, we may have to despair of it—and of European recovery. If we choose to treat it as a sick man, then perhaps, by a judicious admixture of patience and pressure, we can string things out to a better state of affairs.

(2) *Germany.*

The bizonal administration in Germany answered the questionnaires submitted by the Conference in much the same way, I think, as did the other governments: honestly, against the background of present policies, and conceding to the Conference no authority whatsoever to change those policies. On the contrary, while the Conference was in progress, events continued to occur (failure to agree on the use of Benelux ports; failure to agree on purchase of European fish catch; level of industry talks) which made it evident that the chances of the Conference to influence the degree of integration of German economy into that of western Europe in general would remain meager indeed. It had no choice but to accept unquestioning the figures of the bizonal administration, as it accepted the figures of the other countries.

This is not to say that had things been otherwise—had the bizonal authorities participated in the Conference and shown a readiness to adjust their plans to the requirements of a European recovery program—the Conference would have tackled in a constructive and business-like way the working-out of an integrated program, making full and effective use of German economy. French inhibitions and fear of communist criticism would alone have prevented that. But the isolation of Germany from the effective scope of Conference action created an *a priori* block to any genuine attempt to get at the ills of the area—through the major international bottlenecks—and relieved the participants of a responsibility they would otherwise have had at least to bear and to face. In this sense, we share perhaps a portion of the responsibility for the failure of the Conference to meet the demands we ourselves imposed.

(3) *Political conditions.*

The ability of the delegates at Paris to draft a recovery program is no stronger than the ability and readiness of their respective governments to cooperate by measures of internal policy and by the acceptance of new international engagements. These acts require, in varying degrees, resolution, courage, clarity of vision, and ability to enlist popular support. Yet most of these governments are afflicted just at this time with abnormal weaknesses, fears and prejudices. The illness of which the British Government suffers is endemic among all governments in one degree or another. Britain's is an extreme case. But it is not the only severe case among the sixteen nations represented at Paris. And the work of the Conference cannot logically be stronger than the political and psychological fabric of the war-torn, fear-wracked, confused and maladjusted area which is the object of its labors.

Now there is none of these three main difficulties which will not yield to well placed effort over a long period of time. And for that reason the long-term chances for European recovery should not be underrated in the light of present impediments. But, on the other hand, there is none of these three factors which can be corrected within the brief period of grace which still remains before European conditions deteriorate beyond the saving-power of present concepts.

III. HOW HAS EUROPE RESPONDED TO THE HARVARD SPEECH?

The suggestions contained in the Harvard speech were predicated on the underlying thought that unless Europe could make a real effort on her own behalf, she would not be able to make any effective use of foreign assistance. The Secretary's observations had the effect of putting that question to the test.

Today we are in a position to gauge the answer. The answer is that Europe is only partially capable of making on her own behalf and within the time which circumstances will allow the effort which the Harvard speech envisaged—the remainder of the effort she would like to make, and probably will make in large part, given time and opportunity. But she cannot make it now.

Meanwhile the economic situation of two of the leading countries, namely England and France, is deteriorating with terrifying rapidity. If nothing is done for them within two to three months, they both face genuine hunger by winter, and other complications of unpredictable dimensions, with unforeseeable effects in other areas of the world.

IV. WHERE DO WE GO FROM HERE?

(a) First: as to the treatment of the report of the Paris Conference. Here we have the following alternatives:

1. We can let things take their course, receive a report which will not really be satisfactory, review it and reject it in due course, making no further effort to aid.

2. We can make efforts to have the report presented in such a way as to avoid any impression of finality; let it come to us on the understanding that it will be used only as a basis of further discussion; try to whittle it down as much as possible by negotiation; then give it final consideration in the Executive Branch of our Government and decide unilaterally what we finally wish to present to Congress. This would mean that we would listen to all that the Europeans had to say, but in the end we would not *ask* them, we would just *tell* them what they would get.

This last is what some of the more far-sighted of the Europeans hope we will do. They recognize that their report will inevitably be padded. They know that they themselves cannot pare it as it should be pared. As one of them said to me: "You people go ahead and cut it down. We will squawk over every cut. Never mind that. Most of your cuts will be justified, and we will squawk anyway. If any of your cuts are really unjustified, we will set up such a genuine and unmistakable howl that you will know you have made a mistake and you can then correct it." I know of nothing that better illustrates Europe's pathetic weakness, and Europe's consciousness of that weakness, than this remark.

Unquestionably, if we are prepared to recognize that Europe should be aided in spite of herself and if we wish a general aid program put in hand promptly this fall, then this second alternative is the one we should adopt.

(b) Secondly, as to the question of timing.

1. We can try to get an aid program through the next regular session of Congress, leaving ourselves plenty of time to thrash it out, giving Europe no other aid in the meantime, and hoping that it will not come apart at the seams before the aid becomes effective.

2. We can hold a special session of Congress before Christmas and try to jam through it a general aid program, the final dimensions of which would probably have to be determined unilaterally by ourselves as discussed under IV(a)2. Here again we would have to bet on Europe's holding out until the program could be effective.

3. We can attempt to evolve and implement voluntarily and without solicitation from the Europeans, an immediate or early emergency aid program to be administered by ourselves, along the lines of "Food and

Fuel for Europe" or some such slogan, leaving the general program to be dealt with expeditiously but in due course.

My own appraisal of the urgency of Europe's plight leads me to reject alternative No. 1 as giving us no plausible guaranty against a catastrophic deterioration of the world situation.

The choice is between No. 2 and No. 3, and there is much to be said for and against each of them.

On balance I favor No. 3. To evolve a really sound approach to Europe's problems is going to take time. The problems are so grave, so complex, so far-reaching, so critical for the future of our people and the world at large, that they should be dealt with in most orderly and considered manner. This cannot be done if we have the consciousness that people are starving while we deliberate. It cannot be done if the general atmosphere is one of panic and collapse. A short-term aid program would buy us time in which to deal deliberately and carefully with the long-term program. It could be publicly justified on this basis. Put in hand spontaneously by us, without request from Europe, it should do much to offset the vicious propaganda current in Europe as to the motives of our policies toward Europe. It need not constitute a violation of the principle of "no more piece-meal aid", because it could easily be so arranged that it would eventually either be absorbed into any general aid program which Congress might approve or terminate at once if Congress turned such a project down completely.

V. THE BASIC PROBLEM

The main consideration which inclines me to this last alternative is the impression which I am carrying back from Europe with me of the immense seriousness and complexity of the basic problem with which we are dealing. I am not sure that we have come anywhere near to finding the real answers within the scope of our present thinking. At last Saturday's meeting of Mr. Clayton with representatives of the Executive Committee, Sir Oliver Franks stubbornly insisted that he and his colleagues would not be honest, in the light of the data they had before them, if they did not show a small continued deficit at the end of the four-year period. Some of the members of our official family saw in this a violation of the principles on which the Europeans had been asked to approach this matter, and thus a cause for indignation. I could not share this feeling. What Franks was saying was simply that he and his colleagues were not sure that the area in question could really be made "viable" within the four-year period which they had selected for a program of aid. They felt that they were in honesty bound to face this fact.

I think this doubt legitimate. It arises primarily from the component doubts concerning the full efficacy of the present approach as a solution of the problems of England and Germany. In neither of these cases am I sure that we have faced the facts. The replies which were submitted by the bizonal area to the questionnaire sent in by the Paris Conference showed a future German economic development based on several optimistic assumptions. A key assumption, for example, was that the output of steel could be brought within four years to a figure of ten million tons per annum. Another was that adequate export markets would exist and that the terms of trade would develop in Germany's favor. Nevertheless, this reply, too, did not show complete hope of "viability" at the end of the four-year period.

In the case of England, the situation is similar. On the same sort of optimistic assumptions, people in Paris can see Britain at the end of the aid program almost self-sufficient, not quite. If these assumptions should prove to be unsubstantial, the gap would be greater.

But in the case of Britain things are complicated by the process of internal adjustment which is now wracking the British people and Government. We have seen that only the pressure of painful necessity can force a development in the right direction. But we have also seen that if the pressure of necessity gets too great, the result can be a breaking instead of a yielding—a catastrophe instead of an adjustment. For us to attempt to calculate with precision, on a day-by-day basis, the exact position of this point-with-no-return and to utilize the pressure of our foreign aid program to keep the British just close enough to this point without letting them go beyond it, seems to me to demand of us an operating flexibility which we do not enjoy, and therefore to involve tremendous political risks. I am afraid that in this case the whole process of adaptation which the British people must undergo will become fouled up with inevitable psychological by-products of a protracted relationship with us an [as] an object of charity.

And again, I see no guarantee of success. With many of England's traditional sources of income lost I think there is for her no satisfactory economic future, in the long run, which does not include (1) a long-term spontaneous flow of private capital from this country to England, and (2) a considerable freedom of labor and population to emigrate from areas in Britain where their presence is no longer economically justified to other continents, particularly our own. In other words, the problem of England's long-term economic future is one of flexible and fluid adaptation to the economies of this country and Canada.

I do not believe that this process can be successfully brought about by inter-governmental negotiations across the barriers which now divide these countries as independent and sovereign nations. For this reason I am more and more inclined to the feeling that there is no satisfactory solution for England's long-term problems, from the United States standpoint, than some closer form of association between England, Canada, and our own country: something which would involve a sharing of certain of the powers of sovereignty among the three countries. There is no necessity that a move in this direction should take the form of any sudden or abrupt act. It can well be planned as a gradual process, to be completed through a five or ten year program. But whatever it is, it should be threshed out and determined in this immediate period that lies before us, as part of the long-term problem of European recovery. And this, again, requires time for study, time for the preparation of public opinion, and time for careful and highly complicated negotiation.

VI. SUMMARY

In short, the long-term problem before us seems to me to be a deeper, more far-reaching, and more complex one than any of us have realized. We cannot deal successfully with a program of this nature on the spur of the moment or under the abnormal pressure which would be caused by a further deterioration of conditions in Europe.

For this reason, we must undertake at once an interim aid program with which to buy time. If we do this, then both problems—the short-term one and the long-term one—may still be solved. If we do not do it, we shall solve neither the one nor the other.

840.50 Recovery/9–547 : Telegram

The Ambassador in France (Caffery) to the Secretary of State

TOP SECRET PARIS, September 5, 1947—8 p. m.
US URGENT

3610. For Lovett, Thorp, Ness and Nitze from Department Economic Advisers. 1. Present information re conclusion of Conference of European Economic Cooperation work in Paris indicates that technical committee reports will be considered by Executive Committee and approved early next week and general report by end next week. CEEC will probably be convened about September 15 for final action on reports. Some CEEC delegates may not have necessary authorization to approve reports on behalf their governments and transmit to Secretary Marshall. Accordingly, it might be expected that reports will be transmitted to participating governments for consideration and action.

However, present working of general report indicates it is intended for Secretary Marshall. Moreover, Franks and Marris[1] have expressed their hope and expectation that reports will be approved promptly by participating governments in substantially present form and formally transmitted to Secretary. Therefore, Department should not overlook possibility of this outcome and should, in our opinion, consider appropriate course of action. Several possible courses discussed below.

2. Publicity now being given to technical subcommittee reports. Press conferences have been held regarding reports on fuel and energy, and maritime transport. It is apparently intended to hold press conferences on other reports in near future. Franks and Marris have expressed opinion that publication of reports, presumably upon transmission to participating governments or to Secretary, would be desirable. It appears reasonably certain that key CEEC individuals in Paris intend to give widespread publicity to reports.

3. Our present information is that figure for total deficit for entire period is being revised downward from $29.2 billion figure previously reached and mentioned in newspapers. Franks has already indicated aggregate deficit could be reduced by about $5 billion through elimination of capital expansion items. Information is not yet available as to extent of ultimate reduction in aggregate deficit figure or basis on which this reduction will be calculated. We are fairly certain reductions made to date have not thus far been reflected in substantial revision of technical subcommittee reports on net commodity requirements.

We are informed that reductions are being made in aggregate net requirements for food, coal and timber without regard to revision of each country's annual net requirements for those commodities. Adjustments are also being made in dollar price co-efficients for some of these commodities in order to reduce aggregate estimated deficit.

According to present information, balance of payments summary will be for sixteen countries in aggregate without individual country breakdown although it is inconceivable that net deficits by individual countries will not be presented at some point.

4. It is belief of Department Economic Advisers that reports in their present form, and as they will probably be approved by Executive Committee, do not constitute acceptable basis for recommendation to Congress and do not meet US conditions as presented by Clayton August 30 (Embtel 3543, August 31). Reports of technical committees are merely compilations of individual country statements of commodity requirements from outside sources. (These committee reports are now largely unrelated to latest adjusted estimates of aggregate

---

[1] Adam D. Marris, deputy leader, United Kingdom Delegation, CEEC.

dollars deficit and of aggregate net commodity requirements.) These reports reflect little or no mutual criticism and screening. They contain no signs of cooperation by sixteen participants to provide maximum assistance to each other. They evidence insufficient attempt to provide for most effective use of critically scarce resources particularly coal, coke, timber and transport facilities. They indicate no acknowledgement of probable necessity of adjusting standards of living to realities of European situation including capability to produce and possible aid from abroad. Reports fail to distinguish between capital requirements for reactivation of basic industries from capital requirements for longrun projects which should be financed outside of program.

Financial report contains no assurance that effective steps toward internal financial stabilization will in fact be taken.

5. Some CEEC technical experts have acknowledged to us that reports are generally unsatisfactory and also fail to meet US conditions. It is evident that CEEC delegations do not feel their terms of reference permit them to prepare reports along lines which meet US conditions. This situation can be remedied only by new instructions from sixteen governments to their delegations in Paris. Such new instructions will come only, if at all, as a result of vigorous and direct representations by US Govt to other govts concerned.

6. Immediate problem is action, if any, to be taken by US Govt with respect to: (*a*) formal submission of CEEC reports to US Govt and (*b*) formal publication thereof. If US Government takes no action, prospects are that reports in substantially present form will soon be submitted to Secretary as final program of sixteen participating governments in response to his Harvard address. This might conceivably jeopardize acceptance in US of aid program for Europe because it could lead to impression in US of inability of sixteen govts to formulate realistic and defensible program. Consequences of US rejection or prolonged debate might be to embitter European peoples with resulting unfavorable political and economic repercussions. If for these reasons Department determines that positive action respecting (*a*) or (*b*) above is required, immediate approaches to top officials of UK, French, Belgium, Netherlands, and Italian Governments would seem to be necessary in order to assure desired results by tentative September 15 deadline.

7. Most effective way of avoiding consequences outlined paragraph six above would be to take action designed to prevent formal transmission of present reports to US Government and possibly also their publication. Department may accordingly wish to suggest to key governments that reports of CEEC should be submitted to participating governments for consideration rather than directly and formally

to US Government. If steps to assure this result are taken, participating governments should also be urged to issue new instructions to their delegations in Paris enabling them to prepare reports consistent with US conditions. This would have to be done immediately to permit delegations to prepare new reports, preferably by November 1, so as to leave time for examination of reports in Washington prior to submission to Congress. If such developments were assured, present reports could be published as preliminary documents to serve as working papers for second phase of CEEC work. It is believed by Department Economic Advisers that publication under these circumstances would be much less damaging than otherwise. Course of action outlined above would involve vigorous confidential representations to participating governments at this time but would avoid subsequent public rejection by executive branches US Government of unsatisfactory, but European approved program. If completion of program consistent with US conditions extends beyond November 1, or if prolonged Congressional consideration after January is required, Department must of course give immediate attention to question of interim aid.

8. Department may not wish to make representations to participating governments along lines suggested in paragraph seven above since this might appear to violate principle of Marshall address that program should be prepared on European initiative. In that event, US Government should strongly urge participating countries to label reports as tentative and as basis for further exploration of problem by participating countries themselves. This action would at least make subsequent reconsideration easier than if faulty reports are published as final program but would not avoid danger that their formal submission and publication might conceivably prejudice success of entire project.

9. In urging participating governments to adopt new approach and issue new instructions adequate to meet US conditions, US Government should state to them that it is prepared to instruct US military authorities in Germany to cooperate with CEEC countries on same basis and to same extent as participating governments. This would greatly strengthen US position in urging new approach. US control over final distribution of aid (as outlined in Deptel 3195, August 27, 1947 [2]) will enable us to protect position of bizonal area.

Sent Dept 3610, repeated Geneva for Clayton 165, London for Douglas 707.

CAFFERY

---

[2] Telegram 3195, August 26, p. 383.

840.50 Recovery/9–547 : Telegram

The Secretary of State to the Embassy in the United Kingdom

SECRET   WASHINGTON, September 5, 1947—11 a. m.
US URGENT   NIACT

3841. For Ambassador. War and State have agreed that economic plans of bizonal area should be discussed with CEEC with view to integrating bizonal area into a European recovery program.

Before making any announcement to CEEC, agreement with British obviously necessary. Pls take this matter up with Brit urgently to obtain their approval of joint statement to be made to CEEC substantially as follows:

"Answers have already been furnished to CEEC questionnaires covering the bizonal area of Germany administered by the US and UK. In addition, the CEEC has received the revised level of industry plan agreed between the US and UK for the bizonal area.[1] The US and UK recognize that the CEEC, in developing a program for economic recovery, will discuss the various national plans and requirements of participating countries with a view to achieving the maximum European self-help and the most efficient use of existing facilities. The bizonal area in Germany potentially can make a substantial contribution to European recovery. Integration of the bizonal area into a European recovery program carried out by all participating countries will facilitate the contribution which the bizonal area can make while at the same time further the self-support of that area, which is a necessary part of European economic recovery.

The US and UK are therefore prepared to discuss with the CEEC the economic programs of the bizonal area to the same extent that CEEC discusses the plans and requirements submitted by the participating countries. The purpose of such discussions would be to develop recommendations as to the use of facilities in the bizonal area, the priorities in industrial reactivation and in the use and allocation of scarce materials in the same manner as CEEC is considering the same subjects with respect to the participating countries, all with the purpose of achieving an integrated recovery program covering both the participating countries and the bizonal area. The bizonal area cannot fulfill its potential of assistance to European recovery unless the needs of its presently depressed economy are recognized. It is to be understood that such discussions will be on a technical basis. Furthermore, the US and UK must always take into account their special responsibilities as occupying powers and the very large expense now involved in maintaining the bizonal area. Within the above principles, the US and UK are prepared to give careful consideration to recommendations made by CEEC with respect to integrating the bizonal area into a broader recovery program. The US further wishes to emphasize that its participation in such discussions is not to be construed as US Govt approval of any program that may be developed nor as

[1] See footnote 3, p. 332.

any commitment with respect to US aid to carry out any recovery program."

If Brit agree to joint statement,[2] it is proposed that OMGUS representatives who are familiar with level of industry plan and economic situation in bizonal area would immediately join US representatives now attached to Paris Embassy to work on CEEC matters, with perhaps additional staff from War and State. Statement would be delivered to CEEC and arrangements made for prompt consultation.

Will Clayton and Ambs Caffery and Murphy pls send London urgently any comments repeating to Dept. War has agreed to this message.[3]

Sent London, rptd Paris, Geneva for Clayton, Berlin.

MARSHALL

---

[2] See last paragraph, telegram 4951, September 12, from London, p. 429.
[3] Ambassador Murphy on September 8, replied in telegram 340 from Frankfurt as follows: "I concur in text of proposed statement to CEEC. It seems unquestionable to us here that Anglo-American zones of western Germany can and should make substantial contribution to European recovery and without such contribution recovery program is obviously jeopardized. We are also glad to note that alongside question of priorities in industrial reactivation emphasis is also laid on needs of Germany's presently depressed economy. You of course recognize inherent risk in this approach of temptation on part of European countries to obtain indirect financing from US and possibility of an easy tendency to interpret military government commitments in this connection as US Government commitments." (840.50 Recovery/9–847)

840.50 Recovery/9–647 : Telegram

The Acting Secretary of State to President Truman

TOP SECRET WASHINGTON, September 6, 1947—noon.

US URGENT

1025. Eyes Only for the President [1] from Secretary of State. There is every indication that the economic situation in Europe is deteriorating rapidly and seriously. It is now apparent that some of the more important countries, notably Italy, France and England, and possibly some of the others, will be in a dangerous position before the end of the year. This has resulted in part from the factors with which you are already familiar; but the process is being materially aggravated and hastened by the crop failures in Western Europe and by the emergency measures recently taken in England.

Reports along this line are already increasing in Washington, and press and radio are full of comment and speculation about our reaction. As you have seen, Lovett was closely questioned on this subject at his press conference on Wednesday and, while he refused comment on special session or other form of Congressional hearings before end

---

[1] President Truman on a state visit to Brazil had addressed the closing session of the Inter American Conference for the Maintenance of Continental Peace and Security at Petropolis, Brazil. For documentation regarding the Conference, see vol. VIII, pp. 1 ff.

of year, there is no doubt questions at my press conference next Wednesday will continue to center on this point. In the circumstances I feel I should make some type of statement.

There follows text of statement to be made if it meets with your approval:

"We have been following carefully the reports of the economic situation of the various European countries.

"We see the requirements of these countries as falling into two phases of one program: first, some form of interim assistance to meet the immediate threat of intolerable hunger and cold; and second, the general program for rehabilitation of the respective economies.

"The nature of the long-term problem of European reconstruction and our attitude toward it remain basically unchanged. But the short-term problem has become more immediate. Bad droughts, following an unusually severe winter, increasing crop shortages and restrictive financial measures which certain European governments have already been obliged to take, have had serious repercussions and have accelerated the need of some European countries for assistance in reducing hunger and cold this winter.

"In these circumstances this phase of the requirements will clearly have to be given our urgent consideration and cannot await the completion of the broader study which the over-all program demands.

"We expect that, by the latter part of October, we will have available working papers on the basis of which the appropriate Congressional committees could undertake consideration of means to supplement European supplies of food and fuel for the coming winter where it can be shown that every effort has been made locally to meet the critical needs. The majority of the Congressional committees visiting Europe will have returned by that time. We hope that shortly thereafter the complete data for the European Recovery Program can be screened and made available in order that the problem may be faced in its entirety and that any action taken to meet immediate needs may be correlated into the general program.

"The question of how the necessary Congressional authority is to be obtained must await developments of the next few weeks." [2]

[Marshall.]
LOVETT

---

[2] The text of this statement by the Secretary of State was released to the press on September 10.

840.50 Recovery/9–647 : Telegram

The Ambassador in France (Caffery) to the Embassy in the United Kingdom

SECRET   PARIS, September 6, 1947—1 p. m.
NIACT

[711.] [1] For Douglas from Caffery. As indicated last paragraph my 3451, August 26 to the Department, repeated to London as 675, I be-

---

[1] The text printed here is from telegram 3617 to the Department of State, a repetition of telegram 711 to London.

lieve that program European economic recovery will be greatly strengthened by full participation western Germany. I therefore concur in proposed US–UK statement for bizone as outlined Department's 3841, to London, repeated Paris as 3336, Berlin as 1809. I suggest that it would be desirable, in order to assure participation all of western Germany, to ask French Government whether it is disposed to issue a collateral statement re French zone. Department's instructions by telegram requested.[2]

Re foregoing, Benelux representative Executive Committee told me this morning that he believed participation western Germany would strengthen efforts being made to convince Switzerland and the Scandinavian countries that all countries should participate in customs union study group and that conference report should make adequate provision for a continuing organization. In view of fact that conference report is nearing completion, I believe announcement should be made at earliest possible moment.

Sent to London for Douglas as 711; repeated Department as 3617; USPolAd Berlin as 344, copy held for Clayton.

CAFFERY

---

[2] The Department replied in telegram 3365 of September 7, 1947 that once the British agreed to a joint statement, it was "desirable to notify French and inquire whether they wish to issue parallel statement re French zone." (840.50 Recovery/9–747)

840.50 Recovery/9–747 : Circular Telegram

The Acting Secretary of State to Diplomatic Representatives Accredited to Countries Participating in the Conference of European Economic Cooperation and to the United States Political Adviser for Germany (Murphy)[1]

TOP SECRET   WASHINGTON, September 7, 1947—1 a. m.
US URGENT

To certain American diplomatic officers. 1. You are requested soonest and not later than Tuesday to present orally to FonMin or at your discretion to FonMin and Prime Minister substance of following:

2. Admittedly incomplete info received by US Govt as to present content proposed report by Conference on European Economic Cooperation, which they now expect to complete about 15 Sept, is that it has numerous deficiencies which if publicized as final report by Europeans in response SecState's Harvard speech would make it unacceptable to State Dept, would undoubtedly evoke strong criticism in

---

[1] The telegram which went to Paris was addressed to both Ambassador Caffery and Under Secretary of State Clayton.

US and consequently endanger US support of any more reasonable or more realistic European aid program.

3. Indications are that CEEC report may state requirements greatly exceeding potential aid available and that whole program shows little more than lip service to principles of European self help and mutual help.

4. US recognizes political difficulties of participating Govts in conforming national programs and objectives to a cooperative program and subordinating separate national aims where necessary. US believes, however, that recognition this principle essential to US acceptance of program and that political consequences of rejection by US of any aid program immeasurably worse. It was US hope that concept and practice of cooperation would arouse response in European countries as positive approach toward defeating difficulties against which participating countries have been trying to defend selves. As to food, US recognizes political difficulty of Govt's planning for less than satisfactory feeding, and that trimming of program to fit realities of supply situation will come after program submitted and checked against supplies available and possible. Reducing this trimming to minimum, however, should be one objective of drafting program.

5. Under Sec. Clayton is being asked by Dept to take up at once with Exec. Comm., CEEC, a suggested course of action and time schedule aimed at deferring completion present CEEC report by ten days to permit participating Govts to instruct delegates their views as to recasting of report to have it concentrate emphasis on principles, clearly indicate that report is not final but represents completion initial steps of preparing document useful as basis of further discussion, and that initial technical reports require further work by technical committees to correct original deficiencies. (Note: Cable to Clayton being repeated to you for info and background. Please avoid implying interim aid or special session.) [2]

6. US reps at Paris have already communicated to Exec. Comm. of CEEC main essentials which are believed necessary to make program workable and to enhance probability of acceptance. Technical experts of participating countries at Paris possibly may not have communicated these fully to their Govts, and instructions of participating Govts to their reps at Paris may not permit appropriate weight being given these essential aspects in Paris. Hence, US Govt is communicating them directly to participating Govts.

7. Main essentials follow:

a. The achievement within the four-year period of a workable European economy independent of special, outside aid.

---

[2] Circular telegram of September 7, 1947—2 a. m., *infra.*

b. Continuous and progressive reduction in the special outside aid required by the participating countries to the point where it will become eliminated by the end of the period.

c. The participating countries must from time to time during the period of the program show convincing evidence that they have made substantial progress toward the scheduled goals of production of items essential to European recovery, especially food and coal.

d. Long-run development projects should not be allowed to interfere with the reactivation of the most efficient existing productive facilities. The latter must have first priority. The financing of long-term projects must be obtained from sources outside this program.

e. The participating countries to undertake the necessary internal financial and monetary measures to stabilize their currencies, establish and maintain proper rates of exchange, and generally restore confidence in their monetary systems.

f. The participating countries to take concerted steps to facilitate the greatest practicable interchange of goods and services among themselves, adopting definite measures directed toward the progressive reduction and eventual elimination of barriers to trade within the area, in accordance with the principles of the ITO Charter.

g. The participating countries must regard the conditions mentioned above as a common European responsibility and, therefore, should envisage use of some continuing multilateral organization which from time to time will review and take stock of the progress achieved by participating Govts under the program.

8. In communicating these views, US reps made clear that they were not attempting to dictate, and that no commitment by US was involved.

9. US believes that genuine acceptance and vigorous application of foregoing principles and maximization of inter-European cooperation in restoration of production and economic patterns of trade and finance will make possible dynamic program in which Europe, with minimum external aid, can start on path toward healthy economic recovery. When this recovery begins, resources, now latent or hoarded, should emerge and become part of productive effort and further reduce necessity for external assistance.

10. US recognizes that problem of workable European economy independent of special outside aid at end of four years divides into problems of 1) Europe's ability to produce goods and services; 2) Europe's ability to market such goods. While existence of latter problem is recognized, its immediacy is far less than former. First problem and immediate concern of US is production.

11. From point of view of public reaction both in Europe and US, our view is that report should put primary emphasis on positive steps being taken by Europe; the manner in which commodity aid from US can assist positive steps rather than plea for continuing flow of US dollars.

12. In closing presentations to FonMins, points should be made that 1) CEEC to date has perhaps been too much on technical level with delegates unable to cut through instructions so as to concert on and actually apply principles of maximum production and cooperative self-help; 2) opponents of program in US will magnify any indication aid is being requested from US to take up slackness by Europeans; 3) basic chance for success of European recovery program depends on popular European desire to make it work, to which end national approach solely through little understood technical planning will not suffice.[3]

13. For your info, we are now trying to get British concurrence to our proposal to make joint announcement that we will discuss at once bizonal German plans in CEEC with view to integrating into area recovery program. Will advise as soon as cleared. If you receive word before seeing FonMin, it should be incorporated in your oral statement, but you should not delay presentation to await such word as it can be made subject of separate approach.

LOVETT

---

[3] Replies from the American missions indicated that these views received sympathetic consideration by the various foreign ministers. The replies are in file 840.50 Recovery.

840.50 Recovery/9–747 : Circular Telegram

The Acting Secretary of State to Diplomatic Representatives Accredited to Countries Participating in the Conference of European Economic Cooperation and to the U.S. Political Adviser for Germany (Murphy)

TOP SECRET   WASHINGTON, September 7, 1947—2 a. m.
US URGENT

To certain American diplomatic offices. For Clayton and Caffery.
1. Have given careful consideration to action to be taken in light of (a) prospect Paris Conference report will be unsatisfactory as now being drafted, and (b) rapid deterioration of situation France, Italy and U.K. probably requiring action by US before end of year.

2. Department sending instructions (See circtel of this date repeated to you) to U.S. missions in each of participating countries with view of bringing pressure directly on participating governments in effort to secure (a) improvement present draft for issuance as preliminary report, and (b) continuance of conference after such issuance to develop more concrete proposals for mutual and self help and more accurate and thoroughly screened statistics than would be possible in short period of time. Circtel gives Department views on defects of

Paris operation to date and line we assume you will continue to press on Paris conferees.

3. Propose that with aid of this pressure you and staff available in Paris continue to work with Paris Conference in effort to secure report by about September 21st, correct at least as to major policy lines. Department view is that this report be submitted to governments and to US with clear indication that it is preliminary, is intended as basis for further discussions, and is subject to future supplementation and amendment, particularly as to data and concrete implementation of principles. Department believes that it is not feasible to prevent publication of report, but it must contain such covering language as will make its tentative character clear.

4. Department proposes that agreement of Paris Conference and governments of participating countries be secured to a continuance of Paris Conference after publication preliminary report with purpose of screening and coordinating statistics and of translating general policies of self and mutual help into concrete implementation. Understand from Kennan and Bonesteel that you are thinking along same lines

5. Such continuation also necessary to (*a*) supply the detailed information we shall need for screening here in light of U.S. availabilities and justification before Congress as outlined 7 below, and (*b*) permit conference to consider and perhaps adjust its program in the light of results of such screening. As part of this process it will be necessary that data be available on country by country basis. To make continuation effective, conference must give new instructions to working committees. To assist working committees to understand our requirements for screening, presentation and justification purposes U.S. representatives should be available to sit in with Committees on informal advisory basis.

6. Propose that this process of revision and refinement be conducted on time schedule, agreed to by Conference, which will make available final supporting evidence for 1948 and at least revised skeleton presentation for entire period for key items by Nov. 1, 1947, and complete revised presentation for entire period by Dec. 15, 1947. This is for use by U.S. in presentation and does not prevent further revisions as new good or bad conditions arise.

7. Department envisages that program submitted to Congress will in any event have to be retailored from even best probable Paris presentation in the light of potential availabilities in the U.S. which will be far less, particularly as to food, than the minimums which the governments of the participating countries can support domestically as being their requirements.

8. In order to make task outlined in 4 fully effective, it is proposed to announce, subject to favorable response from Douglas on British reaction (See Deptel 3336 to Paris [1]), that Bizonal area of Germany, including U.S. governmental representatives, will take full part in continuing effort to produce integrated program containing maximum mutual help. To aid you in these discussions Clay expected to send personnel from Germany and Department will send representative soon.

9. This schedule for work in Paris is based on tentative thinking that Congressional Committees be called about November 15, and possibility that special session might be called for about December 1–15. If interim assistance is required, as now seems likely to Department, it must be presented to special session as interim installment of Marshall program and be substantiated as directly as possible by data contained in Paris Conference Report and its revisions. Therefore necessary to interim aid not only that report referred to in 3 be available, but that the progress looked for in 4 be on schedule so that presentation can be made to Congress along following lines:

10. Conference completed report correct in principle but inadequate in detail due to short period of time available to date for preparing and analyzing data of great complexity. Though report inadequate in this respect, satisfactory revision and supplementation is in process as evidenced by progress reports received as result of work described in 4. More time is necessary to complete this work, to screen the program in the light of U.S. availabilities, and to permit adequate Congressional review. This fact combined with unexpectedly rapid deterioration of economic conditions in several European countries makes it necessary to adopt an interim assistance program as a first element in the Marshall plan for aiding the recovery of the European economy. This first step can be taken in full confidence that completed program with full details will be available for U.S. action shortly.

11. Believed here that even moderate success for proposed plan of action largely dependent on U.K. attitude. Realize difficult character of decisions involved for U.K. in committing herself to European approach, and difficult internal problems of present government, partly deriving from its own makeup. Would appreciate yours and Douglas' suggestions as to any further steps which might be taken to secure full U.K. cooperation along lines we think will be most conducive to success both in Europe and in U.S.

LOVETT

---

[1] Not printed.

840.50 Recovery/9–847 : Telegram

The Secretary of State to the Embassy in the United Kingdom

TOP SECRET   WASHINGTON, September 8, 1947—9 p. m.
NIACT

3903. For the Ambassador. British opposition, reported by you by phone to Bonesteel,[1] to discussing bizonal area economic program in CEEC with view to coordination with a broader CEEC recovery program focuses attention on problems of utmost seriousness. As stressed in all US communications with CEEC, essence of Secretary's proposals was preparation of program based on maximum European self-help and mutual aid and that such a program could only be prepared if the separate national programs and requirements statements were examined and coordinated so as to produce the greatest European contribution to recovery at earliest moment. Most recent US action along this line is contained in Dept's circtel, Sept 7 (1 a. m.) in which heads of missions to CEEC countries requested to make oral representations stressing that a program developed by CEEC which did not emphasize and show tangible evidence of application of the principle of mutual aid would run serious risk of being unacceptable to US.

Dept's impression as confirmed by reports from Conference and all senior US reps who have had contact with Conference activities is that element of mutual aid and subordination of separate national aims to cooperative approach has been generally lacking.

The force of US pressure to achieve this cooperative approach is seriously weakened if the one European area in which the US has direct responsibility abstains. As pointed out in London's 4552 (repeated to Paris as 469), holding ourselves aloof from mutual discussion of separate programs will only encourage other participants to subordinate the cooperative approach to their individual national objectives. In recognition of this fact, Dept had hoped to include in the oral representations made pursuant to Dept's circtel Sept 7 (1 a. m.) the offer to consider bizonal German plans in CEEC. If British position prevails and we withhold discussion of bizonal area, we can hardly expect to be successful in opposing a French desire to protect Monnet Plan, Scandinavian tendency to withdraw from full participation and other centrifugal forces working against a coordinated area approach.

Dept questions Bevin's statement that bizonal area being adequately discussed. Dept has no evidence that appropriate discussion has taken place and reports from Conference have indicated that Conference

---

[1] In addition to his duties as Special Assistant to Under Secretary of State Lovett, Colonel Bonesteel in September became vice-chairman and executive secretary of the newly-formed interdepartmental Advisory Steering Committee on the European Recovery Program.

considered discussing Germany outside its jurisdiction. (Paris' 3325 [2] and 3327 to Dept, rptd London as number not known and 649) London's 4552 (repeated to Paris as 469) expresses view that in absence of US delegate, UK representatives not considered by CEEC adequate spokesmen for bizonal area.

Provision in CEEC II report [3] of mining machinery exports from bizonal area of only $13 million 1948–51, rough bizonal output expected to reach $1,000 million, suggests lack of adequate discussion of bizonal figures in CEEC. Similar impression from absence in CEEC III report [3] of any net steel exports from Germany after 1947.

Dept analyzes Brit position as reflecting Brit reluctance to coordinate its recovery program with that of western Europe. So long as bizonal area, for which US has direct responsibility, is not correlated with CEEC program, US sanctions exclusion of certain areas of western Europe from program, and this justifies Brit excluding themselves. It appears to the Dept that Brit wish to benefit fully from a European program as suggested by Sec State while at the same time maintaining the position of not being wholly a European country.

Thus the offer of appropriate discussion in CEEC of bizonal program in effect raises question of whether Brit program must be subject to same discussion. Dept does not desire to use bizonal offer as occasion to force the issue with Brit on this matter.

Dept therefore recommends that in your discussion with Bevin and Franks, you explore the Brit position on both the UK and the bizonal area relation to CEEC, that you point out that failure of bizonal area to participate genuinely in CEEC in preparation of program along the line described in Dept's Circular of Sept 7 (1 a.m.) may seriously prejudice the achieving of such a program. You should point out the difficult position of the US if it urges cooperative approach to sixteen nations while withholding cooperation on behalf of the bizonal area. You should urge the Brit to consider the consequences of their reluctance to join with the US proposal regarding the bizonal area and to make every effort to evolve a position which would permit the carrying out of the line of action suggested in Dept's 3841. You might point out that proposed offer to discuss bizonal program is subject to conditions in Dept's 3841 and, pursuant to schedule foreseen in circtel Sept 7 (2 a.m.) would presumably take place in course of revisions to be made after publication initial CEEC report.

Repeated to Paris as 3393.

MARSHALL

---

[2] Not printed.
[3] Reports prepared by CEEC technical committees and circulated as conference documents as basic material for preparation of the final report of the conference.

840.50 Recovery/9–947 : Telegram

The Ambassador in the United Kingdom (Douglas) to the Secretary of State

TOP SECRET   LONDON, September 9, 1947—7 p. m.

NIACT

4888. This afternoon I called on Bevin, Hall-Patch, and Makins [1] present, at the Foreign Office and took up with them the contents of Deptel circular September 7, 1 a.m.

They pointed out that the seven main essentials were not new to them, and that they were trying to incorporate them in the final report of the CEEC. However, they feel that any further attempt at screening now would only tend to slow up the report and that they cannot change the time-table. Bevin feels that it is impossible to postpone the meeting of the Ministers already publicly called, and announced for September 15, to receive the conference report. To do so, the British thought, might cause such dismay that the work of the conference so far made might come to naught. Sir Oliver Franks had, they thought, carried the participating countries as far toward a cooperative effort as is possible. Any effort to press further would, they feared, so impair national sovereignty that many countries would rebel, particularly since the Soviet had already threatened some with withholding coal if they proceeded.

They suggest that the report will give Franks authority to call Committee on Cooperation into session for further discussion and additional work if it seems advisable.

Bevin has not had opportunity to acquaint himself with details of report, but is sending Hall-Patch to Paris with me tomorrow.

In view of the foregoing, it would have been futile to press for a decision on the bizonal statement until after I have had an opportunity to discuss matter with Clayton in Paris and to determine arrangements for continuing work of conference which report may announce. If continuing work is provided for, I will then take up again matter of bizonal participation.

Clayton will attempt to meet with Executive Committee tomorrow at five if he hears from Franks that all members will have heard from their Governments by that time. If not, Executive Committee will meet on Thursday morning.

Sent Dept as 4888, repeated Berlin 429, Paris (for Clayton and Caffery) 506.

DOUGLAS

---

[1] Sir Edmund Hall-Patch, Deputy Under-Secretary of State, and Roger M Makins, Assistant Under-Secretary of State, in the British Foreign Office.

940.50 Recovery/9–1147 : Telegram

The Ambassador in France (Caffery) to the Secretary of State

SECRET

US URGENT

PARIS, September 11, 1947—5 p. m.

3696. For the Secretary and Lovett from Clayton, Caffery, and Douglas. We met yesterday evening with the Executive Committee to outline the key points of the Department's circular telegram of September 7, 2 a. m.

We told them that we considered it highly desirable that the formal conference meeting be postponed pending further work on the report. In view of fact that meeting of Foreign Ministers had already been called for September 15, individual delegates had indicated to us that it would be politically impossible to postpone conference consideration (and probably adoption) of the report.

We then said that our examination of the draft report, plus Departmental scrutiny of conference documents, lead us to conclude that the report in its present form would, if adopted as final, produce an unfavorable impression in the United States and jeopardize the entire program. We strongly urged, therefore, that if it were necessary to issue a report on September 15, it should be so phrased as to clearly indicate that it was of a preliminary or tentative character. If transmitted in its present form, without clear explanation that there would be further work done on it, it was extremely doubtful whether the report could be regarded in the US as a workable program for European economic recovery. As a few examples of weaknesses in the proposed presentation we outlined the following:

1. The balance of payments calculation included large financial provision for capital equipment. From the technical reports we had found that these totalled approximately $2 billion for such items as steel plants, power installations, oil refining and railroad equipment. These items appeared to be outside of the range of such short-term capital equipment as farm and mining machinery and they were properly the subject for consideration by the International Bank or private lending agencies but should not be presented in a form which carried the implication that the United States Government was expected to finance their cost. There were also capital equipment items under category of non-programmed items, outside the work of the technical committees, (approximately $2.5 billion) which had been included in balance of payments estimates submitted by individual countries.

2. The petroleum estimates were prepared on the assumption of no gasoline rationing in Europe. Opponents in the US to the Marshall proposal would be certain to emphasize that the American taxpayer was being requested to pay for European "joy riding".

3. The food and agriculture report had failed to segregate commodity import requirements by sources of supply.

4. The provisions regarding trade liberalization and financial stabilization were in vague form and needed to be "sharpened up" in order to clearly set forth that the participating countries were directing their efforts toward the objectives we had outlined. Chapter on financial and fiscal reforms indicated that no steps could be taken until aid from US had been extended and until production had been substantially increased. This we said was quite unsatisfactory. Franks, after the meeting, told us that our comments in this respect had been most helpful since they strengthened his hand in having the chapter re-written with wholly different emphasis.

The five Executive Committee members then spoke individually and it became apparent that they had previously reached agreement on a joint position which may be summarized as follows:

1. It is not possible to label the report as tentative or preliminary. Such an approach would indicate that the conference was a failure and political repercussions in Europe would be serious.

2. The committee was prepared to indicate in the text that the report was "provisional" in some respects which could indicate that it was expected that some adjustments would be made but would not create the implication that it was to be replaced by a new report. In this connection it was necessary to keep in mind the importance of public reaction in Europe as well as in the US. The Scandinavian delegate (with Russia in mind) emphasized the political as well as the economic difficulties which had faced the conference in its work.

3. A short period of delay would not permit a fundamental change in the structure of the report. It is recognized that the measure of agreement falls short of US essentials in some cases. The difficulties in part arise from the terms of reference of the Conference and in part from national decisions at a Cabinet level. To meet entirely the US conception of a program would require a change in the terms of reference and this would mean a new conference which might not include all of the countries participating in the present work.

4. The Conference during the next few days is prepared to make such adjustments as appear desirable in the report short of major policy changes which would require decisions by the home governments. It is believed that these adjustments can meet some of our criticisms but there is no possibility of the present Conference agreeing on an integrated plan. In this connection, Sir Oliver Franks remarked that some people in the US Government apparently had in mind a form of "dirigisme" under which an overall control agency would plan and regulate the basic economic activity of the individual countries.

5. The Conference was ready to prepare its report in a form which would clearly set forth that the Executive Committee, supported by groups of technicians, was prepared to go to Washington to mutually review the program with us and that the chairman be authorized to reconvene the Conference in the light of the Washington conversations.

6. Sir Oliver Franks told us separately that it had been impossible to obtain agreement on a specific undertaking for the formation of a multilateral organization. He had, however, been able to bring the delegates to the point of agreeing on a statement recognizing that if

the necessary means for carrying out the program are made available, it will be desirable for the participating countries mutually to consult together in order to review the plan's execution and to insure an economic development leading to the realization of the general objectives to which they had pledged themselves.

We made two additional observations re unsatisfactory character of present report:

a. The participants in calculating their requirements had failed to adhere to their agreed assumption of presentation on the basis of a standard of living which they expected to be able to maintain after 1951 without special outside assistance.

b. The report indicates a considerably larger dollar deficit in 1948 than the actual deficit in 1946 and this would be viewed adversely in the US.

On the first point Sir Oliver said that part of the discrepancy had been corrected through elimination of mistakes and adoption of a more reasonable assumption regarding future terms of trade. On the second point he stated that the United Kingdom in 1946 was living on stocks; that it was a period of low industrial activity; and that prevailing commodity prices are much higher than those of 1946. We replied that in some continental countries stocks were being replenished in 1946 and that, in view of fact that we were talking about balance of payments, increased industrial activity should mean larger exports as well as larger imports.

Last night our Department advisers met with conference technicians to review in detail other technical weaknesses in the report.

Separate telegram follows of our conversation this morning with Franks and Hall-Patch.

Sent Department as 3696, repeated London as 722. [Clayton, Caffery, and Douglas.]

CAFFERY

840.50 Recovery/9–947 : Telegram

The Secretary of State to the Embassy in London

TOP SECRET WASHINGTON, September 11, 1947—7 p. m.

3950. For Ambassador Douglas. Reurtel 4888, 9 Sept, it appears that Bevin may have some misconceptions as to the intent of Depcirtel Sept 7, 1 a. m. Read in conjunction with Depcirtel Sept 7, 2 a. m., it will be noted that, in effect, Dept welcomes meeting in Paris of high level representatives of participating countries on or about Sept 15, provided they do not meet for the sole purpose of rubber-stamping initial CEEC report and accepting it as final document. Hope is that final conferring in this phase of CEEC work will permit improvement of report by acceptance in greater measure of major principles involved in "essentials" already given participating governments. If some days' delay in submission of report for this purpose necessary, Dept endorses delay (see paras 3 and 4, Depcirtel Sept 7, 2 a. m.). Most useful course of action by CEEC would, to our mind, be as follows:

a. CEEC composed of Ministers or other top reps meets Sept 15 and revises, so far as is possible or necessary, general report to accept the "essentials".

b. Phraseology of report is changed to make it clear that report is preliminary, intended as basis for further discussion, and will be subject to further amendment, particularly regarding the technical committee reports.

c. If possible, although admitted unlikely, technical reports might be further improved along lines of principles accepted in revised general report.

d. The revised report is published (we suppose about 21 Sept, but earlier if possible) and submitted to participating governments and to US simultaneously.

e. Main CEEC then adjourns but leaves technical working groups, with US technical reps offering friendly aid, in session to take such further action as possible to apply to technical reports the principles agreed in revised general report. This involves screening. In this connection, we hope to have US governmental screening of initial report under way at same time and can soon furnish constructive guidance to US technical reps giving friendly aid. Possible also that we can be using Harriman Committee to check European requirements against US availabilities and make more realistic the guidance offered US reps in Paris. Main CEEC will reconvene at some later date, say Oct 10, to approve and forward final report.

The reaction to Depcirtel Sept 7, 1 a.m., from other governments has in general been very satisfactory and indications are that most reps at CEEC will support US suggestions. Therefore, we are hopeful that if higher level representatives of participating governments meet in Paris on 15 Sept there will be considerable support to the concept expressed above. As for Bevin's remark reference impairing national sovereignties by urging continuing action, replies from other Missions do not seem to have substantiated Bevin's fears.

As for Bevin's remarks that Soviets have threatened some countries with withholding coal, would appreciate any specific information British have in this regard. Department has no knowledge of any specific threats of this nature.

Magowan, British Embassy, queried Dept yesterday at FonOff direction, as to intent behind US activity both as to cirtels and Bizonia offer. He was given full background as to our fears of receiving a final report at this time and, re Bizonia, our belief that by offering Bizonia for limited screening we would induce other nations to submit also. He said he appreciated and understood motives in both cases and his only fears were, on direct approach to govts, that US was embarking on course lessening importance of multilateral Paris meetings. On this point he was reassured and it was explained that we merely wanted govts to reconsider instructions to Paris delegates. His fears on Bizonia were that we were inviting difficult time with French and might be jeopardizing November CFM.[1] These arguments seemed unconvincing in view London discussions on Level of Industry, French interest therein (see Paris Embtel 3650, Sept 9;[2] Paris, please repeat to Douglas if he has not seen), answer given Soviets when they complained London talks and fact that revised Level Industry has been published.

Suggest you approach FonOff again soonest to explain further the broad intent of the cirtel approaches and ask for further sympathetic consideration. As for Bizonia, you should urge agreement on general lines of our offer. If Bevin still is unable to agree inform Dept urgent, since in that event basic reconsideration of bilateral offer must be undertaken.

Repeat to Paris for Clayton and Caffery.

MARSHALL

---

[1] The Fifth Session of the Council of Foreign Ministers met in London from November 25 to December 15; for documentation, see vol. II, pp. 676 ff.
[2] Post, p. 736.

840.50 Recovery/9–1247 : Telegram

The Ambassador in France (Caffery) to the Secretary of State

SECRET   PARIS, September 12, 1947—1 p. m.
US URGENT

3709. For the Secretary and Lovett from Caffery. After Wednesday's unsatisfactory meeting with the Executive Committee, Clayton, Douglas and I held a series of informal conferences with key leaders, including Sir Oliver Franks, Hall-Patch, Ramadier, Bidault and Hirschfeld. Our immediate objectives were:

a. To secure a first report, which would be "correct at least as to major policy lines," Section 3. Dept's circular telegram, September 7, 2 a. m.

b. To obtain, if possible, a short postponement of the conference meeting of Foreign Ministers so that present draft of report could be materially improved.

c. To obtain agreement that original report would clearly indicate that further work was to be done on it.

Our efforts in this direction were aided by the fact that by yesterday delegates were receiving from their home governments information regarding representations made by our missions in pursuance Dept's September 7, 1 a. m. circular.

At a meeting with Franks and Hall-Patch we told them that report fell far short of a program which would prove acceptable to the American people but that we would suggest the following changes which, if adopted, would, we thought, improve their case in the United States:

1. Statement that individual countries should obligate themselves to the group to attain the production targets they had set for key commodities.

2. Revision of financial section to remove threat of thought [sic] that effective stabilization measures could only be adopted after external aid commenced and production substantially increased.

3. Greater emphasis on and sharpening of principles, including commitment to reduce and eventually to eliminate trade barriers among the participating countries.

4. Segregation of capital equipment items (agricultural and mining machinery excepted), with clear indication that conference will look to International Bank and other lending agencies for financing these items.

5. a. Agreement to "recess" rather than "adjourn" the conference.

b. Postponement of formal conference session to September 20.

6. Firm commitment by participating countries that, if assistance is assured, they would form a multilateral organization with powers to review performance of each country.

Franks then consulted with the Executive Committee regarding the foregoing, after which we met with the Committee at its request. Hirschfeld had previously informed Franks that neither Holland, Belgium nor Luxembourg would sign a report which we said would prove unacceptable. At the opening of the meeting Alphand made it clear that the French Government's position had changed from that of the previous day and that it was prepared to proceed along the lines suggested by US. The Scandinavian representative suggested that the conference reach agreement on as many points as possible within 10 days and then issue a final report, leaving other matters of bilateral arrangements between the US and individual participating countries. He said that United Kingdom coal production was something that Norway could do nothing about and that he did not believe that Norway should enter into any obligations concerning such production. Clayton made it clear that the obligation we had in mind was one which the United Kingdom would have towards its fellow participants in return for obligations which they would hold towards it for standards of performance in other matters. There was a mutuality of interest among European nations in economic matters and if this common interest were not recognized, it was difficult to see how progress could be made.

The Benelux representative then proposed the following:

1. The next week would be devoted to making as many improvements in the report as possible.
2. The report would be issued as a "first report".
3. Paralleling US analysis of the report, a number of conference groups (including those on freeing trade barriers, financial experts and several commodity groups) would continue their work.
4. A group from the conference would then meet with representatives of the US to discuss possible revisions.

In view of the fact that this proposal appeared to closely parallel the Dept's timetable suggested its circular telegram September 7, 2 a. m., we concurred in this proposal. The Italian delegate also stated his concurrence.

The understanding which we reached with the Committee was as follows:

1. The Committee would immediately take up the question of postponement of the meeting of Foreign Ministers with a view to informing us of the decision on September 12.
2. The 6 points outlined above would be communicated to the home governments immediately.
3. On or about September 16 we would again meet with the Committee to consider progress made on the 6 points.
4. Our technical experts would continue to meet with the conference people with a view to making other improvements in the first report. Franks indicated that within the time limitations indicated they would give consideration to our further suggestions, pointing out, however, that the new timetable would prevent adjustments in the first report on any additional policy questions, other than those already discussed, which would require consideration by home governments.
5. The future course of action would be mutually decided at the time of the issuance of the first report.

Franks had previously informed us that he believed that points 2 and 4 could be accepted and that he was hopeful that the Executive Committee would agree to point 1. Point 3 had been the subject of concentrated negotiation for 2 weeks and he did not believe that further progress could be made. Points 5 and 6 were political in character and decisions would be based largely on the views of the home governments.

We have checked over the draft of the first report. Assuming that most of our suggestions are adopted, the final draft should appear to the public as neither black nor white but rather as a grey of a shade dependent on whether it is being analyzed relative to our basic essentials or in the perspective of the history of western Europe with its strong emphasis on national sovereignty and the European political situation generally. In any event a beginning has been made and the important consideration is to keep this group moving as rapidly as possible in the direction of our basic objectives.

Sent Dept as 3709, repeated London for Clayton and Douglas as 728.

CAFFERY

840.50 Recovery/9–1247 : Telegram

The Ambassador in France (Caffery) to the Secretary of State

SECRET   PARIS, September 12, 1947—4 p. m.
US URGENT

3714. At a meeting last night of the entire Committee of Cooperation the delegates were informed by Franks of the results of our meeting with the Executive Committee, reported my 3709, September 12, 1 p. m. The Cooperation Committee decided to postpone the formal meeting of the conference called to receive the report until September 20–22, the exact date to be determined later.

Sent Department 3714, repeated London for Clayton and Douglas 729.

CAFFERY

840.50 Recovery/9–1247 : Telegram

The Ambassador in the United Kingdom (Douglas) to the Secretary of State

SECRET   LONDON, September 12, 1947—8 p. m.
NIACT

4950. For the Secretary from Douglas. At meeting with Bevin he orally asked me to transmit to you the following message:

"As Chairman of the Paris Conference, I am much disturbed by the public consequences of the discussions in Paris between the Executive Committee and United States representatives, leading to the postponement of the report pending the consideration of certain points which the United States Government have raised. I fully understand and appreciate the intentions of the United States Government in making this intervention, but the impression has been created that the work of the conference has been unsatisfactory and is now having to be done again under American pressure. This is, of course, not the case but if the impression is allowed to persist it will do untold harm in the European countries and in the United Kingdom. It will provide an opportunity for critics, in Europe and elsewhere, to undermine the progress which the conference has been able to achieve. It may prejudice the final outcome of the conference. This unfortunate result appears to be out of proportion to the advantages which will doubtless flow from the improvement of the report on the points raised by the United States Government.

"There is little I can do here to put this right. The impression can only be corrected from Washington. I therefore hope very much that you may find it possible, by some reassuring statement, to restore the confidence, which has now been shaken, in the work and outcome of the conference and the United States attitude towards it.

"Secondly, I earnestly hope that the United States Government, having made its views known, will not [now] allow the Conference to work upon them and complete its report in an atmosphere of calm and without any feeling of external pressure."

I understand what he means is that the accounts in the press have produced the impression of the situation which he describes and that this public impression can be best rectified by a statement from you in Washington.

Moreover, I do not understand that the last paragraph of this message is intended to imply that during the remaining ten days of this phase of the conference "friendly assistance" should be withdrawn.

DOUGLAS

840.50 Recovery/9–1247 : Telegram

The Ambassador in the United Kingdom (Douglas) to the Secretary of State

SECRET   LONDON, September 12, 1947—8 p. m.
URGENT   NIACT

4951. For the Secretary. 1. Spent Wednesday afternoon and Thursday in Paris with Clayton and Caffery (Deptel 3950, September 11). Two meetings with the Executive Committee of the CEEC were held; the first on Wednesday afternoon, the second on Thursday afternoon. Also two meetings with Sir Oliver Franks and Sir Edmund Hall-Patch, the first prior to the Executive Committee meeting on Wednesday and the second prior to the Executive Committee meeting on Thursday.

2. You should have by now received full cables from Paris reciting the results of these meetings. Nevertheless, the following is a brief résumé of the results of the final meeting with the Executive Committee:

a. Six fundamental considerations inadequately dealt with, or omitted entirely, in the tentative draft report, which we received in Paris, were discussed and emphasized. (These six basic points you should have received from Paris by the time they arrive).[1]

b. Since there was not sufficient time to recast the report along the lines indicated, the members of the Executive Committee agreed, subject to the approval of their governments that the meeting of the

---

[1] See telegram 3709, September 12, from Paris, p. 425.

Ministers on the 15th to receive the report would be postponed until the 22nd.

c. The report when submitted on the 22nd to the Ministers will be labeled "provisional" or alternatively "a first report".

d. After the report has been submitted to the Ministers on the 22nd, the conference will, subject to the approval of their governments, recess and not terminate. Sir Oliver Franks will be given the authority, after the report has been more carefully analyzed by the US, to reconvene the conference for such further work as may be necessary.

3. Bevin indicated this morning when I saw him this procedure was entirely satisfactory to him.

As to the inclusion of bizonal areas—after discussion with Clayton, we concluded that in the light of the difficulties that we had had in persuading the Executive Committee to follow the procedure outlined above, it would only at that time have confused the major issue to bring up the inclusion of bizonal area. Moreover, we felt that it would be more appropriate to ask for the inclusion of the bizonal areas when the conference is reconvened after the submission of the "provisional" or "first report" and press for inclusion during the remaining 8 days of the present phase of the work of the conference.

DOUGLAS

840.50 Recovery/9–1247 : Telegram

The Acting Secretary of State to the Embassy in the United Kingdom

SECRET   WASHINGTON, September 13, 1947—1 p. m.

3987. For Douglas from the Secretary. With reference to Bevin message (urtel 4950), we give you our views below. You are authorized to express orally such portions as you may consider adequately responsive to Bevin's comments.

Bevin's concern is fully appreciated but in light of press stories both here and from Paris quoting Franks and FonOff spokesmen that CEEC will complete "first report" on September 22 (AP and *Times* from Paris, 12 September) there seems little use in a statement from Washington at this time. Dept can not fully endorse CEEC report to date or even projected "first report" of September 22 and, since it is likely that initial report will need some further revision, at least in part, any optimistic comments would be contrary to facts, might take heat off conferees, and would most certainly do harm here. Our understanding is that CEEC has agreed that it will reconvene if necessary to consider further friendly aid suggestions from US after first report is reviewed in Washington (where substantial cuts, particularly in food, may be found necessary). This seems to us desirable way to achieve end result both we and participating nations hope can be achieved.

Dept believes CEEC under Bevin's and Frank's leadership has made much progress in short time it has been at work and taking into account limiting terms of reference. Our friendly aid activities have been motivated solely by genuine desire to help CEEC help itself and in response to appeal from CEEC for our views as to form of report.

All the above may be unnecessary in view of later word on Bevin's attitude contained your 4951 September 12, paragraph three.

If Bevin still concerned we would see no objection your making appreciative statement in London if in your judgment this is wise.[1] In this connection you should give consideration to probable substantial revision of program which must be made here before it can be recommended by us or approved by Congress.

LOVETT

---

[1] In telegram 5129, September 23, Ambassador Douglas stated: "In my judgment it is not now necessary for me to make a statement." (840.50 Recovery/9–2347)

840.50 Recovery/9–1447 : Telegram

The Ambassador in France (Caffery) to the Secretary of State

SECRET   PARIS, September 14, 1947—noon.

3752. In pursuance of the understanding reached at the Executive Committee meeting reported my 3709, September 12, 1 p.m., I reviewed yesterday with Marris details of our working arrangements for the last week of the Conference. The following procedures were established:

1. Departmental advisers are reviewing with Conference people several of the technical reports. New adjustments will be limited (because of the time element) to those which can be made without referral to home governments.

2. Tomorrow Embassy will review with Conference group the entire general report, with a view to recommending revisions of a nonpolicy character.

3. On Tuesday evening Conference will discuss with Embassy the progress which has been made in meeting the six-policy points reported my 3709, plus the two other adjustments, (gasoline rationing and segregation commodity import requirements by sources of supply) reported my 3696, September 11, 5 p.m. A ninth point, commitment re establishment and maintenance of proper rates of exchange, will also be discussed.

4. It is hoped that Clayton and Douglas can join me in Paris on Wednesday for (*a*) joint review of situation relative to one, two and three above, followed (*b*) by a meeting with the Executive Committee.

Sent Department; repeated London for Clayton and Douglas as 740.

CAFFERY

840.50 Recovery/9–1447 : Telegram

The Ambassador in France (Caffery) to the Secretary of State

SECRET   PARIS, September 14, 1947.

3758. Conference yesterday took up with me questions relative to presentation and publication of first report. (Am informed British Embassy Washington is discussing this matter with Department). Provisional plans are as follows:

1. Formal meeting of conference afternoon September 22 to adopt report.

2. 1500 word press release summarizing report on same date. This statement would be made available to Embassy several days earlier for telegraphic transmittal to Department for simultaneous release in Washington.

3. Copy of report signed by sixteen (it is hoped) delegates and addressed to Secretary Marshall would be sent to Washington by courier leaving evening September 22.

4. Simultaneous release Washington and European capitals of entire report for publication morning newspapers September 28.

5. The question raised with me is whether we prefer that presentation of report to Secretary Marshall should be (*a*) through British Embassy Washington on behalf of President of conference (Bevin) or (*b*) by conference in Paris (presumably Executive Committee or Cooperation Committee) to me for transmission to the Secretary. British have suggested procedure (*a*), while some other delegations believe presentation should be by larger conference group to me.

Dept's telegraphic comments requested, with special reference to 5 above.

Sent Dept as 3758; repeated to London for Clayton and Douglas as 745.

CAFFERY

840.50 Recovery/9–1547 : Telegram

The Ambassador in France (Caffery) to the Secretary of State

SECRET   PARIS, September 15, 1947—8 p. m.

3780. For the Secretary and Lovett from Clayton, Caffery and Douglas. Some of the criticisms of the program which is being formulated by the Paris Conference arise, we believe, from the opinion held by a few that the European participating countries should designate without regard to national frontiers the productive facilities that should first be brought into production. This view sounds plausible enough at first but its implications, we think, are far-reaching. First, it inevitably requires for its execution an international organization to select the plants that will be given priority; second, it inevitably requires an international organization to allocate the necessary raw materials for the operation of plants enjoying priority; third, it inevitably requires an international organization to allocate among several or all of the participating countries the products of plants facilities to which priority has been given. The evidence is clear, we think, that the 16 participating countries would not accept this sort of system and organization. Moreover, even if they were prepared to agree to such a system, organization, and procedure, in our opinion, interminable arguments would ensue among many of the participating countries as to which plants would be first brought into production, how raw materials and in what amounts should be allocated to them, and to which countries the products of these plants would be allocated. Finally, such a procedure and organization would, we think, in effect result in a planned economy to a dangerous degree. It is almost certain to lead to international cartels which would stimulate nationalism and tend to frustrate the ultimate restoration of natural economic forces. We believe it much more prudent and much wiser to seek from the participating countries or most of them commitments among themselves and later with US to reduce trade barriers including the establishment of appropriate exchange rates. This course will, in our opinion, more effectively bring about a community of economic interest and responsibility based on natural economic forces.

We realize, of course, that a very limited list of commodities are now being allocated, and must during the period of shortage continue to be allocated, such, for example, as coal and food, but to enlarge the present limited list would, we believe, be impossible to achieve agreement upon and ultimately might produce the situation which we have described.

As to screening of the various nationalistic programs, we think, that not as much has been done by them collectively as might well have been done. We are, however, disposed to the view that the requirement when measured against the available supplies of essential materials inescapably produce[s] the necessary screening.

In our opinion, the most important considerations are those involving the basic principles to which we have referred. [Clayton, Caffery, and Douglas.]

CAFFERY

840.50 Recovery/9–1747 : Telegram

The Ambassador in France (Caffery) to the Secretary of State

SECRET

NIACT

PARIS, September 17, 1947—3 p. m.

4015. For Lovett and Bonesteel from Caffery. CEEC has met or is in progress of meeting points 1 to 5 inclusive, reported my 3709 September 12, 1 p. m. New provisions are satisfactory and in some cases exceed, from the standpoint of the firmness of commitments, our expectations. On point 6 Franks met yesterday evening with Swedish delegate who had just returned from Stockholm. On basis this conversation Franks redrafted multilateral organization provision in a form which is slightly weaker but still meets our condition. He is hopeful that both Swedish and Swiss delegates will approve this new formula, which Clayton, Douglas and I have indicated as satisfactory, but is not certain whether their two governments will approve. Should have definite information this point by tomorrow. Follows summarizing our discussions of yesterday with 18 delegates which was mutually satisfactory and did much to clear the atmosphere.[1]

Sent Dept as 4015, repeated London as 753.

CAFFERY

---

[1] Text as in original record copy; the reference is presumably to telegram 4025, September 17, from Paris, p. 435.

840.50 Recovery/9–1747 : Telegram

The Ambassador in the United Kingdom (Douglas) to the Secretary of State

TOP SECRET

LONDON, September 17, 1947—5 p. m.

5033. For the Secretary and Lovett. 1. Have not answered in detail because course of action reported after meeting with Clayton in Paris and the Executive Committee CEEC on the tenth and eleventh seemed to meet all the points raised. Moreover your cable not received until the twelfth after return from Paris. (Deptel 3950, September 11; Embtel 4888, September 9).

2. As previously reported, Bevin satisfied with course of action and procedure agreed to as result of the meetings referred to in paragraph one above.

3. As to Bevin's remarks that Soviet had threatened to withhold coal from some countries, details are as follows:

About ten days ago, when the Scandinavian countries were meeting to consider a customs union, the Soviet threatened to withhold from them deliveries of coal if they proceeded with their discussions. This information given me from two sources in the Foreign Office and confirmed in conversations Paris yesterday.

4. As a result of several conversations with Bevin and other members of the Foreign Office, am convinced Department's feeling that the British have been "sticky" at the Paris Conference was due to following consideration.

Emphasis which they thought we would place upon a continuing organization for purpose of indicating, without regard to national frontiers, the plant facilities which would first be brought into production necessarily entailed, in their view, the allocation of a relatively large list of raw materials and of the finished products among at least several participating countries. This sort of an undertaking, the British felt, would necessarily mean an impairment of sovereignty and as a result the withdrawal from the conference of several of the member countries. Thus, the British felt the schism in Europe would be broadened and deepened at a particularly inopportune time. Several of the participating countries expressed the same view.

5. Now, however, that the above procedure is not being pressed by the Department, Bevin and the British are completely satisfied and have, I am confident, exerted every effort to persuade the conference to meet, as nearly as is possible among sixteen participating countries, all of the basic principles which have been suggested by us to the conference.

6. Believe it much preferable to press for the inclusion of the bizonal areas after the "first report" has been received and when, should it be necessary, the conference is reconvened for the purpose of either modifying the first report or preparing a second. Can explain this to you fully when we meet in Washington.

DOUGLAS

840.50 Recovery/9–1747 : Telegram

The Ambassador in France (Caffery) to the Secretary of State

SECRET   PARIS, September 17, 1947—7 p. m.

4025. After reviewing latest draft general report yesterday morning, Clayton, Douglas and I met with Sir Oliver Franks to discuss in detail revision sections of report concerned with balance of payments, internal financial stability and freeing of trade barriers.

Subsequently we attended informal meeting Committee of Economic Cooperation September 16, afternoon, arranged to permit discussion with all 16 delegates. Franks opened meeting by referring to draft changes in general report points made by Clayton September 11 (reported Embtel 3709, September 12). French draft proposals (reported Embtel 3762 September 15 [1]) were summarized by Alphand, who indicated they had been generally agreed upon except as regards point six respecting continuing organization. With reference point six, Alphand indicated Swiss had reservations (Swedish delegate arrived later during meeting and later indicated privately to Clayton his government likewise had some reservations respecting French draft on this point).

Clayton on behalf of the three of us congratulated committee on report, referring to magnitude of task and tight time schedule. He indicated that "in their work the representatives of the 16 European nations have blazed a new path in the history of Europe, if not in the history of the world". He expressed appreciation for work done in preparing recent changes in general report, and indicated he had no substantive comments as regards new drafts on points (1) to (3) inclusive. (These points in order given by Alphand were: (1) undertaking on internal stability, (2) undertaking concerning production program, (3) pledge to cooperate). As regards point 4 (measures relating to reduction of trade barriers), Clayton stated he had been informed final draft not ready but indicated his understanding that generally acceptable formula on this point would be reached. With reference point 5 (requirements for equipment), Clayton stated he had been informed final draft not ready but that he understood matter would be taken care of when replies were received to telegram recently sent out requesting information from participating governments as to amount of equipment included in requirement figures submitted on non-programmed items. With respect point 6 (continuing multilateral organization), Clayton stated that paragraph 103 of general report (point 6 Embtel 3762) would, if approved, take care of matter.[2]

Clayton cautioned that while he had no further comments, Washington might have additional suggestions. He emphasized fact that his remarks could by no means be taken as implying any commitment by US Government respecting any part of report, particularly total figures indicated therein. Clayton stated his personal view that report as finally drafted should make favorable impression in US and added that public discussion in US and in participating countries might result in good suggestions being advanced which would merit incorporation in report. It was, therefore, fortunate that first report was to be

---

[1] Not printed.

[2] The material transmitted as point 6 of telegram 3762, September 15, 1947, from Paris, not printed, is substantially that found in paragraphs 111, 113, and 114 of Chapter v, *Committee of European Economic Cooperation*, vol. I, *General Report*, Department of State publication 2930 (Washington, Government Printing Office, 1947).

f a preliminary character. He concluded by stating he expected to ee some members of committee in Washington relatively soon.

Upon invitation by Franks for comment, Danish delegate Vestbirk xpressed appreciation and thanks to US Government representatives or opportunity to discuss questions of concern to committee. He indiated that Denmark was primarily interested in utilizing its agriculural capacity to fullest extent but for this purpose needed feedstuffs vhich for time being could only be obtained in US and elsewhere in Vestern Hemisphere for hard currency. In response, Clayton indicated hat while personally he was fully aware of need for enough flexibility n any program to permit some purchases elsewhere than in US, certain ;roups in US might seek to limit Marshall aid to surplus commodities n US.

Swiss delegate associated himself with thanks to US representatives nd stated his conviction that spirit of solidarity prevailing in comaittee would dissipate effects of divergence of views over paragraphs n continuing organization. He added it was merely matter of finding ight formula.

Sent Department 4025 repeated London for Clayton and Douglas 56.

CAFFERY

40.50 Recovery/9–1447 : Telegram

The Acting Secretary of State to the Embassy in France

ECRET WASHINGTON, September 17, 1947—3 p. m.

3528. Brit Emb Wash, at instance FonOff London, has requested iews Dept on timing and content of material released to press conerning Paris Conf report. Brit feel that with signing of report Sept 22, eaks concerning its contents virtually inevitable. Accordingly, is their ope that official guidance to correspondents on contents report be 1ade available as soon after signing as possible. At same time Brit o not wish do Secretary discourtesy of "reading in newspapers" conents report before it officially received by him.

Consequently they have proposed and Dept has concurred in issu-1ce 1500 word official summary Wash and 16 Capitals at hour agreed) by 16 countries concerned, preferably Sept 22, date of signing.

Brit proposal is that summary prepared by Conf be cabled Wash or Secretary Sept 19 or 20.

Dept, while agreeing utility in prevention distorted leaks, feels :rongly summary should (1) make clear, if such is case, that report is ot final frozen one but tentative in sense of 1st report, and (2) that it adequately and fully presents contents, rather than slanted version to please US reader. We realize delicacy of revision your end but feel you should see in advance copy to be cabled for Secretary.[1]

According present plans time schedule release full report as follows: at least two copies, one for Secretary and one for printing here to be dispatched by Bevin following signing Monday 22nd. As many additional copies as feasible desired. Expected arrival here Tuesday 23rd or Wednesday 24th. To meet our printing schedule copy for printers must arrive Wednesday forenoon at latest. If agreement reached Paris, report to be handed correspondents Wash, London, Paris and presumably other Capitals, Friday, 26 or Sat, 27 for publication morning papers Sun, 28th—i.e. 7 PM EDT, Wash, midnight London and Paris, Sat, 27. Our understanding is report to be in 2 volumes: 1st report itself, 2nd appendices. Date release 2nd volume not now known. Reference point five your 3758, Sept 14, repeated London as 745, Dept feels matter presentation report to Secretary is for decision by Conf itself.

Repeated to London as 4032.

LOVETT

---

[1] For texts of (a) the summary released to the press on September 22 and (b) an accompanying statement by M. Hervé Alphand of France, Rapporteur General of the Conference, see Department of State *Bulletin*, October 5, 1947, p. 681.

840.50 Recovery/9–2447

The Secretary of State to President Truman

WASHINGTON, September 24, 1947.

DEAR MR. PRESIDENT: I have the honor to transmit to you herewith the initial report of the Committee of European Economic Cooperation [1] which I have today received from the Chairman of the Committee, Mr. Ernest Bevin, Foreign Minister of the United Kingdom. The report was signed on September 22, 1947 by representatives of Austria, Belgium, Denmark, Eire, France, Greece, Iceland, Italy, Luxemburg, the Netherlands, Norway, Portugal, Sweden, Switzerland, Turkey and the United Kingdom, who have been engaged in the preparation of the report in Paris since July 12, 1947.

The report is divided into two volumes. The first of these consists of a general statement of the problems of European economic recovery the plans of the European countries concerned to meet these problems and the assistance which these countries believe to be necessary from

---

[1] The report was published as *Committee of European Economic Cooperation* vol. I, *General Report*, and vol. II, *Technical Reports, July–September 1947*, Department of State publications 2930, 2952, (Washington, Government Printing Office, 1947).

the United States and other non European countries and agencies to
restore their economic position. It also contains summary statements
of the position and prospects of the participating countries and western
Germany in food and agriculture, energy sources, iron and steel, transport, timber and manpower as well as in their balances of international
payments and their internal financial situation. These summary statements are drawn from the reports of Technical Subcommittees of the
Conference, which are published in full in volume two.

Faithfully yours,

G. C. MARSHALL

Editorial Note

For the texts of statements issued by Acting Secretary of State
Lovett on September 24 and by President Truman on September 25
regarding the interest and intentions of the United States with regard
to the report, see Department of State *Bulletin*, October 5, 1947,
pages 687, 688. Letters of acknowledgment dated September 25 from
Secretary of State Marshall to Ernest Bevin, Chairman of the Committee of European Economic Cooperation, and to the Committee
itself, are printed *ibid.*, page 689.

III. THE UNITED STATES REACTION TO THE PARIS REPORT, AND MATTERS RELATED TO THE DEVELOPMENT OF A PROGRAM FOR INTERIM AID (SEPTEMBER–DECEMBER)

A. The Washington Conversations on European Economic Cooperation

Editorial Note

The report from Paris of the Committee of European Economic Cooperation was closely examined and evaluated by various committees
within the Executive Branch of the Government with a view to formulating a comprehensive European recovery program for presentation
to the Congress. These committees had been organized in response to a
growing awareness within the Government that European recovery
was proceeding too slowly and too disjointedly. The creation in March
1947 of the SWNCC Committee on Extension of U.S. Aid to Foreign
Governments began the process, and during the remainder of the year
there developed a network of working and study groups, each within
its particular area of competence studying problems, evaluating priorities, and making recommendations. Some of these groups were in the
Department of State, and others were interdepartmental.

The Department of State had organized the Committee on European Recovery Program on June 25, 1947. Meeting regularly on Tuesday and Thursday evenings, the Committee came to focus the thought and energies of the Department as to the needs and priorities of the European countries under study. Through its Executive Secretary, Charle P. Kindleberger, the Committee maintained liaison with the Policy Planning Staff and other offices in the Department, with the Harriman Krug, and Nourse Committees, and with such interdepartmental bodie as the National Advisory Council on International Monetary an Financial Problems and the Executive Committee for Economic For eign Policy.

In addition to formulating and coordinating recommendations fo Departmental policy the Committee on European Recovery Progran undertook to organize the overall framework or concept within whic individual studies could be made and interdepartmental groups coul operate. Several members of the Committee represented the Depart ment of State on the interdepartmental Advisory Steering Commit tee on European Recovery Program (ASC), which was set up i response to Under Secretary Lovett's letters of August 29, *ante.* Th Departments of War, Navy, Commerce, Interior, Treasury, Agricul ture and Labor were represented, as were the Bureau of the Budget the Federal Reserve Board, and the White House. The Committee discussions were confidential; at the first meeting of the Committee o September 9, 1947, Mr. Lovett noted "that in view of the obvious po litical implications of the European recovery program any open dis cussion of this problem would result in extreme repercussions abroad This is the reason for the emphasis on the security aspect at the presen time."

A four-man Correlation Committee consisting of representatives c the State, Treasury, and Commerce Departments, under the chairman ship of Lt. Col. Charles Bonesteel, served as the executive group fo the Advisory Steering Committee, which by pooling technical expert from the interested areas and from different departments create functional working teams to analyze programs and make policy recom mendations. Among the auxiliary groups created was the objectiv subcommittee headed by the Chief of the Policy Planning Staff (Ker nan); its function was to review the broad aspects of the program a it developed. Other specially created subcommittees and their chairme included: the Organization and Administration Group, Mr. Lincol Gordon, Department of State; the Legislative Drafting Group, M Ernest Gross, Department of State; the Financial Policy Grou (which was to prepare balance of payments calculations as a basis fo an appropriations bill in Congress), Mr. Frank Southard, Treasur Department; the Economic Policy Group (to deal with such things a controls to channel aid to Europe, offshore procurement, and the like

Mr. Thomas Blaisdell, Department of Commerce; the Functional and Commodity Analysis Group (to appraise availabilities to meet CEEC's stated requirements), Mr. Paul H. Nitze, Department of State; the Labor and Manpower Group, Mr. Philip Kaiser, Department of Labor; and the Country Analysis Group, Mr. Henry Labouisse, Department of State, which analyzed the potential impact of aid against needs and availabilities.

The Advisory Steering Committee and its subcommittees performed several distinct yet interrelated functions including the holding of discussions on a technical level with representatives of the CEEC (the Washington Conversations); the preparation of a legislative program for presentation to Congress; and the planning of a special interim aid program. Documentation concerning these subjects follows.

840.50 Recovery/9–2047 : Telegram

The Ambassador in the United Kingdom (Douglas) to the Secretary of State

SECRET
US URGENT

LONDON, September 20, 1947—11 a. m.

5094. From Clayton, Caffery and Douglas. 1. At Sir Oliver Franks' request, Douglas and Clayton are meeting with him in London on September 23 for a discussion of the future work and movements of CEEC groups relative to the time schedules outlined Section 6, your circtel September 7, 2 a. m. We would greatly appreciate the receipt by telegram of your advice in this matter before that date and submit the following suggestions for your consideration.

2. We believe it desirable to arrange a series of top level conferences in the Dept immediately upon Clayton's and Douglas's arrival in Washington, October 2 for the purpose of determining policy matters which would serve as a guide to our technical people in their talks with the conference group in Washington.

3. The conference group, which will include the chairman, the rapporteur general, certain delegates from participating countries and a number of technical experts, should be invited to arrive in Washington about October 6 for the purpose of a thorough exploration with our people of the initial, general and technical reports.

4. At the conclusion of these talks, which should be limited to 10 days or 2 weeks, we should be in a position to tell the conference group what additional work we expect from that organization.

5. The chairman would then reconvene the conference in Paris with a view to presenting final supporting evidence for 1948 soon after November 1 and a complete revised presentation for the four-year period by December 15.

6. In the meantime the following utilization of our personnel in Europe is recommended:

a. We are sending observers to London for the meeting Committee of Financial Experts beginning September 23.[1]

b. A conference in Paris of Agricultural Attachés from key European posts beginning September 29 to analyze preliminary work of the Food and Agriculture Committee (reourtel from Paris 3686, September 11, 11 a. m.[2])

c. A conference of economic counselors or chief economic officers in Paris beginning September 29 for the dual purpose of estimating conference technical reports on basis country work done in pursuance Depts circular September 11, noon,[3] and to brief our officers on developments and results Paris conference for their background use in future economic reporting.

d. In view of foregoing plans, we would appreciate early action our recommendation Section 1 our telegram under reference that Ivan White[4] be designated to coordinate the work in Europe. This would formalize the arrangement under which he has been assisting us in this capacity during the past three months. We think it desirable for him to proceed to Washington by air on a short detail arriving there not later than October 6.

7. We assume that in the event you agree with the foregoing suggestions necessary telegraphic travel orders will be issued directly by Dept.

Repeated to Paris as 503. [Clayton, Caffery, and Douglas.]

DOUGLAS

---

[1] The report of the Committee on Payments Agreements, the name chosen by the meeting of financial experts, is printed in the Addendum to the Paris Report, *Committee of European Economic Cooperation,* vol. II, *Technical Reports,* p. 525 This Committee report was not, however, included in volume II as printed by the United Kingdom and France.

[2] In telegram 3686, from Paris, not printed, Clayton and Caffery make a similar recommendation (840.50 Recovery/9–1147). The Department in telegram 4144 September 25, to London, not printed, advised that the calling of the conference of agricultural attachés and economic counselors should be delayed until the Department had consulted with representatives of the CEEC who were coming to Washington to clarify and further explain the Paris Report (840.50 Recovery/9–2047).

[3] Not printed; it asked the American diplomatic missions in countries that took part in the Paris Conference to comment on the replies by the respective governments to the questionnaire by the CEEC. (840.50 Recovery/9–1147)

[4] First Secretary of Embassy at Paris.

840.50 Recovery/9–2047 : Telegram

The Acting Secretary of State to the Embassy in France

SECRET   WASHINGTON, September 20, 1947—3 p. m

US URGENT   NIACT

3604. For Clayton and Caffery. 1. Dept understands from Moore that CEEC delegates and technical experts will leave Paris Sept 2?

after signing report without specific plans for continuance work of technical committees in improving report as was contemplated in circtel Sept 7, 2 a.m., para 4. Moore also indicates your and Embassy Paris belief that in circumstances it would be difficult to press now for continuance technical committee work. Further Dept feels that if US urged, before first report is completed, that plans be made for immediate revision, reaction in Europe and here would be bad.

2. Under these circumstances, Dept desires your urgent comment, and that of Douglas, on following revised schedule of procedure which would not be communicated to delegates now, except for advising Exec Comm of point *b* and, if you wish, point *c*, below.

a. SecState upon receipt of report will make public statement of general character indicating significance of sixteen countries having prepared preliminary report on economic plans and intention of US Govt and Harriman Committee to study carefully with view to formulating recommendations to Congress.

b. Executive Committee would be invited, after receipt of report here, to come to Washington to consult with US Govt officials in early October. Committee would meet with interdepartmental group and with Harriman and other Committees. Meetings would be kept short, small, and attended by minimum publicity.

c. Technical experts would not accompany Exec Comm to US. Dept fearful that gathering such experts in Washington would have effect of reconvening conference here under US supervision and detract seriously from SecState emphasis on European initiative and European character of recovery program. In addition, larger group would require larger US group including technical experts from number US agencies, which would make meetings unmanageable from standpoints of speed and publicity. At your discretion you may indicate to Exec Comm our view that technical experts should not accompany Committee to Washington, and reasons therefore. However, there will be a requirement for further information on some technical reports, particularly from Harriman Committee. Exec Comm should be considering how this will be made available.

d. To extent meeting of Exec Comm with US officials leads former to undertake issuance "supplementary reports" (or revisions of chapters and appendices preliminary report), CEEC, or just working parties, could be reconvened by Oct 20 and one or more technical reports could be amended and transmitted to SecState in time for meeting of Congressional Committees in Nov or for possible special session Congress, end of Nov or early Dec. Reconvened meetings in Paris of CEEC or working Committees would receive US friendly aid, particularly on questions of specifications, availabilities, etc., as contemplated in circtel Sept 7, 2 a. m., and Embtel 3686.[1]

e. Dept presenting to President on Monday proposals for Executive action to meet immediate needs critical countries and for Special Session Congress about Dec 1. Dept must present any request for interim assistance as first installment of assistance under Marshall

---

[1] Telegram 3686, from Paris, not printed, but see reference to it in telegram 5094, *supra.*

Plan or at minimum as temporary assistance required until longer-range assistance under workable European recovery plan can be started. On this account US Govt must be satisfied with present report or be able to point to satisfactory revisions completed or in progress. Being able to point to reconvened CEEC or working parties as evidence of continued European effort would help in this connection, showing that basic of Harvard speech concept, the idea of European initiative, has not been abandoned. Continued active labors by CEEC or working parties essential to preserve underlying principle of Marshall suggestion that European countries primarily responsible for plan. Failure their part continue developing and improving plan would clearly give impression here, which would be fatal, that they attempting to shift responsibility to US.

Re London's 4976,[2] Douglas may wish not to make statement on preliminary report if statement made by SecState. In any event, statement should avoid indicating acceptance by Dept or US of report as satisfactory basis for making recommendations to Congress.

Sent Paris as 3604 for Clayton and Caffery; repeated London for Douglas as 4081.

LOVETT

---

[2] In telegram 4976, September 15, from London, not printed, Ambassador Douglas reported that: "Bevin's concern reported in Emtel 4950, September 12 has abated. He agrees with me that the necessity for a statement has passed but suggests the possibility of a statement by me here in London on the 22nd . . ." (840.50 Recovery/9–1547)

840.50 Recovery/9–2247 : Telegram

The Acting Secretary of State to the Embassy in the United Kingdom

SECRET   WASHINGTON, September 22, 1947—9 p. m.

4103. For Clayton, Caffery, Douglas. Further discussions with Harriman Committee representatives indicate their strong desire to discuss technical aspects of CEEC reports directly with experts who are familiar with underlying data. Discussion would be for the purpose of clarification and further explanation of the report rather than to attempt to revise report in Washington. Accordingly Dept has revised its previous position and now recommends that such technical experts accompany Executive Committee arriving early October.

For your info we believe it will become clear from discussions in Washington that further substantial work by Committees in Paris will be necessary.

For reasons contained Dept's 3604 (repeated London as 4081) to Paris suggest that technical delegation be held to smallest number consistent with adequate representation of each committee or commodity field. Probably one or two from each committee would suffice, if carefully chosen for technical competence. Adequate broad representation from various countries should be taken into account to extent feasible without sacrificing competence.

LOVETT

840.50 Recovery/9–2347 : Telegram

The Ambassador in the United Kingdom (Douglas) to the Secretary of State

SECRET   LONDON, September 23, 1947—3 p. m.
US URGENT

5119. From Clayton and Douglas. After consultation with Caffery, we submit following re questions raised your 3604 to Paris, September 20, 3 p. m.

a. Concur in suggestion for statement by Secretary.

b. Agree on invitation to CEEC group and suggest October 6 as beginning date. Invitation should be addressed to "Chairman, the Rapporteur General, certain delegates from participating countries", terminology used in initial report. (Reason back of this was revolt of smaller participants against "too close control" exercised by Executive Committee. In practice invitation this form would result in Executive Committee plus Greek and Danish delegates appearing in Washington.)

c. Understand from Bonesteel's telephone conversation with Caffery that Department is still considering question presence in Washington of technical experts. We believe European character of program should be maintained and discussions in Washington strictly limited to time period indicated in invitation, say October 4 to 20. In view of time element, however, group of delegates might bring small group of experts, say one for each technical report, for sole purpose of explaining to our experts methods used in compiling reports. If, however, there is to be further work of technical committees, we believe it should be done in Paris and not in Washington.[1]

Principal objective of Washington meeting should be to permit Washington to formulate precise statement of what we want reconvened conference to do. Franks could then use this as basis for reconvening conference and charting its work program.

Reconvening of conference would make most sense to Europeans if it were possible to state publicly that need for revision had arisen from

---

[1] In telegram 5142, September 23, from London, Ambassador Douglas informed the Department that he and Under Secretary Clayton had discussed the above matters with Sir Oliver Franks. They informed him that their "views were tentative and based on preliminary exchange communications with Department," but that they would apprise him when definite instructions had been received. (840.50 Recovery/9–2347)

introduction two new elements: (1) participation western Germany, and (2) need to readjust import and production programs to conform to possible availabilities in 1948.

d. and *e.* In view of rapid deterioration financial, economic and political situations two vital areas France and Italy, we recommend that time schedule calling Congressional committees together and convening special session be advanced to beginning October and beginning November, respectively.

In our opinion, initial report contains enough of the essentials of a workable program to permit Congressional committees to commence consideration of interim aid within its framework by first week October. Our immediate problem is to meet effectively and at once the European crisis so that by spring we shall still have a democratic area upon which to build a complete recovery program.

Sent Department as 5119; repeated Paris for Caffery as 534.

DOUGLAS

Lot 122, Box 19B

The Chairman of the CEEC Washington Delegation (Franks) to the Under Secretary of State (Lovett) [1]

UNOFFICIAL AIDE-MÉMOIRE

TOP SECRET

When I arrived just over a week ago, you were good enough to say that we were engaged upon a common endeavour and that you counted on both of us approaching the problem in a spirit of frankness and in straightforward discussions. I hope therefore you will regard what I have to say today in that light.

I cannot too much stress that the programme which is before you now is important in its political as much as in its economic aspect. The Paris Conference, following so closely on Mr. Marshall's speech, has created a new hope in men's minds in Europe. They feel that the Marshall Plan offers a last chance to Western Europe to recover from the economic and political effects of the war and to lead a way of life which, in its reliance on free political institutions, freedom of speech, equality before the law and the value of the individual to the state, is broadly similar to the way of life followed and enjoyed by the people of the United States. They therefore feel that the initiative taken by Mr. Marshall is, perhaps, the most important single step that any government has taken since the war. For in it they see made manifest

---

[1] A covering memorandum on the file copy indicates that the *"aide-mémoire* was left with Mr. Lovett by Sir Oliver Franks at their conversation on the evening of 22 October."

the interest which the United States has in the solution of their economic problems and in the consequent preservation of the way of life they wish to continue to lead. They therefore look forward with hope and confidence to working with the United States Government to achieve what they believe that Government considers is a common end.

The Paris Conference, furthermore, has made people in Western Europe feel that they have responded successfully and in full measure to the initiative of the United States Government and they are now looking to these discussions in Washington as the next step in the fulfilment of this common endeavour.

If this hope is to be preserved and the new spirit of a common purpose which was such a feature of our work in Paris is to be kept alive, it is essential not only that our present discussions should succeed, but that from them there should emerge a programme which the people of Western Europe believe is likely to lead to a full measure of recovery in a relatively short time. Hopes are fresh and it is vital they should not be disappointed or deferred.

The programme is a *recovery* programme and not a programme of temporary relief. It has therefore to be a large programme and the amounts available under it have to be sufficient to do the job. Otherwise it loses its character, becomes a further instalment of relief, and at its end the people of Western Europe will be on your doorstep again. By then, however, both they and you will be further disillusioned and, more importantly, Europe may have gone so far down the hill that full recovery may have become impossible and the social and political fabrics of Western Europe so altered and strained as to force other solutions than those for which we are both working and hoping. The forging of the recovery of Western Europe can only be done once and it has to be done now.

The programme which is now before you is not perfect and has faults and to remove these faults and to work to something better is certainly desirable: but I should be misleading you if I were not to say at this stage that I am a little disturbed at the way the discussions of the Technical Committees have been going. There seems to be a tendency in these discussions to "chip away" and the risk is that the cumulative effect of this process, if it is allowed to continue, would have the result that the amount the Administration might support before Congress might in aggregate be sufficient only to support a relief programme and not a full programme of recovery.

With few exceptions, your technical people have not questioned the reasonableness of the quantities of the things the programme asks for. The "chipping away" process therefore can only be on availability of supplies or on the assumptions we have made about their cost. In taking a four-year period, one has got to make assumptions on both these points and, in making assumptions, there is naturally plenty of room for difference of opinion. Therefore, what is really important is to decide whether the assumptions we have made are broadly reasonable.

As far as availability is concerned, the quantities in many critical items were cut in Paris below the full statement of requirements. To meet even these reduced requirements would in some commodities call for some physical sacrifice in the shape of exports from the United States. This may well create problems of real difficulty. But if, for example, the cereals programme has radically to be revised over the entire four years, the *whole* programme may be endangered and the date at which recovery in Western Europe will be complete will be seriously delayed. And no one knows how far that process can be pushed without destroying the programme. Even as it is the people of Europe must live to some extent on deferred hope.

As for prices, I think that we have if anything been too optimistic. For example, on foodstuffs, which account for 60% of the total, some of your experts have told us that we have been rash in assuming that food prices will not rise during the next twelve months and will fall during the last thirty-six months of the programme. Already many prices have gone up substantially above the level assumed in the Report. In July wheat was $2.60 a bushel. It is now $3. Fats prices in the United States are now 25% above the level taken in the Report.

For all these reasons, therefore, I hope that the Administration will feel able to support a programme of the order of magnitude which will permit Europe to move forward to recovery within something like the period contemplated in the Report. I do not at all suggest that the Administration should accept the precise amounts mentioned in the Report, but I do venture to suggest that the size of what is recommended should not greatly differ from what the sixteen countries have stated they will need. A few billions of dollars (and I am not suggesting that a billion dollars is a small sum) may make all the difference between success and failure. I fully realise that the combination of political circumstances in this country which you mentioned to me at our first meeting puts the Administration in a position of real difficulty. But this chance will not occur again and I am convinced it is vital that the opportunity be seized and the work begun on a scale to give it the fullest chance of success.

In addition to this main point, there are three others which I would like to mention to you. We have discussed them among ourselves and I feel sure that you have also, but we have not yet had the occasion to talk about them together. I think it is important, however, that we should lest opinion should harden before we have had a chance to explore each other's points of view.

My first point concerns the form which aid might take. I feel sure that you must have discussed whether aid should be given in the form of dollars or in the form of goods. The final decision on this point must, of course, lie with the Congress. But it may nonetheless be useful to give you our views. We would much prefer aid in the form of dollars than in the form of commodities. There are many arguments in support of this.

(i) European recovery as planned in the Paris Report is not possible unless the whole of the deficit with the Americas is covered. If aid were to be limited to supplies from the United States, Europe would be forced to take all steps possible to obtain the supplies and services from the rest of the American Continent that are needed. These steps might well endanger the actual basis upon which the European recovery programme is based. For example, if the United Kingdom had no dollars with which to buy Argentine wheat, it might be forced to send such extra coal as it has available for export not to Europe as contemplated in the Paris Report, but to Argentina. If this happened, the whole fabric of the recovery programme would begin to crumble. In any case, whatever bargains were made with the rest of the American Continent the full supplies needed for the recovery programme would probably not be forthcoming.

(ii) The deficit with the Americas is not made up entirely of commodities. There are many items which appear for the most part among invisibles for which Europe will want dollars, for example, payments for films, service of American obligations, shipping disbursements, etc.

(iii) Although aid given in terms of commodities does not necessarily imply government procurement, it may tend towards this. Government procurement over the whole field of the commodities which the European countries wish to obtain from the United States would introduce rigidities where now there is the flexibility of private trade and we cannot believe that it is in the interests of either the United States or the European countries that this should be so. It must be borne in mind that after the period of the programme Europe will still wish to import from America and pay for considerable quantities of these goods and it is surely wise that so far as possible the normal trade channels should be left available.

My second point is this. It is natural that in an operation of the sort which we are now discussing people should tend to think in terms of the Lend Lease arrangements. I would like to suggest, however, that there are certain dangers in this way of thought. The purpose of Lend Lease was to provide the Allied countries with those foodstuffs, raw materials and equipment which were essential to the prosecution of the war and it was natural, therefore, to attach as conditions to the provision of such supplies restrictions on the use of these materials in the export trade. If, however, restrictions of this sort were to be imposed either on the supplies purchased with any dollars which might be made available or on the use of the supplies themselves, the purpose of the recovery programme would be frustrated for it is the intention of that programme, among other things, to bring about an equilibrium in Europe's balance of payments by a greatly increased flow of European exports.

My final point is this. The organisation and individuals who physically receive the goods and services supplied to Europe from the United States and the rest of the American Continent will naturally pay for them in the local currency of their own country. The United States Government may wish to impose certain restrictions on the use of these funds. For example, it may wish to stipulate that they be not used for financing current expenditure. Such restrictions will tend to be different for each country. But the sums involved will necessarily be large; it is important that the restrictions imposed on their use should not interfere with or prejudice the economic and financial control of the whole economy that must be exercised by the government of each country. In particular, the vesting of these funds not in the government but in some independent organisation might gravely impair this necessary central control.

There are also serious political dangers in such restrictions. The interpretation of them in the future—and a long future—may be a potential source of irritation in the relations between the United States Government and the governments of the participating countries. If the United States decides to support the European recovery programme, it will in the nature of things have an inherent control over it which it will be in a position to exercise without resort to mechanical devices that might cause the irritation mentioned above.

WASHINGTON, 22nd October, 1947.

O. S. FRANKS

Lot 54 D 361 E Box 328

Extract From "Current Economic Developments", October 27, 1947 [1]

SECRET

. . . . . .

BROAD OUTLINES OF PARIS REPORT ACCEPTABLE BUT MOST TECHNICAL ASPECTS NEED REFINING

For the past several weeks technical experts of the Committee of European Economic Cooperation have been in Washington reviewing the Paris report with officials of US Government agencies, members of the Harriman Committee, and special Congressional liaison per-

------

[1] *Current Economic Developments* is a weekly publication circulated within the Department of State.

sonnel. The meetings have been extremely useful in supplying us with background information and providing a general clarification of the concepts underlying the CEEC report.

While in all public statements we have expressed our gratification with the targets and principles of the report, a great number of omissions and discrepancies from the technical point-of-view have been revealed through close examination of the specific commodity chapters. Certain limitations in the report are recognized as unavoidable. Probably the chief limitation is the fact that statistics are based on conditions as of a certain date in the face of rapidly changing situations. Another major handicap in drafting the report was the fact that the amount of government planning varies greatly among the participating states, with some economies having substantial government control and others having comparatively little. The fact that none of the participants have a completely controlled economy, nor desire to have, makes programming more difficult.

We have no argument with the broad outlines of the report, and we recognize that detailed planning for the future is practically impossible. Any program for the recovery of Europe must be flexible enough to meet inevitable changes in conditions and must be regarded more as a blue print than a program.

Even though a great deal of work remains to be done before recommendations to Congress can be finalized, it is deemed inadvisable to reconvene the CEEC in Paris since it is believed that such a conference could not do much to rectify the technical aspects of the report. It is believed it will be more effective for CEEC technicians to continue working with US officials, while additional information is supplied continually by the participating countries. There has been some indication, from reports received from our missions, that a number of the participating countries have been refining the figures which they submitted at Paris. The time schedule also makes a second Paris conference questionable since a report must be ready by November 10 to submit to the joint meeting of the Senate and House Foreign Relations Committees.

One general criticism is that little effort appears to have been made in appraising the submitted national requirements for imported goods and services against their contribution to European recovery as a whole. The work in Washington is aimed at reconciling the requirements with availabilities and world requirements. A Steering Committee [2] has been established to coordinate reports of the working parties, which are divided as follows: agricultural machinery; food, fertilizer; maritime transportation; inland transport; timber; iron

---

[2] Reference here is to the interdepartmental Advisory Steering Committee.

and steel; coal; electric power; petroleum; mining machinery; electricity; and balance of payments. Germany's participation in a recovery program is being fully represented by OMGUS and Departmental officials. In many instances our German program is the focal point of whether or not certain commodities can be made available in the required amounts.

[Here follows a more detailed analysis of the operations and conclusions of individual U.S. working groups reviewing the CEEC technical reports.]

Lot 122, Box 19B

The CEEC Washington Delegation to the Department of State[1]

SECRET   WASHINGTON, October 27, 1947.

AIDE-MÉMOIRE

The Members of the Committee of European Economic Co-operation at present in Washington have, during recent weeks, had important and useful conversations with the Representatives of the U.S. Administration on the problems of aid for Europe.

The European Group is grateful to the U.S. Government for the conditions in which these conversations are being held. In particular they consider that a large number of technical questions which, for lack of time, could not be fully covered in the report of the 16 participating countries have been clarified. The replies to the supplementary questionnaires which have been sent to the respective capitals of the countries concerned will have been of help to the Administration in formulating their views about the character of the programme of co-operation drawn up in Paris, and on the scale of external assistance which is indispensable to ensure the success of that programme. Nevertheless, it has not been possible to give full consideration to certain essential problems although they have been touched on in the course of these exchanges of views. It is therefore necessary for us to set out frankly for the American Government these essential points since they cannot be ignored without the risk of compromising the work of European economic recovery on which all our Governments have set their minds.

These particular points to which we believe we should draw the attention of the State Department concern the amount and period of

---

[1] This was circulated as ASC Document 16, November 3, 1947. A copy i French bearing the penned notation CEEC/W/44, dated October 28, is in fil FW840.50 Recovery/10–2477.

the aid envisaged, its form, its conditions, and, finally, the organisation which should be set up for its administration. The indications in this note are set forth simply as an interpretation of the report prepared in Paris in the belief that they reflect the spirit in which this was drawn up.

I. AMOUNT OF PROPOSED AID

The European Group points out that the figure for the dollar deficit in the balance of payments of the 16 participating countries during the next four years as shown by the Paris Report constitutes an order of magnitude below which the amount of aid should not be reduced without the risk of jeopardising the achievement of the programme which the participating countries have in view. It is certainly not possible to calculate exactly the amount of this deficit which depends on the size of the harvests and therefore on climate, on the movement of prices, on the development of our dollar earnings, on the resumption of trade between Western and Eastern Europe, etc.; but the uncertainty of the factors affecting the figure contained in the Paris Report may lead to revisions upwards as well as downwards. Indeed, some of the favourable assumptions on which the calculation is based may eventually prove to be unfounded and there should therefore be an adequate measure of flexibility in the recommendations which are presented in this respect. The consequences of insufficient availability of certain commodities necessary for the rehabilitation of the European economy must also be emphasised. This factor, far from reducing the global amount of aid necessary, would tend to increase it. The restoration of equilibrium in the balance of payments might, in this case, require a longer period than that envisaged in the Paris Report.

Further, the European group has drawn the attention of the Administration to the particular importance of the year 1948. If certain countries, in the course of this first year, can obtain the resources necessary not only to cover their essential dollar imports but also to ensure their internal economic and financial stabilisation, our task over the coming years will be greatly facilitated. Thanks to the stabilisation policy which it is in any case intended to pursue, resources both material and monetary which are now hoarded will be put into circulation to hasten the recovery of the countries concerned.

II. FORM OF PROPOSED AID

American aid can be furnished either wholly in dollars or wholly in goods, or partly in dollars and partly in goods. The European countries hope that the greatest possible part of the external aid will be supplied in dollars. In carrying out our programme of imports we are anxious that so far as possible the ordinary channels of trade should be used. This condition will be more difficult to fulfil if help is furnished in commodities rather than in dollars. In addition the possibility of receiving dollars rather than goods will permit each of the purchasing countries to procure the types and qualities of goods which are best suited to their needs. Experience during the course of the war has shown the importance of this consideration.

There is no doubt that these dollars will for the most part be used directly in the U.S. themselves which are the principal suppliers of raw materials, foodstuffs and the necessary equipment. Nevertheless, all these commodities which are required will not be able to be obtained on the American market. The European nations will have to place contracts outside the U.S. with producers who will demand payments in dollars. The participating countries will in consequence have to rely on dollars to enable them to pay for these supplies which are indispensable to the execution of the European programme.

We recognise that all necessary steps will have to be taken to limit the inflationary pressure which might result from these dollar purchases. We are ready to examine with the American Government how best we may co-operate in this regard with the American Administration in the common interest.

III. Conditions of Proposed Aid

We have had no clear indication from the American Administration of the possible conditions of the aid that may be granted. The estimated requirements are so considerable that if the aid that is furnished should lead to Europe having to make large transfers, the participating countries would not be in a position at the end of the period in view to ensure a stable equilibrium in their balance of payments.

At the same time, the charges to be paid to service an external debt that is too heavy would make it more difficult to obtain the credits from the International Bank or private banks which will certainly be necessary to pay for long term capital equipment.

The sums in national currency resulting from the sale in the internal market of the products imported in pursuit of the European recovery programme will not in any case, in accordance with the terms of the Paris Report, be used to cover current budget deficits.

The conditions under which these funds may be used will vary from country to country. Consequently the arrangements which will have to be made governing the use of these funds will be different for each country and will lead to individual discussions.

Nevertheless we consider it important to note that these funds should be the property of the recipient European country. This is implied in the way in which the report of the 16 participating countries was drafted.

The question of how these sums should be handled poses a delicate political problem. All those who during recent months have continually opposed the so-called "Marshall Plan" and have announced their intention of using all means to block it, will seek to show that the existence of these funds is capable of conferring upon the U.S. considerable powers infringing the independence of the European countries concerned. Thus these Governments should have these funds in local currency at their disposal and employ them in accordance with whatever arrangements may be concluded. The method which we suggest, while it leaves the ownership of these funds in the hands of the European country produces the desired results: as a result of the conditions which will govern the use of these funds, they will in fact be used to promote the execution of the general European recovery programme and to lighten the task of the United States.

IV. Administration of the Proposed Aid

The European Group points out that in the Paris Report the participating Governments declared their readiness, if the aid necessary for the application of the programme is given them, to set up a joint organisation with two functions:—

*On the one hand to examine and report on the extent to which the programme is being realised,

On the other hand to ensure by joint action, the realisation of the economic conditions necessary to enable the general objectives to which each country has pledged itself to be effectively achieved.

As has been stated, we are ready when the time comes to elaborate the task which would be entrusted to this organisation. It is, however, evident that such an elaboration will depend on the character of the external aid and of the organisations which on its side the American Government deems it useful to set up to ensure the execution of the programme.

In the Paris Report the sixteen participating countries declared their readiness to give, within the framework of the overall programme which they had in mind, a certain number of pledges concerning particularly their production targets, their foreign trade, European co-operation etc. In envisaging these pledges they took into account similar pledges to be given by each of the participating countries. If, however, the scale and the form and the general conditions of the external aid should be substantially different from those we have envisaged it is probable that the participating nations, however willing they might be, would not be able to sustain the pledges embodied in the

---

*The English text of this paragraph differs from the French version which could not be changed in time. It is agreed by the C.E.E.C. Group that the English text is the correct one. [Footnote in source text.]

Report. In particular, the carrying out of these pledges requires that the participating countries should be able to obtain not only in the United States but also in the whole American Continent the raw materials, foodstuffs and equipment which are indispensable.

That is why the Group of the Committee of European Economic Cooperation wished to remit to the State Department this *aide-mémoire*, since it is conscious of the seriousness of the repercussions on the overall plan which would flow from recommendations which did not give sufficient consideration to the essential interests which we have the honour to set out in this paper.

FW 840.50 Recovery/10–2447

The CEEC Washington Delegation to the Participating Governments Not Represented in Washington [1]

CONFIDENTIAL   31st October, 1947.

IMMEDIATE

32. The following is sent to all participating countries not represented in Washington at the request of Sir Oliver Franks.

The calendar of the main events since my second circular telegram was drafted (it was despatched from Washington on October 20th [2]) is as follows:—

a) October 18th	Release of the Krug Committee Report.
b) October 21st	Meeting with Bonesteel Committee [3] on Commercial Policy.
c) October 22nd	Meeting with Bonesteel Committee on European Organisation.
d) October 23rd	Dinner with Mr. Harriman and members of his Committee.
e) October 23rd	Announcement by Mr. Truman of convening of special session of Congress *inter alia* to consider immediate and longer term aid to Europe.
f) October 24th	Meeting with Mr. Lovett.

2. Apart from the above, meetings of the Technical Committees with the American Administration have continued and have been supplemented by meetings between Technical Committees and the International Bank. The latter have asked questions additional to those already discussed in Washington, with the general objective of check-

---

[1] The file copy bears the penned notation CEEC/W/43.
[2] Not printed.
[3] Transcript summaries of this and certain other meetings are in Lot 122.

ing the basic assumptions and consistency of the recovery programme. They have naturally paid particular attention to those portions of the programme such as equipment needs which are likely to be of more direct concern to the Bank. These discussions with the Bank have not involved our approaching participating countries with additional questionnaires and it has been possible to answer most of the questions on the spot.

3. As requested at the second meeting held with the Bonesteel Committee to discuss the General Production Programme, a memorandum [4] has been sent in to the Americans developing further examples of economic co-operation between the participating countries. You will receive copies. At meetings with the Food and Agriculture Committee the Americans queried import requirements of nitrogen fertilisers on the grounds that there was unused manufacturing capacity in the participating countries and that nitrogen production was being used for non-fertiliser purposes. Representatives of the Committee were sent to London where a meeting of interested countries was held to verify the facts. A report of the findings should shortly be available for the Americans.

4. The items in paragraph 1 will now be dealt with seriatim:

a) It will be recalled that the Krug Committee was set up by the President to review the natural resources of the United States with particular reference to the possible effects of their exploitation for foreign aid. President Truman himself summarised the contents of the report in the words "on the whole our national resources are physically sufficient to preserve the national security and the American standard of living and at the same time to support a considerable foreign aid programme." When questioned by the press Mr. Krug admitted that in the writing of the report he had in mind a figure for foreign aid of up to 20 billion dollars. From the point of view of Marshall Aid the Krug Committee findings can be considered generally favourable but the report contains a number of reservations and did not set out to deal with all the relevant economic factors.

b) Commercial Policy. Since all the questions on the American agenda related to intra-European trade, Sir Oliver Franks opened by stressing the importance of viewing such trade in its proper relationship to the wider problem of the necessary expansion of European exports to the rest of the world. In the subsequent discussion Mr. Boland [5] acted as the main spokesman of the C.E.E.C. group.

The Americans asked whether any distinction had been drawn in Paris between essential and non-essential goods in relation to intra-

[4] A copy of this memorandum was printed as part of Advisory Steering Committee Document ASC D–7/3 (Supplement 1), October 31, 1947 (Lot 122).
[5] F.H. Boland, a CEEC delegate representing Ireland.

European trade. It was explained that certain exports were important for the economies of participating countries but that it was recognised that certain countries might not be able to afford to import as much as previously. Bilateral agreements helped to promote the exchange of useful goods and would continue to play a necessary part in the commercial policy of the participating countries.

A considerable part of the discussion was devoted to Customs Unions. American thought is clearly much pre-occupied with the extent to which the reduction or elimination of quantitative restrictions and tariffs might bring benefits to Europe through the creation of a larger domestic market and concentration of productive effort. They appreciate the magnitude and importance of the problem of European trade with the rest of the world, but perhaps not so clearly the limited extent to which Europe's essential requirements from the rest of the world can be affected by a development of intra-European trade.

A question about restrictive business practices of a cartel character was not strongly pressed. The brief prepared for the C.E.E.C. replies will give further information on the whole subject and meeting.

c) European Organisation. In this case also please refer to the American questionnaire [6] and the brief prepared for the delegates. M. Alphand acted as the main spokesman of the C.E.E.C. group and explained the functions of the proposed Joint Organisation on the lines set out in the General Report. The Americans agreed that it was not possible to clarify much further the form and functions of the organisation until more was known of the nature of American aid and any U.S. organisation which might be set up to deal with it. They however indicated that it would probably be of great assistance if the European organisation could make recommendations as to allocations of scarce supplies which were not covered by existing international bodies such as I.E.F.C. or E.C.O. We agreed with them that it would probably be desirable to continue to use these latter organisations for Marshall supplies. The Americans pointed out that they would probably find it necessary to reinstitute in the U.S. some export controls for scarce commodities, but emphasised their desire to maintain existing channels of trade.

We were asked how the Bizone would be represented on the new organisation but reserved our reply. Although the matter was discussed no effort was made to delimit responsibilities as between the new organisation and existing international organisations. Sir Oliver Franks in conclusion stressed that the former would be an advisory and not an executive body.

---

[6] The Advisory Steering Committee developed a series of questions which, in effect, formed the agenda for each of the meetings. Copies of these questions are in series 6 and 7 of the ASC Documents, copies of which are in Lot 122.

d) The dinner given by Mr. Harriman was attended by all the delegates and by nine members of his Committee. An unofficial agenda for discussion had been seen previously and covered a wide field. In fact the discussion after dinner centred exclusively on the different forms the aid might take and the conditions which might attach to the use of the local currency arising from the sale of the goods received under the aid programme. It was clear that the Harriman members were thinking of aid under three heads:

(i) short term consumer goods e.g. food, fuel and fertilisers;
(ii) intermediate goods e.g. raw materials and some types of machinery;
(iii) long term capital investment projects.

They were inclined to think that (i) should be dealt with by grants in aid, (iii) by loans, e.g. from the International Bank. As regards (ii) they felt that it was politically necessary that they should be offered something in return albeit on lines which did not impair the recovery programme. This "contrepartie" might take the form of some sort of control over or participation in the use of the local currency, e.g. for the purchase of strategic raw materials required by the U.S.A. in amounts in excess of their normal imports of such materials.

Replies by C.E.E.C. delegates mainly emphasised the political and economic difficulties inherent in the suggestions regarding category (ii) and particularly how essential it was that governments should retain full control over the local currency proceeds of aid although they were prepared to agree to limitations on their use to non-inflationary purposes on the lines laid down in the Report.

e) You will have seen the full text of President Truman's statement over the radio on October 24th.[7] We welcome the decision to call a special session of Congress on November 17th which will consider action to curb price increases, interim aid *inter alia* to France and Italy, and the speeding up of action on the Marshall proposals.

f) Sir Oliver Franks saw Mr. Lovett on October 22nd to pave the way for the meeting with delegates which took place on October 24th and to suggest that the discussion should cover major outstanding points of policy such as the amount and form of the aid and the proposed continuing European organisation. A brief memorandum on these subjects was left with Mr. Lovett on the 22nd and is being circulated to all participating countries.

During the discussion on October 24th Mr. Lovett indicated that the State Department would endeavour to secure adoption of the general lines of the Paris Report in an enabling act and would ask for an appropriation for 1948. He thought that some return would be required for part of the aid and reference was again made to strategic

---

[7] For references to this and related statements, see editorial note, p. 470.

materials for stock-piling but not at the expense of normal trade. Whilst admitting that supplies from the rest of America were essential to European recovery, Mr. Lovett indicated that it would be politically very difficult for America to provide the full amount of dollars for such purchases. Finally Mr. Lovett pointed out that America would be taking a "calculated risk" in supplying large scale aid to Europe and they would want to know that the European countries were reciprocating by risking something in return—possibly by making some sacrifice of national customs and traditions. This was taken as a reference to the American desire for increased economic co-operation between the participating countries with perhaps particular reference to Customs Unions.

5. It seemed evident at the time of the Lovett conversation that the Administration had not yet reached its own decisions on major points of policy. As the meeting only lasted one hour it was not possible to do justice to these important matters. Accordingly at the suggestion of the Rapporteur General, a memorandum was agreed by the C.E.E.C. group and sent in to Mr. Lovett on October 27th. The memorandum once again emphasises the importance of not whittling down the total amount of aid and thereby converting the programme from one of Recovery to one of Relief, the importance of providing aid to the maximum possible extent in dollars available for the use throughout the American continent and the necessity to avoid conditions which would create future transfer problems or infringe national sovereignties (use of local currencies). As regards the latter point the document states:

"The conditions under which these funds may be used will vary from country to country. Consequently the arrangements which will have to be made governing the use of these funds will be different for each country and will lead to individual discussions."

Finally the memorandum deals with the administration of the proposed aid and the form and functions of the continuing organisation. It is pointed out that the pledges undertaken by the participating countries are dependent on their obtaining not only in the U.S. but also in the whole American continent the raw materials, foodstuffs and equipment which are indispensable.

6. Every effort has been made both in the above memorandum (copies of which are being sent to all participating countries) and throughout the talks to keep within the terms and spirit of the Paris Report.

7. A meeting between delegates and some members of the Cabinet is likely to take place in the near future. Meanwhile the calling of the special session as early as November 17th and the impending publica-

tion of the Harriman and other Presidential Committee reports has thrown a considerable strain on the Administration and curtailed their time for discussion. There seems no reason to change the tentative opinion previously expressed that the work of the C.E.E.C. group would be likely to end by about November 8th. Some Technical Committee representatives may, however, need to stay longer.

8. This telegram is being sent by the Chairman to those participating countries not represented in Washington through the British Missions in the respective capitals, but copies are also being lodged with the representatives of the countries concerned in Washington.

9. Further developments will be reported.

840.50 Recovery/11–347

The Under Secretary of State (Lovett) to the Chairman of the CEEC Washington Delegation (Franks)

CONFIDENTIAL   WASHINGTON, November 3, 1947.

INFORMAL AIDE-MÉMOIRE

In the course of the discussion which I had with you and your colleagues on October 24, I touched upon certain points raised in the unofficial *aide-mémoire* which you presented to me on October 22. An informal indication of present thinking on certain of these points may be helpful to you.

There is no doubt in my mind or in the minds of those associated with me that the program must be designed to achieve genuine recovery; it must not be a mere program of temporary relief. The approach to a solution must be neither half-hearted nor piecemeal.

In my judgment, the report of the Paris Conference is a well reasoned analysis of the problem and presents fundamental lines of action for the achievement of genuine European recovery.

In considering the assistance which the United States might reasonably give in the execution of a specific program falling within that broad framework, we, on our side, must give careful thought to additional factors. The capacity of the United States to continue to export far larger quantities of goods than it imports is strictly limited. We cannot assume unlimited obligations for meeting the balance of payment deficits of other countries. Many of the commodities most essential to European recovery are in critically short supply, not only in Europe and in the United States but in the entire world. If we were to make more dollar assistance available than can be honored in the form of goods, the additional assistance would be purely illusory and would merely contribute to an undesirable inflationary spiral in world prices.

I recognize that the problem of European recovery has both a commodity aspect and a financial aspect. I am hopeful that a program of assistance from the United States can be worked out which will constitute our proper contribution, when considered from either point of view, to a total program which gives real promise of success. But this cannot be merely an American program.

In our opinion it calls for prompt and vigorous steps to restore internal monetary and budgetary stability by the participating countries. As your report points out, (paragraph 65) "the success of the program depends on such stability".[1] Furthermore, the most intense efforts will be required on the part of the European countries, both individually and collectively, to increase their production and their exports if sufficient means of payment are to be found to finance their other requirements. Other countries, especially in the Western Hemisphere, also have a part to play. We recognize the desirability of obtaining flexibility to permit procurement in such countries, in certain circumstances, particularly of commodities not adequately available in the United States, but it is also our hope that means can be found of obtaining at least some share of supplies for Europe from third countries without payment in dollars.

I am hopeful that, even with respect to that portion of United States aid which might be in the form of commodities, procedures can be developed which will preserve to the maximum extent the flexibility of private trade and the preservation of normal trade channels. It is clearly basic to the entire program that exports from the European countries be rapidly developed and that these exports be of a character which can continue and expand after special United States assistance to European recovery comes to an end. Any conditions as to the use of materials supplied by the United States in the export trade of the participating countries must be worked out with this basic objective in mind.

I am in agreement with your point that restrictions imposed on the use of local currency arising from United States assistance should not interfere with or prejudice the economic and financial control of the economy that must be exercised by the Government of each country. It is my hope that formulae can be mutually agreed upon between this Government and the Governments of the participating countries with respect to the use of these funds which will promote and not interfere with the overall objectives of European economic recovery.

---

[1] Reference is to *Committee of European Economic Cooperation*, vol. I, *General Report*.

Although I am sure you are fully aware of the controlling voice the Congress will exercise in these matters I mention this factor again to emphasize that my comments are merely an indication of the present trend in formulating the recommendations of this Department for presentation to the Congress.

[ROBERT A. LOVETT]

FW 840.50 Recovery/11–347

Record of a Meeting Between Members of the Advisory Steering Committee and the CEEC Delegation [1]

CONFIDENTIAL

WASHINGTON, November 4, 1947.

PRESENT

CEEC GROUP

Delegates: Sir Oliver Franks (U.K.)
Messrs. Hervé Alphand (France)
        F. H. Boland (Ireland)
        Campilli (Italy)
        Ole Colbjornsen (Norway)
        H. M. Hirschfeld (Netherlands)
        Verdelis (Greece)

Other: Messrs. Marris (U.K.)
        Marjolin (France)
        Serreulles (France)
        Colonna (Italy)
        Van der Beugel (Netherlands)

U.S. GROUP

Messrs. Averell Harriman, Secretary of Commerce
        Robert A. Lovett, Under Secretary
          of State
        William H. Draper, Under Secretary
          of the Army
        Willard L. Thorp, Assistant
          Secretary of State
        M. S. Szymczak, Governor of Bd. of
          Governors of Federal
          Reserve System
        Charles E. Bohlen, Counselor of
          Dept. of State
        C. H. Bonesteel, Dept. of State
        Lincoln Gordon, Dept. of State
        Melvin L. Manfull, Dept. of State
        Roger Tubby, Dept. of State
        T. C. Blaisdell, Jr., Dept. of Commerce
        Philip M. Kaiser, Dept. of Labor
        Frank A. Southard, Dept. of Treasury
        Dan Wheeler, Dept. of Interior
        J. Burke Knapp, Federal Reserve Board
Colonel R. M. Cheseldine, Dept. of the Army
Lt. Col. Philip Shepley, Dept. of the Army

[1] These minutes, presumably prepared by the staff of the Advisory Steering Committee, were circulated as document ASC D–7/7, December 9, by Mr. Manfull, Secretary of the Committee. The meeting was held in the Department of State at 3:30 p. m.

1. In opening of the meeting, MR. LOVETT stated that, while the United States Executive Branch had now reached the point where the factual basis and the general pattern of the program is quite clear, agreement must be reached on certain basic policy decisions. The majority of these policy questions either cannot be decided on the basis of present information or the alternate courses of action which exist will require extremely delicate evaluation before decisions are made.

SPECIFIC POINTS NOT PREVIOUSLY RAISED BY THE CEEC DELEGATION

2. SIR OLIVER FRANKS stated that, since the CEEC Delegation will be returning to Europe shortly, the members desired to obtain preliminary views of the general policy lines which the U.S. Administration is likely to follow in order that: (*a*) the CEEC can determine how these views will affect the recovery program as conceived by the CEEC at Paris; and (*b*) these views can be taken into account in future work in CEEC and in the individual participating countries. He stated that in addition to the basic points raised in the two *aides-mémoire* transmitted to the State Department by the CEEC Delegation, the CEEC would like an indication of prospective U.S. action with respect to the key items of fertilizers (particularly nitrogen fertilizers) and semi-finished steel, which are of critical importance to the recovery program. He observed that fertilizers in sufficient quantities are essential since they directly affect the rate of recovery in the agricultural production program. Semi-finished steel is essential across the board but affects primarily the programs contemplated by France, the United Kingdom and Italy, in that order. The CEEC is aware that this request might be considered premature in view of imminent publication of the Harriman Committee report. MR. LOVETT replied that general comment on items in short supply would be premature at this time, since the report of the Harriman Committee will prescribe the general limits of availabilities. He inquired whether Secretary Harriman desired to comment on this point.

3. MR. HARRIMAN observed that he occupied a dual position with respect to the recovery program—that of a Cabinet Officer directly concerned with the program and at the same time Chairman of the Harriman Committee of the distinguished citizens appointed by the President to develop recommendations on certain aspects of the program. He requested that the CEEC Delegation keep in mind that the report of the Harriman Committee did not necessarily represent his official views as Secretary of Commerce on the subjects covered therein. With respect to the questions raised by Sir Oliver Franks, he pointed out that a determination cannot be made within the next few weeks since such a determination will be based on a screening process to determine the relative importance of short-supply items to the U.S.

economy as compared with CEEC requirements. In respect to steel, for example, it is a matter of degree, since if too much steel is allocated to meet CEEC requirements it might limit the capacity of the United States to produce.

4. MR. HARRIMAN stated that there was perhaps an aspect of the Harriman Committee report which warranted informal communication to the CEEC Delegation. This aspect relates to food requirements and the food production program. It is the general view of the United States technical experts on the Harriman Committee that the CEEC countries will not obtain the estimated food requirements because of world-wide short supply. Furthermore, it is their feeling that the CEEC has not explored fully the potential sources of supply outside the U.S. within the control of certain CEEC countries; i.e., their colonies and dependent areas. MR. HARRIMAN recommended that the CEEC give consideration to this aspect of the Harriman Committee report since the United States experts on that committee believe that as long as the CEEC countries place abnormal reliance on the United States for fulfillment of food requirements recurrent food crises will probably develop.

POINTS RAISED IN PREVIOUS CEEC "AIDE-MÉMOIRE"

5. MR. LOVETT stated that it might be helpful if he were to indicate the present lines of the thinking in the Department on the points raised in the previous CEEC *aide-mémoire*. For this purpose he had prepared an informal *aide-mémoire* which he would read and make available to the CEEC Delegation. (At this point MR. LOVETT read the informal U.S. *aide-mémoire* of November 3—see copy attached.[2]) In addition the following specific questions merit further comment:

a. *Aid from Latin America and Canada:* MR. LOVETT observed that the United States Government had considered suggesting to the CEEC Delegation that the most appropriate way for the CEEC countries to obtain aid from Latin America would be for them to address an aid request directly to the Pan American Union and that simultaneous action should be taken with respect to Canada. SIR OLIVER stated that, while the CEEC did not desire to comment on the approach to the Pan American Union or Canada at the present time since the CEEC and the governments of the individual CEEC countries would desire to consider the proposal further, the CEEC Delegation would appreciate information on the background developments leading to the U.S. proposal. MR. THORP replied that the proposal stems primarily from the importance of these countries as potential sources of supply for items in critical short supply in the U.S. It is a feeling of some U.S.

---

[2] *Supra.*

experts that the resources of Canada and the Latin American countries in these key items might be somewhat larger than was originally supposed. Therefore, it seems desirable to tap these sources in order to obtain a total amount of commodities which more nearly approximates the total amount necessary for European recovery. Since development of a procedure for procurement of these items would obviously come to a negotiation point at some stage, it might be desirable to bring together representatives of the countries seeking supplies, of the U.S. as the procurement agent, and the supplying country. Efforts should be made to avoid a series of bilateral negotiations.

6. The approach through the Pan American Union was suggested merely as a means of simplifying the procedure since its sub-structure includes an Economic and Social Council consisting of representatives of all Latin American countries and the U.S. Adoption of this procedure would obviate the possible development of a series of direct bilateral approaches.

In this regard SIR OLIVER FRANKS stated that the CEEC Delegation had some concern that if initiative for assistance from Latin America were to come from Europe it might result in the individual CEEC countries becoming involved in a series of bilateral negotiations. For example, it is conceivable that if the U.K. were not able to give Argentina the dollars required for commodities, and if Argentina would not accept sterling, the U.K. might then have to give coal to Argentina at the expense of the European recovery program. MR. LOVETT replied that the proposal did not embrace the possibilities of bilateral discussions with individual Latin American countries but merely a request for economic assistance. He observed that it would be awkward for the U.S. Government to request other American Republics to assist in aid to Europe without their first having received from the CEEC a request for such assistance.

MR. THORP continued that the simultaneous CEEC approach to Canada is an essential element in the proposal because of Canada's major importance as a potential source of supply and the desirability of not creating the impression that a request for assistance from Canada under the program is in the nature of an after-thought.

7. In response to a question as to whether U.S. Government has received any views from Latin American countries on this subject, MR. THORP replied that informally three representatives of three Latin American countries had inquired as to developments regarding a European recovery program and the possible way in which the Latin American countries might fit into the program. He observed that he had indicated to these representatives that there was no question that Latin

American countries would be brought into the picture in the very near future. He added that the Department of State had discussed the question with the U.S. representative on the Pan American Union who feels that a direct CEEC aid request to the Pan American Union would be the most appropriate approach.

b. Off-Shore Procurement: MR. LOVETT stated that current thinking in the Administration is in pursuance of the thesis that, in so far as possible, procurement and trade should follow normal channels of trade. Consequently, Congress will be requested to appropriate funds to the U.S. agency administering the program and an effort will be made to provide for wide flexibility in the allocation and administration of such funds.

He stressed the fact that such an arrangement is dependent entirely upon Congressional action. However, even assuming favorable Congressional action, it should be clear to all that the U.S. public would not permit purchase of commodities in third countries with United States funds at prices substantially higher than those prevailing in the United States. This fact will require some measure of cooperation among the CEEC, the United States, and the supplying country. MR. HARRIS inquired whether this implied that all procurement in third countries would be solely through U.S. Government procurement agencies. MR. THORP replied in the negative, pointing out that in certain cases it might involve only the U.S. making payments on approved transactions.

c. Form of U.S. Aid: MR. LOVETT stated that the general line of thought at present is that U.S. assistance would be partly in the form of loans and partly in the form of grants-in-aid. Only with respect to grants-in-aid does the U.S. Administration see an area for further discussion on the subject of the use of local currency counterparts of U.S. aid. While a division of opinion still exists in the U.S. Executive Branch as to their use, the area of disagreement does not extend to the point where it would render the transfer problems or the capital investment problems more difficult.

MR. BOLAND inquired whether he would be correct in assuming that a general formula had been developed which could be applied in determining whether a certain category of aid would be in the form of a loan or of a grant-in-aid and that specific details for individual CEEC countries would be embodied in the bilateral agreements when negotiated. MR. LOVETT replied in the affirmative.

MR. HIRSCHFELD inquired whether the U.S. envisaged loans of the following types: (1) loans to finance certain types of U.S. aid which would assist in meeting current balance of payment deficits; and, (2) loans from the International Bank or other sources to help finance

the purchase of capital equipment for development projects. MR
LOVETT replied in the affirmative.

d. *Local Currency Counterparts of U.S. Assistance:* Following an
expression of gratitude as to the spirit and manner in which the U.S
has approached the problem of European recovery, MR. ALPHAND
stressed the importance of arriving at a mutually satisfactory arrange
ment for the handling of local European currency counterparts o
U.S. assistance. He stated that in view of the political implications in
volved the CEEC realizes that no final conclusion can be reached
at the present. For example, from the U.S. political viewpoint thi
problem must be considered in light of the requirement for maximun
efficient use of U.S. aid. From the European political viewpoint i
must be considered in light of the recurring reports from certain seg
ments of the public that the European recovery program will result i
U.S. infringement of the national sovereignty of the participatin
countries. While it is recognized that this latter line of reasoning i
clearly overdrawn, it is still necessary to develop a sound and mutuall
agreed formula for handling local currencies.

In this connection MR. LOVETT stated that these were the very con
siderations that create the problem. From the U.S. viewpoint the Eu
ropean recovery program is in a sense a risk both from the economi
and political standpoints if we keep in mind the scale of the aid en
visaged and the internal political factors involved. However, U.S
public opinion in general will require that the European countrie
take a risk commensurate to that undertaken by the U.S. Since there i
a lively recollection in certain sections of the U.S. public of unhapp
past experiences in connection with the use of local currency counter
parts of U.S. aid, it will be necessary under the program now en
visaged to provide adequate safeguards.

MR. LOVETT expressed confidence that a mutually agreeable arrang
ment based on a rule of reason could be developed. He observed the
various segments of the U.S. Government and the U.S. public migl
advance extreme suggestions for the appropriate method of dealin
with this problem which may cause alarm among those persons in tl
CEEC countries not intimately familiar with the U.S. government
processes. He requested that the CEEC Delegation bear in mind, an
transmit to the appropriate persons in their governments, that the
should take their cue on this matter from the U.S. Administration.

e. *Stabilization Loans:* DR. HIRSCHFELD inquired whether the U.S
position with respect to loans to CEEC countries for stabilizatic
assistance had been clarified to the point where preliminary viev
could be given. MR. LOVETT replied that the subject was still und
consideration and no firm decision on the amount or timing for suc
loans had been reached to date.

FURTHER ACTION REQUIRED

8. MR. BONESTEEL stated that pending clarification of Congressional action on the program a mutual problem exists of carrying on the continuing work necessary to obviate a hiatus between possible final authorization for the program and the time when the program can be placed into full operation. This continuing work might include: (*a*) the timing of the review process in CEEC after anticipated U.S. availabilities are known, (*b*) reaffirmation of mutual commitments adopted in Paris and other conditions in the negotiation of the multilateral and bilateral agreements, and (*c*) organization and staffing of the U.S. and continuing European organizations etc. While the U.S. will continue to communicate through the normal diplomatic channels, there appears to be need for some collective action by the CEEC countries on these matters.

9. SIR OLIVER FRANKS stated that it would be helpful to the CEEC Delegation if some indication could be given of a timetable on which the U.S. Administration is currently operating. MR. BONESTEEL replied that definitive information could not be given at present, although it is hoped that the interim aid program would have an over-riding priority in the special session and that consideration of the full-scale program would proceed as soon as possible thereafter. MR. BOHLEN concurred, adding that because of the many variables involved no clear indication could be given until sometime after November 10. He inquired whether the CEEC Delegation was leaving a representative of its Secretariat in Washington who could serve as a contact point for providing continuing information to the CEEC countries. SIR OLIVER replied in the negative but indicated that the embassies of the respective participating countries would forward to the Department of State the names of the representative[s] who will be responsible for reporting to the participating governments on these points. (See ASC D–20 [3])

a. Treatment of U.S. Private Interests Under the Program. MR. BLAISDELL stated that numerous inquiries have been received from private U.S. investors as to their possible treatment under the program. He inquired as to: (*a*) whether in drawing up the Paris Report the CEEC countries had included for balance of payments purposes the U.S. development projects financed wholly or partly by U.S. private capital; and, (*b*) what approach would be used in this regard in the coming years under the program. He pointed out that it was essential to have an agreed U.S.–CEEC view on this subject. SIR OLIVER FRANKS replied that since the practice varied among the individual CEEC countries in their past treatment of such investments, the CEEC

---

[3] Not printed. Various missions subsequently designated certain individuals as their special representatives on matters concerned with the CEEC.

Delegation would prepare a note on this subject and transmit it to the U.S. Government.

Speaking on the behalf of the CEEC Delegation, SIR OLIVER FRANKS expressed appreciation for information on the basic lines of U.S. thinking at present. In particular, the CEEC Delegation was encouraged by the expression of U.S. views on the following points: (*a*) the fact that the U.S. conceives the program in terms of a program for recovery and not relief and the full appreciation displayed by the U.S. representatives on the need for flexibility in the program; (*b*) assurances with respect to the use of local currency counterparts of U.S. assistance; and, (*c*) the views with respect to the possibility of procurement outside the U.S.

B. Development of Programs for Interim and Long-Term Aid

Editorial Note

The need for an emergency aid program to cover short-term needs was pointed out in various documents beginning in August, and on September 9, at the first meeting of the Advisory Steering Committee, Acting Secretary of State Lovett said that it would be "necessary in any event to provide Europe with food and fuel this winter if the major European countries are to remain sufficiently strong that the basis will survive upon which to erect the Marshall Plan (European Recovery Program) in its long-term sense. Therefore, the current thinking in the Department of State is that a European recovery plan should be in two stages: (*a*) an interim emergency program to meet the irreducible minimum subsistence requirements for certain countries, and (*b*) the larger continuing program of rehabilitation and reconstruction. It is believed that these two factors can be integrated under the program." (Lot 122)

The Committee decided at its meeting of September 25 that the "Departments of State and Treasury in consultation with the Army on bizonal items would prepare a paper on measures of Executive Action to meet the emergency aspect of an interim aid program for transmittal to the President for use in connection with his meeting on September 29 with certain Congressional leaders."

At a news conference following this meeting President Truman announced that he was writing to the chairmen of the Senate Committee on Foreign Relations, the House Committee on Foreign Affairs, the Senate Committee on Appropriations, and the House Committee on Appropriations, "requesting that they call their committees together to consider the urgent need for aid to Western Europe." (For texts of this statement and the letters, see *Public Papers of the Presidents of the United States: Harry S. Truman, 1947*, pages 445, 451.)

On October 18 the Advisory Steering Committee was told by its acting chairman, Colonel Bonesteel, that the existing machinery of government needed to be pulled together to prepare the recovery program for presentation to the Congress. It had not yet been decided whether to present the full program or just an interim aid program.

President Truman announced at a news conference on October 23 that he was calling the Congress to a special session beginning on November 17 to consider, among other things, the need for emergency foreign aid. For texts of this statement and of the President's radio address to the American people on October 24, see *ibid.*, pages 475 ff.

Reports were received in this period from the three committees whose formation was announced by the President on June 22, page 264. For texts, see *National Resources and Foreign Aid* (Washington, Government Printing Office, 1947) ; *The Impact of the Foreign Aid Program Upon the Domestic Economy* (Washington, Council of Economic Advisers, processed, 1947) ; *European Recovery and American Aid* (Washington, Government Printing Office, 1947). For comments by President Truman, on October 18, November 1, and November 8, respectively, see *Public Papers of the Presidents of the United States: Harry S. Truman, 1947*, pages 474, 481, and 485. Summaries of the second and third of these reports are printed in Department of State *Bulletin*, November 16, 1947, pages 932, 937.

In November the Correlation Committee on European Recovery Program, which was the executive group of the Advisory Steering Committee, reviewed draft legislation that had been prepared by the Department of State. The three basic proposals were for an interim aid bill, a model agreement to be used for bilateral arrangements, and an overall bill for a European recovery program.

For documentation on the presentation of the interim aid program to the Congress, see *Emergency Foreign Aid: Hearings Before the Committee on Foreign Affairs, House of Representatives* (80th Cong., 1st sess.), and *Interim Aid for Europe: Hearings Before the Committee on Foreign Relations, United States Senate* (80th Cong., 1st sess.). Hearings were held by the House committee from November 10 to 25, and by the Senate committee from November 10 to 14.

For text of a statement by Secretary of State Marshall on November 10 before a joint session of the two committees, see *A Decade of American Foreign Policy, Basic Documents, 1941–49* (Senate Document No. 123, 81st Cong., 1st sess.), page 1270.

Lot 122, Box 13107

Memorandum [1]

SECRET   [WASHINGTON,] September 29, 1947.

IMMEDIATE NEED FOR EMERGENCY AID TO EUROPE

A. THE PROBLEM

1. The emergency needs of certain key countries of western Europe cannot be met without immediate action on the part of the United States. These countries, particularly Italy and France, are without adequate food and fuel supplies for the fall and winter and without sufficient dollars with which to buy them. They cannot, by their own efforts, survive the major crisis which is already upon them. A collapse of France and Italy could initiate expanding economic depression and political repercussions throughout Europe and, potentially, over a wide part of the world.

2. The following sections of this memorandum deal in more detail with the financial, food, and foreign political aspects of the situation.

B. FINANCIAL

3. The slow recovery of European production during this year, especially in production of goods for export, combined with a continuing necessity for imports from dollar countries at rising prices have resulted in a severe drain on the dollar resources of Europe as a whole. The overall drain is estimated for the full year 1947 as being of the order of magnitude of 5 billion dollars.

4. Certain countries such as England still have substantial, but rapidly declining, resources available. France and Italy have now reached the bottom of the barrel.

5. France requires roughly 100 million dollars a month worth of food, coal, and basic supplies which must be paid for in dollars. Her receipts in dollars for goods and services which she exports are running at a rate of 10 million dollars a month.

6. France has been meeting this gap by drawing on credits from the Export-Import Bank and the International Bank, by drawing maximum permissible amounts from the International Monetary Fund, by liquidation of United States securities held by her nationals and by drawing down her gold and dollar reserves.

7. We are informed by the French Government that by October 15 France will have exhausted these resources to a point where she will have to suspend imports even of food and coal for lack of dollars.

---

[1] This memorandum, filed among records of European Recovery Plan committees, presumably was prepared by the Advisory Steering Committee for the use of the President. The memorandum appears to be based on the ASC's meeting of September 25.

8. France still has official gold reserves of 440 million dollars, but these reserves are less than half the minimum of one billion dollars which agencies of this Government and the French have considered necessary to maintain confidence in her currency. Uncontrolled inflation is considered to be as dangerous as a decline in imports of food and coal.

9. A few additional dollar or gold payments will become available to France during the next six months. These include distribution to France of gold looted by the Germans, further liquidation of United States securities owned by French nationals, advance payment of United States Army obligations to France, and a further drawing from the International Monetary Fund at the earliest date permitted by its regulations. With the possible exception of the United States Army obligations, none of these sources will provide finances early enough to meet immediate October requirements. Assuming full use of these last remaining resources France will be short of meeting its minimum dollar requirements for the next six months by from 250 to 300 million dollars.

[Here follows a table showing French dollar requirements October 1, 1947–March 31, 1948, arrived at by comparing expenditures with receipts and resources.]

10. Italy's remaining gold and dollar resources are less than those of France. It is estimated that the Italian Government's unencumbered dollar holdings will be down to about 32 million dollars by October 1. 28 million dollars worth of so-called Fortezza gold [2] and about 30 million dollars worth of European gold looted by the Germans will become available to Italy making a total of 90 million dollars as basic reserves.

11. Italy requires a minimum of 85 to 95 million dollars per month worth of the food, fuel and other essential commodities which have to be paid for in dollars. Her dollar receipts from the export of goods and services are running at somewhat over 20 million dollars per month, leaving a gap of 65 to 75 million dollars per month.

12. This gap will be met in part by U.S. relief shipments and drawings on Export-Import Bank credits. After making full allowance for these items and certain small miscellaneous receipts there remains an uncovered deficit of 20 to 30 million dollars per month during the last three months of this year and 50 to 65 million dollars per month during the first three months of 1948. The total amount by which Italy will fall short of meeting its minimum dollar requirements for the next six months is 210 to 285 million dollars.

[2] Gold uncovered by Allied military forces at La Fortezza in northern Italy on May 6, 1945. For related information, see telegram 5466 of October 10, from London, p. 987.

[Here follows a table showing Italian dollar requirements October 1, 1947–March 31, 1948, arrived at by comparing expenditures with receipts and possible dollar resources.]

C. FOOD

13. Food is one of the fundamental factors in the economic and political problem of western Europe. Reduction or fear of reduction in already low rations is even now having an effect on the political situation, particularly in Italy and France.

14. In these two countries the food problem is double edged. Already existing on minimum scale rations, there are grave fears that actual supplies of grain will not become available in exporting countries in quantities sufficient to satisfy their essential import requirements. Furthermore, without dollars, they will be unable to buy and pay for whatever grain may become available.

15. In Italy the bread (and pasta) ration is now about 290 grams (about 10 ounces) per person per day. This together with the small amounts of other food the average Italian is able to purchase give him 1900 to 2000 calories per day.

16. To maintain this ration the Italian Government has been releasing approximately 400,000 tons of grain per month. It is estimated that some tightening up in the administration of the ration could reduce this to 370,000 tons per month during the remaining nine months of the crop year. The requirement for the full year thus totals approximately 4,500,000 tons.

17. Italian crops are estimated as being so badly affected by this summer's drought and to some extent by the field workers strikes that total Italian grain yields will be 800,000 tons lower than last year. It is estimated that collections from farms will be less than 2,200,000 tons as against 2,800,000 tons last year.

18. To maintain the ration, total imports from all sources of 2,300,000 tons for the crop year would be required. A large part of farm collections in Italy will have been completed by the first of January and collections during the first six months of 1948 will probably not average more than 75,000 tons a month. Imports of nearly 300,000 tons of grains (or equivalent caloric value in substitute foods) a month during that period from all sources would be necessary to maintain the ration. Such quantities are not now in sight. Failure to maintain the ration, however, will undoubtedly have serious political and economic consequences.

19. In France owing to a combination of heavy winter kill from frost and bad weather during the spring, the wheat crop has dropped from about 6.7 million tons in 1946 to less than 4 million tons in 1947. The daily bread ration in France was lowered from 300 grams last

year to 250 grams in the spring and more recently to 200 grams (about 7 ounces) per day. Slightly more other foods are available in France than in Italy and the average Frenchman probably is obtaining some 2100 calories per day. This level of feeding is so low that it has caused widespread demonstrations. Every effort should be made to enable restoration of the ration to 250 grams.

20. Imports of approximately 1,700,000 tons are required if the 200 gram ration is continued. Imports of 2,000,000 tons will be required if the 250 gram ration is to be restored. As in the case of Italy this quantity is not now in sight.

[Here follows a table showing grain requirements of France and Italy.]

D. FOREIGN POLITICAL ASPECTS

21. During this spring and early summer, communist strength in western Europe declined somewhat. It was possible in both France and Italy for governments which excluded the communists to be formed and to maintain greater strength than had been anticipated.

22. The strong reaction on the part of the USSR and the local communist parties against the steps taken by the western European countries to develop a cooperative European recovery program following Secretary Marshall's Harvard speech evidences their fear that the success of such a program would mean their defeat.

23. There is reason to believe that the totalitarian forces have decided to engage in, and have already begun, a militant and concerted effort to subvert democratic governments before such a cooperative recovery program can get under way. They are hoping that the food and financial situation in Europe this winter will produce economic conditions sufficiently serious that they can be aggravated by aggressive communist actions to a point where the position of democratic governments in France and Italy can be made untenable and communist regimes installed.

24. It is believed that the campaign initiated by the USSR against individuals in the United States accusing them of "war mongering" may be designed to lay the necessary psychological foundation to cover militant action by the communists this winter and to reduce the efficacy of reaction by the U.S. to such action.

25. In Italy the communists have already declared open political warfare against the government and the forces of moderation. It is believed that they induced the recent strikes in part to discourage the United States from granting further aid. Unless the Italians acquire the dollar exchange necessary to cover minimum imports, particularly food and coal, it is probable that the resulting hunger and unemployment will enable the communists to gain a dominant if not controlling

position in the government before the winter is over. The Italian government has already drastically curtailed imports, including coal, oil and other basic supplies.

26. In France the story is much the same and, although on the surface there is less turmoil, the situation is in fact as serious as in Italy. The French likewise have been forced to suspend dollar purchases except for limited quantities of food and fuel and a very few other essentials. In the absence of external aid, it is believed that even these limited purchases will have to stop during the fall months. Greatly increased social and political unrest is expected in France this winter. With extremists of the right and left contending for power, there is small hope of there being any degree of political stability in France unless financial aid is given. (In France there is a possibility that the forces of the extreme right, grouped around General de Gaulle, might temporarily seize power. But it is difficult to imagine this taking place without civil war.)

27. It should be borne in mind that if a totalitarian regime, particularly one of the left, obtains control of France, it will be very difficult for us to maintain our position in Germany.

28. On the other side of the ledger, there is every reason to believe that, if we give the people of western Europe timely and adequate financial aid and otherwise help them to meet their minimum requirements, the forces of totalitarianism can be defeated or greatly reduced in those countries. The great majority of the people are strongly opposed to totalitarianism. They want to fight for their freedom. But to have a chance of success during this critical winter, it is necessary that they be enabled, by further aid from us, to maintain the strength to withstand the militant communist campaign.

29. From the viewpoint of the vital interests of the United States, the principal issue in Europe today is whether or not it will be totalitarian. If the virus of totalitarianism spreads much farther, it will be almost impossible to prevent its engulfing all the [of] western Europe. This would mean communist totalitarianism almost everywhere on the continent with the iron curtain moving to the Atlantic.

30. In the event of a totalitarian Europe, our foreign policy would have to be completely re-oriented and a great part of what we have fought for and accomplished in the past would be lost. The change in the power relationships involved would force us to adopt drastic domestic measures and would inevitably require great and burdensome sacrifices on the part of our citizens. The maintenance of a much larger military establishment would undoubtedly be required. The sacrifices would not be simply material. With a totalitarian Europe

which would have no regard for individual freedom, our spiritual loss would be incalculable.

Lot 122

Minutes of the Fourth Meeting of the Advisory Steering Committee on European Recovery Program, Washington, D.C., October 2, 1947 [1]

[Extract]

TOP SECRET

APPROVAL OF MINUTES

1. *Action:* The minutes of the meeting of September 25 (M–3) were approved subject to the communication of any desired revisions to the Secretary.

GENERAL OBJECTIVES AND PROGRESS OF COMMITTEE'S WORK

2. *Action:* It was agreed that it would be advisable insofar as possible to keep the interim aid program distinct from the long-range program for European economic recovery. However, since there is a likelihood that the Congressional Committees will desire to consider aspects of the overall long-range program in conjunction with their consideration of the interim aid program, the Committee should work toward completion of the preliminary appraisal of the CEEC report and integration of the various aspects of a long-range program with the interim program within the next three weeks. To this end the Committee members would inform the Chairman of the various appraisal groups in their respective agencies of the above time schedule.

3. *Discussion:* The Chairman [2] reported that, arising from the President's conference with certain Congressional leaders on September 29, a decision was reached to call the four Congressional Committees to consider the question of interim aid to certain European countries early in November. Certain Congressional leaders have indicated that a possible interim aid program should be considered in relation to the overall long-range program, the reports of the various Congressional Committees surveying conditions abroad, the reports of the Harriman and Krug Committees and other pertinent information. The Committee's previous thinking on a desirable pattern of Government action has been in terms of Executive action on the emergency phase carrying through December, Congressional action on the in-

---

[1] Representatives of the Departments of State, Army, Navy, Commerce, Interior, Treasury, Agriculture, the Federal Reserve Board, the Bureau of the Budget, and the White House were present at this meeting.
[2] Col. C. H. Bonesteel.

terim aid program carrying through March with action on the full-scale program to come at the end of Congressional authority for the interim period. However, in view of the above developments, it might be advantageous to be able to indicate to the Congressional Committees when they convene in November that the Executive branch has completed preliminary work on the basic principles of the full-scale program and that they can go forward with consideration of these aspects of the full-scale program while considering interim aid legislation. Therefore, the Committee should arrange its work so as to begin correlating the various aspects of the program during the next two weeks and place the appraisal groups on notice that a preliminary appraisal is to be completed within the next three-week period.

4. A question was raised as to the anticipated form of presenting the full-scale program to Congressional Committees, it being pointed out that work should commence immediately on the justification for the program. This material might include the CEEC report, the U.S. analysis of the CEEC report, reports of the Krug, Nourse and Harriman Committees, and other pertinent information. In this connection it was suggested that in the interest of expeditious action on the interim aid program it would be advisable to keep it distinct, insofar as possible, from the long-range program, since presentation of an interim program in a manner so as to make decisions on its merits dependent upon decisions on the long-range program would probably delay Congressional consideration of interim aid. Furthermore, it would be inadvisable to present a draft bill for an interim aid program directly to the Congressional Committees. The above suggestions were concurred in by the Committee.

[Here follows material relative to the interdepartmental groups appraising the CEEC report.]

FW 840.50 Recovery/10–1347

Memorandum by the Acting Secretary of State to President Truman

SECRET [WASHINGTON,] October 13, 1947.

Subject: Emergency Financing of French and Italian Requirements.[1]

1. Sixteen European countries have cooperated to produce a program for European recovery and have transmitted their report to the U.S. Government. This report is currently being reviewed for the

---

[1] At the October 10 meeting of the Advisory Steering Committee, Col. Bonesteel stated that "Under Secretary Lovett is presenting the emergency problem to the Cabinet today. It is anticipated that Mr. Lovett will request the Cabinet members to survey the ability of their agencies to contribute and to assist in the development of a definitive plan of action."

purpose of formulating recommendations to Congress. Action by Congress on this program may not take place until March, 1948, or even later. In the meantime, the financial resources of some of the cooperating European countries have so far declined as to threaten economic and political collapse. A downward spiral in economic activity in these countries accompanied by serious deficiencies in food and coal for domestic consumption this winter would lead to explosive political instability. Communism is energetically exploiting and accentuating the present and prospective difficult situation.

2. There are many uncertain factors, both economic and political, which may affect the financial positions of the western European countries during the coming winter months. It is not possible now to forecast exactly what will develop. It is most likely, however, that, pending the appropriation of funds under a general recovery program, interim aid will be needed by some of those countries if their positions are not to deteriorate even more dangerously. Unless these crises are met as they arise, there is little hope that the economic and political foundation on which to build a recovery program will be preserved. In the case of both France and Italy a serious crisis already exists and its dimensions are discernible. The balance of this memorandum is directed to a consideration of the immediate requirements of those two countries.

3. Total minimum dollar requirements for France from October 1947 through March 1948 amount to about 800 million dollars (see attached Tables on France [2]). Current receipts plus other expected availabilities should provide about 450 million dollars leaving a deficit of about 350 millions. If all anticipated sources of revenues were promptly realized and expended, France's needs could be met through December. If France is confined to such resources, however, the lack of any assurance of continued availability of funds would at once compel France to restrict procurement even of food and fuel in anticipation of the uncovered requirements for the first quarter of 1948. Expected current revenues in the first quarter of 1948 amount to less than 50 million dollars. Continuation of dollar deficiencies at the rate shown in the attached Tables would therefore require a further drain on French gold reserves, which at their current level of 440 million dollars are already below the minimum consistent with financial stability. The reserves have declined by 1.4 billion dollars in the last two years.

4. Total minimum dollar requirements for Italy in the same six months period will run about 500 million dollars (see attached Tables on Italy [2]). Available U.S. relief funds, receipts and other probable

---

[2] Tables not attached to file copy.

sources of dollars will provide about 250 millions leaving a deficit of approximately 250 million dollars. Due to the timing of availability of resources, however, the Italians have current funds available to meet less than half their dollar requirements of the present quarter. The basic gold reserve is about 80 million dollars, but this includes 20 millions needed to make initial payment to the International Monetary Fund.

5. Unless there is developed promptly a specific program of action designed to afford some hope that the funds may be available for the most essential items required, not only in the last quarter of 1947 but also in the 1st quarter of 1948, the French and Italian Governments will inevitably, starting almost immediately, further drastically cut essential imports even of food and fuel, and the pipeline will start to empty rapidly. Provision of funds, say in December, without some basis for hope now that they will be available then, would entail a serious risk, since by that time the continuous nature of necessary procurement might have been critically interrupted and irreparable damage done. A special session of the Congress might provide funds before the end of the year, but even if there were a clear indication that the special session would in fact be called, there would be urgently required some other assurance that funds for 1st quarter 1948 procurement would be available, and such assurance in this case could be given in this instance by the Export-Import Bank and the CCC. The financing of these imports is not appropriate for the International Bank or the International Monetary Fund.

6. Financing by the Export-Import Bank of coal and petroleum exports from the United States to France and Italy and by the Commodity Credit Corporation of wheat and cotton exports during the last quarter of 1947 and the 1st quarter of 1948 would involve credits on the order of the following in millions of dollars:

	CCC	EX-IM	TOTAL
To France approx.	150	140	290
To Italy "	100	60	160
	250	200	450

Credits in these amounts, however, would leave uncovered deficits for the six months of about 50 million dollars for France and about 100 million dollars for Italy. Thus the whole problem would not be met and it would be necessary in addition to call upon Congress to provide for the balance of the requirements. It becomes a matter for political judgment as to whether the calling of a special session would be practicable if all but $150 million of the indicated requirements were taken care of by the Export-Import Bank and the CCC, especially in the light of the fact that the items to be covered by the Congressional appropriation would be miscellaneous commodities and other materials which might be considered less vital than food and fuel.

7. The difficulties foreseen in the course outlined above would be overcome if the Export-Import Bank and the CCC could finance the total French and Italian deficit for the period October 1947 through March 1948, or until the Congress could act on the long-range recovery program at the regular session. This would mean that in addition to the $450 million mentioned in paragraph 6 above, the Export-Import Bank would finance the approximately $150 million balance of the total deficit for the period October 1947 to March 1948, since most [of] the items in question would not be of a nature eligible for CCC financing. If assurances of such financing can be given now, this would make unnecessary the calling of a special session of Congress for the particular purpose of meeting the immediate problem in France and Italy. If Congressional action on the European recovery program were delayed appreciably beyond March 31, 1948, further large burdens would have to be carried by these agencies, since, in addition to continuing French and Italian requirements, other European countries would enter equally critical stages at that time.

8. If the program of total support by the Export-Import Bank and the CCC is impossible, there remains the following possibility, which, if successful, would be the one best designed to obtain maximum political advantages abroad. This program would be, in so far as France and Italy are concerned, as follows:

_a._ A special session of the Congress be called to meet in late November. This call should be made as soon as practicable and before the already called convening of certain committees of Congress in early November takes place.

_b._ A two point recommendation be made to the Congress. Firstly that appropriations be authorized to cover the food and fuel requirements of France and Italy through June 1948. Secondly that an appropriate government agency or agencies be authorized to grant credits to the two countries for procurement of other essential imports until the Congress takes action on the European recovery program.

_c._ The Export-Import Bank and the CCC be consulted as to whether, in the light of the critical situation, it would be possible for them to give assurances at once that they will provide credits in the near future to carry France and Italy until the special session appropriates interim aid funds under _b_ above, presumably some time in December.

ROBERT A. LOVETT

840.50 Recovery/11–1847 : Telegram

The Acting Secretary of State to the Embassy in Italy

CONFIDENTIAL   WASHINGTON, November 18, 1947—4 p. m.

2385. For Allen [1] from Dort [2]. Although discussions in Congressional committees have not yet been conclusive present trend would indicate Interim Aid will be handled through existing relief machinery and terms of act will require establishment of mission in Paris. Appears quite possible act may be passed within two weeks. Will endeavor commence French shipments at earliest possible moment. Sent Rome as 2385 repeated to Paris as Depts 4258. [Dort.]

LOVETT

---

[1] Richard F. Allen, Field Administrator, U.S. Foreign Relief Program.
[2] Dallas W. Dort, Special Assistant to the Assistant Secretary for Economic Affairs.

840.50 Recovery/12–447

The Acting Secretary of State to the Secretary of State [1]

URGENT   WASHINGTON, December 4, 1947.

Telmar 35. For Secretary Marshall from Lovett. This is hasty report on present situation regarding interim aid.

The Senate has reported the bill out in full amount and in acceptable form. The House Foreign Affairs Committee reported the bill out at 590 millions, but injected China as one of recipients for 60 million dollars. This therefore represents a reduction of 67 million dollars for the purposes initially covered by the bill. The bill is now on the floor and is being heavily attacked by many members of Congress, notably Congressmen Halleck, Brown, etc., and with defense coming from Bloom, Cox, Vorys, Jackson and others.

Senate Appropriations Committee hearings have been conducted all week with Secretaries of Agriculture, Commerce, farm groups, etc., appearing through Wednesday. State Department went up this morning. Session devoted almost entirely to attacks on lend-lease shipments to Russia, Communism, grain shortage, past relief abuses, German plant dismantling and reparations deliveries, and German currency system. While no direct attack was made on sin, I judge the Committee omitted that feeling that the Department of State was an adequate substitute.

While the ride was rough, it could have been worse and probably will be when I go back tomorrow. The only incident of any real note oc-

---

[1] Secretary Marshall was in London attending the Fifth Session of the Council of Foreign Ministers, November 25–December 15, 1947.

curred in connection with discussion of protection to this country against the continuance of relief aid where the recipient country falls under the control of Communists. This protection is, in our opinion, contained in a mandatory Section 7, Subdivision (b), which provides that the President shall promptly terminate the provision of assistance for any country whenever he finds (b) "by reason of changed conditions, that the provision of assistance authorized by this act is no longer necessary or desirable". Committee wanted to nail this down tight by a specific directive, which I endeavored to persuade them not to do although it was difficult in view of open hearings which prevented any reference UN Resolution of last December.[2] Bridges[3] was particularly insistent in line of question, having indicated off the record that he felt Department could not be relied on in such matters, citing lend-lease again. He then asked on the record for a "direct answer" on U.S. relief policies if these countries "fall under Communist control". I pointed out that Section 7, in those circumstances and in our opinion, would give the President the right to determine whether aid should be promptly terminated. Bridges stated that he wanted an answer as to what the State Department would do. I then replied, according to wire service report, which seems substantially accurate, "I am not in a position to speak for the Secretary of State. In his absence, if I must give a direct answer, it is that I would recommend to the President and his advisers that aid to such countries be stopped if those countries fell under Communist control". While I would like to have avoided the question, it seemed absolutely necessary to meet the situation frankly and the result in the Committee was to stop that line of questioning. The comment may be used for propaganda purposes by the Communists but, as it conforms to the post-UNRRA relief action taken by the Congress in July[4] and is in accord with the National Security Council papers and the opinion of the Department, it seemed better to be frank and decisive rather than to have the line of questioning expanded into an elaborate series of charges by the Appropriations Committee, which probably knew that in executive session the same general answer was given to the Foreign Relations Committee in connection with the Section under discussion.

---

[2] Reference here presumably is to Resolution 48(1) Relief Needs after the Termination of UNRRA (United Nations Relief and Rehabilitation Administration), United Nations, *Official Records of the General Assembly, First Session, Second Part, Resolutions Adopted by the General Assembly during the Second Part of the First Session*, pp. 74–76.

[3] Senator Styles Bridges of New Hampshire.

[4] Reference is presumably to Public Law 271, The Supplemental Appropriation Act, 1948, approved July 30, 1947; 61 Stat. 612. See also Public Law 164, approved July 8, 1947 (*ibid.*, 260), which made certain provisions for liquidation of activities undertaken prior to June 30, 1947, in connection with participation of the United States in the work of the United Nations Relief and Rehabilitation Administration.

New Subject. House Appropriations Committee hearings are scheduled for Monday and I had long work-out with Chairman Taber yesterday morning. He has indicated he does not wish anyone else from the Department to appear before his Committee and states that, if the grain figures hold up under examination, he would hope to have the bill in some form through his Committee by the next night.

New Subject. European recovery program now being completed, with President's message in draft form. On present schedule it is likely to be sent up probably December 10. Strategic materials aspect, with particular reference one item, will be covered by separate cable to you. I am appearing before Hickenlooper's Joint Committee tomorrow morning in endeavor to proceed with negotiations.

New Subject. We are still in business. Best regards.

LOVETT

Editorial Note

The work of preparing the legislative programs and supporting materials continued. On December 9 Acting Secretary Lovett cabled to Secretary Marshall at London as follows: "The basic ERP program is complete and the President's message should be in final draft form the end of this week. As a result of delay caused by violent debate in the House on interim aid measures and flood of amendments offered, it is not likely that there will be action on the enabling legislation and the appropriations legislation before the middle of next week. We have in consequence been advised by our Congressional supporters to delay submission of President's message and ERP. I have passed this word on to the President and am today informed he will call in certain leaders on Monday the fifteenth and discuss matter with them, our concern being to get it in sometime during special session provided it does not jeopardize interim aid action." (To London, Telmar 57, top secret, Eyes Only for Marshall, Dec. 9, 1947, 7 p. m., 840.50 Recovery/12–947.)

On December 15 the Congress completed action on an interim aid bill, which was approved by the President on December 17 as Public Law 389, the Foreign Aid Act of 1947; 61 Stat. 934. Funds were provided by Public Law 393, Third Supplementary Act, 1948, approved December 23, 1947; 61 Stat. 941. (For documentation on interim aid agreements of the United States with France and Italy, see pages 688 ff. and 861 ff.)

The President sent to the Congress on December 19 a special message on the European Recovery Program. For text, see *Public Papers of the Presidents of the United States: Harry S. Truman, 1947*, page 515.

GENERAL UNITED STATES POLICY TOWARD THE EUROPEAN COAL ORGANIZATION (ECO), WITH PARTICULAR REFERENCE TO THE BRITISH COAL SHORTAGE

840.6362/11–2546 : Telegram

The Chargé in the United Kingdom (Gallman) to the Secretary of State

RESTRICTED
URGENT

LONDON, November 25, 1946—4 p. m.

9725. This is Salco 365 from MEA. In view of extremely serious impact long US coal strike [1] would have on economy of many European countries, ECO chairman desires to enquire of Department if statement by him of this situation would be of any possible assistance to US Government. His tentative thought is that if Department sees no objection he would send communication to Department outlining disastrous consequences in Europe of US mine strike, which communication Department could then make public.[2]

We doubt that any appeal by ECO would be of value in this situation, but in view of ECO chairman's responsibility to ECO countries have agreed to refer his enquiry for Department's advice.[3]

GALLMAN

---

[1] The walk-out began November 19.

[2] The Agreement for the Establishment of the European Coal Organization to which the United States was a party was signed in London, January 4, 1946; the life of the ECO was to be one year, and on December 30, 1946 (subsequent to the date of this telegram) a protocol to effect prolongation of the agreement was signed in London; for texts, see Department of State Treaties and Other International Acts Series (TIAS) Nos. 1508 and 1615 respectively.

Relevant reference sources are the European Coal Organization, *The European Coal Organization, 1945–1947; Brief Description and History* (London, 1948) and the Economic Cooperation Administration, *European Recovery Program, Coal and Related Solid Fuels Commodity Study* (Washington, D.C., 1949) ; the latter, though focused on a different aspect of the coal recovery program, has useful information regarding the import requirements, supply, exports, and consumption of the several countries involved.

Representatives of the ECO countries were afforded assistance by the U.S. Government at this time in the procurement of coal in this country through U.S. procurement channels, in which the old lend-lease mechanism and the U.S. Treasury's procurement authority were utilized for the purchase of coal in the United States on the basis of quotas allocated to those countries under authority of the European Coal Organization.

[3] In telegram 7934, to London, Lasco 240, November 27, not printed, the Department of State replied that it recognized the ECO chairman's responsibility to importing countries and that this Government would have no objection to receiving a statement on behalf of such countries outlining the European consequences of a stoppage of U.S. coal exports to Europe (840.6362/11–2746).

840.6362/11–2946 : Telegram

The Chargé in the United Kingdom (Gallman) to the Secretary of State

US URGENT   LONDON, November 29, 1946.

9834. This is Salco 374 from MEA. Reference Lasco 240.[1] ECO has requested MEA transmit following appeal which Department may make public if it deems appropriate:

1. "ECO draws urgent attention of appropriate US authorities to the grave coal situation facing Europe at the beginning of winter.

2. The elements of that situation are: (a) programmed tonnage of US coal represents 60% of the total import availabilities to ECO countries; (b) October and November loadings ex USA fell short of programme by approximately 50%; (c) apart from stoppage of US shipments availabilities ex Germany for December and subsequent months reduced by recent decisions of control authorities whilst transport and other difficulties hamper production and exports of Polish coal; (d) even with full expected imports from US and other sources and counting all indigenous production consumption in ECO countries would average less than 50% of requirements; (e) due to previous shortfalls in imports coal stocks are at or below minimum safety point in many countries and some have already had to increase restrictions on coal use, even for most essential purposes.

3. Immediate situation therefore grave for all European importing countries. Should US stoppage be prolonged situation would become even more critical economically and socially, particularly for countries wholly or mainly dependent on imported supplies.

4. Fully recognizing past US assistance for European relief, ECO nevertheless appeals US authorities to take all practicable measures for earliest possible general resumption of coal shipments to Europe. Meanwhile should local stocks or the quality position in USA permit shipments to be specially authorized they would prove invaluable for European countries in most urgent need."

GALLMAN

---

[1] See footnote 3, p. 485.

840.6362/11–2946

Memorandum by the Under Secretary of State (Acheson) to Mr. Clark Clifford, Special Counsel to President Truman

WASHINGTON, December 5, 1946.

I am attaching a copy of the cable from London [1] transmitting to us the message of the European Coal Organization. There is also a memorandum explaining the composition of the European Coal Organization and a further memorandum explaining why the United

---

[1] Supra.

States loadings in October and November fell short of the program by fifty per cent.[2]

I asked the President whether he wished the Department to make this message public. The President desired to consider making it public in or in connection with his speech on Sunday evening. Unless and until we hear from you, the Department will take no further action.[3]

DEAN ACHESON

[2] Neither attached to file copy.
[3] The walk-out ended December 6, and no radio address was made by the President.

840.6362/12–1046 : Telegram

The Chargé in the United Kingdom (Gallman) to the Secretary of State

RESTRICTED LONDON, December 10, 1946—7 p. m.

10014. Salco 381 from MEA. US coal strike with its immediate effects on many European countries has been seriously damaging to US prestige. European reaction to the coal strike is a forecast of similar response that may be expected if reduction in US coal exports should occur as result of removal of controls essential to effective allocation and maximum shipments. Any significant decrease would be exaggerated and exploited as proof of alleged undependability of US by those who wish to undermine US foreign policy. We warmly approve decision to repatriate German POWS and recognize necessity of curtailing German coal exports.[1] These developments, moreover, emphasize importance of US making every possible effort to export 2 million tons of coal to Europe monthly through 1947.

Gallman requests this cable be brought to attention of the Acting Secretary and Secretary.

GALLMAN

[1] For documentation regarding the German coal question, see vol. II, pp. 909 ff.

841.5019/2–747 : Telegram

The Chargé in the United Kingdom (Gallman) to the Secretary of State

SECRET LONDON, February 7, 1947—7 p. m.

877. 1. Shinwell, Minister Fuel, announced in Parliament today that beginning Monday no power would be furnished industrial con-

sumers in London, southeastern, midland and northwestern areas, and that power to all domestic consumers these areas would be cut off between 9 and 12 a. m. and 2 and 4 p. m. Drastic step taken in order to assure maintenance of power such essential services as sewage, water, lighting, hospitals, bakeries, et cetera.

2. Immediate cause emergency is snow and cold weather of past two weeks which has nearly paralyzed road, rail and coastwise traffic and disrupted coal movement. Basic cause is shortage of coal stocks with which country entered winter on November 1, and which has resulted in steadily worsening crisis ever since cold snap mid-December. (See Embassy's 10027, December 23 [1]). Duration of emergency measures will depend on weather improvements but even after that it will take several weeks to build up coal stocks in order provide general power requirements.

3. Meanwhile, industrial concerns throughout country whose deliveries had already been cut in mid-January to 75% in case of iron and steel and 50% all other industries, are rapidly exhausting their stocks, and press each day carries accounts of new factory close-downs and production curtailment. Although government has not given out figures, in our opinion number unemployed already numbers over 100,000 with considerably larger number on short-time work, and effect of paragraph 1 will be to put several million out of work next week in affected areas. To make matters worse many households have already exhausted their yearly coal allocation which should have lasted until May 1.

4. Although coal traffic has been given priority on all rail lines, traffic disruption has caused shortage of coal cars at the pits and forced serious curtailment coal production. Output in Yorkshire, largest producing area in Britain, is down 50% this week, other areas somewhat less.

5. In our opinion coal stock exhaustion throughout country is now such, that even with improved weather, the country can only limp through until mid-April. For until then country must live on current coal output which is not sufficient to meet winter needs, even if substantial increase in output, which occurred after January 1 when the mines formally passed into public ownership, is maintained when transport again becomes normal.

6. Also in our opinion, government is now facing its first real loss of public support. Failure of production and export drive to forge ahead during past two months has already caused widespread misgivings, and with production and export declines inevitable during next three months in view coal position, we do not see how government can continue maintain popularity at same high levels as during past 19 months. We do not, however, anticipate any government crisis or any

---

[1] Not printed.

attempt to form a coalition and discount all rumours to this effect. Only bright spot for the government is that Labor MP's who led the rebellion against Bevin's foreign policy last fall and meant to renew their attack when Parliament resumed on January 21, have decided hold their fire in view serious domestic situation in order not to embarrass government further.

GALLMAN

840.50 MEA/2–1147 : Telegram

The Chargé in the United Kingdom (Gallman) to the Secretary of State

SECRET LONDON, February 11, 1947—7 p. m.
US URGENT

938. This is Salco 423 from MEA. MEA consulted by MOFP concerning possibility UK coal imports from US, which question under Cabinet consideration. We are informed that there is strong pressure from British industry and within Ministry and Cabinet for imports. We stated that US Government very sympathetic to British plight, but felt US position would be that any UK imports, as distinct from bunkering must be recommended by ECO. We doubt ECO would agree allocation to UK since UK coal position still better than that of any other European country except Poland, unless dollar difficulties may later result in other ECO countries not taking all of US availability. Same view unofficially conveyed by ECO chairman. We believe it probable MOFP will oppose US imports on ground of UK obligation to ECO. We understand also Foreign Office may oppose imports on ground competition for ECO coal would hurt British influence with other ECO countries, particularly France.

GALLMAN

840.50 MEA/2–1347

Memorandum of Telephone Conversation, by Miss Miriam Camp of the Office of the Assistant Secretary of State for Economic Affairs

[WASHINGTON,] February 13, 1947.

Participants: Mr. Paul Porter, Acting Chief, Mission For Economic Affairs, American Embassy, London
Mr. Stinebower and Miss Camp, A–T

I. Paul Porter spoke with Mr. Stinebower [1] and Miss Camp on the telephone at 11:30 a. m. today. He reported that there had been statements in the British press and questions in Parliament about the possi-

---

[1] Leroy D. Stinebower, Special Assistant to the Assistant Secretary of State for Economic Affairs (Thorp).

bility of diversion to the United Kingdom of coal now being shipped from the United States to Europe. Specifically, Mr. Porter referred to statements in the press quoting remarks by Captain Conway [2] and by ex-Governor Lehman.[3] He said that he had been informed by the British that they did not wish for political reasons to buy coal in the United States at present and that they felt these public statements and any more similar statements would have the effect of forcing their hand and making it extremely difficult to withstand the public demand to import coal.

Mr. Porter referred to two telegrams which had been sent from the Embassy, in particular to a telegram of February 11 sent US Urgent,[4] in which it was stated that it was believed both the Ministry of Fuel and Power and the Foreign Office would oppose imports of U.S. coal in view of their commitments to ECO and their feeling that British competition for ECO coal would adversely affect British influence with other ECO countries, in particular France.

Mr. Porter requested Mr. Stinebower to make sure that the British attitude was known at sufficiently high levels throughout the Government so that any further statements which would tend to build up British public pressure to import coal could be avoided.

Mr. Stinebower informed Mr. Porter that he had no knowledge that any action was being contemplated with respect to diversion of coal to the United Kingdom and that he assumed if anything were afoot he would have been informed in view of his responsibility for ECO matters.

Mr. Stinebower further undertook to see that appropriate steps were taken to avoid the issuance of further statements which might prove embarrassing.

II. Following this conversation we learned that a statement had been released to the press from the White House at 10:30 this morning saying that the United States Representative on the European Coal Organization was being instructed to support the United Kingdom Representative if he requested the ECO to authorize the diversion of coal to the United Kingdom.[5]

III. Mr. Stinebower therefore telephoned Mr. Porter to inform him of this action, which had already become known in the United Kingdom.

---

[2] Granville Conway, Coordinator of Emergency Export Programs, formerly Administrator of the War Shipping Administration.

[3] Herbert H. Lehman, former Governor of New York, was the first Administrator of the United Nations Relief and Rehabilitation Administration (UNRRA). Governor Lehman in an undated telegram had appealed to President Truman to send "shiploads" of coal to Great Britain to relieve the coal shortage there; the text of the letter was printed in the New York Times on February 12, 1947.

[4] Telegram 938, Salco 423, from London, February 11, supra.

[5] For text, see telegram 734, infra.

Mr. Porter said that the Ministry of Fuel and Power was disturbed by the announcement and that he (Mr. Porter) was receiving inquiries from the press. He asked whether the diversion of coal would be subject to the agreement of ECO countries, and Mr. Stinebower confirmed that that was his understanding.

Mr. Stinebower explained to Mr. Porter that the press release also contained a fresh appeal by the President for the continuation of the authority of the Maritime Commission to operate Government-owned vessels. Mr. Porter felt this feature of the press release would be welcomed by the British authorities.

Mr. Stinebower said that Mr. Porter would be receiving an urgent telegram giving him instructions to support any British request for coal which might be made to the European Coal Organization and also by telegraph the text of the White House release.

Mr. Stinebower said that no mention of double bunkering [6] was made in the press statement; that he understood that the British had requested double bunkering. He inquired whether Mr. Porter felt a press release on U.S. willingness to provide double bunkering would be useful. Mr. Porter hesitated to give an off-hand opinion and requested us to withhold issuance of a press release until he had had an opportunity to consult with the Ministry of Fuel and Power.

Mr. Porter asked us to find out from Captain Conway what coal there was a possibility of diverting, in particular whether there was any coal now afloat in United States ships for which title had not yet passed to the recipient government. We promised to send this information to Mr. Porter as soon as possible.

Mr. Porter said that he had planned to be in Paris next week for the meetings on restitution of transportation equipment but suggested that it might be better for him to remain in London and for Mr. McClure [7] to handle the Paris meetings. Mr. Stinebower agreed, and undertook to inform Mr. Radius. [8]

IV. Following this telephone call I ascertained from Mr. Lister [9] that the U.S. Coal Committee had already agreed to the double bunkering of British ships and that Mr. Corey Wright (British) had already informed London. Mr. Lister said a press release from the U.S. Coal Committee was already in preparation but that it would be held until he was informed by us that it should be released.

---

[6] Reference is to the bunkering of ships in U.S. ports with sufficient coal to complete a round trip.

[7] Russell S. McClure was U.S. delegate to the International Congress on River Transportation which met at Paris in 1947; in March he was assigned to the Paris Embassy as an attaché.

[8] Walter A. Radius was Deputy Director of the Office of Transport and Communications; in March he was appointed Director.

[9] Louis Lister, International Resources Division.

Mr. Lister also said there was no coal now afloat to which the United States still held title. He undertook to find out and prepare a telegram on the coal now afloat or about to be shipped, giving quantities, ownership, etc.

I have spoken to Mr. Radius, and he agrees that Mr. Porter should not be asked to leave London at this juncture but that Mr. McClure should handle any meetings in Paris. However, Mr. Radius said that he understood the meetings were now to be held in London rather than Paris.

841.6362/2–1347 : Telegram

The Secretary of State to the Embassy in the United Kingdom

US URGENT   WASHINGTON, February 13, 1947.

734. For Paul Porter. Following is text of President's press release re British fuel crisis:

"This Govt stands ready to do everything within its power to relieve the plight of the British people in their present fuel emergency.

"I have directed Captain Granville Conway, Coordinator of Emergency Export Programs, to determine how quickly and in what quantity coal can be landed at British ports. It would take a minimum of 15 days to ship coal from this country to England. Such shipments might very well arrive too late to help England in the present emergency.

"There are, however, a number of colliers at sea in the vicinity of the British Isles carrying coal to other European countries. It may be possible to divert some of these colliers to English ports.

"In view of the present emergency in England, the United States representative on the European Coal Organization which sits in London has been instructed to support a request for a reallocation of the shipments of coal now at sea, if this is the British desire. It is understood, of course, that coal diverted from other countries would be made up as rapidly as shipping schedules can be readjusted.[1]

"A remarkable job has been done in stepping up our export shipments of coal. In Dec, 1.8 million tons were shipped; in Jan, 2.5 million tons; and this month we plan to ship 2.9 million tons. In March, we hope to do even better, for these shipments are vital to the rehabilitation of Europe and other war torn areas.

"To meet these future schedules it is imperative that uncertainty over continuation of the authority of the Maritime Commission to operate Govt-owned ships be dispelled as quickly as possible. This authority, unless extended by the Congress, will expire on March 1.

"On Jan 21, I asked the Congress to adopt a joint resolution extending the authority to June 30. I am gratified that the House Committee

---

[1] The British Government did not request the diverting of coal ships to English ports. In telegram 1028, February 14, from London, Gallman had cabled: "PM informing President his generous suggestion warmly appreciated but UK does not feel it can take coal destined for countries with greater need." (840.50 MEA/2–1447)

on Merchant Marine and Fisheries is holding hearings on this resolution today.

"I cannot emphasize too strongly the need for quick action by the House and the Senate on this legislation because without it our emergency export programs for fuel and grain will break down completely at the end of this month. Every day that action is delayed means further disruption of Feb schedules for shipments of coal and wheat to Europe. Because of the uncertainty now prevailing tanker shipments of fuel oil to the East Coast ports have already slowed down.

"I have every confidence that the Congress will act promptly to extend the authority of the Maritime Commission to operate the ships which are so vitally needed."

MARSHALL

841.6362/2–1747 : Telegram

The Secretary of State to the Embassy in the United Kingdom

RESTRICTED WASHINGTON, February 17, 1947—6 p. m.
US URGENT

785. This is Lasco 276. US will release following press release unless you indicate otherwise within twenty-four hours of date of this cable:

"In furtherance of the President's program to offer to assist the Brit in their present fuel crisis, the US Govt decided, on its own initiative, to offer to bunker Brit ships at US ports for round trip voyages.

"Simultaneously, the Brit Govt through its representative on the Combined Coal Committee, which sits in Washington, presented a request to officials of the US Govt for round trip bunkering privileges. Since the US Govt had already agreed to do so on its own initiative, the UK was informed that its ships may obtain a round trip supply of coal at US ports. The UK Govt has accordingly instructed Brit ships to obtain a double supply of coal at US bunker stations.

"This measure will relieve the UK's fuel shortage to the extent that ships plying between the US and European North Atlantic ports will not need to refuel at Brit ports. It is estimated that the adoption of this practice will relieve the Brit fuel position by 75,000 to 100,000 tons per month.

"The coal for double bunkering Brit ships in US ports will not reduce the volume of export coal because coal shipped to US bunkers does not normally compete with export coal for port facilities."

MARSHALL

840.6362/3–1147 : Telegram

The Chargé in the United Kingdom (Gallman) to the Secretary of State

CONFIDENTIAL LONDON, March 11, 1947—7 p. m.

1566. This is Salco 445. Possibility of UK seeking import US coal still receiving Cabinet consideration. However, we do not anticipate reversal previous decision unless dollar shortages other ECO countries prevent them from taking all US availability. In that case, possible UK may buy surplus for purpose building stocks.[1]

GALLMAN

[1] Chargé Gallman in telegram 1648 (Salco 451), March 14, from London, reported: "British Cabinet decided today request ECO for allocation US coal to UK." (840.6362/3–1447)

840.6362/3–1847 : Telegram

The Ambassador in the United Kingdom (Douglas) to the Secretary of State

CONFIDENTIAL   LONDON, March 18, 1947—8 p. m.
US URGENT

1714. This is Salco 454. Reference Salco 451, March 14,[1] repeated Moscow for USDel as 105.

1. McNeil[2] has asked Porter if US will support request which UK will make to ECO for coal imports. UK probably will request one million tons or more for summer delivery. McNeil said he hoped that the desired import could be obtained from an increased ECO availability, thus avoiding a reduction in delivery to other European countries.

2. MEA confidentially informed that both Foreign Office and Ministry of Fuel and Power opposed imports at meeting Cabinet Fuel Committee and their position was reinforced by cable which Bevin sent from Moscow.[3] Reasons for opposition were UK obligation to ECO and probably adverse effects upon British influence on continent. Fact that these views were overridden indicates serious assessment of Britain's fuel position.

3. Outlook for third quarter makes support for British claim easier to justify than appeared likely month ago.

(a) For second quarter, increased US and German availability and computation French, Belgium, Dutch output on basis probable gross output rather than net merchantable will give these countries approximately 95% pre-war consumption. Authentic production forecast not yet available but being sought by MEA. It is reasonable to compute indigenous production on basis of gross output for these countries in order to establish common basis for comparison with UK consumption.

(b) On basis Ciszewski's estimate of Polish exports and rising Ruhr output, ECO chairman believes third quarter availability from Polish/

[1] See footnote 1, above.
[2] Hector McNeil, British Minister of State.
[3] British Foreign Secretary Bevin was in Moscow for the meeting of the Council of Foreign Ministers. Concerning coal as a general European question and more specifically as a problem of increasing the output of German coal mines, see vol. II, pp. 472 ff. and pp. 909 ff.

German sources will exceed second quarter by 1.4, perhaps 1.8 million tons.

(c) MEA has not encouraged hopes that US exports would be significantly increased over present rate 2.6 million tons per month. Would appreciate your estimate, however, of maximum that may be expected in third quarter. If US exports could be raised to 2.9, believe UK request could be met without serious friction in ECO.

4. On balance, MEA believes US should support British request. Factors which persuade us are these:

(a) British have unquestionably been encouraged by President Truman's offer of February 13 to believe US would support UK proposal for import under ECO allocation, and public pressure for imports has been stimulated by President's offer. MEA convinced US cannot afford seemingly to reverse its position.

(b) Aggravation of Britain's economic plight might have serious economic and political consequences for rest of Europe and ourselves. British economic recovery more decisive in its consequences than that of any other European country.

(c) If ECO allocation denied and if sufficiently hard pressed, UK might take coal from Ruhr, even if this entailed withdrawal from ECO. Case for coal from Germany is that UK is paying large amounts of dollars for food and consumer goods to boost Ruhr production. Almost all European countries except Britain heretofore have benefited from increased Ruhr output made possible by US and UK expenditure. This argument, while not yet widely made in public, is being made privately with much force.

5. MEA aware that recommended course involves some risks for ECO and that other ECO claimants, who feel their need is greater, may object to allocation for UK. We recognize also French will probably use this occasion to again press forcefully for greater exports from Germany than is practical. Nonetheless, we believe President's offer of February 13 overrides other considerations.

6. Foregoing matter discussed with Ambassador, who concurs view expressed in this cable, and urges every possible effort be made to raise US export availability to maximum.

Sent Dept 1714, repeated to Moscow for USDel as 112.

DOUGLAS

840.6362/3–2147 : Telegram

The Acting Secretary of State to the Embassy in the Soviet Union

SECRET WASHINGTON, March 21, 1947—7 p. m.

618. Secdel 1362. London's Salco–454 rptd Moscow for Secdel as 112.[1] Ref prospective Brit request for ECO allocation coal from US following relevant to formulation US position:

---

[1] The Secretary of State was attending the meetings at Moscow of the Council of Foreign Ministers.

Second quarter ECO allocations US coal are on basis 2.6 million tons exports to Europe per month. Achieving this rate requires closest coordination procurement, rail movement and shipping in US and allows no leeway for unforeseen difficulties. Resolving every uncertainty for third quarter in favor of export program US might be able to ship 2.9 million per month to Europe. Dept believes unrealistic to expect such increase because of (a) possible coal strike July (b) present export controls expire 30 June and unless renewed doubtful whether even present export levels can be maintained (c) expiration 30 June Maritime Comm authority to operate pool of ships which may result in inadequate flexible shipping available to move bulk coal and grain cargoes. Therefore only safe to assume that allocation US coal to Brit third quarter would reduce allocations to other ECO importers below second quarter levels. In addition Eire will become regular claimant due Brit inability to supply and probably Iceland. US coal now exported to Norway, Swed, Denm, Neth, Belg, France, Switz, Port Italy, Greece, Finland, all through ECO, also Iceland, Eire. Largest allocations to France and Italy.

Brit statistics show internal consumption availability (production less exports and bunkers) 1946 approx. equal 1935–8 internal availability. Projected 1947 production of 200 million with no exports except expected bunkers will give internal availability 109 percent 1935–8 average. All other ECO importing countries have been and will be in 1947 well below 100% 1935–8 availability. On statistical basis therefore Brit position better than continental. Strain on ECO operation will be severe if Brit request presented.

President's offer Feb 13 was emergency offer to divert cargoes afloat if ECO agreed and was related to internal transport tie-up in UK.

In view effect allocation US coal to Brit in third quarter on other Eur claimants, particularly France, and in view strong position French taking re coal in Moscow and effect on Ger exports of decision on level of industry and reparation, Dept reluctant to take position on matter without comment from Secdel and suggests desirability of discussing directly with Bevin. (Sent Moscow for Secdel, rptd. London for Amb and Porter.)

ACHESON

840.6362/3–2747 : Telegram

The Secretary of State to the Acting Secretary of State

SECRET   Moscow, March 27, 1947—11 a. m
URGENT

1046. Delsec 1354. For Acheson. Personal from Marshall. Reference British request to ECO for allocation of coal from US in third quarter. Department's 618, March 21 (Secdel 1362).

Department should take position that it is reluctant to allocate coal to British as British availabilities from own production without exports are considerably closer to normal availabilities than the quantities available to continental countries.

Transport difficulties make it unlikely that additional coal may be shipped in third quarter and allocation to British could be made only by reduction in allocation to continent. Allocations of US coal to British under these circumstances, unless wholeheartedly supported by ECO importing countries, would lead to misunderstanding and bitterness.

This reply will leave the door open if Bevin desires to appeal to me. I prefer not to initiate discussion with him.

Repeated to London as 108.

[MARSHALL]

840.6362/3–2847 : Telegram

The Ambassador in the United Kingdom (Douglas) to the Secretary of State

SECRET   LONDON, March 28, 1947—7 p. m.
US URGENT

1940. Personal for Acheson. During the last week have taken opportunity to review British coal situation. I fully agree with views of Secretary Marshall, as stated in his 1354 of March 27,[1] that any increase in American coal exports to Europe should be channelled through ECO and that allocations of coal by ECO to UK, unless wholeheartedly supported by ECO importing countries, might have unfortunate consequences on the continent and should not be made.

In the event Mr. Bevin initiates discussions on coal with Secretary Marshall, I am submitting the following estimate of the way in which the Government here is attempting to solve its coal difficulties. On further review this estimate may be altered but at the moment it is my best judgment.

Few steps have so far been taken toward an orderly shutting down of marginal mines. Nor has the wage structure been altered so as to relate miners' compensation to productivity. Only lackadaisical efforts appear to have been made towards providing even temporary housing facilities in the more productive coal fields. No action has been undertaken to increase consumer goods in the more productive areas for the miners and their families. The system of taxation is such that any increased earnings of the miners resulting from increased individual production leaves but a small residue in the hands of the miners. These

---

[1] *Supra.*

steps seem necessary to reduce the present high rate of absenteeism; to induce miners to move from least productive mines, when they are shut down, to the more efficient mines and fields; as incentive to increased individual productivity, and to hasten recruitment of additional men to the mines, which is now proceeding at moderate rate.

There is great resistance to the use of oil in several large electrical generating power stations, which with minor changes are adapted to the burning of oil. This step alone might conserve as much as 3 to 5 million tons of coal annually. The traditional practice of requiring lump coal of substantial size among many large consumers instead of burning the run of the mine product, as is the custom in US is deeply rooted; and no efforts have been made to change it. This has a depressing influence on production.

Mechanical equipment that is available for both open cast and underground mining operating is not being installed as rapidly as might be. The five day week has been adopted. In view of the high rate in absenteeism, this may not have as adverse an effect on coal production during the next six months as might be expected. I recognize that there are many social and political crosscurrents which may account for what appears to be an inadequately vigorous approach to the UK coal issue but I pass on what seem to be the facts for the Secretary's information.

Sent Department as 1940; repeated Delsec Moscow as 142.

DOUGLAS

840.6362/3–2847 : Telegram

The Ambassador in the United Kingdom (Douglas) to the Secretary of State

SECRET   LONDON, March 28, 1947—8 p. m.

1950. This is Salco 465. Reference Dept 1275, London, sent Moscow Secdel 1362 and Delsec 1354 sent London 108. Have informed McNeil and Shinwell that US regards as unrealistic any significant increase in US coal exports to Europe over 2.6 million tons monthly allocated in second quarter. We think UK initiative at ECO general purposes committee meeting March 26 in proposing admission of Eire, Iceland and Faroe Isles to ECO was intended to inform other ECO members indirectly that UK herself would not seek coal outside ECO. In view improbability any increase in US exports we doubt UK will now approach ECO for imports.

Gridley, former ECO Chairman, now Marketing Director, National Coal Board, was prepared go US to discuss procurement arrangements. Trip now unlikely.

Would appreciate Department keeping us informed whether any countries fail to contract all of their US allocation, and any change your estimates.

Sent Department as 1950, repeated Moscow as 145 for Secdel.

DOUGLAS

740.00119 Council/3–2847 : Telegram

The Acting Secretary of State to the Embassy in the Soviet Union

SECRET   WASHINGTON, March 28, 1947—8 p. m.

714. Secdel 1394. Dept with assistance all agencies involved has made full reexamination to determine possibility of US exporting 3.1 million tons coal to Europe (3.7 to all destinations) per month.

Supply: Solid Fuels Admin believes sufficient coal will be available at mines to meet such program although some might be of relatively poor quality. Such availability is subject to possibility strike after 1 July. Strike would immediately severely curtail if not stop exports. Effects of strike would be felt for considerable period after settlement. Impossible to forecast likelihood of strike for several weeks at least. Availability of coal would also be decreased if miners return to 5 day week but probably supply would remain sufficient for export program.

Internal Movement: ODT believes sufficient internal movement capacity to move above program to ports.

Loading Facilities: ODT believes sufficient loading capacity in ports to handle above program. Removal on Apr 1 of quality restrictions on exports will allow export of quality coal through Hampton Roads which will largely constitute a net increase of export capacity over that previously available. There is an outside chance that competition between domestic and foreign demand for quality coal will force reimposition quality controls and consequent loss loading facilities.

Shipping: Sufficient ships to carry above program exist but taking ships out of lay-up and refitting would probably be necessary. Authority of Maritime Comm to operate ships through agents and to use current funds to refit ships expires 30 June. Authority to charter on short term basis to operators expires 31 Dec. Believed assurance of adequate shipping to carry program requires legislation plus reversal of present Maritime Comm policy to liquidate its past operations in anticipation of end of authority in accordance with previous Congressional desire to terminate operating functions. Dept will press for necessary legislation and now discussing matter with Maritime Comm. If Congressional opposition to such legislation develops, carrying out of above program would, as practical matter, be very doubtful. Possibility shipping strike at end summer cannot be forgotten.

Executive Powers: Without already requested extension of export control power,[1] high degree of coordination and control needed to carry out program impossible and no allocations or control over destinations would be possible.

Summary: In the absence of strikes or serious unforeseen contingencies, with renewal export control legislation and sufficient shipping legislation, best estimate that program of 3.1 million tons coal to Europe possible during summer and fall with uncertainties of weather making winter shipments probably lower. This figure probably represents near peak capacity. Best previous shipments Europe since war were 2.4 in July 1946 with only minor use Hampton Roads.

Allocations: Second quarter allocations to Europe made on basis 2.6 million tons per month and followed ECO recommendations. French allocation 787,500 per month, French North Africa 67,500. None to UK. In view possibility that it might be possible to ship more than allocations, each country was issued Apr export licenses for 120% of allocation which makes 3.1 million licensed for Europe. Extra 20% constitutes authority to try to exceed allocations and if successful Apr agreed to overlicense in May and June also. Since second quarter strike unlikely and legislative situation presently satisfactory, quite possible allocations will be exceeded in which case French plus FNA could reach million tons. Rearrangement to cut Brit in for second quarter would mean changing established pattern.

ECO recommendations third quarter made about middle May. By then strike and legislative situation US may have clarified to allow declared availability from US of 3.1. If so, Dept believes ECO allocation million to France plus FNA and 250,000 to Brit possible without forcing down throats other ECO countries. If prospects are less favorable would be difficult to obtain that figure France and any for UK without danger of wrecking valuable cooperation achieved ECO in past 20 months. Any firm quantitative commitment to France from US or Germany would likewise jeopardize not only ECO but also projected Econ. Comm. Europe which ECOSOC has approved and whose terms ref, including takeover of ECO, ECOSOC expected to approve this session. In event conditions necessary for full US program mentioned above not met and US exports fall seriously, quantitative commitment to France would be at expense other claimants, particularly Italy.

Dept recommends (1) Brit withhold request allocation at least until ECO considers third quarter allocations and then request only if

---

[1] President Truman's message to the Congress requesting extension of the Export Control Act was sent on March 19. The President stressed that "This country is the great undamaged center of industrial production to which the whole world looks for materials of every kind. . . . Our international responsibilities cannot be fulfilled without this machinery. . . ." For text of message see Department of State *Bulletin*, April 13, 1947, p. 676.

favorable solution uncertainties appears likely (see Moscow's 1046 to Dept, rptd London as 108). Relevant to note that if Brit miners worked three extra days in 1947 they should produce the 2 million contemplated imports from US and save 16 million dollars cost of coal and probable 24 million dollars shipping cost. (2) French be told US cannot guarantee specific figure but, if third quarter exports expected to reach 3 million per month US will support in ECO 1 million to France plus FNA from US. If third quarter prospects less favorable, US will support proportionate equitable share for France which has in fact done very well relatively in ECO. (See London's 139 to Moscow, rptd Dept 1912, Berlin 221, Paris 229 [2]).

Sent Moscow, rptd London as 1400 and Paris as 1147.

ACHESON

---

[2] Not printed.

841.6362/4–1847 : Telegram

The Ambassador in the United Kingdom (Douglas) to the Secretary of State

SECRET

LONDON, April 18, 1947—1 p. m.

2292. At the request of the Prime Minister [1] I called on him this morning. Subject of the discussion was coal. He asked whether a personal communication from him to the President outlining the needs for an allocation by ECO of coal to the United Kingdom would be an appropriate thing for him to do. I outlined to him in reply what our previous communications to the Dept had contained, told him of the effect of the recent strike upon the availability of coal during the second quarter and of the possibility that with proper cooperation of inland transport and port loading facilities at home the availability during the third and fourth quarters may reach a figure of 3,100,000 tons a month. I pointed out to him that because the possibility of a coal strike on the first of July and other mishaps which might upset close coordination, we could not state precisely what the export availability would be. I informed him of the arrival of Mr. Koenig [2] and of the purposes of his visit. Finally I told him that even though the export availability from the United States to ECO might be substantially increased it was our view that any application of the UK

---

[1] Clement R. Attlee.
[2] Robert P. Koenig, President of Ayrshire Collieries Company, had arrived at the London Embassy to serve as temporary technical consultant on coal to the Ambassador. On June 13 he submitted to Ambassador Douglas a "short analysis and study" of the British coal industry; a copy is in the Department of State file No. 841.6362/6–1347.

for an allocation should stand on its own feet and be voted in the ordinary fashion by ECO. The Prime Minister expressed gratification at what we were attempting to do and concluded that unless I advised him to the contrary he would not now communicate with the President.

Barring a coal strike, it would be helpful to have your current best estimate of the availability of coal for export through ECO.

DOUGLAS

840.6362/4–2347 : Telegram

The Acting Secretary of State to the Embassy in the United Kingdom

SECRET   WASHINGTON, April 23, 1947—8 p. m.

1783. This is Lasco 311. For Douglas and Porter from Acheson.

1. We agree appeal to President would be inadvisable urtel 2292 Apr 18 as it might create impression in ECO that US and UK were willing to consider reaching bilateral understanding committing US to support Brit request.

2. As background to following refer to Secdel 1362 repeated London 1275 Mar 21; to Secdel 1394 repeated London 1400 Mar 28; and to Delsec 1354 repeated to London as 108 Mar 27.

3. May we have your reaction to following suggested points to comprise basis for discussions with UK:

4. US keenly aware of UK's need for coal to attain economic goals. However, since UK 1947 coal supply available for internal consumption is comparatively better than that of other European importing countries (as measured by pre-war rate of internal consumption), UK request to ECO places US in difficult position because UK procurement would reduce availabilities to other countries.

5. In view of this difficulty US believes that it will be able to support UK request in ECO (*a*) only if total exportable coal available to European importing countries from all sources for third quarter reaches level approximating that outlined in Salco 454 para three, including three million tons monthly from US and (*b*) only if allocation to UK is supported by other countries without too much bitterness.

6. Unfortunately US will be unable to give firm estimate of US third quarter availability for some time owing to possibility of coal strike on or after July 1, 1947. Also relevant to mention that US authority to allocate coal exports is dependent upon extension of Export Control Act. US may be unable to determine whether a strike will or will not occur until a very few days before end of Krug-Lewis contract which is presumably 30 June when authority of Govt to operate mines expires. Therefore, US cannot in the meantime make a firm

third quarter estimate of three million tons per month, or, indeed, for any level of exports.

7. If US were to present an optimistic estimate of availability to ECO for third quarter allocation at three million tons or more, then UK may be able to obtain an ECO allocation. If strike should then occur in July actual volume of coal exported will prove to be appreciably lower especially if strike lasts more than two weeks. UK in meantime will have been given authority to compete with other European claimants for a short supply of coal at a level of export availability substantially below three million tons.

8. In the circumstances, US proposes to give ECO two estimates of export availability, probably one estimate at three million tons monthly, at which UK would presumably obtain an allocation and another estimate at 2.6 tons, at which level UK presumably would have a lesser chance of obtaining an allocation. It is presumed that at level of export availability below three million tons, other ECO claimants would be extremely reluctant to share US coal with Britain and that Britain's chances of obtaining an allocation would be reduced with decreasing levels of availability. Note that neither of these estimates is firm in the event of a strike because effect of strike cannot be foretold. However, if a strike occurs the lower estimate is likely to be closer to actual results than the higher.

9. About June 1 US would issue firm allocations for third quarter at 2.6 million tons. If and when union-management and other factors clarify to point where US can adopt a three million ton target for Europe with a reasonable chance of success, US would revise third quarter allocations on basis of ECO's suggested distribution at that level and, assuming ECO has recommended an allocation for UK at upper level of export availability, would try to do everything possible, allocation-wise, to have UK obtain its fair share of US coal for third quarter based upon US export possibilities for that quarter as a whole. It should be borne in mind that if a serious strike does occur, US may be unable to adopt a three million ton program for some time following strike's termination owing to possibility of a serious coal shortage.

10. Foregoing proposals re US export availability are not for submission to ECO but are suggested only for purpose of discussion with UK.

11. If foregoing proposals are acceptable to you, you may proceed with discussions immediately. However, we should by all means preserve our freedom of action within ECO and avoid any bilateral understanding which would commit us to support Brit request, even at three million ton US export availability, in face of stubborn opposition from other claimants. Outcome of proposed Brit discussions with France and Belgium re an allocation might provide material clue to reaction of those countries. Therefore, we suggest you indicate to UK that US believes it inadvisable for US and UK to reach understanding outside ECO and that purpose of your discussion is to acquaint UK of difficulties confronting US. While US would like to

assist UK in its present difficulties, US believes, and is sure that Britain agrees, that serious damage to ECO should be avoided.[1]

Sent to London as Lasco 311, repeated to Moscow Secdel as 1486, repeated to Paris as 1482, repeated to Brussels as 573.

ACHESON

---

[1] In telegram 2407, Salco 482, April 24, from London, not printed, Ambassador Douglas replied: "We agree completely with the proposals contained in Lasco 311 and have informed British Government officials that we cannot be a party to any extralateral understanding which would commit us to support any British claim presented to ECO and we appreciate the possible serious consequences should ECO be damaged." (841.6362/4-2447)

840.6362/5–847 : Telegram

The Ambassador in the United Kingdom (Douglas) to the Secretary of State

SECRET   LONDON, May 8, 1947—8 p. m.
US URGENT

2643. This is Salco 487. Makins [1] and Hall-Patch [2] of the Foreign Office called to inform me of the results of the informal conversations UK delegate to the ECO has had with ECO representatives of governments concerned, covering both the intentions of the UK to submit an application for an allocation of coal and the Polish negotiations as they affect coal. Only the Danish and Swiss representatives on ECO have not so far been acquainted with UK intentions because the former are not available in London but are being informed in Geneva and because the latter is ill and unavailable. When it was explained to the representatives of the remaining countries that the UK's main objective in applying to ECO was to secure an allocation of US coal, general relief and satisfaction was expressed and no opposition was indicated excepting by French. The representatives of Sweden and The Netherlands hinted that they might be unable to afford, for exchange reasons, quantities of US coal in excess of those which they are already purchasing. The views thus expressed were those of the representatives of the respective countries on ECO who have reported to their governments. Further information as to the position of their respective governments may be available later but the Foreign Office believes that they will not differ substantially from the expressed attitudes of the ECO representatives themselves.

---

[1] Roger Makins, Assistant Under-Secretary of State, British Foreign Office.
[2] Sir Edmund Hall-Patch, Deputy Under-Secretary of State, British Foreign Office.

As to France, the French representative was disturbed at the proposed intentions of the UK because of its effects on coal available for France and expressed a hope that the UK request would be spread over as long a period as possible and that the UK might purchase larger quantities of US coal than it required for its own use and resell British coal to Europe. This suggestion the UK declined on grounds of exchange. As a result of the conversations with the French representative on ECO the matter has now been raised to the political level and M. Alphand [3] of the Quai d'Orsay has communicated with the Foreign Office to the effect that he would like to discuss the whole question of the UK application for an allocation, probably coming to London this week-end. The Foreign Office replied that it would not be prepared to discuss the matter with him so soon. It is probable that the discussions with Alphand will take place Tuesday or Wednesday of next week, May 13 or 14. The Foreign Office expect[s] that the French in return for not opposing the UK application for an allocation of US coal will seek UK support on some other issue probably, the Foreign Office suspects, on the proposition that the Saar coal be incorporated in the amount of indigenous French coal and made available for French consumption.[4] This would have the effect of increasing the amount of coal available for France by approximately 200,000 tons a month, with a probable reduction in the amount available for other consuming countries. It will therefore not go unchallenged in ECO.

Makins and Hall-Patch put the following question to me: What will be the attitude of your government should the French oppose the UK application for an allocation of coal?

I replied provisionally that in this case even rather than run the risk of disturbing ECO and of causing bitterness we would be disposed to suggest that the UK application for an allocation be not presented, or if presented, that it be withdrawn, but that we would seek your advice. Inasmuch as the conversations between the Foreign Office and the Quai d'Orsay will be held Tuesday or Wednesday of next week, we urgently request your advice by the tenth if possible but not later than the twelfth.

Sent to Department as 2643; repeated to Geneva for Porter, USDel, ECE, as 32; repeated to Paris as 290.

DOUGLAS

---

[3] Hervé Alphand, Director of Economic Services, French Ministry of Foreign Affairs.

[4] Tripartite agreement was reached among the United States, the United Kingdom, and France at Moscow in April regarding an increase in the production of the coal mines in the Saar, with a concomitant increase in the allotment of coal for France. For documentation regarding this matter, see vol. II, pp. 472 ff.

840.6362/5–1247 : Telegram

The Secretary of State to the Embassy in the United Kingdom

SECRET   WASHINGTON, May 12, 1947—7 p. m.

US URGENT   NIACT

2068. This is Lasco 319. Refer Salco 487. We believe UK has right present to ECO its request for US coal and that we cannot ask UK abstain from requesting coal.

Reasonableness UK request in relation French opposition depends upon total availability coal from all sources. If US export availability rises to point which exceeds effective demand of some countries, UK should have opportunity compete in ECO for US coal. If UK were prevented from getting US coal, France, which evidently has not reached saturation point from dollar standpoint for US coal, would in effect be in position procure by default marginal supply US coal turned back by other countries. Marginal US coal not procurable by some other ECO claimants should not go by default to France in absence other effective demand but should, in effect be allocated by ECO. For that reason US insists US coal be allocated by ECO and within ECO and that France cannot use her presumptive right to a fixed proportion of all US coal at all levels US availability with which to bargain for Saar coal. If French strongly resist UK allocation on ground of equitability, US may be unable support UK in order avoid damage to ECO. But US opposes use US coal for bargaining purposes re Saar.

Recent investigations held here point to prospect exporting possible maximum of 3.4 million tons per month to Europe during third quarter *if there is no strike*. Meeting of US Coal Committee May 15 will discuss this prospect. We may therefore be able give ECO a third level of US export availability at 3.4 million tons in addition other two already given for third quarter.

Sent London as 2068 rptd Paris as 1722 and Geneva for Porter as 355.

MARSHALL

840.6362/5–1647 : Telegram

The Ambassador in the United Kingdom (Douglas) to the Secretary of State

SECRET   LONDON, May 16, 1947—5 p. m.

2777. This is Salco 493. 1. Makins, Foreign Office, just returned from conference with Alphand re British request to ECO for coal allocation. French still eager obtain special concession Saar coal as condition their agreement to British request but Makins says as result preliminary examination French terms less onerous than originally thought. Foreign Office examining them carefully and Makins will inform me details and Foreign Office view bearing in mind US position. I will inform you immediately.

2. British have decided make provisional request ECO coal allocation conditional upon third quarter availabilities. Provisional request permits British withdrawal if opposition develops or French become too difficult. Assume British will make request formally at allocations meeting Tuesday May 20.

DOUGLAS

840.6362/5-1647 : Telegram

The Secretary of State to the Embassy in the United Kingdom

SECRET   WASHINGTON, May 16, 1947—7 p. m.
NIACT

2143. For Douglas. Re Salco 490 [1] and Lasco 319. Please make no commitments on either French or Brit position re UK request for US coal until arrival full details US position by separate tel. Jeffers [2] arriving London Mon and fully acquainted our position.

MARSHALL

---

[1] Not printed.
[2] Charles W. Jeffers, special assistant to the Chief of Mission for Economic Affairs in the Embassy in the United Kingdom.

840.6362/5-1647 : Telegram

The Secretary of State to the Embassy in the United Kingdom

SECRET   WASHINGTON, May 16, 1947—7 p. m.
NIACT   US URGENT

2142. This is Lasco 323. Refer Salco 490 and 491.[1] 1. Urpara 1. Your interpretation correct.

2. We had interpreted Salco 487 to mean that French might reopen Saar question rather than argue against UK allocation on ground of equity. French are in contradictory position in ECO if they (*a*) oppose UK allocation on ground of equity and then (*b*) argue that if UK obtains allocation of US coal, say, at 200,000 tons per month, then, in order to restore equity, France should count Saar coal as indigenous production. As long as France argues on basis of (*a*) alone she may be on strong ground, depending, however, on comparative level of

---

[1] Neither printed.

satisfaction in relation to UK. However, she cannot both defend (*a*) and propose (*b*) as a method of restoring equity, for if (*b*) were adopted, then both UK and France would benefit at expense of rest of ECO. If we were to inform UK to withdraw request simply because French were attempting to reopen Saar coal question we should, in effect, be bowing to French argument whereas French case, in terms of (*b*), does not have any merit *within ECO framework*. Rather than back down, UK should oppose French attempt to bargain US coal. UK should counter French position by pointing to its obvious unfairness to other ECO claimants and to its inconsistency with principles of fair distribution which ECO has been trying to formulate. UK might also indicate to French that US would obviously oppose a bilateral deal outside ECO between UK and France involving US coal.

3. Assuming that UK is opposed to bilateral deal French have in mind, it need not necessarily follow that UK withdraw her request for coal in order to keep French from reopening question of Saar. We assume that if French are informed by UK that no deal on Saar can be made outside ECO, and that UK and US in any case will oppose tripartite settlement of Saar even in ECO, then France will not broach this question in ECO, at least with any success, and that France therefore will have to shift full weight of her opposition to issue of equity, assuming she really wishes to oppose UK allocation in absence of opportunity to bargain for Saar. On this score, strength of her case obviously depends on French level of satisfaction compared with British. UK 1947 level of satisfaction for internal consumption, excluding bunker coal, about 109% of 1935–38 average. French third quarter supply estimate follows (in millions of tons) :

Gross production of clean coal	13.250
Allocation from US	2.700
German availability	.720
Polish availability	.210
Other availability	.130
Total	17.010

Assumptions follow: (1) French output in 1947 53 million tons. (2) US availability 9 million tons and French proportion 30% as in second quarter. At availability of 7.8 from US, French share would be 2.34 million while at availability of 10 million from US, French share would probably be in excess of 3 million. Note however, that US will restrict allocations to 7.8 pending outcome strike threat. (3) German availability and French share assumed to be same as for second quarter. German exports, however, may be reduced in third quarter owing to recent reduction in Ruhr output, and to food shortage. (4) Polish availability to France assumed at second quarter level. This, however, is dependent outcome of Polish-French negotiations and if embargo not lifted France will get no Polish coal. (5) Other imports roughly same as second quarter.

About 80,000 tons should be subtracted as probable exports making probable total net supply of 16.930 million tons on gross production basis without 10% adjustment and without deduction of low grade coal. These deductions have not been made for UK either. French quarterly requirement on 1935–38 base about 17.5 million tons. French therefore, may satisfy about 97% of 1935–38 level of satisfaction. The event may prove supply to be substantially lower than 16.930 or even higher by some 600,000 tons.

While this is below UK level of satisfaction, it does not give French overwhelming basis for argument, especially in view of large UK export trade. Other ECO countries would have much better case for opposition but are apparently not prepared to oppose UK. Furthermore, if at rising levels of export availability, especially from US, some countries reach saturation point for US coal, France will have an opportunity to increase her share of US coal, because from dollar supply position she evidently has higher cut-off point for US coal than other countries. As French share of US coal rises not so much by virtue of allocation formulae alone as by virtue of her willingness to spend dollars for coal, UK chance of obtaining allocation should improve.

4. Depts position as outlined Lasco 311 has not changed. However, imminent possibility that France may try to exercise veto over UK's request has drawn out some implications of our position. While we still believe strongly that UK should not obtain allocation if it leads to bitterness and damages ECO we believe that UK should not necessarily retreat at first sign of resistance on part of France. Reasonableness of French position and lengths to which she is prepared to go in opposing UK, should, if possible, be carefully weighed before British request is withdrawn. While there is danger to ECO in following this course, since UK and France may involve themselves too far in argument within ECO to make graceful retreat, we should use all possible judgment before permitting France to exercise absolute veto power. While our cardinal principle is preservation of ECO, considerations adduced above give us some flexibility in determining whether or not UK should be supported even in face of some opposition. If price for a UK allocation is serious damage to ECO, then we shall not support UK. However, that may not necessarily be case. It will therefore be up to Emb and MEA, who are on spot, to weigh developments and take whatever course seems best in relation to Dept's desire to preserve ECO as working organization. We need neither

favor nor oppose either France or UK in advance but rather should take an objective attitude permitting our final position to be determined by merits of case.

5. US Coal Operating Committee, in considering third quarter coal availability for Europe and North Africa, agreed on May 15 that a third figure of 3.4 million tons monthly should be submitted to ECO. Basis of additional estimate is performance during first 13 days of May, which have run at monthly rate of 3.3 to 3.4 million tons. Loadings through Hampton Rds are in excess of previously estimated movement through that port and account for improved performance.

This leaves US position as follows: Three levels of US availability are submitted to ECO, at 2.6, 3.0, and 3.4 monthly for third quarter. If a serious mine suspension occurs, exports for quarter will probably not exceed lowest figure. If a contract is signed with the Union by July 1, if actual work-week at mines is not cut appreciably, and if there is no maritime strike 3.4 million tons monthly allocation might be adopted here. Please give us soonest pattern distribution at each of three levels. Note that ability to allocate depends on extension of Export Control Act.

6. You may discuss contents para 2 through 5 with UK.

Sent to London as 2142, repeated to Paris as 1803, repeated to USDel ECE Geneva for Porter as 405.

MARSHALL

840.6362/5–1747 : Telegram

The Ambassador in the United Kingdom (Douglas) to the Secretary of State

SECRET   LONDON, May 17, 1947—4 p.m.

2796. Urtel 2142 [1] and Lasco 323 and urtel 2143 [1] very helpful. Please be assured no commitment has been made re French or British position on UK request for ECO allocations of coal. We have consistently informed the British in substance as follows:—(1) We are unwilling to take any position that would cause undue bitterness and damage the effectiveness of ECO. We must be left completely free to judge the merits of the case without prejudice. (2) We object effort to bargain US coal for Saar coal.

Foreign Office is as anxious as we are to preserve ECO as effective instrumentality. It is for this reason UK is submitting provisional application to ECO (see Salco 493) contingent upon availabilities.

Makins gave Embassy his personal views and story of Paris talks and outlined French proposition but emphasized informality because matter had not yet been cleared by Bevin.

---

[1] Both telegrams dated May 16, 7 p.m.

When Makins and Brook arrived in Paris to talk with Alphand, French pointed out that contemplated British request for coal was embarrassing for them from all points of view—psychological, political and economic. They were, therefore, forced to consider some compensating advantage for British request. Alphand suggested semi-officially that as contemplated in the Moscow agreement there should be tripartite notification to ECO that Saar production was to be considered a part of indigenous French production, but that this should be done prior to quadripartite agreement to transfer of Saar.

Makins gave French his personal view that such action might not be possible until questions of Saar frontiers and reparations value of Saar had been settled. He intimated to them that integration of Saar production into French indigenous production and applications of ECO allocations formula thereto probably would result in less coal to other ECO recipients, and therefore opposition by them.

French indicated that they did not require support of UK in ECO to meet possible opposition there. Alphand then outlined a scheme which French considered might avoid opposition. When tripartite notification was given they would undertake to maintain existing Saar commitments to export coal until Ruhr production reached 250,000 tons daily. Until this figure reached they would not benefit from Saar. Thereafter French benefit from Saar would increase *pari passu* with rise in Ruhr production until latter reached 320,000 tons daily. At this point French would receive full benefit arising from consideration of Saar production as part of French indigenous production. Obviously this scheme would cause no immediate loss to ECO pool and might obviate opposition of other ECO members.

French submitted some figures to British of effect of considering Saar production part of French indigenous production; they believed result would be very advantageous to them. British experts considered French figures not entirely accurate and they suggested some changes which are being considered by French. It is expected that both British and French experts will discuss these figures next week.

Makins thinks that British probably will not object to French proposals in principle but he feels that result would not give French as much coal as they believe likely. Matter being considered further by British who intend to communicate with us prior to reply to French.[2]

DOUGLAS

[2] In telegram 2184. May 20, the Department replied:

"Position taken with British (first paragraph urtel 2796 May 17) noted with approval.

"Dept concerned over trend UK–French discussions as reported reference telegram. Pls inform FonOff that US considers premature any discussion in ECO based on the transfer of Saar to France or any ECO allocation predicated on understanding for the treatment of Saar coal as indigenous French output. Any French proposals on Saar should be discussed in first instance at inter-governmental level. Pls advise US member ECO." (840.6362/5–1747)

840.6362/5–2147 : Telegram

The Ambassador in the United Kingdom (Douglas) to the Secretary of State

SECRET   LONDON, May 21, 1947—1 p. m.

URGENT

2848. From Douglas. Yesterday Makins Foreign Office called on me and discussed French proposal relative the Saar and the UK application to ECO for coal. He informed me that the Foreign Office was considering replying to Quai d'Orsay in substance as follows (Deptel 2184 May 20):

1. A recitation of the British understanding of the French proposal.
2. That the statistical basis had not yet been established.
3. That if the Foreign Office clearly understood the French proposal they saw no objection in principle and would be glad to consider the proposal provided the US Government agreed.
4. That they could not, however, further discuss the matter until two questions had been determined: (a) The Saar frontiers and (b) the reparations value of the Saar.

I then informed Makins that the questions of the UK allocation for coal and the proposal relative the Saar were two separate and distinct ones and had no relation to each other. Also informed him that the question of the Saar was one which could be settled only on intergovernmental basis.

This morning Makins informs me that the cable referred to herein from the Foreign Office to the Quai d'Orsay had been sent and that prior to sending it the French had informed the Foreign Office that France would oppose a UK application for an allocation on the basis of US availabilities of 2,600,000 tons a month. Makins said, however, that if the US availabilities rose above 3,000,000 the French opposition might be much weaker and certainly would be argued on less firm grounds.

I repeated to Makins what I told him yesterday, that the question of the Saar and of the UK application were two separate issues and should not be confused and secondly that the question of the Saar could be settled only on an intergovernmental level. He understood our position clearly and replied that the effect of the cable that had been sent to the Quai d'Orsay was to divorce the question of the Saar from the question of the UK application for coal and that he understood thoroughly that the Saar problem could be resolved on the intergovernmental level.

DOUGLAS

840.6362/5–2247 : Telegram

The Ambassador in the United Kingdom (Douglas) to the Secretary of State

RESTRICTED
US URGENT

LONDON, May 22, 1947—4 p. m.

2875. This is Salco 494 from MEA. 1. APC meeting 22 May agreed following scheme third quarter allocations re UK request for US coal:

a. At level US coal 2.6 tons per month previously agreed formula will be used without UK participation.

b. At level 3.0 million tons per month formula will be used but giving UK priority to purchase any coal refused by any country. Other member countries will not have right to compete for this coal.

c. UK to have right to purchase first 200,000 tons over 3.0 million tons.

d. Any further tonnage which will become available above 3.2 to be offered pro rata to all countries receiving US coal. UK to participate according to US pattern for 3.2 million tons availability but without priority in purchasing coal which may be refused by other countries.

2. All countries except France would have agreed to more liberal treatment UK. UK reaccepted [*received?*] this proposal with regret but had received instructions to accept in order to reach agreement without sharp conflict.

3. US distribution at levels 2.6, 3.0 and 3.4 million tons will be forwarded soonest along with detailed recommended allocations.

DOUGLAS

840.6362/5–2347 : Telegram

The Ambassador in the United Kingdom (Douglas) to the Secretary of State

CONFIDENTIAL

LONDON, May 23, 1947—8 p. m.

2915. Salco 498. In conversation with Massigli, the French Ambassador, today he expressed the view that the action of ECO in regard to British application for allocation of coal was a fair and equitable one. As nearly as I can tell from conversation with Foreign Office the British are slightly disappointed that a different formula was not used which would have enabled them to obtain more coal with greater certainty. They are, however, on the whole satisfied with the outcome principally because it provides ECO as an effective instrumentality on the one hand and depending upon the availability of

US coal provides substantial satisfaction of their requirements on the other.

DOUGLAS

Editorial Note

On June 2, the newly-organized Policy Planning Staff of the Department of State completed its second paper, "Increase of European Coal Production". In this study the Staff concluded that the deficient production of coal in Britain and in the Ruhr-Aachen fields of Germany constituted a decisive bottleneck in the rehabilitation of the war-shattered European economy. (The problem of European economic rehabilitation was the subject of the first Policy Planning Staff study.) To overcome this and to reduce the dollar exchange drain in Europe caused by the purchase of American coal, the Staff recommended that the Department of State take energetic steps to bring about measures outside the ECO to overcome the deficiency in European coal production. The Policy Planning Staff believed that it was absolutely necessary to obtain British cooperation at the outset.

As a result, there was some discussion in June and July 1947, at the initiative of the Department, between the United States and British Governments as to the possibility of holding conversations in Washington on the problem of European coal production. This discussion led to conversations in August in Washington between the two governments on German production problems in general. For documentation concerning these talks, see volume III, pages 946 ff.

THE SIGNATURE, RATIFICATION, AND DEPOSIT OF IN-STRUMENTS OF RATIFICATION OF THE TREATIES OF PEACE WITH ITALY, ROMANIA, BULGARIA, AND HUNGARY [1]

740.0011 EW (Peace)/1–2147

The Counselor of the Italian Embassy (di Stefano) to the Assistant Chief of the Division of Southern European Affairs (Dowling)

No. 359/73 WASHINGTON, January 21, 1947.

MY DEAR DOWLING: With reference to our conversation, I quote here below the literal translation of a cable just received from Rome, signed by Mr. Nenni: [2]

"I have to-day delivered to the Ambassadors of the Four Powers an identical message directed to the Four Foreign Ministers in which—after having observed that none of our requests for modification of the clauses of the Peace Treaty has been accepted in its final drafting and that hence the said Treaty, especially in the territorial clauses, deeply hurts the national conscience of the Italian people—I see myself compelled to formulate the widest reservations and to ask that the principle of revision, in the framework of the U.N. and on the basis of bilateral agreements with the other interested States, be admitted and recognized."

I know that you are perfectly aware of the importance that the whole Italian public opinion attributes to the question of an acknowledgment of the possibility of revisioning the Treaty in the framework of the U.N.

I feel that the message does not only interpret on the matter Italy's anxious preoccupation, but as well the feeling of a widespread international principle and necessity, over which Mr. Byrnes evidenced his

---

[1] For documentation on the preparation of the treaties of peace with Italy, Romania, Bulgaria, and Hungary, see the records of the meetings of the Council of Foreign Ministers in Paris, April 25–May 15 and June 15–July 12, 1946; the records of the Paris Peace Conference July 29–October 15, 1946; and of the meetings of the Council of Foreign Ministers in New York, November 4–December 12, 1946, *Foreign Relations*, 1946, vols. II, III, and IV.

[2] Pietro Nenni, leader of the Italian Socialist Party, Minister of Foreign Affairs, October 11, 1946–January 31, 1947. Nenni submitted his resignation in consequence of the split in the Socialist Party's congress of January 9, but his successor, Count Carlo Sforza (Independent), did not take over until January 31 when De Gasperi formed his third cabinet.

515

concern in his letter addressed to Mr. C. L. Sulzberger and published in the *New York Times*, issue of July 6, 1946.

I don't need to stress to you the wide importance and repercussions that a clarification of the point by the United States would have in my country.

Believe me [etc.]　　　　　　　　　　　　　　M. DI STEFANO

740.0011 EW (Peace)/1–2147 : Telegram

The Chargé in Italy (Key) to the Secretary of State

TOP SECRET　　　　　　　　　　　　　ROME, January 21, 1947—7 p. m.

155. Embtel 41 January 7.[1] De Gasperi last evening after cabinet resignation expressed following views to Stone[2] which latter has communicated to SAC:[3]

1. All De Gasperi's information is that Yugos will not sign treaty.

2. Elaborating on statement in his Cleveland speech De Gasperi expressed opinion that Italy also will probably not sign voluntarily although he appreciates that, unlike Yugos position as an ally, Italy as a defeated power can be compelled to sign by the victors .

3. De Gasperi formally asked Stone to inquire of SAC whether Allied Forces in Zone A will be withdrawn from Morgan Line, including specifically Pola,[4] in event treaty goes into effect on R–Day as it can without Yugo signature or ratification.

We understand that SAC will submit De Gasperi's inquiry to CCS. Stone has suggested to SAC that it should be considered on basis that Italy has signed prior to R–Day because it is his understanding (as it is the Embassy's) that treaty will not be submitted to US senate for ratification without signature of Italy.

KEY

---

[1] Not printed; in it Key reported having learned from the British Ambassador that there were circles in the United States who were opposed to the Italian peace treaty as drafted and who were advising Italians not to sign; that both Ambassadors Quarone and Carandini (respectively to the Soviet Union and to Great Britain) had reported that circles in the United States advised against signing the treaty and had suggested as an alternative a bi-lateral Italo-American peace settlement (740.00119 EW/1–747).

[2] Rear Adm. Ellery Wheeler Stone, U.S.N.R., Deputy President and Chief Commissioner, Allied Commission, June 22, 1944–January 31, 1947; then Head of the Italian Military Affairs Section, Allied Force Headquarters, February 1–March 15, 1947.

[3] Lt. Gen. John C. H. Lee.

[4] See footnote 2, p. 518. For documentation on United States interest in the establishment of the Free Territory of Trieste, see vol. IV, pp. 51 ff.

740.00119 EW/1–2247 : Telegram

The Ambassador in France (Caffery) to the Secretary of State

CONFIDENTIAL   PARIS, January 22, 1947—9 p. m.

299. Following is French text of invitation with regard to signing of peace treaties with Italy, Rumania, Bulgaria, and Hungary just received under cover of Foreign Office note dated January 20:

"After the conclusion of the deliberations of the conference held in Paris from July 29 to October 15, 1946, and taking into account its recommendations, the Council of Ministers of Foreign Affairs in its New York meeting drew up the final texts of the peace treaties with Italy, Rumania, Bulgaria, and Hungary.

"These texts have been communicated to the Department of State at Washington through the good offices of the Secretariat General of the Council of Ministers of Foreign Affairs.

"In its meeting of December 11, 1946 in New York, the Council of Ministers of Foreign Affairs agreed that the signing of the peace treaties with Italy, Rumania, Bulgaria, and Hungary shall take place in Paris at the Ministry of Foreign Affairs on February 10, 1947 at 4 p.m.

"The Government of the French Republic, acting in the name of the Council of Foreign Ministers, has the honor to invite the Government of the United States to send to Paris, for the date stipulated, its plenipotentiary or plenipotentiaries for the purpose of signing in its name the treaties with Italy, Rumania, Bulgaria, and Hungary.

"It would be grateful to the United States Government if the latter would be so good as to inform it as soon as possible of the name of its representatives." [1]

CAFFERY

[1] In telegram 386, January 30, 1947, from Paris, not printed, Ambassador Caffery was instructed to accept the invitation on behalf of the United States Government; he was notified that he would serve as U.S. representative in signing the treaties and that his full powers would be sent by courier (740.00119 EW/1–2247). On January 20, the day before James F. Byrnes retired as Secretary of State, he signed the treaties on behalf of the United States. (Department of State *Bulletin*, February 2, 1947, p. 199.)

740.00119 EW/1–2447 : Telegram

The Secretary of State to the Embassy in Italy

SECRET   WASHINGTON, January 24, 1947—6 p. m.

107. Dept has no recent info indicating Yugos might reject treaty, and is still inclined to opinion they will sign. Pls ascertain basis for De Gasperi's contrary opinion.

Failure of Yugos to sign and ratify treaty would of course make Art 89 [1] (old 77 *bis*) operative against them and thus prevent them

[1] Article 89 reads: "The provisions of the present Treaty shall not confer any rights or benefits on any State named in the Preamble as one of the Allied and Associated Powers or on its nationals until such State becomes a party to the Treaty by deposit of its instrument of ratification."

receiving benefits mentioned penultimate para ur 156 Jan 21.[2] It would also render difficult if not impossible implementation treaty clauses re Trieste, and Dept therefore considers consultations this regard among Big Four would be required. In meantime *status quo* would be maintained in Venezia Giulia with Allied forces remaining in present positions. Treaty would however be submitted to Senate for ratification so that peace might be formally concluded and other treaty provisions put into effect.

Foregoing is for your guidance, but may also be communicated informally to Ital Govt as Dept's preliminary views.

MARSHALL

[2] This paragraph read: "With regard to De Gasperi's formal inquiry whether Anglo-American forces in Zone A will be withdrawn from Morgan Line should Yugos not sign, it would seem essential to reply categorically that article 77 *bis* (of old draft treaty) would apply and that Allied troops would remain in disputed area pending other solution. Should treaty go into effect on R–Day without Yugo signature and should its territorial provisions be made applicable along with withdrawal of Allied Forces, Yugoslavia would of course be in position of having received major benefits of treaty without being bound, and could continue pressure of threat of *coup de main* in more advantageous position." (865.00/1–2147)

740.00119 Council/1–2447

The Secretary of State to the Italian Ambassador (*Tarchiani*)

The Secretary of State presents his compliments to His Excellency the Italian Ambassador and has the honor to refer to His Excellency's note 85 D/S of January 24, 1947,[1] inquiring concerning the coming into force of the Treaty of Peace with Italy. It is noted that a similar inquiry was addressed to the Secretary General of the Council of Foreign Ministers under date of January 23, 1947.

Article 90 of the proposed treaty provides that it shall be ratified by the Allied and Associated Powers and also by Italy. It also provides that it shall come into force immediately upon the deposit of ratifica-

[1] Not printed; it stated: ". . . that the Italian juridical experts have been unanimously and constantly interpreting that clause in the sense that the coming into force of the Treaty is subordinated, not only to the signature, but also to the successive ratification on the part of the competent Italian organs.

"On the contrary, according to press reports, a spokesman of the [British] Foreign Office is said to have expressed himself these days in the sense that the Treaties would come into force, not only in case of failure to ratify, but also in case of failure to sign on the part of ex-enemy States." (740.00119 Council/1–2447)

tions by the Union of Soviet Socialist Republics, the United Kingdom, the United States and France.[2]

Article 89 expressly states that the Treaty shall not confer any rights or benefits on any Allied or Associated Power or its nationals until such power ratifies the Treaty.[3]

Although the Treaty itself is silent as to the rights of Italy in the absence of ratification by Italy, it is the view of the United States Government that until the treaty is ratified by Italy, no rights or benefits under the treaty can be claimed by Italy, which would remain subject to the terms of the Armistice.[4]

It is the sincere hope of the American Government that Italy will in its own interest promptly sign and ratify the Treaty.[5]

WASHINGTON, February 1, 1947.

---

[2] Article 90 reads: "The present Treaty, of which the French, English and Russian texts are authentic, shall be ratified by the Allied and Associated Powers. It shall also be ratified by Italy. It shall come into force immediately upon the deposit of ratifications by the Union of Soviet Socialist Republics, by the United Kingdom of Great Britain and Northern Ireland, by the United States of America, and by France. The instruments of ratification shall, in the shortest time possible, be deposited with the Government of the French Republic.

"With respect to each Allied or Associated Power whose instrument of ratification is thereafter deposited, the Treaty shall come into force upon the date of deposit. The present Treaty shall be deposited in the archives of the Government of the French Republic, which shall furnish certified copies to each of the signatory States."

[3] See footnote 1 to telegram 107, p. 517.

[4] In telegram 268, February 1, from Moscow, not printed, Ambassador Smith reported that the Italian Embassy in Moscow had asked the same question of the Soviet Government, mentioning the press statements regarding the views of the British Foreign Office. The Soviet Government's opinion was that in accordance with Article 90 "treaty will be ratified by allied and united powers and must also be ratified by Italy. Article 90 obligates Italy to sign and ratify. Moment when treaty comes into effect depends on exchange of ratified copies by four powers as indicated Article 90." The Soviet Government asked for the views of the United States since the question was within the competence of the Four Powers. (740.00119 EW/2–147)

By telegram 174, February 4, not printed, Ambassador Smith was instructed to explain the United States' view in language almost identical with that of the Secretary's reply to Ambassador Tarchiani and to add that the Department "hopes Italy will in her own interest sign and promptly ratify treaty". The message was repeated to Rome, 164; to London, 567; Paris, 440. (740.00119 EW/2–147)

[5] By telegram 154, January 31, not printed, the Embassy in Rome was advised of the Department's view that Italy's own interest required that it sign and ratify the treaty, that care had been taken to avoid any impression of pressure but the hope had been expressed that Italy would sign and ratify the treaty (740.00119 EW/1–3047).

740.00119 EW/2–647 : Telegram

The Ambassador in the Soviet Union (Smith) to the Secretary of State

RESTRICTED

Moscow, February 6, 1947.

PRIORITY

323. Night of February 6 note was received dated same day from Vyshinski [1] to Ambassador regarding signature satellite peace treaties. Text follows in translation.

On February 2 a note of following text was received by Soviet Embassy in Paris:

"Signature of treaties will take place on February 10 in Ministry Foreign Affairs (Salon d'Orloges) [Salon de l'Horloge].

"Treaty with Italy will be signed in morning. Other treaties—afternoon.

"Messieurs the plenipotentiaries of states signing treaties are invited to appear, having with them their plenipotentiary powers, at Quai d'Orsay at 1100 o'clock for signing of treaty with Italy, at 1500 o'clock for signing treaty with Rumania, at 1600 o'clock 15 minutes for signing treaty with Bulgaria, at 1700 o'clock 30 minutes for signing treaty with Hungary and 1800 o'clock 45 minutes for signing treaty with Finland.

"It is necessary that there be communicated to Ministry as quickly [as possible] as this is important, names of monsieur plenipotentiary and of persons who accompany him, so as to prepare in due time passes to Salon d'Orloges [Salon de l'Horloge], to each delegation will be issued four passes.

"If messieurs plenipotentiaries desire to make declaration before signing, is recommended that they be so good as to transmit its text to the General Secretary of Paris Conference, who at time of these sessions will carry out functions connected with his post, at least 24 hours before beginning of session.

"Protocol will be drawn up according to rules of procedure of Paris Conference. Declarations will be reproduced in it in form of which they are received. With a view to determining before signature place of affixing seal and the ribbons on originals of treaties, plenipotentiaries are requested to be so good as to present their personal seal to General Secretary of Conference (Secretariat of Conference, Minister Foreign Affairs) before February 9, noon."

Minister Foreign Affairs of USSR sent on February 6 following reply to Government of French Republic:

"In connection with note of Minister Foreign Affairs of French Republic of February 2 with regard to forthcoming signing of peace treaties with Italy, Rumania, Bulgaria, Hungary and Finland Minister Foreign Affairs of USSR, on instructions of Soviet Government has the honor to communicate following.

'Soviet Government has no comment of any sort regarding proposal of French Government concerning time of signing each treaty and number of representatives of each party participating in ceremony of signing above mentioned treaties.

'Soviet Government, however, cannot agree to proposal contained in above note of French Government regarding furnishing of opportunity to plenipotentiaries in signing treaty, including plenipotentiaries of former enemy countries, of making in connection with signing of peace treaties any sort of declarations and inclusion of such declarations in protocol. Reference made in note of French Government to effect that protocol would be drawn up according to rules of procedure of Paris Peace Conference, is unfounded, since it is well known that rules of procedure of Paris Peace Conference related only to work of plenary session of conference and its commissions, and did not have relation to signing of peace treaties.

'In opinion of Soviet Government furnishing to plenipotentiaries of former enemy countries right to make any sort of declarations with regard to any pro-

---

[1] Andrey Yanuaryevich Vyshinsky, Deputy Minister for Foreign Affairs of the Soviet Union.

visions of relevant peace treaties, with inclusion of these declarations in protocol might have negative consequences. Moreover, international treaty practice does not know examples of peace treaties signing of which was accompanied by drawing up of protocols expressing views of various signatory states on content of these treaties.

'In view of foregoing Soviet Government cannot agree to procedure for signing peace treaties proposed by French Government, as one not envisaged by decisions of Council of Foreign Ministers. Soviet Government proposes that protocol of signing not be drawn up and gives notice that in signing of peace treaties there must not take place any sort of declarations or conditions on part of defeated countries.

'Soviet Government at same time is addressing to Governments of US and Great Britain an analogous proposal.

'Minister Foreign Affairs requests Embassy to bring foregoing to attention of Government of French Republic.'

"In communicating foregoing, Soviet Government hopes that Government of USA will join in point of view of Soviet Government, set forth in its note of reply to the French Government.

"Respectfully yours, A. Y. Vyshinski." [2]

Sent Department, repeated to Paris as 28, London as 40.

SMITH

---

[2] In telegram 200, February 7, not printed, Ambassador Smith was directed to inform Vyshinsky that the United States Government fully agreed that no protocol of signing should be prepared, and that it did not approve the suggestion of declarations to be made at the time of signature of the peace treaties (740.0011 EW (Peace)/2–647).

In telegram 502, February 7, not printed, Ambassador Caffery was instructed to inform the French Government of this view (740.0011 EW (Peace)/2–647).

740.0011 EW (Peace)/2–947

The Italian Ambassador (Tarchiani) to the Secretary of State

No. 1204   WASHINGTON, February 9, 1947.

The Italian Ambassador presents his compliments to the Honorable the Secretary of State and has the honor to inform him that, according to a communication of the Italian Ministry for Foreign Affairs, the British Ambassador at Rome [1] has handed today, February 9, 1947, to the said Ministry a note stating that, if the Italian Government signs the Treaty of Peace, it is obliged, under Article 90 of the Treaty,[2] to ratify it, and that the Italian point of view, according to which for Italy's signature to be valid there must be the subsequent ratification of the Constituent Assembly, is untenable.

The Ministry for Foreign Affairs in Rome has answered the British Embassy by a note affirming that Italy cannot accept such an interpretation and that the Italian Government affixes its signature subordinating it to the ratification that depends on the sovereign decision of the

---

[1] Sir Noel Hughes Havelock Charles.
[2] See footnote 2, p. 519.

Constituent Assembly, to which the approval of international treaties is conferred by the Italian legislation.

The Ministry for Foreign Affairs in Rome has moreover informed that the Italian Plenipotentiary Delegate for the signing of the Peace Treaty, Marquis Antonio Meli Lupi di Soragna, must, before proceeding to the signature of the Treaty, remit to the Secretary General of the Conference a statement reading as follows:

"The Italian Government affixes its signature subordinating it to the ratification that depends on the sovereign decision of the Constituent Assembly to which approval of international treaties is conferred by the Italian legislation."

The Italian Plenipotentiary has, in addition, been instructed by the Italian Government not to sign the Treaty of Peace if the Secretary General of the Conference refuses to acknowledge the statement quoted above.

A[LBERTO] T[ARCHIANI]

740.0011 EW (Peace)/2–1047 : Telegram

The Ambassador in Italy (Dunn) to the Secretary of State

ROME, February 10, 1947.

301. Reference mytel 297, February 8.[1] De Gasperi presented new government's [2] program to Constituent Assembly Saturday evening.[3] The part concerning foreign affairs was entirely devoted to signing the peace treaty. Prime Minister said that in his long political career no graver or more cruel responsibility had been placed upon him than today. He and his government were faced with two alternatives, (1) to sign the treaty on the government's responsibility, or (2) to obtain a commitment from the Assembly for such step. While the latter would have been more agreeable to the government, the former was more in accordance with the provisions of Italian law. He continued that there

---

[1] Not printed; it mentioned the morning newspaper reports of the departure of Soragna for Paris, and the government's issuance of a communiqué which recognized the need in the circumstances for the Italian Government to sign the treaty (865.00/2–847).
[2] Prime Minister De Gasperi, on returning from his trip to Washington, was met with the declaration by Nenni of his intention to resign as Minister of Foreign Affairs in order to devote himself exclusively to affairs of the Socialist Party. On January 20 De Gasperi announced to the press his intention to resign. The Provisional Head of the State, Enrico de Nicola, by decree of January 28, 1947, accepted the resignation of the second De Gasperi cabinet. The new Ministry was constituted by decree of February 2 and supplementary decree of February 4. De Gasperi remained Prime Minister; Count Carlo Sforza became Minister of Foreign Affairs.
[3] February 8.

was a tendency to over-estimate the importance of the signature and to under-estimate the final approval of the Assembly.[4]

. . . .

Statements on internal program will be reported separately.

DUNN

---

[4] For the full text of De Gasperi's speech see Italy, Assemblea costituente 1946–1948, *Atti*, *Discussioni*, seduta xxxii (Saturday, February 8, 1947), p. 1102.

740.0011 EW (Peace)/2–1147 : Telegram

The Ambassador in France (*Caffery*) *to the Secretary of State*

PARIS, February 11, 1947.

624. Copies of Greek, Yugoslav, Italian, Rumanian, and Hungarian observations on peace treaties, as furnished us by Foreign Office to whom they were addressed, being forwarded airmail.

1. Greek observations include protest over failure of Bulgarian peace treaty to provide satisfaction for Greek claims to adjustment of their frontier with Bulgaria and expression of concern over future security of Greco-Bulgarian frontier owing to lack of effective military control to ensure fulfillment military clauses. With reference to Italian recognition of the sovereignty and independence of Albania, Greeks point out that Article 27 of Italian treaty does not prejudge question of Greco-Albanian frontier, and state that Greek request concerning northern Epirus will remain pending before Council of Foreign Ministers even after signature of treaty.

2. Yugoslav Government observes that the claims and proposals of that country were not given satisfaction in drawing up text of Italian treaty. In this connection it refers to political, military and economic clauses and particularly territorial decisions. They say they are only signing the treaty in order to avoid the responsibility of not according their support to the establishment of peace. They declare however that in signing treaty the Yugoslav people do not in any way renounce their claims to the territories which ethnically are theirs and that the Yugoslav people will not cease to maintain their right over these territories whatever ethnical modifications may be made in them as a result of foreign domination.

3. Italians merely state that "the Italian Government signs the treaty with the reservation that it is subject to ratification which depends on the sovereign decision of the Constituent Assembly to which, under Italian law, the approval of international treaties is subject".

4. Rumanians assert that some obligations imposed are excessive and others unjust and will result in aggravating the country's economic

situation. They express gratification over Transylvanian settlement and indicate that they will enter into direct negotiations with interested states with view to "adapting the clauses of the treaty to present possibilities of the country and to clarifying the provisions which seem ambiguous and contradictory".

5. Hungarian communication deplores absence of guarantees of human rights for Hungarians living beyond Hungarian frontiers and refers specifically to deportations from and harsh treatment of Hungarian nationals in Czechoslovakia. Statement expresses satisfaction over return of full Hungarian sovereignty, prospective return of Hungarian war prisoners, and prospect of joining UN. Government addresses fervent appeal to all signatory powers, particularly Czechoslovakia, for observance of human rights and states its determination to seek the means of closer and friendly collaboration with Hungary's neighbors.

Repeated Rome 37; Belgrade 4; London 118; Moscow 61; USPolAd Berlin 55; Praha 21; Athens 10; Bucharest 15.

CAFFERY

740.0011 EW (Peace)/2–1247

The Ambassador in France (Caffery) to the Secretary of State

No. 7581   PARIS, February 12, 1947.

Subject: Ceremonies Attending the Signing of the Peace Treaties with Italy, Rumania, Bulgaria, Hungary, and Finland

SIR: I have the honor to report, in confirmation of my telegrams on the subject, that the signature of the Treaties of Peace with Italy, Rumania, Bulgaria, Hungary, and Finland took place as scheduled on February 10, 1947.[1]

The ceremonies commenced at 11 a. m. with the signing of the Italian Treaty. Accompanied by Admiral Richard L. Conolly,[2] Mr. James C. H. Bonbright[3] of this Embassy, and Mr. John E. Utter of

---

[1] For the texts of the Treaties of Peace with Italy, Romania, Bulgaria, and Hungary, all dated at Paris February 10, 1947, see Department of State Treaties and other International Acts Series (TIAS), Nos. 1648, 1649, 1650, and 1951, or 61 Stat. (pt.2) 1245, 1757, 1915, and 2065. For the text of the Treaty of Peace with Finland (February 10, 1947), to which the United States was not a party, see British Cmd. 7484.
[2] Ranking Naval Adviser, United States Delegation at the Paris Peace Conference.
[3] Counselor of Embassy in Paris.

the State Department,[4] I proceeded to the Salon de l'Horloge in the Foreign Office, where the delegations of twenty Allied Nations were assembled around the traditional large green table.

The ceremonies were presided over by M. Georges Bidault, French Minister of Foreign Affairs, who opened the meeting with a short message of greeting to the delegates (Enclosure No. 1 [5]). M. Bidault then invited the Italian Delegation, headed by the Marchese Lupi di Soragna, to join the assembled gathering and upon the latter's arrival, addressed to him a few words of welcome (Enclosure No. 2 [5]). The Plenipotentiaries were then invited to go into the adjoining room to affix their signatures to the Treaty. The order of signing followed that set forth in the Treaty itself. The only Plenipotentiary absent was M. Modzelewski, Polish Minister of Foreign Affairs whose train had been delayed, and M. Bidault made the suggestion, to which there was no objection, that he be permitted to sign as soon as he arrived. The proceedings were conducted with unusual rapidity and the signing was completed and the meeting adjourned within forty minutes.

The afternoon session, repeating the ritual of the morning, started at 3 o'clock with the signing of the Rumanian Treaty and continued intermittently until 6:15 when the last signature was affixed to the Finnish Treaty.

The schedule had originally been drawn up to allow for declarations by such delegations as wished to make them. The final decision to eliminate all such declarations resulted in lengthy intermissions between the signing of the different treaties, during which the delegations gathered for conversation in the other salons of the Foreign Ministry.

Inasmuch as the United States was not a signatory to the Treaty of Peace with Finland, I did not remain until the end of the ceremonies, but left at 5:40 p. m. after the signing of the Treaty with Hungary.

In the evening, the President of the French Republic gave a formal dinner for the Plenipotentiaries, followed by a large reception for the delegates and their wives at the Elysée Palace.

In addition to the enclosures mentioned above, I am transmitting herewith copies of the communiqués issued by M. Bidault at the conclusion of the ceremonies. As I have previously reported, these communiqués took the place of the *procès-verbal* which the French Government had originally proposed to draw up and which had been withdrawn at the insistence of the Soviet Ambassador.

Respectfully yours,   JEFFERSON CAFFERY

---

[4] Political Adviser in the Division of African Affairs.
[5] The enclosures, filed with the despatch, are not printed.

740.0011 EW (Peace)/2–1047

Memorandum by the Director of the Office of European Affairs (Matthews)[1]

[WASHINGTON,] February 10, 1947.

When the draft report to accompany the Peace Treaties when they are submitted to the Senate was discussed with Mr. Wilcox, Secretary of the Senate Foreign Relations Committee, in accordance with the suggestion you approved, he suggested that it might be most helpful if this draft could be sent to Senators Vandenberg and Connally.[2] Mr. Wilcox thought that if they were given advance copies of the report they would not only be pleased but might have some helpful suggestions to make as regards the manner of presentation of the Treaties. Accordingly, letters transmitting the draft report are attached for your approval and for the Secretary's signature if you agree that this procedure is desirable.[3]

H. F[REEMAN] M[ATTHEWS]

[Enclosure]

The Secretary of State to Senator Tom Connally

WASHINGTON, February 10, 1947.

MY DEAR SENATOR CONNALLY: As you are aware, when treaties are transmitted to the Senate to receive its advice and consent to their ratification they are usually accompanied by a report from the Secretary of State to the President. A draft of such a report has been prepared and a copy enclosed.

In view of your close association with Mr. Byrnes and the Delegation in the formulation of these Treaties I am sending you this copy in advance and would welcome any suggestions you might care to make in connection therewith.

Sincerely yours,

G. C. MARSHALL

---

[1] Addressed to the Under Secretary and to the Secretary of State. A handwritten marginal notation reads: "I join in this recommendation. D[ean] A[cheson]."

[2] Arthur H. Vandenberg, of Michigan, chairman, and Tom Connally, of Texas, ranking minority member, Foreign Relations Committee, United States Senate.

[3] Enclosure 2, a letter to Senator Vandenberg identical to the enclosure to this document, is not printed. Enclosure 3 was entitled, "Draft of Report to Accompany Peace Treaties When Submitted to the Senate", and was dated February 10, 1947. With two slight changes of wording it went forward as the report of the Secretary of State to the President, February 27, 1947. For text, see Department of State *Bulletin*, March 23, 1947, p. 541.

740.0011 EW (Peace)/2–1147

Memorandum of Conversation, by the Director of the Office of European Affairs (Matthews)

[Washington,] February 11, 1947.

Under instructions from his Government the Italian Ambassador called this afternoon at his request and left with me the attached declaration of the Italian Government concerning that Government's desire for a revision of the peace treaty.[1] He said that he hoped I would agree that the statement was as moderate in tone as could possibly be expected under the circumstances and given the unpopularity of the treaty in Italy. After reading the statement I told him that I agreed.

Mr. Tarchiani then spoke of what he describes as the very stupid British last minute move prior to signature insisting the Italian signature was the equivalent of Italian ratification.[2] This step, he said, caused such indignation in Italy that De Gasperi at the last moment was almost compelled to give up the idea of signing. Tarchiani said that such a position in effect merely made a rubber stamp out of the Constituent Assembly and no self-respecting body could accept it. He expressed confidence that De Gasperi will succeed without much difficulty in obtaining ratification of the treaty by the Constituent Assembly but he had not felt that he could attempt to bind the Assembly before signature.

Tarchiani then referred to yesterday's disturbances in Italy and pointed out what seemed to him a significant fact: neither the French nor the Soviet Embassies were the object of patriotic demonstrations against the treaty in spite of the fact that both the French and Soviet Governments had taken positions with regard to the treaty far more hostile to Italy's interests. He recalled, for instance, how the whole country had been seething at the prospective ceding of Tenda and Briga to France last summer. He felt, therefore, that the demonstrations before the British and American Embassies were largely Communist inspired in order to make the western Allies unpopular. As for the attack on the Yugoslav Legation he attributed that to a curious omission on the part of his Government. Since Italy has no diplomatic relations with Yugoslavia now and that Legation therefore did not appear on the diplomatic list he assumed that the Minister of the Interior had forgotten about it and had stationed no guards there. The Legation building had, however, been inhabited by some members of the Yugoslav Military Mission and it was these people

---

[1] Not printed.
[2] See note No. 1204 of February 9, from the Italian Ambassador to the Secretary of State, p. 521.

who were the objects of the demonstrators' wrath. This group o demonstrators he considered to be "spontaneous nationalists" as dis tinct from the Communist groups at the American and Britisl Embassies.

I asked the Ambassador whether his Government had anythin specifically in mind in its suggestion for a revision of the treaty. H said that three things were, of course, uppermost in their minds: (1 the revision of the eastern frontiers; (2) the military clauses whicl kept Italy in an inferior position vis-à-vis her neighbors and did no permit adequate Italian defense; and (3) the question of the Italia colonies. As to the first, he saw little likelihood of anything being accomplished in the foreseeable future. As to the second, he hoped tha the military inferiority clauses could be revised at some stage. Th most important, however, was the third. Italy had no thought of re gaining her colonies for herself but was anxious that the French pro posal be accepted whereunder Italy would be given some form o trusteeship over the Colonies under the United Nations. He pointee out that this was a matter very dear to Italian hearts and he though it was important to do what we could to keep Italy orientated towarc the western Powers by giving the De Gasperi government as mucl support as possible . . . he fears the results of the next elections whicl will take place either in June or in October. He was emphatic in the need that some further tangible support be given to De Gasperi. I tolc him that as he was well aware we appreciated the importance of help ing Italy but pointed out some of the difficulties in connection witl the Colonies.

H. FREEMAN MATTHEW

740.0011 EW (Peace)/2–1147

The Chairman of the Senate Committee on Foreign Relations (Vandenberg) to the Secretary of State

[WASHINGTON,] February 11, 1947

MY DEAR MR. SECRETARY: This will reply to your letter of Febru ary 10th (identified as SE) containing the proposed draft report tc the President on the Italian and Balkan Treaties. I appreciate your courtesy in submitting the draft for my comment. It would seem tc me that the draft is satisfactory. It must necessarily be confined tc generalities; and I would think that the draft is as adequate as any such paper could be expected to be.

We shall now confront the question of handling these Treaties in the Senate. Unless we are definitely and deliberately to postpone this process until there has been action by other major powers (and I would welcome your Department's judgment on this point) I think we might as well tackle the job *immediately.*

This would permit your own personal appearance as the first witness in the public hearings which our Committee on Foreign Relations will hold.[1]

Then, I respectfully make this suggestion. No one (including Senator Connally and myself) knows these Treaties quite so well as former Secretary Byrnes. It seems to me that it would greatly lighten your burden (and ours) if former Secretary Byrnes were to be invited to follow you upon our witness stand and take over the major responsibility for presenting the issues from his point of view. This is *his* "unfinished business" as well as yours and mine.

If this suggestion meets with your approval, I think perhaps we should send him simultaneous messages because undoubtedly he would wish a direct request from you as well as a formal invitation from me.[2]

With warm personal regards and best wishes,

Cordially and faithfully,   A. H. VANDENBERG

---

[1] Hearings were held on March 4, April 30, and May 1, 2, and 6. Secretary of State Marshall and former Secretary Byrnes testified on March 4 and again on May 6. *Treaties of Peace with Italy, Rumania, Bulgaria, and Hungary: Hearings before the Committee on Foreign Relations, United States Senate, on Executives F, G, H, and I* (80th Cong., 1st sess.).

[2] On February 18 Secretary Marshall addressed a letter, not printed, to the former Secretary of State, James F. Byrnes, asking him to testify (740.0011 EW (Peace)/2–1147).

Byrnes accepted by letter of February 21, not printed (740.0011 EW (Peace)/2–2147).

740.0011 EW (Peace)/2–1147

The Secretary of State to the Italian Ambassador (Tarchiani)

[WASHINGTON,] February 28, 1947.

MY DEAR MR. AMBASSADOR: I have the honor to acknowledge the receipt of your letter of February 11, 1947, transmitting a statement of the Italian Government concerning the Italian desire for an eventual revision of certain provisions of the Treaty of Peace with Italy.[1]

As you know, provision is made in Article 46 of the Italian Treaty for possible future modification of the Military, Naval and Air clauses.[2] Also, it is the view of this Government that means exist under the

---

[1] Not printed.

[2] Article 46 reads: "Each of the military, naval, and air clauses of the present Treaty shall remain in force until modified in whole or in part by agreement between the Allied and Associated Powers and Italy or, after Italy becomes a member of the United Nations, by agreement between the Security Council and Italy."

United Nations Charter for eventual peaceful changes in the provisions of treaties by agreement among the states concerned. Further, as regards provisions of the Italian Treaty which confer on any one of the Allied and Associated Powers rights affecting only that power and Italy, there would surely be no bar to a future modification which might be agreed upon between Italy and the power concerned.

I know the Italian Government will appreciate that this Government cannot at this time appropriately comment upon the possible revision, after the Treaty with Italy has come into effect, of particular clauses of that treaty. I can assure you, however, that in its relations with Italy this Government will be guided in the future as in the past by the principles of international justice and peace which the American people have always cherished.

Sincerely yours, [G. C. MARSHALL]

740.0011 EW (Peace)/3–247

The Prime Minister of Italy (De Gasperi) to the Chairman of the Senate Committee on Foreign Relations (Vandenberg) [1]

[ROME,] March 2, 1947.

MY DEAR SENATOR VANDENBERG: Remembering your friendly personal interest in the future of Italy and your manifestations of sympathy, I am sending you, confidentially, a pressing request.

My Government will meet many difficulties in obtaining approval of the Treaty by the Constituent Assembly. We are counting on the friendly help of the United States to give the Assembly, which is called upon to make a difficult decision, reasons for legitimate hope for the future. [2]

Without prejudicing her commitments to the other contracting parties, America could give us assurances that she will unblock Italian assets in America and hand over to Italian industry, with the obligation of scrapping them, the warships that were assigned to you. Even in our recent conversations in the United States the feasibility of these concessions was suggested to me by the American authorities. The friendship between the two countries requires that these assurances be given now in the immediate common interest and in order to alleviate the harsh peace conditions.

---

[1] This letter in Italian was delivered as the enclosure to a note from the Italian Embassy, No. 1957, March 2, 1947, to the Department of State (740.0011 EW (Peace)/3–247). The translation here printed was prepared in the Department of State and forwarded to Senator Vandenberg by Acting Secretary Acheson on March 4, 1947 (740.0011 EW (Peace)/3–247).

[2] On the same date a similar appeal was sent to Senator Vandenberg, on behalf of the Italian Constituent Assembly, by its President, Umberto Terracini. For text, see *Congressional Record*, vol. 93, pt. 5, p. 6309.

I may remind you that in Paris, at the meeting of May 10, 1946, the American Delegation declared itself in favor of the Molotov-Bidault proposal to entrust the Italian colonies to Italy under a U.N. mandate. It would make an excellent impression if America renewed at this time her declaration of good will and if United States diplomacy encouraged England, which is perhaps coming closer to the idea of a colonial agreement with Italy.

Lastly, many interests in connection with reparations and commercial relations link Italy with the future of Germany. It would be only fair if co-belligerent Italy could for this reason participate in the negotiations concerning Germany. America's support of this request would be greatly appreciated as the first practical result of international cooperation.

I appeal to you as a friend having influence and to the enlightened conscience of the American Senate, which in you and in Senator Connally has two very well-informed members interested in the future of the Italian Republic, and I extend to you in advance my heartfelt thanks.[3]

DE GASPERI

---

[3] Acting Secretary of State Acheson, in a letter dated March 13, 1947, replied to Ambassador Tarchiani on behalf of Senator Vandenberg for forwarding to Prime Minister De Gasperi. He stated that Senator Vandenberg had "now asked me to let you know that he is most sympathetic to the nature of the Premier's appeal" and that he had added "that he shares the anxiety of all of us to aid in the stabilization of the new Italian democracy. He is confident, however, that his friend Signor De Gasperi will understand he cannot make any commitments in foreign affairs other than those which may have been made in the first instance by the President and the Department of State.

"Senator Vandenberg also asks that you repeat to Signor De Gasperi the assurances of his great sympathy for the new Italy, and of his concern for Italy's problems and needs." (740.0011 EW (Peace)/3–347)

740.0011 EW (Peace)/3–347

Memorandum of Conversation, by the Acting Director of the Office of European Affairs (Hickerson)

[WASHINGTON,] March 3, 1947.

Participants: Mr. Vassili A. Tarassenko, Counselor of the Soviet Embassy
A Soviet Interpreter
Mr. John Hickerson, Director, Office of European Affairs
Mr. Francis B. Stevens, Acting Associate Chief, Division of Eastern European Affairs

Mr. Tarassenko came in to see me at 10:30 this morning at my request. I told Mr. Tarassenko that I was now in a position to give him the views of the United States Government on the Italian Treaty question which he put up to me late Friday afternoon. I thereupon in formed Mr. Tarassenko as follows:

The views of this Government regarding the coming into force o the Treaty of Peace with Italy were communicated to the Sovie Government by the American Embassy in Moscow on February 8 1947.[1] These views may be summarized as follows:

Article 90 of the Italian Treaty provides that it shall be ratified b the Allied and Associated Powers and also by Italy. It also provide that the Treaty shall come into force immediately upon the deposit o ratifications by the USSR, UK, US and France. Article 89 expressl states that the Treaty shall confer no rights or benefits upon any Allie or Associated Power or its nationals until such power has ratified th Treaty. Although the Treaty itself is silent as to the rights of Ital under the Treaty in the absence of ratification by that country thi Government is of the opinion that until Italy ratifies the Treaty, n rights or benefits thereunder can be claimed by Italy, which woul remain subject to the armistice regime. This Government therefor hopes that Italy will in its own interest sign and promptly ratify th Treaty.

This Government's views as set forth above were also communicated t the Italian Government.

On February 9, the Italian Minister for Foreign Affairs informed th American Ambassador in Rome that the Italian Plenipotentiary i Paris had been instructed to make clear, at the time of signing th Treaty on February 10, that the Italian signature was subject to late ratification by the Italian Constituent Assembly, and that the Italia Plenipotentiary had been further instructed that if any of the fou great powers objected to this procedure he was not to sign the Treaty It is understood that the Italian Minister for Foreign Affairs similarl informed the Ambassadors in Rome of the USSR, UK and France

Before the ceremony of signature of the Italian Treaty in Paris o February 10, the French Minister for Foreign Affairs read to th Soviet, British and American Plenipotentiaries a note from the Italia Plenipotentiary giving the Italian views as outlined above. Th Plenipotentiaries then proceeded with the signature of the Italia Treaty.

It is the opinion of this Government that although the Italian Con stituent Assembly may be expected to protest the terms of the Treaty o Peace with Italy, it will nevertheless ratify the Treaty as will b recommended by the Italian Government. In view of the prospects fo Italian ratification this Government feels that any public discussio

---

[1] See footnote 4, p. 519.

by the four powers or direct approach to the Italian Government, concerning the extent of Italy's obligation to ratify should be avoided since such action would adversely affect prompt action by the Italian Constituent Assembly. On that account, this Government intends to emphasize to the Italian Government from time to time, as opportunity offers, that it would be in Italy's own interest to ratify the Treaty without delay.

I added that for Mr. Tarassenko's convenience I had written out as an oral message the views set forth above. He expressed his appreciation.

JOHN HICKERSON

740.00119 EW/3–147 : Telegram

The Acting Secretary of State (Acheson) to the Embassy in Italy

TOP SECRET WASHINGTON, March 6, 1947—7 p. m.

322. Department believes Yugos will ratify Ital treaty and therefore feels no action shd be taken now which might delay or complicate ratification by others (ur 444 Mar 1 [1]). If at time treaty is about to come into force, Yugos have still not ratified, Dept anticipates Big Four discussion may be necessary on implementation all treaty provisions re VG,[2] and consideration could then be given to delaying deposit US ratification pending outcome such discussion.

As regards Gen Lee's [3] views re withdrawal US forces from Italy,[4] Dept does not now foresee possibility that ratification by four powers and deposit of ratifications can be completed prior to April 1.

ACHESON

---

[1] Not printed; in it Ambassador Dunn reported: "Military authorities AFHQ are greatly concerned over logistical problems that would be involved in maintaining allied troops in strength in disputed strip between Morgan Line and treaty boundary (French Line) while at same time complying with other provisions of treaty including those pertaining to withdrawal of allied forces in Italy. It is their opinion that even maintenance of troops in disputed area would be wholly impracticable." (740.00119 EW/3–147)

[2] Venezia Giulia; for documentation on U.S. interest in the establishment of the Free Territory of Trieste, see vol. IV, pp. 51 ff.

[3] Lt. Gen. John C. H. Lee, named Commanding General, Mediterranean Theater of Operations, United States Army, and Deputy Supreme Allied Commander, January 3, 1946; succeeded Gen. Morgan as SACMED in April 1947.

[4] Also in telegram 444, Ambassador Dunn stated that ". . . General Lee has indicated to me that in order to assure smooth working of plans for 90 days withdrawal, it is considerable importance to MTOUSA that Senate should not ratify treaty prior to April 1. He states that delay after April 1, if prolonged, might cause military some difficulty, but situation would by no means be as critical as it would be if treaty should come into force prior to that date."

740.00119 Council/3–847 : Telegram

The Acting Secretary of State to the Secretary of State, in Moscow

TOP SECRET   WASHINGTON, March 8, 1947—4 p. m.

427. Secdel No. 1311. For the Secretary from Acheson. Vandenberg called me today and put up to me a suggestion that he propose ratification of the four peace treaties now pending be withheld until a treaty with Austria is signed. He pointed out that while the treaties called for withdrawal of military forces from the countries concerned, they recognize the right of USSR to have some troops to maintain lines of communication to Austria, with the exercise of this right pretty much to Russia's interpretation. Vandenberg said that he believed that his proposal that ratification of the treaties be withheld until treaty with Austria is concluded would strengthen your hand and might be instrumental in at least producing an Austrian treaty out of Moscow Conference.[1]

I told Vandenberg that I would have this matter considered in the Department, consult you by telegraph and try to let him have our ideas by early next week.[2]

It seems to us here that this proposal is inadvisable for the following reasons:

1. Since these treaties and the Austrian settlement were discussed in Paris and we agreed to go ahead with the treaties without awaiting Austrian settlement, it would open us to charges of bad faith.
2. It would not result in better settlements than those provided for in existing treaties but would merely prolong uncertainty and continue for an indefinite period right of USSR to maintain military forces in larger numbers than would be possible under the treaties.
3. The bargaining power of the proposal is probably insufficient to accomplish the desired objective.
4. It would facilitate what may be Soviet tactics anyway; i.e., to make conclusion of Austrian treaty contingent upon German settlement satisfactory to USSR.

May I have your views urgently in order that I can reply to Vandenberg.[3]

I understand that in normal course of events, hearings on treaties will continue for another two or three weeks.

ACHESON

---

[1] See vol. II, p. 139 ff.
[2] Mr. Acheson recorded his telephone conversation with Senator Vandenberg in a memorandum of March 8 to Mr. Hickerson (740.0011 EW (Peace)/3–847).
[3] In telegram No. 731, March 9, 1947, from Moscow, not printed, Secretary Marshall replied: "We are unanimous in our complete agreement with Dept's views expressed in Secdel 1311 and I personally urgently desire ratification of treaties without delay." (740.00119 (Council)/3–947)

740.0011 EW (Peace)/3–847

The Acting Secretary of State to the Secretary of State, in Moscow Relations Committee (Vandenberg)

SECRET [WASHINGTON,] March 15, 1947.

MY DEAR SENATOR VANDENBERG: I have received your letter of March 8, 1947,[1] regarding the possibility of encouraging the Italians in the present situation, and of giving them some hope for eventual revision of the Italian Treaty.

I agree with you as to the desirability of making a few dramatic moves coincidentally with consideration of ratification of the Italian Treaty. There are several steps which we already have in mind, and I am asking the interested officers of the Department to keep your suggestion in mind with a view to determining what else we can appropriately do.

As I believe you know, we intend to explain to the Senate Foreign Relations Committee during the Treaty hearings the position taken by the United States Delegation at the Paris Conference on the return of Italian assets in the United States.[2] Subsequently, we propose to issue a statement on this subject which will give the Italians the official assurances they desire.[3] We have also been giving consideration to the Italian request that Italian naval vessels allocated to the United States be given to them for scrapping. I think this will be done, but it would seem preferable to make no public statement about our intentions before the Treaty has been ratified.[4]

As regards the possibility of future revision of some of the Treaty clauses, I enclose a copy of Secretary Marshall's letter of February 28 to the Italian Ambassador giving the Department's views on this subject.[5] While this letter may not be particularly encouraging, it does hold out some hope to the Italian Government, which appears to be under no delusion as to the difficulty it will face in any eventual move for Treaty revision, and the Department intends to make it public after hearings on the Treaty have been resumed. You may wish to consider

---

[1] Not printed; in it Senator Vandenberg inquired "whether there is *anything*—along the line of De Gasperi's note or otherwise—which we could say to Italy by way of hope for the future, coincident with our consideration of Treaty ratification." (740.0011 EW (Peace)/3–847)

[2] Article 69 of the draft treaty for Italy dealing with Italian Property in Territory of Allied and Associated Powers, which the United States supported at the Peace Conference as an agreed article, is printed in *Foreign Relations*, 1946, vol. IV, p. 31. U.S. statements regarding proposed amendments to Article 69 are printed in the same volume, pp. 399–401.

[3] See Acting Secretary of State Acheson's letter of April 15 to Senator Vandenberg, Department of State *Bulletin*, June 1, 1947, p. 1075.

[4] See the message from the Secretary of State to the Italian Foreign Minister which was released to the press on October 7, 1947, Department of State *Bulletin*, October 19, 1947, p. 769.

[5] *Ante*, p. 529.

incorporating these views also in the statement you will make to the
Senate regarding the Italian Treaty.

I am most grateful for your letter and hope you will let me know
if you have any further suggestions along this line.

Sincerely yours,

DEAN ACHESON

740.00119 Council/4–947 : Telegram

The Acting Secretary of State to the Secretary of State, in Moscow

SECRET   WASHINGTON, April 9, 1947—7 p. m.

867. Secdel 1440. For the Secretary. Ital Amb called yesterday to
say he had been called Rome for consultation primarily in connection
Ital Govt's consideration economic situation which is causing increasing concern. Other matters he expected be asked about were Treaty
ratification and eventual admission Italy to UN.[1]

Re ratification, he said UK was pressing for early Ital action, but
pointed out difficulty of Ital Govt in obtaining Constituent Assembly's
approval prior US Senate action, and assured me Ital Govt would
move promptly once US ratification announced. I told him Senate was
expected resume Treaty hearings end April or first May and while
we expected Italy not to delay ratification unduly we understood Ital
Govt's position.

On Ital admission UN, Tarchiani said US proposal re early application appreciated and he merely wished reassurance US support
when application considered. I replied that assuming treaty would be
in force by time this question arose, Italy could count upon full support US.

Re economic situation, Tarchiani said growing unemployment, grain
shortages, mounting budget deficit and rising prices playing into hands
Communists, which was reflected in increasing Communist pressure
within Govt. He has no doubt De Gasperi and moderate elements
would resist this pressure in every way possible, but he felt Premier
especially would be anxious to know implications for Italy of US
Greek-Turkish policy and extent to which Ital democratic elements
might rely upon US support. I explained to him emergency nature
US assistance Greece and Turkey,[2] reminded him of anticipated assistance Italy under foreign relief program and from Eximbank loan, and
stressed importance stabilizing internal economic situation so Italy
might derive full advantages US assistance and from World Bank

---

[1] For documentation regarding United States policy on applications for membership in the United Nations, see volume I.
[2] For documentation on United States assistance to Greece and Turkey, see
vol. V, pp. 1 ff.

loan which I hope would eventually be available. I said future of Italy was matter of great interest to US, as our attitude in past showed, and we would continue to help where we could, adding I was sure Itals would give their best efforts towards solution their internal situation. Tarchiani said he understood US position and endeavor explain fully in Rome. He emphasized, however, importance in his view of next five months in Italy, since natl elections would be held Oct and Communists are already bending every effort to capturing majority of seats in new parliament. He felt friendship of US must be made very clear to Ital people during this period, and he urged we do everything we could to make apparent value and necessity to Italy of US cooperation. In this regard, he mentioned his personal hope you might visit Rome briefly on way back to Moscow. I promised bring this your attention, but said I knew he realized impossible say anything definite at this juncture.

Sent Moscow as 867 rpt Rome for the Ambassador as 507.

ACHESON

740.0011 EW (Peace)/4–1147

Memorandum of Conversation, by the Acting Secretary of State

[WASHINGTON,] April 11, 1947.

PROCEDURE ON DEPOSIT OF RATIFICATION OF PEACE TREATIES

The British Ambassador [1] called at his request and left with me the attached Memorandum. I told him that I could not answer the questions contained in the Memorandum without thorough study and discussion within the Department. This would be done at once and I would be in touch with him very soon. I made the following interim observations:

1. As a practical matter it would be impossible for the Department, in advance of Senate action on the treaties, to agree to any date for the deposit of ratifications. This came from the obvious fact that we could not know whether or not the Senate would have acted by a particular date and that to attempt to predict the action of the Senate in a note to other Governments would cause resentment on the Hill.[2]

2. In response to a question from him as to the present intentions of the Chairman of the Foreign Relations Committee regarding Senate

[1] Archibald John Kerr Clark Kerr, Lord Inverchapel.
[2] In a memorandum addressed to the British Embassy on April 24 the Department explained that this Government would not be in a position to agree on a definite date for the deposit of instruments of ratification until after the Senate had given its consent to ratification of the treaties; and that it did not consider it necessary to require prior ratification by Italy or other ex-enemy states before ratification by the four Powers (740.0011 EW (Peace)/4–1147).

action on the treaties, I said that my present information was that Senator Vandenberg intended to resume hearings on the treaties after he disposed of the Greek-Turkish bill which might be about the middle of next week. It was possible that, if the Committee considered the treaties and reported them, the Senate might take them up toward the end of April. There was also the possibility that if the House should pass the Post-UNRRA Relief Bill next week, the Senate might act on that Bill before taking up the treaties.

3. In regard to the comments contained in the memorandum on the Italian attitude, which, as I understood it, was that they could not wisely present the treaty to their Constituent Assembly until after our Senate had acted upon it, I had told the Italian Ambassador that I did not regard this attitude as unreasonable. Looking at the matter from the point of view of the Italian Government, it would be in a most serious predicament if it ratified the treaty only to have our Senate either postpone the matter or reject it. I told the British Ambassador that the Italian Ambassador had said that Italian action would be a matter of only a day or two following Senate action and that, therefore, I did not see that this would delay matters.

DEAN ACHESON

[Enclosure]

The British Embassy to the Department of State

MEMORANDUM

CONFIDENTIAL
Ref: 41/162/47

His Majesty's Government in the United Kingdom are anxious to ascertain the views of the United States Government on two matters relative to the ratification of the Peace Treaties with Italy, Hungary, Roumania and Bulgaria.

(*a*) His Majesty's Government in the United Kingdom think it desirable that the United States of America, the Union of Soviet Socialist Republics, France and the United Kingdom should all deposit their ratifications at the same time. Subject to the concurrence of the United States Government, they wish to suggest May 1st as the date on which this should take place.

(*b*) His Majesty's Government in the United Kingdom wish to enquire whether the United States Government think that it would be advisable to inform the enemy governments that the Big Four will not deposit their ratifications until the enemy states have ratified the Treaties.

2. With regard to the first point, His Majesty's Government in the United Kingdom could technically deposit their ratifications of the

Treaties concerned forthwith, but they prefer to postpone action until the Treaties of Peace Bill (which would make the provisions of the Peace Treaties binding in the domestic legislation of His Majesty's Government in the United Kingdom) has been enacted. This should take place by the end of April and His Majesty's Government should therefore be able to deposit their ratifications on 1 May. It is believed that the French Government should be able to deposit their ratification of the Italian Treaty, in which alone they are concerned, by about the end of April. No indication of the Russian attitude has been received. In the opinion of His Majesty's Government the present uncertain position is unsatisfactory because there is a risk that one of the Big Four may try to gain some political advantage either by ratifying in advance of the other Powers concerned or by holding up their ratification. Furthermore, in the case of Italy it is impossible at present for the United States Government and His Majesty's Government to give the Supreme Allied Commander, Mediterranean, and the British and American forces in Italy a definite date on which to start their evacuation. There would therefore appear to be great advantage in endeavouring to reach agreement between the Governments of the United States of America, the Union of Soviet Socialist Republics, France and the United Kingdom that they should all deposit their ratifications of the Peace Treaties in which they are concerned simultaneously and that they should agree as long as possible in advance on a target date when this should take place. They trust that the United States Government will agree to the principle of simultaneous deposit and invite them to name a suitable date. His Majesty's Government for their part suggest that the date of 1 May would be appropriate.

3. With regard to the second point, there is always the danger that the enemy governments will not have ratified the Peace Treaties before the time comes for the Great Powers to deposit their ratifications. The Italian Government are hesitating to seek the approval of the Constituent Assembly to the ratification of the Italian Treaty and are maintaining that it would be easier for them to do so once the Big Four Governments, and in particular the United States Senate, had ratified. Other ex-enemy governments are believed similarly to be delaying matters, apparently in the mistaken belief that the United States Senate, when considering the Treaties, may be able to introduce into them certain modifications to the advantage of the enemy governments. His Majesty's Government and, it is understood, the United States Government have already impressed on the Italian Government the importance of their taking early action to ratify the Treaty. His Majesty's Government intend to continue to stress this point both with the Italian Government and with other enemy governments. In spite

of these representations, however, it may be that these governments will not have ratified the Treaties before the Great Powers are ready to do so, nor can there be any guarantee that the enemy governments will in fact ratify once the Great Powers have done so. For internal parliamentary reasons they may well continue to avoid the issue. It is clearly highly desirable that the enemy governments should ratify the Treaties although such ratifications are not necessary to bring the Treaties into force. If they do not ratify, they may be tempted to claim later that their respective Treaty had been imposed upon them as a "dictat", that they had no sanction from their own public opinion to carry out its terms and that they were therefore justified in trying to escape its obligations. Much might therefore be said in favour of the Big Four letting it be known immediately that they do not intend to deposit their ratifications and thereby bring the Treaties into force until the enemy states themselves have ratified. On the other hand, if, in spite of such a pronouncement, the enemy states still do not ratify, an embarrassing situation will arise. Either the Big Four will have to go back on their pronouncement or the Treaties will not come into force. This would obviously have the undesirable consequence of postponing the end of the state of war and the withdrawal of occupation troops from the countries concerned. His Majesty's Government in the United Kingdom would be grateful for an early expression of the views of the United States Government on the foregoing.[1]

4. A similar communication is being addressed to the Governments of the Union of Soviet Socialist Republics and of France.

WASHINGTON, 11th April, 1947.

---

[1] See footnote 2, p. 537.

740.0011 EW (Peace)/4–1447 : Telegram

The Minister in Hungary (Schoenfeld) to the Secretary of State

SECRET   BUDAPEST, April 14, 1947—11 a. m.

609. President Tildy [1] told me April 12 he hoped US would ratify peace treaty with Hungary as soon as possible since each month's delay costs Hungarian Govt 50 million forint for outlays that will fall away with ratification, this amount being ten times deficit for all other treasury purposes. He pointed out British ratification was already authorized and presumed Soviet ratification will take place more or less simultaneously with ours as had been the case when renewal of diplomatic relations was decided on in 1945.

SCHOENFELD

---

[1] Zoltan Tildy, President of Hungary since February 1, 1946.

740.0011 EW (Peace)/4–1747 : Telegram

The Acting Secretary of State to the Secretary of State, in Moscow

TOP SECRET   WASHINGTON, April 17, 1947—8 p. m.

970. Moskco 68. Personal for the Secretary from Acheson. As I informed you several days ago, Vandenberg had agreed to resumption of hearings of peace treaties April 21 with intention of concluding hearings that day and promptly referring committee report to Senate for action. Yesterday Vandenberg informed me that a considerable number of witnesses were insisting on testifying against the Italian treaty. Among these individuals are Adolf Berle,[1] LaGuardia,[2] Edgar Mowrer,[3] Dorothy Thompson[4] and Antonini.[5] It was clear, he said, that if all the people who want to testify were heard the hearings would drag out over several days. Moreover, he stated, he felt that it would be necessary for adequate answers to be made to their testimony.

Vandenberg pointed out that the principal argument which would be made against the Italian treaty was that it is already obsolete; that is, it was concluded at a time when the policy of the U.S. Govt was to "appease" Moscow, whereas the Truman doctrine has changed that whole policy. He said that in his opinion it will be necessary for you to appear before the committee, in addition to Byrnes, to insure the approval of the treaties by the committee.[6] He went on to say that he was endeavoring to work out with Ed Corsi[7] an arrangement to cut down materially the number of witnesses to appear but that in any event he felt that it would be desirable to postpone the resumption of hearings which had been scheduled for April 21.

I have discussed this matter with Mr. Byrnes who is quite prepared to undertake to answer testimony of opposing witnesses with, of course, assistance from the Dept. Byrnes said he saw no reason why the hearings should be postponed and asked me to urge upon Vandenberg that he go ahead with hearings as scheduled. I thereupon discussed the

---

[1] Adolf Augustus Berle, Jr., Assistant Secretary of State, 1938–1944.

[2] Fiorello H. La Guardia, member of Congress, 1917–1921 and 1923–1933; mayor of New York City, 1934–1945.

[3] Edgar Ansel Mowrer, author and war correspondent; had served with the Office of War Information until February 1943.

[4] Dorothy Thompson, newspaper columnist, lecturer, and radio commentator.

[5] Luigi Antonini, first Vice President of the International Ladies' Garment Workers' Union; President of the Italo-American Council of Labor.

For a complete list of persons who testified before the Committee, see page 3 of the hearings cited on p. 529, footnote 1.

[6] Secretary Marshall testified before the Committee for the second time on May 6, 1947, *ibid.*, p. 172. Cf. footnote 2, p. 545.

[7] Edward Corsi, born in Italy (1896), naturalized in 1921, writer, Commissioner of Immigration and Naturalization, 1933–1934. He testified before the Committee on April 30 in his capacity as Chairman of the Executive Committee, Committee for a Just Peace with Italy, and as State Labor Commissioner of New York State. For his statement, see *ibid.*, p. 31.

matter with Vandenberg who insists on postponement. Vandenberg said that he was still endeavoring to work out arrangement to reduce number of witnesses and in any event could not schedule hearings for April 21. He asked that I consult you and give him your views.

After talking to Vandenberg, I discussed the whole question with the President who wants to do whatever you desire in this matter.

I am confident that it will be necessary for you to appear before the committee on your return and be prepared to answer the question whether in the light of happenings at the Moscow Conference you feel that it is in the interests of the US that the Senate proceed with the approval of these treaties. Incidentally Vandenberg told me today that he feels that in the light of lack of progress made at Moscow the US has very little to gain from the entering into force of these five treaties.

ACHESON

740.0011 EW (Peace)/4–2047 : Telegram

The Secretary of State to the Acting Secretary of State

TOP SECRET   Moscow, April 20, 1947—3 p. m.
URGENT

1481. Kosmos 55. Personal, Eyes Only, for Acheson from Marshall. Reference Moskco 68.[1] I should be deeply concerned if deferment of hearings on peace treaties were construed as decision on our part to make separate peace treaty with Italy and possibly other satellite countries. If treaties are discarded or rejected I do not believe better treaties could be secured by common agreement. Discarding or rejection of Italian treaty would impose prolonged military commitment on us in Venezia Giulia and in view of their economic position, British would probably ask us to take over their share. The leverage (for what it is worth) which the Balkan and Hungarian treaties give us to use against excessive concentrations of Soviet troops in these countries would be gone. Moreover, the effect on the German situation of dropping the proposed treaties cannot be disregarded. While failure to reach agreements with Soviet Government in this Conference should not delay necessary developments under bi-zonal arrangements,[2] it is my thought that we should do nothing to close the door to Soviet cooperation. For that reason we should guard against action which might be construed as definitely closing the door.

According to present indications I expect to be back in Washington within a week or ten days at latest. If hearings on treaties start on

---

[1] *Supra.*
[2] For documentation on this subject, see vol. II, pp. 909 ff.

April 21, I should be back before they close. If President should conclude that he wishes to have hearings deferred pending my return, I hope the deferment may be arranged in a way which will not give rise at this time to talk that we have decided not to proceed with them.

Related subject: reference your Moskco 68, Mr Dulles [3] requests the following be delivered to Senator Vandenberg:

"I am inclined to feel that it is preferable to ratify Italian and satellite treaties but I think there is sufficient doubt so that final decision on policy should await exchange of views after our delegation returns. I agree that any postponement of hearings should avoid impression that any adverse policy decision has already been made."

[MARSHALL]

---

[3] John Foster Dulles, Special Adviser, United States Delegation, Fourth Session of the Council of Foreign Ministers, Moscow, March 10–April 24, 1947.

740.0011 EW (Peace)/4–2647 : Telegram

The Acting Political Adviser (Greene)[1] at Leghorn to the Secretary of State

TOP SECRET LEGHORN, April 26, 1947—8 a. m.

61. Please see Naf 133 [*1313*] [2] of April 25 in which SACMED reviews military problems which will arise if Yugoslavs fail ratify treaty when Big Four do and expresses hope it will be possible avoid these problems by reaching agreement for simultaneous deposit ratifications by Big Four and Yugoslavia.

I understand from my British colleague [3] Foreign Office has proposed simultaneous ratification by Big Four with or after ratification by ex-enemies and that Soviets have agreed in principle. It appears most desirable to eliminate the military and political problems discussed in Naf 133 [*1313*] and in my 57 [4] and 54 [5] of April 18 (reDeptel 24, April 24 [6]) and I therefore hope Department will agree to British

---

[1] Mr. Greene was the Acting United States Political Adviser to the Acting Supreme Allied Commander, Mediterranean (Lee).
[2] Not printed.
[3] William John Sullivan.
[4] Not printed; in it Greene reported that the military authorities were considering the implications of Yugoslav failure to ratify the Italian treaty and that he and his British colleague had been asked to state their views. Greene outlined what he proposed to say. (740.00119 Control (Italy)/4–1847)
[5] Not printed; in it Greene reported that he had said orally that the problem of who would represent the Free Territory of Trieste in the demarcation of its boundaries was under discussion (865.014/4–1847).
[6] Not printed; in it the Department agreed that the Acting U.S. PolAd might advise the military authorities along the lines which he had suggested in his telegram 57 (footnote 4 above) (740.00119 Control (Italy)/4–1847).

proposal and urge its extension to include Yugoslavia in the case of Italian treaty.

Sent Department 61; repeated Rome 23.

GREENE

740.0011 EW (Peace)/5–247

Memorandum by the Chief of the Division of Western European Affairs (Reber) and by Mr. Jacques J. Reinstein, Special Assistant to the Assistant Secretary of State for Economic Affairs (Thorp), to the Under Secretary of State (Acheson)

TOP SECRET   [WASHINGTON,] May 2, 1947.

MR. ACHESON: At the close of the public hearings today Senator Vandenberg asked us to stop for a few minutes conversation with him. He said before the bridges were burned that the Secretary should have one last look at the situation and give serious consideration to determine whether the situation had not so changed as to make desirable a postponement of ratification at least until after the Austrian settlement. He asked that the Secretary's review of the situation take into account the Truman doctrine, the failure of the Moscow Conference and the fact that all testimony so far submitted to Congress would give the impression that only the Communists favor early ratification of the Italian Treaty.

The trend of the hearings has been such as to advance very telling arguments, at least from the American political point of view; that this treaty is not consistent with the Truman doctrine, that it will accelerate Italy's very rapid disintegration into Communism, and that it still represents a policy of appeasement. The Secretary's own remarks to the effect that we should not accept an improper settlement merely to have an agreement on the record have been cited repeatedly to show that we are adopting a different policy with respect to Italy than we are in Greece and in Germany and Austria.

Senator Vandenberg asked the Secretary to consider what effect ratification will have in Italy, whether it will accelerate its progress towards Communism and what effect on our future policy and the negotiation of future peace settlements non-ratification of the Treaty would have. He said that these were questions which must be answered.

The situation was such that a grave mistake might be made in going ahead with ratification and that this was the last opportunity to rectify it if such was the case. We must realize that there is a political danger in this country that if Italy goes Communist there will be a strong current of domestic opinion which will lay it at the door of ratification. He pointed to the unruly situation in the House which could easily take this opportunity to break away from the present bi-partisan Senate leadership in foreign relations.

He said that he himself had some doubts about the Italian Treaty, but if the Secretary, after considering the matter in the light of the above, was satisfied that we should go ahead, he would go along with us. Without a very strong statement from the Secretary answering these questions, however, he thought that the Senate might not give its consent to ratification. He mentioned the fact that most Senators are not primarily interested in the situation in Italy, but are more concerned over the effect of ratification on their constituents. Up to the present all arguments presented by the Italo-American elements have been against ratification except for the one Communist proponent of the Treaty.[1]

Although he did not say so, we got the impression that Senator Vandenberg would welcome an opportunity to talk this matter over with the Secretary. It is also significant, we believe, that when he was asked by Senator Connally when the Secretary and Mr. Byrnes would appear he said the date had not been fixed, thus leaving it open for such discussions.[2]

S[amuel] Reber
J[acques] J. Reinstein

---

[1] Michael Salerno, editor of the New York newspaper, *L'Unità del Popolo*. For his testimony, see *Treaties of Peace With Italy, Rumania, Bulgaria, and Hungary: Hearings before the Committee on Foreign Relations, United States Senate, on Executives F, G, H, and I* (80th Cong., 1st sess.), p. 77.

[2] A handwritten notation at the head of this document reads: "Mr. Secretary. I think that it is important for you & Mr. Byrnes to have a talk with Vandenberg & Connally on Monday & get word to them to this effect on Saturday [May 3]. Do you agree & do you wish to be briefed before such a meeting? D[ean] A[cheson]"

Both Secretary Marshall and former Secretary Byrnes testified for ratification before the Committee on May 6.

740.0011 EW (Peace)/5–1047

Memorandum of Conversation, by the Chief of the Division of Western European Affairs (Reber)

[Washington,] May 10, 1947.

Subject: Statement of policy to accompany announcement of United States ratification of Italian Treaty.

In a conversation with the Italian Ambassador last night, which naturally turned on the approval by the Foreign Relations Committee of ratification of the Italian Peace Treaty,[1] Signor Tarchiani urged

---

[1] On May 9 the Committee had unanimously recommended ratification of the four treaties. *Treaties of Peace With Italy, Rumania, Bulgaria, and Hungary: Senate Executive Report 4, 80th Congress, 1st Session, To Accompany Executives F, G, H, and I*, p. 14.

that, when the time comes to announce final approval of these treaties, any such announcement be accompanied by a statement of policy toward Italy. He hoped that such a statement would include renewed assurances of continuing United States interest in Italy, of its friendship toward the Italian people and its desire to be of all possible assistance to them. He understood that such a statement would be made on the floor of the Senate. He hoped also that the Secretary or the President could make one, as the assurance of executive as well as of legislative interest in this problem would go far, he felt, to allay some of the discouragement which would undoubtedly be felt in Italy when people realized there was no present hope that the treaties would not go into effect. Public opinion in Italy considers that United States action on the treaties will be decisive one, and when the United States has ratified these treaties there will be no delay in their entry into force.

S[AMUEL] R[EBER]

740.0011 EW (Peace)/5–1447 : Telegram

The Ambassador in Italy (Dunn) to the Secretary of State

TOP SECRET   ROME, May 14, 1947—midnight.

1155. I do not feel that we should be bound by a prearranged R–Day as long as there is any question of Yugoslav ratification (see Leghorn's telegram 61 to Department April 26). Furthermore I think we would be putting ourselves in a disadvantageous position if we attempted to include the Yugoslavs with the Big Four in bringing the treaty into force contrary to the spirit of article 90 of the treaty as drafted in Paris last year.

I have shown this telegram to Greene and appreciate the military's desire to secure a fixed schedule for their future movements in this theater. In the final analysis however I feel the best plan is to allow the various ratifications to take their normal course and (Department's telegram 322, March 6) to retain our own liberty of action up to the last.

Sent Department as 1155; repeated Leghorn 37.

DUNN

740.0011 EW (Peace)/5–847

The Department of State to the British Embassy

MEMORANDUM

Reference is made to the British Embassy's memorandum of May 8, 1947, regarding ratification of the Peace Treaties with Italy, Hungary,

Rumania and Bulgaria.[1] The Department of State agrees that upon United States ratification the British, French, Soviet and American Governments should consult together to decide whether, and if so when, the treaties can be brought into effect without further formalities. The Department also shares the preliminary view of the British Government that each of the treaties should be brought into force, through deposit of the necessary Allied ratifications, as soon as possible following ratification by the ex-enemy state concerned.

As regards ratification by the ex-enemy states, the Department questions the advisability of any public statement along the lines suggested, feeling that it would be preferable to continue the informal approach which the American Government has heretofore followed in discussions of this matter with the ex-enemy states.

WASHINGTON, May 28, 1947.

---

[1] In this memorandum, not printed, the British Government referred to the Department's memorandum of April 24, 1947 (ante, p. 537, footnote 2) and recognized that it would not be possible to establish a precise date for the deposit of ratifications until after approval of United States ratification by the Senate; recommended that the British, Soviet, and French Governments agree not to deposit ratifications until after action by the U.S. Senate; suggested that each treaty could be handled separately, that is that the Big Four could act together on each treaty separately; and proposed that after positive action by the U.S. Senate the Big Four make a statement that they consider ratification by the ex-enemy states necessary to bring the treaties into force (740.0011 EW (Peace)/5-847).

740.0011 EW (Peace)/6–647 : Telegram

The Ambassador in Italy (Dunn) to the Secretary of State

TOP SECRET   ROME, June 6, 1947—1 p. m.
URGENT

1437. Now that Senate has approved ratification of Italian Treaty [1] Department may wish to give very careful consideration as to the time when the ratification will be deposited (ref Deptel 322 March 6). A very serious situation would arise (see my 444, March 1 [2]) if the treaty were to go into effect as a result of the deposit of ratification by

---

[1] On June 2, 1947, Senator Vandenberg, having consulted with leaders of both parties, requested the unanimous consent of the Senate that, as in executive session, it take up the Italian peace treaty as "unfinished business". There being no objection, the treaty was read for the second time. The treaty was debated on June 3, 4, and 5. On June 5, by a vote of 79 for, 10 against, and with six senators not voting, the Senate advised and consented to the ratification of the treaty of peace with Italy. *Congressional Record*, vol. 93, pt. 5, pp. 6154–6409.

On June 5 the Senate, having read for the second time the treaties with Rumania, Bulgaria, and Hungary, respectively, passed without debate resolutions recommending their ratification, *ibid.*, pp. 6415, 6420, and 6427.

[2] See footnote 1, p. 533.

the Four Principal Powers and Yugo had not ratified. Commitment made to Italy by military authorized by CCS (see our 752 April 7 [3] and Caserta's 14 January 22 [4]) would be in direct conflict with our strict obligation under treaty to withdraw our troops from all of Venezia Giulia except the Free Territory of Trieste.

It seems most important that if Yugo does not ratify soon Big Four discussions contemplated by Department should be initiated and deposit of ratification be delayed pending outcome of such discussions.

DUNN

---

[3] For text, see vol. IV, p. 68. Telegram 752 reported that an officer of AFHQ had, at the direction of SACMED, informed De Gasperi in a personal and confidential letter that if Yugoslavia failed to ratify the treaty, the Anglo-American forces would remain in Pola and on the Morgan Line.

[4] Not printed; it reported that SACMED had received a formal inquiry from De Gasperi asking whether the Anglo-American forces would withdraw from the Morgan Line, including Pola, if the Treaty were to go into effect without Yugoslavia's signature or ratification, and that SACMED had referred the question to the Combined Chiefs of Staff. (740.0011 EW (Peace)/1–2247)

740.0011 EW (Peace)/6–1147

Memorandum by the Acting Director of the Office of European Affairs (Hickerson) [1]

[WASHINGTON,] June 11, 1947.

Subject: Recommendation to the President for a Statement on Italy

DISCUSSION

Execution by the President of the instrument of ratification of the Treaty of Peace with Italy [2] will afford an opportunity to issue a statement in his name reiterating US views on the treaty as well as US support for a democratic Italy. Through the Italian Ambassador in Washington, De Gasperi has indicated that such a statement would be helpful at this time in securing ratification by the Italian Constituent Assembly. [3]

RECOMMENDATION

That the attached draft statement be transmitted to the President with the recommendation that it be issued by the White House on the

---

[1] Addressed through Under Secretary of State Acheson to the Secretary. A handwritten marginal note reads: "I concur. D[ean] A[cheson]".

[2] Instruction No. 3084, June 18, not printed, forwarded the instrument of ratification to the Embassy in France and directed that it be retained by the Embassy until further instructions were received concerning its deposit with the French Foreign Ministry (740.0011 EW (Peace)/6–1847).

[3] See memorandum of conversation, by Mr. Samuel Reber, May 10, p. 545.

occasion of the execution of the instrument of ratification of the Treaty of Peace with Italy.[4]

---

[4] President Truman concurred in the recommendation. On June 14 he ratified the Treaty of Peace with Italy and issued the statement. For text, see Department of State *Bulletin*, June 22, 1947, p. 1214.

On that same day Ambassador Tarchiani sent a personal letter, not printed, to President Truman thanking him for his statement (740.0011 EW/6–1447).

Two days later, in a note to the Secretary, not printed, Tarchiani asked that a message of thanks from the Italian Foreign Minister, Count Sforza, be transmitted to President Truman.

740.0011 EW (Peace)/6–1247

Memorandum by the Director of the Office of European Affairs (Matthews)[1]

[WASHINGTON,] June 12, 1947.

Subject: Recommendation to the President for a Statement on Hungary, Rumania, and Bulgaria

DISCUSSION

Execution by the President of the instruments of ratification of the Treaties of Peace with Hungary, Rumania, and Bulgaria[2] will afford an opportunity to issue a statement in his name reiterating our views on the oppressive regimes now in power in these three countries, while at the same time indicating the reasons this Government has thought it desirable to conclude peace treaties with such governments. We believe the expression of US disapproval of the Communist-controlled governments of these countries in connection with the ratification of the peace treaties will strengthen those who are still struggling to resist subjugation.

RECOMMENDATION

That the attached draft statement be transmitted to the President with the recommendation that it be issued by the White House on the occasion of the execution of the instrument for ratification of the Peace Treaties with Hungary, Rumania, and Bulgaria, but subsequent to and separate from the release of the statement on Italy. We feel that a differentiation should be made between the ratification of the Treaty

---

[1] Addressed through Under Secretary of State Acheson to the Secretary. A marginal notation reads: "Mr. Acheson concurs. C[arlisle] H[umelsine]".

[2] Instruction No. 1953, June 18, not printed, forwarded the instruments of ratification of the treaties to the Embassy in Moscow and directed that they be retained until further instructions were received from the Department concerning their deposit with the Soviet Foreign Office (740.0011 EW (Peace)/6–1847).

with Italy and the treaties with the Balkan countries, and that this can best be indicated by separating the press releases.[3]

---

[3] President Truman concurred in the recommendation. On June 14 he ratified the treaties and issued the statement. For text, see Department of State *Bulletin*, June 22, 1947, p. 1214.

740.0011 EW (Peace)/6–1447 : Telegram

The Ambassador in France (Caffery) to the Secretary of State

CONFIDENTIAL   PARIS, June 14, 1947—3 p. m.

2349. French National Assembly yesterday ratified Italian Peace Treaty by 500 votes to 0 with approximately 80 abstentions, latter chiefly in Rassemblement des Gauches and PRL. Bidault and MRP speakers defended treaty as best that could be obtained under circumstances and emphasized important part played by France in negotiation. Bidault made many friendly remarks re new Italy and prospectives of close cooperation in future between Italy and France. In reply to question re Fezzan he said there had been no change in French views this territory should be returned to France. PRL criticized treaty as being too harsh, particularly reparations to Soviets and Yugoslavs.

Announcement Rassemblement des Gauches would abstain came as surprise to all, including that party's members in government. De Moro-Giafferri in explaining his group's decision criticized chiefly absence of any consultations with Assembly during negotiation of treaty. Communists voted for ratification but without enthusiasm and were extremely sarcastic re abstention of Rassemblement des Gauches in view criticism of Communists by that party for similar Communist abstentions while members of government.

Treaty now goes to Council of Republic which will presumably ratify during coming week.[1]

Sent Dept as 2349; repeated London 447; Rome 135; Moscow 368.

                                                              CAFFERY

---

[1] In telegram 2416, June 18, from Paris, not printed, Ambassador Caffery reported that the Council of the Republic had ratified the treaty (740.0011 EW (Peace)/6–1847).

740.0011 EW (Peace)/6–1047 : Telegram

The Secretary of State to the Embassy in France

SECRET   WASHINGTON, June 19, 1947— 8 p. m.

2252. Dept favors Brit suggestion simultaneous deposit ratification instruments Ital treaty by Four Powers (ur 2277 June 10 [1]) as well as parallel action by three powers re Balkan treaties. Brit FonOff has now proposed to US, Fr and USSR that deposits be made July 1 provided in each case ex-enemy state had deposited its ratification by that time, and that in event any of latter had not done so those of Four Powers concerned would delay deposit and consider together what action shd be taken.[2]

Subject further consideration implications of bringing one treaty into force before others, Dept intends shortly accept Brit proposal. At same time, other powers would be informed US view that if Yugos were not to ratify prior deposit ratifications Ital treaty by Four Powers, treaty clauses relating to Venezia Giulia could not be implemented and *status quo* that area would have to be continued.

Dept also feels it preferable Itals ratify before deposit ratifications by Four Powers, and is prepared continue informal attempts persuade Itals this course. Dept would not agree however to formal concerted approach Ital Govt this matter by Four Powers as once suggested by Brit, feeling pressure this nature would be seized upon by Ital opponents of ratification.

Sent Paris as 2252 rptd Moscow 1354 London 2642 Rome 959 and Belgrade as 395.

MARSHALL

[1] Not printed; in it Ambassador Caffery reported that the French Foreign Office mentioned its understanding that the United States favored the British proposal of simultaneous deposits of ratifications by the Big Four, and asked for the views of the United States on how the ratification should be made. (740.0011 EW (Peace)/6–1047)

[2] This proposal was made in memorandum 41/246/47 from British Embassy to the Department of State dated June 16, not printed (740.0011 EW (Peace)/6–1647).

In a memorandum of June 24 to the British Embassy, not printed, the Department accepted the British proposal (740.0011 EW (Peace)/6–1647).

740.0011 EW (Peace)/7–547 : Telegram

The Chargé in Yugoslavia (Cabot) to the Secretary of State

CONFIDENTIAL   BELGRADE, July 5, 1947—8 a. m.

753. Despite what Bebler [1] told me Tuesday (Embtel 734 July 1 repeated Rome 72 [2]) I understand Italian Treaty has not yet been ratified by Presidium. Reason given by Foreign Office is that ratification should first be completed for Bulgarian and Hungarian treaties since these are now considered friendly nations.

Sent Department as 753, repeated Rome 78.

CABOT

[1] Aleš Bebler, Yugoslav Assistant Minister for Foreign Affairs.
[2] Not printed; in it Cabot reported that: "Bebler informed me today that Yugos would ratify Italian treaty this afternoon." (740.0011 EW (Peace)/6–147)

740.0011 EW (Peace)/7–847 : Telegram

The Ambassador in Italy (Dunn) to the Secretary of State

CONFIDENTIAL   ROME, July 8, 1947—6 p. m.

1872. We have been informed confidentially by Foreign Minister that Italian Ambassador Moscow [1] has reported to Italian Government in response to its request that according to best information he can obtain Soviet Government is not interested in ratifying Italian treaty at present. According to our informant Brosio reported that in his conversations with US Embassy Moscow Soviet disinclination to ratify at present time had been confirmed. Brosio's telegram plus uneasiness toward Soviet attitude felt in government and Foreign Ministry (see my 1812 of July 3 [2]) caused temporary panic here with result that government last few days has been wavering in its original intention to support and bring to vote treaty approval decree in Constituent Assembly this week (see my 1810 of July 3 [2]).

According to most recent information, however, it is reported that treaty ratification in Assembly will proceed as usual and government will definitely not attempt to obstruct it. Determining factor in government's decision to go ahead regardless of Soviet action [3] is said to be strong telegram from Quaroni, Italian Ambassador to France, pointing out many disadvantages to Italy if government failed to support ratification before Assembly at last moment.

Sent Department as 1872, repeated Moscow 99, Paris 228, Belgrade 88, London 121, copy to Leghorn.

                                                                    DUNN

---

[1] Manlio Giovanni Brosio.
[2] Not printed.
[3] In telegram No. 2357, July 6, from Moscow, not printed, Ambassador Smith reported that he had been informed in strictest confidence that the "Rumanian Ambassador Moscow inquired Soviet Foreign Office probability early ratification Rumanian treaty and was told by Malik that this very difficult question since within province Supreme Soviet. When Ambassador countered that article 49 of Constitution empowered Presidium to deal directly with such matters Malik evidenced patent displeasure and gave Rumanian no satisfaction." Ambassador Smith suggested that "this transparent excuse for nonperformance" was not an encouraging sign for early ratification. (740.0011 EW (Peace)/7–647)

740.0011 EW (Peace)/7–647 : Telegram

The Secretary of State to the Embassy in the Soviet Union

SECRET   WASHINGTON, July 9, 1947—8 p. m.

1434. UK FonOff recently decided approach Soviets again (ur 2357 July 6 [1]) to point out US, UK and France had ratified treaties and

---

[1] See footnote 3, above.

agreed simultaneous deposit ratifications July 1 provided ex-enemy states had ratified by that date; that only USSR had failed respond Brit proposal this regard; and that Brit would therefore be interested in knowing Soviet intentions and whether Soviets desired propose date for deposit ratifications. Although Brit approach[2] was discussed with and concurred in by Dept, no proposal was made re joint US, UK French approach. UK FonOff did suggest at one point that US and French Embassies Moscow might follow up Brit approach, to which Dept replied that it would seem preferable not to give Soviets impression we were all overly anxious for early USSR ratification. If opportunity offers, however, you may in your discretion inquire re Soviet intentions.

MARSHALL

---

[2] See footnote 2 to telegram 2252, p. 551.

740.0011 EW (Peace)/7–1447 : Telegram

The Ambassador in Italy (Dunn) to the Secretary of State

SECRET   ROME, July 14, 1947—6 p. m.
NIACT   US URGENT

1944. Personal for Secretary Marshall from Harriman.[1] Dunn and I saw the President, De Nicola,[2] this morning and later De Gasperi. Both of them talked at great length about difficulty of obtaining ratification of peace treaty by General Assembly at this moment. Each explained there was no doubt of a majority being in favor of eventual ratification but that first vote would be on whether to consider immediate ratification or postponement. On this it appeared vote would go against the government. De Gasperi told us Soviet Ambassador[3] had recently stated Soviet Government would not ratify treaty at present time giving no explanation as to the reasons.[4] In meantime Communists are spreading propaganda to the effect that Russia intends to offer more liberal territorial terms. In this atmosphere there are a number of the assembly who question for internal political reasons the wisdom of Italian ratification until Russia has done so.

De Gasperi is ready to force a vote if British and we insist but indicates there is a real chance of adverse vote in which event his government will be compelled to resign.

Bevin, in forceful terms, told Sforza in Paris that he would insist upon prompt ratification.

---

[1] W. Averell Harriman, United States Ambassador to the Soviet Union, 1943–1946; Ambassador to Great Britain, April–October, 1946; Secretary of Commerce, October 1946–April 1948.
[2] Enrico de Nicola was not at this time President of Italy but was Provisional Head of the State (*Capo provvisorio dello stato*), June 28, 1946–January 1, 1948.
[3] Mikhail Kostylev.
[4] Cf. telegram 1872, July 8, from Rome, p. 552.

Of course, I am not familiar with other side of question but from Rome it would appear a serious risk for us to force the Italian Government to vote at this time particularly as Italian ratification is of no substantive value without Russian action. The wisest course would seem to inform De Gasperi that we of course want earliest ratification possible but would leave to him whether now is right moment to press it.

If this course is decided upon I would suggest that Bevin be informed and urged to take a similar position.

If this government falls over ratification, it would materially strengthen the Communist position and play into the Soviet hands by giving the Communists the possibility of overthrowing the government on a national issue which would place them before the electorate in the position as defending Italian independence against the US and Great Britain.

Reference Embtels 1928 July 12; 1929 July 12; 1930 July 12, 2 p.m.[5]

Repeated to London as 129 for Ambassador. [Harriman.]

DUNN

---

[5] None printed.

740.0011 EW (Peace)/7–1247 : Telegram

The Secretary of State to the Embassy in Italy

SECRET WASHINGTON, July 15, 1947—noon.

1137. Ur 1930 July 12.[1] Dept concurs your opinion re Ital treaty ratification. Since USSR has not ratified and in view reversal position Ital Communists and Nenni Socialists, it would seem unfair urge De Gasperi push Ital ratification to showdown vote at this time, with possible consequences for Govt which defeat this issue would entail. Dept hopes by time Const Assembly reconvenes Aug 20 USSR will have ratified, and situation will be different.

Accordingly, you may inform De Gasperi that in view circumstances and delicate political problem which pressure for immediate ratification would raise for Ital Govt, US does not wish urge that he press for immediate action by Assembly.[2] In response to inquiry, Tarchiani informed in this sense by Dept.

---

[1] Not printed.
[2] In telegram No. 1972, July 16, from Rome, not printed, Ambassador Dunn reported that in Count Sforza's absence he had informed the Under Secretary for Foreign Affairs, Mr. Brusasca "that decision as to whether matter of ratification of treaty is to be pressed at this time before Constituent Assembly is entirely up to Italian Government." (740.0011 EW (Peace)/7–1647)

London and Paris shd inform UK and French Govts, respectively, of Dept's position this matter.[3]

Sent Rome as 1137, London as 3020 and Paris as 2593.

MARSHALL

---

[3] In telegram No. 3893, July 16, from London, not printed, Ambassador Douglas reported that "Bevin bows to our judgment that De Gasperi should not now be urged to push for ratification. This judgment he informed me has been confirmed by the British Ambassador in Rome." (740.0011 EW (Peace)/7-1647)

740.0011 EW (Peace)/7-1847 : Telegram

The Ambassador in Italy (Dunn) to the Secretary of State

SECRET   ROME, July 18, 1947—6 p. m.

1993. The Prime Minister told me this morning he is working on a new formula with respect to ratification of the treaty. He is still anxious to have the Assembly authorize the government to ratify immediately but if that is not possible without running the extreme risk of overthrowing the government he is thinking of proposing that the Assembly authorize the government to ratify the treaty when it becomes effective. This without saying so would mean that Italy will ratify when deposits or [of?] ratification have been made by the four principal governments.

He also told me . . . that Nenni had asked the privilege of making this proposal in order to improve his position with Bevin and the British Socialist Party as he finds the Saragatiani[1] are in better relationship with the British Socialists than himself because of their not going along with the Communists and more particularly now because of their position in favor of ratification.

DUNN

---

[1] Saragatiani, i.e. the followers of Giuseppe Saragat who in January 1947 had formed the Socialist Party of Italian Workers.

740.0011 EW (Peace)/7-2347 : Telegram

The Ambassador in Italy (Dunn) to the Secretary of State

SECRET   ROME, July 23, 1947—11 a. m.
URGENT

2042. Secretary General of Foreign Office[1] sent word to me late last night that the Government's formula re ratification of treaty (see my 2018, July 21[2]) had been defeated in Interparliamentary Committee.

---

[1] Francesco Fransoni.
[2] Not printed.

This unexpected development was attributed to sudden violent reversal of Communists. In discussions among party leaders Togliatti was said to have accused the Government of being "American". Nenni as usual followed Communist lead . . . As was to be expected, the extreme Right faced by the action of the Left had become panic-stricken by prospect of facing elections outdone by the Left on a nationalist issue. Accordingly, all the Qualunquists[3] and most of the Liberals were now opposed to any government action at present time towards even provisional ratification of treaty. Corbin[4] himself was said to have spoken most harshly against Government's proposal and to have urged postponement.

According to our informant, the Prime Minister (whom I shall see later today) was still determined to press for adoption of his resolution despite a considerable defection in his own party led by Gronchi[5] apparently under the influence of Don Sturzo.[6] It remains to be seen whether after his conversations with the leaders today, he will continue on this course (the debate in this Assembly has been postponed to Thursday).[7]

I reiterated our position authorized in Department's 1137, July 15 and it rests entirely with Prime Minister whether he chooses to risk the continuance of his government in office by demanding a vote. It is, of course, most unfortunate that due to the Soviet tactics of delay, the extreme Left have been able to maneuver themselves into taking the initiative as protectors of Italy against premature acceptance of the treaty which all Italians believe unjust and onerous.

DUNN

---

[3] The followers of Guglielmo Giannini whose organ was *Uomo Qualunque* (The Common Man).
[4] Professor Epicarmo Corbino, Deputy in the Constituent Assembly, Minister of the Treasury in the first and second De Gasperi Cabinets (until September 18, 1946).
[5] Giovanni Gronchi, a leader of the Christian Democratic Party.
[6] Don Luigi Sturzo, a Sicilian priest, one of the founders of the Partito Popolare in 1919.
[7] In telegram No. 2065, July 23, from Rome, not printed, Ambassador Dunn reported that De Gasperi had told him and Mr. Clayton that he expected on the morrow (July 24) to go forward with the discussion of ratification of the treaty (740.0011 EW (Peace)/7–2347).

740.0011 EW (Peace)/7–2947 : Telegram

The Chargé in the United Kingdom (Clark) to the Secretary of State

SECRET   LONDON, July 29, 1947—4 p. m.

4116. According to Jebb[1] Foreign Office Soviets have told British Ambassador Moscow[2] that Soviets (1) agree to urgency depositing

---

[1] Hubert Miles Gladwyn Jebb, Assistant Under-Secretary of State and United Nations Adviser in the Foreign Office.
[2] Sir Maurice Drummond Peterson.

ratification treaties; (2) feel deposit ratifications should take place simultaneously Moscow and Paris but that (3) ratifications should not be deposited until satellites and Italy have ratified. In other words, Soviets, through satellites, will determine date effectiveness all treaties.

Sent Dept, repeated Moscow 255, Paris 422, Rome 89.

CLARK

740.0011 EW (Peace)/7–3147

Memorandum by the Director of the Office of European Affairs (Matthews)[1]

[WASHINGTON,] July 31, 1947.

Subject: Suggested Message from the Secretary to the Italian Government to be Transmitted upon the Authorization by the Italian Constituent Assembly of Italian Ratification of the Peace Treaty

DISCUSSION

Premier De Gasperi is making a determined effort to obtain authorization from the Constituent Assembly for Italian ratification of the Peace Treaty. It is anticipated that a vote, which is expected to be favorable, will be taken in the Assembly today or tomorrow.[2]

Italian Ambassador Tarchiani has indicated to me that it would be helpful to the Italian Government, as a measure to counteract the unpopularity of the Government's position in requesting ratification of this treaty, if the Secretary would send a message to the Italian Government as soon as ratification is authorized. De Gasperi's position would be made easier by such a message, holding out hope for ultimate treaty revision along the lines of the President's statement at the time of the United States ratification.

RECOMMENDATION

It is recommended that the attached telegram, instructing the Ambassador at Rome to communicate a message in the foregoing sense from the Secretary to the Italian Foreign Minister for the Prime Minister, be approved for transmission as soon as word is received that the Assembly has authorized ratification.

---

[1] Addressed to the Secretary and the Under Secretary.

[2] In telegram No. 2172, July 31, from Rome, not printed, Ambassador Dunn forwarded a translation of the text of the resolution just passed by the Constituent Assembly: "Tonight the Government of the Republic is authorized to ratify the treaty of peace signed at Paris February 10, 1947, between the Allied powers and their associates and Italy. The ratification of Italy is conditional upon that of all the powers mentioned in Article 90 [i.e., the Soviet Union, the United Kingdom of Great Britain and Northern Ireland, the United States of America, and France] of the treaty of peace above mentioned." (740.0011 EW (Peace)/7–3147)

ATTACHMENT

a) Draft telegram to the American Embassy, Rome.[3]

---

[3] The telegram, which was sent as No. 1287, July 31, forwarded the text of the message of Secretary Marshall to the Italian Foreign Minister, Count Sforza. For this text, released to the press in Washington on August 2, see Department of State *Bulletin*, August 10, 1947, p. 298.

740.0011 EW (Peace)/8–847 : Telegram

The Minister in Hungary (Chapin) to the Secretary of State

CONFIDENTIAL   BUDAPEST, August 8, 1947—4 p. m.
PRIORITY

1332. President Tildy signed legislation ratifying peace treaty August 7.

Sent Department, repeated London 139, Moscow 131.

CHAPIN

740.0011 EW (Peace)/8–1247 : Telegram

The Ambassador in the Soviet Union (Smith) to the Secretary of State

RESTRICTED   Moscow, August 12, 1947—6 p. m.

2628. 1. There follows translation of Soviet note No. 312 dated August 11, regarding peace treaty ratification received this morning:

". . .[1] And with reference to the Embassy's note No. 589 of June 26, 1947, has the honor to inform the Embassy that the Soviet Government on July 21, 1947, sent a reply to the British Government in connection with its proposal for the simultaneous deposit of ratifications of the Italian and Balkan treaties.

"In its reply the Soviet Government stated that it shares the British Government's opinion with regard to the undesirability of postponing the entry into force of the peace treaties with Italy, Rumania, Bulgaria, Hungary and Finland. However, at the present time the fixing of any definite date for the entry into force of these treaties appears premature.

"The Soviet Government stated also that it considers it essential that the entry into force of the peace treaties with Italy, Hungary, Rumania, Bulgaria and Finland, which were drawn up and discussed at the Paris peace conference simultaneously should be timed for one definite moment for all the treaties referred to.

"In this connection the Soviet Government believes that it would be incorrect to postpone the entry into force of the peace treaty with regard to Italy alone until the ratification of this treaty by Italy her-

---

[1] Omission indicated in source text.

self has been completed, as is proposed by the British Government, and proposes for its part that the same procedure should be adopted also with regard to Rumania, Bulgaria, Hungary and Finland.

"Furthermore the Soviet Government stated that when those conditions exist it will be ready in agreement with the Government of Great Britain, France and the US to appoint a definite date for the simultaneous deposit of the instruments of ratification by all the appropriate allied powers upon whom the entry into force of the above-mentioned peace treaties depends.

"In what concerns the ratification by Yugoslavia of the Italian treaty, the Minister of Foreign Affairs does not have any information which would permit of the assumption that Yugoslavia intends not to ratify the treaty."

2. Embassy note No. 589 June 26 referred to above communicated to Soviet Government substance of Deptel 1374 June 24.[2]

3. French Embassy Moscow received similar note from Soviet Government dated August 4 and on August 8 replied along lines of recent British *démarche* (August 4).

SMITH

---

[2] In this telegraphic instruction it was explained that the Department had accepted the British proposal for the simultaneous deposit of ratifications for the Italian and Balkan treaties, but had pointed out that if the Italian treaty were to come into force in accordance with Article 90 prior to Yugoslavia's deposit of ratification, it would be impossible to carry out the cessions of territory in Venezia Giulia to Yugoslavia because of the provisions of Article 89. The Department's view was that the *status quo* in Venezia Giulia would have to continue pending ratification by Yugoslavia. (740.0011 EW (Peace)/6–1947)

740.0011 EW (Peace)/8–1847 : Telegram

The Ambassador in the Soviet Union (Smith) to the Secretary of State

SECRET   Moscow, August 18, 1947—noon.

2665. Soviet delaying tactics regarding ratification of Italian and Balkan peace treaties seem to reflect Soviet estimate that ratification would bring little if any advantage to Kremlin whereas a number of things may be achieved by further postponing entry into force of these treaties.

1. Advantage which Italian treaty designed to bring Russians, withdrawal of Anglo-American troops from Italy, is for time being nullified by lack of progress in finding Governor for Trieste and establishment of FTT Government.[1] On other hand, continued delay in face of self-evident western interest in early ratification may bring with it

---

[1] For documentation on this subject, see vol. IV, pp. 51 ff.

eventual possibility of selling ratification for some new concessions from Western powers in accordance with well-known Soviet proclivity for selling its favors twice. In meantime, maintenance of present precarious political balance would seem desirable from Kremlin viewpoint.

Significant consequences of treaty ratification to Kremlin operations would appear to be obligations (1) to terminate [armistice?] regimes in Finland and ex-enemy Balkan states and (2) to withdraw troops from Bulgaria. The important current preparations for forthcoming Hungarian elections and transitional character of that Government as well as yet uncompleted liquidation of opposition elements in Rumania and Bulgaria are excellent reasons why Kremlin should be reluctant to relinquish rights and direct controls of the several armistice commissions until anti-Soviet forces definitively eliminated and firmly-based Stalinist regimes are squarely in the saddle. Despite continued presence of Soviet occupation troops in Hungary and Rumania following entry into force of treaties, Kremlin contact with its ex-enemy satellites will presumably be mainly through diplomatic and party channels and will require therefore fully integrated satellite administrations if it is to approximate effectiveness of present armistice military controls.

Greece continues to be a main object in Kremlin planning and desirability from its point of view of maintaining Soviet combat units in Bulgaria is self-evident. Even though treaty provides for Soviet forces in Rumania, within easy supporting distance of any point in Balkans, physical presence of Soviet troops in Bulgaria is more effective backing for any Bulgarian aggression against western Thrace, while at same time assuring Bulgarian internal stability and maintaining Soviet pressure on Turkey. Furthermore, in event of American decision to accept possible Greek invitation to despatch troops to Greece to aid in cleaning up local "guerrillas", Kremlin would no doubt prefer to have combat units already deployed in Bulgaria ready to meet any contingency rather than have to send new units to Bulgaria at "invitation" of Bulgarian Government.

In sum as seen from Moscow, there are no apparent reasons why Kremlin should want to ratify treaties at this time, and numerous reasons suggest themselves why it should continue to present negative course.

Repeated to London as 308.

Department pass to Paris as Moscow's 309 and Rome as 72.

SMITH

740.0011 EW (Peace)/8-1547

The Chargé in the Soviet Union (Reinhardt) to the Secretary of State

No. 1547   Moscow, August 19, 1947.
Subject: Ratification of Italian and Balkan Treaties.

The Officer in Charge refers to the Embassy's telegram no. 2629 of August 12, 7 p. m.,[1] and to the Department's telegrams no. 1609 of August 15, 4 p. m.,[2] and no. 1611 of August 16, 1 p. m., 1947,[3] and has the honor to transmit for the records of the Department the following copies of correspondence exchanged between the Embassy and the Soviet Ministry of Foreign Affairs in this connection:

Two copies of letter dated August 18, 1947, addressed to A. Ya. Vyshinski, Deputy Minister for Foreign Affairs, Moscow.

[Enclosure]

The American Ambassador (Smith) to the Soviet Deputy Minister for Foreign Affairs (Vyshinsky)

Moscow, August 18, 1947.

DEAR MR. VYSHINSKI: I refer to the informal discussion which I had with Mr. Molotov on July 11, 1947 relative to the question of the deposit of the ratifications of the peace treaties with Italy and the ex-enemy Balkan States and to the Ministry's note no. 312 of August 11,[4] 1947 which set forth the substance of the Soviet Government's communication of July 21 to the British Government on this subject. In this communication the Soviet Government affirmed its opinion that the deposit of the ratifications of the four Powers should be effected simultaneously and stated that it shared the British Government's view with regard to the undesirability of postponing the entry into force of the several peace treaties. However the communication would seem to infer that the Soviet Government regards ratification by the ex-enemy States as necessary to the entry into force of the treaties.

In this connection I recall that in the Ministry's note of January 31, 1947 regarding the Italian treaty,[5] it is set forth as the opinion of the

---

[1] Not printed; in it Ambassador Smith suggested to the Department that it reconsider its instructions to him to take up orally with the Soviet Government the matter of ratification of the peace treaties and that he be instructed to send a formal note, the proposed text of which he submitted (740.0011 EW (Peace)/8-1247).
[2] Not printed; in it the Department expressed approval of the course proposed by Ambassador Smith (740.0011 EW (Peace)/8-1247).
[3] Not printed.
[4] See telegram 2628, August 12, from Moscow, p. 558.
[5] See footnote 4, p. 519.

Soviet Government that under the pertinent article of that treaty (Article 90) Italy was under the obligation to sign and ratify the treaty as drawn up and that the treaty entered into effect by the deposit of instruments of ratification by the four principal Allied Powers. Inasmuch as the peace treaties with Bulgaria, Hungary, and Rumania contain similar provisions (Article 38 of the Bulgarian Treaty, Article 42 of the Hungarian Treaty, and Article 40 of the Rumanian Treaty) with respect to their ratification and entry into force, the Soviet Government's opinion with respect to the Italian Treaty set forth in its note of January 31, 1947 is equally applicable to the treaties of peace with these three ex-enemy States.

As I informed Mr. Molotov, the United States Government has already ratified the treaties and it is my understanding that similar action has been taken by both the British and French Governments. Furthermore, as you will recall, the several treaties all provide that the instruments of ratification shall be deposited "in the shortest possible time". Accordingly I would appreciate being advised regarding the Soviet Government's plans for its ratification of the treaties and whether it has given consideration to a date for the simultaneous deposit of the ratifications of the four principal Allied Powers.

I am [etc.]   W. B. SMITH

740.0011 EW (Peace)/8–2347 : Telegram

The Ambassador in Italy (Dunn) to the Secretary of State

SECRET   ROME, August 23, 1947—4 p. m.

2475. Re Moscow's 2671, August 18, relayed Rome as 73, August 19.[1] Secretary General Foreign Office confirmed to us that according to opinion prepared by Perassi,[2] Italian Govt is empowered to ratify treaty and deposit ratification provided document contains express reservation stating it becomes effective only upon deposit of ratification by four principal allied powers. According to Perassi opinion Italian Govt has alternative of delaying deposit of ratification until such deposit has been made by the four principal powers. Fransoni stated that the govt had not yet decided which of the above courses to follow nor did it intend to reach a decision until the general international situation with regard to the peace treaties had become a little clearer. He expressed his personal opinion that the govt would be subject to embarrassment internally should it appear hasty in taking

---

[1] Not printed.
[2] Tommaso Perassi, Deputy in the Italian Constituent Assembly (Republican) ; Professor of international law in the faculty of jurisprudence of the University of Rome ; legal adviser to the Ministry of Foreign Affairs.

the formal step of making its deposit of ratification at Paris at this time. Motive for such a move would have to be explained to Italian people and Constituent Assembly who would need to be given reason why govt did not take the second and more obvious alternative. It seems to us that in this delicate situation it would be wise to adhere to policy we have followed so far (Dept's 1137, July 15) of leaving to Italian Govt decision as to timing of its ratification, at least until United States, British and French ratifications are deposited. In our opinion the preoccupation expressed by Secretary General re unfavorable effect on Italian public opinion which immediate deposit would have is entirely justified.[3]

Repeated Moscow 147.

DUNN

---

[3] In telegram No. 1526, August 27, not printed, the Department instructed Ambassador Dunn that the decision regarding the deposit of Italian ratification should, for the time being at least, be left to the Italian Government. The message was repeated to Moscow as No. 1650. (740.0011 EW (Peace)/8-2347)

On August 28 Mr. Raymund T. Yingling, Assistant Legal Adviser for Military Affairs and Occupied Areas, prepared a memorandum, "Termination of Foreign War by the President", which read in part as follows:

"EUR has requested the opinion of this office on whether the war with Italy can be terminated by the President. Such action is contemplated in the event that the Soviet Government fails to ratify the Italian peace treaty within the near future. . . .

"Although the matter is not entirely free from doubt, it is the opinion of this Office that as there are no specific constitutional provisions concerning the termination of war the President, in view of his position as head of the State with plenary control of foreign relations and with power as Commander-in-Chief of the Army and Navy to make his decision effective can terminate a foreign war, at least in the absence of statutory provisions inconsistent with such action." (740.00119 EW/8-2847)

740.0011 EW (Peace)/8-2347 : Telegram

The Acting Representative in Rumania (Melbourne) to the Secretary of State

BUCHAREST, August 23, 1947.

761. Rumanian Communist Political Bureau on August 21 decided to request its parliamentary group to press for peace treaty ratification to take place August 23. Yesterday ratification bill consisting of single sentence "government is authorized to ratify and enforce peace treaty signed in Paris on February 10, 1947 between Rumania and allies and associate parties" was presented to Parliament by Foreign Minister Tatarescu [1] with authentic texts and translations of treaty annexed. Tatarescu stated immediate ratification needed so bilateral negotiations to improve some of treaty clauses may begin. This morn-

---

[1] Dr. Gheorghe Tatarescu, Vice President of the Rumanian Council of Ministers and Minister of Foreign Affairs.

ing, August 23, Parliament unanimously ratified treaty after speeches
by representatives of DPB parties.[2]

MELBOURNE

---

[2] *Bloc al Partidelor Democrate* (Bloc of Democratic Parties).

740.0011 EW (Peace)/8–2547 : Telegram

The Acting Representative in Bulgaria (*Horner*) to the Secretary of State

SOFIA, August 25, 1947.

741. Sobranje has just approved unanimously Cabinet decision ratify peace treaty. Foreign Minister Georgiev[1] who was first speaker extolled Soviet Union and said Bulgaria through UN would seek amelioration treaty conditions imposed as result US and UK pressure. Speakers for other parties including opposition then supported ratification. In conclusion provisional president Kolarov[2] reiterated Bulgaria's intention seeking redress for alleged injustices in treaty especially refusal recognize Bulgaria's cobelligerency, Bulgaria's demand for Greek Thrace and reparations clause.

HORNER

---

[1] Kimon Georgiev, Bulgarian Deputy Prime Minister and Minister of Foreign Affairs since November 1946.
[2] Vasil Petkov Kolarov, Acting President of Bulgaria since 1946.

740.0011 EW (Peace)/8–2647 : Telegram

The Ambassador in Yugoslavia (*Cannon*) to the Secretary of State

BELGRADE, August 26, 1947.

977. Tanjug officially announces ratification by praesidium of Peace Treaties with Italy, Bulgaria and Hungary.

CANNON

740.0011 EW (Peace)/8–2947 : Telegram

The Ambassador in the Soviet Union (*Smith*) to the Secretary of State

MOSCOW, August 29, 1947—11 a. m.

RESTRICTED
US URGENT

2732. There follows Embassy translation Soviet note dated August 28, signed Vyshinski received late last night:

"In connection with your letter of August 18, 1947,[1] I inform you that the government of the USSR has presented to the Presidium of

---

[1] *Ante,* p. 561.

the Supreme Soviet of the USSR for ratification the peace treaties with Italy, Rumania, Hungary and Bulgaria signed in Paris February 10, 1947.

The Soviet Government proceeding from the requirement for the deposit of the instruments of ratification by the Soviet Union, USA and France in Moscow and Paris, as provided for by the corresponding peace treaties, on one and the same day, proposes to deposit the instruments of ratification mentioned in the course of the next 10 to 15 days.

Concurrently with the present note similar notes are being sent to the Embassies of Great Britain and France."

Repeated London 314, Paris 315.

Department pass Rome 76, Sofia 13, Bucharest 13, Budapest 18.

SMITH

740.0011 EW (Peace)/8–2947 : Telegram

The Acting Secretary of State to the Embassy in the Soviet Union

RESTRICTED WASHINGTON, September 3, 1947—noon.
US URGENT

1676. In reply Soviet note Aug 28 (ur 2732 Aug 29) pls inform FonOff this Govt is prepared deposit instrument of ratification of Ital treaty at Paris on Sept 15 and of Bulg, Rum and Hung treaties at Moscow same date provided USSR, UK and French Govts agree simultaneous deposits. Reply shd not be addressed FonOff until your Brit and French colleagues have recd similar instructions. Embs London and Paris shd request UK and French FonOffs instruct their reps Moscow soonest possible if they concur with Dept.

Since Dept and UK FonOff have agreed give SACMED through CCS seven days advance notice of deposit ratifications Ital treaty in order permit final planning withdrawal Allied forces from Italy, Dept is informing JCS contemplated date for deposit is Sept 15. Brit Emb Wash has been requested to inform Brit Staff Mission Wash in similar sense so that necessary CCS directives can be issued SACMED. Shd you receive any indication Sept 15 date not acceptable to Soviet FonOff, pls inform Dept immediately.

Sent Moscow, rptd London 3812, Paris 3301, Rome 1576, Belgrade 579, Bucharest, 538, Budapest 940, and Sofia 341.

LOVETT

740.00119 Control (Italy)/9–447 : Telegram

The Consul General at Trieste (Joyce)[1] to the Secretary of State

SECRET TRIESTE, September 4, 1947—4 p. m.
PRIORITY

86. 1. The unexpected advent and apparent imminence of R–Day has naturally necessitated rapid revision of military plans based on

---

[1] Robert Prather Joyce, appointed Consul General at Trieste, July 1, 1947.

indefinite continuance present status. Quick decisions are being made and there is certain amount of understandable and probably inevitable confusion. I am proceeding Rome tomorrow September 5 for one-day conference G–5 at request senior civil affairs officer here.[2] I shall consult with Embassy and report high-lights from Rome.

2. Have had highly satisfactory meetings with Airey[3] and Carnes and am seeing Moore[4] Monday.

3. American senior military feels Department could and should stall deposit ratification at least until about end September to allow more time implement removal plans. My reply in matters of high policy involving international commitments and our overall interests will naturally govern but feel sure Army problems here being given due consideration by Washington. Would appreciate message on our R–Day policy which I could show General Moore who apparently feels he being left out in cold and not sufficiently advised on broad policy decisions.

Sent Department; Belgrade No. 64; USPolAd Leghorn No. 8.

JOYCE

---

[2] Col. James Jewett Carnes, AUS, Senior Civil Affairs Officer, Allied Military Government Trieste, June 22–October 28, 1947.

[3] Maj. Gen. Terence Sydney Airey, in command of British forces in the Free Territory of Trieste. In March Gen. Lee had announced that the British troops in the FTT would be under command of Gen. Airey, and that no unified command of the national contingents was contemplated.

[4] Maj. Gen. Bryant E. Moore, Commanding General, U.S. Forces, Trieste.

740.0011 EW (Peace)/9–1047 : Telegram

The Ambassador in the Soviet Union (Smith) to the Secretary of State

RESTRICTED   Moscow, September 10, 1947—1 a. m.
URGENT   NIACT   [Received September 9—8 : 02 p. m.]

2812. ReDeptel 1698 September 8.[1] Called yesterday on Acting Foreign Minister Malik.[2]

FonOff called at 0015 today stating Soviet Government agrees exchange ratifications September 15.

---

[1] Not printed; in it the Department notified the Embassy in Moscow that no reply had as yet been received from the Soviets regarding the proposal for the deposit of ratifications on September 15. It was explained that in view of the necessity for providing the Allied military authorities in Italy with the maximum advance notice of the effective date of the treaty, the British had proposed that a new approach to the Soviet Foreign Office be made by the British, French, or American Ambassador at Moscow after consultation among the three. The Department agreed to the proposal. (740.0011 EW (Peace)/9–847)

[2] Yakov Alexandrovich Malik, Deputy Minister for Foreign Affairs of the Soviet Union.

Department please repeat urgently Rome as 80, London as 320, Paris as 327, Bucharest as 16, Sofia as 16, Budapest as 19 and Leghorn and Trieste as unnumbered.

SMITH

740.0011 EW (Peace)/9–1047 : Telegram

The Secretary of State to the Embassy in France

RESTRICTED WASHINGTON, September 10, 1947—6 p. m.
US URGENT NIACT

3417. Pls confirm immediately report that Yugo deposited ratification Ital treaty Sept 4.[1]

MARSHALL

---

[1] In telegram No. 3692, September 11, from Paris, not printed, Ambassador Caffery reported that the French Foreign Office confirmed that Yugoslavia had deposited its ratification of the peace treaty with Italy on September 4 at 4 : 30 p. m. (740.0011 EW (Peace)/9–1147).

740.0011 EW (Peace)/9–1547 : Telegram

The Ambassador in France (Caffery) to the Secretary of State

RESTRICTED PARIS, September 15, 1947—1 p. m.
US URGENT

3761. Instruments of ratification Italian Treaty were deposited at FonOff this morning at 11 a. m. Paris time by France, UK, US and USSR and *procès-verbal* given in my 3740, September 13 was signed.[1]

Italy and then India will deposit ratifications later this morning and Canada this afternoon.

Sent Dept 3761 ; repeated Rome 233 ; Moscow 485.

CAFFERY

---

[1] The Treaty of Peace with Italy was proclaimed by the President of the United States on September 15, 1947, and entered into force the same day ; TIAS No. 1648, or 61 Stat. (pt. 2) 1245. The *procès-verbal* given in telegram 3740, not printed, related to the deposit of ratifications.

740.0011 EW (Peace)/9–1547 : Telegram

The Ambassador in the Soviet Union (Smith) to the Secretary of State

RESTRICTED Moscow, September 15, 1947—7 p. m.
URGENT NIACT

2844. Instruments of ratification Balkan (and Finnish) treaties deposited and respective protocols of deposit signed by Molotov, British Chargé Roberts [1] and myself at 1800 hours today.[2] At ceremony Molotov stated that instruments of defeated signatories were to be deposited 2000 hours this evening. Will confirm tomorrow and report if any other signatories deposit tonight.[3]

Dept please pass Berlin 526; London 324; Paris 333; Sofia 18; Budapest 21; Bucharest 18, Helsinki 24.

SMITH

---

[1] Frank Kenyon Roberts.

[2] The Treaties of Peace with Romania, Bulgaria, and Hungary were proclaimed by the President of the United States on September 15, 1947, and entered into force the same day; TIAS Nos. 1649, 1650, and 1651, or 61 Stat. (pt. 2) 1757, 1915, and 2065. The United States was not a party to the Treaty of Peace with Finland.

[3] Telegram No. 2849, September 16, from Moscow, not printed, reported that the Soviet press of that date carried a Tass statement mentioning that the defeated powers, Romania, Bulgaria, Hungary, and Finland, had deposited instruments of ratification the day before (740.0011 EW (Peace)/9–1647).

Despatch No. 1639, September 20, from Moscow, not printed, reported the receipt of formal notification by the Ministry of Foreign Affairs of the Soviet Union, dated September 18, of receipt of the instruments of ratification from Bulgaria, Hungary and Romania (740.0011 EW (Peace)/9–1647).

THE UNITED STATES PARTICIPATION IN DISCUSSIONS ON DISPOSITION OF THE FORMER ITALIAN COLONIES IN AFRICA

Editorial Note

According to Article 23 and Annex XI of the Treaty of Peace with Italy, signed in Paris on February 10, 1947 (Department of State Treaties and Other International Acts Series (TIAS) No. 1648), the United States, the United Kingdom, the Soviet Union, and France agreed that they would, within one year from the coming into force of the Treaty, jointly determine the final disposition of Italy's former territorial possessions in Africa. The Deputies of the Council of Foreign Ministers were to consider the question of the disposition of the former Italian colonies and to report their recommendations on the matter to the Council. In order to obtain factual information upon which to base their recommendations, the Deputies were to send to the former colonies commissions of investigation to examine conditions in the colonies and to determine the views of the local inhabitants. The documents that follow in this compilation relate to the convening of the meetings of the Deputies for the Former Italian Colonies, the establishment of the Commissions of Investigation, and the views of other interested governments and authorities on the procedure and nature of the final disposition of the territories.

For the documentation on the negotiation of the Treaty of Peace with Italy by the Council of Foreign Ministers at Paris, April–July 1946, and at New York, November–December 1946, as well as at the Paris Peace Conference, August–October 1946, see *Foreign Relations*, 1946, volumes II, III, and IV. For documentation on the signing, ratification, and deposit of ratification of the Treaty, see *ante*, pages 515 ff.

865.014/2–447

Memorandum by the Director of the Office of Near Eastern and African Affairs (Henderson) to the Counselor of the Department of State (Cohen) [1]

[WASHINGTON,] February 4, 1947.

The Italian Prime Minister, during his recent visit to this country,[2]

---

[1] The source text bears the handwritten marginal endorsement "I concur B. V. Cohen".

[2] Italian Prime Minister Alcide de Gasperi visited Washington during January 1947 ; for documentation regarding the visit, see pp. 835 ff.

left with the Department the attached undated, unheaded and un-signed document on the Italian colonial question.[3]

It will be noted that the Italians have requested participation in the commissions of investigation to be sent to the colonies in accordance with Annex XI of the Italian Treaty. Recent telegrams from Paris and London indicate that the Italians have also approached the French and British Governments with the same request. The French are re-ported to be favorable to the request, but the British are said to have informally told the Italians that they foresaw difficulties in any sup-port for the Italian request, which would raise the question of repre-sentatives of other interested states accompanying the commissions.

We feel that we could not support the Italian request without grant-ing similar privileges to all of the other interested parties. These would certainly include Ethiopia and Egypt and perhaps others, in-cluding the Arab League. (The British also mentioned Australia, South Africa and India.) Commissions of this size would be cumber-some and their work almost certainly hampered by the necessity of considering the claims and counterclaims of the representatives of the interested parties. The clear intent of Annex XI is to provide for im-partial, fact finding commissions and the assignment of representatives (or even observers) of Italy, Ethiopia, Egypt, etc. would almost cer-tainly not contribute to this end.

It is our suggestion, if you concur, that the Italians be advised in-formally that we consider that the second paragraph of Article XI contains ample assurance that their views (and those of other in-terested powers) concerning the final disposal of the colonies will be given full consideration by the Four Powers, without the necessity of Italian (or other) representatives accompanying the commissions of investigation.

Loy W. Henderson

---

[3] Not printed.

865.014/1–1147 : Telegram

The Secretary of State to the Embassy in Italy

SECRET   WASHINGTON, March 1, 1947—1 p. m.

297. Rome's 420 Feb 26; Paris' 131 Jan 11 and 820 Feb 22; and London's 438 Jan 21.[1] Dept does not deem it desirable for Italian

---

[1] None of the telegrams under reference here is printed; they dealt with the Italian Government's request that an Italian expert be authorized to go to Libya, Eritrea, and Somaliland and be heard by the Commission of Investigation to be sent to the former colonies. (865.014/1–1147, 2–2247, and 2–2647) A similar re-quest was made by the Counselor of the Italian Embassy, Mario di Stefano, in a letter of February 18, 1947, to Loy W. Henderson, not printed (865.014/2–1847).

representative, observer or expert to accompany Quadripartite Commission of Investigation to be sent to Italian Colonies. However in view importance reconciling Italian Govt and Italian public opinion to any decision on ultimate disposition Colonies, we favor arrangement whereby Italians would be given opportunity consult with Commission, provided similar opportunity given such other interested states as Egypt and Ethiopia which also have immediate interest in problem.

During visit Dept Feb 28, Italian Amb raised with Secy question Italy presenting testimony to Commission. Amb was informed this Govt felt Italy should be afforded opportunity to present Commission with factual evidence considered essential to impartial study Italian claims. Manner and place of presentation not discussed. It was emphasized that any final answer regarding proposed procedure must be made by Deputies who must also extend any invitation to Italian Govt for consultation with Commission.[2]

Sent Rome as 297; Repeated London as 984, Paris as 807, Moscow as 351, Cairo as 284, and Addis Ababa as 26.

MARSHALL

---

[2] The Secretary of State's memorandum of this conversation with Ambassador Alberto Tarchiani, dated February 28, 1947, is not printed (711.65/2–2847). The substance of the views set forth in this paragraph were also transmitted by Loy W. Henderson in a letter to Italian Embassy Counselor di Stefano, dated March 7, 1947, not printed (865.014/2–1847).

865.014/2–1947 : Telegram

The Acting Secretary of State to the Embassy in the United Kingdom

SECRET   WASHINGTON, March 5, 1947—3 p. m.

1041. Urtels 857 Feb 7, 1131 Feb 19, 1370 Feb 28, and 1434 Mar 4.[1] During informal conversation on Feb 15, British Embassy official was informed that Dept inclined to accept London as most suitable place for meetings of Deputies on Italian Colonial question. On further study, however, we thought Geneva might have following advantages: (1) neutral location would obviate criticism which might otherwise result from consideration this question in capital of occupying power; (2) Geneva is centrally located and on direct air route Cairo; and (3) if French or Soviets should object to London, Geneva would appear acceptable compromise.

On Feb 28, British Embassy informed us it had received instructions to transmit note to this Govt suggesting Deputies meeting take place London. Emb also stated FonOff had sent similar instructions Brit Embs Paris and Moscow. We requested Emb ask FonOff to with-

---

[1] None printed.

hold delivery of notes to three powers until we had opportunity to give matter further consideration in view possibility Dept might prefer Geneva.

On Mar 4, we called Brit Emb official into Dept. After acquainting him with our reasons for preferring Geneva as set forth above, we informed him that we would not oppose London as meeting place if British have strong objection to Geneva.

We also discussed following related questions:

(1) As soon as Brit have obtained agreement all four interested powers regarding headquarters Deputies, Dept will immediately take step designate Deputy and Commissioner and hopes other powers will do likewise. Dept considers first meeting Deputies should take place earliest convenient date thereafter in order formulate terms of reference for Commission of Investigation.

(2) Dept agrees with British viewpoint regarding advantages one Commission over two or more. It also agrees with desirability restricting size and duration Commission, but doubts that latter's work can be accomplished in less than six or eight months. In view comparatively short time which would remain for Deputies to agree on recommendation and for Foreign Ministers to arrive at final decision, Dept feels Deputies should be prepared to meet at stated times while Commission is in field. This procedure would give Deputies more time to hear views of other interested states, receive and consider reports of Commission as completed for each territory and discuss other factors entering into final recommendation.

(3) Dept is also anxious ascertain what informal approaches, if any, British have made to French and Soviets regarding meeting place of Deputies and any indications reactions those powers.

Please discuss foregoing with Jebb [2] FonOff and telegraph results.

Sent London as 1041; repeated Paris as 850; Moscow as 385; Rome as 316; Cairo as 299; and Addis Ababa as 29.

ACHESON

---

[2] Hubert Miles Gladwyn Jebb, Assistant Under-Secretary of State in the British Foreign Office; Superintending Under-Secretary, United Nations Department.

740.0011 EW Peace/3–747

The British Embassy to the Department of State [1]

MEMORANDUM

His Majesty's Government in the United Kingdom consider that the Four Powers concerned should now take action to put into effect the

---

[1] Delivered to the Department of State on March 8, 1947.

provisions of the Italian Peace Treaty with regard to the disposal of the ex-Italian Colonies.

2. Under these provisions the Council of Foreign Ministers are to determine the final disposal of the Italian Colonies within one year of the coming into force of the Treaty and their Deputies are to continue consideration of the question, sending out Commissions of Investigation to any of the Colonies to obtain the necessary data and views of the local population.

3. The Council of Foreign Ministers agreed in New York that the Four Powers should nominate their representatives on the Commissions by the date of signature of the Treaty. His Majesty's Government in the United Kingdom have selected Mr. F. E. Stafford [2] as their Commissioner for any territories visited, and would be glad to learn the name of the Commissioner selected by the Government of the United States.

4. His Majesty's Government in the United Kingdom consider that the Deputies of the Four Powers should meet at an early date to draw up the terms of reference of the Commissioners and to decide on the future programme generally. It would also no doubt be desirable for the Deputies to make arrangements for the hearings (after the Italian Treaty has come into force) of the other interested governments in accordance with Annex XI of the Treaty.

5. His Majesty's Government in the United Kingdom consider that in order not to add this question to the Moscow Agenda,[3] where German and Austrian Affairs must have priority, it would be desirable for special Deputies to be appointed. They suggest that these Deputies should meet in London, in view of the fact that, with the exception of a part of Libya under French Military Administration, all the former Italian possessions in Africa are under British Administration, and the information required will be more readily available in London than elsewhere.

6. It will be appreciated that several months will be required to obtain the essential data of the nature indicated in the Treaty Annex on which the Deputies will base their recommendations to the Council of Foreign Ministers, and that it is therefore desirable that the preliminary meeting to set up the Commissions of Investigation should not be delayed.

---

[2] Brig. F. E. Stafford, Egyptian Department, British Foreign Office.
[3] Reference to the agenda for the Fourth Session of the Council of Foreign Ministers, Moscow, March 10–April 24, 1947. For documentation regarding this Council session, see vol. II, Chapter II, pp. 139 ff.

7. His Majesty's Government in the United Kingdom will be glad to learn as soon as possible if the above suggestions are acceptable to the Government of the United States and if the latter could send a Special Deputy to London for discussions in the last week of March. His Majesty's Government in the United Kingdom would also be grateful to learn the name of the Special Deputy appointed. They are for their part appointing Mr. Gladwyn Jebb.

8. A communication in the foregoing terms has also been addressed to the French and Soviet Governments.

WASHINGTON, March 7th, 1947.

865.014/3–647 : Telegram

The Acting Secretary of State to the Embassy in Italy [1]

SECRET   WASHINGTON, March 11, 1947—6 p. m.

335. Only point regarding Italian Colonies on which Secretary gave Tarchiani assurances during conversation of Feb 28 was in connection Italian request representation Quadripartite Commission of Investigation. Secretary stated we favored arrangement whereby Italians would be given opportunity consult with commission, as reported Deptel 297 Mar 1.

Secretary stated further that he was not familiar with various proposals for disposition of colonies but hoped to find time to study them. No assurances, however, were given we would support Italian trusteeship over Italian Colonies, as reported in Rome press (Embtel 457 Mar 4 [2]). In view this fact, Dept not only concerned about leak reported urtel 489 Mar 6,[2] but also with fact that alleged assurances regarding US support Italian trusteeship unfounded in fact.

In your discretion, you may draw this matter informally to attention Foreign Office and suggest that it take steps to correct false impression created in order to avoid raising false hopes Italian people.

ACHESON

---

[1] The substance of this telegram was sent in telegrams 42 to Addis Ababa, 441 to Cairo, 404 to Rome, 1281 to London, 1062 to Paris, and 621 to Moscow, March 22, none printed (865.014/3–1947).

Telegram 412, March 22, to Cairo, not printed, stated that the Department had received a joint telegram from three Tripolitanian political parties (El Kutla, El Watania, and El Horpa) protesting the alleged United States support for an Italian trusteeship over the Italian colonies. Embassy Cairo was instructed to be guided by telegram 411 in taking the necessary steps to correct erroneous reports in the press (865.014/3–1947).

[2] Not printed.

865.014/3–647 : Telegram

The Acting Secretary of State to the Embassy in the United Kingdom

SECRET WASHINGTON, March 18, 1947—11 a. m.

1206. Urtel 1493 Mar 6.[1] Dept has today answered[2] Brit Emb memo dated Mar 7 containing suggestions for putting into effect provisions Italian Peace Treaty re disposal Italian Colonies.

Dept agreeable to preliminary meeting Deputies in London earliest feasible date to draw up terms of reference Commission of Investigation and formulate future program Deputies.

Ambassador Douglas[3] will be appointed Deputy if Soviets and French also agree to London as meeting place. John Utter[4] appointed Commissioner.

Dept would appreciate learning nature Soviet and French replies to Brit note.

Sent London as 1206; Rptd Paris as 1002; Moscow as 551; Rome as 370; Cairo as 371; Addis Ababa as 38.

ACHESON

---

[1] Not printed; it replied to telegram 1041, March 5, to London, p. 571, substantially the same as the British Embassy memorandum of March 7.
[2] Department of State memorandum to the British Embassy, March 18, 1947, not printed (740.0011 EW Peace/3–747).
[3] Lewis W. Douglas, Ambassador in the United Kingdom.
[4] Officer in the Division of African Affairs.

865.014/4–347 : Telegram

The Ambassador in the United Kingdom (Douglas) to the Secretary of State [1]

SECRET LONDON, April 3, 1947—7 p. m.

2069. We are informed by Jebb that Foreign Office is still without reply from Moscow to suggestion deputies to consider Italian colonies meet London.[2] British pressing further Moscow for reply.

Incidentally, in strictest confidence, he said he was meeting Commonwealth High Commissioners today to lecture them on problems involved in disposition Italian colonies. Evatt[3] was continuing to be disagreeable and insisting that Australia be represented on commis-

---

[1] The Secretary of State was at this time in Moscow for the Fourth Session of the Council of Foreign Ministers, March 10–April 24, 1947.
[2] The French Government had earlier agreed to the British proposal for a preliminary meeting of the Deputies in London.
[3] Herbert V. Evatt, Australian Minister for External Affairs and Attorney General.

sion. Evatt also resented what he termed the indignity to which Australia would be subjected in submitting its views to deputies, insisting Australia's views should be presented to Foreign Ministers.

British continue to resist this pressure for membership on commission but are taking the position that if he wishes to defer presenting Australia's views until Italian colonial question is reviewed by CFM, possibly a year hence, British have no objection. Jebb has previously indicated his belief that solution of Italian colonial problem will involve harmonizing multifarious conflicting political desires and conference with Commonwealth High Commissioners may represent active measures by British to obtain prior Commonwealth support for British desiderata.

Sent Dept 2069; repeated Moscow 166; repeated Paris 247; repeated Rome 46.

DOUGLAS

865C.01/4–447 : Telegram

The Ambassador in Egypt (Tuck) to the Secretary of State

CONFIDENTIAL   CAIRO, April 4, 1947—noon.

414. As foreshadowed in mytel 368, March 26,[1] Secretary General of Arab League [2] handed me today a note relative to Libya with request it be forwarded Dept.[3] Note declares that since it is expected Four-Power Delegation may be sent to ascertain wishes of Libyan people on future status, Secretary General wishes remind me he had informed Foreign Ministers of four great powers by identical cable June 11, 1946 that "the League being in virtue of its pact directly concerned with rights and future status of this Arab country and by dint of plenary powers expressly vested in them by Libyan people are positively interested in any decision concerning Libya and in particular in every inquiry to determine future status of that country-and should consequently be represented on any delegation or commission of inquiry in event of such a procedure being adopted." [4]

Note states Sixth Session League Council [5] confirmed Bloudan decision and that "Secretary General cannot help emphasizing in this connection the importance League attach to such a procedure particularly as it corresponds completely with declarations made by Arabs

---

[1] Not printed.
[2] Abdul Rahman Azzam Pasha.
[3] The text of the note under reference, dated March 31, 1947, was transmitted to the Department as an enclosure to despatch 2404, April 5, 1947, from Cairo, neither printed (865C.01/4–547).
[4] The decision quoted here was taken by the Arab League Council at an extraordinary session held in Bloudan, Syria, in June 1946.
[5] The Arab League Council was in session in Cairo at this time.

of Tripolitania and Cyrenaica that they shall disregard any commission of inquiry on which League is not represented".

Full text by pouch, repeated London as 27.

TUCK

865.014/4–347 : Telegram

The Acting Secretary of State to the Embassy in the United Kingdom

SECRET WASHINGTON, April 22, 1947—8 p. m.

1762. Urtel 2069, Apr 3. *Aide-mémoire* of April 10 from Australian Embassy [1] sets forth Australia's desire to participate actively in disposal Italian Colonies. Specific requests made for Australia to (1) discuss with Deputies terms of reference and composition Commission of Investigation (2) participate in actual work Commission as member (3) receive Commission's report in sufficient time to express its views. Furthermore, Australia sought inclusion all interested Govts on Commission, and hearing for Australia before CFM.

Dept has informed Emb it favors affording all interested Govts, including Australia, every opportunity present views to Deputies, and, in appropriate instances, would not object to hearings before CFM. Dept stated, however, that it considers such Govts, with perhaps exception those having direct territorial claims, should deal directly with Deputies rather than Commission on all points raised. Dept opposed participation other interested Govts in work of Commission and pointed out that this body was intended to be quadripartite and would be unworkable if other Govts included. It would not object to Deputies receiving suggestions concerning terms of reference and composition conference from nor oppose furnishing Commission's reports to other interested Govts.

Emb was assured this Govt favored giving every proper consideration to views Australian Govt on final disposal Italian Colonies.[2]

ACHESON

---

[1] Not printed.

[2] The views of the United States described here were conveyed to Australian Minister Alfred Sterling by Acting Secretary Acheson during a conversation on April 10 and in a Department of State *aide-mémoire* to the Australian Embassy, dated April 21, 1947, not printed (740.00119 Council/4–1047).

865C.01/5–347

Memorandum of Conversation, by Mr. John E. Utter of the Division of African Affairs

CONFIDENTIAL [WASHINGTON,] May 3, 1947.

While in New York on a week-end visit, I had an opportunity to renew friendly relations with Azzam Pasha, Secretary General of the

Arab League, at present in that City for the United Nations Assembly session on Palestine,[1] when I called at his apartment at the Essex House late on Saturday [2] afternoon.

As I entered, Azzam was listening to the speech of Mr. Gromyko [3] before the United Nations Assembly defending the hearing of the Jewish Agency before that body. At the end, Azzam remarked that the Soviets were trying to back two horses. He commented with approval on Mr. Austin's [4] previous declaration on the subject and went on to expatiate on the Anti-Communist position of Egypt. According to him, the Egyptian Government wishes no truckling with Communism and rather fancies itself as the bulwark in the Middle East against Soviet expansion. Azzam hoped that an early solution to the Anglo-Egyptian problem would be found and when the question was placed before the United Nations, that the United States would play the role of mediator between the United Kingdom and Egypt. He again repeated to me his desire to see relations between these two countries on a friendly and equal basis and an alliance formed which would also include the United States. Azzam has on previous occasions, talked of a Middle East regional group of Arab states under the United Nations which would include Great Britain because of its extensive interests in that area.

Libya

PARTICIPATION IN COMMISSION OF INVESTIGATION

I then brought up the question of the Italian Colonies and Libya in particular, by referring to the note of March 31, 1947 presented by the Secretary General of the League of Arab States to the United States Ambassador in Cairo.[5] This note referred to the extraordinary session of the League at Bloudan and to identical cables addressed on June 11, 1946 to each of the Foreign Ministers of the four Big Powers stating the League's concern with the rights and future status of Libya, and referring to "plenary powers expressly vested in them (the Arab League) by the Libyan people". Participation in the Commission of Investigation to be sent to that territory by the Deputies of the Foreign Ministers was requested. The note even went so far as to cite a declaration of the Arabs of Tripolitania and Cyrenaica "that they shall disregard any commission of inquiry on which the League is not represented".

---

[1] For documentation on the interest of the United States in the Palestine question in 1947, see vol. v, p. 999 ff.

[2] May 1, 1947.

[3] Andrey Andreyevich Gromyko, Soviet Representative to the United Nations General Assembly.

[4] Warren R. Austin, United States Representative to the United Nations.

[5] See telegram 414, April 4, from Cairo, p. 576.

Azzam did not make quite clear on what basis "plenary powers" were vested in the League by the Libyan people, although I gathered that this originated from the request of supposedly representative leaders of the territory. My main concern was to let Azzam know in an informal and friendly way that we could not favor Arab League participation in the Commission of Investigation. I cited the position that this Government had taken when approached by Italy with a similar request, namely that we would support a procedure whereby governments having direct territorial claims, such as Italy, Egypt and Ethiopia, could present their views and data before the Commission as well as before the Deputies, but would oppose such governments taking an active part in the Commission. As for political groups in Libya disregarding any commission on which the Arab League is not represented, I chided Azzam on such a dog in the manger attitude. The Libyans themselves would be the only losers if they failed to cooperate. He agreed, and said that these people were prompted by the fear that they would not be able to express themselves openly without incurring reprisals from the local governments. Unless there were someone on the Commission who could defend their interests before the world, in case they were coerced either during or subsequent to the visit of the Commission, they might be reluctant to state their views and wishes frankly. I assured Azzam that the vigilant presence of the Arab League should not be necessary. In the first place the British Military Administration was not a Fascist government, ready to pounce on any individual who might express an idea contrary to the Administration's views. Secondly it was my understanding that the representatives of the Four Powers should hear the views of the inhabitants jointly and coercion of any sort would scarcely be tolerated. Publicity would certainly be given to any such coercion if known or reported.

When Azzam inquired whether a representative of the Arab League would be heard by the Deputies, I informed him that this could be done only with the consent of the four Deputies, and it seemed to me doubtful that this could be obtained. The Arab League was not a recognized government, but could as an alternative have one of its member states, an "interested government" act as its spokesman. In that case, Azzam remarked that he could be named by the Egyptian Government as its representative. Due to his knowledge of Libya and close contact with the territory over the last thirty odd years, he considers that he is the most competent Arab to present the Arab point of view with respect to Libya.

FUTURE OF LIBYA

While admitting the unrealistic thesis of immediate independence for Libya, Azzam none the less starts from this point, not only because it is the watchword of the Arab League, but also because the inhabitants of Libya themselves have proclaimed their wish to be free. Next to independence he believes that the Libyans would favor being attached to Egypt. Azzam proceeded to discourse at length on the political, ethnical, religious and economic ties between Egypt and Libya. He stated that there are some six hundred thousand people of Libyan origin who have settled in Egypt over the last 150 years, and the figure could go as high as two million if the migrations of several centuries were taken into account. These people are still closely linked to the tribes in Cyrenaica and Tripolitania. Egypt is a natural market for the cattle, wool, and oil produced in Libya, and it has been customary from time immemorial for the Libyans to drive their herds to the markets in Egypt. I told Azzam that we would be very glad to receive full and authoritative data on the subject of inter-relationship of tribes in Libya and Egypt, and he promised to substantiate his arguments by furnishing facts and figures.

The third possibility for the future of Libya acceptable to the local population might be a United Nations Trusteeship, thoroughly international in character. It should, to be popular, include technicians from Arab states. Egypt, Lebanon and others would be in a position to furnish teachers, doctors, etc.

Finally, Azzam asked if the United States would not be willing to take over the trusteeship. Might this not be a furtherance of the present policy of the United States in the Mediterranean? Azzam said that the Arabs would welcome the United States for they would know that the latter would have the money, specialists and ability to develop the country toward self-sufficiency and the people to self-government. While admitting what he said, I expressed my doubts as to any support of such a proposition in this country.

DIVISION OF LIBYA

Azzam Pasha believes that Libya should not be divided. It might well be a federation and separated into two administrative units, with Cyrenaica under Sayid Idris as Amir, and Tripolitania under its own leaders. Azzam declared himself to be in agreement with Sayid Idris despite reports to the contrary from British sources. Here again, however, the link with Egypt was brought up. Azzam feels that Sayid Idris as well as all of the Senussi confraternity would prefer being under a Moslem rather than under a Christian crown (the British). Under such an arrangement, Azzam still feels that Great Britain could obtain bases in Cyrenaica.

POLITICAL PARTIES

In Tripoli there has been a considerable evolution in the political picture. As I suspected, the solidarity fostered in May 1946 (Discussion of Council of Foreign Ministers) by the danger of that country's being returned to Italian rule has faded. No longer does the United Tripolitanian Front act in unison. Azzam explained that now the factions had broken up into Watania, Kubla, Tripolitanian-Egyptian Union, etc. To realize some sort of unity in the face of the coming investigation of the wishes of the inhabitants, Azzam told me that he had formed a Committee for the Liberation of Libya, representative of all political elements in Libya. As reports from Cairo from British sources have indicated that this Committee was neither representative nor composed of men of political stature, I inquired who were in this group. The following among others were named by Azzam:

Mahmud Bey Muntasser, wealthy land owner, wielding great political influence over untutored Arabs in large areas.
Taher Bey el Morayed, merchant, educated in French Lycée in Cairo.
Ali Regeb, Sheik.
Bechir Saadowi, Tripolitanian Minister to Ibn Saud.
Garagni, also with Ibn Saud.

These are important men but, of course, may be only the cream of the Committee of Liberation. Through this group Azzam hopes to influence the thinking of the Libyans and their answers to the Commission of Investigation. He declares that his only concern is for the future welfare of the Libyan people and would appreciate advice of any kind from us which could help them.

DISCUSSIONS BETWEEN ITALIAN GOVERNMENT AND ARAB LEAGUE

To my surprise, Azzam informed me that exploratory conversations on Libya had been held between an emissary of Nenni,[6] when he was Italian Minister of Foreign Affairs, and himself. According to him, the Italian Government was prepared to relinquish any political claim over Libya, provided that Italian nationals residing in that territory were given equal rights and allowed to participate in the administration. The Arab League's attitude is entirely sympathetic to the principle, and took the position that such Italians could and should become Tripolitanian citizens, just as they adopt the nationality of other states in which they settle. The small Italian farmers in Libya were already appreciated and were closely akin to the Arabs. Azzam believes that the Italians are eager to resume friendly relations with the Arab states and was hopeful that something might be worked out with Sforza,[7] who, he states, is following the same policy as Nenni in this matter. I pointed out that if the Italians through some understanding with the Arabs were willing to renounce political aspirations in Libya in any

---

[6] Pietro Nenni, Italian Foreign Minister, October 1946–February 1947.
[7] Count Carlo Sforza, Italian Foreign Minister from February 1947.

form whatsoever, the French might automatically be faced with the necessity of withdrawing their proposal to place this territory under Italian trusteeship.

ERITREA

When asked whether the Arab League was interesting itself in the fate of Eritrea, Azzam admitted interest though lukewarm in comparison to that shown in Libya. He knew of the formation of the Moslem League in Asmara and said that the Arab League had received petitions for support from this group. Azzam was most vehement in criticizing Ethiopian Government administration, and expressed the hope that guarantees would be demanded from Ethiopia if any part of Eritrea were given to that state. He even went so far as to say that the Eritreans would probably be better off under the Italians than subjected to the reactionary and benighted rule of Addis Ababa. Azzam did, however, feel that Ethiopia should be given an outlet to the sea.

Azzam mentioned the pleasant and interesting talk he had had with Mr. Loy Henderson, and said that he was planning to come to Washington after the present session of the United Nations Assembly. He looked forward to meeting officers in the State Department and to becoming acquainted with the capital of the United States. He also remarked when I was about to leave that he would like to discuss the French North African situation with me, and assured me that he had been counseling patience to the Arabs there as the time was not yet ripe for action and open rebellion could only be deplored and would certainly end in failure and oppression for the North African Arabs. The Arab League, he said, had communicated with the French Government regarding the North African countries under French administration but as yet had received no reply.

Editorial Note

In a statement released to the press on May 29, 1947, the Department of State announced that it had been informed that the Soviet Government had agreed to the British proposal for a meeting of the Deputies of the Council of Foreign Ministers in London to consider the disposition of the Italian colonies. The Department's statement further explained that it was the view of the United States Government that the Deputies should not discuss the actual disposition of the Italian colonies at this preliminary session, but should confine themselves to such procedural matters as the establishment of the Commission of Investigation. For the text of the Department's statement, see Department of State *Bulletin*, June 8, 1947, page 1129.

The British Government proposed and the United States and French Governments had agreed that the first meeting of the Deputies for the Former Italian Colonies should be held in London on June 6, 1947. The Secretary of State designated Ambassador Lewis W. Douglas as his Deputy at these meetings and named John E. Utter, Division of African Affairs, and Foreign Service Officer Philip H. Bagby as advisers to the Ambassador in the forthcoming negotiations. On June 2, the Soviet Government informed the British that it was not prepared to participate in meetings of the Deputies until the coming into force of the Peace Treaty with Italy. Despite the Soviet attitude, Utter and Bagby proceeded to London to carry on consultations preparatory to the meetings of the Deputies.

865.014/5-2947

Memorandum by the Assistant Secretary of State for Occupied Areas (Hilldring) to the State-War-Navy Coordinating Committee

SECRET [WASHINGTON,] May 29, 1947.

Subject: Request of Views of Joint Chiefs of Staff on the Disposition of the Italian Colonies.

According to Article 23 of the Peace Treaty with Italy, the final disposal of the Italian territorial possessions in Africa, i.e. Libya, Eritrea and Italian Somaliland shall be determined jointly by the Governments of the Soviet Union, of the United Kingdom, of the United States of America, and of France within one year from the coming into force of the present treaty. Under the terms of Annex XI of the treaty, a Commission of Investigation, composed of representatives of the four powers mentioned above, is to be sent to the Italian Colonies for the purpose of consulting the wishes of the local inhabitants and of supplying the Deputies with the data necessary to enable the Foreign Ministers to arrive at a decision regarding the future disposition of these areas. In making their recommendations to the Foreign Ministers, the Deputies will take into consideration not only the wishes and welfare of the inhabitants but also the interests of peace and security, as well as the views of other interested governments.

The Deputies may soon resume the consideration of the question, and it is therefore imperative that the United States formulate a general policy which may guide its Deputy during the period of negotiation.

Briefly, the United States Government has advocated trusteeship with the United Nations as the administering authority for these territories, and independence to be granted to Libya and Eritrea at the end of ten years. At the present time, however, the Department is contemplating modification of the ten-year provision for Libya, so as to allow for a longer period of trusteeship, if deemed desirable, as a result of the Commission's findings. Alternative plans for the disposition of Eritrea are also being discussed as there is increasing doubt that this territory can become a viable state within the foreseeable future. This government has also favored a territorial cession of southeastern Eritrea giving Ethiopia access to the sea through Assab.

Although the Department is not informed of the present position, France has not previously wavered in its proposal to place the Italian Colonies under Italian Trusteeship. France has opposed any suggestion that the Colonies be granted independence, even after a period of trusteeship.

On April 29, 1946 the Soviet Union abandoned its demand for an individual trusteeship over Tripolitania, and in May 1946 supported the French proposal. At the present time the views of the U.S.S.R. on the subject of the Colonies are unknown.

While Great Britain has been sympathetic to International Trustee ship, it has not concealed its concern over the future of Cyrenaica Reference has frequently been made by the British to their pledge to the Senussi, that these Cyrenaicans would never again be placed under Italian rule. Great Britain has also indicated an interest in Cyrenaica from a strategic point of view. It is likewise obvious that the disposition of Italian Somaliland is of great concern to the United Kingdom in view of that territory's contiguity to the British East African possessions, which may play an important role in future military plans of the United Kingdom, once the British Army has evacuated Egypt. The British have indicated their sympathy for Ethiopian aspirations in Eritrea.

This memorandum is submitted for the purpose of ascertaining the views of the Joint Chiefs of Staff on the Military implications involved in the disposal of the Italian Colonies, with particular reference to the British requirements for bases in Cyrenaica and perhaps in Italian Somaliland.

JOHN H. HILLDRIN

CFM Files : Lot M–88 : Box 111 : IC Files

Position Paper Prepared in the Department of State [1]

CONFIDENTIAL   [WASHINGTON,] June 2, 1947.

U.S. POSITION ON PROCEDURAL MATTERS AT THE FORTHCOMING MEETING OF SPECIAL DEPUTIES ON DISPOSAL OF ITALIAN COLONIES

THE PROBLEM

The problem is to determine the position which the United States should take in the meeting of the Deputies to be held shortly in London for planning the study of the disposition of the Italian Colonies and for establishing a Commission of Investigation to be sent to those Colonies. According to the terms of Annex XI of the Peace Treaty with Italy, the Deputies shall continue the consideration of the question of the disposal of the former Italian Colonies with a view to submitting to the Council of Foreign Ministers their recommendations in this matter. They shall also send out commissions of investigation to any of the former Italian Colonies in order to supply the Deputies with the necessary data on this question and to ascertain the views of the local population. (See Annex A [2])

The preliminary meeting of the Deputies to determine the organization and terms of reference of the Commission, as well as the future program of the Deputies, is presently scheduled for June 6, 1947.

RECOMMENDATIONS

1. There should be one Commission of Investigation to visit all the Italian Colonies. Representation on the Commission should be limited to the Four Powers primarily concerned and each Power should be represented by one Commissioner, two but not more than four Advisers, and necessary secretarial assistance. A central secretariat and all arrangements for travel and accommodation in the Colonies should be provided by the British Government, the cost to be divided on a

---

[1] Copies of this position paper were taken to London by John Utter and Philip Bagby, advisers to Ambassador Douglas on the disposition of the Italian colonies. The paper was used during discussions with the British and French on the preparation of an agreed set of positions on questions likely to arise at the forthcoming meetings of the Deputies for the Former Italian Colonies. American and British representatives reached general agreement on these questions at the end of September 1947, but all matters became subject to four-power negotiation at the meetings of the Deputies which opened on October 3, 1947.

[2] The Annex, not printed, contained the texts of Article 23 and Annex XI of the Peace Treaty with Italy. For the full text of the Treaty, see TIAS No. 1648.

pro rata basis among the four Governments. The Deputies should request the British and French Governments to communicate with the appropriate authorities of the Italian Colonies in order to facilitate the work of the Commission of Investigation in those territories.

2. The terms of reference of the Commission should be as follows:

A. The Commission, which shall establish its own itinerary, shall have authority to conduct its investigation in Libya, Eritrea and Italian Somaliland in order to examine political, economic and social conditions as they bear upon the problem. Special attention shall be paid to the wishes and welfare of the inhabitants of the Colonies as well as to the interests of peace and security.

The Commission is not authorized to investigate any matter outside the boundaries of the Colonies, except under instructions from the Deputies, who will obtain permission from the Government or Governments concerned.

The views of other interested Governments, as expressed to the Deputies, shall be taken into consideration; the Commission shall be empowered to hear the views of Italy, Egypt, and Ethiopia, and to receive from the representatives of these countries factual evidence bearing on the problem. These representatives may be heard by the Commission in London and, if requested, in one specified place in each of the three Colonies.

B. The Commission shall proceed to the area not later than (date) and shall submit to the Deputies of the Foreign Ministers on or before (date) (N.B. The date to be inserted here should in no case exceed seven months from the coming into force of the Treaty.) reports of the facts disclosed by the investigation. There shall be three separate reports, i.e. one on Libya, one on Eritrea and one on Italian Somaliland. These reports shall include recommendations, it being understood, however, that such recommendations shall not be binding on the Deputies. Separate reports may be submitted, if requested by the Deputies, after the visit to each territory.

The Commission shall, if it deems it advisable or if requested by the Deputies, make special reports to the Deputies.

C. The Commission shall have authority to call upon the Governments, officials and inhabitants of those territories, and to consider the views of competent witnesses, irrespective of nationality, as well as to call upon such other sources as the Deputies may deem necessary, for information relevant to its investigation.

3. As soon as the Peace Treaty has come into force, and while the Commission is visiting the Colonies, the Deputies should hear the views of the other interested Governments. If this work is completed before submission of the Commission's report, the Deputies should adjourn.

4. The term "other interested Governments" should be defined as those Governments having territorial claims in the Colonies, such as Italy, Egypt, and Ethiopia, or those who participated actively in the

war in Africa on the side of the Allies. It is believed that these might include Australia, South Africa, New Zealand, India, Pakistan, Greece, Ethiopia, Belgium, Poland, and Czechoslovakia, but there should be prior consultation with the British in London to determine whether the armed forces of all of these states actually participated actively in the war in Africa.

5. The following general procedure should govern the participation of other interested Governments in the discussion of the disposal of the Colonies:

A. Ordinarily the views of such Governments should be presented to the Deputies.

B. In exceptional and appropriate instances, however, they should be permitted to present their views to the Council of Foreign Ministers, but every endeavor should be made to keep such consultation to a minimum.

C. The other interested Governments should not be permitted to participate in the work of the Commission of Investigation. Moreover, only Italy, Egypt, and Ethiopia should be heard by the Commission. (See Section 2A)

D. The other interested Governments, if they so desire, should be given the opportunity to submit to the Deputies their suggestions on the terms of reference and the composition of the Commission.

E. The reports of the Commission should be made available to the other interested Governments immediately on completion in order to enable those Governments to express their views thereon.

6. There should be no discussions regarding the final disposal of the Colonies until the report of the Commission has been received. When the report is received, the Deputies should proceed to discuss the disposition of the Colonies. Whenever agreement is reached or, if no agreement is reached, ten months after the coming into force of the Peace Treaty, recommendations or the questions at issue should be referred to the Foreign Ministers, unless the latter instruct the Deputies to continue the consideration of the problem.

7. These issues can be taken up at any meeting of the Foreign Ministers which may take place between ten months and twelve months after the coming into force of the Italian Peace Treaty, or, if necessary, at a special meeting.

8. The Deputies should always meet in London except when their presence may be required elsewhere by the Foreign Ministers.

DISCUSSION

Commission of Investigation.

Annex XI of the Treaty of Peace with Italy states that "*commissions* of investigation" shall be sent to the former Italian Colonies. It would appear desirable to restrict the number of commissions to one for the following reasons:

1. The cost and the amount of personnel required to accomplish the Commission's task would be materially reduced.
2. The experience which the Commission would gain in one area would be of assistance to it in the other areas.
3. The weight given to facts and conclusions would be uniform for all three territories.
4. Both the British and the French have indicated their preference for one commission.

It is also thought that the representation of each country on the Commission should be restricted in number to one Commissioner and not more than four Advisers. The British have indicated that the problem of accommodation and transportation of the personnel on the Commission will be difficult and complicated. It is therefore felt that the Commission should be restricted as much as may be consistent with the effective discharge of its task.

Questions may arise from time to time involving territories neighboring on the Colonies. For example, several of the border areas are indefinite and, in other cases, contiguous states have requested border rectifications. It may prove desirable for the Commission to visit these border areas and to enter the territory of contiguous states in order to complete their knowledge of the problem. It is therefore felt that the Deputies should be empowered to obtain the permission of contiguous states for visits of the Commission to such border areas.

Due to the enormous distances which the Commission must cover and the complexity of the problems involved, it is believed that the Commission should be given as much time as possible, consistent with the time limitation of one year imposed by the Treaty, to undertake its investigations. A period of seven months has, therefore, been recommended as reasonable, inasmuch as the Commission must visit three widely separated areas, hear the views of interested governments having territorial claims in these areas, and write final reports for submission to the Deputies.

Although Annex XI appears only to envisage the Commission as a fact-finding body, it is felt that the Commission should submit recommendations to the Deputies in order that the maximum benefit may be obtained from its investigations. These recommendations would be based primarily on the Commission's findings in the territories and would not bind the Deputies, who, in framing their recommendations, would, therefore, be free to take into account other pertinent data.

To provide for a possible eventuality whereby the Commission might be unable to agree on a report covering all three Colonies, it is considered preferable for the Commission to submit a separate report on each of the three Colonies. In this way possible disagreement regarding one area would not prevent or delay the forwarding of the views of the Commission regarding the other areas.

Other Interested Governments.

Due to the limited time (three months) allotted to the Deputies for their consideration of the actual disposal of the Colonies, it would be advantageous for them to hear the views of other interested governments while the Commission is in the field. This procedure should not, however, prevent other interested Governments from subsequently submitting additional views after they had had an opportunity to study the reports of the Commission of Investigation.

It is felt that the term "other interested Governments", which appears in Annex XI, should be given as restricted an interpretation as possible. This end can be accomplished by defining such Governments as those which have territorial claims on the Colonies or those which actively participated in the war in Africa.

This Government is already committed to support the procedure outlined in Section 5 of the Recommendations regarding the participation of other interested Governments in the discussion of the disposal of the Colonies. These commitments have been made in exchanges of communications with the Australian, Italian, and Egyptian Governments. These exchanges of notes constitute Annexes B–F, inclusive.[3]

Recommendations of the Deputies.

In order that the Deputies may give fullest consideration to the findings of the Commission of Investigation, it would be preferable for them not to discuss substantive matters involving the actual disposal of the Colonies until the Commission's reports have been received. A further benefit from this procedure would be that the representatives of each country on the Commission would be available in London as advisers to each of the Deputies.

Assuming that the Commission is allotted seven months in which to conduct its investigations and complete its reports, the most equitable distribution of the remaining five months would appear to be three months for the Deputies to form their recommendations and two months for the Council of Foreign Ministers to make its decision.

---

[3] Annexes B and C were the texts of the Australian Embassy *aide-mémoire* of April 10, 1947, and the Department's reply of April 21, described in telegram 1762, April 22, to London, p. 577. Annexes D and E were the texts of the Italian Embassy Counselor's letter of February 18, 1947, and Loy Henderson's reply of March 7, described in footnotes 1 and 2 to telegram 297, March 1, to Rome, p. 570. Annex F was the text of the memorandum of July 25, 1946, from the Department of State to the Egyptian Legation, not printed, suggesting that the Egyptian Government might wish to make known to the Deputies of the Council of Foreign Ministers its desire to submit its views to any Commission sent to former Italian Colonies (740.00119 Council/7–2546).

865.014/6–1747 : Telegram

The Chargé in the United Kingdom (Gallman) to the Secretary of State

SECRET   LONDON, June 17, 1947—1 p. m.

3300. Itcol 6 from Bagby. Stafford informs me that although the British do not wish to take a definite position on the disposition of the Italian Colonies until commission has submitted its report, their thinking has undergone some evolution with regard to Somalia. They have abandoned the idea of Greater Somalia, due to lack of enthusiasm with which their proposal was greeted in the CFM and the impossibility of inducing Ethiopia to cede the Ogaden.[1] They still believe that British trusteeship would be the best solution and would advocate a rectification of the Ethiopian frontier so that it would follow the boundaries of tribal areas. They believe they can obtain Ethiopian consent to this latter.

They are still thinking of a division of Eritrea between the Sudan and Ethiopia without trusteeship, which they feel would be too complicated for so small an area. He has not yet mentioned British opinions about Libya.

Sent to Dept as 3300, repeated Paris as 333 for Utter. [Bagby.]

GALLMAN

---

[1] Telegram 3419, Itcol 10, June 23, from London, added the following comment on this matter :

"British are still interested in British trusteeship over Italian Somaliland but abandoned idea of joining British Somaliland and the Ogaden with it in a larger trust territory. We now learn that the British Treasury may oppose British trusteeship even over smaller area because of expense." (865.014/6–2347)

865.014/6–2747 : Telegram

The Ambassador in the United Kingdom (Douglas) to the Secretary of State

SECRET   LONDON, June 27, 1947—6 p. m.

3549. Itcol 17 from Utter and Bagby. Reference Itcol 2.[1] As we had heard nothing from the Soviets since the Ambassador's call on Za-

---

[1] Telegram 3185, Itcol 2, June 10, from London, read in part as follows :

"FonOff informed Embassy that [British Secretary of State for Foreign Affairs Ernest] Bevin will see Soviet Ambassador [Georgiy Nikolayevich] Zaroubin today to propose informal discussions and exchange of views between British and Soviets on subject of commission of investigation for Italian colonies preliminary to Deputies meeting. The Ambassador [Douglas], before leaving for weeks visit in Germany, called on Zaroubin this morning and made similar suggestions, explaining that Utter and Bagby are here [and] would welcome exploratory conversations on subject. Zaroubin promised to give matter favorable consideration and said that his Counsellor [of Embassy Georgiy Filippovich] Saksin would get in touch with Utter and Bagby. Similar overtures will be made to the French. Such bilateral conversations should expedite subsequent formal negotiations of Deputies." (865.014/6–1047)

roubin we called on Saksin today. It turned out that he was in charge here during Zaroubin's absence in Paris. (As far as we can find out, the latter has not yet made his proposed visit to Moscow.) We referred to the Ambassador's and Bevin's conversations with Zaroubin and explained that we were anxious to begin preliminary talks with the Soviets in order to save time when the Deputies actually met and so enable the commission to have more time in which to do its job thoroughly.

We added that we were having such talks with the British and had made similar overtures to the French. Saksin confessed that he was completely uninformed on the question and that he had not understood that any agreement had been reached between the Ambassador and Zaroubin about preliminary talks. He welcomed our visit, however, since it would enable him to learn more about the question.

We then showed him the Dept's procedural paper and explained the various questions which would have to be decided before the commission could depart. Saksin showed considerable interest in the problems of the size of the commission and its itinerary and finally said that he would recommend to Moscow that one or more specialists be sent to London at the present time so that they could familiarize themselves with the problems involved and perhaps reach some preliminary understandings through bilateral talks. We took this occasion to suggest that it would be useful if Moscow could send the Soviet Commissioner designated for this purpose.

We were struck with Saksin's cordiality and the frankness with which he confessed his ignorance and we suspect that the delays caused by the Russians in this instance are due more to their lack of understanding of the problem than to any ulterior motive.

[Utter and Bagby]
DOUGLAS

865.014/7–347 : Telegram

The Ambassador in the United Kingdom (Douglas) to the Secretary of State

SECRET   LONDON, July 3, 1947—5 p. m.

3648. Itcol 18 from Utter and Bagby. Stafford has told us in confidence that the British General Staff still feels that British bases in Cyrenaica are absolutely essential to their strategy in the eastern Mediterranean since British troops will have to be withdrawn from Egypt and very possibly also from Palestine. Foreign Office has tried to persuade the General Staff to alter this position, but without success. While Stafford made no definite statement, it appears likely that the British may still seek trusteeship over Cyrenaica. Stafford seems disposed to discourage unrealistic demands for independence by the inhabitants and if this line is accepted by Foreign Office and pushed to its logical conclusion, it would rule out the alternative solution, often mentioned by the British, of an independent Cyrenaica, bound to Britain by treaty of alliance as in the case of Transjordan. Please inform Colonel Bonesteel.[1]

Stafford also said that Bevin had considered proposing, as a compromise to possible renewed Soviet request for trusteeship over Tripolitania, to place Tripoli and the adjoining coastal areas under an international regime similar to that of Tangier, but had been dissuaded by Foreign Office elements who thought such a regime would be impractical and give too great a voice to Soviets. At present Foreign Office is indifferent to the fate of Tripolitania except that they wish to exclude Russians and believe that the Italians could only be reinstated after much bloodshed.   [Utter and Bagby]

DOUGLAS

---

[1] Lt. Col. Charles H. Bonesteel, 3d, previously of the Plans and Operations Division, War Department General Staff, in July 1947 was appointed a special assistant to Under Secretary of State Robert A. Lovett.

865.014/7–847

Memorandum from the State–War–Navy Coordinating Committee to the Department of State

TOP SECRET   WASHINGTON, 8 July 1947.

SWN–5543

Subject: Disposition of the Italian Colonies
        Reference: SWN–5436 [1]

In response to a request from the Department of State forwarded by the State–War–Navy Coordinating Committee in the above reference, the following has been received from the Joint Chiefs of Staff:

"The Joint Chiefs of Staff have considered a memorandum from the State–War–Navy Coordinating Committee dated 2 June 1947 requesting their views on the military implications involved in the disposal of the Italian colonies with particular reference to the British requirements for bases.

"It is in the interest of United States security to prevent any potentially hostile power from obtaining a firm hold in the Middle East and/or Mediterranean areas. Unfortunate and potentially catastrophic

---

[1] Memorandum of June 2, 1947 from the State–War–Navy Coordinating Committee to the Joint Chiefs of Staff transmitting the text of the memorandum of May 29 from Assistant Secretary of State Hilldring to the State–War–Navy Coordinating Committee, p. 583.

though it is, the USSR is our ideological enemy and our most probable enemy should war occur. Further, the USSR, militarily the strongest power in the world today with the exception of the United States, is engaged in improving its strategic position and increasing its military potential by attaching to itself states, peoples and areas to which it has no legitimate claim and to the great military disadvantage of the United States and our potential allies. The United States is now attempting to check this unwarranted expansion of Soviet control. Therefore, it would be contrary to announced United States policy and to United States military interests to accept any disposition of the Italian colonies which gave the USSR either unilateral or joint control of any of the colonies in question, even though this control were obtained in the guise of trusteeship under the United Nations.

"The objections to unilateral Soviet control are too obvious to warrant discussion. The objections to joint control stem from our previous experiences in Germany, Austria, Hungary, Rumania and Bulgaria where the Soviets have not hesitated to negate almost completely the effects of United States participation in joint control by means immoral, contrary to previous agreements with the United States and disadvantageous to the state concerned. If allowed to participate in joint control of any of the Italian colonies, the Soviets would be most likely to employ like tactics to gain for themselves complete control in all but the legalistic sense.

"The Soviets could exercise effective control of any of the colonies if a satellite or a non-satellite communist government were granted control. It would, therefore, be militarily disadvantageous to the United States to allow Italy to resume control of any or all of her colonies unless it had previously become clear that the future government of Italy will be non-communist and affiliated with the Western Democracies. This consideration is over and above the consideration of whether Italy would be able to maintain peace in the colonies, which, in view of the armed forces granted her by the treaty of peace, appears doubtful unless appropriate increases in her armed forces were authorized. In view of the strong ties existing between the various states of the Arab world, armed conflict between Italian forces and Arab forces native to the Italian colonies would threaten world peace.

"The Joint Chiefs of Staff consider Great Britain and her Empire to be our most probable and most important allies, in the event of war with the USSR. A firm hold in the Middle East and Eastern Mediterranean is one of the basic tenets of British strategic policy. Facilities must, therefore, at all times be available somewhere in the area Palestine–Egypt–Cyrenaica which will enable United Kingdom sea, land and air forces to operate effectively in the Middle East and Eastern Mediterranean. The future of Palestine is obscure. The revision of the 1936 treaty between Great Britain and Egypt is deadlocked. Cyrenaica is, therefore, more important than ever for the successful implementation of British strategic policy.

"However, there is doubt that the British can, within the next ten years, deploy sufficient land, sea and air forces in the area to insure, with a reasonable degree of certainty, adequate protection of Anglo-American strategic interests in the Middle East and the Eastern Mediterranean. In spite of this and in view of the great strategic importance of this area to the United States and to the United Kingdom, retention of British forces in the area is, from the security point of view, the least objectionable alternative to

"*a.* Joint United States-United Kingdom responsibility for the military security of the area, or
"*b.* Assumption by the United States of unilateral responsibility for the military security of the area."

For the State–War–Navy Coordinating Committee:
W. A. SCHULGEN
Acting Secretary

865.014/7–1047 : Telegram

The Ambassador in the United Kingdom (Douglas) to the Secretary of State

SECRET   LONDON, July 10, 1947—6 p. m.

3790. Itcol 21. Bonneau,[1] of the French Foreign Office, arrived as planned on July 8 (see Itcol 20 [2]) and after spending the afternoon in discussions with British dined with us. He returned to Paris morning July 9.

He informed us that French commissioner will be Etienne Burin des Roziers, a career diplomat at present in Vienna [3] who speaks excellent English. He is personally known to Utter and should prove most cooperative. Their secretary of delegation will be Féquant [4] who is familiar with CFM work. Bedbeder will continue to be their number two. Their delegation will probably not exceed five and will be completed by the addition of a French-Russian interpreter and a stenographer.

Bonneau said that he had asked one of the Counselors of Soviet Embassy in Paris to call on him about ten days ago and had explained to him in detail the desirability of having preliminary talks about procedure and terms of reference of commission before the coming into force of peace treaties in order to be able to meet time limit of one year. The Russian had apparently understood and agreed to recommend this procedure to his government. He said he hoped to have an answer next day since "half of Soviet Ministry of Foreign Affairs" was then in Paris but nothing has been heard from him since.

---

[1] Gabriel Bonneau, director, Division of African and Levant Affairs, Office of Political Affairs, French Foreign Ministry.
[2] Not printed; it reported that Bonneau would come to London to hold further conversations with the British and American officials (865.014/7–847). Bonneau had earlier meetings with Utter in mid-June.
[3] Burin des Roziers served as Deputy French Representative on the Austrian Treaty Commission which met in Vienna, May 12–October 11, 1947.
[4] Albert Féquant, General Secretariat, French Foreign Ministry.

Bonneau volunteered information that France's chief interest in question of Italian colonies was to ensure restoration Italy to its rightful position in world affairs. While he did not definitely say so we took this to mean that France still advocates the placing of the colonies under trusteeship of Italy. Bonneau added that Scott-Fox [5] in Foreign Office when told this had replied that Britain feared bloodshed especially in Libya if decision were reached to return colonies to Italy but that they might agree to return of Italian Somaliland. When we questioned Stafford later about his last remark he said that some elements in Foreign Office felt that return of Italian Somaliland would be desirable as an encouragement to Italians but that it was unlikely that Britain would propose such a solution or accept it except as a final compromise to achieve unanimity (see Itcol 6 and 10 [6]).

Bonneau also told us he had discussed in detail with Stafford British draft terms of reference and procedural paper and would prepare a draft of his own after his return to Paris. While he would have to give the various questions further study he was agreeable to having a single commission with only four powers represented and to limitation on size of each delegation. He felt that seven months was a reasonable time to allot to commission and he agreed on the whole with Stafford's list of interested governments.[7] (Stafford told us later that Bonneau had suggested omitting Poland and Czechoslovakia at first as a tactical measure and that British would consider this suggestion.)

Bonneau felt that there were really only two matters as far as he could see at this juncture which might cause difficulty. The first was the itinerary. He believed that commission should visit Libya first of all because the inhabitants of Libya were the most easily inflamed by propaganda and as little time as possible should be given for Egyptian and other Arab propagandists to arouse the population. (Stafford said later he had told Bonneau that he felt such propaganda would be continuous during meeting of deputies and therefore it made little difference when commission visited Libya. On the other hand the weather was best in Somaliland in autumn and early winter and commission would do better if it started in this colony which was least

---

[5] R. D. J. Scott-Fox, Assistant Head, Egyptian Department, British Foreign Office.

[6] Telegram 3300, Itcol 6, June 17, from London, is printed on p. 590; regarding elegram 3419, Itcol 10, June 23, from London, see footnote 1 to Itcol 6.

[7] Telegrams 3486, Itcol 14, June 25 and 3487, Itcol 15, June 25, both from London, neither printed, transmitted the texts and commentary on a British Foreign Office paper on procedure and other matters likely to arise at the coming meetings of the Deputies for the Former Italian Colonies. The British paper was based on the United States position paper printed on p. 585. The British list of interested governments" whose views were to be heard by the Deputies included Italy, Egypt, Ethiopia, South Africa, India, Australia, New Zealand, Greece, Poland, Czechoslovakia, and Belgium.

divided politically. We agree with Stafford and would appreciate Department's views.)

The other matter which worried Bonneau was the provision for making separate reports available to interested governments as soon as they were completed (see Itcol 14 and 15, paragraph 5, subparagraph 6). While he had no objection to Commission drafting a separate report after its visit to each colony, he felt any conclusion reached should be kept secret until Commission had left Africa. If reports were given at once to eleven other governments their contents would surely be divulged to the press and an unpopular recommendation (say return to Italy) might lead to disturbances when Commission visited other colonies especially Libya.

Since this original British position was changed by British only under pressure from Dominions, and since it has already been approved by Department (see Itcol 4,[8] paragraph 5 E), we believe we should support French and we withdraw our recommendation in Itcol 15. Please telegraph Department's views.

Department will observe that major preoccupation of French is with danger of nationalist propaganda and disturbances in Libya. Presumably they fear repercussions of such events in French North Africa. Bonneau mentioned several times that Libya of all the colonies was the prime concern of French.

Bonneau said he would like to see us in Paris when he had had time to give all these questions further study and that he would invite us formally through Embassy in Paris at a later date.

Bonneau seems to have been under a misapprehension (due perhaps to a language difficulty) that Scott-Fox has some information to the effect that Russians might not ratify peace treaties. We later checked this with Stafford who was sure that Scott-Fox was merely indulging in some private speculation about possible development of international situation. We mention this in case Bonneau's version is reported to Department by Paris.

Sent Department 3790, repeated Rome 79, Paris 393, and Moscow 241. [Utter and Bagby.]

DOUGLAS

---

[8] Telegram 3213, Itcol 4, June 12, from London, not printed, reported on British Foreign Office comments on the United States position paper printed on p. 585. With respect to paragraph 5 E of the United States paper, the British felt that individual reports by the Commission of Investigation should not be given to the interested governments until the final report of the Commission had been given to the Deputies (865.014/6–1247). The British subsequently reversed themselves on this point and adopted the earlier American position which favored making preliminary Commission reports available to interested governments.

865.014/7–1847 : Telegram

The Secretary of State to the Embassy in the United Kingdom

CONFIDENTIAL   WASHINGTON, July 18, 1947—8 p. m.

3093. Colit 12. ECOSOC at its Mar session requested SYG make field survey, with concurrence govts concerned and at their request, of reconstruction problems Ethiopia and other devastated areas not included reports ECOSOC Temporary Subcommission on Reconstruction Devastated Areas (limited to Europe, Asia and Far East).[1] Accordingly SYG inquired Eth Govt whether it desired field survey made Ethiopia. Similar inquiry addressed UK Govt as occupying power Italian colonies Africa and UK replied Jun 19 it would be glad have such survey undertaken Tripolitania, Cyrenaica and Eritrea. Preparations now being made but no date set for departure field missions. Brit have requested SYG make arrangements for movements of Missions through Maj Gen Cumming, Chief Civil Affairs Officer British Middle East Land Forces.

Dept discussed matter informally with Brit Emb officials here who have telegraphed London suggesting Brit play for time by taking attitude that ECOSOC Commission's surveys in Italian Colonies should not be undertaken independently of or in advance of survey of Ethiopia. This hinged Commission's departure on Ethiopia's acceptance of invitation. Emb further suggested that in event this not acceptable Foreign and War Offices, Brit Govt might take attitude whole question should be carried over to next meeting ECOSOC.

Subsequent to Depts talks with Brit Emb officials, Eth Govt reported to have notified SYG that would renounce UN reconstruction aid "in favor of other member nations more immediately in need of urgent assistance". This action makes impracticable Brit Emb's first alternative suggestion. Dept has now informally suggested to Brit Emb that Brit Govt might instruct Cumming that at such time as SYG might communicate with him re arrangements, he reply that for following reasons, BMA would prefer ECOSOC Commission's survey not conducted until after Quadripartite Commission's field work completed: (1) Simultaneous presence both Commissions in colonies or even separate visits too close together would cause considerable confusion and possibly have adverse effect on work both bodies. Since Quadripartite Commission will be working under time limit, its investigations must

---

[1] For a brief review of the resolution adopted by the United Nations Economic and Social Council at its Fourth Session on March 28, 1947, and the steps leading to a decision by the Secretary General in September 1947 to postpone the survey called for by the resolution, see *Yearbook of the United Nations 1947–1948* (United Nations, Lake Success, New York, Department of Public Information, 1949), pp. 546–547.

take precedence; and (2) two Commissions in areas at approximately same time would prove too great administrative burden on BMA.

Please discuss informally with Stafford and telegraph Dept his and your comments, repeating Addis Ababa.

Sent London at 3093; rptd Addis Ababa as 137. (Re Legtel 175); USUN New York as 318 (for Stinebower [2]).

MARSHALL

---

[2] Leroy D. Stinebower, United States Alternate Representative on the Economic and Social Council; Special Assistant to the Assistant Secretary of State for Economic Affairs.

865.014/7–2247 : Telegram

The Ambassador in the United Kingdom (Douglas) to the Secretary of State

CONFIDENTIAL   LONDON, July 22, 1947—6 p. m.

3992. Itcol 25. See Colit 12.[1] Stafford informs us that original intention of Foreign Office, when UK accepted offer of SYG for ECOSOC field survey in Tripolitania, Cyrenaica and Eritrea, was that General Cumming should be consulted as to when such survey could appropriately be made. Stafford states that, by some unfortunate wording in acceptance, UK appeared to be ready for ECOSOC Commission's survey at any time.

Foreign Office has referred the matter to Stafford, who has made following suggestion, which he is confident Foreign Office will follow:

Postponement of ECOSOC field survey altogether until after four power commission has completed field work in former Italian Colonies, in order to:

1. Avoid possibility of inconvenience and confusion arising from two parties being in field at or about same time and

2. Prevent attempts to use field survey as medium for political activity or intrigue (once Quadripartite Commission's visit is made, this danger will no longer exist).

Moreover, Stafford states that UK delegation at UN will be asked to arrange everything with SYG and Cumming will be out of picture for time being.[2]

We agree entirely with Department that ECOSOC Commission should not visit territories until after Quadripartite Commission's field work is completed.

Sent Department 3992, repeated Addis Ababa unnumbered.

DOUGLAS

---

[1] Supra.
[2] On August 22, 1947, the United Kingdom Government requested of the United Nations Secretary General the postponement of the survey of the former Italian colonies until after the visits there by the Commission of Investigation. On September 15, the Secretary General agreed to the postponement.

865.014/8–1947 : Telegram

The Chargé in the United Kingdom (Clark) to the Secretary of State

TOP SECRET LONDON, August 19, 1947—5 p. m.

4487. 1. When advised that both Utter and Palmer [1] would be in London August 18, Michael Wright [2] expressed a desire to discuss with them most informally questions relating to disposal of Italian colonies, and more particularly Cyrenaica. At luncheon, including Lewis Jones,[3] Wright stressed fact that there is no Cabinet decision in London as to whether British will remain in Near East at all and if they do, whether Cyrenaica is, in circumstances, most desirable base for them. Wright would not predict when these decisions would be taken, but said matter is receiving urgent study by British authorities. He reiterated his personal views as described in Emtel 4398, August 14.[4]

2. Only new information obtained from Wright was his admission that British Government has formulated no views how British base Cyrenaica could be brought into being. Wright said three alternatives under consideration are:

(*a*) Sole British trusteeship;
(*b*) British strategic trusteeship;
(*c*) Independence with understanding between British and Sayid Idriss regarding lease of strategic bases.

Wright made it clear that present trend of British thinking is to regard Cyrenaica, where vital British interests are centered, as separate from problem of Tripolitania and other Italian colonies.

3. Wright said that in his view, this is instance calling for close Anglo-American cooperation and pooling of US and British ideas. He said US views as to how Cyrenaica base might be secured for Britain would be of greatest help to Foreign Office, because "after all, you Americans started this trusteeship business and should be able to think a way out of the present box into which we seem to be placed".

4. Wright will report latest developments to same group (see Paragraph 1) just prior to Palmer's departure for Washington August 30. Meanwhile, it is obvious that Wright hopes that, while time is not yet ripe on British side to discuss this question at high level between governments, all US officials concerned (State, War, Navy, etc.) would formulate the general US view on all aspects this question in preparation for later discussions.

5. Wright's views and fact that he has talked to Embassy so frankly should be closely guarded until British Cabinet takes its decision regarding Near East base and formal US-British talks begin.

CLARK

---

[1] Joseph Palmer II, assistant chief, Division of African Affairs.
[2] Assistant Under-Secretary of State in the British Foreign Office.
[3] George Lewis Jones, second secretary at the Embassy in London.
[4] Not printed.

865.014/9–1947

The British Embassy to the Department of State

No. 513
Ref: 313/–/47

AIDE-MÉMOIRE

His Majesty's Embassy is instructed to inform the State Department that, now that the Italian Peace Treaty is in force [1] and the year has begun within which the four Powers are to determine the disposal of the Italian Colonies, His Majesty's Government in the United Kingdom would welcome an early meeting of the deputies to discuss procedural matters, including the instructions to be given to the Commissioners and to decide on the future program generally.

2. His Majesty's Government therefore suggest that the first meeting should take place in London on the 30th September. His Majesty's Embassy is to inquire whether this date is agreeable to the State Department; if it is, it is hoped that the United States deputy will be instructed accordingly. [2]

3. It is understood that the United States, Soviet and French governments are appointing their Ambassadors in London [3] as their deputies for this purpose. Mr. Jebb has been obliged to proceed to New York for the Assembly [4] and Sir Noel Charles [5] has therefore been appointed as the United Kingdom deputy.

4. His Majesty's Government would be grateful to learn as soon as possible the composition of the United States Delegation and, in particular, the names and ranks of any personnel for whom hotel accommodation, of which there is an acute shortage at the present time, will be required.

5. It is hoped that the United States Government will instruct the United States Commissioner to be present in London when the deputies meet, since time will be saved if the Commissioners can discuss the various technical points regarding their tour concurrently with the deputies meeting.

---

[1] The Peace Treaty with Italy entered into force on September 15, 1947; for documentation on the signing, ratification, and deposit of ratification of the Treaty, see pp. 515 ff.

[2] In an *aide-mémoire* dated September 25, 1947, the Department of State notified the British Embassy that the time and place for a meeting of the Deputies for the Italian Colonies were agreeable to the United States Government.

[3] The French Ambassador in the United Kingdom was René Massigli.

[4] The reference here is to the Second Regular Session of the United Nations General Assembly, September 16–November 29, 1947.

[5] British Representative to the Italian Government with the personal rank of Ambassador, April 1944–October 1947.

6. A similar communication is being addressed to the Soviet and French governments.

WASHINGTON, September 19, 1947.

Files of the Office of Near Eastern, South Asian and African Affairs : Lot 55 D 36

Memorandum by the Director of the Office of Near Eastern and African Affairs (Henderson) to the Secretary of State [1]

TOP SECRET
[WASHINGTON,] October 1, 1947.

PROBLEM

The problem is to determine the policy of this Government concerning the final disposal of Italy's territorial possessions in Africa, namely, Libya (comprising Tripolitania and Cyrenaica), Eritrea, and Italian Somaliland.

RECOMMENDATIONS

It is recommended that the policy of the United States with respect to the future of each of these territories should be as follows:

1. *Libya.* That Libya be placed under the international trusteeship system, with the Government of the United Kingdom as the administering authority, under terms of trusteeship which would provide for the people of Libya to become self-governing at the expiration of a period of ten years from the date of the establishment of such trusteeship, at which time Tripolitania and Cyrenaica would be permitted individually to elect whether they desire to (a) become separate independent states, (b) remain united as an independent Libya, or (c) become federated with other states or territories.

2. *Eritrea.* That Eritrea be ceded in full sovereignty to Ethiopia, except for the area in the northwestern part of Eritrea inhabited by Moslem-Sudanese, which should be incorporated into the Anglo-Egyptian Sudan.

3. *Italian Somaliland.* That Italian Somaliland, together with British Somaliland, be placed under the international trusteeship system, with the Government of the United Kingdom as the administering authority, under terms of trusteeship which would provide for eventual self-government but which would not fix the period of time within which the area would become self-governing.

DISCUSSION

At meetings of the Council of Foreign Ministers concerning the Peace Treaty with Italy, various proposals were made regarding the disposal of the Italian Colonies in Africa. These proposals, as well as

---

[1] The source text was included as Annex XII of a bound dossier of documents entitled "Pentagon Talks of 1947".

what are believed to be the present attitudes of the Governments of Italy, Ethiopia, and Egypt, and of the Arab League, have been summarized in Annex I [2] to this memorandum. The Foreign Ministers were unable to agree upon any definitive solution to the problem. They finally agreed in principle, however, to a suggestion of the United States Delegation that Italy be required to renounce sovereignty over the Colonies, which would be held in trust by the Four Powers for a period of one year from the coming into force of the Peace Treaty with Italy, during which time the Foreign Ministers would endeavor to determine jointly the final disposal of these territories. This principle was incorporated in Article 23 and Annex XI of the Italian Peace Treaty (see Annex II [3]).

In the present international situation, none of the proposals previously made regarding the disposition of the Italian Colonies is satisfactory from the point of view of the United States and the Western World.

It is in the interests of United States security to prevent any potentially hostile power from obtaining a hold in the Middle East, the Mediterranean area, or in Africa. It would, therefore, be contrary to the policy of the United States, and to United States military interests, to accept any disposition of the Italian Colonies which would give the Soviet Union either unilateral or joint control of any of the colonies in question, even if this control were obtained in the guise of a trusteeship under the United Nations. The objections to collective trusteeship are based on our difficulties in obtaining Soviet cooperation in Germany, Austria, Hungary, Rumania, Bulgaria, and Korea.

A decision to grant any of the Italian Colonies immediate independence would result in the creation of weak states which would be exposed to Soviet aggression or infiltration. Moreover, the Soviet Union could exercise effective control over any of these Colonies if their administration should be entrusted to a state in which there is a possibility that a communist government may come into power. For this reason, it would be disadvantageous to the United States to allow Italy to resume control of any of its former colonies unless it had previously become clear that the future Government of Italy will be non-communist and affiliated with the Western democracies. This consideration is over and above the consideration of whether Italy would be able to maintain peace in the Colonies, which appears to be

[2] Annex I, not printed, was largely a review of positions taken by the Soviet Union, United Kingdom, France, and the United States during the Second Session of the Council of Foreign Ministers in Paris, April 25–May 15 and June 15–July 12, 1946. For the records of that Council session, see *Foreign Relations,* 1946, vol. II, pp. 88 ff.

[3] Annex II is not printed.

doubtful in view of the limited armed forces permitted Italy by the Peace Treaty. It is doubtful also that the Italian Colonies in Africa could ever become self-sustaining, and their return to Italy would place an added burden on Italy's already strained economy. Nor would the return of the Colonies to Italy alone solve that country's problem of over-population.

Aside from the foregoing considerations, it is believed that the Arabs in Libya would resist by force any return to Italian rule. In view of the strong ties existing between the various states of the Arab world, armed conflict in Libya between Italian forces and local Arab forces would be extremely harmful to the interests of the United States. Moreover, any action by the United States openly supporting the return of the Colonies to Italian administration would further impair our relations with the Arab states, which are already strained as a result of the Palestine and Egyptian issues. Among other damaging results, a hostile attitude on the part of the Arabs would threaten from the rear the position we are striving to hold in Greece, Turkey, and Iran.

On September 19, an *Aide-Mémoire* [4] was received from the British Embassy stating that, now that the Italian Treaty has come into force and the year has begun within which the Four Powers are to decide upon the disposal of the Italian Colonies, the British Government would welcome a meeting of the Deputies of the Foreign Ministers at an early date to discuss procedural matters in connection with the implementation of Article 23 and Annex XI of the Treaty, including instructions to be given to the Commission, and to decide on the future program generally. It seems highly unlikely, however, that agreement will be reached by the Foreign Ministers. The question of the disposition of these Colonies, therefore, will in all probability go before the General Assembly of the United Nations.

In view of the situation in the Mediterranean area, we cannot wait until the commission of investigation has had time to visit the areas and make its report to decide what our attitude regarding the future of the Italian Colonies will be. It is the opinion of the Joint Chiefs of Staff that Great Britain would be our most probable and most important ally in the event of another war, and it would be extremely unfortunate, from our point of view, for British troops and matériel to be removed from the Near Eastern area. There is already a tendency in certain British circles to withdraw entirely from the Near and Middle East, leaving no great Power established in that area and thus exposing it to Russian aggression or infiltration unless the United States is prepared to fill the vacuum. We strongly believe, therefore,

---

[4] *Supra.*

that Britain should continue to maintain a base in the Eastern Mediterranean area, and that facilities must at all times be available somewhere in the area of Palestine–Egypt–Cyrenaica which will enable the United Kingdom sea, land, and air forces to operate in this area. It appears unlikely that the British can continue to maintain bases in Palestine. Moreover, we believe that British troops should be unconditionally withdrawn from Egypt at the earliest practicable date and that bases in Cyrenaica are the only available substitutes. Cyrenaica is, therefore, more important than ever from the point of view of British and United States strategic interests. It has already been decided that we should inform the British Government that if it would like to transfer its troops and matériel from Egypt to Cyrenaica immediately, we would have no objection thereto; and that we would be disposed eventually to support arrangements for the establishment of permanent British bases in Cyrenaica, when the final disposition of that territory is decided, provided such arrangements could be effected in accordance with the principles of the United Nations Charter and provided the making of such arrangements proves to be practicable in the light of the then existing international situation.

It is accordingly recommended that the United States support the principle of placing Libya under the international trusteeship system with the Government of the United Kingdom as the administering authority. The terms of trusteeship should provide for the peoples of Libya to become self-governing at the end of ten years from the date of the establishment of such trusteeship, at which time Tripolitania and Cyrenaica shall be permitted to elect individually whether they desire to become separate independent states, remain united as an independent Libya, or become federated with other states or territories. By making a definite provision in the trusteeship agreement for self-government at the end of ten years, there would appear to be a good chance that this proposal would be acceptable to the Arab states. It might be possible, particularly in case the friendly backing of the Arab world could be obtained, to rally the two-thirds vote in the General Assembly necessary to give Great Britain a non-strategic trusteeship over Libya. Also, in view of the friendly relations existing between the British Government and the Senussi, an independent state of Cyrenaica, or even an independent Libya, might be willing to give the British Government permanent bases in Cyrenaica.

The Government of Ethiopia has made claims to Eritrea. From exhaustive study given this question in the Department, we feel that there is ample historical, ethnological, linguistic, religious, and economic justification for the cession to Ethiopia, with appropriate safeguards, of the greater part of Eritrea, which would provide Ethiopia with its much needed access to the sea. It has recently been reported from Ethiopian sources that both Great Britain and the Soviet Union have given Ethiopia assurances on the Eritrean question. If Ethiopia is unsuccessful in obtaining this area, one of two courses appears to be likely: (1) Ethiopia will fall into the hands of reactionaries and be set back many years politically, economically, and socially; or (2) Ethiopia may turn towards the Soviets. From a strategic standpoint, Ethiopia is becoming increasingly important to British Empire security and, therefore, to our own security. An increase in Soviet influence in Ethiopia would constitute a direct threat to British control of the strategically important southern entrance to the Red Sea. It is known that the British Government is establishing bases in Kenya Colony and is considering plans for a central African life-line extending from Nigeria to Kenya. We understand that British troops and matériel already are being transferred to Kenya from India. It is in the interest of Great Britain to protect the flanks of this life-line, and it seems obvious to us that a strong, friendly, and peaceful Ethiopia is necessary to achieve this purpose. We recommend that Eritrea be ceded in full sovereignty to Ethiopia, except for the northwestern part, which is inhabited by Moslem–Sudanese who are more closely akin to the peoples of the Anglo-Egyptian Sudan than to the Ethiopians and which, we believe, should be incorporated into the Anglo-Egyptian Sudan.

Because of the strategic location of Italian Somaliland with respect to Kenya colony and the Aden protectorate, we believe that it would be advantageous to the United States and Great Britain for the latter country to assume responsibility for the future administration of Italian Somaliland. It would thus appear that the most desirable solution is for Italian Somaliland to be administered along with British Somaliland as a unit, and for the area so created to be placed under the international trusteeship system with the Government of the United Kingdom as the administering authority. We are opposed, however, to the proposal previously made by Great Britain for joining Italian Somaliland, British Somaliland, and the Ogaden Province of Ethiopia under an international trusteeship. We see no justification for including the Ogaden, which is and should remain a part of Ethiopia. In view of the backward state of development of the Somalilands, no definite time for their attainment of self-government should be specified in the trusteeship agreement, but the agreement should provide for their development toward eventual self-government.

Loy W. Henderson

Editorial Note

The Deputies for the Former Italian Colonies of the Council of Foreign Ministers held 17 meetings between October 3 and November 22, 1947. These meetings, held in London at the invitation of the United Kingdom Government, were in pursuance of the provisions of Article 23 and Annex XI of the Treaty of Peace with Italy which charged the United States, the United Kingdom, the Soviet Union, and France with the task of jointly determining the final disposition of Italy's former colonies in Africa.

Principal members of the delegations at these meetings of the Deputies were:

UNITED STATES

Deputy
  Lewis W. Douglas, Ambassador in the United Kingdom.
Alternate Deputy and Adviser
  Waldemar J. Gallman, Counselor of Embassy, London.
Advisers
  Philip H. Bagby, Foreign Service Officer.
  John E. Utter, Division of African Affairs, Department of State.
  Alfred E. Wellons, Division of African Affairs, Department of State.

UNITED KINGDOM

Deputy
  Sir Noel Charles, former British Representative in Italy.
Advisers
  Frank Edmund Stafford, Egyptian Department, Foreign Office.
  R. D. J. Scott-Fox, Assistant Head, Egyptian Department, Foreign Office.
  I. E. Bell, Egyptian Department, Foreign Office.

SOVIET UNION

Deputy
  Georgiy Nikolayevich Zaroubin, Ambassador in the United Kingdom.
Alternate Deputy and Adviser
  Georgiy Filippovich Saksin, Counselor of Embassy, London.
Adviser
  Ivan Mikhailovich Martinov, Ministry of Foreign Affairs.

FRANCE

Deputy
  René Massigli, Ambassador in the United Kingdom.
Advisers
  Etienne Burin des Roziers, Foreign Ministry.
  Jacquin de Margerie, Conference Secretariat, Foreign Ministry.
  Colonel de la Chapelle.
  Pierre Franckfort, Second Counselor of Embassy, London.

The first 13 meetings of the Deputies, October 3 to November 5, were concerned with determining the matters of procedure for the Deputies and the terms of reference, itinerary, and time-table of the Commission of Investigation to be dispatched to the former Italian colonies. The remaining four meetings of the Deputies, November 12–22, were given over to a hearing of the views of the Ethiopian, Italian, and Egyptian Governments regarding the disposition of the former colonies and to concluding activities of the first phase of the Deputies session. The documentation that follows includes the principal agreements reached by the Deputies and reports on the hearing of the views of Ethiopia, Italy and Egypt. Documentation on the meetings of the Deputies, February–September 1948, and on the Report of the Commission of Investigation is scheduled for publication in a subsequent volume of *Foreign Relations.*

The records of decisions and official documents of the Deputies together with the United States Delegation minutes of the meetings are included in the Council of Foreign Ministers files, Lot M–88, Boxes 110–111. The United States Delegation reported by telegram to Washington on each meeting of the Deputies. These messages together with Department comments, instructions, and related papers are included in Department file 865.014.

865.014/10–747

Memorandum of Conversation, by James J. Durnan of the Division of African Affairs

CONFIDENTIAL [WASHINGTON,] October 7, 1947.

Participants: Mr. Mario di Stefano, Italian Minister
Mr. Joseph Palmer 2nd, AF
Mr. James J. Durnan, AF

Mr. di Stefano, in referring to the meeting of the Foreign Ministers' Deputies in London, stated that he had noted items in the press indicating a disagreement in connection with the definition of the term "interested governments" as used in the Italian Peace Treaty and inquired as to the exact nature of the disagreement. Mr. Palmer informed Mr. di Stefano that the US had proposed the "interested governments" should comprise those countries whose forces fought in Africa on the side of the Allies during the last war and those who have made territorial claims in the former Italian Colonies, i.e., Italy, Ethiopia and Egypt. The British proposed that the term should be unrestricted with any government privileged to submit its views both on procedural matters and on the question of the disposition of the colonies. The Soviet proposal, which had been accepted by the French, would limit the interested governments to the Allied and Associated Powers which had signed the Italian Peace Treaty plus those which had made territorial claims. Asked as to our views on the latter two proposals, Mr. Palmer stated that we would probably support the British proposal, but if this was not found acceptable to the other Deputies we would agree to the Soviet proposal.

Mr. di Stefano then inquired as to our views with respect to the Soviet contention that the peace treaty required two Commissions of Investigation to be sent to the former Italian Colonies. Mr. Palmer stated that we favored one Commission for reasons based largely on economy, difficulty in finding experienced personnel, and uniformity of standards used in evaluating conditions in each colony. Mr. di Stefano referred to a letter received from Mr. Henderson in March 1947,[1] and inquired as to the Department's position with respect to an Italian representative being heard by the Commission in the colonies. Mr. Palmer stated that while we could not give any support to the Italian request for an Italian representative to be attached to the Commission, we would support any request which might be presented to the Deputies for the Commission to hear the views of an Italian representative in the colonies. Mr. di Stefano then inquired as to whether we would present such a proposal at the meeting of the Deputies and was informed that while we would not take any initiative in the matter we would give it support if the question was raised by any other government, including the Italian Government.

Mr. di Stefano discussed at length the long historic ties between Italy and North Africa, the friendly relations which existed and continued to exist between the Italian peasant settlers and Arabs in North Africa, the benefits derived by the Arabs in Libya from Italian administration, and the pressing need for Italy to find an outlet for its surplus population. Mr. di Stefano stated if Libya was disposed of other than as a trust territory under the individual or joint administration of Italy there would be serious troubles in North Africa. Asked to elaborate on this point, Mr. di Stefano stated that unless Italy returned to Libya in some capacity it would have no alternative but to collaborate with the Arabs for the expulsion of France and Great Britain from North Africa. In response to Mr. Palmer's inquiry as to the benefits Italy expected to derive should such an event materialize, Mr. di Stefano was not entirely clear other than to say that Italy had received overtures from the Arabs and would be installed in North Africa on the basis of equality with the Arabs.

---

[1] The reference here is to a letter of March 7, 1947, not printed, from Loy W. Henderson to di Stefano, which repeated the substance of paragraph 2 of telegram 297, March 1, to Rome, p. 570. Henderson's letter was in response to di Stefano's letter of February 18, 1947, not printed, regarding Italian participation in the Commission of Investigation to be sent to the former Italian colonies. (865.014/2–1847)

Mr. di Stefano stated he had heard that the U.S. was considering the acquisition of Libya as a trust territory and inquired as to the accuracy of this report. Mr. Palmer stated that this was one of many press reports expressing different views on the question of the disposition of the Italian Colonies. Asked as to whether the Department had formulated any views on the disposition of the Italian Colonies, Mr. Palmer stated that the matter was being studied and that no decision had been reached as yet. Pressed on the point, Mr. Palmer stated that he did not feel at liberty to discuss the matter further. Mr. di Stefano remarked that he felt certain conclusions might be drawn from the discussion but was informed by Mr. Palmer that it would be a grave mistake for Mr. di Stefano to infer that we had already made up our minds on the question of the disposition of the Italian Colonies. Mr. di Stefano then inquired as to the position of the other Powers and was informed that we had no information on the subject.

Editorial Note

Between October 16 and November 7, 1947, American and British officials held conversations in Washington, referred to as the "Pentagon Talks of 1947", on a variety of political, military, and economic subjects concerning the Middle East and the Eastern Mediterranean. For documentation on these conversations, see volume V, pages 485 ff.; see in particular the undated paper prepared by the Department of State entitled "Disposition of the Italian Colonies", paragraph m, page 543, the undated joint statement of the U.S.-U.K. groups entitled "Assurance of British Strategic Facilities in Cyrenaica", page 586, and the undated joint statement of the U.S.-U.K. groups entitled "Disposition of Former Italian Colonies Other Than Cyrenaica", page 588.

CFM Files : Lot M–88 : Box 110

Instructions from the Deputies for the Former Italian Colonies of the Council of Foreign Ministers to the Four Power Commission of Investigation for the Former Italian Colonies [1]

SECRET   LONDON, 21st October, 1947.
C.F.M./D/L/47/IC/25

I. COMPOSITION

1. The Commission shall consist of Delegations from each of the Four Powers, composed of a Head of Delegation, not more than three

---

[1] These instructions were completed and approved by the Deputies at their 9th Meeting, October 20, 1947.

advisers, a Secretary of Delegation and not more than four interpreters and clerical assistants.[2]

II. Task

2. The task of the Commission of Investigation shall be to collect and supply the Deputies with the necessary data on the question of the disposal of the former Italian Colonies and to ascertain the views of the local population in accordance with the Joint Declaration of the Governments of the Soviet Union, the United Kingdom, the United States of America, and of France, concerning the former Italian territorial possessions in Africa.[3] This shall include data regarding political, economic and social conditions in each colony, as well as the wishes and welfare of the inhabitants and the interests of peace and security.

For this purpose the Commission shall visit each of the former Italian Colonies, i.e. Libya, Eritrea and Italian Somaliland, and carry out investigations on the spot.

3. The Commission shall also carry out any other investigations which may be required by the Deputies concerning such questions as boundary adjustments and any other matters on which information may be required by the Deputies.

4. Upon completion of the investigations in each Colony the Commission shall prepare and submit a report to the Deputies on that Colony, containing such data and information as are called for herein. These reports shall be, if necessary, supplemented or amplified by the Commission on completion of its investigation in all the territories. These reports shall not contain any recommendations on the final disposal of the territories.

III. Procedure

5. The itinerary of the Commission shall be drawn up by the Commission itself, approved by the Deputies, and amended where necessary by the Commission.

6. The Commission shall not investigate any matters outside the boundaries of the former Italian Colonies, except under instruction from the Deputies.

7. The Commission shall have the right to confer with the administration and any officials, organised bodies and inhabitants of the Colonies, irrespective of nationality, as well as to call upon such

---

[2] Heads of the Delegations were: United States—John E. Utter; United Kingdom—F. E. Stafford; France—Etienne Burin des Roziers; Soviet Union—Artemiy Fedorovich Fedorov.

[3] The reference here is to the Joint Declaration constituting Annex XI of the Treaty of Peace with Italy.

sources in the Colonies as they may deem necessary for information relative to the investigation.

8. (i) To the fullest extent possible all sections of the local population are to be given an opportunity of making their views known, and to ensure this the Commission shall visit centres at which the people can most easily be congregated.

(ii) The timetable, local itineraries, and technical arrangements shall be made by the Commission in co-operation with the local authorities.

9. The Commission shall complete its work, including the submission of its reports to the Deputies within a period of not less than six and not more than seven months from the date of the departure of the Commission from London.

10. The work and documentation of the Commission shall be conducted in three official languages: English, French and Russian.

IV. CHAIRMANSHIP AND SECRETARIAT

11. During the Commission's stay in London, the Chairman of the Commission shall be the head of the delegation of the country whose Deputy is for the time being presiding at the meetings of the Deputies.

12. When the Commission is on the spot, the Chairmanship of the Commission shall be held by the heads of delegations, each of whom will act in turn for periods of seven calendar days. The order of rotation shall be the Latin alphabetical order, in the English language, viz. France, Union of Soviet Socialist Republics, United Kingdom and the United States of America.

13. The Commission shall set up a joint secretariat consisting of the secretaries of Delegations, together with such additional clerical assistants and interpreters as it may be found necessary to appoint for this purpose. The Commission shall appoint one of the Secretaries to act as Senior Secretary who will be responsible to the Chairman for the conduct of the work of the joint secretariat.

14. The Commission will keep the following for submission to the Deputies:

(a) summary minutes of the meetings of the Commission;

(b) summary records of the interviews conducted by the Commission;

(c) summary records of the investigations conducted on the spot by the Commission or members designated therefor; and

(d) an index of documentary material acquired by the Commission to which will be annexed any documents which the Commission considers useful to the fulfilment of its tasks.

CFM Files : Lot M–88 : Box 110

Decision by the Deputies for the Former Italian Colonies of the Council of Foreign Ministers [1]

SECRET

LONDON, 21st October, 1947.

C.F.M./D/L/47/IC/27

TIME-TABLE OF THE CONFERENCE OF DEPUTIES AND OF THE COMMISSION OF INVESTIGATION FROM OCTOBER, 1947 TO JUNE, 1948

1. The Deputies shall constitute a Four Power Commission for the investigation of the former Italian Colonies not later than October 20th, 1947.

2. The Deputies shall send out not later than October 20th, 1947, invitations to other interested Governments, as well as to the Governments of Italy and Egypt, asking for a reply within 14 days, enquiring whether they desire to submit their views regarding the disposal of the former Italian Colonies.[2]

3. The Commission shall leave for the field early in November.

4. The Deputies, early in November, will invite other interested Governments, as well as the Governments of Italy and Egypt, which have expressed the desire to present their views, to do so in the order established by the Deputies.

5. During the period early November, 1947, to early June, 1948:

(*a*) The Commission will carry out their investigations in the Colonies.

(*b*) The Deputies will consider the views of the other interested Governments, as well as of the Governments of Italy and Egypt.

(*c*) The Commission will present its reports to the Deputies.

(*d*) Copies of the reports of the Commission will be circulated by the Deputies to other interested Governments, as well as to the Governments of Italy and Egypt.

6. The Commission of Investigation will complete its work early in June.

---

[1] The text of this decision was agreed upon by the Deputies at their 8th Meeting, October 17, 1947.

[2] At their 3rd Meeting, October 7, 1947, the Deputies agreed to define "other interested Governments" as all Allied and Associated Powers, besides the United States, the United Kingdom, the Soviet Union, and France, which signed the Peace Treaty with Italy (Australia, Belgium, Byelorussian S.S.R., Brazil, Greece, India, Canada, China, the Netherlands, New Zealand, Poland, Ukrainian S.S.R., Czechoslovakia, Ethiopia, Union of South Africa, Yugoslavia) and countries that had made territorial claims (Egypt and Italy), it being understood that the definition would include Pakistan. On October 20, 1947, the Secretary General of the Deputies, E. A. Paton-Smith, sent letters to these "other interested Governments" inviting them to express, if they so desired, their views regarding the disposal of the former Italian Colonies. The text of the letter was circulated to the Deputies as document CFM/D/L/47/IC/30, October 21, 1947, not printed.

CFM Files : Lot M–88 : Box 110

Decision by the Deputies for the Former Italian Colonies of the Council of Foreign Ministers [1]

SECRET   LONDON, 21st October, 1947.

C.F.M./D/L/47/IC/29

PROCEDURE FOR HEARING "OTHER INTERESTED GOVERNMENTS" AND THE GOVERNMENTS OF ITALY AND EGYPT

1. Appropriate invitations should be sent to "other interested Governments", as defined by the Deputies, as well as the Governments of Italy and Egypt, asking for a reply within 14 days as to whether they desire to submit their views, in writing or orally should they desire it, regarding the disposal of the former Italian Colonies.

2. The opening date and the chronological order of hearings of the "other interested Governments", as well as of the Governments of Italy and Egypt, by the Conference of Deputies in London shall be decided by the Deputies later, in accordance with paragraph 1, after receipt of replies to the invitations. In drawing up the chronological order of hearing the views of the above-mentioned Governments, the Deputies shall give the first opportunity of stating their views regarding the disposal of the former Italian Colonies to the countries neighbouring these territories, i.e. to Egypt and Ethiopia, as well as to Italy.

3. The Deputies shall study the points of view submitted by "other interested Governments", as well as by the Governments of Italy and Egypt with a view to completing the work by the time the reports of the Commission of Investigation of the Four Powers are received.

4. "Other interested Governments", as well as the Governments of Italy and Egypt should not participate in or be directly connected with the work of the Commission of Investigation of the Four Powers.

The drawing up and approval of instructions, route and time-table of the work of the Commission of Investigation of the Four Powers, as well as the definition of their composition is the prerogative exclusively of the Deputies of the Foreign Ministers of the U.S.S.R., of the U.K., of the U.S.A. and of France.

5. The Deputies shall send copies of the reports of the Commission to "other interested Governments", as well as to the Governments of Italy and Egypt, immediately upon their completion, giving them the right, after examination of the reports, to present supplementary views to the Conference of Deputies either in writing or orally, if they so desire.

---

[1] This decision was agreed upon by the Deputies at their 8th Meeting, October 17, 1947.

6. Any of the "other interested Governments", as well as the Governments of Italy and Egypt may on the recommendation of the Deputies and with the consent of the Council of Foreign Ministers be given the opportunity to present their views directly to the Council of Foreign Ministers at any session on the agenda of which appears the question of the disposal of the former Italian Colonies.

865.014/10–1647

The Director of the Office of Near Eastern and African Affairs (Henderson) to the Italian Minister (di Stefano)

[WASHINGTON,] October 28, 1947.

MY DEAR MR. DI STEFANO: I wish to refer to your letter of October 16, 1947 concerning certain requests of the Italian Government in connection with the meeting in London of the Deputies of the Foreign Ministers.[1] As you are aware, the Deputies of the Foreign Ministers have now agreed upon the terms of reference and the itinerary of the Commission to investigate the former Italian Colonies. It has been decided that the Commission will visit the territories in the following order: Eritrea, Italian Somaliland, and Libya.

With regard to your request that Italian experts be allowed to present their opinion to the Commission in the various areas visited, the terms of reference agreed upon by the Deputies for the Commission preclude hearing official representatives of the Italian Government in the territories. As you are aware, the American Deputy proposed that those states having territorial claims in the area should be afforded the opportunity of sending representatives to present their views to the Commission at certain specified places, but this proposal was not accepted. As the matter stands at present, however, the Commission is empowered to confer with the inhabitants of the colonies, irrespective of nationality, and all sections of the local population are to be given an opportunity of making their views known.

Under the procedure which has now been agreed upon, moreover, the Deputies of the Foreign Ministers will hear the views of the interested governments on the disposition of the former Italian Colonies and, in particular, will hear first of all those governments which have territorial claims; namely, Italy, Egypt and Ethiopia. It is understood that invitations have been sent to these governments to present their views to the Deputies and that after replies have been received hear-

---

[1] Not printed; it stated that the Italian Government was deeply concerned about the serious repercussions that might result should there be protracted delay in the arrival in Libya of the Commission of Investigation. (865.014/10–1647)

ings will be scheduled for the governments concerned. After the examination of the reports of the Commission the interested governments, including the Government of Italy, may present supplementary views to the conference of Deputies either in writing or orally. Furthermore, these same governments may, on the recommendation of the Deputies and with the consent of the Council of Foreign Ministers, be given an opportunity to present their views directly to the Council of Foreign Ministers. In view of these procedures, it would appear that the Italian Government will have ample opportunities to present its views and claims and to have them considered carefully by the Council of Foreign Ministers and its Deputies.

Sincerely yours,

LOY W. HENDERSON

865.014/11–1247 : Telegram

The Chargé in the United Kingdom (Gallman) to the Secretary of State

SECRET   LONDON, November 12, 1947—7 p. m.

6011. Itcol 90. Fourteenth meeting of DepItCol [1] held today 3 p. m. with Zaroubin presiding. Ethiopian Vice Minister Foreign Affairs Aklilou made long speech and presented memorandum on "claims of the Imperial Ethiopian Govt to the return of Eritrea and Italian Somaliland".[2] Speech and memorandum similar to those previously presented to CFM and Paris Peace Conference. Emphasized claim to all of Eritrea and all of Italian Somali. Copies speech and memorandum being forwarded to Dept.

During questioning Zaroubin asked if proposal made at CFM in May 1946 re trading Ogaden for Eritrea was still supported by Ethiopian Govt. Aklilou stalled in replying and asked for text of proposal. Zaroubin said he would raise question again in later meeting after Ethiopia had time to consider. Aklilou then announced that two months ago he had presented British Govt new draft treaty between Ethiopia-UK which contains paragraph which would return Ogaden to Ethiopia.[3]

Since emphasis Ethiopian statement was on Eritrea, questions were asked about Ethiopian claims to Italian Somali. Aklilou said written

---

[1] Deputies for the Former Italian Colonies.
[2] The text of oral and written views of the Ethiopian Government were circulated to the Deputies as document CFM/D/L/47/IC/72, November 12, 1947, not printed.
[3] For an additional report on the subject raised in this paragraph, see telegram 6104, Itcol 91, November 18, from London, *infra.*

statement on Somali would be submitted soonest possible [4] and hoped to present oral statement on Somali at another hearing.

Deputies agreed send Ethiopian speech and memorandum to ItCol Commission with covering letter mentioning important points to be investigated. Letter to be drafted by Secretary-General and approved by Deputies.

Deputies agreed hear views Italy Nov 19 and Egypt Nov 21. Deputies also agreed to reply South Africa in same manner as reply sent New Zealand which says New Zealand will be afforded opportunity express views both before and after ItCol Commission presents reports.[5] Replies to other interested govts are to be drafted in similar vein subject to Deputies' approval.

GALLMAN

---

[4] The Ethiopian Government's communication, dated November 17, 1947, regarding Ethiopian claims for the return of Italian Somaliland was circulated to the Deputies as document CFM/D/L/47/IC/75, November 17, 1947, not printed.

[5] In communications to the Secretary General of the Deputies dated October 27 and October 31, 1947, respectively, circulated to the Deputies as documents CFM/D/L/47/IC/38 and 47, neither printed, the New Zealand and South African Governments protested against the restrictions imposed by the Deputies on the expression of views of Allied Governments which had participated in the war in Africa on all procedural and substantive matters at all stages of the proceedings of the Deputies. The identical replies sent to the New Zealand and South African Governments on November 1 and 13, 1947, respectively, and summarized here, were circulated to the Deputies as documents CFM/D/L/47/IC 57 and 57 *bis*, neither printed.

865.014/11–1847 : Telegram

The Ambassador in the United Kingdom (Douglas) to the Secretary of State

SECRET　　　　　　　　　　　　　　　　LONDON, November 18, 1947—7 p. m.

6104. Itcol 91. Re Colit 50 [1]. Zaroubin's questioning of Ethiopians on possibility Ogaden-Eritrea trade referred to Ethiopian's memorandum dated May 15, 1946 presented Deputies CFM, June 4, 1946, with document CFM (D) (46) 126.[2] Zaroubin quoted part of paragraph three of this memorandum that "it would appear that Ethiopia by giving up one-fourth of her empire, namely the province of the

---

[1] Telegram 4875, Colit 50, November 17, to London, not printed, requested an amplification of paragraph 2 of telegram 6011, Itcol 90, November 12, from London, *supra* (865.014/11–1747).

[2] Not printed. For documentation on the Second Session of the Council of Foreign Ministers in Paris, April–July 1946 and the related meetings of the Deputies, almost exclusively devoted to the preparation of the draft peace treaties with Italy, Bulgaria, Hungary, Rumania, and Finland, see *Foreign Relations*, 1946, vol. II, pp. 88 ff.

Ogaden might receive in return a portion of Eritrea, a land that has belonged to Ethiopia for over three thousand years".

After 14th meeting of deputies ItCol Zaroubin sent above quoted excerpt to Aklilou, Ethiopian Vice Minister FonAffairs. Aklilou replied on November 17 with explanation that Zaroubin had quoted only small part of paragraph three of memorandum referred to. Aklilou transmitted full text of paragraph under reference which he said "should set at rest all doubts in regard to the matter". Full paragraph does not substantiate Soviet allegation and concludes "the Imperial Ethiopian Govt entertain the belief that none of the four great powers will seriously support a suggestion that Ethiopia may regain territories of which she has been deprived by aggression at the cost of paying for the same in other territories of the empire, the use of which she has contributed to the prosecution of the war now victoriously ended".

Embassy today rec'd copies this correspondence between Soviets and Ethiopians with documents quoted above.[3] Zaroubin may also have had in mind British proposal for United Somaliland including Ogaden under British trusteeship made to CFM April 29, 1946, and contained in document CFM (46) 22.[4] British proposal summarized page eight OIR report number 4326 [4] on "proposals for the disposition of the Italian colonies in Africa".

Ethiopians yesterday submitted written statement [5] to Deputies claiming all Italian Somaliland should be returned to Ethiopia. Ethiopian Govt has not requested further oral hearing on Italian Somaliland.

DOUGLAS

---

[3] The correspondence under reference here is included in the working files of the Division of African Affairs, Lot 54 D 464, Box 1640.

[4] Not printed.

[5] CFM/D/L/47/IC/75, November 17, 1947, not printed.

865.014/11–1947 : Telegram

The Ambassador in the United Kingdom (Douglas) to the Secretary of State

SECRET　　　　　　　　　　　　　　LONDON, November 19, 1947—10 p. m.

6123. Itcol 92. Fifteenth meeting deputies ItCol held today 3 p.m. with Massigli presiding. Italian Ambassador Gallarati Scotti read speech in English presenting view Italian Government that all three former colonies should be placed under Italian trusteeship within framework UN Charter.[1] Speech pointed out that because of differences between territories it would be necessary devise suitable form trusteeship for each territory. Bulk speech devoted to praising Italian accomplishments in colonies and claiming great benefits would result from Italian administration in future. Copies of speech being forwarded to Department. Italian memorandum on Eritrea [2] already sent Department. Scotti said today written statement regarding Somaliland would be submitted soon.

During questioning British deputy asked if Italian Government had considered length of time trusteeship should last. Italian adviser Cerruli [3] replied negatively, saying Italian Government had considered only general question of trusteeship.

In response to questions raised by Douglas as to whether the colonies had been economic and financial liability to Italy, Cerruli asserted cost civilian administration met by revenues from colonies but that military and extraordinary expenses including public works had been paid for by Italian Government. Cerruli insisted that in future these capital investments would be benefit to administration. At Zaroubin's suggestion, deputies agreed ask Italian representatives to present data on economic questions.

Since deputies could not agree on whether to send Italian statement to Commission nor on text of draft letter transmitting Ethiopian statement to Commission, it was agreed to discuss disposition statements all three governments after hearing Egyptian views at next meeting.

Deputies discussed draft letters replying to certain interested governments for nearly two hours without agreeing on solution. Secretary-General admitted he had exceeded his instructions in sending letters to Canada and Australia identical with letters previously sent to South Africa and New Zealand. Zaroubin very critical this mistake and refused approval Secretary-General's action retroactively although other three deputies willing to do so. Early in discussion, Zaroubin indicated approval of identical letters to Byelorussia, Czechoslovakia, Poland, Ukraine, and Yugoslavia. After misunderstanding concerning letters to Australia and Canada, Zaroubin refused agree to sending letters to Soviet satellites, although other deputies had approved. Apparently Zaroubin felt Soviet satellites being treated dif-

---

[1] Tommaso Gallarati Scotti, the Italian Ambassador in the United Kingdom. For the text of Gallarati Scotti's speech, see Margaret Carlyle (ed.), *Documents on International Affairs, 1947–1948*, issued under the auspices of the Royal Institute of International Affairs (New York, London, Toronto, Oxford University Press, 1952), p. 250.

[2] The memorandum under reference was circulated to the Deputies as document CFM/D/L/47/IC/70, November 7, 1947, not printed.

[3] Enrico Cerulli, African specialist in the Italian Ministry of State.

ferently from British dominions since text of letters were different although practical effect the same. Texts these draft letters to be discussed again at next deputies meeting.

DOUGLAS

865.014/11–2147 : Telegram

The Ambassador in the United Kingdom (Douglas) to the Secretary of State

SECRET LONDON, November 21, 1947—5 p. m.

6140. Itcol 93. Sixteenth meeting DepItCol held today 10 a. m. with Massigli presiding. Gallman represented United States. Egyptian Ambassador Abdel Fattah Amr presented brief statement in English reaffirming full views set forth in written statement being forwarded to Department.[1] Written statement emphasizes unity of Libya, claims Libya should become independent state immediately, and if Libya should need help during period of readjustment Egypt, either solely or conjointly with other members Arab League, would supply help required. Written statement also calls for rectifications of Egypt's western boundaries and claims all of Eritrea. Statement says Egypt believes people of Italian Somaliland entitled to immediate exercise right of self-determination. Speech added nothing to written views and answers to American questions reaffirmed written claims. United Kingdom deputy asked if Egypt thought it would be just for Ethiopia to have outlet to sea. Answer was if Egypt controlled Eritrea Massawa would be made available to Ethiopia and, besides, other ports could be used by Ethiopia. French and Soviet deputies did not ask any questions.

Deputies continued discussion from last meeting on draft letters replying to certain interested governments for more than two hours without reaching solution. Soviet deputy stated same form of letter should be sent to all these governments (see Itcol 92 [2]) and introduced new draft letter which would [have?] advised these governments to present their views to deputies before reports of commission are received and would have informed these governments they would have right to present supplementary views to deputies after examination of reports if they so desire. Gallman suggested Soviet draft might form basis of replies with certain modifications and additions. British deputy insisted replies should be modeled on letter sent New Zealand. Various compromise suggestions were not acceptable to either British

---

[1] The written statement under reference was circulated to the Deputies as document CFM/D/L/47/IC/76, November 18, 1947, not printed.

[2] Telegram 6123, Itcol 92, November 19, from London, *supra.*

or Soviets. During discussion Zaroubin emphasized his interpretation of agreed procedure (see Itcol 64 [3]) that governments desiring present supplementary views after examining reports of commission must first present views for deputies to study reports of commission received.

British deputy finally suggested sending letters to governments concerned which would be same as letter sent New Zealand on understanding that another letter would be sent to these governments later containing points in Soviet draft which would have to be agreed to by deputies. British deputy agreed make modifications in Soviet draft acceptable to British Government today. Deputies agreed meet tomorrow morning to consider draft letters again and complete other business remaining.[4]

DOUGLAS

---

[3] The telegram under reference, not printed, transmitted the text of document CFM/D/L/47/IC/29, October 21, 1947, p. 613.

[4] At their 17th Meeting, November 22, 1947, the Deputies agreed to send an acknowledgement to the other interested Governments whose communications were awaiting replies and to withdraw the letters which had been sent in error to Canada and Australia on November 13. The Deputies also agreed to transmit to the Commission of Investigation the views presented to the Deputies by Ethiopia, Italy, and Egypt. The Commission was to investigate, in particular, any conflicting statements of fact in the views of the three governments. In pursuance of an earlier decision, the Deputies agreed not to meet again until after the conclusion of the Fifth Session of the Council of Foreign Ministers in London, November 25–December 15, 1947.

INTEREST OF THE UNITED STATES IN THE REPATRIATION OF GERMAN PRISONERS OF WAR IN WESTERN EUROPE; AGREEMENT WITH FRANCE FOR RECRUITMENT OF VOLUNTARY LABOR FOR FRANCE IN THE UNITED STATES ZONE OF GERMANY

740.62114/11–2946 : Circular Telegram

The Acting Secretary of State to the Diplomatic Missions in Belgium, France, Luxembourg, and The Netherlands

TOP SECRET   WASHINGTON, November 29, 1946—6 p. m.
US URGENT

For the Chief of Mission from the Secretary. The President, the Secretary of War [1] and I have decided to begin immediately repatriation of POWs in Am custody or transferred by US to liberated nations. I realize the problems both economic and political which this decision will cause to the Govts of France, Belgium, the Neth and Lux. You should immediately approach the head of Govt to which you are accredited. There follow the lines along which you should speak. Please be guided thereby, using your best judgment as to emphasis most persuasive to head of Govt:

You should base your approach on the pressure being exerted on this Govt by public opinion in the US, with the statement that pressure for return of these POWs is becoming so intensified as to leave this Govt no alternative but to begin immediately a repatriation program. Fortunately, in the case of France, as well as Belgium, the Netherlands and Luxembourg, we are dealing with Govts who can appreciate the force of public opinion in a truly democratic state. In all four cases it is believed that the Govts will appreciate the necessity with which we are faced if they are convinced that public opinion in the US demands this action.

You should then touch on the following points:

(a) A year and a half have elapsed since the end of active hostilities in Europe.

(b) The Geneva POW Convention,[2] both in its letter and spirit, contemplates the repatriation of POWs as soon as possible after the cessation of active hostilities.

---

[1] Robert P. Patterson.
[2] Signed at Geneva July 27, 1929; for text, see *Foreign Relations*, 1929, vol. I, pp. 336–367.

(*c*) The concept of forced labor is repugnant to the American people. The growing feeling in this country, therefore, is that failure to repatriate POWs who are not charged with war crimes or who are not otherwise ineligible for repatriation is indefensible on moral as well as legal grounds.

(*d*) Our position has become more difficult in this connection since the Soviet Govt has announced its intention to repatriate immediately a large number of German POWs in its custody. Added to this is the strong movement in Great Britain which has forced the British Govt to take similar action with respect to POWs under its control.

(*e*) We are, therefore, obliged to announce that beginning immediately we are instituting a program of repatriation applicable both to German POWs transferred for labor to Allied Govts and those remaining under direct American control in Europe. We have, of course, already repatriated most of the German POWs over whom we retained control.

(*f*) We are not, however, unmindful of the economic problems in your country which the labor of these POWs serves in part to ameliorate. Accordingly, our program provides for graduated repatriation over a period ending Oct. 1, 1947, at which time it is contemplated that all German POWs for whom the US is responsible and who are eligible for repatriation will have been returned to their homes. This will provide an opportunity to make gradual adjustments to meet the situation resulting from the departure of this labor. The American military authorities charged with the implementation of the repatriation program will consult with the French authorities with regard to the repatriation of particular occupational groups among the POWs but, of course, it must be understood that repatriation must proceed on a regularly scheduled basis over the period stipulated.

(*g*) Announcement of this program will be made in the US in the near future.

(*h*) A simultaneous notification of our intention is being made to the French, Belgian, Netherlands and Luxembourg Govts by our Chiefs of Mission in those countries.

(*i*) Should Head of Govt suggest that POWs in his country's custody for whom U.S. is responsible be offered the opportunity to accept while still in that country the status of "free laborers", you should tell him that the position is unacceptable to us since it would inevitably lead to charges of coercion. In any case it is in our view in violation of the Geneva Convention, which expressly requires repatriation. As further evidence of our recognition of local economic problems you should offer our cooperation in the recruitment of German labor on a voluntary basis in Germany for immigration to country concerned to supplement available native labor.

Chiefs of Mission please coordinate simultaneous approach to respective Heads of Govt and cable immediately "Niact for the Secretary" when approach to Govt is made.[3]

---

[3] Replies, dated December 3, 1946, from the four Missions, reported acceptance by the four Governments of the United States program, although the French Minister for Foreign Affairs, Georges Bidault, said that he was not happy about it.

Sent Paris as 6239,[4] Brussels as 1404, The Hague as 675, and Luxembourg as 66. [Byrnes.]

ACHESON

[4] The following sentence was added to the cable to Paris: "You will recall that I made similar approach to Bidault last summer and that at his urgent request I reluctantly agreed to defer action until after French elections."

740.62114/1–747

The Secretary of State to the Legal Adviser (Fahy)

[WASHINGTON,] January 7, 1947.

MR. FAHY: Reference is made to your memorandum [1] as to prisoners of war. When I first discussed with Bidault the return of war prisoners and he referred to the shortage of labor, I urged that he take some of the displaced persons. He told me that he could not do so. They did not want the Jews and the Soviets objected to their taking either Slavs or Poles.

Again in New York when I advised Couve de Murville [2] that our message had gone forward to Bidault urging him to take over some of the displaced persons, he said that he did not think it possible for them to do it. However, I urged the matter upon him in the hope that when they were faced with the necessity of returning the prisoners they might change their minds.

Both Bidault and de Murville would take Germans, but they want Germans who are young, physically strong and who were not actively Nazis. I fear the specifications will restrict the immigration.

J[AMES] F. B[YRNES]

[1] Not printed.
[2] Deputy to the French Foreign Minister at the meeting of the Council of Foreign Ministers in New York, November 4–December 12, 1946.

740.62114/1–1647 : Telegram

The Ambassador in France (Caffery) to the Secretary of State

SECRET   PARIS, January 16, 1947—midnight.
US URGENT

210. Following is translation of a note Blum [1] signed immediately upon his return from London about noon today which he has just sent me by hand:

(*Begin translation*). I have the honor to acknowledge the receipt of Your Excellency's memorandum which you delivered to my predeces-

[1] Léon Blum, President of the French Council of Ministers.

sor on December 3 last,[2] concerning the repatriation of the German prisoners of war who have been transferred from the American Army to the French Army.

1. The French Government desires to inform the Government of the United States that it fully appreciates the statements made in the above-mentioned memorandum and according to which there is a close connection between the problem of the release of the German prisoners of war and the present economic situation in France.

In this respect, the American Government's offer to facilitate recruiting, in the American zone of Germany, of volunteers for work in France is very much appreciated. The French Government is convinced that this offer will enable it to lessen the material difficulties which the release and repatriation of the German prisoners of war will inevitably entail for French economy. Moreover, the American Government is fully aware of these difficulties since it has of its own accord—and the French Government keenly appreciates this gesture—postponed the date on which it considers the prisoners captured by its armies and transferred to France should be released. However, the French Government believes it advisable to recall very briefly its vital necessity to have recourse to German labor and the importance to French national production of the contribution of the prisoners of war.

2. Because 720,000 French workers were sent to Germany as forced laborers under the "Service de Travail Obligatoire," because 1,500,000 French prisoners of war were kept in the Reich for 5 years, and because of the forced labor required of political deportees, French labor has suffered a decrease in numbers which, taking into account only the dead and the totally unemployable, represents more than 500,000 persons, to this figure must also be added several hundreds of thousands of persons partially unfit to work whose contribution to French economy can be only a very limited one. These losses, the result of the German action against France, have up to now been compensated for by the labor of the prisoners of war, of whom 220,000 make an indispensable contribution to national agriculture; nearly 150,000 work in various branches of industry, in transportation, on public works and on reconstruction; and 56,000 mine 20 percent of the French coal production. (44,000 as miners in the coal mines, and 14,500 working above ground. Moreover, German prisoners of war are employed in the iron mines and the potassium mines, etc.)

At a time when France is suffering a considerable reduction in its supplies of coal from the Ruhr, when it is obliged to content itself with coal imports from abroad which are less than 50 percent of the coal imports in 1938, when it must do without the labor of tens of thousands of workers of Slav origin, principally miners, who have requested their repatriation and whose departure, followed by that of the German prisoners, would result in a decrease of 25 percent in France's national coal production, the contribution of the German prisoners to its economy, chiefly in connection with the crucial problem of coal, assumes an absolutely vital importance.

3. With a view to reconciling its desire to meet the request of the American Government and the necessities of French economy, the

---

[2] See telegram 6239, November 29, 1946, to Paris, p. 621, for substance of the memorandum.

French Government intends, with the consent of the United States, to offer, in particular to the German prisoners transferred by the American command and who remain under French control, the choice of being repatriated to Germany or of remaining in France as voluntary workers benefiting from a status very similar to that of French workers. With a view to guaranteeing to the American Government that no pressure will be exercised on the German prisoners in question and that these prisoners will enjoy complete freedom of choice in this respect, the French Government intends to invite the International Committee of the Red Cross to designate representatives who will be members of the commissions entrusted with offering the option described above to the prisoners entitled to be released. This measure should enable a considerable number of these prisoners to be released very rapidly under conditions in entire conformity with respect for the individual— and sooner than the date determined by the American Government for the release of the prisoners which it transferred to France.

4. The repatriation of prisoners who do not volunteer for work in France obviously gives rise to questions of various sorts, and particularly of transportation, which, because of the shortage of French coal production, can be solved only with great difficulty. In fact, this shortage has already obliged the French Government to reduce by 22 percent train travel on French railways at a time when freight trains are required to transport additional goods because of the decrease or the cessation of canal transportation, due to the winter.

Furthermore, agreements must necessarily be concluded with the various zones in Germany from which the prisoners came originally, for the repatriation to those zones of those who do not volunteer for work in France.

5. In order to determine as soon as possible the terms of settlement of the prisoners of war problem and to conclude the resulting agreements, a French technical delegation has been instructed to be prepared to meet an American technical delegation, either at Frankfurt or at Paris. The French Government would greatly appreciate learning the date on which the negotiations can begin. (*End translation*)

Blum had very considerable difficulty even with his own Socialist Ministries (particularly Industrial Production, National Economy, Labor and Reconstruction) to get them to agree to foregoing note. The delay in our receiving this note was caused largely by the fact that the above-mentioned Ministries presented two previous drafts (which were shown to me in confidence) which were most unsatisfactory from our point of view. He signed this note in the brief period between his arrival in Paris about noon and his departure for Versailles for the presidential elections at 2 o'clock this afternoon, in the knowledge that if he did not do so, the whole question would have to be reexamined when the new government is finally formed, and a less satisfactory reply might be forthcoming. The official who brought the note said Blum had requested him to tell me in confidence that he (Blum) had done his level best to produce a satisfactory reply for us.

CAFFERY

740.62114/2–547 : Telegram

The Ambassador in France (Caffery) to the Secretary of State

SECRET   PARIS, February 5, 1947—7 p. m.
US URGENT

515. Department's 322, January 24, 7 p. m.[1] I have been told informally by both Foreign Office and International Red Cross that latter does not feel it can accept the French proposal to participate in the option between repatriation and voluntary labor in France to be offered to German prisoners of war.

Foreign Ministry stated that representatives of various interested French governmental agencies are meeting today and tomorrow and an important meeting of the Cabinet will occur the day after tomorrow to consider proposing an alternative solution to US Government. Foreign Office said in confidence that French are considering proposing to US that the UNRRA, Intergovernmental Committee on Refugees, or even perhaps official American representatives replace International Red Cross in supervising the reaction to such possibilities.

Insofar as the meeting of French-American technical experts is concerned Foreign Office hopes to be able to arrange first meeting in Paris during next week so that repatriation program can commence.

CAFFERY

---

[1] Not printed.

740.62114/2–1447 : Telegram

The Secretary of State to the Embassy in France

SECRET   WASHINGTON, February 25, 1947—7 p. m.

743. French Embassy has delivered note dated February 14[1] containing elaborate proposals for disposal German POWs. Department has requested French Embassy have Foreign Office make available copy to you.

Our comments follow. U.S. has recognized the serious position of the French economy in respect to its urgent need for manpower and considers that we have cooperated fullest extent with the French Government in the matter of repatriation of these POWs. In advising the French you should remind them that Secretary Byrnes, at Bidault's urgent request, postponed for 6 months presenting the French with our decision to ask repatriation these POWs. We have, in addition,

---

[1] Not printed.

offered to help recruit DPs and Germans (including liberated POWs) in our zone of Germany and this offer still stands. You should also remind them that both Bidault and Blum personally, and as heads of governments, have agreed in principle with our objectives and have expressed appreciation for our understanding cooperation.

We are obliged to insist upon the immediate initiation in actual operation of a phased and orderly program of repatriation of POWs. To that end we request that immediate discussion begin on a technical level with the American authorities which will result in putting plan into actual operation on a regularly scheduled basis. The question of which groups should move first can be taken up in those discussions. We see no point in discussing question of postponement of date of completion beyond October 1, 1947, when at present no planned repatriation is in actual operation and its numerical aspects can not be judged on basis of performance. We believe that the essential thing to accomplish now is the inauguration of the program leaving the problems of the future to be settled as they arise.

Note unclear in two basic respects: (1) by referring throughout to "liberation on the spot or repatriation". Our position is that unless InterCross reconsiders its reported refusal to supervise free choice by prisoners between repatriation and liberation on the spot (your tel 683, Feb 14 [2]) we must insist on full repatriation; (2) note apparently combined French captured POWs with those turned over by U.S. Our position has to do only with those POWs captured by U.S. forces and we can not consider counter proposal amalgamating the two categories.

Note also states that of the 740,000 prisoners of war transferred to France in July 1945, 290,000 have already been "stricken off the rolls" ("rayés des controles"). While this may not be entirely relevant to present and future problem Department desires breakdown information as to what happened to these 290,000.

Please inform USFET fully.

MARSHALL

[2] Not printed.

740.62114/2-2847 : Circular telegram

The Secretary of State to Certain Diplomatic Officers [1]

SECRET WASHINGTON, February 28, 1947—3 p. m.

(Infotel) See infotels, Feb 6, 2 p.m., and Feb 10, 7 p.m.[2] Caffery reports after discussions with French Internatl Committee Red Cross

[1] Sent to Embassies in Belgium, Netherlands, United Kingdom, and the Soviet Union.
[2] Neither printed.

agreed participate in proposed plan by which German PW's given choice of repatriation or remaining in France as voluntary workers. Internatl Committee issued statement that plan will be carried out under conditions complete freedom and PW's will enjoy guarantees at least equivalent those provided by Geneva Convention. In discussions French reps stated their repatriation plan contemplates return PW's at rate 31,000 a month with no distinction made between PW's captured by French and those received from US.

MARSHALL

740.62114/2–2747 : Telegram

The Secretary of State to the Embassy in France

SECRET   WASHINGTON, February 28, 1947—6 p. m.
US URGENT

797. Our comments follow on InterCross statement urtel 890 Feb. 27.[1] Our original position called for full repatriation these POWs. However, at request French we agreed in principle to permit POWs waive repatriation and elect release from POW status to remain in France as voluntary labor provided InterCross willing accept invitation of French to supervise such option. Our willingness agree such plan based on belief InterCross participation would guarantee free choice and individual rights. Our further conditions stated Deptel 322 Jan. 24.[1] These still stand.

It is our view that with free choice guaranteed POWs waiving repatriation, after having been fully informed status to be accorded them in France, effect termination of their status as prisoners of war and consequently our obligation for them under the Geneva Convention likewise terminates. We are unwilling to agree to any arrangement which continues the obligation of this Govt for such POWs beyond the date of the signing of such option. Any obligation InterCross feels it may have regarding POWs following their release is matter strictly between the French and InterCross. If French agree permit InterCross continue protect interests voluntary workers, we would certainly not object.

Likewise we are not prepared to assume obligation to furnish technical and financial assistance to InterCross in carrying out program. Consider this matter also between French and InterCross. In any event believe additional duties accruing InterCross this connection

---

[1] Not printed.

would not be great since presumably only those indicating a desire to opt need be approached. Additionally under repatriation program contemplated by us InterCross services overall program France would diminish rapidly.

MARSHALL

740.62114/3–1347 : Telegram

The Ambassador in France (Caffery) to the Secretary of State

US URGENT   PARIS, March 13, 1947.

1116. Following is French text of communiqué released this afternoon by French FonOff on agreement on repatriation and liberation of PWs:[1]

"COMMUNIQUÉ TO THE PRESS   March 13, 1947

The American Government requested in a memorandum of December 3, 1946 that the German prisoners of war transferred by the United States to France and still remaining at the present time under French control be repatriated at the latest by October 1, next.

There are at the present time 630,000 German prisoners of war under French control of whom, in addition to the 450,000 transferred by the United States, 180,000 were captured by the French forces.

Of the total of 630,000 prisoners, more than 500,000 are at present employed in the French economy, including 55,000 in the coal mines, 210,000 in agriculture, and the remainder in the various branches of French industry (metallurgy, transportation, construction, etc. . . .).

Calling attention to the fact that the departure from here on October 1 of a total of 450,000 men would be a disaster particularly in French agriculture and coal mines where the prisoners, in the latter economic group, are extracting 20 percent of French coal production, the French Government has requested that the Americans permit the system of liberation on the spot (options) on the same basis as that for repatriation.

On those bases, the American and French negotiators have agreed to the following system:

a) The option will be offered to all the German prisoners with the exception of certain special categories. A period of three months will be granted to the prisoners to whom the option is offered to declare themselves for or against such option.

b) If they declare themselves opposed, the non-volunteers will remain prisoners and will be repatriated following an established schedule, taking into consideration a certain number of priorities.

---

[1] For text of the American press release on the same date regarding the agreement, see Department of State *Bulletin*, March 23, 1947, p. 539. For text of Memorandum of Understanding on Repatriation and Liberation of Prisoners of War, dated at Paris, March 11 and 13, 1947, see Treaties and Other International Acts Series (TIAS) No. 2405; United States Treaties and Other International Agreements (UST), vol. 3 (pt. 1), p. 445.

The repatriation will be made in the beginning at the rate of 20,000 men per month at the minimum.

c) Volunteers for work in France will, on the contrary, be given a work contract to the maximum limit of 25,000 men a month. It is a question of a "text" which will enable the French Government, after a few weeks, to find out whether the prisoners converted to workers and furnished with contracts are still working in France or not.

d) At the end of the period of several weeks indicated above, the two delegations will meet again to take stock of the experiment and to examine the rate of liberation on the spot and of repatriation.

The Agreement provides the American Government with all the necessary assurances with regard to the absolute freedom of choice of the prisoners which will be controlled by the International Committee of the Red Cross which has the full confidence of Washington and Paris.

The two delegations have studied during several meetings the problem of the transfer of wages which German voluntary work in France presents. The French delegation has agreed on this point to give full liberty to German workers who will themselves decide concerning the percentage of their wages which they will relinquish in francs to obtain payments in marks for their families in Germany. To the agreement [garbled] prisoners of war is attached a memorandum concerning the technical terms of the repatriation. This memorandum indicates in particular that the French Government will furnish to the United States the complete statement of the difference between the number of German prisoners of war transferred by the United States to France in 1945 and that of the prisoners who still remain at the present time under French control.

A list of names of the prisoners making up this difference will be furnished.

The two delegations have completed a draft agreement relating to the recruitment of displaced persons in the American zone of Germany. Within a short time, a third agreement relating to the recruitment of free German workers will be completed. The agreement relating to displaced persons and the agreement relating to the recruitment of free German workers for France will be signed simultaneously."

CAFFERY

851.504/3–2447 : Telegram

The Acting Secretary of State to the Embassy in France

SECRET   WASHINGTON, March 24, 1947—7 p. m.
US URGENT

1077. War despatching following cable General Clay:

"From WDSCA. Reurad CC–8312 March; ourade WX 88154, December; and WX 93587, March.[1]

---

[1] None printed.

Since President, SecState and SecWar agreed permit French voluntary recruitment of German labor in US Zone in return French agreement on repatriation German POWs (reourad WX 88154, Dec), US committed to undertake discussions with French relating to recruitment of labor in US Zone Germany. Reurad CC 8362[*8312*?] assumed here and considered necessary qualified representative of yours will be present in Paris beginning March 26 for purpose participating in this phase negotiations. We do not regard quadripartite approval necessary for such discussions, or possible action as result of discussions, within US Zone since recruitment on voluntary basis not inconsistent with US, UK, French views expressed in ACA apropos earlier Russian drafting German technicians. Agree that recruitment must take place so as not to conflict with our obligations to British under Bi-Zonal Agreement.[2]

Negotiations with French arising from US request repatriation US captured POWs began March 4 and resolved themselves into three phases—repatriation proper, recruitment DPs, and recruitment free German labor. Repatriation agreement signed March 13. Re DPs, French willing reach agreement similar that to be concluded with Belgians, but are withholding signing until initiation discussions recruitment voluntary labor US Zone Germany. March 26 date set resumption negotiations last two phases.

Following will be used as basis of negotiations with French on recruitment US Zone:

1. Resettlement DPs has priority for US over recruitment free German labor and will be so treated administratively by US if not possible obtain French agreement this point. In view French Communist opposition to recruitment DPs on political grounds, and recent Bidault declaration Moscow re dispersal German population, doubt French would agree such stipulation in agreement, but we must insist on provision that recruitment German labor shall not interfere with or otherwise affect recruitment among DPs.

2. Recruitment will be directed in first instance at Germans presently unemployed.

3. Recruitment will be conducted under direction of Zonal Commander, and no labor will be recruited without approval of Zonal Commander who will take into consideration need for retention in US Zone of such labor as is strictly necessary to carry out three-year program for achievement self-sustaining economy in bizonal area pursuant to US–UK Agreement.

4. All labor will be recruited on voluntary basis.

5. Arrangements should be made to establish means for German labor voluntarily recruited for service in France and for German POWs electing voluntarily to remain in France to remit support allowances to their dependents in Germany. OMGUS has been authorized to introduce in Allied Control Authority general proposal for quadripartite procedures governing benevolent remit-

---

[2] For text of the Memorandum of Agreement between the United Kingdom and the United States on the Economic Fusion of their Respective Zones of Occupation in Germany, December 2, 1946, see Department of State Treaties and Other International Acts Series (TIAS) No. 1575, or 61 Stat. (pt. 3), 2475. See also *Foreign Relations*, 1946, vol. v, pp. 481 ff.

tances from all countries to Germany. When and if adopted such agreed procedure should also govern remittances by German labor employed in France. Pending adoption general procedures, French should arrange interim procedure for remittances by German labor employed in France to French Zone and arrange with USSR authorities for remittances to USSR Zone by optants. US should undertake to obtain prompt British agreement to interim procedure for remittances to US–UK Zones. In all cases our view that agreement should be sought on acceptance by all Zonal Authorities in Germany of indigenous currency. In case of regular quadripartite procedure as well as interim procedure our view that indigenous currency of remitting country should be accepted without obligation on part of remitting country to convert such currency to dollars or sterling. Foreign currency equivalent of remittances should be available, however, for payment of imports from remitting country. In connection option plan for POWs now in France French Govt has proposed that it be permitted to utilize 1.2 billion Reichsmark acquired in Alsace Lorraine currency conversion and certain other marks or mark claims held by French nationals to make out-payments to beneficiaries of remittances by optants. It is probable French will make similar proposal in connection with remittances by voluntary recruits. Such arrangement as well as French proposal regarding exchange rate reported in AmEmbassy Paris 98 [3] to USPolAd would be unacceptable.

Request confirmation to Paris and Washington that qualified OMGUS representative will be in Paris March 26 to participate negotiations on basis stated above.

Sent Paris as 1077 rptd Berlin as 637 and Moscow for Delsec as 1371.

ACHESON

---

[3] Not printed.

851.504/3–2847 : Telegram

The Secretary of State [1] *to the Acting Secretary of State*

SECRET   Moscow, March 28, 1947—5 p. m.
URGENT

1065. Kosmos 15. For Acheson from Marshall. Your 641, March 24, 7 p. m. [2] We appreciate that US is committed to undertake discussions with French relating to recruitment of labor in US zone Germany. We are also bound by the terms of our bi-zonal agreement with the British. As subject is of major economic importance, we should enter into no

---

[1] Secretary of State George C. Marshall was in Moscow for the meeting of the Council of Foreign Ministers, March 10–April 24, 1947.
[2] This is the same as telegram 1077 to the Embassy in France, *supra*.

agreement with French in the absence of accord with British. In other words, question should be decided on bi-zonal basis and not unilaterally by US, but no objection to preliminary discussion with French to ascertain details French plan. As we understand it, French interested primarily in able-bodied German male skilled workmen and technicians. These are also at a premium in Germany and, of course, directly concern German production and consequently affect US–UK budgetary outlay.

We also do not agree that quadripartite approval is not necessary, and are doubtful of the accuracy of the statement that recruitment on voluntary basis is not inconsistent with views expressed in ACA incident to Soviet deportation of German technicians. Suggest you verify minutes carefully on this point.

Moreover, if we do agree to unilateral recruitment, we should not establish unworkable conditions which would be certain to result in continuing friction between zone Commander and French Government involving repeated appeals to our Government. It does not appear clear how recruitment would prove practical under conditions outlined with respect to priority of displaced persons and need for labor in German economy.

General Clay concurs.

Sent Berlin as 181; Department please repeat Paris as Moscow's 89.

[MARSHALL]

851.504/4–247 : Telegram

The Acting Secretary of State to the Secretary of State at Moscow

SECRET   WASHINGTON, April 2, 1947—7 p. m.

774. Moskco 38. For Secretary from Acheson. As possible factors in your decision on matter subject Kosmos 15 we submit following considerations:

French ability and willingness effect repatriation German POWs conditioned upon internal manpower situation which in turn endangers success of their recovery program under Monnet plan. Extent to which they can effect rapid repatriation in accordance with our wishes dependent in part upon acquisition replacement labor: foreign workers, including Germans; DPs; etc. Under conditions laid down Deptel 641 [1] number and type of German labor recruited by France will be small in comparison with number POWs repatriated and large net gain of workers to Germany will result. Our refusal to facilitate recruitment of Germans for work in France may delay agreement for recruitment

---

[1] This is the same as telegram 1077, March 24, to Embassy in France, p. 630.

DPs, will adversely affect French ability to repatriate POWs and this in turn will result in prolonging German manpower shortage. French have been advised of nature of our commitment to British under bi-zonal agreement to establish bi-zonal arrangement on self-sustaining basis as rapidly as possible. We realize and French should be told that any agreement reached with French must be in harmony bi-zonal agreement.

While we do not find from examination relevant ACA minutes that US is committed to seek quadripartite approval for recruitment voluntary labor at present in US zone, we recognize that in event agreement in Moscow on treatment Germany as economic unit, any recruitment program would have to be subject to appropriate revision.

ACHESON

851.504/7–747

The French Embassy to the Department of State

[Translation]

WASHINGTON, July 7, 1947.

AIDE-MÉMOIRE

The Embassy of France has the honor to refer to its note No. 164 of May 7 and its *aide-mémoire* of June 16 and 18.[1]

During the past months, the French Government has spared no pains in scrupulously carrying out the agreement which it signed on March 11, 1947 [2] concerning the repatriation of German prisoners whose custody was entrusted to it by the American authorities. Between March 1 and July 1, 1947, it succeeded in effecting a total of 87,000 repatriations, 7,000 more than the number set for the same period on the basis of 20,000 repatriations per month. If one adds that, from January 1 to March 1, 15,000 prisoners had already been returned to Germany, this gives a figure of 102,000 men, or nearly one quarter of the total number of prisoners transferred by the United States to France and left under French control, who have been repatriated.

When the French Government agreed to fix the monthly number of repatriations at 20,000, it relied upon the promise contained in the *aide-mémoire* of December 3, in which Mr. Jefferson Caffery indicated that the American authorities in Germany would receive instructions, if the French Government expressed such desire, to cooperate in the recruitment of German workers for France.

---

[1] Neither printed.
[2] See telegram No. 1116 from Paris, March 13, 1947, footnote 1, p. 629.

As a matter of fact, the recruitment of free labor in Germany by the French authorities has encountered long delays on the part of the American authorities and financial terms which were not acceptable to the French Government. In order to overcome these difficulties, the latter proposed to the American Government certain solutions which were, specifically, the subject of the *aide-mémoire* of June 18. It sincerely regrets that there was not greater haste in concluding the agreement sought.

While such agreement failed to materialize the aggravation of the general labor situation only rendered the solution of this problem more difficult for the French Government.

The strikes which have occurred in the coal mines and on the railroads have caused a serious diminution of the raw materials which are indispensable to the French economy.

With the approach of a harvest which is of exceptional importance and seriousness for the country, the French Government, placed under the obligation of improving at all costs, the tragic situation of its wheat supply feels itself obliged not to divert more than a minimum amount of labor from the agricultural population.

The failure of the Italian Government to carry out the commitments made in the labor agreement, in which France took the initiative, has reduced to 5 or 6,000 the recruitment of 17,000 workers per month anticipated in the application of that agreement.

The hiring of displaced persons in Germany cannot give substantial results before harvest time.

If, moreover, in conformity with the Agreement of March 11, work contracts in the number fixed are to be distributed at once to the German prisoners, the transformation of the latter into free workers, by making it easier for them to leave their work and to return to Germany, even in spite of their contracts, entails grave risks for the French economy in the critical period through which it is now passing.

Lastly, the French Government is obliged to permit the workers born in Eastern Europe who formally express the desire to do so, to return to their countries. These elements furnish the French economy with workers who are particularly useful by reason of their specialization in mining and agricultural work. Anxious to lose as few of these workers as possible, the French Government has taken every precaution to make sure that their departure was really voluntary and was not caused by any pressure; it could not, however, oppose the return of these free workers to their countries when they sincerely expressed the desire to do so. While in 1946 these repatriations to the Eastern countries were limited to 7,000 Poles and 2,000 Yugoslavs, or a total of 9,000 workers, the departures amount, during the present year, to much larger figures, which consist of:

> 17,000 Poles, comprising 8,000 employed in coal, iron and potassium mines, 3,000 miscellaneous workers and 6,000 agricultural workers;
> 2,000 Yugoslavs, several hundred of whom are miners, the others being for the most part agricultural workers;
> 10,000 Ukrainians and Byelorussians, chiefly agricultural workers.

To this total of 29,000 workers are added the members of their families, a large number of whom are employed in the French economy.

In the *aide-mémoire* of June 16, the Embassy of France was instructed to state that the recruitment of free German workers conditioned the ability of the French Government to maintain the repatriation of German prisoners of war at the monthly figure contemplated. It stressed the urgency presented for this reason by the conclusion with the American authorities of an agreement on the recruitment of free German workers, analogous to the one which was being negotiated with the British authorities.

The apprehensions of the French Government have become a reality. The situation set forth above places it under the unavoidable obligation, under penalty of causing in the French economy a crisis which may have serious repercussions, to reduce, taking into consideration the provisions of paragraph 3 of the Agreement of March 11, the repatriations of German prisoners from 20,000 to 10,000, during each of the two months of July and August.

The French Government will make every effort possible to compensate for this reduction in the coming months, by exceeding the repatriation quotas established. It is confident that it will succeed in doing so if an improvement in the general labor situation in France can be effected and particularly if the contingents not only of displaced persons but also of German free labor which the French Government has been trying to obtain for several months are received. The French authorities would therefore attach the greatest importance to receiving without delay the reply of the American Government to the offers appearing in the *aide-mémoire* of June 18, a reply which, they very much hope, will be favorable.[3]

H[enri] B[onnet]

---

[3] On July 15 Frances E. Willis, Assistant Chief of the Division of Western European Affairs, gave to Armand Bérard, Minister Counselor in the French Embassy, an *aide-mémoire* expressing regret that the French Government felt compelled to reduce the rate of repatriation during July and August and the hope that it would be possible to compensate for this reduction in the following months. Miss Willis added that instructions had been sent to the American Embassy in Paris to approach the French Government with a view to working out an agreement. (851.504/7–1547)

851.504/8–1247 : Telegram

The United States Political Adviser for Germany (Murphy) to the Secretary of State

SECRET BERLIN, August 12, 1947— 10 p. m.

1935. ReDeptel July 11 to Berlin as 1453, to Paris as 2572.[1] Below is quoted substance of cable OMGUS to War, commenting on proposal contained Dept's reference telegram:

"We appreciate the difficulties of solving the problem of remittances which arise from the agreement of the United States to permit French voluntary recruitment of German labor in the US zone in return for French agreement on repatriation of German prisoners of war. However, we would like to point out that the present proposal is basically no different from the original French proposal except that we have covered up the fact that the French are permitting remittances at $0.10 rate.

"In effect we are agreeing that the French will receive reparations in the form of part payment of the wages of German workers in France at the expense of the German economy.

"If, however, we assume that German workers in France are voluntary workers in a foreign land it would appear that the workers should be permitted to send to their families in their native land any desired portion of their earnings, in which case the foreign currency thus accrued should be at the free disposal of the native country of the worker.

"In the first instance, paragraph 16 C of the revised directive on military govt of Germany would appear to be applicable, and in the second instance, paragraph 18 C of the new directive would appear to be applicable.[2] Both of these paragraphs would appear to be contrary to the position which we are now requested to take. It would also appear that to negotiate on the basis of the position set forth in reference cable would create an undesirable precedent if remittance practices with all other countries had to be adjusted to conform to a formula such as set forth in paragraph 2 C of reference cable.

"We do not propose to agree to the blocking of any portion of the remittances to be made by recruitees now or by optants. We know from the Embassy Paris cable 2899 of 21 July [1] that they intend to refer the matter to Berlin at an early date. We judge that by detailed discussions they refer to the remittance problem as well as the recruiting of voluntary labor."

Sent to Paris as 340, repeated Department as 1935.

MURPHY

---

[1] Not printed.
[2] For text of JCS 1779, July 11, 1947, Directive to Commander in Chief of United States Forces of Occupation Regarding the Military Government of Germany, see Department of State, *Germany 1947–1949: The Story in Documents* (Washington, Government Printing Office, 1950), pp. 33–41.

851.504/8–2147 : Telegram

The Ambassador in France (Caffery) to the Secretary of State

SECRET   PARIS, August 21, 1947—7 p. m.

3382. With reference to conflict between German as opposed to French economic interests in PW repatriation, German labor recruitment and remittance questions reported in Berlin's 2013, August 20,[1] we have repeatedly emphasized in all negotiations these subjects with French, that US must give full consideration to its financial and other commitments in rebuilding a self-supporting German economy, as set forth in revised directive on military government dated July 11, 1947. Primary fact that proceeds derived from remittances must be available to German economy for purchase of imports was clearly stated in our memorandum of July 16, 1947 to French Government setting forth proposals contained in Deptel 2572 of July 11.[1] Blocking of proceeds of such remittances until June 30 or December 31, 1948, would not prohibit their becoming available at later date for purchase of imports in accordance our basic principle. Pending establishment of acceptable franc–mark exchange rate, we fully concur that proportionate payment scheme for reasons outlined in paragraph 2C, Deptel 2572, appears more desirable than agreeing to partial exchange rate such as proposed by French.

In connection with paragraph 2, Berlin's 2013, International Committee of Red Cross submitted detailed breakdown of PW repatriations accomplished by French from March through July 1947 (see Embassy's dispatch 9443, August 14, 1947,[1] copy to USPolAd, Frankfurt and Berlin), which totals 103,101. This figure exceeds original French commitment to repatriate 20,000 monthly during initial phase of agreement. We have requested French to supply us with breakdown of eventual destinations in Germany of these former PWs. It is believed number returning to US and British Zones, however, may represent a considerable proportion based on relative populations of zones. A majority of these repatriates are reported to be able-bodied workers, a factor which will undoubtedly benefit the bi-zonal economy. Conversely, French state they intend to recruit not more than 20,000 workers from US Zone under pending German recruitment program, the families of all but maximum 10 percent of those departing simultaneously from US Zone for French Zone under terms latest French proposal. Thus the financial consideration involved in this aspect of remittance program is relatively slight for reasons given in paragraph D Department's 2572, July 11. Exact number of optants with families

---

[1] Not printed.

in US Zone not known, but information from French indicates many prisoners opting to remain in France are doing so because they are without immediate families in Germany and therefore, would not participate in remittance arrangements.

General principles set forth in reference Deptel are believed to represent most equitable solution and best means of securing early implementation of PW repatriation program, although Embassy welcomes of course, within scope of general proposals which we have already put forward to French, suggestions from interested OMGUS officials as to how proposed agreement can be made more satisfactory to them.

For Department's information, British Embassy Paris states informally British Government desires to conclude as soon as possible an agreement along the lines suggested by French and summarized in my 3326, August 19.[2]

Sent Department as 3382, repeated Berlin as 313.

CAFFERY

---

[2] Not printed.

Editorial Note

Following an exchange of analogous notes at Paris on September 29 and 30, 1947, between the French Ministry of Foreign Affairs and the British Embassy, there was effected by exchange of notes signed on October 25 at Paris an Agreement between the United States of America and the French Republic on Recruitment of Voluntary Labor for France in the United States Zone of Germany. For texts of the notes signed by the Secretary General of the Ministry of Foreign Affairs (Chauvel) and the American Ambassador (Caffery), see Department of State Treaties and Other International Acts Series (TIAS) No. 1878, or 61 Stat. (pt. 4) 4113.

PUBLICATION BY THE DEPARTMENT OF STATE OF "NAZI-SOVIET RELATIONS, 1939-1941"

862.414/9–3047

Memorandum by the Director of the Office of Public Affairs (Russell) [1]

CONFIDENTIAL

WASHINGTON, 9/30/47.

Subject: Publication of the German War Documents Relating to the 1939-1940 Discussions Between the Russians and the Germans, Particularly the Molotov-Ribbentrop Conversations

There are various possibilities with respect to what might be published at this time: [2]

a. The report of November 1940 from the German Ambassador to Moscow of a conversation between him and Molotov, setting forth the conditions upon which Russia would adhere to the Three Power Pact. This document has, as far as we know, never been published or even referred to publicly. It is extremely damaging to the Russian position. It delineates the territories in Europe and the Near East that Russia insisted would have to come under Russian domination and provides for the definite alignment of Russia with Germany, Italy, and Japan.

b. In addition to *a.*, Nazi reports of a series of four conversations between Molotov, Ribbentrop, and Hitler in Berlin in November 1940. These have been referred to publicly on a number of occasions but have never been published in full. These are not as strong in their effect because they portray Molotov as opposing many of the arguments of Ribbentrop and Hitler.

c. The account of Ribbentrop's first visit to Moscow in August 1939 and the text of the Russo-German Secret Agreement of that month. The text of the Secret Agreement has been published unofficially but no mention has been made of the existence of this detailed account of the conversations between Stalin, Molotov, and Ribbentrop which accompanied the signing of the Pact of August 1939.

d. All the important 1939-1940 Russo-German papers might be published. These, in the opinion of the editor of the German War Documents Project,[3] would create a much greater cumulative effect than any selection from the correspondence. They show the length to which

---

[1] Addressed to the Assistant Secretary of State for Occupied Areas (Saltzman), to the Directors of the Offices of European Affairs (Hickerson), of Near Eastern and African Affairs (Henderson), and of Special Political Affairs (Rusk), and to the Legal Adviser (Gross).

[2] For previous documentation on the interest of the United States in the disposition of German Foreign Office archives, captured in 1945, see *Foreign Relations*, 1945, vol. III, pp. 1099 ff., and 1946, vol. v, pp. 200 ff.

[3] Raymond J. Sontag.

Soviet Russia went in aiding Germany on the eve of and during World War II. They cover the period from the spring of 1939 to June 1941.

If no special decision is made at this time, this material would in the normal course of events not be published until around 1950.

The editor of the German War Documents Project would be willing to have *d.* above published as a part of that project. Most of these documents have already been translated. It would take one month to complete the translation and annotations. Under normal procedure it would require another two months to prepare the manuscript for the printer and complete the publishing. Consideration might be given to obtaining Congressional priority in the printing, in which case it might be published within a week or two following the completion of the editing. If publication of *d.* were to be decided upon, although the agreement with the British (to which the French have also adhered)[4] does not require agreement by them to such publication, there is an oral understanding between us and the British and the French that any party will notify the others of its intention to publish any of the documents covered by the Project.

The editor of the German War Documents Project would not approve as a part of the Project the printing of *a., b.,* or *c.* above separately. If publication of these documents were decided upon, they should be released by the Department in some other form, not as a part of the Project.

The Russians have copies of the documents in the German Foreign Office archives. If we print a dozen or so documents, they would undoubtedly print others which would show that Russia at times resisted German pressure. This country might then be accused of giving a one-sided picture.

It will be recalled that the Spanish were able to show that *The Spanish Government and the Axis* did not tell the whole story and thereby to undermine the effectiveness of that publication.[5]

The cumulative effect of all of the documents referred to in *d.* above is very strong and it would be difficult for the Russians to rebut them.

The decision with respect to whether any of the above should be published at this time is, aside from the considerations mentioned herein, purely a political decision. It was decided by Under Secretary Acheson on May 28, 1947 on the basis of political considerations at that time not to publish these documents out of order and apart from the regular program. The appropriate political officers should now make the decision whether supervening events indicate that this de-

---

[4] For information on this agreement, see *Foreign Relations,* 1946, vol. v, p. 200.
[5] For documentation on the release of this pamphlet in March 1946, see *ibid.,* pp. 1042–1043, 1054–1055.

cision should be changed. It should also be taken into account whether such a decision would involve the Department in the necessity of publishing other documents of particular interest, such as those relating to the Grand Mufti.

The Russians are in possession of a great number of German Foreign Office papers and the question might arise whether they would follow any publication of ours by the publication of any embarrassing material in their possession. The editor of the Project states that the material examined so far shows nothing which, if published, would embarrass this government seriously.

F[RANCIS] H. R[USSELL]

[Enclosure]

SUMMARY OF NEGOTIATIONS BETWEEN THE RUSSIANS AND THE NAZI GOVERNMENT 1939–1941

The German documents on Russia become interesting in April 1939 when there began feelers for a political understanding. For some two months, the Germans and the Russians eyed each other suspiciously, anxious to make friends, but each afraid of the other. When it became evident that the British and the French were not willing to allow Russia a free hand in the Baltic, the Russians quite suddenly dropped their reserve and invited Ribbentrop to Moscow. The discussions there are treated in a very long memorandum which recreates the spirit of the occasion very well. As a result of these discussions, there emerged the public pact and an economic treaty for the exchange of Russian raw materials and German armaments. There was a secret agreement dividing spheres of influence, leaving everything in the Baltic north of Lithuania to Russia, together with Bessarabia.

After the Polish campaign, Ribbentrop again went to Moscow. There, the Russians agreed that they would press for a peace favorable to Germany. A new division of the spoils was arranged, Germany taking more of Poland, Russia getting all of Lithuania, except a small region in the south which was to go to Germany. In the succeeding months, there were extended economic negotiations which are of some interest because they show the great contribution which Russia made to the German war effort. Russia greeted in these documents the German invasion of Norway with enthusiasm and relief and applauded the invasion of Belgium and Holland. When, however, the speed and the extent of the German victory became apparent, the Russians moved very rapidly to claim their share of the spoils, while Germany still needed Russian support. The Russian occupation of the Baltic states occasioned some bad feeling, particularly when Russia took the part of southern Lithuania which had been promised to Germany. German resentment was increased when Russia suddenly moved into Bessarabia and, more important, into the Bukovina.

When the collapse of France was complete, the Germans began to strike back at the Russians. They encouraged the Finns to resist new Russian demands, and they aroused the Russians to fury by guaranteeing the new frontiers of Roumania. Russian anger turned into panic on the news of the Three Power Pact between Germany, Italy, and Japan. On receiving news of this Agreement, Molotov abandoned his earlier reluctance to visit Berlin and arrived there in November 1940. He had two interviews with Ribbentrop, and two at which Ribbentrop and Hitler were both present. Hitler and Ribbentrop tried to force Russia to join the Three Power Pact and to accept the Asiatic territory south of Russia to the Indian Ocean as her sphere of influence. On his return to Moscow, Molotov said that he would be willing to join the Three Power Pact if all the territorial demands of Russia were met.

The Germans never replied to Molotov's counter-proposal. Instead, they secretly circulated in December 1940 the first detailed plans for the invasion of Russia.

Through the early months of 1941 the Russians at least outwardly continued to hope for peace and for admission to the Three Power Pact along with [the?] lines proposed by Molotov in the previous November.

Throughout the documents, there are quoted very uncomplimentary Russian remarks concerning the French, the British, and the Americans. It was the opinion of the best informed Germans that Russia would much rather have an alliance with Germany than with the Western democracies.

761.62/10–247

Memorandum of Conversation, by the Assistant Secretary of State for Occupied Areas (Saltzman)

CONFIDENTIAL WASHINGTON, October 2, 1947.

Participants: Charles E. Saltzman–Chairman   Dean Rusk
John D. Hickerson   Fritz Oppenheimer [3]
Llewellyn E. Thompson [1]   Francis Russell
Joseph C. Satterthwaite [2]   C. V. Hulick [4]

The first meeting of the Committee on publication of the Molotov-Ribbentrop papers was held in Mr. Saltzman's office at 3:00 p.m., October 2nd.

---

[1] Chief, Division of Eastern European Affairs.
[2] Deputy Director, Office of Near Eastern and African Affairs.
[3] Special Assistant to the Legal Adviser for German–Austrian Affairs.
[4] Charles V. Hulick, Executive Assistant, Office of the Assistant Secretary of State for Occupied Areas.

Mr. Russell described the progress made by his office in assembling the material and the possible methods of publication. He stated that it would take one month to complete the translation and annotation of these papers and that if the Government Printing Office facilities were used it would require another two months. However, if necessary, much faster service could be arranged through the staff of the Foreign Relations Committee of the Senate. It was agreed that all the important 1939–1940 Russo-German papers should be published.

Mr. Hickerson stated that, in his opinion, these papers should not be published prior to the ending of the CFM Conference, or approximately December 15th.[5] He felt that publication prior to that time would seriously embarrass the U.S. Delegation at the General Assembly of the United Nations and the Secretary of State at the CFM Conference.[6] Mr. Satterthwaite said that Mr. Henderson was suddenly called out of town and was unable to attend the meeting. He said that Mr. Henderson told him that he thought the papers might be published in approximately two or three weeks and that he did not see any strong reason for withholding publication beyond that time. Mr. Rusk supported the view of Mr. Hickerson and raised the question as to whether the publication of these papers at any time would be embarrassing due to the Soviet practice of violent and vituperative retaliation. Mr. Russell stated that a member of his staff had made a detailed examination of the greater portion of these papers and felt that no real embarrassment would be involved.

Mr. Oppenheimer raised the question as to what instructions would be given to the German press and pointed out that existing regulations prohibited the German press from publishing comments which would tend to alienate the Allied Powers. Accordingly, he felt that if the German press published these papers and made any editorial comment that the Soviet member of the ACC would immediately demand that the German editors involved be punished. Mr. Hickerson replied that he felt that we should instruct the German press that extracts of the papers or the papers themselves might be reproduced without editorial comment and that our representative on the ACC be forewarned to resist any attempts on the part of the Soviets to demand punishment. He also pointed out that the Soviets were not observing the provisions of these regulations in their own zone. There was general agreement that no instructions be given to the German press regarding the re-publication of these papers but that our representative on the ACC be advised beforehand and be instructed to resist any attempt on the part

---

[5] For documentation on the meeting at London of the Council of Foreign Ministers, November 25–December 16, 1947, see vol. II, pp. 676 ff.

[6] For documentation on the regular session of the General Assembly at New York, September 16–November 29, 1947, see volume I.

of the Soviets to demand punishment for action taken by the German press.

The Chairman authorized Mr. Rusk to informally obtain the views of Mr. Herschel Johnson [7] as to the effect of the publication during the current Assembly of the United Nations. The Chairman requested Mr. Satterthwaite to convey Mr. Hickerson's views to Mr. Henderson upon his return and find out if Mr. Henderson agrees to withholding publication until approximately December 15th.

It was agreed that a memorandum would be prepared recommending to the Secretary action to be taken and pointing out that it would be necessary to obtain approval from the British prior to publication.

CHARLES E. SALTZMAN

---

[7] United States Representative at the second session of the United Nations General Assembly.

862.414/10–347

Memorandum by the Assistant Secretary of State for Occupied Areas (Saltzman) to the Under Secretary of State (Lovett)

SECRET   WASHINGTON, October 3, 1947.

DISCUSSION

We have an arrangement with the British, to which the French have recently adhered, providing for the publication, after editing by a group of scholars, of the documents contained in the captured German archives. There is an understanding between us and the British and French that any party will notify the others of its intention to publish any of the documents covered by this project. The Russians have not agreed to participate in this work but have independently published some of the captured German documents in their hands.

We have had numerous requests for the publication of these documents, particularly those relating to the Soviet-German pact of 1939. We have heretofore taken the position that we could not publish these documents separately.

The material concerned would in the normal course not be published until sometime in 1950. It is estimated that the ones relating to the Soviet Union could be edited and printed and be ready for release about the first of December of this year.

At a meeting of the interested Officers of the Department held in my office on October 2 it was decided to recommend the publication of these Russo-German papers shortly after the conclusion of the forthcoming meeting of the Council of Foreign Ministers unless developments prior to that time should warrant our withholding them. It was realized that it is probable that the Russians will attempt to retaliate by publishing documents embarrassing to us or more probably the British. On balance, however, it was felt that United States interests would be served by the publication of these papers and that in view of the seriousness of the issues raised by current Soviet policies we would not be justified in further delaying their publication. In this connection it should be noted, however, that some of them have already been published unofficially and that Foreign Minister Bevin in October, 1946, confirmed the authenticity of the publication in a British paper of the secret protocol attached to the Soviet-German non-aggression pact of 1939.

RECOMMENDATIONS

(1) That we inform the British and French of our intention to publish the important captured German documents covering Soviet-German relations from 1939 to June 1941, early in December unless developments at the meeting of the Council of Foreign Ministers should indicate the wisdom of further delaying their publication.

(2) In view of the seriousness of this decision it is suggested that you obtain the approval of the Secretary.[1]

---

[1] Concurrences were shown by Messrs. Hickerson, Henderson, Oppenheimer (for Mr. Gross), Russell, and G. Bernard Noble, Chief of the Division of Historical Policy Research. Mr. Rusk wrote in the following note: "The question of *when* we tell the British and French must be considered by the Secretary in relation to British and French nervousness during present GA session. Otherwise, I concur. D. R."

On October 31 the Executive Officer, Office of Departmental Administration (McWilliams) informed Mr. Saltzman that the Secretary of State had approved the memorandum, in principle, but wished that implementing action be delayed until he had discussed the project with the President and the Cabinet. (862.414/10–3147)

862.414/12–2647

Memorandum by the Chief of the Division of Historical Policy Research (Noble) to the Deputy Director of the Office of European Affairs (Thompson)

SECRET   WASHINGTON, December 26, 1947.

Wednesday morning, December 24, Mr. Sontag and I had conferences with Mr. Henderson of the British Embassy [1] and Mr. Wapler of the French Embassy [2] on the subject of the Department's policy regarding the publication of documents on the Soviet-German relations, 1939–1941. Mr. Henderson and Mr. Wapler were not able to come in at the same time; consequently we met with them separately.

---

[1] John Nicholas Henderson, Second Secretary, British Embassy.
[2] Arnauld Wapler, Counselor, French Embassy.

Mr. Henderson first raised the question whether the understanding between our governments permitted separate publication by the Department of these documents, and he accepted our assurance that it did. He suggested that probably the Soviets would argue that this publication was a violation of the recent "anti-warmongering" resolution adopted by the General Assembly of the United Nations,[3] though he did not apparently feel that this should bar action. His major concern was with the fact that the British Government had not been informed earlier of the intentions of the Department, and he expressed the view that his government might be subject to criticism in Parliament on the ground that the Department of State was in advance of the Foreign Office on the side of open diplomacy. He did not feel that the British Government would raise objections to the publication, though he seemed anxious to inform his government at the earliest possible moment of the Department's proposed action.

Mr. Wapler expressed a good deal of satisfaction over the proposed publication. He said, however, that his government would necessarily have to wash its hands of the enterprise. It would be pleased with the American decision and would be glad not to have to take responsibility for the action. He expressed some satisfaction that his government had not been consulted in advance so that it would not be faced with the necessity of making a decision in the matter.

Copies of the proposed preface and editors' foreword were given to Mr. Henderson and Mr. Wapler. Both of them thought these were well adapted to the needs of the occasion.

---

[3] United Nations, *Official Records of the General Assembly, Second Session*, resolution 110, adopted on November 8, 1947. For documentation, see volume I.

862.414/2–1648

Memorandum by the Director of the Office of Public Affairs (*Russell*)
to the Under Secretary of State (*Lovett*)

CONFIDENTIAL WASHINGTON, February 16, 1948.

As was to be expected, the publication of the German War documents bearing on relations with Russia, 1939–1941,[1] has aroused widespread interest and comment both in the United States and abroad, except in those countries where the "iron curtain" has restricted freedom of expression on the subject.

---

[1] For text of a press release announcing publication by the Department of State on January 21, 1948, of *Nazi-Soviet Relations, 1939–1941: Documents from the Archives of the German Foreign Office* (publication 3023), see Department of State *Bulletin*, February 1, 1948, p. 150.

REACTIONS IN THE UNITED STATES

In the United States the reception has been preponderantly, if not overwhelmingly, favorable. The space given the publication by leading newspapers was probably unprecedented. On all sides, however, the volume was viewed as a propaganda piece in the so-called "cold war" with the U.S.S.R. Nevertheless, most would agree with *Time* that it has "the virtue of sober truth".

Adverse criticism has gradually taken shape. Typical criticisms of one segment of opinion are (*a*) that the documents should have been published earlier; and (*b*) that, in view of the evidence, this Government should not have delayed so long in adopting a "realistic" policy toward the U.S.S.R. Other adverse critics, however, have alleged that (*a*) the release of the documents at this time only accentuates U.S.-Soviet tensions; (*b*) the documents thus presented are out of context and give a distorted picture of events; and (*c*) the Germans will conclude that they lost the war because Hitler made the mistake of breaking his agreement with the U.S.S.R. and that they should return to the Soviet alliance. There is no question, however, that the American public as a whole regards the publication of the documents as appropriate and necessary under the circumstances.

REPERCUSSIONS IN THE UNITED KINGDOM AND FRANCE

When, in December 1947, it was decided to publish the documents, the representatives of the British and French Embassies were informed (on December 24) of the Department's intention to make the documents public. The information was given four weeks in advance of the date on which the documents were released to the press (January 21). When Mr. Henderson of the British Embassy inquired whether the Department's decision was final, he was told that if his Government had important objections to raise these would certainly be taken account of by the Department. Mr. Wapler of the French Embassy was similarly informed.

Both secretaries informed their Governments of the Department's action, and both reported back with replies. The British Foreign Office expressed regret that the "decision" was made without prior consultation, but made no objection of principle.

The French Government made no objection whatever to the publication, though it left the responsibility for the action with the Department of State. Mr. Wapler of the French Embassy informally stated that he was sure his Government would be pleased with the Department's action, but that of course it would have to "wash its hands" of the affair.

In the United Kingdom the incident was not played up significantly in the press, though it received wide notice. Questions relating to the publication were raised in the House of Commons. On January 28, Hector McNeil, replying for the Secretary of State for Foreign Affairs, stated that "H.M. Government are considering whether any useful purpose will be served by issuing these documents separately at an early date", but said that they wanted to avoid issuing "haphazard selections".

On February 4 Mr. Churchill [2] raised the question whether the Government intended to make "a similar separate British publication". Mr. Bevin, in reply, said that his Government had "the matter of a similar separate British publication under consideration". He said he would not, because of its publication in another country, be rushed into "taking out of its context one particular thing without careful study of the rest". He expressed doubt as to whether the American publication was the wisest way of dealing with this problem and said that he had understood that the matter was "going to be dealt with in relation to the other Allies as a comprehensive historical statement", and he had no idea it was going to be published out of its context. He added that, "Whatever happened in 1939–41, I have got to study what is likely to happen in 1948".

The above statements by Mr. McNeil and Foreign Secretary Bevin do not take account of the fact that the Foreign Office had been fully informed in December as to what precisely the Department was proposing to do.

The attitude of the British Government was explained confidentially by Mr. Henderson of the British Embassy, on the basis of a memorandum from the Foreign Office, which stated that Mr. Bevin had no reason to doubt the accuracy of the compilation, "but the fact that these German documents had been published in this way necessarily makes certain people in the United Kingdom suspect that they have been published not so much in the interest of historical accuracy as for an immediate propaganda purpose. Publication in this way also seems to have had the effect of provoking the Soviets into publishing documents directed against Great Britain. This does not especially worry the British Government inasmuch as they are in any case preparing to publish their own documents themselves, but they would have preferred to have been able to publish them first and not to have had the issue forced in such a way as to let the Russians get in first with their highly tendentious version".

In France the publication of the documents was given widespread but not sensational attention. The patriotic press tended to follow the lead of the Government press agency in commenting that the unilateral procedure was not regarded as "normal diplomatic usage", while the

---

[2] Winston S. Churchill, former Prime Minister.

Communist wing branded the documents as "forgeries of the Nazi Gestapo".

Ambassador Caffery reported from France that he had received many inquiries concerning a French translation which he would regard as useful. The French Government has limited itself to stating that it was not consulted prior to publication which, of course, is in line with their previously announced intention to wash their hands of responsibility.

THE SOVIET REPLY

The Soviets began making replies to the documentary publication on February 10 and have issued four statements. The reports of these replies indicate that, while branding those responsible for publishing the documents as "falsifiers of history", they do not challenge the authenticity of the documents themselves. They have rather sought to shift the spotlight by attacking the pre-war and wartime policies of the United States, the United Kingdom and France. The following charges are made:

1. The Allied documents policy was discriminatory against the U.S.S.R.

   a. The claim is made that in the summer of 1945 the British rejected the Soviet request for participation in the study of captured German documents.

   b. It is also claimed that in September 1945 the American officials proposed to the ACA in Berlin that all captured enemy documents in all the zones should be opened freely to representatives of the United Nations, but that this proposal was subsequently withdrawn.

2. The publication is propagandistic. It covers only the period 1939–1941, and it is based exclusively on Nazi documents.

3. The Allies contributed to German rearmament against the Soviet Union. A "golden rain of American dollars fertilized the heavy industry of Hitler Germany", and American industrialists were closely linked with German monopolists. This charge is elaborated at considerable length.

4. The British and French, in the pre-war period, adopted a policy of "appeasing" Hitler Germany while "the Soviet Union came forward as the initiator and champion of collective security".

5. The Anglo-French policy sought to direct German aggression against the U.S.S.R.

6. The Soviet policy during the 1939–1941 period was merely a "fight for time", forced on the U.S.S.R. as a result of its failure to reach an agreement with the Western Powers for a collective security front against Germany.

7. The United States, through Allen W. Dulles, conducted negotiations in 1943 for a separate peace with Germany.

8. The United States and Great Britain deliberately delayed opening a second front in the West in an effort to bleed Russia white and end her role as a world power.

COMMENTS ON THE SOVIET REPLY

The Soviet charges are, for the most-part, red-herrings, employed for the purpose of diverting attention. They will, therefore, not all be considered at this time, although they do merit the attention of the Department in due course. The following comments are immediately relevant:

1. With regard to the charge that the United Kingdom and the United States discriminated against the Soviets in the use of captured German documents:

a. A British Government spokesman has denied all knowledge of a Soviet request in the summer of 1945 for joint exploitation of the documents.

b. On the other hand, the Soviet statement that American authorities proposed in September 1945 that all German archives be thrown open to the governments of all the United Nations is substantially validated by the records of the Department. Such a proposal was made, but the British representative asked for and was granted several delays in order to receive instructions, and the proposal was later withdrawn on the request of the American intelligence authorities in Berlin.

2. As to the charge that the documents are a distortion of the facts because they cover only 1939–41, it is to be regretted that these papers could not have been published as part of the regular series, which would, of course, have given a broader perspective on Nazi relations with all other powers. Time obviously did not permit this to be done. It, nevertheless, remains true that the documents are an accurate account of Nazi-Soviet relations during the 1939–41 period, and the truth which they contain is not obscured by the fact that they come from the German Foreign Office, since they were prepared at the time not for propaganda purposes but as accurate analyses of situations for the confidential use of Nazi authorities.

3. Regarding the charge that the British and French conspired to get Germany into war with the U.S.S.R., the documents thus far cited do not demonstrate the existence of such a conspiracy. Nor have the editors found any evidence of such a conspiracy. It is nevertheless possible that, by a careful choice of parts of documents, the Soviets could present a picture which would be convincing to those desiring to be convinced. It is assumed that the Soviets will attempt to do this.

4. The Soviets have announced their intention of publishing subsequently a collection of documents which will presumably substantiate the charges that have thus far been made. It was to be expected that some such riposte would be forthcoming, and the question arises as to what may be expected. It may be recalled that three volumes of German documents were issued by the Soviets in 1946, bearing on German relations with Turkey, Hungary and Spain. It is the opinion of the American editors of the German War Documents Project that the Soviets may have large parts of one of the higher files of the political division of the German Foreign Office, thereby being in possession of an important cross-section of the record of German foreign relations. The Soviets have not, however, yet shown their hand.

The precise extent of the Soviet holding of documents is not known by the editors, hence no accurate forecast can be made as to possible Soviet action.

IMPLICATIONS FOR UNITED STATES POLICY

The foregoing facts suggest the following considerations of policy:

1. Consideration might be given to offering access to the German Foreign Office Archives to Soviet scholars on a basis of the reciprocal right of access for the editors of the other participating powers to all German Foreign Office documents in the possession of the Soviet Government.

In this connection, a UP report of February 10 stated that a Foreign Office spokesman had invited the Russians to join Great Britain, the United States, and France in publishing without censorship the German Foreign Office documents on Hitler's relations both East and West. This has not been confirmed, and the British Embassy states that the Foreign Office has made no statement that would support such a report.

It is reasonable to suppose that permitting representatives of the U.S.S.R. to join the German War Documents Project would complicate the task of the editors and impose serious delays in publication. This is well illustrated by a statement made by the Soviet reply of February 10 which refers to the alleged negotiations with the British in 1945 and which states that publication of the documents would be inadmissible "without careful and objective verification", which, it stated, would have to be made jointly. The assumption lying behind this proposed "verification", as envisaged by the Soviets, is contrary to the fundamental principle of scholarly objectivity on which the documents project rests. Joint "verification" suggests the right of individual veto for political reasons on the inclusion of particular documents. Serious differences of opinion would doubtless arise and the completion of the project would be jeopardized.

2. The situation clearly calls for the publication at the earliest possible date of the volumes containing a comprehensive record of the crucial years preceding and during the war. It is anticipated that in the Berlin meeting this April the editors will make the final selection of documents covering the period from mid–1937 to the outbreak of war in 1939. Other volumes will follow as soon as possible, bringing the record down through the war years.

The early consummation of this publication program should be pressed, for it will place pre-war and wartime diplomatic relationships in clearer perspective and provide a satisfactory answer to the adverse critics at home and abroad.

3. The Russian statements and documents issued in reply to the Department's documentary publication should be carefully analyzed, annotated, and appraised, and relevant information should be prepared for use as circumstances may dictate.[3]

---

[3] The memorandum was referred to the Counselor of the Department, Charles E. Bohlen, who notified Mr. Russell that he did not think it would be wise to offer access to Soviet scholars but that the other two recommendations were all right. Mr. Hickerson concurred. (862.414/2–2348)

INTEREST OF THE UNITED STATES IN QUESTIONS RELATING TO NAVIGATION OF THE RHINE AND DANUBE RIVERS

[Documentation on this subject, not printed, is in Department of State file No. 840.811.]

654

WESTERN EUROPE

AUSTRIA

(See Volume II.)

BELGIUM

Editorial Note

Documentation on United States policy with respect to procurement of uranium from the Belgian Congo and cooperation with Belgium in the field of atomic energy is included in volume I in the compilation on foreign policy aspects of U.S. development of atomic energy.

AGREEMENT BETWEEN THE UNITED STATES AND BELGIUM SUPPLEMENTARY TO THE GENERAL AGREEMENT ON TARIFFS AND TRADE

[For text of Agreement and Accompanying Letters rendering inoperative the Agreement of February 27, 1935, and supplementing the General Agreement on Tariffs and Trade of October 30, 1947, signed at Geneva, October 30, 1947, see Department of State Treaties and Other International Act Series (TIAS) No. 1701.]

AGREEMENT BETWEEN THE UNITED STATES AND BELGIUM CONCERNING AMERICAN DEAD IN WORLD WAR II

[For text of Agreement, effected by exchange of notes signed at Brussels, June 6 and July 23, 1947, see Department of State Treaties and Other International Acts Series (TIAS) No. 1672, or 61 Stat. (pt. 4) 3352.]

DENMARK

CONSULTATIONS WITH THE DANISH GOVERNMENT ON ARRANGE-
MENTS FOR THE DEFENSE OF GREENLAND AND ON DISPOSITION
OF GERMAN REFUGEES IN DENMARK [1]

811.24559B/1–247 : Telegram

The Secretary of State to the Legation in Denmark

TOP SECRET　　　　　　　　WASHINGTON, January 2, 1947—6 p.m.

4. Top Sec for Eyes of Minister [2] only. Unless you perceive objections please call on Rasmussen in the very near future and say you have
been informed of the substance of my conversation with him in New
York.[3]

You may say you know your Government attaches highest importance to a satisfactory solution of Greenland problem and will, of
course, be interested in learning Rasmussen's personal reaction to the
possible courses of action which I outlined to him; that you are not in
any sense pressing him to reply now but when he has had time to consider the matter further you will be glad to transmit his thoughts to me.

It might be well to take advantage of your visit to lay confidentially
before Rasmussen the info re Spitsbergen contained in paragraph 5
of my tel 924, December 24.[4] The subject might be introduced by your

---

[1] For the text of the Defense of Greenland Agreement, see Department of State
Executive Agreement Series No. 204, or 55 Stat· (pt. 2) 1245 ; for documentation
regarding the conclusion of the agreement, see *Foreign Relations*, 1941, vol. II,
pp. 35 ff. For related documentation on U.S. policy with respect to military bases,
see volume I, compilation entitled "United States National Security Policy".

[2] Josiah Marvel.

[3] In a conversation with Danish Foreign Minister Gustav Rasmussen on December 14, 1946, in New York, Secretary of State Byrnes emphasized the vital
importance of Greenland to the security of the United States. Secretary Byrnes
suggested that American security needs might be met by an agreement giving
the United States long-term rights to construct and maintain military facilities
in specified areas of Greenland or by a treaty with Denmark under which the
United States would undertake to defend Greenland from aggression and would
secure the right to maintain such military installations there as would be necessary. Secretary Byrnes also suggested that possibly the best solution might be
the outright purchase of Greenland by the United States under an agreement
concluded in accordance with the principles and purposes of the Charter of the
United Nations. Secretary Byrnes' suggestions were detailed in a memorandum
handed to Foreign Minister Rasmussen at the close of the December 14 conversation. Foreign Minister Rasmussen appeared to regard the Secretary's proposals as more drastic than may have been anticipated, but he agreed to give
them careful study. Secretary Byrnes indicated that the United States was
willing to continue the *status quo* in Greenland while a solution was being
sought. (811.24559B/12–1646)

[4] Not printed ; in addition to the information concerning Spitsbergen, it transmitted the memorandum handed to Foreign Minister Rasmussen on December 14,
1946, and described in the preceding footnote (811.24559B/12–1646).

saying that during your stay in Denmark you have gained the impression that some segments of Danish public opinion might be fearful of a definitive long-range solution along one of the lines I suggested lest such action inspire a Soviet initiative with respect to, for example, Spitsbergen.[5] You might then proceed as outlined in paragraph 5 of my tel 924 and then go on to say that on the basis of this very confidential info which you have received from your Govt. the thought has occurred to you that Rasmussen might wish to defer taking any steps that might result in leaks and consequent publicity, which might make his own situation more difficult, until after Soviet-Norwegian negotiations re Spitsbergen materialize or at least until the possibility of such negotiations become public. You might say that this thought has come to you as a consequence of your understanding that I have not made formal proposals to him but have only expressed in an exploratory way thoughts re a possible solution which could be made the basis for later more formal discussions after Rasmussen shall have had an opportunity to express his personal reactions.

I think it advisable that at this time you not go beyond limits of foregoing instructions in your conversation with Rasmussen.

BYRNES

---

[5] For documentation regarding the attitude of the United States concerning reported demands by the Soviet Union on Norway with respect to Spitsbergen and Bear Island, see pp. 1003 ff.

811.24559B/1–747 : Telegram

The Minister in Denmark (Marvel) to the Secretary of State

TOP SECRET   COPENHAGEN, January 7, 1947—11 a. m.

9. Top Secret for the Secretary. Pursuant to Deptel 4, January 2 I conferred with Rasmussen last evening. Although I requested his personal views, he volunteered no reaction to the possible courses of action outlined by you except to state that this thinking came as a shock to him and that he believes US greatly over-emphasizes strategic location of Greenland. He was quite relieved to hear suggestion that he defer any action which might result in leaks and disclosure concerning your conversation with him, as he feels that such disclosure would not only be detrimental to Norway but also to Denmark. He agreed to take all steps necessary to prevent any leaks and specifically not to take matter up with Parliamentary Committee until Soviet-Norwegian negotiations materialized or became public. It is therefore important that I be kept advised as to these. He agreed that his understanding

of your conversation of December 14 was only an exploratory one and did not in any way constitute a formal proposal or demand.

In my opinion this understanding most satisfactory as if your suggested courses of action were made known to Parliamentary Committee prompt publicity would be given by Communist members.

MARVEL

859B.20/4–1847 : Telegram

The Acting Secretary of State to the Embassy in Denmark [1]

TOP SECRET   WASHINGTON, April 22, 1947—6 p. m.
U.S. URGENT

219. Although Danes may consider Weather Agreement (TopSec urtel 238, Apr 18 [2]) connected with settlement of question of our long-term military objectives in Green, in our opinion the two questions are totally unrelated. We hope that you will keep this clearly in mind and whenever the point is raised by Danes make every effort to bring Danes to our point of view. As matter of fact even if there were no 1941 Defense Agreement [3] or if we had no long-term military interest in Green we would still have vital interest in continuing and amplifying our cooperation with Danes in Green weather matters not only as contribution to civil aviation generally, but also because of importance of extensive Arctic weather reporting to safety of our military aircraft operating in connection with fulfilment of our obligations in Germany.

It is quite possible that should you be unable thru persuasion to divert Danes from linking the two questions we may have to recommend to War Dept a revision of the desiderata set forth in Deptel 193, Apr 12.[4] This is, however, one of normal hazards of any negotiation and question can be met if and when it arises. Please keep Dept fully informed as discussions proceed.

ACHESON

---

[1] On February 6, 1947, the United States and Denmark agreed to exchange Ambassadors and to raise their respective diplomatic missions in Washington and Copenhagen to the rank of Embassy. The Legation in Copenhagen was elevated to the rank of Embassy on March 18, 1947. Minister Marvel had meanwhile been appointed and confirmed by the Senate as the Ambassador in Denmark.

[2] Not printed; it reported that representatives of the U.S. Army and the American Embassy would shortly commence negotiations in Copenhagen with officials of the Greenland Administration regarding the renewal of arrangements for the operation of certain Greenland weather stations, some of which were owned and operated by the Danes and some of which were owned by the United States but operated by Danish personnel (859B.9243/4–1847). These negotiations were concluded on May 12, 1947, with the signing of memoranda of conversation entitled "Greenland Weather Activities" and "Operation of Thule Facilities". The memoranda, which are not printed, were transmitted to the Department as enclosures to despatch 137, May 16, 1947, from Copenhagen (859B.9243/5–1647).

[3] See footnote 1, p. 657.

[4] Not printed.

859B.20/4–2347 : Telegram

The Acting Secretary of State to the Embassy in Denmark

TOP SECRET   WASHINGTON, April 25, 1947—7 p. m.

230. For your TopSec info only, urtel 253 Apr 23.[1] In informal conversations here Dan Amb Kauffmann has given us impression (whether with authorization of Rasmussen or not we do not know) that (a) Rasmussen is fully aware that while reactions US Govt to his memo of Dec 5 [2] are embodied in Mr. Byrnes' conversation and memo of Dec 14,[3] these do not constitute formal US proposals; and (b) Rasmussen's press statements are not to be considered as Dan reply to Mr. Byrnes' suggestions but as a means of satisfying those segments of Dan public opinion which desire or claim to desire withdrawal of US from Green, while at same time protecting Dan bargaining position if and when formal negotiations eventuate.

Kauffmann has remarked that it is necessary for Rasmussen to give impression to Dan public opinion that discussions are under way although he fully realizes that such is not in fact the case.

ACHESON

---

[1] Not printed; in it Ambassador Marvel reported that since January 1947, Foreign Minister Rasmussen had made several press statements indicating that negotiations with the United States regarding the termination of the 1941 Greenland Defense Agreement were still going on and that Denmark considered the time ripe for such negotiations (859B.20/4–2347).
[2] Not found in Department of State files.
[3] Regarding the conversation and memorandum under reference, see footnote 3, p. 657.

859B.20/5–2347 : Telegram

The Ambassador in Denmark (Marvel) to the Secretary of State

SECRET   COPENHAGEN, May 23, 1947—5 p. m.

347. In lengthy conversation at his request with Prime Minister [1] today Communist resolution (Embtel 344, May 22 [2]) among other subjects was discussed. Prime Minister informed me major parties had indicated support of his or similar resolution. Consequently his Party would be obligated to do likewise. While he felt resolution was Moscow-directed he believed neutral position of Denmark must be maintained. Illness of Foreign Minister and recess of Parliament May 30 might delay Parliamentary action but Prime Minister of opinion some type

---

[1] Knud Kristensen.
[2] Not printed; it reported that the Danish Communists intended to introduce in the Folketing (Parliament) a resolution asking the Government to seek a termination of the Greenland Defense Agreement (859B.20/5–2247). Such a resolution was introduced in the Folketing on May 29. The resolution was, however, withdrawn after Prime Minister Kristensen made a statement of the Government's intention to bring about the termination of the Agreement.

resolution would be passed by Parliament within next week. He stated when such resolution adopted he would do all in his power to have Government move as slowly as possible in carrying out purport of resolution.[3]

MARVEL

---

[3] Telegram 354, May 28, from Copenhagen, not printed, commented as follows regarding the position of the Prime Minister:

"Prime Minister's attitude continues consistently pro-American; but he is faced with lack of majority votes in Parliament; strict adherence to party discipline by each party; and fact each party's action is motivated by local political advantage. It is not acquiescence to Communist attitude but realistic approach to his own political survival which he will not risk by voting against such resolution when by later directing non action thereon he can effectively show his true feelings." (859B.20/5-2847)

859B.20/5-2447 : Telegram

The Ambassador in Denmark (Marvel) to the Secretary of State

TOP SECRET COPENHAGEN, May 24, 1947—2 p.m.

348. Mytel 347 May 23. Purpose of conversation Prime Minister stated by him to discuss general problems. He emphasized his position re So[uth] Slesvig pointing out most important problem there was one of refugees, noting in that area largest concentration of refugees in Germany in relation to indigenous population. Removal of these, immediate separation governmentally from Holstein, and ultimate plebiscite are his aims. He believes Germany has good chance of becoming Communistic and without adoption his plan, Communism, with greatly increased population, would beat Denmark's door and infiltration easily accomplished. He accordingly seeks US aid in writing these aims into peace treaty. He strongly reiterated his hatred of Communism and his belief in western democracies. While stating this was view of govt and majority of people, he pointed out he must maintain for Denmark neutral outward appearance.

I am of opinion (mytel 858, TopSec October 28, 1946 [1]) he would be receptive to arrangement whereby Greenland treaty termination would be delayed pending US active interest in So[uth] Slesvig evidenced by inquiry from Deputy Foreign Minister addressed to Danish Govt for clear cut Danish position re So[uth] Slesvig. He of course is unaware of this opinion and I hesitate to recommend such course of action. I am however satisfied he will successfully meet all immediate local political maneuvers and he and his govt will remain in office barring unexpected crisis until 1949 elections. Consequently sympathetic understanding and some outward recognition of So[uth] Slesvig

---

[1] Not printed.

problem by US, particularly by US Deputy Minister,[2] will go far in slowing down active affirmative action for 1941 treaty termination on party [part?] of present govt. This to me would be more advisable approach than attempt to make deal which in effect would be interference in local affairs, as to make it stick would require similar arrangement with other non-Communist parties.

While Prime Minister has already given word he will drag feet on treaty termination, our showing of interest in So[uth] Slesvig will aid him immeasurably in carrying out promise. If Department sees merit in such approach it might be advisable for me to proceed Berlin and discuss situation with Murphy. Such discussion would be helpful in any event as background for future conversations with Prime Minister which at his suggestion yesterday will take place frequently.[3]

Conference which lasted one hour and half otherwise related to mytel 347, May 23 and local political situation.

MARVEL

---

[2] The reference here is presumably to the United States Deputy for Germany of the Council of Foreign Ministers. The Deputies for Germany met in London, January 14–February 25, 1947, to hear the views of the governments of neighboring Allied States and of other Allied States which participated in the common struggle against Germany which wished to present their views on the German problem. Denmark was one of those states presenting its views to the Deputies. Summaries of the views of the Danish Government on the German problem, including the South Schleswig question, were included in the Report by the Deputies for Germany to the Council of Foreign Ministers, February 25, 1947, vol. II. p. 40.

[3] Telegram 314, May 27, to Copenhagen, replied to Ambassador Marvel's proposal as follows:

"We appreciate PriMin's personal interest Slesvig but while benevolently disposed toward this and other Dan aims most important Green question not be allowed become linked with any other including Slesvig. To do so would introduce factors Green situation beyond our control unnecessarily complicating question which must be settled on own merits without relating it to *quid pro quo* which might prove impossible deliver." (859B.20/5–2447)

859B.20/5–2347 : Telegram

The Secretary of State to the Embassy in Denmark

TOP SECRET WASHINGTON, May 27, 1947—4 p.m.

U.S. URGENT

313. Dept concerned over developments reported urtel 344 May 22 [1] and 347 May 23. Acquiescent attitude PriMin toward Communist resolution (urtel 347) seems inconsistent with attitude reported para 4 urtel 238, Apr 18.[2]

---

[1] See footnote 2, to telegram 347, p. 660.
[2] Not printed; it reported that Prime Minister Kristensen appreciated that Greenland could not be left a military void and that Denmark could not maintain the required facilities. Ambassador Marvel expressed the belief that the Prime Minister would support the maintenance of the Greenland Defense Agreement (859B.9243/4–1847).

May 24 Kauffmann informed public and official opinion in US would be profoundly shocked by passage Communist resolution and should Dan Govt acquiesce in passage we could not avoid conclusion such action carried implied charge US had in some way failed to live up to its international obligation or obligations to Den. He was informed we appreciated steps already taken by Dan Govt to prevent Green issue coming to a head publicly and felt sure it would find some means to move towards solution Green problem other than to fall in with Communist plan for passage above mentioned resolution.

Adverting to reports from various sources that Danes might consider bring Green matter before UN, Kauffmann was told that we were unable to understand what would be the purpose or basis of such action: If it were to be brought forward as question endangering international peace and security this would be tantamount to haling US before UN as guilty of threat to peace and as violating international agreements and accordingly such a step could only be regarded by US as matter of utmost gravity; it would inescapably carry with it conclusion on part US that Den had deliberately chosen associate itself with world forces presently striving in every way embarrass US in its efforts uphold UN and promote peace and security for all nations.

Foregoing is for your info and background use only in event PriMin should take initiative in further discussing matter with you as result of report he may receive from Kauffmann. As events may move rapidly, we do not wish run risk crossing wires by simultaneous conversations Copenhagen and Wash but will continue keep you fully informed content conversations with Kauffmann.

MARSHALL

359B.20/5–3147

Memorandum by the Associate Chief of the Division of Northern European Affairs (Morgan)

TOP SECRET   [WASHINGTON,] May 31, 1947.

CONVERSATIONS WITH AMBASSADOR KAUFFMANN

Subsequent to approval by the Secretary of Mr. Matthews' [1] memorandum of May 28, 1947,[2] Ambassador Kauffmann, on the morning of May 29, informed Mr. Cumming [3] that the Communist resolution introduced in the Folketing on May 21 would be called up for debate on the afternoon or evening of the 29th. In view of the six hours time differential between Copenhagen and Washington, it was obvious that it would be desirable for the Secretary to make some comment at his

---

[1] H. Freeman Matthews, Director, Office of European Affairs.
[2] Not printed.
[3] Hugh S. Cumming, Jr., Chief, Division of Northern European Affairs.

press conference in order that the American point of view might reach the press simultaneously or in advance of the Danish statement. The Secretary's approval was accordingly obtained for the following statement:

"I am informed that the Danish Government will probably publish either today or tomorrow the text of a note requesting the United States to enter into consultations in connection with the agreement regarding the defense of Greenland concluded with the Danish Minister in Washington on April 9, 1941. This agreement, at a time when Denmark was powerless because of the Nazi occupation to act in its own behalf, made it possible to preserve Danish sovereignty over Greenland and prevent the Nazis from gaining a foothold in the Western Hemisphere. German detachments, which had already landed in Greenland were · expelled and adequate defense installations were constructed by the United States on the hitherto defenseless island. In taking this step, the United States acted with scrupulous respect for Danish sovereignty and in the interest of Denmark as well as of this country. The 1941 agreement was unanimously ratified by the Danish Parliament following the liberation of Denmark in 1945. Greenland remains of the greatest importance as a link in the defensive system of the United States and of the Western Hemisphere.

"We have informed the Danish Government that, as stated by Secretary Byrnes, to the Danish Foreign Minister in December, 1945 [*1946*],[4] we are ready actively to explore with his government at any time the basis of some new agreement in keeping with the letter and spirit of the Charter of the United Nations which would take fully into account Danish sovereignty over Greenland and legitimate United States and hemispheric defense requirements."

Ambassador Kauffmann was informally advised by Mr. Cumming of the remarks which the Secretary would probably make at his conference. Ambassador Kauffmann having objected to the reference to "some new agreement" in the last paragraph of the above quoted statement, clearance was obtained from the Secretary for a change in this paragraph so as to read:

" . . . Accordingly, we have informed the Danish Ambassador that, as stated by Secretary Byrnes to the Danish Foreign Minister in December 1946, we are ready actively to explore with his Government at any time the whole Greenland question with a view to finding a solution, in keeping with the letter and spirit of the Charter of the United Nations, which would take fully into account Danish sovereignty over Greenland as well as legitimate US and hemispheric defense requirements."

Mr. Cumming having obtained this approval advised Ambassador Kauffmann that we were not ready at this time to give a written reply

---

[4] For a reference to the meeting of Foreign Minister Gustav Rasmussen with Secretary of State Byrnes on December 5, 1946, at New York, see *Foreign Relations*, 1946, vol. II, p. 1314, footnote 37.

to the Ambassador's note of May 27,[5] but that we had no objection to the publication by the Danish Government of the Ambassador's note. Mr. Cumming then informed the Ambassador that the Secretary would make a statement to the press that afternoon which he was authorized to convey to the Ambassador in advance. This statement might be considered as the interim answer to the Danish Government's request for consultation. Mr. Cumming then read to the Ambassador the press statement as approved by the Secretary, including the alteration in the final paragraph which had been suggested by the Ambassador.

It was subsequently found that due to an inadvertency in the preparation of the material for the Secretary's press conference, the statement as actually read by the Secretary to the press representatives did not contain the alteration to the final paragraph but was read as originally drafted.[6]

The inadvertency was confidentially explained to Ambassador Kauffman by Mr. Cumming who pointed out that for purposes of communication to his Government the Ambassador was entirely authorized to transmit the corrected version as given to him by Mr. Cumming.

---

[5] Ambassador Kauffmann's note referred to various conversations that had taken place during the past year concerning Denmark's desire to terminate the Greenland Defense Agreement and requested, under instructions from his Government, that consultations provided for under Article X of the Agreement be initiated as early as possible. The text of the note was made public in Copenhagen by the Danish Government on May 29, 1947.

[6] For the text of the Secretary of State's statement as released to the press on May 29, 1947, see Department of State *Bulletin*, June 8, 1947, p. 1130.

859B.20/6–647

The Ambassador in Denmark (Marvel) to the Secretary of State

TOP SECRET   COPENHAGEN, June 6, 1947.
No. 182

SIR: I have the honor to refer to the Department's Top Secret telegram No. 318, May 29, 1947,[1] and to previous telegrams relating to the note presented by Ambassador Henrik Kauffmann on May 27, 1947, requesting the initiation of consultations as provided by Article Ten of the 1941 Treaty of Greenland. It may be helpful to the Department if I set forth below certain facts relating to this subject and certain observations made by me during the past months.

The Department has been kept informed of the increasing interest throughout Denmark during the past recent months regarding the

---

[1] Not printed.

status of the 1941 Treaty relating to Greenland. This interest has undoubtedly been accelerated by the present relationship existing between Denmark and Russia. Fear of Russia on the part of the Danish officials is not entirely confined to intangible possibilities. While the Prime Minister, in conversations with me, has often referred to the possibility of the Russians returning to Bornholm and the Foreign Minister has expressed the fear that the Russians might demand bases in the Faroe Islands—both statements being based upon American activities in Greenland—I am assured that no direct threats as to carrying out these possibilities have been made to any Danish official. There are, however, two important phases of Denmark's relationship with Russia which could be acted upon by the Russians immediately, and which would be most detrimental to Denmark. These two phases relate to (1) the debt owed by Russia to Denmark as the result of operations under the Danish-Soviet Trade Agreement and (2) the matter of German refugees in Denmark.

(1) Trade between Russia and Denmark has not materially changed since the situation was reported in the Embassy's despatch no. 871, February 28, 1947.[2] There is, at the present time, owed to Denmark by Russia a balance of approximately 45 million kroner. One effective method of retaliation against Denmark's acquiescence to American activities in Greenland would be the refusal or prolonged delay in making payment of this indebtedness. This is a matter which the Danes realize and is a large factor in their attempt to maintain friendly relations with Russia.

(2) The fear of the Russians' refusal to aid in the removal of the German refugees from Denmark is also a present and realistic reason for the maintenance of Danish effort to continue friendly relations with Russia. The presence of these refugees in Denmark places a large financial drain on the Government. The Russians now are in the process of removing from Denmark 36,000 refugees. Of these approximately 6,000 have already departed and the remainder are leaving Denmark at the rate of 2,000 per week. There is the constant fear on the part of the Danes that any unfriendly act on their part would result in the stoppage of the deportation of the German refugees by the Russians. Even though the commitment as to the 36,000 refugees above mentioned was not affected, the Danes believe no further aid would be forthcoming from the Russians as to the removal of the remaining German refugees.

As the Department is aware, Gustav Rasmussen, the Danish Foreign Minister, has never expressed to me his personal, or Government's reactions to his conversations with Secretary Byrnes on December 14,

---

[2] Not printed.

1946. . . . any negotiations with a view to exploring the basis for some new agreement relating to Greenland undoubtedly must be undertaken with the view that the political leaders of the Danish Parliament must be taken into consideration—a fact which, at times, the Foreign Minister appears to overlook.

As I pointed out in my despatch no. 372, September 4, 1946,[3] it is my view that Ambassador Henrik Kauffmann's views on Danish-American relations carry much weight and will be followed by the Foreign Minister. At the same time, Mr. Kauffmann has considerable influence with Hans Hedtoft, leader of the Social Democratic Party in Denmark. Hedtoft's views were expressed in my Top Secret telegram no. 969, December 27, 1946,[3] and, so far as I know, they have not changed. He then stated that, if Danish sovereignty over Greenland and its citizens were acknowledged by the United States, an agreement for bases for a long-term period could be arranged, so long as emphasis was placed on Greenland being a link between the United States and the United States Forces in Germany. The Prime Minister, Knud Kristensen, holds somewhat similar views but is less explicit and definite than Hans Hedtoft. The Prime Minister will rely almost entirely on the Foreign Minister, Gustav Rasmussen, for his final decision. In fact, he has so stated this to me.

It is, therefore, my view that the key man in the picture is Ambassador Henrik Kauffmann. His views will, in my opinion, be adopted by the Foreign Minister who, in turn, will pass them on to the Prime Minister. At the same time, Ambassador Kauffmann has decided influence with Hans Hedtoft, and the combination of the present Government forces in Parliament with the Social Democrats would assure passage of any agreement approved by these leaders. My view that Ambassador Kauffmann is the key man is fortified by a conversation I had with Director Hvass of the Foreign Office, in the absence of the Foreign Minister who is convalescing from a minor operation, on June 2, 1947. Director Hvass told me that he was awaiting a report from Mr. Kauffmann and that the Danish Foreign Office would take no steps with respect to consultations which were requested in the Danish note of May 27, 1947, until Kauffmann's recommendations were received. I, therefore, cannot stress enough the importance which I give to the manner in which this subject is handled with Ambassador Kauffmann. My own opinion is that he will be amenable to the American viewpoint. . . . I am advised that he expects to return to Denmark in July of this year and, undoubtedly, he will discuss the Greenland situation with me. I accordingly request that I be kept fully advised as to the Department's conversations with him as background in the event

[3] Not printed.

he approaches the subject while here in Denmark, and I again emphasize that the approach to Ambassador Kauffmann must be made with
the present Danish fears of Russian reaction in mind. They cannot be
brushed aside.

Respectfully yours, JOSIAH MARVEL, JR.

859B.20/6–1647

*Memorandum by the Deputy Director of the Office of European Affairs
(Hickerson) to the Secretary of State*

TOP SECRET [WASHINGTON,] June 16, 1947.

DISCUSSION

Ambassador Kauffmann is seeing you to say good-bye before leaving
June 18 for Denmark, and also in order to be able to say to his Govern-
ment that he has spoken with you regarding Greenland. He saw
Mr. Lovett on June 10.

After the release of your press statement of May 29, (attachment 1)[1]
Mr. Kauffmann indicated a desire to have an off-the-record talk with
officials of the Office of European Affairs. In the course of that conversation, which took place Friday, June 6, I reminded him that Secretary Byrnes outlined to the Danish Foreign Minister last December
alternative possible solutions regarding Greenland (attachment 2[2]).
[The alternatives outlined by Mr. Byrnes were: 1. A long-term arrangement for US military facilities in certain unspecified areas of
Greenland, with Danish sovereignty unimpaired and Denmark recognizing the inseparability of Greenland from the defense system of the
United States; or 2. A treaty whereby the United States undertakes
the defense of Greenland in exchange for the right to maintain necessary military installations there, while reaffirming recognition of
Danish sovereignty; or 3. US purchase of Greenland in full accord
with the UN Charter and purposes.][3]

Mr. Kauffmann has just told us that he believes sale to be out of the
question but that it might well be possible to arrange for a joint base
agreement. He believes Danish adherence to such an agreement would
be facilitated by bringing Canada, or even the other American Republics, into the picture, with a view to making it a regional agreement in keeping with the UN Charter. We gave Mr. Kauffmann some

---

[1] The attachment is not printed here; for the text of the statement by the Secretary of State, see the memorandum by Morgan, May 31, p. 663.

[2] Attachment 2, not here printed, was the text of the memorandum which the
Secretary of State handed to Foreign Minister Rasmussen at the close of their
conversation in New York on December 14, 1946; see footnote 3, p. 657.

[3] Brackets appear in the original.

indication that it might be possible to bring Canada into the picture in a new agreement. The Ambassador expressed the desire for additional information regarding the strategic significance of Greenland to the United States in order to enable him to interpret that significance properly to his Government.

In compliance with the Ambassador's request I arranged for him to meet General Lauris Norstad [4] and Vice Admiral Sherman [5] in my office on June 12. They emphasized to him the extreme importance of Greenland to the defense of the United States and of this hemisphere.

Ambassador Kauffmann expects to return from Denmark early in August.

He believes that for Danish domestic reasons consultations should begin shortly after his return here although those consultations need not be hurried after initiation.

RECOMMENDATIONS

It is recommended that the Secretary impress upon the Danish Ambassador the great strategic importance of Greenland to the United States and urge him to persuade his Government of the desirability of concluding with this country an arrangement for joint defense of Greenland.

---

[4] Maj. Gen. Lauris Norstad, Director of Plans and Operations, War Department General Staff.
[5] Vice Adm. Forrest P. Sherman, Deputy Chief of Naval Operations.

859B.20/6–1747

Memorandum of Conversation, by the Secretary of State

[WASHINGTON,] June 17, 1947.

Participants: The Danish Ambassador, Mr. Kauffmann
The Secretary of State
Mr. Hickerson

The Danish Ambassador came in to see me at 12:30 p.m. today. He said that he had asked for an appointment with me to say goodbye before leaving tomorrow to return to Denmark for about six weeks. The Ambassador added that he wished also to discuss briefly with me the Greenland situation.

Ambassador Kauffmann recounted the circumstances in connection with the conclusion of the 1941 Agreement. He said that one of the first acts of the Danish Parliament on the liberation of the country had been to approve that Agreement unanimously. He said that there is now a general feeling in Greenland that the war is over and that the time has come to terminate the 1941 Agreement. It was that state of mind, he said, that led to his being instructed about ten days ago to send us a note proposing consultation in accordance with Article 10 of the 1941 Agreement looking to a termination of that Agreement.

The Ambassador went on to say that he understands fully the American position: That Greenland is physically a part of the Western Hemisphere and that its defense is a matter of vital concern to the United States and the Western Hemisphere. He said that he had been discussing this whole matter realistically with Mr. Hickerson in the Department and that it was his hope that it would be possible to work out a satisfactory solution of the matter. He said that he intended while in Copenhagen to discuss the whole question in detail with his Government and that it was his hope that he would receive instructions which would enable him actively to discuss the problem with the U.S. Government on his return to Washington in August.

Ambassador Kauffmann said that he had been much gratified at the assurances given him by Mr. Hickerson of the State Department, General Norstad and Admiral Sherman of the War and Navy Departments, that the U.S. interest in Greenland was exclusively in defense and that any U.S. installations in Greenland would be of a defensive character. He added that it would be easier for Denmark to deal with the Greenland question along the lines desired by the U.S. if Canada and perhaps the American Republics were to the extent possible brought into the forefront of any new agreement. He said that he had been assured that consideration would be given to this.

I told Ambassador Kauffmann that I had had a good bit of personal experience with the Greenland question and that I could tell him that it is of fundamental importance to the security of the U.S. to keep an enemy state out of Greenland. I told him that we had faced the problem of driving the Germans out of Greenland in World War II, adding that the weather information which they obtained in Greenland had been a material factor in German offensive operations in Europe against us and our Allies. I added that I had had some anxious moments over British naval losses on the Murmansk route and the possibility that the Germans might again be enabled to get into Greenland. I said that relations between the U.S. and Denmark are of course excellent and that our apprehension would be met if we could be sure that our friend, Denmark, was in a position adequately to defend Greenland. I added that the Ambassador would doubtless agree that Denmark is not in such a position. Ambassador Kauffmann readily assented.

I told the Ambassador that I was gratified at the satisfactory nature of his preliminary conversations with U.S. officials on the subject. I said that the U.S. Government would, of course, be glad to endeavor to conclude an agreement along lines which would make it as easy as possible for the Danish Government to answer critics, some of whom would of course denounce whatever action was taken for their own selfish reasons. I said that we would gladly explore any ideas that might contribute to a satisfactory solution. I mentioned an idea which I had advanced for dealing with the Manus situation under which the U.S. would pay a certain sum of money annually to Australia and receive in return rights to use facilities maintained by Australia; the rights would include the rights to conduct maneuvers in peacetime and of course unlimited use in wartime. I said that I did not know whether this would be suitable at all in the Greenland situation.

I expressed my best wishes to the Ambassador for a pleasant trip and said I would look forward to seeing him in August.

840.48 Refugees/6–1947 : Telegram

The Ambassador in Denmark (Marvel) to the Secretary of State

TOP SECRET COPENHAGEN, June 19, 1947—5 p.m.

405. While I appreciate Dept's desire to keep Greenland problem separate and not involved with other Danish problems, nevertheless I feel situation referred to in mytel 403, June 19,[1] could be employed to advantage. There is no obligation upon US to accept additional refugees into US zone. However, as pointed out my Top Secret despatch No. 182, June 6, one effective threat Russians can use in retaliation to Danish acquiescence to American activity in Greenland is refusal to remove refugees in Denmark. If they do so, public reason given by Russians will be failure of other allies to accept 50% of refugees and real reason regarding Greenland situation will not be mentioned.

However, result will be to saddle Denmark with burden of one dollar per refugee per day.

If basis of Russian refusal to accept refugees can be removed, Russians will be faced with difficulty of explaining refusal to carry out Stalin's promise.[2] Consequently, I am of opinion that consideration should be given to receiving additional refugees, say up to 12,000 into US zone when approach is made by Danes.

[1] Not printed.
[2] In June 1946, Generalissimo Josif Vissarionovich Stalin, Chairman of the Council of Ministers of the Soviet Union, promised the Danish Foreign Minister that 100,000 German refugees in Denmark would be accepted into the Soviet Zone of Occupation of Germany provided the other three occupying powers agreed to accept a similar number of refugees. For additional documentation regarding the problem of the German refugees in Denmark, see *Foreign Relations*, 1946, vol. v, pp. 189–193, 196–197.

While Russian pretext for not accepting refugees would thus be removed, Danes would fear such retaliatory action on some other pretext until all refugees were actually evacuated. Hence, no announcement of agreement on Greenland bases could well be made before such covenant completed. However, gratitude toward US for aiding in solving this problem might well fail to outweigh other factors, e.g., fear of other Russian action, national pride, etc., militating against Danish acquiescence in our wishes unless our agreement to accept refugees were based on *quid pro quo* of Danish agreement to accept some settlement assuring our continued control Greenland airfields. Consequently, I believe any offer to accept refugees should be so conditioned.

With this as initial bargaining point, I believe we should emphasize to Danes that the airfields are necessary link in our communications with Germany just as continued Russian activity in Hungary and Rumania is defended as necessary to assure communication with her troops Austria. Moreover, I believe fact airports and alternates are needed for commercial air traffic, particularly in case of SAS as well as AOA, should be stressed, as in case of Iceland. Ultimate solution may then be US commercial aviation operation these fields which, on basis foregoing reasons, might be made palatable to Danish Govt, and which they might well have nerve enough to accept.

Refugees in Denmark present distinct problem from refugees in South Schlesvig, and while above thinking in some respects along lines expressed my Top Secret telegram No. 348, May 24, it does not involve British zone, peace treaty, and other factors which Dept has correctly pointed out might place barriers to effective performance of promises.

MARVEL

811.24559B/6–2647 : Telegram

The Ambassador in Denmark (Marvel) to the Secretary of State

TOP SECRET COPENHAGEN, June 26, 1947—10 a. m.

425. After first hectic day here Kauffmann dined with me alone. He feels approach to Greenland problem must be made slowly, pointing out Communist resolution is out of the way, Parliament is in recess and General Assembly of UN meets in early fall. Consequently discussions on Greenland could appropriately come up thereafter. He suggested that I come to Washington in late fall and believed conversations with the Secretary or Under Secretary Lovett would result in a solution. He emphasized that there was no possibility of a sale. After

he has conferred with Danish officials he will give me more definite views as to Danish course of action.

Above recommendation for schedule of Greenland talks which undoubtedly will be followed by Danish Government makes it difficult to tie in refugees with Greenland problem as suggested my Top Secret telegram 405 June 19. However in view of Danish approach described mytel 422 June 25 [1] it appears advisable to consider receiving immediately additional refugees into US Zone in order to capitalize on fact Russian removal of additional refugees (if such takes place) will be result of US initiative. Consequently urge US agree to accepting 12,000 additional refugees and that Berlin be so advised by direct order from Washington. Most important, if this is done, that it be ordered prior to any Russian commitments (which means immediate action) so that situation will not develop as it did in March when timing of American action largely diluted potential political capital.

Kauffmann departs July 15 and after tour of European capitals and Iceland will arrive back in US August 5.

MARVEL

---

[1] Not printed; it reported that the Danish Government hoped to obtain commitments from the American, British, and French Governments to accept additional refugees into their zones of occupation in Germany prior to requesting the Soviet Government to fulfill its 1946 promise to accept into its zone half of the German refugees remaining in Denmark (840.48 Refugees/6–2547).

859B.20/7–1447 : Telegram

The Ambassador in Denmark (Marvel) to the Secretary of State

TOP SECRET COPENHAGEN, July 14, 1947—10 a. m.

469. Kauffmann informed me July 11 he was to confer later that afternoon with FonMin regarding Greenland. As he was away over week end I have not seen him since conversation. However, FonMin had lunch with me *en famille* yesterday and took the opportunity to express informally his views on a variety of subjects. He feels most strongly in light of recent developments in Europe that Denmark should not now press for settlement of Greenland problem. While Kauffmann will go through motion in calling on the Secretary on his return, such action will be primarily for home consumption and with no thought of pressing matter. Rasmussen feels situation can remain dormant for six months or a year.

Rasmussen departs about September 10 so as to arrive US September 16 to attend UN General Assembly. His decision to be present is based on fact both Norwegian and Swedish FonMin will also be there. He will be in US approximately three weeks. Believe it most advisable particularly for local reaction that Rasmussen not only see the Secretary but also the President. This view was expressed by former Secretary Byrnes in Paris Embtel 4528, September 10, 1946, repeated Copenhagen as 28.[1]

Rasmussen confirmed Kauffmann's statement by Top Secret telegram 425, June 26 that there was no possibility of sale of Greenland. He expressed view that perhaps the solution lay in US control and maintenance of Greenland air fields on basis they are necessary link to communications in Germany and are needed for commercial air traffic (see my TopSectel 405, June 19). While such an arrangement would prompt some Russian reaction he admitted that Russians had only once discussed Greenland situation with him. At the time press carried story of proposed sale of Greenland, Russian Minister called on Rasmussen and requested information whether such sale was contemplated. Rasmussen answered inquiry referring to his press statement to effect that such proposal was absurd.

Emphasize local importance of arranging interview with President for Rasmussen and request Department advise of its concurrence therein.

MARVEL

---

[1] Not printed.

859B.20/7–2247 : Telegram

The Ambassador in Denmark (Marvel) to the Secretary of State

TOP SECRET   COPENHAGEN, July 22, 1947—11 a. m.

494. Last evening Kauffmann had confidential talk with me at residence. He stated that his recommendation for a policy of "going slow" regarding Greenland had been accepted by Danish Government thus confirming views of Rasmussen expressed my Top Secret telegram 469, July 14. Kauffmann feels that time should be taken to thoroughly acquaint Danes here and Americans in Washington as to all aspects surrounding Greenland problem. He feels that an understanding, appreciation and reconciliation of divergent views of Americans and Danes must and can be solved. While he thinks the solution may lie in US control and maintenance of Greenland airfields on ground they are necessary link to Germany and are needed for commercial air traffic he stated this would only be a temporary measure and that he was thinking for a solution along more permanent lines. He indicated that if Denmark could be assured that the Truman Doctrine[1] would

---

[1] For documentation regarding the Truman Doctrine, see vol. v, pp. 1 ff.

be extended so as to protect Denmark from any threatened aggression of Russia a permanent solution could be speedily reached. He felt that within six months or a year the European situation would be clarified to extent that Denmark could take a definite stand with the West. He agreed with me that Denmark was much more inclined this way than either Norway or Sweden but that until Denmark received assurance of protection from Russian aggression the present cautious policy would be pursued. He believes Greenland matter can drag on for some time and that the FonMin can answer, in generalities to effect that negotiations are proceeding, the Communists who in Kauffmann's opinion will be the only party to press the matter in Danish Parliament.

On his return Kauffmann will seek to see Secretary but as heretofore reported primarily for home press consumption. I again emphasize importance of conference with President by Rasmussen in September and recommend he be accompanied to Conference by Kauffmann. Word from the President to effect that Truman Doctrine extends to Denmark would in my opinion go far in laying ground for permanent solution of Greenland problem.

Kauffmann departs early July 23 and, with stops Paris, London, Iceland will return US on schedule August 5.

PrimeMin has invited me to dine with him alone July 24 and perhaps he then will confirm above views of Kauffmann.

MARVEL

859B.20/7–2547 : Telegram

The Ambassador in Denmark (Marvel) to the Secretary of State

TOP SECRET COPENHAGEN, July 25, 1947—7 p. m.

510. At dinner last evening attended by Prime Minister, Minister Federspiel [1] and myself, Prime Minister confirmed Govt's policy of "Going slow" regarding Greenland (see my Top Secret telegram 494, July 22). Conversation lasted more than three hours, was most informal, and covered wide variety subjects but Prime Minister emphasized his interest in South Slesvig problem.

To my surprise he asked point blank whether a permanent arrangement regarding Greenland could not be tied into US active interest in South Slesvig problem (see my Top Secret telegram 348, May 24) pointing out both situations had common factor of defense of respective countries. I informed such proposal involved difficulties and added that [*sic*] the situation eight months hence, during which time the Marshall Plan would develop, the Foreign Ministers Conference in No-

---

[1] Per Federspiel, Danish Minister for Special Affairs.

vember would be held, and perhaps the world situation would be sufficiently clear for Denmark to come out more in siding with Western powers and that then a permanent arrangement regarding Greenland could be concluded. The Prime Minister stated all political parties with exception of Communists had strong and natural feeling for America and he believed tangible actions confirming this view would increase in future but that all-out expression of this view by Denmark was retarded by caution of Norwegians and more particularly Swedes.

As to local political situation he admitted attempt would be made to force elections in fall. He could not forecast now whether such attempt would be successful. In passing he noted that British Embassy here was taking more active interest with Socialists and remarked that currying favor with Socialists appeared to be present British program throughout Europe. I agreed with him that contact between British officials here and Danish Socialists had shown marked increase recently. The Prime Minister thought that while the Social[ist?] political power here would remain about the same it would suffer a setback in Sweden in the next election.

MARVEL

859.00/9–1947 : Telegram

The Acting Secretary of State to the Embassy in Denmark

TOP SECRET   WASHINGTON, September 29, 1947—6 p. m.

596. Dept appreciates interest and friendly attitude shown by Hedtoft (urtel 634, Sep 19 [1]) and appreciates also importance placing our point of view adequately before Parliamentary leader his standing. We believe, however, that this should be done orally as occasion offers and not in manner which he or his opponents could describe as supplying him with material for his use in coming political campaign.

Our thinking re Green problem, as you are aware, is based following points: (1) adequate defense installations in Green continue to be essential to peace and security of Western Hemisphere; (2) as cost of such installations is prohibitive for Den, US is prepared to undertake together with Den responsibility of defending Green and to assume necessary expenses; (3) US entirely willing in cooperation with Den to place defense installations at disposal of UN on request of

---

[1] Not printed; it reported that Ambassador Marvel had a conversation on September 19 with Hans Hedtoft, leader of the Danish Social Democratic Party, who expected to head the new government following Danish national elections in the autumn. Hedtoft thought his government would be able successfully to steer through the Danish Parliament an agreement with the United States under which American bases would be established in Greenland so long as American forces remained in occupation in Germany (863.00/9–1947).

Security Council; (4) as long as US has obligation to maintain control agencies in Ger, airports in Green constitute a necessary link in our communications with Ger; (5) a chain of weather and other navigational aid stations on Green is essential for safety above communications and international sea and air traffic over wide area; (6) US will continue recognize unqualified Dan sovereignty throughout Green and respect all Dan interests there. In reply to allegations that existence US defense installations in Green would constitute an invasion Dan sovereignty, it may be pointed out that Brit with its comparatively large resources has not feared for sovereignty Brit areas in Western Hemisphere which US is defending under 99-year leases.

Above viewpoints may be advanced informally to other Dan officials in your discretion as opportunities arise.

LOVETT

859B.20/10–1047

Memorandum by the Director of the Office of European Affairs (Hickerson) to the Secretary of State

TOP SECRET [WASHINGTON,] October 10, 1947.

PROBLEM

In the interviews which he desires with the Secretary and also with the President, Mr. Rasmussen, the Danish Foreign Minister, will undoubtedly wish to discuss the current consultations concerning the defense of Greenland. He will then be strongly tempted to release for Danish consumption a statement designed to give the impression of having come to grips with the problem. It is to our interest that any such statement by Mr. Rasmussen be couched in generalities.

BACKGROUND

Secretary Byrnes, in a conversation with Mr. Rasmussen on December 14, 1946,[1] emphasized the vital importance of Greenland to United States security and suggested three possible courses of action for Mr. Rasmussen's consideration. A memorandum which includes a brief account of the Byrnes-Rasmussen conversation and summarizes developments as of May 28, 1947 is attached.[2]

The Danish Ambassador, in a note of May 27, 1947, mentioned his Government's wish for termination of the Defense of Greenland Agree-

---

[1] See footnote 3, p. 657.
[2] The attachment is not printed.

ment and requested early consultations as provided in Article X. In the Secretary's press release of May 29, 1947 [3] this Government declared its readiness actively to explore with the Danish Government "at any time the basis of some new agreement in keeping with the letter and spirit of the Charter of the United Nations which would take fully into account Danish sovereignty over Greenland and legitimate United States and hemispheric defense requirements".

The Danish Ambassador stated on August 20 that he hoped that by the time of the visit of the Foreign Minister to attend the General Assembly, sufficient progress might have been made to enable the Danish Government to say without undue exaggeration that consultations under Article X of the Defense of Greenland Agreement had begun and were continuing.[4]

On September 12 I conveyed the following oral statement to the Ambassador:

"With reference to our recent conversation I wish to confirm to you that our current discussions concerning the Agreement of April 9, 1941, for the defense of Greenland are considered by the United States Government as having initiated consultations in the sense of Article X of that Agreement.

"The problems brought up in our discussions with you have been brought to the attention of the other interested agencies of this Government and are being given careful consideration in cooperation with those agencies."

The Ambassador confirmed by letter the receipt of my message and expressed satisfaction.

A committee composed of representatives of State, Army, Navy and Air Force has nearly completed a draft of a new agreement. In my opinion, no such draft should be broached to the Danes until the Danish United Nations Delegation, which includes a Communist member of Parliament, shall have left this country.

RECOMMENDATIONS

That in any conversation with Mr. Rasmussen the importance of Greenland as a link in the defense system of the United States and of this hemisphere be emphasized and that he be told that we are actively studying with the other interested Departments the views which have been put forward by Ambassador Kauffmann and that at a later date we shall pursue the matter further.

---

[3] See the memorandum by Morgan, May 31, 1947, p. 663.
[4] Ambassador Kauffmann's call at the Department of State on August 20, 1947, is reported upon in a memorandum of the same date from the Associate Chief of the Division of Northern European Affairs (Morgan) to Hickerson, not printed (859B.20/8–2047).

840.48 Refugees/10–1047

Memorandum by the Director of the Office of European Affairs (Hickerson) to the Secretary of State

SECRET [WASHINGTON,] October 10, 1947.

PROBLEM

The Danish Government has requested that 15,000 German refugees in Denmark be received in the US Zone of Germany in addition to 12,000 previously accepted. The request, presented in a Danish Embassy note of July 28, 1947, [1] is worded in a manner implying that our Zone will not be asked to take more than the total of both contingents, namely 27,000 refugees.

BACKGROUND

At the close of hostilities nearly 200,000 German refugees, mostly aged people, women, and children, remained in Denmark. The Danes claim to have spent the equivalent of $80 million to support and guard these Germans, and regard them as an intolerable burden.

The British and Soviet representatives on the Allied Control Council in Berlin have never agreed with OMGUS that a decision of the ACC of November 20, 1945 [2] should be construed as obligating the Soviet and British Zones to absorb the great bulk of the German refugees in Denmark.

Despite a promise which Stalin made to the Danish Foreign Minister in June 1946 to admit half of the refugees into the Soviet Zone providing the other three zones would accept the other half, the ACC was unable, because of the Soviet member's refusal to discuss the problem, to work out distribution of the refugees to the various zones.

At loss for a solution, the Danes then appealed to each of the three western zones to accept a contingent of 12,000, and to the Soviet Zone to take 36,000. Actually, the British Zone took 18,000, the French Zone 15,000, and the US Zone 12,000, making 45,000 to the three western zones as against 36,000 to the Soviet Zone. A second contingent of 15,000 has recently been transferred to the French Zone. The British have under consideration a Danish request that their zone take an additional 15,000, and have on their own initiative begun to receive from Denmark German refugees who have relatives in the British Zone to provide shelter. The Danes expect that if the US Zone accepts 15,000 as requested, the USSR will then raise its zone's acceptances to a total matching that of the three western zones. This would have the effect of removing all of the German refugees still in Denmark.

---

[1] Not printed.
[2] For a report on the November 20, 1945 meeting of the Allied Control Council for Germany, see *Foreign Relations*, 1945, vol. III, p. 852; and for the text of the plan approved at that meeting see *ibid.*, vol. II, pp. 1316–1317.

A prompt solution of Denmark's German refugee problem is of vital interest to the United States because of the current consultations regarding the defense of Greenland. If we are not willing to give what the Danes regard as reasonable assistance toward the solution of one of their most serious problems, they are not likely to consider objectively our need for long-term defense rights in Greenland.

ACTION TAKEN

Under Secretary Lovett addressed a letter [3] on September 12 to General Draper, Under Secretary of War, urging compliance with the Danish request and stating that although we can not count on any direct benefits from acceptance of the 15,000 refugees we may be sure that failure to take favorable action will react against us in the Greenland consultations. General Draper departed for Korea before making a decision and has just returned. In the meantime we have learned that General Noce of Civil Affairs [4] is opposed to the Danish request while General Norstad of Plans and Operations is in favor of accepting the 15,000 refugees.

RECOMMENDATION

That in any conversation with Mr. Rasmussen he be told that Denmark's request that the US Zone accept 15,000 German refugees in Denmark is receiving careful consideration.

---

[3] Not printed.
[4] Maj. Gen. Daniel Noce, Chief, Civil Affairs Division, War Department General Staff.

859B.20/10–2247

Memorandum of Conversation, by the Secretary of State

TOP SECRET   [NEW YORK,] October 22, 1947.

Participants: Mr. Gustav Rasmussen, Danish Foreign Minister [1]
                Mr. Henrik de Kauffmann, Danish Ambassador
                The Secretary

In raising the subject of termination of the agreement of April 9, 1941 for the defense of Greenland the Danish Foreign Minister referred to an impression in Washington and London that his Government was subject to Soviet pressure for termination of the agreement. He said that no such pressure had been brought to bear by the Soviet Government, the only time the matter had even been mentioned was on

---

[1] Foreign Minister Rasmussen arrived in New York on October 17 to serve as head of the Danish Delegation to the Second Regular Session of the United Nations General Assembly, September 16–November 29, 1947. The Secretary of State headed the United States Delegation.

one occasion when the Soviet Minister at Copenhagen had asked him as to the truth of press reports that the United States Government was attempting to buy Greenland. He was then in a position to refer the Minister to the public statement Mr. Rasmussen had made a few days earlier to the effect that Greenland was not for sale. The Soviet press and radio had been critical of the United States for continuing to maintain forces in Greenland but had not yet criticized the Danish Government. I observed that the Soviet Government was too astute to use direct pressure when it had at its disposal local means of exerting influence and pressure. Mr. Rasmussen said that pressure for termination of the agreement came from various sections of Danish public opinion [in] addition to the Communists. I recognized that this was a subject on which the Communists could easily get general support. He hoped it would be possible for him to say that the consultations provided in Article 10 of the agreement were making progress, as for example to announce that the weather stations were progressively being transferred from American to Danish hands.

I developed to him forcefully and at some length the importance of Greenland as a vital and vulnerable link in the defense of the Western Hemisphere as a whole. If the Danes could defend it adequately that would be fine but they clearly were not in a position to do so. We could not afford to have it undefended. Enemy occupation of Greenland would not only endanger our whole system of hemispheric defense but would expose our vital industrial areas. I said I had hoped that the Danes would understand its importance to us and be able to make suggestions as to how our defense needs could be met in a form that would be politically possible for them. I had hoped that Ambassador Kauffmann would bring such suggestions on his return from Denmark.

Mr. Kauffmann stated that time was needed to solve the problem and that an improvement in the present international atmosphere would help. Three types of installations were involved: the weather stations, the air fields, and the proposed radar installations in the north. He liked the approach indicated in the Department's press release of May 29, 1947 in which we indicated readiness to explore with the Danish Government the basis of a new agreement "in keeping with the letter and spirit of the Charter of the United Nations which would take fully into account Danish sovereignty over Greenland and legitimate United States and hemispheric defense requirements". He also saw possibilities in a regional defense agreement to include Canada and possibly other countries of this hemisphere.

I indicated that this regional approach including Canada might be explored. Referring again to the imperative need for adequate defense of Greenland, I suggested that the Danish political problem might be met by a formula similar to that which we had been prepared to offer the Australian Government in connection with Manus Island, namely that we would be prepared to make annual payments to the Danish Government to enable it to maintain installations which we had erected in Greenland during the war in return for the right to use those facilities as needed and to station a few men there to look after supplies. I pointed out that we would not be in a position to maintain substantial forces there in peace time.

The Foreign Minister did not reply but the Ambassador repeated that time would be needed to work out an agreement. In the meantime the 1941 agreement continued in effect and the conversations would continue.

(After the conversation had ended Mr. Achilles [2] asked the Foreign Minister whether he considered the suggestion of annual payments in return for the right to use the installations a promising one from the Danish point of view. He replied that he must necessarily speak personally since he was not even sure that he would be in the new government to be set up following the elections on October 28, but that he personally thought the approach a very good one.)

---

[2] Theodore C. Achilles, Adviser to the United States Delegation to the General Assembly.

840.48 Refugees/10–2247

Memorandum of Conversation, by the Secretary of State

SECRET   [NEW YORK,] October 22, 1947.

Participants: Mr. Gustav Rasmussen, Danish Foreign Minister
                Mr. Henrik de Kauffmann, Danish Ambassador
                The Secretary

The Danish Foreign Minister reviewed the problem of German refugees in Denmark and left the attached memorandum.[1] He emphasized particularly his Government's desire that the western zones agree to take an additional 30,000 refugees in order that he might be in a position to ask the Soviets to fulfill Generalissimo Stalin's agreement to take half the refugees in Denmark provided the western zones would take the other half.

He stated that since the memorandum had been written he had discussed the matter in London with Mr. Bevin who had indicated willingness to receive additional refugees in the British zone but suggested

---

[1] Not printed.

that the 30,000 be distributed equally between the three western zones. Mr. Rasmussen planned to take this up with the French.

I told him that the matter was under active consideration by the Departments of State and Army and that I hoped it would be possible to work out something along the lines he desired.

840.48 Refugees/11–547

The Under Secretary of the Army (Draper) to the Under Secretary of State (Lovett)

SECRET   WASHINGTON, 5 November 1947.

DEAR MR. LOVETT: We have given careful consideration to your letter of September 12 [1] with reference to the Danish request that 15,000 additional Germans from Denmark be received by the U.S. Zone.

I have discussed this matter with the Theater Commander [2] who advises me that the U.S. Zone is unable to accept additional refugees. It was on this basis that the additional expellees from Czechoslovakia were refused admittance since conditions of both housing and food are such that for humane considerations no other decision could be reached. This decision could not be justified if an exception were now made in favor of Denmark. General Clay also advises me that Mr. Byrnes, when Secretary of State, personally assured him that if the 12,000 in question at that time were accepted by the U.S. Zone, the State Department would not ask that any more be taken. General Clay's recollection is that Denmark was advised at that time that it would be understood that the 12,000 in question represented the maximum that could be accepted by the U.S. Zone.

One of the considerations at the time the decision to accept the 12,000 Germans from Denmark was made was the desire for U.S. military base rights in Greenland. However, these rights have not been obtained, and there is no assurance, as I understand it, that they would be obtained by acceptance of the 15,000 additional Germans now in question. If definite assurance [were given?] that the base rights would actually be obtained as a result of favorable action on this request, we would be prepared to reconsider the whole question.

The Theater Commander advises me that the American Zone, under the various quadripartite agreements concerned with the acceptance of German refugees and expellees, has already received more than its

---

[1] Not printed.
[2] Gen. Lucius D. Clay, United States Commander in Chief, Europe, and Military Governor for Germany.

proportionate share and more in numbers than any other zone. In view of the present deficit in the U.S. Zone which is being made up by American appropriated funds, acceptance of the Danish request would simply mean that the present costs of supporting these people, which is now being borne by Denmark, would be shifted to our shoulders. Actually, it is indigenous Danish food which they now receive; if they were transferred to the U.S. Zone, they would have to be fed by imported food which we would pay for.

The letter [3] which you enclosed from the Danish Chargé d'Affaires points out that these refugees should no longer be separated from their relatives in Germany. This is, of course, true, but the American Zone has already received all who originally came from that zone so that acceptance of these people would not return them to their families or homes. Under the quadripartite agreement the Russian and British Zones were to receive the residents of the Polish-administered area which formerly was part of Germany. It is my understanding that the German refugees now in Denmark came from this area and the obligation to receive them would therefore rest on those zones. Certainly, as you say in your letter, there is no contractual or other obligation on the U.S. Zone of Germany to receive them.

General Clay informs me that the German authorities in the U.S. Zone were advised at the time arrangements were made for receiving the 12,000 refugees from Denmark that they would not be asked to accept more than that number, and it is obvious what the effects would be if this understanding were now disregarded in view of the present economic conditions in the Zone, particularly with respect to housing and food. We must take into account the effect of any such action on our democratic objectives in Germany.

Therefore, I regret that the Department of the Army cannot concur in complying with the Danish request.

Since writing the above, your letter of November 1 [4] on the same subject has been received, and I have, therefore, taken the occasion to discuss this matter thoroughly with the Secretary of the Army.[5] He has asked me to advise you that he fully agrees with the contents of this letter.

  Sincerely yours,   WILLIAM H. DRAPER, JR.

---

[3] Under reference here is a note dated July 28, 1947, from the Danish Chargé, not printed, setting forth Denmark's urgent desire to be rid of the German refugees brought into Denmark shortly before the German surrender (840.48 Refugees/7–2847).

[4] Not printed.

[5] Kenneth C. Royall.

859.00/11–1547 : Telegram

The Ambassador in Denmark (Marvel) to the Secretary of State

TOP SECRET   COPENHAGEN, November 15, 1947—6 p. m.

772. Hedtoft [1] lunched with me *à deux* today and conversation of two hours covered variety of subjects.

As to local political situation, his policy will be to concentrate on upbuilding Danish economy. No schemes of nationalization of industry or breaking up large estates will be undertaken. Effort will be made to enlarge social reforms such as old-age pensions, workman's compensation et cetera, but with an eye to what budget will bear. In short, policy of prewar Social Democrats will be followed.

As to foreign affairs, immediate announcing of pro-western policy is prevented (1) by present antipathy of Danes towards British and (2) by attitude of Norwegians and Swedes. As to (2) Hedtoft cited cautious and neutral position taken by Swedish and Norwegian Prime and Foreign Ministers at Oslo Conference of Social Democrats last summer. He hopes to persuade them into American viewpoint, but admits difficulties.

In view of Department's decision not to press Greenland treaty here (Department's top secret 665, November 7 [2]), I asked him his views on Greenland generally and whether matter could drag on for some time. He reiterated that joint defense particularly as long as US in Germany was still best solution and pointed out my points on subject (following suggestions of Department's top secret 596, September 29) had been supplied all Social Democrat candidates and uttered by them during campaign. He stated, however, since it was obvious I was not pressing matter, it could be arranged for discussions to be slowed down by taking it up piecemeal, namely, discuss weather stations first, then navigational aids, then air bases, et cetera, which could consume one or two years. This delay he thought could be plausibly explained in Parliament. In fact, he thought this approach would be helpful to Norway and its Spitsbergen problem.

My opinion is government will be favorably inclined towards America and approachable on all problems.

                                                            MARVEL

---

[1] The Kristensen government resigned in October 1947 after a vote of no confidence in the Folketing. Following the election in late October, a new government was formed by Prime Minister Hans Hedtoft.

[2] Not printed. Its operative portion read as follows:

"Green treaty is being negotiated by Dept with Dan Emb here and probably discussions will be accelerated after Kauffmann returns from UN meeting late this month.

"Meanwhile you can assist by evaluating attitude new Dan Govt to problem, and views set forth Deptel 596 Sep 29 [*ante*, p. 676] can be advanced as opportunities arise." (859B.20/11–447)

840.48 Refugees/12–1947

The Acting Secretary of State to the Secretary of Defense (Forrestal)

SECRET [WASHINGTON,] December 19, 1947.

MY DEAR MR. SECRETARY : I should like to bring to your personal attention a matter which may seriously impede our negotiations with Denmark for base rights in Greenland.

The Danish Government has requested the United States to receive in the U.S. Zone of Germany some 8,000 Germans who are refugees in Denmark. The Department of the Army has indicated that it cannot concur in complying with the Danish request. The Danish Government has firmly indicated to the Department of State that Danish feeling in this matter is so intense that refusal by the U.S. to meet the Danish request is likely to make it impossible to obtain the base rights in Greenland which I understand is a matter regarded as highly important from a national security standpoint. In these circumstances I believe the problem is essentially one of weighing the inconvenience and burden which receiving these refugees would place upon the administration of the U.S. Zone against the danger to our negotiations for the Greenland bases which would result from refusing the Danish request. Although it is my own view that the greater interests of the U.S. will be served by agreeing to the Danish request, I feel that the question is one of primary concern to the Department of National Defense. I should, therefore, appreciate your guidance. Because of the interest of the Army, Navy and Air Force in this matter, I am sending copies of this letter to Messrs. Royall, Sullivan [1] and Symington.[2]

The German refugees in question are among some 70–75 thousand who remain from some 200,000 Germans who fled to Denmark during the war. The maintenance of these refugees has been a heavy and distasteful burden upon Denmark, which has repeatedly urged the Occupying Powers to absorb them. The Department of State has been informed by the Danish Ambassador that the Soviet Zone will absorb half of the refugees if the Western Zones will absorb the remaining half. The Western Zones have thus far absorbed some 62,000, of whom 12,000 were taken by the U.S. Zone, although no obligation rested on the U.S. to do so. Of the 70–75 thousand remaining, Denmark regards the Soviet Zone as obligated to take 50,000 and has requested the three Western powers to take 20–25 thousand, the U.S. Zone's share being approximately 8,000.

The Danish Government has stated that the other Western powers are willing to take their share, conditioned upon our agreement to take

---

[1] John L. Sullivan, Secretary of the Navy.
[2] W. Stuart Symington, Secretary of the Air Force.

our share. The British Government has made a proposal in the Coordinating Committee in Berlin [3] to complete the solution of this problem. This matter is now before a subcommittee of the Coordinating Committee and the U.S. must take a position on it in the near future.

This matter has been discussed thoroughly with representatives of the Army Department here and by Ambassador Douglas and Assistant Secretary Saltzman with General Clay in London.[4] The Army's position is based upon the acute housing and food situation in Germany; the effect which affirmative action would have upon the Germans in our zone and upon other countries such as Czechoslovakia and Hungary which have been anxious to send their German population into our zone; the lack of obligation to accept the refugees; and the fact that the U.S. Zone already had accepted the previous group without such obligation. These objections are valid and understandable from the point of view of the administration of Germany. They must be weighed, however, against the effect of U.S. rejection of the Danish request.

The Department of the Army has suggested that if definite assurance can be obtained from Denmark that the base rights would actually be obtained as a result of possible action on the Danish request, it would be prepared to reconsider the whole question. We have considered this suggestion but have concluded that under the circumstances it should not be attempted since its effect would probably be adverse rather than favorable.

Our position will be considerably improved if we are able to give the Danes a favorable reply promptly. I should, therefore, appreciate hearing from you as soon as possible.

Sincerely yours,

ROBERT A. LOVETT
Acting Secretary

---

[3] An agency of the Allied Control Authority for Germany. For documentation on the problems of quadripartite control in Germany, see vol. II, pp. 831 ff.
[4] Lewis Douglas, the Ambassador in the United Kingdom, Charles E. Saltzman, Assistant Secretary of State for Occupied Areas, and Gen. Clay were serving as advisers on the United States Delegation to the Fifth Session of the Council of Foreign Ministers, held in London, November 25–December 15, 1947.

FRANCE

CONCERN OF THE UNITED STATES WITH POLITICAL AND ECONOMIC DEVELOPMENTS RELATING TO FRANCE; MEASURES UNDERTAKEN BY THE UNITED STATES TO ASSIST IN THE PRESERVATION OF DEMOCRATIC GOVERNMENT IN FRANCE [1]

851.00/1–2347 : Telegram

The Ambassador in France (Caffery) to the Secretary of State

TOP SECRET   PARIS, January 23, 1947—7 p.m.

318. My 308, January 23.[2] A most reliable source close to Marcel Paul [3] informs me that latter told him several days ago that the French Communist Party had received instructions from Moscow to get as many Cabinet posts as possible but to enter the Government "even if it only obtained two Cabinet posts".[4] According to Paul the two posts in question were National Defense (this for prestige reasons because of the strong stand the Communists took in December) and Labor. Anything else they could get would be gravy. Paul added that it was of great importance for the Communists to be in the Government during the period preceding the Moscow Foreign Ministers Conference [5] since the results of this Conference would have a vital bearing on the evolution of events in western Europe.

My informant was also told by a Left-Wing Socialist who has very close relations with Pierre Hervé [6] that the latter told him much the same story but added that Moscow has instructed the French Communist Party to behave with moderation in the next several weeks but to be prepared if necessary to create a major political crisis at the end of February or the beginning of March preceding the Moscow conference in case it becomes necessary to "neutralize" French foreign policy

---

[1] For previous documentation see *Foreign Relations*, 1946, vol. v, pp. 399 ff. For documentation on the interest of the United States in nationalist opposition to the restoration of French rule in Indochina, see volume vi.

[2] Not printed.

[3] A leader of the Communist Party in France.

[4] Vincent Auriol, elected President of the French Republic on January 16, selected Paul Ramadier to form a new cabinet after Léon Blum retired. On January 22 Ramadier announced formation of a coalition cabinet that included five Communists, among them Maurice Thorez (as one of two Vice Premiers), François Billoux (National Defense), and Ambroise Croizat (Labor).

[5] For documentation relating to the Moscow Conference, March 10–April 24, 1947, see vol. II, pp. 139 ff.

[6] A leader of the Communist Party in France.

at that juncture. When asked how such a crisis could be provoked Hervé reportedly replied that "the Communists could always find some pretext to withdraw from the Government but in addition could through the CGT create an impossible situation for the present Government".

To protect source I have classified this telegram top secret and request that it be treated with utmost secrecy.

Sent Department as 318, repeated to Moscow as 22.

CAFFERY

851.00/1–2847 : Telegram

The Ambassador in France (Caffery) to the Secretary of State

TOP SECRET   PARIS, January 28, 1947—7 p. m.

372. Bidault [1] told me this morning that the new government is not getting off to a very good start due to the intransigeance of the Communist Ministers who are already fighting the other Ministers at every step. "Unless Moscow changes their directives to the Communist Party here," he said, "this Government is not going to last very long."

He then indulged in a violent diatribe against the Communist Party here; how he has always tried to get along with them even having been occasionally criticized as being too conciliatory; how for a long time he believed it would be possible to live alongside of them but he is doubtful about that now. He has become convinced that the Communists are out to eradicate western civilization as we know it from western Europe. He is particularly worried about Billoux in National Defense. Billoux he considers an extremely able, very likable and extremely dangerous Communist militant. His presence in National Defense bodes no good for the French Army (I agree with Bidault about Billoux).

While on the one hand I believe that Bidault was sincere when he was talking to me about the Communists; on the other hand, I am perfectly aware that for reasons of personal ambition he has frequently "compromised" with them in the past and he will do so in the future when it happens to suit his purpose of the moment. In other words: while Bidault's principles are basically anti-Communist, at the Moscow Conference the Secretary will by no means always be able to count on him; and it is difficult to know in advance when he is going to "compromise" on one of those principles.

CAFFERY

---

[1] Georges Bidault, French Minister for Foreign Affairs.

851.51/1–3047 : Telegram

The Ambassador in France (Caffery) to the Secretary of State

CONFIDENTIAL   PARIS, January 30, 1947—9 p. m.

411. Embassy informed that at Finance Ministry meeting this afternoon under chairmanship Finance Minister Schuman, decision was made for Baumgartner, President Crédit National, to proceed immediately to Washington in connection French application International Bank loan. He is scheduled to take plane this Sunday.[1]

Meeting was reportedly called as result of telephone call this morning from French alternate director International Bank, who reported that McCloy [2] appointment presidence [as president] was imminent.

Mendès-France, French executive director International Bank, is planning to leave for Washington some time next week.

CAFFERY

---

[1] February 2.
[2] The election of John J. McCloy as President of the International Bank for Reconstruction and Development was announced on February 28, 1947.

851.00B/2–1947 : Telegram

The Ambassador in France (Caffery) to the Secretary of State

SECRET   PARIS, February 19, 1947—1 p. m.

741. Remytel 719, February 17, 6 p.m.[1] Viewed from the vantage point of Paris, the "Comintern" gathering at London,[2] timed as it is upon the eve of the Moscow Conference, reflects the highly complex nature of Soviet policy so well orchestrated here through the vast network of the French Communist movement, as well as various Comintern organizations and auxiliaries such as the WFTU, Women's International Democratic Federation, World Youth Federation, and similar groups. The long hand of the Kremlin is increasingly exercising power, or at least influence, in all European countries, largely through its principal lever, the French Communist Party and its fortress the CGT. All these organizations function primarily as public pressure machines designed to promote Soviet aims and ambitions, while attacking the "imperialism" of the Anglo-Saxon "capitalist" powers, and undermining French authority in the colonies.

Posing to the average Frenchman as the strongest defender of his fatherland, especially against the German "menace" and "international

---

[1] Not printed.
[2] The 19th annual conference of the British Communist party was held in London on February 22, 23, and 24, with representatives of various foreign Communist parties present. It was followed by the 1st conference of Communist parties of the British Empire, February 26–March 3.

capital", the Soviet Trojan horse in France is so well camouflaged that millions of Communist militants, sympathizers, and opportunists have been brought to believe that the best way to defend France is to identify French national interests with the aims of the Soviet Union. Accordingly, Moscow is taking the initiative all along the line in utilizing its own auxiliaries like the WFTU and Women's International Democratic Federation for purpose of raising a hue and cry about British and American "imperialism", racial discrimination, promotion of "international trusts", et cetera, and thus diverting attention from the extremely ugly aspects of the Soviet brand of "socialism" in the Soviet Union and its surrounding satellites. Owing to the fact that Paris has become the center of these activities, this city now resembles a veritable hive of Comintern agents with their swarm of followers and dupes, of whom the already large number almost daily increases, and who are endeavoring to "bore from within" international pacifist and idealist organizations like UNESCO and International United Nations Association.

The Comintern "brain trust" here is more active and bolder than at any period since the liberation. One of the Comintern's spokesmen here, Courtade, openly proclaims that Stalin continues to pursue the strategy laid down by Lenin in the aim of exploiting all weaknesses and contradictions arising within the "parliamentary and bourgeois democracies" and asserts that it is absurd to accuse the Soviet Union of pursuing imperialist policies, since imperialism is the outgrowth of "capitalism" and consequently cannot exist in the "socialist" Soviet Union. Courtade insists that the "steps and efforts of a socialist state in the aim of assuring its defense and augmenting its authority are legitimate", and divulges that "even when a conflict arises between a progressive state and one which is not so progressive, it appears normal to us in all cases to support the demands of the progressive state". Basing his thesis on the myth that Soviet Union is really socialist and democratic, Courtade has the effrontery to announce that, "We do not separate our patriotism and the defense of French interests from the defense of the positions already conquered by the socialist revolution."

Courtade's Soviet patriotism and that of other French Communists, such as Thorez, was well tested and found loyal by the Kremlin in 1940, when in support of the Hitler-Stalin pact,[3] he engaged in secret Communist activities designed to disintegrate the French army at a time when his own country was at war with Germany.

---

[3] For text of the Treaty of Non-Aggression between Germany and the Union of Soviet Socialist Republics, signed August 23, 1939, see *Documents on German Foreign Policy, 1918–1945*, series D, vol. VII (Washington, Government Printing Office, 1956), pp. 245 ff.

The real nature of the Soviet advance in Europe is cloaked under the Stalinist doctrine of the unequal development of "socialism", that is, the thesis that the extension of Soviet power depends upon the gradual and uneven breakdown of "bourgeois democracy" in countries situated on the perimeter of the Soviet Union. This thesis is well reflected in the recent remark of the chief spokesman of the Communist parties for western Europe and America, Jacques Duclos, to the effect that "Frenchmen can sleep more tranquilly over the thought that Silesia is no longer in the hands of the Germans". This remark, made on the occasion of the Polish elections on January 19, gave the signal for the French Communists to take an ostensibly French nationalist position on the western frontiers of Poland. Last Saturday, the weekly organ of central committee of Communist Party *France Nouvelle* condemned former Secretary Byrnes' "generosity" at Stuttgart "in proposing the return to Germany of western Polish lands contrary to Potsdam decision",[4] insisted that Silesia should "never" return to Germany.

This publication added that this attitude is based on the "simple principle which should not be forgotten a single moment at Moscow Conference," namely, that "everything which weakens Germany reassures us, so true is it that Germany becomes more or less dangerous according to whether it is strengthened or weakened."

In view of implications of this latest outburst on part of French Communists, it will be interesting to see whether a German delegation will attend the "Comintern" Conference in London, and if so how it will present there the highly "nationalist" line of the German Party. In any event, treatment of German problem at this conference should evoke the greatest possible attention.

Viewed from here, Germany appears as the pivot of power in Europe, and so long as we do not fully exploit the contradictions and weaknesses arising from the fundamental conflict of interests between the Soviet Union and its "fifth columns" in Germany, France, and other countries, the Kremlin will remain in the position simultaneously to pursue its own ends (including demand for heavier reparations) without essentially endangering the position of the French, Polish, and other "nationalist" Communist parties in Europe.

Repeated London 143, Moscow 80, Berlin 61, Rome 41, and Vienna 14.

CAFFERY

---

[4] For text of Secretary Byrnes' speech of September 6, 1946, at Stuttgart, see Department of State *Bulletin*, September 15, 1946, p. 496.

851.00/3–647

The Ambassador in France (Caffery) to the Deputy Director of the Office of European Affairs (Hickerson)

SECRET   PARIS, March 6, 1947.

DEAR JACK: Prior to the Secretary's arrival in Paris this morning I prepared a brief and rather general memorandum on the present French picture as we see it at this juncture. I am enclosing for your information a copy of the memorandum. As I said above, it treats the general aspects of the French situation and represents a symposium of the views of a number of officials and political observers of different political orientation.[1]

With all good wishes,

Very sincerely yours,

JEFFERSON CAFFERY

[Enclosure]

Memorandum by the Ambassador in France (Caffery)

SECRET   [PARIS,] March 6, 1947.

Although the present Government by nature of its broad coalition basis enjoys the appearance of a large parliamentary majority, nonetheless there are a number of critical questions which could lead to serious dissension within this uneasy parliamentary majority. Questions such as wages and prices, revision of the press laws, balancing the budget, French overseas colonial policy (particularly in Indo-China), strictly controlled economy versus economic liberalism, are among the more acute problems on which different elements within the Government are in basic disagreement. A knockdown-dragout fight on some of these issues could easily result in the withdrawal of support by elements which at present are participating in the Government, thus causing a serious political crisis.

For the moment, and particularly until the termination of the Moscow Conference, it is generally believed that none of the political parties participating in the Government will wish to precipitate a serious political crisis because such action would greatly weaken the hand of the French Delegation at Moscow, when critical discussions on Germany, involving French security, are occurring. After the termina-

---

[1] The memorandum was prepared for use by Secretary Marshall as background for his conversations at Paris en route to a meeting of the Council of Foreign Ministers at Moscow. For the record of the Secretary's conversation on March 6 with Vincent Auriol, President of the French Republic, mostly with regard to the forthcoming meeting at Moscow, see vol. II, p. 190.

tion of the Moscow Conference, however, the situation will again become fraught with possibilities, particularly if French economy deteriorates further.

Insofar as the general public is concerned, there is uneasiness and a lack of confidence in the present Government. Reports from many prefectures in France, particularly from those areas where food is scarce and living conditions difficult, indicate that while at present there appears to be no danger of any disorder or trouble originating in such regions, there is considerable discontent, and should there be trouble in Paris there would probably be rapid repercussions in these areas. There is also general discontent with the Government because it seems incapable of governing effectively. This has led in some cases to the development of an unhealthy state of mind to the effect that since democracy as it is practiced in France does not seem to be effective, an authoritative Government is needed.

In this connection it is interesting that de Gaulle [2] has decided to take the initiative and actively reenter the political arena. He has announced that he will make several speeches during the month of March. This decision has resulted in a series of rumors among his opponents of the extreme Left and his supporters of the Right that some form of manoeuver looking to the establishment of an authoritarian Gaullist régime is in the offing. Actually the present Gaullist game is to break down the party discipline of the parties of the Center and Right so that the membership thereof will desert the group to which they now belong and form a coalition headed by de Gaulle which will be anti-Communist in fact but not in name. His chances of succeeding in such a manoeuver in the immediate future do not appear bright but he has unquestionably gained support for the idea recently among the ranks of parliamentarians belonging to the Rassemblement des Gauches, the MRP and the Independent Republicans. Should a situation arise where the French people are given a choice *only* between de Gaulle and the Communists, a majority would certainly back the General. On the other hand, should a crisis of the first magnitude develop it seems probable at this juncture that Blum (who is holding himself on the sidelines) might, because of his recently increased prestige, first be called back to try to solve it, and there is little doubt that Blum and certain elements of the Center have such a possibility in mind. Should Blum fail, the choice might necessarily be between de Gaulle and the Communists.

The Communists, for the moment, are behaving themselves. Apparently on instructions from Moscow they entered the present Gov-

---

[2] Gen. Charles de Gaulle had temporarily withdrawn from public affairs in January 1946.

ernment with a view to influencing the French Government's foreign policy, particularly during the Moscow Conference. While maintaining the outward fiction of being a "Government Party" they continue their undermining and infiltration tactics. What the Communist position will be after the Moscow Conference is not certain and may depend to a considerable extent on what actually transpires at Moscow as well as in France itself.

From the foregoing it should not be assumed that there will be serious trouble or disorder in the period of the next several months. The French people tend to be either over-optimistic or over-pessimistic, and with the advent of Spring, with warmer weather and easier living conditions, their present feeling of pessimism may undergo change. However, this will depend to a great extent on the Government's ability to solve the most critical economic and financial problems in such a fashion that the French people believe that although living conditions are difficult, the Government has a sound financial and economic program through which French recovery may be effected. At this juncture it seems evident that the possibility of adopting a sound economic program depends on gaining real support of the Communist Party and its auxiliary, the CGT. Failing this, it is difficult to see how a serious political crisis can be avoided.

851.00/3–3147 : Telegram

The Ambassador in France (Caffery) to the Secretary of State

SECRET   PARIS, March 31, 1947—8 p. m.

1371. Without question the Socialists as well as the MRP are vastly relieved that the Communists did not leave the government at this juncture because they feared that if they left the government they might make all government impossible by virtue of their control of the CGT which they might launch into a series of strikes all over the country.

This is leading up to say that the CGT is the key to the mystery and while some effort has been made in the direction of removing CGT levers of control from Communist hands a great deal more has to be accomplished before non-Communist labor leaders will be in a position to take hold of the situation. In other words: Non-Communist parties are not yet ready to stage a fight with the Communists over the CGT. While I repeat that much remains to be done I have noticed some encouraging signs of late: For instance a new courage which we now find in non-Communist labor and also the endeavor which is now being made to organize non-Communist groups to confront the presently well-organized, well-disciplined, well-financed Communist groups which will take to the streets in the event of disorder of [*or?*] serious labor difficulties.

In brief: A year ago I was discouraged about the possibility of preventing the Communists from eventually taking over this country; now I have come to believe that they will not take it over; but the process of organizing the genuine democratic forces into an effective machine will be long and tedious; and without a doubt the Communists if they don't take it over will struggle hard to keep it weak and divided.

Sent Department 1371, repeated Moscow for Delegation 202, and London 270.

CAFFERY

851.00/4–347 : Airgram

The Ambassador in France (Caffery) to the Secretary of State

SECRET   PARIS, April 3, 1947.

A–622. André Philip, Minister of National Economy and moderate Socialist, commented to Embassy today that political situation in France was "primarily a battle between the United States and the Soviet Union", and that "before the Socialists could successfully kick the Communists out of the Cabinet" it would be necessary for economic conditions in France to be substantially better than they are today.

CAFFERY

851.5018/4–847

The French Embassy to the Department of State

[Translation]

WASHINGTON, April 8, 1947.

AIDE-MÉMOIRE

On instructions from the French Government, the French Embassy sent to the Department of State on March 31, 1947,[1] a note by which it called its attention to the very precarious situation of the supplying of cereals to France and to the urgent need of obtaining a quick and substantial increase in American shipments, since the United States is the only source of imports on which France can count at the present time.

The reports which have reached the Embassy very recently confirm the gravity of this situation. In spite of the saving realized in North

---

[1] Not printed.

Africa, thanks to the use of a high percentage of barley, and in spite of the energetic measures taken in Metropolitan France to speed receipts, the supplying of flour is already beginning to cause great difficulties, especially in the south of France. For that reason, it has been necessary to draw on the limited stocks of Paris and Lille to assure the supplying of Marseilles and Nice.

These disruptions, which will increase and become more extensive in the course of the coming weeks, are due to several causes: the decrease in receipts in proportion to the resumption of agricultural work; the impossibility, owing to the lessening of the reserve supplies, of assuring the distribution of the available resources throughout the country; and the insufficiency of imports.

It is to be expected that these difficulties will increase considerably at the beginning of May, when shipments within the country will be completely halted as a result of the progressive exhaustion of the supplies.

This situation, the gravity of which was not equaled even in the hardest years of the occupation, imposes upon the French Government, in spite of the weighty political consequences which such a measure involves, the obligation of reducing the bread ration, beginning May 1, to a level which it has never before reached.

This decision, however, will not suffice to solve the problem. It is, in addition, indispensable that France receive, from now until May 31, large supplementary deliveries, and that it receive advance shipment of its June quota if it is desired to prevent, in the great urban centers, the mining areas and other regions, the occurrence of interruptions in the supplying of a ration which has already been diminished and which concerns a type of bread which includes an abnormal proportion of corn.

The French Government has the firm hope that, under these grave circumstances, the Government of the United States will be so good as to lend it its effective and immediate assistance.

851.00/4–1147 : Telegram

The Ambassador in France (Caffery) to the Secretary of State

SECRET   PARIS, April 11, 1947—2 p. m.

1493. De Gaulle's recent political activity, particularly his Strasbourg speech [1] and the threat of more to come, have served further

---

[1] Speech made at Strasbourg on April 7, 1947, commemorating the second anniversary of the liberation of Alsace. In the speech de Gaulle appealed for national unity and spoke on the political, economic, and external problems facing France. The speech was followed by formation of the Rassemblement du Peuple Français (RPF).

to agitate the already troubled French political waters and have created acute uneasiness in all political parties of the Center and Left. This "malaise" stems in large part from the fact that every party (except the Communists) realizes that De Gaulle represents a powerful role of attraction to a substantial part of its membership, and that De Gaulle is actually out to divide and destroy the individual parties as now constituted. (The MRP is particularly vulnerable to De Gaulle's attack because of the basic cleavage between pro-Gaullist and pro-Bidault factions. The Rassemblement des Gauches is equally vulnerable because whereas the leadership of the UDSR is ardently Gaullist, a majority of the Radical Socialist elements would at present probably only support De Gaulle in the event they were given a choice only between him and the Communists). Furthermore there is anxiety concerning the steps by which he intends to seek to return to power and the possible "chain-reaction" his activity may cause.

De Gaulle has not yet decided on his strategy but his general aim is, as indicated above, to destroy the hold of the political parties on their followers so that large parts of their membership, including their parliamentary representatives, will transfer their allegiance to him. Counting on the disintegration of the political parties and his own very considerable public prestige, De Gaulle apparently believes that in the ruins of the present political party system he can rally a substantial majority and construct a strong coalition grouping all anti-Communist forces.

While such a plan of campaign may appear sound to De Gaulle's ardent supporters, its practicality at this particular juncture is open to doubt. In the first place, in order for De Gaulle to succeed in forming a broad and successful anti-Communist coalition, he must have the support of working class elements and particularly of substantial elements of the vitally important trade union movement. As things now stand only Socialists can bring such support to De Gaulle. But the latter by his Bruneval [2] and Strasbourg speeches has served notice on them that he is out to destroy the present government, which is, of course, essentially Socialist (my 1415, April 3 [3]). To defend themselves against this onslaught even strongly anti-Communist Socialists who under certain circumstances would work with De Gaulle have felt obliged for the present at least to make common cause with the Communists (who are determined to fight De Gaulle tooth and nail) on this issue. Thus the Communists who three weeks ago were isolated because of their stand on Indochina (and had in fact pushed the Socialists toward the center parties) now find the Socialists have been driven back into their embrace by De Gaulle's action.

---

[2] The speech at Bruneval on March 30, 1947, marked de Gaulle's return to the political arena in France.
[3] Not printed.

Certain Socialists and a few political leaders of the Center who have been working to establish a strong anti-Communist coalition are unhappy over the results of De Gaulle's recent activity and believe it premature and ill-considered. They think it may set back their work of uniting anti-Communist forces and point out that actually De Gaulle's activity may serve to divide anti-Communist opinion thus strengthening the relative position of the Communists who are not only united but can count at this time on Socialist support on at least this issue. They also fear that if De Gaulle accentuates his present activity the present Communist line of "moderation" may undergo brusque change and the Communists may react forcefully when anti-Communist forces will be not only still unprepared for a final showdown but (as a result of De Gaulle's drive) will be perhaps more divided than ever. They point out that given De Gaulle's deep hostility to both the French Communist Party and the Soviet Union the interests of both would best be served by doing everything possible to prevent him from again taking up the reins of government.

Sent Dept 1493; repeated Moscow for the Delegation 234 and London as 287.

CAFFERY

851.00/4–1847 : Telegram

The Ambassador in France (Caffery) to the Secretary of State

SECRET   PARIS, April 18, 1947—6 p. m.
US URGENT

1623. Mytel 1601 April 17 [1] Discussing the Cabinet session day before yesterday at which the Communists were reported to have walked out because of opposition to rest of Cabinet's stand on the Malgache deputies who were arrested for implication in Madagascar revolt a high Interior Ministry official stated his belief that "although the Malgache are not tied to Moscow as is the Viet Nam in Indo China,[2] there is not the slightest doubt that the Communists prior to the revolt urged the Malgache representatives to resort to illegal insurrectionary action".

My informant said that in leaking to the press what transpired at the Cabinet meeting yesterday "certain Cabinet Ministers including Teitgen" [3] exaggerated somewhat the "menacing" attitude of the Communists with the view of placing the latter in the most unfavorable possible light before French public opinion. For example, the press

---

[1] Not printed.
[2] For documentation on the situation in Indochina, see vol. VI, pp. 51 ff.
[3] Pierre-Henri Teitgen, Vice-President of the French Council of Ministers.

story implied that the Communists walked out in the middle of the meeting threatening quit the government. My source says this not strictly accurate. When the meeting was almost over they withdrew with veiled but not open threats, but Thorez subsequently attended the restricted Cabinet meeting in the afternoon.

Nonetheless it is now clear that the Madagascar problem has become an issue which could lead to the fall of the Ramadier government. While Interior Ministry does not expect a ministerial crisis before the Assembly reconvenes on April 29 it believes that matters will rapidly come to a head immediately thereafter when the debate is opened on the status of the arrested Malgache deputies. My informant believes that if Communist deputies (in opposition to the other parties) do not actually vote against withdrawal of Parliamentary immunity of Malgache deputies they will, as in the case of Indo China, at least abstain. In light of behavior of Communist Cabinet Ministers day before yesterday he believes it possible that they also may abstain or even vote against the government. Such action could entail collapse of Ramadier's government should either the Communists refuse to accept the majority's will or should Ramadier or any of governmental parties refuse to remain in government because of this further violation of the principle of ministerial solidarity. In many respects there is therefore a close analogy between the new impending crisis and that which occurred recently over Indo China.

Speaking of the Communists present tactical position resulting from their stand on the arrested Malgache deputies my informant said that "they are in the difficult position in which they always find themselves when Moscow's orders force them to adopt an anti-nationalist line". He recalled that when Malgache deputies were arrested the Communist Cabinet Ministers did not protest and that for several days thereafter and "pending instructions from Moscow the Communist press played this whole story down and contended itself with simple announcements of the arrest. Subsequently when they received their orders openly to attack the government's stand they obeyed loyally if somewhat unhappily since they know it will hurt them with the French public." He explained their position as follows:

On the one hand Moscow, one of whose cardinal policies is the disintegration of existing colonial possessions not only so that Communists can fill the vacuum but also because it enfeebles the colonial power and makes it an easier prey to ultimate Communist domination, has ordered them to support at all cost colonial independence movements etc., which lead to unrest and weaken France's hold on her overseas empire;

On the other hand by obeying these orders Communist Party (French) tends to isolate itself from the other parties which are firmly behind the present government's policy and weakens its position with the average Frenchman, who although generally apathetic is nonetheless a flag waver insofar as the French Empire is concerned. Furthermore, in this particular instance since the present colonial policy is directed by Socialist Minister Moutet [4] attacks against his policy tend to force the Socialists away from Communists at the very time when the latter have drawn closer on the De Gaulle issue. Such action of course strengthens De Gaulle's hand since the latter has always maintained he is the only one who can save the French Empire.

In summarizing my informant expressed opinion that in the light of this most recent development re Madagascar and the possibility of other important developments in the colonial field (for example when the Algerian statute is debated next month) it is impossible to predict how the internal situation will evolve. This will depend largely on whether or not the French Communist Party receives orders (as he believes it will because of vital importance to Moscow) to support independence movements in French overseas areas even if it means breaking with the government. He said that while the French Communists have a certain liberty of action in choosing tactics to be employed in dealing with internal French problems, "on colonial questions they must follow Moscow's orders to the letter regardless of the immediate damage it may do them with the French public".

I concur with the foregoing estimate of the broad lines of Communist strategy which is shared by other qualified observers (including a former Comintern agent) having intimate knowledge of Communist policy and strategy.

Sent Dept 1623, repeated London 308, Moscow for delegation 257.

CAFFERY

---

[4] Marius Moutet, Minister for Overseas France.

851.6131/4–2347 : Telegram

The Under Secretary of State for Economic Affairs (Clayton [1]) to the Acting Secretary of State

CONFIDENTIAL   GENEVA, April 23, 1947—6 p. m.
PRIORITY

156. For Acheson and Stillwell [2] from Clayton. At Ambassador Caffery's request I saw here today Messrs. Durand, Director of National Cereal Board and Bou, representing Ministry of Agriculture of

---

[1] William L. Clayton was also Chairman of the Second Session of the Preparatory Committee of the United Nations Conference on Trade and Employment at Geneva, April 10–October 30, 1947.
[2] James A. Stillwell, International Resources Division.

France. These gentlemen were accompanied by Thibodeaux our Agricultural Attaché Paris.

France is in a rather desperate position regarding grain supplies. Bread ration reduced from 300 to 250 grams effective May 1st, although not yet published. If unable to get additional help from US they will be compelled to reduce this ration to 200 grams.

French representatives stated that when Tanguy-Prigent, Minister of Agriculture, was in Washington he obtained a promised allocation of 553,000 tons of bread grains for shipment from the US,[3] February, March, April, May and June. However, present program is for shipment only 423,000 tons during this period. France urgently requires shipment of remaining 130,000 tons and in addition 160,000 tons to arrive in July. They could, in case of necessity, take these 290,000 tons in corn and would like to have it shipped half each May and June: in other words, 145,000 tons of corn each in May and June to arrive in France in June and July.

Being convinced of the extreme urgency of this matter I wish to strongly recommend that you go to the President and ask him to request Agriculture to renew the procurement of wheat in the northwest to apply of course against our total export program. I understand Agriculture discontinued the purchase of wheat because of the inflationary effect of further government purchases. This present situation, however, is so critical and the grave social, economic and political consequences which will almost certainly flow from our failure to provide this aid to France seem to me to be compelling reasons for continuing procurement program in spite of inflationary aspect.

Will greatly appreciate your early advice so that we can inform the French.

Sent Department 156, repeated Paris.

[CLAYTON]

---

[3] Pierre Tanguy-Prigent came to Washington in early February 1947 to discuss the cereal situation in France.

851.00B/4–2547 : Telegram

The Ambassador in France (Caffery) to the Secretary of State

SECRET　　　　　　　　　　　　　　　　　　　PARIS, April 25, 1947—3 p. m.

1719. Qualified observers here of the world Communist movement, especially those formerly connected with the Comintern, are increasingly inclined to believe that the French Communists are being directed to accelerate their agitation in the French colonies to the extent even that they may not be able to remain in the government. In this connection the Resident General of Tunisia recently expressed to intimate friends in Paris that he is gravely concerned over the mounting native agitation backed by Communists in Tunis and expects trouble there in the near future.

In the meanwhile the debate continues between the group in the Communist Party leadership favoring passing to opposition to the government and the group which defends remaining therein. My 1364, March 31, 7 p. m.[1] According to a reliable source the real head of the CGT, Frachon, who has remained more or less neutral in this debate up to the present is now tending to join the Mauvais-Fajon block in favor of opposition. Frachon attended the Political Bureau meeting held on April 17 where he stated that an increasing number of Communist militants in the CGT, particularly in the Paris region, no longer willingly accepted the thesis that the Communists should remain in the govt. Frachon insisted that "working class opinion should be taken into consideration, particularly since membership in CGT is falling off owing to the workers failure sometimes to understand Communist trade union policies." This remark probably alludes to recent developments in Paris region where workers and even Communists have revolted against trade union leaders in a few factories.

Great importance is attached by Communists here to Marty's visit to Algeria where he is attending congress of Algerian Communist Party and they expect his report on the situation there to furnish them material in support of the new statutes on Algeria proposed by the Communist Party for discussion in the Assembly.

Sent Dept 1719, repeated Moscow 290, Berlin 146, London 337.

CAFFERY

---

[1] Not printed. It cited "trustworthy evidence available to Embassy" to the effect that the dispute in the French Communist party between the majority opposition group led by Léon Mauvais and Etienne Fajon and the minority led by Thorez, Billoux, and Jacques Duclos concerned tactics and in no way involved "the question of a revolt against Moscow". The telegram reviewed the history of the party since 1920 and concluded as follows: "It must again be emphasized that the very Communists who are now being described in the press as 'Nationalists' have personally performed all the backbreaking somersaults which subservience to Moscow has required of their party in the past. In the circumstances stories to the effect that certain Communist leaders are opposing Moscow; that they are Frenchmen first and Communists second; that Moscow is no longer guiding the general lines of French Communist policy, should all be viewed with the deepest skepticism." (851.00B/3–3147)

851.6131/4–2647 : Telegram

The Acting Secretary of State to the Embassy in France

RESTRICTED WASHINGTON, April 26, 1947—1 p. m.
U.S. URGENT

1530. The French claim that the U.S. Govt promised shipment of 553,000 tons of grain to France in the period February–June 1947 arises from a misunderstanding on the part of the French dating from the time of the visit of Minister Prigent to Washington in February. The misconception was threefold, namely, (*a*) combining of recognized import requirements of Metropolitan France and French North Africa and applying the resultant total to Metropolitan France alone, (*b*) failure to understand that the IEFC recommended figure for shipments to France or any other country applies to total shipments from all sources and does not include specific recommendations concerning the source of such shipments, and (*c*) ignoring of the fact that the United States as a supplying country member of that Council has during the present half-year announced its export programs month by month, not singling out any countries for special consideration by allocation of grain covering longer periods.

The figure 553,000 was combined by Monsieur Prigent himself in a letter of February 18 to the Secretary of Agriculture as follows:

Seed wheat to be shipped from the U.S. in February	17, 000 tons
March program from the United States	68, 000 tons
Balance to be shipped April, May and June	277, 000 tons
Total for Metropolitan France	362, 000 tons
Total to be shipped to French North Africa	191, 000 tons
Total to France and French North Africa	553, 000 tons

There is therefore no basis whatever for the French to talk of a promised total of 553,000 for France itself when they themselves stated that the figure applying to France in this connection was 362,000 which was in harmony with IEFC figures for shipment to France from all sources.

In connection with the Minister's visit the IEFC made an upward revision of the French requirement from 450,000 for the crop-year July 1946–June 1947 to 877,000 which took into account the wheat frost-kill in France and made allowances for 100,000 tons imported for feed use.

In calculating balance still due to France from February forward, IEFC found that known shipments from all sources plus the U.S. March and April programs totalled 600,000 tons (about 500,000 of which had moved during last half of 1946) leaving balance of 277,000 tons to move from all sources. This is balance referred to in Mr. Prigent's letter to Secretary of Agriculture as being expected by French to move to France from United States in addition to already announced February and March programs to make a total of 362,000.

In letter of reply addressed to French Ambassador on March 4, Secretary of Agriculture indicated that February and March programs and also an April program of 123,000 tons to France and French North Africa could be regarded as specific commitments from United States, but that no commitments were yet possible regarding quantities to be programmed from United States in months of May and June, although United States would do its best to furnish as much of balance as possible. Likewise letter made clear that no promise could be made with regard to North Africa.

In actuality the United States with programs as announced through June and including recent emergency allocations of 33,000 and 36,000 tons respectively expects to make available 359,000 tons to Metropolitan France as compared to the 362,000 referred to by Monsieur Prigent in his letter.

This is broken down as follows:

February	17,000
Part of March program moved to France	35,000
Part of April program being moved to France	56,000
May program	100,000
June program	82,000
Emergency programs	69,000
	359,000

Meantime shipments to France from Argentina have brought total known shipments plus U.S. programs to France thru June to a total for the crop year of 960,000 tons, thus actually exceeding the IEFC recommended total of 877,000 tons for France from all sources by 83,000 tons.

As for French North Africa, shipments to this area from United States in March and April will total 92,000 tons. 38,000 were shipped to French North Africa from other sources earlier in the year, making total shipment of 130,000 tons.

The requirement now recognized for French North Africa in IEFC is 207,000 tons. The balance not yet covered is therefore 777,000 [77,000?]. However, this shortfall is more than made up by the excess shipped from all sources to France, namely 87,000 [83,000?] tons. Thus known shipments and U.S. programs through June to France and French North Africa taken together more than meet the total for these areas recommended by IEFC without taking into account additional shipments which will continue to be made from Argentina.

Sent Paris as 1530 rptd Geneva for Clayton as 223.

ACHESON

851.5018/4–2947 : Telegram

The Secretary of State to the Under Secretary of State for Economic Affairs (Clayton) at Geneva

SECRET   WASHINGTON, April 29, 1947—4 p. m.

236. For personal attention of Mr. Clayton. Since telephone conversation with you Apr 23 have been doing everything possible increase shipments grain to France.

No commitment of 553,000 tons from US ever made to French Minister. You will recall we talked with French Minister and Ambassador Bonnet in your office concerning French requirement. We both pointed out that under present demands on US for grain it was not likely we could even ship 423,000 tons referred to by French as now scheduled from US. Present schedule of shipments Jan through June for France now actually amount to approx 461,000 tons, which includes an emergency allocation of 33,000 tons flour for Apr and May shipment announced Apr 15. Also including emergency allocation 36,000 tons wheat and flour for May shipment announced by Secretary Agri Fri, Apr 25. We already had schedule of shipments amounting to 1,500,000 tons a month Jan through June. Our schedule of shipments now Apr through June for over 1,600,000 tons each month. This has created unusual pressure on shipping facilities and also continued pressure on grain market. Entire Cabinet and President are of opinion that any additional demands on grain market at this time will simply further inflate grain market and produce no additional grain for export. Continued pressure from foreign press, particularly claims by French concerning US commitment 553,000 tons, also has inflationary effect on market which tends to drive wheat and corn into hiding.

For your private information Agri officials believe additional corn cn be procured for shipment to France in June, probably amounting to 50 or 60,000 tons.

French officials should be made to understand that we will come as close to the 553,000 ton figure as possible. It is not practical, however, to expect the total to reach more than about 500,000 tons by end of June. Early July shipments to France could more than make up the balance required. French officials also should recognize that further pressure through the press will react adversely and perhaps reduce the quantity of grain available for shipment. French officials should be told only of the 463,000 tons presently scheduled, as mentioned above. Any amounts above that will depend entirely on ability to procure additional corn in present unstable market and continuance of total shipments of more than 1,600,000 tons monthly. Suggest you convey any information herein you deem advisable to Caffery.

MARSHALL

851.5018/4–2947

The Secretary of State to the French Ambassador (Bonnet)

[WASHINGTON,] May 7, 1947.

The Secretary of State presents his compliments to His Excellency the Ambassador of France and has the honor to refer to his note No. 125 of March 31, 1947, his *aide-mémoire* of April 8, 1947, and his note No. 153 of April 29, 1947,[1] referring to the serious situation which has developed in the effort to cover the deficit in bread grains in France and French North Africa.

The Ambassador specifically requested in his note of March 31, 100,000 tons in addition to the April and May allocations which had been announced at that time, and an allocation of 200,000 tons for June. Emergency allocations of 33,000 tons and 36,000 tons of flour wheat equivalent have now been added to the April and May export programs. The June export program also contains 82,000 tons of flour and corn for France. In addition, an emergency allocation of 36,000 tons of corn has just been added to the May–June program for France. These allocations constitute a total of 187,000 tons which have been added since the Ambassador's note was received.

In his *aide-mémoire* of April 8 and his note of April 29 the Ambassador also requested that grain be made available in excess of the present allocations for May and June, and that the June allocation be shipped in advance. Officials of the United States Government have borne constantly in mind the French supply problem and have sought to extend as much help as possible. Efforts are being made to obtain further quantities of grain, but it is not yet certain whether this can be done, and it is only fair to state that any such quantities would be very limited. With respect to the question of shipping the June allocation in advance, the Department is informed that all the flour and grain in that allocation is purchased and shipped through private commercial channels. This Government does not, therefore, make the arrangements for such shipments, but it has already authorized the French to move grain bought through the private trade as fast as contracts will allow and shipping facilities permit.

The Secretary of State wishes to express to His Excellency this Government's great concern with the French grain position and its

---

[1] Notes of March 31 and April 29 are not printed.

earnest desire to furnish as much help as possible. Every consideration will be given to the needs of France, and it is regretted that heavy emergency demands in other parts of the world, together with the limitation of supply and transportation, make it impossible at this time to give the Ambassador assurances of a more definite or extensive nature.[2]

[2] For text of a press release of May 15 on additional grain shipments to France, see Department of State *Bulletin*, May 25, 1947, p. 1042.

Press Release Issued by the International Bank for Reconstruction and Development, Washington, May 9, 1947

The International Bank for Reconstruction and Development announced on May 9 the granting of its first loan, totaling $250,000,000, to Crédit National, a semi-public French corporation created to assist in financing the reconstruction and development of the French economy. The loan is guaranteed by the Republic of France. The executive directors of the International Bank, at a special meeting on May 9, voted their approval of the loan, which originated in a request for a $500,000,000 loan by the French Minister of Finance in an application dated October 8, 1946. The loan agreement was signed for the Bank by John J. McCloy, president, and on behalf of the Crédit National by Wilfrid Baumgartner, president. The guaranty agreement was signed by Henri Bonnet, Ambassador of France.

The loan is being made to assist France in the reconstruction of its war-torn economy and to finance the import of specific goods and equipment necessary to its economic rehabilitation. A portion of the proceeds will be devoted to the modernization of the steel industry, including a modern strip mill. The transportation system is to be improved by the purchase of locomotives and freight cars, cargo ships and canal barges, and commercial airplanes. Coal and oil, essential to industry and transport, figure largely among the prospective purchases, as do industrial raw materials, including semi-finished steel products and nonferrous metals. Under the loan agreement, the Bank will obtain full information concerning the goods to be purchased with the proceeds of the loan and their utilization. France will be free to purchase in whatever markets are most advantageous.

Because of its size and productive capacity, France is pivotal in western Europe. The economic rehabilitation of France will speed the recovery of surrounding countries and, through an expansion of trade, be beneficial to the rest of the world.

The loan is for a period of 30 years and will carry interest at the rate of 3¼ percent. In accordance with its articles of agreement, the

Bank will also charge a commission of 1 percent per annum on the outstanding portion of the loan to build up a special reserve.

The French national recovery program calls for heavy imports during the next five years. Therefore, no repayment of principal is scheduled for this period. Thereafter amortization begins at a modest rate and increases gradually so that the loan will be completely amortized by its due date.

Mr. McCloy states that, although the Bank is not now prepared to make any commitments with regard to a further loan, it will be willing to consider an additional application from France later this year. Any new application will be considered in the light of the funds which the Bank will then have available for lending and of the progress made in carrying out the French economic and recovery program.

851.00/5–1247 : Telegram

The Ambassador in France (Caffery) to the Secretary of State

TOP SECRET   PARIS, May 12, 1947—5 p. m.
U.S. URGENT

1927. French political developments culminating in the recent governmental crisis which resulted in the at least temporary exclusion of the Communists from a Coalition Government for the first time since the liberation have brought us to a point where a thorough analysis of our general policy toward France, and more particularly toward the present Ramadier Government is required. The subject is of great complexity and offers no guaranteed solution. However, its immediate and vital importance in the light of future possibilities is such that I am transmitting my observations by telegram rather than despatch despite their length.

I think it clear that given existing political conditions the party composition of the present government is from our viewpoint the best that could be hoped for. In the first place it excludes the Communists on the extreme left and reactionary elements on the right, and combines the fundamentally democratic forces of the center and left which still represent the views and command the support of a majority of the French Parliament and people despite a general public feeling of disillusionment with governmental fumbling and incoherence. If a really strong democratic France is to be established such a coalition is not only desirable but in fact offers the best chance of success. Furthermore, its component elements are oriented toward us through mutual belief in the new basic conception of liberty and human decency and through deep fear and distrust of ruthless Soviet imperialism. Most important is the fact that the present government is essentially Socialist and is headed by a Socialist. It has thus the support of substantial anti-Communist elements of the vital trade union movement and if it succeeds it will unquestionably gain increased working class support.

While the foregoing considerations lead inevitably to the conclusion that it is in our own very real interest that the Ramadier Government succeed, its chances of so doing without substantial outside support seem very doubtful. Ramadier is faced with crucial economic problems—both immediate and long-range—which must be held to manageable proportions if the economic and hence political situation is not seriously to deteriorate. Conditions of life for the average worker and salaried employee are such that there is very real hardship, with consequent discontent. This makes them vulnerable to exploitation by extremists, particularly the Communists who are artists in this line. Among the government's acutest problems is the food (particularly grain) shortage, which has led to a reduction in the bread ration with a natural deterioration in morale. The period until the harvest is crucial and although some temporary relief may be expected after the harvest the food situation will be critical for at least another year. Furthermore, the price index of foods has risen sharply in the last three months largely as an indirect result of the winter wheat freeze and grain shortage. Lack of coal and low labor productivity both tend to retard the imperative expansion of both industrial and vital agricultural production. The ever present threat hangs over the government of an uncontrolled inflationary spiral which will occur unless the wage level is held and production increased. Administrative inefficiency, unsound control mechanisms encourage a highly developed black market and the tendency to hoard food and consumer goods makes matters worse.

The task facing the Ramadier Government would be difficult enough if all parties, including the Communists, were solidly behind it. But not even this is the case. While the Communists now in the opposition are acting with great circumspection and are not expected in the near future to resort to extreme action which might serve to force the Socialists further away from them and which would lay them open to charges of seriously crippling French economic recovery solely for their own political ends, it goes without saying that beneath the surface they will do everything in their power to torpedo the Ramadier Government. (My 1883, May 8[1].) (Already the Communist press is warning against accepting any further aid from the US on the grounds that this would be at the sacrifice of France's independence.)

---

[1] Not printed.

They are counting, until after the US elections in 1948, on our following a policy of economic retrenchment with drastic budgetary cuts which will not permit adequate aid to our friends and subsequently on an economic collapse which will make later aid impossible. In other words, on our following an economic policy of "too little and too late". It is essential to the Communists that Ramadier fail so that they can prove that France cannot be governed without them and they can subsequently reenter the government with increased authority and influence.

Consequences of a failure of the Ramadier Government on the French internal as well as international situation are too evident to require detailed elaboration. Insofar as the Socialists are concerned, both Ramadier and Blum showed great courage and were largely responsible for the reluctant Socialist decision to head a government excluding the Communists. The fact that they were able to persuade the National Congress of their party, even though by a bare majority, to accept this decision is an encouraging sign and one which certainly would not have been possible six months ago. In this connection the President's policy toward Greece and Turkey was probably one of the decisive factors.[2] On the other hand, there remains a serious division in the Socialist Party on the question of participating in, let alone leading, a government without the Communists. If Ramadier's Government fails, the very strong and vocal left-wing Socialist opposition to the policy of the present leadership will be greatly reinforced. It is almost certain that in such an event the Socialist left-wing will take over the direction of the Socialist Party.

In addition to the lessening of influence of anti-Communist Socialists within the Socialist Party, the fall of the Ramadier Government would almost inevitably weaken the newly-forged ties which for the moment at least link the forces of the center and left in the present government, particularly since both the MRP and RGR would find it infinitely more difficult to cooperate with highly doctrinaire left-wing Socialist leadership. But the major disaster attending a collapse of the Ramadier Government would be the happening [opening] of a division of France into two hostile extremist camps—the Communists on the one side and De Gaulle on the other—with an inevitable struggle to the finish between them.

Too many unknown factors are involved to permit accurate speculation at this juncture on the ultimate outcome of such a showdown between De Gaulle and the Communists, but it is at least clear that the struggle itself would have the most far-reaching and dangerous reper-

---

[2] For documentation regarding the policy of President Truman toward Greece and Turkey, see vol. v, pp. 1 ff.

cussions and from our point of view could not lead to a happy conclusion. If the Communists won, Soviet penetration of Western Europe, Africa, the Mediterranean and Middle East would be greatly facilitated, and our position in our zone of occupation of Germany rendered precarious, if not untenable. If De Gaulle won, France would be headed into a new and unknown adventure which by the nature of the forces generated in such a struggle would make the practice in France of democracy as we understand it difficult if not impossible for some time to come.

It would appear vital to our security to do everything we can to prevent France from falling under Communist domination. Sooner or later we may have to extend such support and the danger of failing to give such support now if it is feasible and warranted is that if the Ramadier Government collapses and a showdown with the Communists follows, we may then be obliged to support French elements which represent infinitely less in terms of democracy and public backing.

With regard to the short range situation, I believe that it is in our interest to continue to make every effort to give material assistance to France (particularly wheat and coal) during this critical period when the Ramadier Government is very definitely on trial. Anything we can do along these lines during the next two months should help to postpone and thereby enhance the chances of preventing the collapse on which both the Communists and De Gaulle are counting.

Our long term studies should include a reappraisal of the Monnet [3] Plan which has been accepted as the blueprint for French recovery. In this connection, it now seems fairly apparent that even if France's financial resources in the next few years held to the level on which the plan was based, the plan itself would not be more than 65% completed by the end of 1950. Actually some of the basic assumptions of the plans were unrealistic in character (notably with regard to labor, assets from immigrant remittances and tourist trade, and a too optimistic view of French agricultural recovery). There has also been an unanticipated deterioration in the economic situation since last October as a result of which important assets have had to be spent on increased wheat and coal imports, etc. In the circumstances, and granting the fact that for political reasons the Monnet Plan must be retained at least as a reflection of the aspirations of the French people which might conceivably be attainable in time, serious study should be given to the question of whether there should not be a complete readaptation of the Monnet Plan to place immediate emphasis on, for example, recovery of agricultural production; increase in production for internal use of goods essential to the masses including housing; and in-

---

[3] Jean Monnet was Commissioner General of the Plan for Modernization and Reequipment of the French economy.

crease of winter coal allocations for household use. France's economic recovery is currently checked by extremely poor productivity. The present Monnet Plan places chief reliance on the remedy of technological improvement of the means of production. The new approach to which I have alluded would give at least equal consideration to greater productivity through the rehabilitation of the physical condition and psychology of France's laboring and small salaried groups. While such a program would further delay the achievement of the position envisaged by the Monnet Plan, it might well enhance the chances of ultimate success by bringing about an early improvement in living conditions which should in turn bring about an achievement in the political atmosphere so necessary if extremist solutions are to be avoided. Further details on this aspect of the program will be submitted by mail.

Sent Department 1927, repeated Geneva for Clayton as 30.

CAFFERY

751.60F/5–1447 : Telegram

The Ambassador in the United Kingdom (Douglas) to the Secretary of State

SECRET London, May 14, 1947—6 p. m.

2737. With reference to possible negotiation of French-Czech and French-Polish pacts, Under Secretary Warner [1] comments that French say that it is the Czechs and Poles who have taken initiative while Czechs and Poles say it is the French. "We have been using such influence as we have with the French", Warner says, "to discourage these pacts on the ground that they are unrealistic." Quai d'Orsay, however, takes position that when eastern European countries hold out a hand to the west they should not be discouraged. Warner surmises that Quai d'Orsay's readiness to undertake discussions with Czechs and Poles results from deal with French Communists at time of Anglo-French pact [2] signature.

To French here in London, Warner says, the unrealistic nature of bilateral pacts with Czechoslovakia and Poland has been especially emphasized. It has been pointed out that bilateral pacts, would be of little if any help against a resurgent Germany. Such a threat the French here have been told can most effectively be met by the Byrnes' draft treaty,[3] which the French have said they favor and the promis-

---

[1] Christopher Frederick Ashton Warner, an Assistant Under Secretary of State in the British Foreign Office.
[2] Treaty of Alliance and Mutual Assistance between Great Britain and France, signed at Dunkerque on March 4, 1947.
[3] During the Second Session of the Council of Foreign Ministers, Paris, April 25–May 15 and June 15–July 12, 1946, Secretary of State James F. Byrnes submitted a draft four-power treaty for German disarmament; for the text of the draft treaty, see *Foreign Relations*, 1946, vol. II, p. 190, or Department of State *Bulletin*, May 12, 1946, p. 815.

cuous negotiation of bilateral pacts serves only to lessen the chances of a treaty along the lines of the Byrnes' draft ever being realized.

Sent Dept as 2737, repeated to Paris as 296, to Praha as 14, to Warsaw as 44.

DOUGLAS

851.00/5–1847 : Telegram

The Secretary of State to the Embassy in France

SECRET   WASHINGTON, May 20, 1947—7 p. m.

1837. Callender *NY Times* story May 19 plays up official "French fears US loans might impair France's independence or sovereignty" with extensive quotations from alleged statements of Ramadier and Daniel Mayer [1] asking whether such future loans would be "dictated by political realities" (Ramadier) and whether "certain American capitalists might not oblige us to act against Russia" (Mayer). Moving into vaguer area Callender speaks of French fears that NY bankers and Pres Truman frown on nationalization and that bankers would demand concessions or trade rights within empire restricting French sovereignty there.

Granting possible erroneous emphasis (story omits Bidault statement on loans penultimate para Embtel 1987 [2]) and traditional if unrealistic fear entertained by doctrinaire socialists of "American capitalism" Dept somewhat concerned effect of Socialist utterances and press stories arising therefrom. If any discreet corrective action appropriate please take it. Any case furnish comments.

MARSHALL

---

[1] French Minister of Labor.
[2] Not printed.

751.60F/5–1447 : Telegram

The Secretary of State to the Embassy in France [1]

SECRET   WASHINGTON, May 21, 1947—6 p. m.

1847. Ref. London's tel 2737, May 14, reptd Paris as 296. Dept agrees Brit views regarding unrealistic nature bilateral French-Czech and French-Polish pacts now being contemplated. Not considered desirable that you make formal representations to French Govt in this respect. You may however reflect this view in informal conversations with French officials adding in our opinion the proposed four power

---

[1] This telegram was repeated to the Embassies in Praha, London, and Warsaw.

disarmament treaty would afford far greater protection to French and such negotiations as contemplated might adversely affect possibility of securing agreement upon the treaty.

MARSHALL

851.6131/5–2247 : Telegram

The Secretary of State to the Embassy in France

WASHINGTON, May 22, 1947—6:28 p. m.

1874. Dept has released following to press:

"The Dept of State is today in receipt of a communication [1] from the French Embassy referring to the additional allocation of 150,000 tons of corn which was made to France on May 15, 1947, to assist the latter in meeting its critical grain shortage. The note states that this supplementary allocation added to more than 500,000 tons of grain already allocated to France within the last several months has been received by the French people with the greatest possible satisfaction, and the French Govt is most grateful for the sympathetic understanding demonstrated by the United States with respect to the situation in France and for the constant effort of American services to permit the delivery of the grains thus allocated."

Understand FrEmb issuing similar communiqué.

MARSHALL

---

[1] Not printed.

851.51/5–2347 : Airgram

The Secretary of State to the Embassy in France

CONFIDENTIAL WASHINGTON, May 23, 1947.

A–809. Recent negotiations in Washington between representatives of the Governments of the United States, United Kingdom, and Canada have resulted in a final agreement on the financial settlement of the combined civilian supply program (Plan A).[1]

As a result of this settlement, the Governments of the United States, United Kingdom, and Canada have presented memoranda to the Government of France, as well as other recipient governments, on May 15,

---

[1] Plan A related to the provision of civilian relief supplies for liberated areas by the combined Allied military authorities in Western Europe and the Mediterranean under financial arrangements agreed to by the United States, United Kingdom, and Canada. For documentation, see *Foreign Relations*, 1945, vol. II, pp. 1059 ff., and 1946, vol. v, index entries under "Plan A". Additional documentation on the settlement, not printed, is in Department of State file No. 841.24 for 1947.

1947,[2] setting forth the respective shares of the three supplying governments in the combined bills for supplies furnished under Plan A. In the case of France, and other northwest European governments, these shares have been determined to be as follows:

To the Government of the United States........ 62%
To the Government of the United Kingdom..... 33%
To the Government of Canada................. 5%

The memorandum from the United States Government to the Government of France states further that it will no longer be necessary for the French Government to maintain a reserve fund of 10% of the combined claim, which was stipulated as a condition of the waiver of the United States share of France's Plan A obligation at the time of the over-all settlement of war accounts between the United States and France in May, 1946.

The United States memorandum was presented to the French Embassy in Washington. It is the Department's understanding that the British memorandum was presented to the French Foreign Office by the British Embassy in Paris, and the Canadian memorandum was presented to the French Embassy in Ottawa.

MARSHALL

---

[2] Not printed.

Editorial Note

On June 10 the Secretary of State informed the Embassy in France that "We are greatly interested" in the "nature of long-range plans French are now contemplating for North Africa", and he described a possible line of action by the United States. For documentation on this subject, see volume V, compilation entitled "Interest of the United States in Communist and Nationalist Activities in North Africa".

851.5151/6–1947 : Telegram

The Ambassador in France (Caffery) to the Secretary of State

SECRET   PARIS, June 19, 1947—6 p.m.

2438. It is now apparent that there is developing in France a recurrence of both the inflationary trends and lack of public confidence in the future of its currency, so noticeable last autumn. Government emphasis in economic policy has gradually been shifting from financial "stabilization" under the Blum experiment to one of "retard the inflation". Symptomatic of these developments are the following:

(*a*) Continuous decline in quotations for government securities to a level so low that plans for a reconstruction flotation have been abandoned for the present.

(*b*) On the other hand, there has been an active demand for investments of the inflation "pegging" type. Common shares on the Paris Bourse advanced last week by 9 per cent. The franc on the black market has fallen in the past week from 225 to 268 per dollar.

The proximate causes of the foregoing appear to be:

(*a*) Government retreat on the wage stabilization front. Although it is not yet possible to measure precisely the impact on wage payments and labor costs, it appears that the government is prepared to permit increases in the neighborhood of 13–15 per cent and that it may be forced by labor organization pressures to even larger concessions.

(*b*) Continued large scale treasury deficit most of which has to be covered by additional note issue which has expanded by 66 billion francs since the end of 1946.

(*c*) Failure of agricultural output and food imports to meet minimum needs at reasonable prices in relation to current wages, especially in the cities.

Although it is hoped that the severe financial measures now under consideration by the Cabinet may prevent a runaway inflation, it is difficult to see how wage and price stabilization can be achieved in France until such time as the effective supply of essential consumers goods is adequate to meet the minimum needs of France's laboring and small salaried groups.

CAFFERY

851.50/7–1147

Memorandum by the Director of the Office of European Affairs (Matthews) to the Under Secretary of State (Lovett)[1]

TOP SECRET [WASHINGTON,] July 11, 1947.

I. PROBLEM

To determine the probable course of developments in France and possible action by the United States in regard thereto.

---

[1] A routing slip from Matthews to Assistant Secretary Armour and to Mr. Lovett, who became Under Secretary of State on July 1, bore the following notations: 'Is this the sort of paper you wanted[?] H. F[reeman] M[atthews]." "Yes L[ovett]." "U—Mr. Lovett: It seems to me this covers the field very well and it is an excellent paper to have on record and for discussion. N[orman] A[rmour]."

The paper was based in part on a memorandum of June 28 by Charles E. Bohlen, Special Assistant to the Secretary of State (851.00/6–2847).

II. DISCUSSION

1. Since the conclusion of the Bidault-Bevin-Molotov [2] discussions in Paris which strengthened the anti-Communist forces in France, there have been two developments which have enabled the Ramadier Government to survive the immediate crisis arising from discussions of the Government's economic program. The Prime Minister received his vote of confidence in the Assembly on July 4 of 331 to 247. The opposition was composed of the Communists and factions of the right-wing parties which are opposed to directed economy. This vote of confidence was followed by a similar vote in the Socialist National Council where Ramadier obtained a majority of 518 votes in his own party as compared with his previous party majority of 404 on May 7th. Even more significant, however, than this vote of confidence in Ramadier was the categorical position taken by the Socialist Council of opposing Communist reentry in the government. Socialists who had heretofore favored agreement with the Communists then stated that the attitudes of the Communist party and of the Soviet Union made the return of the Communists to the government impossible in present circumstances. The MRP has taken a similar stand against Communist participation in the government.

2. These developments have definitely strengthened the position of the present non-Communist government in France and it seems likely that it will hold together until after the parliamentary vacation commences, thus insuring its continuance in office until the municipal elections in September. Nevertheless the basic economic questions which brought on the crisis have not yet been solved and a way must be found to deal with threatened strikes and the chaotic state of wages and price levels. Furthermore, in spite of their setback in France and in the light of current general Communist offensive, it seems likely that the French Communist Party will continue its efforts to demonstrate that no economic stability is possible unless the party forms part of the Government and can utilize its presence there to achieve its ends. The foremost among these will surely be to sabotage the Bidault-Bevin program. Individual strikes in essential industries and services will no doubt continue to be encouraged by the party with little likelihood as yet, however, that they will resort to a general strike. Another possibility might be civil strife resulting from direct action on the part of either the Communists or the extreme Right to seize power. In present conditions these extreme measures are not yet considered likely but they cannot be precluded.

---

[2] Georges Bidault, French Minister for Foreign Affairs, Ernest Bevin, British Secretary of State for Foreign Affairs, and Vyacheslav Mikhailovich Molotov, Minister of Foreign Affairs of the Soviet Union, met in Paris for discussions relating to the European Recovery Plan on June 27, 28, and 30, and July 1 and 2, 1947. For documentation, see pp. 296–308.

3. Although as stated above the Ramadier Government will probably survive for the next few months it has not yet been able to assure economic stability for the country. It was able to weather the recent crisis largely because of the Soviet refusal to participate in the plan for European rehabilitation. This however, was somewhat fortuitous and Ramadier cannot count on other such circumstances in the future. In the event that the Communists are able through their utilization of strikes and similar tactics to bring on another crisis, it cannot be excluded that they would be successful the next time. In such circumstances their aim is clear and they would insist upon joining the government under conditions acceptable to them.

4. Although for the purpose of returning to the government they might be willing to accept fewer Ministries than they held previously, the fact that they would be able to force their return would give them increased power. Regardless of the individual portfolios they would demand, their influence would be exercised on national and foreign affairs not directly related to the Ministries they would hold. We can anticipate, however, that they will wish in particular to control the field of Industrial Production, Labor, Veterans, Agriculture and to have a voice in national defense, whether by claiming the Ministry itself or by seeking one or more of its components, such as War, Navy or Air. Further in accordance with the traditional Communist policy they will seek to obtain Interior and/or Foreign Affairs. In any event their influence within the government would constitute a veto over the conduct of foreign affairs insuring that France does not align itself in major foreign policy issues with the U.S. and Great Britain.

5. In such an eventuality, as previously, we would be confronted with a government in which Communist influence would be so strong as successfully to prevent the French Government not only from adopting an independent foreign policy, but from implementing the initiative which Bidault has taken in the plan for European rehabilitation.

6. This will mean that at international conferences France will be forced to assume positions which in the circumstances will be most advantageous to the Soviet Union. It would certainly restrict France's position and prevent it from participating in any constructive application of any plan in Western Europe. Under these conditions, it is obvious that any program of European reconstruction would be doomed to failure and a policy of piece-meal assistance to individual countries still free from Communist control might have to be followed.

III. RECOMMENDATIONS AS TO U.S. ACTION

A. *Measures to support a non-Communist Government.*

1. Faced with the economic difficulties outlined in this and previous memoranda, in addition to receiving its present allocations of bread

grain from the [*this?*] country, the Ramadier Government may well require further external assistance even before an overall European program can be formulated and implemented by action on the part of the United States. During the critical period of the summer months there are two possible steps which might be taken in support of the non-Communist forces in France. As regards both of these, however, the U.S. Government is not in a position to act alone but should use its influence to secure their approval. The first of these relates to the second installment on the World Bank loan. When the first installment of $250 million was made available to France, the bank agreed to consider in October whether conditions in France would make possible the grant of an additional similar sum. These funds are urgently required by France and it would immeasurably strengthen the position of the government and enable it to withstand many attacks if the U.S. could assist France to obtain some assurance from the World Bank prior to September that its needs in this respect would be met before the winter.

2. The second relates to the question of coal and increased production in the Ruhr and particularly in the Saar coal fields. France has now proposed that Saar coal production be incorporated into the domestic production in France as a preliminary to the definitive incorporation of the territory. The details of this proposal and its relation to the supply of German coal both inside Germany and to other areas are not yet clear and we are endeavoring to ascertain in talks with the French and British experts the full effects of the present proposal. It is clear that no plan which would give France preferential treatment at the expense of other countries can be accepted by this country. It is to be anticipated that the minimum of any French proposal would be to increase the amount of coal France would take from the Saar, thereby reducing its share of Ruhr coal for which it pays dollars. Such an arrangement might cost the bizonal area $20 million a year in export proceeds. Although this might mean a heavy charge upon one administrative budget, on the other hand far more dollars may have to be found by this government in its own interests to support non-Communist elements in France. Furthermore, conversations looking toward the level of increase in German industry are about to result in an agreement between the British and ourselves with benefit to the economy of Germany and may result in decreased coal exports. If France cannot derive some compensating advantage in the reorganization of German economy, it will become a serious political problem for the present government and in this respect add to the difficulties facing it.

3. In another field, U.S. action can be most helpful. In view of the increased distortion by the Communist propaganda machine of the principal motives and objectives of the U.S., it will be necessary to contemplate a highly selective American information program coordinated with a long-range information program from the U.S. by radio. This must be accomplished by intensive cultivation of French newspapers by direct or indirect means.

B. *Action in face of Communist participation in the government:*

1. Should the situation in France develop in such a way that in an effort to reduce economic pressure upon the Government and weaken the Communist hold over the trade unions, the Socialist and MRP Parties might reverse their present stand and agree to a limited Communist participation in the Government. In our opinion this would be a dangerous admission of weakness on the part of the non-Communist elements; but if it is accomplished in such a way as not to give the Communists the control they seek and a virtual veto over French policy, we would not necessarily be obliged to write off France completely just because one or two Communists were in the Government. The situation would however require constant watching and the extent to which our present program of aid should be continued would depend upon developing circumstances.

2. The U.S. would have great difficulty in taking any vigorous course of action since the reentry of the Communists into the government would be substantially a French internal matter and any positive action on the part of this country at that time would no doubt serve to raise the cry of direct interference in French internal affairs and turn large sections of French public opinion against the U.S. In short, the situation created in France, as serious as it would be for U.S. interests, would not be one that would be susceptible of treatment by open official U.S. governmental action. It is a very good illustration of the difficulties we face at present in dealing with the tactics of invisible penetration and eventual capture of a modern democratic state by a resolute and well organized minority.

.   .   .   .

4. On the other hand, should the Communists achieve their end and return to the government in such a way as to exercise complete control over its policies, the U.S. could not continue to afford assistance to a French Government which would be in a position to sabotage any coordinated plan of European recovery. It would in all likelihood be necessary to recommend to the President that no further funds or additional material aid from this country should be forthcoming to assist any such government.

C. *Action in the event of civil strife or complete breakdown of French economy*

1. There are two other possibilities which have not been covered in the foregoing discussions, namely, what should the U.S. do if the government by refusing to admit the Communists is faced with a complete breakdown of French economy induced by increased efforts on the part of the Communists to break the French parliamentary system and render any government incapable of exercising its authority, either through civil strife or complete collapse of French economy. It would be dangerous to state categorically in advance what should be the position of this government in such an eventuality. Should civil strife break out in France, however, as a result of direct action by the Communists in order to gain control of the government the degree of support and effective aid which the U.S. might afford the non-Communist faction would have to be governed by the circumstances existing at that time both in France and abroad. Whether we could afford to give a non-Communist government arms or military assistance which it might request can only be determined by the situation at the particular moment. Such aid should however not be precluded in advance.

2. The reverse of this situation might also occur if a Communist controlled government should be attacked directly by non-Communist elements probably under the leadership of General de Gaulle in a struggle to control France. The question of whether we should aid such a group and [to] what extent will similarly depend upon the circumstances of the conflict, the strength of the movement and popular support both in France and in this country.

3. In any event, consultation with the President, the Joint Chiefs of Staff and Congressional leaders, and in all likelihood, with the British Government should be undertaken immediately upon any such outbreak.

851.00/7–1847 : Telegram

The Ambassador in France (Caffery) to the Secretary of State

SECRET   PARIS, July 18, 1947—5 p. m.
URGENT   NIACT

2866. Last night I saw Maurice Schumann and several other prominent and decidedly friendly Cabinet Ministers and other French politicians. All said they were gravely concerned about effect of "Anglo-American proposals" for Germany [1] on French psychology and

---

[1] Reference is to revision of the level of industry plan for Germany. For documentation on the subject, see vol. II, pp. 977 ff.

on internal political situation; they said: "if the impression prevailing here about your intentions in Germany is not corrected, the Communists will walk away with the October municipal elections".

Yesterday morning André Colin, Secretary General, and Albert Gortais, Delegate General, of MRP, asked to see a member of my staff urgently. While they wholeheartedly back Paris conference and see prompt elaboration of European response to Marshall proposals and implementation of these as essential to preserve a democratic France, Colin and Gortais are extremely worried and alarmed over reports which they are now receiving from grass roots throughout France as to response which current Communist campaign is obtaining. Deploring the chauvinistic point of view of the average Frenchman vis-à-vis Germany, and admitting that they have occasionally catered to this same instinct in the past, they nevertheless point out how deeply it is grafted on average Frenchman after centuries of struggle against first Austria and subsequently Germany, and the consequent instinctive response of many non-Communist Frenchmen to the party's line.

They state that the Communist propaganda now having the most telling effect is not their well-worn saw of the United States desiring to "colonize France economically", but the story that the United States, as after 1918, has poured money into Germany and is interested primarily in rehabilitating Germany rather than France so as to protect American vested interests; that reparations are being abandoned, the Ruhr's resources lost to France, and French security placed in jeopardy. They stressed that the recent decision to increase German steel capacity gives an appearance of truth to the Communist charges, and add: "why was this necessary now, when German production is still well below five million tons?"

These MRP leaders declare that their party, as well as the majority of responsible French leaders, fully support and back the policy of maximum use of German industrial capacity for German reconstruction, as well as for European reconstruction, but beg, repeat beg, that no further measures for German rehabilitation be announced until European plan under Marshall proposals be prepared, when German program can be made to dovetail with it.

Colin and Gortais appeared convinced that should any further proposals on behalf of Germany be announced by the American authorities in the immediate future and prior to the elaboration of the European plan, the Communists would be able, without resorting to any new pressure tactics, to torpedo the Paris conference,[2] merely using the ancestral French hatred and fear of Germany, supported by the false appearances of primary American concern in her defeated

---

[2] For documentation on the conference of 16 European nations, see pp. 249 ff.

enemy rather than in her allies. "The French Government's position will thus be made untenable", concluded Gortais.

Independent newspaper *Combat* in article from London stresses British reluctance to go along with USA in "economic and industrial reorganization of western Germany" while describing Americans as being "very enterprising".

British were painted as reluctant, embarrassed, and as having succeeded in temporarily disengaging themselves "in view of necessities of Paris conference". Paris, thinking of the future and of the "fragility of American assistance to Europe", and London, "loath to close immediately certain doors leading to eastern Europe," are said to be anxious to slow the movement down, while Washington is "eager and insistent". Of course, should this line be followed by French press, it would definitely give the French the impression that the initiative and responsibility for German developments are wholly and only ours.

Politburo minutes published this morning in Communist *Humanité* include the following paragraphs under heading: "Defense of French Security".

"The political bureau has expressed its concern in the face of the new initiatives of American reactionary forces which aim to salvage German war industries and to liquidate the reparations policy, in other words, to endanger France's reconstruction and security.

The Political Bureau has stressed the necessity for our country to return without delay to a foreign policy defending France's security through a just settlement of the German problem and in accord with all her allies, France's independence being respected."

Humanité also features on page one an unsigned article with scare headlines "Washington takes the Ruhr and gives over its management to the men who served Hitler. France excluded from the control of the mines. 'I have come to Europe to reconstruct Germany' declares Averell Harriman".[3]

Article goes on to state Harriman on his arrival in Paris declared: "I have come to Europe to hasten the recovery of German economy. It is necessary that Germany by its exportations shall become an important artisan in European reconstruction". *Humanité* comments this shows clearly it is no longer question of reparations but exports, decided upon by Germans themselves with American advice.

Sent Department 2866, repeated London 555, and Geneva for Clayton via pouch.

CAFFERY

---

[3] Secretary of Commerce.

851.6131/7–2547

The French Embassy to the Department of State

[Translation]

WASHINGTON, July 25, 1947.

AIDE-MÉMOIRE

During the meeting of the Cereals Conference in Paris,[1] the French Government had an opportunity to explain to the American Delegation headed by Mr. Clinton Anderson, Secretary of Agriculture, the gravity of the French cereal situation during the coming crop year of 1947–1948, particularly during the third and fourth quarters of 1947.

In fact, although it still is impossible to give exact figures on the collections that the 1947 harvest will yield, it may be stated definitely that the results will be late and far short of the needs for French consumption.

According to present estimates, the amount of grain for making bread that will be collected in August and September will not exceed 650,000 tons, 150,000 tons of which will have to be used as commercial seed. Since the discrepancy between resources and needs will thus be considerable, the French Government will have to contend with serious difficulties to assure the supplying of the French population even on the basis of a ration reduced to 250 grams of bread per day.

Mr. Tanguy-Prigent, Minister of Agriculture, has therefore submitted to the American authorities a memorandum reporting a deficit during August–September of 450,000 tons for Metropolitan France and 100,000 tons for North Africa. The French Government expresses therein the hope that, in view of this situation, the American Government will be good enough to furnish France, on an urgent basis, in addition to the quotas known at present, and taking into account the expected shipments, 200,000 tons in August and 300,000 in September. Furthermore, the need is there stressed of not in any case permitting to be interrupted the flow of supplies from the United States, which normally stops at the beginning of the month of August, except for urgent shipments.

As regards the fourth quarter, the American Government is requested to support with the Cereal Committee the French requests which will have as their objective a monthly quota for Metropolitan France and North Africa of 340,000 tons from all sources as a minimum, the largest part of which, furthermore, can come only from North America.

---

[1] The Special Cereals Conference at Paris was held July 9–12, 1947.

The French Government expresses to the American Government its thanks for the help which the latter may be good enough to give it.

840.50 Recovery/8–247 : Telegram

The Ambassador in France (Caffery) to the Secretary of State

SECRET　　　　　　　　　　　　　　　　PARIS, August 2, 1947—3 p. m.

3084. For Lovett from Caffery. Reference is made to my telegram 3064, August 1,[1] reporting the statement made by the French to Under Secretary Clayton that, in the event assistance from the United States under the European economic plan now being formulated could not become effective until March next, the exigencies of the situation would require France to curtail severely imports in the interim period and that a situation would certainly develop which would operate against any financial stabilization and which might result in serious political and social problems.

In view of the urgency of this matter, I submit the following comments:

My Agricultural Attaché has today given me a memorandum pointing out that the prospective food shortage in France arising from the winter freeze has been greatly intensified by drought conditions prevailing this spring and summer. I quote from this memorandum:

"The situation has seriously deteriorated since May. In many important agricultural regions there has been continuing drought since the freezes of last winter. The unprecedented heat wave in July has worsened the wheat prospects, and crops generally are now being affected. The wheat crop and other small grains may be said to be past redemption, but unless general rains are obtained in adequate quantities in the near future, reduced yields may be expected for crops generally. As pointed out to the Department in a recent telegram (Embassy's telegram 2988 of July 27[1]) this would mean a reduced availability of domestic food and feed and consequently an aggravated food situation with the beginning of winter. In these conditions it may be expected that the French Government may find it extremely difficult to keep the bread ration at present low levels during this coming winter and spring.

"In short, France is faced with a situation of domestic food shortages during the coming season unless there is a material and timely improvement in weather conditions. The situation may be as difficult as that of the 1945–46 season following the widespread drought of 1945 when approximately 4,000,000 metric tons of direct consumption foods, oilseeds, vegetable oils, and wine were imported during the year beginning 1 July 1945. Of these imports 2,236,000 tons were cereals, including rice. The French are already requesting imports

---

[1] Not printed.

of 2.5 million tons of wheat for the 1947–48 season. If the drought continues, imports of other food items may easily have to achieve levels comparable to those of the 1945–46 season. The implications in terms of the effects of such a situation on French finances, on the economy generally, and on the politics of the country are evident."

In my despatch No. 9327, July 30 [2] I have forwarded information regarding France's prospective international financial position for the balance of 1947 and the first quarter of 1948, which may be summarized as follows:

1. *Sterling area:*

French cash position has increased from sterling equivalent of $51.2 million at end of 1946 to $191 million on June 30, with a possible additional increase of $30 million for second half of 1947. Actual cash position at end of year would be amount indicated above less any amounts of sterling made convertible.

Although trades statistics for franc zone as a whole are not yet available for first six months, it appears that trade of French overseas territories with sterling area was favorable enough to off-set any deficit of Metropolitan France with the same area. Increase in sterling holdings this year has arisen from

(a) Transfer $60 million in gold under 1946 agreement,
(b) Liquidation $72 million in French-owned sterling securities [garbled]
(c) Financing moderate amount of French imports, principally wool, through British banking credits.

The Finance Ministry here is of the opinion that with its cash position and prospective exports, it should be able to finance transactions with the sterling area throughout 1948 without recourse to gold or dollars, unless British financial exigencies require United Kingdom to drastically reduce imports of non-essential items from France.

2. *Payment agreement countries* (principally neighboring European countries) :

France was in a net debtor position equivalent to $197.7 million at end of 1946 and $198.3 million on June 30, 1947. No material change in this item is anticipated for balance of 1947, and no net recourse to gold or dollars should be necessary.

3. *Dollar area:*

The July 15 forecast of 1947 current payments with this area : for expenditures $1,819 million: receipts $343 million: deficit $1,476 million. This represents increase in anticipated deficit over April

---

[2] Not printed.

forecast of $186 million due to shrinkage in export estimates and increased need for wheat imports.

The French assumption in approaching this problem is that it is necessary to maintain a minimum gold reserve of $450 million, plus cash balance in exchange stabilization fund of $30 million. On this basis all except $212 million of $1,476 million prospective deficit is accounted for by such items as:

1. Gold and foreign exchange $335 million
2. Liquidation of private assets $150 million
3. Restitution of German-looted gold $90 million
4. Second Export-Import Bank credit $400 million
5. International Bank credit $250 million
6. Other credits $130 million

The anticipated uncovered deficit of $212 million should be adjusted upward by $30 million to account for difference between estimate of receipts of German-looted gold and probable receipts this year, and reduced by $75 million for Monetary Fund advances made to date and by $60 million for the minimum amount of sterling which the French feel the British will permit to be converted into dollars.

These adjustments would bring prospective uncovered deficit balance of this year to an amount slightly in excess of $100 million,[3] but Finance Ministry estimates have been prepared on assumption of only one million tons wheat imports second half 1947. Such a program would probably in view of agricultural situation described above, require ultimate downward adjustment of bread ration to 200 grams. For the social, humanitarian and political reasons which I have outlined to you in previous telegrams, I would view such a development with concern.

The National Cereals Board, taking into account crop situation and need for 300 gram ration in five winter months, has estimated bread grains imports made second half 1947 at 1,630,000 tons. This approach would require an additional $70 million, increasing 1947 uncovered deficit to neighborhood $117 million.[4] With reference to the first quarter of 1948 it appears that deficit with dollar area may, in view of continued need for heavy imports of wheat and coal, run at rate of $100 million monthly, which might be reduced to neighborhood $80 million if franc devaluation should take place early enough to stimulate exports to the western hemisphere.

My staff has reviewed the foregoing statistics in relation to France's provisions import program for second half 1947, and finds that the latter was reduced from 1.3 billion originally requested by interested ministries, to a sum slightly in excess of $1 billion. Furthermore, a

---

[3] Marginal note: "See despatch $107–117 million."
[4] Marginal note: "See despatch $177–187 million."

prospective savings of $100 million in dollar expenditures was achieved by transferring all possible procurement to sterling and payment agreement areas. The facts available indicate that the prospective deficit through March 1948 of $350–470 million represents a range below which things cannot go without severe underconsumption of food in urban areas and disruption of industrial production.

Mr. Clayton informs me that he will discuss this matter immediately upon his arrival in the Department, but in the interim I would greatly appreciate it if the Department could study the foregoing in the light of the basic situation here with a view to exploring all possibilities. These would appear to include the following:

1. Further reduction in gold reserve of Bank of France, taking into consideration the psychological impact in terms of a further decline in public confidence in French currency.
2. Possibility of suggesting that the British increase the amount of French-held sterling to be made convertible in the event that French dollar problem is of more immediate urgency than is the case with Great Britain.
3. Possibility of requesting IARA, with aid of American occupational authorities, to arrange immediately a German gold distribution based on 80 or 90 per cent of claim, rather than projected percentage.
4. In spite of the disinclination of both the French and Monetary Fund people to utilize short term funds to finance a long term deficit, the emergency may be so great as to make advisable a consideration of possible additional advances by the Fund.
5. Consideration of possible additional credits by the Export-Import Bank or International Bank. It appears that credits from these agencies, to be effective in meeting the commodity import program, would have to be granted on a general purpose basis.

I am fully cognizant of the difficulties inherent in the possible alternatives mentioned above and I suggest their consideration only because of the magnitude of the French financial problem and because of its urgency and implications vis-à-vis the objectives of American foreign policy in this area.

CAFFERY

851.00B/8–747 : Telegram

The Ambassador in France (Caffery) to the Secretary of State

TOP SECRET PARIS, August 7, 1947—5 p. m.

3155. According to a source maintaining close and friendly relations with Communists here, a highly important meeting has just taken place in Paris which was attended by Fried,[1] Stalin's special represent-

---

[1] Eugen Fried, a Czech, had represented the Comintern in Paris in the period 1931–1939.

ative in France, a representative of the Soviet economic expert, Eugene Varga, and other high Soviet officials as well as the most important French Communist leaders. Their decisions may be summarized as follows, according to source:

1. American assistance to Europe, under the "Marshall Plan" will be "too little and too late" to assure effective economic recovery in Europe and accordingly French and other Communist parties must be prepared for "sharpening of conflict between working classes and bourgeoisie". Potential danger of Gaullist movement should not be underestimated and consequently "illegal apparatus" of Communist Party must be reinforced and the "trusted militants" of party should even actively prepare for period when it may become necessary again to "go underground" in the face of "legal persecution".

2. In view of foregoing analysis the Communist Party here must pursue "parallel" policy of building up "illegal" as well as "legal" party groups and accordingly "mass" recruitment of new members should continue.

3. Attacks against leadership of Socialist Party should be intensified, especially against Léon Blum who "persists in favoring American policies". These attacks should be accompanied by intense propaganda campaign aimed at proving that United States, "supported by Socialist leaders," is endeavoring to give top priority over France in assisting "Nazi" Germany to reconstruct its national economy.

4. By pursuing strategy outlined above, party will be prepared for "any emergency" as well as attain success at municipal elections in October.

Sent Department 3155, repeated Moscow 442, London 602, Berlin 288, Rome 201.

CAFFERY

851.00/8–3047 : Telegram

The Ambassador in France (Caffery) to the Secretary of State

SECRET   PARIS, August 30, 1947—6 p. m.

3535. It is manifestly impossible at this juncture to predict with any degree of accuracy how the French political situation will evolve in the coming months—will depend on whether or not there is an economic collapse—but in the absence of unforeseen developments it is generally believed that the present state of latent crisis will continue until after the municipal elections, following which a major crisis may well develop. In such event one fact is increasingly evident and should be kept firmly in mind: namely, that recently De Gaulle's popularity throughout the country has steadily increased to the point where he now is playing one of the leading parts on the political stage.

The reasons for this growing prestige are several. In the first place there is little doubt that the French Communists have, for the moment at least, lost ground both because of their obvious efforts to paralyze French economic recovery by strikes and slow-downs for purely political reasons but even more important because Molotov's walkout from the Paris Conference made it plain to even the least intelligent Frenchman that Soviet Russia and its French Communist stooges do not want to see an independent and prosperous Europe reconstructed. De Gaulle capitalized on this sentiment in his July 27 speech [1] when he bitterly castigated Soviet efforts to "impose a dictatorship on Europe" and admitted that he (De Gaulle) had made a serious error (which by inference he would not again commit) in taking the Communists into the French National Committee in 1943. This declaration was certainly welcomed by the majority of the French who had heretofore held De Gaulle in part responsible for the Communists present position of strength and influence "because of his original sin in inviting them to participate in his govt". Typical of the evolution of a considerable sector of public opinion regarding the possibility of De Gaulle's return to power is the fact that whereas four months ago people often said, "he had his chance, made a mess of it and there is no indication he will do any better". Now the same individuals still criticize his past errors but add, "he has learned and will not make the same mistakes again".

A more important reason, however, for his increased stature than the positive statements he has made is a growing conviction among the public and certain political leaders that whether or not one approves or believes in De Gaulle and his policies, to survive France must have a strong govt. De Gaulle, they believe, is the only figure with sufficient prestige and authority to rally behind him, control and dominate the anti-Communist forces which at present are a definite majority but which are "incoherent and impotent" in govts not only because of the differences which divide them but because of the internal dissensions, jealousies and ambitions within the individual parties themselves.

As a result of the foregoing sentiment many Frenchmen in all walks of life who have thus far hoped for what they call "democratic" solution (that is, a competent, well administered and sufficiently strong coalition govt grouping together the parties of the center and left but excluding the Communists and extreme rightists) are becoming progressively discouraged and disillusioned over such a possibility. They are disgusted with what they consider governmental fumbling, incompetence and irresponsibility. The reduction of the bread ration,

---

[1] Speech at Rennes.

the impending financial and economic collapse unless credits are obtained to shore up the French economic structure and the fact that three years after liberation France is in a more critical position than ever before, have all tended to discredit in the public mind democratic govt in France as practised since the liberation.

To Frenchmen who tend to believe that the present governmental system is unworkable there are only two possibilities—De Gaulle or Communism. At this juncture if faced with such a choice the majority would opt unquestionably for De Gaulle, many with mental reservations but with the feeling that an unknown adventure with De Gaulle is infinitely preferable to the Stalinist police state.

As I stated above, there are too many unpredictable factors to forecast accurately how the situation will develop in the coming months, and what De Gaulle's chances are of returning to power. Nonetheless it is a very definite possibility and will depend primarily on the economic, financial and food situation in the coming months. If an economic and food collapse occurs De Gaulle's changes [chances?] should be considerable despite all the Communists may do to oppose him.

In the absence of some unforeseeable event, I do not believe that De Gaulle himself has any intention of trying to return to power by other than legal means. Persons close to him tell me that from now to the municipal elections it is his intention to concentrate on enlarging and perfecting his RPF machine, naturally keeping himself in the public eye. Subsequently he will base his strategy on the conclusions he draws from the municipal elections and the way the economic situation evolves.

In reporting the foregoing I do not wish to convey the impression that De Gaulle's return is either a certainty or that it is in any way the answer to France's problems. It if [is?] however a possibility which we must bear in mind insofar as the future is concerned.

CAFFERY

851.6131/8–1647 : Telegram

The Acting Secretary of State to the Embassy in France

SECRET   WASHINGTON, September 2, 1947—6 p. m.

3294. Urtel 3298 Aug 16.[1] Figures thousands of tons. US export availability estimated at IEFC Cereals meeting Aug 18–19 Winnipeg 13,500 with reservation allowing for possible further decrease because of reduced corn crop estimates. Latest estimate corn crop made public

------

[1] Not printed.

since Winnipeg meeting 2,436,699,000 bu or about 850,000,000 bu less than last year. This may reduce US availability still farther below last year's approximate export of 15,000. While recognized that greatly reduced indigenous crop France this year compared last year makes larger contribution US necessary, reduced US availabilities and increased requirements other countries such as Germany, Italy, Austria and Greece severely limit volume shipments possible provide for France. Even if were possible make extraordinary shipments France prevent cut rations Sept 1 as suggested by Emb, would appear impossible continue shipments such magnitude remainder year. In fact in view large monthly export programs during early part crop year shipments from US expected taper off strongly last mos year.

In view reduction US availability mentioned above and recently announced great reduction Canadian availability, world exports of grain now estimated IEFC at 29,000 as compared 32,000 at Paris Cereals Conference July. Of this, 7,900 are from non-IEFC sources which considered less certain. For strictly confidential info Emb, pending formal IEFC screening all requirements for year, combined judgment IEFC Secretariat that based on total availability 29,000 share metro France from all sources 1,900, of which 1,100 from US and that Fr No Afr 430 of which 200 from US.

For Emb confidential info also, preliminary computation representing joint judgment IEFC Secretariat indicates 32,250 total shipments needed maintain present rations in world as compared availability 29,000. Consequently reductions rations many countries appear inevitable.

Re total required by France from all sources 1947–48 officials Dept and Agri and some members IEFC Secretariat made preliminary study questionnaire reply French Govt to IEFC with view noting possible savings which might reduce stated requirement of 2,600. Following noted:

Reduction set-aside for wheat seed	150
Reduction wheat for feed	40
Increased use rye for food	100
Increased use barley for food	350
Use corn, buckwheat and other grains for food	100
Saving by increased extraction	100
Reduction final stocks	100
Total reductions	950

Noted from urtel 3293 [2] planned increase barley utilization for food and industry over that indicated in IEFC questionnaire of about 220 and use oats for food about 160 plus some use oats processed foods.

---

[2] Not printed.

Presumably these changes from plan as submitted IEFC questionnaire reflect effect Paris Cereals Conference resolutions on collection coarse grains. Is there also prospect French may use most indigenous rye for food? Emb comments on other savings suggested above invited. It is of course not implied that it is Dept judgment that all savings suggested above will be found possible but seriousness situation requires that no means increasing availability indigenous grain for food be left unexplored.

Sent Paris repeated Clayton FAO Geneva.

LOVETT

851.61311/8–2947 : Telegram

The Acting Secretary of State to the Embassy in France

TOP SECRET   WASHINGTON, September 3, 1947—5 p.m.

3304. In light reports from Paris and Moscow likelihood Soviet offer grain to France at politically propitious moment and suggestions Moscow's 2741,[1] Department planning moves to anticipate such offer. Your comments and additional suggestions requested.

General outline of plan follows: (1) Secretary or Under Secretary will make statement at Press Conference of our grave concern at natural disaster which has made French harvest worst in recent history and of efforts which we are making and will continue to make to alleviate to the greatest degree possible its consequences in light exportable grain surpluses which are expected to be available from this country. He will note that while crop conditions are bad in western Europe, the reverse is generally true in eastern Europe and this led IEFC to estimate that USSR would export two million tons grain in current crop year. He will add that our own estimates indicate even larger Soviet exportable surpluses. He will express hope that in this emergency USSR will share with us burden of feeding western Europe.

(2) OIE will use this statement through all media not only to bring out fact that USSR now enjoys significant exportable surplus but to review in some detail relative contributions US and USSR have made to feeding western Europe since liberation and timing of these contributions.

(3) Full background on US contributions will be supplied to American Press and to Embassy Paris with suggestions to Paris for full and continuing publicity re statistics, ship arrivals and possible ceremonies to be arranged in connection docking of vessel which brings total US shipments to particularly significant or impressive figures, etc., etc.

---

[1] Not printed.

Belief here that if in face this campaign USSR does not offer (or refuses possible French request for) grain, French Communists position will be weakened. If on the contrary Russian grain is offered, US will be in position to take credit for forcing this grain into open while comparative figures for USSR–US contributions will weigh heavily in our favor, whether Russian offer is large or small.

Sent Paris as 3304; Repeated Moscow as 1678.

LOVETT

851.61311/9–447 : Telegram

The Ambassador in the Soviet Union (Smith) to the Secretary of State

TOP SECRET   Moscow, September 4, 1947—6 p. m.

2776. Concur fully in proposed moves to smoke out Soviets and publicize US grain shipments France as outlined Deptel 1678, September 3. Only suggestion is whether advisable to state our own estimates indicate even larger Soviet exportable surpluses than two million tons. Question of Soviet exportable surpluses is very elastic since all grain produced could readily be used domestically. On other hand surpluses could be made available whenever authorities deemed it advisable. Therefore, although perceive no objection indicating may be two million tons surplus this year, statement that they have more to export might boomerang propaganda-wise. They could make countercharge our information not based on facts and was "capitalist trick" to try discredit them.

Since all indications point to fact bread will be derationed here shortly probably in connection with 30th anniversary celebration,[1] advisable prepare to point out in this eventuality either:

1. Soviet indifference and lack of cooperation if they do not offer grain to France and other needy western countries, or

2. If they offer comparatively small amount grain to west play up picture Soviets derationing while western countries, because of adverse weather and other circumstances, still live on very short rations and need extraordinary help which we giving for long time and in large quantities.

Since Communists most adept at rolling with the punch, boasting about black eyes and accusing others of ulterior motives in propaganda campaign, believe it essential to spike French and other Communist guns that we bolster our propaganda offensive with concrete acts. Therefore strongly recommend that in connection propaganda cam-

---

[1] The Bolshevik Revolution of November 1917.

paign we make at least token increase French grain allocations as suggested third paragraph mytel 2741, August 29.[2]

SMITH

---

[2] Not printed.

851.61311/9–647 : Telegram

The Ambassador in France (Caffery) to the Secretary of State

TOP SECRET   PARIS, September 6, 1947—2 p.m.

3621. Our latest information just obtained confidentially from responsible French official is that French Government has submitted an urgent request for bread grains to Soviet Government through Russian Embassy in Paris and French Embassy in Moscow. Reported Russian answer is that request will be studied. Prevailing feeling privately expressed by French officials and implied in Communist press comment is that Russia will send wheat to France only if Communist Ministers are again included in French Government, but there is no confirmation that any such condition has been laid down as yet. An alternative possibility is that USSR may prefer to use wheat as a political weapon later in the season when food situation will be vastly more aggravated than now and when political stakes may be for a complete takeover of power by Communists rather than to use wheat at present for purpose of influencing French municipal elections in October.

Whether or not offer is made, and regardless of its timing, I heartily endorse plan as outlined in your 3304, September 3, and believe that it should be carried out at once.

Sent Department 3621, repeated Moscow 476.

CAFFERY

851.00/9–947 : Telegram

The Ambassador in France (Caffery) to the Secretary of State

SECRET   PARIS, September 9, 1947—11 a.m.

3650. During four-hour evening conversation MRP leaders, André Colin and Albert Gortais, appeared more harassed, tired and worried than ever before. They stated reports were reaching them from their federations throughout France that Communist Party is increasingly major beneficiary of recent disintegration of public morale. They added that quasi-unanimous reaction against our German policy had been and remained important contribution factor to upswing in Communist Party's popularity.

According to them, De Gaulle's RPF is gaining rapidly in Paris and large cities where it is winning over vast majority of bourgeois vote which had supported MRP in past elections. However, in rural areas, villages and small towns, they reported little increased interest in the General.

Requesting complete secrecy, they admitted that MRP had so far failed to attain the fundamental objectives which they and other MRP founders originally set: More efficient government and, generally speaking, a reaction against demagogic and sterile political mores of French Third Republic. Referring to the possibility of an MRP–RPF alliance, they said it was "unthinkable" and explained that "such a group led by staff now surrounding De Gaulle and imbued with its present social philosophy would find itself completely cut off from the world of labor and could not form a popularly accepted government. Furthermore, it is inconceivable that De Gaulle or his entourage would permit any MRP leaders to exert influence in establishing policies."

At present the MRP has not decided on its electoral strategy. Only concrete statement made was that in some areas and more particularly in and around Paris there would doubtless be "many joint MRP–Socialist lists". It was also learned that instructions have been given to local MRP organizations to postpone establishing their lists and making commitments until the last minute.

Throughout talk there ran recurring theme of intense fear of situation now moving so fast that showdown between De Gaulle and Communists could not long be postponed and that at all costs a reprieve had to be given to Center, "to the forces of sanity" so that France could get through the winter "without the irreparable having happened". They literally begged that we be sufficiently magnanimous to overlook the shortcomings of European planning and implement in part or at least confirm in unequivocal terms some stopgap measures of assistance to France and to Europe following lines of Lovett press statement.[1] "Without this breathing spell, anything can happen", they repeated several times.

Furthermore, they declared it essential the US act quickly before October municipal elections, to help scotch present anti-American campaign: "This growing anti-American feeling throughout country

---

[1] In a statement to the press on September 3, 1947, Under Secretary of State Robert A. Lovett warned that if the United States waited until the Marshall Plan could be worked out and put into operation it would be too late to save Europe. Mr. Lovett indicated that he favored the calling of a special session of Congress to deal immediately with the rapidly-deteriorating economic situation, and he suggested that the International Bank for Reconstruction and Development or the Export-Import Bank should extend temporary aid. For additional information on the statement, see the *New York Times*, September 4, 1947.

is serious for reaction to US German policy is based on deep-ingrained traditions and not merely result of Communist and fellow-traveling press campaigns". They hoped that US would stage a real "coup de théatre" by offering to submit bi-zonal plans to conference of sixteen for study and comment: "Thus the US would prove their good faith, set an example of give and take, and would take essential step towards acceptance of new standards of international negotiations and relations needed for inception of real plan of European cooperation, customs union, et cetera."

In purely domestic field, they said situation could also be saved should Ramadier accept to change a few ministers and "start governing, inaugurating immediately overdue fiscal and administrative reforms". For last two weeks they said some MRP leaders had been unsuccessfully attempting to convince Ramadier to replace doctrinaire André Philip, Tanguy-Prigent and Jules Moch, sacrificing an MRP Minister if necessary to save Socialist face. Both were pessimistic, however, about chance of such energetic and decisive government.

CAFFERY

851.6131/8–2247

The Department of State to the French Embassy

MEMORANDUM

The Department of State acknowledges the receipt of the *aide-mémoire* from the Embassy of France dated July 25, 1947 and the memoranda of August 14 and August 22, 1947 [1] in which supplementary allocations totalling 500,000 to 550,000 tons are requested for August and September, and the support of the United States is sought in the Cereals Committee of the International Emergency Food Council for a monthly allocation during the fourth quarter of 340,000 tons for metropolitan France and French North Africa. The Embassy's memorandum of August 22 states an import requirement for France and French North Africa for the half-year period July–December 1947 of 1,450,000 tons as compared to 825,000 tons recommended by the International Emergency Food Council.

The difficulty which France faces by reason of greatly reduced indigenous supplies is fully appreciated and the United States is therefore making relatively large allocations to France beginning in September, whereas allocations from the United States were not made during the previous crop-year in any considerable amount before March. Unfortunately, reduced availability from the United States

---

[1] Memoranda of August 14 and 22, not printed.

and increased requirements in many other countries also afflicted by reduced harvests have not made it possible to meet the French request for large supplementary shipments in August and September.

The matter of the amount of total programs of shipment to France and French North Africa and the share from the United States during the second half of 1947 is related to the recommendation regarding world grain distribution in that period as developed in the International Emergency Food Council's Cereals Committee. The total availability with reference to which that body has to develop its recommendations on distribution has unfortunately been reduced not only because of greatly lowered production of corn in the United States but also by a most serious curtailment of the Canadian wheat crop. It is hoped that the objections or reservations of the French representative as expressed at the Cereals Committee meeting in Winnipeg, both concerning quantities indicated for France and those indicated for military zones of occupation, will be modified as requirements are more fully analyzed and possibly modifications effected in the distribution pattern which has been put forward. The Department understands that the French representative on the Cereals Committee as well as representatives of other countries not sitting in the Executive Committee may be invited to attend hearings held in that Committee on requirements which are recognized to be of especial importance and interest to such representatives. In this way it is expected that the membership of the Cereals Committee will more generally achieve a sense of participation in the important work of evaluating requirements and a more complete understanding of all the factors which must be considered in working out the most equitable distribution which can be realized.

WASHINGTON, September 10, 1947.

851.51/9–1047

Memorandum by Mr. Ridgway B. Knight of the American Embassy in France [1]

MEMORANDUM OF CONVERSATION BETWEEN MR. ROBERT SCHUMAN [2] AND MESSRS. WOLVERTON, MACY, KEOGH, AND MONRONEY [3]

SECRET   [PARIS,] September 10, 1947.

Mr. Schuman, after welcoming the committee, stated that in addition to answering with complete frankness any question which the

---

[1] Transmitted to the Department as enclosure 1 to despatch 9585, September 10, from Paris.

[2] French Minister of Finance.

[3] Members of the Sub-Committee for France and the Benelux Countries, Select Committee on Foreign Aid, House of Representatives, United States Congress.

committee members might care to ask, he would see that complete data and written answers would be supplied on any subject that might be of particular interest to his visitors.

Mr. Wolverton thanked Mr. Schuman for his welcome and indicated the committee's hope that it might be of assistance in helping France in solving the present difficult situation. He reminded the Minister of Finance of American democratic institutions, of the necessity of Congressional approval of any Presidential policy, and also of the fact that in their turn the various Congressmen were answerable to their constituents. With a view to any possible assistance to France, certain major French factors were of particular importance to American public opinion. After consenting to heavy financial sacrifices, the United States had balanced its budget, and the average American would not view with favor aiding a foreign country which had not stabilized its currency and achieved a sane budgetary balance.

Mr. Schuman answered that since he became Finance Minister fourteen months ago, his primary objective has been the balancing of the French budget. He said that considerable efforts had been made and material results obtained, adding that had it not been for the increases in wages and prices, such an equilibrium in France's public finances would have already been attained. As it was, it appears that France's normal budget is "within a few billion francs of being balanced". He then reminded the committee that France had been invaded three times within the span of a single life, and insisted on the vastness of France's losses between 1940 and 1945: destructions, systematic exploitation and pillaging by the Germans, and the less spectacular but important losses due to the fact that French equipment of all kinds could not be maintained properly during those six years. While it was the French Government's policy to achieve a balance of the normal budget, the reconstruction of France, representing capital expenditures, had to be covered by an extraordinary budget. He indicated that such reconstruction budgets would have to cover total capital expenditures of about ten thousand billion francs over the course of the reconstruction period which he mentioned as twelve to fifteen years.

Mr. Schuman went on to declare that while France had made great efforts within the last two years and rebuilt her railroad and road system and her industries so that they were now approaching French pre-war level, the French economy had now reached a point where it was "in neutral" and could not proceed without outside assistance.

Mr. Macy referred to past American aid and said that it was essential that any new assistance not constitute "just another palliative" but lead to a real and constructive solution of the problem. Mr. Schuman expressed his full accord as well as the French Government's agreement with this position.

Mr. Monroney, after commenting favorably on certain results of France's reconstruction efforts which he had been able to witness personally, drew attention to the vital necessity of France's exerting herself to help herself in order to make possible any American assistance. As an example, he raised the wheat problem and the necessity for France to put back under cultivation the same acreage which was planted before the war. Also referring to wheat, he drew attention to the great difficulties of convincing American farmers not to feed wheat to livestock—in view of the short corn crop—if these same farmers could not be assured that this practice had been done away with in France. Mr. Schuman answered that the French Government was fully alive to these problems, that premiums had been offered in the past year to farmers who sowed wheat, but that it had not been possible to accomplish much in this field in view of the low tax receipts from peasant sources. He added that more effective measures—both inducements and penalties—would be added but that, of course, they belonged within the province of his colleague, the Minister of Agriculture. As to the problem of feeding wheat to animals, it was stated that severe penalties had been enacted, but as farm property was over-divided in France (three million farms), measures of control and enforcement were exceedingly difficult.

Answering a question as to the French citizen's willingness to tighten his financial belt and accept heavier taxes, Mr. Schuman said that it had been decided yesterday morning to form a committee of several Ministers in order to reduce Government expenses as much as possible and see to it that these decisions were implemented. Furthermore, Mr. Schuman declared that the entire fiscal policy and tax structure as well as methods of financial administration were under review, and that a bill of complete reform would be introduced into the French legislature in November, doubtless pass before the end of the year, and come into force on January 1, 1948. Mr. Schuman said that in France it was not a question of raising tax rates, which were already so high as to discourage initiative. On the contrary income tax rates had to be revised downward to take into account the devaluation of the franc since 1940 and the [ten-fold][4] increase in living expenses. However, French tax receipts must and will be increased. At present there are vast sectors of French economic life which pay little in the way of taxes: farms, black market operators, the liberal professions, small shopkeepers who are able to dodge taxes. Mr. Schuman said that the French Government's principal objective in the financial field was to plug these holes by simplifying the fiscal set-up dating back to the days of Napoleon and which since then has "grown like Topsy" to a complicated and unrelated whole, impossible to enforce.

---

[4] Brackets appear in the source text.

Answering a question as to the possibility of efficiently administering France's large colonial Empire and thus obtaining assistance for the mother country, Mr. Schuman briefly answered that this was the intent and hope of the French Government.

Mr. MacChesney [5] expressed his pleasure at being once again back on French soil and working on the solution of France's problems. He also drew the Minister's attention to the necessity of France's doing the maximum to help herself in order to convince American public opinion that France should be aided.

Again, while thanking the members of the committee for their interest in France, Mr. Schuman placed his services at their disposal to supply any additional information in writing which they might desire.

RIDGWAY B. KNIGHT

---

[5] Brunson MacChesney, consultant to the Select Committee on Foreign Aid, House of Representatives.

851.51/9–1047

Memorandum by Mr. Ridgway B. Knight of the American Embassy in France [1]

MEMORANDUM OF CONVERSATION BETWEEN MR. LACOSTE, MINISTER OF INDUSTRIAL PRODUCTION, AND MESSRS. WOLVERTON, MACY, KEOGH, AND MACCHESNEY

SECRET   [PARIS,] September 10, 1947.

Mr. Lacoste started by defining briefly the scope of his Ministry, which he said was the Ministry of and for industry. Its primary interests are the basic power generating industries: coal, electricity, gas, motor fuels; but, he added, his Services were also interested in iron and steel, light industries, and even the manufacture of luxury products. He said that domestic commerce also fell within his realm while of course foreign commerce came within the field of the Ministry of National Economy.

Answering a question by Mr. Wolverton as to the measures taken by France to increase her coal output, Mr. Lacoste drew the attention of the Committee to the fact that during the pre-war period French production was never adequate for her needs and that she had had to rely constantly on imports of coal to satisfy one-third of her needs. He said that during the German occupation coal production had been reduced very materially but that since France's liberation production has increased from about 70% of the 1938 figure, to a quantity now slightly in excess. He said that as both financial resources and time

---

[1] Transmitted to the Department as enclosure 2 to despatch 9585, September 10, from Paris.

had so far been lacking to re-equip the mines, the simplest solution had been used : man-power. Miners had been given special food rations and various other incentives. Now, he said, the French miners' output was 75% of the pre-war per capita production "which compares favorably with that of other countries". "Now, unfortunately," said the Minister for Industrial Production, "our available man-power will be seriously reduced. The Polish Government has called upon Polish miners in France to return to Poland, and France is about to lose her German prisoners of war. To counterbalance this state of affairs, the French Government has launched a recruiting drive to obtain additional miners in France. The results have been fairly encouraging, but now France has reached the point where, in order to increase production, she must at last re-equip her mines."

Speaking about equipment of all kinds, Mr. Lacoste drew attention to the fact that France's industrial plant had not only suffered severely during the war when, in addition to destructions, maintenance was impossible; but also that even in pre-war France equipment had a tendency to be antiquated and in poor repair. He said that this unfortunate condition also prevailed throughout the rural areas where the peasants lacked not only modern mechanical agricultural equipment but also chemical fertilizers. "It has been my personal experience," declared Mr. Lacoste, "that French businessmen, workers, artisans and peasants are anxious to work and just as capable as before the war, whenever they have the equipment to do so. What is lacking is this very equipment."

Answering various questions about France's electricity production and requirements, the Minister stated that France had long had a program to increase her generating capacity and that this program was being pushed with the utmost vigor. He drew attention to the new Genessia dam, the largest in Europe, which will start operating this year. In addition to this very large undertaking, he said that the current phase of this program largely centered on the development of a number of hydro-electric sites in the Massif Central and in the Pyrenees. Mr. Lacoste said that now that France's power companies had been nationalized, the various companies were being integrated together for more efficient production. He mentioned that this year it would be possible to release 20% of the personnel. Along technical lines, he said that old plants were being modernized and more particularly that steam generators were being rebuilt to supply more power from the same amount of coal consumed. He mentioned that the peak daily load in 1946 had been 84 million kwh; that in 1947 this had increased to 90 million kwh; and that if capacity could be increased to 100/120 kwh, this would take care of all of France's needs, based on her present industrial and other electric equipment.

With reference to nationalization of French industries, Mr. Lacoste emphatically stated that the French Government's policy was merely to nationalize basic industries considered throughout Europe as "public services": coal, electricity, gas, railroads; and that on the contrary it was French policy not to nationalize all fields calling for competition.

Mr. Keogh then asked whether France's fiscal and tax policies might not be retarding her industrial come-back. Mr. Lacoste answered that for the time being he did not think so, as France's available coal, iron and foreign exchange did not permit re-equipment at a faster rate than the present one. However, he also said that he was sure that these fiscal and tax policies would exert such a retarding influence if the wherewithal was available. "I favor a complete overhaul of the entire fiscal and tax set-up, and, gentlemen, this may be close at hand." Mr. Keogh also asked whether the French Government's wage and price policy did not exert the same influence. Not answering the point directly, Mr. Lacoste said that of course it had been found necessary to increase wages periodically, which put additional masses of paper money into circulation at a time when there weren't sufficient consumer goods to absorb the supply of currency. This in turn resulted in increased prices and in the vicious circle which all have noted in France's economy.

Answering a question by Mr. Macy as to hoarded money, including gold, the Minister said that while of course this was out of his field, it was his belief that gold as well as paper currency was being hoarded throughout the country, and to a large extent by the peasants. "If we manage to stabilize our currency, this will of course result in the return to circulation of these hoards both in paper and in specie."

RIDGWAY B. KNIGHT

EUR/WE Files [1]

Memorandum of Conversation, by the Director of the Office of European Affairs (Hickerson)

SECRET   [WASHINGTON,] September 12, 1947.

Participants: M. Bonnet, French Ambassador
The Secretary of State
Mr. John Hickerson, Director, Office of European Affairs

The French Ambassador came in at 11:30 today by appointment made at his request. The Secretary left the Department for New

[1] Files of the Division of Western European Affairs, Office of European Affairs; Lot 53 D 246, File "Rhineland–Ruhr".

York before this memorandum of conversation could be dictated. I am therefore preparing this memorandum in order that it may be distributed without being forwarded to New York for the Secretary's approval.

M. Bonnet said that he had just returned from Paris and that he had wished to give the Secretary some of his impressions on the general situation. First of all, he said that he had been very much pleased to see that the French Government seemed to be pretty well in agreement with the position of the U.S. Government concerning the work of the CEEC in Paris.[2] He called attention to the fact that on three of the most important aspects of this conference the French Government fully supports what it understands to be the position of the U.S. Government. These are:

1. *Emphasis on production.* The French Government recognizes the full importance of setting production goals and attaining these goals.

2. *Financial reform.* The French Government fully agrees that the countries of Europe must in their own way put their finances in order.

3. *Removal of trade barriers.* The French Government recognizes fully the importance of trade barriers and is prepared even to agree to a European customs union although the French Government recognizes that there are numerous difficulties in the way of a customs union at this time which probably cannot be surmounted.

The Ambassador said that against this background he wished to raise with the Secretary and discuss briefly with him three topics: (1) The French dollar position (2) Wheat and (3) The Ruhr.

The Ambassador said that the French Government was handing to Mr. Caffery a note setting forth their acute financial situation.[3] This boils down to the unpleasant fact that France will run out of US dollars some time between October 15 and October 30. He said that there had been much talk in the US of an interim period in which financial assistance to certain countries in Europe would be necessary. This interim period had been understood to cover that time between the opening of Congress and the voting of funds for a program, presumably about March. The Ambassador said that as regards France there are therefore two interim periods: October 15 until the end of December and January to March. He said that he hoped that if possible consideration would be given by the U.S. Government to this French note.

Next the Ambassador said that France is desperately short of bread grains and must have more wheat if the present inadequate ration

---

[2] For documentation on the Conference of European Economic Cooperation, July–September 1947, see pp. 249 ff.
[3] The note is included in telegram 3725, September 12, from Paris, *infra.*

is to be maintained. He said that he was conscious of the difficulties involved in getting more wheat but that it would have the most serious consequences in France, political and social, if the government found it necessary to reduce the present insufficient ration.

Finally the Ambassador mentioned the French interest in the Ruhr. He recalled the discussions which took place in Paris recently between the French officials and Messrs. Caffery, Clayton and Douglas.[4] At that time he said Mr. Clayton had suggested that the French security apprehensions might be met by a provision in the peace settlement for the establishment of an international board on which Germany would be represented along with France, the UK, US and Benelux to allocate the German production of coal, coke and steel; this board would see to it that enough production was allocated to Germany for a peaceful economy and that the remainder was allocated for export in a fair and equitable manner. The Ambassador said that he frankly felt that this device would not be sufficient to satisfy France's security apprehensions. He said that a control board was all right but that it must be more fully integrated with the economic life of the Ruhr and play a more effective role vis-à-vis management of the mines. He did not elaborate on this.

By this time the Secretary's next caller, the British Ambassador, was waiting to fill an appointment with the Secretary. The Secretary said that he did not have time to do more than comment briefly on the third topic the Ambassador had mentioned, that is, the Ruhr. He said that he must point out to the Ambassador that he is deeply concerned over this whole question and the varying points which are emphasized in the policy of France, the United Kingdom and the United States in regard to the Ruhr question. The Secretary said that he can understand a natural French desire to see to it that adequate security measures are taken to prevent Germany from again menacing France but that he must say that he does not understand how in the present crisis the French can emphasize this to the exclusion of other important factors. The UK Government, a Socialist government, seems to feel that the most important matter in connection with the Ruhr is the early nationalization of the coal mines. The Secretary went on to say that the U.S. Government is frankly interested in achieving at the earliest possible date the maximum production of coal in the Ruhr and favors concentration on the solution of that question now and deal-

---

[4] For reports on the conversations under reference, see telegrams 3239, August 13, 3263, August 14, 3316, August 19, and 3319, August 19, all from Paris, vol. II, pp. 1029, 1031, 1039, and 1041.

ing with the other questions in a fair and equitable manner as soon as the coal begins to roll out of the Ruhr in adequate volume.

The Secretary said that adequate quantities of coal are indispensable to the revival of industry and thus the reattainment of the financial solvency of Europe. The Secretary went on to say that shortage of coal was in the final analysis back of most of France's difficulties including the shortage of dollars. The Ambassador indicated agreement with the Secretary's comments.

JOHN HICKERSON

851.51/9–1247 : Telegram

The Ambassador in France (Caffery) to the Secretary of State

TOP SECRET   PARIS, September 12, 1947—6 p. m.

3725. I have been given the following memorandum by the Minister of Foreign Affairs:

"The Ministry of Foreign Affairs believes it useful to furnish to the Embassy of the United States the following precisions on the dollar situation of France and on its perspectives:

1. In the same way as it follows from the attached technical note, (summarized in Embassy's 3661, September 9 [1]), the reserves in gold or in dollars of the French Treasury will be probably exhausted between the fifteenth and thirty-first of October next. With regard to the gold reserves of the Bank of France, at present reduced to $445,-000,000 it is impossible to deduct again a portion of these reserves for the benefit of the Treasury, because these reserves have fallen to a level very much below the security minimum, and they are besides necessary to cover a certain number of short-term engagements in foreign exchange or abroad. [If?] the French Government could not procure between now and October 15 new resources, it would be obligated to stop the dollar purchases which it has maintained up to the present; namely, purchases of cereals, coal, and fats.

2. On the supposition that France obtains, within the framework of a European program, external assistance permitting it to assure its imports beginning April 1, 1948, the external assistance of which it would have need until that date in order to maintain its current purchases in the American continent would be in the neighborhood of $600,000,000.

In default of assistance of this magnitude, it would be necessary for France to sacrifice a part of its essential imports in raw materials and foodstuffs in the American continent which are indispensable to the functioning of its economy."

CAFFERY

---

[1] Not printed.

851.00/9–1347 : Telegram

The Ambassador in France (Caffery) to the Secretary of State

SECRET   PARIS, September 13, 1947—noon.

3734. A high official of Interior Ministry reviewed for me today in confidence the internal French political situation as he sees it. He began by stating that the French Parliament had not recessed one day too soon and that had it remained in session much longer the Ramadier Government would probably have fallen. He said that Parliamentary nerves and tempers were getting very frayed; "with Parliament in session there was the ever present possibility of some incident capable of precipitating a major crisis particularly in view of the stresses within the Socialist Party resulting from the Lyon Congress coupled with the difference of views between the various parties which compose the present government".

Commenting on Ramadier's position (my informant is close to both Ramadier and Auriol) he said that while several days ago there had been considerable pressure from certain Socialist elements for Ramadier to resign, Ramadier strongly supported by Auriol and Blum is determined, in the absence of some unpredictable development, to continue on until after the municipal elections. He will use this period to try to work out a governmental plan looking to establishment of internal economic and financial stability (balancing budget, adoption of a sound fiscal and tax policy, stabilizing wages and prices, et cetera) for presentation to the Assembly when it reconvenes in November.

My informant believes it is impossible at this juncture to predict what will happen in the period following the elections. While the results of the elections will certainly influence the situation, what happens will in reality be determined almost entirely by the economic and food situation. If France should fail by that time to have the certainty of obtaining sufficient credits (International Bank loan and US credits) to tide over the hiatus period from November until next spring, when the French hope the Marshall Plan will go into effect, the social and political situation will rapidly deteriorate and the Ramadier government will assuredly fall. In such event my source was unable to forecast what would follow but expressed the conviction that while initially the immediate result of such a crisis might appear to strengthen De Gaulle "whose influence and prestige have increased in the past two months, in the final analysis it will be the Communists who profit most". He went on to express the view that if a collapse occurs with an apparently insoluble political impasse it is possible that Auriol "who is as determined as Ramadier to keep the Communists out of the government" might ask De Gaulle to form a government. In such event my source does not believe that the Communists would oppose De Gaulle with insurrectionary action, but would redouble their efforts to paralyze every phase of French national economy with the firm and probably correct belief that if De Gaulle fails again a Communist government would inevitably then take over.

The foregoing possibilities are, of course, based on an economic collapse or serious deterioration of the present situation. On the other hand, if France obtains the necessary credits to stabilize the situation in the interim period prior to the Marshall Plañ taking effect, my informant believes that despite very serious difficulties and grave problems the Ramadier government (possibly with a few Cabinet changes) has a reasonable chance to continue on in office, particularly if a realistic and sound fiscal, tax, wage, and price policy is adopted. He said: "In other words, if we can get sufficient help to prevent the situation from breaking down the chances of either extreme (De Gaulle or the Communists) coming into power will be certainly postponed and there will be a real chance of seeing the present coalition evolve into a reasonably strong democratic government with sufficient prestige and authority to govern. In so far as resisting Communism is concerned, the attitude of both the political leaders and the public has never been better since the liberation. On the other hand, the economic, financial and food outlook has never been blacker. (I agree with this last statement). If a collapse can be prevented it should be possible to maintain and even strengthen resistance to the Communists. If on the other hand, the situation disintegrates, the Communists alone will profit."

While the foregoing opinions are naturally speculative and are in fact more optimistic than the views of some other political observers, I report them at length because of the past reliability of the source and the information to which he has access. I concur with the view that if before the October elections the French see no immediate hope of credits to tide them over the winter months, the Ramadier government is most certainly doomed and grave social and political troubles appear inevitable. I am also inclined to agree that while such a situation might initially appear to benefit De Gaulle, in the long run it would be the Communists who would profit most and who might succeed in coming to power.

Sent Department as 3734, repeated London for Clayton as 734, to Moscow by airmail.

CAFFERY

851.61311/9–1647 : Telegram

The Acting Secretary of State to the Embassy in France

TOP SECRET WASHINGTON, September 16, 1947—1 p. m.

3496. A leak which is being rigorously investigated is responsible for the appearance in Sept 15 issue *Newsweek* (published Sept 11) of article by Edward Weintal revealing Dept's plans outlined Deptel 3304.[1] Consequently it now appears inadvisable to base the plan in first instance on statement by US Govt official. It is thought however that you might inspire in French press (perhaps one of Chipman's [2] friends might be helpful in this regard) an editorial or the statement of some prominent Frenchman calculated to be as arresting and newsworthy as possible in order to receive widest initial coverage in French and world press and provide sound basis for exploitation by Dept and field.

While we shall leave final decision as to theme, medium and exact timing to you it is suggested that theme be centered on surprise and/or indignation that French wheat shortage has not already been alleviated by Russian grain with suggestion that USSR is withholding its wheat until it can be used to greatest political advantage in municipal elections as it did in 1946 when it shipped 500,000 tons of grain largely in American bottoms etc. This performance could be contrasted with American shipments which have been constant and as large as possible based solely on purpose to aid France as much as possible. This could be bolstered with appropriate statistics.

While exact timing is left to you we believe no time should be lost. Please cable us date as far in advance as possible and text as soon as it appears. Dept is furnishing you statistical and background data by separate cable.

Newsweek leak will have alerted Moscow. We must bear this in mind if we proceed in this matter. If in all the circumstances you have doubts about advisability of going ahead with this, telegraph us.

LOVETT

---

[1] Dated September 3, p. 734.
[2] Norris Bowie Chipman, first secretary of Embassy and consul at Paris.

851.00/9–1647 : Telegram

The Ambassador in France (Caffery) to the Secretary of State

SECRET   PARIS, September 16, 1947—7 p. m.

4005. My 3756, September 14.[1] As municipal election campaign swings into high gear it becomes obvious that as usual the Communist Party is by far the best prepared with money, press, films, trained personnel, et cetera, as compared with all other parties, to gain the votes of the masses. Study of this party's "internal" bulletins, as well as public speeches of its leaders, reveals that for the first time since the liberation the Communists have posed France's attitude towards US as one of the main electoral planks. Whether Communist discus-

---

[1] Not printed.

sion touches upon internal or external affairs, our country is constantly accused of menacing France's "independence" and the essential point which is most frequently stressed, as for example in Thorez speech delivered last Sunday at Saint Quentin, is that present government has revealed its complete incompetence by its "gambling on Am aid which will not be forthcoming".

Bread, wheat and coal are the principal subjects of discussion on part of Communists. They portray the US as overflowing with wheat, coal, foodstuffs, etc., which we are withholding until France "capitulates" and becomes completely dominated. *Humanité* harps on "holdup" prices of American wheat and coal and describes the "rage" with which Thorez spoke at Saint Quentin of necessity of "plying [*paying?*] dearly in precious dollars for Ruhr coal". While carefully avoiding discussion of specific aid from Soviet Union, Communists are insisting that American assistance in any event "will be too little and too late" and consequently France should turn to the East. In demagogic fashion they assert that if Thorez had been permitted to head a cabinet "in conformity with will of people" or even if Communists had not been expelled from Cabinet, the present "drift towards abyss" would not be taking place. They are also pointing out that one of the greatest penalties of tying France's fate to American "trusts" will be that Washington will "prevent any extension of nationalization as it has already done in England" and will "impose its investments in our overseas territories".

Appeals to American people to undergo voluntary rationing in order to furnish cereals to Europe such as that made on Monday by our Under Secretary of Agriculture,[2] should prove helpful. Unfortunately, however, that portion of his statement which indicated that large quantities of grain are being fed to livestock in United States was given prominence in this morning's *Herald Tribune* and is sure to be thoroughly exploited by Communists.

To summarize, in their propaganda there is no doubt whatsoever that Moscow and the French Communists are counting heavily on their belief that prior to the October elections there will be no clear and unequivocal indication that the US will supply sufficient help in the coming critical months to prevent famine and cold in France. I feel it of greatest importance that we do everything we can to counteract this propaganda line in the most important pre-electoral period.

Sent Department 4005; repeated Moscow as 487, Berlin 363, London 752.

[CAFFERY]

---

[2] Norris E. Dodd.

851.6131/9–1747 : Telegram

The Acting Secretary of State to the Embassy in France

RESTRICTED   WASHINGTON, September 17, 1947—noon.
U.S. URGENT

3526. Follows background material on French grain situation.

Great concern being expressed throughout US over bad French harvest. US own grain supply greatly reduced because of poor corn crop. 1947 US production all grain together estimated at 10 percent less than 1946. Despite reduced US supply calendar 1947 shipments cereals this country to continental France expected exceed appreciably shipments during calendar 1946 and 1945. First ten months of 1947 US has already delivered or programed 820,000 long tons of grain and grain products. We tentatively plan shipments for last two months which will bring year's total to nearly 1,100,000 long tons. This compares with US deliveries to continental France of 860,000 long tons 1946, and 758,000 long tons 1945.

In addition to US grain shipments to continental France, large quantities have gone directly to French North Africa. For three year period, 1945–1947, direct French North Africa deliveries amounted to almost 1,000,000 long tons.

Altogether, US has already since beginning 1945 supplied or programed a total of almost 3,500,000 long tons of grain for France and French North Africa. If tentative plans for last two months of this year are carried out, total will be raised to some 3,740,000 long tons.

US has also been exporting substantial amounts of mixed dairy and poultry feed to France. It will be remembered that before the war France was not dependent on US for wheat and other grains. Less than 30,000 long tons of wheat were imported from US in each of four years 1937–1940. And France's pre-war wheat flour imports from US were even less than wheat. Same was true of other grain.

US shipments, despite their increased volume, will not alone be adequate to offset the bad French harvest. Therefore, all countries which can make grain available for export ought to join US in its efforts to relieve acute shortage of bread in France this winter.

While harvests in western Europe have been unusually bad this year, in eastern Europe, particularly USSR, they have been good. Cereal Committee International Emergency Food Committee estimated at its Aug meeting in Winnipeg that USSR should have an exportable surplus of 2,000,000 long tons from 1947 crop. Reports from Soviet press indicate estimate is probably conservative. Soviet acreage under cereals was substantially increased this year, and average yield per acre is reported much above both 1945 and 1946. A Soviet paper recently stated that "the outlook for grain yields in principal regions is incomparably better than last year."

Beginning April last year, with a relatively poor crop, USSR shipped, partially in American ships, some 544,000 metric tons of bread grains to France. This grain was sold to France for dollars at prevailing world price. In view bountiful 1947 harvest, it is felt that USSR can this year greatly increase its shipment of bread grain to France.

Soviet shipments to France last year were effected principally during the months of April, May and June. This was first Soviet shipment after war and none has been made since. Total Soviet deliveries of grain to France during post war period thus amounts to date to approximately 544,000 metric tons. This compares with US deliveries of approximately 3,500,000 long tons (3,557,000 metric tons). 1946 Soviet grain was sold to France for dollars and at prevailing world price.

Estimate of a 2,000,000 ton Soviet surplus was arrived at by IEFC after allowance was made for derationing of bread and substantial increase in per capita consumption of bread in USSR.

LOVETT

851.61311/9–1747 : Telegram

The Ambassador in France (Caffery) to the Secretary of State

TOP SECRET   PARIS, September 17, 1947—6 p. m.
US URGENT

4021. Deptel 3496, September 16. I fully appreciate force of the considerations which make the Department reluctant, following the unfortunate leak in *Newsweek*, to have the initial statement on Soviet wheat delivered by a US Government official.

I have given careful thought to the Department's alternative suggestion and my personal conclusion is that in spite of the *Newsweek* story the best method of accomplishing our aim is to ignore it and proceed with the original plan. In brief, this conclusion is based on the following considerations:

1. The French press today is almost exclusively a party press and practically all prominent journalists are first and foremost party men. Even if we could persuade a newspaper or an individual Frenchman of sufficient influence for our purpose to lend his name to such a statement, it is by no means certain that other papers would pick up and develop the story.

2. On the other hand, a statement of this kind coming from an important official of the US Government would carry much more weight here and the task of getting a wider range of French political leaders and writers to comment on it would be greatly facilitated.

3. *Newsweek* has a circulation in France of 7,000 and in Europe as a whole of 50,000. It is possible that Weintal's story will receive little publicity here. In my opinion the effect of the *Newsweek* story in France (and I take it that our main objective is to influence French public opinion) should not be important.

4. I believe that the facts contained in our statement would be sufficiently arresting to outweigh any charges that we were indulging in a political maneuver.

CAFFERY

851.5018/9–847 : Telegram

The Acting Secretary of State to the Embassy in France

SECRET   WASHINGTON, September 19, 1947—6 p. m.

3594. Dept appreciates gravity French food situation as presented your 3649 Sept 8 [1] and earlier telegrams. Govt agencies here have made and are still making every effort to improve exports, but we cannot offer assurance of shipping sufficient grain to restore and maintain French ration 250 grams this winter. While you are already familiar with nature of difficulties in allocating and procuring grain, following offered as possible help to you in understanding situation here. Deptel 3526 Sept 17 was concerned with public info aspects of French grain situation.

1. As already indicated Depts 3294 Sept 2 volume US grain exports will be greatly reduced by small size of domestic corn crop. While wheat crop is 6,782,000 tons more than preceding year, corn crop is 21,250,000 tons less. This deficiency in corn alone is greater than total US exports of all food grains for crop year 1946–47. Result may be that total availability for shipment abroad will not exceed 12,000,-000 tons all types grain as opposed to 14,500,000 predicted earlier in summer.

2. Shortage of corn may unfortunately mean excessive increase in use of wheat to feed livestock. Average Aug price corn last year was 1.91 per bu. Average price Aug this year 2.35. Price Sept 17 2.63. Corresponding figures wheat 1.95; 2.31; 2.69. Only Govt procurement agency is Dept Agri which is obliged to purchase competitively in open market with advance notice. Its buying activities therefore tend to raise prices, and procurement for export has recently been somewhat inhibited by reluctance to stimulate price increases further. There is already widespread concern over food prices, and Dodd and Harriman have spoken publicly of need for voluntary meat rationing

---

[1] Not printed.

to conserve grain. Cabinet Food Committee will meet Sept 22 to consider effect on domestic prices of procurement for export, and decision on policy should be made soon. Govt officials will also consider conservation measures, but obviously doubtful whether they are politically feasible, whether voluntary restrictions would be effective, or whether legislative controls could be established in time to avert food crisis in France this winter.

3. Mentioned above that procurement for export has been inhibited by fear of raising prices. However, while current shipments to all destinations could be larger than they are, they could not be maintained at higher level, or even at present level. Exports at current rate would amount to approximately 7,500,000 tons for period July–Dec 1947. This would leave for export Jan–June 1948 only 4,500,000 tons or more, depending on total availability mentioned Para 1.

4. US is committed to system of allocation through mechanism of International Emergency Food Council. This means that import requirements of all countries are examined and target allocations established by international action. Export programs of participating countries are then planned to meet allocations with which reps of participating countries have agreed in IEFC. System obviously results in comparatively light allocations to many claimants rather than heavy allocations to a few. While US exerts great influence in IEFC, it does not determine allocations single-handed, and it is bound to give some weight to IEFC allocations in its export programs. This makes it more difficult to concentrate large shipments in one area.

5. US exports to other areas cannot easily be reduced in favor of France, aside from considerations relating to IEFC. Estimated here that France would need approximately 50,000 additional tons grain each month from US to restore and maintain 250 gram ration, assuming that domestic supplies and current imports would be sufficient to maintain present 200 gram ration. But France is already largest importer of US grain except occupied areas and Italy. To divert 50,000 tons a month from other destinations would necessitate serious reduction of several smaller allocations, or complete elimination of two or three, such as those to countries participating in CEEC, or to areas in South America or Far East. Such allocations are already limited, and there would be political difficulties in cutting them to extent necessary to satisfy needs of France and Italy. Allocations to eastern Eur have already been shipped, and there are no further allocations to that area which could be cancelled (last para urtel 3593 Sept 4 [2]). With respect to bizonal area it is accepted here that 3,600,00 tons from

---

[2] Not printed.

US will be required to support ration level of 1550 calories, and that this level must be maintained in order to increase Ruhr coal production. Accordingly Dept has joined with War Dept in requesting Dept of Agri allocate 3,600,000 tons produce weight from US to combined zone during current crop year. Best we can do with allocations to other destinations than France is hold shipments to minimum. For example, we are shipping no grain to UK in Nov, and quantities assigned to several Eur countries in US Nov program may result in early reduction of their rations. Already contemplated in IEFC allocations July–Dec this year that rations many countries would inevitably fall, and US programs from Nov on may produce this effect.

Purpose of foregoing is merely to give you background on inability to meet French requirements adequately. We shall continue doing everything to maintain shipments and to increase them if at all possible. Meanwhile will appreciate further info and suggestions from you.

LOVETT

851.51/9–2347 : Telegram

The Ambassador in France (Caffery) to the Secretary of State

SECRET   PARIS, September 23, 1947—midnight.
US URGENT

4135. For State and Treasury from Embassy and Tomlinson.[1] Secretary of Treasury requests following message be brought to immediate attention of Wiggins [2] and Southard: [3]

In conversation on September 22 Finance Minister Schuman listed specific steps in which we might be of immediate assistance in alleviating French dollar payments crisis. I informed Schuman of the sympathy and concern of the Administration with regard to the present situation and assured him that I would do everything possible to expedite attention already being given to these matters.

1. Unutilized balance of Ex-Imbank loan now amounts to 200 million earmarked for purchase of equipment. Schuman suggests terms of loan contract might be changed to permit as close as possible to 100 million of this balance to be used for purchases of coal, cotton, petroleum products and other supplies. Schuman states his relations with Ex-Imbank are excellent but feels that if France negotiates question directly with Ex-Imbank no modification of contract will be possible, at least with necessary speed. He urged that US Administration

---

[1] William M. Tomlinson, representative at Paris of the Department of Treasury.
[2] Archibald L. M. Wiggins, Under Secretary of the Treasury.
[3] Frank A. Southard, Jr., Director of the Office of International Finance, Department of the Treasury.

participate in negotiations to reach favorable solution before October 15.

2. Question of expediting and arranging advance payment on settlement of French claims arising from US Army procurement in France was also raised. Schuman states possibly 50–60 million could be made immediately available from claims outstanding. (Embtel 4088 [4])

3. Schuman urged prompt distribution of "looted" gold recovered to date. He suggested gold be delivered to an Allied central bank to be inventoried, weighed and assayed and that Tripartite Commission in Brussels [5] be directed to go ahead with temporary distribution until technicians could settle exact claims of each country. Question was also raised of approximately 33,000 kg. of fine gold blocked in Bank of Japan and belonging to French Union (Indochina). Schuman asked for assistance of Treasury in reaching favorable solution as promptly as possible.

4. Final question raised by Schuman was problem of mobilization of private French assets abroad, particularly those held in US through Swiss banks and not declared by their owners to French Government. Schuman referred to estimate of 500 million. He expressed hope that Treasury could find some indirect means of assisting his Government in getting these undeclared assets. He acknowledged delicate position of US because of undertakings given to US banks at time of TFR 300 census.[6] Schuman said he did not wish to take strongly punitive measures against French owners but felt some means other than voluntary program would have to be used to obtain desired results. He referred to plan whereby US would announce date for vesting of uncertified assets by Office of Alien Property and expressed view that if concerted with French Government program, such action might bring owners to declare their assets to French. Schuman also referred to plan under consideration by French which would involve certification of assets belonging to French owners without French Government actually learning identity of individual owners. He argued that in most cases such detailed information not necessary to establish non-enemy character of assets involved since largest part of such assets have been held by same owners for long period before the war. He suggested that present certification procedure might be modified to take account of this fact if owners let dollars be used to finance French purchases. [Snyder.]

CAFFERY

---

[4] Not printed.

[5] The Tripartite Commission for the Restitution of Monetary Gold was established by the Governments of the United States, United Kingdom, and France on September 27, 1946. For a statement of the functions of the Commission, see Department of State *Bulletin*, September 29, 1946, p. 563.

[6] A census of foreign-owned property subject to the jurisdiction of the United States was announced by the Department of the Treasury on June 14, 1941. The returns, prepared by banks, corporations, and individuals, were submitted on Report Forms TFR–300.

851.5018/9–2447

Memorandum of Conversation, by the Associate Chief of the Division of Western European Affairs (Wallner)

SECRET   [WASHINGTON,] September 24, 1947.

Participants: The Acting Secretary
               The French Ambassador
               Mr. Wallner

In a conversation lasting over an hour, the Acting Secretary and the French Ambassador discussed the food and financial crisis in France and the possibilities of meeting it within the next few months.

Food was the first subject, and Mr. Bonnet spoke of the absolute necessity for France to obtain further allocations of wheat and his intention to ask the IEFC for 500,000 additional tons. He said that every avenue was being explored but that it had not yet been discovered where the wheat was coming from. Mr. Lovett said he did not know how or where the French could obtain extra allocations of wheat by December. Mr. Bonnet suggested that one place it could be found was in the large amount of wheat earmarked for the British and American zones of Germany, adding that the French people could never understand how it was that the German people were getting larger bread rations than they. Mr. Lovett replied that bread now formed a larger part of the German ration than it did of the French, that the total German ration was much lower than the French and, in his opinion, it would not be feasible to reduce the wheat allocations for the combined German zones. The French Ambassador did not insist further on this point, but he did indicate some skepticism that the Germans would really be worse off this winter than his own people.

Mr. Lovett then referred to the intensive studies now under way in this Government for determining what substitute foods, such as dried fruits, etc., could be procured to take the place of wheat. He offered the information in confidence to the Ambassador that the President was giving serious consideration to calling on the American people for voluntary restrictions, such as two meatless days a week, for the purpose of lowering the prices of meat and poultry and freeing for export the grain that might otherwise be used to feed stock. He assured the Ambassador that the latter's concern over the food crisis in western Europe did not exceed the Secretary's and his and that every means was being looked into to meet the emergency. He added that he could say nothing further at this time since the President had just returned and final decisions had not yet been taken.

Turning to the financial crisis, the French Ambassador reviewed the perilous situation which France would face when she ran out of dollars next month. He said that France had stopped importing raw materials and was using all her remaining dollars for wheat and coal. He said he was hopeful that dollars might be found to continue these essential imports but pointed out that unless the importation of raw materials, such as cotton, etc., could soon be resumed, French industrial production would slow down to almost nothing before the Marshall Plan could be implemented and so affect, as far as France was concerned, the production assumptions upon which the Marshall Plan was based. He said that by adding together all the bits and pieces of dollar assets France might, if she could get an Export Import Bank Loan, be tided over and be able to resume purchase of raw materials before the Marshall Plan came into effect.

Among the bits and pieces he mentioned the German looted gold, unpaid items owed by the US Army to the French Government on procurement account, and finally the earmarked Japanese gold now in Tokyo. Mr. Lovett replied that he thought the first two items were on the way to rapid settlement but that the complications involved in the latter might delay matters so that a decision could not be reached in time to be of any assistance during the interim period. Mr. Bonnet pointed out that the Tokyo gold amounted to more than $37 million and that he must press the Acting Secretary for a rapid decision on this problem. Mr. Lovett promised that the matter would be looked into immediately and requested Mr. Wallner to see that this was done. Mr. Lovett then referred to the Ambassador's suggestion concerning an Export Import Bank Loan and said that to his regret he would be obliged to disappoint him. He explained that he had called upon the directors of the Export Import Bank only last week with the same thought in mind and that he had been turned down. The directors had told him that under the present franchise and their agreement with the Appropriations Committee of Congress they could make no further loans to France, which had received a large amount already from the Bank and which simply had no further collateral to offer.

Mr. Lovett took pains throughout the conversation to impress upon the Ambassador the Secretary's and his awareness and deep concern, which they had set forth at length to the President, regarding the implications for the US and for the world of the food and financial crisis in western Europe.

851.61311/9–2547 : Telegram

The Ambassador in France (Caffery) to the Secretary of State

TOP SECRET   PARIS, September 25, 1947—10 a.m.
US URGENT

4152. Many of our best informed friends, among them publishers-editors of *Ouest France*, largest provincial daily in France, right wing of MRP, Gaullist tendencies, 430,000 circulation, covering 12 departments Brittany and west with 28 regional editions; *Le Maine Libre*, Le Mans daily, Socialist, 80,000 circulation; *L'Ouest Republicain*, Rennes daily, Socialist, 20,000 circulation, are deeply concerned over extremely violent Communist Party propaganda, in view October municipal elections, in rural districts heretofore predominantly anti-Communist, and over danger of Communist gains there as result of this propaganda. Communist campaign is based largely upon current 200 gram French bread ration. Arguments most frequently advanced are:

1. US has sent less cereals than promised;
2. US is now sending less than it could send, in order to aggravate French shortage and at critical moment to send more on condition that France submit to American anti-democratic imperialistic conditions;
3. US sends mildewed corn to France keeping wheat and good corn for German civilians of American zone;
4. US allows German civilians daily bread ration at least double that of France;
5. Ramadier has sold out to Americans and will not procure wheat from Russia although stocks are available there;
6. Severe crop fires in August and September are acts of arson, fires being set by Fascist agents, ex-Vichy militia and Gestapo men, working for reactionary clique, De Gaulle and American interests with Truman's blessing in order to further deplete French stocks and thus the more easily to force France to submit to American conditions.

The journalists mentioned above have all volunteered the opinion that a statement by a high ranking official of US Government re shipments which have been made to France would be most helpful in counteracting Communist efforts in rural areas. They have also expressed the opinion that to obtain the maximum usefulness such a statement should have a "newsworthy peg" and that repetition would greatly strengthen its impact.

These unsolicited views have served to strengthen my own conviction that we should proceed at once with the plan outlined in Deptel 3304, September 3 and that, as indicated in mytel 4021, September 17, the statement should be made by a high American official. My own view is that the statement would carry great weight if made by Under Secretary Lovett who has received excellent press in France in recent weeks as result of his sympathetic approach to question of interim aid.

It is reported in today's press that Ambassador Bonnet has recently made representations to our government for additional allocations of wheat. It seems to me that Bonnet's representations might serve as a suitable "peg" for a statement focused on the French situation, and that he might be called in and given the statement after which it could be given to the press. The statement itself might begin with a reference to Bonnet's representations which would have the advantage of making it appear that the whole matter resulted from French initiative, thereby tending to counteract the Weintal story.

If this is done it would seem best to limit the part of the statement concerning the relative contributions of the US and USSR to France itself rather than have it cover "western Europe" as contemplated in the Dept's original plan. The inclusion of western Europe might also give the Communists here an opportunity to point up their argument that we were sending much more grain to Germany than to France.

An alternative possibility would be to await Clayton's return to Washington and have the statement emanate from him. In my opinion, however, the time element alone is sufficient to favor the first alternative.

CAFFERY

840.50 Recovery/9–3047 : Telegram

The Ambassador in France (Caffery) to the Secretary of State

SECRET   PARIS, September 30, 1947—midnight.
US URGENT

4240. A source close to Ramadier tells me that the latter and other members of the coalition government are deeply disturbed over the news from Washington in regard to the prospects for immediate aid for France. He said that the present government has been progressively orienting its policy toward the US and has continued to oppose heavy Communist pressure to re-enter the government counting largely on the Marshall Plan and interim aid until Marshall Plan can go into effect next spring.

The Communists, who wish at all cost to re-enter the government so that they can further their penetration and influence French foreign, colonial, and domestic policy, have reacted by increasing the violence of their attacks against the present government "for selling out to the US in every field including Germany". The Communist refrain orchestrated by its magnificent propaganda machine, is that the Ramadier Government has been "gambling on the possibility of American aid for France and that France will not only be left in the lurch by the US, but that it also is burning its bridges with eastern Europe which could help it". (The Communists actually believe that we will eventually extend some assistance but are counting heavily on its being too late.)

As reported in mytel 4221, September 30 [1] the Communist press referring to the President's meeting day before yesterday [2] is gloating that "no American aid will be furnished to France and the European countries until next spring at the earliest". We may expect this campaign to continue with growing intensity both prior to and following the elections with a view to completely discrediting the Ramadier Government and demoralizing the French public already discouraged by the prospect of one of the worst winters France has ever had to face.

My informant believes that unless France receives clearer indication that interim aid will be forthcoming the Ramadier Government will probably collapse shortly after French Parliament reconvenes following the municipal elections and that then there will be little, if any, possibility of excluding the Communists from the next government. He said: "Once the Communists get back into the government it is difficult to see how they can again be ejected".

On the other hand, he believes that if the promise of American interim aid is forthcoming the Ramadier Govt has a good chance to survive, since all the parties represented therein (with the possible exception of a few radicals close to Herriot [3]) still "wish with all their hearts to keep the Communists out of the govt" and will, therefore, hesitate to cause a crisis the outcome of which would be uncertain and which probably would benefit the Communists.

CAFFERY

---

[1] Not printed.
[2] For a record of the President's news conference following a meeting with congressional leaders, September 29, see *Public Papers of the Presidents of the United States: Harry S. Truman, 1947* (Washington, Government Printing Office, 1962) p. 445.
[3] Edouard Herriot, President of the French National Assembly.

711.51/10–247

Memorandum by the Under Secretary of State (Lovett) to President Truman

TOP SECRET   [WASHINGTON,] October 2, 1947.

Subject: Call of Mr. Georges Bidault, French Foreign Minister

Mr. Bidault's advisers have indicated that he wishes to talk with you principally about the food and financial crises in France and the prospects for, and extent of, American aid to alleviate them, both immediately and in connection with the European Recovery Plan. He will probably explain their impact on the French political situation, with particular reference to the future of the Government to which Mr. Bidault belongs. It is possible that the French Foreign Minister may also touch on the German question,[1] including the uni-

---

[1] For documentation on the German question, see volume II.

fication of the three western zones and the future status of the Ruhr and the Saar as well as on the November meeting of the Council of Foreign Ministers.[2]

In essence, the several questions which Mr. Bidault will speak to you about resolve themselves into one: the growing split between east and west and the side on which France will find herself. Mr. Bidault will come to you as a member of a Government which represents the middle of the road democratic elements and which in the next few months may well be unable to withstand the pressures from right and left unless the problems of food and coal can be solved.

Recent reports from Ambassador Caffery indicate growing concern on the part of Prime Minister Ramadier and other members of his coalition Government that unless American aid is forthcoming within the next few weeks the Government will collapse and will be replaced by one from which it will be impossible to exclude the Communists. His own political future being at stake it seems likely that Mr. Bidault will paint a grim picture in terms of the alternatives of increased American aid or a Communist France.[3]

Robert A. Lovett

---

[2] For documentation on the fifth session of the Council of Foreign Ministers, at London, November 25–December 15, 1947, see *ibid.*, pp. 676 ff.

[3] No direct record has been found of the conversation between President Truman and M. Bidault on October 2. Telegrams 4293 and 4312 from Paris, October 3 and 5, not printed, review comment in the French press (851.9111 RR/10–3, 10–547).

851.00/10–647 : Telegram

The Ambassador in France (Caffery) to the Secretary of State

SECRET   Paris, October 6, 1947—7 p. m.
US URGENT

4322. There is no doubt that De Gaulle scored a spectacular success yesterday in his speech at Vincennes. (I understand full text has been cabled by American news agencies.) An impressive crowd estimated at between 400 and 500,000 gathered to hear him. While the great majority were middle or lower middle class and white collar workers there were nonetheless a surprising number of workers. The crowd was orderly and it was obvious that it had come to hear what De Gaulle had to say rather than simply for an outing. The applause when he attacked the "Soviet dictatorship", called the French Communist Party "separatists" working in the interest of another country, and paid tribute to the United States, stating that with its strength intact it was opposing Soviet world ambition, was spontaneous and sustained. He said "and there is not a free man in the world who does not think that American policy healthy".

Qualified political observers, including anti-Communist labor leaders, agree that the meeting yesterday was impressive evidence of De Gaulle's popular prestige and that if the present polarization of Communist and anti-Communist forces continues to develop De Gaulle's following may rapidly snowball.

It is interesting that the Communists (as in the case of De Gaulle's Lyon speech last month) endeavored to keep down attendance and destroy effectiveness of speech by resorting to different forms of sabotage including scattering nails on roads approaching Vincennes, sabotaging the loud speaker system (which was rapidly repaired prior to the General's speech) and arranging for "mechanical" interruptions in the service of the only subway which runs to Vincennes.

Copies by pouch to Moscow and London.

CAFFERY

851.00B/10–747 : Telegram

The Ambassador in France (Caffery) to the Secretary of State

SECRET   PARIS, October 7, 1947—1 p. m.

4323. Highly qualified observers here, including one who is close to Duclos,[1] state that the Kremlin's choice of Communist Parties participating directly in new Comintern indicates that latter's battle formation counts on "decisive parties" of Europe. They consider that while designation of French and Italian parties reveals that Moscow regards France and Italy as falling within its "zone of immediate influence", this decision, rather than augmenting Communist prestige in these two countries, is more likely to injure it especially if both France and Italy survive the winter without collapsing economically. Informants explain, and in this I heartily agree, that one of the main sources of Communist strength in France resided in widespread belief on part of general population and even some political circles that the Communists since 1941 were no longer subservient to Kremlin. Consequently, it is believed in anti-Communist circles on the right and left that the "open" operation of Comintern will aid them in providing sufficient evidence during electoral campaign that Communist militants were never anything but Soviet patriots.

The selection of Belgrade rather than Praha as the "transmission belt" leading from Kremlin to Paris strikes these observers as convincing proof that the Soviets feel somewhat isolated and prefer to operate from a "sure GPU and military base". Absence in France of "United Front with Socialists and Radical Socialists" as during pre-

---

[1] Jacques Duclos, a leader of the French Communist Party.

war Popular Front period will greatly handicap, according to same informants, Communists task of convincing people that Moscow stands for peace and anti-imperialism while United States is the bulwark of the "camp of warmongers and imperialists".

Source close to Duclos remarks that "mass Communist Front organizations" will now be directed to reorient their policies by shifting "line" from "anti-Fascism" to anti-Americanism and to stress more than ever view that Moscow is the "bearer of peace".

Source also believes that absence of German party from "open" participation in new Comintern indicates that German question, especially in France, is still too delicate in view of French chauvinism but they firmly believe that even here a new orientation is beginning to take place (reference my 4296, October 3 [2]) and they point to participation of Georges Roucaute at recent Berlin Conference of United Socialist Party.

Socialists militants here also believe that Comintern's attacks against Blum and Bevin are designed "to oblige all Socialists, especially those behind Iron Curtain, to side with Moscow or with 'Social Fascists' like Blum with all the consequences that this decision now entails in Soviet satellite states".

Finally, trustworthy source states that French Communist Party was given task at Warsaw Conference to "direct the Belgian, Dutch, English, Spanish and Swiss Communist Parties". Italian Communist Party will be directed by Moscow via Belgrade. As for North American Continent party work will be entrusted to a "special representative under Manuilski's [3] immediate guidance".

Sent Department 4323, repeated Moscow 495, Berlin 383, Belgrade 49, Rome 254, London 791.

CAFFERY

---

[2] Not printed; it reported that the French Communist press was beginning to extol the administration of the Soviet Zone of Germany and to view sympathetically the efforts of Germans there to create a "new democracy" (740.00119 Control (Germany)/10–347).

[3] Dimitri Zakharovich Manuilsky, Minister for Foreign Affairs of the Ukrainian Soviet Socialist Republic.

851.51/10–847 : Telegram

The Ambassador in France (Caffery) to the Secretary of State

CONFIDENTIAL   PARIS, October 8, 1947—1 p. m.

4338. Independent *Combat* states today that according to well-informed circles Bidault has already obtained formal assurances from Washington "to assist France before October 19". Paper adds that

Bidault will probably make known results of his Washington visit at public MRP rally Saturday night.

CAFFERY

851.61311/10–1047 : Telegram

The Acting Secretary of State to the Embassy in France

TOP SECRET   WASHINGTON, October 10, 1947—5 p. m.

US URGENT

3880. Deptel 3873.[1] Secretary of Commerce Harriman plans to issue Russian wheat statement on Oct. 13 or 14 in course of meeting of Inland Press Association in Chicago. Exact text of statement may not be available in advance but he plans to use following draft as a guide:

This Govt is greatly concerned over the French grain situation. Because of a natural disaster, the French cereal crop this year is the worst in over a century. The US is doing the utmost which circumstances will permit to offset the dire consequences in human suffering of this harvest failure. In spite of our own greatly reduced grain supply, because of the poor corn crop, shipments of cereals from this country to France during 1947 are expected to exceed shipments during 1946. But shipments from this country, despite their increased volume, will not alone be adequate to offset the bad French harvest.

The press has carried statements of an official French spokesman to the effect that the French Government asked the Soviet Government several weeks ago to send wheat to France and that the Soviet Govt has not yet replied to this request. We all know that while harvests in western Europe have been unusually bad this year, in eastern Europe they have been good. Statements in the Soviet press concerning the Russian harvest have lead the Cereal Committee of the International Emergency Food Committee to estimate that the USSR should have an exportable surplus of two million tons from the 1947 crop. Under the circumstances it is hoped that the Soviet Govt will respond favorably to the request of the French Govt and will be willing to share with us the task of relieving the acute shortage of bread this winter both in France and in western Europe generally.

LOVETT

---

[1] Not printed.

851.00/10–1047

The Second Secretary of Embassy in France (MacArthur) to the Associate Chief of the Division of Western European Affairs (Wallner)

TOP SECRET   PARIS, October 10, 1947.

DEAR WOODIE: In view of both international and internal French developments of the past two months, it seems to us that the time has come when a review of the French political situation in the light of future possibilities may prove useful.

You will recall that in my letter of last March 26 [1] we were encouraged by indications that the anti-Communist leadership of the Left and Center was at last beginning to show signs of life and cohesion. We nonetheless felt that the democratic leadership in France still had a long way to go to win the battle against Communism, and among other things we believed that a leader with very considerable prestige and authority was needed if a strong and effective coalition of the democratic forces of the Left, Center and moderate Right was to be formed. Our view that there were encouraging signs in the psychology and outlook of the anti-Communist political leaders was in part justified on May 7 by the exclusion of the Communists from the Government for the first time since the Liberation, by the right wing Socialist leadership supported by the political forces of the Center and moderate Right. Such a development had been considered politically impossible only two or three months earlier.

With the expulsion of the Communists a new phase began. As the Ambassador reported (in his telegram No. 1927, May 12, 1947) the difficulties faced by the Ramadier Government were serious. Nonetheless, given existing political conditions, the composition of the Ramadier Government after May 7 was the best that could be hoped for under the circumstances and, in theory at least, seemed then to offer the best chance of an eventually viable democratic solution.

What has happened since May 7, and where does the Ramadier Government now stand? There is no doubt that Ramadier made a courageous and very real effort to succeed, but in retrospect the task which faced him was, I am afraid, beyond his capacity. There are, of course, a number of good reasons for Ramadier's lack of success and the resultant progressive disillusionment of the French public in his Government.

1. In the first place, the Communists—as had been anticipated—threw the weight of their powerful organization against the Government with a view to overthrowing it and thus proving to the other political parties and to the French people that whether or not they liked the Communists, France could not be governed without them. They unleashed and encouraged a series of so-called "spontaneous" strikes, exploiting the very real hardships and dissatisfaction of the entire working class. While many of the strikes, particularly the railway strike in June, were not an unqualified success from the Communist viewpoint, particularly since they did not succeed in re-entering the Government, nonetheless they forced Ramadier, in his effort to keep his ship of state from capsizing, to jettison ballast in the form of so-

---

[1] Not printed.

called production bonuses, which were in reality nothing more than increased wages. This coupled with the reduction in industrial production caused by the labor stoppages, automatically led to price increases which worked further hardships on low-salaried groups, thus increasing their dissatisfaction.

2. Another important factor in Ramadier's failure could be described as an "Act of God". I refer to the heavy freezes of last winter coupled with an unprecedented drought this summer which greatly reduced the agricultural yield and has resulted, particularly in the past four weeks, in a very serious spiral in French food prices. This is, of course, most keenly felt by small-salaried workers who are at present in a position where it is difficult—in fact almost impossible—for them to obtain sufficient food for themselves and their families for the wages they earn. This situation will unquestionably result in increased pressure (which the Communists will exploit) for increased salaries, which in turn would lead to further inflation.

3. Failure of the Government to achieve budgetary and monetary stability and the ever-expanding note circulation, together with the belated knowledge that France is bankrupt insofar as dollars and gold which are needed to finance vital food and coal imports, have badly shaken the confidence of the entire country in both French currency and in the Ramadier Government.

4. Aside from the foregoing economic and financial considerations there have been important political factors which have worked against Ramadier. The split in his own Socialist Party, as emphasized by the Lyon Congress, as much as any other political development has served to make his task almost impossible. In addition, the differences which divide the various political parties in the present Government— particularly "dirigism versus liberalism"—have tended to make it almost impossible for the adoption of a sound and effective program which all parties will loyally and honestly support before the French public. Such compromise agreements on programs and policies as have been arrived at were often neither fish, flesh nor fowl, and were not based on a meeting of minds but on a common desire to keep the Communists from returning to the Government. To keep the Communists out of the Government is laudable, but once the compromise agreement was reached the political leaders of the different governmental parties at once began publicly and privately to blame another party or the other parties in the coalition for the unpopular features of the program. Such action, of course, served further to discredit the Government in the eyes of the public which progressively began to feel that in reality the present coalition is unable to cope with the task of Government and is devoting its time to political maneuvering rather than to governing France.

5. Finally, the French people themselves are not without blame. There is fatigue, lassitude and apathy which too often lead many of them to prefer to drift along rather than to make any real effort to help themselves by increasing production thus contributing to getting France back on its feet. They criticize the Government for failing to govern but at the same time there is reluctance to support any necessary measures which require some sacrifice but are indispensable for French recovery. In addition, it must be admitted that there has been some corruption and some moral disintegration.

As the prestige of the Ramadier Government has declined, a growing conviction has been developing that the anti-Communist elements, which are the majority in France, will be unable to submerge personal and party differences and ambitions unless they are led by someone with sufficient prestige, authority and popular support to impose on them the discipline and sense of national duty which thus far they have apparently failed to manifest and which is imperative if France is to survive Moscow's drive to take over the country. It is a sad but incontestable fact that France lacks leaders of such stature. At the present time, whether one likes it or not, the only person who stands head and shoulders above the crowd and who could conceivably fill the role is de Gaulle.

De Gaulle, whose prestige as we have reported has continued to increase in the past two months as a result not only of the activity of the French Communists but also because of increased disillusionment with the present Government's ability to cope with the situation, and the growing cleavage between the United States and the Soviet Union, is counting on his popularity snow-balling. He believes the point will finally come when a majority of the French population will flock to his banner. When this time comes, he apparently thinks that he will also be backed by a majority of the Parliament and that his public support throughout the nation will be so strong that the Communists may not resort to insurrectionary action since they would recognize that they would certainly be doomed to failure. While he does anticipate the possibility of a Communist-inspired general strike and localized disorders, he appears to feel that should such a strike be called it will also fail because of lack of public support, even though Gaullists now admit that the General has thus far made little real effort and hence little progress in obtaining any real working class or syndicalist support. Some of them claim, however, that they are giving this aspect of the problem increasing attention.

With the foregoing background in mind, the $64 question is posed— what is going to happen next? Insofar as the Ramadier Government, as now constituted, is concerned there is almost unanimous agreement among the political leaders of the different parties that it has expended its credit and is, as the French put it "used up". Such observers admit that the reluctance of all governmental parties to instigate a crisis, whose outcome is uncertain, works in Ramadier's favor. Nonetheless they believe that shortly after the Parliament reconvenes Ramadier will fall, probably not by an adverse vote of confidence but by the withdrawal of one or more of the component elements of the present coalition. The Socialists themselves might withdraw but their action will to a considerable extent depend on the outcome of the extraordinary session of the Socialist National Congress which has been called for November 22 and 23. The RGR, particularly the Radicals, may withdraw because as you know they are fed up with the "dirigiste" policies of the Socialist left-wing as enunciated by their exponents in the present Cabinet, such as André Philip and to a lesser extent Tanguy-Prigent.

If the Ramadier Government collapses it is difficult to forecast with any degree of accuracy what Government will succeed it. Some observers believe that there will be a further attempt at a "republican solution" in the form of a coalition Government excluding the Communists and having more or less the same composition as the present Government (possibly excluding some or all of the Socialists) but headed by an MRP such as Bidault or Teitgen, or possibly by a Radical. Other observers believe that there may be a new attempt for a non-Communist coalition Government headed possibly by Blum. (At present this is not considered probable.) Still others are thinking in terms of a homogeneous minority Government—MRP or Radical—which would have the limited support of the anti-Communist Parliamentary majority (a formula not unlike the di Gasperi Government in Italy). Should any such Government be formed its life would in all probability be of relatively short duration. It would simply be another interim stopgap.

Our reason for fearing that any "center of the road" coalition is almost certainly doomed and cannot last long is the increasing evidence that until some means is devised of preventing the Communists from sabotaging French economic recovery through their control of the CGT, etc., no Government can succeed in re-establishing economic equilibrium which is a prerequisite of political health and stability. Yet by its very composition no coalition Government that groups the Left, Socialists, Center and moderate Right will dare to adopt the measures which alone can put an end to Communist sabotage and treason. Such measures could amount to imprisonment for sabotage—direct or indirect—and necessarily would seriously infringe on many basic liberties in which we and all other democracies believe. It is painful for me, whose social and political views are considerably to the left of center, to have reluctantly to confess that until France has a more authoritarian regime, with greater power and prestige, it is difficult to see how the Communists are to be prevented from successfully preventing French recovery. In other words, until such time as the Communists can be dealt with by a strong Government, France will almost fatally remain weak and divided.

As things now stand, should such an interim Government be formed and then fall, it would almost inevitably lead to a test of power between de Gaulle and the Communists. Exactly when such a test would come would seem to depend largely on the speed with which the increasing division of France into pro and anti Communist camps proceeds. If this polarization is very rapid as a result of a number of developments, including possible trends evinced in the coming municipal elections (which will not in themselves be decisive), Moscow's recent decision to supplement the Comintern by an "Information Bureau", and an acceleration in the activity of the French Communist Party, the struggle between de Gaulle and the Communists could come to a head in the relatively near future. If on the other hand the polarization occurs more slowly, such a test might take place sometime during the next year. Our feeling is that it is not many months off.

Regardless of whether or not future events develop along the above lines, the time has come when we must face the possibility of the French people and ourselves having to choose only between de Gaulle and the Communists. If the French people are given this *sole* choice the majority will most certainly back de Gaulle, even though many may have doubts and reservations. Under such circumstances, I assume that in our own interest we would make a similar choice. Should de Gaulle come back to power it would certainly be in our interest for him to succeed, for should he fail every possibility of an anti-Communist solution would have been exhausted and the Communists would hold all the cards.

I hope that from the foregoing you will not gather the erroneous impression that we are encouraging de Gaulle or the Gaullists, for this is most certainly not the case. We believe, however, that there is a possibility, and indeed a likelihood, of his return, and it does not seem too soon to give some thought to such an eventuality and to exactly where we stand and what line we would take with him.

De Gaulle has never been and will never be an easy man with whom to deal. On the debit side of his ledger we might list that temperamentally, psychologically, as well as in the realm of practical dealings with people, he is far from the ideal leader. He has had relatively little political experience and lacks a financial and economic background. He is convinced that he alone knows what is best for France, and he has in the past surrounded himself with a small group of advisers, many of whom are not up to their job, and some of whom are extremely ambitious. One reason for his failure after the Liberation was that he lacked able advisers, with real experience and judgment. When he was offered sound advice by men of experience not in his immediate entourage he often not only failed to heed them but gave them a cold brush-off which tended to alienate them from him.

On the credit side it can be stated that he is a patriotic Frenchman who firmly believes that his sole desire is to see France restored. He has more personal prestige than any other leader. He has burned all bridges with Moscow and the French Communist Party, and is their sworn enemy. As such, his orientation is now and at long last definitely toward the United States, for he believes that we are the only country which has the material resources and the will to prevent Soviet world domination. Despite this fact, should he come back to power he would not always be an easy person for us to deal with.

If the situation here evolves into a struggle between de Gaulle and the Communists we do not entirely exclude the possibility that prior to the final culmination of such a test of strength we may be approached directly or indirectly by de Gaulle to ascertain where we stand and what we may be prepared to do in the event he has a real showdown with the Communists. This is all, of course, very hypothetical, but we feel that in these parlous times we should give consideration to the line we may take if we should be faced with such an eventuality. If de Gaulle comes back to power and is to succeed, he will obviously have to make use of more capable men than the limited entourage with which he has in the past been surrounded. For example, perhaps such persons as René Mayer, Mendès-France and other individuals with more common sense and economic and financial background than are presently in the "old entourage". Furthermore, such persons are perhaps more democratically inclined than some of his former équipe, and possibly could aid in giving to a de Gaulle Government a less authoritarian slant than it might otherwise have.

In conclusion, I apologize for the length of this epistle. I have perhaps let myself wander far afield and may have taken up a lot of your time in summarizing a situation with which you are as well acquainted as are we. Once I got started on this, however, I found it difficult to be as succinct as I would have liked. If you, Sam [2] and Jack [3] have any thoughts about all this do let us know.

Yours ever,   Doug

---

[2] Samuel Reber, Deputy Director of the Office of European Affairs.
[3] John D. Hickerson, Director of the Office of European Affairs.

P.S. From what de Gaulle's entourage has let drop it is evident that there are among other things two questions in his mind concerning U.S. policy, etc.:

1) If he comes to power will he (de Gaulle) receive almost immediate "massive" economic and financial aid from us?

2) In the event of a U.S.-Soviet war is our military planning aimed at defending France against Soviet invasion?

Incredible questions but interesting as indicative of the mentality!

851.61311/10–1147 : Telegram

The Ambassador in France (Caffery) to the Secretary of State

TOP SECRET   PARIS, October 11, 1947—noon.
US URGENT

4396. Mytel 4395 October 10.[1] Following is translation Foreign Office communiqué on Russian wheat.

"The French Government had inquired of the Soviet Government whether it would be possible to receive 1,500,000 tons of Russian wheat from the USSR.

On October 8 Mr. Mikoyan, Minister for Foreign Commerce of the USSR, informed M. Pierre Charpentier, French Chargé d'Affaires at Moscow, that the Soviet Government had no objections to the inauguration of negotiations on this subject. He added that the Soviet Government would like to know what products France would be in a position to deliver to the USSR in compensation for the grain furnished. The French Government will examine the list of products which might be of interest to the USSR."

In commenting on above this morning *Figaro* refers to Franco-Soviet commercial accord of December 29, 1945 pursuant to which a list of products was proposed to Soviet Union including notably phosphates, rubber, electrical equipment.

In view of this development Secretary Harriman will doubtless wish to amend statements which he had planned to make on October 13 or 14 (Deptel 3880, October 10).

As was to be expected, this morning *Humanité* headlines event with photo of smiling Russian peasant girl surrounded with sheaves of Russian wheat. *Humanité* stresses point that transaction will not involve need of obtaining dollars. It refers to realization in US of French need for wheat and accuses US of employing French shortage of dollars to strangle France. It is in this situation that "great Soviet Union" comes to aid of France asking nothing in return which could

---

[1] Not printed.

disrupt French finances. Article concludes: "Once again it appears that Communists were right in pointing out that recovery of France cannot be based upon commercial relations which exclude anyone. It must be based on practice of commercial exchanges with all countries. A great hope has now arisen for the French people. It is up to the government to expedite the matter."

Other papers report communiqué without comment.

CAFFERY

851.61311/10–1147 : Telegram

The Acting Secretary of State to the Embassy in France

TOP SECRET   WASHINGTON, October 13, 1947—6 p.m.
US URGENT

3901. Reurtel 4396, Oct. 11. Following, subject minor changes, will form part Sec. Harriman's speech at Chicago, Oct 14.[1]

"Both during and since the war the US has been helping to feed hungry people. During the war we shipped large quantities of food to our allies, including Russia. Last year, for example, we exported nearly 15 million tons of grain and flour alone. Other countries with food surpluses have made important contributions. It is now reported that as a result of favorable weather Russia has an exportable surplus of at least two million tons of grain. I am pleased to note reports in the press that Russia has entered into negotiations to deliver a part of her substantial wheat surplus to France and other countries. The food crisis in all of Western Europe, and particularly in France, is grave. All help that can be given by countries with a surplus is urgently needed.

["]The announcement of the Russian readiness to negotiate for shipment of grain to France has of course been accompanied with great fanfare and Communist activity within France.

["]It therefore should be noted that, as in the case of the last offer of Russian wheat to France, it comes significantly just at the time of an election. Last year they actually delivered wheat. This year they have so far only offered to negotiate. France it appears can entertain the hope of eating some Russian food only at election time.

["]American wheat and other food has been delivered regularly to France throughout the period since the end of the war, as well as to the other needy countries of Europe and the world.

["]In view of the great capital being made by the Communists about this latest demonstration of Russian cooperation, the relative quantities of food which have come from the US and from Russia should be clearly stated. Russia has shipped about 540,000 tons of grain to France, whereas beginning in 1945 we have shipped nearly seven times that amount, or about 3,600,000 tons."

LOVETT

---

[1] For the substance of Secretary of Commerce Harriman's speech, see the *New York Times*, October 15, 1947, p. 22.

851.51/10–1447 : Telegram

The Ambassador in France (Caffery) to the Secretary of State

PARIS, October 14, 1947.

4423. Today's French press gave prominence to following news reports from Washington:

1. *Pre-interim aid.*

a. US agreement to French request that $93,000,000 second Exim Bank loan, be transferred from equipment expenditures to purchase coal and raw materials.

b. Consideration being given by US Government to other sources immediate financial aid, including restitution German and Japanese looted gold, payment for US military expenditures in France and assistance in locating French hidden assets in US.

2. *Committee of European Economic Cooperation.*

Reports quoted an authorized source as stating American Government desired that CEEC conference be reconvened to approve changes in its report regarded by US as necessary before it could be submitted to Congress.

Despatch from London quotes Foreign Office spokesman as saying that other means existed for clarifying the points of the plan which gave rise to the difficulties.

CAFFERY

———————

851.5151/10–1547 : Telegram

The Acting Secretary of State to the Embassy in France

SECRET   WASHINGTON, October 15, 1947—6 p.m.
U.S. URGENT

3941. For Emb and Tomlinson from State and Treas.

1. The President today authorized Army to purchase $50 mil in francs from French Gov. Francs will be used in payment of procurement obligations of Army or for other expenditures of US Gov.

2. Dept of the Army is cabling EuCom info MA Paris directing that purchase be made and transmitting copies of draft letters to be exchanged with French authorities providing that these francs may be used by Army in payment of any of its obligations in France and North Africa and may be transferred by Dept of the Army to any other dept or agency of US for subsequent use in payment for any expenditure of US Gov. In addition French Gov is asked to agree that it will at any time at request of US Gov repurchase against dols at same rate of exchange at which they were acquired any of such

francs held by US. Letters will also provide that this repurchase guarantee will accrue to any agency of US Gov which subsequently acquires any of these francs from US Army.

3. It is assumed that letters will be exchanged between Minister of Finance and appropriate official of EuCom. Dept of the Army requests your assistance in completing details necessary for this purchase. Suggest you communicate at once with EuCom regarding this matter.

[STATE AND TREASURY]
LOVETT

851.51/10–1747

The French Embassy to the Department of State

[Translation]

WASHINGTON, October 17, 1947.

MEMORANDUM

The exchange of views which is taking place in Washington [1] permits the hope that it will be possible to release for the benefit of France the necessary resources in dollars:

(*a*) to meet the expenditures connected with all contracts concluded prior to September 1, 1947;
(*b*) to pay for current purchases of cereals, coal and fats, up to January 1, 1948.

However, the existing credits do not allow the French Government to authorize at present any new purchases of other essential products, such as raw materials for textiles, petroleum products, nitrate fertilizers, siderurgical products, etc.

Unless a remedy is quickly found for this situation, that is to say if imports of these essential raw materials were to cease completely, extremely serious effects would result therefrom for the French economy. Such effects would last for many months, whatever measures might subsequently be taken, the results of which would only be felt much later.

The table enclosed herewith,[2] the figures of which are amounts in round figures, shows the consequences of the stopping of those imports where new contracts could not be concluded before the end of the year.

---

[1] Reference here is to the conversations which took place in Washington between United States officials and the CEEC delegation headed by Sir Oliver Franks, pp. 445–470.
[2] Not printed.

This table is to be understood in the following manner:

—Column (1) indicates the monthly consumption on the basis of the first semester of 1947.

—Column (2) indicates the amount imported monthly from the dollar zone, on the basis of the first semester of 1947.

—Column (3) comprises the total reserve, that is to say the inventory on hand in France and the orders concluded but which have not yet reached their destination.

—Column (4) indicates the minimum requirements below which it is impossible to continue production in the branch being considered.

—The other columns show the development of available amounts in relation to the average consumption of the industries considered, in the first semester of 1947.

Thus, in fields as important as the petroleum, cotton and rubber industries (which latter industry is strictly dependent on imports of carbon black), the repercussions of the stopping of imports will have a catastrophic character as early as the month of November and of December 1947.

The result thereof, beginning with the month of November 1947, will be a lowering of the total of French industrial production which will reach 25 percent at the beginning of 1948, thus taking that production back to the level of the beginning of 1946. Such reduction would have the following principal consequences:

—Reduction of the continuance of work and large-scale unemployment not only in the industries engaged in the conversion of imported raw materials, but also in those industries utilizing semi-finished or finished products (for example, cotton spinning and weaving, working up of fabrics, etc. . . .)

—Necessity for a return to governmental allocations in branches freed from control,

—Appreciable diminution of agricultural production, resulting from the stoppage of imports of certain raw materials, such as nitrate fertilizers,

—General lowering of the standard of living, which would be particularly dangerous in view of the present social climate.

It might seem possible, with a view to maintaining production at the level of the first semester of 1947, to utilize for a certain time the margin between the present inventory and the minimum requirement.

As a matter of fact, this solution is impracticable. Industrialists would naturally tend to equalize their production and, for so long as they had no assurance of a resumption of imports, to make economical use of their inventories by reducing their activity. Furthermore, even before reduction of inventories to their minimum level, serious disturbances would be produced in the process of production.

The repercussions of the stopping of imports of equipment can only with difficulty be stated in detail: Certain articles of equipment would be found to be useless, due to lack of complementary matériel or spare parts. The result thereof might even be the complete shutting down of certain factories.

This is why it is indispensable that as soon as possible and, in any case, before the first days of December, the French Government should be able to be sure of having at its disposal, until the voting of more extensive credits as a result of the Marshall Plan, sufficient sums in dollars to cover not only its purchases of cereals, wheat and fats, but also the resumption of interrupted contracts for the importation of the principal raw materials.

As has been pointed out above, the sums which are indispensable to France amount in 1948 to a monthly figure of 120 million dollars.

H[ENRI] B[ONNET]

851.00B/10–1747 : Telegram

The Ambassador in France (Caffery) to the Secretary of State

TOP SECRET   PARIS, October 17, 1947—5 p.m.
US URGENT

4485. A number of reliable sources of different political orientation (some having definite reservations about De Gaulle) have separately expressed to me in the past several days their belief that while the Communists would, of course, like to return to the government in order better to prevent French recovery, particularly by sabotaging the Marshall Plan, the Communists are now convinced that because of the rapid hardening of anti-Communist sentiment resulting from the recent open reactivation of the Comintern and their all-out efforts to sabotage French economic recovery, the other political parties will not in the near future permit them to reenter a coalition government. Therefore to carry out Moscow's orders to sabotage at all costs French recovery the Communists are necessarily obliged to adopt more "open and revolutionary" tactics than they previously employed regardless of whether or not such action may harm their standing throughout the country at large.

In speculating on what line the Communists may follow after the municipal elections, the above mentioned sources believe that in view of De Gaulle's growing strength "which will be obvious to all from the election results" the Communists are now convinced that a final showdown with the General is inevitable. The question for the Communists is therefore: "When, tactically, is it most advantageous to the Communist cause for the showdown to occur?"

My informants state they have information which indicates that the Communists now feel that the sooner they join battle with De Gaulle, the greater will be their chance of success. That is, they believe that De Gaulle's RPF, although now solidly established in the country, is still not well organized. Furthermore, the Communists know that at present a considerable number of Frenchmen as well as a number of political leaders of the left, center and moderate right, have certain misgivings about De Gaulle and believe that a middle-of-the-road coalition government (such as now exists) is not only the most desirable formula but still has a chance of succeeding. The Communists reason that no such government can solve France's problem chiefly because no such government has the prestige or authority to take the necessary steps to end Communist sabotage. Therefore they feel that persons who now still prefer a center coalition solution will become progressively disillusioned and several months hence will all flock to De Gaulle. In view of these factors, the Communists have come to the conclusion that the showdown with De Gaulle should come now rather than some months hence when the Gaullist organization will be much more firmly established and the General's following and public support throughout France so great that the Communists would not be able successfully to oppose him.

My sources believe that should this estimate of the Communist views be correct, soon after the elections the Communists will increase the tempo of their already violent attacks against the government (particularly through the use of the CGT in fomenting strikes, etc.) with a view to causing the collapse of the Ramadier Government and creating a situation— "not excluding public disorders"—where De Gaulle will make a "premature" attempt to return to power, an attempt which the Communists (posing as "defenders of the Republic") believe they will be able successfully to oppose through use of the general strike, mass demonstrations of force, disorder, intimidation, etc. By defeating De Gaulle now, the Communists would, of course, eliminate from the political picture the one individual who, because of his prestige, represents the most dangerous rallying point of French anti-Communist forces.

While it is possible that events will not bear out the above predictions on Communist tactics, it would be dangerous at this juncture to discount the possibility of such developments particularly in the light of the very definite hardening of the position the CGT has recently taken against the government. While this CGT action is in part for electoral purposes—particularly to permit the Communists to go on posing as the "sole defenders of the working class"—the Communists know that the CGT action such as the present subway and bus strike is alienating the *petits bourgeois* and middle class. It is possible therefore that the present stiffening of the CGT is designed not only for electoral purposes but is also the prelude to stronger action after the elections to bring about a situation which the Communists believe may favor the destruction of the Socialists and the elimination of De Gaulle.

The Gaullists are of course alive to the dangers inherent in this situation and can be counted on to do everything possible to avoid having their hand forced. It is by no means a foregone conclusion that the Communists would be successful in eliminating De Gaulle even if they were able to force a showdown in the immediate future. Nor is it a foregone conclusion that the present coalition government or one like it, will be unable to cope with the Communist tactics. In this connection the strong and successful stand taken by Ramadier in dealing with the metro strike has strengthened his prestige and consequently his position in recent days. If the Communists overplay their hand an increasing part of the population, which thus far has been rather apathetic, may turn actively against the Communists and by less support enable the government to adopt measures to deal with the Communists which thus far have been deemed politically inexpedient.

I need hardly add that hope of American financial and moral support—and the degree of certainty with which that support can be anticipated—will continue to constitute probably the most important force in strengthening the will to resist among all non-Communist Frenchmen whatever their political persuasion.

Sent Department 4485, repeated Moscow 504, to London by pouch.

CAFFERY

851.51/10–1847 : Telegram

The Ambassador in France (Caffery) to the Secretary of State

SECRET PARIS, October 18, 1947—8 p.m.
US URGENT

4496. Mytel 4493, October 18, 2 p.m.,[1] regarding France's dollar position for the October 1947–March 1948 period raises a number of policy problems concerning which I submit the following comments:

1. The last quarter of 1947. On October 1 forward exchange contract of the Bank of France totalled $627,000,000, of which $232,000,000 represent contracts which come due before January 1, 1948, and therefore must be met from the dollar resources of the exchange stabilization

---

[1] Not printed.

fund before that date. The balance of anticipated expenditures during that period of $333,000,000 represent either spot commitments or noncommercial payments which are made on a spot basis. As reported mytel under reference, funds are available or in sight to meet all of these obligations excepting the sum of $104,000,000. According to the Finance Ministry, the forward exchange contracts and other commitments are so spaced that the exchange stabilization fund can now continue operations until the first of December, assuming that potential assets actually become available before that date. This, therefore, narrows the 1947 problem to a sum of $104,000,000 to be expended in the month of December.

The first alternative approach to this problem would be for the Bank of France to cede to the French Treasury an additional sum in the amount mentioned. This would bring the remaining govt resources down to $340,000,000, or approximately 4% of the bank's note circulation. Such a measure is regarded by observers as dangerous, not only because of the low ratio of reserves to note issue but also because such accession, combined with other inflationary factors, would create an adverse psychological reaction which would make more difficult the avoidance of a runaway situation. It is therefore most desirable to avoid this stopgap solution if at all possible. The psychological impact of this measure would, however, be somewhat tempered if its announcement were to come after the French people were informed that actual Congressional consideration in the US was being given to interim assistance.

The other alternative would appear to be an effort to bridge the gap existing to the end of 1947 thru a combination of decrease of dollar expenditures and increase in dollar revenues. As previously mentioned, possibilities savings this year on imports are negligible because commitments have already been made and must be met. This narrows the expenditure problem to the "other payments" category. Opportunities here seem to be limited to (a) continuation moratorium, transfer blocked US motion picture funds and US bank balances ($15,000,000), (b) possible reduction deficit overseas territories (possible by $5,-000,000 or $10,000,000), (c) moratoria on transfer to Belgium under payments agreement, on transfer of dollars to UK Government and on additional contribution to International Monetary Fund, the three totaling $75,000,000. It is believed that to obtain the consent of the other parties to such moratorium arrangements (to continue until long-term assistance became available) would require the firm diplomatic support of the US. If the measures mentioned were successfully employed, the remaining balance of the 1947 gap would be closed either through the transfer of all or part of the Japanese-held gold which France claims ($37,000,000) or possibly through other sources of which the Department may be aware. I believe this short-term problem should be given immediate consideration and, in the event it does not appear possible to meet the December financial requirement through the stop-gap measures indicated, the French Government should be informed prior to the convening of the National Assembly the middle of November. This would give the French Government the opportunity to prepare the necessary draft legislation for an additional gold transfer.

2. First quarter of 1948 as reported mytel under reference France's anticipated uncovered deficit first quarter 1948 is $355,000,000. In conversations the past week, Bidault has emphasized to me the necessity of assuring a continuous flow of imports into France this winter. I concur in this for both economic and political reasons. As the Department will recall, France's productive effort has been disrupted the past three winters: in 1944–1945 because of the transport bottleneck and war ops; in 1945–1946 because of shortages in raw materials and coal; and in 1946–1947 because of the coal bottleneck. Cumulative effect of these periodic disruptions in industrial activity has been (a) that unemployment, or employment uncertainties, have contributed to social unrest; (b) that the supply of goods available to urban consumers or to farmers to be exchanged for their food products has been very limited; and (c) that France's export program has been handicapped. It appears to me that from an economic standpoint, a disruption in the tempo of production this winter may well cost us more dollars over the period of long-term financial assistance. In the political field, a subnormal level of production and employment would facilitate the work of the Communists and help them to capitalize on dissatisfaction. I do not mean to imply by this that we are not faced, under the best of circumstances, with a trying period in the French labor situation this winter. I am convinced, however, that a continued high level of employment, coupled with a 250 gram bread ration, which I am pleased to note the Department has included in its calculations, will minimize the possibilities of success of the Communists' direct action activities.

Furthermore, achievement of the foregoing would provide a firmer basis than presently exists for the French Government to adopt a stronger, more effective economic program.

The conclusion reached from mytel under reference is that France will need external assistance in the neighborhood of $350,000,000 in the first quarter 1948. In order to assure a continuous flow of essential imports, it would be highly desirable for the French Government to know what assistance we are going to provide before beginning of that period. (I know only too well the difficulties in the way of this.) This would permit (a) the Bank of France to engage itself in forward exchange contracts with the knowledge that the dollars would be available when payments became due, and (b) create enough confidence among the New York banks and large commercial companies in the US so that they would provide the credit lines and short-term credits which are the actual dollar counterpart of the Bank's forward contracts.

3. Reciprocal French obligation. From my numerous conversations the past two months with members visiting Congressional committees, I have reached the conclusion that they view with some scepticism the French will or ability to stage an economic comeback. I anticipate that in Committee hearings and on the floor of the House and Senate, French assertions regarding their recovery program will be subjected to close scrutiny and analysis. It seems to me, therefore, that we are entirely justified in arranging here in the near future a series of informal talks with the French Government, at both the policy and technical levels, to review in some detail the current and prospective plans which the French Government has in mind to meet its commitments under the initial report of the Conference on European Economic Cooperation. Such exploratory talks can serve the triple purpose of (*a*) obtaining precise information of the recovery program for Departmental and Congressional use, (*b*) to make the French realize that we are serious in expecting the highest possible standard of performance and (*c*) to provide a factual basis for such friendly suggestions as the Department might want to make. It is my thought that this exploration would be concentrated in the four fields which are essential to French economic delivery [*recovery*] and to a progressive reduction in France's dollar deficit; i.e.

(1) Return to prewar levels of agricultural production.
(2) Internal financial stabilization.
(3) Rapid expansion volume of French exports to dollar areas.
(4) Increase in coal production.

I would appreciate the receipt by telegram of the Department's views in regard to the foregoing.[2]

CAFFERY

---

[2] No reply to this message has been found.

851.00/10–2147 : Telegram

The Acting Secretary of State to the Embassy in France

RESTRICTED
US URGENT

WASHINGTON, October 21, 1947—7 p.m.

4001. Press reaction here on the whole sympathetic to de Gaulle's "victory"[1] and anti-communist aspect of vote invariably stressed.

---

[1] On October 19 the Rassemblement du Peuple Français (RPF), headed by General de Gaulle, won 40 percent of the votes in nationwide municipal elections and displaced the Communist Party as the largest in France.

N.Y. Times calls it "a victory for the western world as opposed to Russian totalitarianism and its communist fifth columns". Much concern reflected over effects of de Gaulle's return on French production, possibility of labor unrest, etc. Allegation that U.S. Govt "not happy" over de Gaulle vote frequently appears. Some editorial speculation over effect of vote on Marshall plan.

LOVETT

851.51/10–2247 : Telegram

The Ambassador in France (Caffery) to the Secretary of State

SECRET   PARIS, October 22, 1947—5 p.m.

4532. The Finance Ministry today conveyed to me the following additional information regarding France's dollar crisis, reported in my telegrams number 4493 [1] and 4496, October 18:

1. Meeting of the Council of the Bank of France was held this week at suggestion of Finance Minister Schuman to consider problem finding dollar exchange to finance additional coal imports during November and December. Coal import program second semester 1947 provided for shipments from US 7.2 million tons, of which 1.7 million to be shipped November and December. French supply ministries have now learned it might be possible to ship 3 million tons under available allocations during those two months. Problem is where to find the additional dollars 26 million required for FOB plus freight costs this additional quantity.

2. No decision has been reached regarding foregoing and decision will probably not be made until beginning of November. This decision will be a part of broader policy question whether to cede additional gold to stabilization fund from remaining reserve Bank of France.

3. Both Finance Ministry and Bank of France are inclined to believe that additional cession, other than the technical one [that?] will be necessary to transfer restituted German looted gold from Bank of France to stabilization fund, would be extremely dangerous, vis-à-vis inflationary trends. They are, therefore, exploring all possibilities stopgap measures mentioned section one my telegram 4496. If combination of measures proves sufficient to meet existing anticipated gap, additional coal imports probably will not be made. Latest information available to Finance Ministry from Washington indicates only remote possibility of obtaining any Japanese-held gold this year. Finance Ministry is exploring, however, possibilities (a) of obtaining increase in ceiling Belgo–Franco payments agreement, which would automatically eliminate need additional dollar payments to Belgium this

---

[1] Telegram 4493 not printed.

year and (*b*) possibility UK waiving dollar settlement item five, section three, my telegram 4493. Finance Ministry remarked that if UK would go ahead with earlier tentative commitment to make convertible into dollars 15 million pounds of French-held sterling, this measure, combined with others mentioned above, would just about bridge the December dollar gap.

4. Finance Ministry concerned over prospective hiatus in commodity arrivals first months 1948 due to inability to place orders closing months 1947. It believes, however, that gap can be reduced once there is definitive affirmative knowledge concerning US financial assistance first quarter 1948. Such knowledge would permit Bank of France to resume issuance forward exchange contracts even though at the moment no dollars were actually earmarked in the exchange stabilization fund for their liquidation.

Tomlinson has seen this telegram and requests that Treasury be informed.

CAFFERY

Editorial Note

For documentation relating to the convening by President Truman of a special session of the Congress to deal with the problems of rising prices and the economic crisis in western Europe, see pages 470 ff. In an address broadcast on October 24 the President stated that the "most imminent danger exists in France and in Italy".

851.51/10–2447 : Telegram

The Ambassador in France (Caffery) to the Secretary of State

SECRET PARIS, October 24, 1947—3 p.m.

4569. With reference my telegrams 4532, October 22, 4496 and 4493,[1] October 18, Finance Ministry has informed me that Cabinet has made following decisions regarding revision import programs:

1. Coal import plan for November and December will remain at 1.7 million tons from US November and December, but 1.3 million of total will be concentrated in November shipments with hope that December shipments can be expanded if external assistance is forthcoming by that time.

2. At insistence of Ministry of Industrial Production that measures were necessary to keep refineries and industries operating, additional imports of $13.6 million were authorized for crude petroleum and $12.4 million additional imports variety of industrial materials, medical supplies and certain essential supplies for overseas territories.

---

[1] Telegram 4493 not printed.

3. Above decisions raised prospective December [?] [2] deficit to $129 million. Finance Ministry is exploring or negotiating on following possibilities for meeting deficit: (*a*) Continuation moratorium motion picture payments; (*b*) deferral monetary fund payment; (*c*) deferral dollar payment to UK Government; (*d*) increase credit ceiling Belgo-Franco payments agreement to avoid further dollar transfers to Belgium; (*e*) possibility UK might agree to make small amount of French-held sterling convertible into dollars; (*f*) additional stopgap administrative assistance from US including availability $37 million Japanese-held gold, Exim Bank assistance and Commodity Credit Corporation assistance.

4. Finance Ministry has been informed by French banks that New York Banks are increasingly restricting their credit lines, which further complicated situation.

5. Finance Ministry and Bank of France continue to hope that new transfer of gold may be avoided but it appears that a large number of the possibilities listed above would have to become realities if this were to prove to be the case.

CAFFERY

---

[2] Query appears in source text.

851.51/10–2447

The Ambassador in France (Caffery) to the Secretary of State

CONFIDENTIAL   PARIS, October 24, 1947.

No. 9801

SIR: I have the honor to transmit herewith a summary of the conversation between Foreign Minister Bidault and members of the Senate Appropriations Committee and of the Revercomb Sub-Committee, on October 17, 1947.[1]

Respectfully yours,   JEFFERSON CAFFERY

[Enclosure]

SUMMARY OF CONVERSATION BETWEEN FOREIGN MINISTER BIDAULT AND MEMBERS OF THE SENATE APPROPRIATIONS COMMITTEE AND OF THE REVERCOMB SUB-COMMITTEE

FRANCE'S TWO PROBLEMS

(a) *The Immediate Financial Crisis:*

Mr. Bidault said that he was the first to deplore the lateness of France's SOS appeal to the USA, and that it had not been possible

---

[1] Chapman Revercomb, of West Virginia, was chairman of a subcommittee of the Judiciary Committee, United States Senate, to study problems of immigration and displaced persons.

to give more warning. "Nevertheless," he added, "it is essential that we not be allowed to be asphyxiated." He said that, while he had "no signed documents or positive promises" to this effect, he was "morally certain" that the United States would find means to assist France during the immediate crisis, and thus permit her to reach the second stage when Congress shall decide on the nature and extent of long-term assistance, based on Secretary Marshall's proposals and on the findings of the 16-power conference.[2] "At the present time," said Bidault, "we are being literally strangled, and I am very specially grateful in this emergency to all the Americans of both political parties whom I saw in Washington, and who were kind enough not to make me feel the humiliation of my position as a beggar for my country."

(b) *Longer Term Assistance to Cover the Three or Four Years Necessary for France's Rehabilitation:*

Mr. Bidault said that the fundamental situation in Europe could be compared to a huge wager between the Communist and anti-Communist forces. The non-Communists, including France and himself, have bet that the Marshall Plan will succeed, and that it will not mean "Germany first", Germany of course to be included but "not first". On the other hand, the Communists have wagered that Germany would "come first" and that the overall plan would be a failure. "I am sure we will win", said Bidault, "but, of course, we can't do so alone."

Referring to the long-term assistance which France will need and to the important sums which this will involve, the Foreign Minister reminded the Senators that France in the past had made considerable loans to other nations and that she had not been repaid. Without giving any assurances of repayment, he said: "This time I hope the United States can make their effort with complete peace of mind that we will do our best." Referring to the plan of European cooperation as an integral part of any long-term United States plan of assistance to Europe, Mr. Bidault declared that France had agreed on her own behalf to the necessary "production commitments", as well as to the other commitments necessary to European and to her own rehabilitation. He mentioned in particular France's efforts to arrive at a customs union with Italy and added: "We and the other 15 nations (of the CEEC) have done what we could and we shall continue to do so."

The Economic Rehabilitation of Germany and Its Achievement "hand in hand" with Europe's

Mr. Bidault said that he understood full well the necessity of rehabilitating Germany's economy "which was an essential part of Eu-

---

[2] For documentation relating to the Marshall Plan and to the 16-power conference held in Paris in July to draw up a cooperative program of European recovery, see pp. 197 ff.

rope's". Nevertheless, he said he could not quite subscribe to the "hand in hand" theory. Germany has coal, France has iron ore. "I think it more appropriate that Germany's coal come first to France's iron ore rather than vice versa." He pointed out that the granting of a priority to Germany's blast furnaces would make it necessary for the Germans to purchase iron ore abroad, be it French or Swedish, and that this will be either a commercial (foreign exchange requirement by Germany) or a sentimental detriment (unfavorable effect on French public opinion). Mr. Bidault begged his listeners to trust the French and "not assimilate them to Germans".

With stop-gap assistance, together with eventual Congressional action on interim funds, can France maintain herself in a sound position free of Communist domination, so that she would be able to participate actively in any Marshall Plan?

The Foreign Minister answered that he wanted to be completely frank, and that the Senators "had come at the worst possible moment". Without wanting to minimize the Communist peril in any way, he did, however, express his personal conviction that regardless of the means which they might have to employ, the anti-Communist forces in France were bound to come out on top: "I don't know what will happen. I have no idea as to the form which coming events shall take. I don't know whether I will long be at this desk. As a matter of fact, I don't think it will be for very long, but, of one thing I am certain, and that is that France shall not be governed by the Communist Party. With reasonable assistance from the United States, and with the help of the mistakes which the Communists make on the internal French level as well as on the international plane, the French anti-Communist forces shall triumph."

Are not the campaigns waged by France in Indochina and Madagascar serious drains on France's manpower, as well as on her national economy?

Mr. Bidault answered that, of course, these campaigns were painful in every respect. "However", he added, "if France's pacification efforts do not succeed, Indochina will have a Communist government, and perhaps Madagascar as well." He added that the Madagascar campaign was "finished" but did not attempt to minimize the difficulties facing France in Indochina, "where we will be very generous with those who deserve it but where it is difficult to be generous with assassins". He concluded with the following statement: "Don't forget, gentlemen, that it is our main desire to finish with these costly and distasteful campaigns."

What incentive is there for the workers to produce as much as possible?

The Foreign Minister answered that in France, as elsewhere, the workers' output was not wholly dependent on governmental decisions.

He did, however, point out that, to his knowledge, France was the only "truly democratic country with a 48-hour work week". He added that other conditions were necessary, such as confidence in the national currency and confidence in general. Concerning short-term confidence, this was dependent on the internal political situation which "is rapidly coming to a climax. Concerning long-term confidence, this is largely dependent on foreign aid and on the willingness of foreign friends to help pull France out of a temporary quagmire. With confidence re-established, the time might come when France might have the wherewithal to pay back."

As one of France's major difficulties seems to be due to the farmers' lack of confidence in the currency, what is the French Government doing to induce the farmer to part with his surplus crops? Are goods being offered instead of cash?

Mr. Bidault said that while "farmers always complain", this year their complaints were justified in view of an exceptionally bad crop year (see Mr. Ramadier's full explanations on this point). He added that the black market had "probably shocked his visitors", but asked them to remember that during the long years of German occupation, non-compliance with the laws of the land had been preached as a patriotic duty: ["]We disobeyed the laws upon advice from London and from the United States. To re-establish a reign of law is difficult when people have become used to disobedience and to do so rapidly we would need a dictatorship". As to payment for farm produce in kind, Mr. Bidault said that it was difficult, in view of the general shortage "of everything". He also pointed out that often "when 10 percent is lacking, it is just as if everything was lacking". Nevertheless, he said that the French Government had made a great effort to earmark as large a percentage as possible of consumer goods for the peasants and that, as a matter of fact, industrial workers and the white-collar classes were jealous of the peasants, feeling they were unduly favored.

Is it correct that, if the United States agrees to help France now, France would be willing to work out conditions leading toward repayment?

Mr. Bidault agreed that he had said "something of the kind", but did not answer the question directly. He indicated that there should be "a business basis for the deal which would be mutually advantageous for both parties". He, furthermore, asked that in making this deal, i.e.—aid to France, "which of course would have political implications", there be no political conditions imposed in view of the unfavorable psychological reaction of the French public.

If Italy goes Communist, what effect will it have on France?

The Foreign Minister refused to admit that Italian political developments could have influence in France. "On the contrary", he said, "I believe that political events in France will have an influence in Italy." "In any event," added Bidault, "I have reasons to believe that the fate of the Communist Party will be the same in both countries."

With the world divided into two blocs, shouldn't Germany be rehabilitated, so that instead of joining the Russians, she will join the Western bloc?

Bidault answered that we should have a better idea of German developments towards the end of 1947, after the London conference [3] and said: "After all, when you think of the numerous times we have been invaded by the Germans, we haven't treated them so badly." He stressed the fact that, because of these invasions and of the Frenchman's traditional fear of Germany, France "needed to be reassured on this point".

What consequences do you think the recent re-establishment of the Comintern will have?

Bidault answered that, in his opinion, this development was only superficial and that, in fact, "it changes nothing".

Would France be satisfied if American aid was in the form of goods instead of an unrestricted loan in dollars?

Mr. Bidault answered that France only wanted dollars to spend in the U.S., and that these dollars would "not stick to France's fingers". He said: "As long as we can have the goods which we need, it doesn't matter what form the transaction takes."

Mr. Bidault concluded not only with an expression of thanks for the Senators' interest but also with the plea that his frankness should not be misunderstood: "I am convinced that ours is a just cause, and it is whole-heartedly that I entrust it to you."

---

[3] The reference is presumably to the 5th session of the Council of Foreign Ministers, at London, November 25–December 15, 1947.

851.00/10–2447 : Telegram

The Acting Secretary of State to the Embassy in France

TOP SECRET   WASHINGTON, October 25, 1947—3 p.m.
US URGENT

4071. Personal for the Ambassador from Armour [1] and Hickerson. We are dismayed by implications Palewski's [2] remarks contained your

---

[1] Norman Armour, Assistant Secretary of State for Political Affairs.
[2] Gaston Palewski, member of the RPF and close associate of General de Gaulle.

4576 Oct 24.[3] We appreciate that Palewski may in this conversation have been expressing only his own views but should these represent the motivating forces underlying any return of de Gaullist group to power in France, we fear the consequences. The press comment in this country while welcoming the anti-Communist polarization of political forces in France has nevertheless expressed extreme concern lest dictatorial methods imputed to de Gaulle will mean the substitution of a dictatorship of the Right for parliamentary methods. Should de Gaulle insist on constitutional changes and concentration of executive powers in his hands alone under the form of full powers as a condition to return to the govt, this will be interpreted here as the first step in this direction, gravely increasing the dangers of civil war and be so reflected widely by the American press thus further complicating the question of assistance to France.

The following represent our preliminary views with regard to the situation created by the municipal elections in France. You may use these in your discretion to persons close to Gen de Gaulle including André Malraux [4] who we hope may be helpful in this connection.

It is vital to the interest of the US that the non-Communist polarization which may have to be centered around Gen de Gaulle succeed. While it is too early to determine the parliamentary and constitutional devices by which the Gen can translate his plurality at the municipal elections into the leadership of a govt, there is little doubt that he will be under increasing pressure from his adherents to return to power in the near future. Assuming the Gen takes power, it is well to review the principal obstacles to his governing effectively.

1. The first and most important of these is French organized labor, which is Communist dominated and even whose non-Communist elements have been in the past flatly anti-de Gaulle. It is not yet known here how many working class votes went to the Gen, but he has made no overtures to that class. A great deal depends on his success in persuading or as a last resort compelling French organized labor, which holds the key to France production and hence to the success or failure of the European Recovery Program. The position of the Socialist Party in this connection is of the greatest importance.

2. To French Communists, whose assigned target is the sabotage of the European Recovery Program, inflation represents a means to that end less dangerous than, if not an alternative to, a halt in production.

---

[3] Not printed; it reported that Palewski had stated that if de Gaulle were asked to form a new government he would insist that the Assembly vote him "full powers" for a specified period to allow him to proceed immediately with the administrative, financial, and economic reforms that were necessary for the welfare of France (851.00/10–2447).

[4] Chief of the press section in the de Gaulle movement.

The Communist dominated CGT has just announced demands for a new round of substantial wage increases for labor, which can only give new impetus to the inflationary spiral, and yet which in less extreme terms all French labor must regard as legitimate in the face of a retail price rise of 26% since July.

3. The promise to maintain public order is one of Gen de Gaulle's strongest appeals, yet production stoppages arising out of Communist inspired or supported strikes for increased wages may bring about disorders not easily suppressed and which if seized upon by either the Communists or Gen de Gaulle as a signal for a showdown, may lead to bloodshed.

It has been clear since the liberation that the isolation and ostracism of the French Communists was essential if France was to remain in the Western orbit. It was equally clear that politically speaking the break must come to the left of or at the very least in the middle of the Socialist Party. Translated into labor terms, the healthy elements of organized labor must be kept in the non-Communist camp. Otherwise the tiny production margin of the fragile French economy would vanish and the ensuing civil disturbances would take on the aspects of class war.

De Gaulle's plurality reflects a thirst to be governed which has caused many of his new followers to abandon their moderate leaders. This thirst undoubtedly penetrates deep into the Socialist and labor union camp but has not been translated into downright adherence because of traditional and doctrinal reservations concerning basic social and political rights. It would seem clearly the part of wisdom for the Gen in the first instance to allay the susceptibilities and suspicions of this vital section of the French public by accepting power, if power is offered him, within the imperfect framework of the present constitution, leaving for the future the decision to insist on constitutional reform in the event that pressures for such reform do not spontaneously develop.

It seems certain that public and congressional opinion here will judge the Gen in the above light. [Armour and Hickerson.]

LOVETT

851.00/10–2647 : Telegram

The Ambassador in France (Caffery) to the Secretary of State

SECRET   PARIS, October 26, 1947— 2 p.m.

4598. Palewski told me last night that De Gaulle has no desire whatsoever to become President of the Council of Ministers until next spring and hopes he will not be forced to do so by Communist maneuvers in the meantime. I warned him that any steps on the General's part headed for anything approaching a dictatorship or looking like they were approaching a dictatorship would be very badly received indeed in the United States and might put an end to our efforts to come to the relief of France. He professed to be in agreement. He declared that De Gaulle understands that it is extremely important for him to capture the goodwill of non-Communist labor, and that he will try to do so.

Palewski said also that when De Gaulle does come into power he will probably offer the Finance Ministry to either Reynaud [1] or Mendès-France; [2] he will ask Ramadier to remain in the government and probably Robert Schuman also. A Cabinet position will probably be offered to Giacobbi [3] and Pleven [4] must be taken care of also. Bidault and Teitgen will not be offered jobs.

I told Palewski that a good many people were apprehensive lest De Gaulle put an end to the present French government's efforts at democratic reform in North Africa. Palewski denied this vigorously. I said they were apprehensive also as to what his attitude to Indochina might be. Palewski alleged that De Gaulle is broadminded there too. I said they are apprehensive as to De Gaulle's attitude to Germany and that he might cause us a lot of trouble. Again Palewski alleged De Gaulle desired only to cooperate with us there too.

I am not inferring that Palewski meant everything he said, but it is interesting to note that he said these things.

CAFFERY

---

[1] Paul Reynaud, formerly French Premier.
[2] Pierre Mendès-France, formerly French Minister of National Economy.
[3] Paul Giacobbi, formerly French Minister of Colonies.
[4] René Pleven, formerly French Minister of National Economy.

851.00/10–2947 : Telegram

The Ambassador in France (Caffery) to the Secretary of State

TOP SECRET   PARIS, October 29, 1947—4 p.m.

4635. For Armour and Hickerson from the Ambassador. I welcomed your 4071, October 25 which parallels so closely our own thinking here and which gave me authoritative backing for the things which I have been saying to some of De Gaulle's people. I shall hammer away at them at every opportunity.

I have not seen De Gaulle personally since the elections, because such a meeting would be publicized by the Gaullists for their own ends and misinterpreted by Ramadier, Bidault and other members of present government. I cannot therefore be absolutely certain that the views which Palewski has expressed to me are shared in full by the

General, but in view of their past relationship and the fact that Palewski's prognostications have usually been confirmed, I think we must go on the assumption that they are substantially correct in the present instance. The statement issued by De Gaulle also tends to bear them out.

I could not agree more with your analysis of the principal obstacles to De Gaulle's governing effectively. But I think that however dangerous the constitutional issue may be, it will continue to rank high on the list of his objectives, for this question lies at the very basis of his philosophy of government and is a matter on which he has repeatedly and publicly expressed the strongest views. For the accomplishment of the task which he will have to face if he assumes power, some revision of the constitution may, as a matter of hard fact, be necessary. I think too that De Gaulle would have some justification for recalling that the present constitution received the affirmative support of only 30 odd percent of the voters, many of whom now favor revision and in fact only voted "yes" last year because they felt that any constitution at that time was better than none.

To my mind the constitutional question as such is probably secondary, at least at this stage to the problem of De Gaulle's relationship with the Socialists, many of whom can be expected at this time to oppose at least such constitutional changes as strike at basic liberties. In this connection, the manner in which De Gaulle acts will be as important as what he does. As I have already reported, the Socialists are in a key position, although torn by the tremendous pressure now being directed against them from the right and from the left. If De Gaulle endeavors to destroy the Socialist Party he may succeed, but he would undoubtedly draw to his camp far fewer followers by such tactics (and would force the rest into an unwished for alliance with the Communists) than he would if he endeavored to reach a working agreement with them. For De Gaulle it is not merely a question of gaining the support of certain Socialist parliamentary leaders, but also the question whether those leaders would be in a position to swing their followers into line. In particular, he must obtain the support of Socialist leaders who are backed by anti-Communist trade unionists.

In view of De Gaulle's temperament and past record, I fear that in spite of these considerations he will favor a frontal attack on the Socialists. The victory which he has just achieved has unquestionably gone to the heads of his followers and cannot be expected to have been without effect on his own thinking.

At any rate this is, I think, the key question at the moment and the one on which I am exerting every particle of influence I can.

I think we have all shared the view that if it could succeed in establishing its authority a coalition government made up of middle of the road parties, such as we have had under Ramadier, guaranteed the best hope for working out in the long run the enormous economic and political problems of France on a democratic basis. For reasons which it is useless recapitulate here, it is now inescapable that this experiment has failed. When faced with the dilemma of De Gaulle or Communism, there is no doubt that the majority of the French people will pick De Gaulle. I assume that in our own interest we will do the same, even though that choice must boil down to the lesser of two evils, since after elimination of middle parties failure of De Gaulle would leave road open for Communists. I think that we should do everything in our power to lessen the shock and to eliminate or reduce the very real dangers which will accompany the return of De Gaulle to power, whether next week or six months hence, and which are a matter of grave concern to many Frenchmen as well as to ourselves. Not the least among the things which need to be done in this connection is for De Gaulle to separate himself from reactionary rightists who have climbed on his bandwagon.

In conclusion, I feel it necessary to add that while De Gaulle may have learned some lessons during the past two years, I think we would be indulging in wishful thinking if we concluded that he had undergone any fundamental change. In the circumstances, I think we must be prepared to anticipate very real difficulties in dealing with him on specific questions; almost certainly in respect to Germany, and very probably in respect to Indochina and North Africa.

CAFFERY

851.00/10-3047 : Telegram

The Ambassador in France (Caffery) to the Secretary of State

SECRET   PARIS, October 30, 1947—7 p.m.

4656. Today's *Humanité* publishes full text of Thorez speech yesterday at meeting of Communist Central Committee (my 4646, October 30 [1]). Speech openly announced CPF transition from tactics employed when it posed as a "government" party to new sharpened methods of struggle and indicates as well abandonment by Communists of serious pretense of patriotism except "defense of France against American imperialism". Speech may be considered as a declaration of loyalty toward Soviet Union and of intention to fight for democratic Government mentioned in party appeal of October 28. Thorez surveys international situation along lines set by Zhdanov [2] and

---

[1] Not printed.
[2] Andrey Alexandrovich Zhdanov, member of the Politburo of the Central Committee of the Communist Party of the Soviet Union.

nine-party conference[3] and in particular savagely condemns American drive for "world domination for which they fought the last war" and the policy of "imperialistic aggression" which the US opposes to the "traditional policy of peace of the Soviet Union which is based on the coexistence of capitalism and socialism for a long period to come". Discussing the situation in France he emphasizes (a) "consolidation of labor and democratic forces around CPF" and (b) disturbing progress and regrouping of reactionary forces around RPF". Main thesis advanced by speech is "American intention to colonize France" which is statedly being accomplished with aid of Socialist leaders (Blum and Mollet) by means of American penetration into French industry and intervention in French domestic affairs. Thorez cites as examples American efforts to oust Communists from Government, aid to parochial schools and establishment in Paris of a bureau "especially entrusted with organization of struggle against the CGT".

Serious self-criticism is likewise prominently featured in speech which dwells on "errors committed by party militants" including failure of Central Committee sufficiently soon "to note and define regrouping of imperialist and anti-democratic forces under direction and for profit of US". According to Thorez, such Central Committee errors have led to "indecision and vacillation" in National Assembly Communist group which opposed "electoral law" with insufficient vigor and failed to vote negatively on questions where such vote was imperative. The hesitations and indecision of the Central Committee and Communist Parliamentary group "retarded the rapid mobilization of the Democratic and Workers masses against the Ramadier Government and its nefarious policy".

Condemnation by Thorez of "sensitiveness of party members toward Socialist and other accusations" that Communist party is prejudicing French recovery, particularly the possibility of obtaining American credits, is of considerable interest as indicating existence of discontent of followers and members with line Communists have been ordered to take. Thorez allusion to opportunist tendencies manifested within party "underestimating labor forces and fearing mass movement" while fully in accord with Zhdanov's report is a clear indication of a planned intensification of "mass" tactics.

---

[3] At a conference held at Wilizia Gora, Poland, September 22–23, 1947, representatives of the Communist parties of Yugoslavia, Bulgaria, Rumania, Hungary, Poland, the Soviet Union, France, Czechoslovakia, and Italy agreed to establish the Communist Information Bureau (Cominform), which was to organize the exchange of information and the possible coordination of activities of the various Communist parties. For documents regarding the founding of the Cominform, see Margaret Carlyle (ed.), *Documents on International Affairs, 1947–1948*, issued under the auspices of the Royal Institute of International Affairs (London, New York, Toronto, Oxford University Press, 1952), pp. 122 ff.

Speech discusses failure of Front Populaire and errors in resistance movements and presupposes creation of a massive Communist led front composed of the forces of the working class, democracy and peace supported by "committee to defend the republic" in all towns and villages (my 4657 [4]) and by unions of workers in all branches of industry to safeguard the republic and protect such industry against American "enslavement plans".

Sent Department 4656, repeated London 820, Moscow 515 and by pouch to Rome, Berlin.

CAFFERY

---

[4] Not printed.

851.00/11–347 : Telegram

The Ambassador in France (Caffery) to the Secretary of State

SECRET　　　　　　　　　　　　　　PARIS, November 3, 1947—6 p.m.

4699. According to sources exercising influence in Socialist and Trade Union movement here "mea culpa" report delivery by Thorez to Central Committee of his party (mytel 4656, October 30) may be regarded as culminating point in series of recent European events which have shaken non-Communist left to extent that even some fellow-travellers and few rank and file Communists (not militants) not to speak of naive and opportunist Socialists, are beginning to take open position against Communist Party. This attitude is in keeping with character of majority of French who are fundamentally nationalist and sincerely patriotic. Thorez' most recent confession of complete Communist Party subservience to Kremlin, as set forth in his statement, has caused many Frenchmen to recall signature of Molotov-Ribbentrop pact in 1939 and Communist efforts, immediately thereafter, to sabotage French war effort against Nazi Germany.

While this latest case of "betrayal of France" is not so obvious and while thus far no prominent Communists have denounced their party, sources under reference insist that Thorez' speech already has produced important repercussions in leftist circles, especially Socialist Party and hesitant elements in CGT. In completely isolating itself on parliamentary, resistance and political level Communist Party is also incurring risk of furnishing ample ammunition to growing anti-Communist resistance in labor movement, particularly among miners, railway and TT[*PTT*] workers. Now, as never before, explain sources, is the moment for independent Trade Unionists to strike hard on labor front and they claim that if existing network of labor opposition within as well as without CGT were adequately financed the isolation and eventual defeat of Communists in labor movement could be effected probably within next year. As indication of way wind is now blowing trustworthy informant reports that last week 400 resignations from France-USSR (Friends of Soviet Union) took place in fourteenth Paris *arrondissement* alone.

According to above sources, Moscovite leadership of party here anticipates that many fainthearted members will fall by wayside as in 1939. Even prior to Warsaw conference it had begun to replace, especially in provinces, hesitant secretaries of cells, sections and federations by hardened Stalinists dispatched from Paris headquarters. Now on defensive the party is tightening its ranks and falling back on its solid core of members who operate directly under guidance of "illegal bureau and who probably do not exceed more than 10,000 militants". Should these Soviet patriots lose the machinery of CGT they would be deprived of their greatest weapon.

Sent Department 4699, repeated to Moscow as 517 and by pouch to London, Berlin and Rome.

CAFFERY

851.5151/11–847 : Telegram

The Ambassador in France (Caffery) to the Secretary of State

TOP SECRET   PARIS, November 8, 1947—1 p.m.

4797. Martin, President Exim Bank, summarized to me as follows talks I arranged for him with Ramadier, Schumann [*Schuman?*], Monnet,[1] Monick:[2]

1. French indicated intention withhold change in franc rate until interim aid in hand (Embtel 4568[3]). (Prospective rate not mentioned but Martin indicated to me that 300 francs to dollar would seem reasonable at this time.)

2. French made half-hearted query whether Exim Bank would consider loan 300 million dollars against 104 million dollars from gold pot[4] and unliquidated securities formerly held by French nationals as security. (Embassy's information indicates value latter far short necessary amount make total security sufficient cover 300 million dollar loan.) Martin replied such operation not normal to his bank, indicated

---

[1] Jean Monnet of the French Planning Commission on October 2, 1947, was made chairman of a special "balance sheet commission".
[2] Emmanuel Monick, Governor of the Bank of France.
[3] Not printed.
[4] The "gold pot" principle "recognizes that the countries whose gold was wrongfully taken by Germany" during World War II "are entitled to its restitution". For explanation of the principle, see *Foreign Relations*, The Conference of Berlin (The Potsdam Conference), 1945, vol. II, p. 938, footnote 4.

would not consider request favorably if made formally and suggested gold and securities be used to meet current French dollar needs. Schumann indicated French would so use gold and securities when liquidation feasible.

3. French intend meet end December obligation to Exim Bank.

CAFFERY

851.51 FC 51/11–1747

The French Ambassador (Bonnet) to the Secretary of State

[Translation [1]]

WASHINGTON, November 17, 1947.

MR. SECRETARY OF STATE: For some time now, the French Government has been seeking to mobilize all the resources at its disposal in order to use them in reviving the French economy. It desires to take every measure that will enable it to effect this mobilization as completely and quickly as possible, so as to make its full contribution at this time when the sixteen nations represented at the Conference of Paris have just submitted their proposals for a program for the economic recovery of Europe and for assistance from the United States during the next few years.

Under present French law all French citizens, whether private individuals or companies, residing in France or in the French overseas territories, must declare to the French Government all their assets abroad, including assets in the United States.

Under an agreement between the French Minister and the United States Secretary of the Treasury, a procedure has been set up whereby these assets may be exempted from the restrictions imposed by the Foreign Funds Control Office upon presentation of a certificate issued by the French Government. Unfortunately these arrangements have resulted in the declaration of only part of the assets in the United States that are thought to be owned by French citizens, and supplementary measures must be taken to mobilize these assets completely and make the corresponding dollars available for the recovery of the French economy.

It is possible that the United States Government may not have considered itself in a position to give the French Government the names of French citizens owning assets in the United States, because this would violate the confidential nature of the information obtained on this subject.

---

[1] Translation made by the Division of Language Services, Department of State.

Consequently, the French Government has carefully examined various plans whereby the mobilization of the assets in question might be effected without disclosing any confidential information. As the first step toward that end, the competent departments of the French Government have prepared and are about to issue a supplementary decree providing for the immediate, automatic transfer to the French Government of title to foreign assets consisting of current accounts receivable, claims, securities, gold, and bank notes, in a number of foreign countries, including the United States, and now belonging to French citizens residing in France or in the overseas territories. The French Government thinks that the mobilization of these assets could be greatly facilitated through joint action of the Government of the United States and the French Government, and to that end it proposes a program of joint action that would comprise the following principal measures:

(1) Under this proposal the President of the United States, acting through the competent United States government department and by virtue of the Trading With the Enemy Act,[2] would order any person in the United States holding assets that belong to French citizens residing in France or in the French overseas territories to transfer those assets to a representative of the French Government. It is understood that this order could be carried out without revealing the names of the present owners of the assets, thereby preserving the confidential nature of the operations which made the preparation of the list of assets possible. It was pointed out to me that the Presidential order could be put into effect through simplified procedures which would make its prompt execution possible.

(2) The French Government would agree with the Government of the United States to take such measures as might be considered necessary for the protection, if need be, of the United States interests by reason of the possible portion of enemy interest in such assets.

(3) The present owners could claim an indemnification in francs under French law now in force. The French Government would also agree to pay in dollars such legitimate claims to these assets as might be submitted by creditors of the present owners in the United States.

I wish to stress two aspects of this proposal which seem particularly important. In the first place, the proposal relates only to assets in the United States owned by French citizens residing in France and does not affect other assets which any other persons might possess in the United States. Furthermore, the proposal would not result in the seizure or confiscation of assets without compensation, since the present owners could claim reimbursement in francs under the provisions of the French laws in force.

I am informed that the implementation of the foregoing joint-action program would result in quickly placing the dollar assets of French

---

[2] Approved October 6, 1917; 40 Stat. 411.

nationals at France's disposal, so that they might be used in reviving the French economy. The rapidity with which the full benefit of this program could be obtained would, of course, be increased if arrangements could be made to open a credit through the Export-Import Bank or some other competent American governmental department on the basis of security or a pledge relating to the assets that would be transferred to the representatives of the French Government.

I have the honor to submit this program for joint action to the Government of the United States for examination as a group of practical measures designed to aid French recovery and help to re-establish French production in such a way that France may make its most effective contribution to the expansion of a free world economy, which is one of the common objectives of our two Governments.

I am happy to have this opportunity to renew to Your Excellency the assurances of my very high consideration.

H. BONNET

840.50 Recovery/11–1547 : Telegram

The Acting Secretary of State to the Embassy in France

SECRET   WASHINGTON, November 24, 1947—5 p.m.

4319. Reur 4905 and 4927 and Depts. 4206.[1] French presentation of interim aid requirements was based on plan for Oct 1947–March 1948 period which, if completely implemented, would have had triple effect of eliminating Bank of France's "short" position of $260 million, operating all new purchases for period on cash basis, and of enabling France to reduce some of her obligations to neighboring countries.

Although this program had much merit from the standpoint of improving France's international financial position, it was clearly impossible for Dept to request an emergency grant-in-aid from Cong on such basis. This approach would have required thorough exploration of France's overall balance of payments situation, and of basic policies

---

[1] None printed. Telegram 4206 to Paris, November 10, informed Ambassador Caffery that the Department of State had found helpful his recent telegrams on France's requirements for interim aid and that $328 million was the amount proposed for France; Caffery was instructed to review the detailed allocations with French officials. Their reaction at a meeting on November 13 was described in telegram 4905 from Paris, November 15, as follows: "In general French merely reiterated requirements previously submitted by them. . . ." Then in telegram 4927, November 17, the Embassy transmitted the text of a note from the French Foreign Ministry confirming statements made at the meeting of November 13, including the necessity of solving the problem of an uncovered deficit of $140–$150 million beyond the $328 million, for "any half-measure . . . would run the risk of compromising the success of the Marshall Plan by creating unfavorable economic conditions in France before the general plan for aid to Europe gets under way." (840.50 Recovery/11–1047, –1547, –1747)

related thereto. Importance of time element, for both France and Italy, dictated approach based on assistance in alleviating conditions of "intolerable hunger and cold and to prevent serious economic retrogression . . ."

Dept has noted French experts are in substantial agreement with estimates commodity import requirements as submitted to Cong. Broader framework of France's balance of payments will, of course, be considered in detail in connection with Congressional examination in coming months of European Recovery Program.

Dept does not believe interim aid estimates presented to Cong are properly subject for diplomatic negotiation. You may, however, in your discretion, use foregoing background material in informal discussions with French Govt at Cabinet levels concerning this matter. Following specific observations may also be of use as background for such observations as you may wish to make concerning the necessity for French authorities to deal with any deficit which they feel may remain.

1. Action by Cong on Interim Aid Bill will not constitute commitment to supply quantities listed in program presented to Cong. Actual supplies wld depend on total funds appropriated by Cong, relative needs of countries included and actual availabilities as determined by US supply authorities from time to time. Dept has assured Congressional committees financial request does not constitute supply commitment. This point being made with other countries concerned.

2. Departmental presentation to Cong was based on assumption obligations already due and payable to Belgium, Brazil and Eximbank should be met. On other hand, future commitments should either be avoided for emergency period or friendly countries should be willing under principle of mutual aid to defer liquidation of such dollar commitments. Latter assumption regarded as applicable to UK war contract problem, particularly in view large French sterling holdings. (Opinion in this country strongly opposed to US assuming entire burden of Western Europe's balance of payments problem.)

3. Any potential deficit remaining after two above could be further reduced or eliminated for the period if France adopts trade policy designed to meet its CEEC target to export from French Union in 1948 $1.56 billion in goods, $325 million of which are projected for dollar areas. If exports in first quarter 1948 only reached 80 percent of this level, extra receipts beyond those anticipated in France's interim aid request would go long way toward meeting any remaining deficit. Methods to be adopted to meet or approach these targets are primarily French internal matter.

4. Finally, Bank of France's forward exchange contracts (uncovered by dollars in Stabilization Fund) are being reduced from $260

million on Oct 1 to estimated $35 million at end of this year. This substantial strengthening of Bank's position would appear give it flexibility needed to deal with any remaining dollar problem for interim period, pending full Congressional consideration of longer-term recovery program.[2]

LOVETT

[2] On November 28 Ambassador Caffery reported in telegram 5119 that he had handed to Robert Schuman, the new Premier, an informal memorandum embodying pertinent portions of telegram 4319.

851.00/11–2947 : Telegram

The Ambassador in France (Caffery) to the Secretary of State

SECRET   PARIS, November 29, 1947—11 a.m.

5120. My 5020, November 22.[1] I had a long conversation with Léon Blum last evening. He began by saying that when [he?] took such a strong stand against De Gaulle before the Assembly last Friday he knew it would probably cost him the Prime Ministership but that he had felt obliged to do so for the following reasons. He said France's possibility of staging an economic, social and political recovery, and at the same time remaining democratic depends to a very great extent on the non-Communist left and, in particular, on the anti-Communist trade unionists. Blum believes that the situation has evolved to the point where it will be possible in the not too distant future to break the Communist control of the CGT, "the Communists' one great weapon". He does not feel, however, that the time is yet ripe, and said it is now of vital importance to support and encourage non-Communist trade unionist elements. In his Assembly speech he had castigated the Communists on the one hand and De Gaulle on the other because had he attacked only the Communists, anti-Communist labor elements would have been profoundly "deceived" and would have gained the impression that Blum's govt had made a deal with De Gaulle looking to the latter's arrival in power. Such an impression, he said, would have seriously compromised the efforts of himself and others to break Communist hold on organized labor. He expressed the strongest possible disapproval of De Gaulle, whose tendencies he believes are not "democratic" and whose action "has seriously hampered the efforts of the real democratic elements in France".

He also referred to the recent visit of Carey of CIO [2] and said that the latter's visit and his statements at CGT and WFTU meetings

[1] Not printed; it reported on Blum's failure to win a majority in the National Assembly on November 21 (851.00/11–2247).
[2] James B. Carey, Secretary-Treasurer of the Congress of Industrial Organizations.

310–099—72——52

coupled with the results of the recent CIO Congress had been "very helpful in strengthening the determination of French non-Communist labor elements".

Referring to the strike situation Blum said he did not have the latest news but his general impression was that the general situation remained about where it had been the last two days. He remarked that while it is serious and the next few days are of critical importance he is not unduly pessimistic and believes a settlement [can be reached?] of this "generalized strike fomented by the Communist influence in the working class, thus aiding the work of liberating French trade unionism from Communist domination". He described the present strike situation as being one of great complexity. He said that on the one hand he believes that for the first time since the liberation a majority of French labor desires to be "liberated from Communist domination". On the other hand, traditional observance of trade union discipline is still an important factor and many workers are now on strike not because they believe in it but because of their habit in observing strike orders from union headquarters. In other cases workers are striking who while opposed to Communist control of the CGT, are either too apathetic to oppose them actively or fear future Communist reprisals if they do not follow the consign of the union leadership.

Despite such circumstances Blum expressed the conviction that the opposition to the Communists in the trade unions is growing daily and said that "for the first time since 1945 the situation is such that there are now good hopes of liquidating Communist control". He mentioned that trade union friends of his who until recently had not believed it possible to break the Communist control of the CGT and who were even opposed in principle to the idea of an ultimate split in the French trade union movement now believe that the Communists can be placed in a minority position and are also now willing to face the possibility that at some future date a split may be necessary.

Sent Dept as 5120; repeated London for Secdel as 878.

CAFFERY

851.00/11–2947 : Telegram

The Ambassador in France (Caffery) to the Secretary of State

SECRET   PARIS, November 29, 1947—2 p.m.

5125. The following observations may be of help in evaluating present situation in France.[1] Moscow and the Communist leadership in

---

[1] On November 24 Robert Schuman took office as President of the Council of Ministers, succeeding Paul Ramadier, who had resigned on November 19 during a wave of strikes.

Paris would of course like nothing better than to be in the position to effect a general strike leading to the complete collapse of the government and the formation of a Communist dominated cabinet that would be subservient to the will of the Kremlin; but it is the opinion of those best qualified to judge these matters i.e., the trade union opposition to the Communists, that as things now stand the French Communist Party is not sufficiently strong successfully to carry out a general strike. First, strong opposition groups are now well organized among the miners, railway workers, PTT, civil servants and even metal workers as well as among other workers of lesser importance. This in itself may well prevent the Communists from fully developing and maintaining the present strikes on a national level in the most crucial sectors of the national economy, especially among the medium sized and small enterprises of which there are so many in France.

The most disturbing factor at the present time arises from the fact that the labor leaders who are resisting the Communist grip on the CGT have not been able (mostly from lack of funds) to organize effective opposition groups within several highly important trade unions, notably among the building trades, dock workers and Merchant Marine. The result is that although a considerable number of persons in 3 unions would prefer to work and perceive in the political nature of the strikes [apparent omission], they do not enjoy a medium of expression, cannot vote secretly for or against the strikes and cannot pass the picket lines.

Most qualified observers here hold the view that the Communists will not succeed in putting over a general strike but unquestionably will succeed in obtaining to a considerable degree their general objective, namely the exertion of great nuisance value at least to the extent of creating disorder, lowering production and in general harming but not completely paralyzing national economy. (In this connection Communist circles here are discussing the visit of Thorez and Dimitrov [2] to Scotchi [*Sochi*] where they are believed to have received instructions from Stalin. These circles state that Stalin has ordered the French Communists to endeavor to sabotage the Marshall Plan as far as it is possible to do so without resort to armed action. They add that within a few days an important meeting of Cominform will take place at Belgrade at which the Italians in particular will be represented in force, and which Thorez may attend.)

Government intervention here against the strikes, especially the use of the army and police, raises a number of delicate problems and should governmental forces be utilized indiscreetly might well act as a

---

[2] Georgy (George) Dimitrov, a leader in the international Communist movement, at one time Chairman of the Presidium of the Communist International.

boomerang against both the government and the anti-Communist forces in the trade unions. Where the opposition to the Communists is strong (as in case of the miners and railway and postal workers) the government may be able to act energetically on the side of the workers who desire to stay on the job; where the opposition is nil or hardly organized the result might be less happy as, for instance, among the dock workers and Merchant Marine. Many observers feel that, apart from providing for secret ballot and strike votes and providing protection for workers who wish to carry on, government should gain time and let the strikers get fed up as is usually the case in France, particularly when as at present general public opinion is strongly against the strikes. Consequently at present juncture indiscreet use of the army might prove as damaging as absence of forcible measures. The Communists in any case are preparing for any eventuality as evidenced by the formation, announced yesterday morning by Political Bureau, of National Strike Committee which is calling upon all party organizations to give moral and material support to the strikers. Qualified observers state that this strike committee is being run behind the scenes by Comintern-NKVD (Soviet) agents who are determined to create the utmost disorder short of armed insurrection.

In reporting the above I do not wish to minimize the extreme seriousness of the situation or to rule out the possibility that the present government may lack the strength and ingenuity to cope with it.

Sent Department as 5125; repeated to Secdel London as 881.

CAFFERY

851.00/12–147 : Telegram

The Ambassador in France (Caffery) to the Secretary of State

SECRET   PARIS, December 1, 1947—5 p.m.

5144. In the course of a conversation with General de Benouville, one of De Gaulle's close advisers, we impressed on him the importance of strengthening the non-Communist left and our apprehension that by his action De Gaulle may alienate this important element which at present is endeavoring to break the Communist control of the French labor movement. Benouville professed to be in complete agreement and while he alleged De Gaulle was working hard to gain the support of the non-Communist left he admitted that the General was by-passing the Socialist leadership. He also claimed that De Gaulle had now made contact with important reformist trade unionists and that under certain circumstances there appeared "a good possibility of De Gaulle reaching agreement with such men as Jouhaux and Bothereau" [1]

---

[1] Léon Jouhaux and Robert Bothereau, French labor leaders.

without having to come to any agreement with political leadership of the Socialist Party. We expressed to Benouville doubt as to the effectiveness of De Gaulle's efforts if he tries to by-pass or crush Socialist leadership.

We also expressed view that what we have heard of De Gaulle's so-called German policy seems very unrealistic. We pointed out that the basic objectives of the US and France insofar as Germany is concerned are identical, and that it would be unfortunate if De Gaulle, as so often had been the case in the past, should begin beating the drums for the benefit of French public opinion with a view of posing as the "defender of France against a resurgent Germany which is being rebuilt stronger than ever by the United States". We pointed out that if De Gaulle publicly takes such a line he will inevitably maneuver himself in a position where, should he come to power, he will have no liberty of negotiation and where not only will he be rendering his country a disservice but he will also be playing the Communist game.

Benouville professed to agree with our line of reasoning and indicated he would speak to De Gaulle. He admitted frankly, however, that De Gaulle was not an easy person with whom to deal and disregarded the advice of even his closest and most intimate advisers. Furthermore, he said that while on many occasions some of De Gaulle's close advisers had talked about how they were going to tell the General that he must do this or that, when actually confronting the General "they seem to freeze and are afraid to say anything which disagrees with his ideas".

Sent Dept as 5144, repeated London for Secdel as 894.

CAFFERY

800.48 FAA/12–247

The Ambassador in the United Kingdom (Douglas) to the Secretary of State

TOP SECRET LONDON, December 2, 1947—6 p.m.
URGENT NIACT

6277. For Lovett from Douglas. Please transmit following to John Vorys,[1] House of Representatives:

"I am sending you this secret message, which you may show Eaton, Chris Herter, Joe Martin,[2] to tell you of Secretary Marshall's grave

---

[1] John M. Vorys, of Ohio, a member of the Select Committee on Foreign Aid, House of Representatives.
[2] Charles A. Eaton, of New Jersey, and Christian A. Herter, of Massachusetts, chairman and vice chairman of the Select Committee on Foreign Aid, House of Representatives; Joseph W. Martin, Jr., of Massachusetts, Speaker of the House of Representatives.

concern over the critical state of affairs in France. This concern is held also by Bevin with whom Marshall privately discussed the matter today.

There is in France a very real struggle for power. Thorez, the French Communist leader has just returned from Moscow, probably with a promise of wheat, which he may make public in the near future at the proper time, in an effort to throw the balance of weight against US.

If we are not to run the serious risk of losing France, we should act promptly. Therefore, if the House is favorable to interim aid, it should approve it at once. Time is of the essence. Hardly a day can be lost. This is not, I promise you, a cry of "wolf, wolf". This we firmly believe is a brute reality.

The situation has moved dangerously far during the last two weeks. Prompt action by the Congress would so encourage and strengthen the favorable forces in France that, in our opinion, they will be able successfully to prevent what is a flagrant attempt to seize power.

You know the far-reaching significance to Germany, Italy, the Mediterranean, North Africa, and to other areas, were France to fall.

Marshall feels the situation is self-evident, and that a message from him might be regarded as a routine administration appeal. Because of the urgency of speed, I disagree, and hope you will use your great influence to expedite action by the House.

I trust you will understand that this intrusion is the result of firm conviction that time cannot be lost if we do not want to run an undue risk of losing the stakes".

DOUGLAS

851.51/12–247

Memorandum by Mr. Ivan B. White of the Division of Western European Affairs

[WASHINGTON,] December 2, 1947.

Subject: French Dollar Position Through March 31, 1948

As projected in its presentation to Congress, the Department estimated that $328 million in assistance, coupled with the complete utilization of France's available resources, would meet France's minimum dollar requirements for the period December 1, 1947 to March 31, 1948.

The French Government, in commenting on this estimate, has informed our Embassy, Paris, that assistance in the amount estimated would still leave France with an uncovered dollar deficit for the period of $143 million.

Examination of the French justification for this estimate indicates that they have included in their expenditures certain items which the Department believed should be deferred. Nevertheless, it appears that there will be some uncovered deficit for the period, arising from the following:

1. *French dollar resources on December 1, 1947.*

The "Blue Book" estimate on this was $153 million. The French Government (Embassy's telegram No. 4905 of Nov. 15 [1]) stated that its actual balance on December 1 would be only $137 million, pointing out that Department's projection made no provision for actual October–November expenditures for administrative and miscellaneous purposes, which in practice amounted to about $16 million.

2. *Expenditures for French zone for other than food imports.*

On grounds the French Government had not given adequate explanation of expenditures for French zone in Germany (other than food), the Bureau of the Budget reduced Department's request by $17 million. In view of the fact that these goods are in course of procurement, France will actually be spending dollars for these items and the amount mentioned will not, therefore, be available to meet other expenditures projected in the Department's presentation as coming from French dollar resources.

3. *Minimum Working Balance.*

The Department's projection assumed that all available French dollar resources would be utilized during the period and that the stabilization fund balance at the end of March would be zero.

The French Embassy here has pointed out that US relief expenditures, other than for Commodity Credit items, are handled on a reimbursement basis and that in the initial step the French must make purchases with their own dollars. This means that during the aid period the French must maintain a revolving fund, estimated at $40 million, to finance initially certain imports included in the US procurement program.

4. *Conclusion.*

The conclusion reached is that, assuming French ability to defer liquidation of certain obligations, there will still remain a minimum need for new money during the interim aid period of $70–75 million if economic retrogression is to be avoided. This uncovered deficit would be increased by the amount that Congress might reduce the interim aid appropriation.

It is suggested that all avenues of possible financing be explored, including a second gold pot distribution and plans to obtain for liquidation French-owned assets in the United States, previously undeclared.

---

[1] Not printed.

851.00/12–347 : Telegram

The Ambassador in France (Caffery) to the Secretary of State

TOP SECRET   PARIS, December 3, 1947—5 p.m.
US URGENT

5186. A high official of the Interior Ministry in strictest confidence expressed last evening very grave concern over Moscow's purpose in inciting the French Communist Party to its present line of action. He said that the Communist generalized strike "ordered by Moscow's Cominform" is not only a failure in that the majority of the French working class is now opposed to it, but that as a result thereof French public opinion is daily crystallizing against the French Communist Party. This, insofar as the French internal picture is concerned, is all to the good and a most desirable and satisfactory development.

"On the other hand," he said, "what deeply worries the French Government is the fact that although the French Communists now know they have lost the strike battle in France, not only are they not modifying their tactics but are in fact hourly taking a more intransigent and uncompromising stand." Reports from the Prefectures throughout France indicate that flying squads of hardened Communist shock troops (my 5132, November 30 [1]) are being shuttled about to combat the police. In the last 24 hours Interior Ministry reports indicate they have not just tried to prevent the authorities from taking over strike-bound factories and services but are deliberately "provoking" the police to fire on them and the crowds they encourage to demonstrate.

(In this connection our source stated that Interior Ministry has information it believes is entirely accurate that when on Sunday certain Communist labor union leaders reported that "the strike battle is lost and a policy should be followed to make a tactical withdrawal which would avoid loss of face", Thorez himself told them that they must not retreat but should step up the tempo of their action.)

A further disquieting sign to the Interior Ministry is not only the action of the Communist group in the Assembly but the fact that in the past three days in many regions of France where previously only Communist labor leaders have been inciting strikers, political leaders including deputies have suddenly injected themselves and have replaced trade unionists as mob inciters.

Our sources said that foregoing developments tend to point to the conclusion that "cost what it may" the French Communist Party has orders to follow a line of action which if carried much further will inevitably call for governmental action against the party not ex-

---

[1] Not printed.

cluding "in extremis" the possibility that the party will be declared "illegal", which would inevitably drive it completely "underground" as in 1939. (In this connection Interior states that in Marseille and at least two other cities, Communist headquarters have received instructions to liquidate their files so that there will be no evidence or lists if the police should seize the headquarters.)

As a result of the foregoing the Interior Ministry, which heretofore has not believed that war between Soviet Russia and the western democracies would occur in the next few years "because Moscow needs at least five to ten years to prepare and the United States would not launch a preventive war", has a very severe case of jitters. Our source said that it is inconceivable to French Government officials who are following closely these developments that Moscow would at this point force the French Communist Party into illegality with all the attendant disadvantages unless it intended to make use of it in the comparatively near future, "say within the next year or two, as an instrument to aid the Soviet Army in an international conflict". He said that the French are baffled as to Moscow's real motives and while they are not entirely certain that "Moscow intends to launch a war in the immediate future, they fear that the tactics pursued by the French Communists may mean that Moscow now intends to adopt a policy, perhaps in Italy and Germany, which involves certain 'risks' —risks which could easily result in war if there is a positive reaction against such a policy by the US and UK."

I report the foregoing at some length not only because of the position the source occupies and his proven sincerity but also as an indication of the line of thinking in the important Interior Ministry.

Sent Department, repeated London for Secdel 909, Moscow 546, Rome 291.

CAFFERY

851.6131/11–1747

The Acting Secretary of State to the French Ambassador (Bonnet)

The Acting Secretary of State presents his compliments to His Excellency the Ambassador of France and has the honor to refer to his note No. 320 of September 23, 1947 and to the Embassy's memoranda of October 24, 1947 and November 17, 1947 [1] requesting that increases be made in the allocations of grain from the United States to France and French North Africa during the present half-year period.

---

[1] None printed.

The Embassy's memorandum of November 17 refers to the monthly allocations as announced from July to December as totalling only about 530,000 tons, as compared to a quantity of 606,000 tons recommended by the International Emergency Food Council for shipment from the United States in this period. While it is true that the total of new programs as announced for these six months is the figure indicated in the Embassy's memorandum, all shipments actually made within the new crop-year, that is, liftings from July 1 forward, must be counted as belonging to the crop-year 1947–48 and are consequently counted against the International Emergency Food Council figure applying to that year. International Emergency Food Council allocations for any period of time are made on a shipment basis. The total of shipments to France from the United States, representing the sum of the carry-over from allocations made before July 1 and the regular six monthly allocations announced for July–December, and allowing for some overage in landings, is expected to be about 620,000 tons. This calculation leaves out of account the considerable imports arriving in France after July 1 but which were lifted before that date.

The American Embassy in Paris has clarified this matter for officials of the French National Cereals Board and reports that there is no disagreement on this basis with the above estimate of 620,000 tons for France and French North Africa as against the International Emergency Food Council recommendation of 606,000 tons.

The Department of State is greatly concerned about the low stock position in metropolitan France which is in prospect by January 1 as the result of heavy diversions of United States exports of grain to French North Africa and the failure to secure a larger flow of imports from other sources to supplement imports from the United States. Conferences in Paris between French officials and American Embassy representatives indicated that stocks might sink to 245,000 tons by January 1. As soon as this position was clarified an emergency allocation of 54,000 tons of wheat and flour (wheat equivalent) was made to supplement the December program of 130,000 tons. It is understood that the four cargoes of wheat can be scheduled at the beginning of December and that the flour, while subject to fumigation because of long storage, is in export position.

While it has not been found possible to assist France at this time to the extent requested by the Embassy, it is considered that the above-mentioned supplementary allocation will give France stocks at least equal to a month's consumption and thus prevent any breakdown in distribution of the present ration.

WASHINGTON, December 4, 1947.

851.00/12–547 : Telegram

The Ambassador in France (Caffery) to the Secretary of State

TOP SECRET   PARIS, December 5, 1947—6 p.m.

5231. The official mentioned in my 5186, December 3, stated in confidence this morning that as a result of information which the Interior Ministry had obtained in the past three days its views on the reasons for Moscow pushing the French Communists to its present line of militant action have undergone considerable clarification since his last conversation on December 2. The Interior now has a report which it believes accurate that Thorez, upon his return from Moscow, outlined the Soviet position along the following general lines:

Moscow is convinced that the Marshall Plan to aid European recovery would serve to promote the formation of a western European bloc which would permit the US under cover of economic aid to expand and organize its zone of influence in western Europe to the point where this zone would prevent extension of Communist influence and would serve as dangerous jump-off place for attacking Soviet Russia. Faced with such menacing possibility Soviet policy requires bold action to neutralize capitalist assistance to France and Italy and to prevent establishment in these two key countries of prosperous regimes and therefore under American influence. Tactics of "legality" followed by French Communist Party since liberation are hopelessly inadequate to cope with the new situation resulting from the Marshall Plan and this is the reason for the adoption of a plan of revolutionary activity which is aimed at destroying American hopes of economic stability in western Europe, thus preparing the way for ultimate Communist control of this area.

According to Interior Ministry reports, the Soviet leadership believes that the reaction of the democratic governments of western Europe (in particular France and Italy) would be too slow and too weak to counteract the revolutionary action of a small group of determined Communist militants and that the US Government would not intervene directly in France or in Italy to prevent or suppress the illegal action of the Communist militants. Therefore the Communists would only be opposed by the existing weak and indecisive governments which are incapable over long period of resisting continuous action against them in the economic, financial, industrial and social fields. Thus the present action of the Communist parties in France and Italy is designed not to grab power by a *coup d'état* at this time but rather to cause the present democratic governments in western Europe to collapse one after another under strong Communist blows against their national, economic and social structures, thus precipitating the abandonment of Europe by the US and leaving the door finally open to Communism. While, according to the report, the Communists realize course of action they have been ordered to take in France and Italy runs the risk of leading to the outlawing of the party, they feel this is not a certainty in view of their parliamentary and electoral strength in both countries. Against the possibility of being outlawed, however, it is necessary to prepare for going underground and such preparations are now in course. Furthermore those services which will engage in sabotage and illegal action must go underground now.

With the foregoing in mind, Thorez reportedly stressed necessity for stepping up the tempo of the party's revolutionary action in the coming period. He also is said to have emphasized that for the time being Communist shock troops should not resort to the use of firearms.

In discussing the implications of the present situation with the militant Communist labor leadership in the CGT Thorez reportedly explained that while Moscow fully realizes that the present tactics might cause serious disaffection among working class elements which have heretofore supported the Communists, such losses must be accepted since if the militant Communists do their job of sabotaging French economy effectively, living conditions of the working class would so deteriorate and there would be such widespread misery that a new and desirable situation would be created which the Communists could exploit and recapture the masses which temporarily had deserted them.

I have reported the foregoing at some length because the Interior Ministry, including Minister Jules Moch, believes it to be an accurate resumé of Thorez explanation of the French situation as viewed from Moscow.[1]

Sent Department 5231, repeated to London for USDel as 930, to Moscow as 552, Rome as 299.

CAFFERY

---

[1] In telegram 5252, December 6, 6 p.m., Caffery added that he had "discussed the present situation in France at length last evening with Interior Minister Jules Moch. He expounded at length his views of Communist reasoning and tactics along the precise lines set forth in my 5231 December 5. Prime Minister Schuman was present and concurred in Moch's analysis." (851.00/12–647)

800.48 FAA/12–1047

The Secretary of State to the Acting Secretary of State

SECRET   LONDON, December 10, 1947.

Martel 57. For Lovett from Marshall. Please give following message to Speaker Martin from myself and Dulles [1] with copy to Vandenberg: [2]

---

[1] John Foster Dulles, special adviser, U. S. Delegation, Fifth Session of the Council of Foreign Ministers, at London, November 25–December 15, 1947.
[2] Arthur H. Vandenberg, of Michigan, chairman, Foreign Relations Committee, United States Senate.

"Certain reported provisions of House Interim Aid Bill give grave concern to French Government and to us. These are particularly: (1) Right to use freely franc equivalent after next June; (2) right to supervise French domestic production of products similar to interim aid. First provision would give United States power to direct or destroy any French fiscal program, and, second would be offensive to national dignity and both would seem to confirm Soviet thesis that US attempting reduce France to status of American colony. Another reported provision is total prohibition export similar goods. This in main unobjectionable but there is small border traffic particularly with Switzerland where coal exchange for food very advantageous for France. Would greatly appreciate your bringing this matter to attention of House conferees. We believe Senate bill in these matters better avoids embarrassing precarious situation in France where struggle by no means ended by initial government victory."

MARSHALL

840.51 FC 51/11–1747

The Acting Secretary of State to the French Ambassador (Bonnet)

[WASHINGTON,] December 10, 1947.

EXCELLENCY: I have the honor to acknowledge the receipt of your note of November 17, 1947, containing the French Government's proposal for mobilizing the assets in the United States owned by French nationals resident in France.

In its present form, the proposal raises certain difficult questions for my Government. However, I fully appreciate the urgency and merit of the underlying purpose of your Government's proposal. I can also assure you that my Government is giving careful consideration to the basic problem for which your Government's proposal seeks to provide a solution, and I will inform you promptly when a decision has been reached.[1]

Accept [etc.]

For the Acting Secretary of State:
WILLARD L. THORP

[1] In a note of March 11, 1948, the Secretary of State informed Ambassador Bonnet that the United States Government had recently formulated a plan that should ultimately achieve the results he sought in his proposals (840.51 FC 51/11–1747).

851.51/12–1447 : Telegram

The Ambassador in France (Caffery) to the Secretary of State

SECRET

PARIS, December 14, 1947—1 p.m.

5379. As soon as Schuman heard of the decision to grant an advance of 150 million dollars for immediate aid, he asked me to express his high appreciation thereof to the Department.

Sent Department as 5379, repeated USDel London as 985.

CAFFERY

851.51/12–1647 : Airgram

The Ambassador in France (Caffery) to the Secretary of State

CONFIDENTIAL   PARIS, December 16, 1947.

A–1742. For State and Treasury. Certain comments by Mr. de Margerie, Assistant Director, Division of Foreign Finance, Ministry of Finance, in a conversation on December 13 may be of interest:

Mr. de Margerie said that he had just surveyed the immediate requirements of the French Treasury for dollars and the balance available in the Stabilization Fund. On the basis of this survey his previous estimate that a payments crisis would be faced soon after December 20, if interim aid did not become available before that date, was not changed. De Margerie said he was encouraged by the reported decision of the House and Senate permitting RFC funds to be used immediately to furnish $150 million of interim aid requirements and the decision making the interim aid program retroactive to December 1. Because of the retroactive aspect it would be possible to release funds earmarked for certain imports as soon as interim aid funds were received. After the interim aid bill is passed De Margerie said they would draw up their requirements for the next few months. At that time he would be glad to review with us the dollar payments picture.

De Margerie stated that he was not in a position to comment on the press reports that Minister Mayer [1] planned to seek agreements with the United States, Canada, Argentina and other western hemisphere countries to bring about an immediate increase of food imports in France. In his opinion, however, all possibilities to achieve the goal would certainly be explored. Many of the officials in the French Government were very concerned over the necessity of increasing availability essential consumption items, particularly food. The necessity of an upward adjustment in wages was acknowledged but it was also recognized that unless there was an accompanying increase in food availabilities the wage increases would soon be merely nominal. The success of any stabilization program obviously hinges on bringing about an increase in the "real income" of the working classes. This can only be done by the maintenance of agricultural prices which in turn depends upon food availabilities.

De Margerie continued that it was a general view that the recent success of the Government in meeting the social crisis has brought

---

[1] René Mayer, French Minister of Finances and Economic Affairs.

about an unusually favorable political situation to lay the groundwork for a solution to the economic and financial difficulties that had long evaded the French Government. The Government, however, must take an immediate advantage of this opportunity. Without doubt, unless there is improvement in economic and financial conditions, it will soon disappear and when it does, conditions may deteriorate very rapidly. For this reason it could be expected that the Government will make every effort to find the resources to take advantage of its opportunity. De Margerie was not certain what form efforts to obtain food imports would take but suggested shifting interim aid funds to obtain a greater proportion of food imports, trade agreements, or perhaps additional credits.

(On the other hand, a high official of the Monnet Plan states that the French Government is under no illusions regarding the possibility of finding additional food imports, in view of world short supply, but he confirmed that everything possible would be done to maximize food availabilities and suggested that something might be done to increase supplies of meat.)

De Margerie was quite alarmed over the newspaper reports that the Senate–House Committee had agreed on amendments providing that not more than ten per cent of the interim aid funds could be used for purchases outside of the United States and that none of the funds could be used for purchases at prices above prevailing U.S. prices for similar commodities. He noted another proposed House amendment which provided that petroleum products should be purchased outside of the U.S. if at all possible.

When asked for a breakdown of sources of imports to demonstrate the difficulties that may arise, de Margerie submitted later the following:

Wheat	—85 percent from US;
	15 percent from Argentina;
Fats and Oils	—50 percent from US;
	50 percent from Philippines;
Coal	—88 percent from US;
	12 percent from Ruhr;
Petroleum	—35 percent from US;
	40 percent from Venezuela;
	25 percent from Middle East;
Fertilizer	—60 percent from US;
	40 percent from Chile.

CAFFERY

CFM Files: Lot M–88: Box 104: Anglo–US–French Conversations

Memorandum of Conversation by the British Foreign Office [1]

[Extract]

TOP SECRET   [LONDON, undated.]

Mr. Marshall paid a farewell call on the Secretary of State [2] at the Foreign Office at 6 p.m. on December 17th. The situation resulting from the breakdown of the recent meeting of the Council of Foreign Ministers and other subjects concerning Anglo-American relations were discussed in a conversation lasting 1¼ hours.

ANGLO-FRENCH MILITARY CONVERSATIONS

The SECRETARY OF STATE said he wished to inform Mr. Marshall that he had already arranged for General Reveres [*Revers*], the Chief of the French General Staff, to come here soon, probably in the New Year, for military talks. He had always wanted to forward the military rehabilitation of France but had been unable to do anything as long as communists were in the French Government. M. Bidault had now assured him that we could talk with absolute confidence. He was doubtful whether we could go so far with the French as we were able to do with the Americans, with whom our military conversations were like those between members of one country. But we must see just how far we could go. France was proud of her Army but it was too big and wrongly equipped for modern needs. It required recasting and reorganizing. He wished, with Mr. Marshall's approval, to test out General Reveres in conversations with Field Marshal Montgomery and Air Chief Marshal Tedder. There would be no publicity, but the possibilities of so far as possible coordinating the French Army with our own air and naval power would be elucidated. We already knew exactly where we stood in this regard both with Holland and Belgium, but they were both nervous of the French. His general idea was to build up a real force in western Europe. These military talks would, however, be kept quite separate from the other official conversations dealing with all the social and economic questions which could be summarised under the heading of Marshall Aid. But France could not be given real confidence unless all facets of French life were brought into play. But he emphasized that these were still his own personal views and subject to Cabinet approval.

Mr. MARSHALL said that his idea was that it was not so much normal staff discussions which were wanted with the French. The French desire, and indeed necessity, was for more equipment.

---

[1] This memorandum was presumably prepared by Frank K. Roberts, personal secretary to the British Secretary of State for Foreign Affairs. For other sections of the memorandum, see vol. II, p. 815.

[2] Ernest Bevin.

The SECRETARY OF STATE said that he was not so much concerned with the equipment side as with the need of shaking up the traditional French conception of a land army which was now out of date. We should of course keep the United States informed, although he presumed they would agree that it was better not to bring the French into our Anglo-American military talks.

MR. MARSHALL said that he took no exception to such Anglo-French talks and fully agreed with the Secretary of State's last point about keeping them separate from Anglo-American talks.

Editorial Note

On December 17 the interim aid program, cited officially as the "Foreign Aid Act of 1947", 61 Stat. 934, was approved. On December 19 President Truman sent to the Congress a special message on the European Recovery Program. Funds for the interim aid program were voted in the supplemental appropriation act of December 23, 1947, 61 Stat. 941. For documentation relating to these developments, see pages 470 ff.

851.00/12–2047 : Telegram

The Ambassador in France (Caffery) to the Secretary of State

SECRET   PARIS, December 20, 1947—1 p.m.

5482. From the point of view of our general interests in Europe as well as from the point of view of our interest in the survival of democracy in western Europe, the *scission* yesterday in the CGT is the most important event that has occurred in France since the Liberation.[1] It is all the more important because it follows on the heels of the failure of the Communist-inspired political strikes; strikes which from an economic point of view were fully justified in view of the prevailing low wages and high prices.

The Department is aware that at the time of the Liberation the Communists seized the levers of command of the trade unions and have been running the unions with a high hand ever since. Some of the non-Communist labor leaders did not support the *scission* mainly because they held comfortable jobs in the CGT, had comfortable offices in the CGT headquarters and money to spend. The leaders of France [*Force*] Ouvrière will not have comfortable jobs, will not have comfortable offices and now have no money to spend.

---

[1] Léon Jouhaux and five other non-Communist labor leaders resigned from the executive committee of the CGT to form a rival group, the Force Ouvrière, also known as the CGT-Force Ouvrière, or CGT-FO.

No one could have foreseen this break a few months ago and a few months ago the young militants who forced the break could not have done so.

They had the courage to do so yesterday for two reasons: The failure of masses of workmen to follow the Communist leadership in the strikes and growing appreciation of what the "Marshall Plan" means to France.

For the past three years non-Communist workmen had been bemoaning their fate to us in the Embassy. They did not like what was going on in the CGT but they were doing nothing about it.

CAFFERY

851.00/12-2347 : Telegram

The Ambassador in France (Caffery) to the Secretary of State

SECRET PARIS, December 23, 1947—4 p.m.

5514. The friends of De Gaulle in the Assembly are bent upon making trouble for the Schuman government. As I reported in my telegrams 5480, December 20 and 5487, December 21 [1] they have been asking for early new elections and they will not be helpful to René Mayer in his attempts to pull France out of the economic morass where she is now floundering.

As I have frequently pointed out, the De Gaullist tactics have been based on the belief that no French Government could succeed this winter in view of the prevailing hardships and that after the inevitable collapse towards the end of the winter De Gaulle would be called back by public acclaim to power. However, they have never allowed themselves to be pinned down as to exactly how they expect this to come about.

Schuman's unexpected success against the Communist strikes amazed them and at this juncture even the bare possibility that René Mayer might succeed fills them with concern.

It is satisfactory to be able to say that I have found recently that some supporters of De Gaulle are becoming disgusted with these tactics.

CAFFERY

---

[1] Neither printed.

800.48 FAA/12-2447 : Telegram

The Ambassador in France (Caffery) to the Secretary of State

SECRET PARIS, December 24, 1947—2 p.m.

5532. Afem No. 13. Re Mefa No. 1. From informal conversations which we have had with French officials it appears that in governmental circles there is apprehension that if the French Government simply signs a draft aid agreement [1] without some explanatory or preparatory statement, it may be vulnerable to attacks that it has supinely agreed to conditions imposed by a foreign power to the detriment of "French National Sovereignty". While the government naturally expects a continuation of bitter Communist attacks along these lines, it is also concerned over the possibility that the Gaullists (who in the past several days have been evincing open hostility) may also be tempted to criticize some provisions of the agreement. With this in mind the French are contemplating drawing up some form of French statement intended to make the point that the aid agreement is being freely entered into by the French and is not being imposed by US.

My initial and very preliminary reaction on the basis of what we have heard is that if such a statement by the French is in no way out of harmony with the foreign aid act and the bilateral agreement and will not introduce any questionable interpretation of the conditions laid down by the American Congress, in principle such a statement would not appear to be objectionable and might even be helpful in cutting the ground out from under elements which are hostile to the United States and to the Schuman government. On the other hand, I believe that any French statement or public comment by French officials which is not in harmony with the letter and spirit of the agreement or which could be interpreted as placing any limitations on any of the provisions of the agreement would be most unfortunate and could create serious complications.

CAFFERY

---

[1] On December 20 the Acting Secretary of State sent to the Embassy in France the draft text of an interim aid agreement with France (telegram 4555, Mefa No. 1, December 20, 800.48 FAA/12–2047, not printed). Similar texts were sent to the Embassies in Austria and Italy.

851.00/12–2647 : Telegram

The Ambassador in France (Caffery) to the Secretary of State

SECRET PARIS, December 26, 1947—5 p.m.

5558. Mytel 5327 December 11.[1] I have been emphasizing to Deputies and members of the Council of State as well as to Cabinet Ministers that it was essential to do something constructive at an early date about the wage price problem because if nothing constructive were done the government's recent victory over the Communists would be nullified and the next strikes would be supported not only by Communists but by non-Communist workers as well. I pointed out also that

---

[1] Not printed.

if nothing were done about wages and prices the main idea behind the Marshall Plan would have no practical application here at all. Everyone agreed; even several supporters of De Gaulle.

Along these lines it is at least encouraging that René Mayer's two projects (one authorizing the issuance of a loan and the other instituting an exceptional levy in the battle against inflation) were voted by the Assembly, for it took courage on the part of the government to force those essentially necessary but fundamentally unpopular bills through. However, those are only first steps and there is much more to be done.

CAFFERY

800.48 FAA/12–2647 : Telegram

The Acting Secretary of State to the Embassy in France

SECRET   WASHINGTON, December 26, 1947—8 p.m.
US URGENT   NIACT

4603. During past few days discussions have been held with Fr Emb concerning the terms of the bilateral draft aid agreement, and minor amendments have been made in an effort to meet the Fr views. Bonnet however informs us that his Govt feels that it must insist upon dividing the nature of the undertakings which it is prepared to assume. Those which deal with mutual arrangements between France and US would be embodied in the agreement and the others that are obligations which France is assuming in respect to its own economy would be contained in an exchange of letters. Bonnet explained his Govt attaches greatest importance to this as indicating the latter arrangements have been freely entered into by France and are not being imposed upon it. There would be no question however that France has assumed these undertakings without reservations.

Although most careful consideration has been given to this proposal, the present situation in this country and the specific terms of Sec 5 of the Foreign Aid Bill [1] are such that we cannot accept this method of handling these undertakings. It would be interpreted as an attempt to make a distinction between the nature of the conditions which Congress considered were essential to the provision of aid. We could of course agree to some preliminary or explanatory statement of the nature described in urtel 5532 Dec 24 and had suggested to Bonnet that his Govt might write preliminary letter stating that it had noted the passage of the bill and reaffirmed its willingness to take these measures which could be then incorporated in the agreement. This letter

---

[1] 61 Stat. 934.

could of course be published before actual signature takes place but the agreement must contain all of the conditions which Congress has attached.

Until this question is resolved we cannot proceed further with aid provisions respecting France. Moreover, it is likely that the agreements with Italy and Austria can be signed without delay. You are requested to urge upon Bidault the urgency of reaching settlement of this problem.

LOVETT

800.48 FAA/ 12–2747 : Telegram

The Ambassador in France (Caffery) to the Secretary of State

SECRET   PARIS, December 27, 1947—4 p.m.

5572. Bidault began by praising in highest terms the recent Congressional action of voting aid to France. He said furthermore he has no basic objection to any of the terms of the bilateral draft aid agreement, but he does have objection to the manner of implementing some of them.

After I described Department's position, he said he would endeavor at once to persuade the government to accept the agreement as it is adding, "I shall almost certainly sign it but that may be the last official act of my career. I am not at all concerned as to what the Communists will do and say, but I am very much concerned about possible attacks from the friends of De Gaulle and other very nationalist elements".

He will study the possibility of writing the preliminary letter suggested by the Department to Bonnet.

CAFFERY

851.00/12–2947 : Telegram

The Ambassador in France (Caffery) to the Secretary of State

SECRET   PARIS, December 29, 1947—7 p.m.

5594. My telegram 5558, December 26. I do not question Robert Schuman's determination to find a solution for the wage-price problem. From everything I hear he is endeavoring to concentrate all his available forces in that fight. Every time I see him he asks my personal opinion as to the possibilities of success of the efforts of his Minister of Finance. He has asked me also personally if I think René Mayer is a competent man for the job and I replied that I have a very high regard for Mayer's ability.

On the other hand the hostility which both the Communists and Gaullists have evinced towards the Schuman government in the Parliament, coupled with the opposition of special interest groups (particularly deputies representing agrarian constituencies) severely limits the government's possibilities to stabilize the situation.

CAFFERY

800.48 FAA/12–3047 : Telegram

The Ambassador in France (Caffery) to the Secretary of State

SECRET

PARIS, December 30, 1947—7 p.m.

NIACT

5606. Bidault informs me that the Council of Ministers authorized him this morning to sign the bilateral foreign aid agreement in the form agreed upon between the Dept and Bonnet at Washington. Bidault showed me the exchanges of telegrams between him and Bonnet in that connection which indicate that original plans for signing the text set out in Deptel 4555, December 20 [1] have been changed. Bidault asked me if the Italian agreement is to be signed at Rome and the Austrian at Vienna. He intimated that he would prefer to have the French agreement signed at Washington, preferring, I assume, not to sign it himself for purely internal political reasons.

As the Dept is aware, in the past we have had difficulty in getting the French press to give adequate coverage to aid received from the United States. If the agreement is signed at Washington it will be extremely difficult to get adequate coverage here (we had made plans in agreement with Foreign Office for unusual coverage by press, radio and newsreels).

Whether agreement is signed in Washington or here, I should appreciate being advised whether the substance of the statement which I had proposed to make, transmitted in mytel 5564, December 26, [1] meets with the Dept's approval. In either event I would appreciate receiving urgently text of revised draft annexes and letters to be exchanged as agreed upon in Washington. [2]

Bidault told me that the entire Cabinet and especially the Minister of Finance were most appreciative of the Dept's sympathetic attitude

---

[1] Not printed.
[2] For text of Agreement Between the United States of America and France, Assistance to the People of France Under Public Law 389, 80th Congress, signed at Paris, January 2, 1948, see Department of State Treaties and Other International Acts Series (TIAS) No. 1690.

in connection with the signing of this agreement and were especially grateful to the Acting Secretary of State for his understanding of the domestic political difficulties of the present French Government.

CAFFERY

ARRANGEMENTS FOR CONTINUED USE BY THE U.S. NAVY OF AIR BASE AND COMMUNICATIONS FACILITIES AT PORT LYAUTEY, FRENCH MOROCCO

Editorial Note

On September 15, 1947, the French Minister of Foreign Affairs (Bidault) and the American Ambassador (Caffery) signed at Paris an agreement providing for the return to French sovereignty of the airfield and seaplane base at Port Lyautey, French Morocco. The construction and maintenance of this base had been provided for in the agreement between Maj. Gen. Mark W. Clark and Adm. François Darlan, signed at Algiers, November 22, 1942 (*Foreign Relations, 1942*, volume II, pages 453 ff.). The new agreement, which was to remain in effect for the period of the occupation of Germany, provided for continued use by the United States of certain facilities, including a radio communication installation operating under the American flag. The text of the Agreement and related documentation, not printed, are in Department of State file No. 811.2351.

AGREEMENT BETWEEN THE UNITED STATES AND THE FRENCH REPUBLIC RELATING TO AIR SERVICE FACILITIES IN FRENCH TERRITORY

[For text of Agreement effected by exchange of notes signed at Paris, May 8 and 17, 1947, amending Agreement of June 18, 1946, see Department of State Treaties and Other International Acts Series (TIAS) No. 1853.]

AGREEMENT BETWEEN THE UNITED STATES AND THE FRENCH REPUBLIC SUPPLEMENTARY TO THE GENERAL AGREEMENT ON TARIFFS AND TRADE

[For text of Agreement and Accompanying Letters rendering inoperative the Agreement of May 6, 1936, and supplementing the General Agreement on Tariffs and Trade of October 30, 1947, signed at Geneva, October 30, 1947, see Department of State Treaties and Other International Acts Series (TIAS) No. 1704.]

AGREEMENT BETWEEN THE UNITED STATES AND THE FRENCH REPUBLIC WITH RESPECT TO AMERICAN DEAD IN WORLD WAR II

[For text of Agreement concerning the interment in France and in territories of the French Union or the removal to the United States of the bodies of American soldiers killed in the war of 1939–1945, signed at Paris, October 1, 1947, see Department of State Treaties and Other International Acts Series (TIAS) No. 1720.]

AGREEMENT BETWEEN THE UNITED STATES AND THE FRENCH REPUBLIC CONCERNING THE RESTORATION OF CERTAIN INDUSTRIAL PROPERTY RIGHTS AFFECTED BY WORLD WAR II

[For texts of the Agreement and a Supplementary Agreement extending certain periods provided for in the former, signed at Washington on April 4 and October 28, 1947, respectively, see Department of State Treaties and Other International Acts Series (TIAS) Nos. 1667 and 1725.]

GERMANY

(See Volume II)

827

GREECE

(See Volume V)

ICELAND

CONCERN OF THE UNITED STATES OVER ECONOMIC AND POLITICAL CONDITIONS IN ICELAND

859A.50/4–1847 : Telegram

The Chargé in Iceland (Trimble) to the Secretary of State

SECRET   REYKJAVIK, April 18, 1947—4 p.m.

174. I had long talk with FonMin [1] yesterday afternoon re present economic situation which he indicated is causing govt great concern. He said tentative agreement had been reached with British at end of last week whereby latter would purchase 12,000 tons frozen fillets—slightly less than one-half estimated production—and substantial quantity of herring oil (40% according to reliable source) at prices somewhat lower than those sought by Iceland delegation London. By a "curious coincidence" news of proposed terms reached Russians within three days. Latter who have been dragging their heels in current Moscow trade negotiations for over two months immediately offered to purchase most of remaining fillets and unspecified quantity herring oil including part of that earmarked for UK. Russian prices lower than those offered by British. They flatly refused to buy any wet salted fish on grounds that no demand for commodity exists in Soviet market where they allege it is practically unknown. Refusal caused consternation among Iceland authorities as government had been counting on Russia buying upwards of 20,000 tons wet salted fish or roughly two-thirds anticipated production. Decision whether or not to accept offer will be taken by cabinet within 48 hours. Iceland reluctant to agree to Russian terms but sees no other alternative as prospects sale of fillets in US highly uncertain. According to report made to Thors [2] Cabinet by former Communist Minister Aki Jakobsson Russian trade representative Semenov had assured him last fall that Soviet Union would buy all wet salted production at high price and was also prepared to purchase all other exportable surpluses. Counting on this govt had therefore guaranteed fish producers price of 17 cents per pound. Efforts by present Iceland negotiators Moscow to communicate with Semenov and obtain a verification of his commitment have been fruitless as he is invariably "indisposed".

---

[1] Bjarni Benediktsson, Icelandic Minister for Foreign Affairs.
[2] Olafur Thors.

Local Communists according to Benediktsson are preparing to attack govt for its failure to follow through on Semenov's "promises". Fon-Min feels cabinet can weather this particular storm by citing true facts in case but must find outlet for wet salted fish in near future, for if economic conditions continue to deteriorate, as seems likely unless fish can be quickly disposed of, general dissatisfaction will inevitably lead to demand that present "weak" govt be replaced by "strong" one capable of solving problems. In this connection Benediktsson pointed out that even certain members of his own party harbor view that present govt lacks strength while Herman Jonasson is becoming increasingly vociferous in his opposition. If a "strong" govt should be formed it would almost certainly include Communist members.

In view of above possibility Benediktsson who appeared extremely worried inquired as to prospects for sale wet salted fish to Army for use in feeding civilian population US zone Germany. I said we had little info on subject but would be glad to inquire into the matter adding however that since cost of feeding Germans is borne by US taxpayers Army must naturally place its orders where prices are lowest. Benediktsson replied he thought price question could be settled satisfactorily but urged preliminary investigation be instituted as soon as possible in view uncertainties present politico economic situation.

As we see it Russians have been stalling on Iceland negotiators since they are counting on continued deterioration economic conditions which would eventually result in fall of govt and replacement by one having Communist representation and were spurred into making foregoing limited offer only because of fear that British would acquire herring oil which Soviet Union apparently needs. Their failure to bid for wet salted fish however seems to indicate that their present offer is an exception to rather than change in policy. Should Soviet tactics be successful local Communists will undoubtedly seek two portfolios in the govt, aviation in order to hamstring AOA operation Keflavik [3] and possibly foreign affairs. If Olafur Thors forms a new govt he would probably refuse to give Communists latter post but might be compelled to let them have aviation portfolio. It is conceivable how-

---

[3] In the Legation's Note 727, April 2, to the Minister for Foreign Affairs, not printed, Trimble informed Benediktsson that "the American Overseas Airlines has been designated under contract to the United States War Department to maintain, either directly or through its subsidiary, the Iceland Airport Corporation, on behalf of the United States Government the services and facilities at the Keflavik Airport extended thereto by the Agreement of October 7, 1946, after the United States military forces have been withdrawn from Iceland." (859A.20/4–2347) For text of Agreement, see Department of State Treaties and Other International Acts Series (TIAS) No. 1566, or 61 Stat. (pt. 3) 2426. Related documentation on the operation of Keflavik airport, not printed, is in Department of State file 859A.7962.

ever that if Herman Jonasson should become PriMin he would be willing to let Communists head both ministries.

Considering implications present situation I strongly recommend Dept and War Dept examine possibilities for purchase wet salted fish by Army for use in Germany or in connection with Greek relief program and furnish me with such preliminary data as may be readily available in order that I may follow up yesterday's conversation with Benediktsson. Prospects for continuance present govt are favorable provided we can help Iceland to dispose of fish. If we cannot and economic conditions continue to deteriorate as they have every likelihood of doing probability is that cabinet will eventually fall. I fully realize course of action Legation advocating corresponds in certain respects with economic warfare practices but consider it necessary from standpoint strategic interests involved.

TRIMBLE

862.5018/8–247 : Telegram

The Chargé in Iceland (Trimble) to the Secretary of State

CONFIDENTIAL REYKJAVIK, August 2, 1947—6 p.m.

298. Department's telegram 200, August 1.[1]

1. With view to increasing Icelandic fish production so as to augment fish content German diet Acheson [2] made following proposals in behalf bi-zonal authorities:

(*a*) Negotiation of residual or open-end contract in which minimum delivery be guaranteed and market established for all possible fish at any time delivered at any German or continental port.

(*b*) Contract renewable annually with reconsideration of prices and terms.

(*c*) Partial payment in terms dollars or sterling with balance reimbursable at such time bi-zonal exports exceed imports on *pari-passu* basis with other participants in German food program including US and UK.

(*d*) Down payment percentage and prices to be discussed upon Acheson's return in two weeks. Latter necessarily conditioned by cost alternative sources of food.

(*e*) Scheme must coincide with any decisions made under Marshall plan.

2. Advantages to Iceland of above:

(*a*) Participation in preview of Marshall plan.

(*b*) No need to alter present trade channels or allocate to US any of Iceland's presently disposable production.

---

[1] Not printed.
[2] Edward C. Acheson, detailed as special emissary from the State Department with the personal rank of Minister to discuss purchases of fish in Scandinavian countries for the bi-zonal German population.

(c) Contract would give "support price" or "floor" to price of fish which would enable Iceland's authorities to develop plans for increased production and at same time provide unique opportunity for long range economic planning i.e. measures to combat inflation.

(d) No intention of bidding up prices thereby enhancing inflationary difficulties.

(e) Opportunity immediately to reestablish normal and natural trade channels with Germany which were of primary importance to Iceland's economy in pre-war period.

(f) Possibility of applying for International Bank loan to finance that part of credit Icelanders feel that they themselves cannot carry.

3. Except for observation regarding bank loan which was based on McCloy statement[3] summarized July 29 radio bulletin aforegoing understood to be in line with instructions Acheson received from General Clay[4] and bi-zonal authorities although I did not see their text.

4. As gesture of good-will Acheson offered to negotiate immediate contract for 1,000 tons wet salted fish for early fall delivery to Greece, reserving balance of funds available for Mediterranean relief for bargaining purposes in connection with bi-zonal discussions upon his return here. However Iceland's negotiators who had been advised by Thor Thors[5] as to amount at Acheson's disposal showed tendency to wrangle over price with result that agreement could not be reached during two and one-half days he was in Reykjavik.

TRIMBLE

---

[3] John J. McCloy, President of the International Bank for Reconstruction and Development, stated that the Bank would correlate its resources for the general stimulation of production, thus supporting the aims of the Marshall Plan.
[4] Gen. Lucius D. Clay, Commanding General, United States Forces, Europe; Military Governor for Germany.
[5] Icelandic Minister in the United States.

Editorial Note

Negotiations for the fish purchase agreement continued through 1947. In October, Trimble was instructed to inform the Icelandic Government that the United States and Great Britain proposed to purchase jointly from Iceland through the British Ministry of Food during calendar year 1948 approximately seventy thousand tons of fish for the bi-zonal area of Germany (telegram 265, October 18, not printed, 862.5018/10–1847). On November 14, Trimble was instructed to inform the Icelandic Government that the British Government had agreed to purchase terms of 100 percent cash sterling, rather than the 75 percent proposed and not accepted in October (telegram 280, November 14, not printed, 862.5018/11–1447). Texts of the purchase agreements are in this same file.

859A.50/9–147

The Chargé in Iceland (Trimble) to the Secretary of State

CONFIDENTIAL　　　　　　　　　REYKJAVIK, September 1, 1947—6 p.m.

323. Benediktsson indicated this morning that government will shortly issue statement showing extremely serious financial situation Iceland now finds itself as result of inflation. This will probably be followed by appeal for voluntary reduction in production costs including wages. Assuming Communists will encourage labor to reject proposal, we "will then have to decide whether to attempt reduction through legislation or take Communists into all-party government on condition that they will induce followers to accept lower standard of living." Latter alternative is in line with Einar Olgeirsson's trial balloon in Saturday's *Thjódviljinn* in which he called on all producing elements—labor, farmers, fishermen, shipowners, et cetera—to join together in seeking solution to current economic problems. Principal objection to it according to Foreign Minister is fact that nearly all non-Communist party leaders distrust Communists. Legislative action on other hand would present material difficulties from standpoint of implementation. . . . Thus it is questionable whether it could enforce legislation in face of strong opposition on part Communist-controlled union. In addition Social Democrats are fearful that enactment legislation while Communists remain in opposition would create serious disaffection among their followers.

There is also third alternative at which Benediktsson merely hinted today (Legation's despatch 979, August 29 [1]) but of which he as a Conservative leader continues to be keenly aware, namely formation progressive-Communist-left wing SD coalition. Such an aggregation could be expected to include in its economic program a measure providing for establishment state-controlled import monopoly, the very thought of which is anathema to the import-wholesale firms which are among the staunchest supporters of Conservative Party.

As soon as he had finished I said inclusion of Communists in reorganized government could not help but have adverse effect on our efforts to assist Icelandic economy, as for example purchase of fish for relief purposes and employment Icelanders by IAC and airport contractor. Furthermore, in my opinion such action would only postpone

---

[1] Not printed.

and thereby render more difficult eventual showdown between Communist minority and overwhelming majority Icelandic people. Cabinet, I said, appeared to have overestimated strength of Communists in labor movement as indicated by its groundless fear that Dagabrun walkout last June would be followed by wave of sympathy strikes.

Foreign Minister said he appreciated validity my observations which tended to coincide with his own views and inquired whether I thought we would stand idly aside in event Communists seize power by *coup d'état*. I replied it was my personal opinion that we would not. Benediktsson concluded conversation with remark that alternative or alternatives he had outlined were still possibilities and any change in government extremely unlikely before Althing at beginning October.

TRIMBLE

ITALY

THE VISIT OF THE ITALIAN PRIME MINISTER, ALCIDE DE GASPERI, TO WASHINGTON IN JANUARY 1947

740.00119 Council/12–946 : Telegram

The Secretary of State to the Acting Secretary of State [1]

TOP SECRET   NEW YORK, December 9, 1946—3 :10 p.m.

Delsec 1102. From the Secretary. Department please relay to Am-Embassy, Rome.[2] As the final work in connection with the treaty of peace with Italy draws to a close and arrangements for the signing of the treaty are being made, it would seem to be of great value to have a discussion with Mr. De Gasperi on matters of mutual interest to our two governments.

Would you, therefore, extend an invitation on the part of the Government of the United States to Mr. De Gasperi as Prime Minister of Italy to come to Washington in the early part of January with a view to discussing the renewal of normal commercial relations between Italy and the United States and also other relevant matters of interest to the two countries. You might tell Mr. De Gasperi that I would be most happy if he could find his way to accept this invitation.[3]

Please also say that if Mr. De Gasperi can accept, I would suggest that any announcement to that effect be delayed until we have worked out a time when there could be simultaneous announcement of his acceptance both in Washington and Rome.

BYRNES

---

[1] Secretary of State Byrnes was in New York for the Third Session of the Council of Foreign Ministers, November 4–December 11, 1946.
[2] Repeated to Rome, December 9, 3 :50 p.m. In telegram 2141, December 12, not printed, the Chargé was instructed to inform the Italian Foreign Minister, Nenni, in general terms of the invitation after it had been extended to the Prime Minister (740.00119 Council/12–1246).
[3] In telegram 4369, December 12, from Rome, not printed, Key reported that De Gasperi was most grateful for the invitation which he hoped to be able to accept; he expected to give a definite decision by December 16 (740.00119 Council/12–1246).

711.65/12–1746 : Telegram

The Chargé in Italy (Key) to the Secretary of State

SECRET   ROME, December 17, 1946—6 p.m.
US URGENT

4406. We have received the following reply through Prime Minister's private secretary [1] (see my 4369 Dec 12 [2]) :

Begin translation.
De Gasperi agrees to leave January 3. He considers it best to defer any public announcement until the last possible moment. Text and date communication will be previously agreed upon and publication will be simultaneous. Better to avoid premature leaks. He will make every effort to keep his appointment but given the upset condition (*stato febbrile*) of country it is not to be excluded that at last moment some postponement or modification departure date may be imposed. (*End of translation*)

Prime Minister hopes begin discussions with Secretary Monday, January 6. He will remain in US for forum of Council of World Affairs at Cleveland (see Dowling's letter to me of November 1 [3]) returning Italy immediately thereafter.

We said we would transmit communication to Department as received but asked Canali to convey to De Gasperi our feeling that public announcement of visit should be made as soon as possible; that such news was bound to leak if postponed any length of time. We also asked that we be given as much time as possible regarding announcement for coordination Rome Washington. Foreign Minister has already been informed of visit of Prime Minister by Tarchiani (see Deptel 2141 Dec 11 [*12*] [4]).

If Department approves our view regarding publicity we should appreciate being authorized to point out to De Gasperi need for urgency in making early announcement to ensure that first news of visit is not presented in unfavorable light by unfriendly elements.

Prime Minister has been upset according to Canali by press despatches from Washington regarding postponement Export Import Bank of consideration Italian application for loan and new unfavorable development in payment $50,000,000 non-troop pay account (see my 4394 Dec 15 [3]). We said that so far as we knew application for loan was still before Bank and that we had had no indication that it was receiving any more or less favorable consideration than formerly. Regarding troop pay we expressed view that it could only be tech-

[1] Paolo Canali.
[2] See footnote 3, p. 835.
[3] Not printed.
[4] See footnote 2, p. 835.

nicalities between War and Treasury Department holding up final transfer of $50,000,000 to Italian account assuring Canali that there could be no doubt that Secretary's assurance to De Gasperi of October 12 would be honored.

KEY

Lot 54–D 328

Memorandum by the Deputy Director of the Office of European Affairs (Hickerson) to the Secretary of State

CONFIDENTIAL [WASHINGTON,] January 6, 1947.

According to the Italian Embassy, De Gasperi will want to talk with you on the following matters:

1. *Italian Colonies:* De Gasperi will again ask US support for the original French plan of an Italian trusteeship over the former colonies when the CFM Deputies meet to discuss this problem.

2. *Surplus Italian Naval Units:* De Gasperi is most anxious that we permit the Italians themselves to scrap the surplus naval vessels allocated to the US.

3. *Yugoslav Attitude on Italian Treaty:* The Prime Minister will endeavor to explain why the Italians feel they can sign the treaty only if the Yugoslavs also sign, and will ask your opinion of the probability that the Yugoslavs will accept the treaty.

These are all questions which have a great influence on Italian public opinion, and De Gasperi feels that favorable answers to them will go far towards pacifying the political uneasiness in Italy, and thus strengthen the moderate element.

In addition, the Prime Minister will probably mention some of the economic matters which he will take up in greater detail with Mr. Clayton:

A. *Eximbank Loan:* To the Italians, this much discussed subject has become a barometer of American confidence in Italy. When the press reported some weeks ago that the loan was off, lira quotations suffered their worst break to date, and rose again only after your statement that the loan was still under consideration. De Gasperi feels that the loan has now acquired an importance far beyond its financial significance, and is therefore the greatest single factor in what we do for Italy.

B. *Purchase of More Liberty Ships:* Italy now desires to buy another 50 Liberty ships, in addition to the 50 already contracted for.

C. *Return of Italian Assets in US:* We are committed to the return of the major part of Italian assets in the US, and there remains only to work out the method by which this will be done, possibly in a general financial settlement between the two governments. It is hoped that we can tell De Gasperi while he is here that we intend to cancel Italian indebtedness for the civilian supply program; that an additional $50 million in the non-troop-pay account is now available for the Italians; and that arrangements have been completed for the use by Italy of the two *Conte* ships for repatriation of prisoners of war and the emigration of displaced persons from Italy to places of re-settlement in South America.

You may wish to suggest to De Gasperi that he discuss with Mr. Clayton the negotiation of a new commercial treaty to replace the *modus vivendi* of 1938 [*1937*].[1] An outline of our proposals can be given to the Italians now, and our draft of a treaty can be presented to them in a few weeks.

Finally, the Prime Minister can be expected to talk to everyone in sight about wheat and coal, which are of prime importance to Italy. Fortunately, the prospects for increased shipments of both commodities seem somewhat brighter, and of course we will do the best we can to meet Italian essential requirements.

JOHN D. HICKERSON

---

[1] See *Foreign Relations*, 1937, vol. II, pp. 435 ff. and 1938, vol. II, pp. 557 ff.

865.50/1-647

Memorandum of Conversation, by the Appointed Ambassador to Italy (Dunn)[1]

[WASHINGTON,] January 6, 1947.

Participants: Secretary Byrnes
Mr. Alcide de Gasperi, Prime Minister
Ambassador Tarchiani
Mr. James Clement Dunn

The Secretary received the Prime Minister of Italy, Mr. de Gasperi, today at 12 noon. Also present were the Italian Ambassador, Mr. Tarchiani, and Mr. Dunn. The Prime Minister expressed the grateful appreciation of the Government and people of Italy to the Government of the United States for an invitation for the Prime Minister to come to this country. He said it was a source of great encouragement to the Italian people to see the friendly attitude displayed by the American Government toward Italy. He said he hoped his visit would result in assistance to Italy as that country was now in the throes of an economic as well as a political crisis. He said the recent disturbances in southern Italy were partly political and partly based upon economic difficulties,

---

[1] Throughout 1946 Mr. Dunn had served as Deputy in the meetings of the Council of Foreign Ministers and in the meetings of the Deputies in the negotiations of the treaties of peace with Italy, Rumania, Hungary and Bulgaria. Although he had been designated Ambassador to Italy on July 25, 1946, he did not present his credentials in Rome until February 6, 1947.

and that the greatest political pressure was being brought at this time by the Communist Party to bring Italy within the orbit of Russian influence. Mr. de Gasperi said that of course his entire effort was to combat this movement as he was of an entirely different opinion.

The Prime Minister then spoke of the need for an increase of 150,000 tons of wheat in the allocations to be granted Italy from now until June, when the new crop in Italy would pick up the slack. He said this would mean an increase in the allocation from 1,450,000 tons to 1,600,000 tons. The food situation in Italy was most precarious; they had no stocks and no reserves, and the delay of one ship in arriving in Italy meant that they were faced with semirevolutionary riots and disturbances in the country.

The Prime Minister also spoke of the need for an increase in the coal shipments from 600,000 tons per month to 700,000 tons per month. He said that formerly coal was obtained from British and German sources but that since the war it had not been possible to obtain them from these sources. There were, he said, about 30,000 tons a month coming from Poland but the deliveries were so tardy that this coal never arrived on time. The Secretary said with reference to both the wheat and coal shipments that of course one of the difficulties was connected with transportation, inland transportation within the United States in the case of wheat as well as ocean transportation, and in the case of coal, ocean transportation and of course strikes we had had in this country. Mr. Byrnes asked Mr. Dunn to call the attention of Mr. Clayton to these matters, and asked that the Prime Minister take these questions up with Mr. Clayton when he saw him; that he was sure this Government would do all it could to assist, but the difficulties were in some respects not entirely subject to our own control.

The Secretary then said that it would be possible to assure Mr. de Gasperi while he was here that Italy would be granted $50,000,000 more of the sum held in suspense account by the Treasury for the payment of supplies and requisitions for the U.S. Army in Italy and that there would possibly be some more on this account which would be made available later but could not be granted at this time. Mr. de Gasperi received this news with satisfaction and gratitude.

The Prime Minister then said that they would like to arrange to secure about 50 more Liberty ships. The Secretary said that Mr. de Gasperi and the Ambassador appreciated the situation regarding the sale of our ships as controlled by U.S. law. He said this was a matter which was subject to the existing conditions, whereupon Mr. de Gasperi said that the Italian Government would be prepared to subscribe to the same conditions under which they made the previous arrangements for ships last autumn. Mr. Byrnes said that in that case that if they were prepared to comply with the same conditions he would see that this matter was gone into with a view to facilitating the arrival at such arrangements as could be worked out for this purpose. He also asked Mr. Dunn to have this matter looked into and a report made to him upon it.[2]

Mr. de Gasperi then spoke of the gold which was captured by the U.S. and British Armies in northern Italy.[3] He said this was Italian gold which he thought should be returned to Italy in much the same manner as Hungarian gold had been returned to Hungary. Mr. Dunn explained that the situation was rather different in the two cases as the United States had no right to retain the Hungarian gold which was found in Germany because any rights to this gold had been waived under the arrangements made at Potsdam. With regard to the Italian gold captured in northern Italy, however, while this Government was very anxious to see this gold returned to the Italian Government, it was understood that there were certain claims against this gold which had to be taken into consideration. Mr. Dunn said that he knew this matter was being looked into and that we would be able to inform the Prime Minister while he was here with respect to the status of this gold.[4]

Mr. de Gasperi then spoke of the post-UNRRA relief program. The Secretary said that a request was being presented to Congress for the allocation of certain funds for the direct relief of countries which were in need of such relief, among which Italy was included. He said that of course no man could say [anything?] now with respect to this request. The present situation was that we had a Republican Congress with a Democratic Administration, and that while there had been full and complete cooperation between the two Parties with respect to foreign affairs, it was not possible at the present time to tell how economic and other matters would be dealt with in the new Congress. He said, however, that it was his hope that this relief would be granted to take the place of the UNRRA program which was expiring and that he would continue to hope so until he found reason to the contrary.

The Secretary had to leave for the White House at this moment because of a request by the President to the Cabinet to assemble at

---

[2] See p. 841.
[3] Discovery and seizure of the gold at Fortezza was reported by Ambassador Kirk in despatch 1885, July 11, 1945, from Rome, not printed (865.515/7–1145).
[4] See telegram 5466, p. 987.

the White House preparatory to proceeding to the Capitol for the
delivery of the presidential message to the new Congress.[5]

[5] In Ambassador Tarchiani's account of this meeting he states that Secretary
Byrnes was cordial but preoccupied, and kept turning to Dunn for confirmation
or information. The Italian Prime Minister and the Ambassador remained quite
puzzled regarding Byrnes' attitude until they learned on the next day, January 7, of Byrnes' resignation and the designation of General Marshall to succeed
him. (Alberto Tarchiani, *America-Italia: Le dieci giornate di De Gasperi negli
Stati Uniti* (Milan, Rizzoli, 1947), pp. 36–37, 55.)

865.5018/1–647

*Memorandum by the Adviser in the International Resources Division
(Stillwell) to the Under Secretary of State for Economic Affairs
(Clayton)*

URGENT   [WASHINGTON,] January 6, 1947.

Subject: US Shipments of Grain and Flour to Italy

In December we loaded at US ports approximately 98,000 tons of
grain and flour for Italy.

For January, allocation has been made to UNRRA sufficient to give
Italy approximately 125,000 tons of grain and out of a total of 100,000
tons of flour allocated to UNRRA, UNRRA has agreed to ship 75,000
tons to Italy making a total of 200,000 tons wheat equivalent for Italy
in January.

We still are having some difficulty with the Department of Agriculture in getting them to actually purchase flour. They have scheduled
none of the above-mentioned flour for actual shipment yet. I am working on this at the present time but may need your help in calling on
Secretary Anderson to take immediate and direct action to see that
these flour allocations are actually translated into procurement and
shipment.[1]

[1] In a subsequent memo of the same day, not printed, Stillwell reported that he
had learned from the Department of Agriculture that its procurement of flour
had been so slow that it was likely that Italy would get no more than half of
what had previously been indicated; that total shipments of grain and flour to
Italy in January would probably be no more that 160,000 tons. He mentioned that:
"It now appears that Agriculture's wheat procurement program is at a complete
stand-still because the Secretary of Agriculture has placed a ceiling of $2 a
bushel at Kansas City on Government purchases." (865.5018/1–647)

Lot 54–D 328

*Memorandum by the Appointed Ambassador to Italy (Dunn) to the
Secretary of State*

[WASHINGTON,] January 6, 1947.

I am told that the Italians should make formal application to the
Maritime Commission for the purchase of an additional 50 Liberty

ships.[1] As soon as the application is in, Mr. Clayton can talk with Admiral Smith and let him know of our support for the Italian application.[2]

You may wish to tell De Gasperi the foregoing when you see him tonight.

JAMES CLEMENT DUNN

---

[1] For the purchase by Italy of 50 Liberty ships in 1946, see the bracketed note, October 31, 1946, *Foreign Relations*, 1946, vol. v, p. 941.

[2] A letter sent by Vice Admiral W. W. Smith, Chairman of the U.S. Maritime Commission, to Under Secretary Clayton on January 21, not printed, refers to Clayton's meeting with the Commission on Friday, January 10; to his urging "that the sale of additional vessels to the Italian Government at this time was of prime importance"; and to the action of the Commission on January 14 approving the sale to Italy of 50 additional ships. (195.2/1–2147)

Editorial Note

According to the account written by the Italian Ambassador, Alberto Tarchiani, *America–Italia: Le dieci giornate di De Gasperi negli Stati Uniti* (Milan, Rizzoli, 1947), page 40, he and the Italian Minister of Commerce, Pietro Campilli, had a meeting on January 6 at 3:30 p.m. with the Secretary of Agriculture, Clinton P. Anderson. No American record of this meeting has been found.

Tarchiani further records (*ibid.*, page 49) that he accompanied De Gasperi and Campilli to a meeting at 9:00 a.m. on January 7 with the Secretary of the Treasury, John W. Snyder, at which it was arranged for Campilli and Donato Menichella, Director General of the Banca d'Italia, to meet next day with experts of the U.S. Treasury Department. No American record of this meeting has been found.

Tarchiani further records (*ibid.*, page 50) that after meeting with Secretary Snyder, he and De Gasperi went at 10:00 o'clock to the Department of State to see Under Secretaries Acheson and Clayton, at which time De Gasperi explained the situation in Italy to Mr. Acheson. No record of the discussion with Acheson has been found in the files of the Department of State.

De Gasperi also conferred with the Secretary of Commerce, W. Averell Harriman, at some time prior to 5:00 p.m. of January 7 at which time Harriman's records indicate that he left Washington for a speaking engagement in the mid-West. This meeting with Harriman is not mentioned in Tarchiani's book, but De Gasperi himself referred to it during his meeting with Secretary Byrnes on January 8 (see page 851) and it is also mentioned in the official communiqué of January 15 (Department of State *Bulletin,* January 26, 1947, page 165).

Tarchiani records a second meeting with Secretary Snyder on January 8 at 4 :00 p.m. (*America-Italia,* page 65) ; a second discussion with Secretary Byrnes on January 14 at 11 :00 a.m. (*ibid.,* pages 123–124) ; and a third meeting with Mr. Snyder on January 14 at 12 : 30 p.m. (*ibid.,* page 125), but no American record of any of these three discussions has been found.

865.51/1–747

Memorandum by the Director of the Office of Financial and Development Policy (Ness) to the Under Secretary of State for Economic Affairs (Clayton)

[WASHINGTON,] January 7, 1947.

Subject: This Morning's Meeting with Premier de Gasperi

You asked on Saturday [1] that I inform you briefly of the status of the matters to be discussed with Premier de Gasperi during his visit here. There are six such major items:

1. *Eximbank loan.* When asked yesterday (Monday) morning whether this credit might be included in the NAC agenda for this afternoon, Mr. Martin said that he wished to think the matter over some more. Accordingly, it is not likely, unless there be a last minute change of thinking, that the application will appear specifically among the agenda items. I have asked the NAC staff to be prepared, however, to bring it up upon our request as "Other Business". As you will recall, Mr. Thorp, Mr. Dunn and Mr. Dowling agreed that it would be better if this credit were not announced during the time the Premier is in this country but that it should be announced on the fifteenth of this month, by which time the Premier would have just returned to Italy.[2]

2. *Post-UNRRA relief.* Here, as you know, we can only assure the Premier of this Government's intention to request funds for food relief from the Congress. The introduction of the legislation during his presence would be a reminder of this intention. We will not, of

---

[1] January 4.
[2] See *Foreign Relations,* 1946, vol. v, p. 942 for the memorandum by the Staff Committee to the National Advisory Council on International Monetary and Financial Problems of November 15, 1946, recommending a loan of $100 million to Italy by the Export-Import Bank. See p. 859 for the approval of this recommendation on January 13, 1947.

course, be able to talk to him about specific sums, but he may wish to have as much assurance as is possible within the foregoing limits.

3. *Emergency revision of UNRRA.* Mr. Wood is now thinking in terms of the second of the two alternatives presented to us last Saturday. This, if finally agreed upon, would involve a net reduction of the allotment to UNRRA on the score that Italy is presently able to finance its emergency needs. You may, at some time during the Premier's visit here wish to acquaint him with this possibility. I would suggest, however, that this "bad news" be held for your meeting on Wednesday afternoon, by which time de Gasperi will have talked to the press.

4. *Non-troop pay account.* The certification of a second $50 million has been completed, and Treasury will be able to effect payment on Wednesday.[3]

5. *Plan A waiver.* Following conversations with the Canadians and British we are now free to announce to the Italians that we are prepared to cancel the American share of the Italian debt for civilian supplies (Plan A).[4] This announcement should, however, be couched in terms which link such cancellation on our part to an over-all settlement with the Italians of war accounts which would be made in conjunction with or after the Italians had signed the peace treaty. This is necessary because, should the Italians fail to ratify the peace treaty, this Government might remain technically subject to claims on the score of requisition by the U.S. armed forces.

6. *Italian assets in the United States.* Italian assets in the United States have been in part vested by the Alien Property Custodian and in part blocked by the Treasury. In Paris Mr. Thorp announced that the United States would return to Italy all such property over and above that needed to meet certain relatively small American claims against Italy. While the Italians would welcome a public statement at this time promising the return of Italian assets in the very near future, it does not appear advisable to go beyond the statements made in Paris for the reason that certain technical difficulties remain to be worked out by the Treasury and also because we will not want to return Italian property until we have secured from the Italians certain commitments respecting our claims against them and possibly respecting Italian pre-war debts, these all to be taken care of in the over-all Italian settlement.

---

[3] For previous documentation on this subject, see *Foreign Relations*, 1946, vol. v, pp. 899–946 *passim.*

[4] Regarding Plan "A", see p. 715, footnote 1.

033.6511/1–747

Memorandum of Conversation, by Mr. George C. McGhee, Special Assistant to the Under Secretary of State for Economic Affairs (Clayton)

[WASHINGTON,] January 7, 1947.

Subject: Meeting between Mr. Clayton and the Italian Prime Minister, Alcide de Gasperi.

Participants: His Excellency Alcide de Gasperi, Prime Minister of Italy
Mr. Donato Menichella, Director General, Bank of Italy
Mr. Carli, Director, Office of Foreign Exchange, Italy
Signor Alberto Tarchiani, Italian Ambassador
Mr. Egidio Ortona, First Secretary, Italian Embassy
Mr. Vincenzo Vogliolo
UE—Mr. Clayton
American Ambassador to Italy, Mr. Dunn
A–T—Mr. Thorp
OFD—Mr. Ness
UE—Mr. McGhee
SE—Mr. Dowling
A–T—Mr. Wood
IR—Mr. Stillwell
CP—Mr. Moore
FN—Mr. Reinstein

After preliminary formalities, the following topics were discussed:

1.) *Grain*

The Prime Minister stated that the availability of grain in Italy had become a political issue of the first order. Italy urgently needed both an increase in grain allocations and better timing of shipments. With the present short stock position, any delay in arrivals creates a serious distribution problem.

Mr. Clayton explained to the Prime Minister that the availability of grain from this country is entirely a question of internal transport. There are adequate supplies of grain and adequate ships to take the grain to Italy, but there was an insufficiency of freight cars and handling equipment. Mr. Clayton pointed out that the United States is not normally a great grain exporting country and that the current rate of grain exports exceeds anything ever before attempted here. He then described measures which this country has taken to alleviate the transportation difficulties, explaining that priorities for grain shipments had been established on the railroads and that an expediter (Captain Conway) has been appointed by the President to coordinate all phases of the transportation problem. Since the same expediter moved 11 million tons of wheat from last year's crop, the movement having been completed only 10 days later than its June 30 deadline, Mr. Clayton expected improvement in present rate of shipment. Mr. Clayton stated that Italy has an allocation of 200,000 tons for the month of January and that although he could not make any commitment, in his judgment this rate could be maintained through June. He advised that he was calling the Secretary of Agriculture by phone later in the day in the Mid-West, to explain the urgency of the situation and to urge that all necessary steps be taken.

The Italian Ambassador stated that Italy was desirous of obtaining an increase in its IEFC grain allocation for the current crop year from 1,450,000 to 1,600,000 tons. He pointed out that supplies available from sources other than the United States are meager. Italy expected only 40,000 tons from Turkey and a small amount from Canada. Supplies from Argentina were very uncertain, there being no assurance that there would be any arrivals from this source before June. The Ambassador pointed out that with elections in Italy coming in June, it would be embarrassing for the present government to cut the bread ration before this time. The ration is already reduced to 200 grams. The Ambassador further pointed out that February and March are expected to be the most difficult months for grain arrivals in Italy. He repeated that Secretary Anderson had advised that he hoped to ship 230,000 tons in February and 250,000 tons in March. The Ambassador said that although Italy would continue her efforts to buy grain in the Argentine and elsewhere, she could rely only on the United States.

Mr. Clayton repeated that he had every expectation that 200,000 tons a month would be shipped from the United States to Italy for the next six months, which, with shipments to date of 400,000 tons, should equal the 1,600,000-ton figure which the Ambassador had requested. He assured the Italians we will do the best we can.

2.) *Coal*

The Prime Minister advised that Italy was currently receiving approximately 600,000 tons of coal per month from this country, but needed an additional 100,000 tons a month in order to achieve a reasonable level of industrial output. He reported that Poland was now furnishing very little coal to Italy, and that both **Germany and UK** furnished some, although both had in the past been large suppliers.

Mr. Clayton agreed that the problem of coal was a serious one both for Italy and for other European countries. He predicted that this would be one of the most difficult of present problems to effect permanent solution. Mr. Clayton asked whether Italy would not prefer coal from other sources than the United States, in view of the high price of our coal. The Ambassador replied that US coal was now actually cheaper to Italy than European coal. Whereas US coal was delivered to Italy for $22.00 a ton, Belgian coal cost $24.00 a ton and Polish coal even more.

Mr. Stillwell advised that a temporary shortage of ships available for coal would make it difficult for the US to fulfill all commitments during the next two months. Mr. Clayton concluded that although he was not in complete possession of the facts and could make no commitments with regard to specific amounts of coal which can be furnished Italy, we understood the gravity of the Italian situation and will do the best we can.

3.) *Additional Liberty Ships*

The Ambassador stated that although Italy has not as yet made application to the Maritime Commission, they would like to have 50 Liberty ships in addition to the 50 already obtained. At the present, their merchant fleet aggregates only 900,000 tons, which is less than one-third of their pre-war fleet of 3 million tons. The 50 additional ships would still give them only 1,300,000 tons. The Ambassador said that the Italian government would purchase the additional ships, in the same way that they had purchased the original 50.

Mr. Clayton promised that he would take this matter up personally with the Maritime Commission on Friday, at which time he would support the Italian request for the 50 additional ships. He suggested that in the meantime applications for purchase of the ships be filed with the Commission. Mr. Clayton observed that he considered it desirable for the Italians to attain their pre-war shipping tonnage level as quickly as possible, in order to alleviate the drain on their foreign exchange.

4.) *Post-UNRRA Relief*

The Ambassador referred to the fact that Secretary Byrnes had indicated to the Prime Minister that the Department would request Congress to appropriate funds for post-UNRRA Relief for Italy and certain other countries. The Prime Minister understood that this represented the policy of the Executive Branch of the US Government only and hoped that the American people, through their Congress, would approve the granting of this relief, which was badly needed in Italy.

Mr. Clayton replied that the Department would give full support to the bill providing for this relief, which he hoped would go forward to the Congress within the next few days. He assured the Prime Minister that he personally and, he hoped, Secretary Byrnes, would appear before Congress in behalf of this bill.

5.) Export-Import Bank Loan

The Ambassador stated that a loan from the Export-Import Bank was vitally needed to assure economic stability in Italy during the year 1947. The Prime Minister observed parenthetically that the loan had attained very great significance in Italy, because of the widespread discussion which had taken place concerning it. The Ambassador continued that the loan had become a political issue. Recent news that the loan would not be forthcoming had produced very serious repercussions in Italy. Particularly because of the large loans which the US has made to the UK and France, the Prime Minister's position would be seriously jeopardized if he should return to Italy without a loan.

Mr. Menichella stated that although the Italian Government had not yet called on the Bank of Italy to issue additional currency to finance its expenditures, the Government may be forced to take this drastic measure at an early date. The Italian people were anxiously awaiting the decision as to whether or not the US would aid in the reconstruction of Italy in addition to their assistance in providing relief for Italy.

Mr. Menichella observed that the Italian people had made a great contribution to their own economic recovery through increased production and through foregoing consumption. He explained that almost everything Italy made was exported, that there was no buying power within Italy. In the opinion of his government, the Italian export prospects justified an Export-Import Bank loan. The loan was of such importance to Italy that he was willing to discuss it on any basis, whether for short, medium, or a long term, if this was necessary to obtain it. He pointed out that technical financial circles in Italy are convinced that Italy deserves the loan, and will be disappointed and puzzled if the loan is not forthcoming. Obtaining the loan is an absolute necessity for the success of the de Gasperi Mission.

Mr. Menichella continued that he had heard informally in Washington that the Export-Import Bank had taken the position that they could not loan money to a country that was at the same time receiving a relief grant. He offered his opinion that there was no relationship between the grant, which was intended to make up for the deficit in food supplies in Italy, and the loan, which could be guaranteed by existing export contracts now held by Italian firms.

Mr. Clayton explained some of the background of the Export-Import Bank, pointing out that although it was enacted under the law of 1934 it is currently operating under an amended charter enacted in 1945, when its capital was raised from $700 million to $3½ billion. As currently constituted, the Bank has five directors, four public directors and the Secretary of State, who is represented by Mr. Clayton. Mr. Clayton explained that the directors are governed by the provisions of law pertaining to the Bank. He stated that although a short-term loan in the order of eighteen months or two years would be easier to negotiate, he did not think such a loan would meet the Italian needs as he understood them. He questioned that the Italian balance of payments position would permit repayment of a short-term loan. Mr. Ness suggested the possibility of making a portion of the loan on a short-term basis, for commodities that could yield foreign exchange quickly, with the remainder of the loan on a longer term basis.

Mr. Menichella replied that he had attempted both to obtain a larger loan than that under discussion and a long-term loan, and that he is willing to discuss a short-term loan only as a matter of necessity. He would, he indicated, be glad to discuss the type of loan mentioned by Mr. Ness involving both long-term and short-term commitments. He pointed out the great psychological boost which would result in Italy, if the Italians could feel that an independent US Agency considered Italy worth a credit risk of $100 million.

Mr. Clayton repeated that he believed the loan must be related to the Italian future balance of payments position, and that he could not disassociate in his own mind any short- and long-term aspects. If short-term proceeds are derived they should probably be reinvested as a method of securing more long-term proceeds. He felt that the directors of the Bank in making their decision as to the loan should be realistic in their approach. He urged that the Italians bring to the attention of the Bank any information not in possession of the Bank which might facilitate a favorable decision on the loan application. It was pointed out that arrangements had already been made for the technicians in the Italian delegation to confer with the staff at the Bank.

Both the Prime Minister and Mr. Clayton agreed that it would be better for all concerned if an attempt were made to secure the loan on a long-term basis. Mr. Clayton, in conclusion, stated that he would do the best he could for the Italians, but that he represented only one of the five directors of the Bank. He added that in the event a long-term loan is secured for Italy, he saw no reason why short-term loans for cotton or other raw materials providing quick returns could not also be made. The Prime Minister expressed appreciation for the consideration which Mr. Clayton and other American officials had shown.

6.) *"Hermitage"* and *"Monticello"*

In closing, the Ambassador raised the question of certain former Italian ships, the *Hermitage* and *Monticello*, which were currently subject to negotiation between the Italians and the Maritime Commission. These ships are to be operated by the Italians on agreed terms under the Panamanian flag. Mr. Clayton advised that he was not fully informed as to the status of these negotiations, but that he would take the matter up with the Maritime Commission on Friday.

The Ambassador stated that there were two points still at issue between the Italians and the Maritime Commission to which he would appreciate Mr. Clayton's giving special consideration. The Italians thought it extremely important from the standpoint of morale of the Italian people that the ships fly under the Italian flag. The Italians also felt that the split of earnings between the Maritime Commission and the Italians should be on a net and not on a gross basis as proposed by the Commission.

In closing, the Ambassador expressed appreciation to Mr. Clayton for the consideration he had shown the Italians in numerous instances, both in connection with his duties as Under Secretary of State and as a United States representative on UNRRA.

033.6511/1–747

Memorandum of Conversation [1]

WASHINGTON, January 7, 1947.

The Prime Minister and the Ambassador of Italy called at 12:00 noon at the White House to pay their respects to the President.

President Truman reaffirmed the American Government's sympathy and full faith in Italy's ability to rehabilitate herself. The President said that it is because of its faith in Italy that America has extended aid in the past and will do what it can in this present critical situation of the Italian people.

Mr. Truman said that he knew the Italians and the situation which they are in and he recalled that one of his beloved war buddy [*buddies*] of World War I was an Italian-American. The interview was general and the President again expressed his sympathy for the Italian people and the Italians in this country.[2]

(The President referred to the remarks that the Secretary of State made at the dinner last night at the Mayflower.)

---

[1] The authorship of this memorandum is not indicated, but presumably it was prepared by Ambassador Dunn or another officer of the Department of State.
[2] Tarchiani's account of this meeting is in *America-Italia*, pp. 51–52.

FW 865.61311/1–1447

The Prime Minister of Italy (De Gasperi) to President Truman

WASHINGTON, January 8, 1947.

MR. PRESIDENT: I was deeply gratified and much comforted by the assurances you kindly gave me in our interview of yesterday regarding the increase of shipments of wheat to Italy.

Unfortunately, this morning an appeal which reached me from my departments in Rome shows that by the 15th of January five or six regions in Italy with dense urban population will be left without stocks.

The inquiries that my officials here have made all day long on the question have brought out so far the following information:

a) no diversion of ships is so far being contemplated in order to satisfy the needs of those areas;

b) while the domestic availability of wheat in the United States would allow the execution of the agreed upon schedule of shipments, in fact:

—out of the 200,000 tons to be loaded in January ships have been named only for about 50–60% of that quantity;

—there exists considerable uncertainty concerning the execution of the planned shipments for February and March in the amount of 230,000 tons and 250,000 tons, respectively, as it has just been outlined to my mission.

I am confident, Mr. President, that you will fully realize the extreme anxiety with which I view these disquieting developments and the keen anticipation with which I am looking forward to receiving the firmest assurances which your departments will be able to give me.

While thanking you wholeheartedly for whatever action you will deem suitable to take in the matter, I wish to renew to you, Mr. President, the expressions of my highest esteem and consideration.

[Alcide] De Gasperi

865.51/1–847

Memorandum of Conversation, by the Appointed Ambassador to Italy (Dunn)

[Washington,] January 8, 1947.

Participants: Secretary Byrnes
Prime Minister De Gasperi
Ambassador Tarchiani
Mr. James Clement Dunn

Mr. De Gasperi came in to see the Secretary this morning to express his deep appreciation of all that Mr. Byrnes had done for him and for all the Department of State and the Government were doing to be helpful in connection with his visit here. The Prime Minister expressed his deep regrets at the news of Mr. Byrnes' resignation as Secretary of State.

Mr. De Gasperi then reviewed the subjects he was interested in while here, stressing particularly the importance of obtaining the $100,000,-000 loan from the Export-Import Bank. He spoke of a new plan he was studying which would support the loan by pledging certain of the Italian industries to the repayment of the loan as well as the Italian Government, thus creating a rather direct relationship between the furnishing of raw materials to these industries and the granting of the loan for industrial purposes rather than reconstruction purposes. Mr. Byrnes then spoke to Mr. Clayton on the telephone and discussed this new plan with him. Mr. Clayton said that he was doing everything he could to promote the loan with the Board of Directors of the Export-Import Bank and with the NAC (National Advisory Council). Mr. Byrnes said that Mr. De Gasperi would be able to go into this matter more fully with Mr. Clayton at the meeting arranged between them for 3:30 this afternoon.[1] Mr. De Gasperi then said he had had satisfactory interviews with Mr. Snyder, Secretary of the Treasury, and with Mr. Harriman, Secretary of Commerce.[2] He said that he was leaving for Cleveland tonight or tomorrow morning but would leave his technical assistants here to continue conversations with the Export-Import Bank, with Mr. Clayton, and with the Treasury, on purely financial matters.

Mr. Byrnes and Mr. De Gasperi then both agreed it would be preferable not to have a communiqué issued today, the last day of the Prime Minister's official visit to Washington, but that it would be better to wait until the end of his visit after he had been to Cleveland and returned to New York, perhaps next Monday or Tuesday, and that if necessary Mr. De Gasperi could come to Washington in order to issue a final communiqué, or it might be arranged by him in New York through the Embassy here. In any event, no communiqué will be issued until Mr. De Gasperi is about ready to leave the United States.[3]

On taking leave, Mr. De Gasperi then again thanked Mr. Byrnes for all he had done and the Secretary expressed his confidence that the results of the Prime Minister's visit would be even better than he had hoped for.

---

[1] *Post*, p. 854.
[2] See the editorial note, p. 842.
[3] For text of the communiqué, released to the press on January 15, see Department of State *Bulletin*, January 26, 1947, p. 165.

611.6531/1–847

Memorandum of Conversation, by the Assistant Chief of the Division of Commercial Policy (Moore)

[WASHINGTON,] January 8, 1947.

Subject: Commercial Policy Discussions with Italian Officials

Participants:

Mr. Campilli, Minister of Foreign Trade
Mr. Menichella, Director General of the Bank of Italy

Mr. Carli, Director, Office of Exchange Control, Ministry of
    Foreign Trade
Mr. Vogliolo, Commercial Counselor
Mr. Sacerdoti, Chief of Italian Technical Delegation
Mr. Ortona, Italian Embassy
A–T – Messrs. Thorp and Reinstein
OFD – Mr. Ness
SE – Mr. Dowling
FN – Messrs. Spiegel and Stibravy
LE – Mr. Boskey
CP – Mr. Moore

Mr. Thorp opened the discussion by outlining in general terms the
present status of the program for expansion of world trade through
reduction of trade barriers. He explained that it was not possible for
the Italian Government to participate in the work of the Preparatory
Commission in view of the limited membership of this body as established by ECOSOC. Although the determination of the countries
which will participate in the world trade conference and the organization of the ITO has not yet been decided, the United States Government will support the extension of an invitation to Italy. Consequently,
the United States Government would be interested in the present view
of the Italian Government on the trade program.

In reply Mr. Campilli stated that the Italian Government had
studied the proposed charter for the ITO and was in accord with the
principles upon which it was based. The importance for Italy of a
program to reduce barriers to world trade is greatly increased by
reason of such factors as the great dependence of the Italian economy
on imports of raw materials. The Italian Government is hopeful that
the program for limiting international restrictions can be extended to
international movement of man power, as well as trade in view of
the difficult problem of unemployment confronting Italy. The Italian
Government has entered into eight bi-lateral compensation agreements with other countries because of the difficulties of developing
European trade by any other means under present conditions. It hopes
that the use of such bi-lateral machinery will be eliminated in the near
future by the adoption of the world wide multilateral trade program
sponsored by the United States.

Mr. Thorp pointed out that the last treaty of commerce and navigation between Italy and the United States was concluded in 1871. Consequently, there is a need for modernization of the arrangements under
which trade between the two countries can be carried on. In the near
future the United States Government would like to submit for the
consideration of the Italian Government, through our Mission in
Rome, a proposed text of a treaty of friendship, commerce and navigation. Mr. Campilli replied that the Italian Government would welcome
an opportunity to negotiate such a treaty, especially since it appears

that trade with the United States will constitute such a large proportion of Italy's total trade in the future.[1]

Mr. Thorp stated that he wished to take this opportunity to call to the attention of the Italian Government the provisions of the proposed ITO charter dealing with international cartels and combines. Mr. Campilli replied that the Italian Government opposed restrictive national business practices, especially in view of its dependence on foreign sources for its raw materials. Mr. Thorp stated that he would also like to take the occasion of the present discussion of commercial policy matters to inquire of the Italian Government as to its plans for the Italian Technical Delegation presently procuring supplies in the United States. Mr. Campilli replied that the Italian Government was in complete agreement with the desire of the United States Government to return trade between the two countries to private channels at the earliest possible opportunity and that he expected the procurement activities of the Italian Technical Delegation to be gradually reduced and eventually eliminated.

---

[1] A new treaty of friendship, commerce, and navigation between the United States and Italy was signed at Rome, February 2, 1948; for text, see Department of State Treaties and Other International Acts Series (TIAS) No. 1965.

033.6511/1–847

Memorandum of Conversation, by Mr. George C. McGhee, Special Assistant to the Under Secretary of State for Economic Affairs (Clayton)

[WASHINGTON,] January 8, 1947.

Subject: Second Meeting Between Mr. Clayton and the Italian Prime Minister, Alcide de Gasperi

Participants:

His Excellency Alcide de Gasperi, Prime Minister of Italy (in part)
Mr. Campilli, Italian Minister of Foreign Commerce
Mr. Donato Menichella, Director General, Bank of Italy
Mr. Carli, Director, Office of Foreign Exchange, Italy
Signor Alberto Tarchiani, Italian Ambassador (in part)
Mr. Egidio Ortona, First Secretary Italian Embassy
Mr. Vincenzo Vogliola
UE – Mr. Clayton
Ambassador Dunn
A–T – Mr. Thorp
OFD – Mr. Ness
UE – Mr. McGhee
SE – Mr. Dowling
IR – Mr. Stillwell
FN – Mr. Reinstein

The Italian representatives stated that as a result of a suggestion made by the staff of the Export-Import Bank, they wished to offer for discussion a new plan for the proposed $100 million Export-Import Bank loan to Italy. They wished to discuss this loan in terms of its being made to a private Italian banking institution, the Istituto Mobiliare Italiano (IMI), which is an investment banking house supported by the leading banks, insurance companies and investment trusts in Italy. IMI has a total capitalization of one billion lira and outstanding loans of eight billion lira. This institution has been selected as the most suitable of all institutions of its class in Italy, because it is engaged in financing both big, medium, and small sized manufacturing businesses of all types. IMI has a good technical staff, has no political associations, and is not dominated by any one industry or group of industries. The Italian representatives explained that this new proposal was being made in order best to comply with the requirements of the Export-Import Bank. The obligation would be undertaken directly by IMI, with the entire loan including the necessary foreign exchange provisions being guaranteed by the Italian Government. It was explained that loans would be made by IMI from the borrowed funds only to firms engaged in the manufacture of goods for export and only for purchase of raw materials. The foreign exchange derived from these exports will be strictly controlled by IMI, so that funds would be available for repayment of the Export-Import Bank loan as required.

Mr. Clayton replied that this was the first time that he had heard of the Italian proposal, and that he would like to explore it a little more fully before making any final decision. He said that there still remained the question of the Italian balance of payments, and he asked when Italy would be in an exchange balance with the rest of the world. Mr. Clayton also asked what the average length of the loan was expected to be.

Mr. Campilli replied that Italy was now producing at 60% capacity and that she expected to be in balance on foreign exchange within five years. If Italy can pay only the interest on the Export-Import Bank loan for the first three years, she can finance the remainder. Mr. Campilli assured Mr. Clayton that all the funds received from the Export-Import Bank would be allocated to purchase of raw materials by firms manufacturing goods for export. He stated that the firms themselves would make the purchases. Although the loan would include both short and long term commitments, depending on the rapidity of turnover of the product derived from the raw materials purchased, the Italians expected the average length of the loan to be between eight and nine years.

Mr. Clayton observed that this loan was not a straight raw materials loan pledged by production derived from the raw materials, as it appeared on the surface to be. Particularly in view of the 3-year delay in starting repayment, there was no assurance that the exchange derived from the sale of the products produced would be used to liquidate the loan. The $100 million was small in comparison with the total amount which would be spent by Italy each year for imports. Mr. Clayton asked whether or not it would be possible for the Export-Import Bank to, under the proposed plan, specify the raw materials to be purchased and to obtain a guarantee that they would go to firms engaged in manufacture for export. The Italian representatives replied in the affirmative.

Mr. Campilli explained that the loan in question was not for the purpose of rehabilitating Italian industry, but for facilitating importation of raw materials. The remainder of the help which Italy will require in reconstruction must come from increased world trade resulting from the International Trade Organization, and from loans from the International Bank. The Italian financial position will be much improved when foreign exchange derived from her exports will be freely convertible, particularly the sterling which she earned from her trade with the United Kingdom, who is one of her best customers. The Italians are placing every emphasis on exports at the expense of internal consumption.

Mr. Clayton observed that after July 15, the United Kingdom will be obligated in accordance with her loan agreement with this country to convert into dollars all sterling earned currently. Mr. Campilli replied that the United Kingdom had indicated that this would not in fact be the case, but that they wished to negotiate with Italy a Trade and Payment Agreement effective July 15, which would provide for use of sterling earned by Italy for raw material purchases in the sterling area. Mr. Clayton stated that this arrangement would, in his opinion, be a clear violation of the British loan agreement. In answer to question as to whether or not the recent British-Argentine Trade Agreement did not also constitute a violation, Mr. Clayton replied that it did, but in a different way. The violation in the case of the Argentine is a theoretical one, since it would occur only in the event of the Argentine's having a favorable balance of trade with the United Kingdom, which is highly improbable. Mr. Clayton promised that he would give consideration to the new Italian proposal before the next meeting of the Directors of the Export-Import Bank. It was pointed out that the Italian representatives planned to discuss this matter further with the staff of the Bank on the day following.

During the preceding conversation, the Italian Prime Minister and Ambassador withdrew from the meeting.[1] Before they withdrew, Mr. Clayton handed to the Ambassador an *aide-mémoire* dated January 8, with regard to transfer of the former Italian ships *Hermitage* and the *Monticello* to the Italian government.[2] Mr. Clayton stated that the *aide-mémoire* did not cover the two questions raised by the Italians in the meeting of the preceding day with regard to this transfer, but that he would take these matters up with the Maritime Commission on Friday.

Mr. Clayton then asked Mr. Thorp to take up any points arising out of his earlier meeting at 2:30 p.m. with certain of the Italian representatives.[3] Mr. Thorp reported essential agreement with the Italians on commercial policy matters. He stated that both sides recognized the need for an over-all financial agreement between the two countries, which he hoped could be ratified at the same time as the proposed Treaty of Friendship, Commerce, and Navigation. It had been agreed that both sides would present a complete list of their claims and counterclaims against the other government in preparation for the over-all agreement.

Mr. Thorp explained that the Italian property in this country which had been seized during the war was still held against claims against Italy. The release of this property was complicated administratively since it involved the Alien Property Custodian, the Department of Justice and other agencies of this Government. Mr. Thorp had assured the Italians, however, that the bulk of their property would be returned except for a small amount to be held against certain limited claims. He added that the United States' claim against Italy for "Plan A" supplies was a substantial one, and that it would be necessary to arrive at some procedure for the settlement of this claim.

Mr. Clayton suggested that this claim be considered along with other claims between the two governments, and that both sides should get together and draft a joint communiqué covering all points under discussion except the Export-Import Bank loan for issue early next week. He suggested that the communiqué constitute a statement of agreements reached so far in the present discussions, and steps to be taken in the future.

---

[1] According to Tarchiani (*America-Italia*, pp. 63, 65), at 4:00 p.m. De Gasperi and he went to see Secretary of the Treasury Snyder who gave them a check for $50 million for the suspense account.

[2] The substance of the *aide-mémoire* was embodied in a press release of January 10, Department of State *Bulletin*, January 19, 1947, p. 136.

[3] See memorandum by the Assistant Chief of the Division of Commercial Policy, January 8, *supra*.

Mr. Dunn reported a conversation between the Prime Minister and the Secretary with regard to an economic survey of Italy. Mr. Campilli added that his government wished the United States to cooperate with the Italians in making such a survey. Mr. Clayton replied that he assumed that the financing for any large-scale reconstruction of Italian industry would come from the International Bank and that the Bank was setting itself up to make the surveys required. He questioned the desirability of the United States and Italy making the survey on a bilateral basis. Mr. Clayton asked the Italians whether or not they had made application to the Bank for a loan. Mr. Campilli replied that the Italians wished to discuss their application with the United States prior to submission to the Bank. Mr. Clayton took the position that this was a matter between the Italian government and the Bank, although we would, of course, be glad to provide such technical assistance as we could. Mr. Clayton stressed the importance of proper documentation of loan applications made to the Bank.

Mr. Menichella expressed appreciation to the United States government for efforts it had made in assisting the Italians in recovering their gold which had been taken over by the Allies during the war. Mr. Thorp summarized the existing situation which he stated was well known to the Italians. First, the gold which was taken by the Germans out of Italy and seized by the Allies in Germany had now become a part of the Gold Pot.[4] Although Italy may be allowed to share in the Pot, decision as to the method of sharing remains to be determined, in fact the procedure for making such a decision has not yet been determined. Secondly, the disposition of the gold seized by the US–UK forces in Northern Italy is a matter for decision by the US–UK governments after consideration of claims put forth by other countries, including France, Yugoslavia and Albania. It is hoped that agreement as to disposition of this gold can be reached at the CFM Deputies Meeting to be held shortly in London.[5]

Mr. Menichella expressed the hope that the 73 tons of gold taken over by the Allies in Germany could be returned directly to Italy, in the same manner that the Hungarian gold had been returned to Hungary. He reported that the Italian government was already in negotiation with the French government in an effort to clear up French claims. Mr. Reinstein commented that there was no possibility of the Italians receiving 100% of the 73 tons of gold taken in Germany, since the most they can expect is to share this with other countries devastated by Germany. Mr. Thorp explained the distinction between the Hun-

---

[4] For an explanation of the "gold pot" principle, see *Foreign Relations*, The Conference of Berlin (The Potsdam Conference, 1945), vol. II, p. 938, footnote 4.
[5] Documentation regarding the Council of Foreign Ministers in 1947 is printed in volume II.

garian gold, which had been seized by the United States forces directly from the Hungarians, and the Italian gold, which had been taken over from the Germans in Germany. The Italian representatives pointed out that they considered the distinction to be in their favor, since the Hungarian gold was taken from the Hungarians while they were still fighting the Allies and was restored to Hungary in an effort to bolster up their currency. The Italians would greatly appreciate the same friendly treatment, since their currency would also be greatly strengthened by an increase in their gold reserve.

Mr. Campilli expressed final appreciation to the American representatives for their consideration. He expressed the hope that the communiqué which would be drafted jointly by the two governments would indicate that positive economic assistance is to be furnished to Italy by the United States government and that the United States will have a continuing interest in the future of Italy. He stated that this was urgently needed in order to give the Italian people hope for the future. Mr. Clayton concluded by assuring the Italians that our heart was in the right place and that we would do all that we could for them under the circumstances.

Lot 60–D 137 : Box 1

Minutes of Fiftieth Meeting of the National Advisory Council on International Monetary and Financial Problems, Washington, January 13, 1947

TOP SECRET

PRESENT

Secretary John W. Snyder (Chairman), Treasury Department
Mr. William L. Clayton, State Department
Secretary W. Averell Harriman, Commerce Department
Mr. Marriner S. Eccles, Board of Governors, Federal Reserve System
Mr. William McC. Martin, Jr., Export-Import Bank
Mr. Orvis A. Schmidt (Acting Secretary)

1. *Reconstruction Loan to Italy*

After discussion, the Council accepted the Staff Committee's recommendation that consideration by the Export-Import Bank of credits to Italy not exceeding $100 million be approved (NAC Document No. 269[1]).

---

[1] See *Foreign Relations*, 1946, vol. v, p. 942.

Action:

The following action was taken:

The National Advisory Council approves the consideration by the Export-Import Bank of credits to Italy not exceeding in the aggregate $100 million.

033.6511/1–1447

Memorandum of Conversation, by Mr. George C. McGhee, Special Assistant to the Under Secretary of State for Economic Affairs (Clayton)

[WASHINGTON,] January 14, 1947.

Subject: Third Meeting Between Mr. Clayton and the Italian Prime Minister, Alcide de Gasperi

Participants: Alcide de Gasperi, Italian Prime Minister
Pietro Campilli, Minister of Foreign Trade
Donato Menichella, Director General, Bank of Italy
Alberto Tarchiani, Ambassador of Italy
Egidio Ortona, First Secretary, Italian Embassy
UE–Mr. Clayton
UE–Mr. McGhee
SE–Mr. Dowling

The Italian representatives proposed certain changes in the draft communiqué covering agreements reached during their present visit.[1] Mr. Clayton suggested they bring these suggestions up in their meeting with the Export-Import Bank later in the day.

Mr. Clayton advised that action on the 50 additional ships requested by the Italians would probably be favorable, although formal approval had not been given either by the NAC or the Maritime Commission.[2] He pointed out that it might not be possible in all cases to obtain the precise type of ships requested, since a few types might not be available.

Mr. Clayton reported that January wheat sailings now appear more unfavorable than had hitherto been expected, and that Italian sailings would probably not exceed 100,000 tons. In view of the difficult Italian supply position, the War Department had, however, diverted to Italy six vessels destined to Germany which carried an aggregate of 50,000

---

[1] The communiqué, released to the press on January 15, is printed in the Department of State *Bulletin*, January 26, 1947, p. 165.

[2] On January 14 the Maritime Commission formally approved the sale of 50 additional ships to Italy (Memorandum by A. J. Williams to James L. Pimper, Acting Director, Large Vessel Sales Division, Maritime Commission, January 15, not printed; File "Application No. 2155: Italian Government," U.S. Maritime Administration Records).

tons of wheat. These ships would arrive as follows: Palermo on the 17th of January; Naples on the 19th; Bari on the 27th; Genoa on the 28th; Naples on the 29th; Genoa on the 1st of February. Mr. Clayton pointed out that the War Department had consented to this diversion only on the assurance that it would be made up from other wheat earmarked for Italy. Although there would result no increase in total supplies going to Italy, there would be an increase in January and early February arrivals. Mr. Clayton promised that we would ship to Italy in February all the wheat we had previously agreed to, and that we would make every effort to pay the Italian diversion back to the War Department in January.

The Italian representatives asked for United States support in the ECO for an increase in their coal allocations to 900,000 tons per month, in the expectation that they would be able to receive 200,000 to 300,000 tons a month from Germany and other sources in addition to the 600,000 tons a month from the United States. Mr. Clayton stated that the Italian request would be given careful consideration and would be taken up with the United States representative on the ECO.

Editorial Note

For text of a letter from President Truman to Enrico de Nicola, Provisional President of the Italian Republic, upon the occasion of De Gasperi's departure from the United States, see *Public Papers of the Presidents of the United States: Harry S. Truman, 1947*, page 105. The letter, dated January 20, was released on January 25.

CONCERN OF THE UNITED STATES WITH RESPECT TO THE MAINTENANCE OF STABLE, DEMOCRATIC GOVERNMENT IN ITALY

Defense Files: Telegram

The Supreme Allied Commander, Mediterranean Theater (Morgan)[1]
to the Combined Chiefs of Staff

TOP SECRET   CASERTA, 28 December 1946.
URGENT

FX 73997. Naf 1253. 1. In view of the progress that is being made on the Peace Treaty it is now necessary for me to plan the rundown of

---

[1] Lt. Gen. Sir William D. Morgan, Supreme Allied Commander, Mediterranean Theater of Operations, 1945 to mid-April 1947.

Allied Force Headquarters, so that final evacuation may be achieved by "R" plus 90 days.

2. In Naf 1242[2] I recommended that my operational role should be modified on "S" day and confirmation of this is urgently required.[3] For planning purposes I have assumed that this modified role will be approved.

3. My plan, based on the assumption that "R" day may be as early as 1 March 1947 is therefore:

a. The Allied Commission should be abolished immediately, its functions being taken over by the G–5 Section of my Headquarters.[4] See Naf 1250.[2] The Service sub-commissions however will have to continue to function under my direct control.

b. By "S" day the G–2 Section Allied Force Headquarters MTOUSA will be reorganized on a national basis, the necessary information being exchanged between Headquarters MTOUSA and General Force Headquarters Central Mediterranean Forces. I shall retain a very small Coordination Section at Allied Force Headquarters until "R" day.

c. By "R" day an Allied Liquidating headquarters on similar lines to Liquidating Agency for SHAEF (CALA) will be established in Rome. A further cable on the detailed organization follows.

d. By "R" day Headquarters MTOUSA will move to Leghorn.

e. By "R" day the Trieste Free Territory Forces must be in position and functioning.[5]

f. On "R" day Allied Force Headquarters should be abolished.

4. Request that approval of my plan be confirmed as soon as possible.[6]

---

[2] Not printed.

[3] R—Ratification; S—Signature.

[4] In telegram FX 74612 (Naf 1272), January 28, from Caserta, not printed, General Morgan reported to the CCS that he was ordering the abolition of the Allied Commission, effective midnight, January 31; cf. *Foreign Relations,* 1946, vol. v, p. 874.

[5] For documentation on Trieste, see vol. IV, pp. 51 ff.

[6] In telegram 3, January 3, from Caserta, not printed, Homer Morrison Byington, Jr., Deputy United States Political Adviser on the Staff of the Supreme Allied Commander, Mediterranean Theater, asked for guidance as to the advice he should give the military, and suggested that a purely national agency for the American forces, and a similar national establishment for the British, each attached to its respective embassy, would be preferable for the intermediate period (740.00119 EW/1–347).

FW 865.24/1–347 : Telegram

The Combined Chiefs of Staff to the Supreme Allied Commander, Mediterranean Theater (Morgan)

SECRET [WASHINGTON,] January 3, 1947.

WARX 88909. Fan 708. This answers Naf 1219.[1]

1. We confirm that you may hold surplus equipment as an interim measure for issue to Italians at later date when suitable governmental agreements have been made, subject to the following conditions:

a. Items held must be of such nature and quantity as to give reasonable assurance that they will, in fact, be desired and required by the Italian Government for the post-peace treaty Italian Army.

b. Equipment held must be from global surpluses and not merely excess to theater requirements. You have already been requested to give the War Office details of main British equipments involved as there may be complications over supply of certain items; e.g., provisions for further maintenance. You should also give the War Department details as to main United States equipment involved in order that necessary concurrence to intended disposition may be expeditiously secured.

c. With regard to British equipment of lend-lease origin, action must be taken without delay, through the War Office, to obtain necessary United States clearance for future transfer to the Italians.

d. No equipment now surplus or which may become surplus, for which sales agreements have been consummated, will be considered as available for retention under this authority.

2. We also agree that this equipment should be held in a depot manned and maintained by Italian Army under supervision of Military Mission Italian Army, but only under the following conditions:

a. In placing stocks in the depot, a definite understanding must first be reached with the Italians that the equipment will remain property of, and subject to withdrawal by, His Majesty's Government and United States Government until suitable agreements have been made, and that final disposal will be made only through normal disposal agencies.

b. Prompt action must be taken, through the War Department and War Office, to secure governmental concurrences for the storing, without demilitarization, in Italian depots of specific items of equipment

---

[1] Naf 1219 (FX 72443), dated September 30, 1946, from Caserta, not printed (FW 865.24/1–347).

and supplies for the purpose of probable future transfer to the Italian Government.

c. Agreement must be reached between the responsible agencies of the owning government and the Italian Government at the time of storage as to quantities of items being stored in order to assure that responsibility for losses rests with the Italian Government.

Lot 60–D 137 : Box 1

Minutes of Fifty-first Meeting of the National Advisory Council on International Monetary and Financial Problems, Washington, January 21, 1947

[Extract]

TOP SECRET

PRESENT

Secretary John W. Snyder, Chairman

Mr. James H. Rorke, Maritime Commission, Visitor

Mr. Walter M. Day, War Assets Administration, Visitor

Mr. William Clayton, State Department

Mr. John P. Young, State Department

Mr. J. J. Stenger, State Department

Mr. Chester M. Carré, Office of Foreign Liquidation Commissioner, State Department

Mr. Thomas C. Blaisdell, Jr., Commerce Department

Mr. Clarence I. Blau, Commerce Department

Mr. Marriner S. Eccles, Board of Governors, Federal Reserve System

Mr. J. Burke Knapp, Board of Governors, Federal Reserve System

Mr. William McC. Martin, Jr., Export-Import Bank

Mr. August Maffry, Export-Import Bank

Mr. Walter C. Louchheim, Jr., Securities Exchange Commission

Mr. Harry D. White, International Fund

Mr. George Luthringer, International Fund

Mr. John Hooker, International Bank

Mr. Joseph J. O'Connell, Treasury Department

Mr. Andrew N. Overby, Treasury Department

Mr. William W. Parsons, Treasury Department

Mr. Joseph B. Friedman, Treasury Department

Mr. Orvis A. Schmidt, (Acting Secretary)

Mr. Andrew M. Kamarck, (NAC Staff)

Mr. Allan J. Fisher, (NAC Secretariat)

1. *Maritime Commission Credits for Ship Sales*

(a) *Request of the Italian Government for Increased Credit.*

Mr. Schmidt recalled that the Council had earlier approved consideration of a credit amounting to $24 million and that a request had been received that this be raised to $51 million to cover the purchase of 104 war-built vessels instead of the 50 originally contemplated. The Staff Committee's study pointed out that a saving of foreign exchange expenditures for freight charges is important to Italy and that the Maritime Commission would not only have a claim on the Italian

Government but also a mortgage on the ships. The Staff Committee, therefore, recommended that the Maritime Commission be advised that the Council had no objection to consideration of the increased credit (NAC Document No. 336).

The Council approved the recommendation without objection.

Action.

The following action was taken:

(a) The National Advisory Council has no objection to consideration by the Maritime Commission of increasing the credit to Italy from $24 million to $51 million to provide for the purchase of 104 vessels, in lieu of 50 as originally proposed.

(b) The Council approves sending a copy of NAC Document No. 336 to the Chairman of the Maritime Commission.[1]

---

[1] The minutes of the 53d meeting of the National Advisory Council, held on February 10, not printed, record that it authorized the Export-Import Bank to take action on a $5 million loan to Italy to finance the purchase of leaf tobacco in the United States (Lot 60–D 137: Box 1).

865.5018/1–2347

Memorandum by Mr. James A. Stillwell of the Division of International Resources to the Under Secretary of State for Economic Affairs (Clayton)

[WASHINGTON,] January 23, 1947.

Subject: January Shipments of Grain and Flour to Italy

I have been needling the Department of Agriculture almost hourly on shipments to Italy this month and now have a firm schedule as follows: 60,899 tons of wheat; 42,099 tons of corn; 38,900 tons of flour. Total 141,898 tons. We must add to this the 50,000 tons which we diverted from Germany, making the total 191,898 tons.

I have contained in this schedule only those ships that have actually been named and loading dates scheduled, but in order to provide some lee-way for possible delays in this schedule I have informed Mr. Ortona of the Italian Embassy that I am confident that at least 118,000 tons of wheat, corn and flour will be loaded and sailed this month, in addition to the 50,000 tons already diverted. I would not like to inform the Italians of the total outlined above until a little later in the month when we can be more certain of the actual sailings.

Defense Files : Telegram

The Supreme Allied Commander, Mediterranean Theater (Morgan) to the Combined Chiefs of Staff

CONFIDENTIAL   CASERTA, 11 February 1947.
PRIORITY

FX 74908. Naf 1277. Subject is liquidation of allied functions after R plus 90 days.

1. Residual allied functions will exist after abolition of AFHQ. As long as MTO and CMF are functioning these allied duties can be performed by integrating the G–5 sections on a cooperative basis.

2. All residual allied functions cannot be completed by R plus 90 days. The Allied Financial Agency (AFA), the Allied Supply Accounting Agency (ASAA), the Allied Forces Record Administration (AFRA) and the Historical Section AFHQ must complete their jobs after R plus 90 days. In addition, it is anticipated that, for an unspecified period after R Day, a considerable volume of residual allied business, which cannot be decentralized to Embassies or other National Agencies, will have to be transacted with Italian Government. Greater part of such business will be connected with Civil Affairs matters.

3. It is proposed that a Military Liquidating Agency (MILA) be organized upon disbandment of AFHQ to ensure the early completion of these functions. Although tentative agreement has been received that AFRA may function under the US/UK Embassies, believe that more effective and expeditious results will obtain if all residual functions are consolidated within a military organization under experienced supervision. Propose that MILA shall be comprised of separate US and UK military units integrated where necessary and maintaining close liaison under Co-equal Commanders who will report directly to War Department and War Office. Direct and intimate contact to be maintained with respective Embassies and their advice and guidance sought on all policy matters. It is clear however, that Embassies are not equipped to take over supervision and control of these residual Allied functions and can in any case do so only if complete self-sustaining staffs are furnished for the various jobs.

4. If MILA is approved, administration, status of individuals vis-à-vis Italian Government and maintenance of personnel will be taken up with US War Department and UK War Office on National basis. There may, however, be certain expenses such as office space, civilian employees, signal services and heat and light which are joint in nature and should be paid on a proportional basis. Excluding housekeeping personnel the combined initial strength of MILA will approximate 40 officers, 90 EM/or and 25 WD civilian employees. Of this total ap-

proximately 8 officers, 45 EM/or and 20 WD civilian employees will be engaged on AFRA duties.

5. Probable all functions MILA except archives and microfilming will be completed within six months after R plus 90 days. Time to complete excepted tasks depends on CCS decisions.

6. The proposal to organize MILA is agreed by CG MTO, GOC in C CMF, and by the US and British Embassies, Rome. Early approval is requested in order that administrative details of national nature may be settled in time for MILA to come into existence at time AFHQ is abolished.

FW 865.248/2-2647

Memorandum by the Commanding General of the Army Air Forces (Spaatz) to the Assistant Secretary of War for Air (Symington)

TOP SECRET WASHINGTON, February 17, 1947.

Subject: Provision of Equipment for the Italian Air Force

1. The State–War–Navy Coordinating Committee (SWNCC) notified the Joint Chiefs of Staff in SWN–5044, dated 9 January 1947, that it had re-examined its views on the matter of the source of equipment for the Italian Air Force and considered that it was desirable, subject to the approval of the Joint Chiefs of Staff, for the U.S. to press for full responsibility to furnish aircraft, together with replacement aircraft, parts and spares, for the modernization program of the Italian Air Force. It was stated that the State Department would take steps, after approval by the Joint Chiefs of Staff, to effectuate an understanding with the British Government to facilitate arrangements for agreement between the United States and Italian Governments on the assistance program.

2. On 22 January 1947, the Joint Chiefs of Staff in SM–7448 advised the SWNCC that no objection from the military point of view was perceived to the views of the SWNCC contained in SWN–5044. The Joint Chiefs pointed out the following: "There is, however, an urgency for reaching an early decision since there is a question as to the capability of the Commanding General, U.S. Forces, European Theater, to meet a delivery schedule which will be politically acceptable. With the passage of time, his capacity to do so continuously decreases".

3. Brigadier General H. Q. Huglin, formerly A–3 of U.S. Air Forces, Europe, has just returned to Hq, AAF for reassignment and on this date, in reviewing the problem of providing the equipment of SWNCC's proposed plan, stated that the major task of placing suffi-

cient aircraft in commission and delivering them to the Italians would necessitate halting all other functions of U.S. Air Forces in Europe and turning all attention to that task. He emphasized the fact that additional delay in reaching a decision reduces the capability of U.S. Air Forces, Europe to meet such a commitment.

4. Working level personnel of the War Department General Staff and Hq, AAF have repeatedly attempted to bring about prompt action by State Department on this matter without apparent success. Further delay in the resolution of diplomatic discussions may place the AAF in the awkward position of being unable to implement a U.S. commitment initiated by the SWNCC.

5. In light of the above, it is suggested that you might wish to bring this matter to the attention of Mr. Petersen [1] with a view toward pressing the State Department for an early resolution.

CARL SPAATZ

[1] Howard C. Petersen, Assistant Secretary of War.

740.00119 Control (Italy)/2–547

Memorandum by the State Member (Hilldring) to the State–War–Navy Coordinating Committee

SECRET   [WASHINGTON,] 19 February 1947.

Subject: Military and Civil Affairs Agreement Between the United States and Italy.

The Department of State has considered the memorandum of the Joint Chiefs of Staff regarding the draft military and civil affairs agreement with Italy, enclosed with SWNCC 271/15 of 5 February 1947,[1] and has concluded that the proposed agreement is unnecessary to ensure to U.S. forces in Italy the facilities necessary for their withdrawal within 90 days from the coming into force of the Treaty of Peace with Italy. Moreover, it is considered from the political point of view that it would be unwise to press the Italian Government to accept an agreement which would undoubtedly be regarded by them as an extension of the armistice regime.

As is known, all functions of the Allied military forces in Italy cease upon the coming into force of the Treaty. From that date, U.S. forces in Italy will require, and will be entitled to, only those facilities which are necessary for their withdrawal within 90 days in accordance with Article 73 of the Treaty. While the primary obligation under this Article falls upon the Allied and Associated Powers, i.e., to withdraw

[1] For previous draft, see *Foreign Relations*, 1946, vol. v, p. 849.

their armed forces from Italy, an obligation is also placed upon the Italian Government by implication and through international comity, to cooperate in the withdrawal of the Allied forces by furnishing for due compensation the services and facilities necessary for such withdrawal.

It is the opinion of the Department of State, therefore, that all facilities which may be required for the withdrawal of U.S. forces in Italy are ensured under the Treaty. Upon the request of the War Department, however, the Department of State is prepared to endeavor to arrange for an exchange of notes with the Italian Government which would provide general assurances that the Italian authorities will cooperate in the orderly withdrawal of U.S. forces from Italy and will make available to them all facilities necessary therefor upon due compensation.

It is understood that the Government of the United Kingdom is also of the opinion that a military and civil affairs agreement is not necessary for the period during which Allied forces will be withdrawing from Italy.

J. H. HILLDRING

865.248/2–2647

The Secretary of War (Patterson) to the Secretary of State

TOP SECRET WASHINGTON, February 26, 1947.

DEAR MR. SECRETARY: The question of modernization of the Italian Air Force, considered in SWNCC 320/5,[1] has become precarious due to the lack of determination as to whether the U.S. or the British shall have the responsibility. The difficulty hinges on ever-decreasing capabilities. It is now apparent that, if the U.S. is to be responsible for equipping the combat element of the Italian Air Force, the determination will have to be made now, or the capability for implementation will no longer exist.

The War Department considers that this matter should be resolved as soon as possible. The earmarking of the equipment has had a disturbing effect on routine operations as well as other considered assistance programs. It appears that we might be seriously embarrassed in many ways if a determination be made that the United States fur-

---

[1] Dated December 12, 1946, not printed; it was an enclosure in a memorandum for the Secretary of State, SWN–5083, January 22, 1947, not printed (865.248/1–2247).

nish the equipment and we find ourselves unable to implement the program.[2]

Sincerely yours,

ROBERT P. PATTERSON

---

[2] Secretary Marshall's letter of March 3, 1947, not printed, acknowledged Secretary Patterson's letter and explained that a reply from the British was being studied by the State and War Departments (865.248/2–2647).

865.00/3–447 : Telegram

The Ambassador in Italy (Dunn) to the Secretary of State

SECRET   ROME, March 4, 1947—midnight.

463. Now that third De Gasperi govt has received its vote of confidence as was anticipated from Constituent Assembly, it can turn its attention to business of govt and implementation of its program (my A–360, February 28 and telegram 428, February 28[1]). Normal opposition extreme right wing and Liberals was supported in this latest test of strength by Republicans and Saragat Socialists. Opposition of latter two groups, however, may be considered more symbolic than real since (1) they could have participated in govt and (2) are not in principle opposed to declared aims and policies of parties comprising present tripartite govt.

On balance we believe De Gasperi emerged from most recent crisis in stronger position though not to degree he had expected when he precipitated crisis. In outgoing govt, ratio was eight Democrat Christians, four Communists, four Socialists, and two Republicans. With elimination and consolidation of ministries, present ratio is Christian Democrats six, Communists and Socialists three each and two Independents. While similar balance between Christian Democrats and Socialists-Communists has been preserved, importance of two Independents positions in Cabinet has been increased by reduction in portfolios. Latter, Sforza[2] and Gasparotto,[3] are most [more] amenable to Prime Minister than were Republicans in previous Cabinet and may be expected to vote with him on important questions. Furthermore, Communists have been eliminated from powerful Finance Ministry and combined portfolio of Treasury and Finance allotted to energetic capable Democrat Christian Minister Campilli. Also in new Ministry of Defense headed by Independent Gasparotto, Democrat Christians have two of four Under Secretaries (my A–272, February 18[4]).

---

[1] Neither printed.

[2] Count Carlo Sforza, Italian Minister of Foreign Affairs in the third De Gasperi cabinet, February 2–May 31, 1947.

[3] Luigi Gasparotto, Italian Minister of Defense in the third De Gasperi cabinet.

[4] Not printed.

While new Cabinet is more compact and, therefore, more manageable political lines therein are most clearly drawn since Socialist representation now comes only from Nenni-Basso remnant of party with its unwavering policy of close cooperation with Communists.

Finally the most recent crisis has bad [*had?*] stabilizing effect on political life of country in that it has brought needed clarification in restless and speculative political atmosphere, (see Embtel 4273, November 25 and 110, January 14 [5]) which had reached its climax on Prime Minister's return from US and proved if nothing more that there is no other workable basis for govt than coalition cabinet comprised of three mass parties. It is, therefore, improbable that there will be any further serious basis for govt crisis during this final interim period leading up to elections for Parliament under new constitution which are obviously predicted between June and October although the continued force[d] cohabitation of the Social[ists,] Communist[s] and Democrat Christians still contains elements for polemics and distrust which existed before.

DUNN

---

[5] Neither printed.

FW 865.248/3–1247

Memorandum by the Joint Chiefs of Staff to the Combined Chiefs of Staff [1]

TOP SECRET [WASHINGTON, March 7, 1947.]

MODERNIZATION OF THE ITALIAN AIR FORCE

The United States Chiefs of Staff have considered the latest British proposal for equipping the Italian Air Force submitted by the Foreign Office to the State Department.

The United States Chiefs of Staff recognize the desirability of assisting the Italian Government in attaining the most effective air force practicable within treaty limitations. The advantages of equipping the combat element of the Italian Air Force with a single type of aircraft make it highly desirable that one country have the responsibility for furnishing such equipment. The United States Chiefs of Staff would like to see the British assume full responsibility for the entire program. They have reconsidered their former position on this matter and are prepared to accept the British proposal as submitted by the Foreign Office provided that the British Government will assume full responsibility for this program.

---

[1] This memorandum, bearing the date March 7, was the enclosure to SWN–5217 of March 12, 1947, not printed. (865.248/3–1247).

The United States Chiefs of Staff do not consider that 136 fighter aircraft would constitute an adequate force. Therefore, if the British are not in a position to augment the 136 Spitfires presently available in Italy, the United States Chiefs of Staff can undertake to make available to the Italian Government up to a total of 60 P-51 aircraft at nominal cost to supplement the British capability.

It is recognized that an immediate decision on this matter is now mandatory if the Supreme Allied Commander, Mediterranean, is to accomplish the modernization of the Italian Air Force prior to the withdrawal of the Anglo-American forces from Italy.

It is requested that advice as to any British requirement for supplementation of their capability be communicated to the United States Chiefs of Staff as soon as practicable.

FW 865.24/7–847 : Telegram

The Supreme Allied Commander, Mediterranean Theater (Morgan) to the Combined Chiefs of Staff

SECRET   CASERTA, 8 March 1947.

FX 75414. Naf 1292. 1. In view of possibly imminent ratification of peace treaty with Italy [1] I forward this review of the situation regarding the equipment of the Italian Army.

2. In accordance with proposals in Naf 1135 [2] we have endeavored to equip Chai [*Italy?*] as far as has been possible from globally surplus British equipment, a force of 5 combat divisions, 10 independent infantry Brigades and 3 Internal Security Brigades. However, when presently earmarked British globally surplus stocks have been turned over to the Italian Army there will still be a deficiency of the following items which cannot be found from British sources in this theater or B.T.A. :

(a) Items	(b) Amounts
rifles .303	35,000
light machine guns Brens	2,300
17 pounder anti-tank guns	25
25 pounder guns	80
25 pounder ammunition	400,000 rounds
300 Browning ammunition	5,000,000 rounds

3. I appreciate that the equipment of the Italian post treaty Army will not be my responsibility. I consider that I should point out, however, that the pre-treaty Army, which was intended for employment, if

---

[1] See pp. 515 ff.
[2] See *Foreign Relations*, 1946, vol. v, footnote 53, p. 917.

necessary, with Allied formations, is lacking in certain essential supporting arms and when Allied Forces withdraw from the country, the Italian Army will be entirely unbalanced with regard to heavy weapons. A certain amount of this equipment is already earmarked and is being held in temporary depots, as authorized in Fan 708. Nevertheless, in order to balance the force referred to in paragraph 2 above, it is considered that the minimum requirements both in addition to those listed above and to the equipment held in temporary depots would be:

(a) Items	(b) Amounts
Piats	400
17 pounder anti-tank guns	40
25 pounder guns	150
40 millimeter anti-aircraft guns	100
3.7 anti-aircraft guns	130
medium artillery (any type)	50
self propelled anti-tank artillery	24
medium tanks	56
light tanks	200
tanks transporters	25
1st and 2nd line ammunition for these items.	

4. It was expected that the 56 medium tanks, 26 of the light tanks and the medium artillery listed in paragraph 3 above, together with certain ammunition, all of which were excess to United States requirements in this theater might be made available for turnover to the Italian Army. However, the United States Joint Chiefs of Staff have agreed that Commanding General Mediterranean should proceed with shipment of the tanks to the United States. Commanding General Mediterranean is reporting to AGWar availability in MTOUSA of surplus and excess equipment and maintenance spares which will include the medium artillery.

5. I consider that the above equipment requirements are the minimum if the Italian Army is to be capable of standing on its own feet when the Allies withdraw. I am informed that no further British globally surplus stocks are available in this theater or BTA and that any further equipment required by the Italians, from the British, must be obtained through their civil import programme.

6. I request to be informed whether any of the foregoing equipment or appropriate substitutes, including maintenance therefor, especially medium or light tanks can be made available without delay from United States sources. I propose, based upon your reply, to inform the Italian Government of the allied position regarding provision of equipment for their Army.

865.48/3–847

The Italian Ambassador (Tarchiani) to the Under Secretary of State for Economic Affairs (Clayton)

No. 2173   WASHINGTON, March 8, 1947.

MY DEAR MR. CLAYTON : I understand that, in connection with the pending authorization bill for $350,000,000 for relief purposes in 1947,[1] the State Department has prepared its own tentative estimates of the extent of the relief needs of various countries.

I have also learned the results of the work of Post-UNRRA relief needs published by the United Nations Special Technical Committee on January 24, 1947.

In this study, the Special Technical Committee estimated Italy's relief needs in 1947 as of the order of $106,900,000. In our opinion, this estimate is far below Italy's actual relief needs in 1947, even if those needs are computed on the basis of the principles employed by the Special Technical Committee.

I have felt that it might prove useful to the Department especially in connection with the discussions pending in Congress on the Post-UNRRA relief, to be acquainted with the study that this Embassy has made on the U.N. Committee Report. I am therefore enclosing a memorandum on Italy's relief needs [2] prepared on the identical principles employed by the Special Technical Committee, with adjustments based on factual information which has become available since the Committee prepared its study. Such memorandum shows a substantial difference from the conclusions reached by the U.N. Committee.

I hope that it will be possible for your staff to give it attention and I thank you in advance for your kind interest in the matter.

Sincerely yours,   ALBERTO TARCHIANI

---

[1] On February 21 President Truman addressed a "Special Message to the Congress Requesting Appropriations for Aid to Liberated Countries," stating : "I recommend that the Congress authorize the appropriation of not to exceed $350 million to assist in completing the great task of bringing relief from the ravages of the war to the people of the liberated countries." He further recommended "that this relief assistance be given directly rather than through an international organization, and that our contribution be administered under United States control." *Public Papers of the Presidents of the United States: Harry S. Truman, 1947* (Washington, Government Printing Office, 1963), p. 149.

By Public Law 84 (Post UNRRA Relief) approved May 31, 1947, the 80th Congress, 1st Session, authorized the appropriation to the President of "not to exceed $350 million for the provision of relief assistance." (61 Stat. 125)

The actual appropriation of funds to enable the President to carry out the purposes of Public Law 84 ($332 million) was not made until the approval by the Congress on July 30 of Public Law 271 (61 Stat. 610).

See also *First Report to Congress on The United States Foreign Relief Program* (For the period ended September 30, 1947), Department of State publication 2985 (Washington, Government Printing Office, 1947), p. 1.

[2] Not printed. It estimated Italy's dollar relief needs in 1947 at approximately $457,098,000.

740.00119 Control (Italy)/3–1047 : Telegram

The Ambassador in Italy (Dunn) to the Secretary of State

SECRET   ROME, March 10, 1947—6 p.m.

509. F 75419 dated March 9 from ComGenMed to War Department [1] transmits new proposed text of detailed agreement to provide necessary facilities for withdrawal of US Forces during 90 day period after R Day (see Embassy's 480, March 6 [2]). General Lee proposes that this agreement might best be effected by exchange of notes between US and Italian Governments. I have informed him that I have no objection to undertaking necessary negotiations should Department so direct me.

Department will note that under paragraph 12 of proposed text it is contemplated that Italian Government will continue to make available all facilities requested by US Forces during 90 days on same basis as in part [past?]. Our and British preliminary conversations with Italians indicate that we may be able to reach an agreement of this sort with Italian Government without too much difficulty. It is my personal opinion that we should endeavor to do so. (Reference Department's 281, February 27.[3]) US military authorities make a very good point when they say that not only do they not have appropriated funds to pay for facilities that they now receive gratis, but also if funds were appropriated they have not necessary personnel to revise their account procedures at this late date. The only remaining solution would be appropriation of a lump sum to be handed over to the Italian Government for dispersal to claimants and it is open to question whether this would be desirable or practical.

DUNN

---

[1] Not printed.
[2] Not printed; in it Dunn reported that the British had submitted to the Italians a draft agreement which Dunn had discussed with General Lee who considered it a suitable basis for a U.S. draft agreement (841.2365/3–747).
[3] Not printed; it reviewed the problem and suggested further informal discussions with the Italians (811.2365/2–2447).

865.5018/3–1347 : Telegram

The Ambassador in Italy (Dunn) to the Secretary of State

US URGENT   ROME, March 13, 1947.

552. All figures thousand metric tons. High Commissioner Cerreti [1] visited Embassy today and urgently requested US immediately furnish 80 wheat or flour by diversion or borrowing from other destinations. Of this 25 should arrive before 1 April. Italians borrowed 15

---

[1] Giulio Cerreti, Italian High Commissioner for Alimentation in De Gasperi's third cabinet.

from AC this week and must repay with first arrivals April. In addition to 80 now requested will need following arrivals to continue present ration until harvest: April 230 US plus 150 Argentina; May same as April; June 100 US and 50 Argentina. Cerreti also asks maximum possible be wheat since US corn difficult.[2]

From 28 February to 20 March, 120 cereals exclusive corn (wheat equivalent) will have arrived according official forecast.

Revised but provisional stock position; (a) wheat and minor cereals and (b) corn follow: February 1 stock, (a) 231 (b) 135; amassing February 18, 16; arrivals February 145, 35; apparent February consumption 246, 71; February 28 stock 148 and 115 (Embtel 432 February 28[3]).

Foreseeable supplies should permit distribution ration 200 grams bread but no pasta normal consumers plus issue bread and pasta for supplements and special classes for average of 29 days from March 1 but because of uneven distribution some places will exhaust supplies by 18 March.

Foreseeable supplies for bread ration at 200 grams including stocks plus shipments en route sufficient to following dates: Sardegna, April 18, Emilia, March, Umbria, Abruzzi, Lucania, March 31, all other regions, March 18–23.

After March 20 no wheat expected for 8 or 9 days and many regions may be forced suspend bread ration. Arrivals from non-US sources will increase late April or May and could be used to repay any wheat that may be diverted now.

Has been widespread unrest from failure to meet ration and from issuance corn in south. Also strikes of millers and demonstrations of unemployed pasta workers. Cerreti says more serious events likely if bread ration has to be reduced.

Embassy urges all assistance possible.[4]

DUNN

---

[2] In despatch No. 319, March 14, from Rome, not printed, a translation of the memorandum which Cerreti left with the Embassy was forwarded to the Department (865.5018/3–1447).

[3] Not printed.

[4] In telegram 427, March 26, not printed, the Department replied that because of insufficient wheat in relation to corn, it was impossible to divert wheat or flour to Italy (865.5018/3–1347).

865.5018/3–1547 : Telegram

The Acting Secretary of State to the Embassy in Italy

CONFIDENTIAL WASHINGTON, March 15, 1947—11 a.m.

364. In view of tight food situation it seems doubtful that sufficient supplies can be obtained to permit Italian imports at a rate which would require $200 million of relief financing by US. It might be

pointed out to De Gasperi that although amount of funds which US can allocate to Italy from $350 million may be substantially below $200 million we are hopeful that it will be sufficient to permit procurement of such part of essential supplies as are available in US which Italy itself cannot finance from other resources. In meantime every effort should be made by Italians to secure help from other countries such as Argentina, Switzerland, Brazil and Canada. Further comments on other questions ur 514 Mar 10 [1] will follow shortly.

ACHESON

[1] In this telegram, not printed, Dunn reported on his first official call on Prime Minister De Gasperi who among other things mentioned "that the $350,000,000 requested by Congress would not seem to provide for Italy the $200,000,000 which had been discussed with him in Washington." (740.0011 EW (Peace)/3–1047)

740.00119 Control (Italy)/3–2147 : Airgram

The Ambassador in Italy (Dunn) to the Secretary of State

ROME, March 21, 1947.

A–458. Reference Embassy's secret A–404, March 7, 1947.[1] Effective 2359 hours, March 15, 1947, Italian Military Affairs Section, AFHQ, was abolished. The Land, Naval and Air Forces Sub Sections have now become Italian Land Forces, Italian Naval and Italian Air Forces Branches of AFHQ, respectively.

Admiral Stone terminated his official connection with AFHQ as Chief of the Italian Military Affairs Section on March 15, 1947.

DUNN

[1] Not printed.

865.00/4–147 : Telegram

The Ambassador in Italy (Dunn) to the Secretary of State

SECRET ROME, April 1, 1947—6 p.m.

696. While fears of violence on Sunday, reported in my 683 of March 29,[1] did not materialize, (see mytel 692, March 31 [1]) Vatican's concern is a reflection of general preoccupation over increase in political violence and disorder in Italy during last few weeks, especially after Togliatti's reference on March 11 in the Constituent Assembly to the possible need of "direct action" on the part of the Communist Party if certain Communist demands were not met (see mytel 692 of March 31). It is also recalled that on February 16 Basso,[2] Secretary of the Socialist Party, violently added that the Basso Socialists were

[1] Not printed.
[2] Lelio Basso.

not above resorting to illegal action in order to further their ends if the elements of reaction should force the issue (see my A–288, February 18 [3]). More recently Saragat's organ *L'Umanita* on March 29 charged that "Red Squadristi" were conducting a campaign of "ideological and physical terror" [to?] prevent the growth of Saragat's party, especially in the region of Emilia and urged its members to defend themselves and their organizations energetically. *Umanita* stated that the Saragat socialists had decided to abandon their policy of passive resistance because the situation had become intolerable. (The Embassy has received from reliable source information to the effect that the Italian police had intercepted orders from Moscow directing Italian Communists organizations to commence disorders immediately in Italy.)

To give the Dept a few isolated examples of recent act[s] of political violence the following incidents are set forth:

(1) A Chamber of Commerce building was burned down several days ago in Bari. The suspected perpetrator was lynched and mobs forthwith devastated the UQ, Demochristians, Monarchist Union and other premises in Bari. *Corriere Della Nazione* and other newspapers labeled the Bari incident as result of direct action.

(2) About a week ago a monarchist meeting in Rome was forcibly broken up by a gang of thugs generally suspected of being Communists or Communist sympathizers.

(3) On March 14 Franco de Agazio, Milan editor of a weekly described in the press as pro-Fascist, was assassinated. The Rome press also linked this murder with Togliatti's direct action. (See my A–445, March 19 [3]).

(4) See Embassy's 582, March 18 [3] relative to acts of violence against certain deputies of the Constituent Assembly.

Repeated Moscow 35.

DUNN

---

[3] Not printed.

FW 865.248/4–747

Memorandum by the United States Chiefs of Staff to the Combined Chiefs of Staff [1]

TOP SECRET   WASHINGTON, [April 4, 1947.]

MODERNIZATION OF THE ITALIAN AIR FORCE

1. The United States Chiefs of Staff have considered the memorandum (C.C.S. 536/12 [2]) by the Representatives of the British

---

[1] This memorandum, not dated, was an enclosure to SWN–5294, April 7, 1947, not printed (865.248/4–747).
[2] Not printed.

Chiefs of Staff wherein the latter agree that the Air Ministry will assume entire responsibility for the Italian Air Force program except for the supply of fifty (50) P–51 aircraft and the associated aircraft maintenance equipment and spares.

2. The United States Chiefs of Staff agree that the plan set forth in Appendix "A", C.C.S. 536/12 should be presented to the Italian Government as an agreed Anglo-American plan, and that the Italians should be invited to discuss details, including finance, with the British and United States authorities in Rome.

3. With regard to the draft message proposed by the British Chiefs of Staff to the Supreme Allied Commander, Mediterranean, in Appendix "B" to C.C.S. 536/12, the United States Chiefs of Staff generally approve the message, but desire to insure that the message will not be construed as a commitment for United States equipment other than the fifty (50) P–51 aircraft, and the specific-to-type aircraft maintenance equipment and spare parts for three (3) years for the P–51's. They further desire the inclusion of a paragraph outlining the cost of the United States equipment to the Italian Government and propose, therefore, that the draft message to the Supreme Allied Commander, Mediterranean be amended as indicated in the Appendix.[3]

4. Subject to the amendments proposed in the Appendix the United States Chiefs of Staff approve the dispatch of the message to the Supreme Allied Commander, Mediterranean, in Appendix "B" of C.C.S. 536/12.

---

[3] Not printed.

865.48/4–947 : Telegram

The Acting Secretary of State to the Embassy in Italy

RESTRICTED WASHINGTON, April 9, 1947—6 p.m.

504. Preliminary conversation held with representatives Italian Govt. March 27 re U.S. relief assistance.

Memo of conversation will be forwarded.

Have delivered tentative draft agreement Italian reps. containing terms operation U.S. and Italy and including restrictions and requirements bill in Congress.[1] Ital. reps. probably will forward Rome draft. Copies draft agreements dispatched today ur info. Send comments immediately.

No agreements will be signed until final passage Congress end April.

Ital reps. asked submit tentative relief import food needs May June, July.

ACHESON

---

[1] The draft text of the proposed agreement was sent to Rome in the Department's telegraphic instruction 895, June 11, not printed (865.48/6–1147).

865.00/4–1247 : Telegram

The Ambassador in Italy (Dunn) to the Secretary of State

SECRET   ROME, April 12, 1947—midnight.
URGENT

797. Recent conversations with officials Foreign Ministry reveal their grave concern over present financial crisis and economic prospects of nation in immediate future (see mytel 763, April 9 [1]). In an informal talk with member my staff some officials of Sforza's cabinet brought up question of US aid to Greece and Turkey. They advanced the view that loans of 100,000,000 to 200,000,000 dollars for Austria, Greece or Turkey, on the basis of relative populations, would indicate that a loan of around 800,000,000 would be needed to ensure similar stability for Italy. A substantial loan of that character would they said enable Italian Government to establish sound basis for recovery (they suggested a 2-year program) which would have a healthy psychological effect upon the Italian people and their cooperation and confidence in making the program work, at the same time providing infinitely more effective propaganda for the US than we now obtain from our present policy of aid in various forms and doses, which, while admittedly lifesaving for Italy and a heavy sacrifice for the American people, has only succeeded in maintaining local economy on a hand to mouth basis year after year.

Implications for Italy of proposed US aid to Greece and Turkey have of course not been lost upon government here. From conversations with Sforza's young men we have impression Italian Government will take every opportunity during next few months to point out similarity of Italian economic and political problems with those of Greece and Turkey and that Tarchiani has been ordered home for instructions (see Secdel 1440, April 9 [2]) principally with that policy in mind.

Sent Department repeated Moscow 42.

                                                          DUNN

---

[1] Not printed.
[2] See telegram 867, p. 536.

Defense Files : Telegram

The Acting Supreme Allied Commander, Mediterranean Theater (Lee) to the War Department

SECRET   LEGHORN, 14 April 1947.

F 75932. Your W 95575 and W 95664 and my FX 75866 refer.

1. Except for American Graves Registration Service, U.S. Troops in this Theater are mainly engaged in providing US share of Allied

United States-United Kingdom Mission as laid down by armistice terms and Combined Chiefs of Staff. Therefore I must make my reply as acting SACMED rather than as Commanding General MTOUSA.

2. General Harding reports and I agree that to maintain law and order in Zone A and to insure reasonable security of Allied communications and living areas in the province of Udine and to provide maximum reserves against a worsening of the internal situation, he requires a minimum of 15 and one half combat battalions for the forward garrison.

3. The foregoing estimate is predicated upon a continuation of present conditions until ratification and excludes the possibility of full scale Jugoslav intervention, military or political, should the ratification proceedings break down completely. In this latter case I would be unable to carry out my assigned mission with the troops at my disposal and must then request additional forces.

4. Allied combat forces now available in the forward garrison area are 7 and one half US battalions and 8 British battalions. General Harding plans and expects to maintain his approximate parity forward with 8 British battalions and necessary administrative backing. Attrition will reduce US forces by approximately 1500, including strength of 1 battalion combat troops, by 30 June 1947. This rate of attrition, i.e., 1 combat battalion each 60 days, if continued without provision for replacements, will very shortly make it impossible for me to fulfill my currently assigned mission. It can be seen that US combat forces cannot be reduced, but must be replaced unless R Day comes before 30 June 47.

5. Of United States troops elsewhere in Italy approximately 11,000 are engaged in administrative backing to 88th Division and in disposal of surplus and excess stocks and are located generally at Base Port Leghorn and along line of communications Leghorn–88th Division.[1]

6. Balance of US forces are engaged in discharge of SACMED's responsibilities important out of proportion to numbers involved. Main responsibilities concerned are:

(a) Allied Military Government in Zone A of Venezia Giulia and Province of Udine.

(b) G–5 activities in Rome, displaced persons, refugees and war criminals.

(c) Italian Armed Forces branches of Allied Force Headquarters. Reorganization and equipping of the Italian Armed Forces and enforcement of the armistice terms.

---

[1] In despatch 1, March 27, from Caserta, not printed, Joseph N. Greene, Jr., Acting U.S. Political Adviser, forwarded a copy of a letter addressed on March 19 by the Acting Chief of Staff, G–5, Col. A. L. Hamblen, to Prime Minister De Gasperi explaining that Allied Force Headquarters would move to Leghorn on April 6, which would permit the closing out of substantially all of the Allied military installations in the Naples-Caserta area. (740.0011 EW/3–2747)

7. Actual current US strength approximately 25,500 against troop basis of 26,000. I can accept a troop basis reduction to anticipated actual strength on 30 June of 22,000 provided I have sufficient funds to hire required civ replacements. Beyond that I cannot go without relief by the Combined Chiefs of Staff of some of my current or contingent responsibilities.

8. Aside from the above, it is hoped that the political significance of a drastic reduction in US troops, which I understand would be paralleled by the British, prior to the coming into effect of the peace treaty, has received careful consideration both by the War Department and War Office as well as by the State Department and Foreign Office. My political advisers are making their views known to their respective Ambassadors.

9. The foregoing is concerned only with the situation prior to ratification of the Peace Treaty. The mission assigned me as acting SACMED by Fan 737 should Yugoslavia fail to ratify the treaty will be impossible of fulfillment under the conditions laid down in Fan 723 with only the TRUST and BETFor forces of 5,000 each.

865.48/4–1547 : Telegram

The Ambassador in Italy (Dunn) to the Secretary of State

CONFIDENTIAL   ROME, April 15, 1947—noon.
US URGENT

810. Reliable ranking Italian official reported in confidence that Sereni,[1] Communist Minister Public Works privately admitted to a Christian Democrat Minister that Communist Party is opposed to post-UNRRA aid to Italy from US for reason that it creates friendship and strengthens ties between the two countries. However, Togliatti and other leaders reportedly prefer that party exert no outright opposition lest such action might encourage the US to give even more relief. In other words, party cannot afford publicly to oppose US aid.

It is not clear whether line of action will be to play up role of Communist Party in obtaining and distributing US goods to workers, to use delaying tactics in making agreements, to foster dissipation or wasting of relief grant by foolish expenditures or wasteful distribution, or to maneuver US into position where difficulties in delivery could be blamed on US.

Apparent food policy of Cerreti,[2] Communist High Commissioner for Food, is to institute differential rationing, to issue food packages

---

[1] Emilio Sereni.
[2] Giulio Cerreti.

to workers as well as pensioners and indigent, to lower prices, and to reduce luxury consumption. It appears also that he and his party favor elimination or reduction of amassing controls as an appeal to farmers and/or as an indirect means of discouraging US aid. Former Under Secretary of Agriculture, Spano,[3] also Communist, reportedly denounced publicly the amassing program in speeches to warn [farm?] groups.

Cerreti has reportedly reorganized Commissariat to include section to handle food packages and has asked Federconsorzia [4] to organize along similar lines with budget of two billion lire annually.

De Gasperi reportedly scolded Cerreti for proceeding with food package proposal (Embtel 780, of April 11, 1947 [5]) without prior approval. Cerreti said proposal was strongly favored by UNRRA and acceptable to US Embassy. Contrary to his purported statement neither UNRRA nor Embassy has expressed opinion.

Embassy has not yet been presented with complete food package proposal but on basis preliminary information submitted disadvantages appear to outweigh advantages. De Gasperi is said to oppose proposal. Main defects appear to be (a) the expense in dollars for processing and packaging; (b) the utilization of US labor for work that could be performed by Italian unemployed; (c) the shifting of the entire food relief burden for specified classes on the US while freeing a portion of Italian indigenous food from control; (d) the distribution of certain processed food items not normally consumed and not always wanted by Italian consumers (i.e. margarine and canned milk); and (e) the possibility of distribution of packages to workers through Communist-controlled organizations.

On the other hand, the advantages seem to be: (a) broadening the base of rationing to the commodities and thereby providing a well-rounded diet for needy and productive classes; (b) easy and quick distribution permitting rapid transfer from one area to another; (c) giving possibility of tighter controls and more easy observation of distribution; (d) possibility of US labels on each package for publicity purposes.

Sent to Department 810, repeated to Moscow as 48.

DUNN

---

[3] Velio Spano, Under Secretary in the Italian Ministry of Agriculture and Forests in the second De Gasperi cabinet, July 1946–January 1947.

[4] Federconsorzia, Federation of Syndicates or Unions.

[5] Not printed; it described the plan for food packages for low-income groups proposed to the Embassy by officials of the Italian High Commission for Alimentation, with the United States supplying up to 10 million completely assembled packages per month which presumably were to be requested as part of the post-UNRRA aid program. The Embassy did not endorse the proposal but asked for full details. (865.5018/4–1147)

865.248/4–2147 : Telegram

The Ambassador in Italy (Dunn) to the Secretary of State

TOP SECRET   ROME, April 21, 1947—midnight.

883. ReDeptel 267, February 25.[1] In conference with Acting SAC [2] this afternoon I was informed that he intends to recommend to CCS that original program for reequipment Italian air force with Spitfires and P–38's be implemented immediately since continued delay in decision to make available P–51's from US is damaging Italian air force program and no longer technically feasible for MTOUSA at this late date because of early close out. I shall alert Department on number and date of Lee's message as soon as it is despatched [3] and meanwhile can only express regret that firm agreement to reequip Italian air force at least in part with modern American equipment understood available in USFET has not yet been reached. In not supplying the P–51 type we are losing an opportunity to establish in Italy a modern air force with American equipment and training which would be adequate to meet any real emergency at least in the initial stages.

Sent Department as 883; repeated Leghorn as 28.

---

[1] Not printed; it informed the Embassy in Rome that SWNCC had on January 9 approved the sale of P–51 aircraft to Italy; that the Department had been discussing the matter on an urgent basis with the British Embassy, but that no reply had been received and the War Department had therefore been unable to instruct the theater (865.248/2–2447).

[2] Lt. Gen. John C. H. Lee.

[3] Leghorn's telegram 62, April 26, not printed, identified General Lee's message as FX 76068 of April 25 (865.248/4–2647). In FX 76068, April 25, not printed, General Lee as Commanding General of the U.S. Forces in the Mediterranean Theater informed the War Department that the austerity standards forced on him did not permit indefinite commitments. He asked for authorization to inform the Italian Government that no U.S. proposal for equipping the Italian Air Force with P–51's had developed; and proposed to suggest that the Italians in their own interest accept the British plan. (Defense Files)

740.00119 Control (Italy)/4–2347

The Secretary of War (Patterson) to the Acting Secretary of State

WASHINGTON, 23 April 1947.

DEAR MR. ACHESON: The delay in ratification of the Peace Treaty for Italy has reached a point where it becomes necessary to consider withdrawal of U.S. forces from Italy irrespective of treaty ratification. This is so because of an increasingly critical situation as regards manpower, the requirement for warning so that withdrawal can be accomplished in the limited period of 90 days and the necessity for funds to cover the prolonged retention of forces in the area.

The understanding of the War Department has been that the national interest required the retention of U.S. forces in Italy until the peace treaty came into effect. In addition to the moral obligation of the U.S. to retain troops in the area until ratification, there is a military commitment with the British to remain in Venezia Giulia jointly until an international settlement is secured.

Informal State Department advice initially estimated that the treaty might be brought into effect by 1 April 1947. This would have permitted the withdrawal of U.S. forces by the 30th of June 1947.

War Department planning has been predicated on no requirement for U.S. forces in Italy after 30 June 1947. In addition, subsequent to agreement by the Council of Foreign Ministers, as regards the Venezia Giulia problem and Trieste, the schedule for troop deployment was revised to provide after 30 June 1947 only the 5,000 troops for U.S. national contingent for Trieste.

The manpower situation is such that the retention of U.S. forces in Italy beyond 30 June 1947 will require either the reduction of U.S. forces available for the European Command or committing a substantial part of the General Reserve. The adoption of either of these alternatives will reduce the respective forces to a level which is considered dangerously low and most unsatisfactory from the military point of view.

The present situation is that the War Department will have, subsequent to 30 June 1947, only the funds necessary to maintain the 5,000 man contingent for Trieste. In order to provide for maintaining forces in Italy after 30 June 1947 and until withdrawal is completed, consideration is being given by the War Department to the impact on the War Department expenditures and its budget resulting from the continuance of U.S. forces in Italy, at least in the initial part of fiscal year 1948.

Unless reasonable assurance can be given that the Italian Peace Treaty will come into force not later than early June this year, thereby permitting the withdrawal of U.S. forces from Italy by September, the course of action concerning the retention of U.S. forces in Italy must now be determined.

It is recommended that every effort be made to secure the earliest practicable consideration by the U.S. Senate of the Italian Peace Treaty. Whatever may be the course of action determined, the War Department assumes that it will have the full support of the State Department in securing necessary funds.

The manpower situation, the advance warning required for withdrawal and the present indefiniteness as regards funds, require early resolution of the problem as outlined. It is hoped that the views of the State Department may be available to the War Department at an early date.

Sincerely yours,

ROBERT P. PATTERSON

865.50/4–2547 : Telegram

The Acting Secretary of State to the Embassy in Italy

SECRET   WASHINGTON, April 25, 1947—8 p.m.
US URGENT

583. A. For Emb's confidential information only, Dept now investigating needs for immediate and longer-run stabilization Ital economy. Basic questions being considered include (1) is stabilization impossible without important changes Ital economic policies, especially toward price and wage stability; (2) is it necessary emphasize production for domestic consumption rather than for export in order to permit most rapid improvement living standards, and (3) what outside financial assistance necessary to facilitate stabilization program over say five-year period and especially to induce adoption sound internal programs and measures.

B. Dept now analyzing Ital political and economic situation, impact of economic assistance already given, and magnitude and nature additional economic assistance required to achieve long-run economic stability if combined with appropriate changes Italy's economic policies.

C. Request Emb give highest priority to submit latest information not previously forwarded on present situation, changes since Liberation and future prospects re following points, assuming no change Italy's policies:

(1) Agricultural and industrial production;
(2) Standard of living, with special reference to (a) per capita availability of principal consumer goods and (b) real wages and the changing distribution of real income among manual laborers, salaried employees, farmers, entrepreneurs etc.;
(3) Investment, with special emphasis on (a) reconstruction activity, (b) investment in new industries and (c) inventories and hoarding;
(4) Relations between domestic prices, world prices and the exchange rate;
(5) Foreign trade and the balance of payments.

D. Request also (1) Emb's evaluation current govt economic policies, (2) detailed suggestions re changes required on economic grounds, and (3) political implications of adoption such changes. Please consider particularly govt policies following fields:

(1) In general;
(2) Taxation;
(3) Currency inflation;
(4) Wages;
(5) Rationing, price control, allocation of raw materials;
(6) Control of foreign trade and foreign exchange;
(7) Public and private investment;
(8) Unemployment.

E. Appreciate magnitude of task inherent preparation detailed replies. Advise if material can be received here by May 20 and advance summaries cabled before May 7.

ACHESON

865.248/4–2947 : Defense Files : Telegram

The Combined Chiefs of Staff to the Acting Supreme Allied Commander, Mediterranean Theater (Lee)

SECRET WASHINGTON, 29 April 1947.

WARX 97147 (Fan 749) Modernization of Italian Air Forces is subject. References Naf's 1235 [1] and 1258.[2]

1. After careful consideration including financial aspect of proposals for reorganization of Italian Air Force put forward by British Air Ministry and U.S. War Department and bearing in mind that our object is to build up an efficient Italian Air Force within the limitations imposed by the Peace Treaty, we have decided that following is the best plan from all points of view.

2. Five fighter-type squadrons to be equipped with Spitfire IXs and two with P–51s all complete to operational role. Supply of fifty P–51 aircraft and specific-to-type aircraft maintenance equipment and spare parts for three years for the P–51s will be the only responsibility of American Government. British Government will assume entire responsibility for provision of all British equipment including ancillary aircraft, ground equipment specialist vehicles, etc., required by the Italian Air Force. Plan will be in essence that prepared by Air Ministry and already submitted to Italian Government with exception that P–51s are substituted for P–38s.

3. You should inform Italian Government that this is agreed Anglo-American plan and that they should discuss details including cost with the British and American authorities in Rome. In view of the early withdrawal of Allied forces from Italy, a decision by the Italian Government is urgently required.

4. For your guidance as regards British equipment, the cost of the Spitfires will be nil, cost of spares and other equipment will be nil so far as these are available from stocks in Italy, one-sixth cost price so far as they are available from surpluses outside Italy and full price

---

[1] Naf 1235 (FX 73372), November 21, 1946, not printed. In this message SACMED mentioned his understanding that there were now available more modern types of combat aircraft than the P–38 and Spitfire 9, and urged that it was essential for the Allies to leave behind the most efficient air force possible within the treaty limits. (Defense Files)

[2] Naf 1258 (FX 74126), January 6, 1947, not printed. In this message SACMED mentioned that pending details of the U.S. plan, the Italian Air Staff had withheld acceptance of the British plan and that reorganization of the Italian Air Force was at a standstill. He urged that delay in the American plan jeopardized the policy of leaving behind an efficient Italian Air Force. (Defense Files)

for such equipment and spare parts as have to be supplied from new production. Air Ministry estimate that about 3 months' aircraft spares plus a considerable proportion of the other equipment required such as MT, special equipment, ammunition, etc. can be provided from surpluses either in Italy or elsewhere but that major part of the spares required for 3 years' backing would have to come from new production. Range and quantity of spares required would of course be for decision by Italians. According to Air Ministry scales of provision of spares total original sterling cost of British equipment is estimated to amount to pounds sterling 4,417,300 of which 2,149,000 worth (including all the Spitfires and a proportion of spares and other equipment) would be supplied free: 1,410,800 worth would be supplied for 305,000 and the remainder would be charged for at full price i.e., roughly about 857,500.

5. With regard to United States equipment, the over-all cost will include a nominal price for aircraft, spares for three (3) years, and associated aircraft maintenance equipment, plus the actual costs incurred in placing the aircraft in operational standard and delivery thereof, and packing, crating, and transporting three (3) years' supply of spares and aircraft maintenance equipment. Due to deterioration in storage, if resolution of arrangements is long delayed, an increase in cost of placing aircraft in operational standard may be expected.

865.248/4–2147 : Telegram

The Secretary of State to the Embassy in Italy

TOP SECRET   WASHINGTON, May 1, 1947—5 p.m.

619. Ur 883 Apr 21. You will have seen WARX 96927 Apr 25 to MilAttaché Rome [1] re P–51 aircraft for Ital air force. You shd inform Ital Govt of availability these planes, parts and maintenance equipment at nominal cost presently estimated at $92,000, and urge that necessary arrangements for acquisition be expedited. Keep ComGenMed informed.[2]

Dept has informed FLC in premises.

MARSHALL

---

[1] WARX 96927, War Department to Headquarters, European Command, Frankfurt, and to Military Attaché, Rome, for information. This message, not printed, directed EuCom to advise FLC, Germany, of the available surplus of 50 P–51's, and to be prepared to fly the planes to Italy on receiving notification that agreement had been reached with the Italian Government. (Defense Files)

[2] In telegram 1044, May 5, from Rome, not printed, Dunn reported that in accordance with Fan 749 (*supra*) General Lee had on May 2 informed Prime Minister De Gasperi of the Allied plan to provide Italy with five squadrons of Spitfires and two of P–51's. He stated he would inform De Gasperi that the cost to Italy would be $92,000 (865.248/5–547).

865.00/4–1747 : Telegram

The Secretary of State to the Embassy in Italy

SECRET   WASHINGTON, May 1, 1947—8 p.m.

622. Personal for the Ambassador. Dept deeply concerned by deterioration Ital political and economic conditions which apparently leading to further increase Communist strength and consequent worsening situation of moderate elements (ur 892 Apr 22 [1]), with Communists becoming more confident and inclined disregard govt authority (ur 973 Apr 29 [1]). Dept would therefore like your estimate at earliest possible date of impact of future course Italy, and particularly implications re October elections, of recent disquieting developments as Communist-Socialist dominance important municipalities (Genoa, Turin, etc); apparent consolidation Communist control of labor (ur A–473 Mar 25 [1]); increase in intimidation and threats of violence (ur 696 Apr 1 [1]); Communist electoral victory Sicily, etc.

Dept also desires your opinion possibility of De Gasperi relinquishing govt leadership (ur 892 Apr 22 [1]) or of attempting form govt without extreme left in hope improving Christian Democrat's chances in October elections. What importance do you attach possible moves form "technician" govt without parliamentary basis (Milan's 24 Apr 17 [1]).

Finally, Dept wishes your views what pol and eco steps if any this Govt should and could take towards strengthening democratic, pro-US forces, having in mind vital importance Italy in relation US policy in Mediterranean, as well as your estimate possible effectiveness any suggested measures.

MARSHALL

---

[1] Not printed.

865.00/5–347 : Telegram

The Ambassador in Italy (Dunn) to the Secretary of State

TOP SECRET   ROME, May 3, 1947—8 p.m.
URGENT

1031. For the Secretary. In response to urtel 622, May 1, 8 p.m. regarding deterioration in Italian political and economic conditions, the lack of confidence in the Govt as present formed of Christian-Democrats, Communists, and Communist inclined Socialist groups has progressed to a point which results in a psychological impediment to effective action by the Govt to correct present economic and financial conditions. I am convinced that no improvement in conditions here can take place under Govt as at present composed. Communists who are represented in Cabinet by second-string team are doing everything possible outside and within the Govt to bring about inflation and chaotic economic conditions. Population generally and particularly more responsible banking and industrial leaders have lost confidence entirely in the Govt and are afraid to venture upon new or expanded enterprises. A flight from the lira is beginning; rise in spiral inflation is unchecked. The pity is that there exists all over Italy a real will to work and there could easily be a general confidence in the future if it were not for the political agitation of the Communists and I doubt if there can be any real effective measures taken to improve the situation as long as the Communists participate in the Government. The Communist Party would, of course, fight hard against any effort to form a Govt without its participation but I do not believe it is too late for a govt to be formed without their participation and there appears to be a growing realization that the Communist Party is not really trying to bring about the restoration of economic stability.

Within the next few days the recently announced program of the Govt in the financial field will be discussed in the Constituent Assembly. We have had reports that strong efforts will be made to pose the question of confidence in the Govt as an underlying factor in the present difficulties. The Prime Minister indicated in a radio address a few days ago his desire that the basis of the Govt be broadened to include representation of more parties and there are many reports current of a possible crisis which will result either in a new composition of the present Government or a different grouping of the Parliamentary representation.

With regard to what political or economic steps we could take in the circumstances I question very much whether any assistance to Italy other than in the form of direct food relief and coal would be advisable at the present time while the Govt is in the hands of the present Cabinet. I do believe that direct relief and coal are of real importance as hunger and unemployment are fertile soil for Communism. There is such a real need of food in the country that responsible men are extremely concerned over the possibilities of a starvation situation arising some time during the next six months, if not all over the country, at least in important sections.

Dept will recall recent indications we have received concerning design on part of Communist leaders to thwart our program to ensure post-UNRRA relief from US to Italy.

There is an important element in the Italian situation which does not manifest itself very sharply when studying the problem. That is that one of the greatest obstacles to the spread of Communism here has been the action of the United States in assisting the economy of the country with food and raw materials and fuel which has provided employment. But we have not accompanied our action with adequate propaganda.

The smooth and deceptive program of the Communist Party has seemed reasonable to a large mass of Italian workers, but if those same people had any idea that adoption of Communism in Italy would cut them off from relations with the US, I feel sure the vast majority would reject the Communist advances. Our practice of holding back from expressing themselves [*ourselves*] on ideological views has given all the advantage to the other side and they have not hesitated to use it and abuse it. With all the efforts which have been made here since the war very little presentation of US policies and position has appeared in the Italian press. (That is why I have been making speeches recently on visits to the important cities and the press has carried them with a good spread.)

We have assumed in the eyes of Italians a passive role as regards the growth of Italian Communism. The vigor and energy of the Communist movement in Italy in particular the efficiency of its organization and propaganda and its penetration of local administrative government ensuring a powerful influence in considerable areas in the distribution of work has contributed to a growing belief among Italians and in many cases fear that the Italian Communist bandwagon is not seriously opposed by the US and it is the one to board. The Embassy is constantly receiving letters from individuals begging the US to take a stand in Italy against this drive towards a totalitarian Communist Italy. All the indications we receive and particularly the trend of local elections throughout Italy show that the Communists are consistently gaining ground and that our policy to assist the development of a free and democratic Italy is losing ground rather than making progress.

In order to bring to the attention of the Italian people therefore a clear indication of what might be the result of their going over to the Communist line and in order to build up a sound resistance to the siren call of the insidious propaganda now being pushed around here, it has occurred to me that perhaps you or the President might consider something along the following lines:

Either voluntarily or in response to a question by a correspondent regarding conditions in Italy and the US attitude toward this country to say that the US has deep and friendly interest in the growth of real democracy in Italy; that we have been happy to assist in the reestablishment of economic stability and will be happy to continue to lend our support to those elements here who have deep and abiding faith in the democratic processes and the preservation of the freedom and liberty of the Italian people and who are opposed to government in Italy by totalitarian regimes either of the extreme right or the extreme left. That we are watching with interest the progress of the Italian nation in solving her difficult economic and political problems and we are ready to lend our assistance to the development of an economic life based upon the liberty of the individual and the protection of his individual rights; and that we are confident that the Italian people will not desire a totalitarian regime which would inevitably break down the close ties that bind together the Italian and American people.

DUNN

740.00119 Control (Italy)/4–2347

The Secretary of State to the Secretary of War (*Patterson*)

TOP SECRET   [WASHINGTON,] May 5, 1947.

MY DEAR MR. SECRETARY: I refer to your letter of April 23, 1947 to Mr. Acheson regarding the retention of United States forces in Italy until the Italian peace treaty comes into effect.

As you know, hearings on the Italian and Balkan treaties were resumed by the Senate Foreign Relations Committee on April 30.[1] I am hopeful therefore that Senate action will be completed at an early date. If no further delays are encountered, it should be possible to bring the Italian treaty into force not later than early June, but you will understand that no definite assurances can be given in this regard at the present time.

The difficulties of the War Department in the situation resulting from the delay in ratification of the Italian treaty are appreciated by the Department of State. In the national interest, however, United States forces should be retained in Italy until the treaty comes into effect, and it seems evident that forces in excess of the national contingent of 5,000 troops for the Free Territory of Trieste could not be withdrawn by June 30. I wish to assure you, therefore, that the War Department will have the full support of the Department of State in securing the necessary funds for the retention of United States forces in Italy beyond July 1, 1947, and during the withdrawal period subsequent to the coming into force of the Italian treaty.

Faithfully yours,   G. C. MARSHALL

---

[1] *Ante*, p. 515.

865.51/5–647 : Telegram

The Ambassador in Italy (Dunn) to the Secretary of State

SECRET   ROME, May 6, 1947—noon.
URGENT   NIACT

1048. For the Secretary. The Prime Minister asked me to come and see him last evening and made a point of trying to keep my visit confidential. He received me at the Colonial Office. He informed me that about a week ago he had sent a letter [1] to President Truman directly and not through the Italian Embassy in Washington telling the President that Italy was in great economic difficulty at the present time and asking the President to request Mr. Clayton to come to Italy from Geneva in order that the Prime Minister and his advisers might have an opportunity to discuss the economic and financial situation here with a view to the adoption of corrective measures, he hoped, with the assistance of the US. Mr. De Gasperi asked that I inform you of this approach and seek your support to his request. I am also informing Mr. Clayton in Geneva of this approach. I believe it would be very helpful at the present time if Mr. Clayton could come.[2]

The Prime Minister then went on to discuss the present political situation. He said he himself considered it advisable to broaden the composition of the Cabinet to include some of the other parties of the center and had discussed this possibility with Togliatti and Nenni. Togliatti had appeared willing on condition that the present program of the three-party government not be changed. Nenni . . . is opposed to enlargement of the government. Mr. De Gasperi said the financial and economic situation was so unstable at the present time that he did not wish to invite a crisis unless he had some agreement among the parties to bring forth another form of government before the present one fell. He said he was afraid of the spiral of inflation and that the fall of the government if it involved any considerable time to find a replacement might result in a financial panic and a real loss of ground in the fight they had been making for return of economic stability.

The Prime Minister then spoke of the lack of confidence in the government. He said he was afraid this was caused largely by his "allies", but he did not think it was wise to attempt to form a government without them at this time unless the Communists were themselves ready to remain out of the government in order to be free to level their criticism

---

[1] Not found.
[2] See despatch 1341, July 25, p. 945.

against it. He said he was continuing his conversations but that he had no intention himself of deliberately provoking a crisis. If this were brought about in the assembly that was quite another thing and he would, of course, accept a reversal in that body. He said various persons had been mentioned as head of a new government; that he himself was ready to retire at any moment that he felt an able and efficient successor could be chosen. He spoke of Signor Nitti as one of those mentioned to succeed him.[3] His own opinion was that Nitti's advanced age and his present physical condition would make it impossible for him to carry on the arduous task of Prime Minister in these present times.

Mr. De Gasperi then spoke of possible assistance from the United States. I said that our Government was deeply interested in the Italian situation and wished to be of such assistance as they could but that it was necessary for us to see some effective measures taken by the Italians themselves to put their house in order before we could give consideration to aid for Italy other than the direct relief. I said that after all it was quite impossible for the US to take the entire burden of assisting Italy to recovery and that it was necessary for the Italians to apply themselves to the solution of their own problems and to take the steps necessary to improve the situation before we convince our people and Congress that we could render effective aid here. Mr. De Gasperi said he was only afraid that assistance might come too late and at a time when it would be extremely more difficult to revive the situation than it would be now to preserve it. I told him (De Gasperi) that we all had the greatest confidence in him personally and that we wanted to be of all the help we could and that we were sincerely hopeful that he would find the means of correcting the present situation and take advantage of the spendid attitude and will to work of the Italian people at this present time.

He asked me to explain to our government that Italy was now in an electoral campaign period and that it was most unfortunate to look forward to financial difficulties, inflation and possible hunger in the country at the same time as the elections. Finally, he made another plea that Mr. Clayton come to Italy with a view at least to talking over the situation and asked me also to convey to you his deep concern over the reduction of the post UNRRA relief fund to $200,000,000 which might drastically affect the possible allotment for Italy.[4]

DUNN

---

[3] Francesco Saverio Nitti had been President of the Italian Council of Ministers from June 23, 1919 to May 21, 1920.
[4] See footnote 1, p. 874.

865.5018/4–1847 : Telegram

The Secretary of State to the Embassy in Italy

CONFIDENTIAL   WASHINGTON, May 7, 1947—5 p.m.

651. Urtel 864 Apr 18.[1] Not found possible make diversions meet critical stock situation Italy early May. Felt here main Italian problem not one of allocation but of prompt movement quantities already allocated. Slipover from early US programs for Italy into Apr totalled about 150,000 tons.

In recent note Italian Emb to Dept request for 60,000 tons additional allocation flour made to help cover June consumption. Claim made that Italian crop not ready harvest before June 20 or 25 thus reducing prospective collections from new crop in June from 150,000 as originally estimated to 65,000, leaving supply inadequate meet ration. Emb requested comment on this claim.

Agri on May 2 allocated 20,000 tons semolina flour to Italy, a quantity representing month's production this flour by US mills.

MARSHALL

---

[1] In this telegram, not printed, Dunn reported that Italian food officials had stated that Italy's cereal supply would be exhausted by May 10 unless there were unforeseen arrivals (865.5018/4–1847).

865.51/5–747 : Telegram

The Ambassador in Italy (Dunn) to the Secretary of State

SECRET   ROME, May 7, 1947—midnight.

1078. This is telegram No. 3.

1. Tasca [1] in accordance with Department's 641 of May 5,[2] is leaving by air for Washington May 8 or 9 carrying the text of the report prepared in response to Department's 583 of April 25. The preliminary summary is therefore not being telegraphed in advance.

There follows however a synthesis of our comments on Section D of Department's outline. For the statistical data called for in Section C reference is made to Embassy's 1013 of May 2.[3] Tasca before departing may be able to assemble some current statistics supplementing those that have already been reported. As Tasca will explain, however, some statistical data, such as inventories, cannot be developed by either the

---

[1] Dr. Henry Tasca, Treasury representative attached to the Embassy in Rome.
[2] Not printed.
[3] Not printed; in it Dunn merely reported that the Italian Cambital (Foreign Exchange) officials were unable to present any new data on exchange availabilities (865.5151/5–247).

Italian Government or ourselves with the means available; many others are suspect and still others, such as trade, will vary according to the government agency which assembles them.

2. The chain of circumstances which have plagued post-Fascist government and have led to the present situation, although familiar, might be summarized for backdrop:

(1) The government[s] since liberation have been composed of parties of widely varying competitive philosophies.

(2) The earliest governments had only token authority during military operations. Since the transfer of full responsibility to the Italians, local and assembly elections, the institutional problem, the constitution and the coming elections for the regular parliament have monopolized the attention of government and politicians. Parliamentary and electoral jockeying has therefore replaced constructive activity.

(3) Party strife and ambitions have resulted in unworkable ministerial organization (witness the separation in the preceding government of the Ministry of Treasury or spending ministry, headed by a Liberal, from the Ministry of Finance or collecting ministry, headed by a Communist.[)]

(4) Incompetence and inexperience, both technical and political, have occurred from the inevitable epuration [of?] so many persons trained in government who were Fascists and from paying-off with political positions of obligations to resistants.

3. The deepening crisis is fundamentally psychological. Other is lack of confidence in the government. This psychological state of mind is reflected in the sudden rise of the lira in the free market yesterday caused by rumors of a government crisis, i.e., "any government is better than this one". Only Draconian measures, and the longer they are delayed the more severe they must be, appear adequate to arrest the drift, which may become a plunge, and to start Italy on the upward path. Such measures will hurt some classes but as things are now done in the fatuous hope of being all things to all men, all of Italy may be reduced to misery.

4. The requirements to meet and vanquish the forces in this whirlpool of disintegration are:

(1) Political leadership both competent and courageous.

(2) Political and economic policy reforms against the opposition of many special interests, including Communist, preference, (a) to prolong the turmoil and (b) to gain time for organizational preparation for the elections;

(3) Effective implementation of policies through fundamental reforms of practices and procedures.

Only the Italians themselves can meet these requirements; outside aid per se will provide neither leadership, confidence, nor courage. What the United States can and should however do is, first, provide wheat, no matter how bad the situation, so as to maintain life and hope; and, second, when the appropriate time comes, to give moral and material support to an eventual competent government who promises some measure of success.

5. Assuming a competent strong government will eventually emerge, we appraise as follows the requirements for Italy to start on the road forward. While we have been mainly guided by technical considerations, we have at the same time tried to remain politically practical by keeping our suggestions within range of attainment.

(1) Restoration of confidence in the government and its ability to direct the economic and financial reconstruction of the country.

(2) Abrogation of political legislation in financial clothing used to intimidate and paralyze strategic economic groups in the country.

(3) Adoption of policies to include: direct block on wages, abandonment of prohibition and work to dismissals [apparent garble], controls over political strikes in key industries.

(4) Adoption of other technical measures with assurance of successful implementation, such as exchange control, credit control, reduction of government expenditures, et cetera.

(5) Extraordinary amounts of foreign aid (government and private if possible) for some time to come.

(6) Strict protection of freedom of speech and assembly against extremist interferences, and restoration of respect in all levels of the population for government and law.

Italian Communist policies have been at direct variance with the above. Therefore, it might be difficult for the Communists to accept participation in a government which would effectively carry out these policies. On the other hand the magnitude of the problems confronting a competent government including increased problems of maintenance of public order of [if?] the PCI were in open opposition and the immense difficulty of its taking the necessary measures we have urged will assuredly require moral and material support and sympathy from the west, meaning more especially of course the US.

DUNN

865.51/5–747

The Ambassador in Italy (Dunn) to the Secretary of State

SECRET   ROME, May 7, 1947.
No. 677

Subject: Recommendations concerning Italian Economic Policies and Needs

SIR: In compliance with the Department's telegram No. 583 of April 25, and with reference to my telegrams Nos. 1022 of May 2,[1] 1030 of

---

[1] Not printed.

May 3,[2] and 1078 of May 7, I have the honor to submit as an attachment a memorandum which may prove helpful to the Department and perhaps to other Government agencies in evaluating current Italian economic and financial policies and in drawing conclusions as to the form and nature of possible long-range American collaboration in Italian reconstruction.

Dr. Henry Tasca, Treasury representative attached to the Embassy, is acting as courier in order to insure expeditious delivery and distribution of the enclosed material within the Department. Dr. Tasca, as the Department is aware, has been recalled to Washington for consultation by the Department's telegraphic instructions of May 5.

Admittedly, conditions are serious, and the present government has not demonstrated its ability to rectify them. With special regard to my views on our policies until such time as an adequate government is installed, I respectfully refer the Department to my telegram No. 1078 of May 7.

Respectfully yours,   JAMES CLEMENT DUNN

[Enclosure—Extract]

CURRENT ECONOMIC AND FINANCIAL POLICIES OF THE ITALIAN
GOVERNMENT

1. *General Appraisal*

The current economic and financial position in Italy reflects the lack of confidence on the part of strategic economic groups in the ability of the Government to direct and control the country. There are four basic interrelated groups of factors accounting for the prevailing forces of financial and economic disintegration:

(1) *Lack of inner consistency in the composition of the Government.*

Since the days of liberation it has been necessary to include in the Italian Government, in varying degrees, representatives of political parties with such widely divergent concepts of social and economic reform that it has been difficult to prepare and execute consistent national plans for reconstruction and rehabilitation. In the field of finance, up until the present Government, the Ministry of the Treasury was in the hands of the Liberal[s]—that is, the spending side of the Government, [—] and the Ministry of Finance—the collecting side— was in the hands of the Communists, with both parties keenly endeavoring to outwit and outmaneuver the other with respect to financial policy. The Communists desired politically spectacular measures designed simultaneously to destroy the dominant property owners.

---

[2] Not found in Department of State files.

The Liberals wished to preserve such classes as the backbone of economic reconstruction. IRI was headed by a Liberal but with left-wing Socialists and Communists in key positions immediately below. The former wished the dissolution of IRI, the latter the transformation of IRI into the central organ for State control of industry. Similar comments may be made with respect to other ministries and to the composition of the Government in general. These conflicts have made impossible the adoption of the sharply defined policies necessary to rehabilitate and reconstruct the Italian economy.

(2) *Political agitation.*

The electoral campaigns in Italy which have taken place, and those which are to take place during the current year, have had the effect of disintegrating such cohesive forces as existed in the Government which might have led to the adoption of viable financial and economic policies. The attempt to build up electoral strength has required a constant process of agitation. Promises, which augment discontent and social unrest, are made and the population is kept in turmoil. Such agitation has been a principal cause in the loss of confidence on the part of the people in their Government.

The agitation of the Communist Party deserves particular attention. It is now a well-known tactic of the Communist Party to remain in the Government and at the same time, particularly through CGIL, to offer corrosive opposition to the Government. This tactic (*a*) provides the Communists with a cloak of respectability for the Party, and (*b*) permits them to infiltrate into key positions. Threats of general strikes have forced the Government to yield on wage policy and expenditures for public works. Sporadic but frequent public disturbances throughout the country frighten business enterprise and accentuate economic difficulties, which in turn provide a tool for the Communists to exert further pressure on the Government publicly and thus seek to obtain further support from the masses.

(3) *Lack of public order.*

The incidents which occurred during the course of one week in Rome and Messina, which in one case involved jostling of and threats to the Minister of Foreign Affairs and in the other case the refusal of a group in Sicily to permit the Prime Minister to speak, could not fail to lower further the prestige of the Government. It has not been possible for a long time in certain zones of Italy for the Government to make effective freedom of speech, as is shown by the inability of a right-wing Socialist leader to speak in the red zone of Emilia. The loss of prestige of the Government incites holders of liquid assets, business enterprisers and people in general to attempt to provide individual economic security and gain in the form of commodity hoarding, speculation, capital flight, etc. This in turn accentuates the gravity of the economic situation. The lack of public order permits extremist elements to disturb public opinion by building up a psychosis of fear which is, in turn, politically exploited. The fear of Communist seizure of power, paradoxically, increases the number of adherents to the Party.

(4) *Technical incompetency.*

The loss of confidence of the strategic groups in the economic system is undoubtedly also to be attributed in part to repeated examples of gross incompetency demonstrated at the ministerial level. To a lesser degree this is also attributable to epuration of top civil servants. For many months the public was kept under the threat of fiscal currency conversion, a threat which finally succeeded in causing holders of currency to dishoard and to lose confidence in the future of the paper lira.

The threat of currency conversion was publicly made over the radio day and night to force subscription to the Reconstruction Loan, with the argument that currency holdings would be taxed as a part of the capital levy program in the process of preparation. The effect of such threats was to emphasize the instability of the lira and to decrease the desire of people to subscribe to the Loan. The interest rate on the Loan, in addition, was low relative to the prevailing interest rate structure. The net result was that the Loan was a failure, and attempts to hedge against the anticipated inflation multiplied to dangerous proportions.

Since currency conversion was supposed to form part of the capital levy, and since those subscribing to the Reconstruction Loan would not, to that extent, be subject to the capital levy, the final decision to abandon currency conversion penalized severely persons who had dishoarded currency to purchase Reconstruction Loan bonds. When the quotations on the stock exchange of the Reconstruction Loan fell to below 80, then the Government stepped in again and raised the interest rate on such securities held by persons who would not be subject to the capital levy. The net effect of the entire operation on the public was to demonstrate an astonishing degree of incompetence.

Another example of incompetency, with a political flavor, was the manner in which extraordinary financing was placed in the forefront, particularly by the Communist Minister of Finance,[3] as the solution of the problem of budgetary deficits. Various types of extraordinary revenue-creating measures were announced and adopted, providing the public with the sensation that such measures would yield sufficient revenue to cover the budgetary deficit. The most recent of these meas-

---

[3] Mauro Scoccimarro, Italian Minister of Finance in the cabinet of Parri (June–December 1945), and in the first and second cabinets of De Gasperi (December 1945–January 1947).

ures has been the adoption of the capital levy, which in its present form will take very many months, if not years, before any substantial flow of revenue can be realized. The declaration of holdings, the examination of such declarations on the part of the appropriate governmental authorities, the assessment of the levy, the possibility of appeals on the part of the tax-payers, as well as the very large number of persons involved in view of the low gross value of 3 million lire subject to the tax, will all consume many months before any significant volume of revenue is collected. When such measures are adopted and the budgetary deficit position not only continues to remain serious but actually worsens, the psychological effect upon the people takes the form of a growing conviction that the most drastic technical measures are insufficient to "save the lira".

A third example, on a smaller scale, has been the establishment by the present Minister of Treasury and Finance of a committee on credit control to study the ways and means of establishing effective credit controls in Italy. In view of the fact that this problem has been under study for many years and in view of the fact that under the 1936 banking act an effective system of credit control had been established, subsequently abandoned in 1944, the matter did not require study at this time. Informed business and financial circles can only believe that the Government is either incompetent or acting in bad faith.

In these circumstances the question arises, how much of Italian disorders and political instability are due to deliberate fomentation and unrest on the part of political elements and how much are due to economic difficulties and the relatively low standard of living. Indices of consumption and real wages would appear to indicate that the position with respect to the masses in Italy has not deteriorated substantially during the last year, and that in fact the probability is that the political agitation is retarding economic recovery rather than economic difficulties retarding the achievement of political stability and equilibrium. This view is of prime importance in connection with the problem of further external aid to Italy.

If it is true that the economic position could be substantially improved through political measures, then aid to Italy perhaps should be based upon the *quid pro quo* of necessary changes in political orientation and policies.

There are presented below a series of concrete recommendations regarding present financial and economic policies of the Italian Government. The recommendations indicate at the same time the defects in existing policies.

[Here follow: II. Recommendations on Tax Policy; III. Recommendations on Government Expenditures; IV. Improvement in Government System of Recording Government Expenditures and Income; V. Recommendations on Exchange Control; VI. Recommendations on Currency; VII. Recommendations on Credit Controls; VIII. Recommendations on Wage Policy; IX. Recommendations on Price Policy; X. Recommendations on Commodity Distribution; XI. Recommendations on Employment; XII. Recommendations on Foreign Trade.]

865.248/5–1447 : Telegram

The Ambassador in Italy (Dunn) to the Secretary of State

TOP SECRET   ROME, May 14, 1947—7 p.m.

1146. ReDeptel 619, May 1 and mytel 1056, May 6.[1] I have now seen War Department WX 97755 of May 9[2] concerning provision of P–51 craft for Italian Air Force. MTOUSA has raised question whether they (reference paragraph 5 A of WX 97755) or Embassy should now carry principal burden of discussion with Italian Government regarding implementation. Since De Gasperi indicated to me that cost would be a principal factor in Italian decision whether to accept, and since details of cost will apparently fall to FLC, I have agreed that Embassy and FLC will negotiate, keeping General Lee fully informed.

Paragraph 5 C of WX 97755 appears ambiguous and leaves open possibility that FLC may charge an amount as yet unknown for the aircraft and spares in addition to $90,000 for packing, crating and transportation, and rehabilitation of aircraft. Please clarify whether remainder of $92,000 figure mentioned Deptel 619 intended cover cost of aircraft. I informed De Gasperi that total is $92,000.

OFLC Rome has no instructions or information regarding program, or manner of payment. (Paragraph 5 E of War Department Signal). Suggest Department instruct FLC Rome, Paris or Washington, or all three, which will handle cost negotiations.

Ruling in paragraph 5 D, namely that Italians will receive no credit toward P–51's for payments on P–38's which they have already bought is likely to prejudice joint nature of program outlined in Fan 749. I am informed contract price for P–38's was $160,000, which more than covers present estimate of P–51 program, and believe it entirely pos-

---

[1] In this telegram, not printed, Dunn reported that he had spoken to Prime Minister De Gasperi on May 5 and had informed him of the proposal in the Department's 619 of May 1. De Gasperi expressed appreciation for the generosity of the U.S. offer. (865.248/5–647)

[2] Not printed; it directed General Lee to explain that the proposal of Fan 749, April 29, was an agreed Anglo-American plan which the Italians should promptly accept, and suggested that USAAF personnel take part along with RAF representatives in discussions with the Italian Air Force. (Defense Files)

sible that if War Department ruling stands Italians might refuse any or all of the Spitfires to be provided by the British, preferring to utilize American craft of both types insofar as treaty limitations permit. Additional factors leading to this conclusion are that British, although intending turn over Spitfires free, apparently intend to charge hard sterling cash amounting about 800,000 pounds for maintenance parts to be purchased out of current British production; furthermore that guns now mounted in Spitfires (reference paragraph 5 F of WX 97755) are Lend-Lease equipment which cannot be sold by British and therefore present additional complicating factor. If, as War Department states, maintenance parts and spares for P–38's are difficult, if not impossible, I suggest that Italians be allowed to return P–38's for scrapping or other disposal and use the credit for the P–51's.

Regarding training of flying and maintenance personnel (paragraph 5 B of War Department Signal 97755) I am informing military through PolAd, in response to their request for views, that important point is that US personnel instruct Italians in use and maintenance of the P–51 craft. Whether this instruction takes place in Germany or Italy I do not consider immediately important, so long as no US military personnel associated with the project remain in Italy after R–Day plus 90.

Sent Department 1146, repeated Leghorn 36.

DUNN

865.20/5–247 : Telegram

The Secretary of State to the Embassy in Italy

TOP SECRET WASHINGTON, May 15, 1947—4 p.m.
US URGENT

695. Reurtel 1021 May 2[1] you shd see WAR 97658 of May 6.[2] Dept has concurred in reference JCS paper and final approval JCS and CCS under urgent consideration.

For your guidance re this transfer and air force equipment (Deptel 619 May 1, Fan 749 Apr 29 and WARX 97755 May 8[3]) difficult financial position Ital Govt fully appreciated. In view overriding importance prompt equipment Ital armed forces Dept considers "scrap price" or "nominal cost" shd insofar as possible be set to conform Ital

---

[1] In this telegram, not printed, Dunn reported having learned that on withdrawal from Italy the Allies would have made inadequate provision for equipping the Italian army; that it now appeared that the British could not take on such a commitment; and he urged that tanks, U.S. artillery and ammunition now in Italy be made available to the Italian forces (865.20/5–247).
[2] Not printed.
[3] Not printed, but see footnote 2, p. 902.

financial and budgetary limitations, since regulations prohibit transfer without some payment. You shd follow negotiations US mil and FLC with Ital Govt and report any serious difficulties which might block or delay implementation programs.

MARSHALL

865.00/5–1647

Memorandum of Conversation, by the Secretary of State

SECRET

[WASHINGTON,] May 16, 1947.

Participants: Ambassador Tarchiani
The Secretary
Mr. Matthews

The Italian Ambassador called this afternoon at his request and gave me his impression of conditions in Italy following his return from a visit there and made some suggestions as to what the United States might do to help. He said that he had seen the President Tuesday, that the President had shown much interest in Italy's situation, and had asked him to talk further with me.[1]

He painted a pessimistic picture of the growth of Communist strength in Italy as evidenced especially by the recent elections in Sicily. He said that in that island, which is essentially conservative, the Communist bloc had polled over a third of the vote. There were two factors in this surprising Communist success: First the general discontent resulting from the poverty of the peasants and second, the extraordinary expenditure of campaign funds by the Communist party. The Communists spent over a billion lire or the equivalent of $2,000,000 which, he said, is an unheard of figure in any Italian election campaign, especially in a small area such as Sicily.[2] This, he thought, proved the importance that Moscow attaches to obtaining Communist control of Italy and presents a gloomy outlook for the elections next October. He said that for the time being Moscow can do little in France since that country is cut off from Russia by the Anglo-American zones of Germany. On the contrary, through Yugoslavia, Italy is in effect directly linked to Russia which makes Communist infiltration much easier. If Moscow succeeds in establishing a Communist Italy it will have gained a highly strategic position. Italy as a base would serve to flank Greece and Turkey, to extend Communist influence north to

---

[1] No record of Tarchiani's conversation with the President has been found.

[2] In a memorandum of conversation with H. Freeman Matthews, Director of the Office of European Affairs, on May 8, not printed, Tarchiani explained that one important source of Communist funds was the Mussolini treasure seized by the Communists at the time of Mussolini's assassination (865.00/5–847).

Germany and Austria and west to France and Spain. It would also facilitate Communist penetration into North Africa, an area to which Moscow is attaching increasing importance.

It was, therefore, he said highly important that Italy should not fall under a Communist regime. The present government crisis, he thought, would soon be solved whether with Nitti as Prime Minister or with de Gasperi.[3] In either case, with the Christian Democrats as the strongest party in the Assembly, de Gasperi would exercise the real power. De Gasperi would do everything possible to prevent the rise of Communism, though whether it would be possible at the present stage to form a government without any Communist participation he could not say. It was important, however, that everything possible be done to assist Italy between now and the elections next October. He did not know when the Italian peace treaty might be ratified, and feels that ratification is a matter between the U.S. Government and the Senate on which he should not comment but if ratification takes place in May or June it will mean the removal of American and British troops from Italy prior to the elections. This, he thought, would be unfortunate. If the Communists do not succeed in coming to power by legal means they may try to take control through insurrection. In the latter case, the Government's position would be serious. The Italian army is disorganized and incapable of resisting and the police have been largely infiltrated by Communists and Socialists. The Carabinieri represent the most reliable force, but there are only 60,000 to 70,000 of them and in villages where only 3 or 4 are stationed they would easily be overpowered. I inquired as to the required date of British-American troop withdrawal which is 90 days after the treaty becomes effective. So far, no country has ratified the treaty but if the four powers ratify by the middle of June, it would in fact mean the removal of these troops before that time. I said that I would give thought to the matter.

I asked whether the exact date for the elections has been fixed. Mr. Tarchiani said no. Both the government and the Communists and Socialists wanted the elections in October, but there was a possibility that the members of the Constituent Assembly might desire to prolong their own political life and not approve the constitution in time to permit elections by that date. This would present various legal complications and the present expectation is that the elections will be held in October.

I said I wanted to assure the Ambassador that I was giving serious thought to the situation in his country and would do all that I could to help. I could tell him that when the new government is formed the

---

[3] De Gasperi submitted his resignation on May 13.

United States Government will issue a public statement expressing its support and its interest in Italy's problems.[4] As to future measures, I will urge that the $100,000,000 Eximbank credit earmarked for Italy be made available.[5] We hope to get ahead with the negotiation of a treaty of friendship and commerce with Italy. I was encouraged by the passage by the Senate of the post-UNRRA relief bill which would assure Italy substantial relief assistance this year.[6] I would likewise press for the early return to Italy of Italian assets in the United States. I asked the Ambassador what these amounted to and he replied about $60,000,000, a substantial proportion of which, however, constitute private bank balances, which while valuable assets would not be available to the government since it did not know the owners. Finally, I said the United States would vigorously support Italy's application for membership in the United Nations. I felt encouraged by the recent trend in Congress which seemed to me a reversal of previous opposition to constructive measures.

The Ambassador expressed his appreciation and said that this brought him to the question of Italy's financial situation. For the next three or four years Italy's unfavorable balance of payments, he thought, would amount to $500,000,000 to $600,000,000 per year. This was due to a number of causes. First and foremost, Italy had lost her most important export markets in central Europe—Germany, Austria, and in large part Czechoslovakia. Only Switzerland remained. Similarly, Scandinavia had reduced its purchases of Italy's principal exports, fruits and vegetables, and Italy had not been able to build up markets in France or England. Fruits and vegetables were now considered as "luxuries" which all those countries could do without and the other important Italian export, textiles, was running into greater competition because of the high cost of Italian production. In order to avoid unemployment Italy's factories are compelled to employ three men for the job of one. Her steel and shipbuilding industries suffer through lack of coal. Furthermore, the Italian merchant marine had been reduced from some 3,600,000 tons before the war—the minimum necessary—to about 600,000 tons. Thanks to American help it is now back to 1,200,000 tons but this is far too small. Atlantic shipping conditions and other factors mean that tourist trade, another important source of revenue, will continue greatly diminished for the next three or four years. On the other hand, Italy is compelled

---

[4] For text of the statement, released to the press by the White House on June 14, see Department of State *Bulletin*, June 22, 1947, p. 1214.

[5] See telegram 1402, June 4, from Rome, p. 917, and memorandum of July 29, p. 951.

[6] Reference is presumably to Public Law 271. The Supplemental Appropriation Act, 1948, approved July 30, 1947; 61 Stat. (pt. 1) 612.

to spend large sums abroad for her two principal essentials: wheat and coal. I asked whether Italy did not desire more ships and whether she had the crews to man them as this seemed to be one possible source of further American help. He said that in addition to the return of Italian ships utilized by the United States during the war, Italy had purchased through Mr. Byrnes' efforts on long term credit 50 Liberty ships and an additional 50 had been granted at the time of Mr. de Gasperi's visit here. I asked why more are not available in view of the large number of Liberty ships which we still have. Mr. Tarchiani and Mr. Matthews replied that they thought the Maritime Commission was reluctant to sell ships to foreign governments owing primarily to the dislike by American shipping interests of foreign competitors who could operate the ships at much cheaper costs. I asked Matthews to explore the possibilities of acquiring further merchant ships for Italy. I asked that tankers be included in such a study since I had this morning considered the sale of tankers to foreign owners and Mr. Tarchiani indicated Italy would like to acquire some on credit.

As to the deficit for the current year Mr. Tarchiani estimated it at $100,000,000 and said that this could be reduced, he thought, to $50,-000,000 if the tentative amount of relief ear-marked for Italy could be increased. He said that he thought it was important that if possible steps be taken to step up food shipments between now and the time of the elections so that the Italian people could be given some material as well as psychological lift. There was one final question about which he had spoken to the President and to Matthews, namely, the importance of issuing a statement at the time of ratification of the treaty. He said naturally the treaty was not popular in Italy and it was important to give the Italian people some counteracting assurances at the time of ratification. I said I thought we could issue a statement at that time. He said that he hoped any statement would contain some specific reference to Italy's "disarmed frontiers" and give some sort of "moral guarantee" by the United States that they would be respected. Opinion in Italy is very sensitive to the fact that Italy has been effectively disarmed by the treaty in the face of an aggressive and well-armed Yugoslavia. For all their talk and oratory the Italians are essentially a realistic people, he said. They think that the United Nations may at some future date become an effective organization for world security but they have little confidence in its ability to defend Italy's frontiers at the present time. I told the Ambassador that I would look into this aspect of the matter. I said that I recognized the importance of aiding Italy from the psychological point of view. I understood Ambassador Dunn was fortunately in "good voice", so to speak and he would be authorized to continue addressing the Italian public. Furthermore, I hoped the programs of the Voice of America to Italy could be stepped up. The Ambassador said both were quite helpful.

865.00/5–2047

Memorandum of Conversation, by the Director of the Office of European Affairs (*Matthews*)

TOP SECRET   WASHINGTON, May 20, 1947.

The Italian Ambassador called this afternoon at his request and read me part of a private very secret message which he had received from de Gasperi. The message was partly in response to reports which the Ambassador had sent following his conversations with the President and with the Secretary. It suggested that the Ambassador make an early approach to Secretary Snyder on Italian financial needs which was in accordance with what Tarchiani said the President had suggested.

While the important part of the message was somewhat vague Mr. Tarchiani interpreted it to mean that Nitti will probably not be successful in forming a government and that de Gasperi will thereupon be asked to do so. De Gasperi seemed somewhat dubious of success and apparently in need of encouragement. Unless he is successful Tarchiani thought a period of uncertainty and disorganization will ensue with eventual Communist success and tragic effects on Italy. De Gasperi asked specifically whether he could count on the moral support of the United States and on additional financial help to enable Italy to meet its financial necessities this year if he undertook to head a new government. The Ambassador asked me to bring this to the attention of the Secretary and to say on his behalf that he felt it important to get some message of encouragement to de Gasperi this evening. I told the Ambassador I would inform the Secretary immediately of his call.

After consulting the Secretary I telephoned the Ambassador by his direction and told him that he might send the following message from the Secretary to de Gasperi:

"You may count on the strong moral support of the United States and that we will make a serious effort to assist Italy in meeting her essential financial needs."

The Ambassador said that he thought this message would give de Gasperi the needed encouragement and expressed his deep appreciation.

The Ambassador emphasized throughout the very private nature of his communications from and to de Gasperi and urged that the matter be kept entirely secret.

H. F[REEMAN] M[ATTHEWS]

865.00/5–347 : Telegram

The Secretary of State to the Embassy in Italy

TOP SECRET   WASHINGTON, May 20, 1947—8 p.m.
US URGENT

726. For the Ambassador. Dept has considered Ital situation in light developments outlined Deptel 622 May 1 as well as info urtel 1031 May 3 and subsequent tels. It is evident any non-Communist govt formed following De Gasperi's resignation must achieve early, visible improvement economic conditions and demonstrate Ital people it enjoys Western support if further progress Italy along democratic lines expected. Foregoing naturally applies also and in almost equal measure to any new govt in which Communist participation is reduced to minimum.

In anticipation of possible request from Itals as to what US support such govt might obtain, following proposals have been formulated and approved:

1) General pledge US support for Italy, to be made upon formation new govt.[1]

2) Consultations to be undertaken UK and French Govts to urge them lend support Ital Govt and take steps provide Ital people tangible evidence this support, including any possible treaty revision in Ital favor. One move would be immediate admission Italy to Tangier regime.[2]

3) Contemplated Italo-US agreements, including commercial treaty, bi-lateral air agreement and trade agreement, to be negotiated soonest possible to derive full psychological value. US to urge Ital Govt take immediate effective steps improve economic conditions.

4) Every available source economic assistance Italy to be utilized, including post-UNRRA relief.[3] Congress to be urged pass promptly enabling legislation for return Ital assets in US, including seized

---

[1] Issued to the press by the White House on June 14. For text, see Department of State *Bulletin*, June 22, 1947, p. 1214.

[2] The Ambassador in France, Caffery, reported in telegram 4171, September 25, from Paris, not printed: "Member of Italian Embassy told us this morning that he had learned from French of our initiative (and French concurrence) in renewed effort to obtain Italy's readmission in international regime at Tangier now that peace treaty has been ratified." (881.00/9–2547)
The British Embassy's note No. 553 of October 13, not printed, gave the Department official notice of Italy's admission under article 11 (b) of the Anglo-French Agreement of August 31, 1945 (881.00/10–1347).

[3] See telegram 1786, July 1, from Rome, p. 930.

ships;[4] Eximbank to be urged expedite availability $100 million earmarked loan; War Dept to be asked expedite final settlement suspense accts.

5) Surplus mil eqpt, recommended by SACMED for transfer to Ital armed forces, to be made available lowest possible cost.[5]

6) Every opportunity to be taken advertise to Ital people US support Italy and US appreciation Ital progress.

Tarchiani told in genl terms of above measures when he called see me May 16, as well as our willingness explore possibility making available additional merchant ships for Italy. He was also informed we contemplate statement of US support for Italy at time treaty is ratified, in addition to friendly statements which I understand will be made in Senate during treaty debate.

In your discretion, you may use substance of foregoing in conversations with De Nicola, De Gasperi or others re formation and future course of new govt.

MARSHALL

---

[4] Regarding the "Memorandum of Understanding between the Government of the United States of America and the Government of Italy regarding settlement of certain wartime claims and related matters", see editorial note, p. 956.

[5] See letter of July 21, by the Deputy Central Field Commissioner for Europe, p. 939.

865.248/5–1447 : Telegram

The Secretary of State to the Embassy in Italy

TOP SECRET　　　　　　　　WASHINGTON, May 21, 1947—6 p.m.

734. Reur 1146 May 14 FLC issuing instructions FLC Rome to negotiate transfer planes at nominal price (Deptel 695 May 15) to be arranged in consultation you.

Figure of $92,000 is total estimate. Final price to be determined by FLC in consultation with you on basis Ital capabilities in accordance Deptel 695.

War Dept has informal reports indicating Itals already forced cannibalize some P–38's to maintain serviceability P–38's presently operational. War reiterates impracticability furnishing maintenance parts spares 38's. You shd therefore discourage any further consideration Itals continued use 38's and urge acceptance overall combined US–UK plan as offered. Dept exploring further with War possibility accept return 38's for credit and will advise soonest.

Contemplated training will be by US personnel in Germany and will involve stationing no US mil personnel in Italy after R plus 90.

MARSHALL

865.00/5–2847 : Telegram

The Ambassador in Italy (Dunn) to the Secretary of State

TOP SECRET ROME, May 28, 1947—8 p.m.
US URGENT

1322. Mr. De Gasperi arranged yesterday for a confidential meeting with me. He said that he was giving serious consideration to the formation of a government by his own party, the Christian Democrats, alone, with the inclusion perhaps of some experts who would not be considered as politically representing any of the other parties. He said he was considerably concerned in making this decision as to whether such a government would be successful in dealing with the economic situation because if it failed, in his opinion the next step would be a government of the extreme Left. He knew that every effort would be made to undermine and discredit the new government by the extreme Left although he felt he could count on sufficient votes in the Assembly to give him parliamentary support.

I took occasion to give him the substance of urtel 726, of May 20, 8 p.m. as no opportunity had presented itself to convey this information because of the discussions regarding formation of a new government. He made very careful notes of each point and discussed them in detail with me. He then said that we could dispense with discussion of the attitude of the US toward Italian situation as he was fully conversant with and fully appreciative of what we had done and the favorable attitude manifested by our government as indicated in the information I had just given him and in conversation which Tarchiani had had with the President and you and R. L. [*J. W.*] Snyder.[1] He said, however, that what he needed for the survival of the new single party government, if he undertook it, was some new and substantial evidence of economic aid which could be applied to the support of the lira and the financial position of the government. He said that in order to provide the basis for economic and financial stability the new government would have to undertake many unpopular measures and it was only by presenting the picture of having the financial strength to effect economic recovery that he could have the necessary program accepted by the country. He said that if he had this new substantial support he was ready to take up the battle against the parties of the extreme Left. He felt that this winning of such a battle was of primary importance to the country because if his party were politically discredited the effort toward preservation of real democracy in Italy would be eclipsed.

---

[1] Records of Tarchiani's conversations with the President and with the Secretary of the Treasury, not found.

My own judgement of the present situation here is that a Democratic Christian government headed by De Gasperi and given economic and financial support by the United States in addition to the matters mentioned in your 726 can turn the tide now strongly favoring the Communists and bring about an increase in the parliamentary representation of the center and left of center, thus strengthening the democratic forces in their development here in Italy. I am fearful however, if the proposed government does not receive some additional financial support that it will not be able to resist the undermining efforts of the extreme Left.

Of course, everyone here has their eyes upon the forthcoming elections which are now expected to be held in October or November and almost every step taken in connection with the formation or actions of the national government is with a view to the representation of the parties which will result from these elections. As the efforts of the other Democratic leaders to form a government have now apparently failed, I believe we have come to the point right now where we should, if possible, give assistance to a Democratic Christian effort should they succeed in forming a government.[2]

In addition to the measures referred to in urtel 726, May 20, 8 p.m. suggested as support for a new government of the kind referred to after consultation with Tasca, strongly urge that consideration be given to additional aid to Italy from the following sources: (a) credit to the Italian Government of a sum of 20 million dollars involved in the prisoner of war credit certificates irregularly taken up by the Italian Government and the elimination of this item from claims by Italy to be cancelled under the financing agreement presently being negotiated; (b) immediate return to the Italian Government of some 20 tons of gold held at Bank of Italy under USFA [US–UK?] custody; (c) transfer of some part of gold pot share ultimately to be transferred to Italian Government at as early a date as possible; (d) modification in administration of Export Import Bank loan to make available the 100 million dollar loan for basic requirements of last six months of 1947; (e) possible addition of further sum to 100 million dollars loan, to be taken from funds allocated to China.

I realize that latter two suggestions involve matters of very high policy, the realization of which may encounter serious difficulties. It should be emphasized, however, that this is the opportunity for the US Government to indicate in bold relief its political support for the first post war Italian Government formed without the Communists.[3]

---

[2] In telegram 1364, June 1, from Rome, not printed, Dunn reported that a government had been formed by Christian Democrats and outside experts, but without Communists (865.00/6–147).

[3] The endorsement of this telegram by the Division of Financial Affairs has the notation: "Memo drafted to Secretary 6–3–47 FN H[enry] R. S[piegel]". See *infra*.

At the same time I was talking to the Prime Minister, Tasca was meeting with Minister of Treasury Campilli with the consent of De Gasperi and myself. Tasca's report of that conversation is contained in next following telegram.[4]

DUNN

[4] Not printed.

FW 865.00/5–2847

Memorandum by the Director of the Office of Financial and Development Policy (Ness) to the Secretary of State

TOP SECRET   WASHINGTON, June 3, 1947.

Subject: Urgent request of Ambassador Dunn for assistance to new Italian government.

DISCUSSION

Ambassador Dunn's telegram No. 1322, May 28, attached,[1] states that it is of great political importance to give de Gasperi's new Democratic Christian Government concrete evidence of U.S. support. The Ambassador feels this is essential if the new government is to survive expected attacks from leftists groups. The Ambassador suggests five possible measures of assistance:

1. Credit Italy with approximately $20 million for prisoner-of-war certificates representing wages and salaries of former Italian POWs.
2. Return immediately to Italy about $28 million worth of captured Italian gold currently in Anglo-American custody.[2]
3. Make an advance transfer to Italy of some part of the share in the German Gold Pool which may ultimately go to Italy.
4. Modify the terms of the existing $100 million Eximbank loan so as to make it available for basic 1947 requirements.
5. Make an additional $100 million Eximbank loan, these funds to be taken from the $500 million earmarked for China.

RECOMMENDATIONS

1. The approximately $20 million available in the POW trust fund account should be transferred. This will require concurrence of and possibly pressure on the War Department.
2. The Department previously attempted to get British agreement to immediate transfer of the gold in custody. The British would agree only to transfer upon the coming into force of the peace treaty. In view of changed circumstances the Department should again seek British concurrence to immediate transfer.

[1] *Supra.*
[2] See footnote 2, p. 987.

3. The Department has engaged in discussions with the British and French looking toward the admission of Italy to the German Gold Pool on the same basis as the other participants. The French, however, insisted that Italy should not share in that part of the German Gold Pool contributed by Switzerland under agreement with the Allies. Until this is resolved it will be impossible even to consider an advance distribution to Italy. In the light of the new political situation in Italy and the French interest therein, a high level attempt should be made to obtain French consent to full participation by Italy in the Pool. If, nevertheless, the French continue to maintain their present position, the Department should agree for the sake of getting prompt action.

4. Since the Eximbank agreed to the $100 million loan to Italy only after vigorous efforts by Mr. Clayton and after the matter had been taken to the White House, it is not believed that Ambassador Dunn's suggestion to seek liberalization of the terms of the loan is feasible. The Eximbank agreed to make funds available only for approved export projects and only if conditions in Italy were stable and Italy's other needs could be met from other sources.

5. It is believed that your decision on May 23 to continue earmarking $500 million of Eximbank funds for China, precludes Ambassador Dunn's suggestion of giving Italy an additional $100 million from this source. The Bank has currently available only about $300 million outside of the funds earmarked for China. In view of the limited resources available a choice must be made between Italy and China or between Italy and other applicants.

6. If the above recommendations meet with your approval they will be communicated to Ambassador Dunn in response to his telegram of May 28.

CONCURRENCES

This action has been concurred in by A–T—Mr. Thorp and EUR—Mr. Matthews.

865.51/6–447

Memorandum of Conversation, by the Director of the Office of European Affairs (Matthews)

TOP SECRET   [WASHINGTON,] June 4, 1947.

Ambassador Tarchiani called this afternoon at his request and read from another private telegram which he had just received from de Gasperi through their private channels (see memorandum of conversation of May 20, 1947). The cable, which was sent before our public statement of June 2,[1] welcomed the assurances which Ambassador Dunn had given de Gasperi (see Dunn's telegram no. 1322, May 28, 8 p.m. and telegram 1323, May 28 [2]) and expressed the hope that a public statement would be made by our Government in support of de Gasperi's new Government. Mr. Tarchiani said that this statement had now been made and that he considered the one which we had issued a very good one, striking just the right note under the circumstances. De Gasperi's cable went on to say that as a result of conversations between Tasca, our Treasury Attaché, and Campilli, the Italian Minister of Treasury, it appeared that Italy's balance of payments for the current year would be in deficit to the amount of some $200,000,000. To meet this de Gasperi urged the importance of further financial assistance in addition to the measures proposed, such as suspense account payments, return of Italian assets in this country, et cetera, now under discussion with Lombardo.[3] Specifically, he wanted to know whether (a) the $100,000,000 Eximbank credit to Italy could not be made available in its entirety to the Government for utilization this year and whether (b) a further $100,000,000 might not be obtained from the $500,000,000 now earmarked for China. Ambassador Tarchiani had been asked urgently to inquire as to the possibilities of obtaining this further assistance. He emphasized that neither Sforza nor Lombardo nor anyone else knew of this personal appeal from de Gasperi and that it must be kept entirely secret. He asked me to look into the matter and let him know the possibilities within the next few days. He said that he naturally did not expect anything approaching a "commitment" in such a brief space of time but would like to know whether or not either or both of the suggested measures were within the realm of possibility. I said that I would look into the question and endeavor to let him know. I asked on what basis post-UNRRA relief for Italy had been figured in arriving at the $200,000,000 deficit. He replied at the "conservative" one of $100,000,000, adding that of course any allotment over that figure would correspondingly reduce the deficit.

He said that de Gasperi has now agreed that elections should be held on the 9th of November and emphasized the importance of them. He said that the new Parliament would be elected for a period of four years and the new Government would be formed on the basis of the November elections. He could not overestimate the importance of doing all that could be done to improve Italy's lot before then and to prevent the Communists, with their apparently unlimited funds, from winning.

Mr. Tarchiani thought that when de Gasperi goes before the Constituent Assembly on Saturday he would come through with a small

[1] For text, see Department of State *Bulletin*, June 15, 1947, p. 1160.
[2] Not printed.
[3] See editorial note, p. 956.

majority which should be adequate. He denied the accuracy of stories reporting that the Communist Partisans were taking to the hills to start disorders. On one road a total of 10 Carabinieri had been stationed but that was all the precautionary measures required in all Italy. The demonstrations in Rome had been quite orderly. In de Gasperi's earlier negotiations, however, the Communists and Socialists had fought bitterly against being excluded from the Government.

I said that as he knew the Italian peace treaty would be voted on by our Senate tomorrow and I asked whether, if we succeeded in obtaining Senate consent to ratification, he believed the Constituent Assembly in Italy would likewise ratify before adjournment on June 24. He said that he felt it would and that he had had Sforza's assurances to that effect. He reverted to his statement to the Secretary on May 16 as to the importance of our issuing a statement promptly on ratification. The statement, he said, should emphasize: (1) the fact that while the treaty is being ratified in the interests of general peace and reconstruction of Europe, its terms did not represent the wishes of the United States which had favored a more generous treaty and (2) that through the usual processes and through the United Nations it is subject to modification.

H. F[REEMAN] M[ATTHEWS]

865.24/6–447 : Telegram

The Ambassador in Italy (Dunn) to the Secretary of State

TOP SECRET   ROME, June 4, 1947—7 p.m.

1398. OFLC, Rome, advise that negotiation of additional credit agreement for $10,000,000 to cover purchases of fixed installations, scrap, YMS vessels, ammunition, combat material and other items not covered by agreement of September 10 [9], 1946,[1] is held up pending further advices from OFLC Paris and Washington, concerning possibility of bulk deal encompassing all these items. These items cannot be included in original bulk deal even though total credit will not be absorbed because prices involved will be considerably less than 18.2% of government cost. Caulkins[2] suggests individual sales contracts covering each class of item using same Three (C) payment terms as bulk agreement and negotiating amendment to bulk agreement to

---

[1] See *Foreign Relations*, 1946, vol. v, p. 932.
[2] Daniel P. Caulkins, Field Commissioner, Office of Foreign Liquidation Commissioner, Mediterranean Theater.

cover additional real estate requirements (reDeptel 734, May 21 and Embtel 1365, June 1 [3]).

In connection with the eventual instructions issued to OFLC Rome for transfer of remaining items to Italy, it is urged that the Embassy together with OFLC be allowed in our discretion to by-pass ARAR. As the Department is probably aware ARAR is constituted as the agent of the Italian Government to receive surplus and to dispose of it on a commercial basis. Because of the commercial aspect of ARAR operations, that organization is loathe to transfer material to impecunious government ministries of which the service ministries are good example. Furthermore, we are inclined to be dubious of the good will toward the US of some of the ARAR personnel. Accordingly, since the sale of surplus ground and air aviation equipment is a nominal sale without commercial aspects, we would be inclined to discuss the proposed negotiations in advance with either the Prime Minister or the new Vice President of the Council, Einaudi, who as Minister of the Budget will have control over expenditures authorized for the service ministries.[4]

DUNN

---

[3] In this telegram, not printed, Dunn pointed out that the program for reequipping the Italian army was not at the same stage as that for the air force for which SAC had received instructions from the CCS whereas none had as yet come regarding the army (865.20/6–147).

[4] In telegraphic instruction 898, June 12, not printed, the Department directed that the negotiations need not involve ARAR; and that Dunn might use his own discretion in dealing directly with the appropriate Italian authorities (865.24/6–447).

865.51/6–447 : Telegram

The Ambassador in Italy (Dunn) to the Secretary of State

SECRET   ROME, June 4, 1947—7 p.m.

1402. Export-Import Bank representatives conversations in Rome ended May 29 and Messrs. Arey and Itana [1] left for visits to industrialists in southern and northern Italy May 30. Subjects of [*subject to*] development of new thinking as a result of this trip, representatives have reached agreement with Italians on memorandum (text by air) to be submitted to board of bank for implementing tentative 100 million dollar credit.[2]

---

[1] Hawthorne Arey, vice president and general counsel, Export-Import Bank. "Itana" is a garble for Tirana. Rifat Tirana was a senior economist with the Export-Import Bank.

[2] The Department's instruction 168, July 28, 1947, not printed, forwarded to Rome copies of the Report to the Board of Directors of the Export-Import Bank, 34 typewritten pages, dated June 23, 1947 (811.516 Export-Import Bank/7–2847).

In summary memo states:

1. Italian Govt will guarantee credits and undertakes to ensure that all qualifying firms will get share of financed raw materials.

2. Credits will be remitted to industries which can most quickly increase Italian exports i.e. improve balance of payments. Italian Govt proposes to limit equipment financing to 15 percent (although needs of individual industries may deviate from this percentage).

3. Credits will be geared to import needs over next one year period.

4. Italian Govt will select the firms (and indicate respective amounts) authorized to contract direct with Export-Import Bank.

5. For smaller manufacturers Italian Govt will draw up an overall program based on one year production and export prospects.
Credit applications for small firm groups will be made by "industrial sectors".

6. Italian Govt proposes to allocate one-half total credit to large firms (about 35) under direct loans and one-half to small manufacturers through IMI.

7. Export-Import Bank proposes to open credits simultaneously for each sector as a whole. Italian Govt suggests following priority of sectors without prejudice to Export-Import Bank's right to examine any application it may receive:

(a) Iron, steel and mechanical;
(b) Electro mechanical;
(c) Chemical; and
(d) Rubber.

8. There shall be no discrimination between term of credit for small firms financed through IMI and "direct loan" firms. Confindustria assumes responsibility to inform firms of terms. Firms belonging to an approved sector may, subject to Export-Import Bank IMI agreement, buy goods from IMI in lire. IMI is responsible for records of distribution of raw materials.

9. Excepting coal and POL materials distributed under credits will not jeopardize right of firms so credited to their normal internal allocations.

10. IMI will cover credits in special dollar accounts guaranteed by dollar value of financed raw material inventories and equipment plus exchange proceeds of exports in sufficient amount to cover deficit.

11. So long as existing exchange regulations prevail dollar exchange to service credits and to enter into IMI cover account is to come from exporters 50 percent share of exchange.

12. Italian Treasury may charge a commission of one and one-half to two percent per annum to borrowing firms.

13. Export-Import Bank will be kept informed of use of credits.

14. Italian Govt should devise methods to reduce number of direct lines of credit (i.e. permit group contracts for each sector or large firms).

15. While the Export-Import Bank emphasizes it is not authorized to discuss terms or interest rates, Italian Govt points to convenience of:

(a) Terms of ten years or more;

(b) Begin amortization only after second year; and
(c) Low interest rates.

16. Export-Import Bank representatives express view that terms and conditions of credit bear direct relation to economic position and export prospects of each sector.
17. Italian Govt has taken note of and has not objected to usual terms included in Export-Import Bank loan contracts.

Throughout conversation Export-Import Bank representatives stressed that discussions in no way modify general conditions set forth in bank's letter of last January to De Gasperi.

DUNN

865.00/6–647 : Telegram

The Secretary of State to the Embassy in Italy

SECRET   WASHINGTON, June 6, 1947—8 p.m.

864. For the Ambassador. Demonstrations organized Rome and other cities show Communists intend charge new Ital Govt as undemocratic, without representation working classes, while attempting portray US as supporting reactionary Ital elements. Dept has no doubt govt program will in time refute these charges but propaganda value of such attacks can not be ignored, either as regards implementation Ital Govt program, some necessary measures of which are bound to be unpopular, or as concerns effectiveness of US assistance.

In view of foregoing, Dept feels that in conversations with Christian Democrats and PSLI [1] leaders you might take occasion intimate some disappointment that agreement could not be reached for PSLI participation in cabinet. You might explain to PSLI leaders, . . . US view that Ital situation requires loyal cooperation all truly democratic elements in nat'l interest. With CD leaders, you might point out need, which applies to all European Govts today, for support of democratic left and of fullest possible representation working classes. To both, you might convey impression of US hope that way may yet be cleared for eventual PSLI participation in govt.[2]

MARSHALL

---

[1] *Partito Socialista dei Lavoratori Italiani*, Socialist Party of Italian Workers, the followers of Saragat who had broken away from the Nenni Socialists because of that party's pact of unity with the Communists.
[2] In telegram 1500, June 11, Dunn reported that he had conveyed this point of view to a principal leader of the PSLI, and he added in telegram 1534, June 13, that a CD leader had reviewed the situation with him and expressed the view that, while widening the cabinet was desirable and might later be possible, for the time being it was likely to provoke an undesirable crisis. Dunn recommended that no further steps be taken. (865.00/6–11, 6–1347)

865.00/6–847 : Telegram

The Ambassador in Italy (Dunn) to the Secretary of State

SECRET   ROME, June 8, 1947—midnight.

1455. While it may be a little early to judge (already 40 deputies are inscribed for interpellations following the new government's statement scheduled for today) there is some justification in expecting the new De Gasperi Government to admit the critical economic facts of Italy, however unpleasant, and to make genuine efforts to adopt and carry out its program accordingly. The bullish reaction of the lira (785 May 13 when Cabinet resigned 725 June 5) since announcement of the new Cabinet is perhaps symptomatic of restrained providence [confidence] and hope.

The participation of Einaudi [1] as Vice Premier and Minister of the Budget over Finance and Treasury; the constitution of a consultative economic planning body (a "brain trust" according to Il Globo) the increasing realism of CIR studies of Italian exchange balance and Italian needs revealed in our current talks on relief, suggest a conscious striving to develop internal measures which inspire confidence among groups, and in countries (i.e. the US) whose contribution to rehabilitation is essential.

In this light, the Secretary's Harvard address [2] is, as concerns Italy, most happy as to both substance and timing. It is what is needed to rally the Cabinet and the majority of the country to support unpleasant restrictions and sacrifices against opposition of special interests. The next few days should prove whether this is indeed the real start up and forward.

DUNN

---

[1] Luigi Einaudi, governor of the Bank of Italy, January 1945–May 1948; later president of the Republic, 1948–1955.
[2] For text of Secretary Marshall's address of June 5, see p. 237.

Editorial Note

On June 9, 1947, by an exchange of notes, signed by Ambassador Dunn and Foreign Minister Sforza, the United States Government agreed to turn over to the Italian Government air navigation, communication, and weather facilities at ten listed air fields where they had been installed by the U.S. military services. For texts of the notes, see Department of State Treaties and Other International Acts Series (TIAS) No. 2127, or 62 Stat. (pt. 3) 4074.

740.0011 EW Peace/6–1147

The Secretary of State to the Chairman of the Senate Committee on Foreign Relations (Vandenberg)

[WASHINGTON,] June 11, 1947.

MY DEAR SENATOR VANDENBERG: You will recall that on April 15, 1947 the Acting Secretary, Mr. Acheson, wrote to you in connection with Italian property in the United States and the Treaty of Peace with Italy. In that letter it was indicated that the policy of the United States had been "firmly directed toward the release by this Government of Italian property controlled by it, whether blocked or vested. It is, therefore, contemplated that arrangements will be made for the unblocking and return of such property".

The letter under reference was designed for inclusion in the record of the Senate dealing with the Treaty of Peace with Italy and, in part, released, during the course of your Committee's hearings, to the public.

Discussions have now for some time been under way with an Italian Delegation which is presently in the United States. Procedures for the unblocking and the return of Italian property here have been discussed with the Italian Delegation and have, with the possible exception of certain drafting changes, been satisfactorily worked out. It appears, however, that further legislative action will be necessary in order to effect the return of such property, previously Italian, as has been vested by the United States Alien Property Custodian.

After conference with the Office of Alien Property, Department of Justice (the successor to the Office of Alien Property Custodian), and the Treasury Department, the Department of State therefore recommends the enactment, by the present session of Congress, of legislation which would enable the executive branch of this Government to enter into arrangements for the return of the vested property under reference. Should such legislation be enacted, the Office of Alien Property will have authority to make returns to Italy or to Italian nationals on exactly the same basis as returns are now authorized vis-à-vis non-enemy countries, such as France, Belgium, etc. I therefore commend to your attention and to that of the Congress the early enactment of legislation designed to accomplish this result.

It may be pointed out that the legislation will, in itself, not actually return Italian property, but will merely authorize the Office of Alien Property to enter into arrangements, safeguarding the interests of the United States, as well as contributing to the welfare of Italy and to the alleviation of the Italian burden under the Treaty of Peace, for the return of such property.

Because of the urgency of the matter this letter has not been cleared with the Bureau of the Budget, to which a copy is being sent.

While the attached joint resolution [1] has been cleared in substance with the interested agencies, it may be necessary for certain language changes to be made prior to its enactment. These changes will be available the early part of next week.

Faithfully yours,   G. C. MARSHALL

---

[1] Not printed; the draft was the basis for Public Law 370, "Joint Resolution: To provide for returns of Italian property in the United States, and for other purposes," approved August 5, 1947 (61 Stat. 784). See also the bracketed note, p. 956.

865.00/6–1747 : Telegram

The Ambassador in Italy (Dunn) to the Secretary of State

TOP SECRET   ROME, June 17, 1947—9 p.m.
US URGENT

1590. Re statistical presentation in my 1579, June 16, midnight,[1] I wish to emphasize following very important qualifications to any interpretation of the data presented:

1. It is likely that the estimates presented, in absence of any substantial US aid in addition to post-UNRRA program will involve a drastic reduction re Italian Govt's exchange reserves. In view of uncertainties attached to problem of financing Italy's requirements in 1948, as well as unfavorable economic developments which may take place during last six months of 1947 it is highly important that Italian Govt maintain sufficient foreign exchange reserves to meet such emergencies as may arise.

2. Dept's attention is also called again to very pessimistic forecast being made at present time with respect to current wheat crop. Until more definitive estimates are available with respect to need for grain imports during next twelve months' period it is impossible to state accurately total foreign exchange deficit which will have to be met during that period.

3. The entire Govt's estimates as revised by Embassy are based upon minimum emergency rations. A primary factor in the instability of any democratic govt in Italy is inadequate food supplies resulting in hunger which provides a fertile field for Communist propaganda and agitation.

4. If the present tide in favor of extreme left is to turn and if a democratic govt of present type is to succeed, its fundamental task

---

[1] Not printed.

must be to shift from present phase of an emergency hand-to-mouth economy to one providing maximum employment and production and their corollary of improved standards of living necessary for eliminating social unrest. For democratic leadership in Italy to survive it must accomplish this position towards a more permanent basic economic reconstruction which offers Italian people concrete hope for a betterment in standards of living in foreseeable future.

The political situation in Italy has reached a point of delicate balance where the outcome between totalitarianism of extreme left and democracy may be decided by the extent to which outside aid will support the democratic elements in Italy who are attempting to meet the heretofore unchecked drive of the Communists. Should the present effort to govern Italy without the Communists fail, the future of democracy in Italy may be most seriously endangered. A victorious Communist Party back in the Govt would face the coming elections in a very strong position with discouraged forces of Center either joining it for self preservation, along with Nenni, or turning in desperation to extreme right.

I urge therefore that Dept give immediate consideration to adoption of measures along lines suggested in mytel 1322, May 28, 8 p.m.

DUNN

865.00/6–1847 : Telegram

The Ambassador in Italy (Dunn) to the Secretary of State

CONFIDENTIAL   ROME, June 18, 1947—9 p.m.

1613. *Avanti* (Socialist) carried this morning brief article to effect that report relative to organization of partisans movements in northern Italy had not been denied by Ministry of Interior. Headline stated that partisans were against the "black market". *Tempo* carried same item adding that center of movement was in province of Asti and its objective was to demonstrate against present government. *Messagero* article on subject referred to movement of opposition to government which parties of extreme left were endeavoring to develop and mentioned speeches inciting armed revolt on part of partisans of Teramo province. In line with above, we have been informed recently by young Socialist that several Communist friends of his had told him that they were bringing out their arms from places of concealment and were getting ready for any eventuality in light of advent of fourth De Gasperi Government. He expressed view, however, that Communists would not push violence tactics to point of civil war on national scale.

There have recently been reports, often from reliable sources, of large potential military and paramilitary formations under Communist control in Italy, especially the north. There is no doubt that Communist Party has military organization based on former Communist controlled partisan formations which are now organized into the ANPI (National Association of Italian Partisans) which is completely Communist controlled. Reported leader of this organization is Luigi Longo, the so-called Minister of War of the party, who was one of the organizers of the International Brigade in Spain. The number of these armed Communist elements has been placed as high as 150,000 men. The Embassy believes that this figure is too high insofar as actually armed elements are concerned. It is of opinion that there are in neighborhood of 50,000 trained men equipped with light weapons and sidearms at disposition of CPI.[1] This does not include, however, unarmed or semi-armed men who might rally to Communist banner in case of insurrection. As example, Embassy has recently received confidential memorandum from a highly reliable source concerning Communist semi-military formations in northern Italy. A copy of this memorandum has been forwarded to Department.[2] It indicates that there are in the provinces of Modena, Reggio Emilia, Parma and Bologna, so-called "Red zone" of north Italy, a total of about 10,000 armed Communist elements, already in active service which, in case of insurrection or direct Communist action, would be supplemented by about 40,000 men organized in the Garibaldi partisan brigades. The 10,000 represent cream of insurrectionary forces, the shock troopers, who would be called upon to undertake the most hazardous tasks as well as to liquidate leaders of opposition.

It is of course quite possible that rumors relative to "direct action" on part of Italian Communists are spread purposely by CPI in order to put country in state of jitters and with view to intimidating the present government. Although we would not be surprised to see an increase in the near future in political violence (a separate telegram is being prepared on this subject), in CPI inspired strikes and in all manner of nuisance tactics aimed at embarrassing government, we are not inclined to believe that Communists will resort to violent methods so long as they feel they may gain control of government through legal means.

DUNN

---

[1] Usually referred to as P.C.I., *Partito Comunista Italiano*, the Italian Communist Party.
[2] Not found in Department of State files.

865.24/6–1847 : Telegram

The Ambassador in Italy (Dunn) to the Secretary of State

SECRET   ROME, June 18, 1947—10 p.m.

1618. For Dowling and Labouisse.[1] We should like to call your attention to the OFLC telegram going out today as Embassy's 1617,[2] proposing in substance that the re-equipment of Italian Ground and Air Forces be brought within the close-out residual surplus negotiations for which Taff, OFLC Field Commissioner Paris,[3] has come to Rome (see our telegram 1398 of June 4 and Department's reply 898, June 12).[4]

As explained in the accompanying OFLC message deliveries under the 160 million dollar credit of the bulk deal of last September,[5] and under surplus contracts entered into before the bulk agreement, will run short a total of 28 million dollars, transfer value. The political advantage of putting into the residual deal (in effect an amendment to the bulk agreement), both non-combat items and all items belonging to the Italian Army and Aviation re-equipment programs are obvious. For example it could prove embarrassing, in fact it might be impossible, to negotiate at a later date an agreement covering only the re-equipment program. Furthermore, it would be easier at this time, considering the present composition of the Italian Government, to reach an agreement which would include the re-equipment (a few weeks ago the Prime Minister said to us P–51 proposal would meet opposition from extreme left in the government). A deal covering solely re-equipment which followed a general formula like that for P–51's would be apt to attract attention and provide a convenient point of attack against friendly government.

We are putting Taff in touch tomorrow with Einaudi to discuss the general purposes of the close-out surplus negotiations, to indicate who the end users should be of certain specific items (this being one of the main reasons for avoiding ARAR at least at this stage), and to suggest to him the setting up of an Italian negotiating group of his and the Prime Minister's confidence. However, the substantive negotiations will necessarily await OFLC's reply to the accompanying telegram and the Department's concurring instructions to us. You will

---

[1] Walter Cecil Dowling of the Division of Southern European Affairs, and Henry Richardson Labouisse, Jr., Special Assistant to the Director, Office of European Affairs.
[2] Not printed.
[3] A. Erich Taff, Deputy Central Field Commissioner for Europe, O.F.L.C.
[4] See footnote 4, p. 917.
[5] See *Foreign Relations*, 1946, vol. v, p. 932.

accordingly understand how useful it will be for us here if you can help expedite the Washington decision.

DUNN

865.24/6–1947 : Telegram

The Ambassador in Italy (Dunn) to the Secretary of State

SECRET ROME, June 19, 1947—8 p.m.

1634. Personal for the Secretary. With the imminent withdrawal of the Allied troops and the end of their stabilizing influence after ratification, the implementation of re-equipment plans of the treaty-size Italian Army and Air Forces becomes a matter of immediate urgency. The general political situation of the Government, and the deplorable inadequacy of the present Italian military forces to assume responsibility for the maintenance of order and even token protection of Italy's northeast frontier, make it indispensable to hasten the Allied program of providing for the transfer to Italian troops of combat material in this theatre. An unobtrusive method would be to include such combat material in a general surplus settlement.

To attain these purposes, the OFLC Deputy Commissioner, Europe, now in Rome, has requested, with our full endorsement, instructions from OFLC Washington in the above sense. (These instructions were requested in this Embassy's telegram 1617, June 18,[1] which was supported by mytel 1618, June 18.)

In view of the foregoing considerations and of the importance of the time factor, may I ask whether you would wish to express your interest in the appropriate quarters to see that the OFLC instructions may be forthcoming without delay in order to expedite negotiation of a single arrangement well before the theatre close-out.

DUNN

---

[1] Not printed.

811.2365/5–2347 : Telegram

The Secretary of State to the Embassy in Italy

CONFIDENTIAL WASHINGTON, June 20, 1947—8 p.m.
US URGENT

972. On 19 June SWNCC approved final draft Military and Civil Affairs Agreement between US and Italy as basis for negotiations by you through an exchange of notes with Ital Govt.[1]

---

[1] On June 20 General Hilldring forwarded to the Department of State a copy of SWNCC 271/21, as approved on June 19, indicating that the Department should initiate negotiations on the basis of the draft (memorandum SWN–5489, June 20, not printed, 740.00119 Control (Italy)/6–2047).

Text agreement approved as in text of annex in ComGenMed tel F 75419 Mar 9 [2] with following amendments:

Para three; second sentence: After "in any case not later than" and before "the coming into force of", insert "ninety days after".

Para eight: After "the United States Forces" insert "and organizations or persons employed by or accompanying these forces".

Para twelve: Delete entire paragraph and substitute following: [3] "The Italian Government will continue to make available all services and facilities required by the United States Armed Forces during this period on the same basis as in the past, in consideration for which the United States Government shall pay to the Italian Government the amount of $250,000, which amount shall be considered as full compensation for all such services and facilities furnished by the Italian Government under the terms of this Agreement. All other financial arrangements in effect between the Armed Forces of the United States and the Italian Government on 1 February 1947 shall continue in effect for the period of this Agreement."

Text of note contained ComGenMed tel F 75419 approved subject to such changes as you might consider appropriate.

Reurtel 1532 June 12,[4] you may, in your discretion, include suggested changes if requested by Itals and agreeable Gen Lee.

Accordingly, you shd undertake appropriate negotiations at the earliest opportunity and inform Dept of date exchange of notes.

MARSHALL

---

[2] Not printed, but see telegram 509, March 10, p. 875. The amendments indicated above were incorporated in the agreement signed at Rome on September 3, 1947; see telegram 2601, September 3, p. 964.

[3] For a summary of the original paragraph 12, see telegram 509, p. 875.

[4] The reference is to telegram 1523, June 12, from Rome, not printed; it listed a series of proposed changes of wording, applicable to the U.S. Forces, on the basis of the text of F 75419 of March 9 (811.2365/6–1247).

865.24/6–2347

The Secretary of War (Patterson) to the Secretary of State

TOP SECRET WASHINGTON, 23 June 1947.

DEAR MR. SECRETARY: In his 1021 of 2 May,[1] Ambassador Dunn states his view concerning 70 medium tanks and 50 105 howitzers which the War Department proposed to be shipped from Italy to the United States since they are needed in connection with War Department programs. General Lee, in messages furnished to the State Department, has recommended that these items of equipment be turned over to the Italian Army.

As to medium tanks, the War Department is querying General Lee since information now available indicates that considerably less

---

[1] See footnote 1, p. 903.

than 70 are required to equip the Italian Army to the number authorized by the peace treaty. Medium tanks of the type of the 70 under consideration are an item of particularly short supply in War Department programs.

There are in the Suez area in British possession over 200 lend-lease medium tanks of a type which the War Department does not intend to retain in its programs. These tanks are available for recapture or re-transfer in connection with foreign assistance programs. Hence, I suggest that in the matter of any additional medium tanks for the Italian Army the State Department take action with the British to utilize those in British possession now in the Suez area.

As to the matter of the 50 105 howitzers, these are in less short supply than the medium tanks. Howitzers are available to fill requirements for the Regular Army, the National Guard and the Organized Reserves, all the programs at present authorized by law. There are inadequate howitzers available for the contemplated needs of Universal Military Training, the Western Hemisphere Defense program and perhaps for the authorized Turkish aid program.

The requirements for this latter program are not available since determination awaits return of the survey group now in Turkey.

From a narrowly military standpoint, the proper action for the War Department is to return the 50 105 howitzers to the U.S. It is apparent that the national interest involved in this matter transcends narrowly military factors and involves international political factors which are the primary responsibility of the State Department.

Your views on the matter set forth in this letter are requested.

Due to the possible early ratification of the Italian Peace Treaty, there is an urgency involved in the problem set forth which requires its resolution by the end of this month. In case the State Department believes that the situation warrants serious consideration of transfer of any of the equipment mentioned above to the Italians, it is requested that the legal and financial considerations involved be taken into account in any action proposed.

Sincerely yours,

ROBERT P. PATTERSON

865.5018/6–2747 : Telegram

The Ambassador in Italy (Dunn) to the Secretary of State

CONFIDENTIAL   ROME, June 27, 1947—8 p.m.

1744. In conversation with Ronchi, High Commissioner Food reported Embtel 1718 June 26,[1] Embassy's Agricultural Attaché[2]

---

[1] Not printed.
[2] Howard R. Cottam.

stressed importance forthcoming IEFC cereals conference and implied by series of questions regarding Italian rationing policy that before making major changes in rations or food controls Italy should bear in mind purpose of IEFC conference and apparent shortage in world cereal supplies (Reurtel 978, June 24 [3]).

At this particular time with new government only 1 week in office since Assembly vote, it would be highly undesirable for US to take responsibility for demanding that government not increase ration. Appropriate place for matter to be acted upon is Paris meeting of IEFC. For US to take action singly now would be a blow to government which expects at least moral support from the US. Pressure for raising ration now is natural result in presence of harvest and it would be extremely damaging to our prestige and support of government for it to take entire responsibility for refusing increase.

Embassy awaits reply to its telegram referred to above before taking further steps.[4]

DUNN

---

[3] Not printed; it directed the Embassy to suggest that the Italian Government postpone any increase of the ration until after the meeting of the various food ministers with the International Emergency Food Council scheduled for Paris in July (865.48/6–2347).
[4] In telegraphic instruction 1045, July 1, not printed, the Department approved the course of action proposed by the Embassy (865.5018/6–2747).

Defense Files : Telegram

The Director of the Plans and Operations Division, War Department General Staff (Norstad) to the Commanding General, United States Forces, Mediterranean Theater of Operations (Lee)

TOP SECRET WASHINGTON, 27 June, 1947.

WARX 81070. From WDGPO MA Rome for Stillwell.

1. Return to Z/I the medium tanks you are holding which originally totaled 70; however, now appear to total 56, and have been subject of exchange of messages. State Department concurs and is considering provision of 20 British lend-lease tanks from the Middle East. References are FX 76636,[1] paragraph 6 of WAR 99303,[2] and F 76195.[3] For your information, the medium tanks are needed to meet established programs of the Regular Army and National Guard and therefore cannot be declared surplus.

2. The 50 105-millimeter howitzers are receiving further consideration by both State and War Departments; instructions are forthcom-

---

[1] FX 76636, June 21, 1947, not printed.
[2] WAR 99303, not found.
[3] F 76195, not found.

ing. We understand that you now have in the depot for turn over to the Italian Army 78 105-millimeter howitzers, M-7, motor carriage, which are US lend-lease items, reference paragraph 3 B of F 76289;[4] plus 5 British pieces of medium artillery, reference paragraph 4 of FX 76636. This total of 83 should equip 3 Italian regiments. Therefore it appears that your action to hold an additional 50 105-millimeter howitzers is to equip 2 more artillery regiments, thus providing the Italians with a total of 5 medium artillery regiments. Is this correct?

3. There are in the European Theater approximately 300, M-18, tank destroyers equipped with 76 millimeter guns which can be declared surplus. Their condition and availability of spare parts are not known. Could 50 of these be used as substitutes for the 50 105-millimeter howitzers you are holding?

---

[4] F 76289, May 15, 1947, not printed.

865.48/7–147 : Telegram

The Ambassador in Italy (Dunn) to the Secretary of State

RESTRICTED   ROME, July 1, 1947—midnight.
URGENT

1786. I expect to sign tomorrow U.S. foreign relief agreement with Italy and I shall notify Department precise time as soon as arrangements are made. I propose to issue following statement at time of signature.

An agreement was signed today at Palazzo Chigi to provide food relief to Italy under recently enacted US foreign relief program. Prime Minister Alcide de Gasperi and Foreign Minister Count Carlo Sforza signed for Italy. Ambassador James Clement Dunn signed for US.

US foreign relief program is designed to alleviate misery of peoples in countries devastated by war. Congress of US has voted 350 million dollars to authorize relief supplies, food and medicines to following countries: Italy, Trieste area, Greece, Austria, Hungary, Poland, and China. This program will remain in operation through 30 June 1948.

Terms of agreement which two governments have signed today are based on an act of Congress of US and are virtually same as those currently being negotiated with other eligible countries.

Amount of funds as well as types and tonnages of supplies to be authorized for Italy and other nations will be determined periodically in joint consultation as the requirements manifest themselves.

In order to insure maximum expenditure for actual relief supplies and to supplement program with donations by American voluntary relief agencies total of five million dollars is set aside in law for expense of ocean transportation and related costs incidental to work of private non-profit American relief agencies. Assistance of these private agencies is expected to augment aid received by Italy considerably.

US relief program will carry on humanitarian work of UNRRA through which US contributed supplies valued at four million dollars to Italy,[1] three quarters of entire UNRRA program, and will give aid to Italian economy while long term measures for rehabilitation of Italy have time to become effective.

This agreement illustrates once again strong sentiments of mutual friendship and sympathy that animate peoples of two countries. Purpose of US foreign relief program is relief on a broad popular scale. It is another indication of desire of American people to assist Italy toward point where her economy can carry on alone with full and unimpeded strength.[2]

DUNN

---

[1] The correct figure of $400 million was supplied on the margin of the working copy in the Department of State.

[2] In telegram 1822, July 4, from Rome, not printed, Dunn reported that the signing took place that day at 11:15 local time with a good press turn-out assuring a good send-off for the strictly U.S. program (865.48/7-447).

Copies of the agreement were transmitted to the Department in despatch 1156, July 4, from Rome, not printed (865.48/7-447) ; for text of the agreement and exchange of notes, see Department of State Treaties and Other International Acts Series (TIAS) No. 1653, or 61 Stat. (pt. 3) 3135.

740.00119 Control (Italy)/6-3047 : Telegram

The Secretary of State to the Acting Political Adviser (Greene) at Leghorn [1]

SECRET   WASHINGTON, July 3, 1947—1 p.m.

55. Urtel 115 June 30.[2] JCS with State concurrence approved Brit proposed reply Naf 1342,[3] authorizing continuance AFHQ during period (if any) between R and RJ days with proviso AFHQ functions vis-à-vis Itals terminate R day.

You shd stress to Gen Lee view this Govt Allied mil in Italy must respect scrupulously restoration Ital sovereignty upon coming into force treaty and abide strictly by that principle in interpretation rights mil and civil affairs agreement.

Dept does not desire approach Yugos re their deposit ratification.

MARSHALL

---

[1] Mr. Greene was Acting United States Political Adviser to the Acting Supreme Allied Commander, Mediterranean Theater (Lee).

[2] Not printed.

[3] In this telegram, June 26, from Leghorn, not printed, SACMED recommended that AFHQ continue to exercise command in the Mediterranean Theater until ratification by Yugoslavia of the treaty of peace with Italy (Defense files).

865.24/6–1947 : Telegram

The Secretary of State to the Embassy in Italy

TOP SECRET WASHINGTON, July 3, 1947—7 p.m.

1063. For the Ambassador. You will have seen numerous War Dept and OFLC tels since urtel 1634 June 19 re reequipment Ital Army.

In letter 1 July SecState has urged SecWar give every possible consideration provide minimum requirements reequipment program.[1] Letter states " . . . I want to emphasize that the Dept of State considers it to be of great importance to the future peace and stability of Italy that the Ital Govt have at its disposal forces adequate to ensure internal order and to discourage aggression against Italy's frontiers and, further, that this factor is considered as being important to the national interest of the United States . . . . "

Re WARX 81070 June 27, it is hoped through substitution or transfer from other areas sufficient equipment may be obtained supply Ital minimum requirements. War Dept urgently considering all possibilities. Dept appreciates urgent requirements other War Dept arms programs but will continue stress importance effective reequipment Ital forces. MARSHALL

---

[1] Not printed.

102.1/7–747 : Telegram

The Ambassador in Italy (Dunn) to the Secretary of State

CONFIDENTIAL ROME, July 7, 1947—6 p.m.

1852. Inform Treasury for Tasca. Several meetings have been held regarding amendment to Corbino Agreement [1] for purchase of surplus property. Apparently a stumbling block is question of valuation of lend-lease material turned over by UK to Italy under April 17 Anglo-Italo financial agreement. (Embassy's despatch 609, April 28, 1947, page 20, of attached agreement [2]) UK apparently stated to Italians at time amount involved did not exceed one million pounds, whereas Italians subsequently discovered 13 to 14 million pounds of US material involved. See Embassy's despatch 988, June 13,[2] containing *procès-verbal* signed in May. Italian Government now reluctant to assume dollar burden involved in such debt. Italians also consider such items as airfields, fixed installations and bridges overpriced. Minister Del Vecchio stated in this connection that he considered the basic Corbino-

---

[1] See *Foreign Relations*, 1946, vol. v, p. 932.
[2] Not printed.

Bonner Surplus Property Agreement unfavorable to Italy, particularly when compared with the Anglo-Italian Agreement for the disposition of surplus property in Italy.

Although Del Vecchio had expressly wished negotiations conducted without the presence of other Ministers, under insistence of Einaudi, a meeting is to be held as soon as possible with the Director General of Economic Affairs of Foreign Office and Del Vecchio, primarily because of the lend-lease item.

Repeated London 118.

DUNN

840.50 Recovery/7–647

Memorandum of Conversation, by the Director of the Office of European Affairs (Matthews)

[WASHINGTON,] July 9, 1947.

The Italian Ambassador called this morning at his request and left with me the attached telegram from Count Sforza to the Italian Embassies at Paris and London, dated July 6, containing the Italian acceptance of the Anglo-French invitation.[1] In connection with the last paragraph, he said that he hoped the pertinent commission of the Italian Constituent Assembly would recommend ratification of the treaty today but seemed a little doubtful. . . . Tarchiani said that he himself feels that it is important that Italy should ratify and I heartily agreed. I pointed out that this would strengthen Italy's case for admission to membership in the United Nations and her position during the forthcoming Paris discussions.

As to news from Italy, he said he felt more encouraged on the political side. There are signs, he said, that the Communists are losing ground. This was in part due to lack of money as well as to lack of patronage and the ability to do favors which comes from participation in the government. I gather that the Italian Government has been weeding out the Communists from positions in the Ministries and the fact that there are no more Communists in high office has strengthened the morale of the police and of government officials. He said it was quite clear that the Communists had been taking considerable sums of money from public funds for their own party purposes and the lack of this money was handicapping their efforts to increase their popularity. He told me a fact which I had not before heard, namely, that through their control of the Government Printing Office the Com-

---

[1] Not printed; regarding Italy's participation in the Conference of European Economic Cooperation, see telegram 2963, July 10, from London, p. 323.

munists had been printing large quantities of lire for their own use without accounting for it. This scandalous state of affairs had, however, been discovered and ended, he said.

He said also that the improved atmosphere following the elimination of the Communists from the Government had resulted in an improvement of the lire rate from some 900 to 600 to the dollar on the open market. He said that unlike France where the peasants apparently have lost confidence in the franc the Government estimates that Italian peasants have salted away some 150 billion lire in their socks. He said this was very fortunate as the inflationary pressure of such a sum if the peasants attempted to dispose of it would be considerable. He emphasized the importance of doing everything possible to continue the improvement and of the vital necessity of American financial aid.

I referred to the suggestion in the attached Italian acceptance telegram for the establishment of a Committee on Emigration and Labor and asked what progress the Italians were making in their negotiations with the French. (There is an agreement that France will import 200,000 Italian laborers.) He said that progress was very slow because of the French unwillingness to grant any economic concessions. I said that we understood that on both the Italian side and the French side all prospective Italian emigrants to France were being carefully screened by the French CGT and the Italian CGIL which labor organizations are Communist controlled. I said that we understood that only militant Communists were being accepted under this arrangement. The Ambassador said he had no knowledge of this and laughingly added it might be good for his country if it could ship its Communists to France. He said that they had tried to send Communists to Argentina but Peron wouldn't have them and wanted only Christian-Democrats. He laughed again and said this would be taking away De Gasperi's voters. More seriously he said that shipping was the bottleneck in getting Italian emigrants off to the Argentine. With an annual excess of births over deaths in Italy of between 400,000 and 500,000, outlets for Italian surplus labor were of great importance.

He asked me the status of the Fortezza gold[2] and I said I understood that we had approached the British suggesting that it be turned over to Italy. He said that this was important as it would give the Bank of Italy at least some gold reserve and strengthen confidence in the lira. He asked again if any progress had been made on the possible sale of Italian fruits and vegetables in Germany and I told him that I understood Italian negotiators were now discussing this in Berlin.

---

[2] See footnote 2, p. 987.

He said that he understood that the Ex–Im Bank's Commission report on Italy was now in and that it was "a good report".[3] I said that I had just received it today and had not had time to read it but that I understood that it was favorable to Italy. He urged that prompt action be taken so that Italy could begin to draw on its earmarked credit.

Mr. Tarchiani said he had heard excellent reports with regard to Ambassador Dunn's trip to Sicily. He thought the visit had been genuinely helpful and that his speeches there had had a real effect. I said I was delighted to hear it and mentioned the Communist article bitterly attacking President Truman which I understood Mr. Dunn had properly objected to. The Ambassador said he was glad Mr. Dunn had spoken of this slanderous article but that the paper itself was of no real importance in Italy. He said that Togliatti's mild and reluctant support for the "Marshall Plan" was rather clear evidence that the enthusiasm for the "Plan" in Italy made it difficult for the Communists to oppose it openly.

In conclusion he expressed the hope, in case Italy now ratifies the treaty, that our Senate would reply to the message on this subject from the Italian Constituent Assembly of last winter. He thought this would have a helpful psychological effect. I told him I would look into the matter and see what could be done.

H. F[REEMAN] M[ATTHEWS]

---

[3] See footnote 2, p. 917.

862.24/7–947 : Telegram

The Secretary of State to the Embassy in Italy

SECRET　　　　　　　　　　　　　WASHINGTON, July 9, 1947—4 p.m.
US URGENT　　　　NIACT

1090. Dept desires your comments soonest possible re Taff's phone conversation with Genl Connolly FLC on 7 July.[1] Understand Taff reported Min of Treas [2] stated Ital Govt not willing agree at this time to amendment Corbino-Bonner surplus property agreement [3] to avoid twenty-eight million downward adjustment in one hundred sixty million settlement figure.

Apparently this development will seriously interfere contemplated arrangements transfer army equipment. In view apparent impossibility Itals undertake even nominal commitment on long range credit basis; impossibility FLC effect transfer gratis under surplus property act;

---

[1] No record of this telephone conversation has been found.
[2] Gustavo del Vecchio.
[3] See *Foreign Relations*, 1946, vol. v, p. 932.

and now obstacle transfer under revision general surplus property settlement, request your recommendations. In your discretion you might wish to point out to Minister Treas or De Gasperi importance of obtaining settlement now in view of substantial concessions by US now being negotiated with Lombardo mission. In view nature certain materials involved in surplus property settlement Dept reluctant to discuss question with Lombardo but you might deem it advisable that tie up with Wash discussions be made by you in Rome. While Dept would not hold up signing agreement with Lombardo unless Ital yielded on surplus property, history of latter discussions indicates Ital refusal at last moment to enter into proposed surplus property agreement may be based on misunderstanding our intentions which might be corrected by reference to substantial concessions we are negotiating in Wash. If you approached Ital you could also point out that settlement now on surplus property taken in conjunction with settlement Wash would constitute complete settlement on all known claims US against Ital. Otherwise, US would, even after signing agreement with Lombardo, have outstanding a claim arising out of retransferred lend-lease property, with original cost 110 million dollars, which has not been made subject for discussion Lombardo, but has been reserved for inclusion in settlement surplus property discussions Rome. For your info OFLC Wash unable concur with Taff's suggestion that title to all remaining surplus Italy be transferred Ital Govt immediately on basis of undertaking by latter to reach agreement on price and payment terms within three months.

For your info only, agreement with Lombardo may be signed middle to latter part week July 14.[4]

FLC deferring further action pending receipt ur views and report results ur discussions Rome, if any.

MARSHALL

---

[4] See editorial note, p. 956.

865.24/7–1247 : Telegram

The Ambassador in Italy (Dunn) to the Secretary of State

SECRET   ROME, July 12, 1947—3 p.m.
NIACT

1932. It is our view that principal obstacles to transfer agreement regarding US surplus property include (*a*) Government's reluctance to burden further Italy's dwindling foreign exchange assets with additional principal and interest payments implied in additional purchases of US surplus property and (*b*) concern regarding burden of Italy's balance of payment when principal payments begin to become due in

1951 (c) Anglo-Italian agreement regarding lend-lease supplies transferred by UK to Italy involve substantially higher figure than Italians had understood at time of agreement. In final analysis all three of above problems could probably be solved by offering Italians sufficiently attractive price with respect to disposal of remaining US surplus property in Italy.

Since it appears to be in US national interest only to complete this agreement as speedily as possible, I recommend that we establish on US side rock bottom price on basis of which we can conclude overall transfer agreement with Italians. Once this is established, I will see De Gasperi and, having in mind recommendations put forward your 1090, July 9, insist this Government conclude transfer settlement promptly.

After conversation with Taff who is sending parallel explanatory cable we believe that settlement with Italian Government might be reached on basis of turning over all remaining surplus property, including lend-lease, in Italy for total sum of 150 million dollars (Corbino-Bonner Agreement contained ceiling 160 million dollars). It is estimated this would mean about 23 percent recovery of original cost which would be above recovery percentages in other countries, such as France and U.K.

Will Department authorize me proceed on this basis or any other lower figure which Department can agree as our rock bottom price?

Please reply urgently.[1]

DUNN

---

[1] In instruction 1138, July 15, not printed, the Department concurred in Dunn's proposal if an over-all transfer agreement could be arranged for a total of $150 million (865.24/7–1247).

865.24 FLC/7–1547 : Telegram

The Ambassador in Italy (Dunn) to the Secretary of State

SECRET   ROME, July 15, 1947—9 p.m.
US URGENT   NIACT

1960. To OFLC. Conversations with Italian Ministers yesterday during Harriman visit [1] indicated a new urgent need for some im-

---

[1] In telegram 1966, July 15, from Rome, not printed, Dunn reported that Secretary of Commerce Harriman arrived in Rome Sunday afternoon, July 13, and was able that evening to discuss matters with Ambassador Dunn and General Lee. He was able next day to meet Italian President De Nicola, Prime Minister De Gasperi, Vice Prime Minister Einaudi, Minister of the Treasury Del Vecchio, Minister of Finance Giuseppe Pella, Minister of Foreign Commerce Giuseppe Merzagora, Minister of Industry and Commerce Giuseppe Togni, and several officials of the Ministry of Foreign Affairs. Harriman mentioned to Dunn "that he had been agreeably surprised and impressed with intelligence and evident high caliber of Ministers in present government whom he had met". (033.1140/7–1547)

mediate gesture on our part in support of present government in view of mounting Communist opposition both to treaty ratification and Marshall plan discussions in Paris. It is possible that in addition to another 100 million dollars credit from Exim Bank which I have already recommended,[2] pending surplus agreement on airfields, fixed installations, mine sweepers, fighter airplanes, combat equipment, lend-lease, scrap, etc., could be turned to advantage along these lines, provided it were divorced from former agreement of September 9, 1946 and presented to Italian public as a new and even more favorable gesture.

It is therefore proposed that the Corbino-Bonner agreement be left untouched and that OFLC endeavor to conclude with Italian Government a new agreement on all items of surplus uncovered by the former agreement on basis of 10% of original cost. In other words, that we agree to sell Italy on 30 year terms approximately 184 million dollars of property for 18 million dollars. Agreement would also include option to obtain up to 10 million dollars in real property and improvements. Aside from retention of the escalator clause in original agreement, this proposal would not alter the total sales price of approximately 150 million dollars as outlined in ourtel 1932[3] (if present estimates on size of underrun prove accurate), but it would have an infinitely greater moral effect by the mere fact of being a new and more favorable agreement with the present government rather than merely an amendment to an agreement made with a former government in which the Communists participated (having in mind that Scoccimaro was present at the signing of the original agreement).

It is my intention, if you agree, to get the utmost news coverage on the signing of such an agreement, however leaving disclosure of the inclusion of combat matériel entirely to De Gasperi as he has indicated that he did not desire it to be known at this time that rearmament of Italian forces with United States equipment was contemplated. To this end wording of the agreement would refer to surplus army matériel, avoiding the use of the words "combat" or "armament" or "ammunition".[4]

DUNN

---

[2] See telegrams 1322, May 28, and 1590, June 17, from Rome, pp. 911 and 922.
[3] *Supra.*
[4] In telegram 1152, July 16, not printed, the Department concurred in the proposal to negotiate a new, separate agreement, and it agreed to omission of the reference to combat material (865.24 FLC/7–1547).

865.24 FLC/7–2147

The Deputy Central Field Commissioner for Europe, Office of the Foreign Liquidation Commissioner (Taff) to the Italian Minister of the Treasury (Del Vecchio)

[ROME,] 21 July 1947.

DEAR MR. MINISTER: The Government of the United States is particularly anxious at this time to aid in every possible way in the recovery efforts of the Italian Government and therefore proposes to transfer to the Italian Government, upon the terms and conditions specified herein, possession of and title to the following listed types of property which have heretofore or will hereafter be declared to the Office of the Foreign Liquidation Commissioner, Central Field Commissioner for Europe, United States Department of State, as surplus to the needs of the Government of the United States. The estimated original cost of the property to be transferred under this Agreement is approximately $184,000,000.

A. United States Army equipment located in Italy. In the event the United States is unable to supply from surpluses located in Italy all of the items which have formed the subject of conversations between our two governments, the United States will endeavor to make suitable substitutions or replacements from surpluses located in other Theaters. The United States Government undertakes to supply such detailed data regarding such equipment as may be desired by the Italian Government.

B. Sixteen (16) United States Government motor minesweepers, type YMS.

C. Fifty (50) aircraft to be designated by the United States Army, together with maintenance equipment and spare parts for said aircraft for three (3) years, which property is presently located in the United States Occupied Zone of Germany.

D. All United States Government property of Lend-Lease origin located in Italy which has heretofore or will hereafter be transferred directly to the Italian Government by the British Government and for which no settlement has been made. The terms of this paragraph "D" are not to be interpreted to apply to property of Lend-Lease origin now in the possession of foreign governments which may be returned in Italy to the United States Government.

E. All interest of the United States in fixed installations located in Italy (which terms include structure or capital assemblies affixed to lands and buildings in a permanent manner).

F. All United States scrap, salvage and waste material located in Italy.

G. All property covered by contracts entered into between the Office of the Foreign Liquidation Commissioner (Central Field Commissioner for Europe) and the Italian Government since 9 September 1946 and for which no settlement has yet been made.

If any property listed above has been sold or is under contract or commitment to any purchaser other than the Italian Government prior to the date of acceptance of this letter, such property shall not be included in the terms of this letter.

For and in consideration of the transfer of surplus property under this Agreement, the original cost of which is estimated to be approximately $184,000,000, the Italian Government agrees to pay in United States dollars to the Treasurer of the United States the sum of $18,000,-000 on the following terms:

1. Beginning on 1 January 1952 and continuing thereafter on the first day of each succeeding year until the balance is liquidated, a sum equal to four percent of the purchase price, together with accrued interest, subject to such pro rata adjustments in annual installments as are provided for below.

2. Interest shall begin to accrue commencing 1 January 1948 on the total amount due under this Agreement and shall be paid on the first day of each succeeding year (the first payment being due on 1 January 1949), at the annual rate of two and three-eighths percent on the balance unpaid as of the first day of each preceding year.

The United States Government reserves the right to receive from the Italian Government, in lieu of the total dollar obligation specified above, Italian currency up to the equivalent of $8,000,000 to be used for the payment of any and all expenditures in Italy of the United States Government, its agencies or Armed Forces, or for educational purposes. However, such acquisitions of Italian currency under this paragraph will be limited to an amount not to exceed $1,000,000 per year.

The United States Government also wishes to acquire and improve certain real properties in which it has an interest and therefore reserves the right to require the Italian Government in lieu of the total dollar obligations set forth above, to enter into negotiations with the United States Government and to use its best efforts to conclude without undue delay appropriate contracts wherein the Italian Government will furnish to the United States the properties and improvements it desires or which its representatives have selected. Representatives of the United States Government may at their discretion conduct discussions directly with owners of property or with contractors for improvements as to fair terms and prices prior to the acquisition of such property or improvements by the Italian Government for delivery to the United States Government. The United States Government agrees, however, that in no event will its acquisitions of real property and improvements made under the terms of this paragraph exceed the equivalent in value of $10,000,000 over the thirty-year period of this agreement.

When any Italian currencies or real properties or improvements are furnished to the United States Government under this Agreement, the Italian Government will be credited (at the exchange rate set forth below) with the United States dollar equivalent of the fair value received. Such credit will be applied first to past due interest, if any, and then pro rata to all remaining unpaid installments of principal.

The exchange rate shall be that established by the International Monetary Fund, provided that, if no such rate exists, the rate shall be that rate which is applicable to all United States Government expenditures under the terms of the Agreement reached between our two Governments on 25 January 1947.[1]

If the proposals contained herein are satisfactory to the Italian Government, would you please indicate the agreement of your Government by signing in the space indicated below and returning this letter to my office.

Respectfully yours,

A. Erich Taff
*Deputy Central Field Commissioner
for Europe*

The terms of the foregoing letter are hereby accepted.

Gustavo del Vecchio
Ministro del Tesoro

---

[1] Not printed.

865.24 FLC/7–2147

The Deputy Central Field Commissioner for Europe, Office of the Foreign Liquidation Commissioner (Taff) to the Italian Minister of the Treasury (Del Vecchio)

[Rome,] July 21, 1947.

Dear Mr. Minister: Reference is made to the Agreement reached this date between our two Governments concerning the bulk acquisition by the Italian Government of certain property surplus to the needs of the Government of the United States.

Under the terms of said Agreement, the Government of the United States reserved for itself the right to require the Italian Government to transfer to the Government of the United States up to the equivalent of $10,000,000 in real properties and improvements thereto over the thirty-year period of the Agreement.

I would like to take this occasion to assure the Italian Government that the United States Government agrees to limit the exercise of this right in such a way and at such times as not to place, in the judgment of the United States Government, any undue financial burden on the Italian economy.

In addition, I wish to remind the Italian Government that the Surplus Property Act forbids the reimportation into the United States of surplus property if it is in the same or substantially the same form as originally produced unless such property is imported for the purpose of reconditioning for re-export. Therefore, all property transferred under the said Agreement will necessarily be subject to this restriction.

Respectfully yours,   A. ERICH TAFF
                                  Deputy Central Field Commissioner
                                           for Europe

865.51/7–2547 .

Memorandum by the Director of the Office of Financial and Development Policy (Ness) to the Assistant Secretary of State for Economic Affairs (Thorp)

CONFIDENTIAL   [WASHINGTON,] July 25, 1947.

Subject: Discussions with the Lombardo Mission of Italy's Financial Needs for Second Half of 1947

1. The Italian balance of payments for the second half of 1947 presented by the Lombardo Mission was screened by ED, FN and DRE in the light of the technical discussions held with the Lombardo Mission by the Department, Treasury, Commerce and Federal Reserve.

The Department's review was based on rather austere criteria, comparable to those used in estimating post-UNRRA relief needs. As has previously been noted in the recent SWNCC paper on Italy, OFD does not endorse these criteria of minimum aid as the basis for continuing United States reconstruction policy toward Italy. In view of the impossibility of obtaining the requisite large-scale financial aid this year, however, it would be pointless in reviewing the Lombardo estimates to adopt economic aid criteria based upon our political objectives in Italy.

While import requirements (c.i.f.) were estimated by Lombardo at $777 million, the Department estimates minimum imports at $702 million. Total payments during the second half of 1947 were similarly reduced from $783 million to $733.5 million. On the receipts side the discrepancies are somewhat larger. Exports for the second half of the year are estimated at $292 million by Lombardo, at $381 million by us. Including invisible items, total receipts were revised upward from $547 million to $650.5 million.

The resulting deficit for the second half of the year, estimated by Lombardo at $236 million, is reduced by the Department's estimate to about $83 million. The major reasons for the differences are summarized below.

2. *Payments*

Coal import requirements stated by Lombardo have been reduced by the 600,000 metric tons which were earmarked for increase in stocks. While it is recognized that such an increase would be not unreasonable and in fact desirable, it is felt that it could be postponed while Italy is in its present critical financial situation. *POL* import requirements have similarly been reduced to eliminate any increase of stocks.

Textile fibers import requirements have also been very substantially reduced to eliminate any allowance of increases in stocks, which now exceed five months' processing requirements for both cotton and wool. A further reduction was made on the assumption that, under present circumstances, it should be possible for the Italian Government to reduce such stocks to a three-month level.

Other imports have been reduced for various reasons indicated in the attached OIR memorandum.[1] On the other hand, miscellaneous industrial materials and miscellaneous supplies (machinery, equipment, ships and commodities which Italy must import under trade or barter agreement) have been increased substantially above the Lombardo estimates to the minimum level necessary to prevent further deterioration of the Italian economy. Payments on capital account have also been increased above the Italian estimates.

3. *Receipts*

Estimated *exports* during the second half of the year were increased from Lombardo's figure of $292 million to $381 million. The latter figure appears to be more consistent with the rate of industrial activity made possible by the volume of imports allowed. Our estimate seems reasonable in view of the most recent information on the level of Italian exports during the first months of 1947.

4. *Conclusions*

(a) On the assumption that Italy will receive during the second half of 1947 $230 million on capital account as indicated in the attached document, paragraph 12, the Italian balance of payments in the last half of 1947 should show a deficit of $83 million. The figure

---

[1] Not printed.

of $230 million includes $25 million of the Eximbank credit; this is the maximum which the Bank's staff feels can be spent in 1947 under the present loan arrangements.

This deficit figure is approximately 40 percent of the deficit indicated by the Lombardo Mission, and constitutes a serious threat to Italian economic and financial stability. Foreign exchange holdings available to the Italian Government as of June 30, 1947 are estimated at $151 million. This appears to be a moderate monetary and contingency reserve for Italy. It should not be drawn on substantially in payment for Italian imports during the remainder of 1947.

(*b*) The Department's screening of the Lombardo estimates assumes that the Italian Government will be able to restrict imports of textile fibers to the screened amounts. Past experience indicates that this will be very difficult for the Italian Government to manage. Similarly, the Department's estimates assume that textile exports can be increased above the Lombardo estimates, which means that some production now going into hoards will be exported. If these two assumptions are not realized, the deficit will be substantially larger.

5. *Recommendations*

In the light of the above, and on the assumption that no further straight financial aid can be granted to the Italians, and if the Italian share of the post-UNRRA relief program cannot be increased, the following is suggested:

(*a*) The Lombardo Mission should be told that the United States is unable to cover Italy's 1947 deficit because no additional financial help can be given until the Marshall plan is put into effect; consequently, it could be informally suggested that the Italian Government exert all its efforts to reduce programmed imports where it is believed that the reduction will do the least damage. As indicated above, postponement of stock increases and reduction of cotton and wool stocks are believed to be possible.

(*b*) The Department should support the immediate granting of a WAA credit which might allow the Italians to finance a small part of their import requirements for equipment, scrap, etc. No important reduction of their deficit could, however, be anticipated from this source.

(*c*) Arrangements should be made immediately to sell additional ships to the Italian Government, to be operated by Italian ship operators for the account of the Italian Government in hauling coal and other bulky materials which Italy is importing from this hemisphere. The time required to put additional ships into operation would, however, preclude any important financial aid from this source during 1947.

(*d*) The Department should explore thoroughly the possibility of increasing grain allocations to Italy from the United States for the 3rd and 4th quarters of this year. Any increase of United States breadgrain available to the Italian population would have obvious excellent political repercussions, and would reduce the cost of breadgrain imports by reducing or excluding imports of high-cost Argentinian wheat.

(e) The importance of utilization of excess inventories and of stronger controls on the use of foreign exchange and of imported raw materials should be pointed out to the Lombardo Mission.

The recommendations summarized above are in line with the recommendations recently received from Ambassador Dunn, especially in cable 1927, July 12.[2]

---

[2] Not printed.

865.50/7–2547

The Ambassador in Italy (Dunn) to the Secretary of State

RESTRICTED ROME, July 25, 1947.
No. 1341

Subject: Report on the visit to Rome of the Honorable William L. Clayton, Under Secretary of State for Economic Affairs

SIR: I have the honor to report that the Honorable William L. Clayton, Under Secretary of State for Economic Affairs, arrived in Rome late in the evening of July 22 and left Rome for Geneva at 5:30 p.m. on July 24.

In the morning of July 23 I took Mr. Clayton to call upon the President of the Council of Ministers, Signor De Gasperi, and the Vice President of the Council of Ministers and Minister of the Budget, Signor Einaudi. I gave a luncheon for Mr. Clayton on that day, which was attended by Signor De Gasperi, Signor Einaudi, Count Sforza, Minister of Foreign Affairs, Marchese Taliani, Chief of Protocol of the Italian Government, and members of the Embassy staff. At five o'clock that afternoon I took Mr. Clayton to call upon Count Sforza, the Minister for Foreign Affairs.

On the morning of July 24 Mr. Clayton was received by the Pope. He held a small background press conference for American correspondents at the Embassy at 11 a.m. and at 12 o'clock attended a meeting in Dr. Einaudi's office composed of Dr. Einaudi, the Minister of the Treasury, Dr. Del Vecchio, the Minister of Finance, Signor Pella, the Minister of Industry and Commerce, Signor Togni, the Minister of Foreign Trade, Signor Merzagora, and the Chief Commissioner of Food, Signor Ronchi.

The President of the Council of Ministers gave a luncheon for Mr. Clayton on that day and in the afternoon Mr. Clayton held a conference with members of the Embassy staff on the subject of the general economic and financial situation in Italy.

In his conversation with Mr. Clayton, Signor De Gasperi touched on the political situation as it related to the matter of the ratification by Italy of the Peace Treaty. He said he anticipated considerable difficulty in the Assembly on this matter but that the Government was determined to press forward with its request for approval of the ratification and intended to leave the responsibility for acceptance or rejection of the Government's position to the General Assembly itself. Signor De Gasperi also spoke of his hope for support of the present Government by the United States, particularly in providing for food grains for the next twelve months. He said that Italy needed to import during the present fiscal year ending June 30 next, 2,900,000 tons of grain in order to maintain the present ration and the Prime Minister remarked that the present Government should not, at least, reduce the ration from that established by the last Government in which the Communists participated. Signor De Gasperi said he hoped to get 700,000 tons of wheat from Argentina, and possibly Turkey, which would make the amount they would ask from the United States 2,200,000 tons. He said the first question was to obtain the allocation of that amount to Italy and the second question was to obtain assistance in the form of credit for purchase of the wheat. He said also that it was important to make an effort to have the delivery facilitated and expedited in order to save the expense of transporting wheat from one section of Italy to another, which was itself uneconomic. Mr. Clayton stated that there was a good crop of wheat in the United States this year, even better than last year, although the corn crop would probably not equal that of last year. He stated further that one of the great difficulties in exporting wheat from the United States was the railway transportation, as the grains had to be carried distances of from 1,000 miles or more to the seaboard and this created difficulties in regard to the rail transportation. He said, however, that the President had granted priorities for the use of cars for the transport of wheat for export and had also granted priorities in shipping so that the problem was now principally one of obtaining the transportation to the seaboard. Signor De Gasperi expressed deep appreciation for all that had been done by the United States for Italy in the past and expressed his confidence that the present Government could meet its difficulties if it had some assistance in meeting its balance of payment.

Signor De Gasperi said that he was faced with a Communist Party in Italy which was under the leadership of a very shrewd politician, Palmiro Togliatti, who had been Secretary General of the Comintern, and he pointed out that with the Soviet suspicion and mistrust of all foreigners, his appointment as Secretary General of the Comintern was an indication of the confidence the Moscow Government had in him.

The Prime Minister asked Mr. Clayton his opinion of the possibilities of the Paris meeting of sixteen nations in connection with General Marshall's proposal. The Under Secretary replied that there was a great opportunity for the European countries concerned to produce a plan for integrating their economy and providing for real recovery in Europe with a minimum of assistance from non-European countries. He called attention to the fact that Europe during the past fiscal year imported coal from the United States to a value of $750,-000,000, which was entirely uneconomic and was more than Europe could normally pay for and at the same time pay for imports of food and other materials.

Mr. Clayton took occasion at this point to suggest to Signor De Gasperi that some thought be given in connection with the Paris drafts to the necessity for restoration of sound currencies in the European countries as a means of promoting exchange of goods and thereby increasing production generally. He said that in his opinion any plan which left out financial and monetary problems as they existed in each country and their relation to the exchange of trade would be incomplete. The conversation ended after a short reference to the position of the Soviet Union with respect to the Paris Conference and the attitude of that country also toward the ratification of the Treaty of Peace for Italy.

In the conversation with Signor Einaudi, Vice President of the Council of Ministers and Minister of the Budget, the subjects touched on were the Paris Conference, the balance of payments position of the Italian Government for the remaining six months of this year and the first six months of 1948, the food situation, and the financial situation of Italy at the present time and in the immediate future. The discussion of the Paris Conference was very much along the same lines as the conversation with the Prime Minister, although Dr. Einaudi did say that he had received a request from Signor Campilli, the Italian representative on the Conference in Paris, for a financial expert to deal with financial and monetary problems. He said he was at the moment endeavoring to send one of the very best financial experts in Italy and hoped that he would be free to go. With regard to the Italian balance of payments, Signor Einaudi handed Mr. Clayton a memorandum,[1] a

---

[1] Enclosure 1, "Deficit of the Italian balance of payments, as a consequence of the war and financial requirements," not printed.

copy of which is enclosed, and the discussion followed the general lines of the information contained in that memorandum.

Signor Einaudi related the food situation also to the balance of payments position and explained how the requirements for an increased import of food this year were due to the poor crop in Italy and the fact that the exports had not yet reached the point where the foreign exchange thereby gained sufficed for the import of necessary materials and fuel and food.[2]

On the financial situation Dr. Einaudi stated that there had been no change in the Italian tariff since 1921 with the exception that some two years ago the ad valorem duty was increased about 3½ times and as the price level had increased 40 or 50 times since the 1921 rate, this meant that the actual ad valorem duty on goods imported into Italy amounted to only 2 or 3% of the value. He said there had been another tax of 5% of the value of the goods as a service charge and this had recently been raised to 10% in order to cover an increase granted by the Cabinet to the salaries of the State employees. Mr. Clayton pointed out that the tariff itself was not always the greatest obstruction in international trade but it was often other restrictions and obstacles which could be just as obstructive as a high tariff.

Dr. Einaudi then explained the taxation system in Italy, stating that the rates of taxation for definite categories of income were in general very high but as they were based on valuations which were very seldom 100% of the value of the income to be taxed the eventual rate of taxation was not as high as was provided for under the law. He said he felt that the tax rates were as high as could be supported by the people at this time but that a simplification of the rates and application of the law could perhaps provide for a more effective collection system.

All the further points covered in this conversation are included in the memorandum Dr. Einaudi handed to Mr. Clayton during his call.

During the call on Count Sforza, Minister for Foreign Affairs, the conversation was rather general in tone, Count Sforza being interested in Mr. Clayton's ideas about the Paris Conference and about the general economic situation in the United States. There was nothing particularly new that came out in this conversation which had not been discussed in Mr. Clayton's previous calls, but Mr. Clayton also took occasion at this time to call Count Sforza's attention to the advisability of having the Paris Conference include a reference to the financial and monetary problems in the European situation.

---

[2] Enclosure 2, "Memorandum on the Production of Cereals in Italy," not printed.

A report on the discussion which took place at the meeting in Dr. Einaudi's office on July 24, which was attended by the financial and economic Ministers of the Cabinet as well as the High Commissioner for Food, is contained in a memorandum by Mr. Walmsley, which is attached herewith.[3] Mr. Byington, Mr. Walmsley, and I accompanied Mr. Clayton to this meeting.

Mr. Clayton, upon leaving Rome, said that while he had had rather full information with regard to the food situation here and the Italian financial situation also before he came to Rome he was interested in meeting the members of the Government and was satisfied that they were an earnest and competent group of officials who were doing their very best in the interests of their country for the promotion of its economic recovery.

I wish to express my appreciation for Mr. Clayton's visit here as it was a source of encouragement to the Italian Government in that they felt they had an opportunity to put their case to an important American official who is concerned with the problems with which they are confronted. Mr. Clayton's tact and interest in dealing with the officials during his visit was deeply appreciated by them and they all expressed themselves as extremely gratified on his informed understanding of the Italian situation.

Respectfully yours, JAMES CLEMENT DUNN

---

[3] Enclosure 3, "Memorandum of Conversation: Italian Food and Agricultural Crisis," July 24, 1947, not printed.

865.5018/7–2647 : Telegram

The Ambassador in Italy (Dunn) to the Secretary of State

CONFIDENTIAL ROME, July 26, 1947—4 p.m.

2109. As evidence of the critical food situation coupled with payments problem fully as serious, which Italy faces this winter, Einaudi, the Vice Premier, on July 24 arranged a special meeting between Mr. Clayton and Italian food experts.

Ronchi, the Food Commissioner, made an excellent statement which followed the lines of my telegram 2014, July 21.[1] He said that he had realistically reduced to 2.9 million tons, "the irreducible minimum", the quantity of foreign bread grains sought over the next twelve months. He emphasized that by September, when fresh vegetables become scarce, and for six months thereafter, it would be essential for

---

[1] Not printed.

humanitarian and political reasons of crucial importance that the bread ration and pasta ration of 235 grams per day and two kilos per month, respectively, be fully met (which at present they are not). In this connection mention was made of the elections which will probably be held by next March.

The plea that Ronchi made was that the American share of Italy's grain imports, amounting to 2.2 million tons be shipped at the full rate of 220,000 tons per month beginning in August. The present strenuous efforts of the government to move domestic grain from surplus to deficit provinces are meeting determined opposition from local authorities, Communists, etc.; it had therefore become imperative to ask the US to expedite this year's movement to Italy.

With regard to Italy's current wheat production problem Segni, Minister of Agriculture,[2] spoke as follows:

(1) Extremely poor growing conditions had seriously reduced this year's harvest per acre; (2) unpopularity of government controls and amassing, among other factors, had reduced overall acreage 10% from pre-war; (3) similar factors had reduced acreage planted this year by 2% compared with last year when crop was 6.3 million tons, equivalent to the 1936 crop, and only about 1.2 million tons less than the 1937–39 average; (4) beginning in 1942 when fertilizers became seriously short, Italian farmland has suffered from the cumulative effect of soil fatigue. It will require three years in Segni's opinion of intensive effort to return Italian wheat production to 7 million tons. One of the most serious difficulties stems, he says, from the payments problem the French are creating over phosphates, an allocation of which Italy has now had to ask from the US under the relief program.

Mr. Clayton assured the Italians that, as a member of the interdepartmental committee of three which examines food requests from deficit countries he would continue to give his most sympathetic attention to all Italian requests. He spoke of the unprecedented success of American efforts to export 16 million tons of bread grains this past crop year and of what this record involved in the way of long hauls within the US, loading and shipping; and yet a world deficit still existed. He urged that it would be easier to continue the high level of American aid if Italy could demonstrate that it is taking every possible measure to stimulate domestic production.

Sent Department 2109, Paris 276, Geneva for Clayton 34.

DUNN

---

[2] Antonio Segni.

811.516 Export–Import Bank/7–2947

Memorandum by Mr. Jerome J. Stenger, Special Assistant in the Division of Investment and Economic Development, to the Director of the Office of Financial and Development Policy (Ness)

[Extract]

[WASHINGTON,] July 29, 1947.

Subject: Agenda for Meeting of Board of Directors Eximbank July 30, 1947.

. . . .

4. *Italian Credits.* The Board agreed at an earlier meeting that, under the $100 million earmarked for Italy, it was prepared to receive separate credit applications on behalf of specific sectors or subsectors of Italian industry engaged in promoting Italian foreign trade. The Bank has received the following applications amounting to $25 million:

(*a*) Fiat, S.A.—$11,000,000
(*b*) Montecatini Soc.—$10,000,000
(*c*) Pirelli, S.A.—$4,000,000.

[Here follows section in which Mr. Stenger reported that the staff of the Bank recommended that the original Fiat application be cut from $11 million to $10 million; that Montecatini's credit be reduced from $10 million to $9 million which would also provide for the possibility of financing by the Bank of applications from other smaller chemical companies; that Pirelli be granted a credit of $4 million in accordance with the wishes of the Italian Government. Mr. Stenger proposed that the Department concur with the recommendations of the staff of the Bank.]

———————

740.0011 EW Peace/7–3147 : Telegram

The Secretary of State to the Embassy in Italy

SECRET WASHINGTON, July 31, 1947—8 p.m.
U.S. URGENT

1288. For the Ambassador. Brit Embassy has informed us that Brit Govt "on financial and manpower grounds" has decided to withdraw Brit troops from Greece and reduce those in Italy to the 5,000 provided for in Annex 7 of the Italian treaty. Brit Embassy said that no announcement foregoing decision is being made.[1]

———————

[1] For the text of the note of July 30 from the British Chargé, see vol. v, p. 268.

War Dept has been informed. Your comments on effect this decision in so far as it applies to Italy are urgently desired.[2]

MARSHALL

---

[2] See *infra*.

740.00119 Control (Italy)/8–247 : Telegram

The Ambassador in Italy (Dunn) to the Secretary of State

SECRET   ROME, August 2, 1947—4 p. m.
URGENT

2191. Dept's 1288, July 31. General Lee is coming to Rome Monday [1] to confer with me and British Embassy re situation arising out of proposed reduction of British troops.

From all information which has come to us here the existing situation in Venezia Giulia in no sense warrants any degree of complacency such as might be inferred from reduction of troop strength in that area prior to going into effect of treaty. Reduction of British troops will inevitably give rise to the question of military commitments in Venezia Giulia which in turn depend on our political commitments. Military commanders here have already expressed themselves as convinced that they are now at an irreducible minimum of troop strength required to fulfill the commitment assigned to them, principally maintenance of *status quo* and prevention of disorder. My preliminary reaction is that we cannot reduce our political commitments concerning Venezia Giulia and that any reduction of troop strength in Venezia Giulia will endanger the carrying out of those commitments.

Sent Dept, Leghorn 80.

DUNN

---

[1] August 4.

740.00119 Control (Italy)/8–447 : Telegram

The Ambassador in Italy (Dunn) to the Secretary of State

TOP SECRET   ROME, August 4, 1947—8 p. m.
U.S. URGENT

2219. For the Secretary. General Lee informs me he has telegraphed War Department on subject of proposed withdrawal of British troops from Italy along following lines:

That a statement should be issued by British announcing decision not to withdraw troops from Italy until Anglo-American commitments here are fulfilled and that US and UK immediately begin studies with a view to reduction of British forces through adjustments whereby US can assist greatly in maintaining supply lines and other administrative functions.

I wish to support General Lee's recommendations. It is extremely important, in my opinion, to maintain the principle of Anglo-American responsibility for maintaining order in Venezia Giulia and preventing any disturbances by either side in connection with establishment of new Venezia Giulia boundary and setting up of Free Territory of Trieste. It would be politically a great blow to Italians and to our position in this area if we were to abandon Pola and perhaps other parts of the Morgan Line to the Yugoslavs. It seems to me that politically any reduction of our commitments in this area would be playing right into the hands of the Communists in Italy and elsewhere in Europe. In this connection, I would refer to position taken by the Combined Chiefs of Staff and the Department as to maintenance of *status quo* in Venezia Giulia until Yugoslavs accept the treaty.

If the British will give us a chance to discuss some readjustments which would permit them to take out of Italy certain contingents not now needed for maintaining the *status quo* in Venezia Giulia, I feel sure that with good will on both sides, we could arrive at an adjustment which would be of substantial help to the British in their home economic situation and we could still present picture of maintaining Anglo-American responsibility in this highly explosive area.

I might also recall that we have not yet succeeded in providing necessary equipment for rearming Italian forces to point where they could with any degree of success meet even first onslaught of forces that in Yugoslavia alone probably exceeds several hundred thousand well armed with Soviet equipment.[1]

DUNN

---

[1] In telegram 1472, August 21, not printed, the Department informed Dunn that it had received assurances that no withdrawals of British troops from Italy would be undertaken without full consultation with the United States (740.00119 Control (Italy)/8–447).

865.24/8–747 : Telegram

The Secretary of State to the Embassy in Italy

TOP SECRET   WASHINGTON, August 11, 1947—2 p. m.
US URGENT

1366. Reurtel 2264 Aug 7 [1] following paraphrase letter Acting SecWar to SecState July 30: [2]

---

[1] Not printed; in it Dunn reported having been informed that, under War Department orders, 31 tanks, 50 105 mm. howitzers, 30 155 mm. howitzers, and 400 rocket launchers were being shipped back to the Zone of the Interior (FW 865.24/8–747).

[2] Not printed.

Lee holding following items recommended as essential complete equipping Ital Army: 31 light tanks, 20 medium tanks, 50 105mm howitzers M2AI, 30 155mm howitzers, and 400 rocket launchers.

Foregoing items necessary meet requirements of planned War Dept programs and therefore cannot be declared surplus but must be returned US. Appears no legal alternative this action in absence legislative authority transfer to Italy US Govt property other than surplus.

War Dept making every effort meet equipment requirements Ital Army, and to this end can make available other equipment as below.

   a. To meet requirement light tanks, 31 light tanks, M–5 available in Germany (an earlier model than those now in Italy; equipped with 37mm gun instead 75mm). Have been stripped of auxiliary armament, radio and fire control instruments and require extensive reconditioning.

   b. To meet requirements medium tanks 20 available in Germany can be made ready issue in five days.

   c. For requirements 105mm howitzers M2AI, in Germany 43 105mm howitzers M–3, require three weeks conditioning. M–3 has range only 8,295 yards as contrasted M2AI's 12,200 yards and for this reason Lee says not suitable substitute. However, since a principal mission Ital Army maintenance internal order, War Dept believes M–3 should be acceptable though not as desirable as M2AI.

War Dept has no available substitute items for 155mm howitzers or rocket launchers.

War Dept has no funds legally available recondition equipment for Ital Army or to transport to Italy from other areas. Every effort made to solve problem within means available to War Dept in view your (SecState's) statement such action considered important national interest US. Appears, however, that unless means found to surmount legal and financial obstacles, best that can be done will be make available at German border substitutes as indicated above in such condition serviceability as may be achieved without appreciable expenditure War Dept funds or use materials which not surplus.

Dept understands from Gen Hyssong, FLC, that he may be able arrange with ETO for transportation to Ital border of such substitute items in Germany as desired for Ital program.

You will have seen ComGenMed tel FX 77066 Aug 6 [3] advising deficit medium tanks being supplied Brit from Austria. Has Gen Lee explored possibility filling other deficits from Brit sources?

As CCS advised SAC in Fan 772 [3] para 4, Brit had advised no Brit equipment available unless demanded and paid for through civil import program. In view FX 77066, it would appear Brit statement inaccurate, however, and possibility may exist finding other Brit equipment suitable Ital program.

---

[3] Not printed.

Pls discuss with Lee status entire reequipment program taking into consideration possible substitutes and all possible Brit sources, and advise soonest.[4]

MARSHALL

---

[4] In telegram 1514, August 26, not printed, the Acting Secretary of State urged Ambassador Dunn to expedite his reply to this message (865.24/8–2647).

Lot 60–D 137 : Box 1

Minutes of Seventieth Meeting of the National Advisory Council on International Financial and Monetary Problems, Washington, August 12, 1947

[Extract]

PRESENT

Secretary John W. Snyder (Chairman), Treasury Department
Mr. Carroll Perry, Maritime Commission, Visitor
Mr. Norman T. Ness, State Department
Mr. J. J. Stenger, State Department
Secretary W. Averell Harriman, Commerce Department
Mr. Thomas C. Blaisdell, Jr., Commerce Department
Mr. M. S. Szymczak, Board of Governors, Federal Reserve System
Mr. J. Burke Knapp, Board of Governors, Federal Reserve System
Mr. William McC. Martin, Jr., Export-Import Bank
Mr. Herbert Gaston, Export-Import Bank
Mr. Hal Lary, Export-Import Bank
Mr. Andrew N. Overby, International Fund

Mr. George Luthringer, **International Fund**
Mr. John S. Hooker, International Bank
Mr. Frank A. Southard, Jr., Treasury Department
Mr. Thomas J. Lynch, Treasury Department
Mr. William W. Parsons, Treasury Department
Mr. Joseph B. Friedman, Treasury Department
Mr. Orvis A. Schmidt, Treasury Department
Mr. Lowell M. Pumphrey, Treasury Department
Mr. Melville E. Locker, Treasury Department
Mr. George H. Willis, Treasury Department
Mr. Harold Glasser (Secretary)
Mr. Allan J. Fisher (NAC Secretariat)

1. *Maritime Commission Ship Sales Credits*

.   .   .   .

(c) *Italy*

Mr. Glasser said that the request was for an increase of credit from $51 million to $68.7 million to permit the Government of Italy to purchase some 15 additional ships. The Staff Committee recommended that the Council express no objection to the increased credit (NAC Document No. 492). The Council approved the recommendation unanimously.

Action.

The following action was taken:

1. The National Advisory Council has no objection to consideration by the Maritime Commission of increasing the credit to Italy from $51 million to $68.5 million to provide for the purchase of 119 vessels in lieu of 104 as previously proposed.

2. The Council approves sending a copy of NAC Document No. 492 to the Chairman of the Maritime Commission.

[Here follow (d) and items 2 and 3.]

Editorial Note

On August 14, 1947, a "Memorandum of Understanding Between the Government of the United States of America and the Government of Italy regarding settlement of certain wartime claims and related matters" was signed by Acting Secretary of State Robert A. Lovett and Ivan Matteo Lombardo, chief of the Italian Economic and Financial Delegation to the United States. For texts of the memorandum and supplementary exchanges of notes, see Department of State Treaties and Other International Acts Series (TIAS) No. 1757, or 61 Stat. (pt. 4) 3962, or Department of State *Bulletin*, August 24, 1947, page 372. A summary of the deliberations was released to the press on August 14, reprinted in the *Bulletin*, page 371, which states: "Highlights of the understandings were the waiver of sizable governmental claims arising out of the war and the establishment of procedures for the return to Italy and to properly qualified Italian nationals of their blocked and vested property, totaling some 60 million dollars, under conditions which assure, among other things, that property in which there are German and Japanese interests will not be returned. Another major feature of the understandings is the provision for the transfer of approximately eight Italian ships which had been seized by the United States before the war, five of which had been purchased from other American republics which had previously seized the ships in their waters, and the transfer of approximately fifteen surplus Liberty ships to replace the Italian ships which had been seized by the United States, requisitioned for war use and subsequently lost. The return of vested property and the return of the ships required Congressional authorization, which was recently given in recognition of the importance to world peace of rendering Italy every possible assistance. . . ."

800.48 FRP/8–2747 : Telegram

The Acting Secretary of State to the Embassy in Italy

CONFIDENTIAL   WASHINGTON, August 27, 1947—4 p. m.

1522. Rap 87. Representatives ItalEmb and Ital Purchasing Mission advised Dept yesterday that because of British suspension pound convertibility Italians have no available dollars to procure Oct coal in US. On basis urgent calls from Rome they requested total Oct allocation coal be included in US relief program. They were advised that since total available relief funds were limited inclusion increased amounts of coal Oct could only result in equivalent decrease relief dollars available for purchase grain or coal at later date and that serious consideration should be given to position Italy would be in at end 1947 or early 1948 re these items before utilizing funds for Oct coal. Dept pointed out that money for Jan grain shipments must be available Nov 15, for Feb shipments Dec 15. We advised however that if after weighing all considerations appeared wise to increase coal in Oct up to 500,000 tons could probably be included in relief program. This being maximum limit which appears to be justifiable for relief purposes in Italy as defined by Relief Act.

Since it is expected matter will be reopened after ItalEmb has communicated with ItalGovt Dept would appreciate ur comments. Commitments for Oct coal will have to be made about Sept 8.

LOVETT

865.51/8–2847

Memorandum of Conversation, by the Acting Secretary of State

[WASHINGTON,] August 28, 1947.

Participants: Ambassador Tarchiani
Mr. Lovett, Acting Secretary
Mr. Dowling, SE

The Italian Ambassador called at his request this afternoon to express the thanks of the Italian Government for US support during the Security Council's discussion of Italy's application for membership in the United Nations.[1] In this connection the Ambassador expressed the hope that when Italy's application is discussed in the General Assembly the American representative would stress Italy's ratification

---

[1] For documentation on the general policy of the United States on the admission of states to membership in the United Nations, see volume I.

of the peace treaty as a factor in the US decision to support Italy.[2] He explained that the Government expected criticism when the Constituent Assembly again meets, especially from the extreme right, since it had urged ratification as necessary to obtain Italy's entry into the United Nations and that it would be helpful if the Government could point out that this action on its part had been of value in obtaining the support of a majority of the Security Council.

I told Tarchiani I was not sure how much stress it would be advisable to place on this factor in any expression of support the US representative might make in the General Assembly but that consideration would certainly be given to it.

Tarchiani then referred to Italy's financial difficulties which he said had been made even more grave by the decision of the British Government to suspend the conversion of sterling funds into dollars. Tarchiani added that he wished to leave with me a telegram from Rome which set forth the Italian position.[3] He pointed out that while the Italian Government realized the difficulties facing the British Government, it felt that its own problems were no less severe. At British insistence the Italian Government had refrained from converting its sterling funds during recent months but had always counted upon the availability of these resources for essential purchases during the final quarter of this year. He showed me another telegram from Rome suspending further purchases of cereals, coal and petroleum pending a reply from the British Government of an Italian request to make available some $10–$15 million monthly from sterling funds.[3] The Ambassador said this action was necessary in view of the fact that present dollar resources were almost exhausted and some months must elapse before additional dollar funds from the troop pay account, POW payments and the return of Italian assets could be expected.

Tarchiani went on to say that it was in this situation that the Italian Government had decided upon an immediate approach to the Export-Import Bank for an additional $100 million loan and to the International Bank for a $250 million loan. He said he had spoken to Mr. McCloy about the International Bank loan and that Mr. McCloy would talk with Italian officials at the London meeting of the Bank and perhaps then go on to Italy for further discussions. He hoped that the Department's support would be forthcoming for both these loans at the proper time.

I told Tarchiani I understood that the British Government would license conversion transactions to the extent possible in the next few

---

[2] For documentation on Italian ratification of the peace treaty, see pp. 515 ff.
[3] Not printed.

months and that I therefore hoped the Italian Government could in this manner obtain at least some of its dollar requirements. I added that we would do what we could to make funds from the American sources he had mentioned available at the earliest possible date. As regards the Export-Import Bank and International Bank loans, I said that as the Ambassador knew, we would give every consideration to the Italian proposals.

865.51/8–2847

The Italian Ambassador (Tarchiani) to the Acting Secretary of State

URGENT
No. 7734

The Italian Ambassador presents his compliments to the Hon. the Acting Secretary of State and has the honor to draw his kind attention to the following:

The seriousness of the Italian financial situation has been repeatedly pointed out to the attention of the competent American Agencies and has been illustrated in detail by the Italian Economic and Financial Mission during the meetings held in Washington during the past months of June and July. In such meetings it was demonstrated how the Italian Government has to face a deficit in its balance of payments of about 236 million dollars, in the second half of the current year, in spite of the generous assistance granted by the American Government, with the troop and non-troop pay funds and the "grant-in-aid" concession.

The recent decision of the British Government, arrived at in the course of the Anglo-American negotiations on the convertibility of the pound sterling, will now deprive Italy of a substantial availability of dollars which had been taken into account among the receipts in the projection of the balance of payments for the second half of the current year.

Such a decision has brought about a complete lacking of dollar availability for the Italian Government, which cannot but view with the utmost seriousness and deep preoccupation the situation which is developing for Italy in the financial field in the coming months.

Due to such severe dollar shortage, instructions have in fact already been sent to the Italian Purchasing Mission in Washington to stop all purchases of coal in September and to utilize the remaining balances available to the Mission only for the payment of the transportation of coal acquired under the grant-in-aid program.

It would be difficult to conceal the very severe consequences in the economic and social fields of any interruption of the flow of basic supplies to Italy. The process of reconstruction in which the Italian Government and people have been so far engaged would receive a fatal set-back and unemployment and hunger would prevail in a very short time in Italy.

The Italian Ambassador finds himself compelled to stress, with the greatest emphasis, the necessity of meeting such a situation with immediate steps, such as to allow the continuance of the flow of supplies to Italy.

In this respect, the Italian Ambassador has the honor to point out that the Italian Government is in these days approaching the British Authorities in order to obtain that the sterling balances accrued in favor of Italy up to August 20th, 1947, be made convertible, in line with the Anglo-Italian agreement of which a most important clause was related to the convertibility of such balances. The Italian Government is, in fact, pointing out in this respect to the British Authorities that the insertion of such clause was the outcome of negotiations relating to the settlement of all pending questions between Italy and the United Kingdom and that, should the convertibility of the said balances not be allowed, this would constitute a very hard blow on the Italian economic situation, which is already very serious.

The Italian Ambassador has the honor to request in this respect that the United States Government kindly give all its support to the action taken by the Italian Government described above. The Italian Government is relying on the understanding of the American Government and on its kind interest and intervention in order to secure the availability, so badly needed, of the dollars corresponding to the balances in question.

Some other steps which could bring, however, minor results but would provide some immediate availability of dollar funds, could also be taken, i.e.:

—further consideration could be given as urgently as practicable to the possibility of making available to the Italian Government the balance of the "suspense account".

—Consideration could be given to the possibility of making available to the Italian share under the grant-in-aid program, an increased dollar allocation in order to make it possible to have during the coming months a larger amount of coal shipped to Italy and the related necessary freight expenses paid out of the same "grant-in-aid" funds.

—UNRRA is now considering the refund to various countries of advances made by them for the procurement of essential raw materials at the time when, for administrative reasons, UNRRA had no available funds. So far, with the liquidation of its administration, UNRRA has refunded out of the 22,7 millions disbursed by Italy for the reasons above mentioned, only an account of 2,1 million dollars. UNRRA could be urged to refund the highest possible balance with the utmost speed.

The steps which the Italian Ambassador has deemed it fit to suggest above, are, however, related to the problems of the immediate dollar availability.

While the Italian financial situation is already presenting itself under the most precarious circumstances in the present impact, making it necessary to take recourse to emergency measures, no favorable prospects can be envisaged also for the following months and the next year 1948.

In fact the deficit already foreseen for the second semester of the current year will be far greater in the next year, when the income of certain proceeds, like the troop and non-troop pay and the grant-in-aid, will not recur.

Moreover, the difficulties so far encountered by Italy in receiving essential basic supplies, like coal, from central Europe, the persistent need of obtaining wheat supplies from the Western Hemisphere, the practical impossibility of restoring normal trade relations with the German market, will characterize again the structure of the Italian economic situation in the future.

The Italian Government has taken note with the greatest appreciation of the suggestions brought up by the Secretary of State in his Harvard speech, and has tried, with constructive proposals, to give its utmost contribution to the work entrusted to the Conference of the 16 European countries in Paris.

The Italian Government is, however, aware that, even if the problems which the Conference will bring to the attention of the American Government will receive a favorable solution, there will be a considerable lapse of time before any suggestion for assistance to the European countries will be put into practise.

The Italian Council of Ministers has therefore decided to take the following steps, in order to obtain the dollar funds which are necessary for maintaining the present rate of production, so that the process of recovery be not undermined:

—an application has been filed with the International Bank for obtaining an interim line of credit of 250,000,000 dollars. This loan is being now negotiated with a view of assisting Italy in continuing and increasing the maintenance, development and reconstruction of productive facilities and activities. In such negotiations the Italian Government will try to focus on the financing of projects of national importance.

—steps are being taken in order to ascertain the possibility of obtaining from the Export-Import Bank of Washington a second line

of credit of 100 million dollars, for satisfying the request of the qualified Italian industries, engaged in export activity, which will not benefit of the credit granted under the first line of credit of 100 million
dollars.

—consideration is being given for the filing of applications with the
competent American Agencies for the purchase of surplus materials
both in the United States and in Germany.

The steps above mentioned are meant not only to provide the necessary dollar funds for the purchases of supplies essentially needed but
also to give to the Italian Government a breathing space for increasing
the chances of a satisfactory development of the budgetary situation,
through the receipts in lire accruing from the utilization of such
credits.

Such decisions have been taken by the Italian Government in the
intent of avoiding any collapse of the economic situation in the coming
months and in the awareness that, without the assistance accruing from
the implementation of such requests, it would be difficult to avoid a
deterioration of the psychological situation in Italy and a further
increase of the inflationary process.

The Italian Ambassador, in calling the kind attention of the Acting
Secretary of State to the seriousness of the conditions described above,
requests his kind assistance for obtaining that the applications filed
or to be filed by the Italian Government and the steps which will be
taken in their connection, receive all possible support and assistance by
the United States Government.

The Italian Ambassador thanks in advance the Hon. the Acting
Secretary of State for his kind interest in the matter.

WASHINGTON, August 28, 1947.

A[LBERTO] T[ARCHIANI]

865.6584/9–347

The Italian Ambassador (Tarchiani) to the Acting Secretary of State

No. 7885

The Italian Ambassador presents his compliments to the Honorable
the Acting Secretary of State and has the honor to draw his kind attention to the following.

In the meetings held in Rome between the Under Secretary of State
for Economic Affairs, Mr. Clayton, and the Chiefs of the Italian Economic Agencies,[1] and in the interview, which took place in Paris, between the United States Secretary of Agriculture, Mr. Anderson, and

---

[1] See p. 945.

the Italian Minister of Agriculture, Mr. Segni,[2] the Italian cereals situation for the period July 1947–June 1948 was illustrated in detail.

It was then pointed out by the Italian Representatives that the need for importation of supplies of cereals would have been, on the basis of the IEFC questionnaire pattern, of 3.400.000 tons in the above said period, but that such figure could be reduced to the smaller amount of 2.900.000 tons in view of the following facts:

a) in the month of July 1947 and even in the present month, the consumption has been reduced for failure of distribution with some consequent savings, (which however raise increasing opposition and unrest and cannot obviously be continued indefinitely);
b) the Italian Government is planning to exercise the utmost pressure on the farmers for obtaining the maximum results from the amassments (as in fact the July amassment has already shown the original target for that month having been surpassed);
c) the Italian Government hopes to be in a position to waive a part of the allocation by cutting the end stock requirements, in case some advance crops in the southern regions would be possible.

It was pointed out to the American Representatives that, of the above said amount of 2,9 million tons, 2,2 million tons should have come from the United States at the rate of 220 thousand tons a month beginning from the month of August included, the remaining part of 700 thousand tons having to be imported from Argentine, Canada, Near East. Moreover the necessity was stressed of obtaining such allocation of 220 thousand for the month of August in view of the fact that in the present period of the year the imports from the Near East would not be forthcoming immediately and that already towards the end of September, the Italian Government has essentially to rely on imports in order to obtain all the supplies needed for the distribution.

The Honorable the Acting Secretary of State is aware that a meeting of the Cereals Committee of the I.E.F.C. took recently place in Winnipeg. In such meeting the general situation of the allocations was reviewed and a resolution proposed by the United States delegate was approved, according to which, among other decisions, Italy should receive an allocation of 775.000 tons of cereals in the period July–December 1947, of which 540.000 should come from the United States. To this resolution the Italian Delegate strongly objected voting against.

Should such resolution in fact be adopted, Italy would receive in the months between July and December, from the United States, an amount of cereals which is less than half of what was previously asked to the American Representatives above mentioned. This would entail

---

[2] No record of this meeting has been found.

unforeseeable consequences in the present Italian situation: the working classes have already indicated their strong concern for the limitation of the cereal supplies distributed to them and for the inflationary spiral that such shortage of cereals is entailing. Moreover, the Italian Government, which is constantly faced with the problem of shifting from the producing provinces to the others the amounts needed for the distribution of the minimum ration, will have to fight against insolvable difficulties to achieve such distribution, as various provinces have already shown their reluctance to comply with the Government orders in the awareness that cereal supplies will become even shorter in the near future.

The Italian Ambassador has the honor, therefore, to invite the most serious attention of the Honorable the Acting Secretary of State to the gravity of such a problem, asking him to explore any possibility in order to arrive at an increase in the allocation to Italy in the future months to come.

The Italian Ambassador realizes the present shortage throughout the world but cannot but stress the great concern of the Italian Government for the consequences that inadequate provisions in the field of cereal supplies would entail for the social and economic situation in Italy.

The Italian Ambassador thanks the Honorable the Acting Secretary of State for his kind interest on the matter.

WASHINGTON, September 3, 1947.   A[LBERTO] T[ARCHIANI]

740.00119 Control (Italy)/9–347 : Telegram

The Ambassador in Italy (Dunn) to the Secretary of State

ROME, September 3, 1947.

2601. Following official press release by Italian Foreign Ministry today:

"There was signed today at Chigi Palace by Minister Sforza and Ambassador Dunn, an agreement in the form of an exchange of letters for facilitating the withdrawal of the American armed forces from Italy and for regulating the status of same during the period of evacuation in which the armistice regime shall have ceased to be in force.[1]

This agreement provides further that the United States High Command shall immediately prepare, in conjunction with the appropriate Italian authorities, for the substitution, with Italian personnel, of

---

[1] For text, see Department of State Treaties and Other International Acts Series (TIAS) No. 1694, or 61 Stat. (pt. 4) 3661.

the American personnel now serving with the Allied Military Government in the areas to be given back to Italian administration.["]

Sent Secretary of State 2601, Leghorn 111, Trieste 52.

DUNN

Editorial Note

On September 4 the Department of State reiterated to the Embassy in Rome its policy of supporting impartially all moderate political elements in Italy. It stated that the United States would welcome support for participation in the Italian Government of the greatest possible number of moderate left, center and right groups prepared to work together in harmony, without regard to narrow party differences, for the best interests of the Italian people. The Department further stated: "Obviously, we shall not support extremists, but it must be clear also that we cannot support those who, while not themselves of extreme left or right, make common cause with extremists to detriment of general welfare." (Telegram 1593 to Rome, September 4, 1947; 865.00/8-2847)

865.51/9-1147

Memorandum of Conversation, by the Assistant Secretary of State for Political Affairs (*Armour*)

[WASHINGTON,] September 11, 1947.

Participants: Ambassador Tarchiani
Mr. Armour, A–A
Mr. Dowling, SE

When the Ambassador called at his request this morning he said that in a brief conversation with the Acting Secretary yesterday [1] Mr. Lovett had requested any suggestions which the Ambassador might have regarding assistance for Italy. The Ambassador said that unfortunately he had been unable to think of any concrete measures which would not require Congressional action, although it was clear by now that Italy would run out of dollars long before any action which Congress might take. He said Italy would be able to finance her requirements this month and it might be possible to pay for October requirements, but there would be nothing at all left for November

---

[1] No record of this conversation has been found.

imports. He said he had not received complete figures from Rome but his own estimate was that within the near future Italy had in sight only some $37 million; this figure would have to be reduced proportionately if there were any delay in final settlement of the Army accounts, from which Italy expected to realize approximately $4 million, or in the POW account totalling perhaps $5 million. On the other hand, his estimate of Italy's needs to the end of December was $120 million. As he understood it the only immediately available source of assistance was the relief program for Italy which is generally expected to total about $120 million. Of this amount, about $35 million had been committed in the present quarter, leaving about $85 million for the balance of the program. He understood further that it was contemplated that about half of this amount would be spent in the final quarter of the year and the rest in the first quarter of 1948. He hoped, however, we would give consideration to stepping up shipments in the final quarter, in anticipation that funds under the Marshall Plan would be available for the first quarter of next year. He said the essential commodities for Italy were, of course, wheat and coal; he realized there were difficulties in procurement and transportation, but if Italy's requirements for these two items could be covered under the relief program he felt that they would get along somehow.

I told Tarchiani that we would give consideration to his suggestion and that we would see what could be done in this connection.

After thanking me, the Ambassador turned to the question of Italy's admission to the UN. He said that of course none of us knew what the Soviet attitude on Italy's application would be, now that the treaty was coming into effect, but he feared the USSR would continue to oppose Italy unless the other ex-enemy states were also admitted. He added that he knew and sympathized with our attitude in this matter, but that he hoped if we could admit some of the ex-enemy states Italy could also get in. I said we had particularly grave doubts that Albania, Bulgaria and Rumania were willing to carry out the obligations of the Charter and that I did not see how we could vote for all of the ex-enemy states. At the same time, Italy could count on the same warm support for the Italian application which we had already given in the Security Council. The Ambassador said that the Italian Government was most grateful for this support and he knew we would continue it.

Referring again to the coming into force of the Italian treaty on September 15, Tarchiani said there were two matters to which he hoped we would give special consideration. One was the delimitation of the Italo-Yugoslav frontier. He said the Italian Government had not accepted the Four Power Boundary Commission's recommendations, which he felt deviated from the treaty provisions and made too many concessions to Yugoslavia. The area involved was not great, but it meant a great deal to the Italian people, and he hoped this unfavorable frontier would not be imposed on Italy. The second matter was the possible return to Italy of the US share of Italian naval vessels distributed under the treaty. He said he understood we did not want to use these ships, and he felt their return to Italy for scrapping would make a tremendous impression on the Italian people. He said the scrap metal was needed for Italian industries, and the return of the ships, perhaps for some specific purpose like the production of agricultural machinery, would be a gesture which would capture the Italian imagination.

In conclusion the Ambassador said he hoped very much that any action we might take in regard to these matters could be announced before September 23 when debate began in the Constituent Assembly on the motion of no confidence introduced by Nenni. He said De Gasperi would surely be hard-pushed in the debate; the Communist-instigated strikes were becoming increasingly grave; Togliatti had just threatened the use of violence if necessary to overthrow the Government; and every effort would be made to charge De Gasperi and his pro-Western policy with responsibility for all of Italy's ills. He felt the vote would be extremely close, and further evidence of American support and assistance might be the deciding factor.

I promised Tarchiani that I would look into all these questions immediately, adding that as he knew we would be as helpful as possible.

N[ORMAN] A[RMOUR]

865.24/9–1147 : Telegram

The Ambassador in Italy (Dunn) to the Secretary of State

TOP SECRET   ROME, September 11, 1947—3 p. m.

2718. Deptel 1366, August 11. Decisions on outstanding matters of equipment for Italian army have been delayed while Italian army staff considered which of available items they wish accept under terms of July 21 surplus agreement and while allied and US authorities examined availabilities from surplus stock.

In meeting with Italian chief of army staff [1] September 1 General Lee after consultation with us offered the following equipment:

(a) 110 105mm howitzers, M–3 of which 99 in EuCom and 11 in Italy. All of these weapons are in poor condition having been stripped of fire control instruments and those in EuCom prepared for demili-

---

[1] Gen. Efisio Luigi Marras, Chief of Staff of the Italian Army.

tarization; further we do not consider them substitute for 105 howitzer M-2 A-1 weapons. General Lee offered them to General Marras as scrap thus leaving open for possible future fulfillment the commitment of the July 21 agreement to provide substitute items and General Marras accepted.

(b) 20,000 rounds of ammunition for the M-3 available in EuCom; General Marras accepted.

(c) 39 light tanks M-5 available in EuCom. Since these tanks have been stripped of radio and fire control and auxiliary armament and require extensive reconditioning, they were also offered not as substitute items but as "scrap". General Marras was informed they are believed suitable for training purposes and said he would send a representative to inspect them before giving final answer.

(d) 20 medium tanks M-4 and M-4-1 available in EuCom. (This offer made even though medium tanks had been supplied from British troops Austria to meet earlier deficit (FX 77066 August 6 to War Department from ComGenMed [2]) in accordance with our belief that all possible equipment should be offered to Italians regardless of limits of "balanced force", which in any case refer only to minima. We also interpret treaty limitations to refer only to material in operative condition). Italian representative will inspect these before final answer given.

(e) 89 57mm anti-tank guns for which ammunition may not be available. General Lee undertook to query EuCom availability ammunition there and General Marras said he would take weapons if ammunition available. (Subsequent to meeting MTO staff reported 30,000 rounds ammunition available in Italy after R–Day).

(f) Assorted grenades, mines and small arms ammunition available in Italy.

In line with Deptel 1441, August 19 [2] General Lee stated equipment located in EuCom would have to be accepted "as is", and that he hopes arrangements can be made to transport it to German border without cost to Italy.

I have informed General Lee that I am communicating with Hyssong [3] at Paris on question of arranging transport from present depots to German border.

Re possibility that additional British equipment may be found available for Italian program understand that British decision to make such equipment available only against payment has not been altered in principle. However, British troops Austria have been ordered to close down their depots by 30 September and War Office has approved shipment to Italy equipment which Italians may want, in preference to its abandonment inside. Financial arrangement to be worked out subsequently.

---

[2] Not printed.
[3] Brig. Gen. Clyde Lloyd Hyssong, central field commissioner, Office of Foreign Liquidation Commissioner.

Majority of equipment available this source comprises personnel and munition carriers, armored scout cars and similar vehicles.

My understanding is that when all equipment referred to above has been delivered to the Italian army, the latter will still be lacking the following items in good condition required to establish minimum level of balance force.

200 light tanks; 230 field artillery pieces (105mm); 50 medium artillery pieces (155mm); 140mm anti-aircraft guns; 130 3.7 inch anti-aircraft guns; 400 rocket launchers, and 65 17 pounder anti-tank guns.

I have informed General Lee of my understanding that under July 21 transfer agreement US still committed endeavor supply Italy with equipment called for, or suitable and acceptable substitutes. Since agreement specified no time limit for fulfillment this obligation I have informed General Lee I believe intensive search should be continued to obtain items still deficient from whatever source for delivery to Italian army.

I hope the Department will agree that the US should make every effort to see that the reduced Italian forces are as well equipped as possible.

Dunn

865.51/9–1647

Memorandum of Conversation, by the Acting Secretary of State

[Washington,] September 16, 1947.

Participants: Ambassador Tarchiani
Mr. Lovett, Acting Secretary
Mr. Dowling, SE

The Italian Ambassador called this afternoon to bring to my attention data on Italian financial requirements for the final quarter of 1948. He referred to his recent conversation with me [1] and said that additional figures were being received by mail from Rome but that he believed the essential facts were shown in the memorandum which he was leaving with me.[2]

Tarchiani also left with me a note regarding the IEFC grain allocation to Italy [3] and urged that this allocation be increased if at all pos-

---

[1] This brief conversation, for which no record has been found, took place on September 10, for it is referred to as of "yesterday" in Tarchiani's conversation with Armour and Dowling on September 11 (*ante*, p. 965).
[2] Note of Italian Embassy, No. 8275, *infra*.
[3] Note of Italian Embassy, No. 8274, p. 972.

sible. He said that contemplated shipments in the next few months would leave Italy with little more than a month's supply of grain on January 1.

I told Tarchiani I was glad to have these figures and inquired whether there would be any objection to making them public if it seemed desirable. He replied there would be no objection, adding that most of the information had been made available to other countries participating in the Paris talks on the Marshall Plan.

The Ambassador then discussed the present situation in Italy. He said the recent wave of strikes, coming as the treaty entered into force and Italy's economic resources were practically exhausted, were of course part of the overall strategy of the Italian Communist Party to force the De Gasperi Government out of office. He added that he did not believe Togliatti could overthrow the De Gasperi Government by parliamentary vote. If Togliatti failed, however, he might then attempt to set up a Communist government in Northern Italy which would undoubtedly receive recognition and assistance from Tito. The Italian Government in this event would take all possible measures to defend itself and to regain Northern Italy, but the armed forces permitted Italy under the Treaty were small, and even with the support of a majority of the population, a situation would exist akin to that in Greece today. He was still hopeful, though, that De Gasperi could win through, and that the Communist drive could be checked by means short of civil war.

After expressing the opinion that developments in Italy were related to general Soviet moves in Europe, Tarchiani said he felt the Soviets were pushing ahead in Italy rather than elsewhere since Greece and Turkey were now under "direct US protection", both in a military and economic sense, whereas Allied troops were being withdrawn from Italy and the economic situation there was growing worse. He added that while he felt sure the Italian Communists could count on Yugoslav and Soviet support he wondered what assistance the Italian Government would obtain.

I commented that Italy could proceed under Article 51 of the United Nations Charter, pointing out that Italy's right to defensive action thereunder was not subject to the veto. Tarchiani agreed, but seemed doubtful that the Italian Government could hold out while appealing to the United Nations; he reiterated, however, that the Government would do everything possible to maintain and defend itself.

In conclusion Tarchiani said that his views were based on his own estimate of the situation; he had received no direct word from De Gasperi, he said, but if he did, he would let me know.

840.50 Recovery/9–1647

The Italian Ambassador (*Tarchiani*) *to the Acting Secretary of State*

No. 8275 WASHINGTON, 16 September 1947.

DEAR MR. LOVETT : Following our conversations of the other day,[1] I enclose herewith some tables [2] which show the magnitude of the problem of the Italian requirements for the next months.

The tables here submitted are the following :

a) Table n. 1 *reflects the immediate problem* confronting the Italian Government for the purchases to be made in U.S.A. from now to the end of 1947. No funds are at present available to the Italian Government for such purchases. Should funds not be forthcoming and said purchases not be effected, a complete breakdown of the Italian economic system would occur. The table in question includes the amounts of basic essential commodities, like coal, cereals and P.O.L. products, in excess of those now being financed under the grant-in-aid program as within the limits so far indicated by the American competent authorities, plus other items absolutely indispensable to maintain the minimum production level of Italian industries in the above said period. The total requirement for these undeferrable purchases amounts to approximately *190 million dollars*, for four months, or an irreducible minimum of more than *47 million* dollars per month. I wish to point out that this figure does not include purchases to be made in other countries, for which payment in dollars is required.

b) Table n. 2 estimated balance of payments for the second semester 1947 showing a deficit for such period of approximate 236 million dollars.

This figure was however calculated when the decision of the British Government on the nonconvertibility of the pounds sterling had not been taken. Such figure therefore must be considerably increased, as approximately 15 million sterling pounds of receipts corresponding to net trade balances are not usable for the time being.

What is very clear is that the deficit in the balance of payment for 1947 is such that Italy without additional assistance can not meet the irreducible minimum requirements of more than 47 million per month, as set forth in paragraph a) above.

c) Table n. 3 shows the estimated projection of Italian balance of payments in the year 1948 as submitted to the Paris Economic Conference of the 16 European countries. It indicates a total deficit of 852 million dollars, i.e. a monthly deficit of approximate 70 million dollars. In the calculations of such balance of payments no considera-

---

[1] See footnote 1, p. 969.
[2] None printed.

tion was at the time given to the possibility that the pounds sterling accruing for Italian export into the sterling area might not be convertible. In this respect it may be useful to recall that the Italian Government estimates that Italian export in the sterling area will exceed imports to that area for an amount of 1,5 million pounds sterling per month. Therefore should the nonconvertibility be maintained, the actual deficit within the dollar area would considerably increase.

With respect to the above, I wish to stress the absolute necessity in which the Italian Government finds itself to obtain the necessary funds to finance the undeferrable essential purchases in the U.S. market, in the present moment. I venture to suggest that an immediate increase of the grant-in-aid program for Italy would be a practical solution to meet the present emergency.

I hope that you will give all your kind and careful consideration to the data submitted herewith and I thank you very much for the attention which you will give to the matter.

Yours sincerely,   ALBERTO TARCHIANI

865.6131/9–1647

The Italian Ambassador (Tarchiani) to the Acting Secretary of State

No. 8274   WASHINGTON, [September 16, 1947.]

The Italian Ambassador presents his compliments to the Honorable the Acting Secretary of State and has the honor to refer to his previous note No. 7885 of September 3rd, 1947.

In such note the Italian Ambassador deemed it necessary to draw the utmost attention to the Honorable the Secretary of State on the very serious consequences which the present insufficient grain allocation for Italy would have entailed.

Since the presentation of the note above mentioned, the Italian Ambassador has been again urged by his Government to point out to the competent American Authorities that, should the allocations in question be not increased, no stocks would practically be available to Italy at the end of the year or a further drastic cut in the rations would now be needed.

A table is attached to the present note with the aim of giving an illustration of the extremely dangerous situation confronting the Italian Government.[1]

As specified in its footnotes, such table is to be considered as an exploratory approach to the situation as it would develop for Italy in the months up to next January, if no prompt and adequate pro-

---

[1] Not printed.

visions were taken to increase wheat shipments in the immediate future.

The depletion of stocks before next year will also mean that Italian food administration will be soon faced with the impossibility of maintaining an orderly bread distribution.

On the other hand it cannot be easily conceived how in the present moment in which the Italian Government is faced with riots and widespread strikes, it would be possible for them to announce and enforce a reduction in the bread rations.[2]

---

[2] In letter No. 8641, September 24, not printed, Tarchiani told Armour of a new, urgent, personal appeal from Prime Minister De Gasperi for the Secretary of State, urging an increase in the wheat allocation for Italy (865.6584/9–2447).

865.5018/9–1747 : Telegram

The Ambassador in Italy (Dunn) to the Secretary of State

TOP SECRET   ROME, September 17, 1947—3 p. m.

2772. ReEmbtel 2633, September 5 and 2651 and 2652 September 6 [1]. In submitting my recommendations to ship wheat to Italy at the expense of other commodities under the relief program, we made a choice that was forced upon us, and in which we were guided by humanitarian as well as political arguments of special importance to Italy. Aside from the preponderance of cereals in the Italian diet (normally two-thirds of the caloric intake), we would be poor managers indeed of relief program if Russia, by timing rather than generosity, were afforded the opportunity to make good the Italian deficit at a critical political moment, say March.

The choice of wheat is almost entirely at the sacrifice of coal, the commodities under USFRP already having been virtually eliminated. Whether we supply all of the wheat and none of coal, or half of wheat and half of the coal, there remains a wide gap which Italy must fill with foreign exchange. The gravity of this decision to Italian economy is clear.

Italian economy normally used about one million tons of foreign coal a month. However, Italian industry operates on a narrow margin as regards both fuel and raw materials; the proportion of coal allocated to public services here is considerably greater than is the case in countries with heavy industries. Therefore, proportional cuts of coal receipts affect Italian production to a greater degree than production of most of its neighbors.

---

[1] None printed.

The Italian Government has been counting among its exchange resources some 20,000,000 of sterling, most of which would have been used for US coal purchases. The suspension of convertibility leaves the Italian Government in a critical exchange position—according to statements of Governor of Bank of Italy [4] and Minister of Foreign Trade,[5] the net dollar position is between 13,000,000 and 15,000,000. While by scraping the bottom of barrel, Italian Government may possibly find some small sums of additional dollars, it is very undesirable for it to consume the last of the meager resources, and placing the government before end of year in a most vulnerable political position. (The Embassy is making a careful inquiry into such additional US tapped [*additional untapped?*] sources of dollars as may exist—for instance, suspension of 50% exchange retention legislation—and hope to be able to report at end of the week.)

It can be frankly said, therefore, that Italy is on verge of a dollar crisis, which if allowed to break, will inevitably so restrict production, transportation and employment as to cause an inflation, with attendant political upheaval, so far unmatched in Italy. If it does not break in a few weeks, it cannot be held off for long.

While the Marshall plan is still a light of hope on the dismal road Italy walks, it is a dim and distant one for the weary traveller.

I appreciate from the messages we have been receiving and particularly from the Under Secretary's statement of September 3 and yours of September 12, that our government is anticipating the measures to take in order to meet the gathering forces of despair in western Europe. However, as the situation in Italy is giving signs of starting to move rapidly, I have felt constrained to risk the error of repetition by presenting the above picture. By the same token I submit for what it may add to the Department's material, some of the possible emergency devices which might be considered.

1. An advance of dollars against Italy's sterling as collateral.
2. A stabilization loan similar to the recent one to Mexico, if the Italian case fits the requirements.
3. Expediting the opening of credits under the Export-Import Bank 100,000,000 dollar credit, of which only some 30,000,000 have been formally committed and none used.
4. Making a public commitment now, with a view to negotiation of an agreement as soon as possible, of a new Export-Import Bank loan of at least $100,000,000 available for purchases of raw materials without conditions as to the export trade it could develop, the present formula of "political stability", etc. (While such an operation would depend upon a change of bank's policy, I imagine that, in the absence of other US loan funds for foreign countries the interim use of the

[4] Luigi Einaudi.
[5] Giuseppe Merzagora.

Export-Import Bank for the critical period in Europe is under general examination.)

5. Exploring the possibility of an International Monetary Fund and Bank operation in favor Italy. Despite the long term nature of the bank's loans public commitments to an Italian loan should have a splendid psychological effect at once.

Patently, these are all emergency measures to meet a new, and the worst, emergency; the definitive solution to Europe's ills must be built of constructive planning at Paris which will sell itself on its merit to the American people and Congress. The suspension of controvertibility has rapidly accelerated economic deterioration. There was a time not long ago when I believed Italy would pull through, at least until the first of the year. Such is no longer the probability. In a short time, perhaps a very short time, it will be question no longer whether this government or even a broadened one can survive; it will be a question when Communists find it suits their purpose to seize initiative, which is passing to them, to assume the Government by legal means.

The present or a similar type of government is one which we should support with substantial assistance now if we really want to avoid Italy going Communistic. Without assistance this government will fall and the only alternatives are either a coalition including the Communists or a government of Communists and non-Socialists [*Nenni Socialists?*]. Either of course would mean the end of democracy in Italy.

Sent Department, repeated Paris 365.

Repeated Paris for Clayton.

DUNN

740.00119 Control (Italy)/9–1747 : Telegram

The Acting Political Adviser (Greene) at Leghorn to the Secretary of State [1]

LEGHORN, September 17, 1947.

173. From MTOUSA to SecState, info AmEmb Rome AmEmb Belgrade US PolAd Hq AMGVG Trieste US PolAd Frankfurt. Effective with abolition AFHQ September 17, US PolAd Leghorn closes. Correspondence relating to US military establishment in Italy should now be addressed to AmEmbassy Rome.

British PolAd also closes same date.

---

[1] Mr. Greene was Acting United States Political Adviser to the Acting Supreme Allied Commander, Mediterranean Theater (Lee).

Sent Dept 173, repeated Trieste 15; Rome 83; Belgrade 30; Frankfurt unnumbered.

GREENE

865.00/9–2247 : Telegram

The Ambassador in Italy (Dunn) to the Secretary of State

TOP SECRET   ROME, September 22, 1947—1 p. m.
URGENT

2871. For the Secretary and Under Secretary. On Saturday evening (September 20) during meeting with member of Embassy staff, Prime Minister de Gasperi expressed his deep concern with respect to outcome of vote on Socialist-Communist motion of lack of confidence in present government, expected to take place at end of next week. He stated that vote, in any case, would be very close and that he would have to mobilize every possible support in order to pull through. Loss of vote of confidence, he added, would undoubtedly mean his departure from government and the formation of a government which would include those left-wing forces which brought about his defeat.

Immediate measures of support of the present government, prior to the vote of confidence, may be the decisive factor. I recommend strongly therefore, that the following measures be taken by the US Government prior to the vote of confidence: (1) Immediate availability of the dollar counterpart of prisoner of war certificates, estimated at 20 million dollars, (2) immediate certification by War Department of remaining dollars forming counterpart of American lire spent in Italy, (3) immediate restitution of 24 tons of Fortezza gold which it has now been agreed is to be restored to Italy, (4) transference to Italian Government under surplus property agreement of July 21, 1947, of three wrecked ships lying in Italian territorial waters which Maritime Commission propose offering generally on sealed bids.

I strongly recommend that the US Government announce these measures, involving some 50 or 60 million dollars, together in one press release prior to the vote of confidence.

DUNN

Executive Secretariat Files

Memorandum by the Policy Planning Staff

TOP SECRET   [WASHINGTON,] September 24, 1947.

The Problem: Possible Action by the U.S. to Assist the Italian Government in the Event of Communist Seizure of North Italy and the Establishment of an Italian Communist "Government" in That Area.

FACTS BEARING ON THE PROBLEM

1. The Communists were excluded from the Italian Government in June, 1947. Since then, their rapid increase in strength and power appears to have been checked, and their influence seems to have declined, although they remain the strongest single force in Italian politics.

2. Resenting their exclusion from the Government, and alarmed at the initial success of this first attempt since liberation to govern without them, the Communists have exerted increasing pressure through propaganda, popular demonstrations and strikes by constituent unions of the Communist-dominated General Labor Confederation to bring about the downfall of the De Gasperi cabinet and the formation of a new government with Communist participation.

This pressure has recently been intensified. Following the introduction of a motion of no confidence before the Constituent Assembly, Communist propaganda has alternately threatened De Gasperi with defeat and pled with him to resign for the good of the country. Strikes have been increased in number and size, and a nation-wide "hunger" demonstration was held on September 20 in an attempt to intimidate the cabinet and Assembly before debate begins September 23 on the motion of no confidence. For the first time, the Communists have threatened the use of force to overthrow the government.

3. Following the signature at Paris of the Italian Peace Treaty on February 10, 1947, small US and UK forces have been maintained in Italy, primarily for reasons of stability and to ensure an orderly and peaceful transfer of Italian territory ceded to Yugoslavia under the treaty. The Italian treaty having come into effect on September 16, these forces must be withdrawn within ninety days of that date under the provisions of Article 73 of the treaty.

4. Annex VII of the Italian treaty, however, provides that 5,000 US troops shall remain in the Free Territory of Trieste, together with 5,000 British and 5,000 Yugoslav troops, until such time as the Governor of the Free Territory shall declare to the Security Council that their services are no longer required. Maintenance of the security and territorial integrity of the Free Territory is a direct obligation of the Security Council.

5. US policy towards Italy has been directed toward the support of a friendly, democratic regime in that country in order to safeguard US security aims in the Mediterranean.

DISCUSSION

6. There can be no question of the ultimate aim of the Italian Communist Party; this aim is the complete subjugation of Italy to Soviet control. There is, however, some question as to their immediate objective. It may be that they expect and desire no more at present than

participation in the Italian Government, in the belief that the increased power and prestige to be derived from this participation would enable them to win the national elections in March 1948. A possibility exists, however, that they may have decided upon an immediate attempt to seize full power.

7. While consideration of their participation in the Government as the Communists' immediate objective is beyond the scope of this paper, it should be said that it seems doubtful they could now overthrow the De Gasperi government by parliamentary means unless economic conditions grew worse. If conditions do worsen, discontent and disorders may well rise to a point beyond the ability of the Government to control with the limited armed forces permitted it under the treaty, thereby enabling the Communists to achieve their ultimate aim of full power.

8. If the Communists are persuaded they cannot succeed by constitutional means, and are convinced that with US assistance economic conditions will improve rather than worsen, it seems probable they will intensify still further their efforts to disrupt economic life and undermine the authority of the Government. The plan will be to reduce the country gradually to a state of chaos in which local and national administration will collapse and in which "peoples' councils" can be set up in Communist-dominated areas as spontaneous expressions of the popular will. Any effort in this direction would be facilitated by the virtual control which the Communists and Nenni Socialists already exercise over the municipal governments of Milan, Turin, Genoa, Bologna and other smaller cities in the North.

Once established, these "peoples' councils" could be joined together to form a Communist national "government," whose authority might be expected to cover initially most of North Italy as far south as Florence. Appeals would then be issued to Italian regions in the south to recognize this "government" as truly representative of the Italian people.

9. In this situation, the Italian Government can be expected to exert every effort to maintain its authority in Rome and throughout Southern Italy, where the Communist Party is weaker and less well organized than in the north. Above the Po Valley, the Government might attempt to hold Venice, where the Christian Democrats are strong, and around which the greater part of US and UK forces will probably be concentrated while awaiting withdrawal. Its main effort, however, would have to be directed towards consolidating its position in the south, and even there it could not hold out for long without appreciable assistance from abroad. Cut off from industrial production of the north, and deprived also of the agricultural produce of the Po Valley, southern Italy would soon be almost wholly dependent upon imports

for its very existence. Though assistance under the United States relief program would be used for the 20 million people in South Italy, rather than for the entire population of 46 million as at present, additional assistance would be required for an improvement in present living standards if stability were to be insured.

10. North Italy would likewise require foreign assistance. It is possible that basic food requirements might be met from domestic sources for an initial period, but coal and primary raw materials would be required almost immediately to maintain production and employment in urban centers. Communications with Yugoslavia would, however, provide means as well as a source for many essential materials. These same means would also serve for military assistance from Yugoslavia and the USSR; such assistance would most probably be extended covertly, with overt Yugoslav action limited to seizing for itself the border areas, notably the province of Udine, claimed during the Italian treaty negotiations.

11. The rise of Communism to power in Italy would seriously menace US interests. Apart from the influence this development would have on the future of Western Europe and the repercussions to be expected in South America, a Communist regime in Italy could nullify the achievement of US objectives in Greece and Turkey. On the other hand, failure of the Communist moves in Italy could only cause most favorable reactions throughout the Mediterranean and Europe, giving courage to the peoples of those areas in their own efforts to resist Soviet pressure.

CONCLUSIONS

12. It is evident that the Communists are exerting the greatest possible pressure to obtain their renewed participation in the Italian Government by parliamentary means. It is not equally evident that they are prepared at present to resort to force to obtain their aims before the final withdrawal of Allied forces from Italy. This possibility cannot be excluded, however, and plans should now be made for action by the US in the event that Communist seizure of North Italy appears imminent. Soviet control of the Italian peninsula would jeopardize US interests in Europe and the Mediterranean, and the National interest would require that the greatest possible support be given the Italian Government in its efforts to maintain itself and eventually to regain the territory seized by the Communists.

Communist seizure of North Italy would probably be presented as purely domestic in character, without foreign aid or intervention. In the event that Yugoslavia seizes Italian border territory, the US should if possible treat this as a separate matter, bringing Yugoslav aggression to the attention of the United Nations and making it clear to the Italian people that we are acting in the interest of the Italian nation as a whole, regardless of the fact that Yugoslav aggression is against territory held by an illegal Communist regime.

13. It is believed that plans now formulated should apply to the period of ninety days within which US and UK forces must be withdrawn from Italy in accordance with the treaty. If action has not taken taken by the Communists in the near future, but appears likely to be taken after the final withdrawal of US forces, these plans should be reviewed not more than sixty days from now in order to determine the course of action to be followed by the US in the circumstances which may then exist.

RECOMMENDATIONS

In the event of Communist seizure of North Italy, the following plan of U.S. action is recommended:

a. The Italian Government should inform the Four Ambassadors (US, UK, USSR and French) in Rome (with the request that they notify the other signatories of the peace treaty) that it is no longer able to maintain effective authority in North Italy and that it consequently cannot accept responsibility for the execution of the terms of the peace treaty in that area.

b. The Italian Government should inform the U.S. and, so far as may be applicable, the British Government, that in the light of the situation which has arisen in North Italy it is no longer able to guarantee order along lines of communication across Italy from Leghorn for the support of US forces in Italy and in Trieste; that it must therefore leave it to the U.S. to take suitable measures to protect legitimate American interests in that area; and that in this connection it remains prepared to render to the United States Government, within the limits of its ability, all possible assistance in servicing US forces in Italy and in meeting US obligations to the UN with respect to the Free Territory of Trieste.

c. The US should immediately express concern publicly over the fact that disorder has broken out in Italy so soon after the entry into force of the peace treaty and should notify the Italian Government and the UN that in the light of this situation it has become necessary to suspend the withdrawal of US forces from Italian territory.

d. The US should inform the Italian Government that in view of the situation which has arisen it will require additional military facilities for the time being and arrangements should be made to that end.

e. The US should announce the suspension of aid to North Italy under the US relief program, at the same time making it clear that this aid will be continued for areas under the jurisdiction of the Italian Government.

f. If the Italian Government makes a request to the US for direct military assistance, our reply should be that we are not disposed to intervene with US armed force in what appears to be a civil conflict of an internal nature in Italy but that we will continue to recognize the Rome Government as the legitimate Government of Italy and will regard all of our existing undertakings with respect to aid to that Government as still in effect.

g. If, in the foregoing situation, Yugoslavia should make incursions into or seize Italian border territory, the US should vigorously take up this aggression against Italy with the appropriate body of the United Nations.

h. These recommendations are designed to apply only to the period between now and December 12 (the expiration date of the period during which we are entitled to have forces in Italy). They should be reviewed in the latter part of November, and revised to fit the circumstances which will prevail after December 12.

865.51/9–2547

Memorandum of Conversation, by the Assistant Secretary of State for Political Affairs (Armour)

SECRET [WASHINGTON,] September 25, 1947.

Participants: Ambassador Tarchiani
Mr. Armour, A–A
Mr. Dowling, SE

The Italian Ambassador said he had asked to see me to continue our conversation of some days ago [1] regarding Italy's present situation. He said that he had just received a telegram from De Gasperi, which he wanted to read to me, and which in substance said that the continued existence of a non-Communist government in Italy would be determined primarily by the assistance which Italy might receive during the next few months. De Gasperi seemed reasonably confident that the Communist-Socialist motion of no-confidence in the government would fail, and he was firmly disposed to resist Communist demands for their inclusion in the government. He (De Gasperi) did not believe that the Communists would succeed in any attempt to overthrow the government by violence so long as the government was able to maintain essential supplies, principally wheat and coal. Italy's current dollar resources, however, were down to approximately $2 million, while existing commitments totaled $6 million, and there was

---

[1] See p. 965.

no hope that the government could continue purchases in October without assistance.

In this connection, Tarchiani said he wanted to leave with me a copy of a telegram summarizing Vice Premier Einaudi's conversation in London with Messrs. Snyder and Clayton regarding interim aid,[2] and to urge upon the Department the importance of making available to Italy every possible amount of assistance. He said that in the existing situation every dollar would help, and he therefore hoped it would be possible to expedite the return of the Fortezza gold, payment of the balance of the suspense account, and settlement for the POW certificates.

I told the Ambassador we would certainly do what we could, and that I would immediately bring his suggestions to the attention of the Departmental officers concerned.

The Ambassador then said he wanted to leave with me a letter urging an increased IEFC allotment of grain for Italy,[3] adding that he appreciated the difficulties confronting us in this matter, but that if it became necessary to reduce the present low bread ration in Italy he did not believe the government could survive.[4]

[Enclosure—Memorandum]

Text of the telegram received from Premier De Gasperi by Ambassador Tarchiani:

"Vice President Einaudi and Menichella have presented in London to Mr. Snyder and Mr. Clayton a memorandum on the Italian financial situation pointing out that if within the next few weeks no extraordinary help in dollars will be granted to Italy the collapse of the Italian economy will be inevitable. Such immediate help cannot be found in loans from banking institutions due to the slowness of the procedure and the finalities of the aims of such institutions, which are mainly devoted to the reconstruction of industries. No concession whatsoever was obtained in London by the British Government on the question of the convertibility of sterlings. Einaudi has proposed to Mr. Snyder an advance on the amount of the grant-in-aid to be recovered at a later date out of other extraordinary appropriations to be decided or an advance of forty million dollars on the frozen pounds. Both proposals could be combined. Snyder pointed out difficulties, but

---

[2] See enclosure to this document.
[3] See footnote 2, p. 973.
[4] A typewritten, attached memorandum, without date or signature, reads: "Questions which could be examined with the War Department:—Immediate concession of the balance of the suspense account. —Speedy solution of the granting of the dollars for the scrips of the prisoners of war.—Consideration to the possibility of granting to Italy some dollar amounts against requisitions effected by the United States Armed Forces in Italy."

promised to examine this and other suggestions although mentioning necessity of Congress' decision for definitive solutions."

WASHINGTON, September 24, 1947.

865.24/9–1147 : Telegram

The Acting Secretary of State to the Embassy in Italy

TOP SECRET WASHINGTON, September 27, 1947—11 a. m.
US URGENT

1863. Army Survey Group (ASGI) under Col Bathurst [1] proceeding Italy Sept 27 to undertake thorough review reequipment program Ital Army and also to study all aspects possible desirability and practicability establishment US Military Mission Ital Govt. Decision send Group largely result consideration, in consultation with Dept, points urtel 2718 Sept 11. Mission has full support Gen Lee who discussed matter with Group yesterday. Col Bathurst will advise you his instructions and will undertake survey in closest consultation you and Emb staff. Army informing MA who will give you further details ASGI mission.

Re establishment US Mil Mission Italy, Dept has formulated no firm position but will appreciate your views desirability from political point of view after you have considered recommendations ASGI report.

LOVETT

[1] Col. Charles R. Bathurst, executive officer, Organization and Training Division, General Staff.

865.24/9–2947 : Telegram

The Ambassador in Italy (Dunn) to the Secretary of State

SECRET ROME, September 29, 1947—3 p. m.

2987. US Army in Italy desires to turn over direct to Italian Army sufficient surplus of Quartermaster, Signal Corps, Medical Corps, Transportation and Ordnance supplies to properly equip the force provided by Article 61 of the treaty as part of combat equipment included in Taff-Del Vecchio agreement of July 21, 1947. General Hyssong, central field commissioner, OFLC,[1] objects to such transfer, stating that Taff-Del Vecchio agreement comprises a specified list of actual combat equipment which did not include vehicles, clothing,

[1] Brig. Gen. Clyde Lloyd Hyssong.

medical supplies or communications equipment which, when surplus, should be turned over to army under Bonner-Corbino agreement of September 9, 1947 [*1946*]. His position is that transfer of this additional surplus under Taff-Del Vecchio agreement, which had no escalator clause, would reduce net return to US and that he cannot approve without instructions from Foreign Liquidation Commissioner.

Unfortunately MTOUSA Leghorn did not understand that Taff-Del Vecchio agreement was limited to arms and ammunition and have informed Italian Army and Cingolani,[2] Minister of Defense, that these other items would be included with result that De Gasperi has issued a protocol stating that Italian armed forces are authorized to receive these additional items direct from the US Army under the Taff-Del Vecchio agreement.

Total value at government cost of these additional items will be about 20 million dollars, which will reduce return on Taff-Del Vecchio agreement from 18.2 percent to about 15 percent. However, political and strategic factors at this time would appear greatly to outweigh this monetary sacrifice. For both political and economic reasons present government in no position to properly equip Italian Army. This fact has lowered effectiveness and morale of the force.

I, therefore, strongly urge that FLC, Washington, immediately instruct Hyssong to allow transfer under Taff-Del Vecchio agreement.

Repeated Paris for OFLC 384.

DUNN

---

[2] Mario Cingolani, Italian Minister of Defense in the fourth De Gasperi cabinet (until December 15, 1947).

865.24/9–2947 : Telegram

The Acting Secretary of State to the Embassy in Italy

SECRET   WASHINGTON, October 4, 1947—3 p. m.

1951. Ur 2987 Sept 29. In view Dept following three procedures possible effect transfer equipment Ital Army:

1. Amend two agreements as follows:
Such non-combat equipment and supplies as are required for equipment and maintenance Ital Armed Forces, and for which transfer to Itals provided Bonner-Corbino Agreement, may be transferred directly Ital Army upon declaration as surplus by US mil in accord transfer procedures provided Taff-Del Vecchio Agreement.

Upon the final computation of value of surplus property transferred under Bonner-Corbino Agreement in application escalator clause, to the value of the property transferred under that agreement will be added cost of additional property transferred under procedure Taff-Del Vecchio Agreement in accordance above paragraph.

2. Amend agreements to add to the total Ital payment due under Taff-Del Vecchio Agreement the value of the additional equipment and provide for transfer under Taff-Del Vecchio rather than Bonner-Corbino as latter agreement now provides.

3. Amend agreements to allow transfer under Taff-Del Vecchio procedure instead of Bonner-Corbino without requiring additional compensation from Itals for additional equipment under Taff-Del Vecchio and at same time allowing credit under escalator clause Bonner-Corbino.

We consider first procedure most desirable in that it would permit direct transfer equipment without substantial alteration existing agreements. Second course also acceptable. If third proposal adopted would necessitate statement by SecState to effect gratis transfer made in consideration substantial benefit received by US. We would be most reluctant pursue this course, particularly since necessity not apparent to us.

You are authorized negotiate necessary agreement to effect either first two proposals after consultation Hyssong. Final draft amendment shd be submitted Dept and Hyssong for approval prior signing. OFLC concurs.

(Sent Rome 1951 rpt Paris 3807 for Hyssong)

LOVETT

865.6131/9–1647

The Secretary of State to the Italian Ambassador (*Tarchiani*)

The Secretary of State presents his compliments to his Excellency the Ambassador of Italy and has the honor to acknowledge his notes of September 3 and September 16 in which an increase in grain allocations to Italy from the United States is requested and attention is called to the serious political and social consequences which might result from any reduction in rations in Italy. Specifically, the request is made for allocations of 220,000 tons a month. Reference is made in the note of September 3 to savings effected by reduction of consumption in July and August and to efforts to effect maximum collections of indigenous grain.

The United States Government regrets that it is unable to make allocations to Italy in the magnitude requested and thereby to remove uncertainty regarding adequate supplies to meet the present ration. Careful thought has been given to what the United States can make available to various countries for the entire crop-year. The export program during the first part of the year must not be so large that little or nothing would remain to be shipped in the winter and spring when the impact of this year's unprecedented deficit is expected to be most keenly felt. It is quite clear that no such quantity as 220,000 tons a month can be sustained for Italy and it would be unwise to lay plans regarding procurement and consumption levels with such an expectation in mind.

The successful progress of the Italian amassment has been watched with interest and gratification. However, the increase in consumption which is known to have occurred in July and probably also August, when controls on distribution are understood to have been in part relaxed, has been a matter of concern because of the vital necessity of conserving supplies to meet the difficult winter and spring period. This development is the more disquieting in view of the projection of Italy's grain position attached to the Ambassador's note of September 16 indicating that monthly consumption is expected to continue throughout the present semester at the increased rate of 400,000 tons reached in July. This is in strong contrast to reductions in rations which are taking place in other countries in recognition of the necessity of making adjustments to conserve supplies because of the great grain deficit known to exist. It is hoped that means are being found to reestablish effective controls of distribution so that the most careful use can be made of all available resources.

WASHINGTON, October 8, 1947.

865.24/10–947 : Telegram

The Ambassador in Italy (Dunn) to the Secretary of State

SECRET   ROME, October 9, 1947—midnight.

3159. Del Vecchio, Minister of Treasury, interviewed this morning and given letter proposing amendment to Bonner-Corbino and Taff-Del Vecchio agreements as in suggestion No. 1 in Deptel 1951 October 4. Although Del Vecchio said he would study matter nevertheless he made it quite clear that such procedure was entirely contrary to wording and spirit of Taff-Del Vecchio agreement which he says was final clean-up of all army surplus and that first sentence Paragraph A "U.S. Army equipment located in Italy" refers to any Army equipment of whatever nature to be turned over directly to Italian Army. When reminded that this sentence referred only to specific list of combat equipment Del Vecchio answered that no such list formed part of this agreement nor was it his understanding that such equipment was limited to arms and armament. He did not apparently recall that this list was not made integral part of agreement for political reasons.

We will advise as soon as reply to our letter received but it may be assumed that in view of Del Vecchio attitude we will have to fall back on suggestion No. 3 in Deptel 1951. In this event it is considered that you can substantiate a statement that gratis transfer is in consideration of benefits to the US inasmuch as Italian Army now has sole responsibility for defense of new eastern frontier, a task it could not perform without the proper equipment, and enabling it to assume internal and external security so that US Army may withdraw under treaty terms. The Italian Government cannot appropriate funds for such equipment in its present precarious financial situation. If transfer is made under Bonner-Corbino Agreement, a covering appropriation to Italian Army would have to be made and any such proposal at this time would undoubtedly precipitate another government crisis as the Left parties are united in opposing any additional funds for defense.

Sent Department, repeated Paris 393 for Hyssong OFLC.

DUNN

865.51/10–1047 : Telegram

The Chargé in the United Kingdom (Gallman) to the Secretary of State

SECRET   LONDON, October 10, 1947—noon.

US URGENT

5466. ReDeptel 4217 [*4207*], September 30, to London, repeated Rome 1884.[1] Fortezza[2] protocol signed on schedule 11 a. m. London time by Gallman for US, Bevin for UK and Italian Chargé B. Migone.[3]

Text follows that quoted Embstel 5353, October 3, repeated Rome 120, Paris 5361, October 4, repeated Paris 555, Rome 121, October 6 and Embstel 5391, October 7, repeated Paris 559, Rome 123. US copy being forwarded cover air despatch immediately.[4]

Sent Department 5466; repeated Paris 562; Rome 128.

GALLMAN

---

[1] Not printed.
[2] In telegram 1442, May 29, 1945, from Rome, not printed, Ambassador Kirk reported that the gold discovered by U.S. troops at Fortezza, valued at approximately $25 million, had been identified as a portion of the gold reserve of the Bank of Italy, apparently removed to northern Italy by the Fascist Republican government. (865.515/5–2945) In the memorandum by Ness of June 3 (*ante*, p. 913), the value of the gold was estimated at $28 million. For additional information, see Department of State *Bulletin*, October 19, 1947, p. 770.
[3] Bartolomeo Migone.
[4] None printed; for text of the Protocol, "Transfer to Italian Government of Gold Captured at Fortezza", see Department of State Treaties and Other International Acts Series (TIAS) No. 1658, or 61 Stat. (pt. 3) 3239.

865.00/10–1047 : Telegram

The Ambassador in Italy (Dunn) to the Secretary of State

SECRET   ROME, October 10, 1947—noon.
US URGENT

3168. Our analysis of results of votes of confidence on October 4 fortified by information we have since obtained in conversations and from press is summarized as follows:

1. De Gasperi's personal prestige was greatly enhanced more so than that of his party.

2. De Gasperi's leadership within his party was strengthened. (During debate on no confidence motions it is reported that Gronchi,[1] Demochristian, had approached Nitti proposing combination with him of "dissident" Christian Democrats to overthrow the government and presumably make use of Nitti's prestige for formation of new government with Gronchi in prominent role. Nitti did not take to this maneuver as his attitude in debate showed and even it is reported informed De Gasperi of it.)

3. The extremist Marxian Parties emerged not only proportionately weaker, in parliamentary terms, but also somewhat discredited in absolute terms vis-à-vis the public. Three motions were voted upon: the further to the left the origin of the motion the greater the majority for the government (see despatch 1701, October 8[2]). The total supporting votes remained virtually the same on all three counts while the votes against were (1) on the Nenni motion 178 with 63 abstentions; (2) on the Saragat motion 224 with 17 abstentions; and (3) on the Republican "order of the day" 236 with one abstention.

Immediately upon the completion of the vote on the Nenni motion Togliatti withdrew the Communist motion; undoubtedly he preferred not to risk a greater defeat of the Communist motion than that suffered by the Fusionist motion.

4. The course of the vote should now strengthen De Gasperi's bargaining position with the small moderate Leftist parties for admittance into the government to broaden its base (the Prime Minister in fact confirmed to me night before last that he planned to negotiate with these small parties after seeing results of Rome municipal elections October 12).

The most important result, however, of last week's test may not come to light for a time although the new Communist manifesto setting up the Belgrade information bureau may hasten realignments and momentous decisions. (In accompanying telegram 3145, October 9[2] Lombardo's program for Italian Socialism is amply reported. Present telegram should be examined jointly with that one.)

---

[1] Giovanni Gronchi, one of the founders of the *Partito Popolare* in 1919.
[2] Not printed.

In a meeting a few days ago with members of the Smith-Mundt Committee the Prime Minister, commenting on the present situation, averred that the next big undertaking on his program is the breaking up of the Fusionist Socialists; the time and the tactics must be adopted to the end that segment remaining in Communist camp be as small as possible. (Again it should be mentioned that Communist tactics from Belgrade may influence De Gasperi's and Lombardo's timing.) It is surely not entirely coincidence that in the present Rome municipal campaign (see mytel 3117, October 7 [3]) the Communists are directing their violence against Saragat Socialist meetings only.

The reconstitution of single Socialist party aside from the problem of size of Left-Wing group which would merge with Communists is also, however, beset by problems of personalities. Saragat has advantage deriving from having split first but both in his group and in the center and right of Nenni group there are personalities with individual followings who may be expected to contend for leadership of reunited party.

There seems to be a move within bureaucratic circles in favor of getting Lombardo into the government soon as possible; but Lombardo himself notwithstanding his talent would not greatly strengthen government until he can speak for a mass following.

Despite the brighter prospects in Italy now of reunited moderate Socialist mass party allied with social democracy of Demochristians much if not all of progress toward moderation in Italy may be lost by election time, if this alliance is identified this winter with bread riots. This serves to point up the tremendous importance of continued support by us of forces of moderation; without promise of our long-term support and with ever present possibility of timely Russian shipment of wheat into Italy this winter the Communist party's chances of gaining control of Italian Government through legal means would be immeasurably increased.

Sent Department 3168; repeated London 230; Paris 395; Moscow 160.

DUNN

---

[3] Not printed.

865.20/10–1047 : Telegram

The Ambassador in Italy (Dunn) to the Secretary of State

TOP SECRET ROME, October 10, 1947—midnight.

3185. Re Deptel 1863, Sept 27. Colonel Bathurst and his associates called on me and members of my staff October 8 and we had most useful exchange of views. In view of confusion which has arisen re aid to

Italian army, I was particularly glad to see how thoroughly AGSI [*ASGI?*] has gone into matter, and believe their trip will prove well worth while.

In our discussion, I told Colonel Bathurst that my comments would be restricted to political aspects of question, on assumption that General Jaynes' staff at MTOUSA had covered purely military aspects, on which I did not in any case feel competent to speak. I said that I considered it of utmost importance that we continue our efforts to assist Italy to establish and maintain a balanced army which would be capable of insuring both internal security and local defense of frontiers against guerrilla incursion or attack incident to an operation less than formal war. Colonel Bathurst agreed, and also agreed that the balanced force to which we refer should be as recommended by SAC and approved by CCS.

I also emphasized that Italy in its present state is not economically or politically able to provide required materials for itself, nor are the British able to assist. Colonel Bathurst pointed out that some of equipment considered necessary to establish balanced force is not available from US Army surpluses, and that legislation would in all probability be required to permit War Dept make such equipment available. He also noted difficulties of procurement in US at this time.

Re military mission, I said I consider such a mission highly undesirable from political viewpoint, in that its presence in Italy under present circumstances would, I believe, be source of embarrassment to and consequent weakening of present Govt. I added that my objections to military mission do not extend to possibility of assigning a few specialist officers to Military Attaché to instruct Italians in care and use of US equipment which we may make available to them.

In any case, any project for mission would have to have concurrence of Italian Govt; of course, if Italian Govt itself should unexpectedly ask for mission, situation would be materially changed. Colonel Bathurst said he believed that mission could be set up under President's emergency powers, but that when these expire, legislation (as contemplated in military mission bill now before Congress) would be required.

Colonel Bathurst and I agreed that immediate consideration should be given to inviting Italian officers to attend staff, technical and tactical schools in US, possibility in which Minister of Defense and Chief of Italian Army Staff have already expressed great interest. Colonel Bathurst felt, however, that legislation would be required to permit any significant number of Italian officers to attend our army schools in US.

We discussed together question of Congressional approval in three matters mentioned above, and I expressed view that it would be most undesirable at this time to initiate debate in Congress confined to our military policies in Italy. Such debate might well upset the trend toward stability which De Gasperi Govt is beginning to show and might well defeat the very purposes it was intended to fulfill. Of course, if general legislation, without specific reference to Italy, were to be introduced and debated in Congress, this objection need not apply.

Throughout the discussion I emphasized both that my views are based entirely on present political circumstances, and that any program of military aid must be considered as part of an overall program of aid, of which AUSA now forms the most important and most obvious part. I said I do not believe the situation in Italy today is now analogous to that in Greece or Turkey but that of course crucial period will come during the winter. If De Gasperi Govt is unable to get over hump of winter distress, we may well be faced with serious deterioration of Italian political climate, necessitating a complete revision of our plans and procedures. AGSI pointed out that considerable time must elapse between initiation of emergency military planning and its implementation; accordingly, we agreed that it is desirable for our planning staffs at Washington to begin now to study and formulate plans including active military assistance, should need arise in Italy next winter or spring.

Colonel Bathurst also asked my views on possible desirable revisions of the peace treaty. I said that I do not believe it necessary or desirable in view of economic situation to seek at this time modification of the treaty limitations on Italian ground forces, although an upward revision might later become necessary if, for example, trusteeship of any of the colonies is assigned to Italy or aggression from outside were threatened. As regards air force limitations, I expressed view that present ceiling of 200 fighter planes is inadequate for minimum requirements of air defense and support of army, a situation which is both intrinsically bad and which may well adversely affect the morale of the army and air force. Accordingly, I believe we should sponsor modification of treaty designed to permit Italy additional fighter aircraft and to remove completely limitations on training planes. Air force personnel ceilings would have to be revised upward appropriately, and the US would, as in the case of the army, have initially to provide material assistance.

DUNN

865.5018/10–1147

The Italian Ambassador (Tarchiani) to the Acting Secretary of State

No. 9313   WASHINGTON, October 11, 1947.

MY DEAR MR. LOVETT: I have received with deep concern the note of the Department dated October 8, 1947, regarding the grain allocations to Italy from the United States. I have particularly given full attention to what is stated in the note regarding the considerations of the Department as to the increase of consumption of grain which has occurred in Italy during the month of July and as to the fact that the table attached to my note of September 16, indicates a monthly consumption up to the present semester at a rate of 400,000 tons.

I deem it necessary therefore to clarify the situation of the needs for grain in Italy.

It is known that Italy, as well as other European countries, has suffered this year from a very poor season and as a consequence has grown less crops.

The import requirement for the consumption year of 1947–1948 had been estimated at 2,900,000 tons. On the other hand all possible sources of supply from abroad are becoming more and more limited: in fact it is now almost certain that Canada, as a result of a very low production, will be unable to supply the quantity of 100,000 tons as it was estimated in the Italian Government's plans. Supplies from Argentina are being received at a very low rate, and it is doubtful, owing to transportation difficulties, that the estimated amount of 500,000 tons will be provided. There are no other sources from which the Italian Government can hope to receive substantial shipments of cereals.

The allocations from the United States having been limited to 115,000 tons monthly, it has been necessary for Italy, in order to meet the rations required, to draw at a dangerous rate from the local sources which are rapidly running towards exhaustion.

Regarding the estimate of consumption of 400,000 tons of grain monthly during the current semester, it is necessary to remark that during the month of July there was in Italy an increase of cereal consumption due to the infractions of government regulations and to a rush movement of wheat from producing to consuming provinces, and it was feared that the same conditions would have prevailed during the immediate future months.

However, the prompt and strong action taken by the Government, through severe punishment of violators and through a widespread persuasive campaign had immediate results. Final returns of consumption during the month of August have shown that the situation is again under control and consumption has dropped to 382,000 tons. Provisional returns for the month of September indicate even better results, since consumption is estimated to be further lowered and reach 370,000 tons, which means not only a full compliance with rationing requirements, but also some savings in distribution losses.

As to the Department's remark concerning the contrast between Italy's consumption previsions and the reductions which are taking place in other countries, I must emphasize that Italy has preceded other countries in reducing the already extremely low rations, since she was forced to reduce the "pasta" ration by 50% as of December 1946 and has been unable ever since to restore it. Furthermore, the bread ration had to be modified in order to make the maximum possible use of coarse cereals. The bread ration now being distributed is composed of 200 grams of bread, containing from 15% to 20% coarse cereals, and of 35 grams of corn flour.

At the same time the hardships suffered by the Italian people should be fully measured, namely by appraising the meaning of cereals in the Italian food consumption. In fact, cereals represent from 60% to 70% of the Italian diet. Italy ranks foremost in cereal consuming countries, and the effects of a reduction in her cereal intake cannot be compared with those occurring in countries where diets are based mainly on foods other than cereals.

I have therefore the honor to call again your kind attention to the extreme serious situation developing in Italy.

I voice my confidence that further consideration will be given to Italy's need for cereals, with the hope that the food savings campaign so generously undertaken in the United States will make available larger supplies in the immediate future so that allocations to Italy be brought as far as possible nearer to 200,000 tons monthly.

Please accept [etc.] [1]   ALBERTO TARCHIANI

---

[1] No reply was made to this note. A memo by Leo I. Highby, International Resources Division, dated January 5, 1948, not printed, indicates that the note went first to IR, and was then borrowed by another division and not returned until December 30 by which time a formal reply would have been "awkward", and in any case there had been frequent consultations between officials of the Department and of the Italian Embassy on the problem. (FW 865.5018/10–1147)

865.51/10–2047

Memorandum of Conversation, by the Acting Secretary of State

[WASHINGTON,] October 20, 1947.

Participants: Ambassador Tarchiani
                Pietro Campilli, Chairman of the Italian
                      Inter-Ministerial Committee on Reconstruction
                Mr. Lovett, Acting Secretary
                Mr. Ness, OFD
                Mr. Dowling, SE

The Italian Ambassador called at his request this afternoon to present Mr. Campilli and to leave with me a memorandum giving figures on Italy's immediate financial needs which Mr. Campilli had brought from Rome.[1]

The Ambassador said that on the basis of the latest information which Mr. Campilli had received from Rome this morning by telephone Italy had some $9 million on hand with something over $10 million in obligations which had to be met immediately. He added that the memo would show Italy's needs to December 31 amounted to some $180 million. Mr. Campilli explained that this sum represents not only supplies needed for the rest of the year but also supplies which the Italian Government must purchase within the very near future for consumption in January and February. He pointed out that a firm commitment must be made by November 5 for the small amounts of grain available to Italy from Turkey, Syria and Argentina; otherwise this grain would be sold to other countries or would be available to Italy only at greatly increased prices. He said too that additional coal supplies were needed because of a shortage in hydroelectric power in Italy.

I told the Ambassador and Mr. Campilli that I would ask Mr. Ness to look over these figures and that I would also examine them personally. The Ambassador thanked me and said that he knew we realized the extent of Italy's needs but he wished to urge that we do everything possible to obtain funds at once for these immediate needs.

---

[1] *Infra.*

865.51/10–2047

The Italian Embassy to the Department of State

No. 9535

Memorandum

In the course of the last few months, the Italian Government have several times called the attention of the United States Government to the rapid deterioration which was and is taking place in the Italian situation with regard to dollar exchange and to vital supplies.

The Italian Government have participated wholeheartedly in the Conference for European Economic Co-operation which has met in Paris this summer, and which following the lead given by the Secretary of State of the United States in his Harvard speech in June last, has made every effort to elaborate a constructive plan for global European recovery over the next four years. Equally an Italian Delegation is now taking part in the Washington conversations on the same matter. The Italian Government and people fully recognize that the

United States can extend their support to each European country on the scale and for the time which will be necessary only if such support is part of a series of constructive measures, beginning with national and intra-European self-help. Also Italy is vitally interested in the re-establishment of the economic health of her European neighbours, which for deep-seated reasons of economic history and structure have been in the past and must be in the future amongst her principal customers and suppliers.

The Italian Government and people, which through great efforts had already achieved some measure of success in the work of economic and financial reconstruction, had hoped that the generous aid already extended to Italy by the U.S. in 1947 would have been sufficient to meet the essential requirements of the Italian economy until such time as the new plan of American aid to European reconstruction would come into force.

An accurate survey which has been again made by the Italian Government clearly shows that even with the mobilization of all possible dollar credits standing in favor of Italy, like balance of suspense account, redemption of P.O.W. scrips, a very serious gap is developing at present in relation to dollar availabilities of the Italian Government. In fact for reasons which are well known to the United States Government and in spite of the severe measures already taken by the Italian Government for reducing its purchases abroad, Italy's meager resources in dollar exchange and in basic imported commodities are now exhausted to all practical effects.

According to the last data (October 8th) the Italian Exchange Office had in hand and with "agent banks" less than $9.000.000 corresponding roughly to a few days of the country's imports to be paid for in dollars.

It is therefore imperative for the Italian Government to find ways and means in order to face its dollar requirements in the period between now and the coming into force of the Marshall plan.

The requirements and the receipts in the period between October 1st, 1947 and March 31st, 1948 are stated in a letter of the Italian Technical Delegation (copy attached under #1 [1]), which has been handed to the Chief of the Economic Development Division of the Department of State, entrusted with the study of this matter.

As shown in said document, the difference between requirements and receipts for the period mentioned is in the order of U.S. $334.000.000. This figure has been arrived at, after taking into full consideration the necessity of reducing the import requirements to the minimum possible extent.

---

[1] Not found in Department of State files.

In effect the figure is based upon estimates of grain requirements which do not take into account the fact that after March 1948, the remaining requirements would represent almost 100% of the rations; this would exceed by far practical possibilities. Also the above figure does not include U.S. $41.000.000 of general commodities which would be in themselves extremely useful for the working of the Italian economic machinery on the present low level. Neither does it include the re-establishment of a minimum operating reserve of U.S. $50.000.000, which appears necessary in view of the exhaustion of the Italian Government's exchange reserves, which have been absorbed in part by the lack of external financing during the first weeks of October.

If the President of the United States convenes Congress to a special session for the examination of this problem, the Italian Government will be anxious to submit all the additional data which may be required. However, as the procedure involved for such examination would certainly take some time, and the above said needs are indeferrable, the Italian Government consider it their duty to stress the necessity of obtaining the immediate availability of some funds in order to avoid a breaking down of the economic and social structure in Italy.

A break-down of the global figure per months as shown in Table 5 of Attachment 1, shows that the indeferrable needs between now and the end of December 1947 amount to $182.000.000. This is due to the fact that in these months the Italian Government must not only provide the funds to meet engagements already incurred into and make the purchases which are immediately necessary, but must also place the orders and open the credits for the arrival in the first months of 1948. If this is not done in time, it may be impossible to obtain the necessary goods or a much higher price will have to be paid for them.

The Italian Government venture to ask the American Government if they consider practicable that the appropriate Italian Authorities should apply to the following United States Agencies, who may already have funds at their disposal:

a) The purchase of coal, POL and a part of industrial materials could perhaps be financed by the Import-Export Bank over and above the credits to Italian industries now being perfected. As such purchases would be made to maintain the level of industrial production and therefore of exports from Italy, it would appear that a request from the Italian Government for such a credit would fall within the Bank's field of operations.

b) The Italian Government could perhaps also apply to the Commodity Credit Corporation for obtaining funds for the purchase of grains and other agricultural products in the United States of America. As such operations would fall within the sphere of action of the Corporation, no legal obstacles seem to stand in the way.

c) There remains a third category of expenses, i.e. purchases of grains in other countries than the United States, as well as the payment of freight on some purchases in the United States. For this third category of expenses, the Italian Government strongly appeals to the United States Government for reconsideration of the problem of the granting to Italy of the dollars corresponding to the requisitions effected by the United States Army in Italy. Should this not appear as a sufficient or workable solution, the Italian Government venture to suggest that recourse be made to the Stabilization Fund of the United States Treasury.

A part of the funds needed could also be obtained if ways and means were found to mobilize, in agreement with the British Government, the sterling balances owned by and gradually accruing to the Italian Government.

WASHINGTON, October 20th, 1947.

811.516 Export-Import Bank/10–2447

The Acting Chairman of the Export-Import Bank (Gaston) to the Secretary of State

WASHINGTON, October 24, 1947.

MY DEAR MR. SECRETARY: I think you may be interested in the enclosed release telling of the Bank's action on credits to Italy. It is our belief that these individual credits will have a substantial effect in promoting the revival of Italian industry.

Yours very truly,   HERBERT E. GASTON

[Enclosure]

Press Release Issued by the Export-Import Bank, October 23, 1947

The Board of Directors of the Export-Import Bank today approved credits in the amount of $36,500,000 to Italian industries through Istituto Mobiliare Italiano, thus bringing to $97,300,000 the aggregate of credits approved under an earmark of $100 million made in January for the purpose of reactivating Italian industry and foreign trade.

The credits granted today are in two groups, as follows:

1. Credits in favor of Istituto Mobiliare Italiano for the account of the leading Italian iron and steel mills in the following amounts:

a) $7.5 million for the account of Ilva, Alti Forni e Acciaierie d'Italia, Societa per Azioni;

b) $3.0 million for the account of "Terni", Societa per L'Industria e L'Elettricita;

c) $1.0 million for the account of Dalmine, Societa per Azioni;

d) $1.0 million for the account of Societa Italiana Acciaierie Cornigliano;

e) $2.0 million for the account of Acciaierie e Ferriere Lombarde Falck, Societa per Azioni.

2. Credits in favor of Istituto Mobiliare Italiano, aggregating $22 million, for the account of small industrial concerns within the four industrial sectors eligible for financing:

a) $4 million for small chemical concerns;
b) $2 million for small rubber concerns;
c) $6 million for small electro-mechanical concerns;
d) $10 million for small metallurgical and mechanical concerns.

Credits approved earlier under the January 1947 earmark include:

a) $23 million for the account of the Fiat automobile and machine works, Montecatini chemical and mining industries, and Pirelli rubber and cable manufacturers—August 4, 1947; [1]
b) $5.8 million for four leading Italian shipyards—October 1, 1947;
c) $32 million for 60 medium-sized metallurgical, electrical, chemical and rubber firms—October 16, 1947.

The steel mill credits approved today are designed to enable the Italian steel mills to purchase solid and liquid fuels and certain amounts of equipment in the United States with a view to sustaining and increasing their production of steel to meet urgent internal Italian requirements and to supply materials to other Italian concerns engaged in manufacturing for foreign markets. Italy had built before the war an iron and steel industry which took care of a large part of its needs. Capacity was reduced by war damage and removals, but there has been a notable recovery. The five steel mills benefiting from today's credits should be able to produce an aggregate of well over 1,000,000 tons of steel in the coming year.

The credits for the small industrial concerns supplement the $32 million previously approved by the Board for the account of 60 medium-sized industrial concerns.

In Italy, as in several other European countries, medium and small-sized industrial concerns play a very large role in the economy of the country as well as in its foreign trade. They range in size from a labor force of as few as 10 workers to 250 workers. Before the war, and especially under the Fascist regime, there was an increasing tendency toward monopoly, with the small industrialists either being absorbed or squeezed out of business. With the liberation of Italy the small industrialist is making successful efforts at a comeback. The credits approved by the Board today are designed to furnish the small indus-

---

[1] See memorandum by Mr. Jerome Stenger, July 29, p. 951.

trialist of Italy with essential raw materials and equipment to enable him to resume the place he formerly occupied in the Italian economy and in foreign trade.

Following the decision to earmark $100 million the Bank,[2] at the request of the Italian Government, early in May sent two representatives to Italy for exploratory discussions and to survey industrial conditions.[3] In July the Board of Directors reviewed the findings of its representatives and informed the Italian Ambassador of its readiness to receive and consider separate credit applications. The Bank started receiving applications in July.

The credits granted have been of varying maturities and conditions in accordance with the merits of each application, the ability of the applicant to earn foreign exchange readily convertible into dollars, and the general economic welfare of Italy. Though the credits are for specific purposes and for given industrial concerns, the lines of credit, for the sake of convenience and expediency, have been established in favor of the Istituto Mobiliare Italiano. This is an Italian public credit institution engaged in medium-term industrial financing, which will act both as banker and as trustee. The credits granted by the Bank to named industries will permit these industries to establish definite production and export programs free from uncertainties which have had a general restraining effect on Italian recovery.

---

[2] See minutes of the 50th Meeting of the National Advisory Council, January 13, p. 859.

[3] See telegram 1402, June 4, from Rome, p. 917.

811.2365/11–1247

The Ambassador in Italy (Dunn) to the Secretary of State

SECRET   ROME, November 12, 1947.
No. 1855

Subject: Transmitting Text of Note to Foreign Ministry Regarding Liquidation of Residual Military Matters in Italy.

SIR: With reference to my telegram no. 3637 of November 12, 1947,[1] I have the honor to enclose herewith a copy of a note which I handed to the Secretary General of the Italian Ministry of Foreign Affairs[2]

---

[1] Not printed; in it Dunn reported having handed the note here printed to the Secretary General of the Foreign Ministry who said that the proposal appeared to be satisfactory (811.2365/11–1247).

Rome's despatch 1996 of December 9, not printed, forwarded an English translation of Sforza's note No. 2032 of December 5 which constituted acceptance of the American proposal (811.2365/12–947).

[2] Francesco Fransoni.

on November 11, 1947 relating to liquidation of residual military matters in Italy after December 15, 1947, in accordance with instructions in the Department's telegram no. 2287, of November 5, 1947.

I would suggest that the contents of this note be reclassified from "Secret" to "Restricted".

Respectfully yours,

For the Ambassador:
J. WESLEY JONES
First Secretary of Embassy

[Enclosure]

The American Ambassador (Dunn) to the Italian Minister for Foreign Affairs (Sforza)

F.O. No. 590   ROME, November 11, 1947.

EXCELLENCY: Acting on the instructions of my government, I have the honor to refer to the withdrawal from Italy of United States military forces, which is now in progress and which, as contemplated in our exchange of notes dated September 3, 1947, is to be completed on or before December 15, 1947.

After the latter date there will inevitably remain a few residual matters relating to the former United States military establishment in Italy. I am to inform you that these matters will be liquidated as quickly as possible after December 15 by the Office of the United States Military Attaché, to which office it will be necessary temporarily to attach certain additional military and civilian personnel and facilities.

As soon as possible, the names of these additional personnel will be communicated to the Ministry of Foreign Affairs. I trust that they will be accorded the usual immunities and privileges ordinarily extended to members of the Embassy staff, and that they will receive such assistance from appropriate Italian authorities as may be necessary.

In this connection, I would draw to your Excellency's attention that limitations of space within the buildings now occupied by the Embassy preclude that the temporary additional staff contemplated above be provided offices therein. As your Excellency is perhaps aware, negotiations have been in progress through a representative of the Ministry of Foreign Affairs to provide suitable office and dormitory space in the Foro Italico, in consideration of an appropriate rental, I shall be grateful if the Ministry of Foreign Affairs can use its good offices to the end that these negotiations are speedily concluded to the mutual satisfaction of those concerned.

Accept, Excellency, the renewed assurances of my high esteem.

[JAMES C. DUNN]

AGREEMENTS BETWEEN THE UNITED STATES AND ITALY

[For a reference to the text of the Treaty of Peace with Italy, see page 524, and for references to the texts of other agreements, see pages 920, 931, 956, 964, and 987.]

Editorial Note

Documentation on further developments with regard to Italy at the end of 1947 was not available in time to appear in this volume. This documentation is scheduled for inclusion in a subsequent volume of the series.

NETHERLANDS

AGREEMENT BETWEEN THE UNITED STATES AND THE NETHERLANDS SUPPLEMENTARY TO THE GENERAL AGREEMENT ON TARIFFS AND TRADE

[For text of Agreement and Accompanying Letters rendering inoperative the Agreement of December 20, 1935, and supplementing the General Agreement on Tariffs and Trade of October 30, 1947, signed at Geneva, October 30, 1947, see Department of State Treaties and Other International Act Series (TIAS) No. 1705.]

AGREEMENT BETWEEN THE UNITED STATES AND THE NETHERLANDS RESPECTING MUTUAL AID SETTLEMENT

[For text of Agreement, signed at Washington, May 28, 1947, see Department of State Treaties and Other International Acts Series (TIAS) No. 1750.]

AGREEMENT BETWEEN THE UNITED STATES AND THE NETHERLANDS RELATING TO AMERICAN DEAD IN WORLD WAR II

[For text of Agreement, effected by an exchange of notes signed at The Hague, April 11, 1947, see Department of State Treaties and Other International Acts Series (TIAS) No. 1777.]

1002

NORWAY

ATTITUDE OF THE UNITED STATES REGARDING REPORTED DEMANDS BY THE SOVIET UNION ON NORWAY WITH RESPECT TO SPITSBERGEN AND BEAR ISLAND [1]

857.014/12–1146 : Telegram

The Chargé in Norway (Huston) to the Secretary of State

SECRET   OSLO, December 11, 1946—5 p. m.

724. Foreign Minister Lange informed me today he had two talks with Molotov [2] in New York recently (Embtel 716 December 5 [3]) during which Molotov pressed for early negotiations regarding Spitzbergen and Bear Island on basis of exchange notes of January 1945 (despatch 158 July 26, 1945 [3]). Lange indicated his willingness to proceed with negotiations since his government considers it cannot disregard commitment made by a previous government in 1944 and 1945, but declared he could not actually enter into such negotiations before consultation with his government and the Storting.

Lange says he maintained position that (*a*) Norway considers itself bound by 1920 treaty, (*b*) Norway cannot enter into abrogation of treaty except in consultation with other signatories, (*c*) any agreement regarding common defense is subject to approval by Security Council and (*d*) entire procedure must be governed by provision of UN charter notably article 43.

This question has not been considered by government nor discussed in Storting since Foreign Minister's return from New York although Foreign Affairs Committee has been informed that early consideration in secret session will be necessary in order "to determine line to be taken". As present Storting ends its work December 14 question will not receive parliamentary attention until after new Storting is convened January 11. While Lange believes proposal for negotiations must be kept secret during government and Storting consultations, he does not wish to maintain secrecy indefinitely and believes that Nor-

---

[1] For previous documentation on this subject, see *Foreign Relations*, 1945, vol. v, pp. 91 ff. For the negotiation of the Treaty relating to Spitsbergen between the United States and other powers, signed at Paris on February 9, 1920, and subsequent questions concerned with it, see *ibid.*, 1920, vol. I, pp. 73–87, with text of the treaty at p. 78; 1924, vol. I, pp. 1–6; and 1925, vol. I, pp. 201–209.

[2] Vyacheslav Mikhailovich Molotov, Minister for Foreign Affairs of the Soviet Union.

[3] Not printed.

way should not actually engage in negotiations "without letting Norwegian people know what we are talking about". He had hoped, he says, that the Spitzbergen question could be allowed to "sleep indefinitely" but he is now convinced that early negotiations cannot be avoided and may take place toward end of January or beginning of February.

Lange endeavored see Secretary Byrnes just prior his departure from New York but as this was not possible he had prepared memorandum regarding his talks with Molotov and given it to Ambassador Morgenstierne with instructions to inform Secretary fully in Washington at earliest opportunity. He has so far heard nothing on subject from Morgenstierne and hopes that, if he has not already done so, he will be able to see Mr. Byrnes at early date for his [*this*] purpose.

Sent Dept 724; repeated Moscow 26.

HUSTON

861.24557H/12–2346

Memorandum by the Director of the Office of European Affairs (Matthews) to the Secretary of State

[WASHINGTON,] December 23, 1946.

MR. SECRETARY: Norwegian Ambassador Morgenstierne is coming to see you at 10 o'clock this morning to inform you, on instructions from Norwegian Foreign Minister Lange, of the present status of Soviet-Norwegian conversations on the revision of the 1920 multilateral treaty regarding the status of Spitsbergen (which includes Bear Island and may be referred to by the Ambassador under its Norwegian name Svalbard).

There is attached a telegram dated 11 December from our Embassy in Oslo on this subject.[1]

We have learned from Mr. Morgenstierne that the Soviets have proposed bilateral Soviet-Norwegian negotiations looking to the abrogation of the 1920 Treaty and the subsequent negotiation of a new multilateral treaty. The Soviets propose that such 1920 signatories as Italy and Japan, and possibly others, be dropped from the new multilateral negotiations when they take place, and that Finland be included.

So far as we can gather, the fundamental points in the Soviet proposals to Norway are: (1) Elimination of those clauses of the 1920 Treaty which demilitarized Spitsbergen; (2) Joint Soviet-Norwegian defense installations in Spitsbergen (which, by the way, is only something over 500 miles from the northeast coast of Greenland); (3) Special Soviet economic privileges with respect to fishing and hunting

---

[1] See *supra.*

rights and the exploitation of the Spitsbergen coal mines which produce roughly 700,000 tons of coal a year and are the sole source of coal within Norwegian territory; (4) The new Treaty to be within the framework of the Charter and to take the form of a regional defense agreement under Article 43 of the Charter.[2]

For your general information, the 1920 Treaty was the culmination of many years of international negotiation over the sovereignty of Spitsbergen (in which the US had economic interest due to American ownership of a coal mine there). Previously, Spitsbergen had been generally considered *terra nullius*—the 1920 Treaty gave the sovereignty to Norway under the conditions laid down in the Treaty.

The conversations with Norway looking to special Russian privileges in Spitsbergen were initiated by Mr. Molotov in the autumn of 1944 and therefore antedated by some months any US initiative for long-term overseas bases with the exception of the 1940 destroyer-base arrangements with the United Kingdom.[3]

The Joint Chiefs of Staff about a year ago indicated that the US had no special military interest in Spitsbergen [4] but I understand that the problem is to be re-studied in the light of our recent Iceland Agreement [5] and the proposal which you recently made to the Foreign Minister of Denmark [6] with regard to Greenland.

My suggestion would be that we refrain at this time from commenting on what Mr. Morgenstierne may communicate to you but that we make it clear to him that any Norwegian-Soviet negotiations regarding Spitsbergen should, of course, take into account the position of the US as a signatory of the 1920 Treaty.

The Soviet Union has ratified the 1920 Treaty.[7]

H. FREEMAN MATTHEWS

[2] In his conversation with the Secretary, Ambassador Morgenstierne did discuss the subjects here indicated. He told about the two talks between the Norwegian Foreign Minister Halvard M. Lange and Foreign Minister Molotov at the New York sessions of the General Assembly of the United Nations in November. Lange had informed Molotov that he would have to confer with his government and parliament on the proposals, and that no abrogation of the 1920 treaty could occur without the full consent of the signatories. The Department informed the Embassy in Norway of Morgenstierne's visit in telegram 7 to Oslo, January 6, 1947, noon, not printed (861.24557H/1–647).

[3] *Foreign Relations*, 1940, vol. III, pp. 49–77.

[4] For a more precise expression of the views of the Joint Chiefs of Staff with regard to Spitsbergen, see *Foreign Relations*, 1945, vol. V, pp. 96–97.

[5] For the text of this agreement, "Termination of Defense Agreement July 1, 1941 and Provision for Interim Use of Keflavik Airport", effected by exchange of notes signed at Reykjavik, October 7, 1946, see Department of State Treaties and Other International Acts Series (TIAS) No. 1566, or 61 Stat. (pt. 3) 2426.

[6] See footnote 3, p. 657.

[7] With respect to a note from the Soviet Government of February 16, 1924, to the Norwegian Government wherein it was stated that "from now on the Government of the Union recognizes the sovereignty of Norway over Spitzbergen, including Bear Island, and therefore will not hereafter make any objection with respect to the Spitzbergen Treaty of February 9, 1920," see the note from the Norwegian Minister to the Secretary of State of March 20, 1924, in *Foreign Relations*, 1924, vol. I, p. 1. *De jure* adherence to the treaty by the Soviet Union came by the decree of February 27, 1935, and entered into force on May 7, 1935.

861.24557H/1–1047 : Telegram

The Ambassador in Norway (Bay) to the Secretary of State

OSLO, January 10, 1947.

14. Foreign Office has issued following statement published in afternoon press concerning alleged Soviet approach to Norwegian Government regarding military bases in Svalbard (Spitsbergen):

"In autumn 1944 Government of Soviet Union approached Norwegian Government which was in London on question of revision of Spitzbergen treaty. Soviet Union has particular interests at Spitzbergen and treaty came into existence without participation of Soviet Government. In fall 1944 and spring 1945, subject was taken up for preliminary discussion between two governments. During negotiations both parties realized that an alteration of Spitzbergen treaty could not take place without approval of signatory powers (except signatory powers who fought with Germans against Allies) and it was also agreed that final solution could not be reached until Norwegian Government returned to Norway and Storting again was functioning. Committee of Foreign and Constitutional Affairs and Storting have been informed regarding negotiations which have taken place. With consent of Soviet Government principal Allied nations, US and Great Britain, and later France, also have been informed."

BAY

861.24557H/1–1147 : Telegram

The Ambassador in Norway (Bay) to the Secretary of State

SECRET   OSLO, January 11, 1947—6 p. m.
US URGENT

18. Embtel 14, Jan 10. Foreign Minister Lange received me this afternoon and told me Norwegian Govt was not responsible for news leak in London regarding Soviet proposals for establishment of military bases in Svalbard. British Ambassador [1] had, he said, informed him that he had received assurances by telephone from Foreign Office, London, that reports had not come from British official sources adding suggestion may have originated in Norwegian circles, London.[2] Lange remarked smilingly to me that it was possible to imagine disclosure at present time might seem good idea in British quarters, allowing inference he felt British circles at least as suspect as Norwegian.

In course of hour's discussion Foreign Minister reviewed developments since 1944, including presentation by Norwegians of draft joint

[1] Sir Laurence Collier.
[2] Responsibility for the leak in newspapers was admitted by the London correspondent of the Oslo *Arbeiderbladet*, who informed the (London) *Times*.

declaration (despatch 158, July 26, 1945 [3]) to which Russians have never replied and repeated previous assertions of his declared position that (*a*) Norway is bound by 1920 treaty; (*b*) abrogation or modification thereof can be effected only in consultation with other signatories; (*c*) any mutual defense arrangement must be elaborated within framework of UN and have approval Security Council; and (*d*) negotiations can be undertaken only after consultations with Norwegian Govt and Storting.

When I asked him extent to which he felt bound by 1944–45 Commitment, Lange said that he obviously could not ignore commitment made by previous Govt, altho terms of proposed declaration could not be considered binding, as it had never been accepted by Soviet Govt. He reminded me that initial discussions occurred in war period, when Russians were occupying northern part of country and London Govt felt it had at least to accede to Soviet request that Norway agree to need of abrogation or modification of treaty. At that time, he emphasized, Soviet Govt was making outright claim to Bear Island and making condominium [*sic*] over Svalbard.

Lange expressed belief that other signatories would not agree to abrogation of 1920 treaty or modifications proposed by Russians. He also mentioned that Norwegian people would be greatly opposed to granting Russia special economic rights in Svalbard, particularly as Spitzbergen is Norway's only domestic source of coal.

Foreign Minister seemed rather fatalistic regarding future developments, feeling that Norway is in stronger position today than when original commitment was made in 1944; and that particularly now that militarization projects have recently been further discountenanced by UN adoption of disarmament resolution,[4] Norway will be rescued from any serious effects of Russian designs by double check of other signatories to treaty and of second [*Security?*] council. He gave no clue to any indications he may have received regarding Soviet reaction to news leak. He evidently believed the Soviet Govt hoped that regardless of results of consultation with other signatories Norway could be induced to declare its agreement with Soviet view that 1920 treaty should be abrogated and new arrangements made.

Most Norwegians, including many high officials, seem genuinely surprised at news of Soviet proposals regarding Svalbard and preliminary reaction is marked by grave concern, if not by shock. Press

---

[3] Not printed.
[4] A resolution on Principles governing General Regulation and Reduction of Armaments was adopted unanimously by the General Assembly at its 63d plenary meeting on December 14, 1946. For text, see *Yearbook of the United Nations 1946–47*, p. 142, and for documentation on this subject, see *Foreign Relations*, 1946, vol. I, pp. 712 ff.

has devoted considerable space to yesterday's announcements, together with pictures, historical sketches and other background; but more studied editorial comment will probably appear during next few days.

Sent Dept as 18; repeated London as 2; Moscow as 2.

BAY

861.24557H/1–1647 : Telegram

The Ambassador in the Soviet Union (Smith) to the Secretary of State

Moscow, January 16, 1947.

100. Translation follows Tass item published Soviet press January 15.

"Question of Spitzbergen (Svalbard Archipelago):

Statements have appeared in recent days in Norwegian press as well as in press of certain other foreign states concerning negotiations which have taken place between Soviet and Norwegian Governments regarding Spitzbergen (Svalbard Archipelago). Authoritative Soviet circles [1] and informed Tass as follows concerning these negotiations:

At end 1944 and beginning 1945 negotiations took place between Soviet and Norwegian Governments concerning Spitzbergen Islands, Soviet side having raised question of necessity for revision of treaty on Spitzbergen concluded February 9, 1920 in Paris.

This treaty, which introduced radical change in status of Spitzbergen Islands which had previously been considered no man's land whereas Bear Island included in Spitzbergen Archipelago group was actually Russian island, was signed without knowledge of Soviet Union and without its participation. Moreover as states which had fought against Allied powers were among signatories of this treaty this treaty cannot preserve its validity.

This treaty did not take into consideration USSR security interests in north as well as important economic interests of Soviet Union. As regards question of security of USSR, as Second World War particularly showed, Spitzbergen Islands, where lies western exit to ocean, have in this connection exceptionally important significance for Soviet Union in north. In economic sense significance of Spitzbergen Archipelago to Soviet Union is apparent from fact that before Second World War northern regions of USSR and Soviet fleet in north were supplied with coal acquired by Soviet organizations on Spitzbergen Island in approximate amount of 400,000 tons annually as compared with general coal output for Spitzbergen Island of 600,000 to 650,000 tons.

During Soviet Norwegian negotiations mentioned understanding was reached concerning necessity for joint defense of Spitzbergen Islands. It was also envisaged that consultation be achieved with per-

---

[1] Apparent omission.

tinent Allied governments concerning revision of 1920 treaty. But negotiations were not concluded.

In November 1946 during General Assembly session in New York exchange of views in spirit of preceding negotiations took place on this question between USSR Foreign Minister V. M. Molotov and Norwegian Foreign Minister Lange.["]

Sent Department as 100, repeated Oslo as 1, London as 12.

SMITH

861.24557H/1–1747 : Telegram

The Ambassador in Norway (Bay) to the Secretary of State

US URGENT   OSLO, January 17, 1947.

31. Following is abbreviated translation of Norwegian Foreign Office communiqué on Spitzbergen published here this morning:

"Contrary to will of Norwegian Government there appeared in world press during last few days reports of certain discussions which took place during war concerning Spitzbergen, Spitzbergen Archipelago.

Since these discussions were confidential Norwegian Government hitherto has considered itself unable report on them officially. However, because of nature of afore-mentioned newspaper reports Foreign Office feels it necessary issue following statement:

In fall 1944 Soviet Government broached to Norwegian Government, which was then in London, question of revision of Spitzbergen treaty of 1920. It pointed out that treaty was concluded without participation of Soviet Union and that it did not satisfactorily provide for either Soviet Union's security or its other interests. Treaty was signed by two countries which fought on Germany's side against Allies, namely, Italy and Japan.

War had disclosed importance of protecting supply routes over Arctic Sea and Soviet Union, therefore, wished to discuss, together with economic questions, question of joint measures concerning security of these areas. Soviet Union could not agree that treaty continued to remain in force.

Soviet Government stated it intended take question of revision up officially in regular manner but it felt obligated first to notify Norway which had sovereignty over islands. It was necessary to settle in entirely just fashion these questions which involved Norway's and Soviet Union's common defense interests as well as their economic interests. Regarding economic interests it was stated Norway would suffer no loss.

Norwegian Government in reply stated it was desirous of reaching solution which could contribute to strengthening still further good relations which had always existed between Norway and Soviet Union and which war had deepened. It was pointed out further that Norway had met with understanding declaration of Soviet Government, after

Spitzbergen treaty was signed in 1920, that it could in no way recognize as legally binding any solution of Spitzbergen question which was put into effect without Soviet Union's participation. It was recalled further that not until Soviet Union had in its note of February 16, 1924 [1] announced it recognized Norway's sovereignty over Svalbard, including Bear Island, and therefore it would take no future exceptions to Spitzbergen treaty and organization of mines, that Norwegian Government asked Storting on February 22, 1924 to approve treaty so it could be ratified by Norway. In 1935 Soviet Union adhered to treaty without reservations.

It was clear to Norwegian Government that powerful political interests were involved. In defense of this region Norwegian and Allied ships were regularly traversing these waters and suffering heavy losses. Norwegian Government stated its understanding of viewpoint that war had put situation in new light.

However, under international law, defense dispositions could not be taken until treaty was revised. Article 9 in treaty binds Norway not to establish or permit establishment of naval bases or to build any fortifications in area which treaty covers and which must never be used for belligerent purposes. Norwegian Government stated, therefore, its belief, which it assumes other Allied powers which were parties to Spitzbergen treaty share, that article 9 either should be dropped or be replaced by new article which would permit military utilization of islands as regional link in universal security organization.

Norwegian Government declared itself willing to consider, together with Soviet Government, possibilities of agreement between Norway and Soviet Union on military utilization of islands. After further discussions between Soviet Foreign Minister and Norwegian Ambassador in Moscow [2] Norwegian Government, in April 1945, stated it was willing to sign provisional joint declaration on matter. This would state, among other things, that Norwegian and Soviet Governments desired, with full maintenance of Norway's sovereignty over Spitzbergen, to bring about joint arrangement for defense of islands which would serve to promote security of two countries and which could become link in development of international security organization.

Qualification was made that this arrangement should not come into effect until it received approval of American, British, Danish, French, Dutch and Swedish Governments. Norwegian Government also made reservation that arrangement must be accepted by Storting.

During discussions Norwegian Government maintained that for constitutional reasons it could not consider arrangement which might result in changing sovereignty of islands and Spitzbergen treaty could be abrogated only in accordance with international law. During provisional negotiations it was determined that two governments were agreed that any change in or abrogation of Spitzbergen treaty could take place only with consent of other signatory powers.

No joint declaration was signed. Great Britain and United States have been kept informed by Norway, with knowledge of Soviet Union, of negotiations between two countries and have given no expression of any reaction in connection with case.

---

[1] See footnote 7, p. 1005.
[2] Rolf Otto Andvord. In 1947 he was Secretary General of the Norwegian Foreign Office.

After end of war there were no negotiations of any kind between two countries on Spitzbergen question until Foreign Ministers of Norway and Soviet Union conferred on matter in Paris in August 1946 and in New York in November 1946. After this Denmark, France, Holland and Sweden were informed as signatory powers.

During conversation in New York Foreign Minister Molotov expressed wish to take up negotiations. Case therefore is now under consideration in government and Storting."

Repeated Moscow as 7.
Pass to War and Navy.[3]

BAY

[3] This message was relayed to the War and Navy Departments on January 17, 1947, at 11 : 15 a. m.

861.24557H/1–1647 : Telegram

The Secretary of State to the Embassy in Norway

SECRET   WASHINGTON, January 18, 1947—9 a. m.
U. S. URGENT

26. Urtel 30 Jan 16.[1] As previously indicated we are interested Spits question as party 1920 Treaty and because of general security considerations. We desire to be kept informed and expect any agreement between Norway and Soviet Union concerning Spits will be subject approval other signatories. Last week's communiqué Norwegian FonOff apparently satisfactory on these points and no action on our part seems necessary at this time.

Brit Emb Wash has been in touch with Dept and has been informed along above lines.

Sent to Oslo as 26, repeated Moscow as 85 and London as 297.

BYRNES

[1] Not printed.

861.24557H/1–2947 : Telegram

The Ambassador in Norway (Bay) to the Secretary of State

SECRET   OSLO, January 29, 1947—6 p. m.

52. ReEmb 47, Jan 28.[1] Foreign Minister Lange told me today that second meeting of Storting had not yet been held and may be delayed one or two weeks while Lange goes to hospital for check-up. He is apparently not seriously ill but health has been sub-par since return-

[1] Not printed.

ing from US in November. Lange expects that following Storting consideration Norwegian Govt will inform Soviet Govt that (*a*) situation is different today in light of UN Charter and objectives in conformity with which Norway's present policy is opposed to bilateral military action between Norway and Russia or between Norway and any other power and (*b*) Norway is satisfied with *status quo* and present terms of 1920 Svalbard treaty but if Russia should initiate request that treaty be submitted to signatories for any purpose whatever Norway will not oppose in principle such submission.

Lange told me that he put question squarely before Molotov in New York as to what Russia objects to with respect to her economic interests, pointing out that Russia has equal economic rights with every other signatory. Presumably Molotov did not answer this question. Lange also told me that since principal economic interests in Svalbard are now divided between Norway and Soviet Union, if Russia wishes to bring to Norway's attention any matters which may presently be disturbing to Russia in economic field Norway would be happy to explore such situation but if any question arises in such exploratory discussion which may be of concern to any other signatory question must be submitted to other signatories.

Lange informed me that he has not told Soviet Ambassador [2] during recent informal call his expectations re Norwegian communication to Moscow as set forth above.

Sent Dept 52; repeated Moscow 9; London 6.

BAY

---

[2] Nikolay Dmitriyevich Kuznetsov.

861.24557H/2–447

The Secretary of War (Patterson) and the Secretary of the Navy (Forrestal) to the Secretary of State

TOP SECRET   WASHINGTON, 4 February 1947.

DEAR MR. SECRETARY: There is inclosed a statement [1] of the views of the Joint Chiefs of Staff on the military implication of a change in the status, under the Treaty of Paris of 1920, of the Spitzbergen Archipelago.

We wish to reinforce these views by stating that in our opinion it would seriously impair the overall security interests of the United States to accede to any substantial Soviet demands with respect to Bear Island and the Spitzbergen Archipelago. Even in open negotiation among all non-enemy powers signatory to the Treaty of 1920, we

---

[1] Not printed.

would recommend that the United States oppose any Soviet gains which could be interpreted in this country or abroad as appeasement of the U.S.S.R.

Sincerely yours,

FORRESTAL
Secretary of the Navy

ROBERT P. PATTERSON
Secretary of War

861.24557H/2–447

The Secretary of State to the Secretary of the Navy (Forrestal)

TOP SECRET   [WASHINGTON,] February 18, 1947.

MY DEAR MR. SECRETARY: I have received the letter of February 4, 1947 signed jointly by you and Secretary Patterson, together with the statement of the views of the Joint Chiefs of Staff, on the military implications of a change in the status of the Spitsbergen Archipelago as established by the Treaty of Paris of 1920.

The Joint Chiefs of Staff correctly state the facts regarding Soviet approach to the Norwegian Government looking to a change in the status of the Spitsbergen Archipelago with particular reference to Soviet participation, in some form not entirely clear, in the military use of the Islands. No change in status can however legally take place without the concurrence of the United States (and such concurrence would require action by the Senate), and of all non-enemy powers signatory to the 1920 Treaty. No proposal for a modification of the 1920 Treaty has been received from Norway or the Soviet Union or any other party to the Treaty.

I have noted the conclusions of the Joint Chiefs of Staff that the Soviet Union can advance some plausible military arguments for a share in the defense of Spitsbergen, and that Spitsbergen "in the hands of an aggressive Soviet Russia, would have an offensive potential against the United States, but not sufficient from the purely military point of view to justify military action by the United States to prevent a measure of Soviet control".

I have also noted the opinion expressed by you and Secretary Patterson that agreement to any substantial Soviet demands with respect to Bear Island and the Spitsbergen Archipelago would "seriously impair the overall security interests of the United States", and your joint recommendation that the United States oppose any Soviet gains which could be interpreted as appeasement of the USSR. If and when any question involving such considerations with respect to Spitsbergen arises, I will, of course, discuss the question with you, the Secretary of War and the President.

I realize that in determining the treatment of the Spitsbergen question we will have to keep in mind United States' long-term objectives with respect to military rights in Greenland and Iceland. On the one hand, if the Soviet Union pursues its apparent objectives in Spitsbergen the possession of military rights in Greenland and Iceland will become correspondingly more essential to our national defense. On the other hand, if at this juncture we press ahead with negotiations for military rights in Greenland and Iceland, we might well stimulate the Soviet Union to take positive action in Spitsbergen which might otherwise be avoided or at least postponed.

In this latter connection, I think that two points merit serious consideration:

(1) Now that Soviet objectives in Spitsbergen have come into the open, it is unlikely that either Denmark or Iceland would at this time be willing to grant us long-term military rights if, while asking for such rights, we oppose any change in the status of Spitsbergen;

(2) Maintenance of the *status quo* (which the Joint Chiefs of Staff recommend as the most desirable solution to the problem) would not preclude clandestine Soviet military activity in Spitsbergen under the guise of development of the extensive Soviet coal mine properties in the Islands.

In these circumstances, I take it that no action by the State Department is necessary at this time except to continue to follow the situation closely and to work on it in the closest possible touch with the War and Navy Departments as in the past.

I am addressing a similar letter to the Secretary of War.

Sincerely yours,   G. C. MARSHALL

861.24557H/2–1947

Memorandum of Conversation, by the Chief of the Division of Northern European Affairs (Cumming)

TOP SECRET   [WASHINGTON,] February 19, 1947.

Mr. Middleton [1] called on me this afternoon to say that the British Embassy had received, with instructions to communicate the contents to the Department for information, a copy of a telegram sent by the Foreign Office to the British Embassy in Oslo.

The British Ambassador in Oslo had been instructed to apprise the Norwegian Government that the legal position of the British Government remains as in the past, namely, that any legal change in the 1920 Spitsbergen Treaty can only take place with the consent of all the signatories except Japan; that whether or not the consent of Italy would be required is uncertain, but that the British Government inclines to the view that Italian consent would have to be obtained. The

---

[1] George Humphrey Middleton, first secretary of the British Embassy.

Ambassador was also instructed to express the hope that in any discussions that may take place between the Norwegian Government and the Soviet Government the Norwegians will reserve their position in accordance with the foregoing, and will not "spring anything" on the British Government unexpectedly. He was further instructed to inform the Norwegians that the British Government is keeping in touch with Canada and the United States with regard to the Spitsbergen question.

Mr. Middleton also told me that the Embassy had received an expression of the views of the British Joint Chiefs of Staff which, in summary, were that a modification of the Spitsbergen Treaty to permit of legal Soviet military activity in Spitsbergen would have no direct influence on the security of the United Kingdom but would directly affect the defense interests of Canada and the United States.[2] Mr. Middleton added that it was his understanding that the British Joint Chiefs would get in touch with the United States Joint Chiefs of Staff with regard to the matter if they had not already done so.

H[UGH] S. C[UMMING, JR.]

---

[2] In a communication of March 20, 1947, to Mr. John D. Hickerson, the Deputy Director of the Office of European Affairs, the Canadian Ambassador, Mr. Hume Wrong, conveyed the viewpoint of the Canadian Chiefs of Staff: "They consider that this might constitute a threat to the security of North America, with the employment of new weapons of increased range and power. In consequence, they have recommended that every effort should be made by diplomatic means to secure the maintenance of the conditions laid down in the Treaty of 1920, to which Canada is a party, which provided that the establishment of military fortifications or bases on Spitzbergen and Bear Island should not be permitted." (861.24557H/3–2047) This information was sent in letters to Vice Adm. F. P. Sherman, Deputy Chief of Naval Operations (Operations), Department of the Navy, and to Maj. Gen. Lauris Norstad, Director of Plans and Operations, War Department General Staff.

861.24557H/2–1947 : Telegram

The Ambassador in the Soviet Union (Smith) to the Secretary of State

SECRET　　　　　　　　　　　　　　　　Moscow, February 19, 1947—6 p. m.

PRIORITY

462. Norwegian Ambassador [1] informs me report that Secretary General of Norwegian Foreign Office visited Moscow is incorrect.[2] Offi-

---

[1] Hans C. Berg.
[2] Ambassador Smith relayed the information to the Department in his telegram 435, February 18, 1947, 5 p. m., not printed, that Secretary General Andvord had arrived in Moscow on the night of the 17th to discuss the question of Spitzbergen (861.24557H/2–1847). By telegram 470, February 20, 11 a. m., not printed, he advised the Department that telegram 462 was highly confidential and requested that the news contained in it should not be passed on in an information telegram nor given wide distribution within the Department itself (861.24557H/2–2047).

cial was a secretary of Foreign Office carrying in a sealed envelope for Mr. Molotov, reply of Foreign Office after consultation with Storting on the matter of Spitsbergen. In event this reply has not been communicated to the Department from Oslo, gist is that Norwegian Government finds it impossible to consider revision of present treaty on bilateral basis and that any changes would of necessity be made as result of consultation among all signatories. Also that any modification of military aspect would presumably be considered within the framework of UN.

SMITH

861.24557H/2–1947 : Telegram

The Ambassador in Norway (Bay) to the Secretary of State

SECRET   OSLO, February 19, 1947—6 p. m.

84. Reference Embassy's 47 and 52, January 28 and 29.[1] Foreign Minister Lange called me to Foreign Office today and handed me copy of resolution adopted by Storting secret meeting February 15 re Svalbard. Verbatim text resolution being forwarded following numbered telegram.[2] Lange informed me he had forwarded copy of resolution with personal letter to Molotov because of personal nature of recent discussions with Molotov in New York. He informed Molotov that copies of resolution would be handed Chiefs of Mission of signatory nations now and about week later to Norwegian press. Lange indicated government and Storting made offer to continue nonmilitary discussions largely as friendly gesture to mitigate Norwegian refusal to negotiate bilaterally on military aspects.

Lange added that only Norway and Russia have been concerned with active economic development of Spitsbergen during recent years and therefore perfectly reasonable for Norway and Russia to discuss bilaterally economic aspects of treaty. I asked Lange whether Norway felt satisfied with general provisions of treaty 1920. He answered that while Norway is satisfied with the demilitarization provision, nevertheless Norway would not object to and might even favor certain changes in treaty. He stated for example that Norway has felt that it assumed under the treaty all the obligations of sovereignty without acquiring corresponding benefits.

---

[1] Former telegram not printed.
[2] Not printed. Ambassador Bay informed the Department in telegram 103 of March 4, 1947, 5 p. m., not printed, that all newspapers had published on that day a Foreign Office statement that this resolution by the Storting had been approved by a vote of 101 to 11. The minority of 11 had supported a Communist proposal in favor of joint Norwegian-Soviet defense measures (861.24557H/3–447).

Sent Department as 84; repeated Moscow as 10; London as 9; pouched to Stockholm.

BAY

861.24557H/3–1147 : Telegram

The Ambassador in Norway (Bay) to the Secretary of State

SECRET   OSLO, March 11, 1947—noon.

115. ReEmb's 84, and 85, February 19, and 86, February 20.[1] In visit with Mr. Andvord, Secretary General Foreign Office, on March 8, I asked him whether Norway has yet received a reply from USSR to Norwegian note on Svalbard. He stated that Norway had received no answer.

To clarify that part of the Storting resolution reading, "Storting never forgetting assistance given to Norway by Soviet Union, agree that discussions with Soviet Union, state which, besides Norway, has particular economic interests on Svalbard, otherwise should be continued concerning preparations for revision of Spitsbergen treaty 1920 with view to making it more satisfactory," I asked him whether Norway is presently dissatisfied with any major provision of the treaty and desires on its own account to call a meeting for revision, to which he replied in the negative.

I asked what the Norwegian Govt meant by that phrase, and he stated with a smile that if USSR initiates request for meeting to revise the treaty that Norway would like to take up certain minor provisions on its own account, but that none of these provisions has anything bearing upon the military or defense aspects of treaty. He made it clear that Norway would not initiate a request for revision of treaty, but would be willing to join such request if USSR should initiate request.

My conclusion is that Norway desires to reject USSR proposals for treaty revision, but wishes to do so as graciously as possible.

BAY

---

[1] Last two telegrams not printed.

861.24557H/3–2847

The Ambassador in Norway (Bay) to the Secretary of State

SECRET   OSLO, March 28, 1947.
No. 810

SIR: I have the honor to report that after a dinner at the French Embassy on the evening of March 22, Mr. Andvord, Secretary General of the Foreign Office, told me in private conversation that the Norwegian Government had not yet received any reply from the U.S.S.R. to its note (reference Embassy's telegram No. 86, February 20[1]) communicating the resolution adopted by the Norwegian Storting with respect to Svalbard. He then told me that a Soviet representative to the United Nations had recently stated to the Norwegian representative to that organization—the names of these representatives were not given—that "Norway need not have been so prompt about sending the note". I asked Mr. Andvord how he interpreted this and he said that, on the basis of his experience during his term as Norwegian Ambassador to the U.S.S.R., as well as upon his general knowledge of Soviet methods, it was his definite belief that the Soviet remark was inspired from Moscow. I asked if he had any idea as to why the U.S.S.R. was disappointed in receiving the note "so promptly", and he stated as his personal opinion that the U.S.S.R would possibly have preferred not being on notice to the effect that their request for Svalbard militarization had been rejected by Norway; that the Soviet receipt of such rejection at the beginning of the Foreign Ministers' Conference in Moscow would possibly put a brake on similar Soviet plans for other areas (possibly meaning the Dardanelles).

Respectfully yours,

C. ULRICH BAY

---

[1] Not printed.

861.24557H/5–1948 : Airgram

The Chargé in Norway (Huston) to the Secretary of State

SECRET   OSLO, May 19, 1948.

A–273. Embtel 115, March 11, 1947. FoMin Lange told Ambassador Bay yesterday, in reply to a question, that there have been no developments whatever in the Spitsbergen question since the despatch of his letter to Molotov last year conveying Norway's refusal to enter into negotiations looking to the joint defense of the archipelago. Mr. Lange indicated that he considered the subject "dead", at least for the time being.

HUSTON

PORTUGAL

**NEGOTIATIONS BETWEEN THE UNITED STATES AND PORTUGAL RE-
GARDING A NEW AGREEMENT GRANTING TO AMERICAN MILITARY
AIRCRAFT TRANSIT RIGHTS THROUGH LAGENS AIRFIELD IN THE
AZORES FOR THE DURATION OF THE OCCUPATION OF GERMANY
AND JAPAN** [1]

853B.7962/3–1447

*The Acting Director of the Office of European Affairs (Hickerson) to
the Under Secretary of State (Acheson)*

SECRET   [WASHINGTON,] March 14, 1947.

You will recall that last June we completed an agreement [2] with
the Portuguese by which ATC could continue to operate through the
Azores using the field at Lagens. That agreement was for 18 months
and will expire December 2, 1947. The Azores are vital to our lines of
communication with Germany and for that reason a new accord or
an extension of the present one is required. If negotiations are to be
undertaken, they should be started well in advance of the date the
present agreement expires. The Army is anxious to have these discussions opened about the middle of May. Paul Culbertson [3] has done
the previous negotiations and it is my thought that he would go to
Lisbon on his way to Madrid, arriving in Lisbon about the middle of
May. We would like to ask the War Department to assign General
Kissner to assist in these negotiations. Before we get any deeper into
our discussions with the War Department I would like to have your
approval for going ahead with these negotiations.

JOHN D. HICKERSON

---

[1] For previous documentation relating to United States interest in the airfields
in the Azores, see *Foreign Relations*, 1946, vol. v, pp. 962 ff. For related documentation on U.S. policy with respect to acquisition of military bases and air
transit rights, see volume I, compilation entitled "United States National Security
Policy".

[2] See telegram 480, May 30, 1946, from Lisbon, *Foreign Relations*, 1946, vol. v,
p. 996.

[3] Paul T. Culbertson was assigned to the Embassy in Spain where, on April 15,
1947, he became First Secretary.

853B.7962/6-347

The Secretary of State to the Ambassador-Designate to Portugal (Wiley) in New York

SECRET   WASHINGTON, June 3, 1947.

SIR: The United States Government is now prepared to open discussions with the Portuguese Government for the purpose of negotiating a new agreement under which United States military aircraft serving American forces of occupation abroad would enjoy transit rights at the Lagens airfield in the Azores for the duration of the occupation of Germany and Japan. The Department wishes you to initiate negotiations to that end as soon as you think it wise to do so after your arrival in Lisbon. The essential elements of the proposal to be made to the Portuguese Government are contained in the attached draft Note for delivery by you to the Portuguese Foreign Minister at an early appropriate opportunity.

The War Department has designated Brigadier General A.W. Kissner as military adviser to assist you in these negotiations. General Kissner is continuing his present duties in Washington, but is prepared to proceed to Lisbon promptly as soon as you indicate the need for his presence there. General Kissner's instructions authorize him to speak for the War Department except in cases where a major change in existing War Department policy is involved. Discussions have been held in Washington with General Kissner and other representatives of the War Department. They have agreed to the presentation of the objectives in the form of the attached draft Note. Depending on the development of your discussions with the Portuguese Government, you will of course be free to recommend changes, having in mind the objectives of the War Department with which General Kissner is familiar.

You will note that the draft proposals contain no *quid pro quo* on the part of the United States Government and it is not intended that there should be given any form of political assurance such as might be suggested by the Portuguese Government in exchange for the concession of military base rights. The War Department is, however, prepared to make certain commitments in connection with assistance in the training of Portuguese military and civilian personnel, in making available surplus military aircraft, in the construction of certain facilities and in the assumption of certain maintenance responsibilities. General Kissner will inform you of these in detail.

In view of past experience, it is felt that the Portuguese Government would be unwilling to agree to a mere extension of the time limitation contained in the May 30, 1946, agreement.[1] It is therefore considered

---

[1] For text of Agreement, effected by exchange of notes May 30, 1946, see Department of State Treaties and Other International Acts Series (TIAS) No. 2345; United States Treaties and Other International Agreements (UST), vol. II, (pt. 2), p. 2201.

important that, although the purpose of the new agreement is substantially the continuation of present facilities and privileges, the Portuguese Government should be given every indication that it is intended to negotiate an entirely new agreement to take effect upon the expiration of the May 30 agreement.

As to the duration of the new agreement, it should be for the period of occupation of Germany and Japan, since the entire premise of the agreement is the need for the facilities to which the occupation gives rise. If that is not obtainable, provision for termination under certain conditions after a lapse of five years, as in Paragraph 12 of the United States-Iceland Agreement of October 7, 1946,[2] might then be sought. A copy of Despatch No. 713 of October 7, 1946,[3] from the American Legation at Reykjavik, containing the text of the agreement just mentioned, is enclosed.

Discussions with the Portuguese Government last year on long term arrangements for joint use and maintenance of military base facilities in the Azores were discontinued early in September 1946. The Portuguese Government showed great interest in the matter but attached conditions which were unacceptable to the United States Government. At the conclusion of the discussions, the Portuguese Government was informed that they were being recessed rather than terminated. In the light of the interest shown by the Portuguese Government, you may, if you think it desirable to do so, refer to those discussions and emphasize our continuing interest in coming to an agreement of that nature. The uncertainty of present world conditions suggests, however, the desirability of postponing further discussions along those lines, which could be resumed at a later date at the initiative of either Government, and of confining present arrangements to the immediate need for transit facilities to service occupation forces in Germany and Japan.

The British Embassy in Washington was informed on May 22, 1947 [4] of the intention to open these negotiations and was assured that the British Government would be kept informed of their progress. Emphasis was laid on the necessity of secrecy at this stage of the negotiations. The hope was expressed to the British Embassy in Washington that the British Ambassador at Lisbon would be given instructions enabling him to lend prompt support to your negotiations, should that be necessary. You should keep the British Ambassador at Lisbon [5] informed of the progress of the negotiations. A copy of the Depart-

---

[2] For text of Agreement, effected by exchange of notes October 7, 1946, see Department of State Treaties and Other International Acts Series (TIAS) No. 1566, or 61 Stat. (pt. 3) 2426; for documentation on the negotiation of the Agreement, see Department of State files 859A.20 and 501AA.
[3] Not printed.
[4] Note of May 22 not printed.
[5] Sir Nigel B. Ronald.

ment's note of May 22, 1947 to the British Embassy in Washington is enclosed.

Very truly yours,

For the Secretary of State:
JOHN HICKERSON
Acting Director
Office of European Affairs

[Enclosure]

Draft Note From the American Ambassador to the Portuguese Minister for Foreign Affairs (Caeiro da Mata)

EXCELLENCY: I have the honor to refer to the negotiations which were conducted last year between the Governments of the United States and Portugal with respect to the use of facilities in the Azores Islands for the transit of United States aircraft serving the forces of occupation in Germany and Japan.

The Government of Portugal recognized the need of the United States Government for these facilities and, in an agreement of May 30, 1946, authorized for a period of eighteen months the passage in transit through Lagens airfield of United States aircraft serving American occupation forces. For its part, the United States Government has conscientiously carried out its obligations under the spirit and letter of that agreement. This authorization expires on December 2, 1947. However, the responsibilities of the United States to the other members of the United Nations and, in fact, to all nations of the world for the occupation of the ex-enemy nations still continue. The United States as one of the occupying powers must therefore continue to look to friendly governments for such cooperation as they can give in assisting the United States and the other occupying powers in carrying out their responsibilities for the occupation of Germany and Japan.

The facilities which the United States Government has enjoyed in the Azores have been a vital link in the line of communications with the American forces of occupation, and its need for such facilities will still exist at the date of expiration of the agreement of May 30, 1946. In view of the consistently cooperative and friendly attitude of the Government of Portugal in providing essential facilities in the Azores during the war and in recognizing the need for transit facilities during the subsequent period of the occupation of Germany and Japan, the Government of the United States is encouraged to anticipate a renewed cooperation of the Portuguese Government in providing for the continuation of facilities in the Azores after December 2, 1947, for the transit of the United States aircraft serving the forces of occupation. The need for these facilities has been recognized in the agreement of May 30, 1946, as a clear and unavoidable consequence of the responsibilities of the United States Government as one of the occupying powers, and the United States Government feels certain that it can depend upon the Government of Portugal to provide this assistance so essential to the successful discharge by the United States of its responsibilities in the occupation of Germany and Japan.

The United States Government would therefore appreciate an early opportunity to negotiate a new agreement to meet the foregoing requirements and to take effect upon the expiration of the agreement of May 30, 1946, which will include the following essential elements:

1. Lagens airfield on Terceira Island in the Azores to be available for regular and scheduled passage in transit of United States military aircraft serving the forces of occupation in Germany and Japan.
2. The United States to maintain such American personnel, facilities and installations at Lagens airfield as are necessary for controlling, maintaining and serving United States military aircraft.
3. Santa Maria airfield to be available to United States military aircraft for emergency use in the event of adverse weather conditions at Lagens.
4. A mixed commission to make periodic inspections of the two airports and to advise the Portuguese Government on any improvement of conditions, services and equipment necessary to maintain both airfields at a high standard.

853B.7962/6–1847 : Telegram

The Secretary of State to the Embassy in Portugal

SECRET WASHINGTON, June 18, 1947—3 p. m.

428. Referring to Dept's note of May 22 outlining our proposed negotiations with Portugal Brit Emb has given Dept note substance as follows:

"It is understanding of HMG that US proposals are substantially those contained in memo from Byrnes to Bevin of 19 Aug 1946 [1] and that no new requirements are now under consideration. On this understanding, HMG are prepared to instruct their Ambassador Lisbon to support US approach to Port Govt if he should be asked to do so by his US colleague or if he should be consulted by Port Govt.

HMG wishes also to make clear that their support of US proposals will be given on understanding that facilities for which US is asking are not exclusive, i.e. that nothing in any arrangement which US may make with Port Govt would prevent HMG should an emergency arise,

---

[1] Not printed. Ernest Bevin, British Secretary of State for Foreign Affairs, and Secretary of State James F. Byrnes were at that time attending the Paris Peace Conference.

from seeking such military facilities in Azores as they might consider necessary for protection Brit military interests.

Finally HMG attach importance to Brit participation in any mixed commission set up to supervise upkeep of two airfields in accordance with Point 4 of US proposals. It is hoped that US Ambassador at Lisbon may be instructed to include proposal for Brit participation in mixed commission in his approach to Port Govt."

We have assured Brit that understandings in first two quoted paragraphs above are correct and have given assurance that we have no objection in principle Brit participation mixed commission. We said that since functions of mixed commission would be developed during course negotiations we would find appropriate time take up this point with Portuguese. However, we said in initial stages we would prefer not to introduce this additional factor as it might seem to relate our approach to long-term base question which we wished to avoid.

Brit Emb cabling our assurances FonOff with recommendation that Brit Amb Lisbon be given appropriate instructions promptly.

MARSHALL

853B.7962/6–2047 : Telegram

The Ambassador in Portugal (Wiley) to the Secretary of State

SECRET   LISBON, June 20, 1947—7 p. m.

451. For Reber.[1] Saw British Ambassador today and acquainted him with substance of your No. 428, June 18. He replied that his instructions already received from Foreign Office differed only in that he was to broach to Portuguese Government the question of British participation in mixed commission as soon as I started conversations. I pointed out that question of best timing to raise this question was impossible to foresee at this moment, that it might be better for me to keep him currently informed of progress of conversations and then we could together work out the best moment for this step. He acquiesced entirely. He gave evidence of earnest and sincere desire to be as helpful as possible going so far as to suggest that wherever I might encounter obstacles (for example, Mathias [2]) he would then go into action as indicated by me.

I expect to make preliminary calls on Foreign Minister [3] and Political Director soonest and will promptly thereafter initiate conversations.

WILEY

---

[1] Samuel Reber, Chief of the Division of Western European Affairs.
[2] Marcello Mathias, Portuguese Minister-designate to France; formerly Director General of Political Affairs in Ministry of Foreign Affairs.
[3] Dr. José Caeiro da Mata.

853B.7962/7–347 : Telegram

The Ambassador in Portugal (Wiley) to the Secretary of State

SECRET LISBON, July 3, 1947—7 p. m.
US URGENT

500. For Reber. Mytel 493, of July 2.[1] By appointment I called on the Foreign Minister at 12:30 today. The Minister, as a result of my off the record talk with Teotonio Pereira, Ambassador designate to the US, was of course forewarned of the purpose of my visit, namely to present the Azores note. There was a marked atmosphere of nervous expectation.

I spoke to the Foreign Minister along the following lines; I told him that we are very grateful for the collaboration we have received in the past from Portugal in respect of the Azores and, to allay current rumors, I assured him that I had not been sent to Portugal only to work out this or any other particular question. I foresaw a broad and continuing field for collaboration between us. We appreciate the special ancient relationship which exists between Portugal and England and I assured him we had no desire to see it weakened in any way. I reminded him that there has also been a very special relationship for a long time between Great Britain and the United States, based on realities rather than the written word. I hoped that collaboration on the same basis between the United States and Portugal might close the triangle.

I then referred to previous conversations for a long range agreement with Portugal and the inadvisability either for US or for them to pursue the matter further at this time. With this the Foreign Minister expressed entire agreement.

I handed our note to the Minister which he read carefully. He stated that a new agreement according US essential facilities in the Azores was necessary not only for the United States but also for Portugal. He recognized that the presence of American military occupation forces in Germany and Japan was of the greatest value to all.

He went on to say that there had been a very important meeting of the Cabinet (this presumably resulted from my conversation with Teotonio Pereira), in which Dr. Salazar [2] had called on him to discuss the world political situation. He repeated to me the gist of his remarks at that time which were in brief as follows: He lamented the fact that Great Britain, which in the past had been the central pillar of Portugal's economic and financial structure, had now become a

---

[1] Not printed.
[2] Dr. Antonio de Oliveira Salazar, President of the Portuguese Council of Ministers.

debtor nation to "little Portugal", was fatigued from the war and could no longer play its traditional role. Portugal has always looked upon France as a great political force in Europe but it too could no longer play its traditional role. The infiltration of Communism in many countries of the world and the Soviet control of Eastern Europe, he viewed with the greatest alarm and said that he felt that another war was inevitable. He was not sure that it would not be both advisable and necessary. I replied that another war would be a universal disaster and the United States could be counted upon to do everything humanly possible to avert any such calamity.

The Foreign Minister repeated that we would get in the Azores what we needed and he expressed great satisfaction that we had included the paragraph on the Mixed Commission. In making arrangements to meet European requirements, however, he said that we must work out a formula which would permit the Portuguese Government to reassure Portuguese public opinion that there was no infringement of Portuguese sovereignty. He said that he was convinced that we could readily work out such a formula and he implied that whatever the formula might be we would have what we want.

The Foreign Minister stated he would see Dr. Salazar today but he was confident that he would encounter no difficulties with him.

I asked the Foreign Minister to let me know when it might be timely for me to pay my respects to Dr. Salazar. He said he would mention the matter [to] Dr. Salazar at once.

These conversations have opened under what appear to be very favorable circumstances. The Foreign Minister, however, has the reputation of being at times too optimistic and Dr. Salazar is, of course, known to be very legalistic. I think we can expect to encounter snags in connection with the formula. While I am convinced of the good intentions of the Foreign Minister, there are resolute die-hards in key positions here. This business is not yet in the bag and we may still encounter serious difficulties.

After my conversation with the Foreign Minister, I fully informed the British Ambassador. He told me that he had been alerted to be prepared in the immediate future to make representations to the Portuguese Government together with the French Minister in connection with the Paris meetings on the "Marshall Plan". He promised to take that occasion to tell the Foreign Minister privately that he had learned with great satisfaction that my representations had received such a favorable reception, and he will make clear the interest which his government feels in seeing a solution satisfactory to all concerned.

WILEY

853B.7962/7–1447 : Telegram

The Ambassador in Portugal (Wiley) to the Secretary of State

SECRET LISBON, July 14, 1947—2 p. m.
US URGENT

536. For Reber. My wife and I spent weekend motoring through northern Portugal as guests of Foreign Minister. After dinner Saturday night I informed him briefly of the recent visit to Lisbon of Colonel Warren and of the interviews Colonels Warren and Tibbets [1] had with the Minister for War [2] and General Cintra.[3] The Foreign Minister was very interested and said he would immediately confer with Minister of War and would see Cintra upon latter's return from Azores where he now is; the Foreign Minister would then see me.

I told Foreign Minister that we had certain practical problems in the Azores that I would like to work out in principle with him, namely, certain repairs were needed in connection with gasoline storage installations, and that it was very desirable during the few remaining summer months to bring in and store the winter's supply of gasoline because of weather conditions in the Azores after October 1. The Foreign Minister seemed slightly upset about this and referred to the great Portuguese susceptibilities and the need of finding a "formula". I was able, I think, considerably to reassure him. He promised also to discuss the question with me shortly.

The following day, Sunday, seated in the back of the car, the Foreign Minister raised the Azores question at great length with my wife. He insisted on his great desire to consolidate Portuguese relations with the United States. He is convinced that war is inevitable and that in this critical period collaboration of all nations sharing the same moral aims is indispensable. He thought that in foreign relations there were issues that must be kept above the bargaining level. There were many with small minds everywhere who considered international agreements as purely business propositions and thought only of what they could derive therefrom in a material way. Happily, however, Dr. Salazar was in complete agreement with him that concessions Portugal might grant to the US in the Azores should not be on the basis of a *quid pro quo*.

Dr. Salazar, he went on to say, wanted very much to see me as soon as possible. He, the Foreign Minister, was anxious to have this interview take place while he was still in Lisbon. (He departs the twentieth for Paris by motor.)

---

[1] Col. John W. Warren, Commanding Officer, ATC personnel at Lagens; Col. Gene H. Tibbets, U.S. Air Attaché in Portugal.
[2] Col. Fernando dos Santos Costa.
[3] Gen. Antonio Cintra, Portuguese Director of Civil and Military Aviation.

Foreign Minister then discussed colonial questions: Macao means nothing in a material sense to Portugal; it is a small, inconsequential spot that is an economic outlet to nothing and is in no sense a political bulwark. Yet the historical tradition in Portugal is such that if Portugal's precarious position there is worsened the repercussions in Portugal would be very great. Exactly the same situation applies to Goa and the two other Indian colonies. Moreover, there was much importance attached in Portugal to the role of the Patriarch of the Indies now in Portugal on the eve of returning to his ecclesiastical duties. On the subject of the Indian colonies he had made, a month ago, very strong representations. He considered the matter so delicate that he was keeping them entirely secret so as not arouse public opinion or popular emotion in Portugal. He showed great concern over the foregoing.

I am reporting this since it is tied in so closely with our Azores conversations. The coincidence is unfortunate that Portuguese colonial alarm should be so aroused at this particular moment since it makes their susceptibilities just so much more acute. It is obvious that we shall be obliged to use the utmost tact in every step in order to achieve our essential objectives.

WILEY

853B.7962/7–2647 : Telegram

The Ambassador in Portugal (Wiley) to the Secretary of State

SECRET   LISBON, July 26, 1947—noon.

582. For Reber. I was requested to call at Foreign Office yesterday afternoon by Dr. Faria, Director General of Political Affairs. He told me that great consideration had been given to our note of July 3 on the subject of the Azores, and that the Prime Minister and other members of the Portuguese Government were quite agreed to according US transit facilities for Army aircraft servicing American occupation forces in Germany and Japan. Before communicating a note formally to me, however, he desired to acquaint me with the position of the Portuguese Government. He then produced an unsigned document dated July 25 which reads in translation as follows:

"1. Within the spirit of friendly understanding which has animated the Portuguese Government in its relations with the Government of the United States regarding the facilities granted in the Azores to American aviation, and having in mind the situation resulting from the expiration on December 2, 1947 of the agreement of May 30, 1946 the government is disposed to grant for a period to be determined upon, to North American airplanes of the ATC servicing occupation troops in Germany and Japan the right of transit through the Lagens airdrome.

"2. It is known that the execution of the program resulting from the technical agreement negotiated between the military authorities of the two countries for the carrying out of the May 30th agreement is well advanced and it will be practically terminated on the date of the expiration of the latter agreement. For this reason all of the services of control, maintenance and technical aid should be turned over to and exclusively executed by Portuguese services of the Lagens base which will be in a position to render the necessary assistance.

"3. In order to carry this out it is necessary that there be ceded, under whatever arrangement, the American material which is at present in Lagens and which material the United States Government undertakes to provide substitution or replacement.

"4. The Government of the United States should take for its own account warehousing of aviation spare parts for the airplanes in transit and to maintain civil personnel for the maintenance of the airplanes in a number to be agreed upon.

"5. For the execution of this concession the Portuguese Government would like the Government of the United States to agree to: (*a*) Authorize the contracting by Portugal authorities of some American personnel which may still be necessary, and during the indispensable period, to serve on the base; and (*b*) to advise through the intermediary of its technicians the Portuguese Government regarding improvements which may be desirable to introduce in the field or in its services.

"6. The concession granted to the Government of the United States under the new agreement will be extended for the same period to the British Government.

"7. The Portuguese Government would appreciate it if the American Government would take under consideration the eventual competition which the airplanes of the ATC may be giving to private companies whose airplanes utilize the airdrome at Santa Maria." Portuguese text follows by air pouch.

Dr. Faria in conversation amplified somewhat the text of the foregoing document. With regard to paragraph 2, he quoted the Minister of War as being definitely of the opinion that the Portuguese could take over all the technical services on December 2. I replied that I disagreed entirely with regard to the ability of the Portuguese to take over the aforesaid services. Dr. Faria pointed with pride to the operation of the Lisbon airport. I replied that the Lisbon airport was the cause of consternation to the American airlines; it did not even have equipment for a blind landing. ATC would never be satisfied with conditions like those in Lisbon. Concerning Paragraph 3 Dr. Faria stated that the Portuguese Government was willing to take over American equipment in the Azores either by purchase, loan or lease. With regard to 4, I expressed great doubt that the American Government had any civilian personnel that could be provided. Also I told him

ATC would require its own personnel, maximum 677, minimum 382. They would have to be in uniform and could not and should not be disguised as civilians. With regard to 6, I expressed complete satisfaction that the Portuguese Government should extend whatever concessions it might wish to the British. With regard to 7, I denied that there was any competition worth mentioning between ATC and private airlines.

My interview with Dr. Faria lasted one hour and five minutes. I gave him all the orthodox arguments for Portugal's collaboration with the US in the conformation of the American war effort in Germany and Japan. Since the explanation by Dr. Faria made it more than clear that the Portuguese concept is that everything in the Azores shall be completely Portuguese operated and controlled without any American military personnel or responsibilities, I told him that the formula, as tentatively proposed, would be in my opinion, utterly unacceptable. Indeed I was convinced that ATC would infinitely prefer to leave the Azores rather than to remain there on anything that even remotely resembled the present proposition. Dr. Faria talked about Portuguese susceptibilities. I told him we had susceptibilities too. I asked him why there was no reference to the suggestion of a mixed commission. He replied that this was approached indirectly in five ways. The approach seems very indirect.

After my reiterating the complete unacceptability of the present Portuguese formula, he expressed the hope that I would nevertheless communicate it to my government and in the meantime he would communicate my objections to the Prime Minister.

I think there are two schools of thought in the Portuguese Government with regard to the Azores problem. One, represented by the Foreign Minister and Teotonio Pereira, Ambassador designate to Washington, is conciliatory. The other, headed by Athias [*Mathias*] and probably by the Minister of War and perhaps with the legalistic and sympathetic support of Dr. Salazar, is one of most reluctant acquiescence to anything. The Foreign Minister left July 20 for Paris. Dr. Mathias, who is now Minister designate to Paris, was to have accompanied him. Apparently Mathias stayed behind and left only yesterday. I think the document and what Dr. Faria said were the fruits of his labor. It was understood between me and the Foreign Minister that the question of the Azores would be suspended until his return. Thus, this interview today came as a surprise. My suggestion is that as soon at Teotonio Pereira arrives in Washington the Department talk to him frankly and that any instructions to me be postponed until the return of the Foreign Minister, probably about the middle of August. I think we can proceed faster and better in this matter by making haste slowly.

WILEY

853B.7962/8–1347

Memorandum of Conversation, by Mr. William B. Dunham of the Division of Western European Affairs

SECRET [WASHINGTON,] August 13, 1947.

During his call on me this afternoon, Dr. Rocheta [1] said that the Ambassador had asked him to state, in connection with his discussion with Mr. Reber and me yesterday, that the Embassy had just received the pouch from Lisbon which contained a copy of the Portuguese Memorandum of July 25.[2] The Ambassador's judgment was that this did not represent an official document but merely constituted a written record of an informal conversation. He felt that, while we might be dissatisfied with the "formula" contained in this paper, nevertheless the opening paragraph did indicate that the Portuguese Government was quite willing to permit the US the continued use of the airfield at Lagens. It now remained to agree upon a time period and the formula.

I explained to Dr. Rocheta that we understood that this Memorandum was merely informal. One of the things which troubled me about it, I said, was the fact that Ambassador Wiley had been assured by the Foreign Minister that the two of them would conduct the discussions. However, shortly after the Foreign Minister left Lisbon, Ambassador Wiley was handed this Memorandum by a lower official of the Foreign Office.

I also told Dr. Rocheta that we were disturbed by the formula which this Memorandum contained. I told him that with all due respect to the abilities of the Portuguese Air Force, the Portuguese Minister of War had agreed at one time in the recent past with our Military Attaché for Air and our commanding officer in the Azores that the Portuguese personnel at Lagens were not yet capable of taking over the many services which must be rendered there to our aircraft. The training of Portuguese personnel was going forward, but as he knew this was a long process and until their personnel was trained up to our standards, our Air Force people would not wish to consider turning over the essential services rendered our aircraft; they would wish to perform these services themselves.

---

[1] Manuel Rocheta, Counselor of the Portuguese Embassy.
[2] Presumably reference is to the unsigned document quoted in telegram 582, July 26, 1947, *supra*.

I also explained to Dr. Rocheta that we were under an obligation, in view of our current agreement, to begin by September 2 making our plans for the evacuation of Lagens and that it would, of course, be desirable, if possible, to reach some firmer agreement in principle before that time if the evacuation was to be unnecessary.

Dr. Rocheta indicated that he understood these problems and said that the Ambassador, who was still without instructions on the subject, was writing to Lisbon for further information.

853B.7962/7–2647 : Telegram

The Acting Secretary of State to the Embassy in Portugal

SECRET   WASHINGTON, August 13, 1947—6 p. m.

575. We have delayed replying your recent telegrams pending opportunity discuss your negotiations with Pereira yesterday after he had presented credentials. We gave him copy of Memorandum (urtel 582 July 26) and repeated objections you have already made.

Pereira had not seen Memo and has not heard from his Govt about negotiations since his departure. He obviously did not understand this turn of events and was surprised by contents of Memo and to learn FonMin was not expected in Lisbon before end of month. He said he would cable Lisbon to express our views and request information.

Pereira gave no indication of part he expected Bianchi [1] might play in negotiations but did suggest he would be appropriate person to talk with in FonMin's absence. We discussed negotiations with Bianchi prior to his departure and while he was sympathetic with our objectives he seemed more interested in winding up his personal affairs.

War Dept has expressed great appreciation for effective manner in which you countered points raised in Portuguese Memo. They and we concur fully in all points you made and you are authorized, whenever you consider it desirable, so to inform FonOff.

It has occurred to us as it probably has to you, in connection with urtel 582, that Portuguese may be purposely using widespread shift in FonOff personnel as means of delaying negotiations. In view of FonMin's extended absence and fact that you will probably have to begin all over again if you deal with Bianchi, you may wish to consider desirability of approaching Dr. Salazar as Acting Minister of Foreign Affairs. We have not discussed such an approach with Pereira.

Following details have arisen out of examination of Memo and are set forth for your info:

Portuguese use of phrase "North American airplanes of the ATC" indicated misconception of type of traffic we wish to have serviced at

---

[1] Dr. João Antonio de Bianchi was succeeded by Mr. Pereira as Portuguese Ambassador to the United States.

Lagens. This would for instance exclude occasional administrative and transport flights of Navy aircraft and might well exclude transit of combat aircraft. Furthermore name of Air Transport Command might be changed at some future date. Our inclination is therefore to describe aircraft which we wish to transit Lagens as "aircraft operated by or on behalf of the United States Government" (phrase used in Iceland Agreement).

In connection with personnel, War Dept states it would not be able to find qualified civilian personnel who would be willing to settle at Lagens and War Dept cannot of course "authorize the contracting by Portuguese authorities" of American military personnel. If present Iceland Agreement should be raised as precedent in connection with use of civilian personnel you may say that it has proved most unsatisfactory in operation (i.e. through contract arrangement with private company) and that we hope for much more satisfactory arrangement with Portuguese Govt.

Assume Col Warren had satisfactory info on current number and use of personnel. If you desire further briefing on this please advise.

LOVETT

853B.7962/8–1447 : Telegram

The Ambassador in Portugal (Wiley) to the Secretary of State

SECRET   LISBON, August 14, 1947—6 p. m.

MOST IMMEDIATE

630. Embtel 588 July 28.[1] Following suggestion Carvalhaes,[2] I lunched with General Cintra today. I showed him "oral statement" and also gave him detailed personnel information obtained from Warren. Cintra apparently is member of school of thought which believes Portuguese able operate Lagens for ATC albeit with certain specialized American technical assistance. When expressing foregoing he added that without such assistance "formula" would have to be reworked thus implying Government might then be disposed reconsider matter.

I frankly told Cintra formula utterly unacceptable and ATC would prefer withdraw rather than operate under basis proposed. I also told him Lagens facilities great convenience to US but not indispensable, but that I considered Lagens question most important as point of departure for US-Portuguese relations in general and that without such point of departure I could only be very pessimistic.

Cintra asked if I had discussed matter with Salazar. I said not as yet but hoped, in view of time element to do so soonest. Concluding I stressed fact that present instructions call for last American flights

---

[1] Not printed.
[2] Col. Esmeraldo Carvalhaes, Protocol Officer in Portuguese Ministry of War.

through Lagens October 2. I told Cintra quite a story about our getting out of Galápagos [3] and subsequent chagrin of Ecuador.

WILEY

---

[3] For documentation regarding return by the United States of military bases in the Galápagos Islands to Ecuador in 1946, see *Foreign Relations*, 1946, vol. XI, pp. 836 ff.

853B.7962/8–1447 : Telegram

The Acting Secretary of State to the Embassy in Portugal

SECRET   WASHINGTON, August 15, 1947—6 p. m.
US URGENT   NIACT

588. We have had very helpful discussion with Wayne C. Taylor [1] today. War Dept and we agree that formula which you have devised is acceptable. Redraft of formula incorporating few suggested changes is being telegraphed separately. We feel we should avoid, in first paragraph, impression that we are seeking only extension of old agreement. We believe for tactical reasons, that it might be wise to include in second paragraph statement that Lagens Airfield will remain under full control of Portuguese authorities but leave this to your judgment. We agree fully that it is wise to include a statement that similar privileges are being extended to British.

We will take no action here to obtain British support for your approach to Dr. Salazar next week (urtel 631 Aug 14 [2]) unless you specifically request it since we believe British Ambassador has adequate instructions and that you will in any case wish to arrange with him timing of his approach.

War Dept and we entirely agree with statements you made to Gen Cintra (urtel 630 Aug 14 [3]). In connection with question of Portuguese ability to take over technical services at Lagens we would be interested in significance you attribute to change in War Minister's view on this subject since Tibbets and Warren spoke with him on July 11 (Embtel 531 July 12 [2]).

Summary of timing situation is now as follows:

If by Sept 2 we do not have strong indication of favorable outcome of negotiations, War Dept will begin issuing instructions to staff agencies to initiate evacuation Lagens. By Oct 2 transit flights through Lagens will be discontinued. Thereafter flights will overfly Azores and/or use Iceland route.

---

[1] Member of Advisory Committee to Secretary of State on International Aviation.
[2] Not printed.
[3] *Supra*.

Since we are anxious to have, by Sept 2, some indication of eventual outcome of negotiations we are somewhat concerned about stressing Oct 2 deadline to Portuguese. In April and May of 1946 the Portuguese purposely delayed negotiations in order to take advantage of approaching firm deadline June 2. If they now believe that Oct 2 is a similar firm deadline it is possible they would delay negotiations beyond Sept 2 and War Dept would thus be forced to begin evacuation.

We have just spoken to Pereira and have again repeated our dissatisfaction with Portuguese proposal. We stressed our desire to get on with negotiations and told him of your plan to see Dr. Salazar. He has received a letter from Faria with copy of July 25 Memo. He assures us that this Memo represents merely Faria's notes for his conversation with you and is not official document. He says Faria told him first paragraph of Memo shows they have accepted idea of our continued use of Lagens and that balance of Memo according to Pereira represents primarily War Minister's thoughts. We again reviewed with him necessity for presence of ATC personnel at Lagens to operate many technical services. Some of these services ATC must operate themselves at all times but others we are quite willing Portuguese personnel should take over as they become competent to do so. We however pointed out that these technical questions could be arranged in Lisbon after basic agreement reached.

LOVETT

853B.7962/8–1547 : Telegram

The Acting Secretary of State to the Embassy in Portugal

SECRET WASHINGTON, August 15, 1947—6 p. m.

US URGENT   NIACT

589. Following contains suggested revisions in text of "formula":

In view of the termination on December 2, 1947 of the agreement of May 30, 1946 granting transit privileges at the Lagens airport to United States Government aircraft serving United States forces of occupation in Germany and Japan, the Government of Portugal, animated by the spirit of international cooperation is prepared to grant transit privileges at this airport to US Government aircraft serving the US forces of occupation for the period of the occupation, provided that if this period exceeds ten years the question of further use of these facilities shall then be subject to further agreement between the two governments.

The foregoing privileges are granted on condition that the competent American authorities will accept full responsibility for all technical installations and services, maintenance and repairs having to do with the passage of US Government aircraft. The airport at Lagens will of course remain under the full control of the Portuguese authorities.

The Portuguese authorities will be disposed fully to collaborate in the discharge of the foregoing responsibilities and, when deemed opportune, will favorably consider assuming part or all of the aforesaid responsibilities.

The Portuguese Government is extending similar privileges to the aircraft of the British Government.

LOVETT

853B.7962/8–2047 : Telegram

The Ambassador in Portugal (Wiley) to the Secretary of State

SECRET   LISBON, August 20, 1947—10 p. m.

654. Saw Dr. Salazar for hour and half this evening. Gave him our formula and fullest background. He told me that he understood our difficulty in supplying civilian personnel and seemed to accept idea that any new agreement would permit ATC to remain on. During whole discussion Dr. Salazar never mentioned question of wearing uniforms and seemed to attach no particular importance to question.

Dr. Salazar stated that he was mistrustful of over-rapid intelligence of his own people and of possible over-confidence in their ability to take over technical aspects of aviation. Nevertheless, they had made considerable progress and the passage of planes through Lisbon exceeded in number those transiting Lagens. He wanted therefore to approach new agreement on basis factual determination of what responsibilities the port authorities could assume now and, on basis of further preparations, at a later date.

He insisted that he attached the greatest importance to collaboration between the United States and Portugal; that he would work with US with complete good will; and that he had no thought of any kind of ulterior motives or hidden designs on our part.

I mentioned to him the date line of September 2 and that the mechanism for withdrawal would then have to be put in motion, explaining that this would involve considerable work and some confusion. He replied that we could disregard the September 2 date line. He then mentioned December 2. I queried him closely on this so that there would be no misunderstanding. It ended up by his saying that if agreement was not reached promptly, and he implied that no new agreement would be forthcoming immediately, that we could have one month, or two or three or four months or—with sweeping gesture of hand—whatever was necessary during which time we could carry on as usual; he was not approaching the question in any narrow spirit.

I am asking Colonel Tibbets to request appointment with Minister War to repeat foregoing, in order to make absolutely sure that there is no misunderstanding.

Dr. Salazar spoke with great appreciation of the manner in which the American authorities had complied with agreement and with their commitments, of absence of incidents, and of cordiality which characterizes American-Portuguese relations at Lagens. I told him of General Huglin's [1] availability to advise me on technical matters. He replied that he did not think it would be necessary for the General to come for the present, perhaps not at all. I told him, nevertheless, that the General would remain alerted and requested Dr. Salazar to inform me whenever it might be timely for the General to come. He promised to do this.

In our conversation I suggested to Dr. Salazar that we take a trip together to Lagens and look the place over. He sidestepped quickly but amiably.

I got impression from Dr. Salazar's remarks that he wishes to await the return of Caeiro da Mata (now scheduled for early September) before proceeding further with matter.

The way things now appear to stand is that we have reached an agreement on broad question of principle that the technical details must be worked out on a factual basis and that further conversations will be with Foreign Office and not with Dr. Salazar.

WILEY

---

[1] Brig. Gen. Harold Q. Huglin, Deputy Commander of Air Transport Command.

853B.7962/8–2547 : Telegram

The Ambassador in Portugal (Wiley) to the Secretary of State

SECRET   LISBON, August 25, 1947—6 p. m.

671. Faria told me last night immediately subsequent to interview he had with Salazar—he gave same story to Zanthaky [1] the previous day following an earlier interview with Salazar—that the Doctor was pleased with our talk August 20 (Embassy's telegram 654, August 20). Faria stressed fact that he is convinced that an agreement satisfactory to US will be reached but stated it could not be exactly like the May 30 agreement but that the new agreement would have to be "attenuated". For example he mentioned matter of reduction in American personnel and substitution by Portuguese, and said that even on this point the Portuguese did not wish to hinder our efficiency and safety at Lagens

---

[1] Apparently the reference is to Theodore Anthony Xanthaky, special assistant to the Ambassador in Portugal.

and that they will base their estimates on a "factual" study of Portuguese possibilities in furnishing Portuguese personnel wherever possible.

Faria apparently uses the term "May 30 agreement" loosely (the gist of that agreement is of course contained in article (B)) and what he really means is the ancillary Kissner-Cintra document of September 7.[2]

Department will recall that under numbered paragraph 13 of that document the US undertook to lessen drastically our technical staff at Lagens and although the Portuguese have been unable to effect replacements (Embassy's telegram 531, July 12 [3]) our army nevertheless accepted at that time the broad principle of reduction of our personnel and substitutions by Portuguese—which incidentally we agreed to train—and this tenet is now coming home to roost.

Department's attention is also invited to numbered paragraph 8 of this document which stipulates that operations, services, et cetera, including radar would function under control of Portuguese authorities.

Salazar apparently is harping on our commitments under existing agreement and insists on tying them into any new agreement. I expect to see Bianchi shortly and shall reiterate that new agreement shall indeed be "new".

WILEY

---

[2] See telegram 794, September 7, 1946, from Lisbon, *Foreign Relations*, 1946, vol. v, p. 1020.
[3] Not printed.

853B.7962/8–2547 : Telegram

The Acting Secretary of State to the Embassy in Portugal

SECRET   WASHINGTON, September 5, 1947—6 p. m.

648. Urtel 671 Aug 25. In connection with US commitments under May 30 Agreement and Kissner-Cintra Agreement following comments from War Dept may be useful to you in future conversations with FonOff:

A. The US has generously and conscientiously fulfilled spirit Kissner-Cintra Agreement as cordial relations prevailing at Lagens indicates.

B. In July 1945 US military complement in Azores was 2600. At time Kissner-Cintra Agreement concluded US detachment at Lagens was 440 military and 661 civilians (latter preponderantly Portuguese nationals). By Jan 1947 US military personnel had been reduced to 345 military and 590 civilians. Experience demonstrated this number inadequate to handle normal base functions, aircraft maintenance, technical facilities and creditably discharge training commitments. By

July 1947 number was therefore necessarily increased to 550 military and 780 civilians.

C. Para 1 of Kissner-Cintra Agreement accomplished according to schedule; para 2, sale of supplies and equipment concluded to great financial benefit of Portuguese; para 3, assistance of US technical personnel at Santa Maria upon initial occupancy by Portuguese after US withdrawal was made freely despite critical US personnel shortages; paras 4 and 5, terms scrupulously observed including removal US flag from pole in soil to building at Portuguese request; paras 6 and 7, wholehearted cooperation between US and Portuguese authorities and mechanical training continues; para 8, US has submitted to over-all Portuguese control and yet bears major burden for operation of technical facilities; para 9a and b, operations conducted and training obligations being fulfilled; by June 1 it was recognized by all that training of weather reconnaissance personnel was insufficiently advanced to justify assumption of this responsibility by Portuguese military; para 9c, fully and generously fulfilled over and beyond letter of commitment, including better model aircraft than specified, and one-year supply spare parts; paras 10 and 11, scrupulously observed; para 12, full cooperation including assistance to Portuguese Navy in sea-rescue not specified; para 13, recognized by all that Portuguese training insufficiently advanced to adopt substitution for US personnel on scale envisaged this para; para 14, minor technical modification by local agreement; para 15, no comment; para 16, full cooperation.

Question of large-scale substitution of Portuguese for Americans is dependent upon continuous active training and cooperative effort over long period of time. As training for various functions completed gradual substitution of Portuguese for American personnel can of course take place. Estimated however some years will be required to complete training of sufficient number Portuguese up to required standards and to build up reserve pool adequate to guarantee sustained operation of field by Portuguese. Hence realistic approach to duration new agreement must take this into account and not contemplate a temporary expedient of 12–18 months.

Particular reference paras 8 and 9a and b USAF has spent three decades perfecting techniques and training personnel in highly technical matters but is willing to be placed under Portuguese control as long as ultimate responsibility for strictly technical functions rest with US personnel. Is further anxious to make available its skill and knowledge to Portuguese Air Force to indoctrinate its personnel over period of years until adequate number Portuguese reach general level of efficiency and experience to insure uninterrupted airport operation under all circumstances at standard comparable to those required by CAA.

Col Warren estimates 600 US military and civilians are required to guarantee sustained operations with current average work load and to continue to conduct present training. This figure is minimum consistent with our obligations. Since Lagens is vital link US air transport chain supporting occupation forces, it must be maintained at reasonably safe, efficient level. USAF must daily and hourly be prepared to reinforce occupational units, both in personnel and supplies. This may result in abnormal traffic loads. Peak loads can also arise from contingencies of weather and maintenance. Personnel, supplies and facilities must be predicated on anticipated maximum work load rather than average. If US capability cut due to unwise personnel reductions to point where unable to handle peak loads, such conditions would constitute direct and heavy financial and manpower burden on Portuguese.

Capabilities of present operation and servicing personnel means maximum of only six to eight modern four-engined aircraft can be handled in any twenty-four hour period. These are normally scheduled transports, weather reconnaissance and locally based aircraft. In event diversions are made from Santa Maria by commercial aircraft due to weather or USAF special missions by squadrons or groups are required to be handled in same twenty-four hour period, capability this personnel will be exceeded and backlog will develop.

Present stockpiles of US matériel and supplies, many of which are in critical shortage category, cannot be adequately preserved and safeguarded without sufficient personnel. . . . Health of community as well as aircraft maintenance and cooperation of technical services dependent upon regular measures to prevent deterioration of food, water and supplies.

US desires Port Govt be under no financial burden as result of use of transit privileges at Lagens by USAF or of imminent necessity rebuild housing and technical edifices in restricted area now used by US personnel. Only by continued US participation in operation of Lagens can assumption of financial burden by Portuguese be avoided.

LOVETT

811.24553B/10-847

Memorandum of Conversation, by the Director of the Office of European Affairs (Hickerson)

TOP SECRET   [WASHINGTON,] October 8, 1947.

Participants: The Portuguese Ambassador,
                Mr. Hickerson,
                Mr. Reber.

The Portuguese Ambassador called this afternoon at my request to continue the conversation which he had had with Mr. Armour [1] on September 27. I explained that I wanted to take this occasion to give him some of the background of our thinking and policy with respect to base and transit rights in the Azores as I had been closely associated with the formulation of the U.S. position in this matter. There are two separate aspects of the problem which had become confused and thereby might be creating some misunderstanding in his mind and possibly that of his government. I explained that I wanted to talk to him as frankly as he had talked to Mr. Armour and, as it were, off the record.

---

[1] Norman Armour, Assistant Secretary of State for Political Affairs.

The matter which was now under discussion in Lisbon related only to our requirements for transit facilities for the period of occupation of Germany and Japan. We have suggested that the agreement last ten years in order to be sure that we could justify necessary expenditure in maintaining the facilities for which we were asking the Portuguese Government. No one at the time knew how long the occupation of Germany would last but these transit rights were required only in that connection.

The other aspect of the problem was the long-term base rights which we would like to obtain in the Azores and eventually in the Cape Verde Islands. These rights would in all likelihood provide joint operation by Portuguese and U.S. Governments. The facilities we would require might be similar to those which we had obtained from the British Government in some of the islands and which in no sense were considered a derogation of British sovereignty there. We fully understood the Portuguese preoccupation in this respect and had every intention of working out an arrangement with them fully safeguarding their sovereign rights.

In 1946 Mr. Byrnes had decided in connection with the long-term problem to send Mr. Russell, who was then Assistant Secretary of State, to Lisbon in order to explore this question with Dr. Salazar and the members of the Portuguese Government. Recognizing the Portuguese difficulties in respect to any such matter but also their interest in Atlantic security arrangements, we proposed at that time to give an assurance to the Portuguese Government to the effect that any threat to the territorial security of Portugal would contribute a threat to the security of the Atlantic. Should Portugal be the victim of aggression the U.S. by reason of the commitments under the United Nations is obliged to use force against any aggressor. Should the United Nations fail for any reason to act the U.S. would be prepared immediately to consult with Portugal in regard to the solution.

Dr. Salazar seemed profundly interested in this offer but the definite response of the Portuguese Government was disappointing. The Portuguese Government at that time had replied that any agreement on this subject should be limited to five years and that the desired base rights could only be granted in time of war and even then only if the United Kingdom were actually in the war on the same side as the United States. I explained briefly to the Ambassador why these conditions were not acceptable. It had then been decided in the light of this reply and of conditions existing at that time that it would be preferable to postpone further discussions with the Portuguese Government on this subject until a more appropriate time. We felt that both in our own interests and in the interests of the Portuguese Government such delay would be advantageous but that we still believed that some such arrangement was important and would be glad to talk to the Portuguese Government at some later date which both governments considered opportune.

I then referred to the suggestion which the Ambassador had made to Mr. Armour concerning possibility of an arrangement with Portugal in line with the provisions of Article 51 of the Charter.[2] As the Ambassador was aware, there has been discussion in the press of this country as to agreements which might be reached probably on a multilateral basis to carry out the provisions of this article and that the matter was under study by the U.S. Government. We do not yet know what the result of this study would be. Personally it seemed to me to offer the best chance of providing the security which we had originally hoped the Charter itself would give when it was not expected that the veto would be used to nullify it. When this government had reached a decision on the matter I could state that Portugal's suggestion in this matter would be given most sympathetic consideration.

The Ambassador said that he welcomed this frank explanation of U.S. position which would be most helpful indeed to him. He recognized that with regard to the long-term security problem which would involve the base rights this must now await the results of this year's General Assembly. He was frankly concerned by its trend and feared that it might mark a very crucial point. He was worried that the American position had not been sufficiently understood in certain countries and that its leadership which was so important to the safety and security of the smaller countries was not being given the full recognition which it merited.

JOHN HICKERSON

[2] Charter of the United Nations, June 26, 1945; for text, see Department of State Treaty Series No. 993, or 59 Stat. (pt. 2) 1031.

853B.7962/10–2247 : Telegram

The Acting Secretary of State to the Embassy in Portugal

TOP SECRET WASHINGTON, October 22, 1947—6 p. m.

784. We have learned from Emb here Portuguese most disappointed Azores discussions not resumed same basis Russell proposal (Embtel 615 July 16, 1946 [1]) and Portuguese have not fully understood or accepted explanation our inability resume discussions that basis. Portuguese furthermore disappointed and disturbed we are minimizing importance transit facilities we have requested. While facilities may seem relatively unimportant to us they maintain granting them presents problem first importance to Port Govt since it will then be

[1] *Foreign Relations*, 1946, vol. v, p. 1004.

at least indirectly associated with US policy generally. They feel US should indicate greater appreciation importance to Portugal this question. They apparently would welcome indication from us now we would send them, when agreement concluded, letter of appreciation for their assistance and cooperation.

While appreciating Portuguese position we wish avoid overemphasizing importance facilities in order avert possibility Portuguese then seeking obtain unrelated concessions, or commitment such as contemplated in Russell approach, which we cannot make.

LOVETT

853B.7962/10–2347 : Telegram

The Ambassador in Portugal (Wiley) to the Secretary of State

TOP SECRET LISBON, October 23, 1947—7 p. m.

869. Am most surprised to learn Portuguese disappointed because conversations re Azores not initiated same basis Russell proposal (Deptel 784, October 22). Am further surprised that they have not understood or accepted "explanation" (what explanation?) our inability resume on that basis since question has never in any way been raised with me.

I have repeatedly emphasized that facilities at Lagens represent important point of departure for American-Portuguese collaboration, but without suggestion of any *quid pro quo* on our part. Dr. Salazar perfectly understands that we entirely unable to give Portuguese any "empire guarantee", etc, etc.

Since comments set forth in Deptel do not tie in with realities of situation as they appear here, I would be interested in knowing source of Department's information; was it the Ambassador? [1]

WILEY

[1] The Department in its telegram 791, October 24, 1947, to Lisbon, not printed, identified the source as the Counselor of the Portuguese Embassy (853B.7962/10–2347).

853B.7962/10–2447 : Telegram

The Ambassador in Portugal (Wiley) to the Secretary of State

SECRET LISBON, October 24, 1947—9 p. m.

875. Have seen Foreign Minister. I told him in detail my trip Azores, of excellent impression I received there; that I doubted if in entire world there was a more happy example of international collaboration and that I doubted if one would find more satisfactory formula than conditions as now exist. I discussed with him conditions there in detail. I referred to Portuguese susceptibilities. I told him I thought these

susceptibilities were limited to very few Portuguese indeed and that I myself would not call them susceptibilities but superstitions.

The Foreign Minister told me *inter alia* that although Dr. Salazar had promised to show him the report of General Cintra he had not done so. He felt very much as I did about the Azores but regretted to say that Dr. Salazar's views were more rigid than his although he added that Dr. Salazar was most anxious that a mutually acceptable agreement be reached.

Dr. Salazar, the Foreign Minister explained, felt that the time had come for us to get on a technical basis. The [*They?*] thought that this was the moment to bring over one of our generals. I replied that I was perfectly agreeable to anything Dr. Salazar desired. If he, the Foreign Minister, wished I was ready to telegraph that a general proceed immediately to Lisbon. Personally, however, I thought suggestion was premature. I was running the negotiations here; we had established an atmosphere of mutual confidence but, so far, we had not reached an agreement in principle. I thought that we were not yet ready for small details. The Foreign Minister asked what I proposed. I suggested that it would be valuable indeed if he, Dr. Salazar and I, with ample time at our disposition, could sit down around a table and talk things out. The Foreign Minister replied that he thought idea was excellent. He would communicate with Dr. Salazar in that sense tomorrow. He feared very much that interview would not be feasible until after Wednesday, October 29. There were American naval vessels here, the Portuguese military celebrations and the Canadian Minister of Commerce. Just as soon after Wednesday as possible interview would be arranged.

During the course of conversation I talked about psychological misinterpretation and informed him re nomenclature Lagens that name was being changed to "Azores Air Transport Station".[1] He seemed very pleased.

WILEY

[1] The Air Force had taken action earlier to designate Lagens as the "Azores Command" (853B.7962/10–1747).

853B.7962/10–2447 : Telegram

The Acting Secretary of State to the Embassy in Portugal

TOP SECRET   WASHINGTON, November 1, 1947—2 p. m.
US URGENT

815. We have had most useful discussion with Wagner[1] today. Fundamentally important fact has emerged which will probably have direct bearing on your next talk with Salazar.

[1] Joseph J. Wagner, second secretary and vice consul at Lisbon, temporarily in Washington.

We believe that Salazar and FonOff are fearful that US, under guise of request for innocuous transit facilities, is attempting to obtain substance of long term base rights, as proposed by Russell, without giving *quid pro quo* of type he outlined. We are still definitely interested in long term arrangements for joint use and maintenance of military and naval base facilities in Azores (see para 6 Dept instr. June 3, 1947 re Azores). It is essential that Portuguese understand such arrangement is still a matter of interest to us but is entirely separate from present request for transit facilities. When long term discussions ended last year Portuguese were assured talks were being recessed but not terminated. From Portuguese point of view particularly, Russell proposal is not extraneous issue. They attach great importance to long term arrangement but should understand foregoing.

You may inform Salazar accordingly.

We believe Portuguese suspicion we are attempting obtain substance long term base rights without necessity giving them *quid pro quo* may be basic reason for their procrastination, reluctance to conclude agreement and for Pereira's effort (perhaps under instructions from Salazar) to obtain reassurance that US is still interested in Russell proposal.

We will see Pereira Tuesday, bring him up to date (urtel 873, Oct 24 [2]) and express anxiety long delays in negotiations.

LOVETT

---

[2] Not printed.

853B.7962/11–347 : Telegram

The Ambassador in Portugal (Wiley) to the Secretary of State

SECRET   LISBON, November 3, 1947—10 p. m.
NIACT

910. I saw Dr. Salazar for 1 hour 35 minutes this evening, discussed Lagens with him in greatest detail. He reverted to familiar theme song about necessity for finding "formula". I asked him what he had in mind. He replied that he hadn't reached a decision; that he would immediately confer with Minister War on latter's return Wednesday and would talk to General Cintra. He insisted that he wanted agreement that would permit no possibility of misunderstanding with US; he attached greatest importance to Portuguese relations with US and didn't want them jeopardized; in formula it must be shown that Portugal had made "progress" from last agreement; that Portugal would be able to take additional technical services. He will communicate with me in course of present week.

I urged continuation of present ideal situation existing in Lagens, insisted that exaggerated importance was being given to question of formula, as when he raised question of Portugal susceptibilities (this always comes up) I suggested these were limited to a very few men in or near his government and did not preoccupy Portuguese public opinion. He replied this was true because public opinion had confidence he would take best decision to safeguard Portuguese interests. I replied that Portuguese public opinion had confidence in US. I repeatedly brought up December 2 deadline. He said and reiterated that he would try to work out acceptable formula as rapidly as possible. He hoped it would be done before December 2 but if he could not we could forget about December 2 and if we could not agree on a formula we could have "six, eight or twelve months, or whatever time we needed" for evacuation.

I made strong plea for American personnel at Lagens to be able to bring families.

My conclusions are that in course of next week Salazar will gently place Azores baby in lap of General Cintra and will want an American general to come over in order to engage in long and very detailed negotiations. Salazar, I think, would prefer our staying in Azores for next millenium if Portuguese Government could dodge responsibility definite decision.

There is not the slightest manifestation of interest on part of Salazar with regard to any political guarantees (he is, I think, bright enough to know from realities of world situation Portugal already has in fact all guarantees in that he [*that we?*] could possibly give them). So far he has not shown the slightest interest in any agreement "for long-term base". (ReDeptel 815, November 1, 2 p.m.)

Salazar has excluded Foreign Minister from his conversations with me and has not even given Foreign Office copy of Cintra report.

(ReEmbtel 889, October 29 [1]). I therefore urge that Department observe extreme reticence in talking with Pereira.

Would like to have Col. Warren informed of foregoing thru ATC and also that it may be desirable Major Hammond [2] remain here some time.

WILEY

---

[1] Not printed.
[2] Maj. Mahlon B. Hammond.

853B.7962/11–1947 : Telegram

The Ambassador in Portugal (*Wiley*) *to the Secretary of State*

SECRET   LISBON, November 19, 1947—1 p. m.
URGENT   NIACT

949. Attention Dunham WE. Had occasion to talk briefly to Foreign Minister at dinner last night. I told him I had received very nice

letter from Dr. Salazar informing me he thought he had found "formula". Foreign Minister replied, "Yes, we have just finished working over this formula today and I think you will find it satisfactory. Dr. Salazar's point of view has become much less rigid." He then added that he wanted to talk to me about it but explained he was not feeling well. He gave me impression that it would be perhaps several days before he could receive me.

I then had occasion to talk to Faria. He volunteered that a satisfactory formula had been found that he was sure I would like. Bianchi too was there. He said the formula provided for continuation without renegotiation for, he added, perhaps twenty years or even longer. (This probably means an "escape clause".) He said that he was sure wives and children of American personnel could come to Azores.

Please inform Colonel Warren through ATC of foregoing telling him I am going to shoot hard to make it possible to get at least a few families to Lagens for Christmas. He should make tentative plans.

WILEY

853B.7962/11–2747 : Telegram

The Ambassador in Portugal (Wiley) to the Secretary of State

SECRET   LISBON, November 27, 1947—8 p. m.
NIACT

960. Following is formula mentioned mytel 958, November 27 [1]

"I have the honor to communicate to Your Excellency that the request of the Govt of the US relative to the continuance of transit facilities granted to the airplanes of the ATC under the agreement of May 30, 1946 has been considered attentively and in the most friendly spirit. The Portuguese Govt believes that the following formula will give satisfaction to the interests in question:

The Govt of Portugal and the Govt of the United States:

Considering that the facilities granted for the transit of airplanes of the ATC servicing the occupation troops in Germany and Japan terminate on December 2, 1947 under the terms of the agreement of May 30 of the preceding years;

Considering the manifest utility to the Govt of the United States, given its international responsibilities with which at the moment it is burdened, in continuing the transit thru Lagens of the referred to airplanes;

Having in mind the advantages which those facilities will achieve for the security of Europe and for the reestablishment and consolidation of world peace as well as the indirect value which the same may bring about for the common defense and security;

---

[1] Not printed.

Examining the execution of the program agreed upon for the carrying out of the May 30 agreement between the Portuguese military authorities and the ATC command in the Azores:

Agree:

That the Portuguese Govt will continue to grant to the Govt of the United States transit facilities for American aviation (ATC) thru Lagens airdrome in the following terms:

(A) The granting of facilities refers to period of three years beginning December 2, 1947, tacitly extendable from year to year for two years more, if not denounced by the Portuguese Govt with three months' notice. The Govt of the US may denounce the agreement and relinquish the facilities at any moment.

(B) There shall not be due, for the utilization of the aerodrome and of the various installations, the payment of any tax or rental; and for the purpose of customs and other facilities the special character of the airplanes in transit will be respected. The Govt of the US will, however, be responsible for the expenses which may have to be made for those improvements of the aerodrome which are not necessary for the utilization by the Portuguese services as well as the eventual substitution of deteriorated installations which are destined to the services or living quarters of its personnel, it being understood that all constructions shall be immediately considered property of the Portuguese Government.

(C) The Govt of the US will continue to furnish the necessary facilities for the apprenticeship and training of Portuguese personnel having in mind the perfect functioning of the services of the air base including those utilized by the ATC during the three year period mentioned in para A, as well as the acquisition by the Portuguese Govt of material deemed indispensable for the services of the base.

(D) The special conditions of a technical nature necessary for the carrying out of the present agreement will be stipulated between the Portuguese military authorities and the authorities of the ATC and will be subject to confirmation of the Minister of War in Lisbon, as well as a periodic revision at the request of either of the parties. It is understood, however:

(1) The personnel of American nationality normally in service may not exceed the minimum reached during the last 12 months, except in case of emergency communicated as far as possible in advance to the Portuguese Govt and there then can be authorized the entry and utilization of personnel necessary to the anticipated traffic.

(2) Among the material the acquisition of which will be facilitated the material needed for the new control tower will be given urgent consideration.

(3) There may be authorized the residence in Praia da Victoria of persons of the families of the personnel on service and there will be granted as a consequence of this authorization the necessary facilities.

(E) The Portuguese Govt reserves the right to grant the Govt of Great Britain transit facilities identical to those mentioned in this agreement.

In case the govt of the United States accepts the formula mentioned above the affirmative reply of Your Excellency will constitute with this the agreement of the two govts concerning this matter, which will enter into force together with the arrangements contemplated in item (D) above."

WILEY

853B.7962/11–2747 : Telegram

The Ambassador in Portugal (Wiley) to the Secretary of State

SECRET   LISBON, November 27, 1947—9 p. m.
NIACT

961. Foreign Minister today handed me Portuguese "formula" covering our continuance at Lagens, and English translation thereof is being telegraphed separately (Emtel 960).

During Foreign Minister's conversation with me, he mentioned that Portuguese would consider any modifications which we might wish to make in their formula. I replied, that, concerning the number of US personnel at Lagens, we might have to add to such complement during times not of an "emergency" nature, to take care of new types of aircraft et cetera, and said that I believed that this feature should be provided for, suggesting the use of the words "in order to meet technical exigencies". He reacted sympathetically.

The Foreign Minister also said that after Salazar had relaxed his rigidity, he, the Foreign Minister, had had great difficulty with the Minister War, who tried to insist that the formula be limited to one year, and who also fought stubbornly against the admission of families of American personnel. The Minister War eventually relaxed to the extent of accepting the idea of admitting 10 families, then 20 and finally the Foreign Minister was able to arrange the formula without any limitation on numbers.

The Foreign Minister also told me that we should interpret the formula to mean that we will enjoy the use of the facilities for the full five years.

I think it notable that the Portuguese have dropped any demands to show "progress" in the new agreement, and have similarly dropped all requests for their forces to take over any of the technical functions at Lagens.

Furthermore, I think that the Foreign Minister has done a grand job on our behalf, in the face of stiff and resolute opposition.

I discussed with the Foreign Minister the substance of Deptel 855, November 25.[1] He is immediately calling in Faria, in order to prepare a press release which could simultaneously be given out in Lisbon and Washington.

---

[1] Not printed.

I think that the foregoing will give all that the ATC want at this time. However, we are going to work immediately to see if the requirement that families be stationed at Praia da Victoria (the small town near the airfield) can be eliminated since ATC desires to remodel existing quarters to accommodate families; and to dilute word "emergency" in respect to increase of personnel and that ATC aircraft be changed to US Government aircraft.

Subheading D of formula suggests that ATC now send me very competent technical adviser.

Please inform Colonel Warren of formula through ATC. Please also brief Major Hammond on Department's reaction to formula and return him here.

WILEY

853B.7962/12–147 : Telegram

The Ambassador in Portugal (Wiley) to the Secretary of State

SECRET   LISBON, December 1, 1947—2 p. m.
NIACT

973. Yesterday had very intimate and off-the-record conversation with Bianchi. After thinking things over, have reached conclusion that in view of Portuguese susceptibilities re formula, it is wiser to accept it as is and not run risks inherent in reopening conversations. I propose therefore, when I see Foreign Minister tomorrow afternoon, to congratulate him on statesman-like and friendly solution which he and Dr. Salazar evolved. I shall then, unless instructed to the contrary, say that formula is entirely acceptable and is accepted. Only after this shall I seek modifications. In meantime, suggest Department draft very affable expression of appreciation which I can include in my formal note of acceptance (see last paragraph of formula). Please instruct me soonest.

WILEY

853B.7962/12–147 : Telegram

The Acting Secretary of State to the Embassy in Portugal

SECRET   WASHINGTON, December 1, 1947—5 p. m.
US URGENT   NIACT

862. Agree formula may be accepted in principle subject to minor modifications. (Urtel 973, Dec 1.) Hope you can postpone any final decisions with FonMin on modifications we desire until arrival Ham-

mond who is full briefed on our views and who is due to arrive Lisbon probably with Warren Dec 3.

Briefly, we would like language modifications made (urtel 961, Nov 27) but do not wish to insist, if Portuguese have strong substantive objections, in view liberal interpretation they are giving formula. Believe you are best judge of what is feasible and acceptable this respect. However, we do wish to insist on removal requirement dependents must live at Praia da Victoria. Hammond advises conditions there are so bad this requirement constitutes, in effect, prohibition on presence of families.

Instead of including expression of appreciation in formal note of acceptance, we suggest you send FonMin separate letter, under instructions from your Govt, along lines of draft enclosed with Dunham's letter to you Oct 28.[1]

LOVETT

---

[1] Not printed.

853B.7962/12–247 : Telegram

The Ambassador in Portugal (Wiley) to the Secretary of State

SECRET   LISBON, December 2, 1947—7 p. m.
US URGENT

977. Saw Foreign Minister this afternoon. Expressed sincere gratitude for his and Dr. Salazar's statesmanlike solution.

I told him that formula was acceptable and was, in principle, accepted [;] only then I went into matter of modifications. Concerning "American aviation (ATC)" I pointed out (1) that ATC might change its name at some future date and (2) that US Government planes other than ATC aircraft transit Lagens and inquired if wording of formula would present any legalistic hindrances. He categorically said that terms used meant all American Government aircraft, including Navy. I told him that his interpretation was sufficient. I then suggested that perhaps a synonym could be found for word "emergency" emphasizing that the word had taken on a special connotation in the English language. He said that he had thought of this himself, and that he considered "unforeseen necessities" would be a better expression of what was intended. I agreed entirely.

I thereupon raised the proposed residence of dependents at Praia da Victoria. The Foreign Minister quickly replied that this feature had been most difficult for him to work out. He said Dr. Salazar had at times been most rigid on the point, and that attitude of Minister War had been adamant. The Foreign Minister finally suggested that he would see what could be done about allowing some dependents at

Lagens, perhaps families of officers. I made strong appeal to get some dependents out for Christmas. He jumped at this and said that it would give him a good talking point with Dr. Salazar.

The interview, which was most friendly and characterized by sincere desire of Foreign Minister to assist us, ended by his assuring me that he would see Dr. Salazar this evening and also contact Minister War.

To recapitulate: from conversation with Foreign Minister it is clear that all US Government aircraft can transit Lagens; that probably a satisfactory synonym for "emergency" will be found and, finally, that part of the dependents (officers families) will be permitted to reside at Lagens. On subject of getting all dependents at Lagens I went all out but attitude of Dr. Salazar and Minister War is such that I don't think we can accomplish this immediately. I think however that we have our foot in the door. I might add that Foreign Minister suffers from no illusions that we can rent premises at Praia da Victoria; he realizes that we have to build. Surely building a few beaverboard houses in neighborhood of Praia, which is very near Lagens, would involve neither great expense nor inconvenience. In any event the women and children would spend their days at Lagens. From my visit there I would say that living in vicinity of Praia would present no more inconvenience than for State Department personnel to reside in vicinity of Dupont Circle.

I gave Colonel Warren and Major Hammond tremendous buildup and also hinted that Colonel Matalo should be brought over from Lagens to work on operating agreement.

WILEY

Editorial Note

An agreement between the United States and Portugal granting American aircraft the right to continue using transit facilities in the Azores was effected by an exchange of notes signed at Lisbon February 2, 1948; operative retroactively to December 2, 1947. For text of Agreement, see Department of State Treaties and Other International Acts Series (TIAS) No. 2351; United States Treaties and Other International Agreements (UST), volume 2 (pt. 2), page 2266.

AGREEMENT BETWEEN THE UNITED STATES AND PORTUGAL ON AMENDMENT OF THE ANNEX TO THE AIR TRANSPORT AGREEMENT CONCLUDED DECEMBER 6, 1945

[For text of Agreement effected by exchange of notes signed at Lisbon, June 28, 1947, see Department of State Treaties and Other International Acts Series (TIAS) No. 1656, or 61 Stat. (pt. 3) 3185.]

SPAIN

ATTITUDE OF THE UNITED STATES WITH RESPECT TO THE FRANCO REGIME IN SPAIN [1]

852.00/1–347

Memorandum of Conversation, by the Chargé in Spain (Bonsal) [2]

[MADRID, January 2, 1947.]

Following a conversation on other subjects the Foreign Minister [3] and I discussed the Spanish political situation and the regime's foreign relations. The Foreign Minister stated that the recent resolution [4] approved by the General Assembly of the United Nations in New York with regard to Spain constituted a set-back for those members of General Franco's [5] cabinet, including himself, who desired to secure some sort of evolution here. The attitude generally prevalent in the cabinet at present is that nothing which the regime could conceivably do internally would be apt to improve Spain's international position. This applies not only to political developments but also to such matters as repatriation, SAFEHAVEN, etc. which involve concessions to the requests of the United States and Great Britain. (See other memoranda of this same date.[6])

The Minister said, however, that he himself had every intention of continuing to press for evolutionary changes here since he is strongly of the opinion that the Government, in order to achieve stability, must rest upon institutions rather than upon one man, i.e., General Franco.

The Minister then spoke with considerable indignation of the way in which the Spanish problem has been handled in the United Nations. He said that it had been a sort of cat's paw in the struggle between the Soviet Union on the one hand and the United States and Great Britain on the other. Whenever the relations between East and West became tense the Spanish issue was apt to be dragged out and the Western powers were apt to make concessions to the Soviet in the form of attacks on the Spanish regime.

---

[1] Continued from *Foreign Relations*, 1946, vol. v, pp. 1023 ff.
[2] Transmitted to the Department as an enclosure to despatch 3315, January 3, from Madrid, not printed; received January 15, 1947.
[3] Alberto Martin Artajo.
[4] Resolution on Spain adopted by the General Assembly of the United Nations on December 12, 1946; see *Foreign Relations*, 1946, vol. v, pp. 1080–1090.
[5] Francisco Franco y Bahamonde, Spanish Chief of State.
[6] Not printed.

In reply to this I endeavored to raise the larger issue of the attitude in general of the peoples of the Western countries and especially of Great Britain and the United States toward the Spanish regime. I said that we all considered that Spain belongs to our civilization and that therefore a regime which denies the basic freedoms considered essential to that civilization cannot hope for good relations with us. I pointed out that, viewing the situation wholly objectively, the recent action of the United Nations was merely a further step in a process which, if it were allowed to continue, could only result in a still greater isolation of Spain from the rest of the western world. I also ventured the thought that the longer this isolation continued the more apt would be the extremists to win out in Spain.

The Minister replied that he frankly no longer believed that there was anything within the power of the present Spanish regime to perform which would improve public opinion in general in the United States and Great Britain. He said, however, that he believed that in Spain's own interest some sort of evolution is necessary. He said that he had been in frequent contact with General Franco on the subject and that he himself was advocating the preparation of a constitutional law which would set up a ["]Consejo del Reino" (Council of the Realm) which would provide for an orderly succession in the leadership of the State as well as public participation on a moderate scale in the work of Government. The Minister said that it was his idea that this constitutional law would be subjected to a popular referendum.

The Minister then referred to the demonstrations of December 9 against foreign interference in Spanish affairs. He said that the importance of this matter had been wholly and willfully neglected by the foreign press and that this neglect was a further contribution to misunderstanding of Spanish realities. He said that the Monarchists had been amazed at the evidence of the regime's strength afforded by the demonstrations and he took occasion to say that he thought orthodox Monarchists rather weak and ineffective.

The Minister said that there was some sentiment in Government circles for the holding of a plebiscite in order to register support for Franco. In his opinion General Franco would win such a plebiscite overwhelmingly, particularly if Giral [7] were to be placed on the ticket. However, the Minister said that in his own opinion it would be undesirable to have such a plebiscite since the objective toward which Spain should work, i.e., institutional normality, would not be furthered by voting at this time on personalities.

The Minister then returned to the handling of the Spanish question in the United Nations. He expressed great indignation at the difference

---

[7] José Giral y Pereira was President of the Spanish Republican "Government-in-Exile" until his resignation on January 27, 1947.

between the treatment accorded the Soviet Union and her satellites and that meted out to Spain. I said that we were endeavoring to carry out our obligations in regard to Poland, Rumania, Bulgaria, etc. He said, however, that it was a farce for us, in view of our attitude toward the Soviet Union to maintain that we had fought and won a war for the overthrow of totalitarianism and that this justified our attitude toward the Franco regime. He said that there was considerably more personal liberty in Spain than in countries which we had mentioned.

The Minister then described the actual voting in the United Nations regarding the Spanish problem. He referred to the vote at San Francisco in the spring of 1945 when Spain was not even mentioned by name and when all of the members of the United Nations voted in favor of a vague condemnation of regimes brought into power with Axis assistance. He then referred to the General Assembly meeting in London in February [8] of this year [1946] and pointed out that although the resolution on Spain obligated no one to take any action two American republics have voted against it. He then said that considering the prestige of Great Britain and the United States and the pressures which he assumed had been brought to bear that it was well worthy of notice that the resolution which had been voted in New York last month had received the negative votes of six countries and fourteen had abstained. He said that he himself had received the visits of certain representatives of countries which had voted in favor of the resolution and they had indicated that their delegates had had no choice in the matter although deploring this infringement of the principle of non-intervention. The Minister said that it was his own impression, apparently derived from the return from the United States of such travelers as the Bishop of Ciudad Rodrigo, that our public opinion was becoming more favorable or at least less hostile toward the regime and that with a Republican victory in Congress some change might be expected in our Spanish policy.

In closing the conversation I returned to the theme of the impossibility of Spain's maintaining indefinitely a regime based upon principles wholly in disaccord with those which have been worked out by the countries whose civilization Spain shares and to which Spain has made important contributions. I again said that it seemed to me the longer the present situation lasts the more certain would be a violent overthrow. The Minister of course reaffirmed his own feeling as to the popular support of the regime. In the course of the discussion I had said that it seemed to me that the objective of evolution here would be to close the wounds of the Civil War and to establish a political system

---

[8] For text of the resolution on Spain adopted by the General Assembly on February 9, 1946, see *Foreign Relations*, 1946, vol. v, p. 1033, footnote 16.

within which both sides in that conflict might have some possibilities of free expression. The Minister conceded this to be a desirable objective and he agreed with me that the Government could not indefinitely be the sole property of those who won the Spanish Civil War. However, he made the point that the United Nations so far is being conducted by and for the benefit of those who won the World War.

852.00/2-647

Memorandum of Conversation, by the Chargé in Spain (Bonsal)[1]

[MADRID,] February 1, 1947.

This conversation took place at my home on the evening of February 1. General Beigbeder was accompanied by Señor Tomás Peyre who represents moderate Republican sentiment and is reported to be close to the Socialists. Mr. Maffitt of the Embassy was also present, and this account reflects our joint recollection of what took place.

After the customary amenities, General Beigbeder said that as we were all aware he had replaced General Aranda in negotiating on behalf of the Monarchist parties with the Republican groups for the setting up of a provisional government which would be broadly representative of the opposition to General Franco within Spain. The plan is to form a cabinet consisting of seven Monarchists, seven Republicans and either three or four military men. General Beigbeder's responsibility is apparently confined to discussions with Republican elements of the A.N.F.D.

General Beigbeder said that he did not know when or if these negotiations might be successful. He said that there was at least a chance that agreement might be reached within the next few days. He said that he wished to inform me about this so that the Government of the United States could be thinking over the matter and deciding what its attitude would be. He said that he felt that the prospective government came within the objectives set forth in the tripartite statement of March, 1946[2] of the British, French and American Governments.

At first General Beigbeder implied at least the hope that the formation of this new provisional government would be followed by a rupture of relations on the part of the British and ourselves with the Franco regime. However he did not insist on this point. He did say that the success of the new organization would depend in large part

---

[1] Transmitted to Department as enclosure 1 to despatch 3500, February 6, from Madrid, not printed; received February 19, 1947.
[2] Joint statement by the United States, United Kingdom, and France on their relations with the Franco Government, released to the press on March 4, 1946. For text, see Department of State *Bulletin* March 17, 1946, p. 412.

upon the "calor" or warmth with which it was received in Washington and London. He made it clear that in the absence of such warmth it would soon fall apart and "Franco might last for thirty years". He also said that he hoped that as soon as the new government was set up, it would be possible for "agentes oficiosos" or semi-official representatives to be received in Washington and London.

In reply to all this I stated that while our attitude toward the Franco regime was well known, it was difficult for us to define beforehand the action we would take in any particular set of circumstances. I set forth some of the considerations involved in the recognition of a new government, taking as a minimum basis the requisites of the so-called Estrada doctrine.[3] I said that while there had been cases in which our Government had continued to recognize governments after they had been driven into exile by foreign invaders, I did not know of any cases where we had recognized organizations which had never held executive power.

Although General Beigbeder concentrated entirely on his own negotiations with the Republicans within Spain, I gathered that those Republicans are in pretty close touch with various groups outside of Spain and even with Martinez Barrio, the so-called President of the Spanish Republic.

It is General Beigbeder's thought that as soon as the new provisional government is formed about half of its members will be arrested here and the other half will be able to reach Tangier where they can set up operations. A period of conspiracy and underground activity will ensue, the success of which will be greatly dependent upon the support which the new organization is able to obtain from abroad.

The purpose of the interim government, once it has secured the elimination of General Franco, will be merely to hold elections on the fundamental question of whether Spain is to be a Republic or a Monarchy. It is General Beigbeder's idea that these elections will be held shortly after the assumption of power and that conditions prevailing in the interim and on that occasion will include strict censorship, a continued state of war, the suspension of the right to strike and very limited scope for political propaganda. In fact, General Beigbeder envisages statements on the matter at issue only by members of the new Ministry, i.e., the seven Monarchists, seven Republicans, and three or four generals. Once the country has decided on

---

[3] In 1930 Genaro Estrada, the Secretary of Foreign Relations in the Mexican Government, announced that when a new government was established in another country by means of a *coup d'état*, Mexico would continue its diplomatic relations with that country without regard to the legitimacy of the new government. For discussion of the doctrine, see Instituto Americano de Derecho y Legislación Comparada, *La Doctrina Estrada* (Mexico City, 1930).

either a Monarchy or a Republic, all parties will be pledged to accept this decision and to work loyally under whatever system is achieved.

852.00/2–447 : Telegram

The Chargé in Spain (Bonsal) to the Secretary of State

SECRET   MADRID, February 4, 1947—1 p. m.

97. Gen Beigbeder has just called on me to say that it is possible negotiations between Monarchist groups (which he represents with approval of Pretender Don Juan [1]) and Alliance of Democratic Forces including certain Republican elements, Socialists, UGT and CNT may possibly not certainly result in agreement within next few days. Beigbeder said purpose of giving information was to enable US Government to ponder its possible attitude toward new provisional government. He said that its eventual success would depend on "warmth" with which it was received abroad principally in Washington and London. He said he hoped that unofficial agents of this new organization when formed would be received in friendly manner in Washington and London. Other than stressing our policy regarding Franco regime I was non-committal. Full report being despatched.

It is my belief that if agreement reached on governmental slate including representatives of conservative classes largely Monarchists, Republicans and major labor organizations, important step forward would have been taken here. Difficulty is that of ascertaining representative character of self-styled leaders of various groups.

Repeated Paris 20, London 15.

BONSAL

---

[1] Juan de Borbón y Battenberg.

852.00/2–747

The Chargé in Spain (Bonsal) to the Secretary of State

SECRET   MADRID, February 7, 1947.
No. 3506

SIR: I have the honor to submit below certain considerations regarding the policy which the Department might adopt in the matter of recognition of any new Spanish government which might emerge as a result of political developments within the country.

It is assumed that the recognition issue would not arise unless the new government fulfilled at least the minimum requirements of the so-called Estrada doctrine. However, as I have already indicated (see the Embassy's telegram 85 of January 31 [1]), the opinion has been expressed by some members of the opposition to the Franco regime that in the event that a "paper" government is formed which is deemed truly representative of the Spanish people, recognition should be forthcoming even in the absence of the removal of the present regime. This is an interpretation of the tripartite statement of March, 1946 for which I can see no basis. The question of the attitude to be observed by the Department with regard to any opposition organization or self-styled government prior to the removal of the present regime will be the subject of other communications to the Department.

There is no doubt that the prospects of anti-Franco groups or coalitions within Spain are becoming more promising. Therefore, the attitude which the British and ourselves may assume in the matter of recognition in the event that such groups or coalitions manage to achieve power is becoming of increasing urgency and should be defined. In fact, it is my belief that not only should the policy be defined but that this Embassy should be authorized in its discretion, following consultation with the British Embassy and perhaps also with the French Mission here, to make it known at an appropriate time to opposition leaders. Those leaders are, of course, much concerned with the matter and we will eventually, in fairness to them and in furtherance of our own stated policy toward Spain, have to express a point of view particularly if and when a practical agreement is reached among opposition groups. (See, for example, the Embassy's telegram 97 of February 4.)

My recommendation in the matter involves a separation between the two principal aspects of the matter:

1) the recognition of a new government and maintenance of diplomatic relations with it, and
2) cooperation with the new government in economic and political matters, appointment of an American Ambassador to Spain and advocacy of Spain's admission into the United Nations.

Recognition should in my judgment be accorded as soon as in our judgment the new government appears to control the situation, to enjoy the at least passive acquiescence of the people and to have pledged itself to the performance of its international obligations. The added condition might be injected that it should pledge itself as soon as possible to ascertain the will of the Spanish people regarding the constitutional future of the country. Whether to add this condition would depend very much upon circumstances. Such a statement would

---

[1] Not printed.

in all likelihood be made in any case. I assume that this matter of recognition of any new Spanish Government would be handled individually rather than through the United Nations.

The second phase of the problem would then be subject to developments here. We might wish to make it clear that economic and political cooperation, the designation of an American Ambassador to Spain and support of Spain's admission into the United Nations would depend on the reestablishment in Spain of fundamental individual freedoms. On the other hand, circumstances might be such that we would find it desirable to bolster the new government (which would undoubtedly find itself in a position of considerable difficulty from the economic point of view) without exacting any very specific pledges. It is my opinion that we would wish to make no statements or commitments which would unduly tie our hands and take away from us the possibility of action designed to further our own best interests in Spain.

Those interests clearly lie in the direction of the appearance here as soon as possible of a government of moderate tendencies able to steer a course between the extremes of rigid dictatorship of the reactionary and fascist elements on the one hand and on the other the social revolution advocated from Moscow. In order to promote such a situation we will obviously not find it possible to apply too rigid a series of definitions and conditions but will have to be guided by our estimate of the practical possibilities of Spanish politics at the time we are called on to make our decisions.

In conclusion I wish to emphasize that I believe that a time may come when the activities of the opposition to Franco, especially among military and middle class circles here, will be stimulated and facilitated if the leaders of those elements could be given a general idea of the recognition policy which would be followed by our Government and by the British Government. I should appreciate receiving the views of the Department on the matter.

Respectfully yours,   PHILIP W. BONSAL

711.52/2–2847 : Telegram

The Chargé in Spain (Bonsal) to the Secretary of State

CONFIDENTIAL   MADRID, February 28, 1947—1 p. m.

166. Immediately preceding telegram contains text signed editorial appearing this a.m.'s Falange organ *Arriba* with highly of-

fensive statements re US Govt (see especially last two paragraphs).[1] I have orally indicated to high Foreign Office official for transmission to Ministry that I must regard this article as official statement of Spanish Govt since it appears in organ of single party, of which Franco is head, and I added that I was sending text to Dept for instructions as to any action which might be desirable.

In my judgment opportunity is afforded to press Foreign Office to oblige Falange organ to publish humiliating apology.

Dept's views and instructions would be appreciated.

BONSAL

---

[1] Not printed. The penultimate paragraph of telegram 165, February 28, 1947, referred to Braden's "Hispanophobia" and included the following sentence: "How long are there to be let loose through the world those degenerates and criminals who stain all that they touch and dishonor wherever they enter?" (811.00B/2–2847)

711.52/2–2847 : Telegram

The Secretary of State to the Embassy in Spain

CONFIDENTIAL WASHINGTON, March 3, 1947—8 p. m.

194. We are wholly in accord with prompt action you took Embtel 166 Feb 28. You are authorized to take such further measures in this connection as you deem appropriate, including request for public retraction of references to Asst Sec Braden.

MARSHALL

711.52/3–1047 : Telegram

The Chargé in Spain (Bonsal) to the Secretary of State

CONFIDENTIAL MADRID, March 10, 1947—6 p. m.

208. Note protest sent Foreign Minister re *Arriba* editorial (Embassy's telegrams 165 [1] and 166, February 28) and latter discussed at some length with him March 8. Foreign Minister takes position insulting adjectives do not grammatically apply Mr. Braden. This seems to me quibbling with only slight foundation and I have refused Foreign Minister's suggestion that I withdraw my note. He is consequently sending me a reply [2] disclaiming any unfavorable intention of Spanish Government in matter.

Despatch follows.

BONSAL

---

[1] Telegram 165, not printed.
[2] Not printed.

852.00/3–1047

Memorandum of Conversation, by the Acting Director of the Office of European Affairs (Hickerson)

[WASHINGTON,] March 10, 1947.

Participants: Dr. Salvador de Madariaga [1]
Mr. John D. Hickerson, Acting Director, EUR
Mr. Paul T. Culbertson, Acting Deputy Director, EUR
Mr. Samuel Reber, Acting Chief, WE
Mr. Outerbridge Horsey, Division of Western European Affairs

At the suggestion of Mr. Francis B. Sayre,[2] Mr. Hickerson received Dr. de Madariaga. Mr. Hickerson said that Mr. Acheson[3] had expressed great interest in knowing Dr. de Madariaga's views but regretted that pressure of work, particularly on the Greek situation, made it impossible for him to see him. Mr. Hickerson invited Dr. de Madariaga to outline his views on the political situation in Spain.

Dr. de Madariaga thought that, from the point of view of the Spanish people only, the longer Franco continued in power, the better. The Spanish people had so often resorted to civil war during the past century that they ought to learn the hard way the evils of that practice. However, from the point of view of the Western powers, particularly vis-à-vis the USSR, the continuation of Franco in power was a disaster. This situation prevented the completion of an Atlantic system of security; it continued the economic stagnation in Spain since the US was prevented from extending economic aid to the Franco regime; and in addition, there was the propaganda advantage to the USSR of placing the Western powers on the defensive by picturing them as defenders of fascism and reaction. The last thing the USSR wanted was the replacement of Franco by a moderate regime. Dr. de Madariaga thought that what was strengthening Franco was not the fact of the USSR attacking, but the fact that the US and UK hung back and were obviously opposed to international pressure on Franco. This enabled Franco to say to the generals, on whose support he must rely, that the Anglo-Saxons did not really want to get rid of his regime.

As to the means of getting rid of Franco, the first and most important step was a determination on our part that Franco *must* go, and that all the means necessary to accomplish that end would be employed,

---

[1] Salvador de Madariaga, Spanish historian and diplomat; Ambassador to the United States in 1931, and to France in 1932–1934.
[2] Formerly Assistant Secretary of State; on February 28, 1947, he was sworn in as United States Representative on the Trusteeship Council of the United Nations.
[3] Dean Acheson, Under Secretary of State.

including the use of force if necessary. For example, an embargo on petroleum and cotton exports to Spain would, he thought, be immediately effective. But before taking coercive action, we should send a secret emissary of international standing, such as Winston Churchill, who would speak for the UK and the US, and who would communicate to Franco the decision that he must go. At the same time, the Army chiefs would be told of our decision and of our intention to use all necessary means. We should not, however, lay down the details of what kind of Government should follow Franco. That would be resented by the Spanish people. We should confine ourselves to a statement of certain general principles which, if followed by the new government, would enable us to support it economically and politically. For example, we should specify that the government should rest on the consent of the governed and that it should guarantee fundamental freedoms. We should not, however, enter into details on the forms, as for example, whether suffrage should be universal or direct, etc. To do this would be to create resentment. Success depended on not arousing political passions in Spain as the activities of other political exiles were constantly doing. The initial approach to Franco should be secret and should include arrangements for his own personal safety. If the secret approach failed to produce results, the pressure would become public and would be continued until the objective had been achieved.

As to the form of the new government, Dr. de Madariaga favored the restoration of the Monarchy under Don Juan. Since it was the Generals who would hold effective power upon Franco's departure and since they were opposed to the idea of a republic and favored a monarchy, the latter was the logical form to expect. He had talked with Don Juan and believed that he would be a sound constitutional ruler. Moreover, Dr. de Madariaga thought that the sooner Don Juan came in, the better. He thought that, without the stabilizing influence of the Monarchy, there was the risk that the period of preparation for elections would degenerate into chaos. He thought that an interim group of mixed Republicans, Monarchists and Generals, all acting, as it were, in their personal capacities [would?] have great difficulty in commanding allegiance and maintaining order. Moreover he thought that it would be hard for such a group to accomplish the delicate task of bringing back political exiles and reintegrating them into Spanish life. He thought the superior authority of the Monarchy was important for this purpose. He thought that, in the elections, the Monarchy would meet with the approval of the majority of the people. Under the Republic, the popular following of the Right and Left had alternated on a 40%–60%, 60%–40%, 40%–60% basis and he thought that the pendulum had now swung in favor of the Right so that the Monarchy would probably get 60% or 70% of the vote. Dr. de Madariaga thought that many Republicans would be willing to support the restoration of the Monarchy. The CGT [*UGT?*] and CNT (labor federations under the Republic, now outlawed, but maintaining clandestine organizations) had both agreed to suspend strikes for the duration of the interim period until elections had been held and were apparently not averse to having the Monarchy in power during this interim period provided there was to be opportunity for a free choice between the Republic and the Monarchy in the elections.

Instead of an interim government representative of all political complexions, Dr. de Madariaga favored interim rule by two or perhaps three persons. The "two" would be a Republican and a Monarchist and the "three" would include a supporter of Franco. This latter scheme, if suggested to Franco, would put him "on the spot", for he affects to have popular approval. Moreover, it would have the result of dividing the vote of the Right between Franco and the Monarchy, thus favoring the Republic in the eventual elections. However, Dr. de Madariaga recognized that neither the Spanish Left nor opinion abroad would look with much favor on the inclusion of Franco on the ballot.

Economic and political support of the interim regime by the Governments of the US and UK would be an important element in its success.

Mr. Hickerson said that, although in England there was a general attachment to the Monarchical principle, that was not the case in the United States, as Dr. de Madariaga well knew. Accordingly, public opinion here would not be predisposed in favor of the immediate return of the Monarchy. We would take no action influencing the choice of the Spanish people. A Monarchy could look for active economic and political aid from us, only *after* it had received approval in public elections.

As to the strength of the Communist Party in Spain, Dr. de Madariaga was not sure how it was now. In any case it was useless to fight that type of totalitarianism with Franco's type of totalitarianism. Our interests required the development of healthy political conditions in Spain.

Concluding the talk, Mr. Hickerson thanked Dr. de Madariaga for a most valuable exchange of views and assured him that they would be brought to the attention of Mr. Acheson.

852.00/4–147 : Telegram

The Chargé in Spain (Bonsal) to the Secretary of State

CONFIDENTIAL   MADRID, April 1, 1947—5 p. m.

276. Franco's broadcast and the project of law of succession [1] follow expected lines and in my judgment contain no real concession whatever in sense of liberalizing regime here. Full texts being airmailed soonest. It is assumed there has been ample press coverage.

Proposed law must now be discussed by Cortes, meeting date of which unannounced. Passage of law presumably certain. It will make no practical change in present situation except to constitute new Council of Realm (a body of twelve government appointees directly or indirectly) and to give Franco right if he sees fit to designate a successor or rather to submit such designation to approval as provided in law.[2] Machinery provided in project mainly designed for event Franco's incapacity or death and as such regardless its merits it fills long felt constitutional lacuna. There is no evidence any intent on Franco's part voluntarily to give machinery opportunity to function.

Project states Spain is kingdom to be ruled either by a person of royal blood (male over 30) or by a regent who would be selected similarly by machinery provided. Reliable information is that project has been conveyed to Pretender in Lisbon by official emissary of Franco but evidence so far at hand is strongly against thought that it represents any agreement with Pretender; in fact it may be anticipated anti-Franco Monarchists will strongly oppose project.

Proposed law is logical development of ideas consistently expressed by Franco, especially in speeches of July 1945 and May 1946 (opening of Cortes) and involved no change in basic principles of so-called national movement and much less any tendency to submit those basic principles to any sort of public discussion. Franco's concept is of Catholic kingdom of corporative nature devoted to social and material advances through a mechanism of so-called organic democracy in which the individual finds expression not as member of political party but as member of family, vertical syndicate, municipality or provincial organization.

---

[1] Gen. Franco, in his broadcast of March 31, 1947, announced that Spain was to become a monarchy with a regency council and himself as the head of state. In case of the death or the incapacity of the chief of state the regency council would propose a king or regent who must be accepted by a two-thirds majority of the Cortes. This "Law of Succession" was approved by a referendum vote on July 6, 1947.

[2] In reply to a question at a press conference on April 4, Acting Secretary of State Dean Acheson stated that the establishment of a Regency Council in Spain "does not change our attitude with regard to Spain at all". (852.00/4–447)

More detailed comments and reactions will be sent as available.
Sent Department 276; repeated Paris 58; London 33; Lisbon 17.

BONSAL

852.00/4–747 : Telegram

The Acting Secretary of State to the Embassy in the United Kingdom

TOP SECRET   WASHINGTON, April 7, 1947—7 p. m.

1531. For the Ambassador. From point of view of US and UK, it must now be clear that as long as Franco remains in power, the Spanish situation is dangerous. In substance Franco's latest decree providing for succession does not improve situation since it seems intended merely to consolidate the regime regardless of person of Chief of State.

As long as Franco, or a successor appointed in accordance with new decree, continues in power there can be no real improvement of economic stagnation in Spain. We will continue to be blocked from providing the effective assistance which would make possible the economic reconstruction of that country and thereby build an effective barrier to civil strife and communist domination.

It further becomes increasingly clear that Moscow not only is interested in keeping Franco in power until political and economic distress in Spain reaches the point of revolution, but also derives considerable propaganda advantage from the present situation by placing the Western powers on the defensive as defenders of fascism and of reaction. Franco's new decree is apparently motivated by a necessity for meeting a growing desire in Spain for some change, need for which is emphasized by inability of present regime to solve Spain's economic problems.

Further, there is already evidence that movement in direction of action by UN against Spain will not be altered by new decree. It may be expected to grow and to lead to increasingly serious action. If more forceful measures against Spain are recommended or called for by the UN, US and UK might be obliged to join in such measures in spite of doubts which we might have as to their wisdom.

Our reports both from inside and outside Spain indicate increased political activity by non-communist anti-Franco groups looking toward some governmental organizational change in the country. While there are, to be sure, many fears and other factors tending to maintain the *status quo* (fear of communism, fear of renewed civil war, disillusionment, weariness and apathy), nevertheless, there is sufficient evidence to indicate that some other form of change might be brought about.

The attitude which the US and Grt Brt should assume has therefore become urgent and must be defined. It is clear that Franco and any regime perpetuating the principles of his control must go. Although action involves certain risks, nevertheless it appears to us that the time has come when the US and UK should agree upon a positive policy which would act as an inducement to Span elements to bring about another form of change themselves and thereby render possible extension of our assistance in creating healthy economic and political conditions in the country. Such action by the US and UK would not be contrary to but would aid in bringing about the objectives sought by the UN.

If at this particular juncture the US and Grt Brt could make this policy known in Spain this would, in our opinion, materially assist the efforts of the non-communist elements to compose their differences and to agree upon some interim regime which could maintain order and enjoy the acquiescence of the people and which would not merely continue the objectionable characteristics of the present form of government. In order to receive our support such regime should assume a public obligation to preserve freedom of speech, of press, of religion and of public assembly and to hold free elections, and should provide amnesty for political prisoners and allow the return of political exiles. A precise indication of the nature and degree of support which a regime accepting the foregoing obligations could expect from the US and UK would, we believe, go far in giving confidence to those who desire a change, particularly in the Army, but who have so far been restrained by doubts as to our intentions.

There might be two stages in our relations with any new regime of this character. The first stage concerns the interim period which must of necessity last for sufficient time to prepare for the elections, during which we would enter into more friendly political relations and eliminate without delay the unilateral economic restrictions now imposed on Span trade and commerce by the US and Grt Brt. We would expect that our action in this respect would be followed by other members of the UN.

As soon as elections had been held and a government formed in Spain with the consent of the governed, the second phase could begin and fuller measures of economic and political support could immediately be contemplated. These would include our backing for Spain's admission to the UN and a greater degree of positive aid for economic development and industrial modernization.

We would hope that conditions during the first stage would make possible economic assistance going further than the mere elimination of existing restrictions but this would of course be influenced by the character of the provisional regime and by the degree of support which it secures from the Span people. In our opinion such additional aid in the first stage would be difficult if Franco's departure immediately led to the restoration of the Monarchy. We do not wish to impose any form of govt upon the Span people, which should of course be made clear, and would be willing to accept their choice when freely expressed. Immediate restoration of the Monarchy, although possibly gaining greater immediate allegiance and better able to maintain order, would, however, in our opinion, have too great an influence upon the results of the elections and it would be difficult for public opinion in this country and for this Govt to give it the necessary support during the interim regime. The Monarchy could only look for active economic and political aid from the US if as a result of the elections it is the clearly expressed choice of the people of Spain.

Should this policy be agreed we feel it should immediately be made known secretly to Army chiefs since Army support is essential to peaceful change, to opposition leaders and to Franco himself. We feel that the approach to Franco should be an important element in the settlement. Our resolve that we can no longer deal with him and our conviction that his proposed plan for succession is unsatisfactory should be made clear and an opportunity afforded him to depart in safety.

You are requested to seek an early opportunity to bring this matter to the attention of the FonOff and to state that, as part of our over-all security arrangements, we attach importance to the Span phase of the problem and we hope it will be possible for the Brit Govt to concert with us in achieving our common end, namely the restoration of a democratic Spain. The latest developments in Spain point to the necessity of adopting some positive policy lest events in the country itself get out of hand and we be faced with the appearance of a change which does not alter the inherent difficulties in the present situation.

We should be glad to receive UK Govt views at an early date. We are prepared to discuss this matter in detail either in London or Washington and would of course wish to avoid publicity at this stage.

ACHESON

852.00/4–1047 : Telegram

The Ambassador in the United Kingdom (Douglas) to the Secretary of State

TOP SECRET   LONDON, April 10, 1947—7 p. m.

2160. Personal for Acheson. Called on Sargent [1] this morning and discussed contents urtel 1531, April 7, 7 p. m. He indicated gratification

---

[1] Sir Orme Sargent, British Permanent Under-Secretary of State for Foreign Affairs.

over fact that Department was reviewing policy toward Franco and said that Foreign Office had been doing the same thing. He agreed that from evidence in possession Foreign Office it was to Moscow's advantage that Franco be kept in power, thus increasing the economic and political confusion in Spain and providing propaganda advantages. He agrees further that there is some danger that even at the special meeting of the UN action might be taken which, unless US and UK have developed by then a positive policy, might prove to be embarrassing to both of us.

Sargent considers the method of implementing a positive policy to be extremely delicate, requiring utmost skill, and that key generals of army should probably first be tapped for without their support the venture might, and probably would, fail. A meeting is being held in the Foreign Office this afternoon to discuss the matter. He defers judgment for the time being as to whether further discussions should be held in Washington or London.

DOUGLAS

852.00/4–1947 : Telegram

The Ambassador in the United Kingdom (Douglas) to the Secretary of State

TOP SECRET　　　　　　　　　　　　　LONDON, April 19, 1947—6 p. m.

2314. Personal for Acheson. Meeting Foreign Office Thursday, April 17. Present McNeil,[1] Sargent and Victor Mallet, British Ambassador to Spain who was recalled pursuant to resolution [2] of UN Assembly. Have delayed reporting on it until I had received résumé of telegram from His Majesty's Chargé d'Affaires [3] at Madrid dated 15 April 1947 on the political situation in Spain. It has just come and is as follows:

"As I understand them, the main differences between suggestions under consideration by United States Government and His Majesty's Government respectively are:

(1) That American proposal is for an Anglo-American approach which would involve a promise of material aid to a government which seemed to comply with provisions of tripartite declaration, and

(2) That British proposal is for tripartite approach to opposition elements inside and outside Spain, to Generals and to Franco.

---

[1] Hector McNeil, Minister of State in the British Foreign Office.
[2] Resolution of December 12, 1946; see *Foreign Relations*, 1946, vol. v, p. 1083.
[3] D. F. Howard.

"To deal with the second point first. It must, I fear, be admitted that French prestige is very low here. Internal opposition in France is generally considered most undefined and the French Government are believed to be dangerously open to Communist influence. Moreover, French policy toward Spain, in particular the closure of the frontier and the toleration of extremist exiles near the Spanish frontier, is violently resented by the Spanish Government and also, I have no doubt, by Spanish Generals. I am, therefore, convinced that association with the French Government in any approach to them would prejudice this from the start and in the last resort it would, I think, be better for the United States Government to act alone if their relations with the French Government make it impossible for His Majesty's Government to take any joint *démarche* without the French.

"Indeed even before the receipt of your telegram I had decided it would be better not to discuss the questions involved with my French colleague. I realize, of course, that if the United States Government and His Majesty's Government agree upon departure in their policy towards Spain it might well be necessary to secure French concurrence but I would strongly recommend that we should not disclose to the French Government the lines on which we are thinking until we have reached our own conclusions particularly where any secret *démarche* is involved.

"As regards financial aid to the new government I assume the reason why this does not form part of the British proposal is that there is not much that His Majesty's Government could do in that direction. Promise of such aid is, however, clearly complementary to warning of likelihood of sanctions and in following comments I have for convenience dealt with the two plans together.

"Bill of succession has I think left matters much as they were. It is unlikely to win any favourable support for the regime. Don Juan's declaration of April 7th [4] will in my view likewise fail to shake allegiance of Franco's supporters though it seems to have been generally welcomed by a moderate Left as well as by loyal Monarchists. On the other hand, the implications in statements attributed to him in the *Observer* interview published on April 13 that he would insist on returning to Spain before the plebiscite is held will, I fear, impede the agreement with the Left especially with Llopis' [5] Government who have I believe announced that in no circumstances will they agree to the restoration of the Monarchy prior to the plebiscite or election.

"Although it is too soon to judge the effect which Franco's bill, Don Juan's declaration and his *Observer* interview will have on Right-Left negotiations, it may nevertheless fairly be assumed that in time the movement to bring them together stands good chance of success provided neither side meanwhile sees better way of reaching power— the Left by the hope of outside support particularly from United Nations Organization for revival of Popular Front and the Right as a result of concessions by Franco.

---

[4] Don Juan on April 7 issued a personal message to the Spanish people in which he reasserted his hostility to the Franco regime.

[5] Rodolfo Llopis, head of the Spanish Republican "Government-in-Exile", at Paris. Giral had resigned on January 27, 1947.

"In my view Army is fundamentally loyal to Franco. General A [6] has throughout been doubtful on the subject and we have always doubted whether he could count on any appreciable support from Army officers. Many senior officers profess Royalist sentiments but they are hypnotised by 'Communist menace' against which the regime must seem to them to offer the best defence and even if they do not approve of it in all its aspects they prefer it to any leap in the dark. They also have to consider their own material comforts and vested interests which they owe to Franco and which they naturally wish to preserve. There is therefore, in my opinion, no reason to think that the Generals are ready to desert Franco now or that they would do so in the future unless they were very seriously alarmed indeed about the consequences of his continuance in power and were also satisfied that there were alternatives ready at hand which would not lead to anarchy.

"This is also true of industrialists and leading businessmen.

"Commission of the Cortes which has been nominated to consider the bill for succession consists of servile followers of Franco mostly old members of Falange, and there is no likelihood of the bill meeting with opposition in the Cortes. I understand Cardinal Archbishop Toledo who was nominated in the bill to serve on the Regency Council has declined to do so and that Bishop of Madrid who was likewise nominated to serve on the Regency Council in his capacity as head of the Spanish Academics and who is a member of the Cortes Commission has been summoned to Rome by the Vatican. Any boycott on the part of the Church is, however, unlikely to deter Franco; Cardinal Archbishop of Seville who was likewise without his consent appointed member of the Cortes some years ago and who promptly declined to sit has nevertheless continued to receive summonses to attend its sessions.

"Knowledge that United States aid would be forthcoming for the democratic government would, of course, be great stimulus to those working for the coalition of the moderate Left and Right. On the other hand we cannot be sure that prospective drastic action by United Nations Organization might not actually hamper negotiations by suggesting to moderate Left that of the two alternatives open to them, revival of the Popular Front offered the best chance of success.

"Effect on present supporters of Franco of approach on lines suggested should not be over-estimated. United States proposal at least seems based on the assumption that the economic situation of Spain is critical. The deterioration which was so marked last summer and autumn has slowed down and despite maladjustment caused by the rise last year of over thirty percent in general price level and the continuance of basic inflationary trends, there seems no reason to suppose Spanish economy is likely to break down this year in the absence of any unexpected developments of which the economic sanctions would, of course, be one. Food situation though still very difficult has in some respects improved and the outlook for crops is not unpromising. Industrial production should increase as a result of better supplies of electrical power. Moreover, the picture of the outside world presented to the Spanish public suggests that only in some former neutral coun-

---

[6] Presumably reference is to Gen. Antonio Aranda, a monarchist.

tries and perhaps Belgium is the economic position less difficult than in Spain and that in many countries which have the sympathy of United States Government and His Majesty's Government the position is actually much worse than here. Much as the Generals, businessmen and Government officials would welcome economic aid from outside, I do not therefore think that in order to secure this they would think themselves compelled to adopt the course which on other grounds seemed to them undesirable or dangerous, while a warning or threat of sanctions might in my view well be more likely to exasperate than to intimidate them. Such a clear case of foreign intervention as the suggestion from the United States Government and ourselves that they should unite to throw out the head of the state, whom they have all sworn allegiance to, would hardly incline the Generals to listen favourably to any proposals that we might make. I do not think, therefore, that we should count on any practical help from these quarters.

"Such chance as there is of securing the removal of Franco on the line suggested in these proposals seems to me to lie rather in combined approach to Franco himself. I should hesitate to rule out altogether the possibility that he might decide to surrender power if faced:

1. With alternative government which offered reasonable prospects of stability and which would receive generous United States aid.
2. With some guarantee as to his own personal safety, and
3. With the probable certainty of economic sanctions if he remained in power.

"But if this possibility cannot be ruled out altogether it must, I fear, be regarded as extremely remote. Nothing that he has done gives any indication that he will take this line. On the contrary the bill of succession in itself shows that he is at present prepared to yield up nothing of his real power. Nor is this an experiment which can be tried without expense. If as United States Government propose we told Franco 'that we can no longer deal with him' we should surely have to abide by our word. In the same way, especially in view of possible leakages to the public, even to hint at the probability of our having to agree to sanctions might make it much more difficult for us to oppose their imposition by United Nations Organization if Franco remained in power.

["]Indeed the course of action under consideration seems to me open to very serious objections. Both United States Government and His Majesty's Government have constantly acclaimed that they are opposed to intervention in Spanish internal affairs which must be settled by Spaniards themselves. If once they depart from this principle they may, I fear, find themselves forced, step by step, to more and more extreme forms of intervention which might in the end not stop short of armed force—all this in violation of the United Nations Charter. The serious consequences to the United Kingdom of economic sanctions were set out fully in your despatch number 27. But at the risk of wearying you I would repeat that such pressure is also calculated to defeat its own object by splitting the moderates and leading to a situation where Franco and the extreme Left would remain face to face in an atmosphere of growing ultra-violence and anarchy. Such a situation is opposite to everything for which we and the Americans stand. It should, on the other hand, suit the Soviet Government very well—much better than the present state of affairs—and it is no doubt for this reason that they continue to press for direct action by UNO.

"If His Majesty's Government and the United States Government stand by the United Nations Charter and refuse to tolerate outside intervention in Spanish affairs, there are at least good prospects that under the stress of circumstances Franco's moderate opponents on the Left and Right will finally come together. I confess that I am unable to hold out any hope that Franco's early disappearance can be achieved on these lines, but they seem to offer in the long run the only satisfactory solution of the problem and surely even temporary continuance of Franco in power (which so far as I know does not directly threaten any vital British or American interests) is a lesser evil than those outlined in preceding paragraph."

The article in the Sunday *Observer* is being sent airmail.

Discussion indicated that if action were now taken France should at least be informed. Serious doubt was expressed by Mallet and Sargent of the success of any approach that we might now make or action that we might now take. A tentative view was expressed that the matter should, therefore, now probably be dropped. McNeil, however, dissented from this view on the ground that he was not convinced that we should do nothing and that if we pursued a do-nothing course it was not unlikely that the UN Assembly, possibly at the forthcoming special meeting, would make recommendations to impose sanctions or to take other steps in the internal affairs of Spain which we could not decline to follow without seriously weakening the prestige of the UN.

It was suggested that the matter be considered further. These further discussions will probably be held within two or three days.

If your information differs from the information contained in telegram quoted herein from His Majesty's Chargé d'Affaires or if you have any additional information it would be most helpful if you would let me know.

DOUGLAS

852.00/4–1947 : Telegram

The Acting Secretary of State to the Embassy in the United Kingdom

WASHINGTON, April 25, 1947—7 p. m.

1818. Personal for the Ambassador. There are some points brought out in Embtel 2314 April 19 which we feel can be clarified.

In proposing these discussions with British we proceeded on assumption that Brit Govt would agree with us that continuation of present situation in Spain serves Moscow's interest and that longer Franco remains in power the more dangerous situation becomes and more certain the eventual disintegration. Brit Govt has failed to comment on this assumption and has merely pointed out, through its Chargé in Madrid, that our approach will probably not work. We feel strongly that although there are prospects of temporary economic improvement as indicated by Brit Chargé nevertheless dangers inherent in present situation are such that some positive action should be taken very soon.

Our plan of action was put forward only as one method of achieving our end. If Brit agree with our premises we of course would consider any other scheme which they may desire to advance.

We agree with Brit Emb Madrid that for obvious reasons French should not be brought into this plan at present time.

We note that British seem to think we are proposing intimidation in order to achieve our objective. We agree that emphasis on this point would produce little result and we would not threaten application of economic sanctions. On other hand we should have to point out trend in the UN and emphasize our determination to support UN even if recommendations are made with wisdom of which we were not entirely in accord. We assume that Brit Govt is in the same position.

Furthermore with reference to emphasis placed by Brit Emb Madrid upon approach to Franco himself, we also in our previous telegram had indicated we considered this an essential element of plan. This approach must be made and it presents a possibility which has not yet been thoroughly explored. We recognize that it may not be successful but if no such direct approach is made Franco might well be justified in continuing to believe his own propaganda to effect that US-British opposition to his regime is nominal, and that insofar as US is concerned recently announced policy of President [1] would indicate that we are prepared to shift our policy in regard to Franco and support any noncommunist regime in Spain, including his own.

ACHESON

---

[1] Apparently a reference to President Truman's Special Message to the Congress on Greece and Turkey, March 12, 1947; for documentation on this message, see volume V.

852.00/5–147 : Telegram

The Ambassador in the United Kingdom (Douglas) to the Secretary of State

TOP SECRET   LONDON, May 1, 1947—7 p. m.

2547. Personal for the Secretary and Under Secretary Acheson. Deptel 1531, April 7; Embtel 2314, April 19; Embtel 2399,[1] April 24; Deptel 1818, April 25.

---

[1] Telegram 2399, not printed.

Sargent informed me this afternoon that he had communicated with Bevin [2] while he was in Berlin and after his arrival here had discussed with him the tentative proposals in regard to Spain. Bevin concluded and the Foreign Office concurred that the matter was too dangerous to take up now.

The reasons for this conclusion are as follows:

1. The Spanish economic situation is improving. The generals of the Army are solid in their support of Franco. The general attitude in Spain is that the present regime, such as it is, is preferable to the risk of a civil war. Accordingly the chance of succeeding along the lines proposed is now considered to be slim if there is any chance at all.

2. Tentative proposals whether successful, which is considered to be most unlikely, or unsucessful, which is considered to be almost a certainty, would if followed be characterized as unilateral voluntary intervention in the internal affairs of another country which had not sought the intervention and would therefore constitute a precedent which to our disadvantage might justify similar intervention by the Soviets in the internal affairs of other countries.

3. The proposals as followed might give rise to a complaint that might be made by some other nation, perhaps Argentina, before the United Nations that we had violated if not the letter at least the spirit of the Charter.

For all of these reasons, Bevin had concluded that the matter was now too hazardous to broach. Sargent indicated that they had come to this conclusion regretfully but that the facts made it, they thought, inescapable.

He discussed the reasons for the action taken by the Assembly recommending the withdrawal of Chiefs of Mission and reposing in the Security Council the authority to consider further steps if the situation in Spain warranted it. This action he felt had been taken because the Polish representative and others had done such effective advance lobbying that there was no alternative on our part to the acceptance of the recommended action of the subcommittee of the Assembly.

He therefore threw out the suggestion for whatever we considered it to be worth, that we and the British now commence quietly to solicit the support of appropriate members of the Assembly of the United Nations against any further action by it in regard to Spain, thereby preventing any recommendation which would be unpalatable to us both. He spoke of this suggestion as defensive lobbying.

Would appreciate your advice as to whether the matter should be pressed further with the Foreign Office here.

DOUGLAS

---

[2] Ernest Bevin, British Secretary of State for Foreign Affairs.

852.00/5–647 : Telegram

The Chargé in Spain (Bonsal) to the Secretary of State

SECRET   MADRID, May 6, 1947—6 p. m.

417. On balance it is my belief that surface developments from announcement March 31 of Franco's succession bill have favored regime and that Franco has shown skillful understanding of local political situation.

Government propaganda during April was concentrated upon following:

1. Revival of memories of civil war horrors. Bloody shirt was waved enthusiastically and effectively.
2. Pretenders alleged trafficking with elements identified with Reds who lost civil war and whose return to political power would allegedly result in return to civil war conditions.
3. Raking up of unfavorable aspects of Bourbon history over past centuries.
4. An obscure and reportedly discredited Grandee Marques de Villamagna has signed articles in Falangist organ purporting to prove that rightful claimant to throne is not Don Juan but infant son of his elder brother Jaime (Jaime is ineligible personally because he is approximately deaf and dumb and he renounced his rights on contracting morganatic marriage).
5. Theme that whole world now recognizes Franco was right about Soviets is being worked very hard.
6. Principles of national movement with emphasis on Christian social justice have been stressed.

As a result certain conservative elements have shuddered closer than ever to Franco. Traditionalist Monarchists and others have been displeased at liberal tone of Don Juan's manifestoes published here. And Communists whose disinterest in any sort of moderate or immediately practical solution should be self evident by this time have viewed with alarm negotiations between Monarchists and democratic alliance. All this has strengthened Franco temporarily by stressing divisions of opposition. He can probably confirm his advantage by admitting certain amendments to succession law project allegedly reflecting consideration varying opinions. Thus appearance of certain amount of give and take will have been given.

Above factors, however, are in my judgment of short term importance. Regime continues slow deterioration previously described and evidenced among other things by great difficulty of securing outstanding men to serve it. Long delay Cabinet changes probably attributable this factor.

Furthermore, there is some inflammable political material lying about. Labor difficulties or sensational political crime may set it on fire and thus jolt key elements, especially in army, to practical recognition of necessity for change. This is, however, still only remote possibility and regime looks stable over next few months.

Over long term I believe Monarchists prospects have been improved by refusal of Don Juan and those around him to make deal on Franco's terms. At least monarchy is still in running against time when system conforming to political thought of modern western Europe is established in Spain.

BONSAL

852.00/5–1047 : Telegram

The Ambassador in the United Kingdom (Douglas) to the Secretary of State

TOP SECRET LONDON, May 10, 1947—2 p. m.

2678. Personal for Acheson. Sargent gives me the following information relative to Spain. A member of the Foreign Office who had recently discussed Spain with the Belgian Chargé d'Affaires in the absence of the Belgian Ambassador here is reported to have said the Foreign Office had been considering the Spanish situation and was glad that it had not been placed on the agenda official meeting of the United Nations Assembly. To this the Chargé d'Affaires replied that Spain [*Spaak?*] would have been pleased had it been included on the agenda for he (Spaak [1]) had a personal grudge against Franco.

The member of the Foreign Office took this occasion to point out to the Belgian Chargé d'Affaires the consequences of economic sanctions against Spain. It would, he is reported to have said, involve the re-establishment of controls, the blockading of the Iberian Peninsula with warships and that Belgium would be asked to participate. Moreover, he said, economic sanctions would seriously affect the UK position and would have unfavorable consequences in other directions. For example, Spain was the principal source of pyrites for the UK. If the imports of this type of iron ore were prohibited it would mean a lower steel production in Britain, even though Swedish iron ore were substituted, since Swedish ore is of lower grade and requires more coal for its metallurgical benefaction. UK would probably, therefore, be compelled to seek steel from Belgium. Certainly however, he said, this situation would impel the UK to request larger allocation of coal from ECO, with corresponding diminished amount of coal to other coal consuming countries.

---

[1] Paul-Henri Spaak, Belgian Prime Minister and Minister of Foreign Affairs.

The Chargé d'Affaires seemed to be impressed with this statement of the consequences of economic sanctions against Spain.

Sargent then showed me communication from the British Embassy in Portugal in response to a request from the Foreign Office as to whether Portugal would cooperate in economic sanctions, and as to their effect on Portugal. The Embassy in Lisbon has replied in substance as follows:—that economic sanctions against Spain would require the re-establishment of the controls of economic warfare that had been abandoned, that they would have unfortunate consequences in Portugal and that it would be impossible to make economic sanctions effective against Spain without Portuguese assistance, which it was stated categorically Portugal would not provide. Therefore if they were to be made effective they would necessarily have to be applied against Portugal also. This step would seriously impair friendly relations between Portugal and the UK and among other things might adversely affect the strategic advantages already obtained in the Portuguese islands (the Azores) and elsewhere.

DOUGLAS

852.00/5–147 : Telegram

The Secretary of State to the Embassy in the United Kingdom

TOP SECRET   WASHINGTON, May 15, 1947—2 p. m.
US URGENT

2110. For the Ambassador. Feeling that the British had perhaps drawn wrong impression on nature of our proposed approach on Spanish question (urtel 2547 May 1 and previous) we thought it might be useful to go over whole background with Brit Emb here and accordingly did so May 13.

Brit Emb quoted from FonOff telegram to Bevin in Moscow to effect that FonOff did not agree with our basic premise that longer situation continued more likely was solution to be violent and detrimental to our and Spanish interests. FonOff said to Bevin that any alternative non-communist regime would continue to be attacked by USSR and implied that little would be gained from this point of view by disappearance of Franco.

We said that continuance of Franco means that US and UK cannot give Spain political and economic support which in our opinion is essential to creation healthy political conditions there. We agreed that there had been a temporary alleviation of food and power shortages thus reducing economic pressure for a change. We said we were nevertheless convinced that Franco's system, both politically and economically, offers no prospect whatever of long range stability. We believed that political and economic conditions will get steadily worse and final result will be resort to violence by extremist elements both sides, which could have serious consequences for both US and UK.

We said that FonOff apparently thought our approach necessarily involved threats and actual execution of joint US and UK economic sanctions and that this was not what we had in mind. We agreed with British that such action would be contrary to UN Charter and would have grave consequences to UK economy specifically and to overall political and strategic situation in Atlantic. Our approach envisaged more of an objective explanation of our views to Franco, the Generals, the opposition and all interested Spaniards, urging necessity of change. In other words we would show Spaniards the gains accruing from a change in regime rather than emphasize the penalties of failure to make the change. We said our approach would of course include emphasis on fact that nature and timing of changes was entirely up to Spaniards and would avoid giving grounds for Spanish resentment against "foreign intervention".

We said we would in our approach to Spaniards call attention to trend in UN and increasing demands for further action such as economic sanctions with implication that despite any disagreement by us on desirability such measures we might be forced to follow recommendations of UN. We felt that such a line of action would not preclude our opposing economic sanctions in UN if these should, as we thought likely, be proposed later this year. In this connection we pointed out evidences of interest on the part of other states in reviving Franco issue in UN at an early date.

We mentioned that we did not know how far British had gone in talking to French although we had had reports from Paris that fairly extensive conversations had been conducted. For your confidential information this information was contained in a CIG report from Paris which we asked CIG to have repeated to you and it is contrary to indication contained in urtel 2473 of Apr 29.[1] We said that we would of course want at later stage to tell French of our joint position but for obvious reasons believed it better not to associate them in any approach in Spain.

Under circumstances we have outlined in this exchange of messages, we feel that subject has not yet been sufficiently explored and hope that British will agree on value of common positive approach in near future. We would of course consider any alternative proposals they may make. A recent INS press despatch from Paris to effect that US and UK were discussing joint economic sanctions against Spain em-

---

[1] Not printed; it stated that it appeared clear that the official in the British Foreign Office concerned with Spanish affairs "had no knowledge of any approach by British to French concerning solution to Franco problem before UN meeting in autumn". (852.00/4–2947)

phasizes our request that no publicity be given to our discussions at this stage.

Brit Emb here is reporting conversation to FonOff and we suggest you take early opportunity to develop foregoing with them.

MARSHALL

852.00/5–2047 : Telegram

The Ambassador in the United Kingdom (Douglas) to the Secretary of State

TOP SECRET   LONDON, May 20, 1947—8 p. m.

2840. For the Secretary and Under Secretary. Deptel 2110, May 15. Bevin away on vacation, therefore discussed Spanish question with Sargent FonOff this morning.

He had received long despatch from British Embassy recounting conversation there with Reber. Explained to him our view.

Over a considerable period, we believed, Spain, under the present regime to which we could offer neither political or economic assistance, would experience progressive deterioration and finally violence invoked by the extremist elements on both sides. In order to dispel any misunderstanding of our previous discussions, pointed out that we not proposing action which would involve joint US and UK economic sanctions but that our proposal was that an objective expression of our views be presented to Franco, the Generals of the Army, industrialists, and the opposition documenting the necessity for a change by pointing out the advantages rather than by suggesting threats. The timing of any change was to be determined by the Spaniards.

Referred also to the growing disposition of the United Nations to invoke economic sanctions despite any opposition by US to their imposition.

Sargent had not discussed the matter with Bevin and was therefore speaking informally and personally when he said that he could find no fault with the argument. He raised the question, however, as to how the approach to Franco, etc., was to be made. Having withdrawn the heads of the British Mission and our mission it was not likely that Franco would receive the Chargé d'Affaires.

Two alternative methods of achieving the objective were discussed. First, a public announcement. This Sargent felt might give encouragement to the intransigent members of the UN who are anxious to have US invoke economic sanctions. As a defense it was suggested that in any public announcement the disadvantages to many countries resulting from economic sanctions might be explained. This, however, he felt would be construed as an anticipation of the discussion of economic sanctions which properly should take place in UN. He was, therefore, doubtful about the wisdom of his own suggestion that a public statement would be an appropriate method of approaching the interested parties and groups in Spain. Second method contemplated the appointment of special emissaries representing the US and the UK respectively, who would explain our position to Franco and to other groups. This method, however, Sargent thought could not ultimately be kept from the Spanish press and would therefore lead to much publicity which Franco could capitalize for his own benefit were the proposal for a change to be unfavorably received by him and the parties supporting him.

Sargent thought that either of these two methods, should our suggestions be rejected, would be interpreted by Franco for Spanish consumption as intervention by foreign powers in the domestic affairs of Spain. They might therefore have the effect of strengthening Franco instead of furthering the objective we have in mind.

The solitary question in Sargent's mind was how and by whom the approach to Franco and other Spanish parties can be made without running the risks which he informally and personally indicated he thought would be implicit in our proposal, and which he was confident Bevin would want to avoid. He will give matter further thought.

Please give us your advice covering the methods by which the type of approach we have in mind may best be made.

Sargent assured me that there have been no discussions with the French. Massigli, the French Ambassador, has inquired of him on several occasions whether consideration was being given to the possibility of taking any action, vis-à-vis, Spain. Sargent has consistently refrained from giving him any indication that the matter was in the discussion stage.

Impressed upon Sargent the need for greatest secrecy and in this connection referred him to the article in the London Sunday *Observer* of May 11. He assured me that he had no knowledge of the source of this information and would take every possible step to guard with greatest discretion the conversations on the Spanish question.

DOUGLAS

852.00/5–2247 : Telegram

The Secretary of State to the Embassy in the United Kingdom

TOP SECRET WASHINGTON, May 22, 1947—4 p. m.

2218. For the Ambassador. We are very pleased note from urtel 2840 May 20 that there now seems to be better understanding on part Brit in respect our suggestions re Spain.

As possible channel approach to Franco we suggest similar but not identic letters might be addressed by Pres and Mr. Attlee [1] to Franco. These communications could be sent our Chargés d'Affaires Madrid who would ask for appointments, preferably separately, in order present them to Franco. If Franco refuses receive Chargés letters could then be handed Span FonOff for delivery. Such approach would have double advantage of avoiding adverse effects of publicity and of preventing Franco from distorting oral approach to benefit his own position.

MARSHALL

---

[1] Clement R. Attlee, British Prime Minister.

711.52/7–647 : Telegram

The Chargé in Spain (Culbertson) to the Secretary of State

CONFIDENTIAL   MADRID, July 6, 1947—2 p. m.

627. Accompanied by Maffitt, I saw Foreign Minister Thursday at Ministry at my request and again last evening at his residence at his suggestion. On Thursday we discussed SAFEHAVEN, *Readers Digest*, repatriation of Spaniards in Germany and Germans in Spain, the bill for oil supplied to Italian vessels, and our interest in matter of political prisoners. I indicated my hope that by a bit of give and take on both sides these lesser problems could be settled. Artajo agreed. I then said that while I thought we could settle the lesser questions I was not sanguine about the major problem. It was then two o'clock and Artajo suggested coming to his residence last evening where we could continue our talk. Artajo measures out his soda first and that is a bit the way the two hours conversation went since we never did exactly reach the scotch. Joaquin Ruiz Gimenez, Spanish Culture Institute head, was present for last evening's talk and did most of the interpreting.

Artajo opened emphasizing special viewpoint of those who underwent civil war on Franco side and proceeded to hew closely to the present party line saying that Spain is basically pro-American; is together with us in opposition to Communism and would surely be with us in any future conflict against Communism. Spain was undeniably neutral in war, at great risk to herself; cannot understand our hostile attitude toward Spain which although at first by force of circumstances authoritarian not totalitarian is now slowly developing own democracy in own way, while at same time we continue relations with totalitarian governments like Russia, Yugoslavia, etc.; feel that Roosevelt's 1942 letter [1] to Franco and secret promises Churchill and

---

[1] See *Foreign Relations*, 1942, vol. III, p. 306.

Eden [2] allegedly made to Ambassador Alba about same time have not been fulfilled; if US had put as much effort into understanding Spain as we have into attacking her, our relations would be much better today and that today's referendum will demonstrate to world that Spanish people give full support to Franco and that he is free choice.

My end of conversation was limited largely to factual, historical presentation except for remarks about today's "free" election, and sharp distinction we draw between Spanish people and Franco. I told Artajo frankly that we did not and would not consider the result of the referendum as free expression of will of the people. It was by then ten o'clock and meeting had to break up. Artajo suggested we meet again soon. Hope to reach the scotch next time and would appreciate guidance on what if anything might be said along lines of policy being well developed prior my departure from Washington.

Sent Department 627, repeated London 62.

CULBERTSON

[2] Anthony Eden, British Secretary of State for Foreign Affairs, 1940–1945.

852.00/7–947 : Telegram

The Secretary of State to the Embassy in Spain

US URGENT WASHINGTON, July 9, 1947.

589. At press conference today Asst Secy Armour was asked for comment on election results in Spain. He said that there was no evidence that there had been any press freedom or relaxation of press restrictions prior to referendum and that there had apparently been little opportunity for any public discussion among Span people on alternative forms of govt which they might prefer. He said that nothing which happened in Spain last Sunday would in any way change the position of this govt which of course had been made entirely clear in our relations with the regime in Spain.

MARSHALL

852.00/7–2147

Memorandum of Conversation, by the Assistant Secretary of State (Armour)

SECRET [WASHINGTON,] July 21, 1947.

Participants: Señor Don Germán Baraibar, Spanish Chargé d'Affaires a.i.
Mr. Norman Armour, Assistant Secretary of State
Mr. Outerbridge Horsey, WE

Mr. Baraibar called to pay his respects. He mentioned the recent referendum in Spain on the law of succession as evidence of Franco's strong position. While admitting that there was widespread opposition to Franco, Mr. Baraibar said that the general feeling was that he was the only alternative to Communism. Mr. Armour recalled that, speaking personally, he had suggested to the Spanish Foreign Minister as long ago as November 1945,[1] that there was a third alternative which was for Franco to turn back power to the generals from whom he received it in 1936, who would be in a position to maintain order and to return the country to representative government.

Mr. Baraibar thought that the most important feature of the referendum was that the ideas of Falange had now been suppressed entirely since the "26 points" of Falange were no longer part of the constitutional basis of the Government. The basic laws are now the Bill of Rights, the Labor Charter, the Constituent Law of the Cortes, the Referendum Law and the new Succession Law. Mr. Armour commented that the Bill of Rights was all very well but its importance lay in whether or not it was implemented. Mr. Baraibar expressed confidence that the referendum was a sign of real evolution in the Government. He thought it would soon be followed by municipal elections. Mr. Armour expressed hope that this was indeed so. Mr. Armour recalled that municipal elections had been promised over two years ago and had not yet materialized. Mr. Armour called attention to the bad effect created by continued political oppression and by restrictions on the freedom of foreign press correspondents. In conclusion, Mr. Baraibar offered his cooperation and assistance in any way in which it might be needed.

N[ORMAN] A[RMOUR]

---

[1] See telegram 2438, December 1, 1945, from Madrid, *Foreign Relations*, 1945, vol. v, p. 695.

852.00/7–2447 : Telegram

The Ambassador in the United Kingdom (Douglas) to the Secretary of State

TOP SECRET   LONDON, July 24, 1947—1 p. m.

4029. When in London recently, Hickerson [1] discussed Spain with Sir Oliver Harvey,[2] who promised obtain review British position. In absence on leave of Harvey, Warner [3] tells us British have explored

---

[1] John D. Hickerson, Deputy Director of the Office of European Affairs.
[2] Deputy Under-Secretary of State, British Foreign Office.
[3] Christopher Frederick Ashton Warner, Assistant Under-Secretary of State, British Foreign Office.

all aspects our proposed action and are convinced plan will not work. He says (1) British are confident Franco is less interested in Spain and Spanish people than in maintaining power in his own hands and that therefore he would refuse under any conditions voluntarily to step down and (2) leaks would most surely occur with resulting embarrassment which would be seized upon by Soviets or others to make our position in respect of Spain at UN more difficult and worse than it is.

Accordingly, British Embassy Washington is being instructed to renew to Department previous proposals for soliciting support friendly nations to prevent further UN action on Spain.

As FonOff dossier indicated Harvey had not presented Hickerson arguments very forcibly, we suggested possibility of having Ambassador see Sir Orme Sargent once more but Warner thought such action would be ineffective, saying that Bevin had himself taken position outlined above.

If therefore Department desires this matter pursued further in London, it will likely be necessary that I go direct to Bevin.

DOUGLAS

852.00/7–2747 : Telegram

The Chargé in Spain (Culbertson) to the Secretary of State

SECRET   MADRID, July 27, 1947—1 p. m.

687. For Hickerson or Reber. Father Molina Spanish with first US papers now at Catholic University favorably known to Embassy during war called on me week ago at which time we had off-the-shoulder exchange views. He knows Franco personally, has church approach to regime but seems honestly interested in solution Spanish question. He asked whether I had seen Franco. I said no, that I was merely a Chargé and had nothing to say to Franco although if Franco wanted to see me and I could speak freely a meeting would be O.K. by me. At San Sebastian [1] on Thursday I learned from Embassy Madrid Franco wished to see me at 6:30 yesterday afternoon. I returned to Madrid yesterday by Embassy plane. Molina and I went to Pardo in Molina's car. No one else was present at the meeting which lasted two hours. Molina interpreted. Franco was extremely friendly and the talk was carried on very informal basis.

Franco opened up with discussion complexities Spain and need for people know Spanish history both old and recent past in order understand present situation in Spain. He explained his position and that of

---

[1] Spanish summer capital.

Spain in recent war step by step, frequently citing conversations with or remarks made to Ambassador Hayes. He laid considerable stress, as did Artajo on July 3, on promises they claim Churchill and Eden made in 1940 provided Spain remain neutral. These promises according to Franco involved territorial adjustments in North Africa at expense French. He said that Spanish Government has documents in connection with this matter but will not use them because to do so would complicate British-French relations. He said also that Germans had offered make French border readjustments, including Andorra but that Franco had refused this offer. He did not mention the Roosevelt letter of November 1942. His attitude and words were to effect that he could not understand why Spain was now being penalized by rest of world, particularly the US since Spain had retained real neutrality during war and had given allies benefits for which Spain now receives no credit. He discussed at very considerable length the problem of communism in Spain going back in his historical development as far as 1922. More particularly however he discussed a "revolution" in Asturias in 1934 at which time he was called back by the then government from the Canaries to put down this revolution. He touched only lightly on infiltration communism into Spain during civil war. He discussed problem Spaniards outside of Spain mentioning briefly the Monarchists but more particularly the other elements. He explained that these people were all free come back Spain and cited case of Lerroux [2] and also mentioned fact that Hazana's [3] son had recently left the country but on leaving declared that he would and wanted return.

Franco went into considerable detail on economic and social program of regime stressing point that he is anxious develop educational system in Spain in order that there may be not only educational advancement but a resulting political and civic development of people.

While Franco did most talking I was able to get in a number points with regard our general position and I found that Franco took my remarks without any resentment even though he did avoid getting into a direct discussion on such things as lack of political liberties here in Spain.

I stressed several times during conversation that while I appreciated his feeling that rest of world must understand Spain's position, Spain and her government must likewise understand reasons for policies toward Spain which have been adopted by US and other countries.

At the end of our conversation Franco indicated an interest in our

---

[2] Alejandro Lerroux was the first Foreign Secretary of the Spanish Republic. He returned to Spain from exile by permission of the Franco Government.

[3] Presumably this is a misprint and the reference is to a son of Manuel Azaña, formerly Premier of the Spanish Republic.

meeting again near future and in carrying on in informal way in which discussion went yesterday afternoon. On coming back town Molina mentioned another meeting and I told him that if Franco raised question with him again I would be quite happy continue talk but that initiative would have come from Franco himself.

The one impression I got from this meeting was that Franco is sincere and honest with himself. He is convinced that what is now being done in Spain is in the best interest of Spain and the Spanish people. He thinks that Spanish people are being lifted up both economically and socially and he will not lightly relinquish his position to anyone else unless he is convinced that whoever takes over will maintain stability and order and will continue what he considers to be present progressive evolution and education Spanish people.

Culbertson

852.00/7–2847

The Counselor of the British Embassy (Allen) to the Chief of the Division of Western European Affairs (Reber)

SECRET WASHINGTON, July 28, 1947.
Ref. 35/ /47

Dear Reber: We have learned from the Foreign Office that they had conversations on the subject of Spain with Hickerson on the 3rd July and with a member of the United States Embassy on the 23rd.

It appears that at the latter conversation the Foreign Office explained why, after full consideration, they had come very reluctantly to the conclusion that there was nothing that our two Governments could do to improve the position inside Spain and that we must both fall back as a second best on action to prevent further intervention by the United Nations. You will remember that we last discussed this latter question on the 13th June, when you expressed the view that any general approach to a large circle of governments should be postponed until rather nearer the date of the United Nations Assembly. The Foreign Office, who were informed of your views at the time, now tell us that they hope that the State Department will agree that it would be unsafe to delay action much longer and that they accordingly wish to suggest August 8th as the target date upon which our two Governments should take coordinated action.

Perhaps you would let me know whether the United States Government are ready to fall in with this proposal. In that event, I could perhaps come down and have a further talk with you about details so that, in particular, we might agree upon the list of Governments to be approached.

As regards the content of our approach, our view is that, provided the action of our respective representatives in the various capitals concerned is closely co-ordinated, particularly as regards timing, it is unnecessary for both of us to take exactly the same line.

I shall look forward to hearing from you as soon as you are ready to discuss the matter further.

Yours sincerely,

DENIS ALLEN

852.00/10–2347 : Telegram

The Chargé in Spain (Culbertson) to the Secretary of State

TOP SECRET   MADRID, October 23, 1947—9 p. m.

904. At his request I called this evening on José Erice, Director General Foreign Policy Spanish Foreign Office. He showed me copy of note which Spanish Foreign Office delivered yesterday evening to British Embassy here protesting fairly mildly and in somewhat injured tone against Bevin's action in having received Prieto [1] and Gil Robles.[2] First paragraph of note quoted statement allegedly made by Prieto upon leaving Bevin's office to effect that Bevin agreed with his (Prieto's) program. Note called attention to fact that British Foreign Office had issued no denial of accuracy of Prieto's statement.

Erice then showed me copies of telegram received by Foreign Office from Duke of Alba, then Spanish Ambassador in London. There were three of these telegrams, one each in 1940, 1941 and 1942. First of these telegrams gave account of conversation between Alba and Eden in which Eden expressed British friendship for Spain and called upon Spain to do nothing more than keep Germans from entering or transiting Spain. This telegram also contained assurances by Eden that England would not permit Spanish refugees to operate in Great Britain.

Second telegram quoted Eden as promising British consideration of Spain's desire to have Gibraltar as well as to assist Spanish aims in other territorial adjustments.

Third telegram gave account of alleged proposal by Eden to Alba with regard to Britain's desire for Spain to move in on French zone of Morocco, a subject which Spanish Government required Alba to take up with Churchill. Churchill confirmed this proposal, adding

---

[1] Don Indalecio Prieto, leader in Spanish Socialist Workers' Party.
[2] José Maria Gil Robles, Catholic Action Party leader.

that once war had been won by British, France would owe Britain much and Britain would owe France nothing; that Churchill expected obtain naval aid from United States which would assist her in Mediterranean fight; that at end of war ships and other aid would be given to Spain and that although he, Churchill, had made public statement favorable to Spanish Government, he would make another one.

Erice then showed me memo of conversation between Ambassador Hayes and Foreign Minister in 1943 in which Ambassador Hayes is said to have asked Spanish Government to permit United States to use port of Barcelona for evacuation of Allied wounded and sick and also to use that port for sending into France for use of civil population food and other materials. Memo stated that Ambassador's requests were granted.

Erice then elaborated to some extent how seriously Government takes fact that Bevin had seen Prieto and Robles in his capacity as Foreign Secretary, adding that he personally could understand gasoline embargoes and that sort of thing but that for Bevin not to deny Prieto's statement as mentioned above placed very substantial strain on present relations between two Governments, and Erice again called attention to telegram in which British were supposed to have promised that Spanish refugees would not be permitted to operate on British soil.

Erice assured me that this resentment was not purely his but also that of Franco and Foreign Minister and government as whole. He expressed hope to me that my government might find it possible to bring to attention of British Government the strength of feeling which this Prieto-Bevin conversation has had and that we might suggest to British utility of at least denying accuracy of Prieto's statement. I naturally told Erice that all I could do would be to submit his request to my government.

Erice also dwelt at considerable length on position of Spain in event of war between Western Powers and Russia. He said there could be no question as to eventual position of Spain in event of such war but that should Spain by reason of her weakness remain neutral for even as much as three months, Russian armies could then easily have reached Pyrenees and probably North Africa. He pointed out that because of Spain's present inadequately equipped army and because of Spain's almost complete lack of airdrome facilities, she could not in spite of her interests undertake to oppose Russia, and in view of inadequate airport facilities, Western Powers would not be able to send in their air forces and airborne troops. He rather appealed to me in hope that something in way of policy modification could be found, protesting that Spain did want to liberalize and did want to evolve toward more liberal situation. He asked me at lunch other day and again this evening whether I could not define to him just what we mean by evolution. I did not endeavor to correct him by saying that our policy had not envisaged evolution under Franco.

I appreciate that it is hardly up to us to approach British in this matter but I do hope Department can give me early guidance for use in any future discussions which I may be called upon to have with Spanish officials on this subject. I do not know whether Department in light of world developments as they are envisages possibility of policy modification or not. I personally feel that this is not opportune moment to develop antagonisms between United States and Spain or to in any way upset applecart here regardless of number of rotten apples in cart.

Sent Department 904, repeated London 75.

CULBERTSON

852.00/10–2347 : Telegram

The Acting Secretary of State to the Embassy in Spain

TOP SECRET   WASHINGTON, October 24, 1947—7 p. m.

830. You should tell Erice that matter seems to us entirely between Span and Brit Govts and one in which we cannot intervene. You should add we know nothing of alleged commitment by Eden (second para Embtel 904 Oct 23 rptd London 75) but that for our part, in absence of any specific and binding agreement on question with foreign govt, we would feel free to get info on conditions abroad from any and all available sources.

In your discretion you may inform your Brit colleague fully Erice conversation and your reply for info FonOff.

Sent Madrid 830 rptd London 4560.

LOVETT

852.00/10–2447

Memorandum of Conversation, by the Assistant Chief of the Division of Western European Affairs (Horsey)

TOP SECRET   [WASHINGTON,] October 24, 1947.

Having called ostensibly on one or two unimportant matters, Mr. Sanz-Briz [1] then said that their Embassy had been told by Madrid of the conversation of Mr. Culbertson at the Foreign Office at Madrid,

---

[1] Angel Sanz-Briz, second secretary, Spanish Embassy.

reported in Madrid's telegram 904 of October 23. He asked me whether we had yet heard and what my personal reaction was.

I said that we had received a report of Mr. Culbertson's conversation and that we were giving it consideration. The matter seemed to me, personally, to be entirely between the Spanish and British Governments. I said that we knew nothing whatever about the alleged commitment made by Mr. Eden not to permit activities of Spanish political refugees in England, but that we felt strongly on the question of the general principle involved. As far as we were concerned, I said that we would not consider limiting ourselves, in the case of any particular country, to persons considered inoffensive by the government of the country concerned. I said that we would consider ourselves free to talk to anyone we wished in assembling all possible information on any given problem and that this action would not necessarily imply official agreement with the views of any one particular person.

Mr. Sanz-Briz said that they would not mind the British and us talking to relatively unimportant Spaniards, such as Negrin and Albornoz, but that the case of Prieto was different. I suggested that this meant that, in their eyes, Prieto had a following in Spain and that his opinions on the Spanish political situation were of some significance. It therefore seemed to me all the more important to have his views as a contribution to the total picture.

My impression was that the Spanish Embassy here had received instructions to repeat to us the protests which they have already made to both Embassies in Madrid, and that Mr. Sanz-Briz was sent in to get a preliminary reaction as to how such a protest would be received.

As to Mr. Bevin's failure to deny press reports that he had given his blessing to Prieto's activities, I suggested that they were taking this a little too seriously and that, for our part in a parallel case, we could not undertake to confirm, deny or correct every statement about our activities appearing in the press.

711.52/10–2847

Mr. George F. Kennan of the Policy Planning Staff to the Secretary of State and the Under Secretary of State

TOP SECRET   [WASHINGTON,] October 24, 1947.

At the suggestion of Mr. Armour, the Policy Planning Staff has looked into the question of our current policy toward Spain. I attach a Staff paper on the subject.

You will note that the paper brings out the following points:

(1) While the Staff does not feel that it should make suggestions concerning current operations, nevertheless it has serious doubts as to

the results to be expected from the Department's efforts to eliminate the Franco regime by bringing international pressures to bear.

(2) The Staff believes that in the National interest the time has come for a modification of our policy toward Spain with a view to early normalization of U.S.-Spanish relations, both political and economic.

(3) This will involve some modification in the instructions under which our U.N. delegation is now operating.

I recommend that if you approve this paper, it be transmitted, in confidence, to Mr. Armour for his guidance.[1]

GEORGE F. KENNAN

[Annex]

TOP SECRET   [WASHINGTON,] October 24, 1947.
PPS/12

U.S. POLICY TOWARD SPAIN

The Policy Planning Staff has studied the question of our relations with Spain, which are unsatisfactory not only from the political point of view but from the viewpoint of our military planners. On the one hand, we have hoped to bring about the replacement of the totalitarian regime of General Franco by withholding from his government the benefits of international political and economic relationships. On the other, we are confronted with the fact that General Franco remains firmly in power and that his regime has actually been strengthened by demonstrations of international hostility.

At present, our relations with Spain are governed in part by the United Nations Resolution of December 12, 1946, recommending that member states withdraw their Chiefs of Mission from Madrid and that Franco Spain be excluded from organizations connected with the U.N. For example, the U.S. recently took an active part in the expulsion of Spain from ICAO, and in various other ways we have affirmed our opposition to the Franco government on ideological grounds. In the economic sphere we are withholding all forms of Government assistance; Government credits have been refused, sales of surplus Government property to Spanish buyers have been prohibited, and

---

[1] The memorandum, which had been initialled "L[ovett]" by the Under Secretary, and the annex were returned by the Secretary to Mr. Kennan with the notation: "Approved as indicated G C Marshall." A filing notation on the copy retained by the Policy Planning Staff indicated that the paper was approved by the Secretary of State on October 24 (Lot 62D1, Box 2529).

Government purchases in Spain cut to a minimum. This official policy has had the effect of discouraging private U.S. credits and trade and has contributed to the increasingly serious economic situation in Spain.

The Policy Planning Staff agrees that it would be highly desirable to bring about the replacement of Franco by a regime fully representative of the Spanish people, if it were possible to do so without violent internal or external repercussions. It would be desirable if a plebiscite could be held and some form of coalition government established which would restore to the Spanish people the freedom and rights of which they have been deprived by the totalitarian police methods of the present government. Unfortunately, there is no evidence of effective opposition to Franco, either within or without Spain, which could bring about an orderly change in government.

By adroit maneuvering, occasional concessions, and relentless police persecution, the Franco government has forestalled action by its opponents. There is no indication that the Army, on which the strength of the regime rests, is disposed to withdraw its support. Spokesmen for the old Republican, Socialist and Monarchist parties have been unable so far to compromise their differences or to agree on any program of joint action. Except for the Communists, the opposition parties are divided and disorganized; a concrete political ideal or a leader able to capture popular imagination is lacking.

The Department last Spring initiated conversations with the British with the object of agreeing upon a joint plan of action to eliminate Franco and to replace his regime with one based on democratic lines. The approach contemplated was an objective explanation to Franco of the views of the United States and British Governments, emphasizing the gains which would accrue to Spain from a change in regime. Our explanation was, in addition, to be directed to high ranking Generals, members of the opposition, and to all interested Spaniards, upon whom we would urge the necessity of change. It was contemplated for us to point out that the nature and timing of the change was entirely up to the Spaniards themselves, thus avoiding grounds for Spanish resentment against foreign intervention.

The British have indicated that they do not consider this plan workable, on the ground that: (1) Franco's interest in maintaining his own power would lead him to refuse, under any conditions, voluntarily to step down, and (2) leaks regarding the suggested action would undoubtedly occur, with resulting embarrassment and difficulties. The Department plans to raise the question again with the British at the conclusion of the present General Assembly of the U.N. At the same time, consideration may be given to a suggestion that the Vatican might be persuaded to take an active part in bringing about the retirement of Franco, a possibility which is actually being explored by members of the Spanish opposition.

While the Policy Planning Staff does not feel that it should make suggestions concerning current operations, it nevertheless has serious doubts as to the results to be expected from such a course. The Staff remains unconvinced that the leaders of the present regime in Spain would accept the proposal or that a sufficiently cohesive opposition exists to take over the government successfully. Even if the plan should be accepted with the consequent retirement of Franco, there would seem to be a strong probability of an ensuing political struggle leading only to internal chaos and resultant advantage to the Communists with all its ominous implications.

However, in the unlikely event that one or more of the contending opposition groups should eventually gather sufficient strength to be in a position to take over the functions of government, and in the event that our political support is sought by one of these groups, we should decline. On the other hand, we should be prepared to make available our good offices, in the event they are requested by two or more of the opposition parties, for the purpose of bringing these parties together.

The Staff believes that, in the National interest, the time has come for a modification of our policy toward Spain. The net result of our present policy has been: (1) to strengthen the Franco regime; (2) to impede the economic recovery of Spain; and (3) to operate against the maintenance of a friendly atmosphere in Spain in the event of international conflict.[1]

It is the recommendation of the Policy Planning Staff that instead of openly opposing the Franco regime, we should work from now on toward a normalization of U.S.-Spanish relations, both political and economic. Insofar as possible this should be done in such a way as not to strengthen the Franco regime. While no public announcement should be made of our views, we should have in mind the objective of restoring our relations to a normal basis, irrespective of wartime ideological considerations or the character of the regime in power.

The Staff feels that the principal step now open to the United States is a relaxation,[2] on our own initiative and entirely aside from our U.N. position, of our restrictive economic policy with regard to Spain. Steps should be taken whereby the various controls we have imposed are quietly dropped, so that normal trade may be resumed between the two countries. Elimination of official restrictive measures as such would naturally be followed in a short time by the opening up of

---

[1] Marginal note referring to this paragraph and the next two, in Marshall's handwriting: "OK GCM."

[2] In the margin Marshall wrote "Yes" with reference to the words "is a relaxation".

private trade and the possibility of financial assistance in the rehabilitation of the Spanish economy. Thus, instead of contributing to the rapid deterioration of the economic situation, as we are doing at present, we would provide the opportunity for Spain to develop its resources and play a normal part in the revival of world commerce and industry.

Before any economic measures can be taken, the question of Spain is expected to come up in the United Nations. Spain is on the agenda of the Political Committee and we may be called upon to take a position in respect to one aspect or another of the problem. The Staff is of the opinion that at the present session of the General Assembly, this Government should do everything possible to minimize discussion of the Spanish question. We should endeavor to discourage any action, whether under the Resolution of December 12, 1946, or in the form of a new resolution. In particular, we should refrain from any mention of our previous support of the action of the United Nations in condemning the Franco regime. The Department's position paper on this subject states that we should reaffirm such support. This, the Staff believes, should *not* be done.[3]

In the event that a resolution is introduced seeking to impose economic sanctions, break diplomatic relations, or otherwise strengthen last year's resolution, we should oppose the proposal. On the other hand, if a resolution should be introduced recommending that the provisions of the December 12, 1946, resolution now be rescinded, we could either vote in its favor or abstain. The Staff is inclined to the opinion that, in line with its recommendation for a change in our policy toward Spain, we should support such a resolution,[4] stating that the measures opposing Franco have not proved efficacious and that their continuation does not appear warranted by circumstances.

[3] In the margin Marshall wrote "I agree GCM" with reference to the words "should *not* be done".
[4] In the margin Marshall wrote "I agree GCM" with reference to the words "should support such a resolution".

Editorial Note

On November 17, 1947, a proposed reaffirmation of the resolution of December 12, 1946, failed to receive the necessary two-thirds majority of votes in the United Nations General Assembly. The United States voted against the proposed reaffirmation but voted in favor of a resolution, which was adopted, expressing confidence that the Security Council would exercise its responsibilities under the Charter as soon as it considered that the situation in Spain so required (U.N. document A/P.V. 118).

852.00/12–1847 : Telegram

The Acting Secretary of State to the Embassy in Spain

TOP SECRET   WASHINGTON, December 18, 1947—7 p. m.

903. Dept has carefully reviewed policy toward Spain and has reached conclusion that our primary objective at this time should be gradually to bring about normalization of relations, both political and economic, between Spain and western democracies, particularly US. Full normalization would be difficult if not impossible without substantial political and economic changes within Spain.

Fundamental and lasting improvement in regime can be brought about only by Span people themselves, not by interference from abroad. Our delegation at recent UNGA session emphasized this view, which appeared to be shared by majority of delegations other than those of Soviet bloc.

Primary desire of Spanish people, other than extreme leftists, is unquestionably for stability and avoidance of recurrence of civil strife. We emphatically do not desire to see Spanish state weakened to point at which disorder and civil strife might ensue. On other hand, indefinite continuance of present authoritarian repression serves to increase underground pressure which may eventually become explosive unless relieved in gradual and orderly manner.

For these reasons this Govt will seek to encourage orderly and peaceful evolution of Spanish Govt toward free and democratic regime representative of freely expressed will of Span people. We are convinced that such evolution must be both orderly and real (rather than any mere window dressing for present regime) if it is to serve best interests of Span people.

We consider choice as between monarchial or republican form of govt purely one for Span people themselves, provided they have opportunity freely to choose. Question of Franco's removal from all connection with Span Govt also one for Spaniards alone to decide, but removal would obviously result in more substantial improvement in Spain's international position than would liberalization of regime with Franco still participating.

We fully recognize need for broadest possible agreement among Spaniards on both objectives and procedures. Recent Robles-Prieto conversations are encouraging but only short preliminary step. Sincere agreement more far reaching and widespread within Spain will be necessary. We are of course mindful of difficulties impeding agreement including passions remaining from civil war, inherent instability of Spanish politics, complacency and support of present regime by various Rightist groups and present repression of political expression. We nevertheless wish to encourage such agreement and orderly evolution in any way we can without giving cause for charges that we are unwarrantably interfering in internal Spanish affairs.

Insofar as US attitude can have influence within Spain, we hope to convince Rightist elements now supporting regime, particularly Army and Church, that we do not favor foreign intervention in Spain and are not seeking to reverse outcome of civil war, but that we do hope to see orderly evolution toward democratic govt under which their legitimate interests would not suffer, whose permanence would rest upon support of Span people rather than upon repression, and which would restore Spain to full political and economic place in international community. We hope center and non-Communist Left will recognize that such evolution will afford better chance of genuine attainment of their objectives than revolution.

In economic field this Govt contemplates gradual and unobtrusive relaxation of existing trade restrictions. No direct governmental financial assistance now contemplated. When consulted on private trade credits Dept will express no objection on political grounds, but leave economic risk to judgment of American interests concerned. (Economic housecleaning in Spain is apparently prerequisite on purely commercial grounds to any substantial increase in trade.) We would expect, however, to coordinate any positive economic assistance with political developments in Spain and to utilize it (not economic compulsion) to encourage democratic evolution. Possibility of Spain becoming internationally "respectable" in time to secure measure of assistance under European Recovery Program should be important influence.

Foregoing is for your general guidance but not for any specific *démarche* in absence of further instructions.

We are repeating this to AmVat instructing Parsons [1] to communicate our general line of thought to Vatican with view to obtaining its reaction and possible exertion its influence in Spain along similar lines. We are not yet communicating our line of thought to anyone else.

Sent Madrid 903 rptd AmVat 19.

LOVETT

---

[1] James Graham Parsons, Foreign Service Officer at Vatican City.

852.00/12–2647 : Telegram

The Chargé in Spain (Culbertson) to the Secretary of State

TOP SECRET   MADRID, December 26, 1947—7 p. m.

1047. American policy toward Spain is based on opposition to Franco and his concept and practice of government. It looks to his complete withdrawal. Comment on Deptel 903, December 18 would be easier if I knew whether Department prepared deal with Franco subject his adopting gradual, effective (not "window dressing") economic political liberalization. (Last part paragraph 2 Embdesp 4337, November 25 [1]). Franco's removal is question for determination Spanish people (or Spanish army) but fact is he is "in" and the "outs" are of two distinctly different breeds of cat—monarchists and left, each completely disorganized and each basically opposed each other vis-à-vis ultimate political control and means determining expressed will of people. This despite any eventual Robles-Prieto agreement. Since our published policy says Franco must go completely he will hang on and is not likely adopt substantial effective modifications government except possibly in immediate face economic disaster and then measures, if any, may well be too late. While majority Spaniards oppose Franco regime (not necessarily Franco himself) majority also fear results his precipitous removal and this passive support enough keep him in. If we, England *et al*, Vatican, monarchists, the left would adopt policy trying find, with Franco, cooperative solution in interests Spain and western countries. I think pressure would be so great Franco would liberalize and in time be eased out of power, particularly if we prepared accept restoration monarchy and monarchy prepared accept gradual transition from present complete Franco control to liberal democratic monarchy. I see trouble in abrupt transition.

If positive policy of cooperation feasible in place present kick-Franco-out-now-policy, US contribution to solution Spanish problem would be (*a*) sell all elements including Franco on practicability of cooperative solution and long term democratic results and (*b*) economic assistance, both governmental and private. (I recognize (*a*) not easy but believe possible.)

Increasing jitteriness here over economic situation indicates moment relatively opportune use economic assistance as leverage obtain modification and liberalization. Uncoordinated piecemeal private credits, probably in limited amounts because of risk involved, not likely have effect on economic policy and certainly none on political. My suggestion therefore we implement policy outlined reference telegram by willingness consider now governmental assistance coordinated with private credits.

CULBERTSON

---

[1] Not printed.

711.52/12–3047 : Circular telegram

The Acting Secretary of State to Diplomatic Representatives in the American Republics

RESTRICTED   WASHINGTON, December 30, 1947—8 : 15 a. m.

Representatives of Colombia, Brazil, Peru and Salvador have asked us informally whether we now intend to send an Ambassador to Madrid.

The UN General Assembly resolution of 12 December 1946 included a recommendation that "all members of UN immediately recall from Madrid their Ambassadors and Ministers Plenipotentiary accredited there". With the exception of Argentina, UN members who then had Chiefs of Mission in Madrid withdrew them. We attach importance to scrupulous compliance with UN recommendations as a matter of major principle. Although a motion to reaffirm the 1946 resolution failed at the 1947 session to get the required two-thirds majority (US being among those opposing reaffirmation on ground it had been ineffective), 1946 resolution was not repealed and our opposition to reaffirmation indicates no change in our policy respecting a Chief of Mission in Madrid. Consequently, we contemplate no change in the status of our diplomatic representation in Madrid at this time.

Although you should take no initiative, you may reply along foregoing lines if FonOff should approach you, reporting any such conversations to the Department.

LOVETT

852.00/12–3047

The Chargé in Spain (Culbertson) to the Secretary of State

TOP SECRET   MADRID, December 30, 1947.
No. 4402

SIR : I have the honor to refer to the Embassy's telegram No. 1047 of December 26, sent in response to the Department's telegram No. 904 of December 19.[1]

It was with considerable hesitation that I finally let the reference telegram go; first, because I was not satisfied with its presentation and, second, because the suggestion of an attempt to obtain a cooperative effort on the part of the major Spanish factions probably looks like, and may be, daydreaming. Nevertheless, I am naive enough to think it has a possibility of modest success.

---

[1] Telegram 904, not printed.

The opposition elements inside and outside of Spain have been living in the false expectation that we and the other powers would unseat Franco and place them in control. None of these elements has ever seemed to figure out the mechanics of this change. In fact, they have probably never tried. They have lived on negative opposition to Franco and have kept in the forefront of international condemnation of Franco. In my estimation Don Juan has played more for international reaction and approbation than he has to the internal situation in Spain. Gil Robles and Prieto cling to the hope of positive international action against Franco. Visions of sanctions and sugar plums dance through their heads. The destruction of Franco has been so uppermost in their minds they have failed to see in the situation a possible development resulting in the destruction or near destruction of Spain herself, economically and possibly politically.

On Franco's side, he has been cursed and condemned by all the world. No loophole has been left for him in any of the announced policies of the United States or other powers. With nothing but opposition to confront him, Franco has had two alternatives: one, to commit suicide or, two, to pull in and tighten the dictatorial reins. He is not going to commit suicide, unless it be in the form of pulling the temple down on himself and thus on the Spanish people.

Our policies, for whatever reason adopted, have failed and continue to fail to obtain material political and economic liberalization for the Spanish people. We say, quite rightly, that it is for the Spanish people to determine what they want. At the same time our policies tend to exclude those people who, for whatever the reason may be, support Franco and who are not prepared to plunge into the unknown.

I am not up much on Vatican attitude toward Spain but I am willing to wager that deep down the Vatican is going to be most reluctant to take any step which will open the door to the return of a situation such as existed under the Republic. I am sure that even those elements in the Spanish church which object to Franco would object to the Vatican taking such a step. The Vatican may move toward Monarchy. If it moved to tell Franco he must go at once, I can see division within the Spanish church. Were the Vatican to urge upon Franco, the Church and the Monarchy the need, in the general interest of Spain, for cooperative efforts, such action would eliminate, at least to some degree, the Vatican taking a step which might well develop or accentuate division, especially within the Church.

I doubt whether Prieto could be brought to the point of any kind of cooperation with the present regime, and I am inclined to think it would be a mistake even to try. Not only Franco but lots of people in Spain would find it difficult to accept Prieto. (Even the country laborer who carried my gun on a partridge hunt last week expressed violent objection to Prieto.) There are, however, some men of the Left here in Spain, and after all they mean more in the future evolution of Spain than all of the exiled Republican leaders put together. One of those here in Spain (Señor Tomás Peire) has already expressed to an officer of the Embassy his growing conviction that cooperation with Franco seems to be the only remaining solution.

"Evolution" as opposed to "revolution" (last sentence, paragraph 7, Deptel 903 of December 18) should mean, as I see it from here, evolution *of* the present, *from* the present to a future improved governmental structure. If I see it correctly, cooperative effort in place of antagonism is the only possible solution and it is worth a try.

In order to obtain cooperation from the opposition, those gentlemen will have to swallow some pride and, at the start, subordinate some of their ideological thinking. I doubt whether that would be a very great task for Gil Robles, for instance.

Franco, on the other hand, is called upon to give a bird in the hand for two in the bush and he will at least want to see the color of the birds in the bush. If one glitters with gold and the other is the blue of friendliness, I think he will come along. No man is likely to refuse a friendly hand that would lift him from the international pit where Franco now rests, and this in spite of the fact that Franco seems to feel that he has been chosen by a higher power to lead Spain and the Spaniards out of the wilderness. I have a hunch he will come down to earth. He is very likely to do so if, in the face of an economic crash, real economic aid will be given to Spain and thus economic, as well as possible political, disaster can be avoided.

On the question of economic policy I feel I've got to stick my neck out by saying that the easing up of present economic and financial restrictions, as outlined in the ultimate paragraph of the Department's telegram No. 903, will in my estimation have practically no effect (*a*) on the economic situation in Spain or (*b*) in bringing about evolution politically or governmentally. For that reason I suggested in the Embassy's telegram No. 1047 the implementation of our policy by present willingness to consider direct governmental assistance. I appreciate that such action may be out of the realm of the practical from the standpoint of problems in Washington, but I suggest it as the practical one for Spain if we want to keep Spanish economy from going to pot.

Respectfully yours,

PAUL T. CULBERTSON

SWEDEN

AGREEMENT BETWEEN THE UNITED STATES AND SWEDEN ON QUANTITATIVE IMPORT RESTRICTIONS IN RECIPROCAL TRADE MODIFYING TEMPORARILY THE AGREEMENT OF MAY 25, 1935

[For text of Agreement, effected by exchange of *aide-mémoire* dated at Washington, June 24, 1947, and exchange of letters, see Department of State Treaties and Other International Acts Series (TIAS) No. 1711, 61 Stat. (pt. 4) 3745.]

AGREEMENT BETWEEN THE UNITED STATES AND SWEDEN RESPECTNG EXCHANGE OF OFFICIAL PUBLICATIONS

[For text of Agreement, effected by exchange of notes signed at Stockholm, December 16, 1947, see Department of State Treaties and Other International Acts Series (TIAS) No. 1688, 61 Stat. 3605.]

INDEX

INDEX

Abbott, Douglas, 117*n*, 123*n*, 124, 128, 131
Abdullah, Sheikh, 180, 188
Acheson, Dean G.: Arctic region, territorial claims in, 135; British financial situation, 7, 27–28, 34*n;* Canada, 113–114, 117, 118*n;* coal problem, 486–487, 496–497, 499–504; European Recovery Program, 197–198, 199*n*, 202, 219–220, 223, 232–233, 236, 241–242, 247*n;* France, 701, 703–705; German war documents, publication of, 641; German war prisoners, repatriation of, 621–623, 630–632; Greenland, 659–660; India, 136–137, 151–152; Italian colonies, 571–572, 574–575, 577; Italy, 535, 536–537, 835, 842, 876–877, 879, 884, 886–887, 921; Newfoundland, 94; peace treaties, 526*n*, 530*n*, 531*n*, 533–536, 541–542, 544, 545*n*, 548*n*, 549*n;* Portugal, 1019; Spain, 1062, 1064, 1065*n*, 1066–1069, 1073–1074, 1077, 1080
Acheson, Edward C., 831–832
Achilles, Theodore C., 682
Afghanistan, 37, 160–161, 181
Agriculture Department, 440, 477*n*, 702, 754, 841, 865
Airey, Maj. Gen. Terence Sydney, 566
Aklilou Abte Wold, Ato, 615–617
Alba, Duke of, 1083, 1088
Albania, 37, 858; Greek claim to Epirus, 523; Italian recognition of, 523; U.S. views on membership in the United Nations, 966
Albornoz, Alvaro de, 1091
Algeria, 701, 703
Ali, Asaf, 147–149, 167–169
Ali, Laik, 173
Allen, Denis, 1087–1088
Allen, Richard F., 482
Allen, Ward P., 234*n*
Alling, Paul H., 175–177
Alphand, Hervé, 308–309, 315–316, 333, 393–395, 426, 436, 438*n*, 458, 463, 468, 505–506, 511
Alsop, Joseph, 241
Alsop, Stewart, 241
Amberley (Australia), air service facilities at, 102
American Overseas Airlines (AOA), 830
American Republics, 23–24, 27, 207, 269, 275, 288, 362, 465–467, 668, 670, 681

Amr, Abdel Fattah, 619
Anderson, Clinton P., 164, 482, 704, 725, 841–842, 846, 962
Andorra, 1086
Andvord, Rolf Otto, 1010, 1015*n*, 1017–1018
Anglo-Egyptian Sudan, 590, 601, 605
Ansiaux, Hubert, 338
Antigua, 94
Antonini, Luigi, 541
Arab League. *See under* Italian colonies *and under* French North Africa.
Arab states, 159
Aranda, Gen. Antonio, 1056, 1071*n*
Arctic region, territorial claims in, 135
Arey, Hawthorne, 917
Argentia (Newfoundland), 99
Argentina, 2, 11–12, 25, 29, 52, 56, 165, 232, 269, 271–272, 276, 278, 324, 449, 466, 705, 816–817, 846, 856, 877, 934, 946, 963, 992, 994, 1075, 1099
Armour, Norman, 717*n*, 790–793, 965–967, 973*n*, 981–982, 1040, 1042, 1083–1084, 1091–1092
Army, Department of, 477*n*, 683–684, 686–687, 775–776
Army Transport Command (ATC), 1019, 1028–1030, 1032–1033, 1035–1036, 1046–1048, 1050–1051
Arnold, Elting, 75
Arnold, Gen. of the Army Henry H., 245
Artajo, Alberto Martin, 1053*n*, 1054–1056, 1061, 1082, 1086, 1089
Atherton, Ray, 97, 111–113, 116–117, 121–123, 125, 127–128, 135
Attlee, Clement R., 52, 59*n*, 88, 143–144, 155–156, 181, 186–187, 189–192, 271, 273, 282, 492*n*, 501–502, 1082
Auriol, Vincent, 688*n*, 693*n*, 748
Austin, Warren R., 578
Australia:
Italian colonies, disposition of, 570, 575–577, 587, 589, 595*n*, 612*n*, 618, 620*n*
Marshall Plan, source of food for, 232
United Kingdom: Food imports to, 276; sterling balances, 11–12, 16, 57
U.S. relations with, 102–103; air facilities agreement, 102; naval base at Manus Island, 102–103, 671, 682
Austria, 655, 723, 880, 906, 954; economic situation in, 220*n*, 362; European Recovery Plan, 264, 311, 314,

1128 INDEX

Tedder, Air Chief Marshal Sir Arthur,
818
Teitgen, Pierre-Henri, 699, 770, 793
Terracini, Umberto, 530n
Terrill, Robert P., 367, 382
Theotónio Pereira, Pedro, 1025–1046
passim
Thibodeaux, Ben H., 702
Thompson, Dorothy, 541
Thompson, Llewellyn E., 260, 643, 646
Thompson-McCausland, L. P., 2–3, 64
Thorez, Maurice, 688n, 691, 700, 703n,
751, 795–797, 805, 808, 810, 813–814
Thorp, Willard, 38–39, 53, 55, 124, 202,
235, 243, 256n, 267, 405, 463, 465–
466, 489n, 544, 843–845, 853–854,
857–858, 914, 942
Thors, Olafur, 829–830
Thors, Thor, 832
Thurston, Ray L., 175n, 176–179
Tibbets, Col. Gene H., 1027, 1034, 1037
Tildy, Zoltan, 540, 558
Tirana, Rifat, 917
Tito, Marshal (Josip Broz), 970
Tobey, Charles W., 93
Togliatti, Palmiro, 556, 877–878, 882,
893, 935, 946–947, 967, 970, 988
Togni, Giuseppe, 937n, 945
Togoland, 42
Tomlinson, William M., 756, 775, 785
Towers, Graham, 116–117, 119–120
Trade Agreements Act, 129
Trading with the Enemy Act, 800
Transjordan, 592
Treasury Department, 198, 231, 371–372,
440, 470, 477n, 837, 842, 844, 921,
942, 997
Treaties, conventions and agreements
(*see also under individual coun-
tries*):
Anglo-Argentine Agreement (*1946*), 3,
11–12
Anglo-Egyptian Treaty (*1936*), 593
Anglo-French Agreement regarding
Tangier regime (*1945*), 909n
Belgium-France, payments agreement,
781, 784, 786
Bretton Woods Agreements, 5–6, 293
Convention of St. Germain-en-Laye
(*1919*), 42
European Coal Organization, agree-
ment for establishment, and
protocol (*1946*), 485n
French-Soviet commercial accord
(*1945*), 773
General Agreement on Tariffs and
Trade (GATT), *Oct. 30*, 54, 60,
100–101, 126–127, 131–134, 656,
825, 1002
Geneva Convention (*1929*), 621–622,
628
Hyde Park Agreement (Roosevelt-
King) (*1941*), 110
Land-Leathers Agreement (*1944*), 101

Treaties—Continued
Peace treaties *Feb. 10*, with Bulgaria,
Finland, Hungary, Rumania,
524n; with Italy, 43, 524n, 569,
573, 575, 583, 585–588, 593, 600,
602–603, 606–608, 610n
Potsdam Agreement (*1945*), 273, 692,
840
Soviet-German treaty of non-aggres-
sion (*1939*), 640, 645, 691n, 797;
secret protocol, 646
Spitsbergen treaty (*1920*), 1003–1005,
1006–1017
Three Power Pact between Germany,
Italy and Japan, 643
Trade agreements between U.S. and
Belgium (*1935*), 656; Canada
(*1938*), 126–127, 130–135; France
(*1936*), 825; Italy (*1938*), 838;
Netherlands (*1935*), 1002; Swe-
den (*1935*), 1102
Trusteeship agreements for Cam-
eroons, Togoland and Tangan-
yika (*1946*), 42
United Nations Monetary Fund
Agreement (*1944*), 5–6, 293
Trevelyan, Humphrey, 159
Trieste, Free Territory of, 277, 518, 533n,
543n, 548, 559, 862, 885, 892, 930,
953, 977, 980
Trimble, William G., 829–834
Trinidad, 94
Tripartite Commission (Anglo-Ameri-
can-French) for the restitution of
monetary gold (1946), 757n
Tripolitania. *See under* Italian colonies:
Libya.
Troutman, Harry L., 377–379
Truman, Harry S.: Aid to Greece and
Turkey, 197–198, 216–217, 224, 243,
1074; Bulgaria, 549–550, 550n;
Canada, 108–109, 110n, 112–113,
113n, 125; coal shortages in Europe,
486–487, 490n, 492–493, 495–
496, 501–502; China, 202; conversations with: Asaf Ali, 147, 147n,
Mackenzie King, 108–110, 110n, De
Gasperi, 850, Tarchiani, 904, 907–
908, 911; European Recovery Program, 232–233, 264–266, 308n, 331n,
356, 363, 375, 389, 390n, 410, 410n,
438–439, 443, 456–457, 459, 464,
470–471, 472n, 477–478, 483–484, 762,
819; export controls, continuation
of, 214, 500n; foreign affairs, responsibility for conduct of, 531;
France, 702, 706, 714, 721–722, 758–
760, 762, 763n, 775, 785, 800; German prisoners of war, repatriation
of, 621, 631; Greenland, 674–675;
Hungary, 549–550, 550n; India, 164,
169, 171–172; Italy, 546, 548–549,
549n, 557, 785, 850–851, 861, 891, 893,
904, 907–908, 911, 935, 996; Maritime Commission 491–493; message